BRITISH COLUMBIA

A BEST PLACES® GUIDE TO THE OUTDOORS

JACK CHRISTIE

SASQUATCH BOOKS
SEATTLE

RAINCOAST BOOKS
Vancouver

Dedication

For Shirley Suttles (Lesley Conger)
For Charmien Johnson and Suzanne Westphal
For Charles Campbell

Acknowledgements

Thanks to Team Inside Out BC: Kate Rogers, Trent Ernst, Corene McKay, Naomi Pauls and Theresa Best. Thanks to contributors Maggie Paquet, Steve Threndyle, Kathryn Fowler, Grace Hols, Eileen Delahanty Pearkes, Murphy Shewchuk, Barbara Maryniak, Gordon Long, Tony Eberts, Peter Tyedmers, Suzie Simms, James Evans, and Betty Pratt-Johnson.

Printed in the United States
Published in the United States by Sasquatch Books
Published in Canada by Raincoast Books, Ltd.

First Edition

00 99 98 6 5 4 3 2 1

Library of Congress Cataloging in Publication Data
ISSN: 1097-6000
ISBN: 1-57061-133-5

Canadian Cataloguing in Publication Data
Christie, Jack, 1946–
Inside Out British Columbia
Includes index.
ISBN: 1-55192-131-6
1. Outdoor recreation--British Columbia--Guidebooks. 2. British Columbia--Guidebooks.
I. Title
FC3807.C57 1997 917.1104'4 C97-910861-6
F1087.7.C57 1997

Cover Photo: John P. Kelly/The Image Bank
Cover Design: Karen Schober
Interior Design: Lynne Faulk, Vashon Island, WA
Maps: GreenEye Design, Seattle, WA
Copy editor: Catherine Bennett, Vancouver, BC
Proofreader: Kris Fulsaas, Seattle, WA
Composition: Patrick David Barber Design, Seattle, WA
Indexer: Miriam Bulmer

Important Note: Please use common sense. No guidebook can act as a substitute for experience, careful planning, and appropriate training. There is inherent danger in all the outdoor activities described in this book, and readers must assume responsibility for their own actions and safety. Changing or unfavorable conditions in weather, roads, trails, waterways, etc. cannot be anticipated by the author or publisher, but should be considered by any outdoor participants. The author and the publisher will not be responsible for the safety of users of this guide.

The information in this edition is based on facts available at press time and is subject to change. The author and publisher welcome information conveyed by users of this book, as long as they have no financial connection with the area, guide, outfitter, organization, or establishment concerned.

Sasquatch Books, 615 Second Avenue, Suite 260, Seattle, WA 98104, (206)467-4300
email: books@SasquatchBooks.com www.SasquatchBooks.com

Raincoast Books, 8680 Cambie Street, Vancouver, BC V6P 6M9, (604)323-7100
email: info@raincoast.com www.raincoast.com

Contents

Introduction v

How to Use This Book vi

BC Outdoor Primer viii

About Best Places® Guidebooks xvi

Lower Mainland 1

Greater Vancouver 3
The Fraser Estuary 40
The Fraser Valley 61
The North Shore 107
Whistler and the Sea to Sky Highway 142
Pemberton and Lillooet 189
The Sunshine Coast 208

Vancouver Island and the Gulf Islands 235

Greater Victoria 237
Sooke Basin and the West Coast Trail 262
Nanaimo and the Cowichan Valley 276
Tofino and Pacific Rim National Park Reserve 295
Parksville and the Comox Valley 314
Nootka Sound and Strathcona Provincial Park 331
North Vancouver Island 342
Southern Gulf Islands 354
Northern Gulf Islands 374

Central and Northwest Coasts 387

Inside Passage and Discovery Coast 389
Queen Charlotte Islands (Haida Gwaii) 403

Southern Interior 413

The Trans-Canada Highway 415
Manning Provincial Park 435
Crowsnest Highway: South Okanagan Valley 441
The Coquihalla Highway 450
Okanagan Valley 458
Kettle Valley 478

The Kootenays 483

Crowsnest Highway: The West Kootenays 485

Slocan Valley and Upper Arrow Lake 502

North Kootenay Lake and Selkirk Valleys 517

Crowsnest Highway: The East Kootenays 522

Columbia River Valley 529

Northwest Interior 543

The Bella Coola Road (Highway 20) 545

The Bulkley and Skeena River Valleys 560

Fraser Plateau 572

Central Interior 589

The Cariboo Highway 591

The Yellowhead Highway 602

The Far North 613

The Northeast 615

The Stewart-Cassiar Highway (Highway 37) 639

Index 653

Introduction

Rock and ice, salt spray and rain forest, desert and taiga: When you have as large a patch of land as that covered within British Columbia's borders—bigger than the states of Washington, Oregon, and California rolled into one—you need simple, rugged words to describe it. The magic of BC's wilderness is encapsulated in each of these elements, and nowhere else on the continent prepares you for the range of outdoor adventure to be found here.

Don't be deceived by the cozy but thin veneer of civilization that has been thrown up around the wilderness. Even in the southwestern corner of the province where half of BC's population resides, those who do not respect the neighbouring wilds often face uncompromising consequences. Here's the natural truth about BC: Venture much beyond sidewalk's end and you come face to face with a landscape shaped by the girth of glacial ice that until quite recently covered the entire landmass. So strong was the force exerted by this miles-thick crush that, as it retreated, it cast a ragged impression in the bedrock.

Those who devote themselves to adventurous exploration of Canada's western coast eventually make their way here to hike trophy trails, ski trophy peaks, and paddle trophy waters. Fortunately, most travellers don't have to resort to extremes in order to get an inside look at these fantastic features. Although your explorations will brush up against the churning natural forces still at work in the aftermath of the most recent ice age, with proper preparation and a confident spirit you can negotiate your way in and around the landscape, emerging with untarnishable memories of your encounter with the natural world. The land persists and is there for each of us to discover anew. The farther afield you venture, the more appreciation you'll develop for its staggering abundance.

—*Jack Christie*

How to Use This Book

We have tried to make *Inside Out British Columbia* an entertaining, informative, and easy-to-use guidebook. The province's geographical regions were divided into eight sections. Basic reference maps are featured at the beginning of each section. Each section is then subdivided into smaller, more manageable areas (or chapters) that are represented in the following manner.

Introduction

The introduction to each chapter offers a general description of the area and its primary towns and features. These sections should provide you with a sense of place and history, as well as give you an idea of what to expect when you visit. Directions to the area and transportation information are included in the **Getting There** sections, which are followed by **Adjoining Areas** to your destination that are found in this book.

inside out

The Inside Out sections make up the bulk of the book. We go to great pains to discover what the best year-round options are for outdoor activities in each area. We talk to locals, forest service officials, guides, and outdoor store owners to get the scoop on the most popular trails, lakes, stretches of river, climbs, ski slopes, and more. And we reveal some lesser-known gems as well.

These sections are divided into individual sports and activities, listed in order of prominence and appeal. Most chapters include **Hiking, Biking, Fishing, Camping, Skiing,** and **Rafting/Kayaking**—things that can be enjoyed in many parts of the province. Other chapters feature specialized activities, such as **Windsurfing, Caving,** and **Hang Gliding.** Here, you can select your adventure and discover how to get out into the wilderness, outside, out-of-doors, just out!

The BC Outdoor Primer, beginning on page viii, also provides safety tips and essential information on outdoor recreation and travel.

outside in

After a long day spent enjoying the outdoors, you need to know where to go for some inside fun. The **Attractions** sections tell you about museums, hot springs, shops, and other sights in the area that will distract the kids, get you out of inclement weather, or are just plain interesting places.

The **Restaurants** and **Lodgings** sections provide star-rated reviews of the best places to eat and sleep. (See the About Best Places® Guidebooks segment on page xvi for a description of how we rate and choose our restaurants and lodgings.)

More Information

Finally, we wrap up each chapter with a list of useful phone numbers specific to that area. Forest Service districts, parks, city infocentres, visitors centres, and more are all included for your convenience.

BC Outdoor Primer

Despite the toll inflicted on the land by urbanization and the extraction of natural resources, there are still corridors and tracts of BC wilderness to revel in. The purpose of *Inside Out British Columbia* is to guide you to and through these areas. Follow these pages and you'll soon be soaking in a thermal spring, biking along a historical gold-rush trail, or paddling with loons in the serenity of a sunset. Some adventures will be of the remote, once-in-a-lifetime variety. Others, once the way is known, will occur as often as you can arrange a visit. This book offers you an inside line on the myriad ways around BC. We suggest places and people to consult who will help you make your way. With this assurance you can plot your own course and design an adventure that suits your style. Every effort has been taken to pack as much detail as possible into these pages. Your challenge—and your ultimate reward—will be to discover the language of the land, to get inside British Columbia. Following are some general tips.

Roads and Ferries

Finding your way around BC can be perplexing at times, even for locals, particularly in regions like the Kootenays where a warp-and-weft of highways weaves through tightly packed mountain ranges. Along the coast, much of the rhythm of travel is determined by the BC Ferries schedule. If you're from out-of-province, it will take a day or two to familiarize yourself with the way things run here. For example, many first-time visitors are surprised to find that there are no freeways in the city of Vancouver. Somehow the 600,000 residents have found a way to survive without them. Negotiating through the province's largest city—and the gateway for many travellers to the rest of BC—requires patience, acuity, the assistance of a good navigator, and, the most precious of all ingredients, time. Budget plenty of it, especially when connecting with the two nearby ferry terminals.

For information on schedules and fees for all **BC Ferries routes,** call (888) 223-3779. For 24-hour information on **road conditions** throughout the province, call (604) 299-9000, code 7623; (900) 565-4997 or (800) 550-4997.

Weather

Current weather information is available from Environment Canada; for an **automated weather menu,** call (900) 565-5000, and for information on weather **services,** call (604) 664-9032. For recorded weather **forecasts** for Greater Vancouver, call (604) 664-9010, and for the Fraser Valley, Howe Sound, and Whistler Village, call (604) 664-9021. To receive a weather **fax,** call (900) 451-3007, or for one-on-one live weather **consultation,** call (900) 565-5555. On-line weather information is available from Environment Canada's **Web site:** www.weatheroffice.com

Generally speaking, November and February are the two wettest months in **coastal British Columbia.** May and September are the two most enjoyable months to explore the coast; not only are there fewer travellers, but the weather also tends to be at its best. Cold weather blankets much of the **BC interior** from October to April, with northeastern BC frequently cool and overcast through July. The best months to travel here are August and September after the first frosts have brought an end to insect season.

Camping

Travellers can reserve campsites in over 40 campgrounds throughout BC's **provincial parks,** up to three months in advance of a visit, and can stay as long as 14 days. The **BC Parks reservation line**—(800) 689-9025 throughout Canada and the United States, or (604) 689-9025 in Greater Vancouver—operates daily between March 1 and September 15; for detailed information, call between 7am and 7pm Pacific time, Monday to Friday, and between 9am and 5pm Pacific time on Saturdays and Sundays. If you are reserving on one of three long weekends in summer, there is a minimum three-day charge. Long weekends in BC during reservation season occur on Victoria Day (the Monday nearest May 24), BC Day (the first Monday in August), and Labour Day (the first Monday in September). At present, a surcharge of $6.42 per night is added to the regular camping fee of about $15 per night, with a maximum surcharge of three nights even if you are reserving for a longer stay.

With the exception of Gwaii Haanas National Park/Haida Heritage Site in the Queen Charlotte Islands, a fee is charged all visitors to the five **national parks** situated in BC. (Note: Reservations, however, *are* required of those entering Gwaii Haanas unaccompanied by a private operator.) Call **Parks Canada, (800) 748-7275,** for more information about fees and services, and to order advance passes. Parks Canada offices are located in Vancouver, Victoria, and Kelowna, as well as at the visitors centres in each of Pacific Rim, Mount Revelstoke, Yoho, Glacier, and Kootenay National Parks. A day-use fee as well as annual passes are available in a variety of price ranges, depending on your age, the size of your group, and the length of your stay. Note: Campground reservations for

Green Point Campground in Pacific Rim National Park may be made with the BC Parks reservation line (see above).

There is no charge for camping at any of more than 1,000 recreation campgrounds maintained by the **BC Forest Service** throughout the 42 provincial forest districts. Detailed maps of each district may be obtained by calling (800) 331-7001 in Nanaimo, and at Tourist InfoCentres and regional and district Forest Service offices in towns throughout BC. Phone numbers and addresses for many of these offices are given at appropriate points in the text.

For general information on both public and private campgrounds, consult the *Super Camping Guide for British Columbia* and the *British Columbia Accommodations Guide BC,* both published by Tourism BC and available at most Tourist InfoCentres throughout the province, or by calling (604) 945-7676 to request a copy. For private accommodation reservations throughout the province, call Tourism British Columbia, (800) 663-6000.

Hiking

When planning a hike, carefully consider your trip and what to pack. Conditions have a habit of changing quickly in this mountainous province, and it pays to be prepared for any eventuality. Every hiker should carry along the **"10 essentials,"** a tried-and-true list of equipment that can save a life in an emergency:

- **Map:** Make sure it's of the area you're visiting and that you know how to use it. Also bring along any relevant guidebooks.
- **Compass:** An orienteering class is the best way to learn how to use a compass.
- **Sunglasses and sunscreen:** You need these even on cloudy days, especially in alpine areas.
- **Extra food:** Bring enough food that doesn't require cooking to last an extra day; high-energy foods such as nuts and raisins are always a good bet.
- **Extra clothing:** This should include rain gear, hat, mittens, and extra warm layers (preferably not cotton). Consider carrying it in a plastic bag inside your pack for assured dryness.
- **Flashlight:** Even if you're sure you'll return before darkness, it's comforting to know you have a light along. Bring an extra bulb and a set of backup batteries.
- **First-aid kit:** Everyone should bring a basic kit, which can be purchased prepackaged in pharmacies or outdoor stores; a larger group should carry a more extensive kit. Know what's inside and how to use it.

- **Fire starter:** Candles, burning paste, or fire pellets work well, but if you're spending a lot of time on snow, nothing beats a camping stove.
- **Matches:** Carry them in a waterproof container.
- **Pocket knife:** A Swiss Army knife, complete with the usual assortment of bells and whistles, can deal with most trail emergencies. Pocket tools are becoming increasingly popular, too.

It's also important to carry plenty of **water,** usually a minimum of 1 quart (roughly 1 litre) per person per day. Other items that are a good idea to have along, especially for emergencies, include a whistle and a large plastic bag or space blanket. File a **trip plan** with someone reliable as to your exact destination, the time you plan to return, and the licence plate of your vehicle. An informative, pack-sized guide to have handy is *Outdoor Safety and Survival* by Judi Lees.

Bear Advisory

Finding bear scat at the door of your tent is an electrifying way to greet the day in the backcountry. Being dragged into the bush by a hungry bruin is a manifestation of an altogether different order. The former is a warning, while an outright attack serves notice that in the arena of the great outdoors, all bets are off. The unfortunate truth is that every year in BC a few people are seriously mauled or die from unprovoked bear attacks.

Today, many hikers carry a can of **bear spray** on their hip. There are two caveats to relying on spray: test your spray with a short blast (outdoors!) at least once a season to insure that the can is still pressurized, and learn how to use it accurately at close range (no small feat). Most importantly, however, before heading out into bear country, familiarize yourself with **common-sense practises** to avoid confrontation. Consult a guide such as *Backcountry Bear Basics* by Dave Smith. Subtitled "The Definitive Guide to Avoiding Unpleasant Encounters," Smith's book is an easy read to which every backcountry-user should refer. The information contained in it is well researched and helps separate factual evidence from half-baked research and uninformed opinion. For example, the speed with which bears move means that even track stars should never flee from a bear or attempt to scale a tree. That's one race you'll never win. If a bear spots you in the backcountry, generally you should back away slowly and talk quietly. But different tactics are recommended for black bears or grizzlies and in different situations. Always check with local authorities before entering bear habitat. The rarity of bear predation on humans is a sign that we don't often fit their prey image like marmots, mice, and salmon do. Still, most knowledgeable wildlife biologists such as Dave Smith are unwilling to dismiss predation as an unnatural act or the desperate deed of a starving or slightly crazed bear.

Signs posted at regular intervals along BC highways warn drivers of the possible presence of moose, elk, mountain goats, bighorn sheep, and even livestock on the road, but no mention is made of bears. Yet, as you drive these routes, it's possible you'll lose track of the number of black bears spied grazing beside the highway. Food-conditioned bears pose the most dangerous threat to humans. Once a bear has tasted food prepared by humans, all else in its diet pales in comparison. Travellers in the wilds of BC are reminded that "a fed bear is a dead bear." Eight hundred black bears and 50 grizzlies, so-called "nuisance bears," are shot each year in BC; for their well-being and your own, only use roadside trash barrels that are bear-proofed. Most garbage containers in provincial and national parks are sturdily designed, but many others found on the highway are so flimsy that they function as much as food banks for bears as they do for drop-off spots for odour-weary travellers.

Mountain Biking

The difference between cycling and mountain biking is often subjective. For some, mountain biking means riding on a road that isn't paved. For others, it's just not a challenge if the path doesn't go straight down a mountain and involve hopping the bike over rocks, boulders, and fallen trees. For the purposes of this book, mountain-bike trails usually involve at least the possibility of singletrack, which is just a fancy term for a trail that's only wide enough to fit one bike on it at a time. Mountain-bike trails seem to congregate and proliferate in certain areas. *Inside Out British Columbia* doesn't attempt to list all trails but we have tried to describe those broader areas where mountain biking is welcome. Because mountain biking has gained such popularity in so short a time, few land managers have amended their land-use plans to include mountain biking. Very few legal, or open, trails exist. Despite this, many land managers tolerate the respectful use of their trails by mountain bikers. It is important to maintain good trail etiquette when riding. Some trails are officially closed to mountain bikers. In the name of good relationships with land managers and other trail users, please stay off these paths. There are many alternatives, including virtually all Forest Service roads, most dike systems, most cross-country ski trails, and many abandoned railways. If in doubt about an area, get in touch with a local club or bike store, or call the appropriate land manager before riding. In provincial parks, all trails are officially closed to mountain bikes unless otherwise posted.

Fishing

Freshwater

There are so many fishable lakes in BC that even if you managed to try a different one each day of the year, you would have to start young and have a long life (and maybe a floatplane) to visit them all. Hundreds of pleasant lakes are easily reached and fished with simply a vehicle with good ground clearance, a car-top or inflatable boat or float tube, and the right tackle. Several good sources to consult before you set out are *Best of BC Lake Fishing* by Karl Bruhn, *Kamloops: An Angler's Study of the Kamloops Trout* by Steve Raymond, *Irresistible Waters: Fly Fishing in BC Throughout the Year* by Art Lingren, and the *BC Fishing Directory and Atlas*. It's a given that local store operators will know about the lakes and streams in their areas and will be able to recommend what flies or lures to try according to the season.

Once onsite, ask other anglers if they've spotted hatches of insects, from tiny chironomids to muscular sedges, and examine the lake bottom in shallow areas to see what kind of fish food is swimming about. In shallow, muddy-bottomed lakes, a leech imitation is often a good bet. If you have a favourite "attractor" fly that resembles nothing in the surrounding environment, give it a try. Trout are curious and can occasionally be charmed into taking a shot at a foreign import.

Catch-and-release with a single barbless hook has become the official operative byword for those anglers fishing ocean-bound streams and rivers in BC. Once hooked, do not overly tire your catch or mishandle it when landing, causing abrasions that can lead to disease. Simply grasp the shank of the hook and lift the hook-bend upwards for the most effective release. Attitude means a lot in fishing. Remember that the essence of sport angling is to try to hook a fish on the most sporting terms you can handle, from light tackle with artificial lures, barbless hooks, and delicate leaders to a belief that a trout is much more valuable as a living challenge to your skill than as part of a meal.

For general information on fishing regulations, contact the BC Fish and Wildlife Regional Office, (604) 582-5200 or (800) 665-7027.

Saltwater

Salmon are the sportfish of choice in BC's marine waters. Depending on the time of year you'll find chinook (also called king or spring, or tyee if over 30 pounds/13.5 kg), coho (also called silver, blueback, or northern), sockeye, or pink (also called humpy). There are two main methods to catch salmon: trolling and mooching. Mooching means fishing with bait, often live anchovy or herring, from a boat that is anchored, drifting, or only occasionally using a motor. Usual tackle is a long, flexible mooching rod and an ounce or two of lead to sink two small hooks, single or treble, near the bottom where fish lurk.

Trolling is the more common method. Unless salmon are feeding on or near the surface, use a downrigger (a lead ball on a wire cable, mounted on a small windlass affair) to get bait or lure down to fish that are often in 100 feet (30 m) or more of water. When a salmon strikes, your line snaps away from the downrigger so you can play the fish with little interference. In this way you can use very light, sporty tackle. Trollers use bait and an assortment of artificial lures such as little octopus-like, soft plastic "Hootchies," torpedo-shaped plugs, and metal spoons. Large shiny "flashers" are often located some distance ahead of the lures to get the attention of salmon at a distance. Coho aren't the biggest salmon but are the most sought after, as they jump and fight like trout. They are usually caught in late spring and early summer as bluebacks (immature fish of 3–5 pounds/1.5–2.5 kg) or in late summer and early fall as northerns (upwards of 20 pounds/9 kg). Sockeye are the tastiest salmon of all and average about 6 pounds (3 kg) and are usually plentiful when heading upriver to spawn in late summer and early fall. Pinks are similar in size but not as tasty.

It's a mystery but fish—oceangoing and freshwater alike—are hungriest just as a slack tide is beginning to fall and for an hour thereafter. That's just some of the fishing lore that you'll encounter when tossing a line in BC waters. Another well-considered tip is that the best time to fish in ocean waters is an hour before and after both high and low tides.

Kayaking

With BC's more than 10,000 miles (16 000 km) of coastline, you could spend several lifetimes sea kayaking your way around. *Wave~Length Paddling Magazine*, (250) 247-9789, runs an all-purpose Web site packed with information on sea kayaking in the province, with links to guides and outfitters, clubs, parks, routes, etc. Their address is http://www.wie.com/~wavenet/. A comprehensive general manual to consult is *Sea Kayaking* by John Dowd.

Skiing/Snowboarding

Each year an increasingly large number of Americans, Europeans, and Asians come to BC on ski and snowboard holidays. Visitors shouldn't assume, however, that Whistler/Blackcomb is the be-all and end-all of winter resorts. For example, Sun Peaks, Silver Star, Big White, and Apex Ski Resorts in the interior are where Vancouver residents who ski Whistler regularly go with their families on winter holidays.

Internationally, the word is out that Canada is *the* place to learn to ski and snowboard. According to Olympic champion Nancy Greene Raine of Sun Peaks Resort near Kamloops, who hosts clinics of her own for intermediate and advanced skiers, the quality of teaching here accounts for much of the world's reawakened interest in winter recreation in BC. After all, in the 1930s, Canada was perceived as one of the best places to take a vacation by rail to Banff, Jasper, and—yes—even Whistler, then called Alta Lake. And these days Whistler/Blackcomb teaches more people how to ski and snowboard than any other resort in North America. The halo-effect of Whistler/Blackcomb having been crowned the number-one winter destination by all three major winter sport magazines in the US is also creating more interest in smaller BC resorts.

Backcountry winter adventuring is a whole other league. Before you head out into the backcountry anywhere in BC, prepare yourself for any eventuality. Learn to handle demanding winter camping conditions and discover how to anticipate and avoid avalanche hazards. The Canada West Mountain School, a division of the Federation of Mountain Clubs of BC, has been offering **mountain safety instruction** since 1982 and has expanded considerably in the past several years to include introductory backcountry courses for snowboarders and ice climbers as well as skiers. Weekend ski treks for novices begin in early January and continue through March; avalanche safety programs for skiers and snowboarders begin in early December and also continue through March. For more information on the Canada West Mountain School, contact the Federation of Mountain Clubs of BC, #336—1367 West Broadway, Vancouver, BC V6H 4A9, (604) 737-3053 or (888) 892-2266, or visit their Web site at http://home.istar.ca/~fmcbc/fmcbc.htm. Once you're comfortable with backcountry winter conditions, consider making an extended foray in March and April. **Spring snow conditions** are generally the most favourable of the year, which is why many skiers and snowboarders plan backcountry expeditions as the sun strengthens and provides longer daylight hours.

The **Alpine Club of Canada**'s Vancouver section posts information about trip schedules plus a variety of other useful listings and links, including weather reports and road conditions, at their Web site, www.bivouac.com. Their email address is ACC@bivouac.com.

About Best Places® Guidebooks

The restaurant and lodging reviews in this book are condensed from *Best Places* guidebooks. The *Best Places* series is unique in the sense that each guide is written by and for locals, and is therefore coveted by travellers. The best places in the region are the ones that denizens favor: establishments of good value, often independently owned, touched with local history, run by lively individuals, and graced with natural beauty. *Best Places* reviews are completely independent: no advertisers, no sponsors, no favours.

All evaluations are based on numerous reports from local and travelling inspectors. *Best Places* writers do not identify themselves when they review an establishment, and they accept no free meals, accommodations, or any other services. Every place featured in this book is recommended, even those with no stars.

Stars

Restaurants and lodgings are rated on a scale of zero to four stars, based on uniqueness, loyalty of local clientele, performance measured against goals, excellence of cooking, value, and professionalism of service. Reviews are listed alphabetically.

☆☆☆☆	The very best in the region
☆☆☆	Distinguished; many outstanding features
☆☆	Excellent; some wonderful qualities
☆	A good place
no stars	Worth knowing about, if nearby

Price Range

All prices are in Canadian dollars, and are subject to change; contact the establishment directly to verify.

$$$	Expensive (more than $80 for dinner for two; more than $100 for lodgings for two)
$$	Moderate (between expensive and inexpensive)
$	Inexpensive (less than $30 for dinner for two; less than $70 for lodgings for two)

Directions

Basic directions are provided with each review; contact each business to confirm hours and location.

Cheaper Eats and Cheaper Sleeps

The listings under Cheaper Eats and Cheaper Sleeps are for the budget-conscious traveler. While they are not star-rated, each establishment is recommended and is generally in the inexpensive price range (see above). These listings do not provide directions; call ahead to confirm location.

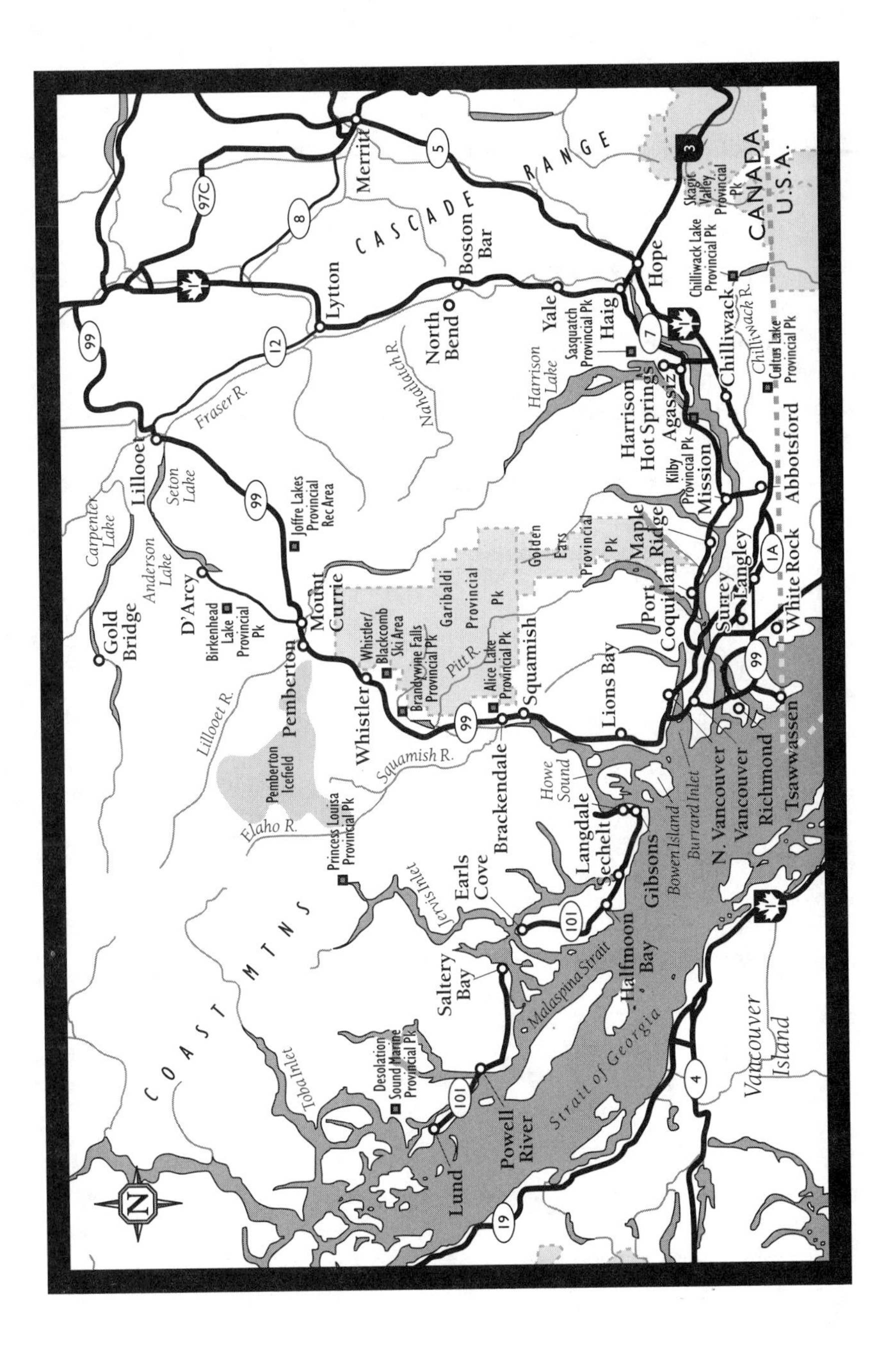

Lower Mainland

Greater Vancouver 3

The Fraser Estuary 40

The Fraser Valley 61

The North Shore 107

Whistler and the Sea to Sky Highway 142

Pemberton and Lillooet 189

The Sunshine Coast 208

Greater Vancouver

Vancouver, Burnaby, New Westminster, Port Moody, and Belcarra, including Stanley Park, and Pacific Spirit and Belcarra Regional Parks.

About the only thing Vancouverites seem to enjoy doing more than being outside is complaining about the weather. If you can't take a joke, why live in the rain forest? As for the price residents pay to live here, it helps to think of Vancouver as a destination resort. Fortunately, one of the trade-offs for paying your dues in "Lotus Land" is the wonderful array of public gardens, parks, and beaches where residents and visitors alike frolic. You can always count on there being enough room for you to play somewhere around town. Here are a few pointers on where to find the action, and where to avoid the crowds.

To begin, it's important to understand the layout of the city. In 1792, when Captain Vancouver first sailed into English Bay and Burrard Inlet, he found a sheltered, deep-water harbour. (One discovery he overlooked was the mouth of the Fraser River. That remained hidden from Europeans until Simon Fraser and his crew of transcontinental adventurers completed their voyage to the Pacific Ocean by canoe in 1808.)

Not long ago, it used to be easy to distinguish Vancouver from its neighbours. Bridges spanned Burrard Inlet and the Fraser River to connect with communities to the north and south, while buffer zones of undeveloped land defined where the "Big Smoke" left off and all else to the east began. By the 1970s, such distinctions had blurred to the point where one hardly noticed a transition from one city to the next, particularly between Vancouver, Burnaby, New Westminster, and Port Moody. Today, Vancouver is just one swatch in a quilt of 23 cities, municipalities, villages, districts, and even a township. Although each still maintains its own history, flavour, and relative autonomy, together they form the Greater Vancouver Regional District (GVRD).

There is a vast amount of green spaces and outdoor activities to take advantage of in this little corner of the province. From Bowen Island (prosaically called Electoral Area C in government-ese) to Matsqui, the GVRD covers a swath of land 30 miles (50 km) long from the Strait of Georgia east into the Fraser Valley, and about the same distance wide from the North Shore Mountains to the Canada-US border. Among its many duties, the GVRD stewards 22 parks that range in size from diminutive Grant Narrows to massive Lynn Headwaters. Include the GVRD's Seymour Demonstration Forest in the tally, and the total protected area is more than 41,480 acres (16 800 ha). At the same time, BC Parks, the provincial parks department, also maintains a considerable presence around Greater Vancouver. For example, Cypress Provincial Park in West Vancouver is the busiest in the province, hosting more than a million visitors a year. The range of activities that visitors can pursue inside these parks encompasses all possible modes of exploration—biking, fishing, hiking, skiing, paddling, swimming—even driving!

Many people—residents and visitors alike—view Greater Vancouver as a staging area for adventures in the wilder territories of the province. This region contains one of the most urbanized areas in Canada, with all the attendant benefits and drawbacks that implies. Even so, it's surprisingly easy to get around the metropolitan core, which teems with parks, beaches, and cycling and walking destinations. On every corner, it seems, there is a pocket of green space. In the midst of concrete and glass will be an oasis of trees and grass. From the famous Stanley Park to the infamous Wreck Beach, Vancouver is awash with outdoor possibilities. Add to that its world-class restaurants and attractions, and you have enough activities to keep you in this corner of the universe forever. Vancouver is one of the most desirable cities on the planet to explore. It's time you checked it out for yourself.

Getting There

Greater Vancouver occupies the southwestern corner of British Columbia. The Canada-US border marks the southern boundary line. Travellers clear customs from Washington State into British Columbia at any of four locations (Canada Customs, (604) 666-0545 or (800) 461-9999 in Canada only; US Customs, (360) 332-5771). The busiest locations are the two crossings in Blaine, Washington, where Interstate 5 links with Highway 99 at the Peace Arch crossing and leads north into Vancouver, a distance of 30 miles (50 km).

Nearby, a short distance east of Peace Arch, is the crossing at Douglas. Follow well-signed Highway 15 north to Highway 99 via Eighth Avenue. A third crossing is located north of Bellingham at the junction of Washington's Highway 539 and British Columbia's Highway 13, just south of Aldergrove in the Fraser Valley. Farther east, Washington's Highway 9 links with British Columbia's Highway 11 at the Sumas/Huntingdon crossing just south of Abbotsford, also in the Fraser Valley. BC Ferries, (604) 277-0277 or (888) 223-3779 in Canada only, sails from Swartz Bay on Vancouver Island to Tsawwassen in Delta, and from Nanaimo to Horseshoe Bay in West Vancouver. Crossing time is under 2 hours and Vancouver is a 30- to 45-minute drive from either terminal. Approach the Lower Mainland from the east on Highway 3 (Route of the Crow) from Princeton, or Highway 5 from Merritt. From the north, take either Highway 1 (Trans-Canada Highway) west from Kamloops, or Highway 99 south from Highway 97 near Cache Creek.

Airline passengers arrive at the Vancouver International Airport, (604) 276-6101, on Sea Island in Richmond. Vancouver lies on the north side of the Fraser River's North Arm, adjacent to the airport, and is easily reached via the Arthur Laing Bridge. Bus and train passengers arrive at the Pacific Central station located in downtown Vancouver at 1150 Main Street. Public transportation is available from both terminals. BC Transit, (604) 521-0400, encompasses Vancouver's bus system, as well as SkyTrain, an elevated light-rail rapid-transit system, and SeaBus, catamarans that shuttle passengers between downtown and the North Shore. Fares range from $1.50 (one zone) to $3 (three zones), and bus transfers are available for SeaBus or SkyTrain.

Adjoining Areas

NORTH: **The North Shore**

SOUTH: **The Fraser Estuary**

EAST: **The Fraser Valley**

WEST: **Southern Gulf Islands; Greater Victoria**

inside out

Parks

Stanley Park

Vancouver wouldn't be half the city that it is without its extensive roster of parks and gardens. Stanley Park is the centrepiece, one of the largest parks (1,000 acre/405 ha) in any urban centre in North America. For many residents, the park is the green heart that beats in the core of urbanity, the ecological holdout amid glass and concrete. Situated on a peninsula and surrounded on three sides by water, its popularity is both a blessing and a curse. After all, Vancouver's fame as one of the most beautiful cities in the world is tied to Stanley Park's popularity. But visitors looking to get away from the madding crowd for a brief while will often find thousands of others in Stanley Park looking to do the same. It is not a refuge so much as a showcase for the natural beauty that surrounds the city, a quasi-wilderness for those who like nature to be well tended. The **Vancouver Parks and Recreation Board** offices are headquartered in Stanley Park at 2099 Beach Ave, (604) 257-8400, a good place to pick up maps and information on this and all of the city's parks.

So firmly is love for Stanley Park rooted in the citizenry's soul that in an annual survey carried out by the *Georgia Straight*, a free weekly paper, readers repeatedly choose the park as the best place in town to take a romantic stroll, watch the rain fall, experience bliss, have sex, break up, and take visitors. It's certainly got our vote as one of Vancouver's best outdoor places to write about! As well, readers voted the park the best local tourist attraction, the second-best place to be in an earthquake, and the third-best place to get married.

What all this heady praise really testifies to is the park's miraculous ability to absorb and reward visitors while being situated adjacent to the West End, one of the most densely populated neighbourhoods in North America. True, you will meet others as you make your way around the perimeter on the park's 6.5-mile (10.5-km)-long **seawall,** or on the trails that cross through its dense rain-forest interior. Still, it's the very best we offer.

Miles of wide gravel paths lead through the wilder sections of the park and around **Beaver Lake** and **Lost Lagoon,** resting places for hundreds of migratory birds such as Canada geese, swans, and ducks. Many enjoy the park's ambience so much that, once here, they never leave. The park is also home to large populations of raccoons, squirrels, skunks, and coyotes. The raccoons and squirrels are used to the large crowds of people and habituated to handouts, despite numerous notices that warn visitors *not* to feed the animals.

Height is not Stanley Park's long suit. **Prospect Point** is a mere 210 feet (64 m) above sea level, so expect an easy go of it along the majority of paths and trails. Even the most fleet-footed, intrepid explorer will need at least a day to see everything the park has to offer. If possible, time your visit for earlier or later in the day, particularly on hot summer weekends. You'll find far fewer people in the park at these off-peak times. As well, begin exploring from some of the more remote areas of the park, such as the segment of the seawall to the east of the Lions Gate Bridge near

Prospect Point. (If you arrive by car, you'll find ample roadside parking here.) Walk west to **Third Beach** on the seawall, then back to Prospect Point following the well-marked forest trails (on the way back, watch for a giant hollow red cedar 56 feet/17 m around). The views of the inner and outer harbour and the **North Shore** are superb along this section. As you pass under the bridge, look up at the orderly columns of volcanic basalt on the hillside of Prospect Point, rising sharply above. This is a reminder of the region's turbulent past at the end of the most recent ice age, about 10,000 years ago. Small distance markers along the seawall keep you posted on your progress. **Lions Gate Bridge** (kilometre 5) is approximately the halfway point around the park's perimeter. Other markers to watch for between here and Third Beach include the final stone that completed construction of the seawall on September 26, 1971. A plaque affixed to the hillside near Siwash Rock honours James Cunningham, the single-minded master mason who dedicated 32 years of his life to the construction of the seawall from 1931 until his retirement in 1963. Numerous park benches along the seawall provide places to rest and enjoy the views. Occasionally, a harbour seal will haul up on one of the nearby rocks and sit as still as a piece of sculpture.

Although there are dozens of places where the seawall can be accessed around the rim of the park, if you're exploring **by bike** or on in-line skates, you should begin at the southeast corner of the park off Georgia St. Because of the popularity and the sheer number of people who go forth around the Stanley Park seawall's 10.5-km pathway, bike and in-line skate circulation is restricted to a counterclockwise direction. The seawall has many points of interest along the way, including Deadman's Island, the Nine O'clock Gun (whose loud report can be heard throughout much of the city), the Brockton Point Lighthouse, the *Girl in a Wet Suit* sculpture, the *Empress of Japan* figurehead, Prospect Point, and **Siwash Rock,** an offshore monolith that the Squamish people who once lived in Stanley Park believe to be a symbol of "clean fatherhood."

A Squamish legend, told to Mohawk poet Pauline Johnson-Tekahionwake by Chief Joe Capilano in the early years of the 20th century, has it that a young chief and his wife came to Prospect Point for the birth of their child. In order to be clean and vicariously impart purity to their baby, the couple went swimming in the ocean. Custom deemed that only when they were so clean that wild animals could not detect their scent were they fit to be parents. When the mother went ashore to give birth, her husband remained in the water. As the chief continued to swim, a canoe with four supernatural giants (the Transformers, emissaries of Tyee, the Creator) came upon him. When asked to move out of their way, the chief refused for the sake of his unborn child. The four, who were impressed by the chief's fearless commitment, transformed him into Siwash Rock to stand as a permanent example of "clean fatherhood." So that he not be separated from his wife and child, the Transformers changed them into two rocks, a larger one side-by-side with a smaller, which is in the forested hillside above Siwash Rock.

If you'd like to clean up *your* act, the **west side of the peninsula,** from Siwash Rock to the southwest corner of the park at Denman St, features three popular ocean beaches (see Beaches, below). By midsummer the water is usually delightfully warm.

Typical of urban green spaces, Stanley Park is dotted with man-made attractions, including the Vancouver Aquarium, a pitch-and-putt **golf course,** (604) 681-8847, **tennis courts,** aging totem poles at Brockton Point, as well as monuments to England's Lord Stanley (for whom the park is named), Queen Victoria, and Scottish poet-laureate Robbie Burns, and a cairn that contains the ashes of legend-gatherer Pauline Johnson-Tekahionwake. Natural wonders include **towering trees** (Canada's tallest bigleaf maple and red alder both grow within the park) and acres of well-kept **gardens,** including over 3,000 types of roses.

Bordering the south side of the park, particularly along Denman St, is an area rife with coffee shops and bike and in-line-skates rental emporiums, occasionally all rolled into one! Among the major routes in the West End that lead directly to Stanley Park are Georgia, Robson, Nelson, and Davie Sts, and Beach Ave. **By car,** the park is best reached from either Georgia St or Beach Ave, though finding parking once you get there is often more challenging than it's worth. One alternative is to catch the #19 Stanley Park **bus** that deposits riders at the Georgia St entrance to the park. The #3 and #8 buses drop passengers near the park at the corner of Robson and Denman Sts. All these routes connect with the Main St Sky-Train station. On weekends and holidays from April to October the #52 **Around the Park** bus provides hourly service between 10am and 7pm to points along the scenic road that circles the park. Call (604) 521-0400 for more information on all bus routes.

Other Parks

Stanley Park's "counterpark" in Vancouver is **Queen Elizabeth Park,** (604) 257-8400. While Stanley Park is at sea level, surrounded on three sides by water, Queen Elizabeth is completely landlocked, sitting atop the so-called Little Mountain, an extinct volcano and the **highest point in Vancouver** at 500 feet (150 m). From here, visitors have sweeping views in all directions across the city to such faraway places as Mount Baker to the southeast, the Gulf and San Juan Islands to the southwest, Vancouver Island to the west, and the Coast Mountains to the north. This 131-acre

(53-ha) park is home to the **Bloedel Floral Conservatory,** (604) 257-8584, a triodetic domed greenhouse that resembles a steel and Plexiglas cherry atop a sundae. A well-groomed array of colourful flowers occupies the cone of the ancient volcano. It is quite deservedly the most popular spot for wedding photos in Vancouver. Pathways circle the park, but it is best known as a place to revel in the cultivated beauty of the conservatory, or engage in recreational activities like tennis, disc golf (played with a Frisbee), and pitch-and-putt, (604) 874-8336. When it snows, the slopes of the little mountain become a toboggan haven. The park is spread out between 33rd and 37th Aves, and between Main and Cambie Sts.

Vanier Park, (604) 257-8400), in Vancouver's Kitsilano Point neighbourhood, is the home of the Vancouver Maritime Museum, the H. R. MacMillan Planetarium, and the Centennial Museum. From early spring until fall, Vanier Park's open fields west of the Burrard Bridge attract **kite fliers.** The Vancouver Children's Festival is staged here during the last week of May, as is a summer-long Shakespearean festival, Bard on the Beach. Large tents are erected to house the performances at both **festivals.** The main entrance to the park is located on Chestnut St north of Cornwall Ave.

Tucked away on the north side of False Creek is **Discovery Park** on Pacific Blvd beside the Plaza of Nations. The park was opened with fanfare that far outweighed its size in April 1986, at the beginning of the World Exposition held in Vancouver that year. Today, this little gem sprouts up on the east side of one of the last remaining structures from Expo 86, the BC Pavilion. A tranquillity prevails here unlike anywhere else downtown, with the obvious exception of Stanley Park. It must be the presence of so many **trees and shrubs** native to the province that does it—red cedar, western hemlock, Douglas fir, vine maple, and alder push up to heights of almost 60 feet (20 m). A perimeter of evergreen and deciduous trees shelters the winding pathway that leads past rhododendron, azalea, holly, fern, and even devil's club. Water hasn't flowed in the rock-walled streambed that descends through the middle of the park since Expo closed; the little sandbar in its middle is a soft place to sit and listen to the wind whistle in the boughs. Shafts of sunlight find their way through the dense canopy, illuminating the park's sheltered east point. One of the park's most delightful features is that visitors almost always have it to themselves.

The largest green space in Vancouver is located in **Pacific Spirit Regional Park,** which adjoins the University of British Columbia (UBC) on the city's west side at Point Grey. Although the 1,885-acre (763-ha) park is still in its "formative" stage, visitors have been enjoying its trails and beaches for decades before its designation as a Greater Vancouver regional park in 1989. (Prior to the creation of the park, this area was considered part of the UBC Endowment Lands; longtime residents still refer to it as such.) Pacific Spirit Park is particularly popular with cyclists, as well as dog owners, horseback riders, joggers, walkers, and bathers. The explosive popularity of mountain biking in the 1980s suddenly brought cyclists into conflict with those partaking in the more traditional ways of exploring the park. The park managers have tried to mitigate the problem by designating certain trails as multi-use and others exclusively for walking and hiking. Currently, there are **21 miles (35 km) of mixed-use trails,** and a further 12 miles (18 km) for foot traffic. Most trails are gentle and offer visitors the opportunity of a quick getaway from the pace of the city.

Within minutes of entering Pacific Spirit Park, visitors find themselves in another realm. Although this land was exhaustively logged in the early part of the 20th century, much of the forest has regenerated into a rich mix of coniferous and deciduous trees. A hush falls upon the place as you explore its lush interior. A dozen varieties of ferns carpet the forest floor. Underfoot, decades of accumulated mulch softens your steps. Choose from over 30 trails that crisscross the park like a game of Snakes and Ladders. Some, such as the **Sword Fern Trail,** run for almost the entire length of the park.

One of the park's most interesting natural features is **Camosun Bog,** a remnant of the most recent ice age. Bogs generally are an undervalued resource and act as the lungs and kidneys of the earth, cleansing the atmosphere by capturing and storing carbon in peat moss. Until recently, the draining of land adjacent to the bog for development caused the water level in Camosun Bog to decline. A group called Friends of Camosun Bog has made efforts to stabilize the bog's health and promote increased awareness of its invaluable contribution to city residents. A system of boardwalks allow visitors to tour the bog and enjoy the delicacy of this specialized environment, where the western bog laurel's pink flowers intermingle with the stiff green leaves of Labrador tea.

Native settlement in Pacific Spirit Park has been carbon-dated to 3,000 years ago. All of the park lies within the traditional home of the X'muzk'i'um, or Musqueam nation. Over the millennia, they've watched the river delta take shape from their riverfront homes. When they first settled here, Sea Island had not yet formed. Today, it's the site of the Vancouver International Airport. For an insight into the richness of the cultural heritage of the tribe, visit the nearby UBC Museum of Anthropology (see Attractions, below) beside Gate 4 on Marine Dr.

The best way to approach the park is to make your way to its centre, on 16th Ave just west of Blanca St. There's plenty of parking here. You can just as easily take the #25 UBC bus, which stops next to the park centre at

4915 W 16th Ave, a short distance west of Blanca St. Pick up a trail map here and begin exploring. For more information on the park call (604) 224-5739.

True to its name, **Central Park** is situated in a key location on the Burnaby side of Boundary Rd (the dividing line between Vancouver and Burnaby). The park is a popular place for tennis, jogging, pitch-and-putt, cycling, picnicking, or just wandering about. The numerous paths make the 222-acre (90-ha) green space seem larger than it actually is. A dense stand of towering Douglas fir blocks most of the noise from the three main thoroughfares that constitute the park's north, south, and west borders. Central Park is located in the rectangle formed by Boundary Rd, Kingsway, Patterson Ave, and Imperial St. Parking lots are located off all roads except Patterson Ave, where street parking is allowed. For more information, call (604) 294-7450.

City planners around the Lower Mainland seem to have deliberately placed parks bordering on major roads, perhaps to attract passersby, perhaps to contrast the natural and the artificial. For instance, Hwy 1 (the Trans-Canada Highway) runs through Burnaby's largest green space, formed by Deer Lake Park, Burnaby Lake Regional Park, and Robert Burnaby Park. **Deer Lake Park** was once a popular swimming destination, but poor water quality has forced the Burnaby Parks Board to keep the area closed for nearly a decade. Still, it is an attractive picnic area or a good place to drift about in a canoe, rowboat, or sailboat for a few hours. (A Squamish legend tells of an underground river that runs from Deer Lake to False Creek.) The Deer Lake area is home to the Burnaby City Hall (including the **Burnaby Parks and Recreation Dept** at 101-4946 Canada Way, (604) 294-7450, a good place to pick up maps and information on municipal parks), the Shadbolt Centre for the Arts, the Burnaby Village Museum, and the local Royal Canadian Mounted Police (RCMP) detachment. Parking is off Sperling Ave. Deer Lake Park has a pleasant, grassy picnic location: one look at the lake is enough to cool anyone down. Too bad there's no swimming. **Robert Burnaby Park** is located about a mile (1.5 km) east of Deer Lake. A good place to start stretching your legs is at the corner of Edmonds and Fourth Sts, at the southwest corner of the park.

Burnaby Lake Regional Park is on the north side of Hwy 1 across from Deer Lake, and is a blend of highly developed recreational facilities alongside a completely undeveloped wildlife sanctuary. Special features in this 740-acre (300-ha) park include both the Nature House (open mid-May to Labour Day), and a BC Wildlife Watch viewing tower at the Piper Ave entrance. A easygoing 6-mile (10-km) walking trail circles the lake. There are three main access points to Burnaby Lake park, including two off Winston Ave and another off Sperling Ave. All are well marked. For more information on Burnaby Lake Regional Park, call (604) 520-6442.

Queen's Park, in New Westminster, is located on the site of a converted fairground and is as old as Stanley Park. The fact that it doesn't receive the same recognition as a destination makes it even more valued by local residents. Although not as large as Stanley Park, it features a number of similar attractions, including a water park for the kids, a petting zoo, sports and picnicking facilities, and beautifully groomed gardens to wander through. Queen's Park is bordered by Sixth and Royal Aves, McBride Blvd, and First St. For more information, call New Westminster Parks and Recreation, (604) 526-4811.

Beaches

Although there are some lovely beaches along a 10-mile (16-km) stretch of Vancouver's outer harbour, principally along English Bay, many of them have come into being only in this century. Some, like Wreck Beach, Spanish Banks Beach, Locarno Beach, and Jericho Beach on Vancouver's west side, receive regular deposits of sand courtesy of the Fraser River's silt-laden plume, which arches around Point Grey into English Bay. Sand has been trucked in to create the beaches in the West End on English Bay, including those in Stanley Park. For summer information on all Vancouver beaches, call (604) 738-8535, June to September.

The sand at Stanley Park's **Third Beach** is noticeably coarser and brighter in texture and colour than at either **First or Second Beach.** A large, freshwater swimming pool is located next to Second Beach. All three beaches are located on the west side of Stanley Park, just off Stanley Park Dr.

Of all the outdoor swimming areas in Vancouver, **Kitsilano Beach** is one of the most festive. Kitsilano Beach Park's enormous, heated, saltwater pool stands outdoors beside a wide stretch of beach opposite Cornwall Ave. On bright summer days the atmosphere at Kits pool is one of controlled frenzy, while action on the beach is more characteristically mellow, a reflection of this neighbourhood's laid-back reputation. More than a dozen volleyball courts and nets are arranged on the beach. Both organized and informal games rule here in the heat. As at all city beaches, there are hot showers and change rooms. Located on the north side of Cornwall St between Arbutus and Vine Aves, Kits Beach also features several dozen tennis courts. Most visitors like to congregate in this area. However, the farther north you walk along the broad beach, the less crowded it becomes. A tall stand of trees shades nearby **Kitsilano Point** at the north end of Arbutus St, the best place to picnic in hot weather. Splash in the modest surf while the barbeque fires up. Kits Point is also a prime spot to watch the international fireworks competition held in July on English Bay. At such times the Kits Point neighbourhood (as well as much of the West End) is closed to vehicle traffic. Come early in the evening to get a good view. Rounding Kitsilano Point, the beach continues east to Vanier Park (see Parks, above).

Jericho Beach Park, Locarno Beach, and Spanish Banks Beach might well be considered as one since they connect to each other along Point Grey's 3.7-mile (6-km) shoreline. For the past two decades, the three-day **Vancouver Folk Festival** has been held in July in **Jericho Beach Park**'s lush, weeping willow–draped grounds. During the day, musicians from around the world entertain on small stages in intimate settings. Passersby can tune in for free to the evening performances held on the main stage, as amplified melodies waft over the security fence and onto the beach. Just park yourself on one of the driftwood logs that dot the beach and revel in the waves—wave lengths, that is—which don't recognize any borders. Farther west lie tennis courts, a viewing pier that attracts anglers and crab fishers, and the Jericho Sailing Centre (see Kayaking/Canoeing, below). Watch for the wild bunnies of Kitsilano, which make the bramble bushes on the hillside above the beach their home. They play a constant game of "catch me if you can" with the local coyotes. Jericho Beach is easily reached from Fourth Ave west of Alma St in the Point Grey neighbourhood. Just west of Jericho, Fourth Ave heads uphill towards UBC while NW Marine Dr leads downhill to Locarno and Spanish Banks. The two roads reconnect at the UBC campus. The #4 bus travels this route.

Locarno Beach begins just north of the Jericho Sailing Centre. A pedestrian and cycle path runs beside the beach from here west to **Spanish Banks Beach.** If you're looking for seclusion, there are more tucked-away places along Spanish Banks' sheltered beach than at Locarno's open expanse.

When the tide goes out between Jericho and Spanish Banks, it goes *way* out. This is a good place to explore the sand flats and get a closer look at the freighters anchored offshore. At low tide, skim boarders gather here to play in the tide pools.

At this point the forest closes in as the hillside begins to rise towards the University of British Columbia. The border of Pacific Spirit Regional Park lies on the south side of Marine Dr. Pacific Spirit Park's corridor of protected land (see Parks, above) stretches from the North Arm of the Fraser River to **Acadia Beach** at the mouth of English Bay. In addition to its forested environment, a shoreline perimeter of rock, pebble, and sand beach rings Point Grey between Acadia Beach and Wreck Beach.

The atmosphere is definitely different at **Wreck Beach,** Vancouver's official clothing-optional beach. "Bare as you dare" is the byword here, and most bathers wear little more than smiles and sunscreen. Owing to the steep hillside that surmounts the beach, visitors have to make their way down to it from Marine Dr at one of three approaches on the UBC campus: Trail 3, Trail 4, or Trail 6 (the numbers correspond to the entrance gates to the university along Marine Dr, which encircles the university). Allow 10 minutes to make the descent, which is often slippery at wet times of the year. Trail 6 leads to the kookier part of the beach, where at the height of summer strolling, vendors proffer a variety of mood-altering substances, from frozen daiquiris to headier fare. Traditionalists will enjoy the more tranquil side of Wreck Beach, reached via Trails 3 and 4. (Note: "Wrecked" Beach is regularly patrolled by members of UBC's Royal Canadian Mounted Police detachment.)

You can also walk around to Wreck Beach from Spanish Banks. It's a lengthy stroll, made more difficult by the soft sand and piles of driftwood, particularly when the ocean crowds up against the hillside at high tide. Along the way you'll pass an old concrete gun emplacement, left over from defence preparations during World War II. The views from the beach, and from some opened sections of trail in the forest, are of the Coast Mountains as they run along the North Shore and along the Sunshine Coast. From Point Grey the views expand out across the Strait of Georgia towards Vancouver Island. The nature of the shoreline changes as it rounds the point and begins to follow the mudflats beside the North Arm of the Fraser River. **Booming Ground Trail** (3 miles/5 km return) follows the river from the UBC Gate 6 and 7 entrances east towards the Musqueam Indian Reserve. There's always plenty of activity to watch on the Fraser, from herons stalking the beach to a constant parade of boats, particularly on weekends. The occasional harbour seal will pop its head up to check you out. There's a tranquillity here and also a feeling of great release as the muddy Fraser rolls out into the strait, its momentum finally spent.

Burnaby's **Barnet Marine Park** is located on the site of an old logging community that flourished in the first half of the 20th century. All that remain are the massive concrete towers and a squat scrap burner hunkered on the broad beach. Burnaby has replaced the old wharfs with a pier from which visitors can scan Burrard Inlet for marine and birdlife. A large boomed-off swimming section fronts the hard-packed sandy beach. Picnic tables with barbeque stands are shaded by tall poplars. There's also a boat launch here (see Kayaking/Canoeing, below). A level pathway leads west of the park and runs for much of the distance towards the Ironworkers Memorial Second Narrows Bridge. It provides visitors to Barnet with a chance to walk or cycle on those overcast days when the beach is not the exclusive reason for visiting this charming site. To find the park, drive east from Vancouver on Hastings St towards Port Moody. This route leads to the

Barnet Hwy. In 1.6 miles (2.5 km) you'll see the signed entrance to Barnet Marine Park on your left. Thick foliage hides any view of the park from the road, and railway tracks obscure the shoreline. Park and walk across the tracks to reach the beach. (Note: Dogs are not allowed in the park.)

Although **Belcarra Regional Park and Buntzen Lake Recreation Area** are both located directly across Burrard Inlet from Barnet Marine Park, it will take you 30 minutes to drive around the end of the inlet to reach them. Follow Hastings St east through Burnaby to its junction with the Barnet Hwy, then east to Port Moody. As you enter Port Moody, turn left onto St. John's St; six stoplights later, turn left again onto well-marked Ioco Rd. In hot months the beaches at Belcarra's **Sasamat Lake** and at nearby Buntzen Lake are so popular that park information signs, which appear immediately after you turn onto Ioco Rd, will tell you if Belcarra and Buntzen are full. (You can probably sense this on a hot day before you even leave the house. On weekends, unless you get an early start for their beaches, look elsewhere for a destination.) Ioco Rd soon turns left at an intersection marked by a green GVRD sign pointing the way to Belcarra. The route to Buntzen lies straight ahead at this well-marked intersection along Heritage Mountain Rd.

Once at Sasamat Lake, follow the signs to White Pine Beach. There's plenty of parking here on a benchland above the sandy beach. There's one critical difference between this beach and nearby Buntzen Lake: although the sun shines equally warm on both, the water in Buntzen is far colder than in Sasamat.

There are two beaches at Buntzen Lake, one at each end. You can drive to South Beach, where there is a boat launch (nonmotorized only) but you'll have to paddle, or walk or cycle along a gated access road the 1.8 miles (3 km) from the parking lot to North Beach. Whereas South Beach has a gentle incline, the lake drops off sharply at North Beach. One of the lake's attractive features includes a small island offshore from South Beach, a magnet for stronger swimmers.

Vancouver and Burnaby both have beaches on the Fraser River's North Arm, and both are named **Fraser River Park** (see Hiking/Walking, below). Watching activity on the Fraser is the main attraction from both beaches. The beach at Burnaby's Fraser River Park lies at the south end of Byrne Rd off Marine Dr in Burnaby. Vancouver's lies at the corner of 75th and Angus. Although wading in the Fraser is refreshing, full immersion is a dicier proposition and not recommended.

Hiking/Walking

There's plenty of action afoot around Vancouver and neighbouring areas, especially in city parks and beaches (see Parks and Beaches, above). You can "walk till you drop" along the **Stanley Park Seawall** and along **Pacific Spirit Park**'s 33-mile (53-km) trail network, 12 miles (18 km) of which are set aside exclusively for those on foot. Vancouver's **Queen Elizabeth Park** and New Westminster's **Queen's Park** feature particularly eye-pleasing pathways bordered on all sides by intensely planted gardens. At certain times of the year the colours and perfumes are almost overwhelming.

Vancouver and Burnaby both have trails that run beside the Fraser River. Vancouver's **Fraser River Park** is located at the south end of Angus Dr and 75th Ave. Take 72nd Ave west of Granville St and watch for the large wooden sign that will direct you to the park. There's always plenty of activity on land, sea, and air to watch as you stroll the shoreline trail here (easy; 1 mile/0.6 km return). One of the most interesting features of the park has been the ongoing restoration of intertidal marshland. Interpretive signs explain the function of a system of weirs that regulate the flow of water through the park. Boardwalks and bridges lead beside the river and make walking a delightful pastime even in wet weather.

There are also river trails in Vancouver's **Riverfront** and **Gladstone-Elliot Parks,** as well as the paths in **Everett Crowley Park** (see Mountain Biking, below) just uphill from Riverfront. To find them, head along SE Marine to Kerr St, then south to Kent Ave. Park here and begin exploring Riverfront Park with its broad pier, twin walking/cycling/in-line skating trails (easy; about 4 miles/6 km return), a beach, and a children's play area. Walk west along this stretch of waterfront that eventually reaches Gladstone-Elliot Park, which has its own pier, perfect for river viewing.

One good stretch with a forested feeling is the **Burnaby River Trail** (easy; about 6 miles/10 km return). This hard-packed, cedar-lined dirt pathway runs east beside the river from the south foot of Boundary Rd near Marine Way towards New Westminster. Parking is available beside the trailhead on Boundary Rd. An alternate approach to the trail is at **Fraser River Park**, located at the south end of Byrne Rd off Marine Way. Here in the park, the log booms that line the shoreline beside much of the trail give way to a long stretch of open beach. One of the most attractive sights along the trail is Mount Baker's snow cone, framed by the spires and guy wires of two bridges, the Queensboro and the Pattullo. For more information on the trail and park, contact the Burnaby Parks and Recreation Department, (604) 294-7450.

The **Sasamat Lake Loop Trail** (easy; 1.5 miles/2.5 km return) circles

Belcarra Regional Park's Sasamat Lake (see Beaches, above). Follow it around from White Pine Beach as it leads south to a floating boardwalk that crosses the lake. Two small docks for fishing and swimming are located along the walkway. The road that leads to the heart of Belcarra Park begins just before Sasamat Lake. Follow the signs to reach the main parking area. Detailed maps of Belcarra Regional Park are available year-round from the park's concession stand nearby. (Note: There is no public parking in the village of Belcarra, so it is imperative to follow the road that leads to the park's main parking area.) Belcarra has a tradition of being a summer picnic destination. Boats once brought day trippers from Vancouver's Coal Harbour to Belcarra for the day. Belcarra's picnic area has reservable picnic shelters and even a reservable wharf. Call (604) 432-6352 for more information. **Admiralty Point Trail** (easy; 3 miles/5 km return) begins from the main parking lot and heads south through second-growth forest and over a naturally cobblestoned trail to several good viewpoints. A 30-minute walk will have you at Admiralty Point and the Maple Beach picnic area. Even on cloudy days you'll find the open shoreline on Burrard Inlet is bright. Rocky outcroppings occur at points like Cod Rock, a perfect place to sit and watch the tide. Besides the view of Barnet and Mount Burnaby, you can also see Cates Park and Deep Cove to the west, and Mount Seymour rising above the entrance to Indian Arm, a fjord that stretches 11 miles (18 km) north. **Cod Rock Trail** (moderate; 4 miles/7 km return) leads inland through tall second-growth forest from Cod Rock to Sasamat Lake and links with the Sasamat Lake Loop Trail (see above). Yet another pathway, the **Jug Island Trail** (moderate; 3 miles/5 km return), begins beside the covered picnic shelter in the heart of the park. Much of the way along the trail is either up or downhill, with a series of wooden staircases for assistance in the steepest sections. Although there are few views along the way, there is a branch of the trail that leads out to an opening beside Bedwell Bay. From here you look east to the slopes of Eagle Ridge and the broad flank of Coquitlam Mountain. Depending on your pace it will take you between 30 and 45 minutes to reach pleasant cobble-and-sand **Jug Island Beach** from the Belcarra picnic grounds. (Jug Island actually lies offshore at the north end of a narrow peninsula.) For more information on Belcarra park's trail, phone (604) 432-6359.

Cycling/In-Line Skating

The character of a city is often defined by the vision of exceptional individuals. One of Vancouver's first park commissioners, Matthew Logan, championed the idea of a pedestrian seawall that would eventually ring the entire harbour, from Stanley Park to False Creek. It took 55 years to complete (see Parks, above), and today there is an almost seamless route that covers much of the distance (about 12 miles/20 km), certainly more than most of us can traverse in the course of a morning or afternoon's outing. Each year the **Stanley Park Seawall** and the **Seaside Bikeway** are thronged with an ever-larger number of walkers, joggers, in-line skaters, and cyclists. Experiments in blending the various groups have yielded the present system, which with its restrictions is still less than satisfactory to all. Just take your time, exercise caution, and wear a smile and you'll do fine. Some stretches are busier than others. Unless you're an ardent people-watcher, see if you can adjust the time of your visit to avoid the crowds that predictably descend on the seawall on Sunday afternoons. Good starting points for exploring the seawall on wheels include Brockton Point in Stanley Park and First Ave between Cambie and Main Sts for the seaside bikeway. Parking is plentiful at both locations. Bikes and blades can be rented from a number of shops that border the park, including Action Rentals, 1793 Robson St, (604) 683-7044; Bayshore Bicycles and Rollerblade Rentals, 745 Denman St, (604) 688-2453; Bikes n' Blades Rentals, 718 Denman St, (604) 602-9899; Spokes Bicycle Rental, 1798 W Georgia St, (604) 688-5141; and Stanley Park Cycle, 1741 Robson St, (604) 608-1908.

One of the best places to begin exploring the paths in **Pacific Spirit Regional Park** (see Parks, above) is at the park headquarters at 4915 W 16th Ave, (604) 224-5739. You can pick up a free map here that will outline all the trail options available to walkers, cyclists, and even in-line skaters. You'll have to bring your off-road in-line skates with you, as most of the park trails are unpaved, although many are compact enough for skinny-tire cyclists to enjoy. A paved pathway does parallel much of 16th Ave as it passes through the park. (Off-road in-line skates are available for rent from Outa-line Inline Sports, 1231 Pacific Blvd, (604) 899-2257.)

For a cycle tour of Vancouver's **docks,** begin from the corner of Powell and Commissioner Sts in east Vancouver where the Princeton Hotel, established in the early 1900s, is one of the most prominent heritage establishments. Cycle north from the Princeton on Commissioner St, across the Canada Pacific Railroad (CPR) tracks. Past the container terminal—where cedar trees once stood so thickly, they concealed all view of the ocean—Commissioner is a largely untravelled waterfront street, with wide shoulders for cyclists to enjoy a long, lazy, rubber-necking, thirst-building ride. A boulevard of grass between the street and the rail line softens the environment on one side; a string of industrial and marine-related companies line the harbour on Commissioner's west side. Follow it far enough—a 1.5-mile (3-km) ramble—and you reach **New Brighton Park.** You'll find the entrance to it on Wall St. Go east of

Commissioner on Yale St, then Wall St, to New Brighton Park, the site of Hastings Mill, the first European settlement in Vancouver. Your reward for reaching the park will be one of the best views of the Lions from anywhere in Burrard Inlet. In summer, the park's open-air swimming pool is a big attraction for eastside families.

Rocky Point Park in Port Moody is a place that will appeal to those with wheels to spin. The distance from the Vancouver-Burnaby boundary to Port Moody is 9 miles (15 km), an easy 30-minute jaunt by car at off-peak times. Drive along St. John's St, Port Moody's main drag. Watch for signs that point to Rocky Point Park. Turn north on Moody St and follow it to an overpass that leads to the park. A scenic, paved pathway wraps itself around the east end of **Burrard Inlet** and runs for several miles to **Old Orchard Park.** Paralleling it is a pedestrian-only walkway through the park. Rocky Point Park also has a lengthy pier running out into the shallow waters of Burrard Inlet's eastern end. There's swimming here, both in the ocean and in a freshwater pool. A boardwalk section of the walking trail passes over a marshy area of Burrard Inlet around Rocky Point. In spring and fall this is an excellent location for bird-watching.

Other cycling trails of interest include the **7-11 Trail** (easy; 25 miles/40 km return) that follows the SkyTrain route between New Westminster and Vancouver's Clark Dr. Vancouver's **Riverfront Park** (see Hiking/Walking, above) has a lengthy, paved cycle and in-line skate pathway beside the mighty Fraser River. Throughout Vancouver, cyclists enjoy 30 designated bicycle commuter routes on streets such as Adanac, 37th Ave, and Point Grey Rd (all east-west), and Ontario, Heather, and Cypress (all north-south). Cyclists and in-line skaters also benefit from designated sections of sidewalk when crossing the Burrard and Cambie Bridges. The best guide to cycling in Vancouver is the GVRD Commuter Cycling map. Call (604) 432-6375 to request a free copy. The map also provides useful urban cycling information on bridges, tunnels, and ferries throughout Greater Vancouver. Another good source of information on cycling around Vancouver is Better Environmentally Sound Transportation (BEST), a non-profit organization located at Terminal and Main Sts under the Main St SkyTrain station, 195 Terminal, (604) 669-2453. Other useful contacts include the Bicycle Hotline (City of Vancouver only), (604) 871-6070; Cycling BC, (604) 737-3034; and the Cycling BC Hotline (special events and race information), (604) 290-0455.

Mountain Biking

Although the seat of extreme mountain biking lies just across the Lions Gate and Second Narrows Bridges from Vancouver and Burnaby on the

North Shore, Vancouver itself has very little in the way of challenging fat-tire trails, aside from those in **Pacific Spirit Regional Park** (see Parks, above).

Everett Crowley Park is located in Vancouver's Champlain Heights neighbourhood. Although the park has been in existence only since 1987, it has already gained a reputation as a place to ride a bike, be it skinny tire, fat tire, or BMX. In July 1997, the park served as the venue for the mountain-bike races for the BC Summer Games. Burnaby actually won the right to host the games, but as cycling is prohibited in all its parks, the city refused to sanction a location for the mountain-biking events, even though, for example, Burnaby Mountain is a latticework of trails and would have made the ideal choice. In casting about for a site as close to Burnaby as possible, games organizers arranged for the use of Everett Crowley Park, which lies just a few handlebar lengths inside Vancouver near Boundary Rd and SE Marine Dr. Named after the founder of Avalon Dairy, who was also president of the Vancouver Parks Board in the 1960s, the park occupies what for years was the Kerr Rd dumpsite and is splendidly overgrown with brambles and alder. The focal point of the park for mountain bikers is a steep-sided mound of compacted soil dubbed Mount Everett. As seen from the top of this lone, cone-shaped promontory, Boundary Bay's intertidal surface glitters to the south. To the west across the Strait of Georgia, the ghostly forms of Malahat Ridge on Vancouver Island seem pencilled into the horizon. Not far below, the Fraser River flows by, flat as a plate. The mound is treetop tall and is covered in Scotch broom. There is an interesting demarcation that can only be discerned from the top of the mound. Most of the open ground below is completely overgrown with evergreen blackberry, which meets the forest head-to-head but goes no further. It makes you wonder if there is an eternal contest between the two to gain the upper hand. The single-track bike trails that weave through the thickets leave little room for pilot error. If you were to tumble into the blackberries, you'd burn for sure.

Easy riders (and easy walkers) don't have to concern themselves with suffering a similar fate. The bark-mulched pathways are broad and level, and loop around the 96-acre (39-ha) park, touching on several viewpoints along the way. At one, a handmade sign nailed to an old tree trunk points to Mount Baker. You'll find enough trails in Everett Crowley Park to keep you content for more than one visit. If you aren't completely satisfied, bike a short distance downhill on Kerr St to Riverfront Park (see Hiking/Walking, above). You can see the park's piers, which jut out into the Fraser from Everett Crowley. Bike paths run a long way west beside the river but provide little of the views that make its counterpart up the hill so special. The entrance to Everett Crowley Park is located on the east side of Kerr St near

E 63rd Ave across from Fraserview Golf Course. There's room for a dozen cars to park beside the unassuming trailhead. Riverfront Park is located nearby at the intersection of Kerr and Kent Ave E and extends west to Gladstone St.

The trails on **Burnaby Mountain** (elevation 1,340 feet/403 m) are not open to mountain bikes, but try telling that to the mountain bikers who regularly make their way along one of the dozens of trails that criss-cross the mountain. Its high usage stems in part from the fact that students attending Simon Fraser University at the top of Mount Burnaby want alternate paths up to and (especially) down from school other than the two roads that wend their way up Mount Burnaby (more often referred to as Burnaby Mountain): Gaglardi Way from the east, and Curtis St (which becomes University Dr) from the west.

The use of the challenging trails around **Buntzen Lake** (see Beaches, above) by those on mountain bikes is currently under discussion by a mixed group of hikers, equestrians, and mountain bikers. Some trails are open, such as the service road along the east side of the lake, while others aren't. The wheel's still in spin, as it were. For more information on Buntzen Lake and the mountain bike scene in general around Vancouver, contact **EMP (Extreme Mountainbike People),** a nonprofit organization dedicated to promoting healthy lifestyles through mountain biking and to developing, preserving, and restoring areas to ride; 5008 St. Catherines St, Vancouver, BC V5W 3E8, or email the organization at emp@ultranet.ca. Their Web site is http://members.xoom.com/emp.

Well-known local riders Joan Jones and Liz Earles are the directors of the **West Coast School of Mountain Biking,** which offers mountain-bike instruction on weekday evenings and weekend afternoons at a variety of community centres, including the Belcarra YMCA Outdoor Centre. This school is an excellent place to learn technique and find out more on the routes on the challenging north side of Burrard Inlet, directly across from Mount Burnaby. They also operate the West Coast Mountain Biking Club, which offers members guided monthly tours of all the hot spots. For more information, phone (604) 931-6066, or visit their Web site, home.bc.rogers.wave.ca/wcsmb.

There are so many good, knowledgeable, and friendly mountain-bike shops around Vancouver that it hardly seems fair to single any of them out. A good place to begin is on the Internet. Check out the mountain-bike listings at http://bcyellowpages.com for a complete listing of shops in Greater Vancouver and throughout the province. Among Vancouver's oldest bike retailers are **Caps Bicycle Stores,** which began in New Westminster in the 1930s and now have locations throughout Greater Vancouver, including their flagship store (with its heritage bike collection), 450 E

Columbia St, New Westminster, (604) 524-3611, and **West Point Cycles,** 3771 W 10th Ave, Vancouver, (604) 224-3536.

For a detailed description of the trails around Vancouver, see *Mountain Bike Trails in the Lower Mainland*, by Christine Boehringer, and *Mountain Biking British Columbia*, by Darrin Polischuk.

Kayaking/Canoeing

Burrard Inlet lies both west and east of Stanley Park's Prospect Point (see Parks, above) where it is spanned by the Lions Gate Bridge at First Narrows. This aging, three-laned structure connects Vancouver with North and West Vancouver. The inlet expands into Coal Harbour, where much of the commercial marine activity is centred. It contracts again at Second Narrows where the Ironworkers Memorial Second Narrows Bridge links Vancouver and Burnaby on the south with North Vancouver on the north. Just beyond Second Narrows, Burrard Inlet divides and branches east to Port Moody and north up Indian Arm, a slender, steep-sided fjord.

Vancouver's outer harbour is composed of English Bay and Burrard Inlet and acts as the holding area for large, oceangoing freighters. You often see as many as 20 ruddy-coloured ones floating high in the water as they await their turn to take on cargoes of prairie grain, lurid yellow sulfur, raw logs, sawdust, and finished lumber. When they come to load, each is guided to the inner harbour by a tugboat that possesses the muscle of a nightclub bouncer combined with the finesse of a maître'd. Their antics are fun to watch from a beach or the Stanley Park Seawall trail. All this heavyweight activity allows very little room for recreation in the inner harbour, other than the rowers, whose sculls venture out at dawn and sunset from the Vancouver Rowing Club in Stanley Park. Strong currents that churn through First Narrows restrict small boats to the calmer waters except at slack tide.

Burrard Inlet does make a concession to recreation—it's called **False Creek.** (In fact, False Creek is much more like a narrow bay. In England, the word "creek" applies to a small indentation on the coast. Since it was named by Captain Richards of the Royal Navy in the late 1850s, we'll have to live with it.) The ocean slips in under the Burrard Bridge and balloons past residential housing that in the past two decades has replaced the light industry that once soiled the shoreline. Gone are the battery recyclers with their lead and the barrel makers with their creosote. Ocean Cement is one of the last tenants of its kind here; its lease on Granville Island expires in 1999. The occasional tugboat still makes its way in and out of False Creek with a load of sand for the city works yard, but otherwise this sheltered backwater is the playground of kayakers and canoeists, and provides moorage for fishing boats at the federal dock and sheltered anchorage for sailboats. The Cambie Bridge arches above False Creek's midpoint. The polished stainless-steel dome of Science World marks the creek's eastern perimeter.

It's easy to think that False Creek has always been the watery playground of the inner city. Most evenings, primarily from April to October, the sheltered finger of Burrard Inlet teems with a mix of canoes, dragon boats, kayaks, sculls, sailboats, tugboats, and stinkpots. Until the 1986 World Exposition on Transportation was held on its north shore, however, False Creek had been shabbily treated for decades. Its condition today as one of the cleaner waterways in Vancouver is a testimony to the recuperative powers of nature. Come see for yourself. You can launch your own hand-carried boat from the wharf in front of the False Creek Community Centre, 1318 Cartwright St, (604) 257-8195, on Granville Island. Head for the loading zone beside the centre's Cartwright St entrance, then carry your boat past the tennis courts and down the ramp to Alder Bay. From here it's a steady 30-minute paddle to Science Centre at the east end of False Creek. It's an equally long paddle west to Sunset Beach in the West End, though through choppier waters as you cross beneath the Burrard Bridge. You can rent a kayak from EcoMarine Ocean Kayak Centre, 1668 Duranleau St, (604) 689-7575, one of several canoe and kayak stores on Granville Island. (EcoMarine also operates from the Jericho Sailing Centre, 1300 Discovery St off NW Marine Dr, (604) 224-4177, in Jericho Beach Park, from June to September.) If you have time, drop by **Feathercraft Products,** 1244 Cartwright St, close by the False Creek Community Centre, to admire their finely built folding kayaks.

Barnet Marine Park (see Beaches, above) has a paved driveway that can be used to launch canoes, kayaks, or sailboats in Burrard Inlet. No motorized boats can be launched from here. **Belcarra Regional Park** lies enticingly close across Burrard Inlet to the north. On a calm day, paddle over to explore the area around Belcarra's **Admiralty Point.** Just be mindful of the occasional large freighter that may be gliding slowly into one of the nearby oil terminals.

If you're looking for a place to begin a paddle on the **Fraser River,** Vancouver and Burnaby's **Fraser River Parks** (see Hiking/Walking, above) are two good sites to launch out onto the river in a hand-carried boat. If you have a day to spare, consider paddling between the two, a distance of about 7 miles (11 km) one way. In order to pull this off, you should arrange transportation between the two sites in advance. Leave a vehicle at each park or arrange to be picked up once you've completed your journey. The ideal time to run the Fraser is a Sunday morning when commercial traffic on the river's North Arm is light. On weekdays, tugboats and other large vessels create a mishmash of wakes that might swamp an open canoe. Enjoy a few quiet hours on the Fraser, and you'll thrill to the site of blue herons, sandpipers, and dabbling and diving waterfowl going about their business along the shore. A thrill of a different kind is experienced as you pass beneath all of the major bridges that link Vancouver and Burnaby with Lulu and Sea Islands (see The Fraser Estuary chapter). If you're fortunate to catch the tide flowing with you, a gentle current will carry you along. Check the tide tables in Vancouver's daily newspapers to determine the optimum time to make this journey. Allow six hours to make the trip one way. Places to go ashore for a break include Vancouver's **Riverfront** and **Gladstone-Elliot Parks** (see Hiking/Walking, above). For an abbreviated adventure, you can paddle between one of these parks and Burnaby's Fraser River Park, about 3 miles (5 km) round trip. You'll miss much of the activity around the bridges, but will be spared having to arrange land transportation between sites.

You can arrange to rent a canoe on **Buntzen Lake** (see Beaches, above) at the nearby Anmore Grocery, (604) 469-9928. There is a boat launch (nonmotorized only) at the park's South Beach.

Fishing

You'll need a saltwater fishing licence before you toss a line into the waters around Greater Vancouver. Licences are available at most sport-fishing stores, some of the better-known of which are **Ruddick's Fly Shops,** with two locations, 1654 Duranleau St, Granville Island, (604) 681-3747 (ask for Cathy Ruddick; she's as knowledgeable and as friendly as they come), and 3726 Canada Way, Burnaby, (604) 434-2420; and **Turner's Fly Shop,** 3519 Kingsway, (604) 434-7716, in east Vancouver. Perhaps the most respected source for information on fishing in Greater Vancouver is in Surrey, **Michael & Young Fly Shop,** 10484 137th St, (604) 588-2833. Call their free fly-fishing report for advice on the latest conditions, (604) 299-9000, extension 3597. Granville Island's **Maritime Market** in downtown Vancouver features numerous marine supply stores, principally on Duranleau St. **Granville Island Charter Centre,** 1808 Boatlift Lane, (604) 683-1447, offers guided fly-fishing and charter-boat fishing service from False Creek. **Granville Island Boat Rentals,** 1696 Duranleau St, (604) 682-6287, will set you up with a boat as well as arrange sportfishing charters for you. **Stanley Park Boat Rentals,** 1525 Coal Harbour Quay, (604) 682-6257, rents sportfishing boats for those who would like to explore angling in the inner harbour or the adjacent North Shore.

Anglers and crabbers use the dock at **Belcarra Regional Park** and the pier at **Jericho Beach** (see Beaches, above) as an excuse to spend some time in the outdoors. Water quality at both locations is often suspect, especially for its effect on bottom feeders, but this doesn't keep fishermen from enjoying their catch. Smelt fishers cast their filigree nets from the waters of Jericho and Kitsilano Beaches.

The seawall at Stanley Park (see Parks, above) is another popular angling location, particularly around the kilometre 6 marker at Siwash Rock. The water is sufficiently deep here to allow the possibility of landing a salmon, especially when a run of pinks returns to Burrard Inlet at the end of summer.

For general information on fishing regulations, contact the BC Fish and Wildlife Regional Office, (604) 582-5200 or (800) 665-7027.

Photography

Perhaps decades ago it was possible to tell where Vancouver left off and Burnaby began. Today, visitors seamlessly pass between the two cities. **Burnaby Mountain** (properly called Mount Burnaby) is Vancouver's eastern neighbour's tallest landmark. Simon Fraser University sits on top, a crucible of learning designed by architect Arthur Erickson (who also put his imprint on the Provincial Courthouse on Howe St and the Museum of Anthropology at the University of British Columbia). Simon Fraser's campus is surrounded by **Burnaby Mountain Park.** The park is a warren of trails that cut through deciduous second-growth forest. Most visitors come to visit the **Playground of the Gods,** a home away from home for 50 or so totem poles carved by Japanese artist Nubuo Toko and his son Shusheo. The Tokos are members of the Ainu culture, Japan's first inhabitants. Installed on the top of an open slope looking west over Coal Harbour, the poles honour the ties between Burnaby and its Japanese sister city, Kushiro. The spectacular setting inspired Toko to imagine it as Kamui Mintara, or Playground of the Gods. The poles represent the story of the gods who descended to earth to give birth to the Ainu. Animal spirits such as whale, bear, and owl adorn the tops of the slender poles that are bunched together in groups of twos and threes. A killer whale and a brooding raven stand apart from the rest, looking west across the Strait of Georgia towards Vancouver Island (and Japan). This is a stunningly beautiful setting, one of the best examples of art in a public place in the Lower Mainland. You'll want to photograph it, especially at sunrise or sunset, to take away with you as a memory of Vancouver. In June, a formal rose garden nearby perfumes the air and makes the environment appear even more like the Elysian Fields. A grassy slope descends the mountain below the totems, contributing to the open feeling of this part of the park. The most convenient way to reach Burnaby Mountain Park is on Centennial

Way as the highway climbs Mount Burnaby. The park is at the end of Centennial Way and is well marked. For a map and further information on the trails of Burnaby Mountain Park, call the Burnaby Parks and Recreation office, (604) 294-7450.

Sailing/Windsurfing

The winds and waves at **Jericho Beach** (see Beaches, above) have been familiar to local Native people for a mighty long time. Thick middens of clamshells on the nearby hills testify to where the Musqueam people once maintained a seasonal residence. Now wild bunnies and coyotes cavort among the brambles, while on the beach windsurfers and kayakers get their kicks being blown around. Jericho Beach is one of the few beaches in Vancouver where, on a big wave day, you run the risk of getting tumbled "in the washing machine," as they say in Hawaii. The Jericho Sailing Centre Association maintains an old Royal Canadian Air Force office building as a staging area for anyone wishing to swallow some seawater. The centre is located at 1300 Discovery off NW Marine Dr, (604) 224-4177; for sailing lessons, call (604) 731-5415, and for windsurfing lessons, (604) 224-0615.

Diving

Belcarra Regional Park (see Beaches, above) is the place to head for underwater exploration in Indian Arm. As well as wading in from the beach beside Belcarra's pier, there's a small street-end park at **Whiskey Cove** on Coombe Rd where divers also put in, located a 5-minute walk east of the picnic area. Other popular dive sites include nearby **Indian Arm Provincial Marine Park's Racoon and Twin Islands.** Farther up Indian Arm, **Croker Island,** a proposed regional park, is yet another. For more information, including excursions, contact Diversworld, (604) 732-1344; Rowand's Reef SCUBA Shop, (604) 669-3483; and the Diving Locker, (604) 736-2681, all of which are located in Vancouver.

outside in

Attractions

Vancouver is Canada's fastest-growing metropolis and a city of magical contradictions—from rough-and-tumble Hastings St, where timeworn brickwork still exudes a wild, beer-for-a-dime, seaport-town atmosphere, to trendy Robson St, with its futuristic Japanese noodle houses and haute couture. Vancouver has long touted itself as Canada's gateway to the

Pacific Rim, and for decades, waves of immigrants have broken on its shore. Vancouver, its residents are fond of saying, is one of the few cities in the world where you can go skiing and sailing on the same day. How remarkable, then, that it should also be one of the few where, sitting outside a Neapolitan cafe, you can eavesdrop on an impassioned argument in Hungarian and see graffiti in Khmer. The city seems living proof that a benign environment will produce an easygoing disposition. Below is a brief overview of the city; for a more in-depth look, refer to our complete city guide, *Vancouver Best Places*.

Visual arts. Vancouver is a festive city, and art is everywhere. Visitors who fly into Vancouver and enter through the international terminal building are greeted by an astounding display of the rich culture of the Musqueam people, the Coast Salish inhabitants of the lands around the airport. The focal point of the new terminal is pre-eminent Northwest Coast Native artist Bill Reid's magnificent bronze sculpture *The Spirit of Haida Gwaii, the Jade Canoe*, displayed on a bed of polished jade-coloured marble. Downtown, Francis Rattenbury's elegant old courthouse is now the Vancouver Art Gallery, which holds more than 20 major exhibitions a year and whose permanent collection includes works by Goya, Emily Carr, Gainsborough, and Picasso; 750 Hornby St, (604) 662-4719. Across the street from the VAG, tucked behind the impressive facade of Cathedral Place, is the Canadian Craft Museum, Canada's first national museum devoted to crafts; 639 Hornby St, (604) 687-8266. Many of the city's commercial galleries are located on the dozen blocks just south of the Granville Bridge; and Granville Island, site of the Emily Carr Institute of Art and Design, has a number of potteries and craft studios. The Museum of Anthropology at the University of British Columbia, 6393 NW Marine Dr, (604) 822-3825, has an extensive collection of artifacts from Native American cultures of coastal British Columbia (including an impressive display of totem poles), as well as artifacts from Africa and the Orient.

The main branch of the Vancouver Public Library is now located in the dramatic Library Square complex (Robson and Homer Sts, (604) 331-4000). Designed by world-renowned architect Moshe Safdie (he's also responsible for the Ford Centre across the street), the library is a marvel.

Shopping. Vancouver has always been bursting with storefronts. In Yaletown, brick warehouses have been transformed into chic shops that are the destination of choice when shopping for exciting and eccentric fashion for oneself and one's home. Robson St is the meeting place of cultures and couture, as *tout le monde* can be found strolling among its many boutiques and restaurants every day. Downtown is full of outstanding shops. In poor weather, head underground for the Pacific Centre and Vancouver Centre malls, with shops like Holt Renfrew, Eaton's, and The Bay.

South Granville, the area from the Granville Bridge in the north to 16th Ave in the south, is rich with an abundance of specialty shops full of high-end merchandise. At Granville Island Public Market, on the south shore of False Creek, you can get everything from just-caught salmon to packages of fresh herbs to a wonderful array of fresh produce. Or visit the lesser-known public market at Lonsdale Quay in North Vancouver, with two levels of shops and produce, right at the North Shore SeaBus terminal. (It's a 15-minute SeaBus ride from the terminal near Canada Place across Burrard Inlet.) Gastown is a restored 1890s precinct, once touristy, now anchored by some really good shops that are of use to locals as well. Book Alley, the 300 and 400 blocks of W Pender, has bookstores specializing in everything from cookbooks to radical politics to science fiction.

Ethnic Vancouver. The oldest and biggest of Vancouver's ethnic communities is Chinatown. The 200 block of E Pender is the main market area; to get started, try Yuen Fong for teas or the Dollar Market for barbequed pork or duck. Many Asians have moved into Richmond, as evidenced by the increasing number of outstanding Chinese restaurants and the New Aberdeen Centre, where you can get ginseng in bulk or durian from Thailand, and eat home-style Chinese food while you bowl. Italian commercial and cultural life thrives in the distinctive neighbourhood around Commercial Dr, east of downtown. A second, less-discovered Italian district is on Little Italy's northern border—the 2300 to 2500 blocks of E Hastings. Vancouver's 60,000 East Indian immigrants have established their own shopping area, called the Punjabi Market, in south Vancouver at 49th and Main Sts, where you can bargain for spices, chutney, and sweets. One of Vancouver's longest-established groups of ethnic inhabitants, the Greeks, live and shop west of the intersection of MacDonald and W Broadway; and a large Iranian population has settled in North Vancouver, as the many Iranian markets and saffron-scented restaurants attest.

Music. Over the last decade, the city has witnessed a renaissance in the proliferation of classical, jazz, and world music. The Vancouver Symphony Orchestra has reached new heights of artistic splendor under the leadership of Maestro Sergiu Comissiona. The main season starts in October at the Orpheum, an old vaudeville theatre, 884 Granville, (604) 876-3434. The Vancouver Opera puts on five productions a year at the Queen Elizabeth Theatre, Hamilton at W Georgia, (604) 683-0222; the program is a balance of contemporary and traditional. The sets are spectacular and the artists are of international calibre. The du Maurier International Jazz Festival attracts crowds of more than 250,000 jazz lovers (held in June; call (888) GET-JAZZ for details), and the annual Vancouver Folk Music Festival is extremely popular as well; (604) 602-9798. For information about any musical event, call Ticketmaster, (604) 280-4444.

Theater. The Vancouver Playhouse Theatre Company explores contemporary and classical theatre, offering six plays each season, October to May, in the Vancouver Playhouse, Hamilton and Dunsmuir, (604) 873-3311. Contemporary theatre in Vancouver is largely centred in the Vancouver East Cultural Centre (known to locals as The Cultch), 1895 E Venables St, (604) 254-9578. Vancouver's home of the megamusical is the Ford Centre for the Performing Arts, 777 Hornby St, (604) 602-0616; its two most striking features are the intimacy of the 1,824-seat auditorium and the visual power of the seven-storey, mirrored-wall grand staircase that unites all levels.

Gardens. At Queen Elizabeth Park, dramatic winding paths, sunken gardens, and waterfalls skirt the Bloedel Conservatory; Cambie St and 33rd Ave, (604) 872-5513. The University of British Columbia campus boasts several superb gardens—the Botanical Garden, Nitobe Memorial Gardens, and Totem Park—along with the Physick Garden, which re-creates a 16th-century monastic herb garden, and the Food Garden, an amazing example of efficient gardening; UBC, SW Marine Dr; (604) 822-9666. The Chinese Classical Garden within Dr. Sun Yat-Sen Park is a spectacular reconstruction of a Chinese scholar's garden, complete with pavilions and water-walkways; 578 Carrall St, (604) 662-3207. Near Queen Elizabeth Park, the VanDusen Botanical Garden stretches over 55 acres (22 ha); 5251 Oak St, (604) 878-9274.

Set in beside the False Creek Community Centre on Cartwright St is the **Granville Island Waterpark,** one of the most imaginatively built, warm-weather playgrounds in the city. From the end of May to early September, water spews from hydrants and overhead archways, and from geysers mounted in the concrete surface that can be activated with the push of a button. A bright-yellow water slide thrills youngsters. The local community centre employs a summer staff of young supervisors to run the water park. Games and creative activities are offered free-of-charge to visitors throughout the summer. Hours are 10am to 6pm daily from the Victoria Day long weekend in May through Labour Day in September.

Nightlife. On a warm summer night, the music spilling out from Vancouver's clubs and bars ranges from down-and-dirty R&B at the suitably raunchy Yale Hotel, 1300 Granville, (604) 681-9253, and the rollicking Blarney Stone Olde Irish Pub, 216 Carrall St, (604) 687-4322, where you see entire families partying together, through local alternative bands at the Town Pump, 66 Water, (604) 683-6695, and disco thump at Richard's on Richards, the yuppie meat market, 1036 Richards, (604) 687-6794). To find out who's playing where, pick up a copy of the *Georgia Straight* or Thursday's *Vancouver Sun*. Another fun option is to get out of town on the Pacific Starlight Dinner Train, which passes along part of the famous Sea-to-Sky Route beside Howe Sound (June through October), (604) 984-5500 or (800) 363-3373.

Spectator sports. The Canucks, Vancouver's hockey team, haven't managed to win the Stanley Cup yet, but they've come close a few times (GM Place, (604) 899-4625). The Vancouver 86ers, the local soccer team, has a devoted following (Swangard Stadium, in Burnaby, (604) 273-0086). Visiting baseball enthusiasts should try to catch the minor-league Vancouver triple-A Canadians game at the Nat Bailey Stadium, (604) 872-5232, a venue New York Yankee stalwart Roger Maris once called "the prettiest ballpark I've ever played in." For information, contact Sport, BC, 1367 W Broadway, (604) 737-3000.

Restaurants

Allegro Cafe ☆☆☆ This restaurant has become a hot spot for the young urban set. Partly it's the great '60s modern decor, but mostly it's the excellent food at more-than-reasonable prices. The Allegro offers Mediterranean dishes with a West Coast panache. *1G-888 Nelson St (between Hornby and Howe), Vancouver; (604) 683-8485; $$.*

Bacchus Ristorante (The Wedgewood Hotel) ☆☆☆ Bacchus's superb cooking is Northern Italian with an emphasis on fresh and simple, using the bounty of BC's local products. At lunchtime, Bacchus attracts the "legal beagles" from the neighboring courthouse for penne with Gorgonzola, pizza rustica, or Il Taitano. *845 Hornby St (at Robson), Vancouver; (604) 689-7777; $$.*

Bishop's ☆☆☆☆ No restaurant is as personal as this minimalist Kitsilano space. The rack of venison with goat cheese fritters and the ginger-steamed halibut (in season) are standouts. Everything bears the trademark of subtly complex flavours and bright, graphic colour. *2183 W 4th Ave (between Arbutus and Yew Sts), Vancouver; (604) 738-2025; $$$.*

The Bread Garden ☆ The Bread Garden is Vancouver's original bakery/cafe and is still its most successful. As the franchise grows, the deli cases keep expanding, stuffed with salads, sandwiches, and ready-to-nuke fare such as quiches, frittatas, and vegetable lasagne. *1880 W 1st Ave (between Burrard and Cypress), Vancouver (and branches); (604) 738-6684; $.*

Bridges ☆☆ One of the city's most popular hangouts has a superb setting on Granville Island. Bridges is actually three separate entities: a casual bistro, a pub, and a more formal upstairs dining room. The bistro's offerings are the best bet. *1696 Duranleau St (Granville Island, on the waterfront), Vancouver; (604) 687-4400; $$.*

Caffe de Medici ☆☆☆ The high molded ceilings and serene portraits of members of the 15th-century Medici family create a slightly palatial feeling that is businesslike by day, romantic by night. Skip the soups and order the beautiful antipasto. Pasta dishes are flat-out magnifico. *1025 Robson St (between Burrard and Thurlow), Vancouver; (604) 669-9322; $$$.*

The Cannery Seafood House ☆☆ Serving "salmon by the sea" for 25 years, The Cannery resides in a building that has been cleverly refurbished to look and feel even older than that. On any given day, you'll find a baker's dozen of high-quality seafood choices on the fresh sheet. *2205 Commissioner St (near Victoria Dr), Vancouver; (604) 254-9606; $$$.*

Century Grill ☆☆ Although the steak is the star here, salads and pastas are perfectly respectable. This place is very popular with the trendy set, whom you'll see smoking cigars at what's shaping up to be the city's hottest bar scene. *1095 Hamilton St (at Helmcken St), Vancouver; (604) 688-8088; $$$.*

Chartwell (The Four Seasons) ☆☆☆☆ Chartwell evokes an upper-class English men's-club atmosphere. A pre-theatre dinner menu with valet parking is an outstanding value. The wine list is an award winner, and the winemaker dinners are the most popular in the city. *791 W Georgia St (at Howe), Vancouver; (604) 689-9333; $$$.*

CinCin ☆☆☆ CinCin is a hearty Italian toast, a wish of health and good cheer, all of which is implied in this sunny Mediterranean space. Noodles are made fresh daily. This is a great place to sip wine with the gang in the lounge (food's served until 11:30pm). *1154 Robson St (between Bute and Robson), Vancouver; (604) 688-7338; $$$.*

Cipriano's Ristorante & Pizzeria ☆☆ This compact pasta-pizza house is an institution of basic and plentiful portions. Straightforward Italian home cooking arrives at your table, preceded by fabulous garlic bread, dripping with butter and deluged with Parmesan. *3995 Main St (at 24th), Vancouver; (604) 879-0020; $$.*

Diva at the Met (Metropolitan Hotel) ☆☆☆ An airy multi-tiered space with an exhibition kitchen has set the stage for imaginative, well-executed cooking at what's sure to become one of the finest hotel restaurants in the city. *645 Howe St (between Dunsmuir and Georgia Sts), Vancouver; (604) 602-7788; $$.*

The Fish House at Stanley Park ☆☆☆ Here, seafood rules (salmon, sea bass, shellfish of all kinds). The chef's vegetables aren't an afterthought; each is a discovery in itself: red cabbage with fennel, spaghetti squash with poppy seeds, and buttermilk mashed potatoes. *2099 Beach Ave (entrance to Stanley Park), Vancouver; (604) 681-7275; $$.*

Five Sails (Pan Pacific Hotel) ☆☆☆ The drop-dead gorgeous harbour view at the Five Sails may lure diners here for the first time, but it's chef Cheryle Michio's imaginative ways with fresh fish, soups, duck, and more that bring them back. *999 Canada Pl (between Burrard and Howe Sts), Vancouver; (604) 891-2892; $$$.*

Grand King Seafood Restaurant ☆☆☆ The menu here is a creative assimilation of Chinese regional cuisines with innovative touches gleaned from Japanese and other Asian cooking styles. Local ingredients become new classics in dishes like pan-fried live spot prawns in chile soya. *705 W Broadway (in the Holiday Inn, at Heather), Vancouver; (604) 876-7855; $$$.*

Griffins (Hotel Vancouver) ☆☆ The eminently respectable Hotel Vancouver houses a bright and lively bistro. Three meals a day are served à la carte, but the buffet meals are the way to go. Work your way through the entrees and take a run or three at the pastry bar. *900 W Georgia St (between Hornby and Burrard), Vancouver; (604) 662-1900; $$.*

Herons (Waterfront Centre Hotel) ☆☆ Herons is a multi-purpose bistro and restaurant with an open kitchen. The menu changes weekly, and there's a daily fresh sheet of contemporary Canadian cooking with a fusion flair. Everyone appreciates the emphasis on healthy cuisine. *900 Canada Pl (between Howe and Burrard), Vancouver; (604) 691-1991; $$.*

Il Giardino di Umberto ☆☆☆ Stars, stargazers, and movers and shakers come to Umberto Menghi's Il Giardino to mingle amid the Tuscan villa decor for dining alfresco (no better place in summer). The emphasis is on pasta and game, with an Italian nuova elegance. *1382 Hornby St (at Pacific), Vancouver; (604) 669-2422; $$$.*

Kalamata Greek Taverna ☆☆ Not just your usual souvlakia-and-pita spot, Kalamata serves up excellent Greek classics with a modern touch. Fluffy zucchini rice and delicious roasted vegetables take the edge off the usual meat-heavy menu. *478 W Broadway (at Cambie), Vancouver; (604) 872-7050; $$.*

Kamei Sushi ☆☆ Kamei's simple, Westernized dishes make it one of the most popular Japanese restaurants in town. The luxury-class Kamei Royale on W Georgia Street seats more than 300, with open and private tatami rooms. Robata dishes are the focus at the Broadway Plaza location. *1030 W Georgia St (at Hemlock), Vancouver (and branches); (604) 687-8588; $$.*

Kirin Mandarin Restaurant ☆☆☆ Of all the vastly different (and well-executed) regional cuisines at Kirin's, the Northern Chinese specialties are the best. The second, equally fine outpost is in City Square. *1166 Alberni St (between Bute and Thurlow), Vancouver; (604) 682-8833; $$$.*

Le Crocodile ☆☆☆☆ France without a passport—that's Le Crocodile. Salmon tartare and sautéed scallops in an herb sauce are both showstoppers. The well-thought-out wine list and European atmosphere make a dinner at Le Crocodile an affair to remember. *100-909 Burrard St (at Smithe), Vancouver; (604) 669-4298; $$$.*

Le Gavroche ☆☆☆ Arguably the most romantic restaurant in the city, Le Gavroche is one of the city's leading French kitchens (with a Northwest influence) complete with blazing fire and glimpses of the harbour and mountains. Service is formal but friendly. *1616 Alberni St (at Cardero), Vancouver; (604) 685-3924; $$$.*

Liliget Feast House ☆ This downstairs West End space originated 20 years ago as Vancouver's only First Nations restaurant. You'll sample dishes you never dreamed of—pan-fried oolichans, toasted seaweed, and wild blackberry pie with whipped soapolallie berries. *1724 Davie St (between Denman and Didwell), Vancouver; (604) 681-7044; $$.*

Lola's Restaurant ☆☆☆ Lola's is a glamorous eatery—a ménage of adventurous cooking, an opulent building, and an incredibly baroque atmosphere. French classics are prepared with nuances of the West Coast and Pacific Rim. *432 Richards St (between Hastings and Pender), Vancouver; (604) 684-5652; $$$.*

Lumière ☆☆☆ The minimalistic elegance of this room on the ever-expanding Broadway corridor showcases both the chef's exquisite creations and the Armani-clad clientele. There always seems to be a perfect balance of flavours and textures. *2551 W Broadway (between Larch and Trafalgar), Vancouver; (604) 739-8185; $$$.*

Montri's Thai Restaurant ☆☆☆ Why go anywhere else for Thai food when Montri's is simply the best in town? The Tod Mun fish cakes blended with prawns and chile curry are excellent, as is the salmon simmered in red curry and coconut sauce. *3629 W Broadway (between Dunbar and Elma), Vancouver; (604) 738-9888; $$.*

Nat's New York Pizzeria ☆☆ Nat's serves up some of the best thin-crust pizza around. Have it delivered or ask for it three-quarters baked and cook it crisp at home. Or pull up a chair under the Big Apple memorabilia and sink your teeth into a loaded pie. *2684 W Broadway (between Stephens and Trafalgar), Vancouver; (604) 737-0707; $.*

900 West (Hotel Vancouver) ☆☆☆ After a multimillion-dollar renovation, the fusty old Timber Club has been turned into one of the most fashionable rooms in the city. There's a wine bar area, an open kitchen, and live entertainment that keeps the action churning. *900 W Georgia St (at Burrard), Vancouver; (604) 669-9378; $$$.*

Olympia Seafood Market and Grill ☆ The Olympia purveys some of the best fish and chips in the Lower Mainland. Whatever is on special in the store, which might be halibut cheeks, scallops, or catfish, is the day's special at the 12-seat counter. *820 Thurlow St (between Robson and Smithe), Vancouver; (604) 685-0716; $$.*

Phnom Penh Restaurant ☆☆☆ This restaurant wins a steady stream of accolades from sources as diverse as local magazine polls and the *New York Times*. The decor is basic, but the menu ranges from its original rice-and-noodle focus to the cuisines of China, Vietnam, and Cambodia. *244 E Georgia St (at Main St), Vancouver; (604) 682-5777; $.*

Piccolo Mondo ☆☆☆ This exquisite Italian restaurant is one of Vancouver's best-kept secrets, a place where the setting is calm and elegant, the food absolutely authentic, and the wine list phenomenal. Each dish is packed with the intense flavours of Northern Italy. *850 Thurlow St (at Haro), Vancouver; (604) 688-1633; $$$.*

The Pink Pearl ☆☆ Tanks of fresh fish are your first clue that the Cantonese menu is especially strong on seafood. A good dim sum is served every day. This is a great place for kids. *1132 E Hastings St (at Clark Dr), Vancouver; (604) 253-4316; $$.*

Planet Veg ☆☆ There's hope for the slender wallet at Planet Veg. This new, mostly Indian fast-food spot is located in the heart of health-conscious Kitsilano and serves the juiciest veggie burger in BC. *1941 Cornwall Ave (between Cypress and Walnut), Vancouver; (604) 734-1001; $.*

The Red Onion ☆☆ Forget drive-ins and head to Kerrisdale for the best double dogs, cheeseburgers, and fries (with a sour cream and dill dip) in town. The menu is designed to please everyone (we like the hot chicken salad; others pick the veggie soup). *2028 W 41st Ave (between Arbutus and Granville), Vancouver; (604) 263-0833; $.*

Sophie's Cosmic Cafe ☆☆ Where "Leave It to Beaver" meets Pee Wee Herman—this funky diner-cum-garage-sale is a fun place to be. People rave about the huge spicy burgers and chocolate shakes, but the best thing here is the stick-to-the-ribs-style breakfast. *2095 W 4th Ave (at Arbutus), Vancouver; (604) 732-6810; $.*

Sun Sui Wah Seafood Restaurant ☆☆☆ The splashy Vancouver branch is the talk of the town. This is the place for dim sum, and being named the best Cantonese restaurant in the Lower Mainland by a Canadian Chinese radio poll only serves to firmly set the jewel in the crown. *3888 Main St (at 23rd St), Vancouver; (604) 872-8822; $$.*

The Teahouse at Ferguson Point ☆☆ This stunning location in Stanley Park is a magnet for tourists, but a faithful following of locals attests to the consistency of fare. The rack of lamb in fresh herb crust is a perennial favourite—even without the view attached. *7501 Stanley Park Dr (in Stanley Park), Vancouver; (604) 669-3281; $$.*

Tojo's ☆☆☆☆ Tojo Hidekazu is one of the best-known sushi maestros in Vancouver. Japanese menu standards like tempura and teriyaki are always reliable, and daily specials are usually superb. The dining room has a view of the stunning North Shore mountains. *202-777 W Broadway (between Heather and Willow), Vancouver; (604) 872-8050; $$$.*

Victoria Chinese Restaurant ☆☆ This upmarket, well-maintained, professional restaurant is a downtown favourite. The older sister restaurant, East Ocean Seafood Restaurant, at 108-777 W Broadway, was among the very first of the new-style Chinese dining rooms to cross the Pacific from Hong Kong. *1088 Melville St (Royal Centre), Vancouver; (604) 669-8383; $$.*

Vij's ☆☆ A civilized change from ersatz curry houses, Vij's dishes up home-cooked Indian fare that evolves at whim. The seasonal menu changes every three months but almost always includes a mean curry or a killer saag. The prices are civilized too. *1480 W 11th Ave (at Granville), Vancouver; (604) 736-6664; $.*

The William Tell (The Georgian Court Hotel) ☆☆☆ This is special-occasion dining at its very best— it's also an elegant spot for drinks before the theatre or late-night dessert. A revitalized menu ranges from the traditional to the light and flavourful. The desserts are pure decadence. *765 Beatty St (between Robson and Georgia), Vancouver; (604) 688-3504; $$$.*

Cheaper Eats

Accord Accord serves excellent Cantonese seafood and a handful of Chiu Chow specialties. It's open till the wee hours so ask for the midnight snack menu. *4298 Main St, Vancouver; (604) 876-6110; $.*

Hon's Wun Tun House Headquartered in one of Chinatown's newer retail complexes, Hon's decor may now be urbanly chic, but the lines, rock-bottom prices, and basic menu remain the same. Soups are a major draw—standard wonton, and 90 or so other variations—all in a rich, life-affirming broth. *108-268 Keefer St, Vancouver; (604) 688-0871; $.*

Milestones Mega-servings of inexpensive food (and booze) are the draw at this spot which, despite being a chain restaurant, manages to consistently impress with its witty takes on West Coast food trends. Breakfasts are outstanding. *1210 Denman St, Vancouver; (604) 662-3431; $.*

Nazarre BBQ Chicken The chicken here is basted in a mixture of rum and spices, slowly cooked on the rotisserie, and delivered with mild, hot, or extra-hot garlic sauce. There are a few other goodies on the menu but the chicken is your best bet. *1859 Commercial Dr, Vancouver; (604) 251-1844; $.*

Tang's Noodle House You'll find locals rubbing elbows with those who have trekked in from the distant 'burbs for the 100-plus options that include barbequed duck, chicken, pork, or brisket; warming hot pots; and vegetarian dishes. *2805-2807 W Broadway, Vancouver; (604) 737-1278; $.*

Tokyo Joe's Here's the best spot in Vancouver for inexpensive sushi: prices start at $2 a roll. There's also a reasonably priced lunch box served all day with chicken teriyaki, vegetable tempura, salad, and rice. *955 Helmcken St, Vancouver; (604) 689-0073; $.*

Lodgings

Coast Plaza at Stanley Park ☆☆ Situated just off the main artery in the vibrant West End, this former apartment tower offers 267 large rooms, including 170 suites. Many of the rooms have complete kitchens, making this a great place for vacationing families. *1733 Comox St (at Denman), Vancouver, BC V6G 1P6; (604) 688-7711 or (800) 663-1144; $$$.*

English Bay Inn ☆☆☆☆ The owner devotes meticulous attention to his romantic five-room inn, and he has proven himself to be a top-rated innkeeper, year after year. Stanley Park and English Bay are just minutes away by foot. *1968 Comox St (a few blocks off English Bay), Vancouver, BC V6G 1R4; (604) 683-8002; $$$.*

The Four Seasons ☆☆☆☆ The upscale chain of Four Seasons hotels is well known for pampering guests, and the Vancouver hotel only enhances that reputation. Although it is located smack-dab in the centre of high-rise downtown, many of the guest rooms offer surprising views of the city. *791 W Georgia St (at Howe), Vancouver, BC V6E 2T4; (604) 689-9333 or (800) 332-3442 (from the US only); $$$.*

Hotel Vancouver ☆☆☆ One of the grand French château-style hotels owned by the Canadian Pacific Railway, the Hotel Vancouver dates back to 1887. The 508 rooms are popular for conventions and tour groups; nonetheless, service remains quite good. *900 W Georgia St (between*

Hornby and Burrard), Vancouver, BC V6C 2W6; (604) 684-3131 or (800) 441-1414; $$$.

Metropolitan Hotel ☆☆☆ Located in the heart of downtown's business and financial district, this richly appointed, 197-room hotel was built in time for Expo 86. There are 18 palatial suites; all other rooms are deluxe, with balconies, peekaboo views of the city, and elegant contemporary appointments. *645 Howe St (between Dunsmuir and Georgia), Vancouver, BC V6C 2Y9; (604) 687-1122 or (800) 667-2300; $$$.*

Pan Pacific Hotel ☆☆☆ No hotel in Vancouver has a more stunning location, a better health club, or a more remarkable architectural presence. The Pan Pacific juts out into Vancouver's inner harbour with its five giant white signature sails. Standard guest rooms are among the smallest in any of Vancouver's luxury hotels, but the spectacular views make up for any shortcomings. *300-999 Canada Pl Way (between Burrard and Howe), Vancouver, BC V6C 3B5; (604) 662-8111 or (800) 663-1515 from Canada, (800) 937-1515 from the US; $$$.*

The Sutton Place Hotel ☆☆☆☆ Vancouver's most elegant hotel would rank as a top lodging in any European capital. All 397 soundproofed rooms in this sumptuous residential-style hotel look and feel like part of a beautiful home. Maids appear twice a day with all the amenities one could wish for. *845 Burrard St (between Robson and Smithe), Vancouver, BC V6Z 2K6; (604) 682-5511 or (800) 543-4300; $$$.*

Sylvia Hotel A favourite for price and location, this ivy-covered 8-storey historic brick hotel is a landmark adjacent to English Bay, Vancouver's most popular beach and strutting grounds. All 119 rooms (some quite small) have baths. Families or small groups should request the one-bedroom suites. *1154 Gilford St (at Beach Ave), Vancouver, BC V6G 2P6; (604) 681-9321; $.*

The Wedgewood Hotel ☆☆☆ Located in the heart of Vancouver's finest shopping district, and across the street from the art gallery, the Wedgewood offers Old-World charm and attention to every detail of hospitality. This is the only luxury hotel in the city where you'll hardly ever find tour buses unloading swarms of visitors. *845 Hornby St (at Robson), Vancouver, BC V6Z 1V1; (604) 689-7777 or (800) 663-0666; $$$.*

West End Guest House ☆☆ Don't be put off by the blazing pink exterior of this early-1900s Victorian home, which is located on a residential street close to Stanley Park. The eight rooms (each with private bath) are generally small but nicely furnished. *1362 Haro St (at Broughton), Vancouver, BC V6E 1G2; (604) 681-2889; $$$.*

Westin Bayshore Hotel ☆☆ This is the only downtown hotel that resembles a resort (children love it here). Rooms look out over a large outdoor pool, with Coal Harbour's colourful marina as a backdrop and the North Shore mountains beyond. *1601 W Georgia St (at Cardero), Vancouver, BC V6G 2V4; (604) 682-3377 or (800) 228-3000; $$$.*

Cheaper Sleeps

Hostelling International Vancouver This hostel on Jericho Beach is Canada's largest. Formerly the barracks of the Canadian Air Force, the hostel has 286 dormitory bunks and private rooms for families and couples. *1515 Discovery St, Vancouver, BC V6R 4K5; (604) 224-3208; $.*

The New Backpackers Hostel This hostel has larger rooms than other Vancouver hostels. Some units have full kitchens. The location near Gastown makes it a prime choice. No parking. *347 W Pender St, Vancouver, BC V6B 1T3; (604) 688-0112 or (604) 687-9837; $.*

Shaughnessy Village The one-room studios at the centrally located Shaughnessy are like cabins on a cruise ship, with a fold-down double bed, microwave oven, fridge, and colour TV. There are two lounges, a health club, pools, a sauna, and a restaurant. *1125 W 12th Ave, Vancouver, BC V6H 3Z3; (604) 736-5511; $.*

Simon Fraser University From May 1 until August 31, Simon Fraser rents student accommodations to visitors. Single and twin rooms are available, and groups can rent four-bedroom townhouses complete with bathrooms and kitchen. *McTaggart-Cowan Hall, Room 212, Burnaby, BC V5A 1S6; (604) 291-4503; $.*

YWCA Hotel/Residence Although its name suggests it's for young women only, this Y welcomes everyone else, too—including couples, families, groups, and men. The 155 units vary in size from single rooms with shared baths down the hall to family suites that have private baths. *733 Beatty St, Vancouver, BC V6B 2M4; (800) 663-1424 (from BC or Alberta only) or (604) 895-5830; $.*

More Information

BC Ferries: *(604) 277-0277 or (888) 223-3779 in Canada only.*
BC Transit Information: *(604) 521-0400.*
Burnaby Parks and Recreation Department: *(604) 294-7450.*
City of New Westminster Parks and Recreation: *(604) 526-4811.*
City of Port Moody Parks, Recreation and Culture: *(604) 469-4555.*
City of Vancouver Web site: *http://www.city.vancouver.bc.ca.*

Greater Vancouver Regional District (GVRD) Parks Department: *(604) 432-6350.*
Port Moody and Coquitlam Infocentre: *(604) 464-2716.*
Vancouver Parks and Recreation Board: *(604) 257-8400.*
Vancouver Tourist InfoCentre: *(604) 683-2000.*

Mountain Equipment Co-op, 130 W Broadway, (800) 663-2667, locally (604) 876-6221, anchors a strip of outdoor equipment stores on Broadway between Cambie and Main Sts. Shoppers must join the co-op before making purchases. A lifetime membership is $5. The store is a good source of information on self-propelled outdoor recreation in British Columbia, including maps and knowledgeable advice and directions.

Between them, **World Wide Books and Maps,** 736A Granville St, Vancouver V6Z 1G3, (604) 687-3320; and the **Geological Survey of Canada,** Suite 101, 605 Robson St, Vancouver V6B 5G3, (604) 666-0271, are almost certain to carry the detailed maps needed for any area of the province. The two stores are a block apart, so if one doesn't have the map you're searching for, the other probably does.

The Fraser Estuary

Richmond, Delta, Surrey, and White Rock, including Boundary Bay, Deas Island, Iona Beach, and Tynehead Regional Parks.

The term "Lower Mainland" came into currency among Vancouver Island settlers in the 19th century. Early immigration into the Crown Colony of British Columbia from Asia, Australia, Hawaii, Newfoundland, Europe, the United States, and Mexico spilled over from Vancouver Island into the lush farmland of the Fraser Estuary and Fraser Valley. "Mainlanders" became a term used by island residents to emphasize the separation, and perhaps the feeling of superiority, between the two. The Strait of Georgia that divides Vancouver Island from the Lower Mainland represents a psychological schism as much as it does a physical split.

Just as Vancouver is blessed by its proximity to the North Shore mountains, so too is it graced by the Fraser River's union with the Pacific Ocean. Riverside trails, intertidal wetlands, a delta of low-slung islands and a catalogue of wildlife accompany the mighty waterway. As you make your way through the Fraser River Estuary you are always aware of the silent weight of the Fraser, to which the landscape owes its existence. Much of the estuary has come into being only in recent times—geologically speaking—a fact attested to in the oral history of the Musqueam people, whose ancestors witnessed the islands at the mouth of the Fraser take shape. As the estuary silts in at a regular annual rate, it's as easy to gauge the increase in its size as it is to measure the growth of a tree. In an age of diminishing expectations, it's reassuring to know that in the Fraser Estuary, at least, there's an expanding quantity of soft, rich soil and broad, muddy water to explore!

Getting There

Highway 99 links Richmond, Delta, and Surrey with Vancouver. Travelling in a north-south direction, Highway 99 crosses Lulu Island from the Oak Street Bridge through Richmond to the George Massey Tunnel, which conveys highway traffic under the South Arm of the Fraser River into Delta. Highway 99 gradually swings east around Boundary and Mud Bays and crosses into Surrey just east of the Highway 91 interchange. The Canada-US border is 10 miles (16.5 km) south of here.

Highway 91 is an alternate link between Delta and Richmond via the Alex Fraser Bridge that spans the South Arm of the Fraser River. In Richmond, Highway 91 leads east-west, with interchanges at Knight Street and Highway 99. The Knight Street Bridge spans the North Arm of the Fraser and links Richmond with Vancouver. Highway 91A leads east from the Alex Fraser Bridge and connects Richmond with New Westminster via the Queensborough Bridge.

Highway 99A (the King George Highway) runs north-south from the Canada-US border and links Surrey with New Westminster via the Pattullo Bridge, which spans the Fraser River. From its western junction with Highway 99A, Highway 1A (the Fraser Highway) links Surrey with Langley and the South Fraser Valley to the east.

Highway 1 (the Trans-Canada Highway) links Surrey (and the South Fraser Valley) with Coquitlam, New Westminster, Burnaby, and Vancouver via the Port Mann Bridge, the most easterly bridge in the Fraser Estuary and Greater Vancouver.

Travellers arrive from Vancouver Island and the southern Gulf Islands at BC Ferries' Tsawwassen terminal in Delta. Highway 17 links the terminal with Highway 99. This interchange lies just south of the George Massey Tunnel.

In order to avoid confusion, it's important to note that reference is often made to former villages such as Whalley, Newton, Cloverdale, and South Surrey, which have all amalgamated into the city of Surrey. Other examples include Ladner and Tsawwassen, which are now part of Delta, and Steveston, which is part of Richmond. White Rock is an exception, a small, independent community surrounded by Surrey. Most adventure destinations listed in this chapter lie within an easy 30-minute drive of each other.

Adjoining Areas

NORTH: **Greater Vancouver**

EAST: **The Fraser Valley**

WEST: **Vancouver Island and the Gulf Islands**

Parks/Beaches

There are many things to experience on and around the Fraser River, but bathing isn't high on the list. The river rarely warms up to a comfortable temperature, even in summer. Due to fast-flowing currents in spring, and the fact that industries still find the river a convenient place to dump waste, swimming in Big Muddy is not recommended. There are exceptions, such as at Deas Island or Iona Beach Regional Parks, where wading in the river is a refreshing way to cool off. Water-skiers in Deas Slough and Ladner Marsh, for example, are willing to brave the chill waters, though many of them wear wet suits.

Fortunately, a trio of bays on the Pacific—Boundary, Mud, and Semiahmoo—provide miles of shoreline beaches to explore, almost all of which lie within parkland, and they offer saltwater swimming, too! There is such a diversity of wild, natural rhythms at play at each beach year-round that there is no reason to wait for warm, sun-filled weather to visit them. Their moods change with the season. The skies out here are brighter than in nearby Vancouver and provide more expansive views than in the city.

Boundary Bay Regional Park

There aren't many places in the world where you can *swim* between two countries with such ease as at **Boundary Bay.** A metal-scaffolded tower marks the place where the 49th parallel slices across the sandy beach. In summer, when the bay is a bathtub of sun-warmed seawater, you can make like a dolphin as you skip back and forth between Canada and the United States. When you're ready to dry off, stroll the beach and experience the same thrill.

Visitors can't venture far into the United States. From the town of Point Roberts, Washington State's portion of the beach—known locally as **Maple Beach**—peters out to rock and cobblestone as it nears an escarpment. (Note: Although there is public access to Maple Beach, almost the entire beach is privately owned. For adventures in Point Roberts, see Cycling, below.) In summer, many swimmers gather near the border tower. The swimming is better here, especially at high tide when the bay fills to a greater depth than elsewhere. (In 1792, the Spanish explorer Galiano named this Ensenada del Engaño, **Mistake Bay,** since he made the mistake of thinking there was a way inland from the end of the bay.)

When a low tide drains Boundary Bay, its sandy bottom is as mottled as the moon. Little pools of seawater are trapped in sandy depressions and reflect the sky in an endless array of mirrors. Walk out and explore the expanse but be sure to keep an eye on the shoreline where you may have left your picnic basket. It's easy to lose track of your spot unless you have a landmark such as a large umbrella or a distinctive piece of driftwood.

The temptation is to stroll far out at low tide into the middle of the bay, where some of the most interesting wildlife features are revealed, either in the pools, beneath the sand, or on the shoreline. Thousands of birds—dunlin and sandpipers, herons and brants—follow the twice-daily rise and fall of the ocean as it rinses the bay. You can walk so far out into Boundary Bay that the vapour rising off the sand obscures the horizon and you feel very remote from land indeed. If you are here later in the day, sit back and watch the setting sun colour Mount Baker's snow cone to the southeast, the most visible landmark on the horizon. Plan to be here in the days leading up to and immediately following the full moon, to watch it rise from behind the semi-dormant volcano. After dark, Boundary Bay Park is a great place to count stars. Although the park remains open throughout the night, if you plan to linger, make sure that you leave your vehicle outside the nearby park gates that close at dusk.

To reach Boundary Bay, follow Hwy 17 south from Hwy 99 in Delta and head in the direction of the BC Ferries terminal. Turn left at 56th St (also called Point Roberts Rd) where signs point to Tsawwassen's town centre. Drive into Tsawwassen, turn left on 12th Ave and continue to Boundary Bay Rd, which leads south around the bay to the park entrance. Beach amenities, including changing facilities, showers, and restrooms, are located here. For more information on Boundary Bay Regional Park, call (604) 520-6442.

Crescent Beach Park

Crescent Beach lies on the east side of Boundary Bay in Surrey, directly across the water from Boundary Bay Regional Park. Although the bay almost empties at low tide, don't expect to be able to walk between the two. The distance is so great that, as seen from Crescent Beach on a sunny day, the western and northern shorelines of Boundary Bay appear to be just a thin strip of land.

The contrast between the two beaches is best highlighted by the proximity of nearby housing. Except at its extreme south end, a buffer zone of fallow agricultural land separates Boundary Bay Regional Park from the surrounding Tsawwassen neighbourhoods. At Crescent Beach, summer homes overlook the water along O'Hara Lane, which parallels the beach. A walkway separates the homes from the beach and is a popular promenade.

Stores and restaurants are clustered around the entrance to the beach on Beecher St, Crescent Beach's main drag. Even on rainy days it's hard to get much of a head start on the crowds that throng the walkways here. The fish-and-chip stands on Beecher St do brisk business year-round, as do the ice cream vendors. (So plentiful are dogs at this South Surrey beach that it seems as if there's an unwritten bylaw that you must be accompanied by one.) Parking is scarce near the beach on hot summer days, but at other times there is plenty of room. Even if you do end up parking a few blocks away, part of the fun of visiting Crescent Beach is walking the back streets, along which you'll find some lovely permanent residences as well as a sprinkling of well-kept summer homes.

Once on the beach, turn your back on the thin veneer of commerce and enjoy the broad, sandy expanse. Find a piece of driftwood to use as a backrest. **Swimming** is best on sunny summer days when the hot sand warms the incoming tide. Offshore you'll spy sailboats, windsurfers, and water-skiers, while in the sky above, ultralight airplanes move along at improbably slow speeds as they battle the wind currents. All of this activity may seem a trifle hectic when all you plan to do is relax.

Crescent Beach is located at the western end of Crescent Rd in South Surrey. Take Hwy 99 to the Crescent Beach–White Rock exit and follow Crescent Rd west from its intersection with King George Hwy (Hwy 99A.) For more information, call the Surrey Parks and Recreation Department, (604) 501-5050.

Semiahmoo Park

Semiahmoo Park is located in White Rock, a residential community that clings to the slopes above Semiahmoo Bay's expansive beach. White Rock shares the bay with the nearby border town of Blaine, Washington. (There is also a small Semiahmoo Park on the Washington side of the bay, although you'll have to drive or cycle 20 miles (32 km) around Blaine's Drayton Harbour to reach it.)

To find Semiahmoo Park, take the 8th Ave exit west from Hwy 99 and drive into White Rock. Marine Rd takes over from 8th Ave as it passes the intersection with Stayte Rd. The well-marked entrance to Semiahmoo Park is located on the south side of Marine Dr. If the parking lot is full, don't be discouraged; someone is always leaving. A raised railway bed shields the bay's wide expanse of beach from view. Walk up the embankment with your barbeque, your beach toys, and even your dog—they're welcome here. There is room for everyone on this broad beach, even on the hottest summer days, and the reason they all come is to wade a long way out into the warm water of the shallow, sandy-bottomed bay. For more information, contact Surrey Parks and Recreation, (604) 501-5050.

White Rock Beach

As you walk the beach east of Semiahmoo Park (see above) you soon reach White Rock Beach. A boardwalk runs almost the entire length of the beach in front of Marine Dr. Near the train station a long pier marches out into Semiahmoo Bay. From here you can look back to shore and identify the famous white boulder from which the town takes its name. Native legend has it that the rock marks the spot where the Transformers, emissaries of the Sagalie Tyee, the Creator, once passed. Another legend holds that the white rock marks the landing spot of a stone that was hurled across the Strait of Georgia by a young Indian chief. It was said that he and his bride moved there from Vancouver Island to make a home together. If this was the case, they started a migratory trend that continues to this day, albeit among retirees moving to the west coast from cooler parts of the country. (White Rock is also called *Wrinkle* Rock by some of its residents, a reference to the fact that the majority of its citizens are of retirement age.)

White Rock has a reputation as one of the sunniest locales in the Lower Mainland, a fact borne out by meteorological statistics that show it receives 20 percent more sunshine than does Vancouver. Small wonder that the beach here is so popular with swimmers, windsurfers, anglers, and joggers. Visitors in search of picnic tables should head to the west end of the beach, where there are a number of them grouped together on a grassy hillside overlooking the bay, each with its own small barbeque.

Iona Beach Regional Park

The Fraser River's constant flow is responsible for filling in the shoreline of the Strait of Georgia with silt. Two expansive tracts of tidal marshland front the delta—Sturgeon and Roberts Banks—without providing much in the way of beaches. Instead, the shoreline is characterized by tall stands of bulrushes and lies strewn with driftwood. Iona Island's 12 miles (20 km) of sandy shoreline beside Sea Island is an exception.

Finding your way to Iona Beach Regional Park involves first crossing **Sea Island,** which can be tricky. Sea Island is the home of the Vancouver International Airport; follow the street signs in Richmond (or Vancouver) as if you're headed there. The Arthur Laing Bridge in Vancouver, and the Moray, Dinsmore, and No. 2 Rd Bridges in Richmond, all link with Sea Island. If you cross the Arthur Laing, take the Richmond exit to the right as soon as you reach the south end of the bridge. Follow the off-ramp towards Miller Rd, staying in the left-hand lane as you approach the stop sign. From there, a green Greater Vancouver Regional District (GVRD) sign points left to Iona Park. In Richmond, head west along Sea Island Way, cross the Moray Bridge, and turn north onto Grauer Rd. Follow the signs from here. The Dinsmore and No. 2 Rd Bridges both connect with

Russ Baker Way on Sea Island, which in turn connects with Miller Rd. Turn east on Miller, then immediately north on Grauer, and follow the signs for Iona Beach Park from here. To request a map with complete information on all of Iona Beach's attractions, call the GVRD at (604) 224-5739 or (604) 432-6359.

As the backroads lead to Iona, you pass the somewhat misnamed **McDonald Beach** (see Fishing, below). At low tide a small beach is revealed here but it is hardly the place you'd want to spread out a towel (the wake put up by passing marine traffic on the Fraser River would soon send you running for higher ground). Iona Beach Park is really where you want to head if you are looking for a place to stretch out beside some driftwood. There is a wildness here on the western perimeter of the delta that defines Iona's unique personality. Two lengthy jetties shelter the beach as they stretch out into the Strait of Georgia. The banks of Iona Jetty are lined with concrete riprap, while North Arm Jetty is much sandier.

If you're looking for an ideal spot to do some **stargazing,** Iona Beach Park is it. The park is far away from the lights of nearby Richmond or Vancouver, and out here the night sky is as black as bean sauce. Just make sure that you leave your vehicle outside the nearby gates if you plan to be in the park after closing time, unless you're attending one of the special stargazing evenings offered throughout the year by GVRD Parks. (Note: Although the gates to the park close at dusk, visitors may still enter on foot.)

Cycling

Early European and Asian settlers in the Fraser River Estuary quickly learned the importance of dike building to hold back both the ocean's high tides and the river's annual floodwaters. **Lulu Island,** the largest in the delta and home to the city of Richmond, is embraced by all three arms of the Fraser. Seven bridges and the George Massey Tunnel connect it to the rest of the Lower Mainland. One of the first dike trails constructed in the Fraser Estuary was on Lulu's south shore at London's Landing. Today, the island is ringed by 48 miles (77 km) of dikes topped by easygoing walking and cycling trails. As these trails are level, you can cover a lot of ground in an outing while soaking up the island scenery.

Begin your jaunt at any one of numerous places along the dike. Two of the more popular starting points are **Terra Nova,** at the northwestern corner of the island, and **Garry Point Park,** on the southwestern tip. The Terra Nova trailhead is located at the west end of River Rd. To get there, head west of Hwy 99 on Sea Island Way. Turn south onto No. 3 Rd and drive to the next major intersection, Cambie Rd. Turn west onto Cambie, which immediately blends into River Rd. Follow River Rd west to its end beside the Terra Nova lands. Park here. An observation platform and picnic tables are located nearby. At this point you can choose to head in several directions. If you want to explore the open marsh, take the 3-mile (5-km) West Dyke Trail. If you are more inclined to watch the action on the Fraser River, try the Middle Arm Trail, which runs an equal distance east along Moray Channel. All trails are well signed with distances indicated in kilometres.

The **West Dyke Trail** connects Terra Nova with Garry Point Park. A cycle trip can just as easily begin from one point or the other. Garry Point Park lies 3 miles (5 km) south of Terra Nova in the fishing community of Steveston. The park entrance and trail are located at the west end of Chatham St. Take the Steveston Hwy W exit from Hwy 99 to reach Steveston.

The **South Arm Dyke Trail** begins at the foot of No. 2 Rd, just east of the Steveston harbour, and runs 3 miles (5 km) to Woodward's Landing Park beside the George Massey Tunnel and Hwy 99. Along the way, you'll pass numerous interpretive signs that outline interesting aspects of natural history, such as bird and fish migrations, as well as heritage sites. This section of trail offers a variety of stops for visitors to explore. You can pause for a look around at London Farms, picnic on the pier at the foot of No. 2 Rd, and check out the old river homes on Finn Slough at the foot of No. 4 Rd. For a map of all the Richmond trails, contact the City of Richmond Parks and Leisure Services, (604) 276-4107.

Sea Island's backroads are a good place to cycle while watching planes or eagles, osprey, and heron, take off and land. A good place to begin is Iona Beach Regional Park (see Parks/Beaches, above). A causeway links Iona Island with Sea Island. Plan on taking 45 minutes or so to pedal the lengthy 7.5-mile (12-km) stretch of paved backroads that lead across Sea Island along Grauer, McDonald, and Ferguson Rds. If the backroads don't completely satisfy your will to wheel, tack on another 5.5 miles (9 km) by riding out to the end of Iona's jetty and back. By then you'll be saddle weary, for sure!

An impressive stretch of dike trail runs beside Mud and Boundary Bays in Delta, Richmond's neighbour to the south. The **Boundary Bay Regional Trail,** which includes the **East Delta Dike Trail,** winds around both bays, skirting the mudflats that once extended much farther inland. Today's dike is a much sturdier version than the crude ones built at the turn of the century. You can put in a full day cycling 12 miles (20 km) one way between the Surrey-Delta border and Boundary Bay Regional Park in Tsawwassen. There're always shorebirds to entertain you, and towards evening the sky around Mount Baker lights up in the southeast. Access points to the dike trail include the entrance to Boundary Bay Regional Park (see Parks/Beaches, above) at the east end of 12th Ave in

Tsawwassen, the south end of 64th or 72nd St off Dewdney Trunk Rd, and the south end of 96th, 104th, or 112th St off Hornby Dr near Dewdney Trunk Rd's intersection with Hwy 10.

Point Roberts is located on the extreme southern tip of the peninsula that defines Boundary Bay's western shoreline. Cyclists must cross the Canada-US border on Point Roberts Rd in Tsawwassen to enter or leave the tiny enclave. Except for a steep hill south of Maple Beach, exploring Point Roberts makes for a mostly level, 2-hour tour by bike. The roads blend into one another in a simple rectangular grid and are easy to follow. Whatcom County, Washington, of which Point Roberts is a part, maintains **Lighthouse Park,** a delightful and often overlooked park at the extreme southwestern point of the mainland. From this windswept point, cyclists are rewarded with some of the best views on the entire Fraser Estuary: Haro Strait and the Strait of Juan de Fuca as well as the Strait of Georgia open up on three sides.

There's even more cycling to be had along the dike at **Brunswick Point,** about 3 miles (5 km) west of Ladner in Delta. To find the entrance to the dike, head west on Ladner Trunk Rd from downtown Ladner. Ladner Trunk Rd soon becomes River Rd W. About 2 miles (3 km) west of Ladner, River Rd W passes the bridge over Canoe Passage, which links Delta with Westham and Reifel Islands (see Wildlife, below). The road continues past the bridge for another 1.5 miles (2.5 km) as it winds its way to a gated cul-de-sac. There is parking here, beside the dike. Mount up and pedal off.

A branch of the South Arm of the Fraser River spreads out beside the dike. It seems so relieved to have finally accomplished its long run to the ocean that it emits a contented gurgle. As the river narrows between Westham Island and Delta, it forms **Canoe Passage.** From the parking area, the dike trail leads west and then south as it curves around Brunswick Point. Canneries once thrived here at the turn of the last century, as attested to by the orderly rows of creosoted pilings that march like a doomed army out towards **Roberts Bank.** Suddenly, the city seems very remote. In the distance, a wall of Coast Mountains runs down the Sunshine Coast, crosses the North Shore, and then heads towards the Golden Ears, the distinctively shaped twin peaks of Mount Blanshard in the north Fraser Valley. The Strait of Georgia expands west to Vancouver Island. This scene is painted with broad brush strokes indeed. One of the joys of such an easygoing trail is that you can ride with your head up. You can do as much rubbernecking as you please without worrying about a mishap.

It will take you 30 minutes to ride the 4.5 miles (7 km) from the Brunswick Point trailhead to the beginning of the **Roberts Banks coal port causeway,** which juts out onto the bank. Freighters load coal brought here in railcars from southeastern British Columbia. You can ride out on the lengthy causeway for a look back at Brunswick Point and add another 4.5 miles (7 km) to your journey. The **Tsawwassen Indian Reserve** begins just south of the causeway. If the gate is open, you can extend your ride to the **BC Ferries Tsawwassen terminal causeway,** about 2 miles (6 km) farther south. By now you will be several hours from where you began. Along the way you will pass viewpoints and places where you can park your bike and rest atop a driftwood log. There's always plenty of wildlife along the shoreline, where herons stand on guard while rafts of waterfowl drift offshore. For more information on this and other cycling trails in Delta, contact the Corporation of Delta Parks and Recreation, (604) 946-3300.

Barnston Island in Surrey has the flavour of both the Fraser Estuary and the Fraser Valley rolled into one. A protective dike rings the diminutive island, which has a distinctly agricultural air (and aroma). Dairy farming is the main focus these days, as the soil is infested with iron worms, a nasty predator that attacks root crops. Recently, a park was created at Robert Point on the northwestern tip of the island. A small barge operates between the Surrey mainland and Barnston Island, which lies east of Surrey Bend (see Kayaking/Canoeing, below), and just beyond sight of the Port Mann Bridge. There is no charge to use the **ferry,** which takes less than 5 minutes to cross Parsons Channel. To reach the ferry dock, take the 104th Ave exit off Hwy 1 and follow it east until it ends. Take 176th St if you're approaching from the east. It meets 104th at the ferry dock. The free ferry runs on demand from 6:20am every day until midnight. Although much of the island is private property, there are access points to the river, particularly at Robert and Mann Points. From the north side of the island, the view is out over the Fraser River across log booms and open water to the far shore, where light planes buzz around the Pitt Meadows Airport. In the distance some familiar landmarks loom, such as the knolls in the Pitt River Valley and the Golden Ears to the northeast. For most of the time you spend cycling on Barnston, your attention will probably turn away from the river and towards the mighty contented cows, pigs, spring lambs, and ponies in nearby fields. The best view of the island is from the ferry landing as you arrive. Look east past the farmhouses across the fields. In the distance is Mann Point, the site of an old orchard where you can sit with your legs hanging over the high bank and watch families of Canada geese. In springtime, goslings are strung out in a row behind their parents on the water, with their legs pumping against the current to keep up. There are no tricks to this 6-mile (10-km) loop road that rings the island. The choice of directions is simply left or right from the ferry dock. If you head right and wish to reach the slippery shoreline south of Mann Point, watch for a trail that leads down the embankment just before an especially well-kept farm. Walk from here to the point for a look at the eagles, herons, and geese that enjoy the protection of the Barnston shoreline. Facing the island on the Surrey side is a typical Fraser River industrial scene, but the island itself has no commercial development. In addition to the loop road around Barnston, a secondary road leads through the farm fields at mid-island.

Kayaking/Canoeing

One of the best ways to get a feeling for the Fraser Estuary is from a small boat such as a canoe or kayak. Although the Fraser River powers its way through the estuary in three main channels, there are numerous backwaters where the current is not as strong nor the wakes from passing tugboats and freighters as intimidating. Try launching at **Deas Slough** and explore the nearby **Ladner Marsh** area. There are two approaches, one from Deas Island Regional Park and the other from the public boat launch at the north end of Ferry Rd on the outskirts of Ladner. (Ladner, together with Tsawwassen to the south, is where the majority of Delta's population resides.) Both approaches are equally well suited to exploring Deas Slough. Deas Island Park lies 1.5 miles (2.5 km) east of the Hwy 99/Hwy 17 interchange. A small causeway links the island with River Rd. Car-top boats can be launched at the east end of Deas Slough beside the Delta Rowing Club. From here, the entire length of the slough stretches before you, an open invitation to steal away. For more information on Deas Island Park, call (604) 520-6442.

The **boat ramp** on Ferry Rd at the west end of Deas Slough is vehicle accessible. This is where anglers, water-skiers, jet boats, canoes, and kayaks launch. To reach Ferry Rd, take the Ladner exit immediately south of the George Massey Tunnel on Hwy 99. Drive west on River Rd to Ferry Rd. Turn east on Ferry and drive to the launch ramp. From here, Deas Island's rocky-pointed snout is only a quick paddle away. The full girth of the Fraser River's South Arm lies on the far side of Deas Island and should be paddled only at slack tide. During falling tides, currents in the Fraser can reach almost 7 miles (11 km) per hour, although you won't experience these conditions in the backwater on Deas's south side. The heart of the slough is equidistant from either Ferry Rd or Deas Island Park. (Note: The gates at Deas Island Park close at 9pm; leave your vehicle outside them if you decide to linger longer than that. The short portage this necessitates is more than rewarded by the delight of drifting in the slough's sleepy backwater as night falls.)

If you want to expand your journey beyond the slough, investigate the secluded channels of **Ladner Marsh** and the **South Arm Marshes Wildlife Management Area** that begins west of the Ferry Rd boat launch and includes all of the delta between Deas and Westham Islands (see Wildlife, below). There's also a private marina beside the public boat launch on Ferry Rd that provides private moorage. Contact Captain's Cove Marina, (604) 946-1244.

There's more to do at Crescent Beach (see Parks/Beaches, above) in South Surrey than simply get sand between your toes. Although swimming is *the* big attraction in summer, you can launch a car-top boat and explore the coastline of **Boundary and Mud Bays,** as well as the **Nicomekl River,** which channels into Boundary Bay east of Crescent Beach year-round. For larger boats, there's a ramp just east of the Burlington Northern railway tracks in Crescent Beach. There's also a drive-in boat launch nearby on the Nicomekl at Surrey's **Elgin Heritage Park** on Crescent Dr near 35th Ave.

Although there's no boat launch at **Semiahmoo Park** (see Parks/Beaches, above), if you've arrived with a car-top boat or an inflatable raft, park as close to the end of the parking lot as possible, beside a baseball diamond. Launch in the nearby **Campbell River** and drift downstream from here. Note: Paddle out onto **Semiahmoo Bay** underneath a Burlington Northern Railroad bridge and gaze down through the clear water to the golden sand below. This is a dreamy location. Campbell River is intertidal, and thus more shallow at certain times than others.

One of the best ways to explore **Surrey Bend Park** is in a small boat. Use the boat launch beside the Barnston Island ferry slip at the foot of 104th Ave and 176th St in Surrey (see Cycling, above). Paddle west along **Parsons Channel,** hugging the south side of the Fraser River. Make your way into the park on Central Creek, which flows into the Fraser River at Surrey Bend a short distance west of the dock. Once in the backwaters of Central Creek, paddlers are guaranteed hours of enjoyment as they investigate its meandering course through shaded second-growth forest. This is a unique, West Coast river environment. As Surrey Bend was given park status only in 1995, there are few visitor services in place. For the moment, visitors are expected to make their own way around the park. What better natural path than a meandering creek?

Wildlife

Of all the wildlife viewing areas in the Fraser Estuary, none surpasses the **George C. Reifel Migratory Bird Sanctuary.** Located on the western fringe of the estuary in Delta, Reifel Island and its companion, Westham Island, provide wintering grounds for 230 species of **birds.** Many of these are nesting residents, such as **Canada geese, ducks and teals, marsh hawks, coots, blackbirds, gulls, and doves.** Some stay year-round, while others head north to their summer nesting grounds. For example, 20,000 **snow geese,** one of the largest birds at Reifel, winter here from October to March before heading to Wrangel Island (Ostrov Vrangelya), off the coast of northeastern Siberia. Fall and winter are the best seasons to visit the Reifel sanctuary, before the bird population begins to thin out. A simple network of trails leads around the island and connects with a series of blinds from where you look on in hushed silence as the birds go about their business. For a peek at the action from on high, seek out the 3-storey observation tower at the north end of the island. As you may find the breeze out here a touch chilly, the sanctuary thoughtfully provides a warm-up cabin next to the entrance, where a cheery fire blazes in colder months.

The sanctuary's entrance fee is $3.50 for adults and $1 for seniors and children ages 2 to 14. Visiting hours are from 9am to 4pm daily. For more information, contact the B.C. Waterfowl Society, which operates the sanctuary, (604) 946-6980. Reifel and Westham Islands are in Delta, about 6 miles (10 km) west of Ladner. Follow the signs to Ladner from the Hwy 99/Hwy 17 interchange. A roadside marker on Hwy 17 S indicates the turnoff to the Reifel Sanctuary on Ladner Trunk Rd (48th Ave). Turn right here. Once you reach the heart of Ladner, stay on the Ladner Trunk Rd as it crosses Elliot St (also called 47A Ave) and leads to River Rd W. Follow along this diked road past floating houses and marinas to a small wooden bridge that leads to Westham and Reifel Islands. Traffic etiquette when crossing the one-lane span gives those driving onto the island the right of way.

With **Canada geese** populations very much on the rebound these days, it's hard to believe that they were threatened in the 1960s. One of the places where the honkers began recolonizing the Lower Mainland was at Serpentine Fen, located at the east end of Mud Bay in Surrey. (On the geological evolutionary scale, fens lie between swamps and bogs.) Watch for a tall wooden observation tower that stands out on the east side as Hwy 99 passes over the Serpentine River. Farther east you can see yet another of these. Exit Hwy 99 at Crescent Beach and head north on Hwy 99A (King George Hwy) for a short distance to 44th Ave. A garden nursery is located at this junction. Turn left and drive in to the parking lot and picnic area. The towers aren't hard to find because they are the tallest structures on the fen. Together, the two observation towers are located at the **Serpentine Wildlife Management Area,** (604) 589-9127, where Ducks Unlimited released 260 Canada geese in 1972. A series of trails loops around ponds that were created with funds from the Sportsmen of Northern California and the British Columbia government. The refuge provides sheltered nesting grounds for the fat ducks and geese that winter locally. A grove of trees protects several picnic tables from the breeze that often blows in off nearby Mud Bay. The main trail begins here and leads out to the nearby observation towers.

Tynehead Regional Park is a refuge for local wildlife such as **coyotes, rabbits, and salmon fry** in rapidly developing Surrey. It's easy to find and easier still to explore. As Hwy 1 leads east of the Port Mann Bridge, take the 176th St exit south and make the first turn west on 96th Ave. From here you have a choice of two approaches. Either turn right at the next major intersection, 168th St, and drive to a park entrance at the road's north end, or continue west on 96th Ave to another entrance beside the Tynehead Hatchery. Operated by the Serpentine Enhancement Society, a volunteer organization, this is the site of a fish release that occurs each spring as part of the Salmonid Enhancement Program. (For information on the dates of the release, to which the public is invited, call (604) 589-9127.) Come fall, you can see salmon migrating to spawning beds in the park. Another section of the park features a garden that is designed to attract butterflies. Hedgerows line the borders of the park's more remote corners, excellent locations to look for some wildlife stalking in the tall grass. For more information on Tynehead Park, call (604) 530-4983.

Salmon also spawn in Surrey's Campbell River in autumn. Visit the Campbell River fish hatchery in September and October for an intimate insight into the effort being made to restore declining salmon runs (you can see salmon being milked for their eggs). The hatchery is on the east side of 184th St between 16th and Eighth Aves.

If it were summer year-round, Boundary Bay Regional Park (see Parks/Beaches, above) in Delta might lose some of its seasonal appeal to **migratory birds.** The bay is one of the most important stops on the Pacific Flyway. Each spring and fall, more than 250,000 birds pass through the area—between 20,000 and 30,000 brant alone. Together with the sight of the annual salmon migration in the nearby Fraser River, this north-south passage is one of the most stimulating natural events in the region. Throughout the year, the Friends of Boundary Bay run numerous natural-history interpretive programs in the vicinity of the bay and nearby Burns Bog. For more information and a brochure, telephone (604) 940-1540.

A dike trail follows the perimeter of the bay from Boundary Bay Park east to Mud Bay. There are many good viewpoints for birding along the way. Drive to the south end of 64th or 72nd Ave from Ladner Trunk Rd, and walk up onto the dike from here. This is the Boundary Bay Regional Trail (see Cycling, above), all 12 miles (20 km) of which is public park. In winter, watch for **snowy owls**—they are often seen sitting motionless on fenceposts. Or a pair of oval-faced **barn owls** may fly overhead. There's always magic at work on the shoreline and in the skies above Boundary Bay.

Just as at Boundary Bay, the birdlife viewing at Iona Beach Regional Park in Richmond (see Parks/Beaches, above) is exceptional, with its own resident population of **rare birds** such as the **burrowing owl** and the **yellowheaded blackbird.** In fact, more rare birds are seen here than anywhere else in the province. Walk through the sand dunes that characterize much of the island, keeping your binoculars at the ready. You're bound to spot great blue herons as they stalk the shore of McDonald Slough or in the marshy areas of the island. Throughout the year, GVRD Parks offers special bird-watching programs. For information, call (604) 432-6359. Group tours with a park naturalist can also be arranged by calling (604) 224-5739.

A whale observation tower at Lighthouse Park (see Cycling, above) in Point Roberts, Washington, rises above an interpretive display on **orcas.** There are three black-finned pods that frequent the park's offshore waters from May to October. Even if the pods aren't passing at the time of your visit, you can still learn a lot about the locals from the display.

Photography

At sunny times of the year, **Peace Arch Provincial Park** in South Surrey attracts almost as many photographers as it does motorists who must wait patiently for their turn to cross the border. The main attraction here is the imposing white monument called the Peace Arch, a unique symbol of peace and friendship between Canada and the United States. The floral landscaping in the park is another reason that visitors come here with cameras in hand. On sunny days, particularly when the long afternoon sun begins to drop towards Vancouver Island, Semiahmoo Bay dazzles with its powerful reflection of light. This a good location for big sky shots of the fiery variety. To find your way to the park, take Hwy 99 south almost to the Canada Customs and Immigration Building, then turn west onto Beach Rd, next to the duty-free store, and watch for a sign pointing the way to Peace Arch Provincial Park.

Plexiglas shelters are located at the midway point and the far end of the pipeline at **Iona Beach Regional Park.** Not only do they provide a break from the cool winds that often blow across the ocean, but these are also ideal locations from which to snap a sunrise or sunset shot. The most prominent features in the panoramic vista are Mount Baker to the east, the Coast Mountains to the north with Pacific Spirit Regional Park (see Greater Vancouver chapter) in the foreground, and the open water of the Strait of Georgia with a profile of the Vancouver Island Mountains to the west.

Picnics

Almost all of the parks and beaches in the Fraser Estuary are ideally suited for picnicking. Some simply provide picnic tables while others have covered shelters, barbeques, and playing fields.

In Delta, **Deas Island Regional Park** (see Hiking/Walking, below) has two picnic areas, one near the park entrance at the Riverside picnic area and the other at the west end of the park access road at Fisher's Field picnic area. A large picnic shelter is located at Fisher's Field and is available for rent to groups of up to 100 people. Advanced booking is recommended for large groups; call (604) 432-6352 for reservations. Several picnic tables are located at the entrance to the **George C. Reifel Migratory Bird Sanctuary** (see Wildlife, above). You're bound to have ducks waddling up for handouts, so hold onto your sandwiches. (Do *not* feed bread to birds. Instead, bring birdfood. Small bags of grain may be purchased at the entrance for a modest fee.)

In Surrey, a large picnic shelter is located on both sides of the border at **Peace Arch Provincial Park** (see Photography, above). On the Canadian side, the dining area has room for 150 people. The kitchen has five double hot plates and sinks with hot and cold running water. The shelter in the state park has similar equipment. In addition, 41 picnic tables are scattered throughout the park. Note: The picnic shelter on the Canadian side of the park, with its natural wood finish and picturesque setting, is quite popular. It's open from 8am to 9:45pm daily. No reservations for its use are accepted and no group has exclusive use of the shelter. However, it is advisable for groups of 20 or more to notify the park office in advance. Contact the park supervisor at (604) 531-3068 between 9 and 10am.

Windsurfing

In **Tsawwassen,** on the south side of the BC Ferries causeway that carries travellers out to the ferry terminal, is a beach that attracts anglers and windsurfers. Best time to catch the breeze here is following a storm blowing from the south. Although this small bay empties at low tides, at other times you can rip out here. Take Hwy 17 south to the beginning of the causeway, then follow the service road that parallels the causeway. You'll find portable toilets for changing and rough picnic spots where you can build a fire to dry out. For wind conditions, call Environment Canada, (900) 565-5555.

Also in Tsawwassen is **Boundary Bay Regional Park** (see Parks/Beaches, above) located on the east side of the isthmus. The winds can blow just as hard across its surface as out by the BC Ferries jetty. A good place to launch is the vehicle-accessible ramp at the east end of 1A Ave via 67th St, several blocks south of the park's main entrance.

Hiking/Walking

Between dips in the ocean at **Crescent Beach** (see Parks/Beaches, above) search out viewpoints south of the sandy beach area. (If you are not planning to visit the beach, leave your car at a small parking area at the intersection of Bayview and McBride just south of Beecher next to the Burlington Northern Railway tracks.) Pick your way along the rocky shoreline and head south towards distant Kwomais Point, around which the railway tracks curve east past Semiahmoo Bay and White Rock Beach. Gravel and riprap make walking more difficult at water's edge than beside the tracks. (A warning notice posted near the parking area informs track walkers that they do so at their own risk.)

Kayakers pass by offshore, balanced on the waters of the bay with much greater ease than those poised above on the steel rails. The tracks hug the hillside, curving gracefully along the embankment. Looking south from one of the curves, you can just make out the sandstone bluffs that rise above Birch Bay in Washington State. Along the way, various rough trails lead down the steep embankment, none of which are very inviting to explore. The charm here lies in the quiet isolation of the beach as the less adventuresome throngs are left behind.

Watch for the **"1,001 Stairs"** that lead from the beach to the neighbourhood situated above that is all but unseen from below. The clue to finding them is the appearance of a very small trestle bridge. A trail runs from the beach beneath the bridge and then leads south along the embankment behind a mesh metal fence. In minutes you'll come upon a wooden staircase that climbs the hillside. Numerous landings interrupt the flow of stairs, places where you can pause to catch your breath while taking in the views of Tsawwassen and Point Roberts on the peninsula to the west across Boundary Bay. (As hard as we've tried, we've only counted 233 steps.)

Deas Island Regional Park in Delta (see Kayaking/Canoeing, above) is interlaced with over 3 miles (5 km) of forested walking trails that run beside the Fraser River on the north side and Deas Slough on the south. Walk across the island to a small beach near the west end where the Fraser laps at the shoreline as large, oceangoing freighters glide past. The overwhelming girth of these vessels dwarfs those of the small fishing boats that also ply the Fraser. Eagles perch in the branches of the tall black cottonwood trees that overhang the trails. There's even a 2-storey observation tower from which you can look out over the island at treetop level. Nearby is a lovingly restored heritage home, a schoolhouse, and an agricultural hall. For information and a map (also available at the park) that outlines the walking trails in Deas Island Park, call the GVRD at (604) 432-6359.

Expect to find extended walking on any of the estuary dike trails cited in Cycling, above, including **Brunswick Point** and the **Boundary Bay Regional Trail** in Delta, and all the dike trails in **Iona Beach Regional Park** in Richmond.

Fishing

McDonald Beach on Richmond's Sea Island (see Parks/Beaches, above) features a boat launch, a bait shop, and several picnic tables arranged on a high bank beside the Fraser River's North Arm. There's also fishing in Richmond near **Steveston,** where a municipal pier juts out into the Fraser at Gilbert's Beach beside the South Arm Dyke Trail (see Cycling, above) at the foot of No. 2 Rd, just east of the Steveston harbour.

Anglers can catch salmon, trout, and numerous other species from the shores of **Deas Island Regional Park** (see Kayaking/Canoeing and Hiking/Walking, above). The Riverside picnic area is one of the most popular areas from which to fish. A "Tidal Waters Sports Fishing License" is required by all anglers and available at most fishing shops.

Perhaps the most respected source for information on fishing in Greater Vancouver is in Surrey. Michael & Young Fly Shop, 10484 137th St, (604) 588-2833, provides a free fly-fishing report for advice on the latest conditions: call (604) 299-9000 and dial extension 3597. Other informative sources for fishing tackle and licences in the Fraser Estuary include Berry's Bait and Tackle, 14651 Westminster Hwy, Richmond, (604) 273-5901; Nikka Industries, 3551 Moncton, Steveston, (604) 271-6332; Steveston Marine, 3560 Moncton, Steveston, (604) 277-7031; and Stillwater Sports, 4849 Ladner, Delta, (604) 946-9933.

For general information on fishing regulations, contact the BC Fish and Wildlife Regional Office, (604) 582-5200 or (800) 665-7027 (toll free).

Camping

Camping is difficult to find close to Vancouver. In the Fraser Estuary, look for **Bayside Camping,** 16565 Beach Rd, White Rock, (604) 531-6563, which offers quiet, family-oriented camping by the sea in summer. There's also camping in Point Roberts, Washington, at **Lighthouse Park** (see Cycling and Wildlife, above); call (360) 945-4911 for details, or contact Whatcom County Parks and Recreation, (360) 733-2900. Group tent-camping is available at **Deas Island Regional Park's Muskrat Meadow** (see Hiking/Walking and Fishing, above). The setting is an open field in a forest. Up to 40 people can be accommodated here, and the location includes a fire ring, drinking water, a playing field, toilets, picnic tables, and a cookstove and fireplace. Organized school and community groups can reserve for a fee by calling (604) 432-6352.

outside in

Attractions

The **Gulf of Georgia Cannery National Historic Site** in Steveston, on Fourth Ave directly behind Canfisco, is operated by a group of community members and representatives of the local fishing industry and contains relics from the past, when the canneries operated day and night. A model of a 1930s production line is set up along one long L-shaped counter. Murals of fish and trawlers cover the walls; showcases full of glass net floats from Japan, various shiny salmon tins, and model boats help convey a sense of Steveston's heritage. Mountains of fishing gear and nets are arranged outside. The interpretive centre is open from May to mid-October. Visiting days vary; call ahead if you wish to ensure a tour: (604) 664-7908. Family admission is $7.50 and includes a 20-minute film presentation in the Boiler House Theatre.

Also located in Steveston at the south foot of Railway Ave is the **Britannia Heritage Shipyard.** Visitors can take a self-guided walking tour of this National Heritage Site. Britannia is one of the few surviving examples from Steveston's rich past, when a mix of canneries, net lofts, boatyards, residences, and stores defined the neighbourhood. Restoration of the site is in the development stage, and over the coming years much of its former glory is slated to be restored. At present, the Britannia Shipyard augments a walking or cycling tour of the Steveston harbour. For more information, contact the Britannia Heritage Shipyard Society, (604) 718-1200.

Cloverdale, one of Surrey's five central hubs, lies just north of the 168th St Bridge. If you're out for a leisurely drive, this is an excellent area in which to buy fresh vegetables and fruit from roadside stands, particularly along 152nd and 168th Sts between Hwy 10 and 40th Ave. Also, on the west side of 168th St between 50th Ave and Colebrook Rd, watch for a most unusual display of hubcaps affixed to the side of a large barn and on two tall poles at the entrance of a farm north of the bridge over the Nicomekl.

Many farms on Westham Island also feature fresh fruit, vegetables, and flowers from June to October. You can hand-pick berries, or purchase vegetables and fresh flowers from a number of roadside stands. Watch for **Westham Island Herb Farm**'s prominent sign soon after you begin your trip across Westham Island. The Ellis family has been farming on Kirkland Rd since the turn of the century. Dried flowers, herbs, and vegetables are for sale from late May to early November; call (604) 946-4393.

See Attractions in Greater Vancouver chapter for additional highlights from this area.

Restaurants

Floata Seafood Restaurant ☆☆ The largest restaurant in Vancouver to date, the cavernous room of the Floata seats 1,000 (yes, 1,000). A brisk dim sum trade ensures fresh and very good nibbles for those who are there to enjoy this popular Chinese roving lunch-hour feast. *1425-4380 No. 3 Rd (Parker Place Shopping Centre), Richmond; (604) 270-8889; $$.*

Giraffe ☆☆ This delightful, elegant neighbourhood restaurant with a view of Semiahmoo Bay strongly believes in the three Gs of California-style cooking—garlic, goat cheese, and grilling. Be sure to graze the dessert menu. *15053 Marine Dr (across from the pier), White Rock; (604) 538-6878; $$.*

La Mansione Ristorante ☆ There's a menu of mixed delights in this handsome mock-Tudor mansion with a warm fireplace for winter evenings. Specialties include chateaubriand, rack of lamb, and veal scaloppine Sergio. *46290 Yale Rd E (near Williams St), Chilliwack; (604) 792-8910; $$.*

Top Gun Chinese Seafood Restaurant ☆☆ A visit to Top Gun is never just a culinary experience, it's also a crash course on Pacific Rim cultural immersion. The dinner menu is generic Cantonese, but specials can be quite interesting. *2110-4151 Hazelbridge Way (Aberdeen Shopping Centre), Richmond; (604) 273-2883; $$.*

Lodgings

Delta Pacific Resort ☆☆ This is one of two Delta hotels in the vicinity of Vancouver International Airport. Both are well run and offer a wealth of recreational facilities. The free shuttle service goes to and from the airport as well as to major nearby shopping centres. *10251 St Edwards Dr (at Cambie), Richmond, BC V6X 2M9; (604) 278-9611 or (800) 268-1133; $$$.*

Radisson President Hotel and Suites ☆☆ This new airport hotel is a class act, offering everything from Cantonese cuisine to shopping. Customer service here is prompt and friendly. Rooms are spacious and well appointed. *8181 Cambie Rd (from Hwy 99 S, take No. 4 Rd south to exit 39A, turn west on Cambie Rd), Richmond, BC V6X 3X9; (604) 276-8181 or (800) 333-3333; $$$.*

River Run Cottages ☆☆ Located in historic Ladner, 30 minutes south of downtown Vancouver and quite near the ferries to Victoria, the cottages are set among a community of houseboats and offer closeness to nature. The complex features one floating cottage and three on shore. *4551 River Rd W (west on Hwy 10 to Ladner Trunk Rd, which becomes River Rd W), Ladner, BC V4K 1R9; (604) 946-7778; $$.*

More Information

City of Richmond Community Services: *(604) 276-4107.*
City of Surrey Parks and Recreation: *(604) 501-5050.*
City of White Rock Parks Department: *(604) 541-2179.*
The Corporation of Delta Parks and Recreation: *(604) 946-3300.*
Greater Vancouver Regional District (GVRD) Parks: *(604) 432-6350; Web site address, www.gvrd.parks.com.*
Gulf of Georgia Cannery National Historic Site: *(604) 664-7908.*
Whatcom County (Washington) Parks and Recreation: *(360) 733-2900.*

The Fraser Valley

The north and south Fraser Valley, including Coquitlam, Port Coquitlam, Pitt Meadows, Maple Ridge, Mission, Harrison Hot Springs, Hope, Chilliwack, Abbotsford, Matsqui, and Langley, and featuring Golden Ears, Rolley Lake, Sasquatch, Skagit Valley, Chilliwack, and Cultus Lake Provincial Parks.

The wide, fertile Fraser Valley, yet another aspect of the Lower Mainland's landscape, is spread between the Coast and Cascade Mountains, parallel with the Canada-US border. The valley runs more than a hundred miles inland from the Pacific to the small town of Hope at its eastern end. You can drive from one end of the Fraser Valley to the other in about two hours. You can just as easily spend a lifetime exploring the 93 miles (150 km) between Vancouver and Hope. With half the population of British Columbia living in or within easy driving distance of the Fraser Valley, the question of where to head in advance of the crowds is a challenging one. From an explorer's perspective, Forest Service recreation sites and provincial parks pick up where Greater Vancouver Regional District (GVRD) parks leave off. Except for the cities of Maple Ridge and Mission on the north, and Abbotsford and Chilliwack south of the Fraser River, this is a prairie realm where cowboy boots and Stetsons aren't out of place. Almost all of the fertile land is rural and supports a blend of farming, forestry, and outdoor recreation. Fraser Valley residents are just as keen on using these parks and trails as their neighbours in the GVRD. One of the benefits of living out in the valley is knowing the best spots and having a head start in reaching them, especially on summer weekends. If you can be on one of the many backroads by 3pm on Friday, you're well on your way to securing a campsite. Rest assured that at other times of the week you will have your pick of sites.

Since the 1980s, the population explosion in the Lower Mainland has exerted considerable pressure on the Fraser Valley. Fortunately, much of the lush farmland is protected under the provincial Agricultural Land Reserve Policy instituted in the 1970s. Demographic analysis of growth patterns from now to the mid-21st century suggests a continual erosion of this rural landscape. With this in mind, in the mid-1990s the provincial government accepted a committee's recommendation that almost 14 percent of the land base be set aside for parks. This was welcome news for outdoor enthusiasts, many of whom actively supported the preservation of critical wilderness corridors found in places such as the Skagit Valley in the south Fraser Valley and the Pitt Lake region in the north. The signing of the provincial Protected Areas Strategy Accord in October 1996 signalled a victory for conservationists who had worked for the protection of such pristine areas since the mid-1970s. Now it's time to get out there and enjoy the 14 percent solution.

Getting There

The Fraser River flows down the middle of the Fraser Valley and, by the very nature of its broad, deep, muddy girth, forces road travellers to choose either its north or south side. River crossings are limited. East of the Port Mann Bridge, which links Coquitlam on the north with Surrey on the south, travellers must rely on the Albion Ferry between Maple Ridge and Fort Langley, the Mission-Matsqui Bridge (Highway 11), or the Highway 9 Bridge east of Chilliwack that links Agassiz with Rosedale if they wish to journey from one side of the Fraser Valley to the other.

Two major highways cut east-west routes through the Fraser Valley, and link Vancouver with Hope. Highway 7 (the Lougheed Highway, or Broadway in Vancouver) traverses the North Fraser Valley parallel with the Fraser River. As Highway 1 (the Trans-Canada Highway) heads east of Vancouver, it crosses the Fraser River on the Port Mann Bridge and leads through the South Fraser Valley. Whereas Highway 1 is a divided freeway designed to deliver travellers to their destination as quickly as possible, in most places Highway 7 is a conventional roadway and doubles as the main street for the towns through which it passes.

As you become familiar with the geography of the valley, you'll be better able to decide which route to take for the quickest access to the destination of your choice.

Adjoining Areas

NORTH: **Whistler and the Sea to Sky Highway**

EAST: **Crowsnest Highway: South Okanogan Valley; The Trans-Canada Highway**

WEST: **Greater Vancouver**

inside out

Camping/Parks

North Fraser Valley

As you approach Vancouver, campsites get as rare as courtesy in rush-hour traffic. Out in the Fraser Valley, where folks have more breathing space and arguably better manners, there are a number of stunningly beautiful public campgrounds.

Golden Ears Provincial Park in Maple Ridge is a destination with many possibilities. Once there, you can fan out through the park to explore on foot, by boat, by bike, or on horseback. But the first order of business is to find a pad. There are 343 well-spaced vehicle/tent campsites at two locations inside the park, at **Alouette Lake** (205 sites) and **Gold Creek** (138 sites) **Campgrounds,** as well as wilderness campsites dotted throughout the park's backcountry. All drive-in sites are nestled beneath tall stands of sheltering hemlock and fir. This canopy helps protect campers from the rain that is not uncommon here, even during summer heat waves. Hot showers are especially welcome after a day of "liquid sunshine." So's dry wood—pack some kindling as a fire starter, just in case. The wilderness sites at sandy **North Beach** require a 15-minute walk from the Gold Creek parking area. The open beach in front of the forested sites is a great place to watch meteor showers in early August. A note of mild caution: because of its semi-remoteness, North Beach sometimes attracts rowdies, particularly on graduation weekends in June.

Golden Ears is a remarkably popular camping destination. Reserve ahead through Discover Camping for a vehicle/tent site if you plan to stay here between late May and early September; (800) 689-9025 or (604) 689-9025 in Greater Vancouver. For more details, see the BC Outdoor Primer. For those who head out on the spur of the moment, BC Parks keeps a number of sites at Golden Ears park available on a daily, first-come basis (turn-over time is noon). A camping fee of about $15 per day is charged between April and October for regular campsites; wilderness campsites charge $6. There is a sani-station for recreational vehicles near the entrance to the park. Call BC Parks, (604) 463-3513 or (604) 924-2200, for more information and a map of the park.

Golden Ears Provincial Park lies about 7 miles (11 km) north of Maple Ridge. Take either of two approaches from Hwy 7 in Maple Ridge, or from Hwy 7 east of Maple Ridge in Albion. As Hwy 7 enters the municipality of Maple Ridge from the west, it intersects with the Dewdney Trunk Rd. Drive east on Dewdney Trunk Rd, then north on 232nd St. Follow provincial park signs from here. If you approach Maple Ridge from the east on Hwy 7, turn north on 232nd St. The route from Albion begins at the Fraser River ferry slip.

A large carving of a mountain goat greets visitors at the park gates. Stop at the visitor information kiosk located just inside the gate to pick up a map. Although it's always a relief to reach this point, there is still another 7 miles (11 km) to drive into the park before you arrive at the entrance to Alouette and Gold Creek Campgrounds. Along the way you'll pass the entrances to day-use areas at Alouette Lake (see Beaches, below) and Mike Lake (see Hiking/Walking and Mountain Biking, below).

As you drive north from Hwy 7 towards Golden Ears Provincial Park, the route follows 232nd St, then turns east on Fern Crescent. Here it passes **Maple Ridge Park and Campground** (40 vehicle/tent sites), a lovely forested municipal campground and also home to an imaginatively designed water park that is open on sunny days from the end of May until early September. The sound of the Alouette River is pleasant backdrop. For more information, call or visit the Maple Ridge InfoCentre, 22238 Lougheed Hwy (Hwy 7), (604) 463-3366.

East of Maple Ridge, the countryside becomes noticeably less populated. The well-marked turnoff to **Rolley Lake Provincial Park** is at the mill town of Ruskin and lies 6 miles (10 km) north of Hwy 7. Before reaching Ruskin, the highway passes beside the small river towns of Albion and Whonnock. A ferry service links Albion with Fort Langley on the south side of the Fraser. Although much more modest in size than Golden Ears Provincial Park, Rolley Lake Provincial Park's 65 vehicle/tent campsites are more spaciously laid out. Special features include hot showers and darling Rolley Lake nearby. There is a camping fee of about $15 per night, which includes firewood. You can reserve a campsite here between March and September by calling (800) 689-9025 or (604) 689-9025 in Greater Vancouver.

A third major park worth investigating for overnight camping in the North Fraser Valley is **Sasquatch Provincial Park** (see Canoeing/Kayaking/Boating, Fishing, and Wildlife below). The park, named for the elusive Big Foot reputed to inhabit this densely wooded region, is located on the east side of Harrison Lake, almost 4 miles (6 km) north of Harrison Hot

Springs (see Attractions, below). Harrison Hot Springs lies 4 miles (6.5 km) north of the junction of Hwys 7 and 9. Rockwell Dr leads out to the park and winds beside chilly Harrison Lake's east side to the park's **Green Point** day-use area (see Picnics, below). Warmer waters are found in the three small lakes located several miles inland from Green Point. Two of them—**Hicks** and **Deer Lakes**—feature a combined 177 vehicle campsites spread out near their shores. On summer evenings, natural history talks are presented at the amphitheatres at both sites. Hicks is the larger of the two lakes. The facilities at diminutive Deer Lake are geared more towards families with young children. There is a fee of about $10 charged for an overnight stay from April to October. Campsites may be reserved in advance by calling (800) 689-9025 or (604) 689-9025 in Greater Vancouver.

There's camping west of Harrison Lake on **Harrison Bay,** where 38 vehicle/tent campsites are located just south of Hwy 7 beside the beach at **Kilby Provincial Park** (see Beaches, below). A fee of about $10 is charged April to October. The setting is lovely, but there's not much privacy between sites here. For information, contact BC Parks, (604) 824-2300.

South Fraser Valley

Derby Reach Regional Park near Fort Langley is the only Greater Vancouver Regional Park that offers overnight vehicle/tent camping. (There are group campgrounds at several other locations such as Deas Island and Campbell Valley. Call the GVRD for more information; (604) 432-6350.) The 38 riverfront sites here are allocated on a first-come basis, and there is a charge of about $11 per night, with a maximum stay of three nights. The park is situated on the original townsite of Fort Langley, the oldest continuously settled European community in British Columbia. Tall black cottonwoods shelter the campsites and support the nests of a colony of blue herons. To reach the park from Fort Langley, head south on Glover to 96th Ave. Turn west on 96th and follow it to where it joins McKinnon Crescent, and follow McKinnon to Allard Crescent, where you turn right to Derby Reach Park.

A series of three provincial parks at Cultus Lake, Chilliwack Lake, and in the Skagit Valley offer camping in the South Fraser Valley. The scenery at each is startlingly rugged, as tall Cascade peaks rise above broad, watery surfaces that reflect the mountains' glory. Cultus Lake is the easiest to reach, and along a paved road too. Chilliwack and Skagit both make you kick up some dust along their gravel approaches.

Cultus Lake Provincial Park, on the east side of Cultus Lake, lies nestled in the folds of the Cascade Mountains, about 7 miles (11 km) south of Hwy 1. Follow either of two signed exits as the highway passes through Chilliwack. During summer months the gatehouse at the entrance to the park is open 24 hours a day; (604) 858-4515. If you are seeking camping space, register here. At other times of the year simply choose your own site. There are four campgrounds within the park, at **Entrance Bay, Clear Creek, Delta Grove,** and **Maple Bay,** with a combined total of 296 vehicle/tent sites. The sites at Delta Grove are the closest to the lake. All campgrounds have very clean facilities, though the amount of hot water for showering depends on the time of day and the number of visitors competing for it. Firewood is supplied at the campsites. An overnight camping fee (about $15) is charged from April to October; at other times camping is free but services are limited. You can reserve a site here by calling (800) 689-9025 or (604) 689-9025 in Greater Vancouver. For information and a map of the park, call (604) 824-2300.

Chilliwack Lake Provincial Park is located about 30 miles (50 km) east of Cultus Lake. Take the Chilliwack Lake exit (exit 104) south from Hwy 1, then go 9 miles (14 km) south on No. 3 Rd to Chilliwack River Rd, and finally 26 miles (42 km) to the lake. The pavement gives way to a well-maintained gravel road for the last 7.5 miles (12 km). Situated on a bluff at the narrow lake's north end, the park has 100 vehicle/tent sites, the most attractive of which are located beneath some large ponderosa pines at lakeside. A wide, sandy beach spreads out below the bluff while, high above, the snowfields of Mount Corriveau present themselves like the Great Wall of China. There's a soothing sound from the nearby Chilliwack River, which drains north out of the lake and immediately turns to whitewater. The lake and river form the park's southern and western perimeter, respectively. An old trail follows the river to its confluence with **Post Creek.** Bootprints keep the path smooth in summer, while in winter these trails are popular with cross-country skiers. A fee of about $10 is charged from April to October. For more information, contact BC Parks, (604) 824-2300.

There are also rustic Forest Service recreation sites near Chilliwack Lake at **Post Creek Campground** (see Hiking/Walking, below) and at the lake's midpoint at **Paleface Creek Campground.** (Note: Of the two, Paleface is less prone to rowdies, though there are no guarantees at any of these unsupervised sites.) For a map of recreation sites in the Chilliwack Forest District, call (604) 660-7500.

If you look at a map of the **Skagit Valley** prior to the 1960s, you will notice that a road once ran through here into Washington State. Seattle City Light power company logged the Washington side of the valley and flooded it in the late 1960s to provide hydroelectric power. Although the Skagit's headwaters lie east of here in Manning Provincial Park (see Manning Provincial Park chapter), the river flows south into Ross Lake. Assuming its river form again at the lake's south end, it flows through Washington's own Skagit Valley to meet Puget Sound near La Conner.

There are three campgrounds located along the road into the Skagit Valley, which begins off Hwy 1 just west of the town of Hope at the eastern end of the Fraser Valley. Take the Hope Business Rd exit and drive a short distance to the well-marked Silver-Skagit Rd turnoff. A sign posted here for the benefit of American visitors indicates "Hozameen 38 Miles." (Hozameen—or Hozomeen, as it's spelled in Canada—is the site of a US ranger station at the north end of Ross Lake and the only road access to the lake.) Silver-Skagit Rd is paved for only a short distance south before turning to well-graded gravel for most of its 43.5-mile (70-km) length. Watch for **Silver Lake Provincial Park,** 3.7 miles (6 km) past the bridge over Silverhope Creek. A small campground is located here with several dozen vehicle/tent sites. A fee of about $9 is charged for camping between April and October. Although not within the Skagit Valley itself, the rugged landscape that rises above this campground gives a flavour for what lies ahead. For more information, call BC Parks, (604) 463-3513.

As the road leads south of Silver Lake, it passes beside some of the best fishing streams in the Lower Mainland (see Fishing, below). There are many small wilderness campsites visible from the road beside Silverhope Creek, and the Klesilkwa and Skagit Rivers.

Just south of the entrance to **Skagit Valley Provincial Park** is **Silvertip Provincial Campground** which, along with the **Ross Lake Provincial Campground** 15 miles (25 km) farther south, provides the best sites for camping. There are 50 well-spaced vehicle/tent sites at Silvertip, the prettiest of which are located on the banks of the Skagit River. The forest here is a thick mix of Douglas fir and western red cedar. The wind whistling through their branches, combined with the Skagit's rushing water, soundproofs the environment around each campsite and gives campers a sense of privacy. Mount Rideout rears up behind Silvertip, at 8,029 feet (2447 m) so tall (and the campground so close) that its peak is obscured from view here by its lower ridges. You only get a true sense of its grandeur when you look up as you journey farther south towards Ross Lake. Ross Lake Provincial Campground has 88 vehicle/tent campsites on the lake's north shore. Some sites sit in an open area beside the lake, while the majority are set back in the shelter of the nearby woods. Although not as cozy a setting as Silvertip, the views from here are stunning, as several major peaks rise above the lake. Owing to their height, the tops of these Cascade Mountain peaks escaped the most recent period of glaciation and boast a more rugged, less rounded appearance than their Coast Mountain counterparts to the north.

A fee of about $10 is charged at both campgrounds from April to October and includes firewood. Bring your own dry supply of kindling, especially early in the season when the firewood is often still wet. For more information on camping in Skagit Valley Provincial Park, call BC

Parks, (604) 463-3513.

A short distance south of the Ross Lake campground is another extensive campground at **Hozameen,** Washington. Just past the ranger station's A-frame residence is a boat launch, beach, and dozens of campsites beside the lake. On a benchland above the lake are several dozen more sites, most of which remain unoccupied except on American long weekends in summer. There is no charge for camping at Hozameen.

Beaches

Two mountain ranges hem the Fraser Valley: the Coast Mountains to the north and the Cascades to the south. In the folds of each are numerous lakes (for the most part bone-chillingly cold), the largest of which are Pitt and Harrison to the north, and Cultus and Chilliwack to the south. Ross Lake in Skagit Provincial Park is also a contender. Although most of Ross Lake's basin is located in Washington State, the easiest access to it is from the Canadian side in the Fraser Valley. The excellent beaches at most of these big lakes are easily reached, with steep-sided Pitt Lake being the one exception. You'll need a boat to reach those.

North Fraser Valley

Undoubtably the most popular beach in the North Fraser Valley is at **Alouette Lake** in Golden Ears Provincial Park (see Camping/Parks, above). You can drive right to the beach at the lake's south end, or take 15 minutes to hike to **North Beach** from the Gold Creek parking lot. Water temperatures in the dammed lake warm up quickly, and by the middle of May there's bound to be a melee of bodies stretched out in the sun here. It's a far different picture in winter when water levels (and temperatures) drop, but the mood is still magical. The forested slopes of the steep-sided valley are reflected on the lake's surface, although you have to paddle out onto it in order to truly appreciate the sight of the surrounding peaks. The longest stretch of beach is located at the Alouette day-use area near the park entrance; the approach is gentle, and is suited to wheelchairs and strollers. Farther north, **Campers Beach** lies beside the Alouette Campground. Campers Beach is near a hillside, so a short walk down a pleasant path and staircase is necessary to reach it.

There's a small beach at **Rolley Lake Provincial Park** (see Camping/Parks, above) near Ruskin, perfectly in keeping with the scale of the diminutive lake itself. It's a welcome feature when camping in the park. However, for a bigger beach experience, head to **North Beach** on nearby **Hayward Lake,** where the broad shoreline is dotted with picnic tables. Action at the beach runs hot and cold: good weather brings out the crowds, while at other times the beach can be so deserted that you'll have its centrepiece—a gracefully constructed gazebo—to yourself. Trails lead south from the beach along the reservoir and to a viewpoint on a nearby bluff. To find your way here, follow the signs north of Hwy 7 at Ruskin, a small mill town on the Fraser River between Maple Ridge and Mission, to the **Hayward Lake Reservoir Recreation Area.** For more information and a map of the recreation area, contact BC Hydro, (604) 528-7815.

The beach at **Kilby Provincial Park** (see Camping/Parks, above) is particularly popular with water-skiers. But don't forget your wet suit. Water temperature in the park's Harrison Bay is influenced by outflow from the chilled fjord waters of nearby Harrison Lake and rarely warms up above 70°F (20°C). The beach is also popular with anglers, trumpeter swans, and a thousand or more eagles that come here to feast on the annual salmon run in late autumn. There's a wonderful pioneer history associated with the Kilby Historic Store (see Attractions, below) situated next to the park. The beach is located just south of Hwy 7, about 20 miles (33 km) east of Mission.

Green Point picnic area lies just north of Harrison Hot Springs where a wide swath of grassy lawn rolls down to the shores of Harrison Lake. Here in the day-use area of Sasquatch Provincial Park (see Camping/Parks, above) you'll find picnic tables (many with barbeques), an open play area, and a beach with great exposure to the afternoon sun. **Harrison Hot Springs** is fronted by a long stretch of municipal beach, so perfect for building sand castles that an annual international competition is held here in September (see Attractions, below).

South Fraser Valley

Life on the Fraser River is often best viewed from a beach. Unfortunately, many of the river's best beaches (or "bars") are leased to lumber companies for logging booms. Several exceptions lie on either side of Fort Langley, at **Derby Reach** (see Camping/Parks, above) and **Glen Valley Regional Parks.** The hard-packed beaches at Derby Reach's **Edgewater Bar** and Glen Valley's **Two Bit, Poplar,** and **Duncan Bars** (see Fishing, below) are wide, gently sloping stretches of sand, perfect to stroll on while watching the river flow. Blue herons glide by above, while in the river a seal will occasionally poke up its head to check *you* out, sometimes with a fish in its mouth. Although 30 miles (50 km) upriver from the mouth of the Fraser, tidal action in the river is still powerful enough to leave more (or less) of the beach exposed, depending on the time of your visit.

The warm waters of **Cultus Lake** (see Camping/Parks, above) have attracted visitors to frolic and splash on its beaches for decades before the establishment of a provincial park on the lake's east side. Small private cabins clustered around **Cultus Lake Municipal Beach**'s maze of swimming wharves testify to this tradition. The warm water is so clear that at midday the gold sand on the bottom of the lake perfectly complements the colour of the summer sun. A small slide mounted on one of the wharves gives users of all ages a youthful thrill. All the amenities of beach life are found here: barbeques, a picnic gazebo, tennis courts, washroom facilities, and even a boat rental are close at hand. To reach the municipal beach, take the Cultus Lake Provincial Park exit from Hwy 1 in Chilliwack and follow the signs. Turn right at the large wooden public parking sign as you enter the town of Cultus Lake and drive the short distance to lakeside. In between dips, stroll past nearby cottages, some sporting names such as "Bide-a-wee," "Laffalot," and "Dunroamin." Mounted atop one beachfront cabin are several pairs of ancient homemade water-skis equipped with cut-off rubber boots, signs of earlier, more ingenious times.

Drive a short distance south of the municipal beach into the provincial park. **Entrance Bay, Spring Bay,** and **Maple Bay** all have a beach and picnic day-use area, where neatly trimmed grass lawns roll down to the shoreline. Tall cottonwoods shade the banks of the beach and the narrow pathways that traverse the shoreline. No matter what time of year you visit here, the setting bespeaks long, hot, breezy summer days.

Just as at Cultus Lake, you'll find a series of beaches on the eastern shoreline of **Chilliwack Lake,** beginning at the provincial park located here (see Camping/Parks above). Three more beaches front the Forest Service recreation sites located along Chilliwack Lake Rd at **Paleface** and **Depot Creeks,** and at **Sappers Park** at the south end of the lake, perhaps the prettiest of them all. The sand here is a very fine quality, which is a good thing because you'll spend more time stretched out on it than in the chilly waters of the big lake. No matter which beach you choose, there are awesome views on all sides as the ramrod-straight fir forest rises to ice-fields and scissor-cut peaks.

Kawkawa Lake Provincial Park has a large picnic area, beach, and boat launch in a forest setting, 1.5 miles (2.4 km) north of Hope. The word *kawkawa* is a poetic Native term that means "much calling of loons." Repeat it often enough and you'll get the picture. Many people journey here as part of a visit to the Othello-Quintette Railway Tunnels, 2.7 miles (4.4 km) farther north (see Crowsnest Highway: South Okanagan Valley chapter). For more information, call BC Parks, (604) 824-2300.

Picnics

North Fraser Valley

The tranquil Blue Mountain Forest in Maple Ridge provides a soothing setting for picnicking in **Kanaka Creek Regional Park** (see Canoeing/

Kayaking/Boating, below). Tables are spread about in a sunny location just above **Cliff Falls.** Come June, the salmonberry bushes are laden with ripe fruit, in brilliant shades of red and gold. They both taste the same (the yellow ones are rarer) and provide a sweet, juicy accompaniment to whatever else you have on your menu. The picnic site is several minutes' walk downhill from the parking area at the 252nd St entrance off Dewdney Trunk Rd. There's also picnicking in the park farther upstream at the **Bell-Irving Kanaka Creek Fish Hatchery** (see Wildlife, below). This open setting beside the main fork of Kanaka Creek (the two forks merge below Cliff Falls) lacks some of the mystique of Cliff Falls, but none of the calm (except in April, when schoolchildren gather for the annual release of fry from the hatchery). For more information and a map of the park, call GVRD Parks, (604) 432-6350.

Picnic shelters are located at **Alouette Lake**'s popular day-use area in **Golden Ears Provincial Park** (see Beaches, above). A strong breeze blows here in the afternoon, so pack a full hamper to help anchor the tablecloth. The open setting looks east across the lake towards the far shore, where a future expansion of the park is planned. They just can't build this beach big enough! And such a beach.

If you're on a "picnic crawl," journey the short distance between Hayward Lake and Mission on the Dewdney Trunk Rd for a peek in the backwoods. It's a change from the river scenes presented along Hwy 7, the more popular route. Both roads lead to Mission, where you'll find good picnicking with some of the best views in the Fraser Valley at **Fraser River Heritage Regional Park.** Turn north off Hwy 7 on either Stave Lake Rd or May St, then turn east on Fifth Ave. Mount Baker's snowcapped visage beams down on you from the distant horizon, while below the park the Fraser River makes a sweeping elbow turn on its way to the Pacific. One look at the wide-open spaces in this park and you'll see why this is a wonderful place to enjoy a picnic, especially towards the end of July when the park is the venue for the Mission Folk Festival. Just come prepared to do battle with the bugs. If you get too baked in the hot summer sun, seek out the cool refuge provided by a ravine that cuts through the nearby forest. Also within Mission's city limits is **Hatzic Park,** a colourful place to picnic from May to October. The park overlooks the fields of flowers that surround **Ferncliff Gardens** and is a good place to picnic after a visit to the gardens. To find it, turn north off Hwy 7 on Dewdney Trunk Rd at the Hatzic Esso station. The park entrance is on Draper St.

A third picnic park in Mission is nearby **Neilson Regional Park,** located on the west side of Hatzic Lake, an easy five-minute drive from Hatzic Park. Follow the signs to the park from Edwards St. Picnic tables dot the open field that slopes down to the shore of Hatzic Lake from the parking lot.Your reward is a view of Westminster Abbey's bell tower, which graces the skyline above the park. In October, salmon spawn in Draper Creek, which cuts through the park.

Another waterfront to admire while you picnic in the North Fraser Valley is **Kilby Provincial Park** (see Beaches, above) east of Mission, a short distance off Hwy 7 on wide-mouthed Harrison Bay. Winds blowing off the bay can have a chill edge to them, so find a sheltered table or keep a sweater handy. This is the open heart of the valley. Chilliwack lies unseen on the south side of the Fraser.

Finally, if you're headed for Harrison Hot Springs with a picnic hamper in hand, visit the **Green Point** day-use area picnic grounds just north of town on Rockwell Dr at the entrance to Sasquatch Provincial Park. There are several dozen picnic tables arranged along the lakeshore in the shade of a cottonwood grove.

South Fraser Valley

One of the best picnic sites in the south Fraser Valley is located at **Campbell Valley Regional Park** in Langley (see Hiking/Walking, below). An unspoken welcome permeates the atmosphere. Eat a little, explore a little, eat a little more—you know the routine. Choose from any of three tabled sites or simply bring a blanket and spread yourself beneath the arms of the Hanging Tree, an imposing bigleaf maple in the valley bottom beside the Little River Loop Trail. Picnic tables and toilets are located at the North Valley and South Valley entrances, as well as at the **Campbell Valley Downs Equestrian Centre** (see Horseback Riding, below). The park can be reached from either Hwy 1 or 99. From Hwy 1, take the Langley City–200th St S exit (exit 58) and travel 9 miles (14.5 km) south. Turn east on 16th Ave for the North Valley entrance and the Campbell Valley Downs Equestrian Centre. Or turn east on Eighth Ave for the South Valley entrance. From Hwy 99, take the Eighth Ave E exit (exit 2), travel 4.7 miles (7.5 km), and follow the park signs. There's also a group picnic area located at South Valley Entrance's **Old Orchard.** For reservations, call (604) 432-6352.

Matsqui Trail Regional Park (see Cycling/In-Line Skating, below) has picnic tables arranged beside the Fraser River. Most of the year these are on high ground, but during spring runoff the tables may be covered by several feet of muddy water. Fortunately, the tables are well secured and should still await you once river levels recede. Here on the Matsqui prairie you'll find many grassy areas between the river and the dike where you can spread a blanket and let the Fraser lull you with its slow but steady rhythm.

Canoeing/Kayaking/Boating

North Fraser Valley

Over the past decade, an increasingly large amount of land has been opened to the public as park in the region around **Pitt Lake** at the northwestern corner of the Fraser Valley. Today, Grant Narrows, Widgeon Marsh, and Minnekhada Regional Parks straddle both sides of the Pitt River as it carries water from the intertidal lake to the nearby Fraser River. All of this abundantly rich land is the traditional territory of the Katzie people. The four reserves that they now occupy include one at the outlet of Pitt Lake adjacent to Grant Narrows. The recently created Pinecone-Burke Provincial Park borders the reserve and encompasses much of the western side of the lake, while Golden Ears Provincial Park's boundary (see Camping/Parks, above) is the eastern shore.

It's easy to see why the Katzie have always spent most of their time around the south end of the lake. In times gone by, sturgeon, salmon, and eulachon flourished in the river, while berries and wapato (a potato-like tuber) grew in the sloughs where ducks, geese, and sandhill cranes foraged. The abundance was staggering. Occasionally, a Katzie hunting party would venture up the east side of the lake in search of mountain goats. Only in summer do the surefooted animals descend the steep slopes of the fjord in search of drinking water. Ancient pictographs still visible on the sheer rock face above the southwest side of the lake detail such hunting scenes. Although you'd have to make like a goat to reach them, the red ochre shapes are clearly visible from the lakeshore.

Several superb locations await paddlers searching for freshwater adventure and wildlife in this region. From May to September there are canoes for rent at both Grant Narrows and Alouette Lake, so you don't need your own boat to share in the experience. **Grant Narrows Regional Park** at the south end of Pitt Lake is the starting point for river exploration of a large, intertidal marsh that includes nearby Widgeon Creek. In Pitt Meadows, turn north off Hwy 7 at the Harris Rd stoplights east of the Pitt River Bridge where a large sign points to Pitt Lake. Harris Rd meanders north, then east. Turn north again at Neeves Rd. Once across a narrow bridge over the Alouette River, the road becomes rougher and its name changes from Neeves to Rennie. Deep ditches line each side of the road as mountains begin to rise before you. You are now in Pitt Polder, travelling beside the broad Pitt River north towards Pitt Lake. Grant Narrows Park lies at the end of the road. Although Grant Narrows is a pocket-sized park, it serves as the gateway to several adjacent wilderness areas, such as the **Pitt-Addington Marsh Wildlife Management Area** (see Wildlife, below). By far the most popular feature in the park is the boat launch. There is a charge of $3 for trailer-mounted boats; car-top boats launch for free. The Greater Vancouver Regional District has set aside a large area of the marsh at the mouth of Widgeon Creek, where it flows into the Pitt River, as a wildlife reserve. The GVRD offers seasonal nature programs that involve paddling in the **Widgeon Marsh Reserve;** call (604) 432-6359 for more information. The Ayla Canoe Company rents canoes at Grant Narrows most days during the summer; call (604) 941-2822 for hours and rates.

Widgeon Creek is the destination of choice for most paddlers who sprint across Grant Narrows to reach its protected backwater. The distance isn't great, and it should take only 10 minutes of hard paddling to cross the open water. Strong winds spring up on nearby Pitt Lake in the afternoon and can kick up whitecaps that will intimidate novice paddlers. (Note: Paddling on Pitt Lake is not recommended because of the winds. Even experienced powerboaters on the lake treat it with respect.) A safe approach is to launch as early in the day as possible. In fact, to get the most out of your visit here, explore near sunrise or sunset when wildlife is most active and the scenery divine.

Widgeon Creek is helpfully marked by a wooden signpost that rises up above the water of the marsh. Follow upstream, bearing to the left early on where another signpost points towards the Forest Service recreation site located an hour's paddle northwest of Grant Narrows. (If you follow the branch to the right, you enter a series of secluded backwaters perfectly suited for wildlife observation and fishing.) Late in the summer, when water levels are at their seasonal lows, you may have to hop out to float your canoe across a sandbar or two. Wear a pair of old running shoes that you can slip into and out of easily. The shoes will also come in handy when launching from Grant Narrows' muddy shore. You don't have to venture far upstream before you find the first of many fine sandy areas, suitable for sunning and picnicking. Tall cottonwood, hemlock, and solitary Sitka spruce shade the shore as Widgeon lazily winds its way into the folds of the nearby mountains. A silence envelops you. The Forest Service recreation site features a rough canoe pullout beside a broad, grassy field, where both an old road and a trail begin. Follow either to reach **Widgeon Falls.** (The old road is a holdover from the days when miners followed this route north into the upper Pitt River valley. Today, it serves as the southern terminus of a lengthy 8-day hiking trail through Pinecone-Burke Provincial Park.) The hiking trail to Widgeon Falls (2.5 miles/4 km return) is a winding affair, with several steep staircases. The road leads gently uphill to the falls and covers approximately the same distance as the trail, but for the most scenic approach, take the trail as it follows emerald-hued Widgeon Creek for half of the journey. Widgeon Falls tumbles over and through a series of smooth granite boulders. When water levels drop, it's possible to walk out on the rock shelf beside the creek for a better look. On sunny days you may even find a small pool for a quick dip. The best feature of the falls is the relentless, roaring white noise it emits, a powerful sound that clears and cleanses the mind.

Rather than follow the crowd to Widgeon Creek, take advantage of the log booms that line the Pitt River and float south along its banks. The booms help cut the wake of passing motorboats. Osprey nest on the tops of the mooring posts. In these quiet waters you'll have the best chance of observing them as well as herons, swans, and perhaps even exotic sandhill cranes, whose nesting ground lies nearby in the polder. (Polders are low-lying sections of land near rivers and oceans, dried by using a technique perfected in Holland.) Cross over to explore the backwaters along the western side of **Siwash Island,** which conceals the true riverbank at the foot of Mount Burke. The channel between the two is shallow. In summer, the wild smell of marsh marigolds in bloom perfumes the air.

If you're fortunate enough to get a ride up Pitt Lake on a powerboat that also has room to carry or tow your canoe or kayak, June is the best time to spend a few hours exploring the intertidal waterways of **Red Slough** at the north end of Pitt Lake. That's when water from freshets, combined with semi-annual high tides, makes navigation easiest. Broad arms of the slough invite paddlers back into the folds of the mountains. Lurid yellow lichen cling to the glistening, black granite walls, creating an effect as striking as an abstract expressionist painting.

Kanaka Creek Regional Park in Maple Ridge is a long corridor of protected land that stretches almost 7 miles (11 km) inland from the Fraser River. To explore the park by canoe or kayak, head for the car-top boat launch in a section of the park located near Kanaka and the Fraser's confluence. Take Hwy 7 (Lougheed Hwy) a short distance east of Maple Ridge. Just after the highway crosses the Kanaka Creek Bridge, a green GVRD sign indicates the way to Kanaka Creek Regional Park's **Riverfront** entrance. Turn south onto River Rd, cross the railway tracks, and drive to the west end of the parking lot. The boat launch is located a short distance from here. You can spend an idyllic 30 minutes paddling a mile or so upstream to a fish counting station beside the 240th Street Bridge (only open from October through mid-December). Shallow water north of here choked with blowdowns makes paddling more difficult—better to float back downstream through Kanaka's oxbow bends with your binoculars at the ready. Lazily explore the last few bends made by Kanaka between the boat launch and the Fraser. The atmosphere in this section is one of protective solitude, with only a hint of a breeze. Tall stands of evergreens and cottonwoods shade much of the creek. From their branches, hawks eye the herons who have flown across from their colony in Derby Reach Regional Park. Thick stands of green vegetation are so perfectly mirrored in the creek's languid surface that at times it is difficult to tell where the true growth leaves off and the reflection begins. In places along the creek, mauve, helmet-shaped penstemon flowers tower above the shoreline.

Golden Ears Provincial Park's **Alouette Lake** (see Beaches, above) provides a big-lake paddling experience. Head for the day-use area where a drive-in boat launch is nestled beside the picnic area. Canoe and kayak rentals are available at lakeside from June to September; the going rate is about $30 per day. The best time to explore the length of the 10-mile (16-km) lake is early or late in the day. Strong winds often arise at midday, which make paddling a tough proposition. As Alouette is a flooded lake (there's an unobtrusive earthen dam at its south end), the forest descends to the waterline. You'll find only a few good landing spots in case of trouble; the lake's east side is particularly rough.

If you wish to explore the less-visited northern half of Alouette Lake, you can save yourself an hour or more of paddling time by portaging your canoe or kayak from the Gold Creek parking lot to **North Beach** (see Beaches, above). A service road leads from the parking lot to a dock at the beach, a 15-minute hike. As you approach **Moyer Creek** two prominent features stand out on the skyline, Mounts Nutt and Gatey. You'll find much to admire as you paddle north towards wilderness campsites at Moyer Creek, a two-hour, 2.5-mile (4-km) paddle one way. In summer, several small beaches stand revealed on the lake's west side, perfect places to pause for a break in the paddling while you enjoy a dip.

If you're planning a visit to modest-sized **Rolley Lake** (see Camping/Parks, above), you can launch a small boat or inflatable raft from the beach. Powerboats are not allowed on Rolley Lake and tranquillity prevails here. Bring binoculars for wildlife viewing, and perhaps a fishing rod.

A companion site to the BC Hydro recreation site at Buntzen Lake (see Greater Vancouver chapter) is located at the dam that separates **Stave** and **Hayward Lakes** near Mission. As at Buntzen Lake, only hand-powered boats or boats with electric motors are permitted on Hayward Lake. (Canoe rentals are available on a seasonal basis from Clarke's Estate General Store, (604) 462-8065, in nearby Stave Falls.) Larger, more powerful boats should launch on Stave Lake at a site 0.6 mile (1 km) north of the North Beach turnoff. The boat launch for Hayward Lake is just beside the North Beach parking lot and has its own driveway down to the lake. Although a paddle on the lake can be enjoyable, there are almost no places along the shoreline to find shelter should you encounter strong winds.

East of Mission's **Hatzic Lake,** where you can launch a car-top boat at Neilson Regional Park (see Picnics, above), the Lougheed Hwy runs through the small town of Dewdney and then crosses a bridge onto Nicomen Island. Just before the bridge, River Rd leads off to the right and follows the shoreline of Nicomen Slough past a pub and a number of wharves to **Dewdney Nature Park,** where there's a vehicle boat launch. The Fraser River flows past just beyond sight, a short distance south of the boat launch. This is a languid section of the river where a series of sloughs forms backwaters away from the river's main course. **Strawberry Island** lies at the east end of **Nicomen Slough.** (In the 1930s, strawberries were a major cash crop in the Hatzic area.) This is one of the quietest backwaters between here and the eastern end of the Fraser Valley.

Kilby Provincial Park (see Beaches, above) is located east of Mission, a short distance off Hwy 7 on wide-mouthed Harrison Bay. There is a paved boat launch here, particularly popular with water-skiers.

Weaver and nearby **Morris Creeks** are excellent locations to explore when paddling the **Harrison River** as it flows from Harrison Hot Springs to Harrison Bay, about 12 miles (18 km) in total. You can do it point-to-point if you have two vehicles. Leave one at the boat launch at Kilby Provincial Park on Harrison Bay and another beside the public boat launch at the west end of the municipal beach in Harrison Hot Springs. Paddling is one of *the* best ways to see the languid side of the Harrison system. Wildlife lingers here—why shouldn't you?

Chehalis Lake, the source of the rugged Chehalis River, is cupped in the round folds of the mountains west of Harrison Lake. Although not nearly as large as Harrison, it is surrounded by many smaller lakes beside which you'll often find a modest Forest Service recreation site with a picnic table or two. The Forest Service sites on Chehalis Lake, complete with their own vehicle boat launches, are far grander than most others in the Fraser Valley. Unfortunately, the steepness of the hillside surrounding the lake makes reaching these sites a challenge. Chehalis Lake is typical of the long, narrow trenches scoured out by glaciers, work that these icy tongues still carry on nearby at higher elevations. Hemmed in by mountains on both sides, the scenery here is not as dramatic as elsewhere in the Coast Mountains. Only snowcapped Mount Fletcher really impresses. Its peak is best viewed from the middle of the lake, one good reason for paddling here. Another is the clear, deep, pale-green colour of the water. The southern half of the lake is prettiest as it has not been as affected by logging. Chehalis is perfectly suited to canoeing because it is not as prone to strong winds as other North Fraser Valley lakes such as Alouette or nearby Harrison. A dozen small creeks flow or fall into the lake and chill its waters.

Boat-launch ramps are located at the Chehalis Lake South and Skwellepil Creek Forest Service campsites. To reach these sites, watch for the Sasquatch Inn on Hwy 7, just north of the Harrison River Bridge. This is where you begin the 20-mile (32-km) journey to Chehalis Lake via paved and gravel roads. Two roads branch north here, one on each side of the inn. They both link up at an intersection behind the inn and continue as the Morris Valley Rd. A short distance farther, the Chehalis Valley Forest Rd branches north and leads to Chehalis Lake. A second approach to the lake is via the Fleetwood Forest Rd that begins on the east side of the Chehalis River Bridge. A medium-sized Forest Service recreation site is located on the east side of the bridge. (If you follow paved Morris Valley Rd farther east it divides: one branch leads east to Weaver Creek and the other north to **Hemlock Valley** (see Skiing/Snowboarding, below). Both Chehalis Valley and Fleetwood Forest Rds are gravelled roads that serve as active logging routes. Watch for information signs posted regarding their use. Drive with your headlights on and exercise extreme caution, especially on weekdays. The two roads merge near marker 13. There is a Forest Service site with vehicle boat launch at the south end of the lake. The approach to both this site and the one at **Skwellepil Creek** is rough and steep. It's often best if someone gets out to check road conditions before attempting a descent. The first views of the lake occur at marker 15.

In spring and early summer, when water levels are at their annual high, there's challenging river kayaking and **rafting** on both the **Chehalis** and **Chilliwack Rivers.** The Chilliwack and the Chehalis are both geologically young rivers, prone to changing their course from one spring runoff to the next. Be as mindful of sweepers as of boulder gardens. For a thorough, rapid-by-rapid examination of the Chilliwack and Chehalis Rivers, consult Betty Pratt-Johnson's *WhitewaterTrips British Columbia, Volume 2.*

The **Chehalis River** flows south from Chehalis Lake into the Harrison River. Whitewater adventurers seek out the Chehalis in May and June when water levels are high. Experienced paddlers put their canoes and kayaks in at an obscure point just above the river's confluence with Statlu Creek near marker 14. The presence of vehicles beside the road is a tip-off. Unfortunately, the Chehalis's red-rock canyon, waterfalls, and caves are hidden from sight by dense stands of scrub forest. You must run the river to view them. For information on guided rafting and kayak trips on the Chehalis, contact the Mission InfoCentre, (604) 826-6914.

Sasquatch Provincial Park (see Camping/Parks, above) near Harrison Hot Springs touches on four lakes, two of which—Deer and Hicks—are well suited to exploring in small boats. (Electric motors only on Deer Lake's diminutive surface, and 10hp is the maximum permitted on Hicks.) There are boat launches at both Deer and Hicks. Paddle to isolated Sandy Beach at Hick's south end, well worth the journey. It's always less crowded than the beach beside the campground. Two small islands also lie offshore in Hicks Lake and make for easygoing exploring.

South Fraser Valley

The **Chilliwack River** is better known than the Chehalis, which lies almost due north on the opposite side of the valley. A challenging section of the Chilliwack is used as a race course and training site for Canada's national kayak team. Watch for the metal flags strung above the river east of the Vedder Crossing Bridge that outline the kayak slalom course. In total, there are almost 22 miles (33 km) of the Chilliwack to run. Conditions on the river are more demanding in some sections than others. Only advanced kayakers should attempt to paddle the entire length when the river is at full flow. For paddlers in search of an intermediate-level outing, try the section between the Chilliwack River salmon and steelhead fish hatchery and the Vedder Bridge, a distance of about 12 miles (20 km).

To reach the Chilliwack River, take exit 104 from Hwy 1 in Chilliwack towards the provincial parks at Cultus and Chilliwack Lakes. Once you've made the exit you are on No. 3 Rd. South of Yarrow is the small river settlement of Vedder Crossing. Turn east here on the Chilliwack Lake Rd. Numerous Forest Service recreation sites are sprinkled beside the Chilliwack River and afford launch and rest areas. Several rafting companies, such as Hyak River Rafting, (604) 734-8622, offer guided rafting tours in May and June. Other good sources of information include the Chilliwack InfoCentre, (604) 858-8121, and the Chilliwack Forest District office, (604) 794-2100.

Cultus Lake is a popular location for waterskiing and jet-boating, but one of the most enjoyable ways to visit here is in the tranquillity provided by a canoe or kayak. You don't have to paddle far out from the undulating shoreline to get a good look at International Ridge, which rises above the east side of the lake. In fall, the ridge blazes with colour.

Beach Buoy Leisure Rentals, (250) 858-8841, housed in an old wood-frame building set back above the water at **Cultus Lake Municipal Beach** (see Beaches, above), rents out canoes, rowboats, and paddle wheelers. Both **Jade Bay** and **Maple Bay** in nearby Cultus Lake Provincial Park (see Camping/Parks, above) have a boat launch.

Cycling/In-Line Skating

North Fraser Valley

The **PoCo Dike Trail** ribbons the western shore of the Pitt River. Similar to dike trails throughout the Fraser Estuary, the PoCo trail provides a broad, level surface on which to cycle, with plenty of room for all. The difference between the estuary and the Fraser Valley is that the mountains are much closer to the towns of Port Coquitlam (also called PoCo) and its neighbour, Coquitlam. Here at the northwestern end of the Fraser Valley a feast of eye-catching peaks rises up on both sides of the little prairie that the dikes protect from seasonal floods. On the dike, the challenge is horizontal, not vertical. On the PoCo Trail you can easily log 30 miles (50 km) round trip; double that if you tie your ride in with the **Alouette River dike trails.** (The Alouette is a tributary on the east side of the Pitt River and has a series of dike trails of its own that leads east from Pitt Meadows towards Maple Ridge. Cross the Pitt River Bridge to reach them from the PoCo Trail.)

Travel through Port Coquitlam on Hwy 7. Turn north on Dominion Ave or Coast Meridian Rd, just west of the Pitt River Bridge. (If you turn at Coast Meridian, turn east onto Prairie Dr.) Go east on either Dominion or Prairie until it reaches the dike, and park on the shoulder where permitted. There's not much to see from the road, but as soon as you climb up to the trail you get a panoramic view. Once you get your wheels rolling, lift up your eyes and enjoy the scenery. Motion in the Pitt River sets the pace: log booms line sections of shoreline, while in places such as De Boville Slough, open areas attract anglers. The PoCo trail heads inland for a short distance in order to skirt the slough. North of here the trail becomes rougher as it enters Coquitlam. The slopes of Mount Burke are suddenly much closer at hand. The trail reaches its northern terminus at the foot of Minnekhada Knoll. A wooden picnic gazebo welcomes visitors and provides them with a view of Addington Point and the Pitt-Addington Marsh Wildlife Management Area (see Wildlife, below). A rough trail not well suited for cycling curves out through this wildlife reserve and passes two observation towers positioned beside the river. There's another viewpoint from the summit of Minnekhada Knoll. A trail leads to it from behind the kiosk, a steady 1-mile (1.6-km) hike.

Nicomen Island is a short distance east of Mission, on the opposite side of the Fraser River from Matsqui Trail Regional Park (see South Fraser Valley, below). Entirely rural and level-surfaced, the lengthy **dike trails** (at least 10 miles (16 km) each way) around the perimeter of Nicomen Island are as sleepy as it gets. This is a pretty route to cycle or in-line skate in autumn, when the champion-sized bigleaf maples turn golden. After Hwy 7 passes Hatzic Lake, it runs through the small town of Dewdney and then crosses a bridge onto Nicomen Island. Leave your vehicle beside the bridge at Dewdney and use your bicycle to explore as far east as the rustic town of Deroche, located where Hwy 7 crosses from Nicomen back onto the mainland. (If you're looking for even more easygoing riding on a paved road, a backroad leads west of Deroche along Nicomen Slough.)

South Fraser Valley

Throughout the 1990s, the municipality of Langley has been one of the leaders in the Fraser Valley when it comes to developing trails for cycling and in-line skating: the **Langley Bike and Rollerblade Trails.** This means that in many places you'll find generous, paved shoulders on both the backroads and some of the principal routes that lead through this largely rural environment. Several routes lead from Fort Langley and Aldergrove Lake Regional Park (see Mountain Biking, below). For more information and maps of the entire Langley recreation bike network routes, contact the Township of Langley, (604) 533-6082, or stop by the municipal office, 4914 221st St (at Fraser Hwy) in Langley.

The valley land between the Fraser River and the Canada-US border ripples away like the wake behind a troller. Early settlers didn't have an easy go of it; the land was boggy and *thick* with mosquitoes in summer. But having come this far, they dug in, cleared the trees, farmed the land, and, in season, hunted and fished for wild game. You can still get a scent of those years as you pedal the backroads along the border of **Surrey** and **Langley.** Make **Campbell Valley Regional Park** (see Picnics, above), off 200th St in Langley, your hub. Take Hwy 1 to the 200th St exit and drive 9 miles (14.5 km) south to either the 16th or Eighth Ave entrances. Or, from Hwy 99, take the Eighth Ave E exit and travel 4.7 miles (7.5 km) to the South Valley entrance. (Note: Bicycles are not allowed on park trails.)

Begin your ride from either of the Campbell Valley Regional Park entrances on 16th or Eighth Ave, head to 200th St, then south to Zero Ave, which runs along the Canada-US border. (Surprisingly, there aren't any fences or signs forbidding crossings, just a dense scrub forest and one lone concrete marker.) Cycle west on Zero Ave to 184th St and then turn north. You are now on the Halls Prairie Rd. Immediately watch for one of the most gracious (and spacious) pioneer farm homes on the east side as the road drops down into the Hazelmere Valley. Perched on the hillside, the view from here of the North Shore is captivating, particularly when the clouds part. From here, head to Eighth Ave and then east to return to Campbell Valley Regional Park, for a total distance of 9 miles (14 km) round trip.

Paved shoulders on the Langley backroads around **Aldergrove Lake Regional Park** (see Mountain Biking, below) provide the extended length that you wish you could find everywhere for cycling and in-line skating. They are wide and smooth and, best of all, there is only a hint of traffic along most of the route. As you ride or skate along, you can relax and let your eyes drink in the views of the surrounding farm fields with Mount Baker towering over them. Park at the entrance to Aldergrove Lake Regional Park at Eighth Ave and 272nd St and begin from here. The paved shoulders nearby on 272nd St have been installed by the district of Langley for cyclists and in-line skaters. Signs posted by the district of Langley point out the route to follow. A note of caution: Although you can in-line skate in the park, a steep hill dropping down to the lake will prove too challenging for novice skaters.

Matsqui Trail Regional Park's level dike trail runs for over 6 miles (10 km) beside the Fraser River's south shore across from the town of Mission. It offers good views of the Fraser and the quiet farms that border it, as well as the snowcapped Cascade Mountains. The main trailhead can be a little tricky to locate. It sits under the south end of the Mission Bridge, which links Hwy 11 in Abbotsford and Matsqui with Hwy 7 and Mission to the north. Turn west off Hwy 11 onto Harris, then north on Riverside, which will take you right to the park's Mission Bridge picnic area.

There're always a few fisherman here casting from a nearby sandy fishing bar (see Fishing, below). Industries crowd the riverbanks west of Mission, but thin out as the trail leads east of the bridge. Several old riverboats are tied up at the Canadian Pacific Railway dock. Nearby fields are dotted with black-and-white Holsteins. The trail runs beside these fields and has long stretches where the full capabilities of a bike can be tested. Paths lead down off the trail to picnic spots beside the river.

Rounding the last major bend before the trail reaches Sumas Mountain and the Page Rd trailhead, you finally look out at wilderness on all sides. Mission's famous Westminster Abbey (see Attractions, below) presides on a ridge to the northwest. The town of Hatzic is directly across the river. Strawberry Island is the large sandy expanse to the east on the far side of the Fraser. All signs of industry are beyond view downstream. This is the mighty Fraser as it should be: big river, big landscape, big fun. The Matsqui trail ends at an old quarry on the side of Sumas Mountain.

Riding time both ways from the Mission bridge is about one hour. With so many places to pull off and watch the river flow, it just might take you longer. In fact, you can expand your ride by tacking on the 4-mile (6.6-km) round trip between the west side of the bridge and the park's **Glenmore Road** trailhead. This stretch leads past Gladwin Pond, and it's rougher in places than the dike trail—skinny tires will definitely be a disadvantage here in wet weather. The backroads that lead west from the Glenmore Rd trailhead pass through Bradner, Glen Valley Regional Park (see Beaches, above), Fort Langley, and Derby Reach Regional Park (see Camping/Parks, above). The Pemberton Hills present a smoldering challenge to cyclists along the way. The best map to consult for cycling this region is *Fraser Valley,* published by World Wide Books and Maps, 736A Granville St in Vancouver, (604) 687-3320.

One of the most laid-back rides in the South Fraser Valley takes riders along a section of the Canada-US border near Cultus Lake (see Beaches, above). Drive (don't ride) along the Columbia Valley Hwy as it heads south past Cultus Lake Provincial Park (see Camping/Parks, above) onto the benchland above the town of Lindell Beach, a small lakefront village similar in flavour to Cultus Lake. Leave your vehicle here and begin to ramble by bike through the **Columbia Valley.** In contrast to the narrow shoulders and highway traffic running the length of Cultus Lake, the roads south of Lindell Beach are much quieter and ideal for cycling.

Columbia Valley Hwy divides south of the town's golf course. Follow either one. Both Frost Rd and Columbia Valley meet near the border after looping through the valley. Along the way, several side roads lead off into the far reaches of the valley. Avoid any that are posted "No Exit" and you will have no trouble finding your way.

Both major roads level out soon after cresting on the benchland above Lindell Beach, and run 7.4 miles (12 km) to the Canada-US border. The border is marked by one small obelisk and a narrow 40-foot (12-m) cut visible on the hillside above the valley. Near the border, on the valley's east side, the waters of Frost Creek run towards Cultus Lake. Canyon Rd is a pleasant, albeit narrow, gravel road that leads down to a bridge spanning the creek, then back up to Frost Rd.

Mountain Biking

North Fraser Valley

If you're a mountain biker looking for an aerobic workout, head for trails on **Burke Mountain** (more properly called Mount Burke) in Coquitlam. You'll be in good gearhead company here. The mountain is a network of old skidder trails and logging roads and some more recent singletrack, including the in-your-face Sawblade, which is comparable to even the nastiest technical riding trails on the North Shore. To find the trailhead, from Hwy 7 go north on Coast Meridian Rd. Instead of heading for the PoCo trail (see Cycling/In-Line Skating, above) continue on almost to the end of Coast Meridian and turn right on Harper. Follow Harper as it climbs Mount Burke. Park beside a gate next to the Coquitlam Gun Club and begin pumping uphill from here. Follow **Woodland Walk Trail** on your left. It soon divides, with the beauty-view **Coquitlam Lakeview Trail** heading off to the right. Both Woodland and the Lakeview trail are crossed in several places by the rough—and renowned—**Sawblade Trail.** An alternate route is the **Galloway Trail.** To find it, stay right at all turns as you cycle east from the gun club. Watch for the Galloway trailhead on your right before the road passes beneath some power lines. Although the trail begins with a steep descent, it soon moderates to an intermediate singletrack with a sweet drop to paved Galloway Rd. Turn right on Galloway, which leads back to Harper.

Looking north from **Grant Narrows Regional Park** (see Canoeing/

Kayaking/Boating, above) on Pitt Lake's south shore, visitors peer out at the long lake whose surface is tightly hemmed in by the surrounding mountains: Burke to the west, Alouette and Blanshard to the east. If you arrange a boat ride up the lake, you enter a much less visited region that attracts mountain bikers as well as anglers, hikers, and paddlers. Two companies that provide transportation and guided tours of the Upper Pitt River region are Pitt Lake Legendary Adventure Tours, Ltd., (604) 942-9350, and the Pitt Lake Resort, (800) 665-6206.

The J. S. Jones Timber Company has a log-sorting yard beside the wharf where you land. Head north from here along the **Upper Pitt River Logging Road.** It's a relief to trade the throbbing boat engine for the whistle of wind through the vents in your helmet. The voice of the Pitt River sings through the woods to the west of the road as it flows south from its headwaters in Garibaldi Provincial Park, 30 miles (50 km) north of the lake. The Mamquam Glacier's massive wall of snow and ice stands like a fortress on the skyline when seen from here. Olive-coloured moss cloaks the arms of the sturdy vine maples, some of the largest in the Lower Mainland, that line the road. Solitary Sitka spruce rise from the wetland of Red Slough to the east.

Knobby tires come in handy as you cycle the rough logging roads that parallel both sides of the river. The road divides at marker kilometre 5 on the Pitt River Rd. If you follow the east side, the road leads past the small settlement of Alvin, where these days only a logging-company caretaker is in permanent residence. Alvin lies about 2 miles (3 km) north of the road's divide. A short distance beyond Alvin is one of the oldest fish hatcheries in the province, run by members of the Katzie band. It's worth a stop here just to see the waters of Corbold Creek charge through a narrow canyon before spilling onto the gravel spawning bar below. Once the snow leaves the ground, cyclists can enjoy a 10-mile (16-km) ride north of the hatchery to the Pitt River wilderness hot springs. Ask at the Pitt Lake Resort, (800) 665-6206 or (604) 520-1796, located at the kilometre 7 marker on Pitt River Rd, for directions and current conditions.

On the opposite side of the Upper Pitt River from the fish hatchery lies the narrow **Boise Valley.** To make your way there, follow the west branch of the logging road where it divides at the "kilometre 5" mark. Cross a nearby log bridge over the Upper Pitt and head north. The Boise Logging Rd is much more challenging than its counterpart on the opposite side of the valley. This is where conditioning counts, particularly where the road climbs for about 2 miles (3 km) towards the Cougar Lakes. Follow the road another 5 miles (8 km) to its end, at which point a hiking trail through the Boise Valley section of Pinecone-Burke Provincial Park begins.

There are two good mountain-bike rides for the taking in Golden Ears

Provincial Park (see Camping/Parks, above). A paved road leads west from the parking lot at **Mike Lake** into the **UBC Research Forest.** Although bikes are not allowed in the forest, they are permitted on the rough **Alouette Mountain fire access trail** (12 miles/20 km return) that begins from the paved research forest road a short distance north of Mike Lake. This is a quiet, forested stretch, far removed from the crowds at nearby Alouette Lake (see Beaches, above). A good intermediate hiking trail that intersects with the Alouette Mountain fire access trail at several points leads from Mike Lake to Lake Beautiful and the summit of Alouette Mountain (12 miles/20 km return). Lake Beautiful is located at approximately the halfway point between Mike Lake and the top of Alouette Mountain itself. The diminutive, lily-pad-covered lake is a bit of a letdown, overgrown and sheltered as it is by the surrounding virgin forest of mountain hemlock and yellow cedar. Uphill from Lake Beautiful the trail becomes all but impassable to mountain bikes. (Tell that to the rogue who left a tire tread in wet cement beside the cairn at the top of Alouette Mountain.) The thrilling descent down the Alouette Mountain fire access trail takes half the time. For more details, call the UBC Research Forest at (604) 463-8148, or BC Parks in Golden Ears at (604) 463-3513. The other mountain-bike trail in Golden Ears is the **East Canyon Trail,** which begins from the Gold Creek parking lot. For a description of this route, see Hiking/Walking, below.

Blue Mountain, in the municipality of Maple Ridge, is a victim of its own popularity. The soft loam that forms much of the area's trails has been severely rutted by years of motorbiking. This Forest Service area is still a great place to ride for the technically proficient. For every rutted route, there's a soft, fresh trail to be had. One of the more popular trails is the **Humphill Downhill,** but with the number of side trails, it might take you a while to figure it out. It's not a long ride, though, and once you've found the right line, you'll want to ride it a few more times, just for the thrill of it. Another popular trail is the **Muzz,** complete with wooden sidewalks, or corduroys, to get you over the really muddy sections. For trail information, drop by one of the bike stores in Maple Ridge, such as Westridge Sports Stop, (604) 465-1156; High Gear Bicycles, (604) 466-2016; or Maple Ridge Cycles, (604) 463-4823. To reach Blue Mountain, travel east of Maple Ridge on Dewdney Trunk Rd, then turn north on either 256th St or McNutt Rd. Trails begin from the gates at the end of each. Detailed descriptions of all rides, including Humphill Downhill and Muzz, are included in *Mountain Biking British Columbia* by Darrin Polischuk.

As Dewdney Trunk Rd heads northwest of Mission, watch for the Forest Service recreation trails on **Bear Mountain** and **Red Mountain.** Signs appear as the road nears Stave Lake's Ruskin Dam (see Fishing, below). Don't park on Rod 'n Gun Club property, even though you have to bike through it to get to Red Mountain, a loop with some side trails to explore, depending on your mood. Red Mountain is the site of an annual race, and the trails are fast yet also moderate. Not so with the companion Bear Mountain, just across the road, which is a *bear* of a ride. But even it can't compare to the **Mount Mary Ann Trails,** near Westminster Abbey. Park in the Fraser River Heritage Regional Park (see Picnics, above), just off Stave Lake Rd on Fifth Ave in Mission. (You might want to get the Benedictines to administer last rites before you make any attempt on these. This is technical riding at its most difficult: fast, steep, and out of control.) Local mountain-bike contacts in Mission include Wenting Cycle Shop, (604) 826-1411, and Golden Ears Cycle, (604) 820- 2454.

Miles of old logging and hydro power roads run through the hills surrounding Hicks and Deer Lakes in **Sasquatch Provincial Park** (see Camping/Parks, above), perfect for a moderately challenging but lengthy mountain-bike ride. Bear Mountain (not to be confused with the *other* Bear Mountain near Stave Lake) lies just outside the park to the south. Take Rockwell Dr from Harrison Hot Springs around the east side of the lake, almost to the Green Point picnic area (see Picnics, above). As Rockwell climbs a steep hill, watch for a rough side road that leads off to the right. This is where the Bear Mountain Trail begins. Park here. A series of old roads climbs from the Bear Mountain trailhead beside Harrison Lake for almost 6 miles (9 km) with an elevation gain of 3,300 ft. (1000 m). Head uphill on an old road that skirts a fenced mining-company property and joins an active logging road. You'll have to bike-and-hike in places, or stash your two-wheel chariot for a final ascent on foot. Catch your breath as you drink in panoramic views of the Fraser Valley and peaks to the south, with mountain scenery on the other three sides.

Also in the Harrison Lake region, the **Green Mountain Trail,** near Agassiz, rates a mention. Talk it up with one of the local bike stores, such as Brad's Skate and Cycle in Abbotsford, (604) 858-0017; or Pedalsport, (604) 795-2453, and Central Cycle, (604) 792-2565, both in Chilliwack.

The folks over at **Hemlock Valley** (see Skiing/Snowboarding, below) have opened their clear-cut hillsides in the summer to mountain bikes. Come ride the trails, but on hot days make sure you pack two water bottles *and* a camelback, as there's precious little shade. Just give those hemlocks another few decades to get growing again. Call High Roads Mountain Bike Company, (604) 797-4411, in Agassiz, or Hemlock Valley Ski Area, (800) 665-7080, for more information.

South Fraser Valley

When measured by the amount of fun that trail riding provides, diminutive **Aldergrove Lake Regional Park** outperforms its size. Located on the dividing line between Langley and Abbotsford, a network of easygoing trails, about 7 miles (12 km) in total length, lead through the wooded park and lend themselves to exploration by bicycle. Mount Baker's snow cone towers above the valley and is best appreciated when seen from a viewpoint along the **Rock N' Horse Trail.** To reach Aldergrove Lake Regional Park, take the 264th St exit south from Hwy 1 (Trans-Canada Hwy) to Eighth Ave (Huntington Rd), and then turn east to reach the main park entrance at the intersection of Eighth Ave and 272nd St. (There are equestrian and pedestrian entrances on the west and east sides of the park, 272nd St and Lefeuvre Rd, respectively.) Another approach is to drive east from Hwy 99 on 16th Ave, enjoying the countryside along South Surrey's historic North Bluff Rd as it heads to the park.

Vedder Peak, just off Parmenter Rd near Cultus Lake (see Camping/Parks, above) is rife with bike trails. Brad's Skate and Cycle Shop, (604) 858-0017, in Abbotsford can give you pointers on which trails are right for you. Most of the trails split off from the **Vedder Ridge Loop,** a technically easy cardiovascular workout that offers some great views and some stiff cranking on the side trails.

Mountain-bike trails climb the sides of **McKee Peak** near Clayburn Village in Abbotsford. There are two approaches. From Hwy 1, turn north on Sumas Way to Old Clayburn Rd, right on McKee, and park just past the golf course. From Hwy 11, turn southeast on Sumas and then along as above. The trail runs off to the right of the golf course and leads up to McKee Peak along an old Forest Service road. There are a couple of side trails that will lead you back down, but if you don't make it to the top for the view of the Fraser Valley, you've missed the whole point. For more information on local trails in the Abbotsford area, contact The Bike Shop, (604) 852-2883; Hub Sports, (604) 859-8316; Life Cycles, (604) 859-2453; or Caps, (604) 852-4770.

Fishing

North Fraser Valley

Some of the best fishing in the Fraser Valley is found on the **Upper Pitt River** (see Mountain Biking, above) as attested to by the frequency with which steelhead strike at the barbless lures of fly-fishing anglers. (Fishing is strictly catch-and-release on the Upper Pitt.) The Pitt Lake Resort is an excellent source of information (call or fax (604) 520-1796 or (800) 665-6206) as are any of the local Travel InfoCentres.

Along Fern Crescent between Maple Ridge Municipal Park and Golden Ears Provincial Park (see Camping/Parks, above), you'll often see anglers patiently casting for trout from smooth boulders beside the fast-flowing **Alouette River.** River access is from Fern Crescent at one of two municipal locations. Contact Maple Ridge InfoCentre, (604) 463-3366. If you visit Golden Ears park with a car-top boat, you can launch from a small wharf next to the parking area at **Mike Lake** and enjoy a quiet paddle. The wharf is also a good place to toss in a fishing line.

At **Rolley Lake Provincial Park** (see Camping/Parks, above), anglers have as much competition from blue herons as from each other. You can toss in a line from many points along a trail that runs around the perimeter of the lake, beginning from a modest beach and boat launch in the day-use parking lot. (Powerboats are not allowed on Rolley Lake.) Docks jut out into the lake at several locations, from which anglers can toss in a line. Although the lake is well stocked early in the season with rainbow and cutthroat trout, it is often fished out by late summer. The catch limit is two per day.

Kanaka Creek is one of the healthiest sportfishing channels in the North Fraser Valley. Steelhead, sea-run cutthroat trout, and chum and coho salmon are all found below the 240th Street Bridge (see Canoeing/Kayaking/Boating, above) where a fish-counting fence is located. Angling is not permitted upstream from this point. A provincial freshwater fishing licence is required on this section of the creek and a federal tidal-fishing licence is needed to fish the Fraser from the mouth of the creek.

Coho and chum salmon spawn in the **Stave River** in late October and November, a good time for visiting and viewing. Wide spawning channels have been dug on each side of the river. The best place to begin is the **Ruskin Recreation Area.** To reach it, take Lougheed Hwy (Hwy 7) east of Maple Ridge to the small Fraser River town of Ruskin. Turn north as if heading to Rolley Lake Provincial Park. Drive a short distance to the Ruskin Dam. Follow Ruskin Rd east across the top of the dam and descend 0.6 mile (1 km) down to the site gates. A gated boat launch is on your left as you enter; car-top boats can be launched here. A short trail leads to the Stave River, where a wooden footbridge leads across the gravelled spawning channel onto the banks of the river itself. Looking downstream from the recreation site, you can see Ruskin's sawmills beside the Fraser River's brown expanse.

Both **Deer** and **Hicks Lakes** in **Sasquatch Provincial Park** (see Camping/Parks, above) near Harrison Hot Springs are ideal for angling from a small boat. (Powerboats are restricted to electric motors on Deer Lake and 10hp is the maximum permitted on Hicks.) Trout fishing is popular at both stocked lakes, and also at aptly named **Trout Lake** closer to the park entrance. There are boat launches at both Deer and Hicks, whereas only a rough trail leads downhill from the park road to Trout

Lake. If you don't have a boat, try casting from the shoreline beside the camping area at Hicks Lake.

South Fraser Valley

Crescent Island lies on the opposite side of the Fraser River from the Stave River, and shelters **Glen Valley Regional Park**'s fishing bars from sight. (A fishing bar is an expanse of riverbed that lies exposed at low tide.) Glen Valley lies 4.3 miles (7 km) east of Fort Langley and, together with Derby Reach Regional Park, offers some of the best saltwater fishing on this section of the Fraser River. Head east from Fort Langley along 88th Ave: **Two-Bit Bar** is located at the intersection of 88th Ave and 272nd St. Follow River Rd east of Two-Bit Bar to reach **Poplar** and **Duncan Bars,** a total distance one way of about 2.5 miles (4 km) between the three sites. Of the park's three fishing bars, Poplar Bar is the largest and offers the most interesting options. You can fish, launch a car-top boat, and explore several riverside trails.

Derby Reach Regional Park (see Camping/Parks above) sits across the Fraser River from the entrance of Kanaka Creek. The park's **Edgewater Bar** is a big attraction to anglers of all ages who come to set their lines for salmon and watch the Fraser River flow by. Fishing bars that were once prevalent along the Fraser have more recently been usurped by log booms, which makes Edgewater even more valuable. What gives this park top billing are the squares of melmac inlaid at the corner of each picnic table. This is the officially sanctioned place to clean your salmon. Just the sight of it raises one's hopes.

Anglers congregate near the south end of the Mission Bridge in **Matsqui Trail Regional Park** (see Cycling/In-Line Skating, above). This is the great divide in the Fraser River. Upstream from the nearby Canadian Pacific Railway bridge anglers must carry a provincial freshwater licence, while downstream from it the feds want you to carry a tidal-fishing licence. Take your pick or carry both. Sturgeon, coho and chinook salmon, steelhead, and cutthroat trout await your cast. The GVRD requests that anglers *not* use the picnic tables to prepare bait or clean fish (no melmac inserts here yet).

With the autumn rains comes the rising of water levels in Lower Mainland rivers and creeks. Then the welcome mat is out for schools of salmon that have been waiting for just such a seasonal occurrence to begin the journey upstream to their spawning grounds. As you drive the Chilliwack River Rd, you pass beside the **Chilliwack River** (see Canoeing/Kayaking/Boating, above). At these times you'll encounter riverbanks lined with expectant fishermen waiting to intercept them. There are frequent Forest Service recreation sites along the road where anglers can park and easily reach the river. The Royal Canadian Mounted Police station themselves by the bridge at Vedder Crossing, carefully scrutinizing the contents of cars for violations of the four-coho-per-day catch limit. A fish hatchery is located beside the river, 13 miles (21 km) east of the Vedder bridge. Fishing is not allowed in the river between the hatchery and Chilliwack Lake.

Owing to **Chilliwack Lake**'s year-round chilly water (see Camping/Parks, above), it attracts serious anglers in pursuit of various species of surface-feeding trout, including rainbow, cutthroat, kokanee, and dolly varden char. Be cautious when out in a small boat as Chilliwack Lake's sparkling waters are prone to being whipped up by winds that funnel out to the coast. Lakeside casting is possible from the sandbars at Paleface and Depot Creeks on the lake's east side.

The **Skagit River** (see Camping/Parks, above) is one of the premier rainbow trout rivers in Western North America. Angling is particularly popular along the Silver-Skagit Rd between **26-Mile Bridge** day-use area and **Chittenden Bar** day-use area. In addition to these two sites, there's off-road parking and quick access to the Skagit along the Silver-Skagit Rd at **Shawtum, Rhododendron Bar, Strawberry Bar,** and **Nepopekum** day-use areas for both riverbank and float angling. A BC freshwater-angling licence must be purchased before arriving in the park. These are available locally in Hope and Silver Creek. Fishing is strictly catch-and-release with barbless hooks on the Skagit River.

For general information on fishing regulations, contact the BC Fish and Wildlife Regional Office, (604) 582-5200 or (800) 665-7027.

Hiking/Walking

North Fraser Valley

Minnekhada Regional Park in Coquitlam (see Wildlife, below) has almost 5 miles (8 km) of trails, most of which are of the gentle-walking variety. These trails lead through a wooded area surrounding two large marshes. You can walk the perimeter of the park in two hours, experiencing the moods of the seasons. For those with enough energy, **High Knoll Trail** will get your heart rate up in a hurry. Although not a long trail, its ascent is steady from the marsh to the viewpoint that overlooks the Pitt and Fraser Rivers and the farm fields. From Hwy 7 in Port Coquitlam, turn north on Coast Meridian Rd, travel 1.5 miles (2.5 km) to Apel Dr, from where signs direct visitors the remaining 3 miles (5 km) to the park's Quarry Rd entrance.

Although the best way to experience the lower section of **Kanaka Creek Regional Park** is by boat (see Canoeing/Kayaking/Boating, above), for an easygoing walking tour, follow **Riverfront Trail** on foot as it leads out to Kanaka's confluence with the Fraser from the Hwy 7 trailhead. Along the way, climb the three-storey observation tower beside the creek, which provides an overview of the landscape here. Bring your binoculars, as this quiet refuge sustains a host of fascinating flyers. The creek and river close in on both sides of the nose of land as you follow the trail west. Decaying pilings offer mute testimony that fishing boats once tied up in this sheltered backwater. From an observation deck that overhangs the riverbank, you get broad views of the Fraser. Farther along, a gracefully arched bridge spans the mouth of the creek.

This is as far as you can explore in the riverfront section of the park, but you can log an hour's more walking time around the **Cliff Falls** area of the park, a 10-minute drive inland. Turn west onto Hwy 7 from River Rd, cross the Kanaka Creek Bridge, then turn immediately north on Kanaka Creek Rd. This route takes you past the Kanaka Creek Fish Fence to 240th St. (The fish-counting fence is worth visiting in autumn, when spawning salmon school here. See Fishing, above.) Just north of the fish fence, turn left on 240th St and follow it to Dewdney Trunk Rd. Turn right and follow Dewdney Trunk east to 252nd St, where park signs indicate the entrance to Cliff Falls. Walk down a short trail that leads to the first of two bridges that span the twin waterfalls conjoining the separate arms of Kanaka Creek. Another trail leads down to the north fork of the creek. Rock-hopping the streambed in either direction is not difficult when water levels are low. In summer, this is a lovely environment in which to cool off. Small pools have been worn in the creekbed, not big enough for swimming but ideal for giving overheated feet a treat. Wooden staircases and sturdy bridges lead through the nearby forest, which rises and falls dramatically in places. Trails lead east from Cliff Falls to the Bell-Irving Salmon Hatchery (see Wildlife, below), an easy half-hour walk. For a map of Kanaka Creek's trails, contact GVRD Parks, (604) 432-6350.

Golden Ears Provincial Park (see Camping/Parks, above) offers more walking and hiking close to Vancouver than any other single destination. Over a dozen trails lead to various destinations throughout the park, including a lengthy 8-mile (12-km) one-way journey to the Golden Ears themselves.

Adjacent to park headquarters, tiny Mike Lake (see Mountain Biking, above) is the starting point for the **Alouette Mountain Hiking Trail** (12 miles/20 km return) trek to the summit of Alouette Mountain. Although there aren't many open views along the way, once on top you have a panoramic perspective south across the Fraser Valley into Washington and west across the Strait of Georgia to Vancouver Island. Shorter excursions in Golden Ears Provincial Park include the 2.6-mile (4.2-km) **Mike Lake Trail.** Search the understorey for signs of old logging equipment and wildflowers such as the delicate pink azalea, with petals shaped like five-pointed stars. By the beginning of summer, clusters of bright red elderberries hang from the branches that droop overhead. A month later, devil's club, a relative of ginseng, with broad maple-shaped leaves, puts forth red berries from the ends of its pointed—and very prickly—stems.

In addition, two more walking trails begin from the park's Alouette Lake day-use area. The **Lookout** and **Loop Trails** each take walkers on a 1.5-mile (2.5-km) round trip from lakeside to an elevated viewpoint. Allow an easy hour to complete the loop, just time enough to dry off between swims. The **Spirea Nature Trail** is a short walk that winds through the woods adjacent to the park's main road and introduces visitors to the fascinating variety of flora in the forest understorey. The trail begins from the parkway near the entrance to Alouette Lake.

Two trails begin from the Gold Creek day-use area parking lot, located at the north end of the park's main road. Both lead to a set of waterfalls on Gold Creek. The Lower Falls Trail (easy; 3.5 miles/5.5 km return) is one of the most popular walks in Golden Ears Provincial Park. The East Canyon Trail (moderate; 17 miles/28 km return) is much rougher. One of the benefits of taking either route to the falls is the views of the Golden Ears and other peaks in this group that stand revealed on the skyline above Gold Creek.

Lower Falls Trail is a gentle, cedar-bark trail that winds through a mixed forest of mature vine maple and conifers. This is an especially pretty walk in autumn, when pancake-size bigleaf-maple foliage blazes red and reflects in the golden waters of the aptly named creek.

East Canyon Trail runs along the east side of Gold Creek and leads to the upper falls and far beyond. At first the trail follows a service road from the Gold Creek parking lot, past a metal gate, then left where it divides. (If you stay right, this road brings you to Alouette Lake's North Beach in 15 minutes. See Camping/Parks, above.) The road, signed with orange markers, climbs gradually uphill. Although you can't see Gold Creek, its voice filters up through the surrounding forest. Moss-covered limbs of gracefully bowed vine maple frame the road. Large cedar stumps attest to the size of the ancient forest that once stood here. The rubble from runaway creekbeds, prone to flooding during heavy storms, cuts across the roadway in several places. At the "2.5 km" sign lies the wreckage of an old log bridge that has been swept aside. A short distance beyond, watch for a rough trail, part of which is a broad, dry creekbed, that leads downhill to a dramatic view of the thundering falls. Mind your step here.

If you want to explore the far reaches of Golden Ears Provincial Park, hike the **West Canyon Trail** (easy; 6 miles/10 km return), which links with the **Golden Ears Trail** (moderate; 10 miles/20 km return) to eventually reach the summit of the north Ear, part of the two horn-shaped granite formations easily spotted from as far away as Washington and the southern Gulf Islands. An alpine cabin sits below the summit on Panorama Ridge and sleeps eight. In summer, many climbers use Panorama Ridge as their base to make an approach to the Golden Ears, which form the twin peaks of Mount Blanshard. A note of caution: Weather patterns in the region may change rapidly. Storm clouds smoke up the valleys so quickly that hikers on exposed sections of the trail may have little time to shelter. Hypothermia is always a threat, even on the hottest days. Plan (and dress) accordingly. For more information and a map of park trails, contact BC Parks, (604) 463-3513, or pick up a map of the park at the information kiosk located just inside the park gates.

A gentle walking trail runs around the perimeter of **Rolley Lake** (see Camping/Parks, above), part of which includes a boardwalk that crosses a wetland at the lake's west end. An astounding variety of birds can be spotted if you wait patiently here. Other good viewing spots are from the docks that jut out at several places around the lake.

Another easy walking trail loops around **Hicks Lake** in **Sasquatch Provincial Park** (see Camping/Parks, above) near Harrison Hot Springs. Budget an hour or two to complete the 2.5-mile (4-km) round-trip route. One of the rewards is that the trail passes Sandy Beach at the south end of the lake. Far less visited than the beach beside the campground, this is a pleasant resting place. You may also wish to explore the **Beaver Pond Interpretive Trail** beside Hicks Lake, an easy 20-minute walk. Another mostly level trail winds its way around **Deer Lake** nearby. Watch for osprey, who swoop down on unsuspecting fish as you explore the lake's south side. For a map of the trails in Sasquatch Provincial Park, contact BC Parks, (604) 824-2300.

South Fraser Valley

The hillside above the campgrounds at **Cultus Lake Provincial Park** (see Camping/Parks, above) is crossed by the **Edmeston Road Trail** (easy; 8 miles/12 km return), once used as a logging road. The trail begins from Edmeston Rd south of Columbia Valley Rd and east of the Entrance Bay campground. As it nears Teapot Hill, the Edmeston Rd Trail merges with the Road 918 Trail, and together they lead to a fine viewpoint at the top of Teapot Hill. The **Road 918 Trail** (3 miles/5 km return) begins on the Columbia Valley Hwy across from the park's Honeymoon Bay group campground and provides a shorter, albeit steeper approach to Teapot Hill's viewpoint, from where you look west across Cultus Lake and south into Washington. Because the slopes of International Ridge are forested with an eye-pleasing mix of evergreen and mature deciduous trees, the hillside burns with colour in the fall and gleams with fresh green in early spring. Salmonberry bushes are plentiful in this lush, ferned environment. Picking is usually best in June. For more information and a map of the park, contact BC Parks, (604) 824-2300.

There's no more thrilling a sight while hiking than an ancient forest cloaking the sides of a mountain range. Hiking trails in the Chilliwack Lake region (see Camping/Parks, above) lead to magnificent stands of western red cedars at both the north and south ends of the lake. The alpine scenery here is so enchanting that you may be tempted to head above the tree line altogether.

Radium Lake lies cupped on the side of craggy Mount Webb, which overlooks Chilliwack Lake. As the Chilliwack Lake Rd nears Chilliwack Lake, watch for Paulsen Rd. Turn west on Paulsen and drive past a group of cottages to lot 24. Park here and follow a short distance to Post Creek's confluence with the Chilliwack River. A rough bridge spans the creek while a sturdy suspension bridge conveys hikers across the adjacent river. The **Radium Lake Trail** (moderate; 8 miles/12 km return) begins on the far side and to the right of the bridge. From here the trail climbs to a small Forest Service cabin beside Radium, one of several alpine lakes uphill from the Chilliwack River. Use the cabin as your base for mountaineering on the slopes of Mount Webb. For more information and a trail map, contact the Chilliwack Forest District office, (604) 820-2055, or the local Forest Service office in Rosedale, (604) 794-2100.

A Forest Service campsite is located beside the Chilliwack Lake Rd at Post Creek, a short distance north of the entrance to **Chilliwack Lake Provincial Park** (see Camping/Parks, above). The entrance to it may not be marked, as signposts to favourite campsites in the Fraser Valley vanish with irritating regularity. The steep turnoff to the recreation site's parking lot is on the east side of the road. Post Creek is the trailhead for a popular Fraser Valley route that leads to both Lindeman and Greendrop Lakes, which have recently been given provincial-park status. Along the way, the moderately difficult 8-mile (12-km) round-trip hike leads past some of the largest stands of old-growth forest left in the Fraser Valley. Plan on five to six hours round trip to complete the route to both lakes. By itself, **Lindeman Lake** is a strenuous 3-mile (5-km) round-trip hike. A wide path begins to climb beside Post Creek's south side. As if to test your resolve (and your fitness level) the steepest part of the trek to the lakes is at the outset. Cool sounds from the creek and shade from the massive Douglas firs help distract you from the demands of exertion. After a half-hour ascent through the shaded forest, Lindeman Lake's brilliant blue-green surface suddenly unfolds before you beneath the open sky. The rocky shoreline doesn't provide much of an approach. Pause on the wooden staircase at the far end of the lake to marvel at the beauty. This scene is characteristic of the Cascade Mountains, which run from here into California.

For some, reaching Lindeman Lake will be rewarding enough. If you have the stamina, carry on to **Greendrop Lake** where more awe-inspiring sights await. Along the way, the trail passes through a typical coastal rain-forest environment of prickly devil's club fed by snowmelt well into summer, so be sure to wear waterproof boots. All the slogging is worth it when you finally catch sight of the towering western red cedars that anchor the mountain slope above the lake. In places, their roots drape like pipelines into Greendrop Lake, feeding shaggy trunks that taper skyward 200 feet (50 m) or more. Biomass never looked—or smelled—better, as gracefully draped skirts of cedar boughs perfume the fresh air. Find a blowdown to rest on beside the lake and inhale your fill. For more information, contact BC Parks, (604) 824-2300.

Elsewhere around Chilliwack Lake the contrast in the skyline between the nearby Fraser Valley and the lake is remarkable. Lumpy mountain ridges abruptly give way to rugged Cascade Range peaks. This geographical transition is so immediate that you feel as if you've entered another world hidden behind the valley's pastoral veneer. Strong winds gust across Chilliwack Lake's grey-green surface and cool even the hottest days. As the sun drops behind the western skyline, long shadows drape the upper slopes. Patches of snow tucked into north-facing folds feed subalpine streams throughout the summer. Orange and yellow bracket fungi and red amanita mushroom caps provide colourful relief from the otherwise green monotone. And stands of western red cedar that line the banks of the **Upper Chilliwack River Trail** (moderate; 18 miles/30 km return) add auburn to this palette.

This level riverside trail leads to a flourishing grove of them in a provincial ecological reserve at Chilliwack Lake's south end and beyond into the United States as it follows the Chilliwack River to its headwaters in Washington's North Cascades National Park.

A 6-mile (10-km) portion of the trail makes a satisfying round-trip hike through the international area and provides a good look at the ancient forest. The Upper Chilliwack River trailhead lies 9 miles (15 km) south of Chilliwack Lake Provincial Park. The two-lane gravel Chilliwack Lake Rd is level for much of the way as it runs beside or just above the lake, turning inland briefly to cross bridges over Paleface and Depot Creeks. A hefty pile of boulders brings vehicles up sharply just before the road reaches the Forest Service recreation site on Chilliwack Lake's south shore. Over time, the Upper Chilliwack River has deposited a fan of fine sand here at one of the most undisturbed beaches in the Lower Mainland. Hikers are rewarded with beautiful views of rugged Mount Lindeman directly to the west, and farther north of Mount Macdonald and Mount Webb. A well-worn track leads behind the beach towards the banks of the Upper Chilliwack River. Watch for a large brown wooden stake on the left side of the old road, which marks the beginning of the Upper Chilliwack River Trail. Enormous old-growth cedars surround you almost as soon as you begin walking the well-maintained pathway. Groves of these giants, some of them 10–13 feet (3–4 m) in diameter, feed on the steady supply of water from the nearby river, which usually crests by late June. The river gurgles pleasantly along past the ecological reserve, the boundaries of which are marked by signs posted high on the sides of several leviathans. It's not a large area, less than 2 miles (3 km) long, and stretches to the Canada-US border, which is readily identified by a 40-foot-wide (12-m-wide) clearing that runs up the slope on the west side of the river.

South of the border, crudely fashioned logs convey hikers across some of the marshier sections of the trail. Persevere and you'll soon find yourself back out on the banks of the river, ready for an encounter with another grove of graceful cedar. The Little Chilliwack Campsite is located here, one of three on the way to Hannegan Pass and eventually Washington's Mount Baker Hwy. If you have time, follow this trail for another 6 miles (9 km) to the next campsite. Along the way you will not only pass through groves of western red cedar but also several stands of giant Douglas fir at higher elevations. This is one of the most enjoyable hikes in the Fraser Valley region and one on which you're guaranteed to see more wildlife than fellow hikers. Note: A backcountry permit is required to make the full two-day hike and can be obtained at no charge from the ranger station in Glacier, Washington. If you are making the journey from Canada and intend to camp overnight in North Cascades Park, you must call ahead to the Glacier Public Service Center, (360) 599-2714, to pre-register.

The historic **Skagit River Trail** in Skagit Valley Provincial Park (see Camping/Parks, above) was blazed in the 1850s during the feverish stampede to the Cariboo gold fields in central British Columbia. In an attempt to do an end-run around the colonial government's customs and excise tax collectors stationed at the mouth of the Fraser River, American entrepreneurs constructed a trail that ran from Whatcom, Washington (now Bellingham), to the Thompson River. For all the underhanded effort, the trail lasted for only two months before it was abandoned: the upkeep was too taxing. A moderately challenging 9-mile (14.5-km) section of the trail persists between 26-Mile Bridge near Silvertip Provincial Campground (see Camping/Parks, above) and **Sumallo Grove** in Manning Provincial Park. Sumallo Grove is situated on the south side of Hwy 3, 16 miles (25 km) east of Hope, just inside the park's western boundary. This is a forested route, where rare wild rhododendrons bloom in places beside the trail as it follows the Skagit River. A provincial ecological reserve adjacent to the kilometre 9 marker protects a tall stand of western red cedar and Douglas fir that dominates the southern bank of the river. In late summer, watch for bears in the kilometre 11–14 section where the trail passes beside low-lying huckleberry and blueberry bushes. The best time to make this journey is from midsummer on, once water levels in a number of small creeks that must be forded have receded. Allow four to six hours to cover the trail one way. Although it's possible to complete the round trip in a day, the **De Lacey Wilderness Campsite** 2.5 miles (4 km) along the Skagit River Trail from Sumallo Grove welcomes hikers. Hikers may find that access to the Whatcom trail is easier from Manning Provincial Park than Skagit Valley Provincial Park, as this approach is via paved rather than gravel road.

Another hiking trail between Skagit Valley and Manning Provincial Park is the 14-mile (22.5-km) **Skyline II Trail.** Skyline II's well-marked trailhead in the Skagit Valley is just north of Chittenden Meadows (see Wildlife, below) on Silver-Skagit Rd, and at either Strawberry Flats or Spruce Bay Campgrounds in Manning Park. This trail has received considerable upgrading recently from BC Parks, and although that hasn't reduced the amount of hiking time, it does make the hiking less difficult in places. As with many long-distance routes, you don't necessarily have to cover the entire route in order to find rewarding vistas, such as from Hozomeen Ridge above Ross Lake. An alternate route to Hozomeen Ridge begins from the Hozomeen Campground (see Camping/Parks, above). Check the map at the US Park Service ranger station at the entrance to the campground for details. There's overnight camping midway along Skyline II Trail at Mowich Creek in Manning Park. For a map of Skagit Valley Park's hiking trails, contact BC Parks' Fraser Valley office, (604) 463-3513. A time-tested guide to these and other hiking trails in the region is *103 Hikes in Southwestern British Columbia* by David and Mary Macaree.

You can lose yourself without getting lost on **Campbell Valley Regional Park**'s (see Picnics, above) miles of walking trails. The landscape here is so welcoming that you won't feel isolated or alone. At every twist and turn along the pathway, a bird will call, a squirrel will chatter, and fellow walkers will offer a smile. Little Campbell River bubbles along its meandering course. Follow the 1.4-mile (2.3-km) **Little River Loop Trail** through the meadows and forested slopes of the valley bottom. Pause at the Listening Bridge to listen. Spend an hour or more exploring the gentle contours of the park along the **Ravine Trail,** where former owners once farmed. Wander around the Annand/Rowlatt farmstead, whose sturdy barns, sheds, chicken coops, and home have all been well maintained. Peek in the windows of the old, one-room Lochiel Schoolhouse nearby that's been relocated to the park. For a longer stroll, follow a portion of the **Shaggy Mane Trail** that makes a grand 8.7-mile (14-km) sweep around the park's perimeter. Horseback riders also use this trail for their workouts (see Horseback Riding, below), so mind your footing. The Shaggy Mane Trail does not connect with many other trails in the park, so the best idea is to walk a portion of it before retracing your steps. For example, walk up into Cottonwood Meadows from Little River Loop Trail's junction with Shaggy Mane to reach the Campbell Valley Downs equestrian centre. For more information on Campbell Valley Regional Park, contact the GVRD's East Area office, (604) 530-4983.

As you approach Derby Reach Regional Park's Edgewater Bar entrance (see Camping/Parks, above) west of Fort Langley, the road passes the Houston House and nearby Karr/Mercer historic barn, recent additions to the park. The easygoing 2.5-mile (4-km) **Fort-to-Fort Riverside Trail** begins across the road from the farmhouse. At present, its use is restricted to walkers, although in the future it may open to cyclists, too. Trails through the wooded countryside to the west of the Houston House are for walkers and horseback riders only.

If you're exploring **Matsqui Trail Regional Park** (see Cycling/In-Line Skating, above) on foot, the 6-mile (10-km) round-trip walking time will be about two hours. The trail is level for its entire length, which makes it an ideal destination for those who like to chat with friends while walking. The most interesting time to visit is in late spring when water levels in the Fraser are at their highest.

Wildlife

North Fraser Valley

Tranquillity reigns in Coquitlam's Minnekhada Regional Park (see Hiking/Walking, above), a haven just beyond the urban sprawl that threatens to engulf much of the lower south-facing slopes nearby on Mount Burke and Coquitlam Mountain. Tucked in behind several large knolls on the west side of Pitt River, Minnekhada Regional Park shares a common border with the eastern portion of the **Pitt-Addington Marsh Wildlife Management Area.** Rural charm flows easily from one into the other. Minnekhada is characterized by two large marsh areas that are bisected by a dike and surmounted by two distinctive, rugged knolls. Trails ring the marshes and thread through the surrounding forest. In fall, this is a moody environment. The forested slopes of nearby Mount Burke capture clouds that often don't burn off until late in the day, if at all. Patches of bright red and gold leaves flare against this pale backdrop. To reach Minnekhada, turn north off Hwy 7 in Port Coquitlam at Coast Meridian Rd. A GVRD sign near the intersection with Apel Dr points the way to the park, a 10-minute drive. There are three entrances to the park. On its south side, Oliver Dr passes through farmland to a formal gate where it looks as if a sentry should stand on guard. Minnekhada was once home to British Columbia Lieutenant-Governor Eric Hamber, who built a Scottish-style hunting lodge on the hillside above one pond in the 1930s. An information kiosk is located next to the lodge, as are several picnic tables. A short distance farther east on Oliver Dr is another approach to the park on the PoCo Dike Trail beside the Pitt River (see Cycling/In-Line Skating, above). The western entrance to the park is located on Quarry Rd. (Quarry is a continuation of Victoria Dr, reached via Apel.) This approach quickly brings you to the midmarsh area of the park. The nearby ponds are a natural draw with the more than **60 species of birds** that pass through the marsh during spring and fall migrations. Don't forget your binoculars. For more information on Minnekhada Regional Park, call (604) 520-6442. Guided nature walks of the park are offered on a regular basis. To receive a brochure, contact GVRD Parks, (604) 432-6359.

When you visit Kanaka Creek Regional Park (see Canoeing/Kayaking/ Boating, above) in Maple Ridge, you may choose to begin from the **Bell-Irving Salmon Hatchery,** at the 256th St entrance off Dewdney Trunk Rd. An open playing field and picnic tables border the main arm of the creek. The flow of water here is modest compared with that below Cliff Falls, where the creek's main and north forks merge. Signs at the hatchery detail the work carried on here to rebuild fish stocks in the creek. Since the hatchery opened in 1983, about two million salmon fry—most of them **chum,** with some **coho**—have been released. Contact the hatchery at (604) 462-8643 for information on this annual spring event.

Cliff Falls lies about 0.6 mile (1 km) downstream from the hatchery. As there are trails along both sides of Kanaka Creek, make a round trip of it. You'll find one trailhead directly across 256th St from the hatchery and the other a short distance north next to privately owned Kanaka Lodge. Along the way to the falls you'll discover many inviting approaches to the creek, especially on the north side The trail that follows the south side of the creek involves steeper climbing. Both trails lead through the sheltering forest. **Woodpeckers** are drawn to this environment, as are a variety of **songbirds** that feed on the juicy salmonberries. Small amphibians such as **rare tailed frogs** can be spotted along fern-draped banks of the creek.

The **Pitt-Addington Marsh Wildlife Management Area** occupies both sides of the Pitt River, adjacent to Minnekhada Regional Park on the west in Coquitlam and Grant Narrows Regional Park (see Canoeing/Kayaking/ Boating, above) on the east in Pitt Meadows. Trails into the wildlife reserve begin from both Minnekhada and Grant Narrows Parks. Observation towers are strategically positioned along the trails in both. Among the rarer species to be seen are the **sandhill cranes** that nest in the east side of the wildlife reserve. For more information, contact British Columbia Wildlife Watch, a Ministry of Environment, Lands, and Parks program designed to promote wildlife viewing opportunities throughout the province; (604) 582-5200.

The **fish hatcheries** at Weaver Creek and Morris Creek near Harrison Bay (see Canoeing/Kayaking/Boating, above) are good staging areas for viewing wildlife such as **bald eagles** and **trumpeter swans** in winter, and spawning **salmon** in autumn. This is one of the most unique geological zones in the Lower Mainland. The rounded mountain tops are actually millions of years older than adjacent ranges of the Cascade and Coast Mountains. To reach the hatcheries on Weaver and Morris Creeks, turn north off Hwy 7 at Harrison Bay on the Morris Valley Rd. Follow paved Morris Valley Rd east to where it divides: one branch leads east to Weaver Creek while the other leads to Morris Creek. Both hatcheries are well signed.

If you camp at Deer Lake in Sasquatch Provincial Park (see Camping/Parks, above), watch for white-coated **mountain goats** on the steep-sided slopes of Slollicum Bluffs that rise above the lake's north side. Early in the morning is the best time to see them as they pick their way along the bluffs. During the hottest times of the year they may even descend to drink from Deer Lake. And keep your eyes open, too, for the park's namesake.

South Fraser Valley

Skagit Valley Provincial Park (see Camping/Parks, above) finally got its due in 1996 when it was granted full park status. The struggle to save critical sections of the park began in the early 1970s. William "Curly" Chittenden, a Fraser Valley logger and one of the chief proponents for conserving the valley, lived just long enough to receive word of the Skagit's official protected designation before his death at age 88. A special section of the valley, Chittenden Meadows, honours his commitment to save a rare stand of **ponderosa pine trees** located here. A self-guided nature walk leads through the meadows. An informative guide is provided at the kiosk located beside a nifty suspension bridge that takes visitors across the Skagit River to Chittenden Meadows. You can learn more about wildlife in the Skagit Valley at the park's entrance. An interpretive information sign posted there describes in detail the importance of the Skagit to **more than 250 species** of animals, including mammals, reptiles, and birds. The unique topography of the valley, where the Coast and Interior biogeoclimatic zones converge, is also explained. One of the more intriguing species of wildlife to watch for is the **rubber boa constrictor.** True to its name, the harmless little boa, the size of a small garter snake, resembles a coiled piece of inner tube, rounded at both ends.

Horseback Riding

North Fraser Valley

Golden Ears Provincial Park has a network of trails earmarked for horseback riding. As you head north from either of the two park signs that appear on Hwy 7 in Maple Ridge, horses and riders will begin to appear in the vicinity of **Maple Ridge Municipal Park** (see Camping/Parks, above). Unless they are privately owned, the horses most likely come from the Golden Ears Riding Stable at 232nd St and 136th Ave, north of Fern Crescent; call (604) 463-8761. Open daily from 9am to 6pm, the stables are quite busy on weekends. The riding trails in Golden Ears Provincial Park are some of the most extensive in the Lower Mainland.

South Fraser Valley

The riding paths in **Campbell Valley Regional Park** are located east of 200th St in Langley. Before this was parkland, Langley riders maintained the bridle trails that run east towards Aldergrove. Since September 1979, when the GVRD took control of the 2-square-mile (535-ha) valley, these trails have come into greater public use. Today, Campbell Valley Regional Park is one of the easiest places for visitors to satisfy a desire to ride a horse. The **Shaggy Mane Trail,** which rings the park, runs 6.8 miles (11 km), an easy two-hour ride. Campbell Park Riding Stables, located at one of the neighbouring farms directly across from the park equestrian centre at **Campbell Downs,** provides horses and guided tours of the trail on a one- or two-hour basis. Costs are about $20 an hour or $35 for the two-hour round trip during the week, $25 and $40 on weekends. Since riders often encounter park visitors who are exploring the trails on foot, they must be escorted for the first several visits. Once riders qualify, however, they can set out on their own. Only 40 horses are available at the Campbell Park Riding Stables, so advance booking is a must, especially on weekends; (604) 534-7444. To reach Campbell Valley Regional Park, drive south from Hwy 1 on 200th St to either the 16th or Eighth Ave entrance. Or from Hwy 99, take Eighth Ave east and travel 4.7 miles (7.5 km) to the South Valley entrance.

Gliding/Hang Gliding

At the east end of the Fraser Valley, the Hope-Flood Airport is home to the Vancouver Soaring Association. The club flies out of this small municipal airport to take advantage of the favourable winds that funnel through the Fraser Valley from the west and come sweeping up the sheer ridges of nearby Mounts Hope and Ogilvie. These winds also bring a freshness to the air that you can almost taste. As seen from the quiet soaring of a glider, the geography of the region is dramatically—and graphically—laid out below. A 20-minute flight costs about $60. Call (604) 521-5501 for bookings. To reach the airport, take the Hope-Flood exit from Hwy 1, just west of Hope.

Mount Woodside on the east side of Harrison Bay (see Beaches, above) is a favourite with hang gliders in the valley. A rough road leads to the summit on the north side of Hwy 7 east of the Kilby Provincial Park turnoff (see Beaches, above). The road is passable to two-wheel-drive vehicles. Even if you aren't planning to launch yourself from one of the ramps, the views from here are some of the best in the valley.

Windsurfing

The beach at **Paleface Creek** on **Chilliwack Lake** (see Camping/Parks, above) is an ideal staging area, and windsurfers love the winds that are almost guaranteed to blow across the lake daily. (There's also a sturdily constructed boat launch with an entrance located just north of Paleface Creek.)

Along the Silverhope Rd west of Hope, windsurfers search out **Silver Lake Provincial Park** (see Camping/Parks, above). The same strong winds that prove so favourable for gliders here at the east end of the Fraser Valley also power windsurfers across this lake's chilly surface. Wet suits are recommended year-round.

Skiing/Snowboarding

Hemlock Valley Ski Area is located 8.5 miles (14 km) north of Hwy 7 from Harrison Bay. This is a small, regional winter recreation destination that is also beginning to develop its trails for summer use by mountain bikes (see Mountain Biking, above). Because of its low elevation and close proximity to the ocean, Hemlock Valley fares better in some years than others. The depth of its snowpack depends on a pattern of sustained cold weather. Despite Hemlock Valley Ski Area's low elevation, local skiers and snowboarders make the most of its three chairlifts (one triple, two double), which access its rolling, contoured bowl—when it's open. The season here runs from December to March. For information on opening hours, call (800) 665-7080.

There's good **cross-country skiing** in the woods surrounding **Post Creek** near the north end of Chilliwack Lake (see Hiking/Walking, above). Signs nailed high on the trunks of fir trees indicate the routes. One particularly good one runs beside the Chilliwack River between Post Creek and the provincial park at Chilliwack Lake.

outside in

Attractions

Throughout British Columbia, several historic 19th-century forts have been preserved as reminders of how the west was originally settled by Europeans. **Fort Langley National Historic Site,** a Hudson's Bay Company post that has been preserved and restored, is open year-round. It, too, is a delightful reminder of yesteryear. Call (604) 888-4424 for information. To start your visit, ask to see a video depicting the early history of the fort. The 10-minute production can be viewed in a theatre next to the reception office and gift shop, with a soundtrack of your choice in any of five languages: English, French, German, Cantonese, and Japanese.

Train tracks run along the riverbank below the fort. Nearby is the **Fort Langley Railroad Museum** on Glover Rd, with a restored station from the 1920s era, a Canadian National Railway caboose, and an operating model railway. It's well worth a visit as you explore the town in the vicinity of the fort. Glover Rd, Fort Langley's main street, features a variety of shops, many of which are housed in well-maintained heritage buildings. Stop at the large interpretive map of Fort Langley displayed at the railroad historical site. It outlines a **heritage walking tour** of the town. The large community hall, for example, has been lovingly preserved.

From Hwy 1 take either the 200th St S or 232nd St S exit and follow the signs to Fort Langley. For information on special events, group tours, school programs, or hours of operation at the fort, call (604) 888-4424.

Kilby Historic Store is adjacent to Kilby Provincial Park (see Camping/Parks, above). It's well worth a look through the restored boarding house, post office, and general store to get a feel for life on the Fraser River at the turn of the century, when steam wheelers linked small towns like Harrison Mills with the docks downstream at Mission and New Westminster. There is a small admission charge to view the store, which is open from May to October and at Christmas each year.

If you're in the south valley around Easter weekend, plan to attend the **Bradner Daffodil Festival,** held here annually since 1928. To get to Bradner, take the 264th St N exit from Hwy 1. Turn immediately east on 56th Ave (Interprovincial Way) and continue to Bradner Rd. Turn right here. Cross the railway tracks, and watch for the Bradner Community Hall on the west side of the road next to the school. The daffodil festival is held here, complete with its legendary bake sale, and more than 400 varieties of daffodils bloom in the surrounding fields. The small park across the road from the Bradner General Store, complete with a gazebo, is one potential picnic location, as is nearby Glen Valley Regional Park.

Mission (population 31,500) is the largest town in the North Fraser Valley. Watch for the Travel InfoCentre, located on the north side of Hwy 7, just east of Mary St, where you can obtain a Mission Visitors Guide with detailed street maps of the area. Mission is tied historically to the Cariboo gold rush of the 1850s, and there is still a strong Native presence in the region. Each year in July, the **Mission Powwow** draws drummers, singers, dancers, and spectators to a three-day festival, held just east of the Travel InfoCentre. **Westminster Abbey,** home to a Benedictine monastery, crowns the skyline and occupies a ridge overlooking the Fraser River Valley. From Hwy 7, take Stave Lake Rd to Dewdney Trunk Rd. Turn right and go east along Dewdney. Watch for the abbey on your right just past the intersection of Dewdney and Goundrey Sts. Visiting hours at the monastery are weekday afternoons from 1:30 to 4:30, and 2 to 4 on Sundays. A 30-minute choral vespers service begins at 5:30pm on weekdays and 4:30pm on Sundays.

Xa:ytem Longhouse Interpretive Centre, Mission, BC, bills itself as the oldest dwelling site in the province. Carbon-dated at between 5,000 and 9,000 years old, the centrepiece of the ancient village site is an enormous boulder dubbed the Transformer Stone (more prosaically called Hatzic Rock). The Sto:lo Nation has recently erected a longhouse at the site where, between June to September, visitors can learn more about traditional First Nations' culture and history. Hours of operation are 10am to 4pm daily. For more information write to the Xa:ytem Longhouse Interpretive Centre, 35087 Lougheed Hwy, Mission, BC V2V 6T1.

Maple Ridge wildlife educator Chris Laustrup leads photography, nature-observation, mountain-bike, and boat tours of Pitt Lake. He also operates the **Widgeon Valley Hideaway resort.** For more information, contact Pitt Lake Legendary Adventure Tours, Ltd., 3368 David Ave, Coquitlam, BC V3E 3G8, (604) 942-9350.

Situated at the southern end of Harrison Lake, **Harrison Hot Springs** is a small, quiet row of low buildings facing the sandy beach and lagoon. The hot springs themselves are in a strangely enclosed temple, with sulfur steam billowing out and an occasional Coke can strewn along the bottom of the pool. But don't be dismayed; the public soaking pool (which has cooled hot-spring water pumped into it) is large and wonderfully warm (100°F or 37°C, average). In addition, there are sailboards and bikes to rent, hiking trails nearby, helicopters to ride, and a pub or two. There's also an annual world championship sand sculpture competition that takes place in September. Call (604) 796-3425 for information.

Restaurants

Bedford House ☆ A lovely place with a picturesque view of the Fraser River, this restored 1904 house is furnished with English antiques and has a pleasant, countrified elegance. The menu is rich, with fancy continental cuisine. *9272 Glover Rd (on bank of Fraser River, downtown), Fort Langley; (604) 888-2333; $$.*

Black Forest ☆ Bavarian food seems a staple in BC, and here's an authentic restaurant serving more than just schnitzel. This is also the place for goulash soup and beef rouladen. Be sure to make a reservation. *180 Esplanade Ave (1 block west of Hwy 9), Harrison Hot Springs; (604) 796-9343; $$.*

Lodgings

The Harrison Hotel This legendary hotel on the shore of beautiful Harrison Lake is a better place to view than to visit (staying here is expensive). Our advice? Use the place for a short stay, arrive in time to enjoy the excellent hot pools, and then head down the street to eat. *100 Esplanade Ave (west end of Esplanade Ave), Harrison Hot Springs, BC V0M 1K0; (604) 796-2244; $$$.*

More Information

Abbotsford InfoCentre: *(604) 859-9651.*

BC Forest Service: Central Fraser Valley, *(604) 820-2055;* **Chilliwack Forest District,** *(604) 794-2100;* **Upper Fraser Valley,** *(604) 794-3361.*

BC Parks: Fraser Valley Office, *(604) 463-3513;* **Lower Mainland Office,** *(604) 924-2200.*

BC Wildlife Watch: *(604) 582-5200 or (250) 387-9796.*

Chilliwack InfoCentre: *(604) 858-8121.*

Coquitlam Leisure and Parks: *(604) 933-6000.*

Fort Langley InfoCentre: *(604) 888-1477.*

Fraser Valley Auto Body: *(604) 795-3454 (emergency road service on Chilliwack Lake Rd).*

Greater Vancouver Regional District (GVRD) Parks: *(604) 432-6350;* **East Area Office,** *(604) 530-4983; Web site: www.gvrd.bc.ca.*

Harrison Hot Springs InfoCentre: *(604) 796-3425.*

Hope InfoCentre: *(604) 869-2021.*

Langley InfoCentre: *(604) 530-6656.*

Maple Ridge InfoCentre: *(604) 463-3366.*

Maple Ridge Parks and Leisure Services: *(604) 467-7346.*

Mission InfoCentre: *(604) 826-6914.*
Pitt Meadows Chamber of Commerce: *(604) 465-7820.*
Port Coquitlam Parks and Recreation Department: *(604) 927-7900.*
Township of Langley Parks and Recreation: *(604) 532-7529.*
UBC Research Forest: *(604) 463-8148.*

The North Shore

North and West Vancouver, from Deep Cove to Horseshoe Bay, including Cypress and Mount Seymour Provincial Parks, Lynn Headwaters and Seymour Demonstration Forest Regional Parks, and Lighthouse and Whytecliff Marine Parks.

There's an old saying that if you can see the North Shore from Vancouver, it's about to rain, and if you can't, it's raining. Rain is part of the price residents on the steep-sided slopes of West and North Vancouver pay for living on the "wild side" of Burrard Inlet. Clouds bump up against the forested mountainside, become ensnared in dense stands of Douglas fir and hemlock, and linger long after skies have opened over Vancouver. This is a moody locale. On a clear day, few skylines can compete with the one composed of the Shores' six peaks—Black, Strachan, Hollyburn, Grouse, Fromme, and Seymour Mountains. After a rainstorm, the brilliant black-green hue of the North Shore shines with freshness. When snow coats the slopes, they sparkle so perfectly your heart sings at the sight.

Before the construction of the original Second Narrows Bridge in 1925, the North Shore was a world apart. Ferries once linked Ambleside in West Vancouver with Vancouver. From Ambleside, hikers in summer and skiers in winter would make their way up the side of Hollyburn Mountain, at first on foot or by wagon, later by car and bus. Cabins were constructed, trails brushed out. Grouse and Seymour Mountains developed in much the same way, though Grouse has always been the leader in commercial development. Mountain tops were the perfect places to get away from "dirty old Vancouver," especially in cool weather. Before the Second

World War, sawdust was the fuel of choice in many Vancouver homes, darkening the air with its soot.

Much has changed since Navvy Jack Thomas became the first European to permanently settle on the North Shore in the 1880s. Today, thousands of visitors walk and hike where Chief Joe Capilano first guided poet and outdoorswoman extraordinaire Pauline Johnson, the most popular Canadian entertainer of her time, along the ancient North Shore trails. Johnson, the daughter of a Mohawk chief and an Englishwoman, wrote *Legends of Vancouver*, published in 1911, two years before her death. The tales she transcribed still bear repeating, such as the story of the two sisters who, long before Captain George Vancouver sailed into English Bay, brought peace to the Native communities of the region and who were subsequently honoured by being transformed into the twin peaks that dominate the North Shore skyline. Today, these peaks are widely known as the Lions.

No matter how far up the mountainside neighbourhoods have crept, the wilderness still influences the North Shore. Black bears and cougars prowl backyards on the perimeter of habitation. Hapless hikers, skiers, and snowboarders routinely lose their way and wait (and pray) to be saved by the North Shore Rescue Team, a volunteer group who selflessly put their own lives at risk to track down missing adventurers.

Despite the outward appearance of urbanity, the North Shore contains some of the most rugged terrain in the province. The mountainous topography represents the forward perimeter of land pushed out to the coast by the mile-thick glacial ice pan that held sway 12,000 years ago. The Coast Mountains, which begin on the North Shore and sweep north along the British Columbia coast and through Alaska, are the tallest range in North America and among the most heavily glaciated.

Due to the North Shore's steep incline, much of the outdoors activity that takes place here will get your heart rate up within minutes of starting out, whether you adventure on foot, by bike, or on skis or snowboard. Pothole lakes are the refreshing reward for those who explore the higher reaches in summer. Just as prized are the rugged beaches on Burrard Inlet that await those who prowl the shoreline. Rain or shine, you can always count on finding shelter beneath the broad branches of the ancient and second-growth forests.

Getting There

The North Shore is reached by travelling west on Highway 1 (Trans-Canada Highway) across the Ironworkers Memorial Second Narrows Bridge. Highway 1 (or the Upper Levels Highway, as it is called on the North Shore) crosses North and West Vancouver to Horseshoe Bay, site of the BC Ferries terminal that connects the North Shore with Nanaimo on Vancouver Island, Langdale on the Sunshine Coast, and nearby Bowen Island. Travellers from downtown Vancouver journey west on Georgia Street (Highway 99) to the Stanley Park causeway, then cross the Lions Gate Bridge to Marine Drive. Depending on your destination on the North Shore, you can choose to enter either North or West Vancouver from the north end of the bridge. From Marine Drive, Taylor Way in West Vancouver is a continuation of Highway 99 and intersects with the Upper Levels Highway at the junction of Highways 1 and 99. Highway 1/99 continues west to Horseshoe Bay from here. From Horseshoe Bay, Highway 99 (Sea to Sky Highway) links the North Shore with the upcountry communities of Squamish, Whistler, Pemberton, and Lillooet. BC Transit's SeaBus links Lonsdale Quay in North Vancouver with the Vancouver terminal, located at the foot of Granville Street at Cordova, a 15-minute crossing.

Adjoining Areas

NORTH: **Whistler and the Sea to Sky Highway**

SOUTH: **Greater Vancouver**

EAST: **The Fraser Valley**

WEST: **Nanaimo and the Cowichan Valley**

inside out

Hiking

The first recreational hiking trails on the North Shore were opened almost a century ago. You can still walk some of these trails today, including the original **Grouse Mountain Trail,** blazed by members of the Vancouver Mountaineering Club in 1900. (Several years later the club changed its name to the British Columbia Mountaineering Club to reflect its expanded horizons.) If you're looking for company, there are several well-established clubs that host walking and hiking outings on a regular basis for both members and nonmembers. Among these are the North Shore Hikers, (604) 988-9525, and the North Vancouver Outdoor Club, (604) 983-6543, ext. 2966. For more information, visit the Federation of Mountain Clubs of British Columbia's Web site: http://mindlink.bc.ca/fmcbc.

Getting to the trailhead is the easy part of many of these rambles. Once on the trail the challenge is to stick to your route as, typically, many other fainter trails intersect with the one you're following, be these old logging roads or newer mountain-bike routes. All the trails outlined below are well marked, usually with bright orange metal disks affixed to the trunks of sturdy trees. Do not make the mistake of using coloured plastic surveyor's tape as your guide: the mountainsides are strung with it.

By far the longest route on the North Shore is the almost 30-mile (48-km) **Baden-Powell Trail,** the thread that knits the North Shore together into one continuous strand. The trail runs between its western terminus at West Vancouver's Horseshoe Bay and Deep Cove on North Vancouver's eastern perimeter. Along the way, it climbs and descends a well-trodden route that passes through both Cypress and Mount Seymour Provincial Parks. You can devote days to discovering it bit by bit, or push yourself to your limit in a day. As hard as it is to believe, five hours is the time in which top-shape runners cover the trail in the annual North Shore Knee Knacker competition held in July. Altogether there are 12 entrances to the Baden-Powell Trail; most are located conveniently close to public transportation. The trail is well marked, with route maps, distances, and estimated completion times posted at trailheads and important junctions along the route.

A note about Robert Stephenson Smyth, the first Baron Baden-Powell: Anyone familiar with the scouting movement will recognize the name of its founder, who along with his sister Agnes also headed up the Girl Guides in 1910. In 1971, to commemorate British Columbia's provincial centennial and honour the memory of their founder, Boy Scouts and Girl Guides of the Lower Mainland constructed and maintained their worthy endeavour, the Baden-Powell Trail, for the next 10 years. Once you encounter the wooden staircases and bridges that assist hikers along the route, you'll realize this was no small undertaking. In recent years, maintenance of the trail has shifted to local municipalities and Adopt-a-Trail groups such as the North Shore Hikers, members of the Federation of Mountain Clubs of British Columbia, and even the occasional Scout or Guide troop.

This overview follows the Baden-Powell Trail from west to east. The western trailhead lies on the east side of Hwy 99 in Horseshoe Bay close to the BC Ferries terminal at the north end of Eagleridge Dr. Look for a clearing that usually contains at least one parked car. The eastern trailhead begins on Panorama Dr a short distance north of Gallant Ave in Deep Cove. There's ample parking nearby. Allow two to four days to complete the entire 30-mile (48-km) route. A free map of the Baden-Powell Trail is available from Scout House, 664 W Broadway, Vancouver, (604) 879-5721.

The most challenging section of the Baden-Powell Trail crosses **Eagle Ridge** on **Black Mountain** near the western terminus, a distance of 5.3 miles (8.5 km). Plan on taking five hours to make the journey one way, as the elevation gain is almost 4,000 feet (1220 m). Eagle Ridge's bare face rises above Horseshoe Bay and Eagle Cove, and only those in good physical condition should attempt it. (You know who you are.) Several delightful viewpoints of Howe Sound appear as you enjoy an easy walk for the first 1.75 miles (2.85 km), then the going gets tough along the approach to Eagle Ridge. You'll have a much better idea of where you are when you finally gaze out from Eagle Ridge over the Lower Mainland: the view ranges from Mount Baker in the southeast to Victoria and Vancouver Island in the west, and from Texada Island in the northwest to the San Juan Islands in the south. It's not unusual to find snow on Black Mountain (elevation 4,012 feet/1224 m) and at comparable elevations on most of the North Shore's other peaks well into June. Although ice may not coat the surface of the Cougar Lakes (a nest of pothole lakes beside the trail just above the ridge), a swim here on a hot August day quickly reveals that icy conditions lurk just beneath the surface in these pleasant, heavily forested pocket ponds. You'll emerge breathlessly refreshed. (More snow falls on Black Mountain than any other local mountain, including Whistler and Blackcomb. Winter storms moving inland from the Pacific encounter cold outflow winds on Howe Sound, and the result is that 10 feet (3 m) or more of snow falls annually here.)

The next section of the Baden-Powell Trail runs from the downhill ski area on Black Mountain in **Cypress Provincial Park** to Grouse Mountain, a distance of about 7 miles (11 km) one way. The well-marked trail leads east across the slopes of **Mount Strachan** and **Hollyburn Mountain** and joins with a series of cross-country ski trails on Hollyburn Ridge (see Skiing/Snowboarding, below). Although it's rarely level—not much is, on these steep slopes—the trail is only moderately challenging. Small lakes appear at intervals and the open skies above them brighten the environment until you plunge back into the shaded forest once again. A series of creeks splashes down from unseen headwaters above: Lawson and Brothers Creeks are two of the major ones you'll encounter. Once you reach West Vancouver's British Properties neighbourhood, you'll have to pick your way along several residential streets before the Baden-Powell Trail begins to descend to **Capilano Regional Park** and beyond to the foot of **Grouse Mountain** (see Skiing/Snowboarding, below) at the north end of Capilano Rd in North Vancouver. This last portion is a more picturesque stretch, as the Capilano watershed opens in front of you. As you cross the Capilano River, the great divide, you pass from West into North Vancouver.

From Grouse Mountain to Deep Cove, hikers are able to connect with BC Transit buses that will help you make a loop of your journey. Up to this point there have only been two possible transit connections, at Horseshoe Bay and the British Properties. There is no regular bus service to Cypress Provincial Park.

From Grouse Mountain east to **Lynn Canyon Park, Mount Seymour**

Provincial Park, and eventually **Deep Cove,** the Baden-Powell Trail begins an almost uninterrupted 18-mile (30-km) ramble. You can break the journey up at Lynn Valley Rd, about 6 miles (10 km) east of Grouse, or at the Mount Seymour Pkwy, about 15 miles (25 km) east of Grouse. Bus routes to consider for round-trip transportation or to reach trailheads in North Vancouver from elsewhere in Greater Vancouver are the Queens (#232), which runs between the Phibbs Exchange and Grouse Mountain, the Westlynn (#229) bus from Lonsdale Quay to Upper Lynn Valley Rd, and the Seymour (#211) and Dollarton (#212) routes, which run between the Phibbs Exchange and Deep Cove. Call BC Transit for schedule information; (604) 521-0400.

Along the way between Grouse Mountain and the Baden-Powell Trail's eastern terminus in Deep Cove, hikers cross the trail's longest bridge, which spans aptly named **Mosquito Creek,** walk beneath miles of towering second-growth forest whose understorey is a mass of ferns and fungi, pass beside earth-shuddering waterfalls in Lynn Canyon (see Parks, below), and encounter some of the best views of the entire trail as it nears Deep Cove. From the hillside above Deep Cove, Indian Arm spreads out with all the charm that Howe Sound presents near Eagle Ridge at the western terminus.

Cypress Provincial Park, a 7,400-acre (3000-ha) provincial park in West Vancouver, was born out of controversy in the 1960s and 1970s after clandestine logging, carried out under the guise of cutting ski trails, devastated much of the landscape. The clear-cut can still be seen from Vancouver. Today, commercial development in Cypress is still a hot issue. To see why groups such as Friends of Cypress Park and the Sierra Club of Canada oppose any further logging in the park, take a hike on one of the park's more moderate trails, such as the Hollyburn Mountain Trail. At 4,350 feet (1326 m), Hollyburn Mountain is one of the three peaks easily reached from the Cypress Pkwy. The others are Black Mountain to the west (see Baden-Powell Trail, above) at 4,016 feet (1224 m), and Mount Strachan (pronounced *strawn*) to the north at 4,770 feet (1454 m). Much of the unique old-growth forest on both Black and Strachan was thinned, if not wiped out completely, by logging. The subsequent cutting of trails for downhill skiing eliminated even more.

Hollyburn Mountain's slopes have lured hikers and skiers to West Vancouver since the 1920s. Vintage log cabins sequestered in the forest around First Lake attest to this tradition. In more recent years, Hollyburn's trails have become the preserve of cross-country skiers in winter. In summer months these trails are overgrown with berry bushes where they are not tramped down by hikers on the Baden-Powell Trail or on the route that leads to Hollyburn's summit. This is a particularly pleasant hike, well suited for a warm day in late summer once the threat of insects has waned. Otherwise, come prepared to do battle with the bugs!

The well-marked Cypress Provincial Park exit from the Upper Levels Hwy in West Vancouver leads uphill to the Hollyburn Ridge parking lot. The **Hollyburn Mountain Trail** (4 miles/6 km return) begins here. Walk a short distance uphill beside a string of power lines on the Powerline Rd to its junction with the Baden-Powell Trail. Follow the Baden-Powell uphill past the warming hut at Fourth Lake, at which point the Baden-Powell Trail links with the Hollyburn Mountain Trail. The summit of Hollyburn Mountain (4,345 feet/1325 m) lies 1.3 miles (2.1 km) uphill from here. Along the way you'll pass a number of pocket lakes that act as reflecting ponds for the forest's paintbox. Wear sturdy boots and watch your footing. As on many of the trails on Hollyburn, much of the way is over exposed roots that ripple around the base of the thick firs. You'll immediately notice the grandeur of the forest, one of Hollyburn's most attractive features. The last easily accessible stand of giant hemlock in the Lower Mainland between Garibaldi Provincial Park and Chilliwack is located here. Add to this the fact that it hasn't been touched by forest fires for at least 1,000 (and possibly 4,000) years, and you have a unique subalpine, old-growth rain-forest environment that many regular visitors passionately wish to preserve. (Rings on a stump atop Mount Strachan indicate it was nearly 1,200 years old when cut in 1988 as part of a commercial expansion.)

A well-placed rope helps hikers ascend the last steep rock section before the top. From the summit you look west to the top of the chairlift on Mount Strachan, past Black Mountain to the waters of Howe Sound and over to Gibsons on the Sunshine Coast in the distance. The majestic Lions, or Two Sisters, soar above Capilano Lake to the north. From Hollyburn's open summit, hikers are also rewarded with views of the mountain ranges to the north not visible from the city. Retracing your steps, you'll be treated to views over the Fraser Estuary as far south as Boundary Bay.

For a more extensive hike on Hollyburn, follow the Baden-Powell Trail downhill past Fourth Lake to the **Wells Gray Trail** and First Lake. Follow the **Burfield Trail** from the lake back to the parking lot. For added variety, and a chance to walk some of the cross-country trails, continue hiking east from First Lake on the **Mobraaten Trail** to its intersection with the **Grand National Trail,** and continue around on Grand National about 0.5 mile (0.9 km) to West Lake. (Both Wells Gray and Mobraaten start from the warming hut at Fourth Lake and both intersect with Grand National.) Part of an old chairlift that operated until the 1950s can still be seen at the north end of West Lake. Return to the parking lot along the Burfield Trail, which passes beside a nest of old cabins, some of which date from the 1920s. BC Parks plans to restore the classic Hollyburn Lodge as a park interpretive centre so that Cypress, the busiest park in BC, with over a million visitors a year (a third of them skiers), will be a showcase for the province.

Additional hiking trails in Cypress Provincial Park begin from the traihead beside the Cypress Bowl parking lot located a short drive past the turnoff for Hollyburn Ridge at the top of the Cypress Pkwy. The **Yew Lake Trail** covers only about a mile but leads to a very picturesque location. The view of Black Mountain from here indicates what the entire bowl was like before logging began. Amazingly, considering the numbers of visitors to the park, you'll often have the trail (and lakeside picnic table) to yourself. Recent upgrading has made this trail wheelchair-accessible.

The most challenging trail—hands-down—in the park is the 18-mile (29-km) **Howe Sound Crest Trail,** which traverses the spine of ridges and peaks from Cypress Bowl north to **Porteau Provincial Park.** Along the way, this rugged trail crosses the top of suitably named Mount Unnecessary, skirts the base of the Lions, then crosses the ridges of Mounts Harvey and Brunswick before descending past Deeks Lake to a trailhead on Hwy 99 near Porteau Cove. This hike is only for those who are experienced and well equipped. A cleared area suitable for camping is located at the outlet of Deeks Lake; otherwise, there are only emergency huts at Magnesia Meadows and Brunswick Lake. Note: Campfires are forbidden. With a couple of exceptions, views are limited for much of the way between Cypress Bowl and Mount Unnecessary; snow often covers parts of the trail well through June. The best time to attempt the Howe Sound Crest trail is between mid-July and October. If you want to get a feel for the trail, try the first 3.4 miles (5.5 km) between the Cypress trailhead and St. Marks Summit viewpoint. Allow two hours one way. Along this way you'll be treated to a view of the Lions from Strachan Meadows (1.6 miles/2.6 km) and then of Howe Sound at St. Marks Summit. Some hikers prefer to use the Howe Sound Crest Trail as a route to the Lions, then descend along the **Lions Trail** to Lions Bay. From Cypress Provincial Park to Lions Bay is a strenuous 11 miles (18 km). Allow nine hours to complete this hike one way. Allow two full days to complete the entire Howe Sound Crest Trail, a 15-hour trek one way. Note: Trail markers on open sections of Mount Unnecessary and other exposed sections are often difficult to follow even in good weather. Do not attempt this route unless you are confident in your pathfinding abilities. Consult topographic map 92G/6 (North Vancouver), available from the Geological Survey of Canada, Suite 101, 605 Robson St, Vancouver, BC V6B 5G3, (604) 666-0271.

Other trails to pursue in Cypress Provincial Park include the **Black Mountain Loop Trail,** a moderately difficult, 1.6-mile (2.5-km), two-hour tour of the mountain's subalpine meadows and pocket lakes, complete with a terrific viewpoint on top. The loop trail ties in with the Yew Lake Trail, both of which begin at the base of the Black Mountain chairlift.

For more information and to request a map of Cypress Provincial Park, including a detailed description of the Howe Sound Crest Trail, contact BC Parks Zone Office at Mount Seymour Provincial Park, (604) 929-4818 or (604) 924-2200.

As you drive the 5-mile (8-km) **Cypress Parkway** in West Vancouver, you'll notice cars parked at its four switchbacks and elsewhere along the road. Their occupants have probably headed off along one of the many trails that crisscross the lower slopes of Black and Hollyburn Mountains. An easygoing route leads west from the first switchback (just past the road-maintenance yard) towards **Cypress Falls Park,** an enjoyable 4.5-mile (7-km) round-trip excursion. (Part of the trail covers the old Cypress Creek Logging Rd that rambles 4.7 miles/7.6 km up the mountain from here to Cypress Bowl.) Although not as challenging as other hikes found higher up the slopes, the lower section that leads past Cypress Falls has the advantage of being open almost year-round. Snow rarely accumulates for any duration this close to sea level. In fact, winter is one of the most bewitching times to visit the falls. During those months, snow often blankets the outer boughs of the dense evergreen forest that surrounds Cypress Creek; water vapour thrown up by the splashing creek gels in icy formations. It takes 30 minutes to walk beyond the logging road gate to reach the boundary of Cypress Falls Park, a distance of almost 1 mile (1.5 km). As you reach the park, pick up the **Cypress Falls Trail** that loops for 2.5 miles (4 km) around the creek's lower and upper falls. Watch for the entrance to the trail on the south side of the logging road as it nears a BC Hydro substation. The hiking trail is a steep singletrack at the outset but quickly widens and becomes much more inviting. It will take you an hour to complete. Bright green bracken fern line the trail year-round. Majestic hemlock, Douglas fir, and western red cedar tower above. A rustic, moss-covered wooden bridge conveys hikers across to the west side of Cypress Creek. Just downstream from the bridge is a view of the creek as it pours into a canyon below. The trail follows the west bank of the creek towards the upper falls. In places there are openings where you can clamber down and do some rock hopping. The hillside becomes steeper above the big cedars as the trail approaches the upper falls. You'll have to peer through the forest to catch a glimpse of its foamy white veil. A short distance beyond this viewpoint the trail meets pavement. Bear right and follow along until it connects with the old logging road. A wooden bridge crosses Cypress Creek above the upper falls, but views from here are restricted by dense second-growth forest. The logging road loops past the municipal yard and back towards Cypress Pkwy. The most enjoyable section of the hike lies behind you now but the satisfaction derived from your visit to the falls persists. (For an alternative approach to the park, take the Caulfeild-Woodgreen exit from Hwy 1. Once on Woodgreen, follow around to the third street on the right, Woodgreen Pl. Drive to the end of this cul-de-sac. There's parking in an old quarry next to some tennis courts and a playing field. The trail to the falls begins here.)

If you're searching for some shade when the temperature hits unusually high readings (anything above 77°F/25°C is considered *hot* in the Lower Mainland), head for the **Brother's Creek Trail** in West Vancouver. There's no need to break out the sunscreen as you explore beneath the sheltering arms of mighty western red cedar and Douglas fir trees on the mountainside above the British Properties neighbourhood. This hike is moderately difficult and your heart rate will get a real boost during the 5.5-mile (9-km) round trip. It will *really* flutter at the sight of the two small lakes near the creek's headwaters. Allow six hours to complete this hike. The trailhead is located at the top of Millstream Rd, reached via Taylor Way (Hwy 99) and Eyremont Dr. Watch for a wooden signpost that announces Brother's Creek. There's room here for several cars to park beside a yellow gate. Nearby is a bus stop. If you travel on foot, catch the British Properties (#254) bus, which leaves Park Royal Shopping Centre on Marine Dr at 20 minutes before the hour. Check with West Vancouver Transit, (604) 985-7777, for more details. To reach the Brother's Creek Trail, hikers must first ascend a rough fire road that intersects with the Baden-Powell Trail a short distance above Millstream. Distances and estimated hiking times to a variety of destinations are inscribed on metal trail markers here. It's up to you which side of the creek you wish to ascend. Make a loop by going up one side and down the other. Bridges span Brother's Creek in three places and are located approximately 0.6 mile (1 km) apart. Hikers can either follow the fire road to the Second Bridge, a 1.25-mile (2-km) journey, or head west along the Baden-Powell Trail for about a mile to the First Bridge crossing. A trail leads uphill from First Bridge along the west bank of the creek. Watch for a stand of massive western red cedars that shelters the trail as it leads towards Second Bridge. Hefty Douglas fir dominate the forest on the east side of the creek between the fire road and Second Bridge. Mightier still are the cedar and fir that grow beside the fire road as it approaches Third Bridge. **Blue Gentian** and **Lost Lakes** lie 1 mile (1.6 km) uphill from Third Bridge. Allow between 15 and 30 minutes to reach them. Lost Lake is the larger of the two and on a hot day is a refreshing place to take a quick dip. Two picnic tables hug Blue Gentian's shoreline. The West Vancouver Historical Society publishes a detailed map and forestry heritage walking guide to Brother's Creek, entitled "Shakes, Shinglebolts and Steampots." For a free copy, contact the Parks and Recreation Department, (604) 925-7200.

Capilano River Regional Park and its waterfront partner, Ambleside Park, are among the most sociable gathering places on the North Shore. Visitors come to stretch their legs and exercise their dogs while taking in the view of others doing the same across First Narrows on the Stanley Park Seawall (see Greater Vancouver chapter). Although most of the leisure activity takes place close to the Capilano River's confluence with the ocean, Capilano River Regional Park's hiking trail runs 5 miles (8 km) north from Ambleside Park to Capilano Lake.

Ambleside Park is easily reached from numerous entrances along Marine Dr, including the south end of Taylor Way. (Taylor is the first major intersection west of the Lions Gate Bridge.) There's usually a buzz of marine activity offshore from Ambleside beneath the Lions Gate Bridge. On Saturday evenings in summer this is a picture-perfect place to watch gaily lit cruise ships power their way out of port. When salmon are running in the Capilano River in September, you can count on seeing dozens of small pleasure craft drift-fishing just offshore. Upstream at such times, residents of the Capilano Indian Reserve, on whose land Ambleside Park and the north end of the Lions Gate Bridge are located, will also be fishing along the riverbank. Tidal currents ripple the surface of First Narrows, but the water at Ambleside's sandy beach is predictably calm. Skip a stone, toss a stick, talk to your neighbour: it's that kind of park.

As you follow the Capilano River Trail upstream from Ambleside Park (a short section of the trail is also signed as West Vancouver's **Town Trail**), it will lead you through a residential neighbourhood around the Park Royal Hotel before reaching the wilder side of the park. From this point north there's easy access to the boulder-filled river. For many visitors, this sea-level section of the park provides enough exploring to take up an entire visit. For others, there's a long ribbon of trail to follow as the **Capilano-Pacific Trail** leads along the west side of Capilano Canyon to the Fish Hatchery and Cleveland Dam. Allow three to four hours to complete the round trip from Ambleside Park.

As you make your way north from Ambleside, the banks of the Capilano River begin to narrow. Near Hwy 1, the trail climbs away from the river and follows Keith Rd for a short distance north beneath the Upper Levels Hwy Bridge. If your plan is simply to hike the forest trail and explore some of the pools in the Capilano River Canyon, this is the best place to begin. By car, take Keith Rd east off Taylor Way and drive to its end. Park here near the trailhead. A Greater Vancouver Regional District (GVRD) signpost indicates the start of this section of the Capilano-Pacific Trail. At this point the trail has the appearance of a charming country lane. The nearby forest is interlaced with old logging roads. In 1926, once logging ended, Capilano became one of the first municipal parks on the North Shore. Occasionally a short secondary trail leads downhill into the Capilano River's narrow canyon. The one to **Ranger Pool** is moderately steep in places, but worth the effort to enjoy the view of the canyon from its riverbed. The overstorey of tall evergreens, combined with a mass of ferns that carpet the forest floor, imbue the environment with a uniform green essence year-round. One of the great joys of visiting here is the quiet that permeates the atmosphere. Even when it's raining, the branches of the forest are so sheltering that much of the moisture never reaches the ground. You'll find a good spot to take a break at one magnificent viewpoint, where the canyon can be seen dropping away sharply to the river below. A conveniently placed bench sits beneath towering Douglas firs here. Just south of this viewpoint, a short trail leads down to the **Sandy Point Pools.**

North of the viewpoint the Capilano-Pacific Trail leaves the river for a while and crosses two major creeks. At Houlgate Creek, a branch of the main trail leads higher up to the **Shinglebolt** viewpoint. Explore the Shinglebolt on a clear day when the trail isn't too muddy. As seen from the viewpoint, Capilano Lake spreads towards the Lions, and the landscape looks wonderfully composed. A warren of trails winds through the woods here. Despite logging, some beautiful old trees remain along the trails on the west bank. Easygoing **Rabbit Lane Trail** (2.5 miles/4 km return), which loops through the forest and links with the Capilano-Pacific Trail in several places, was the route used by the Capilano Timber Company railway and accounts for the gentle grade. Nearby is Capilano River Regional Park's North Vancouver entrance.

There are several entrances in North Vancouver to Capilano River Regional Park, all within a short distance of each other. If you are travelling on Hwy 1, take the Capilano Rd N exit (exit 14) to reach the park. Capilano Rd can also be reached from Marine Dr in North Vancouver, a short distance east of the Lions Gate Bridge. Four parking lots are located near the fish hatchery in Capilano River Regional Park; another is at the picnic site beside Cleveland Dam. You can also catch the Grouse Mountain (#236) bus from North Vancouver's Lonsdale Quay, which stops at the fish hatchery and Cleveland Dam. Call BC Transit, (604) 521-0400, to check times on bus routes. For a map of the 16 miles (26 km) of hiking trails in Capilano River Regional Park, call GVRD Parks's West Office, (604) 224-5739.

Lynn Headwaters Regional Park in North Vancouver is a hidden jewel, located just out of sight of the uppermost homes on Lynn Valley Rd. Within minutes of entering the park, all vestiges of nearby habitation drop from sight. Even the sounds of the city evaporate and are replaced by the constant rhythm of water splashing on boulders in chilly Lynn Creek. Hiking trails begin at the entrance to the park, just beyond the caretaker's cottage (please don't disturb, except in an emergency). An information kiosk located on the east side of Lynn Creek acquaints visitors with the area and reminds hikers of the importance of advance preparation. The weather in the narrow valley through which the creek runs is volatile and can quickly change from welcoming to threatening. Hikers are asked to self-register at the kiosk. A series of trails leads visitors into the headwaters region. You can choose a relatively gentle, half-day creekside walk along the **Headwaters Trail** (9.5 miles/15.5 km return) to Norvan Creek, or a full-day trip to either Lynn Lake (15 miles/24 km return) or the top of Grouse Mountain on the rigorous **Hanes Valley Loop** route (9 miles/15 km one way) via Crown Pass.

Lynn Headwaters Regional Park has been welcoming a steadily increasing flow of visitors since it opened to the public in 1985 after being kept off-limits for decades as part of the extensive North Shore watershed system. To reach the park, take Lynn Valley Rd in North Vancouver to its uppermost end, following the signs to Lynn Headwaters GVRD Park. Public transit to the park's doorstep runs from the SeaBus terminal in North Vancouver; catch the Lynn Valley (# 229) bus.

Although Lynn Headwaters Regional Park is characterized by a rugged landscape, there's no need to feel that every hike has to be in the thigh-burning category. Far from it. Two gentle trails, **Lynn Loop Trail** (1 mile/1.7 km) and **Cedar Mill Trail** (1.3 miles/2.1 km) follow the creek for much of the way towards Norvan Falls. Pick the length and degree of difficulty that best suit you. All trails begin at the visitor registration kiosk. An ancient logging road serves as a trail and leads off into the park along first the Lynn Loop and then the Cedar Mill Trail. A network of steep staircases on the suitably named **Switchback Trail** links the valley floor with the midelevation Headwaters Trail. From bottom to top this short but demanding ascent will send your heart rate climbing at a pace equal to the elevation gain. Once at the top you can head back to the park entrance on the Lynn Loop Trail or begin the long hike north to the headwaters. If you don't feel that you need an aerobic workout, stay beside Lynn Creek and follow the Cedar Mill Trail north to its junction with the Headwaters Trail. The round trip is 5.8 miles (9.5 km). Plan on taking three hours to cover the entire distance. Along the way are a variety of places to pause and enjoy the sequestered, boulder-filled valley bottom. Boulders in Lynn Creek are round and smooth from years of being tumbled by rainy-season runoff. Owing to the steepness of the valley, only the top of Mount Fromme is visible from the creek. The park's more rugged formations, such as the Needles and Coliseum Mountain, only begin to reveal themselves as you make your way along the Headwaters Trail to Norvan Creek. Signs of logging camps that flourished here a century ago crop up along the trails: old boots, kettles, and blue glass jars decorate the forest where they've been unearthed. Trunks of sturdy second growth thrust up through the chassis of abandoned vehicles. A short side trail leads up to a viewpoint of Norvan Falls from the Headwaters Trail as it nears its northern terminus. Eminently fine views abound here. Beginning in late summer, the forest floor is dotted by the colourful caps of a dozen or more species of fungi.

In summer, when water levels in Lynn Creek are at their lowest ebb, experienced hikers can follow the **Lynn Lake Route,** which otherwise lies sequestered in the northern extremities of the park, isolated by the fact that part of the trail—the creekbed itself—lies underwater. On the park map (available at the information kiosk at the entrance to the park) a small notation makes mention of the fact that the trail to the lake is incomplete. Although that is the case in places, yellow metal tags affixed to trees and red tape tied to branches identify much of the route. As there is no camping allowed in the park and the time required to do the 7.5-mile (12-km) hike to Lynn Lake is five hours one way, you should be at the park gates when they open at 8am. If you wish to get hiking before then, park beside the gate and walk into the park from Lynn Valley Rd. Note: Walking into the park on the access road tacks on another mile to your journey; come the end of day, you may not wish to take one more step than is absolutely necessary. Carry plenty of drinking water, wear sturdy high-top footwear for support when negotiating the boulders, and consult with a GVRD attendant for final words of wisdom before setting out. One is often on duty near the registration kiosk at the park entrance.

The **Hanes Valley Hiking Route** (9 miles/15 km one way), a 7- to 8-hour grunt through Lynn Headwaters, presents a level of difficulty equal to that of the Lynn Lake Route. In places there are few signs of a trail, and hikers must be wary if visibility deteriorates. The route is well marked to the foot of a treacherous scree slope beside Hanes Creek. Beyond this, there are no trees on the rocky incline to which markers might be affixed. Bamboo poles wrapped in reflective tape help show the way to Crown Pass at the top of Hanes Valley. From the pass you look west to Howe Sound and north to the distinctively shaped outcropping called the Camel beside Crown Mountain. Crown Pass epitomizes the extreme ruggedness of the North Shore. The mountain slopes away on each side with dizzying rapidity. From Crown Pass the trail becomes much easier to discern and less demanding on leg muscles as you head for Grouse Mountain via Little Goat, Dam, and Goat Mountains. At the end of this journey, make your descent into North Vancouver on the Grouse Mountain Skyride. It costs about $5 and is worth it. The alternative, a descent on the Grouse Grind Trail (see below) is probably more than most hikers' knees are willing to endure. If you need to return to Lynn Headwaters Regional Park to retrieve your vehicle, catch the Lonsdale Quay (#236) bus from Grouse Mountain and transfer to the Lynn Valley (#229).

A third strenuous hike in this wilderness park climbs Lynn Peak. Although the hiking time is shorter than that required for either the Lynn Lake or the Hanes Valley routes, the 4.5-mile (7.2-km) round-trip journey to the peak (elevation 3,021 feet/921 m) is equally demanding. Your rewards are two splendid viewpoints and a visit to one of the last stands of ancient forest in the park. The approach begins from the park kiosk via Lynn Loop Trail. Watch for the well-marked turn away from this main trail onto the rougher **Lynn Crest Trail** (also referred to as the **Lynn Peak Trail**). The trail begins to climb sharply uphill, following the course of a small streambed in places. Depending on the season, this route may be wet or bone-dry. Bring plenty of drinking water, as the effort required to ascend this trail will dehydrate you at any time of the year. The first viewpoint appears after 1.2 miles (2 km). Catch your breath as you gaze east across the Seymour River Valley. The sound of the river rises from below, reminding you that Lynn Creek's familiar voice faded away as you climbed. Farther along, you pass through the Enchanted Forest, where the high sound of wind in the boughs will have you guessing whether it's created by the breeze or the creek. You can tell when you've reached the ancient grove, as the understorey begins to thin out. Far less nourishing sunlight reaches the forest floor here; the towering trees don't even begin to put out branches until 100 feet (30 m) or more above the ground. As the final viewpoint of Lynn Peak is only 0.3 mile (0.5 km) farther along, you have plenty of time to linger here and appreciate the majesty of the location. Allow two to three hours to complete this challenging hike. (Note: The clearing in which the highest viewpoint is located was the site of a blimp logging operation carried out here in the early 1970s.)

For an update on current trail conditions at any time of the year in Lynn Headwaters Regional Park, call (604) 985-1690. For a map of hiking trails, contact the GVRD Park's West Office, (604) 224-5739. A detailed topographic map of North Vancouver (Geological Survey of Canada map #92G/6) is helpful. These are available from several sources in the Lower Mainland, including Worldwide Books and Maps, 736A Granville St, (604) 687-3320, and the Geological Survey of Canada, 605 Robson St, (604) 666-0271.

Almost 25 miles (40 km) of roads and trails run through the **Seymour Demonstration Forest** in North Vancouver. Sandwiched between

Lynn Headwaters Regional Park and Mount Seymour Provincial Park, the Seymour Demonstration Forest is operated by the Greater Vancouver Regional District and has a status akin to a regional park. Hiking trails in the forest here are lengthy but easygoing. The most challenging ones are the **Homestead, Twin Bridges,** and **Fisherman's Trails,** which lead down into the Seymour Valley and follow the Seymour River. The Seymour Demonstration Forest is located at the north end of Lillooet Rd. Take exit 22 from Hwy 1 at the north end of the Ironworkers Memorial Second Narrows Bridge. Trails head off in all directions from the parking lot's gatehouse. It's a 1.4-mile (2.2-km) walk down to the Seymour River, from where the Fisherman's Trail heads north and Twin Bridges south. The winding Fisherman's Trail leads to the Mid-Valley Bridge, a distance of about 3 miles (5 km). Plan on taking two hours to complete the distance one way. You can choose to retrace your steps, or return along the paved **Seymour Mainline Rd** (see Cycling, below).

Walk the **Forest Ecology Loop Trail** in the Seymour Demonstration Forest (0.25 mile/0.4 km). You'll find it on the north side of Rice Lake, a short walk from the parking lot. Tie in this short walk with a more wide-ranging exploration of the demonstration forest. Maps and an interpretive brochure are available at the gatehouse. For more information on the Seymour Demonstration Forest, including a trail map, contact the GVRD, (604) 432-6286.

If you enjoy hiking to viewpoints, there is a wealth of moderate hiking trails in **Mount Seymour Provincial Park** in North Vancouver. Use extreme caution when exploring its open summit, especially in the region around **Mount Bishop,** at 4,947 feet (1508 m) the tallest peak in the park. Weather conditions change quickly during storm season, and the route between peaks can become obscured. Each year this mountain gobbles an unwary hiker or two. To reach the park, travel east on Mount Seymour Pkwy from the Ironworkers Memorial Second Narrows Bridge.

For an easygoing introduction to Mount Seymour Provincial Park, explore the 3-mile (5-km) section of the Baden-Powell Trail (see above) that runs east-west through the park near the base of the mountain. Watch for its well-marked trailhead and picnic area where it crosses Mount Seymour Rd. If you wish, begin from the parking lot just inside the park entrance and follow the **Old Buck Logging Road Trail** uphill to reach the Baden-Powell route, a distance of about 1.5 miles (2.3 km). In total, Old Buck leads 3.4 miles (5.5 km) up the side of Mount Seymour to a junction with the **Perimeter Trail.** The lower section of Old Buck has recently been upgraded for biking (see Mountain Biking, below), which also makes for easier hiking.

In summer, once the snow has melted, short hiking trails lead from the parking lot at the top of Mount Seymour Rd to **Dinky Peak** and **Goldie, Mystery, and Flower Lakes.** Distances to these spots aren't great, the elevation gain is minimal, and hikers are rewarded with views of Greater Vancouver that are among the best in the Lower Mainland.

For a more extended hike, try the **First Lake Trail** to Dog Mountain from the parking lot at the top of Mount Seymour Rd. Plan on taking two hours to complete the 3-mile (5-km) round-trip journey. Wear waterproof boots, as this trail is often soggy. If you set your sights on reaching Mount Seymour's summit, try the moderately difficult 2.5-mile (4-km) hike to Mount Seymour's **First** and **Second Pump** peaks. The trail traverses Brockton Point on its way to the peaks. Owing to the panoramic view from here, this is a very popular trail. Other hiking routes on Mount Seymour include the 10-hour, 9-mile (14-km) round-trip trek to **Elsay Lake.** The initial section of the trail covers the same route as used to reach First Pump Peak. From there the trail to Elsay Lake passes Gopher Lake, then narrows as it enters the most exposed section of the mountain. Trail markers are often difficult to locate in bad weather along this rugged portion of the trail, and hikers should not hesitate to turn back. Only experienced, well-equipped hikers should attempt this difficult trail. An emergency shelter is located at Elsay Lake. For more information and a map of Mount Seymour Provincial Park, call BC Parks at (604) 924-2200.

Other hiking routes to explore on the North Shore include the **Grouse Mountain Trail,** better known as the **Grouse Grind.** The first hiking trail up the side of Grouse Mountain was brushed out by the Vancouver Mountaineering Club in 1900 when a journey to the North Shore from town involved a boat ride, then a hike on foot or horseback to the base of the mountain. Almost a century later, Grouse continues to be a magnet for Vancouverites in search of a challenge—and companionship. The Grouse Grind, billed as the world's biggest stair-climb, is *the* outdoor venue these days to work out and meet new friends. During summer months, hundreds of trim, fresh-faced hikers ascend the steep-sided mountain from its trailhead on the east side of the Grouse Mountain parking lot at the north end of Capilano Rd, usually in groups of twos and threes. A typical opening line once on top is, "What's your time?" (If you complete the 1.8-mile/3-km climb with a elevation gain of 2,760 feet/842 m in less than an hour, you're doing better than average. If you beat 32 minutes for men, or 36 minutes for women, you're the champ!) A workout on the Grouse Grind is excellent preparation for a backpacking trip. This is a quick way to stretch your lower calf muscles (the ones you rarely call upon except with a 50-pound/22.5-kg pack on your back) into shape. If you're hard-core, you'll do the trail both ways. Otherwise, it's a $5 ride down in the Grouse Mountain Skyride gondola. Other trails on the side of

Grouse Mountain include the **BCMC Trail** (2.2 miles/3.5 km one way; allow two and a half hours), which begins from the same location as the Grouse Grind. You don't need a car to participate; call BC Transit, (604) 521-0400, to check times on the #232 and #236 bus routes to Grouse Mountain. For information and a hiking brochure, call Grouse Mountain, (604) 980-9311 or (604) 986-6262.

Cycling

Although the North Shore has increasingly become identified with mountain biking, road riding has enjoyed a longer, though less lustrous, appeal. Alex Steida, the first Canadian cyclist to wear the yellow jersey in the Tour de France, trained on the North Shore in the 1980s. Here are a few smooth routes to roll your skinny tires on.

You'd think they designed the paved **Seymour Mainline,** which runs for 8.7 miles (14 km) through the Seymour Demonstration Forest (see Hiking, above), with bicycles (and in-line skates and strollers, for that matter) in mind rather than logging trucks. With the exception of one moderately steep hill at its midpoint, this is an easy ride to the walls of the Seymour Dam. (Depending on the time of year, a torrent or a trickle of water will be spilling from the dam's gates. Note: There's no water available along this route, so in warm summer months bring plenty.) Along the way you'll have one of the best views of Mount Seymour's deceptively gentle-looking peaks. There's one drawback: on weekdays during working hours, all but the first 1.25 miles (2 km) of the road are closed to recreation. Even when the weather is at its hottest in Vancouver, there's always a soft breeze blowing through the valley. In summer, combine a bike ride here with a splash in the Seymour River (see Beaches/Swimming, below), and you have the makings of a perfect recipe for recreation. The entrance to the Seymour Demonstration Forest lies at the north end of Lillooet Rd, reached by taking the Mount Seymour Pkwy exit (#22) off Hwy 1 in North Vancouver near the Second Narrows Bridge. A large green GVRD sign at the intersection of the parkway and Lillooet Rd points straight ahead on Lillooet to the Seymour Demonstration Forest. The last section of the road is unpaved. A tipoff that you're on the right road is that you'll often see groups of cyclists well before you reach the park.

Both the 5-mile (8-km) **Cypress Parkway** in West Vancouver and the 7.4-mile (12-km) **Mount Seymour Road** in North Vancouver have wide paved shoulders for those cyclists who enjoy the challenge of a lengthy ascent. Cypress Pkwy climbs through four switchbacks from the Upper Levels Hwy (Hwy 1) to the parking lot at the foot of Cypress Bowl's downhill ski runs. Hard-core cyclists lash skis and poles to their frames in winter when making their way here. Mount Seymour Rd provides a similar challenge. Riders on both routes are rewarded with viewpoints midway up each mountain, and the scream of wind in the vents of their helmets on the way down. Check your brakes!

Mountain Biking

The North Shore is rightfully renowned for some of the most challenging off-road mountain-bike trails in the world. Most of these have only recently been constructed as the popularity of single-track riding has outpaced road riding. These routes are cut by ad hoc groups of cyclists desperate for some quality singletrack to call their own, often without permission from municipal or provincial governments. Clandestine trails are not well signed, but in most cases you won't have any problem finding them. The best directions can be obtained from bike shops such as the Cove Bike Shop, one of the North Shore's oldest mountain-bike centres, 4310 Gallant Rd in North Vancouver's Deep Cove neighbourhood, (604) 929-1918; the Bike Cellar, 94 Lonsdale Ave, in North Vancouver near the SeaBus terminal, (604) 985-2213; or Ambleside Cycle, 1852 Marine Dr in West Vancouver, (604) 926-6242. Cyclists would also do well to consult Christine Boehringer's *Mountain Bike Trails in the Lower Mainland* and Darrin Polischuk's *Mountain Biking British Columbia,* both of which are comprehensive guides. William Rosenthal's *Mountain Biking the Lower Mainland* features many of the less technical rides, while David Godwin's *Greater Vancouver Extreme Ride Guide* is exactly as advertised.

One of the attractions of the North Shore slopes, particularly at lower elevations, is that trails stay snow-free throughout most of the winter. This is a prime reason why many of Canada's elite mountain-bike riders live and train in North Vancouver.

A myriad of off-road trails leads through the **Seymour Demonstration Forest** (see Hiking, above). True to its name, part of the largely second-growth forest is a manicured showcase for the logging industry. Much of the undergrowth has been brushed out in places near the park entrance, which makes for smooth trail riding. Several of the hiking trails here are also open to mountain bikes, including **Twin Bridges, Riverside,** and **Fisherman's.** Tie in a trip around the Seymour Demonstration Forest with an off-road spin through nearby **Lynn Canyon Park** (see Parks, below), located immediately south and west of Seymour's parking lot. Main trails are all well signed to avoid confusion. For a map of trails in Seymour Demonstration Forest, call GVRD Parks, (604) 432-6286; also check the mountain-bike listings at their Web site: www.gvrd.bc.ca. Trail maps of Lynn Canyon Park are available at the Lynn Canyon Ecology

Centre at the entrance to the park, (604) 987-5922.

Mount Seymour Provincial Park (see Hiking, above), near Deep Cove in North Vancouver, has several trails on which mountain biking is sanctioned. In turn, these link with many unofficial ones outside the park's boundaries, including the infamously challenging and colourfully named **Severed Dick Trail.** To reach it and many others, follow **Old Buck Trail** as it climbs steadily beneath a forest canopy for almost 1.5 miles (3 km) to a BC Hydro service road. Old Buck Trail begins on the west side of Mount Seymour Rd just inside the park gates. This former logging road has been reinforced to withstand the rains that often soak the mountainside and to absorb the impact of knobby bike treads. (Old Buck is the site of the start/finish area for the annual Hell of the North mountain-bike race held each July.) Short stretches of single-track trails crisscross the mountain both above and below the service road. The well-marked **Baden-Powell Trail** (see Hiking, above) runs east and west through the park and is always a good touchstone with which to orient your scrambled senses; however, it's more suited to walking than riding. Severed Dick is reached by heading west on Baden-Powell from its intersection with Old Buck. Where the Baden-Powell changes from a wide pathway to rough single-track, watch for the entrance to Severed Dick on the left. Severed Dick eventually connects with the **Bridle Path Trail.** Bear left here to return to Old Buck. Along the way, granite outcroppings amid a second-growth Douglas fir forest provide twisting drops over loose, loamy soil. The maze of trails here is so dizzying that you may quickly lose your bearings. Maps are scarce. Try these trails with a friend who knows the topography, and ask directions wherever you go.

Additional trails in the vicinity of Mount Seymour Provincial Park can be reached from the north ends of Riverside Dr and Berkley Rd, both of which intersect with Mount Seymour Pkwy immediately east of the Seymour River. Anglers and horseback riders also use these trails, so be cautious as well as courteous. Cross the Seymour River north of Riverside Dr at Twin Bridges to connect with the lengthy **Fisherman's Trail** in the Seymour Demonstration Forest (see Hiking, above).

Cypress Provincial Park in West Vancouver has only one official trail, named **BLT** (boulders, logs, and trees), which begins just north of the entrance to the old logging road at the first switchback on the Cypress Pkwy. Another entrance is from the maintenance yard above the fourth switchback. BLT may be the only trail, but at least it's got length (10 miles/16 km return) in its favour. There are a number of trails just outside the park, ranging from the idyllic **Fern Trail** to the psychotic **Sex Boy,** both of which link with BLT. Fern Trail begins where BLT meets Cypress Bowl Rd's third switchback. Entrances to upper and lower Sex Boy occur along BLT north of a BC Hydro substation and the third switchback. Mountain biking elsewhere in the park is illegal (rigorously enforced). Expect fines or bike confiscation (as well as scorn and ridicule from park authorities) if caught. Another series of trails is found at the second switchback higher up Cypress Pkwy. These trails, including **Skyline, Panorama, No Stairs Allowed,** and **My Friend the Stupid Grouse,** run through the forested British Properties neighbourhood. Although they haven't been officially sanctioned, they haven't been officially condemned, either.

Grouse Mountain and its companion peak to the east, **Mount Fromme,** sport a number of trails that are open to mountain biking, most of which intersect with Old Grouse Mountain Hwy. The gravel-surfaced road once carried busloads of visitors to the top of Grouse Mountain. It's long been closed to vehicles—but not hikers or bikers—on the slopes above North Vancouver's Lynn Valley neighbourhood. To reach the gated trailhead, head to the north end of Mountain Hwy, one of the principal streets that intersect with both Lynn Valley Rd and the Upper Levels Hwy. The Old Grouse Mountain Hwy begins climbing first the side of Fromme, then Grouse, from here. Keep track of the switchbacks to locate pioneer mountain-bike trail builder Ross Kirkwood's **Seventh Secret,** which descends from the seventh major bend. **Griffen, Roadside Attraction, Leopard, Crinkum Crankum, Cedar, Egg,** and **Dweezil** are trails open to mountain bikes. You'll find them spread along the north (uphill) side of the road soon after beginning the climb. Other trails, almost all of which descend to the Baden-Powell Trail (see Hiking, above) from the road beyond the fifth switchback, are not open to mountain bikers.

In summer, Velo-City Cycle Tours, 2256 Chapman Way, North Vancouver, (604) 924-0288, Web site: www.velo-city.com, offers **guided mountain bike descents** of Grouse Mountain along the Old Grouse Mountain Hwy. Although the 15.5-mile (25-km) route is off-road, it appeals to those cyclists who would rather enjoy the scenery than see how much punishment their bodies and equipment can absorb. It's also a good way to practise your "death grip," as much of the trip is spent braking. Velo-City also offers guided tours of off-road trails on Grouse Mountain.

A 20-minute ferry ride from Horseshoe Bay lands you on **Bowen Island.** Bowen is a paradise of trails, from relatively easy loops around Killarney Lake in Crippen Regional Park (see Parks, below) to the burning climb up Mount Gardner. The island is a world unto itself, so take the time to explore and revel in Bowen's sedated pace. Although the tempo may be relaxed, mountain bikers will find the roads that ring the island demanding, with few level stretches and even fewer beach-access points for well-deserved breaks. For a map of Bowen Island, stop at the island's gas station near the ferry dock. For a trail map of Crippen Regional Park, contact the GVRD, (604) 224-5739.

Parks

By a twist of fate, the dark background provided by a stand of old-growth rain forest on Point Atkinson's shore in West Vancouver turns out to be its saving grace. If it weren't for the contrast that it provides for a powerful lighthouse beacon built here in 1888, this primarily Douglas fir forest would have been logged long ago. As it stands, **Lighthouse Park** contains the largest uncut, coastal-elevation trees in the Lower Mainland. And what a beautiful environment in which to view them. Waves crash against an outcropping of granite as the ocean breeze whistles through the boughs above. All this within a 10-minute walk of the parking lot. The trees are so large and, in places, poised at such precarious angles to each other that one walks past them with bated breath. The sight of an occasional bench hewn from the trunk of a downed predecessor helps to steady one's nerve. Pause here under the shelter of their moisture-trapping limbs (some cloaked with an estimated billion or more needles) and marvel at the lushness of the understorey. Follow along the seaside trail, part of a 3-mile (5-km) network of pathways, from the lighthouse to **Jackpine Point,** where you're sure to find a smooth rock on which to pause again, beneath the polished, mahogany-coloured branches of a strawberry madrona, or arbutus as this broad-leafed evergreen tree is known in Canada. In late summer, paper-thin scrolls of bark peel off and drift with the tide, revealing a smooth, red trunk. Visit here on an autumn day to experience the Zen-like peace that pervades this oceanside scene. Lighthouse Park is tucked away off Marine Dr in West Vancouver at the south end of Beacon Lane. To reach it, travel west on Marine from the heart of West Vancouver. The park turnoff is marked by a wooden sign; turn south on Beacon Lane and drive to the parking lot. There is regular bus service from Park Royal Shopping Centre to the park; take the Horseshoe Bay (#250). An interpretive sign at the end of the parking lot provides a large map of the park and some natural-history notes. A concise map of park trails is also available here, complete with a suggestion for a self-guided walk to some of the more significant natural features in the park. For information, call West Vancouver Parks and Recreation, (604) 925-7200.

If it weren't for the fabulous canyon that Lynn Creek smashes its way through, there would hardly be reason to mention **Lynn Canyon Park** in the same breath as its oversized neighbours, Lynn Headwaters Regional Park and the Seymour Demonstration Forest (see Hiking, above). As it is, this triad of parks comprises one of the most exciting and integrated networks of protected land in the Lower Mainland. Lynn Canyon's contribution is its marvellous suspension bridge from which visitors cast cautious glances at the water 150 feet (50 m) below, where it turns from placid emerald green to whipped-up whitewater in an instant. Despite the sturdy steel cables there's always a slight feeling of dread, an uncertainty as to whether the footings will hold. This crossing is not for the timid, as the bridge bounces and sways. Trails follow both sides of the canyon and lead upstream to 30 Foot Pool and downstream to Twin Falls Bridge. A tall wooden staircase assists walkers and cyclists to venture north through the park from 30 Foot Pool to its borders with the Seymour Demonstration Forest. One trail to follow when exploring Lynn Canyon is a section of the **Baden-Powell Trail** (see Hiking, above) that winds through the park on its long journey across the North Shore. To find Lynn Canyon Park, take either the Mountain Hwy or Lynn Valley Rd exits off the Upper Levels Hwy (Hwy 1) in North Vancouver, close to the Second Narrows Bridge. Both roads intersect near the park. From there, follow Lynn Valley Rd to Peters Rd, where a large sign points the way to Lynn Canyon Park. The suspension bridge, an interpretive centre, and a concession stand are next to the parking lot at the end of Peters Rd. Stop at the **Lynn Canyon Ecology Centre** to pick up a map of the park. If you enjoy looking closely at the landscape, spend time upon arrival at the Ecology Centre as part of your visit to Lynn Canyon Park. You'll come away with a much clearer understanding of the natural history of the park. Admission is free, as are many of the natural history programs presented here and by the centre in neighbouring parks throughout the North Shore. Daily summer nature walks leave the centre at 2pm during July and August. The Ecology Centre's hours are 10am to 5pm on weekdays, noon to 4pm on weekends and holidays. Call (604) 981-3103 for information on seasonal programs.

Feel like taking a short sea cruise? The ferry ride from Horseshoe Bay to **Crippen Regional Park** on Bowen Island aboard BC Ferries' *Queen of Capilano* only takes 20 minutes. You'll be following a long-standing tradition if you do. Ferries once brought revellers from Vancouver for day and overnight outings to Bowen. One of the delights of visiting the island at the mouth of Howe Sound is that you're in the park as soon as you step onto the dock. Upon arrival, check in at the restored Union Steamship Company store just uphill. The Greater Vancouver Regional District houses its park reception centre here where you can pick up a map of Crippen, as well as a historic walking-tour guide. Across Government Rd is a row of shops, including a bakery and two pubs (featuring Bowen Island brew). Uphill at the corner of Government and Miller Rds is a gas station, a good source for a map of the island. Bowen Island's Snug Cove is part of Crippen Regional Park. You can rent one of the restored Union

Steamship Company cabins here if you wish to spend the night,on the island. Call (604) 947-0707 for rates.

If you're only here for a short visit, follow the waterfront promenade from the ferry dock around to Snug Cove's wide beach. A steep trail leads up the hill on the far side of the spacious picnic area to **Dorman Point.** There's a great view of Howe Sound and the Howe Sound Crest mountains from here as you look down into aptly named Snug Cove.

Even though the ferry ride and a stroll on the beach make an entirely satisfactory trip in themselves, the best way to appreciate Crippen Regional Park is over the course of a half-day or more. Head inland to **Killarney Lake** to explore the quiet side of Bowen Island. As you walk or bike (see Mountain Biking, above) uphill from the ferry on Government Rd past the Union Steamship store, trails marked by a green park signpost lead off to Killarney Lake. Allow 30 minutes to walk the 1-mile (1.6-km) Killarney Creek Trail to the lake. Take one of two routes to reach the Killarney Lake Trail. One trail leads past a pair of fish ladders that climb the hillside above a small lagoon. Alternatively, walk down past the Memorial Garden to a causeway that crosses the mouth of the tranquil backwater. On the opposite side of the lagoon, follow left on Melmore Rd to Miller Rd, where a yellow gate across from St. Gerard's Church marks the entrance to the Killarney Creek Trail. The first third of the trail is on level ground padded by years of fallen leaves and needles, then it begins to rise gently through second-growth forest. Huge cedar stumps testify that these graceful giants once predominated here. At the halfway point to Killarney Lake, a path leads off to the left and across a small bridge over Terminal Creek. Horses exercise in a paddock nearby. Once at the lake, the Killarney Loop Trail (2.5 miles/4 km) circles its perimeter somewhat erratically, passing a picnic area and a small beach along the way. A lovely stretch of boardwalk spans a marshy area at the north end of the lake. Crippen Regional Park comprises everything visitors hope to find in a park.

Telephone BC Ferries, (604) 669-1211, for sailing times on the *Queen of Capilano,* which carries 85 vehicles. The round-trip fare for foot passengers is currently $4.25 per person, and there is an extra charge of $1.50 for bicycles, much more reasonable than the $14.50 fee for cars. You can travel to Horseshoe Bay by bus (#250). Call West Vancouver Bus Transportation at (604) 985-7777 for schedule information.

Beaches/Swimming

Going to the beach is a far different experience on the North Shore than across Burrard Inlet in Vancouver (which, interestingly, is *never* referred to as the South Shore). Over here it's rugged from tideline to skyline. Cobble beaches and rocky outcroppings make beaches on English Bay look positively *cushy* by comparison. That being said, a few soft pockets do exist in places such as **Caulfeild** and **Ambleside Parks** in West Vancouver, and **Cates Park** in North Vancouver's Deep Cove neighbourhood. All are extremely popular with families on weekends and yet can be almost deserted on weekdays. Cates has a forested ambience that leads out to Roche Point, while Ambleside and Caulfeild are open, windswept expanses. No matter which you choose, the views of English Bay and Burrard Inlet are terrific. Caulfeild Park offers the most variety of sandy beach and shoreline trail, and is located on Pilot House Rd. Turn off Marine Dr at Piccadilly South, then turn again on to Dogwood Lane, which connects with Pilot House. Ambleside Park is located south of Marine Dr between the Capilano River and Keith Rd. Cates Park is on the south side of the Dollarton Hwy, 5 miles (8 km) east of the Ironworkers Memorial Second Narrows Bridge. There is a vehicle boat launch at Cates Park. On several weekends during the summer, Native canoe regattas are held here.

Whytecliff Marine Park's rugged shoreline and cobble beach lie in West Vancouver's Horseshoe Bay neighbourhood. To find your way to the park, take the Upper Levels Hwy west to Horseshoe Bay. Turn west onto Marine Dr, just before the BC Ferries toll booth. Signs point the way to Whytecliff at all major intersections from here. The entrance to the park is at the western end of Marine Dr. (If you're in no hurry, enjoy the scenic route by taking Marine Dr through West Vancouver rather than the Upper Levels Hwy.)

Beside the beach, interpretive signs explain in words and pictures the variety of marine life to be found beneath the waves. Although you have to take most of it on faith, occasional life forms do bob to the surface, such as the head of a curious **seal** or a school of divers. (See also Wildlife, below.) The setting here at the mouth of Howe Sound is dramatic, with the vastness of the Strait of Georgia spread out to the west. Ferries serving Vancouver and Bowen Islands and the Sunshine Coast glide in and out of nearby Horseshoe Bay. As the wake from the larger boats hits the shoreline, it creates surf. Modest though it is, it's an unusual sight in these sheltered waters.

On all but the busiest summer weekends, visitors can usually find a secluded spot with a driftwood log for a backrest. Follow one of the rough but well-trodden trails that run along the top of the cliffs. Small sets of rock stairways lead here and there. (See also Wildlife, below.) A rocky breakwater leads out to nearby Whyte Islet. At low tide you can clamber up its steep slopes and find a sheltered spot beneath a lone shore pine. Keep one eye on the progress of the tide. It's a cold swim back to shore!

In the heat of a summer day the only element debatably more precious than a swimming hole is cool, fresh air. When you find both together, it's heaven. One of the best places to find such swimming holes is on the **Seymour River** in North Vancouver. Unlike many other streams and lakes on the North Shore, water in the Seymour is several degrees warmer owing to the large 12-mile-long (20-km) reservoir backed up behind the dam, from which a steady volume is released downstream in order to sustain fish habitat.

Not only does the Seymour register just the right reading for refreshment but you are almost always assured of a constant breeze blowing through the valley to wick off moisture without need of a towel. Yet another benefit is the proximity of the GVRD's **Seymour Demonstration Forest** (see Hiking, above), through which much of the Seymour River flows. From the entrance to the forest, take the well-marked **Homestead Trail** (0.6 mile/1 km) to the river. You can hear the river to the east of the trail before you see it. Follow north along Homestead until it comes into view, then make your way down the embankment to the river's boulder-filled channel. Although water levels in summer are at their annual lows, you'll quickly find that there are plunge pools galore; there'll be one that's just the right size for you. Remember to wear an old pair of running shoes or sandals to negotiate your way over the boulders, some of which are made slippery by algae. You may find that you are sharing the river with the occasional group of anglers; however, the Seymour is of proportions generous enough for all. It would be surprising if, after a quick look around, you couldn't find a quiet place to yourself. After all, the Homestead Trail merges with the Fisherman's Trail (see Hiking, above) and meanders upstream for almost 9 miles (15 km); somewhere along its length, there's bound to be a swimming hole with your name on it.

Kayaking/Canoeing/Boating

Deep Cove in North Vancouver is one of two jumping-off points for exploring **Indian Arm,** a steep-sided, 18-mile (30-km) fjord that branches north from Burrard Inlet just east of the Ironworkers Memorial Second Narrows Bridge. Kayakers (and the occasional canoeist) also launch from Belcarra Regional Park (see Greater Vancouver chapter) on the east side of Indian Arm. You can explore the south end of Indian Arm, including the islands that comprise **Indian Arm Provincial Marine Park,** in the course of a day, or set out on an extended two- to four-day circumnavigation of the coastal inlet. The best time to paddle here is between April and October. During monsoon season, Indian Arm (and the North Shore generally) often receives twice as much rain as nearby Vancouver.

In addition to the convenience of having such a wilderness paddling environment so close to the city, Indian Arm is also a fairly sheltered environment in which to try ocean kayaking. However, don't let its proximity to the city fool you into thinking all is peaches and cream. Strong winds funnel down the inlet from Garibaldi Provincial Park and can quickly turn a relaxing paddle into a fight to stay afloat. On busy summer days, powerboats also kick up a mishmash of waves that toss smaller craft around. The farther north you go, the steeper the walls of the inlet become, providing few places to beach in a hurry. Always exercise caution and respect the speed with which conditions may change during a paddle trip here.

Some of the places where you'll want to pause and stretch your legs along the way include **Racoon Island** and **Twin Islands,** which make up Indian Arm Provincial Marine Park (not to be confused with recently created Indian Arm Provincial Park, a large tract of undeveloped land along the west side of the inlet). These are among the very few islands that dot Indian Arm; from Deep Cove you'll have to cross over to the inlet's east side to reach them. If you'd like to spend the night, there are wilderness campsites on Big Twin Island. Water is scarce, so pack along whatever you think you'll need. The best beaches on the inlet are located north of Deep Cove on the inlet's west shore. As you make your way into the more remote, northern half of Indian Arm, stop to explore **Granite Falls Regional Park** on the east shore. Although there is no development in the park, there are plenty of signs of past logging activity around the falls. Indian River enters the extreme north end of the inlet and creates a marshy delta that attracts wildlife. Active logging carries on nearby; a Forest Service road leads from here to Squamish. For more information on paddling Indian Arm, including guided trips, contact the Deep Cove Canoe and Kayak Centre, 2156 Banbury Rd, North Vancouver, (604) 929-2268.

What's amazing about paddling the **Capilano River** is how distant the well-ordered world nearby suddenly feels as you enter its 3.5-mile (5.6-km) drop-and-pool course. This is an enchanted canyon and should only be attempted by those who can handle its powerful spell. Opinion is divided as to whether this should be attempted in an open canoe. Certainly not before consulting knowledgeable sources, such as Walter's Ski Shack, 1637 Marine Dr, North Vancouver, (604) 988-3937. Opinion is united on one necessity: have a guide with you when you put in for the first time. By July, water levels begin to drop and the river becomes more technical. Even in summer this is most definitely a wet suit-and-helmet river. There's only one put-in, at the top of the canyon beside the fish hatchery (see Hiking, above). The Cleveland Dam's presence is a reminder that water levels on the river can fluctuate daily, depending on the amount of water released from the dam (and the sky above). A water gauge at the west end of the weir near the salmon pools indicates the difficulty of the water: 2–3 feet (0.6–0.9 m) equals easy; 4–6 feet (1.2–1.8 m) equals difficult; above 6 feet (1.8 m) equals expert only. On rainy days this river calls to local intermediate and expert paddlers, who treasure its proximity to home. One such fan is Betty Pratt-Johnson, who wrote the endo-by-endo description of the Capilano in her biblical *Whitewater Trips for Kayakers, Canoeists and Rafters, Volume Two*. Track it down; then, welcome to the washing machine.

The other river on the North Shore is the **Seymour,** a river of a whole different hue. About the only thing the two have in common is that they're both dammed. The Capilano stole the Seymour's thunder when challenges were being handed out (but don't tell that to someone learning to paddle here). There's not a canyon in sight, just a shallow boulder-and-rock garden riverbed, with a small patch of fast water just before the river passes under the Seymour Creek Bridge near its confluence with Burrard Inlet. An old weir creates a sudden drop at this point. Hang onto your paddles. Best places to put in on the Seymour are either at Riverside Park at the intersection of Riverside Dr (East) and Chapman Way or at the west end of Swinburne Ave off Riverside. The take out is downstream from the BC Rail bridge over the Seymour at the west end of Spicer Rd off Riverside Drive (West).

Paddlers began journeying to **Horseshoe Bay** long before the arrival of the first Europeans. For Native people, Horseshoe Bay was a traditional meeting place, used both as a seasonal fishing encampment and a place to spend a night when travelling between villages on the Squamish River and Burrard Inlet. The sheltered bay was called *ch'xáy* or Chai-hai, after the swishing sound made by schools of little fish stirring up the waters of Horseshoe Bay. (In 1991, it was discovered that Horseshoe Bay Park stands atop an ancient shell midden.) Boaters launch from the federal dock next to the park. If you want to join the throng, you can rent one from Sewell's Marina. The Sewell family have operated a marina at Horseshoe Bay since the 1920s. Powerboats, available for about $20 per hour, are popular with salmon fishermen. The waters around the mouth of Howe Sound are usually dotted with their boats. Call Sewell's at (604) 921-3474.

Bowen Island Sea Kayaking, (800) 605-2925, offers **guided kayak tours** around a nest of islands at the mouth of Howe Sound. Explore Bowen's extensive shoreline as well as nearby Gambier and Keats islands. They also rent kayaks, as well as dispense advice to those adventurers who arrive under their own steam.

Wildlife

The **Capilano River Fish Hatchery** in Capilano River Regional Park (see Hiking, above) teems with **piscicultural activity** year-round. The best part about it is that visitors get to spy on the fry through glass walls that surround their tanks. It's like a giant aquarium set in a rock canyon.

The **Seymour River Hatchery** in the Seymour Demonstration Forest (see Hiking, above) has ponds full of **coho** and **steelhead** fry beside Hurry Creek. You'll have to make your way almost to the Seymour Dam to see them. By then you'll need a break. Follow the trail from the hatchery to the river, where you'll discover a sweet little beach offshore by which the fry school when first released in spring. Come summer, you can even take a dip with them!

In 1993, **Whytecliff Marine Park** became Canada's first Marine Protected Area. Harvesting or collecting any marine life beneath the waters of this sanctuary is prohibited. (Although there are many provincial marine parks in BC, there is very limited protection for the marine life within these areas. Whytecliff is a municipal park.) Upwards of 200 marine animal species, with exotic names such as the **speckled sanddab** or the **sunflower seastar,** call these waters home yet pay no property taxes, despite living in Canada's most affluent community. (For directions to the park, see Beaches/Swimming, above.)

Fishing

As there are few places to shore-cast on the North Shore other than the lower reaches of the Capilano River in Capilano River Regional Park (see Hiking, above), anglers would do well to head to the boat-launch ramp at **Cates Park** in North Vancouver (see Beaches/Swimming, above), Seycove Marina at the north end of Panorama in **Deep Cove,** (604) 929-1251, or **Mosquito Creek Marine Basin,** at the south foot of Forbes, (604) 987-4113, also in North Vancouver. One of the best sources for information on fishing on the North Shore is Castaway Tackle, 1388 Main St, North Vancouver, (604) 980-1621.

There's a public boat launch at **Horseshoe Bay** beside the BC Ferries terminal. Sewells Marina, 6695 Nelson Ave, Horseshoe Bay, West Vancouver, 604-921-FISH (3474), established in 1931, rents powerboats and dispenses expert angling advice at dockside. A short distance east of Horseshoe Bay, Thunderbird Marina, (604) 921-7434, is located on Marine Dr in West Vancouver's Eagle Harbour neighbourhood.

Skiing/Snowboarding

Hollyburn Ridge in Cypress Provincial Park is the domain of cross-country skiers. Hollyburn's 10 miles (16 km) of groomed and track-set trails, as well as skating lanes, are cut through some of the most challenging terrain in Western Canada. The tradition of skiing is an old one here, dating well back into the 1920s. Evidence of this can be seen in the many rustic cabins that dot the woods. There are trails here to suit all skill levels.

Downhill skiers and snowboarders have their pick of **Cypress Bowl** (25 groomed runs, 1,750 feet/537 m vertical, 3 chairlifts) in West Vancouver's Cypress Provincial Park; in North Vancouver, **Grouse Mountain** (22 runs, 1,200 feet/365 m vertical, 4 chairlifts) or **Seymour Snow Country** (20 runs, 600 feet/200 m vertical, 3 chairlifts) in Mount Seymour Provincial Park. Intermediate- and advanced-level skiers and snowboarders gravitate to Cypress and Grouse, while Seymour has the distinction of being the place where three-quarters of Lower Mainlanders learn to ski, and it's got 5,000 pairs of rental skis (and snowboards) to prove it.

No one mountain has an edge on the others when it comes to chairlifts. This isn't Whistler, so don't expect state-of-the-art, high-speed lifts with protective bubbles to keep out the elements. Slow but steadily up the mountain is the pace on the North Shore. Some days half the crowd (or more) will be on snowboards. All three mountains have snowboard parks—Cypress has a dozen or more sprinkled around its slopes—which is a big draw for those who like to practise their moves as they launch off the top of an old school bus and other props that have been positioned to create jumps and chutes. Caution: Perfect powder conditions do occur on the North Shore and, day or night, that's the time to hurry up the mountains to catch winter at its best. Unless you have winter (not all-season) tires, don't attempt to drive to Mount Seymour or Cypress in a snowstorm. The roads are plowed frequently but can still be hair-raising, even with a good grip on the road. Grouse Mountain's gondola is the safest bet during a snow dump. Because of the moderating influence of the ocean, the texture of the snow that drops on the North Shore is heavier than that which falls inland. Coast Cement is not just the name of a local concrete company! Still, on those days when the temperature drops low enough, you will discover light, fluffy flakes of magic on the trails. Sometimes it snows all night then clears at first light: that's when being a member of the crack-of-dawn club pays dividends. All three mountains open early (8–8:30am) and close late (11pm), and all have lighted trails with specially priced lift tickets after 4pm.

For more information, including seasonal transportation, contact Cypress Bowl Ski Area, PO Box 91252, West Vancouver, (604) 926-5612, snow report, (604) 926-6007; cross-country (Hollyburn Ridge), (604) 922-0825; Grouse Mountain, 6400 Nancy Greene Way, (604) 984-0661; snow report, (604) 986-6262; and Seymour Ski Country (Mount Seymour), 1700 Indian River Rd, (604) 986-2261, snow report, (604) 879-3999.

More informal, though no less fun, are the trails in **Lynn Headwaters Regional Park,** North Vancouver (see Hiking, above). Cut your own cross-country tracks along the **Lynn Loop Trail** (2 miles/3.5 km return) and **Cedar Mill Trail** (2.5 miles/4 km return), both of which run beside Lynn Creek with only limited elevation gain. Cross-country skiers also head for the **Seymour Demonstration Forest** (see Hiking, above). The wide swath of the **Seymour Mainline Road** (17.4 mile/28 km) isn't plowed in winter. The route has limited elevation gain for the first 3 miles (5 km), then one major hill to negotiate.

Snowshoeing is enjoying a renaissance. If you can walk, you can snowshoe. You can rent a pair on either Seymour Snow Country or Hollyburn Ridge, or from a number of sports shops in the Vancouver area, including Carleton Recreation Equipment, 3201 Kingsway, (604) 438-6371, and Coast Mountain Sports, 2201 W Fourth Ave, (604) 731-6181. Snowshoeing is permitted on designated trails on all three mountains.

Diving

As you make your way along the beach at **Whytecliff Marine Park** (see Beaches/Swimming, above), you'll probably see wet-suited figures emerge from the embankment and make their way towards the ocean. After a day at the office, scuba divers come to experience a little weightlessness as they float off into the nether world just offshore, where temperatures matter little year-round, provided you dress appropriately. Although the majority of park visitors prefer gum boots over wet suits, Whytecliff Marine Park has become a magnet for local divers. A list of rules of conduct, prominently displayed in the parking lot, are directed primarily at the divers, who are encouraged to change in the washrooms and to keep their language clean! For more information about diving on the North Shore, and to arrange to participate in a **group tour,** contact the Wet Shop Diving and Water Sports Centre, 6371 Bruce St, West Vancouver, (604) 921-6371; the Great Pacific Diving Company, 1236 Marine Dr, North Vancouver, (604) 986-0302; Aqua Sapiens, 1386 Main St, North Vancouver, (604) 985-3483, Web site address: www.aquasapiens.com; and the Deep Cove Dive Shop, 4342 Gallant St, North Vancouver, (604) 929-3116. A good descriptive guide to diving the waters around the North Shore is *141 Dives in the Protected Waters of Washington and British Columbia* by Betty Pratt-Johnson.

Picnics

Picnic sites are plentiful on the North Shore. In West Vancouver, you'll find picnic tables and covered shelters in **Whytecliff Marine Park** (see Beaches/Swimming, above), **Lighthouse Park** (see Parks, above), and **Ambleside Park** (see Hiking, above). All these sites have scenic ocean vistas. For a map, contact West Vancouver Parks and Recreation, (604) 925-7200.

Sightseers make their way into the 7,400-acre (2,996 ha) **Cypress Provincial Park** from the Upper Levels Hwy in West Vancouver along a 5-mile (8-km) paved highway. Although most visitors ride up on four wheels, others make do with two (see Cycling, above). There are four major switchbacks on the way to the top where the road ends at Cypress Bowl (see Skiing/Snowboarding, above). The **Cypress Park Viewpoint** is at the second of the switchbacks. This is one of the most frequently visited locations in the park There is ample room here and an accompanying interpretive sign identifies the geographical landmarks laid out before your eyes.

One of the best places to view **the Lions** is from the viewpoint (where, conveniently enough, picnic tables are also located) beside Capilano Lake in **Capilano River Regional Park** (see Hiking, above) in North Vancouver. The entrance to the picnic site is on Capilano Dr, just north of the Capilano River Fish Hatchery (see Wildlife, above). Another dramatic picnic setting is beside Lynn Creek at the entrance to **Lynn Headwaters Regional Park** (see Hiking, above). Just inside the park you'll find four well-spaced picnic tables on a grassy slope above the creek. This is one of the noisiest locations in the park as the creek splashes past at a furious rate. (Unrepaired damage to a flood control dam here suggests the futility of trying to contain Lynn Creek when it is swollen by spring runoff or winter monsoons.) A short 15-minute walk east of the picnic tables on a connector trail leads to several more picnic tables at **Rice Lake** in the **Seymour Demonstration Forest.**

Of all the regional parks on the North Shore, **Crippen Regional Park** (see Parks, above) on Bowen Island holds the crown as the king of picnic grounds. The latest addition to the park's **Snug Cove** picnic shelters are two electric barbeques. Picnic tables are also arranged elsewhere in the park beneath the sheltering arms of a cedar grove at **Killarney Lake,** a 30-minute walk from Snug Cove.

Both **Cypress** and **Mount Seymour Provincial Parks** have special areas set aside for picnicking. In Cypress, it's the tables beside **Yew and First Lakes** that offer the prettiest ambience. Yew is an easy 15-minute walk from the parking lot at **Cypress Bowl** (see Skiing/Snowboarding, above), while First Lake is the same distance from the parking lot at **Hollyburn Ridge** (see Skiing/Snowboarding, above).

In Mount Seymour Provincial Park you'll find a picnic area as soon as you arrive at the **Kilometre 0** parking lot, a good place to begin or end a mountain-bike ride through the park. Soon afterwards there's another, prettier picnic site where the **Baden-Powell Trail** (see Hiking, above) crosses Mount Seymour Rd. You can also picnic at two impressive view-points along the 7-mile (12-km) Mount Seymour Rd. Drive to the second switchback to reach the **Vancouver Lookout,** and then on to the fifth switchback for the **Deep Cove Lookout.** It's difficult to overstate how sweeping the panorama is from either of them.

outside in

Attractions

The magnificent front doors of the **Boathouse Restaurant,** a large wooden-sided building on the far side of Sewell's Marina on Nelson Ave in Horseshoe Bay, are well worth a look. Carved by Nisga'a artist Norman Tait in traditional West Coast style, the two large panels rival those at the entrance of the University of British Columbia's Museum of Anthropology.

See Attractions in Greater Vancouver chapter for other highlights from this area.

Restaurants

The Beach House at Dundarave Pier ☆☆☆ First opened as a teahouse in 1912, this heritage building is a waterside favourite, only metres away from Dundarave Beach. The Beach House offers fine West Coast dishes including superb cornmeal-crusted Fanny Bay oysters. *150 25th St (waterfront at Dundarave Pier), West Vancouver; (604) 922-1414; $$.*

Beach Side Cafe ☆☆☆ With its creative approach to regional cuisine, this little Ambleside haunt has become the area's most serious kitchen. The summertime deck rates among the city's best, with views of Stanley Park and Kitsilano across the water. *1362 Marine Dr (between 13th and 14th), West Vancouver; (604) 925-1945; $$.*

Café Norté Mexican Restaurant ☆☆ Of the too few Mexican restaurants in Vancouver, Café Norté reigns supreme. For diehard traditionalists, the refried beans are great and the margaritas perfectly slushy. Check out Norté's sibling Cafe Centro in Kits; (604) 734-5422. *3108 Edgemont Blvd (at Highland Blvd), North Vancouver; (604) 990-4600; $$.*

Corsi Trattoria ☆☆ The Corsi family ran a trattoria in Italy, and the old-country touches still show. Twenty-odd homemade pastas include the house specialty, rotolo—pasta tubes stuffed with veal, spinach, and ricotta and topped with cream and tomato sauces. *1 Lonsdale Ave (across from Lonsdale Market), North Vancouver; (604) 987-9910; $$.*

La Cucina Italiana ☆☆ Stuck rather incongruously in the middle of North Vancouver's strip of car dealerships, La Cucina has a rustic character that overcomes its surroundings. Fish specials are usually good. Don't leave without sampling the homemade ice cream. *1509 Marine Dr (between MacGowan and Tatlow), North Vancouver; (604) 986-1334; $$.*

La Toque Blanche ☆☆ This cozy, '70s retro-woodsy retreat is still a well-kept culinary secret. Prices are almost a bargain by today's standards—especially considering the quality, detail, and presentation. *4368 Marine Dr (at Erwin Dr), West Vancouver; (604) 926-1006; $$.*

The Salmon House on the Hill ☆☆ Northwest Coast Native artifacts reflect the origins of the Salmon House menu. The hallmark dish is BC salmon cooked over green alderwood—certainly worth the drive. Check out the annual salmon festival in October. *2229 Folkestone Way (21st St exit off Hwy 1), West Vancouver; (604) 926-3212; $$$.*

The Tomahawk ☆ The Tomahawk is a 70-year-plus institution, famous for its hungry-man-size meals. Everyone comes for the eye-opening Yukon Breakfast. For lunch, there are several hamburger platters (named after Native American chiefs), fried chicken, and even oysters. *1550 Philip Ave (at Marine Dr), North Vancouver; (604) 988-2612; $.*

Vivace! ☆☆ This fun and lively spot is a good place to take the family or a group of friends for huge servings of excellent pastas, tasty grilled meats, and hearty appetizers. *60 Semisch Way (at Esplanade St), North Vancouver; (604) 984-0274; $$.*

Lodgings

Laburnum Cottage Bed and Breakfast ☆☆ This elegant country home is set off by an award-winning English garden. The main house, furnished with antiques and collectibles, features four airy guest rooms with private baths and garden views. *1388 Terrace Ave (6 km from downtown, 1 block from Capilano; call for directions), North Vancouver, BC V7R 1B4; (604) 988-4877 or (888) 686-4877; $$.*

Lonsdale Quay Hotel ☆ The pleasant Lonsdale Quay Hotel, located inside the enjoyable Lonsdale Quay market and across the harbour from downtown Vancouver (yet only 15 minutes away via the SeaBus), gives you a comfortable place to stay (as long as you don't need to be pampered). *123 Carrie Cates Ct (at Lonsdale Quay), North Vancouver, BC V7M 2E4; (604) 986-6111 or (800) 836-6111; $$$.*

Park Royal Hotel ☆☆ The Park Royal is nestled into its own little forest of mature greenery just yards away from one of Vancouver's busiest freeways, but traffic noise never seems to intrude. We like the genuinely friendly housekeeping staff, and the legendary hospitality of owner Mario Corsi. *540 Clyde Ave (just off Marine Dr at Taylor Way, then Clyde Ave on right), West Vancouver, BC V7T 2J7; (604) 926-5511; $$.*

Cheaper Sleeps

Capilano RV Park The Squamish Nation owns much of the North Shore waterfront and operates this first-class, 208-site camping facility on the north end of Lion's Gate Bridge, just minutes from downtown. There are showers and laundry facilities, too. *295 Tomahawk Ave, North Vancouver, BC V7P 1C5; (604) 987-4722; $.*

More Information

BC Parks: *(604) 924-2200.*
District of North Vancouver Parks: *(604) 990-2450.*
Geological Survey of Canada: *Suite 101, 605 Robson St, Vancouver V6B 5G3, (604) 666-0271. Store hours are 8:30am–4:30pm, Mon–Fri.*
Greater Vancouver Regional District (GVRD) Parks' West Area Office: *(604) 224-5739; general information, (604) 432-6350; Internet address, http://www.gvrd.bc.ca/parks.*
Municipality of West Vancouver Parks and Recreation: *(604) 925-7200.*
North Vancouver Recreation: *(604) 987-7529.*

Whistler and the Sea to Sky Highway

Highway 99, the Sea to Sky Highway, through five distinct biogeoclimatic zones, from coastal rain forest at Horseshoe Bay, and including Squamish, Garibaldi Provincial Park, and the Resort Municipality of Whistler.

Intensely scenic, the Sea to Sky Highway (Highway 99) crosses paths with two historic routes, the Pemberton Trail and the Gold Rush Heritage Trail, which linked the coast with the interior in the days before the automobile. Along these ancient pathways, generations of Coast Salish people traded with their relations in the Fraser Canyon, while in the 1850s, prospectors stampeded north towards the Cariboo gold fields. In 1915, the Pacific Great Eastern railway began service between Squamish and the Cariboo. For those in search of outdoor recreation, the railway proved an ideal way to reach trailheads in Garibaldi Provincial Park and fishing camps such as Alta Lake's Rainbow Lodge, situated at the foot of London Mountain. By the mid-1960s, the prospect of skiers heading from Vancouver to the fledgling trails on London Mountain—by this time renamed Whistler Mountain—prompted the provincial government to open a road north from Horseshoe Bay through Squamish to Whistler. Space being at a premium along steep-sided Howe Sound (North America's southernmost fjord), the road and railway parallel each other for much of the 28 miles (45 km) between Horseshoe Bay and Squamish at the head of the sound. By 1975, the highway was pushed through to Pemberton, and by 1995 the last stretch of gravel road was paved between Pemberton and Lillooet. (Highway 99 and the railway part company in

Pemberton but link up again at Lillooet.) Today, vehicles breeze along the entire route in five hours, the time it took in the 1960s to make the journey just from Horseshoe Bay to Whistler.

Both the railway, which now departs from its southern depot in North Vancouver, and Highway 99 have helped introduce visitors to the backcountry region in the Sea to Sky corridor. (The 12-hour train trip between North Vancouver and Prince George in the Central Interior is one of Canada's most scenic rail journeys. Travellers can choose to disembark or be picked up just about anywhere along its route.) Certainly, Whistler's success as a resort destination has propelled development, both commercial and recreational, in other parts of the region, particularly Squamish and Pemberton. So too has the popularity of the mountain bike and the sport-utility vehicle. The pace of mountain-bike trailblazing carries on today with the same zeal once devoted to the creation of new ski runs, while logging roads no longer intimidate drivers in search of backcountry getaways as they once did. And it's not just the proximity to Greater Vancouver that drives this expansion. The landscape itself just happens to be some of the most ideal terrain for outdoor activity in British Columbia.

Squamish (population 16,000) is a relief. Smaller than Vancouver, larger than Whistler, and equidistant from them both, Squamish is the envy of the south coast. It has so many things going for it—location, geography, wildlife, weather—that as forestry declines as the town's major employer, tourism and outdoor recreation have taken on greater importance. Travellers have *always* been drawn to Squamish, from the days of the Coast Squamish people, who journeyed between Burrard Inlet and *STA-a-mus* at the mouth of the Squamish River, to more recent times when steamships began ferrying anglers, climbers, and picnickers here over a century ago. There's a rich history to the Squamish region, and the best way to experience it is through a favourite outdoor activity. No matter what your pleasure, you'll follow paths laid down by fellow admirers who've cleared the way.

Something magical happens when you arrive at the summit of the small valley that contains Whistler. A cluster of little lakes is gathered here, reflecting the outline of the mountains high above. Alta Lake is the great divide in the Sea to Sky corridor. Water flowing from its south end reaches the Pacific via the Cheakamus and Squamish Rivers, while water flowing from its north end in the River of Golden Dreams eventually reaches the ocean through the Harrison watershed and the Fraser River. No other valley in the Sea to Sky region has such a wealth of small and medium-sized lakes. No other lakes have scenery quite like this to mirror. When you let your eyes rise from the reflection to admire the real thing, the contours of the ski runs on Blackcomb and Whistler Mountains pattern the forested slopes. Above the tree line, you can still see remnants of the most recent ice age in the glaciers that encrust the highest peaks. Take a deep breath of the freshest air imaginable.

Getting There

Horseshoe Bay in North Vancouver is the southern terminus of Highway 99. Lillooet, about 190 miles (310 km) north, is its northern twin. From Lillooet, a recent extension of Highway 99 (formerly called Highway 12) leads almost 47 miles (75 km) farther north and east to its conjunction with Highway 97 at Hat Creek. The southern terminus of the Sea to Sky Highway (Highway 99) is reached via the Trans-Canada Highway (Highway 1) at Horseshoe Bay. The northern terminus lies at its junction with Highway 97, about 7 miles (11 km) north of Cache Creek. An alternative approach near its northern terminus is Highway 12's junction with Highway 99 at Lillooet. Despite major improvements over the past 30 years, such as rock scaling, bridge reinforcement, and frequent passing lanes, sections of this predominantly two-lane road can still be extremely treacherous in foul weather. Drive cautiously but not so slowly as to frustrate those who are more familiar with the route. All exits and trailheads are well marked, with adequate room for off-road parking.

Adjoining Areas

NORTH: **Pemberton and Lillooet**

SOUTH: **The North Shore**

EAST: **The Coquihalla Highway**

WEST: **The Sunshine Coast**

inside out

Parks/Camping

Camping space is limited along the shores of Howe Sound. Wherever you decide to overnight, be prepared to share it with sounds from the nearby highway and railway. So close do freight trains come to the sites in **Porteau Cove Provincial Park** that you might imagine they're rolling right through your tent. Take heart in the thought that it's a notch more attractive than having a bear charge through, which is not unheard of elsewhere in the woods of BC. Porteau Cove is located near Howe Sound's midpoint, 15 miles (24 km) north of Horseshoe Bay on Hwy 99. As you approach it, the beach and jetty are what first catch the eye. Only in winter, once the leaves are down, is it possible to see through the surrounding forest into the little cove itself, where 59 campsites are located, 15 of which are walk-in sites. (It takes only several minutes to reach them.) As this is the only provincial campground on the Sound, campsites are in constant demand from late May to early October. If you're intent on staying here, arrive early in the afternoon or phone ahead for reservations, (800) 689-9025, or locally (604) 689-9025. A sign posted on Hwy 99 informs travellers when the park is full. Although the vehicle/tent sites go quickly throughout the summer and on Friday and Saturday nights at other times of the year, there is usually a good chance of getting one of the walk-in sites even if you arrive late, except in the months from June to August. A user fee is collected from April to October: about $15 for drive-in sites and half that for walk-ins. As soon as you enter the campground, bear right to see if any of the oceanfront sites are vacant. In the middle of the campground is a washroom facility complete with showers. The walk-in sites are located at the far end of the campground road. An amphitheatre is located between the drive-in and walk-in campsites. Interpretive displays are presented here on summer evenings, one of the most scenic locations in the park. Because there is so little level land, most sites are relatively closely spaced compared to other provincial parks. Tucked in behind the walk-in sites is the cove itself. A stone wall on the west side is one of the few remaining signs of a small settlement that once stood here. There's a charming sense of formality where an open lawn is laid out beside the cove and a small bridge spans the narrow backwater. For information on Porteau Cove Provincial Park, call BC Parks, (604) 898-3678.

For climbers (and those who cheer them on) there's a provincial campground at the base of Stawamus Chief Mountain in Squamish. You'll find 15 spiffy drive-in sites and 48 walk-in sites in **Stawamus Chief Provincial Park.** Watch for the turnoff from Hwy 99 at the large roadside interpretive area at the south end of town. The forested campground is located at the south end of a rough road that hugs the base of the mountain. A fee of about $7 per site per night is charged while the vehicle campsites are open, usually from late May to mid-September. A gate restricts vehicle access at other times of year, and only the walk-in sites are accessible. For more information, contact BC Parks, (604) 898-3678.

Alice Lake Provincial Park, 8 miles (13 km) north of Squamish, is tucked away east of Hwy 99, just far enough to be buffered from traffic sounds. A short approach road leads to the park gates where signs direct visitors to 88 vehicle/tent campsites. An overnight camping fee (about $15) is charged May to October. A hush prevails over this lushly forested campground. In part this is due to the thick canopy of western hemlock that shelters much of the park. If you're lucky, one of the sites near both the lake *and* the hot showers will be vacant. Bear right at the entrance to reach them. Successive rows of pleasantly spaced campsites spiral up the hillside from the lake. At night, stars are reflected in Alice Lake's still surface. Best viewing of the open sky and cosmic wonders (such as a moonrise over the peaks in nearby Garibaldi Provincial Park) is done from the beach. Alice Lake Park is predictably busy in summer. It is possible to book ahead. Call BC Parks reservations, (800) 689-9025. You won't have nearly as much difficulty from September through May (yes, there is winter camping here). For more information on the park, contact BC Parks, (604) 898-3678.

There are three Forest Service recreation campsites in the Squamish region, at **Cat** and **Brohm Lakes** (see Swimming, below) located just north of Alice Lake, and **Ashlu Creek** in the Squamish Valley. These are no-frills locations, with few amenities. If you get one with a picnic table, count your blessings. (To its credit, the Forest Service builds the sturdiest log-and-plank tables found anywhere in the province.) Although Cat and Brohm Lakes are easily reached from Hwy 99, Ashlu Creek is farther afield in the Squamish Valley. Follow signs to the Squamish Valley Rd west of Hwy 99 opposite the entrance to Alice Lake Provincial Park. Ashlu Creek flows into the Squamish River about 14 miles (22 km) north of the road's origins in Cheekye. The last 3 miles (5 km) to the campsites are gravel. Cross the Ashlu Creek Bridge and drive down to the river, where there are a number of natural campsites. A short distance farther along is another bridge, beside which are several more open sites. To request a free map of BC Forest Service recreation sites in the Squamish Forest District, call (604) 898-2100. There is no fee charged for camping at these sites.

One outdoor essential that's in short supply around **Whistler** is campsites. This is surprising, given the number of visitors that floods through the Whistler Valley each summer. In its defence, the valley floor is little more than 0.5 mile (less than 1 km) across at its widest point; that doesn't leave much level space on which to build campsites. You'll notice this deficiency if you overnight at **Brandywine Falls Provincial Park,** which is girdled by Hwy 99 on the west and the BC Rail line on the east. Still, the 15 vehicle/tent sites here are in constant use in warm weather. Once snow falls, the campground closes for the winter. Brandywine Falls is located about 6 miles (10 km) south of Whistler on Hwy 99.

A modest brown sign marks the entrance to the campground at **Cal-Cheak Forest Service Recreation Site,** 2.7 miles (4.3 km) north of Brandywine Falls Provincial Park. Visitors must cross the railway tracks, then journey a short distance beyond to reach the first of three small locales around which rustic campsites are grouped in a pleasant, heavily forested location. The sound of the Cheakamus River and Callaghan Creek, which merge beside the sites (hence the site's hokey, hyphenated name), helps drown out traffic noise from Hwy 99 and the BC Rail line.

Just north of Cal-Cheak, on the west side of Hwy 99, is the beginning of the **Callaghan Forest Road.** Although the road is rough in places, particularly in spring when frost heaves the ground, if you take it easy it leads to two Forest Service recreation sites. One small campsite is at **Alexander Falls,** located 4.3 miles (7 km) along the road; a nest of similar sites have been fashioned by years of campers on the shore of **Callaghan Lake** 9.3 miles (15 km) west of Hwy 99. Of all the campsites in the Whistler region, the view from Callaghan Lake is the best. Too bad there's no one to monitor activity at the site; partying can carry on well into the night here.

Garibaldi Provincial Park

There's a roadside viewpoint in Squamish at the town's lower limits, about 1 mile (1.6 km) south of Shannon Falls on Hwy 99. A plaque here honours the memory of the great 19th-century Italian leader Giuseppe Garibaldi, for whom distant Mount Garibaldi (8,918 feet/2678 m) is named. Fittingly, it is mounted on a large piece of granite quarried from nearby Stawamus Chief Mountain. On a clear day, pause here to admire the remarkable series of geographical formations laid before you: Shannon Falls, BC's third-highest waterfall, the smooth granite features of the Chief, with Mount Garibaldi and craggy friends on high in the distance. The scene will put you in the same frame of mind as the anonymous crew member on the English Navy survey ship *Plumper* who christened it in honour of the headline-making freedom fighter in 1860. (Members of the Squamish First Nation call it *Chuckigh.* The settlement of Cheekye near Brackendale is a variation on this spelling.) In 1927, after vigorous lobbying by the BC Mountaineering Club, the Vancouver Natural History Society, and others who had explored and named many of the most prominent geological features in the alpine region around Mount Garibaldi, a 480,000-acre (195 000-ha) park was created by an act of the provincial legislature.

There are five main entry points to the park: Diamond Head, Garibaldi Lake, Cheakamus Lake, Singing Pass, and Wedgemount Lake. More trails, such as Black Tusk, Musical Bumps, and Helm Creek, lead hikers back into the park. All approaches are from the west side of the park, and the trailheads are all well marked along Hwy 99 between Squamish and Whistler. The turnoff to **Diamond Head** is just north of the Mamquam River Bridge, and a 10-mile (16-km) drive is required to reach the trailhead. Hikers benefit from this approach as the road climbs for much of the way to an elevation of just over 3,000 feet (914 m). The turnoff to **Black Tusk** and **Garibaldi Lake** is just south of Daisy Lake, 12 miles (19 km) from Whistler. A paved road runs 1.6 miles (2.5 km) east to a large parking lot beside Rubble Creek. A 5.6-mile (9-km) trail to Garibaldi Lake begins here. **Cheakamus Lake** is reached by following the 5.3-mile (8.5-km) Cheakamus Lake Rd (also known as Eastside Main). The turnoff is located across from Whistler's Function Junction neighbourhood. The road that leads to the **Singing Pass** trailhead begins next to Whistler Village. Follow the signs from Hwy 99 that direct you along Village Gate Blvd to Blackcomb Way. The access road begins next to the BC Transit interchange and runs uphill for 3 miles (5 km), across the north base of Whistler Mountain. Finally, the **Wedgemount Lake** trailhead is located 2.5 miles (4 km) north of Whistler's northernmost neighbourhood, Emerald Estates, just beyond the Whistler town sign. Turn east off Hwy 99 and cross the Green River Bridge, then turn left and head uphill about 2 miles (3 km) on a dirt road. There are signs at each divide pointing the way to the lake's trailhead.

Although much of the park's terrain is rock and ice, there are lush stands of mature hemlock, fir, and cedar in places such as Cheakamus Lake. Southwestern slopes around Diamond Head are thickly carpeted with heather, which bears pink and white blossoms in summer, and blueberry bushes which turn every shade of yellow and red imaginable in fall. For a comprehensive map of the park, contact BC Parks, (604) 898-3678.

There is backcountry camping along the Diamond Head Trail near Squamish in Garibaldi Provincial Park (see below), at **Red Heather Campground** (3 miles/5 km from the trailhead; moderate; 1 hour), at **Elfin Lakes Campground** (7 miles/11 km; moderate; 3 hours), and at remote **Mamquam Lake** (13.6 miles/22 km; strenuous; full day). In addition, there's a heated overnight shelter with 34 bunks and cooking facilities at Elfin Lakes. The cost is $4 per night, year-round. To reach the Diamond Head trailhead, turn east off Hwy 99 in Squamish where a BC Parks' sign indicates "Diamond Head (Garibaldi Park)." This access road runs 10 miles (16 km) to the parking lot at the trailhead. The first 2.5 miles (4 km) is paved, passing through the southern outskirts of Garibaldi Estates. The remainder is along gravel-surfaced Mamquam Rd, which climbs gradually above the Mamquam River Valley. The final 2.5 miles (4 km) of road covers a series of switchbacks. Only at the last one does the view of the Squamish Valley open up. This is a good place to stop and look south to Howe Sound, the Stawamus Chief, and Sky Pilot Mountain on Goat Ridge. Across the valley to the west is Cloudburst Mountain, and south of that is the broad body of glaciers around Mount Tantalus. For a detailed map of campsites in Garibaldi park, including Diamond Head, contact BC Parks, (604) 898-3678.

Camping at **Garibaldi Lake** in Garibaldi Provincial Park is restricted to two designated areas—Taylor Meadows and the west end of Garibaldi Lake. The hiking distance to both locations is the same, about 5.6 miles (9 km) from the Garibaldi Lake/Black Tusk trailhead, located 2.5 miles (4 km) east of Hwy 99, 12 miles (19 km) south of Whistler. A common trail leads to within 0.6 mile (1 km) of each, then divides. Tent pads and a covered cooking shelter are located at each. Campers must bring their own stoves and be prepared to pack out all refuse. During summer months, there is a camping fee of about $7 per night per site. When water levels in Garibaldi Lake are high, be prepared to wade a short distance along the shoreline to reach the 36 campsites on its west side.

There are also wilderness campsites at three locations on **Cheakamus Lake** in Garibaldi Provincial Park. The easiest one to reach is at the west end of the lake, while those at **Singing Creek** and **Castle Towers Creek** are more remote. You'll need a boat (and a couple of hours' paddling) to reach the primitive site at Castle Towers from the launch at the lake's west end, which almost guarantees that you'll usually have the site to yourself. From the trailhead, located about 4 miles (7 km) south from Hwy 99 on Cheakamus Lake Rd, it's an easy 2-mile (3.5-km) hike to reach the first sites at Cheakamus Lake, situated beneath a sheltering old-growth forest. The sites at Singing Creek are a further 2 miles (3.5 km) of moderate hiking along the north side of the lake. Castle Towers Creek enters Cheakamus Lake directly across from Singing Creek.

Elsewhere in Garibaldi Provincial Park, there are wilderness campsites at **Russet Lake,** 1.2 miles (2 km) east of Singing Pass, and at the northwest end of **Wedgemount Lake** (see Hiking/Backpacking, below). In addition, an alpine hut with room for eight is located at each site. For more information on wilderness camping in Garibaldi, contact BC Parks, (604) 898-3678.

Picnics

If you are just visiting **Porteau Cove Provincial Park** for the day, park beside the jetty. This is a wonderful place to enjoy the spectacular views of Howe Sound while watching wet-suited divers enter or emerge from the cold waters of the Sound. Eat your picnic at one of the numerous tables spread around the broad, driftwood-littered beaches on both sides of the jetty. Aptly named Anvil Island sits to the southwest, while the glaciated peaks of the Tantalus Range rise in the northwest. Take a walk to the viewpoint on the trail that leads west from the walk-in campsites and up onto the forested bluff. Stunted shore pines (a coastal variety of lodgepole pine) and stately Sitka spruce provide shelter on the point, from where you can look down on the cove or out across the waters of the sound. This is a quiet place in which to enjoy the surroundings, especially in the early or late hours of the day, or to stop for an off-season breather from the pressures of the highway.

Murrin Provincial Park enjoys a placid lakeside location about 2 miles (3 km) north of Britannia Beach, on the west side of Hwy 99. The waters of **Browning Lake** lap the shoulder of the highway. Picnic tables dot the far side of the little lake, some sheltered in the forest, others in the open. This is a good place to stop for a snack while you check the road or trail map.

With almost a half-million visitors annually, **Shannon Falls Provincial Park** is one of the most popular picnic spots in the entire Sea to Sky corridor. Located on the east side of Hwy 99 just south of Stawamus Chief Mountain (see Hiking/Backpacking, below), extensive picnic grounds surround the base of BC's third-highest waterfall (1,105 feet/335 m). In summer months the parking lot is full by noon, with half of the visitors arriving by tour bus. Picnic tables are located beside Shannon Creek and in the Loggers Sports Field nearby. A boardwalk leads to a viewing platform near the base of the roaring falls. From here you can gaze up the smooth sides of the granite walls over which the falls foam and tumble. At low flow, the falls does little more than veil the rockface. In feistier seasons, when the falls gives off an almighty roar, its spray will drench you if you get too close. Some people (the cold shower types) don't mind and follow a rough trail that leads from the viewing platform to the base of the falls. Often the best time to picnic here is on the first warm days of spring and the last ones of fall, when water levels in the falls are running strong.

As befits a region that receives over a million visitors a year, equally divided between summer and winter and all equally focused on enjoying the outdoors, there are plenty of idyllic picnic sites around Whistler/Blackcomb. Special mention should be made of both Rainbow and Meadow Parks. Picnicking at these sites is done on a grander scale than the rest. **Rainbow Park** has many tables dotted beside a group of heritage cabins on the west side of Alta Lake. Some of the log structures have been relocated to the property, while others are all that remain from the days of the Rainbow Lodge, for years Whistler's premier accommodation. **Meadow Park,** in Alpine Meadows, has a delightful picnic location on the banks of the River of Golden Dreams (see Canoeing/Kayaking/Boating, below), with a combined view of Blackcomb and Whistler Mountains that is one of the best in the valley. **Lakeside Park** occupies an open area on the southeast side of Alta Lake. A lawn runs down to the beach with its two L-shaped docks. There are six well-spaced picnic tables here, most with their own barbeques.

Hiking/Backpacking

Of all the natural features in the Lower Mainland, none have greater visual presence than **the Lions** (or **the Two Sisters,** as they are called by local

Native peoples). Geologists believe that these two peaks—the West Lion stands at 5,401 feet (1646 m) and the East Lion at 5,245 feet (1599 m)—are the remnants of a volcanic cone. There are two main approaches to them, both of which require a strenuous hike. As the route from the Cypress Provincial Park trailhead (see The North Shore chapter) begins at a 3,000-foot (980-m) elevation, it's not as vertically challenging as the approach from sea level at Lions Bay. However, it is lengthier (6 miles/10 km one way from Cypress, 5 miles/8 km from Lions Bay). When you put your body to a test like this, you're thankful for every little energy-saving shortcut you can find. The optimum time to do this hike is in late summer or early fall. Not only will the weather favour you but also you'll be blessed with better views as the broadleaf maples begin to shed their foliage. Budget four hours to climb from the trailhead in Lions Bay to the ridge below the **West Lion.**

Passing through Lions Bay, travellers get a glimpse of the West Lion from Hwy 99 as the highway crosses Harvey Creek. Finding your way to the trailhead is a challenge in itself. Take the Oceanview entrance to Lions Bay from Hwy 99. Follow the signs pointing left towards the convenience store. Turn right on Centre, left on Bayview, left on Mountain Dr, and finally left again on Sunset. As you climb through the neighbourhood you'll pass the elementary school, next to which is a parking lot. If you arrive at the trailhead and find that all parking spaces there have been taken, you can park at this overflow lot, but before descending back to the school, check to see if there is any space on Sunset south of Mountain Dr. If there is (the parking restrictions are well marked), you will save yourself an extra 10 minutes each way.

Don't let the overall challenge of reaching the Lions deter you. Perhaps all you'll wish to experience are the viewpoints that appear at intervals for the first 2 miles (3 km). Several stone arrows point the way at important junctions as you follow first an old logging road, and then the orange and silver metal markers affixed to the sides of trees as you ascend a narrow hiking trail. Horseshoe Bay is surprisingly close, while modest-sized Bowyer Island lies offshore. Along the way are several sturdy old-growth Douglas fir trees on the steep slope bordering the trail. Rudimentary wooden steps assist hikers across a tricky section near Harvey Creek. The best time to cross the creek is in late summer, when it's at its lowest point; during rainy spells, crossing the rushing waters can be perilous. The boulders in the creek are popular spots on which to sunbathe and catch your breath. (Note: Harvey Creek provides water for the Lions Bay community, so please be extremely careful not to pollute it in any way.)

Massive old-growth forest surrounds the trail as it climbs above Harvey Creek, and you head towards the best viewpoint yet of Howe Sound.

Now all of Gambier Island is revealed, as is the nest of smaller islands between Bowen and the Sunshine Coast. Footing becomes trickier as you hop from boulder to boulder up the last incline to the ridge, where a better path establishes itself and you can walk at a more leisurely pace. In late summer the narrow gullies are filled with a low ground cover of heather turning a burnt red and blueberries.

The **Howe Sound Crest Trail** begins in Cypress Provincial Park in North Vancouver (see The North Shore chapter) and runs almost 18 miles (30 km) across ridges and mountains—including the Lions—while skirting pocket lakes to reach the shores of Howe Sound near Porteau Cove. Phew! Without a doubt this is *the* way to see as much of Howe Sound as any hiker could wish, but it comes with a price tag: a real grunt. Then again, so are most hikes on the slopes of Howe Sound. There are few breaks in this demanding climb (and punishing descent), and often you can't see the ocean for the trees. When you do, all else is momentarily put aside. The northern terminus of the Howe Sound Crest Trail is at Hwy 99, 6.7 miles (11 km) north of Lions Bay. There's a pullout on the west side of the road where you can leave your vehicle. (Note: Be wary when crossing the highway to reach the trailhead.) For more information on the Howe Sound Crest Trail, including a detailed map, contact BC Parks, (604) 924-2200.

The **Deeks Lake Trail** (strenuous; 8 mile/13 km return; 3–4 hours each way) leads hikers up a steep rock-and-roots trail that passes through lush evergreen forest. The occasional stream or waterfall provides cool encouragement to overheated brows (and other body parts). Deeks Lake is skin-tighteningly frigid, year-round. If you don't exist on a daily regime of cold showers, you needn't pack your bathing suit. What it lacks in heat, it makes up for in passion. This is a sublime location, far above the hum of traffic. You'll want to linger as long as possible, as much to revel in the landscape as to put off the inevitable descent. There are two trailheads from which this hike can begin, both located along Hwy 99 north of Lions Bay. The more scenic route begins about 4 miles (6 m) north of Lions Bay, where Deeks Creek empties into Howe Sound. Watch for a pullout on the west side of the highway. If you miss it heading north, drive on and then double back when possible. The trail, indicated by orange metal markers, begins beside the creek. An alternative route is from the Howe Sound Crest Trail's northern terminus located beside Hwy 99, about 3 miles (5 km) north of Deeks Creek. A large wooden kiosk marks this approach.

One of the reasons that there's such a large parking lot at Murrin Provincial Park (see Picnics, above) is that directly across Hwy 99 and a short distance north is the entrance to a favourite Howe Sound hiking trail to **Petgill Lake** (7 miles/11 km return). Everything you should know is posted on the little kiosk at the trailhead. What they don't tell you (but we will) is that you don't need to go the full distance in order to enjoy the scenic viewpoints from this well-marked trail. Just surmount the first steep, hand-over-fist pitch, and Howe Sound will be laid out before you. The higher you go (total elevation gain is only 1,968 feet/600 m), the better the views of the mountains to the east and north, including unmistakable Sky Pilot and Mount Garibaldi. Sections of this trail can be boggy, so wear waterproof boots.

Stawamus Chief Mountain is a strenuous, 4- to 7-mile (7- to 11-km) return hike, depending on which of three summit routes you choose. There are several approaches to the base of this mass of granite. For the first, leave your car in the lot beside **Shannon Falls Provincial Park's Logger's Sports Area** (see Picnics, above). Look for the orange and red markers affixed to a large cedar tree by the Federation of BC Mountain Clubs at the north end of the sports area, which point the way. Travel time to the base of the Chief is 15 minutes on this 0.6-mile (1-km), well-maintained trail, which features several good viewpoints and close encounters with the cool, smooth rock face where the trail runs beside it.

An alternative approach allows you to drive to the base of the Chief itself at the interpretive viewing area on Hwy 99 just north of Shannon Falls. Take the dirt road that leads up the embankment in the middle of the viewpoint (it's not as badly eroded as the others). It links up with a section of the old highway that runs north and south as it hugs the base of the Chief. When you stand next to the Chief here, you look up and up at a wall of smooth granite. It's awe-inspiring. You can see why this monolith has become internationally famous among climbers and has graced more than its share of magazine covers. To reach the trailhead, turn south onto the old road above the viewpoint, continuing on to its end. Hiking from here to the Chief's south summit is a 2-mile (3.5-km) ascent and takes about 90 minutes; add another hour if you choose the longer Centre and North summit route (3.5 miles/5.5 km one way). Both routes share a common beginning, then divide above Oleson Creek. (Note: The trail from Shannon Falls joins this approach at Oleson Creek, a short distance uphill.) Altogether there is a 1,980-foot (600-m) elevation gain on this hike; you will be climbing almost constantly until the top. This trail is the most popular with hikers (upwards of 50,000 a year), but it is only one of several possible routes on the Chief. For a detailed description of these and other hikes in the region, consult *A Guide to Climbing and Hiking in Southwestern B.C.* by Bruce Fairely. Even if you don't plan to hike, be sure to stop at the Stawamus Chief Mountain viewpoint on Hwy 99 in Squamish, a short distance north of Shannon Falls Provincial Park. An interpretive display will acquaint you with the mountain and some of the history of the region. Get out your binoculars and scan for climbers high up on the sides of the Chief.

When you are on a tour of the outdoors, especially in the Sea to Sky corridor, downtown Squamish may seem like an odd place to begin. However, the walking trails around the **Squamish Estuary** will convince you of just how sensible an idea this is. In Squamish, turn north off Hwy 99 at the Cleveland Ave stoplights. Drive along the town's main drag to Vancouver St, turn right, and drive three blocks to the trailhead. A wooden sign bears a detailed map of the estuary and the dike trail that rambles west from here. Plan on taking an hour to cover a 2.5-mile (4-km) round trip. Along the way, the grass-covered trail leads past channelled waterways, home to a resident population of raptors and a host of migratory birds; bring binoculars. Trumpeter swans overwinter here before flying north to their nesting grounds come spring, as do bald eagles.

Out in the estuary, the already uncluttered view *really* opens up. The smooth granite walls of Stawamus Chief Mountain form the centrepiece. Equally arresting, should the skies be clear, is the dagger point of Atwell Peak, with its broad-shouldered companion, the Dalton Dome. Together, they dominate the skyline of Garibaldi Provincial Park to the north. A cool breeze often blows across the marshy sloughs of Howe Sound's shoreline, so dress accordingly. In summer, the white stalks of pearly everlasting rival Shannon Falls' snowy tress, visible as it cascades down the slopes to the south of the Chief.

This portion of the estuary trail ends at a log-sorting yard. Another section follows a long finger of the estuary whose east side is diked by the Squamish Spit (see Windsurfing/Sailing, below), but is too distant to reach on foot.

Lakeside and hillside trails await visitors in **Alice Lake Provincial Park** north of Squamish (see Parks/Camping, above). In keeping with the park's easygoing nature, you can make as much of them as you care. One trail blends into the other in a pleasing fashion, and you're never far from a viewpoint and one of four lakes—Alice, Stump, Fawn, and Edith—found within the park. The **Four Lakes Loop Trail** (7.5 miles/12 km) is the longest and threads by them all. **Lakeshore Walk** is a short but pretty walking trail that leads along the north side of Alice Lake and links the campground with the lake's two picnic beaches. The **Stump Lantern Interpretive Trail** offers another short walk through the forest at the north end of Alice Lake. After a visit here, you'll have learned to identify creeping liverwort, lady fern, skunk cabbage, and devil's club when you spy them carpeting the forest floor elsewhere in your travels. **DeBeck's Hill** presents the steepest challenge in the park. An old logging road winds its way for about a mile up DeBeck's Hill from the south end of Alice Lake. Follow it to the top and in less than an hour you'll be treated to a great view of the Squamish region, including Howe Sound, the Tantalus glaciers, and the Cheakamus River boring its way through a steep-sided granite canyon.

Other hikes in the Squamish area include two very demanding ones in the Squamish Valley. In order to reach **Lake Lovely Water Provincial Park,** you'll first have to arrange to cross the Squamish River to reach the trailhead, about 7 miles (11 km) north of Squamish. A rough and sometimes obscure trail leads upwards from the west bank of the Squamish River to Lake Lovely Water. This is a strenuous 8.5-mile (14-km) eight-hour round-trip hike with few views to reward the weary until you've reached the lake. Once there, the world's your oyster! Lake Lovely Water lies cradled between the peaks of Alpha and Omega Mountains at a 4,000-foot (1310-m) elevation. After all the effort you expend reaching the lake, you may wish to camp. The Alpine Club of Canada maintains a locked cabin beside the lake. You can make arrangements to get the key if you call in advance, (604) 687-2711; there is a modest fee for nonmembers. The best bet is to pack along a tent. For more information, call BC Parks, (604) 898-3678. Consult Geological Survey of Canada topographic map 92G/14, "Cheakamus River."

Farther along the Squamish Valley Rd is the start of the **High Falls Creek Trail** (difficult; 4.5 miles/7 km return). The trade-off for making the demanding hike is the reward of seeing the Squamish River spread before you, surmounted by the Tantalus Range, one of the most inspiring vistas in the Coast Mountains. Until you've seen it yourself, a description will just be so many words on a page.

Be forewarned: This hike is not for the fainthearted. Strategically placed ropes help hikers up some of the steeper stretches, but in other sections you'll have to call on all of your wits to clamber still higher. To find the trailhead, follow the signs to Squamish Valley from Hwy 99, directly across the road from the entrance to Alice Lake Provincial Park. A bridge crosses the Cheakamus River at Cheekye, and on its far side the road divides into the Squamish Valley Rd to the left, and the Paradise Valley Rd to the right. Bear left and follow this road for almost 15 miles (24 km). Just past a hydroelectric powerhouse, watch for High Falls Park on the right side of the road. The trail begins here.

There's probably more ground to cover on foot than you can explore in one visit, which makes the **Brohm Lake Interpretive Forest** (see Mountain Biking, below) an ideal destination for repeat visits. Although the lake itself is the main magnet, particularly in summer, the more remote forest trails have a quiet charm of their own. A 2-mile (3-km) walk from the parking lot, starting on the **Alder Trail** and then branching to the **Cheakamus Loop Trail,** leads to two viewpoints that look across Paradise Valley to the glacier-clad peaks of the Tantalus Range—including

Mount Tantalus itself as well as Alpha, Omega, Zenith, Pelion, and Serratus Mountains. A series of staircases assists visitors up the steepest stretches between the two viewpoints. A covered lookout shelter sits atop a rocky bluff and overlooks the Cheakamus River flowing past far below, with the Squamish waterfront visible in the distance. The entrance to the Brohm Lake Interpretive Forest is located 2.5 miles (4 km) north of Alice Lake Provincial Park on the west side of Hwy 99.

One of the best-preserved sections of the old **Pemberton Trail** passes between Brandywine Falls Provincial Park and the Cal-Cheak Forest Service Recreation Site (see Parks/Camping, above). This is a gentle, well-worn pathway, and although there are several up-and-down sections, staircases assist walkers in the most difficult places. The distance between Brandywine and Cal-Cheak is 2.5 miles (4 km). The most entertaining section of the walk is crossing Callaghan Creek on a wooden suspension bridge. The bridge is located next to the Forest Service campsites and may be a bit difficult to locate when the campground is full. Look for the trail to the suspension bridge midway around the road that loops through the north campsite.

A short walking trail leads from the parking lot at **Brandywine Falls Provincial Park** (see Parks/Camping, above) to an observation platform at the top of the falls. Cross the bridge over Brandywine Creek and then follow the trail to the right, which in 10 minutes will bring you to a clearing beside the falls. Along the way the trail passes close to Brandywine Creek beneath some towering fir trees, crosses the BC Rail tracks, and then reaches the viewpoint. Daisy Lake spreads out below as the monolithic Black Tusk probes the skyline. Depending on the time of year, dammed Daisy Lake may be more or less at "full pool." Spray from the 218-foot (66-m) falls coats the sides of the gorge into which it plummets with ice in winter and nourishes lush growth in warmer months.

Hiking is one of the most popular outdoor recreation activities in the Sea to Sky corridor. You could easily fill up every weekend in summer with a different trail, beginning at lower elevations in spring and gradually heading higher as the snowpack melts. Although the distances seem great, most hikes are only moderately demanding. Some, such as **Garibaldi Lake** (moderate; 11 miles/18 km return) and **Black Tusk** (extreme; 8.7 miles/14 km return from Garibaldi Lake), are so popular that the route seems as congested as Hwy 99, particularly near the end of the day when everyone is making a hurried descent to be in the parking lot before dark.

In most cases, the viewpoints in the Whistler region are not easily reached by car. One of the exceptions is the short drive east of Hwy 99 to the Garibaldi Lake/Black Tusk trailhead parking lot. Head this way near sunset to view the rock formation called **the Barrier.** As the late light of day strikes the red volcanic rock face, many shades of colour are revealed. This is the site of a massive landslide that occurred in the mid-1850s, several years prior to the arrival of the first European explorers. Squamish Indian guides led two Hudson's Bay Company employees past the site as they crossed the ancient trading route later known as the Pemberton Trail. Evidence of the slide can still be see in the boulder fields that line Rubble Creek and in the rock fields beside Hwy 99 near the turnoff. The Barrier holds back water in the Garibaldi Lakes system that would otherwise flash down into the valley. The possibility of such a drastic failure is the reason that much of the immediate region is posted as "No Stopping." For the sake of the view, take a chance!

Occasionally one trail will serve as a springboard to lengthier jaunts. For example, the **Cheakamus Lake Trail** (easy; 4 miles/7 km return; see Mountain Biking, below) connects with **Singing Creek** (easy; 4 miles/7 km return from Cheakamus Lake) and **Helm Creek** (moderate; 15 miles/24 km return) **Trails.** In turn the Helm Creek Trail links with the Black Tusk Trail and provides an opportunity to make an overnight, point-to-point excursion. Such trips require advanced planning for return transportation. Another such route is the **Madley Lake to Rainbow Lake Trail** (moderate; 11 miles/18 km return), which links at lakeside with the **Rainbow Falls/Rainbow Lake Trail** (moderate; 10 miles/16 km return). Madley Lake lies just north of Callaghan Lake (see Parks/Camping, above). Follow Callaghan Lake Rd past Alexander Falls. The road to Madley Lake is on the right just beyond the bridge that spans Madley Creek. The trailhead for Rainbow Lake is on the west side of Alta Lake Rd in Whistler, a short distance north of Rainbow Park (see Picnics, above). It's a short, moderately steep hike to the base of the falls, then a long half-day hike to the lake as the trail follows the creek to its source. The views on this trail are better coming out on this trail than going in, as you have many good views of the peaks between Whistler and Wedge Mountains. For a full description of these and other hikes in the Whistler region, consult *103 Hikes in Southwestern British Columbia* by David and Mary Macaree.

For those with less time to explore, shorter excursions such as the **Loggers Lake Trail** (moderate; 3.7-mile/6-km loop) and the **Whistler Interpretive Forest Trails** (easy; 7.5 miles/12 km return; see Mountain Biking, below) will give your body and soul a good workout. A large map of these trails is displayed at the entrance to the Cheakamus Lake Rd on the east side of Hwy 99 across from Whistler's Function Junction industrial park. For a map of the Whistler Interpretive Forest, contact the BC Forest Service office in Squamish, (604) 898-2100.

If you walk the entire 9.3 miles (15 m) of the **Valley Trail** (see Cycling/In-Line Skating, below), you'll not only come away with a comprehensive idea of the layout of the resort, but also you'll have seen most of the important landmarks from a variety of perspectives. Because the mountains fold into each other in tight succession and rise so sharply from the valley floor, you'll see varying profiles of them from different parts of the valley. For example, when you're standing at the south end of the trail near Alpha Lake, none of the bare rock that forms Blackcomb Peak is revealed. Walk 2 miles (3 km) north along the Valley Trail and you can spy not only Blackcomb but also all its companion peaks in the Spearhead Range. (Note: Although Blackcomb is sometimes referred to as a mountain, the formation itself is, in fact, a peak. The terrain referred to as Blackcomb Mountain is in the western reaches of the Spearhead Range, where winter recreation trails have been cleared.) This is just one of the advantages of taking several hours to walk as much of the trail as possible. You can begin exploring the Valley Trail from numerous points throughout Whistler. One of the most scenic stretches occurs between Meadow Park in the Alpine Meadows neighbourhood and Rainbow Park on Alta Lake. The trail follows the River of Golden Dreams (see Canoeing/Kayaking/Boating, below) for much of the time, and you'll find park benches placed at various scenic viewpoints along the way. Also watch for the **Lost Lake Nature Trails,** which loop away from the Valley Trail for short distances near the south end of Lost Lake. The Valley Trail extends as far north as Emerald Estates at the north end of Green Lake; however, as this section of the trail runs along the shoulder of Hwy 99, it loses much of its pastoral charm.

Fitzsimmons Creek carves a deep trench through the heart of Whistler Village. Looking into the mountains from the village, you can trace its channel to the flanks of Tremor Mountain and Overlord Glacier. Trails such as **Singing Pass** (moderate; 7.5 miles/12 km return) and **Musical Bumps** (moderate; 7.5 miles/12 km return) lead into the alpine area east of **Whistler Mountain** (easy; various distances). Across the valley to the north, trails through **Blackcomb**'s alpine (easy; various distances) give hikers a view of their compatriots on these extended routes. For a map of the hiking trails on Whistler Mountain, including the Musical Bumps, call (604) 932-3434; for information on Blackcomb, contact (604) 932-3141. Note: All Whistler Mountain summer activities will be moved to Blackcomb Mountain for the summer of 1998 because of construction on Whistler.

The alpine flower display at **Singing Pass** is legendary. The timing of the height of the blooming season depends on the amount of snow remaining from the previous winter, but it usually occurs during the first two weeks in August. Singing Pass stands in the headwaters region of Fitzsimmons Creek, a 15-mile (24-km) round trip from Whistler Village. BC Parks has signs to mark the turnoff to the trailhead on Hwy 99 at Village Gate

Blvd. A dirt road that leads to the pass begins beside the BC Transit loop on Blackcomb Way and runs along the north side of Whistler Mountain. Follow the road uphill past the "Singing Pass 4.8 km" sign, as the Whistler Express gondola passes overhead. The narrow road to the Singing Pass parking lot climbs relentlessly uphill; use caution and sound your horn at blind corners. You'll have to scramble up a rocky section at the outset of the trail as it leads for almost 2 miles (3 km) to the boundary of Garibaldi Provincial Park (see Parks/Camping, above). The well-groomed trail to the pass gains elevation at a gradual pace as ever-improving views of Blackcomb and the Spearhead Range provide a riveting spectacle. You'll know that you are close to Singing Pass when flowers begin to appear beside the trail. From June to August, the slopes are alive with colourful blossoms. Yellow glacier lilies begin blooming in June, followed by white Sitka valerian, yellow fan-leaved cinqefoil, orange Indian paintbrush, tall yellow western pasque flowers, and blue lupines.

Note: As of 1997, a landslide has kept the road to the parking lot at Singing Pass closed. To check on the current condition of the Singing Pass road, call BC Parks in Squamish at (604) 898-3678.

If you visit the Whistler Museum you'll be astounded by some of the archival photographs. The shoreline around Alta Lake, for example, was almost completely clear-cut in the 1930s. Alta and nearby Green Lake were used as booming grounds, and throughout the summer the lakes' surfaces were choked with logs. That was then; this is now. Vibrant second-growth has replaced much of the damaged landscape, but the impact of more recent logging is still visible above the Alpine Meadows neighbourhood and in many hidden places such as the Soo River Valley (see Mountain Biking, below). Although much of the lower-elevation, old-growth forest has been removed around Whistler, a pocket of western red cedar remains near the summit of Cougar Mountain (see Mountain Biking, below) that will enchant you.

The **Ancient Cedars Trail** (easy; 2.5 miles/4 km return) loops through the forest and provides not only an introduction to the trees but also to an undisturbed cross section of growth clustered around a nourishing stream. As summer lengthens, so too does the astounding size of the leaves on prickly devil's club (its Latin name, *Oplopanax horridus*, provides a clue as to its nasty side), which can grow here to widths of 14 inches (35 cm). Judging by the familiar shape of the leaves, you'd think it was a member of the maple family; in fact, devil's club is related to ginseng. The root of this pernicious shrub is prized by Native peoples throughout BC for its anaesthetic properties, and they esteem the plant as a whole as one of the most medicinal on the coast. Western red cedar, some as wide as 9 feet (3 m) in diameter, and devil's club enjoy damp conditions as much as do the ferns and fungi that carpet the forest floor. (An excellent backpack-sized reference book on West Coast botanicals is Pojar and MacKinnon's *Plants of Coastal British Columbia.*) There's a wonderful ambience here, heightened by a small waterfall near the beginning of the trail. To reach the Ancient Cedars Trail, follow the Showh Lakes Forestry Rd west of Hwy 99. The turnoff occurs 0.6 mile (1 km) north of Whistler's Emerald Estates neighbourhood. Take the two-lane gravel road that rises uphill on west side of Hwy 99. A short way in you pass a brown Forest Service sign marking the beginning of the road along 16-Mile Creek. Just past the Forest Service sign is a widening on the right (north) side of the road where snowmobilers, snowshoers, and cross-country skiers park in winter. Snow is not cleared past this point. If you wish to do the entire 12.4-mile (20-km) journey by bicycle or on foot in summer, you can leave your vehicle here, or you can drive halfway to Cougar Mountain (beyond the halfway point are ditches that may be too deep for most cars to negotiate). Nearby are several buildings on the north side of the road. Proceed past them, ignoring the road branching off to the left (it leads along the recently logged south side of 16-Mile Creek). For the first 1.2 miles (2 km) the road proceeds along a level part of this small valley with the creek on its right side. A log bridge spans 16-Mile Creek and the road begins to climb a ridge above the creek on the valley's north side. Beside the bridge is another good place to leave your car; from here on the road is often rutted by runoff. (The ditches offer added excitement when you're going downhill on a bike.) From the bridge to the Showh Lakes is about 2 miles (3 km), an easy hour's walk. Take something to drink when you set out on a warm day; there is no water until you reach the lakes. Just before the lakes the road divides. The road to Cougar Mountain heads uphill on the right. For the best access to the Showh Lakes, take this road. It continues uphill for 1.2 miles (2 km). The larger of the two lakes appears below you halfway along. Watch for the trail to its shoreline on your left, leading down through stumps and blueberry bushes. The road climbs to its end 0.6 mile (1 km) past the larger of the Showh Lakes. The Ancient Cedars Trail loop begins here.

When you feel that you're in top shape, tackle the most northern entrance into Garibaldi Provincial Park (see Parks/Camping, above) along the trail to magical **Wedgemount Lake** (extreme; 8.6 miles/14 km return). This is one tough climb, with hardly a level spot to rest on. Total elevation gained is about 3,935 feet (1200 m). Once you've made the effort of climbing to the lake, where the tongue of Wedgemount Glacier is stuck in the turquoise-coloured water, it's a shame to spend the day here only, especially as much more hiking beckons above. Mount Weart and Wedge Mountain (at 9,527 feet (2904 m) the highest point in Garibaldi Provincial Park) are close at hand, as is the Armchair Glacier surmounted by two scoured granite fans, part of a volcanic ridge called the Owls. A small, stuffy cabin sleeps eight, but most visitors prefer to camp by the lake. (One bizarre feature here is a pit toilet in a metal-sheathed outhouse that's shaped like a silver bullet.) To reach the trailhead, turn east off Hwy 99, 2.5 miles (4 km) north of Whistler's northernmost neighbourhood, Emerald Estates, and cross the Green River Bridge, then turn left and head uphill about 2 miles (3 km) on a dirt road. There are signs at each divide pointing the way to the lake.

Downhill Skiing/Snowboarding

Whistler Mountain (elevation 7,160 feet/2182 m) and **Blackcomb** (elevation 7,494 feet/2284 m) competed with each other for two decades before merging in the spring of 1997. Competition between the two led to their status in the minds (and hearts) of many skiers and snowboarders as the premier North American winter resorts. Their union merely confirmed the impression that, for most visitors, Whistler is a seamless valley. You can just as easily explore one mountain as the other. Each offers a complimentary perspective on its companion and each has a loyal following of ski and snowboard devotees. The best answer to the question "which is best?" is that when you're in heaven, it doesn't matter which side of the street you walk on. Both have been around long enough (Whistler since 1965, Blackcomb since 1980) to have developed trails over a combined total of 7,071 acres (2864 ha) that over the seasons have been shaped, groomed, and gladed to hold snow and reduce obstacles. Some of the lengthier trails on Whistler Mountain include the **Dave Murray Downhill,** one of the world's premier downhill race courses, and **Franz's,** named for Franz Wilhelmsen, one of the founders of the Garibaldi Lift Company, who originally developed the trails on Whistler. Over on Blackcomb, **Couloir Extreme** and **Blackcomb Glacier** are two of the more renowned runs, both of which originate in the high alpine region of the mountain. Each year more runs are added. Even for those who have spent many years visiting the two mountains, constant change makes each new season seem like the first.

Whistler Mountain hosts World Cup ski and snowboard races at the beginning of the season, while Blackcomb is the site of World Cup freestyle competition in early January. (One of the novelties of summer is to watch freestyle skiers practise their routines at the foot of Blackcomb in a specially designed outdoor swimming pool.) Both mountains share a common statistic: an average annual snowfall of 30 feet (9 m).

A total of 3 gondolas, 17 chairlifts, and 4 T-bars ascend both mountains from three separate locations in Whistler. **Creekside** (elevation 2,140 feet/653 m), at the south end of town, is the site of the original Garibaldi Lift Company operation. The Creekside gondola runs up the west side of Whistler Mountain to Midstation (elevation 4,265 feet/1,300 m). From here, skiers and snowboarders make their way higher up the mountain on the Orange and Big Red Express chairlifts or head back downhill to either Creekside or Whistler Village. From the heart of the Whistler Village (elevation 2,215 feet/675 m) the Excalibur gondola links with the Excelerator Express chairlift on Blackcomb, while the Whistler Village gondola runs to Olympic Station at midmountain (elevation 3,346 feet/1003 m) and continues up the north side of Whistler Mountain to Pika's and the Roundhouse (elevation 6,069 feet/1850 m). The Wizard Express quad-chair runs from the Blackcomb Day Lodge in the **Upper Village** (elevation 2,247 feet/685 m) and connects with the Solar Coaster Express quad-chair to take skiers, snowboarders, and sightseers to the Rendezvous Lodge (elevation 6,102 feet/1860 m). A new, high-speed quad chair called The Peak is replacing the current left of the same name in the summer of 1998, which will carry skiers to the summit in less than 4 minutes. All lifts from the village connect with a multitude of lifts higher up each mountain, allowing skiers and snowboarders to fan out across the slopes. The longest lineups are at the base of the mountains. The farther uphill you go, the more dispersed the crowds become, and lineups predictably shrink. T-bars and chairlifts transport skiers and snowboarders to the summit of each mountain.

It takes 30–60 minutes riding a combination of interconnecting gondolas and/or chairlifts to reach the upper slopes of each mountain from its base. If conditions permit, you can easily spend that much time making your way to the bottom. Snow-making equipment installed on lower slopes helps maintain an adequate covering so that, with the exception of the beginning and end of the winter season, you should be able to reach the bottom without downloading on one of the lifts. One caution: During mild weather, icy conditions may persist at lower elevations. Unless you have razor-sharp edges and energy to burn, download rather than ski out at the end of the day. As attractive as the idea of skiing or snowboarding on both mountains in a single day may be, in reality you'll spend more time riding lifts than you will enjoying the outdoors. Better to explore one mountain per day and savour every moment you can.

One of the best introductions to each mountain is provided by Whistler's Mountain Ambassadors and Blackcomb's Mountain Hosts. Stop by guest relations at Blackcomb's Daylodge, Rendezvous Lodge, or Glacier Creek Lodge, or the Whistler Village gondola station, the Creekside gondola station, or the Guest Satisfaction Centre on Whistler Mountain to arrange for a complimentary guided tour. Local volunteers will lead you around the mountain and introduce you to runs that suit your abilities. It's a good way to get an insider's look at the mountains and to learn more about Whistler in general. Whistler Mountain has slightly more terrain developed for beginners than Blackcomb (20 percent versus 15 percent). Both mountains devote about 55 percent of their trails to intermediate-level skiers and snowboarders, with the remainder considered the domain of the expert (25 percent on Whistler, 30 percent on Blackcomb). (These numbers may change, however, with the work being done in the summer of 1998 to improve alpine routes and shape them into routes more accessible to non-expert skiers.)

Both mountains have special areas set aside for snowboarders. Blackcomb was the first of the two mountains to welcome snowboarding, and as a result maintains more appeal for younger boarders. Glacier ice still cloaks the peaks of both mountains, but Blackcomb's is much larger. Come summer, skiing and snowboarding carries on without a pause right through August on the Blackcomb glacier. What sets Whistler Mountain apart from Blackcomb is its series of wide alpine bowls: Bagel, West, Whistler, Harmony, Symphony, Sun, and Burnt Stew Bowls define the upper reaches of the mountain. Because they are tucked away at high altitude it's difficult to appreciate their magnificence from the valley.

Lessons and rentals can be arranged at the day lodges of both mountains. In addition, there is a proliferation of rental shops throughout Whistler Village. Lift ticket prices are about $55 per day for adults. The best bargain is a five-day pass for about $265. For more information on Blackcomb and Whistler Mountains, contact guest relations, (800) 766-0449 toll free, (604) 932-3434 in Whistler, (604) 664-5614 in Vancouver; Web site: www.whistler-blackcomb.com. For current snow conditions, call (604) 932-4211 in Whistler, (604) 687-7507 in Vancouver.

Cross-Country Skiing

As soon as the snow begins to fall at higher elevations around Squamish, cross-country skiers head for **Diamond Head** in **Garibaldi Provincial Park** (see Parks/Camping, above). Chances are that, beginning in late October and lasting through May, you will find snow covering the 7-mile (11-km), intermediate-level route that runs from the trailhead at the 3,000-foot (900-m) level to the cabin at **Elfin Lakes** (4,900 feet/1485 m). Allow four hours to make the trek one way. Bring your skins, as it's a steady uphill for the first three hours as far as Paul Ridge before the trail levels and then makes a gradual descent to Elfin Lakes. If you're just here for a day trip, the day shelter at **Red Heather Meadow**, a 2-mile (3-km) climb, may be as far as you wish to go, whereas continuing up the trail to the Elfin Lakes is more appropriate for an overnight excursion.

Diamond Head is also the approach to a vast backcountry region in the southwest corner of the park. Skiers should come prepared for sudden changes in weather. Diamond Head is the southern terminus of the **Garibaldi Névé Traverse,** a classic 26-mile (42-km) ski trek to **Garibaldi Lake** (see Hiking/Backpacking, above). Although this tour has many extended moderate sections, do not attempt it without a guide experienced in glacier travel. For more information, contact the Canada West Mountain School in Vancouver, (604) 737-3053, Web site: home.istar.ca/~fmcbc/. The best maps of the route are Geological Survey of Canada topographic maps 92G/14 and 92G/15.

If there's fresh snow, stop at **Brandywine Falls Provincial Park** (see Parks/Camping, above) for some ungroomed, cross-country trekking. You'll have to cut your own track in to **Swim Lake** from the parking lot but the rewards are worth it. Follow the trail markers intended for summer hikers. This isn't a long trek, about 2 miles (3 km) return. Crossing the bridge over Brandywine Creek is an adventure in itself, especially if the snowpack is so deep that you ski at the same height as the top railing. Pause in the shelter of a cedar grove at lakeside to admire the Black Tusk (see Hiking/Backpacking, above), gone white with snow. From there, retrace your tracks to Brandywine Creek and head along the trail to the falls. Cross the BC Rail tracks and ski a short distance to the observation platform beside **Brandywine Falls**. In winter, the sound of Brandywine Creek tumbling onto the exposed boulders below is remarkably similar to that of a jet streaking high in the sky above. All this glory, and you may have the place to yourself, too.

A gentle cross-country route runs between Brandywine Falls Provincial Park and the whistle stop of **McGuire** near the Cal-Cheak Forest Service Recreation Site. From Brandywine Falls Provincial Park, the trail follows a BC Hydro access road to McGuire (population: 1) near the Forest Service's **Cal-Cheak** campground (see Parks/Camping, above). This 5-mile (8-km) round trip is perfect for a smooth bit of cruising, a genuinely relaxing stretch past frozen pothole lakes with the sight of the Black Tusk on high. To find the trail, turn left immediately after crossing the bridge over Brandywine Creek from the parking lot in Brandywine Fall Provincial Park. (Swim Lake and the falls lie to the right.) You'll have to do a short bit of hill climbing at the outset before reaching the level part of the trail. Inexperienced skiers should be very cautious when descending this hill on the return journey: bend the knees, mind the trees.

Cross-country skiing in **Whistler** is all about relaxation. There's no pressure to get in line because there are no lineups. There are several styles of cross-country trails around Whistler. The **Valley Trail** is a designated winter ski trail. You don't have to worry about any errant golf balls heading your way during this season, either. This mostly level loop route runs for almost 10 miles (16 km) and passes many of Whistler's neighbourhoods and Lost Lake. The trail can be accessed from any number of places, including the Whistler Golf Course on Hwy 99 in Whistler Village, the Meadow Park Sports Centre on Hwy 99 in Alpine Meadows, and Rainbow Park on Alta Lake Rd. The Valley Trail also passes through Lost Lake.

The 18-mile (29-km) network of packed and tracked trails around **Lost Lake** is easily located. Just drive into Whistler Village on Village Gate Blvd and turn left onto Blackcomb Way, then right into the parking lot directly across from the municipal offices and medical clinic. This is where the trail to Lost Lake begins. Shortly after starting out, you will come to a log chalet, where you must pay a fee (about $10 during the day, $4 in the evening, no charge after 9pm) for use of the Lost Lake trails. Skiing around the lake will take a quick 60 to 90 minutes. The selection of approaches ranges from beginner to expert, marked like downhill runs.

Lost Lake often freezes in a way that makes it appear still to be open water. The wind sweeps the snow into small drifts that look like whitecaps. The setting sun reflects pink off the clouds onto the icy surface below. An added bonus is that night skiing is also possible at Lost Lake on the 2.5-mile (4-km) Lost Lake Loop Trail.

There are several other locations near Whistler where cross-country skiers head. At the north end of Green Lake on the west side of Hwy 99, the road up **16-Mile Creek** to Cougar Mountain is used by snowmobilers, with advantages for skiers too. This is also a particularly good place to snowshoe in dry and powdery conditions.

Watch for cars pulled off at places like the **Callaghan Lake Road** or **Brandywine Mountain Forest Road,** about 3 miles (5 km) south of Whistler on the west side of Hwy 99. These are ungroomed roads in winter and are quickly packed down by cross-country skiers and snowmobilers, which often share the same route. The Mad River Nordic Centre, (604) 932-5629, is located in the upper part of the Callaghan Valley and offers **hut-to-hut snow touring** in spring months on groomed trails.

Winter Sports

Snowmobiling is many things, including noisy, but in Whistler one thing's for certain: it's big. For years the Showh Lakes Forestry Rd has been the winter location for Whistler Snowmobile Guided Tours, (604) 932-4086, or Web site: www.snowmobiles-bc.com. Snowmobiles can be rented from Squamish Snowmobile, (604) 892-9221 in Squamish, or (604) 938-1280 in Whistler. Visit their Web site: www.mountain-inter.net\sqsnowmobile.

Guided snowmobiling tours in Whistler can also be arranged with Blackcomb Snowmobiling, (604) 932-8484; Garibaldi Snowmobile, (604) 905-7002; and Canadian Snowmobile Adventure, (604) 938-1616.

Heli-skiing/boarding in Whistler can be arranged with Whistler Heli-Skiing, 3-4241 Village Stroll, (604) 932-4105; Town & Country Heli-Boarding, 8545A Drifter Way, (604) 938-2927; Mountain Heli-Sports, 4340 Sundial Crescent, (604) 932-2070; and Blackcomb Helicopters, 9990 Heliport, (604) 938-1700.

To those with an aversion to flight (unless it's off a cornice) **sno-cat skiing/snowboarding** can get you into the untracked backcountry around Whistler just as effectively as heli-skiing/boarding. For more information, call Powder Mountain Snowcats, (604) 932-0169; Sea to Sky Snowcats, (604) 932-7754; or West Coast Cat Skiing, 9615 Emerald Pl, (888) 246-1111 or (604) 932-2166 in Whistler.

Sleigh rides put the jingle bells into outdoor winter fun. To hitch a ride, call Blackcomb Horse-Drawn Sleigh Rides, (604) 932-7631, in Whistler. If you'd rather mush that giddy-up, call Husky Kennels, 8046 Parkwood, (604) 932-5732, to go **dogsledding.**

If you can walk, you can **snowshoe** (and your knees and back will thank you). Some of the most inviting trails in Whistler are those in the forest surrounding Olympic Station on Whistler Mountain. For information on rentals and **guided tours,** including evening outings on Blackcomb, contact Canadian Snowshoe Adventures, (604) 932-0647, or visit their Web site: www.iias.com/outdoors.

Paragliding is certainly the most graceful way to make a descent of a mountain. There's only one bump to contend with, and that's when you touch down. Paragliding is a long-standing tradition on Blackcomb Mountain's Seventh Heaven zone. For instruction and more information, call Parawest Paragliding, (604) 932-7052, in Whistler.

When it's cold enough, out come the snow shovels to clear a place for **ice skating** on Alta Lake in Whistler. Head for Rainbow Park (see Picnics, above) on Alta Lake Rd to find it (and don't forget your shovel). Indoor ice skating is a sure bet at the Squamish Civic Centre, 1009 Centennial Way, (604) 898-3604, in Squamish's Brackendale neighbourhood, or at the Meadow Park Sports Centre Arena/Leisure Pool and Fitness Centre, 8107 Camino Dr, (604) 938-3133, in Whistler's Alpine Meadows neighbourhood. Skates are available for rent at both.

Rock Climbing

Steep but easily accessible cliffs that rise on the west and north sides of 60-acre (24-ha) **Murrin Provincial Park** (see Picnics, above) make it a popular destination for novice rock climbers who wish to work on their technique. Climbing trails branch off from the main trail to Petgill Lake (see Hiking/Backpacking, above), located north of Murrin's parking lot.

At last count there were 180 routes to climb on **Stawamus Chief Mountain** (see also Hiking/Backpacking, above) in Squamish, all of which begin from the base of one the largest free-standing granite monoliths in the world. Estimated to be 93 million years old, the Chief is one of the senior members of the local landscape, parts of which were laid down as lava a scant 12,000 years ago. Advanced and novice climbers alike look for appropriate routes on "The Chief," "The Squaw," and "The Apron," which together form the main climbing area. The best barometer of the Chief's international reputation is to check the wide range of licence plates on the cars parked in the climbers' lot at the base of the mountain, and to eavesdrop on the languages being spoken here in the staging area, where as many as 25,000 climbers gather annually. The climber's parking lot in Stawamus Chief Provincial Park is located on the east side of Hwy 99 at its junction with the Stawamus River Forest Rd, just north of the Stawamus Chief roadside viewpoint. Information on these routes and others in the Squamish region can be gleaned from Kevin McLane's *The Rock-climber's Guide to Squamish.*

As you travel north of Stawamus Chief Mountain into Squamish, keep your eyes on the bare-faced bluffs that rise above the Mamquam Blind Channel on the east side of the highway. These are the **Smoke Bluffs,** a novice and intermediate climbers' delight. The bluffs get their name from the mist that rises from them when lit by morning sunlight. Not nearly as imposing as the Chief, the Smoke Bluffs receive more direct sunlight than their renowned neighbour, and thus routes here, although shorter, dry much faster. There are two approaches to the Smoke Bluffs. The easiest one to find is on Loggers Lane. Turn right off Hwy 99 onto Loggers Lane at the Cleveland Ave stoplights, across from a string of fast-food franchises. Drive a short distance to the top of the Mamquam Blind Channel. There's plenty of parking in a clearing here that is often occupied by pieces of heavy equipment. The north end of the Smoke Bluffs Trail begins along a gated service road. An alternative approach begins from the traffic lights just north of the Stawamus Chief. Turn right at the lights, then left, and drive past the hospital to the top of Vista Crescent. A map posted in the parking lot here details the various approaches to the bluffs and shows the locations of several good viewpoints. The solid granite on both the Chief and the Smoke Bluffs is prized by climbers; at present, there are about 200 climbing routes from which to choose.

The trail north around the base of the Smoke Bluffs descends onto an open plateau and below to the bank of the Mamquam Blind Channel.

Wood and rock staircases lead up to one section called the **Octopus's Garden.** Farther along, the loop trail narrows as it curves between two granite walls. Watch for wooden stairs leading down to **Pixie Corner.** This 2-mile (3-km) loop trail brings you out at the notice board near Vista Crescent. Even if you don't come to climb, a walk around the Smoke Bluffs will provide plenty of inspiration.

Mountain Biking

Alice Lake Provincial Park (see Parks/Camping, above) is almost as much a favourite with mountain-bike riders as the Stawamus Chief is with climbers. Because it seldom occurs, mountain bikers get a warm feeling when invited to ride trails in public parks. It is hoped that this helps foster a better rapport between cyclists and those on foot. This is the scenario at Alice Lake Provincial Park north of Squamish. Although not large when compared to neighbouring Garibaldi Provincial Park (see Parks/Camping, above), at 980 acres (397 ha) Alice Lake is just the right size for a rock-and-rolling 7.4-mile (12-km) trail that *everyone* can enjoy 10 months of the year. In July and August, campers take precedence in the park, and the **Four Lakes Loop Trail** is closed to mountain bikers. It's cool. Everyone understands. Time to play elsewhere. But as soon as "noncrunch time" (BC Parks' terminology) at Alice Lake Provincial Park returns, so do the bikers.

Trying to keep up with the rapid pace of mountain-bike trail building in the Sea to Sky corridor is enough to drive any cyclists to distraction, but pleasantly so. Some of the best new single-track trails are being built by the Ministry of Forests at their **Brohm Lake Interpretive Forest** beside Hwy 99, 2.5 miles (4 km) north of Alice Lake Provincial Park, near Squamish. Trail maps are available from the prominent information kiosk at the entrance to the site. An extensive network of new trails, some of which are still not complete, cuts through the forest to the south and west of **Brohm Lake.** The best approach to the mountain-biking trails is at a gated entrance about 0.6 mile (1 km) south of the lake's main paved parking area. There's plenty of room to pull off Hwy 99 here, and the trailhead is marked with a large, brown Forest Service sign, beside which is the covered box filled with trail maps. The sounds of the highway quickly fade away as you begin riding. At several places the 7 miles (11 km) of connecting trails divide, offering a choice of directions to cliffside viewpoints. At present, the trails around Brohm Lake itself are unsuitable for mountain bikes. Keep your eye out for improvements as the Forest Service continues work on the site.

The **Paradise Valley Road** connects with a section of the **Pemberton**

Trail, one of the oldest trails in the Lower Mainland. This trading route linked Native communities on the coast with the Thompson Plateau in the Central Interior. It was along this route that the first Europeans were guided, beginning with fur traders and later with adventurers in search of good fishing in the Alta Lakes region. Parts of the old trail are still faintly visible on the hillside above the North Vancouver Outdoors School, located 1.2 miles (2 km) north from the Cheekye Bridge on the Paradise Valley Rd. Today, mountain-bikers follow the intermediate-level route beginning from the bridge through Paradise Valley. To find it, watch for the signs to Paradise Valley on Hwy 99 opposite the entrance to Alice Lake Provincial Park. Travel 2.5 miles (4 km) west of Hwy 99 on the Squamish Valley Rd to the Cheekye Bridge. The Paradise Valley Rd branches off the Squamiush Valley Rd here and runs for 7 miles (11 km) through Paradise Valley. The road is paved for the first 3 miles (5 km) and parallels the Cheakamus River for much of the way. A 3-mile (5-km) section of the Pemberton Trail begins at the north end of Paradise Valley Rd and leads to Hwy 99. At first it ascends along a rocky service road to the BC Rail tracks. This is a difficult section to ride clean; don't be surprised if you have a short hike with your bike over the roughest sections. Beyond the railway tracks the trail smooths out as it makes a gradual ascent above the Cheakamus Canyon, passes Starvation Lake, and finally links with Hwy 99 near the north end of the canyon. Turn back here and enjoy the descent, along with views of the Tantalus Range on the western skyline.

There aren't many trails in **Garibaldi Provincial Park** where mountain bikes are allowed, but one of the best is the 7-mile (11-km) trail to **Elfin Lakes** in the Diamond Head region of the park (see Parks/Camping, above). Plan on taking several hours to ascend the old service road, then enjoy a thrilling though not technically challenging descent. For a map of mountain-bike trails in Garibaldi Provincial Park, contact BC Parks, (604) 898-3678.

For more information on mountain-bikes trails in the Squamish region, contact the Squamish Off-Road Cycling Association, (604) 898-5195. Bike shops in Squamish include Corsa Cycles, 38128 Cleveland Ave, (604) 892-3331; Vertical Reality, 38154 Second Ave, (604) 892-8248; and Tantalus Bike Shop, 40446 Government Rd, (604) 898-2588. Tantalus also rents mountain bikes. Good trail guides to consult include *Mountain Biking British Columbia* by Darrin Polischuk.

Mountain biking may trace its origins to the 1970s in northern California, but it didn't take long to make its way to Whistler. By the early 1980s, North America's longest point-to-point mountain-bike race, the **Cheakamus Challenge** (about 30 miles/50 km, from Brackendale to Whistler), was already underway. Held on the last weekend in September, the race attracts a thousand riders, from elite pros to ordinary janes and joes, who take anywhere from 2 to 5 hours to complete the course. Much of the distance covers the same route as the **Sea to Sky Mountain Biking and Hiking Trail** that runs between Squamish and D'Arcy, a distance of 93 miles (150 km) by road. When complete, it's expected that the Sea to Sky trail will cover twice that distance as more use is made of off-road trails, deactivated logging roads, and BC Hydro access roads. For a map of the entire Sea to Sky route, call the Whistler Chamber of Commerce, (604) 932-5528.

Some of the best single-track mountain-bike trails in the Whistler region are found at the south end of the resort in the **Whistler Interpretive Forest.** The trailhead is located at the beginning of the Cheakamus Lake Rd on the east side of Hwy 99, directly across from the entrance to Whistler's Function Junction industrial park. The over 7.5 miles (12 km) of well-constructed trails in the interpretive forest lead along both sides of the Cheakamus River and onto the ridges at higher elevations around **Loggers Lake** (see Hiking/Backpacking, above). Maps are available from a dispenser at the trailhead; just reach underneath to get one, or contact the BC Ministry of Forests, Squamish Forest District, (604) 898-2100, or the Resort Municipality of Whistler, (604) 932-5535. Most trails are suited to intermediate-level riders.

You can ride a mountain bike on the trail that leads to **Cheakamus Lake** in **Garibaldi Provincial Park.** This is one of only two places in the massive park where cycling is allowed, Diamond Head being the other. Follow the Cheakamus Lake Rd, which begins 6 miles (10 km) south of Whistler Village, east from Hwy 99. The road runs uphill for most of the way to the park boundary, a distance of 3.7 miles (6 km), from where a rock-and-rolling trail leads 2 miles (3.5 km) through old-growth forest to Cheakamus Lake. This is a good trail for beginners. For a map of Garibaldi Provincial Park, contact BC Parks, (604) 898-3678.

One of the biggest developments in mountain biking recently in Whistler has been the opening of the **Whistler Mountain Bike Park.** Located below the Olympic Station on the north side of the mountain and accessible from Whistler Village by the Whistler Mountain gondola, the self-guided single- and double-track trails provide for all ability levels. Guided descents of the mountain are also available. Call (604) 932-3111 for a map and more details. (Note: All Whistler Mountain summer activities will be moved to Blackcomb Mountain for summer of 1998 because of construction on Whistler Mountain.)

One of the longer off-road routes runs along the east side of **Green Lake** and passes through the ghost-town of **Parkhurst,** once a thriving logging community in the 1940s and 50s. This 14-mile (23-km) return journey follows a BC Hydro access road north from the Valley Trail (see Cycling/In-Line Skating, below), where Fitzsimmons Creek enters Green Lake. Instead of following the Valley Trail down to Green Lake, take the rugged road that leads north beside the hydro towers. Instead of riding this section "clean," you may have to push your bike until you reach the crest of the slope. From here north is the most enjoyable section. As the access road nears the lake's north end, watch for a side road that leads to Parkhurst, the only such side road you'll encounter on this ride. The access road eventually crosses the BC Rail line near the approach to Wedgemount Lake (see Hiking/Backpacking, above) on the east side of Hwy 99. You can either retrace your tread marks or loop back to Whistler on Hwy 99.

Just north of Whistler is the route to **Cougar Mountain** and Soo River. The road to Cougar Mountain begins at the north end of Green Lake, 0.6 mile (1 km) past the entrance to Whistler's Emerald Estates neighbourhood. Take the two-lane gravel road that rises uphill on the left (west) side of Hwy 99. A short way in you pass a brown Forest Service sign marking the beginning of the road along 16-Mile Creek. From here the road and then an enchanting section of single-track trail lead explorers on a 12-mile (20-km) jaunt through clear-cut fields choked with blueberry bushes to the **Showh Lakes,** and from there to a grove of old-growth cedars near the summit of Cougar Mountain on the **Ancient Cedars Loop Trail.** For an extended mountain-bike tour of the base of Cougar Mountain, follow the **Soo River Forest Road.** Stay to the left when the road forks around the Showh Lakes rather than follow the well-marked road uphill to the Ancient Cedars Loop Trail. Beyond here the road becomes rougher as it heads north towards the Soo River Forest Road, which loops east to Hwy 99.

A number of detailed trail guides for mountain biking in Whistler are currently available. Among the best is the one published by the Whistler Off-Road Cycling Association, the *Whistler Off-Road Cycling Guide* by Charlie Doyle and Grant Lamont. For information, call (604) 938-9893. For a preview of mountain-bike trails in Whistler, visit the Radical Multimedia mountain-bike cyberguide, whose Web site address is http://www.rideguide.com. Radical Multimedia also publish the *Sea to Sky Mountain Bike Guide,* a comprehensive listing of mountain bike trails in the Squamish-Whistler-Pemberton region, as well as providing information through their Web site on mountain biking in other parts of BC.

Cycling/In-Line Skating

There's a long, level 12-mile (19-km) stretch of the **Squamish Valley Road** that makes for a mellow cycle ride. The route begins at the Cheekye Bridge.

Follow the signs to Squamish and Paradise Valleys from Hwy 99 north of Squamish, directly across from the entrance to Alice Lake Provincial Park. Or you can cycle out along Government Rd from downtown Squamish, a rambling 6-mile (10-km) route with charm of its own. As the Squamish Valley Rd heads northwest from the Cheekye Bridge through the long, narrow valley, it parallels the Squamish River for much of the way. The road is overhung with the sheltering branches of tall broadleaf maple trees that blaze with colour in September. The road passes through several Indian reserves on its way to Cloudburst, a small community where the pavement ends. Along the way you'll be treated to more staggeringly beautiful views than you can imagine. One of the best ones occurs at the Pillchuk Creek Bridge, about 8 miles (13 km) from the Cheekye Bridge. This route also features many places to pull off and take a break beside the river.

Possibly the most vital transportation route through the Whistler Valley, after Hwy 99 and the BC Rail line, is Whistler's **Valley Trail.** Paved for much of its 10-mile (16-km) route, the trail links almost every neighbourhood between Alpha and Green Lakes. Snowshoers, cross-country skiers and warmly shod hikers are the principal users in winter; once the snow melts, cyclists and in-line skaters, as well as walkers, joggers, and strollers, vie for space. Although cyclists should be able to cover the entire loop, in-line skaters will have to avoid unpaved sections around Lost Lake, at least for the time being. Community opinion is split over the merits of blacktopping the entire trail. Be that as it may, there is plenty of ground—mostly level—to explore. You can join the trail at numerous places throughout the valley, including the Whistler Golf Course, directly across Hwy 99 from Whistler Village, and use it to reach any of the seven parks, five lakes, several creeks, and a river along the route. For a map of the Valley Trail, contact the Resort Municipality of Whistler, (604) 932-5535.

The *really* big cycle and in-line skate journey around the valley is the 22-mile (35-km) section of **Highway 99** that links Whistler and Pemberton. Some folks use this as a commuter route, while others simply cover sections of it before turning around. How long it will take you and how far you go depend on your conditioning. There's always the choice of returning on the private bus service that operates frequently throughout the day, but you'll have to ship you bike back separately as freight. In places, Hwy 99 parallels the Green River, as well as Rutherford Creek, both cheery companions whose rolling motion is an encouragement to pedal harder. Hills will challenge you no matter which direction you're travelling. Be particularly cautious in the narrow section between Nairn Falls Provincial Park and the BC Rail bridge that spans the highway south of the falls. Although you'll find paved shoulders along much of Hwy 99, there are none in this tight section.

Canoeing/Kayaking/Boating

When flat-calm, **Howe Sound** is an inviting place to paddle, but beware the outflow winds that build on summer days. The Sound is a channel for winds drawn out to the ocean from cooler inland regions. Kayakers will have an easier time of it than canoeists when the winds rise. It's worth heading offshore to enjoy the views of the Howe Sound Crest and Britannia ranges that are not revealed from land. The 1.2-mile (2-km) paddle north from Porteau Cove to **Furry Creek** is a pleasant workout. Watch for pictographs painted on the rock face on the north side of the small bay just past Furry Creek. (Keep an eye out for errant golf balls that may shank your way from the nearby golf course.) **Porteau Cove,** about 15 miles (24 km) north of Horseshoe Bay, is also a designated provincial marine park, with sheltered moorage. The boat launch at Porteau Cove Provincial Park (see Parks/Camping, above) is the only public one accessible from Hwy 99 between Horseshoe Bay and Squamish. There is a private boat launch at Sunset Marina, (604) 921-7476, 3 miles (5 km) north of Horseshoe Bay at Sunset Beach, and at Lions Bay Marina, (604) 921-7510, 3 miles (5 km) north of Sunset Beach.

For an extended trip, launch from Lions Bay Marina and head 3 miles (5 km) across Howe Sound to nearby **Gambier Island.** Tucked away from view just inside its sheltered southeast corner is **Halkett Bay Marine Park.** A government wharf lies at the end of the bay where a thick fringe of hemlock and second-growth fir shield the shoreline from view. If you walk into the shade of the trees, you'll discover a series of clearings linked by old logging trails that have assumed the character of sedate laneways. You could camp here where there are several formal sites or on a small island just offshore in the bay. The island boasts a small beach, above which stands a clearing large enough for one tent. While on Gambier, follow the old logging road that terminates beside the campsites at Halkett Bay west to Camp Fircom, a half-hour walk. At first the road leads through the forest, but it descends to the shoreline as it nears the camp, with a pleasing view south of Bowen Island's Hood Point.

Four rivers merge into one at the northern outskirts of Squamish. The Cheakamus and Cheekye join forces in quick succession, then the Mamquam swells the volume in the Squamish just before its confluence with Howe Sound. There's good sea kayaking and canoeing on the **Squamish River** almost year-round, though you must be wary during high-water volumes. These traditionally occur during autumn storms and spring snowmelt. Two of the best locations for launching and taking out are beside the Squamish River dike on Government Rd in the Brackendale neighbourhood and at the federal dock at the west end of Loggers Lane in downtown Squamish on the Mamquam Blind Channel. To reach it, follow Cleveland Ave south from Hwy 99 through downtown Squamish to Vancouver St. Turn left and drive two blocks to the dock. The advantage of launching from the dike is that you have the current in the Squamish running in your favour. Drift downstream past the **Squamish Spit** (see Windsurfing/Sailing, below) into Howe Sound with your binoculars at the ready. There's always something to see along this stretch. If you launch from the federal dock, be prepared to do some steady paddling around the Squamish Estuary (see Hiking/Backpacking, above) to reach the Spit. The afternoon winds tend to kick up quite a chop. Those with open canoes should avoid Howe Sound during these times.

Of the four lakes in **Alice Lake Provincial Park** (see Parks/Camping, above), Alice is the one most suitable for paddling, especially canoeing (motorized boats are not permitted on any of the lakes). There are launch sites at each end of the lake beside the picnic areas.

Rough and ready **Brohm Lake** (see Mountain Biking, above) has a boat launch for hand-carried boats only, located a short distance from the parking lot on Hwy 99. This diminutive lake is ideal for a quick paddle and is primarily used by anglers.

Lakes in the Whistler region are often hemmed in by thick forests. Paddling out on their open surfaces reveals views that are restricted from shore. In fact, some of the best views in the area are reserved for paddlers. On a clear, calm day, the surrounding peaks are so perfectly mirrored on the lakes that you would be hard-pressed to tell the reflection from the original. The best example of this is **Callaghan Lake** (see Parks/Camping, above). Drive to the end of the Callaghan Lake Forest Rd and launch from the rough approach at lakeside. Within minutes you'll have left the hubbub of the campsite behind and be drifting over the deep, emerald-hued lake. Water temperatures are so frigid that algae barely blooms, which accounts for the lake's exceptional clarity. It takes 30 minutes' solid paddling to reach the far end of the lake (about 1.2 miles/2 km), much of which is not visible until you round a point of land in the lake's middle. You'll spend most of that time with your mouth hanging open. (Fortunately the insect population is sparser here than on shore.) Looking across the lake to the east, you'll see a panorama of peaks that extends from Whistler Mountain south to the Black Tusk and beyond to the glaciated slopes of Mount Garibaldi near Squamish. This is without question the most expansive mountainscape to be found in Whistler. To the south is a formidable barrier of snow-clad mountains that separates the Squamish and Callaghan Valleys. Chief among the peaks is Powder Mountain, whose icefields form an unbroken white mantle. The flanks of Callaghan and Rainbow Mountains dominate in the northwest and north, respectively. One or two locations around the lakeshore suggest places to take a break, but the bugs, at least until late August, will soon have you back on the water.

Equally enthralling are the peaks and glaciers that reflect in **Cheakamus Lake** (see Hiking/Backpacking, above), though the lake itself is more difficult to reach. If you have a lightweight canoe or kayak you'll have no trouble making the 2-mile (3.2-km) portage from the parking lot to the lake, particularly if you have a folding kayak or a two-wheeled dolly. The trail is only moderately difficult and as it is suitable for mountain bikes, you should have little difficulty wheeling through the forest with a canoe or kayak in tow. About 4 miles (6 km) long, Cheakamus is the largest lake in the Whistler region; having gone to this effort, consider overnighting at Castle Towers Creek or Singing Creek Campsites (see Parks/Camping, above). Both of these streams enter the lake near its east end, several hours' paddle from the rough launch and campsite at the lake's west end. Paddling is also the only means of exploring the Cheakamus River's braided headwaters and sandy-shored delta. Watch for a giant, hollow black cottonwood sticking up at the southeast corner of the lake. Looking up from the lake you can easily pick out features such as the avalanche chutes on the south slopes of Whistler Mountain. These are the same treacherous pitches that, when snow-covered in winter, lure unsuspecting skiers and snowboarders out of bounds. Follow along the bumps of Piccolo, Flute, and Oboe summits—the Musical Bumps—as they lead to Singing Pass (see Hiking/Backpacking, above).

Placid paddling on the **River of Golden Dreams** is a tradition that links today's visitors with Whistler's past. The "river," also called **Alta Creek,** was named by Alex Philip who, with his wife, Myrtle, ran the Rainbow Lodge at the whistle stop of Alta Lake, the first commercial attraction in the valley. From modest beginnings in 1915 until the Philips sold the business in 1948, Rainbow Lodge established Alta Lake (which officially changed its name to Whistler in 1966, and became the Resort Municipality of Whistler in 1984) as the pre-eminent recreation destination west of Jasper in the Canadian Rockies. Ever the romantic, Alex renamed the creek and sent many a honeymooning couple paddling down the gentle stream to Green Lake and back. This is still an attractive and mildly challenging canoe paddle, particularly when water levels are high. In summer, short portages may be necessary to cross shallower sections. The fastest-flowing sections of the river occur at midpoint, where the creek flows beneath the **Valley Trail's Twin Bridges**—paddle hard in the sweeping S-turn that follows—and north of the Hwy 99 bridge as the creek makes several sharp bends before entering Green Lake. This last section is a pretty sight, indeed. A put-in/takeout is located beside the **Valley Trail's River of**

Golden Dreams Bridge, downstream from the hwy. A large parking area and public phone are located beside the pedestrian bridge. If you are not planning to paddle back to Alta Lake, this is a good place to arrange to be picked up. Another plan is to leave a bicycle here before you start; drive your vehicle and boat over to **Rainbow Park** (see Windsurfing/Sailing, below), paddle downstream to Green Lake, then ride back along the **Valley Trail** (see Cycling/In-Line Skating, above) to reclaim your vehicle, returning to retrieve your boat by driving west on Alta Lake Rd to Hwy 99, a short distance north of the River of Golden Dreams. Alternatively, Town and Country Taxi, (604) 932-7788, offers canoe and passenger transport, as does the Whistler Sailing and Water Sports Centre, (604) 932-7245. Canoes are available for rent at Alta Lake at both **Wayside** and **Lakeside Parks** (see Swimming, below), and at the Edgewater Lodge, 8841 Hwy 99, (604) 932-0688, on Green Lake near the outlet of the River of Golden Dreams. If you're looking for a little lake to practice rowing or paddling on, boats and canoes are also available at **Alpha Lake Park,** a family-oriented site in the Creekside neighbourhood.

Green Lake Park (see Swimming, below) has a sandy beach from which to launch a canoe or kayak. The park is located on Lakeshore Dr in the Emerald Estates neighbourhood near the north end of Green Lake. Follow the signs to the boat launch on Summer Lane from Hwy 99, then turn on Lakeshore to reach the park. (The vehicle boat launch is also a good place to begin exploring Green Lake but lacks the ambience of the park.) Water in Green Lake is often opaque due to the silt carried into it by 19-Mile and Fitzsimmons Creeks, two of its major tributaries. When ice-free, the lake is a pronounced shade of green on all but the greyest days. Paddle directly across the lake from the park to reach **Parkhurst** (see Mountain Biking, above), the site of an abandoned logging community. Follow south to reach some of the best beaches on Green Lake, located north of Fitzsimmons Creek. The Green River drains out of the north end of the lake. Its exit isn't that noticeable until you are almost drawn into it. Avoid being caught in its current as this is a dangerous, swift-flowing river from the get-go.

As it flows through Paradise Valley, the **Cheakamus River** is a clear emerald colour, except in those places where it billows with whitewater. The total length of its run is just under 7 miles (12 km) from the put-in at the north end of Paradise Valley Rd (see Mountain Biking, above) to the take-out just above the Cheekye Bridge on the Squamish Valley Rd. Except for a rough, Class III section at the midpoint where Culliton Creek enters the river, this is a consistent run with a predictably steady, Class II descent. Water levels in the river are controlled by a BC Hydro dam farther upstream on Daisy Lake near Whistler. A steady flow is guaranteed, as much for the health of fish stocks in the river (a debatable point with local anglers) as for paddling. The takeout at the bridge is next to the SunWolf Outdoors Centre on the east bank of the river. Caution is suggested should you wish to paddle below this point. Boulders pushed into the river from the nearby Cheekye River have created a drop below the bridge that may be more than less-experienced kayakers or rafters can handle.

Guided rafting tours are offered on the **Elaho and Squamish Rivers.** The SunWolf Outdoors Centre, 70002 Government Rd, (604) 898-1537, Web site: www.mountain-inter.net/sunwolf, in Cheekye is the base for most of this activity. The Sea to Sky Kayaking School in nearby Brackendale conducts tours of the Cheakamus River and other whitewater sources around Squamish. Call (604) 898-5498.

The best whitewater kayaking around **Whistler** happens on the Cheakamus River. Put-in points include the upper section of the river accessed from the Cheakamus Lake Rd and the Whistler Interpretive Forest's Riverside Trail (see Mountain Biking, above), as well as on lower stretches of the river near its confluence with Callaghan and Brandywine Creeks near the Cal-Cheak Forest Recreation Site (see Parks/Camping, above). Consult Whistler River Adventures, (604) 932-3532, for information; also, Captain Holidays Kayak and Adventure School, (604) 905-2925. To join a guided rafting tour in Whistler, contact Blackcomb Whitewater Adventures, (800) 789-6111; Extreme Whitewater, (800) 606-7238; or Wedge Rafting, (604) 932- 7171.

Windsurfing/Sailing

Oregon has the Columbia Gorge, Squamish has the Spit. Although not as well known, the **Squamish Spit** is the launch pad for windsurfers, who rely on its predictable wind, known as a "squamish," which blows each afternoon. So strong is the force of the breeze that carries across Howe Sound that unwary windsurfers in the waters off the spit often can't right themselves if they get dunked. An emergency rescue service is on standby to pluck such hapless types from the water. The spit is a long breakwater located at the mouth of the Squamish River. On busy summer weekends, there can be more than a hundred cars parked here. At the very end of the spit is the windsurfer launch area; you can drive to a drop-off point beside it, unload your board, then park. To find your way to the spit, turn west off Hwy 99 on Cleveland, then north on Buckley, which blends into Government Rd. The gravel road to the spit starts on Government Rd's west side, just north of the Squamish Valley Feed Supply store. It is almost 3 miles (4.5 km) from the unmarked turnoff to the end of the spit. Turn left just before the road climbs up on the dike and follow along south to the very end. The spit is administered by the Squamish Windsurfing Society. Launch fees are currently $10 per day or $75 for a season's pass. (For information on daily wind conditions from May to October, dial (604) 926-WIND in Vancouver, or the society's Wind Talker phone line in Squamish, (604) 892-2235.)

For years, windsurfing on **Alta Lake** was the pastime of choice for many ski buffs in the off-season. Then along came the mountain bike. Windsurfing is still popular, although you'd be advised to wear a wet suit as the lake's glacier-fed waters are always bracingly cold. **Rainbow Park** on the west side of the lake is one of the best places to launch. There's even a section of the beach here set aside specifically for windsurfers. Take Alta Lake Rd west of Hwy 99 to reach the park. Other launch sites include **Lakeside Park** on the east side of Alta Lake. The turnoff to the park is indicated on the west side of Hwy 99. Windsurfers are available for rent here during summer months. For more information, contact the Escape Route in Whistler, (604) 938-3338.

Even though Whistler lies over 30 miles (50 km) inland from the Pacific, the ocean stills exerts an influence. As water in the Strait of Georgia evaporates and rises in summer months, cooler air is drawn towards it from the interior. Wind channels out to the strait through valleys such as Whistler's and creates ideal afternoon conditions for sailing and windsurfing, as well as keeping pesky biting insects down. Those interested in sailing should check out **Wayside Park** (see Swimming, below), a pocket of greenery at the south end of Alta Lake. Smaller than nearby Lakeside Park, Wayside Park has an open lawn that fronts a strip of beach on which stands a small boathouse. Laser sailboats and canoes are available for rent here. On Sunday afternoons during the spring and summer months, sailing races are held at Wayside, following a slalom course to the north end of the lake and back. You can either rent a Laser or take your own if you wish to enter. A dozen or so Lasers usually chase each other during the races, often led by a windsurfer.

Swimming

A pebble beach slopes gently into Howe Sound in **Porteau Cove Provincial Park** (see Parks/Camping and Picnics, above). On summer days when the tide is low and the sun high, the warm rocks heat the incoming waters, making swimming here a pleasure. For those who brave the ocean, there are hot showers nearby in the changing rooms. For some freshwater dipping, head to **Browning Lake** in Murrin Provincial Park (see Picnics, above).

Squamish is close to sea level, which means that the small lakes in the area actually warm up during summer months. **Alice Lake** (see Parks/Camping, above) is the biggest and has a sandy beach at both ends, changing rooms, and hot showers, but other sites are a bit of a letdown. Not that the Forest Service recreation sites at Cat, Brohm, and Levette Lakes won't satisfy; it's just that they're rustic by comparison. **Cat Lake** has a well-earned reputation as a place for swingers—rope swingers, that is. You can tell where the rope is by following the whoops made by those who arrive ahead of you. Makeshift rafts, free for the commandeering, are secured at several places around the shoreline. Pull out on one into the sunshine. The Cat Lake Forest Rd is on the east side of Hwy 99 north of Alice Lake Provincial Park. Watch for a highway sign that says "Whistler 44 km" and make the next right turn. Cat Lake lies 1.2 miles (2 km) from here. Note: On weekends, a gate blocks vehicle access near the lake. You'll have to walk a short distance uphill from the parking area.

Brohm Lake (see Mountain Biking, above) is just north of Cat Lake, on the west side of Hwy 99. Although its south end is quite marshy, it's north half is clear and deep. For the easiest approach, follow the trail from the parking lot down to the boat launch. Otherwise, head north along the rocky perimeter and find a spot to dive (or swing) in.

Levette Lake is a local favourite with those whose vehicles can make the climb. There's a very steep section just before the lake. Take it easy and you'll do fine. The road begins across from the North Vancouver Outdoors School on Paradise Valley Road (see Mountain Biking, above). Along the way you'll pass Evans Lake, site of a private forestry camp.

Aptly named **Swim Lake** in Brandywine Falls Provincial Park (see Parks/Camping, above) is a refreshing place to take a plunge. You'll have to make your way along a rough trail around the lake's perimeter to a somewhat marshy clearing at the far end. This is the most suitable location for swimming. The setting is glorious. Dagger-shaped Black Tusk dominates the skyline, while cool green smells waft out of the surrounding forest.

There are six parks in Whistler where you'll find beaches and diving docks. **Alpha Lake Park** is one of the smaller ones, as is **Green Lake Park** in the Emerald Estates neighbourhood. **Lakeside, Wayside** (a dock is moored just far enough offshore to make swimmers appreciate reaching it after a plunge in the cold waters of Alta Lake), and **Rainbow Parks** on Alta Lake and the beach at **Lost Lake** are the most popular by far. You'll find discreet clothing-optional bathing at Lost Lake, at the opposite end of the lake from the beach. For a map of the resort's parks, contact the municipality at (604) 932-5535.

Diving

As you turn into **Porteau Cove Provincial Park** (see Parks/Camping, above), you pass information signs, directed at divers, that detail the location of several marine vessels scuttled offshore specifically for underwater exploration. The first of these boats was sunk in 1981 when the park was opened. Marine life is attracted to such wrecks, making a dive even more exciting. (Note: Fishing is not permitted within the park.) Small floats positioned offshore help divers orient themselves. Affix a flag to one of these to warn boaters to stay well away. This is not a challenging dive but is an interesting introduction Howe Sound nonetheless.

For information on diving trips at Porteau Cove, consult *101 Dives from the Mainland of Washington and British Columbia* by Betty Pratt-Johnson or call Diversworld, (604) 732-1344, in Vancouver.

Fishing

You almost always see someone fishing in **Browning Lake,** Murrin Provincial Park's (see Picnics, above) most prominent feature. The lake is well stocked with rainbow trout each spring but gets fished out in a hurry. Still, that doesn't stop anglers, particularly small fry, from trying. This is a safe environment to test out flotation equipment such as inflatable rafts, float tubes, and belly boats.

For saltwater anglers there are boat launches at Sunset Marina, (604) 921-7476, 3 miles (5 km) north of Horseshoe Bay; Lions Bay Marina, (604) 921-7510, 6 miles (10 km) north of Horseshoe Bay in West Vancouver; and Sewell's Marina in Horseshoe Bay, (604) 921-3474. Sewell's also rents boats.

Freshwater lake fishing from the dock at **Alice Lake** may not be everyone's speed but there is a chance you'll hook a trout in these stocked waters, especially in May and June. There's also a boat launch at the north end of the lake (no motors) if you'd like to improve your chances by paddling to some of the less-accessible parts of the lake.

Freshwater river fishing happens on the **Cheakamus River** almost year-round. Fishing is strictly catch-and-release on all the rivers and creeks in the Squamish region. Unlike the nearby Squamish River into which it flows, water in the Cheakamus is clear year-round. Anglers cast from the banks of the Cheakamus for coho salmon in October and November, for steelhead from late February to April, and for dolly varden char year-round. Best access to the banks is from the north end of Paradise Valley Rd. Head west of Hwy 99 on Squamish Valley Rd to reach Paradise Valley Rd.

For **guided fishing trips** in the Squamish region, contact Neil McCutcheon, (604) 898-4139, or Steve's Scenic and Fishing Guided

Tours, (604) 892-5529, in Squamish, or Red Wind Trail Rides, (604) 898-2812, in Garibaldi Highland. Sources for information and guided fishing trips in the Whistler region include Whistler Backcountry Adventure, (604) 932-3474, Whistler Fishing Guides, (604) 932-4267, and Trout Country Fishing Guides, (604) 905-0088.

Wildlife

In spring and fall, the **Squamish Estuary** (see Hiking/Backpacking, above) provides a rest stop for migratory birds. In winter, the moderating influence of Howe Sound's ocean waters keeps much of the estuary ice-free. Elegant **trumpeter swans** spend the winter here, as do regal **bald eagles.** Bundle up and take a walk to see them.

Winter is the best time to walk the dike trail in the **Brackendale Eagle Reserve,** located farther north on the Squamish River. Short days and low light create an austere atmosphere. Eagles gather in the bare branches of the black cottonwood trees that tower above the Squamish River. The trees stand some distance away on the far shore, across the wide, milk-grey waters. Some trees are decorated with a dozen or more eagles, mute and motionless. As your eyes scan the forest perimeter, you can make out hundreds of such shapes. Although many of the eagles will head north in summer, others nest here year-round, as the bundles of twigs that bulge out near the tops of some of the cottonwoods attest. Equally at home here are the skittish **glaucous gulls.** If it's a lean winter, their carcasses are just as likely to be on the menu as the salmon carrion left from late fall coho runs on the Squamish River. In the early morning hours, before the daily arrival of bird-watchers, eagles frequent the banks on both sides of the river. Once the admirers appear, the eagles put the river between themselves and the gawkers.

Over the past 20 years, Brackendale sculptor Thor Froslev has led the fight for the protection of the Squamish winter eagle habitat. Six of his large wooden carvings, on which the aristocratic profile of an eagle is represented, stand at strategic points in the vicinity of the birds' winter home, including on Hwy 99. In 1996, the BC government announced the creation of a 1,482-acre (600-ha) sanctuary for the eagles, which can number more than 3,769 in winter. Froslev has now turned to monitoring the health of the Squamish River. Without healthy salmon runs, there would be far fewer eagles drawn to feed in this relatively small but vital stretch of water. Froslev maintains his vigilance from his home in the Brackendale Art Gallery, which he established in 1969. Located on Government Rd several kilometres north of the dike where most eagle viewing takes place, he has assembled a coterie of artists to conduct workshops and concerts, with the eagles and river as the core theme. As well, the Brackendale Gallery offers daily walking tours, led by naturalists, of the prime eagle-viewing areas. The gallery also arranges river tours that give visitors a chance to see eagles in more secluded habitats such as nearby Baynes Island. For more information, call the gallery at (604) 898-3333.

Photography

As Hwy 99 heads north of Squamish, it climbs a long hill, the top of which is one of the most stunning viewpoints in the province—a big claim. Once you've seen the skyline from the **Tantalus Viewpoint,** you'll want to stop whenever you're passing by and snap a few more shots of its ever-changing moods and snowfields. There are pullouts on each side of the highway, which eliminate the worry of having to cross this busy section of road for the best angle. An immense sheet of ice grips the upper slopes of the Tantalus Range year-round. Its 11 peaks, from Mount Thyestes to Pelion Mountain, are clearly outlined as seen from here.

Horseback Riding

If you'd like to explore the Squamish region on horseback, call Cheekye Stables, (604) 898-3432, which is on the Squamish Valley Rd 1 mile (1.6 km) east of Cheekye. In Whistler, contact Whistler Trail Riding, (604) 932-6623. The stables are located on Mons Rd on the east side of Hwy 99, 1.5 miles (2.4 km) north of Whistler Village.

outside in

Attractions

The good times roll year-round in **Whistler,** with daily street entertainment, and many festivals from June to September. Call (800) WHISTLER and ask in particular about the Whistler Mountain Music Festival.

Restaurants

Caramba ☆☆ For great food, upbeat atmosphere, and value in Whistler, you really can't beat this fun, boisterous, Mediterranean-influenced restaurant. Kids and adults both love the platter of three-cheese macaroni after a strenuous day on the slopes. *12-4314 Main St (in Village North), Whistler; (604) 938-1879; $$.*

Il Caminetto di Umberto ☆☆ Few things can top fresh pasta and a bottle of red wine after a day on the mountains. The less expensive Trattoria di Umberto in the Mountainside Lodge, (604)932-5858, appeals to the more informal crowd for pasta and rotisserie items. *4242 Village Stroll (across from Crystal Lodge), Whistler; (604) 932-4442; $$.*

Joel's Restaurant at Nicklaus North ☆☆ Joel's is quickly becoming the restaurant to escape to; here (a few miles from the Village) you can still get a last-minute reservation and a buttery beef tenderloin so good that you'll find yourself forgiving the few flaws in the appetizers. *8080 Nicklaus North Blvd (5 km/3 miles north of Village at Nicklaus North Clubhouse), Whistler; (604) 932-1240; $$–$$$.*

La Rua (Le Chamois) ☆☆☆ The food at this stylish but comfortable restaurant is nuova Mediterranean with Asian tweaks—and some of the best in Whistler. No one makes better lamb and there's always an unforgettable vegetarian dish. *4557 Blackcomb Way (Upper Village on Blackcomb), Whistler; (604) 932-5011; $$$.*

Quattro at the Pinnacle ☆☆☆ This cornerstone restaurant in the Pinnacle Hotel is upbeat and innovative. The Italian passion for food comes through here in dishes that are simple and uncomplicated. Desserts are stunning. *4319 Main St (in Village North Town Plaza), Whistler; (604) 905-4844; $$$.*

Rim Rock Cafe and Oyster Bar ☆☆☆ Filled to the rafters with a hip local crowd, this cozy cafe has been dishing out great food for years. The freshest seafood appears on the specials sheet in all sorts of lovely incarnations. *2101 Whistler Rd (just north of Creekside, in Highland Lodge), Whistler; (604) 932-5565; $$$.*

Ristorante Araxi ☆☆ The Italian menu at Araxi speaks with a decidedly West Coast accent—the chef does an excellent job with fresh fish, free-range fowl, and house-made pastas. The wine list is impressive (though pricey). *4222 Village Square (central Whistler Village), Whistler; (604) 932-4540; $$$.*

Sushi Village ☆☆ A civilized hush hovers over this refreshingly modest Japanese eatery, where the staff is knowledgeable, gracious—and familiar year after year. Consistently delicious sushi and sashimi plates are prepared by animated experts at the counter. *4272 Mountain Square (2nd floor of Westbrook Hotel), Whistler; (604) 932-3330; $$.*

Val d'Isère ☆☆☆ Whether you want to impress or be impressed, you can't go wrong in this sophisticated dining room. Reserve a window seat and start with a slice of onion pie, a dense, smoky specialty, or warm smoked salmon in a horseradish cream. *4433 Sundial Pl (upstairs in St. Andrews House in Whistler Village), Whistler; (604) 932-4666; $$$.*

Wildflower Restaurant (Chateau Whistler Resort) ☆☆ Splashy Chateau Whistler's restaurant melds a big, formal space with folk-arty touches. The menu uses local Northwest products—free-range chicken, wild salmon, and organic produce—to create inspired dishes. *4599 Chateau Blvd (at base of Blackcomb Mountain, in Chateau Whistler), Whistler; (604) 938-8000; $$$.*

Cheaper Eats

Auntie Em's Kitchen Small, cozy Auntie Em's (she's not in Kansas anymore) is tucked away in the Marketplace Mall and offers hearty breakfasts and healthy soups, salads, and sandwiches. *129-4340 Lorimer Rd, Whistler; (604) 932-1163; $.*

Gone Bakery & Soup Company After you've gone skiing or hiking, Gone Bakery is a welcome spot for refuelling. In the morning there are croissants and muffins; at lunch, expect hearty soups with hot loaves of bread; and at night, it's just desserts. *4205 Village Square, Whistler; (604) 905-4663; $.*

Hoz's Creekside Cafe & Pub Hoz's Creekside is a friendly and casual neighbourhood joint that locals give the nod for the best and biggest burger. Families are welcome and the bar menu is available until late at night. *2129 Lake Placid Rd, Whistler; (604) 932-4424; $.*

Mallard Bar (Chateau Whistler) Those on a budget can confidently stride into Chateau Whistler's Mallard Room, ease down into a plush loveseat by the huge river-rock fireplace, nurse a plate of nachos and a pint of Black Tusk Ale for an hour or so after skiing, and feel like the sultan of Oman. *4599 Chateau Blvd, Whistler; (604) 938-8000; $.*

Mondo Pizza When you're dining on a budget, there's always pizza. At Mondo, the pies arrive hot and huge from the brick oven, and you can save even more dough by checking for discount ads in *The Pique*, Whistler's weekly magazine. *Village Marketplace, Whistler; (604) 938-9554; $.*

Mongolie Grill Select your combination of seafood, meat, and vegetables, as well as one of the Mongolie's 18 sauces. The food is weighed and then cooked in a wok in front of your eyes. The prices are right, and the place is very kid-friendly. *201-4295 Blackcomb Way, Whistler; (604) 938-9416; $.*

South Side Deli The ingredients in the omelets at this local hangout are considerably more exotic than what you'll find at other British Columbia roadside breakfast joints. In addition, the produce is always fresh and the portions are generous. *1202 Lake Placid Rd, Whistler; (604) 932-3368; $.*

Thai One On You might have a hard time finding this place, tucked into a corner of Le Chamois in Blackcomb Village, but keep searching for it, because the Thai cuisine is respectable and, most important, reasonably priced. *4557 Blackcomb Way, Whistler; (604) 932-4822; $.*

Lodgings

Chateau Whistler Resort ☆☆☆ This Paul Bunyan–sized country mansion is the place to see and be seen on Whistler—where a valet parks even your ski gear. The health spa is especially swank: a heated pool flowing both indoors and out, allowing swimmers to splash away under the chairlifts or soak in the Jacuzzi under the stars. *4599 Chateau Blvd (at base of Blackcomb Mountain), Whistler, BC V0N 1B4; (604) 938-8000 or (800) 606-8244; $$$.*

Delta Whistler Resort ☆ It may not be as grand as Chateau Whistler nor as chic as Le Chamois, but this resort, one of the oldest and largest hotels in the area, offers nearly 300 rooms, restaurant and bar, exercise room, swimming pool, and dome-covered year-round tennis courts. *4050 Whistler Way (Whistler Village); PO Box 550, Whistler, BC V0N 1B0; (604) 932-1982 or (800) 515-4050; $$$.*

Delta Whistler Village Suites [*unrated*] Big is in here, and big this place will be, with 207 suites and mini-condos at the edge of Village North (which, if Delta Whistler has a say in the matter, will no longer be on the edge of town). Plans for plenty of shops, three restaurants, and perhaps Whistler's biggest nightclub. *4308 Main St (in Village North), Whistler, BC V0N 1B4; (800) 268-1133; $$$.*

Durlacher Hof ☆☆☆ This legendary Austrian pension, complete with edelweiss, is a short ride from the base of Whistler-Blackcomb. The owners' painstaking attention to detail is evident in the cozy après-ski area and the immaculate rooms (some suites) with hand-carved pine furniture. *7055 Nesters Rd (call for directions); PO Box 1125, Whistler, BC V0N 1B0; (604) 932-1924; $$$.*

Edelweiss ☆☆ This nonsmoking Bavarian-style guest house, run in a European fashion, is one of our favourites of its kind (there are many around Whistler). The eight rooms are simple and spotlessly clean, with down comforters and private baths. *7162 Nancy Greene Dr (1 mile/0.6 km north of Whistler Village in White Gold Estates); PO Box 850, Whistler, BC V0N 1B0; (604) 932-3641; $$.*

Edgewater ☆ While many Whistler accommodations make the most of every priceless square foot of space, the 12-room Edgewater sits in solitude on its own 45-acre (18-ha) Green Lake estate. It's probably the only hotel in Whistler where you see more wildlife than life that is wild. *8841 Hwy 99 (3.75 miles/6 km north of Village, across street from Meadow Park Sports Centre); Box 369, Whistler, BC V0N 1B0; (604) 932-0688; $$$.*

Howe Sound Inn and Brewing Company ☆ This one-of-a-kind inn (and what we like to call the roadhouse for the 21st century) is a perfect stop on the way up (or down) from Whistler. The 20 rooms are simple, warmed by the use of wood and window seats. *37801 Cleveland Ave (at south end of town); PO Box 978, Squamish, BC V0N 3G0; (604) 892-2603 or (800) 919-ALES; $$.*

Le Chamois ☆☆ This inviting six-storey condo/hotel, though somewhat dwarfed by its gargantuan neighbour, the Chateau Whistler, has a sleek, refined air. Single bedrooms are built to accommodate 4 people; each includes a living area with either a fold-out sofa bed or a Murphy bed (and every room has a view, though views of the mountain cost more).*4557 Blackcomb Way (at base of Blackcomb Mountain), Upper Village; PO Box 1044, Whistler, BC V0N 1B0; (604) 932-8700 or (800) 777-0185; $$$.*

Pan Pacific [*unrated*] The Pan Pacific's first resort lodge has nabbed one of the most desirable locations in Whistler/Blackcomb, just a few paces from the base of each world-class mountain. Each of the 121 suites has a fireplace, kitchenette, and all the amenities we've come to expect in a top-rated hotel chain. *4320 Sundial Crescent (at base of Whistler and Blackcomb gondolas), Whistler, BC V0N 1B4; (604) 905-2999 or (800) 905-9995; $$$.*

Timberline Lodge ☆ This is the kind of spot where you feel at home clomping into the lobby in your ski boots to warm your toes by the enormous fireplace. Timberline's 42 rooms are simple and rustic; some rooms have fireplaces, others have balconies, and a few have both. *4122 Village Green (adjacent to Conference Centre in Whistler Village), Whistler, BC V0N 1B4; (604) 932-5211 or (800) 777-0185; $$$.*

Cheaper Sleeps

Fireside Lodge This big, comfortable lodge has 12 private rooms, a dormitory that sleeps 31, and a large stone fireplace in an impressive living room. It's run on a cooperative basis: bring your own groceries, bedding, and towels, and do your own cooking and cleaning. *2117 Nordic Dr (Nordic Estates), Whistler, BC V0N 1B2; (604) 932-4545; $.*

Garibaldi Inn Slumbering in Squamish is not as nice as staying in Whistler, but there are plenty of reasonably priced lodgings, including this small 25-room inn. Nine of the rooms even have kitchenettes, which might save you from blowing your wad in too many restaurants. *38012 3rd Ave, Squamish, BC V0N 3G0; (604) 892-5204; $.*

Rainbow Creek Bed and Breakfast Almost taller than it is wide, this three-storey log home is reminiscent of a terrific tree house. The B&B has three guest rooms (two with a private bath) and a spare fridge for storing your food. *8243 Alpine Way (PO Box 1142), Whistler, BC V0N 1B0; (604) 932-7001; $.*

Southside Lodge This "lodge" is more like a back entrance to six low-key rooms with baths. It's primarily for the young at heart. And the longer you stay, the lower the rates. The location is great—especially if you don't have wheels. *2101 Lake Placid Rd (Whistler Creek), Whistler, BC V0N 1B0; (604) 938-6477; $.*

Steelhead Inn This historic inn, located on the Thompson River just off the Trans-Canada Hwy, is one of the few notable lodgings along the Coast Mountain route. Fork over an extra $10 for one of the four rooms with a private bath so you won't have to fight over the two potties shared by the eight units without. Reasonably priced dinners are offered in the restaurant. *PO Box 100, Spences Bridge, BC V0K 2L0; (250) 458-2398; $.*

Sunwolf Outdoor Centre Sunwolf offers 10 recently refurbished guest cabins scattered along the Cheakamus River. Cabins boast hardwood floors, four-poster beds, *and* a single day bed. Whitewater rafting tours are offered in summer, eagle viewing in winter. *70002 Government Rd (PO Box 244), Brackendale, BC V0N 1H0; (604) 898-1537; $.*

Swiss Cottage Bed & Breakfast White Gold Estates is turning into B&B heaven—and this cottage in a quiet cul-de-sac is one of its gems. Lost Lake trails are just outside the inn's door, and the walk to Blackcomb is easy. *7321 Fitzsimmons Dr (PO Box 1209), Whistler, BC V0N 1B0; (604) 932-6062; $.*

Whistler Hostel Aside from being 15 minutes south of Whistler Village, this former fishing lodge makes a primo base for windsurfing on Alta Lake. The eight bunk rooms (four bunks to a room) are upstairs, and one private double is available. *5678 Alta Lake Rd, Whistler, BC V0N 1B0; (604) 932-5492; $.*

More Information

BC Forest Service, Squamish Forest District: *(604) 898-2100.*

BC Parks, Garibaldi-Sunshine Coast Regional Office, Alice Lake Provincial Park: *(604) 898-3678.*

Blackcomb Mountain: *(604) 932-3141; Web site address: www.blackcomb.com.*

Geological Survey of Canada (maps): *Suite 101, 605 Robson St, Vancouver, BC V6B 5G3, (604) 666-0271. Store hours are 8:30am–4:30pm, Mon–Fri.*

Pemberton Chamber of Commerce: *(604) 894-6175.*

Squamish Chamber of Commerce: *(604) 892-9244.*

Whistler Activity and Information Centre: *(604) 932-2394.*

Whistler Chamber of Commerce: *(604) 932-5528.*

Whistler Mountain: *(604) 932-3434; Web site address: www.whistler-mountain.com.*

Pemberton and Lillooet

North of Whistler from Pemberton to Lillooet in the northeast corner of the Lower Mainland, including Nairn Falls, Birkenhead, Joffre Lakes, and Stein Valley Nlaka'pamux Provincial Parks.

For over a century, Pemberton existed in something less than splendid isolation from the rest of the Lower Mainland. Travel in and out of the valley was regulated by the railway. When a highway was finally punched through from Whistler in 1975, the long period of separation ended. At first, there was only a trickle of traffic along this stretch of Highway 99, mostly logging trucks southbound for Squamish and the occasional carload of climbers headed north to Joffre Glacier. In the past decade, the pace of tourism has accelerated. The 1986 World Exposition in Vancouver kick-started bus tours to Whistler and beyond; in subsequent years, the paving of the Duffey Lake Road made the corridor between Pemberton and Lillooet a breeze to explore. (Until then, the standing joke was that this former logging road was always under two feet of mud and four feet of snow.)

Today, Pemberton is experiencing a growth in both visitors and new arrivals who are taking up residence in this agriculturally and recreationally rich valley. Quick access to hiking, climbing, mountain biking, and backcountry ski-touring routes is one of the main reasons for the surge in popularity. Unlike Whistler, very little of this activity is centred in the small town, the population of which is estimated at between 500 and 4,000, depending on who you consult. Instead, a variety of wilderness outfitters, guides, and ranches are located throughout the 30-mile (50-km) stretch between the head of Lillooet Lake and the north end of the valley. This is the traditional territory of the Lil'wat Nation, who today are headquartered in Mount Currie and D'Arcy, with smaller communities sprinkled along Lillooet Lake. From the time of their first contact with Europeans, the Lil'wat have always been characterized by their friendliness towards visitors. Although such openness hasn't always worked to their advantage (they are now involved in complex treaty negotiations with the provincial government), you'll be welcomed at events such as the Lillooet Lake Rodeo, held each May in Mount Currie, and at the salmon festival in D'Arcy in August.

As the Sea to Sky Highway winds between the Cayoosh Pass, Lillooet, and Hat Creek, it passes through the most notably varied terrain of its entire length. Transitions between the other biogeoclimatic zones are more subtle. Here the change from coastal temperate zone to aridity occurs abruptly. Much of this area lies in the rain shadow of the Coast and Cascade Mountains. By the time the last moisture in the clouds has been raked off by the peaks around Cayoosh Pass, there's little left to water the countryside to the east. Ponderosa pine and sage take over from western hemlock and devil's club.

Getting There

As the Pemberton Valley opens up, so too does the number of roads leading off from Highway 99 that will be of interest to those seeking backcountry adventure. The main link between Pemberton and Lillooet (60 miles/100 km) is Highway 99 (the Duffey Lake Road), which runs in a vaguely east-west direction. Alternatively, the paved Pemberton Valley Road runs 16 miles (26 km) west through the valley, then links with the gravel-surfaced Lillooet River Road. In summer, the Hurley-Donnely Road leads north from Lillooet River Road to Gold Bridge and Bralorne, the entrance to the south Chilcotin backcountry. (Note: Neither of these roads is plowed in winter.) Highway 40 connects Gold Bridge with Lillooet and Highway 99. The D'Arcy–Anderson Lake Road is paved and leads 25 miles (40 km) north from Mount Currie and Highway 99 to the small community of D'Arcy on the shore of Anderson Lake.

Adjoining Areas

NORTH: **The Cariboo Highway**

SOUTH: **The Fraser Valley**

EAST: **The Coquihalla Highway**

WEST: **Whistler and the Sea to Sky Highway**

inside out

Parks/Camping

There are two provincial parks in the Pemberton region with well-organized campgrounds. **Nairn Falls Provincial Park** (88 vehicle/tent sites) is located just south of Pemberton beside Hwy 99, and features captivating views and day-use areas. As it flows through the park, the **Green River** carves its way through a mass of granite at the foot of Mount Currie. Having picked up volume from the Soo River and Rutherford Creek on its way from Green Lake in the Whistler area, it swirls and crashes its way along until it reaches a fracture in the granite. Suddenly, its broad shape is transformed into a thundering column of whitewater as it drops 197 feet (60 m) at **Nairn Falls.** As abruptly as the theatrics begin, the river reverts to its former character and hurries on towards Lillooet Lake. Unlike Shannon Falls or Brandywine Falls (see Whistler and the Sea to Sky Highway chapter), Nairn Falls does not drop down a sheer pathway but instead boils through several frothy cauldrons. Over the centuries, silt carried in the water has scoured out bowls in which the whitewater churns momentarily before surging to the rocks below. Clouds of spray are jettisoned above the maelstrom in random patterns that are pleasant and hypnotic to watch. This is one of the most (hydro)dynamic sites in the Whistler region. If you're just visiting for the day, park at the picnic area just inside the park gates beside Hwy 99. The 1.1-mile (1.8-km) trail to the falls is smooth and only moderately difficult to walk. Fine views of Mount Currie present themselves along the way. Once at the falls, a wire-mesh fence keeps visitors back from the edge while still permitting a good view of the river's violent action.

Birkenhead Lake Provincial Park (103 vehicle/tent sites, including 9 double sites) is somewhat more remote, an hour's drive north of Mount Currie near D'Arcy. It also has mountain-biking trails and paddling and fishing options on the lake (see those sections, below). The gravelled Blackwater Forest Service Rd leads 10.5 miles (17 km) west from the D'Arcy–Anderson Lake Rd to Birkenhead Lake. The park has a wilderness camping area situated 1.2 miles (2 km) from the vehicle/tent sites at the northwest corner of the lake. You can either walk to it along a pleasant trail, or paddle in from the boat launch. (Watch for a large red marker affixed to one of the sturdy trees that surround the wilderness site, indicating where to land.) This is a delightful, arm's-length approach to camping at Birkenhead.

Both Birkenhead Lake and Nairn Falls Provincial Parks fill up quickly on summer weekends. Signs on the D'Arcy–Anderson Lake Rd inform visitors when the Birkenhead campsite is full so that travellers don't make the 21-mile (34-km) round trip in vain. A fee of about $10 is charged at both parks. For a map of provincial parks in the Lower Mainland, contact BC Parks, (604) 929-1291, in North Vancouver. For more information on Nairn Falls and Birkenhead Lake Provincial Parks, contact BC Parks in Squamish, (604) 898-3678.

There's camping at a variety of Forest Service recreation sites sprinkled throughout the valley and along Lillooet Lake. The **Owl Creek** sites are located 4 miles (7 km) north of Mount Currie on the D'Arcy–Anderson Lake Rd. There are two separate sites on opposite sides of Owl Creek, where it meets the Birkenhead River (see Canoeing/Kayaking/Boating, below). Farther north towards D'Arcy you'll find four campsites beside noisy **Spetch Creek** in a pleasantly forested location off the D'Arcy–Anderson Lake Rd.

Recreation sites on Lillooet Lake are located along gravel-surfaced Lillooet Lake Rd at **Strawberry Point** (road marker "6 Km"; see Beaches/Swimming, below), **Twin Creeks** (marker "10 Km"; see Canoeing/Kayaking/Boating, below), **Lizzie Bay** (marker "15 Km"), **Driftwood Bay** (marker "16 Km"), and at **Lizzie Lake** (see Hiking, below) on a logging road 7.5 miles (12 km) east of Lizzie Bay. Lillooet Lake Rd begins 9 miles (15 km) east of Mount Currie and runs south off Hwy 99. For a map of Forest Service recreation sites in the Squamish Forest District, contact the BC Forest Service in Squamish, (604) 898-2100.

Residents of the Pemberton Valley have been camping at **Tenquille Lake** since the 1920s. An old cabin that was constructed there in 1940 is now best left to the pack rats, but it still provides shelter if needed. Access to the lake, the starting point for exploring the surrounding peaks, is from either a trailhead beside the Lillooet River Bridge at the north end of Pemberton Valley, or from a trailhead that begins about 10.5 miles (17 km) north on the Hurley River Rd, followed by another 1.2 miles (2 km) on the Tenquille Lake Logging Rd. Either way, count on a demanding 7.5-mile (12-km) hike to reach the lake. A step-by-step description of the trail appears in *Best Hikes and Walks of Southwestern B.C.* by Dawn Hanna.

Due to the extremely rocky terrain, wilderness campsites at **Joffre Lakes Provincial Recreation Area** (see Hiking, below) are difficult to find. For those who plan to overnight in this park, follow the hiking trail on the southwest side of Upper Joffre Lake to where the alpine forest provides some slight shelter. There are no facilities here other than an outhouse and a few rough camping spots that have been cleared over the years. Campers are expected to remove all traces of their visit. Joffre Lakes Provincial Recreation Area is located on the Duffey Lake Rd section of Hwy 99, about 14 miles (22 km) northeast of Mount Currie.

There is less likelihood of being rained out when camping in the Lillooet region than there is farther west in the Coast Mountains. As Hwy 99 leads from Duffey Lake to Lillooet, a provincial park campground and several small Forest Service recreation sites suitable for camping appear beside the lake and along Cayoosh Creek. At the forested east end of **Duffey Lake,** a provincial campground with 6 rough vehicle/tent sites is the best-organized site and also one of the most scenic, with views across the dark lake to Mount Chief Pascall and the Joffre Glacier Group (see Hiking, below). The biting insects here are bothersome during much of the summer and are so aggressive that even a steady breeze doesn't deter them. Several smaller sites are located along Hwy 99 at **Roger, Cottonwood,** and **Cinnamon Creeks** beside Cayoosh Creek as it flows towards Lillooet. For a map of Forest Service recreation sites in the Lillooet area, contact the Ministry of Forests, (250) 256-1200. For information on Duffey Lake Provincial Park, call (604) 898-3678.

One of the most extensive campsites in the region is BC Hydro's **Seton Lake Reservoir** recreation area, 3 miles (5 km) west of Lillooet on Hwy 99. Located on the south side of the road, 47 vehicle/tent sites are spread out in a forested location beside Cayoosh Creek and are open between May and September. One of the campsite's more unusual features is an old Chinese stone oven, a remnant of the gold-rush days in the 1800s. A marker points to its location near the east end of the campsite. For information on Seton Lake and other BC Hydro recreation sites throughout the province, call (604) 528-1812 or visit BC Hydro's Web site: www.bchydro.com.

Attractively situated **Marble Canyon Provincial Park** (see also Rock Climbing, below) lies 22 miles (35 km) northeast of Lillooet on Hwy 99. Limestone cliffs tower above the campground's 34 vehicle/tent sites, while the placid waters of Turquoise Lake reflect the sky. A waterfall on the opposite side of the lake pours forth a steady stream; the sound helps mute all else. There is a charge of about $10 per site from May to September. For more information, contact BC Parks, (250) 851-3000.

As you travel west to east through the Sea to Sky corridor between Pemberton and Lillooet, you enter a transition zone. Coastal terrain gives way to that of the interior, and in the process the alpine tundra biogeoclimatic zone becomes more accessible. Around Pemberton, you may have to hike to an elevation as much as 2,000 feet (630 m) higher to reach the alpine than you would an hour's drive farther east. A good example of this is at **Blowdown Lake,** where you'll find wilderness camping on the alpine perimeter at the 6,700-foot (2044-m) elevation, well below the benchmark of 7,382 feet (2250 m) in Pemberton and Whistler. Gott Peak rises above the lake to the north, while several equally rugged companions flank the lake to the south. Although much of the perimeter of the lake is marshy or touched by snow even in July, there are campsites on higher ground at the south end of the lake. One of the advantages of camping here is that the nearby alpine zone is easily reached for exploring with a lightweight pack. The approach to Blowdown Lake begins from Hwy 99, 2.2 miles (3.5 km) east of the Duffey Lake Provincial Campground (see above). A logging and mining road climbs more than 10 miles (16 km) from Hwy 99 to Blowdown Pass. Most vehicles can make it as far as 6 miles (10 km) up the road before parking at a level area next to an abandoned metal-and-wood structure. If you have a four-wheel-drive vehicle, it's possible to go farther, but deep ditches and washouts will eventually halt all but the most hard-core drivers. On foot, it's a 3.5-mile (6-km) hike to the lake from the metal-and-wood structure, and another 1.2 miles (2 km) to the pass. The lake and camping area lie a short distance from the road.

The **South Chilcotin** wilderness, one of the most pristine and least protected backcountry areas in the region, is reached via Gold Bridge, about 55 miles (90 km) west of Lillooet or northwest of Pemberton on the Hurley-Bralorne Rd. Over 90 miles (150 km) of trails begin from **Gun** and **Spruce Lakes** and lead through mountain lakes, midelevation grasslands, timbered slopes, and subalpine meadows surrounded by spectacular mountain peaks. Over 20 routes and 18 Forest Service recreation sites are detailed in a guide map ("Spruce Lake Trails Area") published by the Lillooet Forest District. To obtain a copy, call (250) 256-1200.

Hiking

One of the oldest hiking routes in the Pemberton Valley leads 7.5 miles (12 km) from the trailhead off the Hurley River Rd to **Tenquille Lake** (see Parks/Camping, above). During the first half of the 20th century, miners used pack-horse routes to reach the subalpine region surrounding Tenquille and Owl Lakes. More recently, some of these overgrown trails have been reopened for hiking and mountain biking. An alpine trail system that links Tenquille and Owl Creek, as well as the original horse trail from Tenquille to Barber's Valley and Ogre Lake, has been constructed. The revitalizing of the trails around Tenquille, coupled with those around nearby Birkenhead and Blackwater Lakes, makes this region one of the best destinations for experienced hikers and mountain bikers. For trail information, consult Spud Valley Sports, (604) 894-6630, or High Line Cycles, (604) 894-6625, in Pemberton. For an outline of these trails, consult the Squamish Forest District Recreation Map. Call the Ministry of Forests at (604) 898-2100 or the Squamish Chamber of Commerce, (604) 892-9244, to request a copy.

Farther north, a rough trail follows the Lillooet River into the **Upper Lillooet Headwaters** (see Wildlife, below), a sublime wilderness region that has recently become a provincial park. Plan on a 2.5-mile (4-km) hike from the trailhead at **Salal Creek** to reach broad sandbars that stand revealed in late summer on more open sections of the Lillooet River. To reach the trailhead, follow the Pemberton Valley and Lillooet River Rds 30 miles (50 km) northwest of Pemberton. Turn left immediately after the road crosses Salal Creek and drive about 0.6 mile (1 km) to the trailhead at the end of a rough but passable range road.

Lizzie Lake (see Parks/Camping, above) marks the western trailhead of an extended 40-mile (60-km) hiking route that transects **Stein Valley Nlaka'pamux Heritage Park.** Allow a week or more to cover the entire length to the park's eastern boundary near Lytton. For those without much time but who still wish to get a look at the Stein, try the day hike from Lizzie Lake to the Lizzie Creek Cabin in the subalpine zone (4 miles/6 km return). For a complete overview of Stein Valley Nlaka'pamux Heritage Park, including detailed hiking and climbing routes, consult the *Stein Valley Wilderness Guidebook* by Gordon White and *A Guide to Climbing and Hiking in Southwestern B.C.* by Bruce Fairley. Note: Extensive damage was done to parts of the Stein's landscape by a forest fire in 1996, making some hiking routes difficult to distinguish, particularly west of Scudamore Creek to the midpoint in the upper canyon. For more information on current trail conditions, contact BC Parks, (250) 851-3000.

The **Gold Rush Heritage Trail** is a slice of British Columbia's colonial history, a remnant of the Cariboo gold rush in the late 1850s. Short sections of the trail—actually an old road built by Royal Engineers—can still be discerned in places along the east side of Lillooet Lake. The biggest challenge is simply finding traces of the trail. One of the best places to begin is from **St. Agnes Well Hot Spring,** located 30 miles (50 km) south of Hwy 99 on the Lillooet Lake Rd. The turnoff to the springs and the heritage trail is directly across from hydro tower marker "68.2." To find the Gold Rush Heritage Trail, begin walking north beside the swift-flowing Lillooet River from the hot springs. Another section of the trail can be seen on the hillside above Rogers Creek, about 2 miles (3 km) north of the turnoff to St. Agnes Well. You can easily hike up to it from the bridge over the creek. A good source of information is the Squamish Forest District Recreation Map, available from the Forest Service, (604) 898-2100, or the Squamish Chamber of Commerce, (604) 892-9244.

At present, one of the most complete sections of the **Sea to Sky Trail** (see Whistler and the Sea to Sky Highway chapter) runs between Gramsons, 10.5 miles (17 km) north of Mount Currie on the D'Arcy–Anderson Lake Rd, and the trail's northern terminus (and the road's) in D'Arcy. The jewel in this well-marked, picturesque 25-mile (40-km) one-way stretch is Birkenhead Lake. If you'd like to get right to the heart of this hike, a good place to begin is **Birkenhead Lake Provincial Park** (see Parks/Camping, above). Pick up the trail next to the boat launch and follow it south as it climbs above the shoreline for about 4.5 miles (7 km) towards Gramsons. For a map of the Sea to Sky Hike and Bike Trail, contact the Whistler Chamber of Commerce, (604) 932-5528. (Note: The section of the Sea to Sky Trail described here is part of the 31-mile/50-km loop route described in Mountain Biking, below. What has been omitted for hikers is the 6-mile/10-km portion on the D'Arcy–Anderson Lake Rd.)

Perhaps the toughest but most rewarding hike in the region is to Upper Joffre Lake in the **Joffre Lakes Provincial Recreational Area** (see Parks/Camping, above). The three lakes in this subalpine chain are strung like a turquoise necklace on the mountainside below the massive Joffre Glacier Group. It's a short walk from the parking lot beside Hwy 99 to Lower Joffre, but a stiff 5-mile (8-km) hike to Middle Joffre and another 2.5 miles (4 km) to Upper Joffre, a total distance of 15 miles (24 km) return. Expect wet trail conditions throughout the year, particularly as you approach Middle Joffre. You'll have to scramble in places where loose soil conditions make for treacherous footing. The reward of reaching Upper Joffre cannot be overstated: an amphitheatre of crevassed, blue-hued ice rises directly above the lake's south end and embraces most of the mountainside in a sweep from Mount Taylor to Joffre Peak and Mount Chief Pascall. Cool winds blow down from the icefield; you'll begin looking for shelter from the breeze almost as soon as you arrive at Upper Joffre.

Blowdown Pass (see Parks/Camping, above) is one of the approaches used when hiking into **Stein Valley Nlaka'pamux Heritage Park.** Hikers are assisted by a logging and mining road that leads 9 miles (15 km) to the pass from Hwy 99 and then descends towards Cottonwood Creek. Plan on taking five to seven days to complete the 32-mile (52-km) moderately difficult hike from Blowdown Pass to the Stein trailhead near Lytton. For those with their sights set a little lower, there's good alpine hiking around Blowdown Pass itself. **Gott Peak** (elevation 8,350 feet/2545 m) is an easy 2.5-mile (4-km) round-trip scramble from the pass. However, watch the loose footing and also the weather, which is prone to change quickly. Great views of surrounding peaks and wildlife are guaranteed on clear summer days. For a complete description of this trail and hiking routes around Blowdown Pass, consult Gordon White's *Stein Valley Wilderness Guidebook.*

Mountain Biking

North of Pemberton the **Sea to Sky Trail** (see Whistler and the Sea to Sky Highway chapter) has received some of the most concentrated attention, as trail builders fine-tune the route between Mount Currie and D'Arcy. At present, a 31-mile (50-km) loop runs between D'Arcy (the trail's northern terminus) and the whistle stop of Gramsons on the BC Rail line south of Birkenhead Lake (see Parks/Camping, above). Quite a variety of terrain is up for grabs along the way. Decide which section best suits your skill level. For beginners, the 4.3-mile (7-km) trail that leads around Birkenhead Lake is a good route on which to practise. Much of it is level as it follows an old fire road along the west side of the lake. Only one section is so steep that you'll need to dismount. A more challenging section lies between Birkenhead Lake and D'Arcy, particularly the steep descent on **Smell the Fear,** a short but technically demanding piece of singletrack. For those who wish a gentler approach, a power-line road is an alternative. The Sea to Sky trail is well marked along this route, which passes beside the Forest Service recreation site at Blackwater Lake near the halfway point between Birkenhead Lake and D'Arcy. A 6-mile (10-km) intermediate-level section of trail runs between the south end of Birkenhead Lake and Gramsons. At Gramsons you can either retrace the route or follow the D'Arcy–Anderson Lake Rd (see Cycling, below) north to where you began. For a detailed map of the Sea to Sky Trail, contact the Whistler Chamber of Commerce, (604) 932-5528.

Aside from the Sea to Sky Trail, the heart of mountain biking in the Pemberton region is centred around **Mosquito** and **Ivey Lakes.** The two lakes are tucked in behind a knoll on the north side of the valley between Pemberton and Mount Currie. A dozen or more trails wind in and out of each other; principal among them are the **Mosquito Lake Trail, Ridge Loop,** and **Lake Loop Trails.** Although much of the fun is concentrated around Mosquito Lake (where a Forest Service recreation site is located) and on the east side of Ivey Lake Rd, the most challenging trails—**Psychopath, Indy 500,** and **Blood, Sweat, and Fear**—run along the west side of the BC Hydro power-line grid. More placid rides include the **River Trail,** which follows a dike along the east side of the Lillooet River for a considerable distance. Easiest access to the trails is from Hwy 99 between Pemberton and Mount Currie, just east of the Lillooet River Bridge. The River Trail begins beside the bridge. To reach the majority of the trails, turn north off Hwy 99 at the first road east of the bridge, beside an impressively landscaped log home. Follow this road as it crosses the BC Rail tracks and then begins climbing the knoll. Watch for trails as you ascend Ivey Lake Rd. There are usually other mountain bikers on the road to question about routes. An alternative approach to Mosquito Lake is on the west side of D'Arcy–Anderson Lake Rd, just north of Mount Currie. It's a 1.2-mile (2-km) ride from here on a gravel access road to the Forest Service recreation site. Massive Mount Currie dominates the landscape, and the views from the knoll are sublime. Equally absorbing are the clouds of mosquitoes for which the valley is renowned, particularly in late spring and early summer. For detailed information (and perhaps even a map), contact High Line Cycles in Pemberton, 1392 Portage Rd, (604) 894-6625. High Line also rents mountain bikes.

One of the most extensive network of trails in the Lillooet region is the more than 100 miles (162 km) of routes in the South Chilcotin Mountains around **Spruce Lake** (see also Parks/Camping, above), which are also utilized by hikers and horseback riders. The weather around Lillooet is much drier and hotter than elsewhere in the Sea to Sky region, so be prepared to consume a lot of liquid as you pedal along the trails. For more information, contact Camelsfoot Sports, (250) 256-7757, or Winner's Edge, (250) 256-4848, in Lillooet. For **guided mountain-bike tours,** contact Kevin Aitken, (250) 256-0075, or Pat Ansdell, (250) 256-7947. A good map of the region is in the *British Columbia Recreational Atlas* (Ministry of Environment, Lands and Parks).

Cycling

The Pemberton Valley is a natural for cycling: mostly level, lightly trafficked, it's a pastoral setting with incredible mountain views. Beginning from the town centre, the **Pemberton Valley Road** runs north and links with **Pemberton Meadows Road.** Both roads are paved and run farther than you'll probably care to pedal in the course of a day, about 28 miles (45 km) one way. Follow Prospect St for a short distance past the Pemberton Pioneer Museum (see Picnics, below), to where Pemberton Valley Rd begins. From here north the road gently meanders past rich farmland, much of which is cultivated with seed potatoes. Miller Creek and Ryan River empty down off the slopes of the mountains to the west into the nearby Lillooet River. North of Ryan River the road subtly changes its name to Pemberton Meadows Rd, and carries on north for the next 23 miles (38 km). An important intersection to watch for is the **Lillooet Lake Road,** which begins slightly more than 4 miles (7 km) north of the Outward Bound Centre (a wilderness-survival-training organization). Follow Lillooet River Rd for about 1 mile (1.5 km) to the Lillooet River Forestry Bridge, a good place to take a break. At this point you are 16 miles (26 km) northwest of Pemberton and will have a great view back down the valley. The trailhead to Tenquille Lake (see Parks/Camping, above) is located on the north side of the bridge. If you choose to follow Pemberton Meadows Rd north of the Lillooet River Rd intersection, there are few approaches to the Lillooet River; the road eventually peters out as the mountains crowd in on both sides of the river.

When you cycle the **D'Arcy–Anderson Lake Road** to Mount Currie (50 miles/80 km return) you are also covering the same ground as that of the Gold Rush Heritage Trail (see Hiking, above). The road runs through a narrow valley and follows the course of the Birkenhead River for much of the way. It a tight squeeze to fit hydro towers, the BC Rail line, and the two-lane paved road side by side. Fortunately for cyclists, the road is not heavily trafficked. The scenery makes this cycle trip special: high peaks straddle the valley, while the river, aided by various creeks, bubbles along the forested floor. Unless you're really hard-core, you'll want to do this ride from north to south. The elevation gain between Mount Currie and D'Arcy is 924 feet (280 m), as the road climbs to the Pemberton Pass; most of that gain is between Mount Currie and the pass. The road is fairly level between the Pemberton Pass and D'Arcy. You may wish to ride the morning passenger train to D'Arcy with your bike, and then cycle back as far as you wish. For more information, call BC Rail at (604) 894-6980 in Pemberton, or (604) 984-5246 in North Vancouver. Bikes travel on a space-available basis, and there is a charge of $10. The passenger fare from Pemberton or Mount Currie to D'Arcy is about $11.

Cross-Country Skiing/Snowshoeing

Whistler grabs all the press for winter sports in the Sea to Sky corridor, leaving the region between Pemberton and Lillooet for those who enjoy the quiet of a backcountry ski or snowshoe excursion. It's often colder here than in Whistler, which makes for lighter, fluffier snow conditions. Tall peaks shadow the valleys. Places such as the north end of **Pemberton Meadows** hardly receive a ray of sunshine from December to February. Up top, there's nothing to block the sun or whatever marine system blows in from the ocean across the **Pemberton Icefield,** a vast frozen pan that stretches from the headwaters of the Squamish River to the upper Lillooet River. This covering is a remnant of the most recent ice age. The Varsity Outdoors Club maintains the Julian Harrison hut on Mount Overseer as a staging point for those who undertake a ski-touring trek here. There's no charge to use the hut, which sleeps six to eight people comfortably. For information on the hut, call (604) 822-2228. Rather than make the 36-mile (60-km) ski-in along the Lillooet River Forest Rd, you may decide to helicopter in from nearby Pemberton Meadows and ski out via **Ring Creek.** Contact Pemberton Helicopters, (604) 894-6919. Consult detailed maps of the area, particularly *North Creek* 92/J11, *Ryan River* 92/J6, and *Pemberton* 92/J7, available from the Geological Survey of Canada. A comprehensive guidebook is *Exploring the Coast Mountains on Skis* by John Baldwin.

There's tamer terrain at lower elevations, but in these steep-sided valleys the threat of avalanches is always real. Better to explore as part of a group with knowledgeable leadership and come equipped with snow shovels, probes, and location indicators. Several places where you can explore comfortably on skis or snowshoes in the region without these aids, although still on ungroomed trails, are around **Blackwater Lake** (easy; 2.5 miles/4 km return; see Mountain Biking, above); and **Birkenhead Lake** (moderate; 8.5 miles/14 km return; see Parks/Camping, above), near D'Arcy. **North Joffre Creek** (easy; 4.3 miles/7 km return) on the Duffey Lake Rd is another possibility. The parking lot for North Joffre Creek is located on the west side of the Duffey Lake Rd (Hwy 99), about 2 miles (3 km) south of Joffre Lake Provincial Recreation Area (see Parks/Camping, above). A good source of information on these routes, as well as a source for **guided backcountry trips for skiers and snowboarders,** is the Federation of Mountain Clubs' Canada West Mountain School in Vancouver, (604) 737-3053. Visit their Web site for information on backcountry ski and snowboard touring, as well as rock climbing, backpacking, mountaineering, wilderness hiking, peak ascents, mountain rescue, custom guiding, backcountry leadership, and wilderness first aid: http://home.istar.ca/~fmcbc/.

Wildlife

Sweet and petite, **One-Mile Lake** (see Beaches/Swimming, below) in Pemberton has a boardwalk that runs across its marshy north side. From here, it's possible to quietly watch birds, particularly during migration season. This can begin as early as April, when larger birds such as **trumpeter swans** make an appearance. For the most part, though, it's **mergansers, mallards,** and **loons,** while in the surrounding forest, **songbirds** and **hummingbirds** work the woods.

Beginning in late August and early September, **spawning salmon,** which have made their way up the Fraser, Harrison, and Lillooet Rivers, begin the last part of their journey in the **Birkenhead River.** The sockeye run is particularly spectacular: the river turns red with them. The sight is so remarkable that at first you can hardly believe your eyes. Salmon also run in **Gates Creek,** which flows into the south end of Anderson Lake in D'Arcy. The Birkenhead River is easily spotted from either Hwy 99 as it passes through rural Mount Currie or numerous places along the D'Arcy–Anderson Lake Rd, including the Owl Creek Forest Service site (see Parks/Camping, above).

The **Upper Lillooet Headwaters** (see Hiking, above) is now a protected area, which must come as a relief to the wildlife that have been pushed farther and farther north as logging destroyed lower stretches of critical shelter. Without the forest, animals that come down from higher elevation cannot survive the coldest days of winter. **Moose, deer, bear, wolf,** and others leave their prints on the silty sandbars that stand revealed at low water levels, and slip mutely through the fir, cedar, and pine forest. Although the occasional bear might leave a paw print outside the door of your tent as a calling card, most wildlife prefer to remain well out of sight. Don't let that stop you from looking for signs of their presence in the landscape. They're there!

Canoeing/Kayaking/Boating

There are four lovely lakes in the Pemberton region—Birkenhead, Anderson, Lillooet, and Joffre—that paddlers will find attractive. Joffre is the junior member, while 3.5-mile-long (6-km) Birkenhead is somewhat larger. The other two are much bigger, and *much* breezier. All of them are sequestered among the peaks that range through this heavily mountainous area. Of the four, **Birkenhead Lake** is the most welcoming for a quiet sojourn around its shoreline. Launch from the dock at Birkenhead Lake Provincial Park (see Parks/Camping, above) and paddle south. A surprise awaits you, as it does on many mountain lakes: Tenquille Ridge's white-walled flank, hidden from view at the dock, begins to reveal itself to the west, while the mountains that hem Anderson Lake begin to appear in the north. Late spring, when the surrounding snow-topped peaks reflect on the lake's surface, is one of the best times to visit here.

Nearby **Anderson Lake** lies at the north end of the D'Arcy–Anderson Lake Rd (see Cycling, above). There's a boat ramp here next to **Heritage Park** (see Picnics, below), where those with boats on trailers can put in. Steel-grey Anderson is a large, rather forbidding lake to paddle, with few places to land, particularly along its west shore, where the BC Rail line runs. **Lillooet Lake** is equally large, but has a friendlier appearance. It must be the colour that makes a difference: milky green when seen in full sunlight, a deep jade colour towards dusk. There's a boat launch at the **Twin One Creek Forest Service Recreation Site** (see Parks/Camping, above) about 6 miles (10 km) south of Hwy 99. An alternative approach is to launch a hand-carried boat from a rough site beside the Birkenhead River Bridge (see Fishing, below) on Hwy 99. The river flows into the north end of Lillooet Lake, where a delta of soft silt is steadily deposited by the nearby Lillooet River. An attractive destination to head for is the sandy beach at Strawberry Point Forest Service Recreation Site (see

Parks/Camping, above). Allow an hour to make the 2.5-mile (4-km) paddle journey one way.

High above Lillooet Lake are the three small **Joffre Lakes.** Two of them require a challenging hike to reach, but Lower Joffre Lake is just minutes from Hwy 99 at the Joffre Lakes Provincial Recreation Area (see Parks/Camping, above) trailhead. Not many visitors make the effort to carry a small boat through the forest to the lake, but those who do are treated to the finest landscape surrounding any lake in the region. Not only is the lake fantastically coloured—shades of turquoise and aquamarine—but it is also surmounted by the massive Joffre Glacier Group. On a clear day, time seems suspended as you paddle here in absolute stillness.

The Lillooet and Birkenhead Rivers have been providing sport for whitewater kayakers since the invention of fibreglass. The Lillooet can be treacherous, owing to the numbers of submerged sweepers brought down into the river as a result of logging and slope instability, particularly in the Meagre Creek drainage. The Birkenhead is much more predictable and also more pleasantly landscaped.

The **Lillooet River** system runs for almost 120 miles (200 km) with Class II–III water throughout. Runs include a 3-mile (5-km) stretch on the Upper Lillooet River (see Hiking, above) between the put-in at riverside on the Upper Lillooet Forest Rd north of Pebble Creek and the takeout beside the Meagre Creek Forestry Rd bridge. A lengthier stretch of paddling runs for 9 miles (15 km) between the bridge and takeouts at the km 23 or km 25 markers on the Upper Lillooet Rd.

The **Birkenhead River** provides more challenging Class III–IV kayaking in tighter confines as the river runs for about 3 miles (5 km) between the narrow bridge over the Birkenhead north of Owl Creek (see Parks/Camping, above) on the D'Arcy–Anderson Lake Rd and another bridge near Mount Currie on the road that leads to the Pemberton Sportsmen's Wildlife Association fish hatchery. To find the takeout, turn east onto a gravel road on the south side of the train tracks as the D'Arcy–Anderson Lake Rd leaves Mount Currie. A good source to consult is *Whitewater Trips for Kayakers, Canoeists and Rafters, Volume 2,* by Betty Pratt-Johnson. For more information, call Whistler River Adventures, (604) 932-3532.

There are many terrific rivers for whitewater paddlers to play in around Lillooet, and one of the very best is the **Bridge River.** Featuring Class III+, IV, and V water, with easy portages around the headiest sections, the Bridge demands that those who paddle here be advanced kayakers. The put-in is at the confluence of the Yalakom and Bridge Rivers north of Lillooet, from where it's a 16-mile (26-km) ride to the Fraser River. The Bridge offers everything an expert paddler can hope to find: fast water, raging rapids, hair-raising drop-offs, and challenging technical stretches. For more information, consult the Lillooet Forest District Recreation Map. To obtain a copy, call (250) 256-1200.

Fishing

The clear **Birkenhead River** melds with the murky green waters of the **Lillooet River** just as the two empty into the north end of Lillooet Lake. Beginning in August, successive runs of sockeye salmon enter the Birkenhead from the lake, having made their way this far from the Pacific via the Fraser River and Harrison Lake. When they do, the river runs red with the stock returning to spawn. This is a stunning sight, an autumn treat that rivals the changing colours in the forest along the riverbank. Although the salmon aren't feeding, you can sometimes fish for the rainbow trout that follow in their wake. The best place to launch is beside the more northerly of the two Birkenhead River bridges on Hwy 99, at the head of Lillooet Lake. You'll often see anglers casting from the banks of the Birkenhead beside the D'Arcy–Anderson Lake Rd (see Cycling, above). **Birkenhead Lake** (see Parks/Camping, above) is a popular fishing spot (even in winter), particularly at the mouth of Sockeye Creek. Try gang trolling using a wedding band or flatfish. **Tenquille Lake** (see Hiking, above) lies west of Birkenhead but at much higher elevation. Pack a fly-fishing rod and a "Royal Coachman" for the best chance of hooking a rainbow trout.

A knowledgeable person to consult is professional **freshwater guide** Neil McCutcheon (catch-and-release only), who drift-fishes from a Mackenzie boat, the pride of the Pacific Northwest. Call (604) 898-4139. Other sources to consult include Whistler Backcountry Adventure, (604) 932-3474 or (888) 932-9998, and Whistler Fishing Guides Ltd., (604) 932-4267.

Both **Lower** and **Middle Joffre Lakes** (see Hiking, above) have been stocked with rainbow trout that are now reaching maturity. Owing to the frigid conditions in these two lakes, the size of most fish is smaller than you'll wish to keep. However, given the setting, a paddle on Lower Joffre offers as many rewards as does landing a trout.

Rainbow trout dominate the 40-odd lakes, rivers, and streams around Lillooet just as salmon and sturgeon rule the Fraser. There are even a few locations—such as **Mowson** and **Pearson Ponds** west of Lillooet on Hwy 40 near Gun Lake, and **Lake Lamare** on the Yalakom River Rd north of Hwy 40 at Moha—where you can cast for brook trout. **Anderson, Seton, Duffey, Carpenter,** and **Gun Lakes** are all big, with strategically placed boat ramps located along Hwy 40 west of Lillooet. As well, there's a dock at the BC Hydro recreation site on **Seton Lake** beside Hwy 99 just west of Lillooet (see Parks/Camping, above) where you can cast for rainbow trout, steelhead, and dolly varden up to 15 pounds (6.75 kg). Come fall, there's a chinook and coho run. Use at least a large 5-ounce spoon—Kitimats or Crocodiles work well—when casting into the lake and let your line drift by the dock. Be sure to retrieve your lure before it gets lost in the Seton River's swift current at the outlet of the lake. Nearby, **Texas Creek** south of Lillooet on the West Fraser Canyon Rd is loaded with rainbow trout, "old-time fishing at its best" as the locals say. Also, as you drive Hwy 99 between Duffey and Seton Lakes, try your luck for rainbows at the Forest Service recreation sites at **Downton** or **Melvin Creeks,** where they enter **Cayoosh Creek.** Fly-fish with a small spoon, such as the dependable "Deadly Dick," favoured by area anglers. An excellent source of information on fishing in the Lillooet region is Camelsfoot Sports, 633 Main St, Lillooet, (250) 256-7757.

Horseback Riding

A number of horseback-adventure companies operate from Pemberton, including Adventures on Horseback on Pemberton Meadows Rd, (888) 894-7433, and Pemberton Stables near Hwy 99, (604) 894-6615.

There's no finer source of information on horseback riding in the Pemberton–Mount Currie region than Wayne Andrew, who operates the **WD Bar Ranch.** Andrew, former world saddle-bronc champion, was raised in Mount Currie and now rents horses and guides backcountry pack-horse treks from his ranch. For information, call (604) 894-5669.

For information on exploring the **South Chilcotin** wilderness (see Parks/Camping, above) with pack horses, contact Chilcotin Holidays, (250) 238-2274, in Gold Bridge or visit their Web site: www.chilcotinholidays.com/guide.

Picnics

One sign that spring has arrived in Mount Currie is the blooming of the apple trees at the **Owl Creek Forest Service Recreation Site** (see Parks/Camping, above). It's a miracle that these old trees still blossom at all. They're at least 60 years old and have endured the coldest winters of the century. Picnic tables covered with white petals await travellers in May, though they are just as appealing at other times, particularly when the sun shines and the creek sings. There's an adjacent site on the opposite side of the creek in a more heavily forested section favoured by kayakers.

Farther up the road from Owl Creek is D'Arcy's **Heritage Park** on the shore of Anderson Lake. Tables dot this grassy site, which is exposed to the cool wind that often blows off the lake on even the hottest days. This same wind *really* helps keep down the bugs, the bane of any picnic.

D'Arcy is a easygoing town, which is evident by the cattle that are allowed to range freely around the park and on nearby roads.

You can enjoy a picnic in a log-cabin setting at the **Pemberton Pioneer Museum.** These are not the smooth, round-log homes that are now constructed in Pemberton, but the rough-hewn timber models that served early settlers so well. It's a delight to examine their thick walls and peer through the windows at their snug interiors, even if you find that the museum itself is closed. The picnic tables are always available, as is the view of imposing Mount Currie that rises before you. The museum is located at the corner of Prospect and Camus Sts, a short distance north of Hwy 99 in the heart of Pemberton.

The limestone canyon in which **Marble Canyon Provincial Park** (see Parks/Camping, above) is located is a rather rare geological formation in British Columbia. That's what makes picnicking here such an unusual experience. You can sense there's something different: the white, chalk-faced slopes are certainly not composed of granite as are the nearby Coast Mountains. And the weathered peaks, surmounted by the remarkable **Chimney Rock** (see Rock Climbing, below), have the appearance of a crumbling castle wall. This canyon was once part of a Pacific island chain, another section of which lies in the northwest corner of the province. Thanks to continental drift, they got *around.* Keep this thought in mind as a waterfall on the far side of suitably named Turquoise Lake reminds you of the power of the elements to eventually wear all things down.

Beaches/Swimming

There are few places around Pemberton where you can stay in the water for any great length of time—it's just *too* cold. The exception is **One-Mile Lake** (see Wildlife), a small park beside Hwy 99, complete with a beach and dock. Later in the summer the lake can become choked with algae, but attempts have been made to improve the drainage, which may help restore clarity.

The best beach in the Pemberton region is on Lillooet Lake at the **Strawberry Point Forest Service Recreation Site.** Drive 4 miles (6.5 km) south of Hwy 99 on rough-surfaced Lillooet Lake Rd to reach Strawberry Point. A short trail leads from the parking lot to a wide swath of sand. The beach is remote enough that you'll often have it to yourself. Lillooet Lake is broad and deep, and its waters never really have a chance to warm up. However, swimming is possible for short plunges before retreating to your blanket.

It's a shame that for a region renowned for *seriously* hot summer days and for exquisite lakes and rivers, so few are warm enough to even consider swimming in them. At least the beaches are inviting, which is what makes the BC Hydro recreation site at **Seton Lake** (see Parks/Camping, above) such a hit. Even if you don't go in the water, your eyes will be bathed in colour. Seton Lake is a rare shade of green, and it's complemented by the rugged, mineral-hued mountainside that rises nearby to the north.

Rock Climbing

The limestone walls of Marble Canyon northeast of Lillooet are easily reached from Hwy 99. Dozens of routes have been opened by Lower Mainland climbers over the past decade in this area, which has come to be known as the "Cinderella of BC rock," because of its still relatively undiscovered beauty. A maze of canyons runs off on both sides of the main canyon, through which the highway makes its way as it passes beside the brilliantly hued Turquoise, Crown, and Pavilion Lakes. **Chimney Rock** (known as Coyote Rock by members of the Fountain Band First Nation) dominates the crenellated skyline. The best description of routes such as the Headwall and the Great Gully are found in *Central B.C. Rock* by Lyle Knight, a comprehensive climbing guide to routes in the Lillooet region north through the Central Interior and east through the Okanagan and West Kootenays.

According to that rare breed of mountain cat—the ice climber—Lillooet is *the* centre for **ice climbing** in British Columbia, and **Marble Canyon Provincial Park** (see Parks/Camping, above) has one of the best and most easily accessed icefalls in the region. Good ice is also found in several places beside the **D'Arcy–Anderson Lake Road** (see Cycling, above). Owing to the ease with which nearby glaciers can be reached, the Joffre Glacier Group in **Joffre Lakes Provincial Recreation Area** (see Hiking, above) has been visited by novice and expert ice climbers alike for decades and its popularity continues to grow. Beware exploring the glacier. Even knowledgeable climbers run the risk of falling into a crevasse. A good topographical map to consult is 92 J/8, *Duffey Lake*. For more information, see *The Climber's Guide to West Coast Ice* by Serl and Maclane.

Attractions

Two hours north of Whistler, you'll happen upon the 1850s town of **Lillooet**—mile 0 of the Cariboo Gold Rush Trail. The best thing about Lillooet is getting there (via either car or train). The BC Rail line between

Lillooet and Vancouver is a vital link to the outside world for the loggers, miners, and farmers who live in remote areas of the Coast Mountains. It's also one of the most scenic stretches in British Columbia, along pretty Howe Sound and into the jagged mountains. The route links Vancouver with Whistler, Lillooet, and Prince George; call BC Rail at (604) 984-5246. Also, check out the old suspension bridge (built circa 1913) that spans the Fraser River at the north end of town.

Restaurants

For recommended restaurants, see Adjoining Areas to this chapter.

Lodgings

Tyax Mountain Lake Resort ☆ In the wilderness of the Chilcotin Range about 160 kilometres (100 miles) north of Vancouver, floatplanes are seen dropping incoming guests off at Tyaughton Lake's dock. There are 29 suites in the freshly hewn spruce-log lodge. We prefer one of the large chalets, especially for longer stays. Don't own a floatplane? Take the train from Vancouver to Lillooet—the resort will pick you up. *Tyaughton Lake Rd (off Carpenter); mail: General Delivery, Gold Bridge, BC V0K 1P0; (250) 238-2221; $$$.*

Cheaper Sleeps

The Log House B&B This new, 5,000-square-foot (450-m^2) log house looks slightly out of place on its residential street, but the space inside—and on the wraparound deck with a wraparound view—is wonderful. Each of the three large guest rooms has its own TV and reading chairs. Daily buses make ski travel a cinch. *1357 Elmwood (PO Box 699, General Delivery), Pemberton, BC V0N 2L0; (800) 894-6002 or (604) 894-6000; $.*

More Information

BC Forest Service, Squamish Forest District: *(604) 898-2100.*
BC Hydro Recreation Sites: *(604) 528-1812; Web site: www.bchydro.com.*
BC Parks, Garibaldi/Sunshine Coast District: *(604) 898-3678.*
BC Parks, Thompson River District: *(250) 851-3000.*
BC Rail: *(604) 894-6980 in Pemberton; (604) 984-5246 in North Vancouver.*
Geological Survey of Canada (maps): *605 Robson St, Suite 101, Vancouver, BC V6B 5G3, (604) 666-0271. Store hours are 8:30am–4:30pm, Mon–Fri.*
Lillooet Chamber of Commerce: *(250) 256-4308.*
Pemberton Chamber of Commerce: *(604) 894-6175.*

The Sunshine Coast

The Sunshine Coast shoreline and mountain slopes, from Howe Sound north along the Sechelt Peninsula to Jervis Inlet and along the Malaspina Peninsula to Desolation Sound, including Roberts Creek, Porpoise Bay, Tetrahedron, Skookumchuk Narrows, Saltery Bay, and Okeover Bay Provincial Parks.

The world's longest highway, the Pan-American (also named Highway 101 in parts of the United States and Canada), stretches 9,312 miles (15 020 km) from Castro on Chile's south coast to Lund on BC's Sunshine Coast. The 87-mile (139-km) stretch of Highway 101 between Langdale and Lund outperforms its size. Dozens of parks with biking, hiking, and ski trails; canoe and kayak routes; beaches; and coastal viewpoints are easily reached from the highway. Campsites are plentiful, and except in July and August and on long weekends from May to September, you won't have any difficulty in finding a place to pitch your tent or park your RV.

The Sunshine Coast lives up to its name. With an annual total of between 1,400 and 2,400 hours of sunshine—that's an average of 4 to 6 hours per day, depending on where the measurements are taken—bright days outnumber gloomy ones by a wide margin. The Sunshine Coast benefits from a rain shadow cast by the Vancouver Island mountains, which catch most of the moisture coming in off the Pacific Ocean. In winter, clouds regroup in the Coast Mountains to the east of the Sunshine Coast and provide sufficient precipitation in the form of snow to coat trails for cross-country skiing. The remainder of the year it falls as rain, British Columbia's "liquid sunshine," which nourishes the temperate rain forest.

The Sunshine Coast is split into two portions on either side of

Jervis Inlet. Roughly speaking, the southern half between the ferry slips at Langdale and Earls Cove occupies the Sechelt Peninsula, while the northern half between the ferry slip at Saltery Bay and Lund sits on the Malaspina Peninsula. The coastline is deeply indented by the Pacific Ocean at Howe Sound, Jervis Inlet, and Desolation Sound. Jervis and Desolation are of such fjordic proportions that they attract a steady stream of marine traffic throughout the summer months, when brilliant sun shines on the countless cataracts that cascade down the sheer-sided slopes. Come moodier months, the clouds become ensnared in the snaggle-toothed peaks, making you feel just as pleased to stick to the sunnier coastline.

Getting There

The Sunshine Coast is accessible from the rest of the Lower Mainland only by boat or airplane. Travellers aboard BC Ferries leave Horseshoe Bay in West Vancouver for a 9.5-mile (15.5-km), 45-minute ride to Langdale on the Sechelt Peninsula. Highway 101 links Langdale with Earls Cove, 50 miles (80 km) north. Another ferry crosses Jervis Inlet to Saltery Bay, a 60-minute ride. Highway 101 makes the second leg of this journey 37 miles (59 km) north to Lund. BC Ferries also connects Powell River on the Malaspina Peninsula with Comox on the east side of central Vancouver Island. For more information on schedules and fares, contact BC Ferries, (604) 669-1211, in Vancouver, or on the Sunshine Coast in Saltery Bay, (604) 487-9333, and Powell River, (604) 485-2943; or visit their Web site at www.bcferries.bc.ca/ferries.

A note about travel times: One of the most enjoyable aspects of visiting the northern Sunshine Coast in the off-season from September to May—particularly if you travel midweek—is being able to catch the ferry both from Horseshoe Bay to Langdale, and then from Earls Cove to Saltery Bay, without experiencing interminable lineups. You'll still have to allow six hours to reach the Malaspina Peninsula from Horseshoe Bay, but you can do it without hurrying, enjoying the travel time just as much as the play time once you arrive.

If you can't travel midweek to avoid lines, at least leave Vancouver early Friday afternoon or late Saturday morning and return early on Monday. Those travelling up the entire coast or returning via Vancouver Island should ask at the Horseshoe Bay terminal about special fares (which can save you up to 30 percent) for the circle tour (four ferry rides).

Adjoining Areas

NORTH: **The Bella Coola Road (Highway 20)**

SOUTH: **Southern Gulf Islands**

EAST: **Whistler and the Sea to Sky Highway**

WEST: **Parksville and the Comox Valley**

inside out

Camping

There are three major provincial campgrounds located along the Sunshine Coast. Two of them are on the southern portion of the Sunshine Coast: **Roberts Creek Provincial Park,** (604) 885-9019, has 24 vehicle/tent sites, including 1 double, and straddles Hwy 101, about 9 miles (14 km) west of Gibsons. **Porpoise Bay Provincial Park,** (604) 898-3678, has 84 vehicle/tent sites, including 8 double units, located 2.5 miles (4 km) north of Sechelt on East Porpoise Bay Rd. (Note: In addition to the vehicle/tent sites there are also 6 bike-in sites for those who are cycle-touring the region.) A third, **Saltery Bay Provincial Park,** (604) 898-3678, has 42 vehicle/tent sites, including 3 double units, and sits beside the BC Ferries' Saltery Bay terminal on Jervis Inlet south of Powell River. A camping fee of about $15 per site per night is charged at all of these parks between April and October. Although Roberts Creek and Porpoise Bay fill up quickly in summer months, you'll stand a much better chance of squeezing into Saltery Bay Provincial Park, owing to its more remote location, which requires an additional ferry ride from Earls Cove. To guarantee a campsite, you can make reservations at both Porpoise Bay and Saltery Bay Provincial Parks by calling (800) 689-9025.

In addition to these three major provincial parks, there's also camping at **Smuggler Cove Provincial Marine Park,** (604) 898-3678. Located about 9 miles (15 km) northwest of Sechelt, this small, sheltered marine park with 5 walk-in campsites serves as a jumping-off point for paddlers wishing to explore several offshore islands in what is arguably the most scenic location on the Sunshine Coast. Watch for the well-marked approach to the park on the south side of Hwy 101, between Halfmoon Bay and Secret Cove. Follow Brooks Rd 3 miles (5 km) to the parking lot, from where you can either paddle in or walk a 1-mile (1.6-km) trail to the campsites.

Okeover Arm Provincial Park, (604) 898-3678, near Lund on the northern Sunshine Coast, is another small campground frequented by paddlers. This park is the choice of those intent on exploring Desolation Sound. Except in the busiest summer months, you'll probably have your pick of any of the 5 vehicle/tent sites and 4 adjacent walk-in sites in the forest beside Okeover Arm, a long neck of water along the east side of Malaspina Peninsula, 3 miles (5 km) south of Lund. There's a federal dock and boat ramp here and, unlike in Lund, plenty of parking, should you be heading out for an extended paddle. The park lies 3 miles (5 km) east of

Hwy 101 on Malaspina Rd. For information on Okeover Arm and other provincial parks of the Sunshine Coast, call BC Parks, (604) 898-3678.

There are more Forest Service recreation sites concentrated around **Powell River** on the northern Sunshine Coast than in almost any other similar-sized area in British Columbia. This is a testament not only to the dozens of lakes surrounding the town but also to the amount of logging that has taken place here for the past 70 years. Where there is logging, there are Forest Service recreation sites. Much of the forest is still in recovery, particularly at higher elevations, but where industry first cleared the easiest-to-reach trees, the second growth is beginning to re-establish itself. One of the best sites includes **Dinner Rock.** The entrance to the site is on the west side of Hwy 101, 2.5 miles (4 km) south of Lund. Drive slowly as you approach Lund and watch for the sturdy wooden campground sign at the entrance to a dirt road that leads 0.5 mile (1 km) downhill to a dozen beautifully positioned sites. (Note: A gate bars access to the site October 15–April 15.) With plenty of firewood, freshwater, and a car top boat launch, this is where you want to be when a full moon lights up Malaspina Strait and shooting stars strafe the night sky.

Along forest roads east of Powell River, you'll find more good camping at Forest Service sites at **Inland Lake,** including award-winning cabins designed for people with disabilities (see Beaches/Picnics, below). South of Powell River there's camping at **Lois Lake** (9 sites) at the start of the Powell Forest Canoe Route (see Kayaking/Canoeing/Boating, below), at **Khartoum Lake** (16 sites), also on the canoe route, as well as at **Nanton Lake** (25 sites) and at **Dodd Lake** (12 sites), both located on the Welwood Mainline Forest Rd. For a map of Forest Service recreation sites on the Sunshine Coast, call the district office, (604) 485-0700, or pick one up at 7077 Duncan St in Powell River at 1975 Field Rd in Sechelt.

Other public campsites along the Sunshine Coast include Katherine Lake Regional Park, near Garden Bay and Irvines Landing, and Haywire Bay Regional Campground, near Powell River. To find **Katherine Lake Regional Park** (20 vehicle/tent sites, (604) 885-2261), turn west off Hwy 101, about 3.4 miles (5.5 km) north of Madeira Park. Follow Garden Bay Rd about 2.5 miles (4 km) west of the highway to Katherine Lake, the smallest of four lakes ringed around Pender Harbour. For more information, contact the Pender Harbour InfoCentre, (604) 883-2561 (seasonal). **Haywire Bay Regional Park** (43 vehicle/tent sites, (604) 483-3231) is reached by driving east of Marine Ave (Hwy 101) in downtown Powell River on Duncan Ave, north on Manson, and east on Cassiar to Yukon. Follow Yukon to Haslam. Turn east on Haslam, then north on Inland Lake Rd. Haywire Bay Rd branches west of Inland Lake Rd and leads in short order to the campsites.

Beaches/Picnics

Sechelt Peninsula

By the time you reach **Roberts Creek Provincial Park** (see Camping, above), about 7.5 miles (12 km) west of Gibsons, located on both sides of Hwy 101, the highway will have taken up its gentle rising and falling rhythm as it ribbons through lush second-growth forest, a rhythm that is played out for much of its length along the coast. This is the setting for the park's picnic grounds and beach, the entrance to which lies south of the campground on Elphinstone Rd, where you'll find two dozen tables arranged beside the ocean. Bring your beach shoes, as bare feet may find the cobblestoned coastline too rough on tender tootsies.

Davis Bay, about 14 miles (22 km) north of Langdale, is one of sandiest and most accessible beaches on the Sunshine Coast. Just pull off beside Hwy 101 at a likely looking spot and let the picnicking begin. The sweeping views here across the Strait of Georgia to Vancouver Island are unbroken by any offshore islands, and are a rarity along the otherwise sheltered coastline. A pier juts a long way out from the beach, a good indication of how shallow the water is. In summer, when the tide rises over the beach exposed to the warmth of the summer sun, the ocean warms up as it absorbs all that solar energy and provides swimmers with a Mediterranean-like setting. Purple-hued sand dollars add to the ambience; their shells fade to a bleached white when their life cycle is complete.

Snickett Park and **Pebble Beach** in Sechelt are good places to head once you've packed the picnic hamper full of goodies. In case you've forgotten anything, you'll find it at one of the shops on the Boulevard just off Hwy 101 in downtown Sechelt. If you're in a hurry (a contradiction if there ever was one in this laid-back environment), park yourself on Snickett's Pebble Beach on Trail Bay adjacent to the Boulevard. If not, head 3 miles (5 km) north of Hwy 101 on E Porpoise Bay Rd to the sandy shores at **Porpoise Bay Provincial Park** (see Camping, above) on the Sechelt Inlet. As you'd expect from a park this size, rows of picnic tables dot the beach, which is sheltered by wistful willows.

Sargeant Bay Provincial Park north of Sechelt features a sandy beach that's ideal for swimming and picnicking. At the moment, few visitors know about this diminutive park on Redroofs Rd, so you're most likely to find yourself sharing it with local bird-watchers who come down to explore the nearby marsh (see Wildlife, below). Don't be disappointed when you first arrive: as you walk south along the bay, the cobblestone beach changes to more hospitable sand, which is where you'll want to spread out and listen to the lapping of the waves and the laughing of the gulls. Farther north along Redroofs Rd is **Coopers Green Regional Park,**

where you'll find a beach with a mix of rock and sand, and offshore islets. Enjoy a picnic supper while watching the summer sun sink offshore as it lights up the picturesque cove.

Katherine Lake Regional Park (see Camping, above) in Garden Bay is a freshwater treat in a region dominated by saltwater locales. The sandy beach at this small lake will appeal to both swimmers and picnickers. If you like to take an early-morning plunge after a night spent sleeping under the stars, this is where to do it.

Just east of Earls Cove lies the Forest Service recreation site at **Klein Lake,** as well as **North** and **Waugh Lakes** close to Egmont. All three are beautifully clear, freshwater lakes with tiny little fish that will nibble your toes if you stand still. North and Waugh Lakes are situated beside Egmont Rd, and access points are easily spotted. Klein Lake is reached after a short drive along well-marked North Lake Forest Rd from Hwy 101 near Earls Cove.

Malaspina Peninsula

If you haven't already enjoyed your picnic lunch while sitting out on deck of the BC Ferry that brought you across Jervis Inlet from Earls Cove, stop in at the **Mermaid Cove** picnic grounds in **Saltery Bay Provincial Park** (see Camping, above). At both the campground and the Mermaid Cove site there are three dozen picnic tables, many of which sit atop mounds of sun-bleached mollusc shells left from precontact times when Native peoples picnicked and feasted here. You can see why they chose this spot: shellfish cling to the rocky shoreline, while in the deep, dark waters of the inlet, whales, seals, and sea lions cavort in pursuit of schooling fish.

Valentine Mountain in Powell River requires just a short stair-climb to reach the top and the first of several viewpoints. It's as if you're standing in an observatory: as you make your way around the circumference, you see enough landmarks and reference points to bring any map to life. Islands and inlets, mountains and lakes lay spread below you. Picnic tables have been secluded in several places on Valentine's 853-foot (260-m) summit, which is reached by following Duncan Ave east of Marine Ave to Manson Ave. Turn north and follow Manson to its end at Cranberry St; turn east on Cranberry, then north on Crown Ave and follow it to the trailhead, which begins at the end of the road.

Of all the 32 lakes in the Powell River region, **Mowat Bay Park** on Powell Lake is the beach of choice. The biggest challenge is finding the park. Powell River's road grid is such that it takes a turn or two to reach most of the recreation destinations tucked in the slopes of the Coast Mountains that rise gently from the shoreline. Mowat Bay Park is no exception, and is even a little easier to locate than some others. From Hwy

101 in downtown Powell River, follow Duncan St east to Manson Ave, then turn north and follow Manson to its junction with Cranberry St. Turn east on Cranberry, then north on Mowat and follow this to the beach.

Inland Lake is ringed with cottonwoods, which makes it a delightful place to picnic in autumn, when the leaves change from pale green to bright yellow. Picnic tables are located within an easy distance of the parking area. From there a splendidly constructed 8-mile (13-km) trail follows the shoreline (see Cycling, below). More picnic and bathing sites appear as you walk the trail. This recreation site is the pride of the BC Forest Service. All visitors, no matter what their abilities, will feel welcome here. So successful has it been that in 1989 it won a provincial handicap-access design award for Powell River's Susan Jersak. To reach the lake from Hwy 101 (Marine Ave), follow a series of city streets through Powell River to Inland Lake Forest Rd. Briefly, from the harbour take Duncan St east of Marine Ave to Manson Ave. Turn north on Manson and drive towards Cranberry Lake. Turn east on Cassiar, north on Yukon, and finally east on Haslam St, which leads to Inland Lake Rd. The lake is about a 15-minute drive from here.

You'll also find picnicking and swimming at **Haywire Bay Regional Park** (see Camping, above) on Powell Lake near Inland Lake. The turn-off to Haywire Bay Regional Park is from Inland Lake Rd south of Inland Lake Park. One of the treats of visiting this beach is swimming the short distance to nearby Honeymoon Island.

Kayaking/Canoeing/Boating

Several **provincial marine parks** are located along the Sunshine Coast, most with undeveloped facilities. Boaters may find freshwater at the occasional one but should always bring their own. Much of the coastline is sheltered, which provides good protection for those in small paddlecraft or motorboats. Marine parks along the Sechelt Peninsula include **Simson, Buccaneer Bay, Smuggler Cove** (see Camping, above), and **Garden Bay.** Simson Marine Park enjoys a particularly pretty location on South Thormanby Island, with a blend of sandy beaches, forested slopes, and tranquil coves. Spyglass Hill at the north end of the island is a prominent landmark to watch for after launching from Halfmoon Bay north of Sechelt. Marine parks around Malaspina Peninsula include **Desolation Sound** (British Columbia's largest marine park, and which now includes the Curme Islands), the **Copeland Islands, Roscoe Bay, Walsh Cove,** and **Teakerne Arm.**

Sechelt Peninsula

If it weren't for a small neck of land less than a half mile wide, a large portion of the peninsula north of Sechelt would be an island, cut off from the mainland. This wedge of sand backs ocean water, which flows from the northwestern entrance to the inlet near Egmont, into three inlets: Sechelt Inlet (the largest), and Salmon and Narrows Inlets, which branch east from Sechelt Inlet. **Sechelt Inlets Provincial Marine Recreation Area** is a narrow, fjordlike environment where old-growth forest plummets down the sides of the Caren Range mountains to the ocean. Beaches are limited, and where they do occur you'll find small park sites suited for rest stops or overnighting. Given the rocky shoreline of much of the Sechelt Inlet and its two branches—Salmon and Narrows Inlets—you'll be relieved to reach one of the sites when the wind rises and makes paddling extremely difficult. It takes the better part of a day to paddle the 22 miles (35 km) from the federal dock in Sechelt to Egmont at the north end of the inlet via **Skookumchuk Narrows** (see Hiking/Walking, below). You can reduce the paddle time by launching at Porpoise Bay Provincial Park (see Camping, above) or private Tillicum Bay Marina, a good place to leave your car if you're going on an overnight paddle. Both the park and the marina are located on E Porpoise Bay Rd (Sechelt Inlet Rd) in Sechelt. It's only about a 2-mile (3-km) paddle from the marina to the first marine-park site at Tuwanek Point. Two of the trickiest sections involve crossing the mouth of Salmon Inlet, where strong winds can quickly turn a leisurely paddle into a maddening fight, and navigating Tzoonie Narrows in Narrows Inlet where, unless you enter the narrows at a favourable tide, you're in for a battle against the current.

There are 8 marine-park campsites located on both sides of Sechelt Inlet and along Narrows Inlet in Sechelt Inlets Provincial Marine Recreation Area. Wilderness sites with basic amenities are located at **Halfway, Tuwanek, Nine Mile Point, Kunechin Point,** and **Piper Point.** Undeveloped sites are located at **Tzoonie Narrows, Thornhill,** and **Skaiakos Point.** Most sites are located within a mile or two (2 to 3 km) of each other and provide welcome resting places, particularly when strong winds funnel through the inlets on summer days.

For more information on paddling Sechelt Inlets Provincial Marine Recreation Area, call BC Parks, (604) 898-3678. For **guided kayaking tours** and paddling supplies, consult Pedals and Paddles Adventure Sports in Sechelt, (604) 885-6440. The best navigation chart of Sechelt Inlet is NTM L/C 3512, Strait of Georgia/Central Portion.

Simson Marine Park enjoys a particularly pretty location and occupies much of South Thormanby Island. It's only a 2-mile (3-km) paddle from the public boat ramp in Halfmoon Bay across Welcome Passage to the east side of South Thormanby, the larger of two similarly named islands. Paddlers can not only explore Simson but also **Buccaneer Bay Marine Park,** on the west side of North Thormanby Island, as well as many bays and headlands around **Smuggler Cove Marine Park,** just north of Halfmoon Bay.

There's lovely freshwater paddling on **Ruby Lake,** which most folks only get to admire from their vehicle as they pass by. Stop at Don Bosch Regional Park on Ruby Lake, where you'll find just the place to launch, as well as picnic and swim. If you need a boat, nearby Ruby Lake Resort rents them. Call (604) 883-2269.

Boat-launch locations on the south Sunshine Coast include public ramps at Gibsons, Chapman Creek, Sechelt, and Cooper's Green Regional Park in Halfmoon Bay, and private ramps at Halfmoon Bay, Secret Cove, Madeira Park, Garden Bay, and Irvines Landing in Pender Harbour, at Sakinaw Lake, and in Egmont. For more information on paddling the south Sunshine Coast, contact the **outfitters** Tzoonie Outdoor Adventures in Sechelt, (604) 885-9802; Rising Sun Kayak Adventure in Egmont, (604) 883-2062; or Sunshine Kayaking, (604) 886-9760, in Gibsons. Kayak, canoes, and motorboats can also be rented from the Peninsula Market, (604) 885-9721, in Davis Bay; Lowes Resort, (604) 883-2456, Sunshine Coast Resort, (604) 883-9177, Mount Daniel Resort, (604) 883-9569, and Malaspina Ranch Resort, (604) 883-1122, in the Madeira Park area; and Fishermans Resort, (604) 883-2336, and Duncan Cove Resort, (604) 883-2424, in the Garden Bay area. **Boat and kayak rentals** are also available in Egmont from the Egmont Marina Resort, (604) 883-2298, and the Bathgate Store and Marina, (604) 883-2222.

Malaspina Peninsula

Since it was completed in 1983, the **Powell Forest Canoe Route** has come to be recognized as one of the more significant paddle routes in the province, right up there with the Bowron Lakes in the Cariboos (see The Cariboo Highway chapter). Whereas the Bowron Lakes presents an extended 7 to 10 day, 72-mile (116-km) canoe and kayak route through six major lakes linked by portages, and requires reservations, the Powell Forest route can be done in small or big bites. There's room for everyone on this eight-lake journey, and paddlers can attempt it whenever the feeling moves them. The full-on, 48-mile (80-km) trip requires five to seven days to complete and includes almost 7 miles (11 km) of portages. A shorter 7.75-mile (12.5-km) route takes three days and includes about 3 miles (5 km) of portages. You can avoid the portage between Lois and Horseshoe Lakes by putting in at Nanton Lake, but then you'd miss one of the most scenic stretches of original forest in this region that has been so methodically flooded and stripped of coastal old-growth. Canoe racks are provided in many places along the portages, which not only gives paddlers a chance to rest their shoulders but also provides an opportunity to look around the interior of the forest where remnants of old logging activity persist in many places. It's important to acquaint yourself with the lakes in advance of setting out. Each has its own characteristics: some are deep, others are exposed to strong winds. Altogether, there are 20 campsites sprinkled along the route, good places to hole up while waiting out a blow. The Forest Service publishes a detailed map and description of the Powell Forest Canoe Route. Contact the Forest Service's Sunshine Coast district office in Powell River, (604) 485-0700, for a copy or pick one up from one of their Sunshine Coast offices, 7077 Duncan St in Powell River, and 1975 Field Rd in Sechelt.

Other lakes well worth paddling in this extensive network include **Inland Lake** (see Beaches/Picnics, above) and newly protected **Confederation Lake,** which, along with Haslan Lake, comprises a complete watershed with extensive recreation values. Confederation Lake lies north of Inland Lake and can be reached by following Inland Lake Forest Rd. (Note: Access to Haslam Lake, part of the municipal watershed, is restricted.)

Desolation Sound Marine Park possesses a magical magnetism that draws boaters and paddlers from distant shores. Most of those who arrive aboard "stinkpots" tend to congregate in popular anchorages, such as Prideaux Haven, Tenedos Bay, and Grace Harbour, much as "fifth-wheelers" converge on RV parks. Be a little more imaginative and you'll find plenty of isolated bays and campsites throughout Desolation Sound's more than 37 miles (60 km) of coastline. One of the prime attractions of these waters is their warmth in summer months, which makes them ideal for swimming and snorkeling. The scenery is less severe than many of the other sheer-sided waterways along the central coast, although just as majestic. Snow-capped peaks of the Coast Mountains soar from the tideline to heights of 7,875 feet (2400 m). Boaters and paddlers will discover an environment nearer in spirit to the protected waters of the southern Strait of Georgia. What Desolation Sound provides that the southern Gulf Islands don't is an astonishing breeding ground for shellfish, principally oysters. Whoever penned the time-honoured expression "When the tide is out, the table is spread" must have been inspired by these nutrient-rich waters.

There are two approaches to Desolation Sound, either from Lund or nearby Okeover Arm Provincial Park (see Camping, above) at the head of the inlet. A boat ramp is located at each location. Paddlers will find less marine traffic in Okeover Inlet than along the west side of Malaspina Strait. For more information, consult *An Explorer's Guide: Marine Parks of British Columbia* by Peter Chettleburgh.

Public **boat ramps** on the northern Sunshine Coast are located at Saltery Bay Provincial Park, at Okeover Arm Provincial Park, and in Lund. Private ramps are located in Powell River. For **rentals, guided trips,** and more information, contact Powell River Sea Kayaks, (604) 483-2410, or Eagle Kayaking Adventures, (604) 483-3454 or (604) 483-4012, in Lund. Canoes and kayaks are available for rent from Ocean Kayak Rentals and Accessories, (604) 483-3223, in Lund; and from Powell River Boat Rentals, (604) 485-7322, and Sunshine Coast Fitness & Sports, (604) 485-6969, in Powell River.

Cycling

Sechelt Peninsula

Although shoulders on the winding highway can be narrow, cyclists will find that **Highway 101** is a challenging but often scenic route. Avoid peak traffic times, such as the surge that follows the arrival of a BC Ferry, and you'll have long stretches of the highway to yourself, particularly as you pedal north of Sechelt. One consideration: You don't have to cycle Hwy 101 all the way, all the time. There are a few backroads, such as **Lower Roberts Creek Road,** that travel in roughly the same direction while providing a more tranquil ambience. Lower Roberts Creek Rd loops away from Hwy 101 north of Gibsons and rejoins it north of Roberts Creek, for a total distance of 5 miles (8 km).

Hwy 101 rises and falls as it parallels the coastline for much of its length. One of the steepest hills is on the north side of Sechelt. **Redroofs Road** is a delightful 6-mile (10-km) side road that loop-dee-loops along the coast off Hwy 101. The southern entrance to Redroofs is located about 4 miles (7 km) north of Sechelt. The northern entrance is just north of Trout Lake. Note: In recognition of cyclists, **Porpoise Bay Provincial Park** (see Camping, above) in Sechelt has 6 ride-in campsites.

Malaspina Peninsula

Just as a backroad took cyclists away from Hwy 101 around Roberts Creek on the southern half of the route, so too does a series of roads that leads from Hwy 101 at the south end of Powell River through **Paradise Valley,** a lush agricultural area. As Hwy 101 approaches Myrtle Point, follow Centennial Dr to Padgett Rd, which eventually links with Duncan St. Head west on Duncan to reach Marine Ave (Hwy 101), which parallels Powell River's inner harbour.

Cyclists heading north of Powell River as Hwy 101 covers the 14 miles (23 km) to Lund will be confronted with one major hill. The highway makes a wide switchback as it climbs above the dam on Powell River. Catch your breath at the dam, from where you get a picturesque view of the boathouses on Powell Lake. Once you reach the Native community of Sliammon, the road levels out for the remainder of the journey.

An easygoing, ultrascenic cycling path runs along the **Willington**

Beach Trail. This route was originally a railway bed but has now been converted into a simple network for walking and cycling. The trail begins in the Powell River Municipal Park beside Willington Beach, just north of the central harbour.

Inland Lake (see Beaches/Picnics, above) is tucked into the hillside behind Powell River. It is the site of an ambitious program to make the municipal park located here as friendly and useable to people in wheelchairs as to those on foot. A wide, limestone pathway encircles Inland Lake and provides an excellent 8-mile (13-km) cycle route, with the gentlest of grades. You'll enjoy it so much you might want to do it twice.

Mountain Biking

Sechelt Peninsula

The Sunshine Coast is its own little world, a place where things happen that defy expectations. One example is **Sprockids Mountain Bike Park,** a designated mountain-bike area in Gibsons designed with the younger generation in mind. Located at the north end of Stewart Rd just off of the Gibsons Bypass, the park provides almost 9 miles (14 km) of trails that will appeal to mountain bikers of *all* ages.

With such a progressive attitude towards mountain biking, is it any wonder that the Sunshine Coast is a maze of mountain-bike paths? North of Gibsons, the area around Roberts Creek is a great hangout for the serious mountain biker. Three major loop trails—**Roberts Creek** (18.5 miles/30 km), **Clack Creek** (7.5 miles/12 km), and the **Brodie Race Trails** (4.5 miles/7.5 km)—will wear the tread off any tire and introduce riders to shorter technical routes such as Three Steps, the Mexican Jumping Bean Trail, Black Tower, and Portage, all accessed from B&K Rd (Roberts Creek Forest Rd), just east of Roberts Creek Provincial Park (see Camping, above). All trails begin a short distance up the road at the BC Hydro power line. Each route is marked with a bike symbol and a different shade of paint.

In Sechelt, an area with some good intermediate/expert trails is the **Angus Creek Bike Loop,** between the Sechelt landfill and the Gray Creek Forest Rd, about 6 miles (10 km) one way. A number of interconnected forest service roads will lead you to the singletrack. The Angus Creek route is marked with a biking symbol and orange paint. The steep approach on the Sechelt-Crucil Forest Rd will test your ability to ride clean.

North of Sechelt, the area around **Trout Lake** has a plethora of trails for all skill levels to choose from. Look for trails such as **Little Knives** (also called the **Trout Lake Trail;** easy; 7.5 miles/12 km return) and **Redroofs** to the south of Hwy 101, as well as **Shakecutters, Hydroline, Crowston,**

Wormy Lake, and the **Microwave Tower Trails** to the north. The trailhead for routes on the north side of Hwy 101 is on Trout Lake Rd about 6 miles (10 km) north of Sechelt. The Trout Lake Loop Trail (moderate; 9 miles/15 km) is marked with biking symbols and yellow paint. Trails on the south side of Hwy 101 begin at the south end of Trout Lake. An alternative approach to Little Knives (Trout Lake Trail) is from Redroofs Rd in Sargeant Bay Provincial Park (see Beaches/Picnics, above). The trail begins opposite the yellow gate that marks the entrance to the beach.

Other lengthy loop trails reached from the Trout Lake and Halfmoon Bay Forest Rds include the **Carlson Lake Loop** (moderate/difficult; 13 miles/21 km), which is marked by orange paint, and the **Lyon Lake Loop** (difficult; 10.5 miles/17 km), marked by yellow paint. North of Trout Lake, the **Homesite Creek Bike Loop** (moderate/difficult; 5 miles/8 km) follows the Homesite Creek Forest Rd. The entrance to the road is obscure, so watch carefully for an orange "Trucks Turning" sign about 3.5 miles (5.6 km) north of Trout Lake on the north side of Hwy 101, just past Homesite Creek. The 5-mile (8-km) intermediate/expert trail is marked by biking symbols and blue paint. The biggest reward on this loop is an extended downhill after a taxing opening ascent.

One of the most ambitious mountain-bike trail projects, the 20-mile (33-km) **Suncoaster Trail,** opened in the mid-1990s. At present, it extends between Homesite Creek, near Halfmoon Bay, through the foothills of the Caren Range to Klein Lake near Earls Cove. Along the way, it passes abandoned rail lines, BC Hydro service roads, old-growth forests, and rocky promontories, and near its northern terminus has incredible views of Ruby and Sakinaw Lakes. Although mostly gravelled singletrack, the trail follows Hwy 101 for short distances where necessary. The shoulders on the highway have been broadened to comfortably accommodate cyclists in these places. Eventually, the trail will extend to Langdale. One of the most scenic spots is beside a waterfall where a 68-foot (21-m) bridge spans Sakinaw Creek. For more information, contact the Suncoast Trails Society, (604) 883-9043.

There are several good sources of mountain-bike **information** and **rentals** on the Sechelt Peninsula, including Pedals and Paddles Adventure Sports, (604) 885-6440, Seasport SCUBA and Mountain Bike Rentals, (604) 885-9830, Psycho Cycle, (604) 885-0850, and Trail Bay Sports, (604) 885-2512, all in Sechelt. In Gibsons, check out The Real Bicycle Shop, (604) 886-7192. The Ministry of Forests publishes detailed **maps** and comprehensive directions for many of the mountain-biking trails described above. For a free copy, call the Sunshine Coast district office in Powell River, (604) 485-0700, or pick one up from 7077 Duncan St in Powell River, or the ministry's office at 1975 Field Rd in Sechelt.

Malaspina Peninsula

The Upper Sunshine Coast area is well documented as having some of the best trails in the province, most of which are clearly marked with a white mountain-bike symbol and double bands of various-coloured paints, making the routes a breeze to follow.

The riding starts as soon as you get off the ferry at Saltery Bay, with the **Elephant Bay Loop,** a 30-mile (48-km) ride that will take you all day. Just follow the symbols. Except for a challenging ascent at the beginning, this is not a hard ride, but it is a long one.

An area rife with trails is along **Duck Lake Road** off Hwy 101 in southern Powell River. To name all the trails would not do the area justice; to describe them all would take another book (or at least the better part of a chapter). Best talk to the folks at Taws Cycle and Sport, (604) 485-2555, or Suncoast Cycles, (604) 487-1111, in Powell River.

A ride of epic proportion—the **Bunster Hills Loop**—is found about halfway between Powell River and Lund. It starts along Wilde Rd on the north side of Hwy 101, is marked by orange paint and white biking symbols, and gains 2,460 feet (750 m) over the first 7.5 miles (12 km), but the views—and the 13.6-mile (22-km) ride down—make the effort worth it. Another extended route still under development is the **Malaspina Trail,** between Powell River and Lund. One of the more scenic sections of the trail passes through Dinner Rock Forest Service Recreation Site (see Camping, above).

For a detailed account of many of the single-track mountain-bike trails on the Sunshine Coast, consult *Mountain Biking British Columbia* by Darrin Polischuk. Its well-drawn maps (with some exceptions around Sechelt that can be misleading at first) are a valuable resource to discovering off-road trails. The Sunshine Coast Forest Service District has done a remarkable service for mountain bikers. Pick up any of the Forest Service mountain-bike maps and take some time to explore. To obtain a free copy, call (604) 485-0700, or stop by 7077 Duncan St in Powell River.

Hiking/Walking

Sechelt Peninsula

The **Soames Hill Trail** (moderate) is Gibsons' answer to North Vancouver's Grouse Grind, a 40-minute stair-climb that seems to last forever, at the top of which you're rewarded with a view that just won't quit of Howe Sound and the Strait of Georgia. To reach the trailhead, take North or Reed Rd to Chamberlain Rd, then east on Bridgeman Rd to its end.

Much lengthier hiking trails in Gibsons can be found on Mount Elphinstone, which dominates the northwestern entrance to Howe Sound.

The **Mount Elphinstone Heritage Trails** have been developed only in the past decade and take advantage of numerous logging roads that had become overgrown when the timber supply was exhausted. All the trails are well marked with both colour-coded surveyor's tape and metal disks. The **K2 Trail** (moderate) ascends the side of Mount Elphinstone (4,137 feet/1261 m) from the end of Wharf Rd. To find the trailhead, follow the Port Mellon Hwy a short distance north of the ferry terminal at Langdale to Wharf Rd. As the pink-taped K2 Trail ascends, it meets with the blue-taped **Waterfall Trail** (easy), a much shorter, lower-elevation hike that leads to a waterfall viewpoint on Langdale Creek. The trailhead for the Waterfall Trail begins at the north end of Stewart Rd. Take either North Rd or the Gibsons Bypass to reach Stewart Rd. Red-taped **Tramway Trail** (moderate) follows the path of two tramways that once ferried supplies to loggers at higher elevations. The trailhead is located only after following several marked and unmarked roads. Take North Rd from either Gibsons or Langdale to Cemetery Rd, then follow Cemetery, which leads past a—you guessed it—cemetery, to Keith Rd. Watch for a road opposite the Boothill Ranch, which will deposit you in front of a yellow gate. Hike a short distance from here to the trailhead, which is marked with a red aluminum tag.

Three postage-stamp-size remnants of old-growth forest on **Mount Elphinstone** have recently been designated as provincial park. A prolific number of mushrooms, some of which have yet to be properly identified, grow here. Tread carefully and take only photographs.

Pender Harbour is a tough part of the Sunshine Coast to get a handle on. If you try to figure it out as you pass by on Hwy 101, you'll have only a half-baked notion of where freshwater lakes end and saltwater coves begin. This place is a geographical mess. Even if you take the plunge and begin exploring the roads that connect the three oceanside communities that comprise Pender Harbour—Madeira Park, Garden Bay, and Irvines Landing—you'd be hard pressed to keep your bearings. You'd probably do just as well if you were blindfolded and spun around three times. Fortunately, two hiking trails lead to viewpoints that will explain everything. **Pender Hill** (758 feet/231 m) rises sharply from the *saltchuk* (a Native term for water) above Irvines Landing, while **Mount Daniel** (1,375 feet/419 m) sits above Garden Bay. Both present moderately difficult, unrelentingly steep hiking. Packing a water bottle (or two) is a must. If time is of the essence, choose the Pender Hill Trail (moderate; 2 miles/3 km return) where a 30-minute cardiovascular workout will have you at the top. Plan on 90 minutes to reach the top of Mount Daniel (moderate; 5 miles/8 km return). Take a map to make sense of the view; NTS 92G/12 is the most detailed. Mount Daniel is too diminutive to be identified on most maps (tell that to someone who's just made the ascent) but the surrounding lakes and bays are. Mount Daniel is west of Hwy 101 on Garden Bay Rd. Drive some 2 miles (3.5 km), watching for a trail sign on the left side of the road. Park here and hike a short distance along a dirt road to the trailhead. To find the trail for Pender Hill, stay on Garden Bay Rd to Irvines Landing Rd, then along to Lee Rd. Watch for a sign on the right side of Lee Rd—and a turquoise-coloured telephone pole—that announces the trailhead.

The hiking trail between **Ruby Lake** and **Klein Lake** is also part of the **Suncoaster Trail** system (see Mountain Biking, above). At 2.5 miles (4 km), the trail is not overly long but is quite steep as it climbs north between the two lakes. Park at Don Bosch Regional Park beside Hwy 101, just north of Ruby Lake Resort. The trailhead at Klein Lake begins near the south end of the lake opposite the Forest Service recreation site. If you have a four-wheel-drive vehicle you can drive to the Klein Lake trailhead; if you don't you may have to add 0.6 mile (1 km) to the hike where the road around the lake grows impassable. To reach Klein Lake, follow Hwy 101 north to Egmont Rd, then drive 1 mile (1.6 km) to the North Lake Forest Rd. The rough road follows the shore of North Lake, then climbs towards Klein Lake. Use your discretion as to where to park and begin hiking. When you reach Klein Lake, take the left fork and follow the road as it leads around the lake, staying right at each subsequent fork until you reach the well-marked trailhead. Allow two to three hours to make the round trip.

One of the greatest natural shows in British Columbia occurs twice daily in **Skookumchuk Narrows Provincial Park** in Egmont at the north end of the Sechelt Peninsula. One of the largest saltwater rapids on Canada's West Coast, **Skookumchuk Rapids** boils as huge volumes of water force their way through Skookumchuk Narrows at the north end of Sechelt Inlet ("Skookum" is a Native word for strong and "chuk" means water). A 2.5-mile (4-km) walking trail leads from the outskirts of Egmont to viewing sites at North Point and Roland Point. This is an easy-going ramble without much diversion except where it skirts Brown Lake. Depending on the motion of the ocean, viewing is at North Point during a falling tide and at Roland Point during a flood tide. The two points are separated by only a short distance. At low tide, the bays around both points display astonishingly colourful and varied forms of marine life. Giant barnacles, colonies of starfish, sea urchins, and sea anemones thrive in the nutrient-rich waters, whose strong tidal currents cause these creatures to grow to extravagant sizes. In order to fully appreciate the scene, plan your visit to coincide with the change in tides. The most dramatic motion, when billions of gallons of water are sucked into cavernous whirlpools and whipped up into standing waves, occurs an hour after slack tide when the ocean is rising. Consult tide tables to determine the timing of your visit. You'll find these posted at tourist information centres around the Sunshine Coast, on BC Ferries, and at the trailhead, or call Bathgate's Store and Marina, (604) 883-2222, or the Sechelt Visitor Info-Centre, (604) 885-3100.

Malaspina Peninsula

The **Sunshine Coast Trail** is an ambitious program to create a route from the ferry terminal in Saltery Bay to Okeover Inlet and the western end of the peninsula at Desolation Sound. Trail building began in the early 1990s, and it will be a few more years before the entire 112 miles (180 km) is complete. For more information on the existing route and hiker-friendly accommodations along the way, contact the Powell River Visitors Bureau, 4690 Marine Ave, (604) 485-4701.

Other, more moderate hiking routes include the **Lang Creek Trail** (easy; 3 miles/5 km return) and **Sweetwater Trail** (moderate; 4.3 miles/7 km return). To reach the trailheads, turn north off Hwy 101 on the Duck Lake Forest Rd, which is about 14 miles (23 km) north of Saltery Bay. The Lang Creek trailhead begins on the right side of the road in about 7 miles (11 km). To reach the Sweetwater Trail, carry on farther to Duck Lake, turn right over the bridge, and continue on for another 2 miles (3.2 km), then turn left and drive a short distance to the traihead. The loop trail begins here and climbs through an enchanting stand of old-growth western hemlock past MacGregor Falls and returns along an old railbed.

Several hiking trails originate in the lake country north of Powell River. You can walk through old-growth forest as you explore the landscape around Powell, Inland, and Confederation Lakes. **Confederation Lake** is part of the new provincial park that also includes the Haslam Lake watershed. The moderate, 7.4-mile (12-km) round-trip hike leads around Mount Mahoney to Confederation Lake and will take the better part of a day to complete. To reach the trailhead, follow directions to Inland Lake (see Beaches/Picnics, above). Instead of turning in at Inland Lake, continue on, take the next road on the right, and drive another mile. Leave your vehicle at the pullout here and walk up a deteriorating road to the next fork. Take the right-hand route up a washed-out road, which soon narrows to a trail that is indicated by strategically placed metal markers. Make the rustic cabin on Confederation Lake your destination, although a rough trail does lead farther on from there to Powell Lake. With the exception of one steep section where a ramp and staircase assist hikers, most of the trail is easily negotiated.

A 2.5-mile (4-km) moderately difficult hiking trail connects the regional park at **Haywire Bay** (see Camping, above) on Powell Lake with the west side of **Inland Lake** (see Beaches/Picnics, above). Along the way this up-and-down, forested route passes diminutive Lost Lake. Short lake-side hiking trails also run along the shores of Powell Lake from **Mowat Bay Park** (see Beaches/Picnic, above) and Haywire Bay Regional Park.

North of Powell River you'll find a lengthy hiking route along the **Marathon-Appleton Trail** (moderate; 7.5 miles/12 km return). Some of the values of these routes include fine viewpoints at the Gibraltar and Gentle David lookouts, located off the Marathon Trail, as well as picnic sites at Rieveley's Pond and Appleton Creek. To find the trailhead, head north of Powell River through Sliammon (see Wildlife, below) to Southview Rd, which begins on the east side of Hwy 101. Travel almost 3 miles (5 km) on Southview to the well-marked trailhead. One of the beauties of this trail system is that you can choose to do all or part of it and still find significant rewards. An alternative approach to the Forest Service recreation site at Appleton Creek, where a stand of old-growth forest is located in Appleton Canyon, is via Wilde Rd, which begins on the east side of Hwy 101 in Sliammon. Wilde connects with the Theodosia Forest Rd, which climbs for more than 7 miles (12 km). The well-marked **Appleton Creek Trail** begins about halfway up the forest road on the left.

Powell River's **Inland Lake Trail** (see Cycling, above) is a lengthy walk, with plenty of places to rest along the way. There's something so *exhilarating* about the 8-mile (13-km) loop around the lake that some folks we met here were on their second time around.

The **Powell River Greenways Trail,** part of the Sunshine Coast Trail, passes along the hillside above the Forest Service recreation site at Dinner Rock (see Camping, above). A quiet 2-mile (3-km) walk here provides lovely views of Malaspina Strait and nearby Savary Island. You'll find the trail partway down the Dinner Rock Rd on the west side of Hwy 101. (Note: There are two roads named Dinner Rock. Take the one marked by a Forest Service sign.) The road is gated from mid-October to mid-April. Park and walk in if you arrive during these times.

Maps and **trail descriptions** are free for the asking from the Ministry of Forests' Sunshine Coast district office in Powell River, 7707 Duncan St, (604) 485-0700.

Fishing

Sechelt Peninsula

If you like to pick mussels and oysters, the beach at **Roberts Creek Provincial Park**'s picnic grounds (see Camping, above) is a good place to visit at low tide. Just check for red-tide warnings and harvesting closures beforehand at the entrance to the park.

The sandy beach at **Davis Bay** (see Beaches/Picnics, above) less than

2 miles (3 km) south of Sechelt may yield clams, but your best bet is casting from the pier here for salmon. So successful has the rearing program been at nearby **Chapman Creek** that it is the only stream on the Sechelt Peninsula where anglers can keep coho and chinook salmon. It's still best to check local regulations beforehand. While the hatchery has been experiencing good returns, fish stocks in the Strait of Georgia and Malaspina Strait have been steadily declining in recent times.

Secret Cove, about 10 miles (16.5 km) north of Sechelt, has three private marinas, which along with the marinas in **Pender Harbour** have some of the best fishing charters in the Lower Mainland. As successful lures, hot spots, and biting times vary so greatly in the convoluted waterways around Pender Harbour and nearby **Jervis Inlet,** it's important to drop by one of the marinas for the inside line, plus charts, licences, restrictions, and limits. Fishing is what they do best here, and patience is their long suit with visitors—all that sunshine has a profoundly positive effect on residents' attitudes.

March is one of the few months on the fishing calendar when anglers get to stay home and tidy their tackle boxes, or tie on a fly and try for surface-feeding trout at **Garden Bay Lake, Hotel Lake,** and **Mixal Lake,** which are located beside Garden Bay Rd, Irvine Landings Rd, and Hotel Lake Rd, respectively, west of Hwy 101.**Trout Lake** is the easiest to locate, as it lies on the north side of Hwy 101, 6 miles (10 km) north of Sechelt.

For more information, contact Hemstalk Hunting and Fishing Supplies in Sechelt, (604) 885-4090. **Fishing charters** can be arranged at many marinas and **boat rental** locations along the Sunshine Coast, including Garden Bay Marine Services, (604) 883-2722, Madeira Marina, (604) 883-2266, and Pelagia Marine Services, (604) 883-2280, as well as Ketchalot Charters, (604) 883-9351, Rainbow Voyage Charters, (604) 886-4938, Rogue Charters, (604) 883-1113, and Sunshine Charters, (604) 883-9362, all in the Pender Harbour region.

Malaspina Peninsula

Powell River may be one of the world's shortest rivers but it connects with a string of lakes—Powell, Goat, Windsor—that characterize much of the inland region. Fishing for cutthroat trout is possible year-round in milder years, as waters in the area rarely experience a freeze in any but the coldest winters. One of the best places to begin is at any of the access points to the Powell Forest Canoe Route (see Kayaking/Canoeing/Boating, above).

South of Powell River, some of the best ocean fishing is found in the **Lang Creek Estuary,** about 13.5 miles (22 km) north of Saltery Bay on the west side of Hwy 101. Beach casting is popular here for spring salmon from mid-September through late October. Owing to the shallow water of the creek's outlet into Malaspina Strait, use lures that don't sink quickly. If you use a spin rod, try spoons in a variety of colours to match the clarity of the water, with a light line. Salmon here are in the range of 20 to 50 pounds (9 to 23 kg). Farther up the coast near Lund you'll soon discover why a small, offshore island is named **Dinner Rock** (see Camping, above): ling cod and salmon frequent these waters. For more information on angling, contact Marine Traders in Powell River, (604) 485-4624. There are several dozen **charter boat** and **rental** businesses on the northern Sunshine Coast, including Malaspina Charters, (604) 485-6386, Dave's Boat Rentals, (604) 483-3667, and Jason Charters, (604) 485-4857.

Diving

Sechelt Peninsula

The Artificial Reef Society of BC scored a major coup for divers when it was given the go-ahead to scuttle HMCS *Chaudière,* a retired Canadian Forces destroyer escort, off **Kunechin Point** in **Sechelt Inlet.** The *Chaudiére* now rests on its side in deep water (66–130 feet/20–40 m). Several descent lines lead divers to the 387-foot (118-m) hull of the ship and assist as guides to the surface. Kunechin Point, in Sechelt Inlets Provincial Marine Recreation Area, is also the site of a marine park campground (see Kayaking/Canoeing/Boating, above) and can be reached by boat from either Sechelt or Egmont.

Another popular dive site in Sechelt Inlet is at **Tuwanek Point Beach,** where fish are so varied and numerous that you may think you're snorkelling in Hawaii. (The chill of the waters in the inlet will quickly disabuse you of that notion.) To reach the site, head north on Sechelt Inlet Rd from Hwy 101 via Wharf and Porpoise Bay Rds. Bear left in Tuwanek where the road divides (the Gray Creek Forest Rd leads off to the right). Swim out from Tuwanek Point Beach to the nearby Lamb Islets to visit the "aquarium."

North of Sechelt the popular spot for diving begins in the waters of **Halfmoon Bay** at Coopers Green Regional Park (see Beaches/Picnics, above). Follow Redroofs Rd (see Cycling, above) as it loops west of Hwy 101 from either of two entrances. The relatively shallow water on the east side of the bay provides good beginner and intermediate diving as well as snorkelling. A note of caution: Divers must be mindful of boaters in the water around Coopers Green Regional Park and Halfmoon Bay in general.

The maze of coves, bays, and islands around **Pender Harbour** make it the most popular diving spot on the Sechelt Peninsula. You'll need a boat to reach the four most popular sites at **Fearney Bluffs, Nelson Rock,** and **Anderson** and **Charles Islands.** See Fishing, above, for a list of charter and boat rental locations in Pender Harbour.

The northeast corner of the Sechelt Peninsula is also the entrance to the Sechelt Inlet. Boat dives originate from the village of **Egmont,** a cluster of homes gathered around Secret Bay, a short distance east of the BC Ferries terminal at Earls Cove. Three of the many possible dive sites close to Egmont (which include the sunken *Chaudière* at Kunechin Point in Sechelt Inlet) are in the waters of **Jervis Inlet** off Foley Head, in **Agamemnon Channel**, and the Park Wall off North Point at the **Skookumchuk Narrows** (see Hiking/Walking, above). A combination of wind and tidal currents makes diving at these sites both exhilarating and dangerous.

Arrange a **charter dive trip** with the Egmont Marina Resort, (604) 883-2298, Destination Egmont, toll-free 1-888-292-9999 or (604) 883-0251, or Lowe's Resort in Madeira Park (Pender Harbour), (604) 883-2456. For more information, also check with Seasport SCUBA and Mountain Bike Rentals, (604) 885-9830, in Sechelt. The definitive dive book to consult is *101 Dives from the Mainland of Washington and British Columbia* by Betty Pratt-Johnson.

Malaspina Peninsula

Powell River is deservedly known as one of the premier winter diving locales on the west coast of North America. The clarity of the water and strong currents in **Malaspina Strait** are the two factors that anchor this claim. More than 100 dive sites attract SCUBA divers from around the world. One of these sites is the breakwater formed by a ring of 10 concrete-hulled Liberty ships that were sunk offshore in 1947 to protect the deep-water harbour in front of the MacMillan-Bloedel pulp mill. In addition, relics of sailing ships and sunken tugboats provide a refuge for marine life, such as the wolf eels and giant octopi that inhabit the deep offshore waters. A beautifully sculpted bronze mermaid sits in 60 feet (20 m) of water offshore from **Saltery Bay Provincial Park** (see Camping, above) in Mermaid Bay. For more information on diving in Powell River, contact Wolf's Den Diving, (604) 485-2010. **Charter services** for divers as well as many other amenities are available from Beach Gardens Marina, (604) 485-6267, or toll-free (800) 663-7070.

Wildlife

Sechelt Peninsula

California and Steller sea lions and **harbour seals** gather during winter months at mouth of Chapman Creek south of Sechelt. Walk out onto Mission Point for the best views. The best approach to the point is from the beach at Davis Bay (see Beaches/Picnics, above).

The marshland around **Sargeant Bay Provincial Park** is an important stopover for waterfowl such as **harlequin ducks, Canada geese**, and **trumpeter swans**, as is the upland area for a host of **migratory songbirds.** Local volunteers have undertaken an ambitious project to restore wildlife habitat around the bay. To reach the park, follow Redroofs Rd west of Hwy 101, about 3.6 miles (6 km) north of Sechelt. You'll have to watch carefully for the road sign as it is not prominent. Follow Redroofs to Sargeant Bay Park Rd a short distance to the undeveloped shingle and sand beach, and begin stalking from here.

Some of the oldest yellow cedar and western hemlock in western Canada grow in the Caren Range. Home to the **marbled murrelet,** a drab, starling-size seabird whose numbers are in as precipitous a decline as the old-growth western hemlock on which it depends, these mountains form the backbone of the Sechelt Peninsula. Although most murrelets nest in cliffs and rock walls, the marbled murrelet, having evolved beside the majestic, ramrod-straight, temperate old-growth forest, lay their eggs on the hemlocks' broad, moss-draped limbs. A bittersweet victory was gained here when the last of the great Caren forest was recently protected as **Caren Provincial Park,** but not before some of the oldest trees in Canada—in excess of 2,000 years old—were cut, then left to waste. You'll have to drive a long way through open hillsides before you reach the shade of the park, but the tranquillity you'll experience there will be a grand reward. Look for a paved road that begins 8 miles (13 km) north of Sechelt on the east side of Hwy 101, marked by a Wildlife Rehabilitation Centre sign. Drive a farther 8 miles (13 km) up what soon turns into the Caren Mainline Forest Rd. Parts of this road are deteriorating, and those with a four-wheel-drive vehicle will have the easier go of it. At the three-way fork in the road, take whichever direction seems best suited to your vehicle. Each leads to the forest, still some distance above. For information on Caren Provincial Park, call BC Parks, (604) 898-3678.

Malaspina Peninsula

Come fall, many of the streams that feed into Malaspina Strait teem with spawning **salmon.** Depending on the year and the spawning cycle, **Lang Creek Hatchery and Spawning Channels,** about 13.5 miles (22 km) north of Saltery Bay, will be thick with returning salmon. The best viewing is right next to the well-marked pullout on Hwy 101.

As sure as salmon return to spawn in late summer, so too do raptors and bears follow. Although black bears in the Powell River region tend to frequent the backwoods logging roads, **osprey** and **eagles, otters,** and **pine marten** have no fear of approaching the coastline around Sliammon Creek in search of carrion. Occasionally, even a **black bear** will put in an appearance. One particularly good viewing spot of both predator and prey is near the Sliammon fish hatchery, about 3 miles (5 km) north of the Powell River bridge. Sliammon is the site of a native village that has been in continuous habitation for the past two millennia. To reach the hatchery, follow Klahanie Rd, which begins beside a Native handicrafts store of the same name on the south side of Hwy 101. Watch for an enormous eagle's nest in one of the trees as you near the strait.

Cross-Country Skiing

Sechelt Peninsula

The Sunshine Coast's long suit is brightness, which, when combined with winter whiteness, produces a dazzling effect. Hang onto your ski poles! Cross-country skiing is the choice of winter recreation pursuits. Snow often remains in the forest well into June, by which time most visitors have wisely headed for the beaches.

The best winter recreation is near Sechelt, where you'll find 12 miles (20 km) of well-developed cross-country ski trails on **Mount Steele** in **Tetrahedron Provincial Park.** The Tetrahedron Ski Club built the trails as well as the four sturdy, 12-person, first-come-first-snooze cabins that lie at a variety of locations throughout the park. To find your way to the trail-head from Hwy 101 in Sechelt, follow Sechelt Inlet Rd for almost 6 miles (10 km) to Tuwanek. Turn right on Upland Dr, then right onto Carmel Place to reach the Gray Creek Logging Rd. Drive about 7 miles (11 km), following the ski signs affixed to trees along the way. The road is plowed as far as a parking area in winter. Cabins with wood-burning stoves are located at Batchelor Lake, Edwards Lake, McNair Lake, and near the summit of Mount Steele. All but the expert 3.8-mile (6.2-km) return trail to Mount Steele are rated as intermediate runs. Bring your skins, as many of the approaches climb the steep-sided, clear-cut hillsides to Gilbert and Edwards Lakes. Trails lead from the cabin at Edwards Lake up to the Mount Steele cabin above or down to the cabin near McNair Lake. A popular loop route runs from the parking lot to Edwards Lake and then returns via the cabin at Bachelor Lake.

For more information on these trails as well as to obtain a **trail map,** contact the Forest Service district office in Powell River, (604) 485-0700, or stop by the Forest Service field office in Sechelt, 1975 Field Rd, (604) 740-5005, to obtain a free copy of *The Trails of the Lower Sunshine Coast.* Contact BC Parks for a trail map of Tetrahedron Provincial Park, (604) 898-3678. The Tetrahedron Ski Club is another good source of information; (604) 886-9411. The club also operates a **snow phone** during winter months; (604) 885-9167. For experienced, avalanche-prepared skiers, there's backcountry ski touring in the Panther Peak section of the park. The best map of the region is NTS 92 G12.

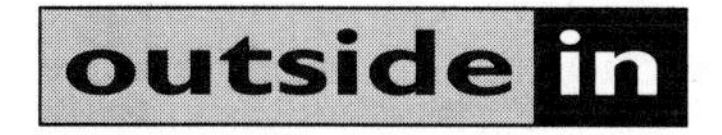

Attractions

Gibsons, just west of Langdale, became widely known years ago as the setting for *The Beachcombers,* a once-popular TV series, and has not been slow to cash in on its fame. The harbour is everything it should be (and the BC Ferries' dock in nearby Langdale isn't), chock full o' boats, with an atmosphere as thick as fog on a fall morning.

Treat yourself to a walking tour of the harbour. At times, you'll find fresh seafood for sale right off the side of a working fisherman's vessel moored at the government wharf. A stroll on the Seawalk will introduce you to both the commercial and the natural sides of the harbour.

Seventeen kilometres (10.5 miles) farther up Hwy 101 is **Sechelt,** one of the fastest-growing towns in Canada. It's also home to the Sechelt Nation's cultural centre, the **House of Hewhiwus,** which houses an art centre and the Raven's Cry theatre; (604) 885-4597. Turn off the main highway and you discover a scattering of small coastal communities where life still unfolds at a leisurely pace. **Roberts Creek,** between Gibsons and Sechelt, is a favourite haunt of painters and craftspeople.

Pender Harbour, north of Sechelt, was once the winter headquarters of the Sechelt Nation, and on nearby Mount Daniel you can see the remains of moon rings (stone circles built by Sechelt girls as they entered womanhood); Sechelt **pictographs** mark the cliffs above Sakinaw Lake. Garden Bay is a scenic small village on the north side of Pender Harbour; the deck of the pub at the Garden Bay Hotel is a fine place to while away a summer afternoon.

Powell River, home to about 18,000 people, has been dependent on the logging industry for its survival since about 1911. Tourism is developing quickly, however, thanks in part to an abundance of sun and clear water. It is also the ancestral home of the Sliammon First Nation.

The pristine waters of Desolation Sound are surrounded by steep evergreen mountains, all teeming with the wildest of wildlife. The Sound sits at the end of British Columbia's Sunshine Coast, the northernmost terminus of Hwy 101 (which begins 14,880 miles/24 000 km south in Chile). Here, the tiny hamlet of **Lund** is only 95 miles (153 km) north of Vancouver, but it takes five hours (including two BC Ferries' rides) to get there. It's worth the drive from Powell River just to sample the blackberry cinnamon rolls at Nancy's Bakery on the town pier; (604) 483-4180.

Restaurants

Blue Heron Inn ☆☆ One of the nicest places to dine on the Sunshine Coast is the Blue Heron—partly for the waterfront view (and the blue herons, of course) and partly for the food (fresh clams, roast loin of veal, grilled salmon). *Porpoise Bay Rd (turn right at lights at Wharf St and right at Porpoise Bay Rd), Sechelt; (604) 885-3847 or (800) 818-8977; $$.*

Chez Philippe ☆☆ The menu is French-inspired, with Northwest influences. The best choices on the menu are the seafood entrees. The dining room is elegant, with a crackling fireplace and views towards the water. *1532 Ocean Beach Esplanade (outside Gibsons, at Gower Point), Gibsons; (604) 886-2188; $$.*

The Creek House ☆☆ Situated in a house with a view of a tree-filled garden, the restaurant is decorated simply with flowers on the tables and original art. You may choose from 10 entrees that change seasonally, such as wild boar, rack of lamb Provençal, or locally caught rabbit. *1041 Roberts Creek Rd (at Beach Ave), Roberts Creek; (604) 885-9321; $$.*

Gumboot Garden The Gumboot Garden is an old maroon house with a simple sign: Cafe. Inside, a terra-cotta sun radiates warmth and the menu shines with a strong Mexican influence. Breads and cheesecakes are baked daily, and organic produce is used when possible. *1057 Roberts Creek Rd (junction of Lower Rd), Roberts Creek; (604) 885-4216; $.*

Howl at the Moon This spot frightens away hunger pains with Tex-Mex staples augmented by steaks, burgers, and six imaginative chicken dishes. We suggest you stick with the Tex-Mex. *450 Marine Dr (on 1st block of Marine Dr going toward Langdale), Gibsons; (604) 886-8881; $.*

jitterbug cafe ☆ The jitterbug cafe is a stylish little place that's open only during the high season, but it's a fine stop for a simple meal based on local ingredients (and some wonderful homemade breads). *4643 Marine Ave (in the Wind Spirit Gallery, on west side of Hwy 101), Powell River; (604) 485-7797; $$.*

Lodgings

Beach Gardens Resort ☆ Sitting on a protected section of the Strait of Georgia, the Beach Gardens Resort is a mecca for scuba enthusiasts, who come for the near-tropical clarity of the water and the abundant marine life. The rooms are comfortable: nothing sensational, except the views of all that water. Divers prefer the less expensive cabins without views. *7074 Westminster Ave (0.5 hour north of Saltery Bay ferry on Hwy 101), Powell River, BC V8A 1C5; (604) 485-6267 or (800) 663-7070; $$.*

Bonniebrook Lodge This simple yellow clapboard house on the water has been a guest house since 1922. Its combination of inn with campground and RV sites is not for everyone. Of the four rooms, we prefer either of the two facing the Strait of Georgia. *1532 Ocean Beach Esplanade (outside Gibsons, at Gower Point); mail: S10 C34, RR4, Gibsons, BC V0N 1V0; (604) 886-2887; $$.*

Country Cottage Bed and Breakfast ☆ There are two lodging options here. You can stay in a pretty one-room cottage or, better, in the supremely comfortable Adirondack-style cedar lodge (sleeps six), complete with huge fireplace and adjacent wood-fired sauna. You're a five-minute stroll from a sandbar beach. *1183 Roberts Creek Rd (14.5 km/9 miles from ferry, off Hwy 101), Roberts Creek, BC V0N 2W0; (604) 885-7448; $$.*

Halfmoon Bay Cabin ☆☆ This rustic yet luxurious retreat has everything you might want, from a massive stone fireplace to an outdoor shower on the deck. Surrounded by an English country garden, it sits on a hill overlooking its own beach, complete with private cabana. *8617 Redroofs Rd (3.75 miles/6 km north of Sechelt), Halfmoon Bay; mail: No. 502 - 1290 Burnaby St, Vancouver, BC V6E 1P5; (604) 688-5058; $$$.*

Lord Jim's Resort Hotel ☆ Lord Jim's aspires to be *the* resort on the Sunshine Coast but the overall impression is closer to utilitarian motel. Still, its location on a quiet cove is prime, and the facilities include a restaurant and an outdoor pool. Fishing, scuba diving, and kayaking can be arranged. *Turn left on Mercer Rd off Hwy 101 north of Sechelt; mail: RR2 Ole's Cove Site, C-1, Halfmoon Bay, BC V0N 1Y0; (604) 885-7038 or (888)757-FISH; $$.*

Rosewood Bed & Breakfast ☆☆ The Rosewood is an Edwardian-style mansion filled with light. Of the two rooms, the suite with the bay-window bath looking out to the sea is the better. Breakfast can be pretty much whatever the guests would like. *575 Pine Rd (Pine Rd starts at Lower Rd turnoff from Hwy 101, about 4 miles/6.5 km west of Gibsons); mail: S46 C21, RR2, Gibsons, BC V0N 1V0; (604) 886-4714; $$.*

Ruby Lake Resort ☆ Near scenic Ruby Lake is this collection of 10 units facing a private lagoon. The cottages are nicely furnished and have full kitchens and TVs. It's a great place to bring the kids. Plan to come in time for the eagle feeding at 6pm each evening. *Hwy 101 north of Madeira Park; mail: C65 S15, RR1, Madeira Park, BC V0N 2H0; (604) 883-2269 or (800) 717-6611; $$.*

Cheaper Sleeps

Cattanach Bed and Breakfast This cozy two-room B&B offers a rock fireplace, a guest living room, and a wood-burning stove. Guests share the bathroom. *RR 2, F18 C7, Roberts Creek, BC V0N 1V0; (604) 885-5444; $.*

The Old Courthouse Inn The historic courthouse in the Powell River Townsite has been converted into an inviting, inexpensive, 10-room inn. Five rooms share bathrooms and are rented by the night; the other five rooms have private baths and are only available for stays of a week or longer. *6243 Walnut St, Powell River, BC V8A 4K4; (604) 483-4000; $.*

Sundowner Inn Housed in a former hospital built in 1929, the Sundowner offers recently renovated rooms with a view of Garden Bay (off Pender Harbour). The rooms that share a bath are the least expensive. Closed in winter. *4339 Garden Bay Rd (PO Box 113), Garden Bay, BC V0N 1S0; (604) 883-9676; $.*

More Information

BC Ferries: *general inquiries, (604) 669-1211; Saltery Bay, (604) 487-9333; Powell River, (604) 485-2943.*

BC Forest Service, Sunshine Coast Forest District, Powell River: *(604) 485-0700.*

BC Parks, Garibaldi/Sunshine Coast District: *(604) 898-3678.*

Gibsons Tourist InfoCentre: *(604) 886-2325.*

Powell River Regional District: *(604) 483-3231.*

Powell River Tourist InfoCentre: *(604) 485-4701.*

Sechelt Tourist InfoCentre: *(604) 885-0662.*

Sunshine Coast Regional District: *(604) 885-2261.*

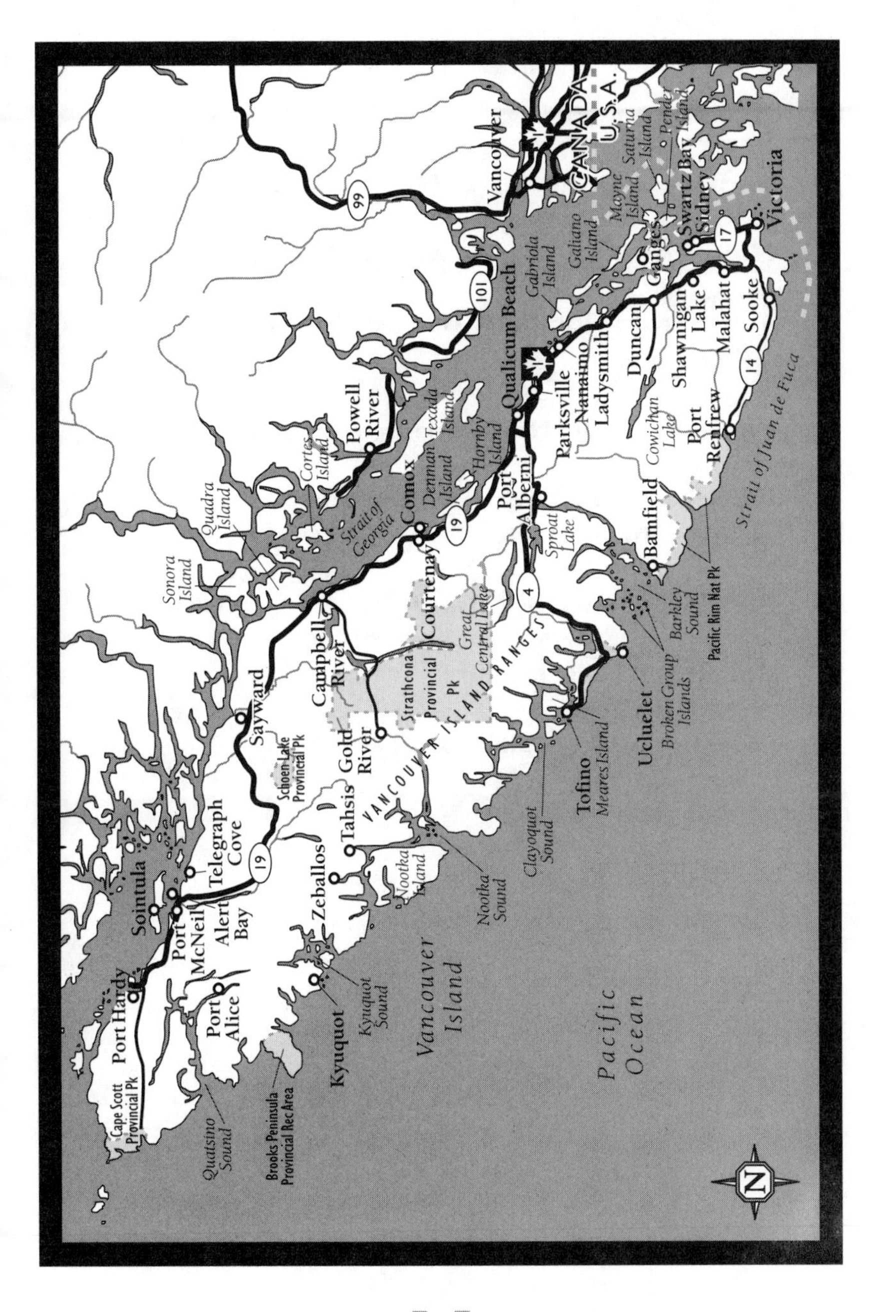

Vancouver Island and the Gulf Islands

Greater Victoria 237

Sooke Basin and the West Coast Trail 262

Nanaimo and the Cowichan Valley 276

Tofino and Pacific Rim National Park Reserve 295

Parksville and the Comox Valley 314

Nootka Sound and Strathcona Provincial Park 331

North Vancouver Island 342

Southern Gulf Islands 354

Northern Gulf Islands 374

Greater Victoria

The extreme southern end of Vancouver Island, including the Saanich Peninsula, Victoria, Esquimalt, Colwood, Metchosin, and Sooke, and featuring Goldstream Provincial Park, Galloping Goose Trail Regional Park, and East Sooke Regional Park.

Almost half of Vancouver Island's population of 670,000 lives within the Capital Regional District (CRD) around Victoria at the southern end of Vancouver Island. There is a rich diversity of landscapes within the cool Mediterranean climate of the region, ranging from the Douglas fir forests along the coast to the drier, exposed conditions of the higher, rockier elevations, which support arbutus (madrona) and Garry oak forests. Flowers bloom year-round in Victoria, which makes exploring the outdoors here enjoyable in any season. Ferns and lichens colour the forest floor throughout the winter; come spring, an explosion of trilliums and calypso orchids heightens the effect before giving way to bushes lush with huckleberry, salmonberry, trailing blackberry, salal, and Oregon grape. Such profusion is a reward for migrating birds that make the Victoria region a semi-annual stop-over point. Bald eagles, ospreys, turkey vultures, herons, shorebirds, belted kingfishers, dippers, winter wrens, and many species of migratory ducks, geese, and swans flock to the delightfully benign environment.

Victorians display their love for the natural world by cultivating flower gardens at every turn. As you'd imagine in a region where a large urban population interacts with such a delightful natural tableau, a vast network of walking, hiking, and biking routes leads through the many parks with which the city is blessed. In fact, the very first property to be donated to the provincial park system—

John Dean Provincial Park—is located in the middle of Greater Victoria's Saanich Peninsula. Throughout the 1990s, a string of new parks have been set aside in the CRD, including the almost 3,000-acre (1200-ha) Gowlland Tod Provincial Park and the 37-mile (60-km) Galloping Goose commuter walk and cycle trail.

Although the mountainscape on the southern end of Vancouver Island is not as rugged as the North Shore mountains that rise above Vancouver, this actually mitigates in favour of hiking, as the physical demands for reaching viewpoints is not as great. On the other hand, the views are as panoramic and breathtaking as anywhere in the province. It's easy to imagine how sweet life was for Native Canadians who once had this all to themselves. Beacon Hill Park in downtown Victoria was the site of a village that had been inhabited for thousands of years prior to the arrival of the colonial settlers in the 1840s. A tangled web of events since then has displaced the original dwellers, but their history is evident in the petroglyphs that adorn the shoreline and in the middens of seashells mounded up beside the beaches on Strait of Juan de Fuca. Totem poles new and old stand as proud reminders of this heritage. To gain a fresh appreciation for the talents and skills of First Nations peoples, combine a visit to the outdoors around Victoria with a stop at the Royal British Columbia Museum, a world-class repository of native artifacts. With the enriched perspective that such a visit will bring, you'll look at the landscape with new interest and appreciation. The figures on the totems will no longer be static representations from a mythological age. Instead, combined with the presence of killer whales, seals, eagles, ravens, salmon, and other species that are as vibrant in the landscape today as they were in the past, you'll enter a timeless realm and, in the process, discover a new place in nature for yourself.

Getting There

Victoria lies on the southern tip of Vancouver Island and is linked with the rest of the 280-mile-long (450-km) island by the Island Highway (Highway 1), whose southern terminus begins at Douglas Street in downtown Victoria. Visitors from the Lower Mainland travel to Victoria via BC Ferries' Tsawwassen terminal in Delta. Sailing time to the Swartz Bay terminal, located on the northeastern tip of the Saanich Peninsula, 20 miles (32 km) north of Victoria on Highway 17, is about 90 minutes to cover the 27-mile (44-km) distance across the Strait of Georgia. Call (604) 277-0277 in Greater Vancouver, or (250) 386-3431 in Greater Victoria, for a detailed recorded message on seasonal sailing times and fares.

Visitors from the United States can journey to Victoria via ferry from either Anacortes in northwestern Washington, from Seattle, or from Port Angeles on Washington's Olympic Peninsula. The Anacortes ferry arrives in

Sidney, at the Washington State Ferries terminal, 2499 Ocean Road, 3 miles (5 km) south of Swartz Bay; (250) 381-1531. The Black Ball ferry from Port Angeles (call (360) 457-4491 in Port Angeles, or (250) 386-2202 in Victoria) arrives in Victoria's Inner Harbour, as does Clipper Navigation's catamaran service to Victoria from Seattle's Pier 69, (800) 888-2535, or (206) 448-5000 in Seattle, or (250) 382-8100 in Victoria. The Olympic and Saanich Peninsulas are separated by the Strait of Juan de Fuca, a 17-mile (27-km) stretch of (almost) open ocean.

By air, visitors arrive at either Victoria Harbour by float plane or Victoria International Airport on the Saanich Peninsula, about 17 miles (27 km) north of Victoria.

Adjoining Areas

NORTH: **Nanaimo and the Cowichan Valley**

WEST: **Sooke Basin and the West Coast Trail**

inside out

Parks/Camping

Goldstream Provincial Park (150 vehicle/tent sites, including 9 double sites) offers visitors to Victoria better camping than provided in any other urban centre in British Columbia. This is a showcase for provincial parks, and many visitors fortunate to stay a day or two here end up wishing they could take up permanent residence. The campsites are well spaced, close to all park amenities, including hot showers, and within easy walking distance of Goldstream River. As well, the campsites are separated from the day-use area of the boot-shaped park by a network of hiking and walking trails that provides a further degree of privacy, particularly in early fall when thousands of day trippers converge on the north end of the park to witness an annual salmon run. Goldstream Park's campground is located to the west of the Island Hwy (Hwy 1) and is reached via Sooke Lake Rd, about 10 miles (15 km) west of central Victoria. To book a site here from March 1 to September 15, call BC Parks' campground reservation service, (800) 689-9025. Detailed maps of the park are available at both the entrance to the campground and the day-use area. For more information, contact BC Parks, (250) 391-2300.

McDonald Provincial Park (60 vehicle/tent sites) is located beside the BC Ferries terminal at Swartz Bay in North Saanich. Although you'll find a lot of marine traffic swirling around the area during the day, in the evening the pulse slows to a sleep-inducing rhythm, especially once the last ferries have sailed or docked for the night. The campground is tucked in between the Pat Bay Hwy (Hwy 17) and the shoreline of Canoe Bay. Although this location doesn't guarantee complete privacy, it admirably suits most travellers' purposes. With its eastern exposure, you're sure to be roused by sunrise. For more information, contact BC Parks, (250) 391-2300.

Sidney Spit Provincial Marine Park (27 walk-in sites) is located at the north end of Sidney Island, just far enough offshore from the Saanich Peninsula to seem remote. You'll share the park with thousands of shorebirds that populate the extensive tide flats and salt marshes, which sustain an astonishing spectrum of plant and animal life. You won't find a softer surface on which to camp than the park's white sand. Like that of many neighbouring islands, the topography is a blend of level ground and steep-sided bluffs. Much of the park is situated on a spit of land more or less revealed by the rise and fall of the tides, while a more sheltered upland section of the park lies south of the beach. Campsites are located within an easy walk of the federal dock. The island is accessible only by boat, a 3-mile (5-km), 15-minute ride by ferry from Sidney. Ferry service runs from mid-May to mid-October. Call (250) 727-7700 for information; see also Beaches/Picnics, below. There is a charge of $9.50 per night for use of the campsites. Unlike the majority of marine parks, fresh drinking water is available here but is high in sodium, so bring your own if you have health concerns.

Ferry service from Sidney to **Princess Margaret Provincial Marine Park** on Portland Island, about 2.5 nautical miles (4 nautical km) from Sidney, is also available for groups of 10 or more. The price for this 50-minute trip is $16 for adults. You may find that the experience of visiting Portland Island is well worth the cost. Wilderness campsites are located at three places on the island. Freshwater is available from a hand pump located at the old Youth Crew camp. Note: Raccoons are numerous on Portland Island; be sure to secure all food supplies in containers (a tent is not a secure container!). For more information and a map of the park, contact BC Parks, (250) 391-2300. For information on ferry service, call (250) 727-7700.

Beaches/Picnics

One of the glorious things about the Victoria region is that you can picnic here year-round, something that much of the rest of the province (and rest of the country!) has always envied. Each season has its unique character, and life is always assuming new forms. Spring and fall migrations of birds and fish animate the landscape. Evergreen forests brighten a winter landscape that otherwise lies unveiled once deciduous trees drop their summer foliage. Even snow makes the occasional appearance, though it rarely remains for long. Summer droughts and winter rains determine the songs sung by rivers and creeks. Through it all, the picnic ground at **Goldstream Provincial Park** (see Parks/Camping, above) beside the Goldstream River provides a welcome. A lot of lunches get consumed here during the fall salmon migration, when hundreds of nature-loving onlookers come to the park to watch fish have sex. (If you want to keep your drive alive, this is the outdoors place to be.) The picnic grounds (43 tables and counting) are located just off Hwy 1 about 11 miles (18 km) west of Victoria, midway through Goldstream Provincial Park.

Without doubt, **Sidney Spit Provincial Marine Park** (see also Parks/Camping, above) has the finest beaches of any park in the Victoria region. The hitch is that visiting this park requires a boat ride. Ferry service to Sidney Island runs during summer months; otherwise, you must make your own arrangements to get here. The trip takes 15 minutes one way. There is a $9 charge for adults, with reduced rates for seniors and children ages 12 years and under. Ferry service begins at 9am on weekdays and 10am on weekends. The boat holds 35 passengers and leaves from the Sidney Marina just north of the Beacon St dock. For information, call (250) 727-7700.

Island View Beach Regional Park is located on the east side of the Saanich Peninsula in North Saanich. Follow Island View Rd east from Hwy 17 a short distance to this gentle cobble- and driftwood-strewn beach. Good views of James and Sidney Islands, and beyond to Mount Baker, make this a pleasant, no-charge alternative to taking the ferry to Sidney Spit Provincial Marine Park. An unbroken string of small islands seem to fold into each other offshore. If you get bored watching the action from the shore, there's wildlife viewing in the open fields behind the beach. The best access to the beach is at the entrance to the park and from the parking lot on the north side of an adjacent private RV park. (Note: The entire beach is public.) Locals use the beach area north of the park fronting Indian reserve land for discreet, clothing-optional tanning. The beach leads a long way north to the tip of Cordova Point.

Several picnic tables stand beneath the spreading trees next to Eagle Beach in **Elk and Beaver Lakes Regional Park,** but visitors will find the sound of traffic on nearby Hwy 17 hard to ignore. A stand of tall Douglas firs shelters North Beach and the beach around Cowquitz Creek at the south end of nearby Beaver Lake from traffic. Picnicking here is much more pleasant. The turnoff from Hwy 17 to Beaver Lake is well marked.

Coles Bay Regional Park, a small park on Saanich Inlet, has a rough, barnacle-covered rock beach typical of the peninsula's west side. Bring along a pair of beach shoes to best enjoy the environment. The water in this deep fjord is always invigorating. The park is located on Inverness Rd off Ardmore Dr, a short distance west of Hwy 17A (West Saanich Rd).

Picnic tables are thoughtfully placed in the forest above a pond in **John Dean Provincial Park** (see Hiking, below). Beside the tables rises a small but stately stand of virgin Douglas fir. This is a good place to have a snack before exploring farther in the park. Follow the right-hand trail from the parking lot as it leads downhill, and bear right at a junction that it makes a short distance farther. The picnic tables are located here as the trail continues downhill towards another stand of fir beside the pond. For the most dramatic effect, continue on around the pond, which acts as a mirror for the tall trees.

Three small lakes dot the slopes of **Mount Work Regional Park.** Depending on your mood, the weather, and the season, freshen up in **Durrance** or **Pease Lake** on the north side of the park once you've completed the hike to the top of the mountain, or just relax at lakeside and enjoy the woodland ambience. **Fork Lake** lies at the south end of the hiking trail to the summit of Mount Work. To reach Durrance Lake, take Wallace Dr west of Hwy 17A, then follow Willis Point Rd until the lake appears on its north side. Pease Lake is a short distance father west. Follow Willis Point Rd to Ross Durrance Rd and head south to the lake. Fork Lake is reached by following Millstream Rd north of Hwy 1 west of Victoria, then turning northeast on Munnis Rd.

Thetis Lake Regional Park lies on the west side of Victoria, about 7 miles (12 km) from the city centre in View Royal. Sandy beaches front the park's two heavily indented lakes, which are connected by a thin canal. If you have a canoe or kayak, you can reach some of the more remote beaches (see Kayaking/Boating, below); otherwise, enjoy yourself within an easy walk of the parking lot. To reach Thetis Lake, head west of Victoria on Hwy 1 and watch for signs that point the way north of the highway to the park. Note: Although several hiking trails originate from Thetis Lake Rd, the beach is reached by following West Park Lane, about 6 miles (10 km) from the city centre.

Witty's Lagoon Regional Park (see Wildlife, below) west of Victoria offers yet another perspective on the coastline. A long swath of sandy beach curves gently along Strait of Juan de Fuca, protecting a crucial marshland from the full force of waves and wind. Find a sturdy piece of driftwood and shelter from the constant breeze, which even in summer has a fresh edge to it. From this vantage point, you can look across the strait to the towering heights of the Olympic Mountains in Washington and its signature glaciated formation, Hurricane Ridge. The shallow beach makes for a pleasant warm-water swim after the tide rises over sun-heated rocks. There are several entrances to the park. For quick access to the beach, take Hwy 14 west of Victoria, then turn south on Metchosin Rd. The well-marked trailhead at Sitting Woman Falls is located opposite the Metchosin Golf Course. Allow 10 to 15 minutes to walk from the parking lot to the beach.

Sooke Potholes Provincial Park is located north of Hwy 14 and just east of Sooke. The Galloping Goose Trail (see Biking, below) runs past this small day-use park. Swimming in the potholes that have been carved in the sandstone in the Sooke River provides ideal refreshment on hot summer days. This site has been luring picnickers from the Victoria region for years, so don't be surprised by the controlled mayhem when you arrive. Picnic tables line the river next to the parking area, and the potholes are just steps beyond.

Kayaking/Boating

A public boat launch is located beside the federal dock at the north end of Lands End Rd at **Swartz Bay.** This is a good place to put your boat in the water and head for any number of nearby islands or to explore the coastline of the Saanich Peninsula. Those in open canoes should be cautious of the wash from BC Ferries' boats and larger marine traffic around Swartz Bay. To reach the boat launch, take the MacDonald Dr exit east from Hwy 17 just south of Swartz Bay, then turn north on Lands End Rd.

Launch from either the boat ramp or wharf in **Sidney** and head across the channel to **Sidney Spit Provincial Marine Park** or **Princess Margaret Provincial Marine Park** (see Parks/Camping, above). To locate the launch, drive to the east end of Beacon Ave.

James Island shelters the waters of Cordova Channel in front of **Island View Beach Regional Park** (see Beaches/Picnics, above). A boat ramp is conveniently located at the entrance to the park. Paddle over to nearby James Island (about 0.6 mile/1 km), and from there to Sidney Island (about 2 miles/3 km) and beyond.

The Elk Lake Rowing Club operates from Eagle Beach in **Elk and Beaver Lakes Regional Park** (see Beaches/Picnics, above) where a public boat launch welcomes those with small outboard motors of 10 horsepower or less. Water-skiers with more powerful boats have the northwestern corner of Elk Lake reserved for this activity. The boat launch is located on Brookleigh Rd east of Oldfield Rd. (Note: No swimming is permitted in the waterskiing area.)

Thetis Lake Regional Park (see Beaches/Picnics, above) in View Royal provides freshwater paddling for those with hand-carried boats. Launch from the main beach and explore the many bays and small islands that characterize the lake. A narrow channel connects the two halves of the lake system, just wide enough for a canoe or kayak.

Matheson Lake Regional Park in Metchosin is set in a steep-sided, heavily forested environment, 16 miles (26 km) southwest of Victoria, at the foot of Mount Matheson. The park is a paddling destination for those seeking a serene, cloistered environment. From Hwy 17, follow the well-marked entrance off Rocky Point Rd to reach the lake. It's a short walk from the parking area to the beach, where hand-carried boats may be launched.

The Gorge in Victoria is a meandering waterway that leads from Victoria's upper harbour through a landscaped urban environment, before finally widening into Portage Inlet. A daily tidal surge occasionally creates near-whitewater conditions in the narrowest passages, a thrill that kayakers will particularly enjoy. The best place to launch is the dock at Gorge Park near the intersection of Hwy 1A (Gorge Rd) and Tillicum Rd, just west of downtown Victoria. There's more paddling here than you can explore in one day, which guarantees a return visit.

Fishing

Sidney is the place to head for **charters and fishing information** in the Greater Victoria region. Try Westport Marina, 2075 Tryon Rd, (250) 656-2832; Van Isle Marina, 2320 Harbour Rd, (250) 656-1138; and Port Sidney Marina, 9835 Seaport Pl, (250) 655-3711, all in Sidney. Sportfishing charters can be arranged with Corey's Fishing Charters, 847 Woodcreek, (800) 949-4689; Sunrise Salmon Charters, 10288 Rathdown Pl, (250) 656-5570; or Affordable Fishing Charters, Port Sidney marina, (250) 655-3229, all in Sidney.

Try casting for salmon in **Finlayson Arm** from the shores of Goldstream Provincial Park (see Beaches/Picnic, above). You'll need a tidewater licence. Consult the BC Tidal Waters Sport Fishing Guide for information on catch limits. Call the Fisheries and Oceans field office in Victoria for more information, (250) 363-3252, or try the 24-hour sportfishing information line, (604) 666-2828.

Next to the fall salmon run at Goldstream Provincial Park, the spring herring run in Victoria's **Gorge** waterway (see Kayaking/Boating, above) is one of the major events of the year in local waters, with the bonus that the fat, sardine-like fish are easier to catch.

In the Sooke region you'll find excellent salmon fishing in the **Sooke River,** where the annual salmon run is best viewed from Sooke Potholes Provincial Park (see Beaches/Picnics, above) just north of Hwy 14 in Sooke.

Biking

Even though Whistler prides itself on being the mountain-biking mecca of British Columbia, Victoria is truly the centre of cycling in the province. Riders from across the country—cyclists and mountain bikers alike—come to the Commonwealth Training Centre for coaching. As well, the Capital Regional District's **Galloping Goose Trail Regional Park** represents one of the most successful rail-trail initiatives in any Canadian city. Although it's not yet complete, there's more riding here than most bikers can fit into a day. Your best approach is to break up the trail into manageable chunks and tackle each one separately.

The Saanich Peninsula extension's **northern trailhead** of the Galloping Goose is on the Sidney waterfront and runs a considerable distance south from the intersection of Lochside Dr and Beacon Ave in North Saanich to Quadra St near Victoria. The Lochside section is rougher and less well marked as it passes through urban neighbourhoods, but highly enjoyable as it leads through rural Saanich. Along the way it passes near Island View Beach Regional Park (see Beaches/Picnic, above), a good place to take a break. The trail becomes obscured by city streets as it nears Quadra.

As the trail leads through Victoria west to Colwood, it functions largely as an urban commuter and recreation trail. The Swan Lake/Christmas Hill Nature Sanctuary (see Wildlife, below) near the Quadra St entrance provides a pleasant rest stop; however, bikes are not permitted on the nature-sanctuary trails. You'll find parking for three cars, as well as an interpretive display just off Quadra, south of Mackenzie Ave.

The Galloping Goose Trail officially begins in the middle of the trail on the west side of the Johnson Street Bridge in downtown Victoria. It crosses three major trestles on its way west to the abandoned mining community of Leechtown, including the old Selkirk Bridge across the Gorge waterway. Eventually it will link Swartz Bay in North Saanich with Port Renfrew at the north end of Hwy 14. At the moment, the trail runs for approximately 37 miles (60 km) from Sidney to Sooke.

One of the most interesting rural sections of the Galloping Goose Trail runs for about 12 miles (20 km) from **Roche Cove Regional Park** to **Sooke Potholes Provincial Park** and Leechtown. You can pick up the trail south of Roche Point on Rocky Point Rd, just east of a donkey farm. Watch for a parking area just west of Rocky Point's intersection with Malloch Rd. Trail markers indicate that this is the "Km-29" (Mile-18) point west of the Johnson Street Bridge. Such markers occur at regular intervals to acquaint you with your progress. Trails to Matheson Lake (see Kayaking/Boating, above) lead down the steep hillside above the lake. (Note: No bikes are permitted on the Matheson Lake trails.) Although the trail is mostly a level grade, it covers bumpy but solid ground with the exception of stretches of gravel near several bridges. The parking area beside Roche Point Regional Park occurs at "Km 35" on the east side of Sooke Basin. From here views begin to open up to the west, and the temptation is to pause beside the clear blue-green ocean water to enjoy the view. Along this stretch, a number of rough picnic spots can be reached by a short scramble downhill. The forested environment features broadleaf maple that burn gold and red in autumn. Snowbrush scents the air and its white clusters of flowers provide a rich contrast to the evergreens. You'll encounter light traffic wherever you go along this portion of the trail, where butterflies often outnumber bikers.

The **Mountain Bike Park** (also known as the **Hartland Surplus Lands**) in Saanich is located next to the Hartland Ave Disposal Site. Park to the right of the gate before entering the landfill. This site is so new that trails are just in the process of being mapped out. Short, technically challenging trails begin on the opposite side of the road from the parking area beneath the power wires. Rough singletrack feeds off into the forest from the power service road. To find the trailhead, drive to the west end of Hartland Ave off W Saanich Rd (Hwy 17A), 20 minutes from downtown Victoria. Even though the area is designated multi-use, mountain biking is the primary activity. It even sports a bike wash-down facility.

A series of rough roads and dike trails doubles as bike pathways in the marsh inland from **Island View Beach Regional Park** (see Beaches/Picnics, above). Just begin pedalling out along one of the trails that lead from the beach into the marsh. Some of the trails eventually lead through the marsh back out onto the north end of the beach. Unfortunately, once there you won't make much headway, as your tires sink in the sand.

An amazing maze of mountain-biking trails crisscross the hillsides of **Millstream Highlands,** 11 miles (18 km) from downtown Victoria. Take Hwy 1 west of the city centre to Millstream Rd, then go north for almost 2 miles (3 km) until you see concrete barriers and a steel gate where power lines cross the road. There are both double-track and single-track trails to challenge every skill level. Novice riders will want to head for the top, as the trails here are smoother and more level. It takes 30 minutes to bike up the hill on good double-track road, but it's worth the effort for the view from the top of Skirt Mountain. More experienced mountain bikers will want to play on the steeper, more technical singletrack on the lower north-facing slopes, where the terrain is often wet. Note: Once at the top of Skirt Mountain, make sure to descend across the southeast face of the mountain to avoid a steep hill climb in advance of your return to the trailhead on Millstream.

Limited cycling is permitted in **Goldstream Provincial Park** (see

Parks/Camping, above) along the short trail that runs between the day-use parking lot and the Freeman King Visitors Centre. Although brief, the trail does lead through a breathtaking grove of broadleaf maple trees that blaze in fall, as well as some large western red cedar that thrive on the water from the nearby Goldstream River.

Some good sources of mountain-bike information around Victoria include The Bike Seller, 721 Yates St, (250) 380-7060; Fort St Cycle, 1025 Fort St, (250) 384-6665; and Rider's Cycles, 1092 Cloverdale Ave, (250) 381-1125. You can also try Brentwood Cycle & Sport's locations in Brentwood Bay close to Mount Work Park, (250) 652-4649, and in Saanich close to Hartland Mountain Bike Park, (250) 652-5614; Russ Hay Cycles' locations in Sidney at the northern terminus of the Galloping Goose Trail, (250) 656-1512, and in Victoria, (250) 384-4722; and Sooke Cycle in Sooke near the southern terminus of the Galloping Goose Trail, (250) 642-3123.

Walking

It's a pleasure to stroll around Victoria, not just to admire the city but also to let your eyes drift across the landscape in places such as **Beacon Hill Park** near the harbour. A delightful quiet envelops this sunny spot, where walking trails link with neighbourhood streets that lead down into the busy hum of commercial activity. Main entrances to the park are located east of Douglas St (Hwy 1) between Southgate St and Dallas Rd.

Farther afield, near Goldstream Provincial Park, **Francis/King Regional Park** offers 6 miles (11 km) of secluded trails where the forest buffers the hum from the nearby Island Hwy. The park's Elsie King Trail boardwalk is pleasant, but is closed until fall of 1998 due to decay. Francis/King Regional Park is located on Munn Rd in Saanich, 8 miles (13 km) west of downtown Victoria. Follow Hwy 1 to Helmcken Rd. Turn north on Helmcken, west on W Burnside, then north on Prospect Lake Rd to Munn Rd.

In **Goldstream Provincial Park** (see Beaches/Picnics, above) you'll find five interconnecting nature walks and trails between the day-use parking lot, the picnic grounds, the Freeman King Visitors Centre (see Wildlife, below), and the south shore of Finlayson Arm. The natural beauty of the environment, including a lush ancient forest and a little waterfall on Niagara Creek, makes this a special place to explore at a leisurely pace. You can easily spend an hour strolling through the impressive old-growth rain forest that thrives here. Black cottonwood and broadleaf maple border the trail to the visitors centre, where fascinating natural history displays are on view. Western red cedar, some as much as

600 years old, shade the trails beside the picnic ground.

Elk and Beaver Lakes Regional Park (see Beaches/Picnics, above) has 11 miles (19 km) of meandering walking trails, including a gentle ramble that links the two lakes. Although traffic sounds from the Pat Bay Hwy intrude at Elk Lake, Beaver Lake is much quieter, thanks to its tall stand of fir.

If you approach the beach at **Witty's Lagoon Regional Park** (see Wildlife, below) from the Sitting Woman Falls entrance, you find an enjoyable 15-minute walk, with several places at which to pause, including a viewpoint of the falls that tumble through a cleft in the granite, thickly laden berry bushes in summer, and a vibrant marshland lined with gnarly Garry oak and arbutus trees.

Hiking

Just as Victorians can be proud of their lengthy Galloping Goose Trail (see Biking, above), so too can they brag about the beauty of the **Coast Trail.** The 6-mile (10-km) trail, which runs beside the Strait of Juan de Fuca in East Sooke Regional Park near Victoria, is the ideal testing ground for a longer journey such as the West Coast Trail (see Sooke Basin and the West Coast Trail chapter).

It takes about seven hours to cover the Coast Trail round trip, which runs through the thickly forested rolling hills that rise above the strait between Becher and Iron Mine Bays. The shoreline, as rugged here as anywhere farther up the coast, forced the trail builders to deal with everything from windswept bluffs to rain-forest ravines. Occasionally the trail descends to sea level, allowing a hiker's eyes the chance to range across the strait to the peaks of Washington State's Olympic Mountains that dominate the southern horizon. You don't have to traverse the entire length of the Coast Trail in order to enjoy a visit to this large 3,500-acre (1420-ha) park. Watch for one of the trail's most exotic features, a large petroglyph that is carved into the rock face at **Aldridge Point,** a 1.2-mile (2-km) ramble from the east entrance to East Sooke Park at Becher Bay. Once you reach Aldridge Point, the large sea-lion petroglyph is easy to locate. An interpretive marker is fixed on the hillside directly above the rock face on which it is inscribed. According to a Native legend, the petroglyph represents a supernatural animal like a sea lion that was responsible for the deaths of many of the Becher Bay Indians when they ventured out in their canoes. The tribe became nearly extinct; the remaining members were afraid to go out on the water, until one day a mythical man caught the sea lion and turned him into the stone representation seen on Aldridge Point.

Although it's helpful to have an incentive such as an ancient rock carving to draw you out along the trail, the natural beauty of the environment is enticement enough. Wild rose blossoms perfume the breezes that blow among the gnarled, smooth-skinned limbs of arbutus trees. Some of the park's best beaches are located in several small coves around the bay at Creyke Point, about 0.6 mile (1 km) east of Aldridge Point.

Follow the well-marked Coast Trail about a mile west of Aldridge Point to **Beechy Point,** where the ocean swells beat against the craggy shoreline. The old-growth forest is marvelously shaped by years of spindrift driven on the wind by winter storms. Far off in the west you can just make out where the trail ends at **Iron Mine Bay.** Shoulder your pack and head that way if you wish, or simply retrace your steps to Becher Bay and drive about 7 miles (12 km) along East Sooke Rd to reach it. In fact, if you are intent on exploring the entire length of the Coast Trail, it would be helpful to go in two parties and leave a vehicle at each end, trading keys when you meet up in the middle.

East Sooke Regional Park and the Coast Trail trailheads are located approximately 25 miles (40 km) west of Victoria. Take Hwy 14 to its intersection with Gillespie Rd just west of the historic 17-Mile House Pub. At this point you are almost 20 miles (30 km) west of Victoria. Drive south on Gillespie to East Sooke Rd. Follow the signs from this point east to Becher Bay Rd or west to Pike Rd, where the respective east and west trailheads are located. Although there is no camping permitted in the park, private campgrounds are conveniently located at the Lions Club Marina at Becher Bay or the Sunny Shores Resort in Sooke. In addition, there are many bed-and-breakfast homes to be found in the region around the park. For more information on East Sooke Regional Park and the Coast Trail, call Capital Region Parks at (250) 478-3344 in Victoria.

Seven main hiking trails run the length of **Goldstream Provincial Park** (see Parks/Camping, above), including an ascent of Mount Finlayson. With the exception of the **Prospectors Trail** (moderate; 6 miles/10 km return) and the **Mount Finlayson Trail** (strenuous; 1,375 feet/413 m; 3 miles/5 km return), all of the trails run along the upland region of the park to the west of Hwy 1. The trailhead for all hiking routes (except for Mount Finlayson) is located in the campground area of the park, as opposed to the walking routes, which begin in the day-use area. The Prospectors Trail links both areas of the park. The trailhead for Mount Finlayson is located on the east side of Mount Finlayson Rd, just past the day-use parking lot and the bridge over the Goldstream River. The Prospectors Trail also emerges here. The trail to the top of Mount Finlayson may not be lengthy but it is steep and rugged. Cautions when hiking this trail include sticking to the marked trail at all times, wearing appropriate clothing (including sturdy footwear), and packing lots of water on warm days.

Other trails include the **Arbutus Ridge Trail** (moderate; 6 miles/10 km return), which begins from campsite #40 and climbs uphill through the drier upland regions of the park, where a profusion of wildflowers accompanies hikers from April to June, the finest season to enjoy this hike. The **Upper Goldstream Trail** (easy; 2.5 miles/4 km return) passes through some the largest groves of trees in the park as it heads to Goldstream Falls. The trailhead is beside the campground gatehouse, where trail maps are also located.

You can reduce your hiking time in the park by beginning from the hiker's parking lot located on the west side of Hwy 1, halfway between the campground and the day-use areas. Arbutus Ridge lies south of the parking lot, while the **Gold Mine Trail** (easy; 4 miles/6 km return) leads north to Niagara Creek. Highlights include evidence of old-time resource extraction, a tall falls that depending on the season may or may not have any water in it, and a short side trip to view an impressive wooden railway trestle still in use by the Esquimalt & Nanaimo Railway. The day liner passes over the trestle twice daily, Monday to Saturday, so if you're here by 8:30am or 5:15pm you stand a good chance of seeing it whisk by.

The hiking trail (easy; 2 mile/3 km return) in **North Hill Regional Park** in North Saanich leads to one of the highest viewpoints at the top of the Saanich Peninsula. It climbs gradually through a semi-arid forest to the summit of North Hill. From here you have splendid views of the Gulf and San Juan Islands, Mount Baker's volcanic cone, Hurricane Ridge's scissor-cut profile, and all of the Saanich Peninsula and Inlet laid out before you in stark relief. This is a good hike to do as soon as you arrive at BC Ferries' Swartz Bay terminal. You can stretch your legs, taste the island air, and orient yourself for further exploring. To find the park, head west on Wain Rd from Hwy 17, just south of Swartz Bay. Follow signs pointing north on Tatlow Rd to the parking lot and trailhead. You'll often have this trail to yourself.

When you hike the trails in **John Dean Provincial Park** in North Saanich, you are following some of oldest in the provincial park system. You are also following in the footsteps of the local First Nations people who, legend has it, rode out the great flood atop Mount Newton (1,007 feet/302 m), or *Lau Welnew,* "the back of a whale." There is great hiking here for those who admire old-growth forests. At heart of this park are some the largest Douglas fir that remain on the south coast of Vancouver Island, as well as a mix of grand fir, western red cedar, Garry oak, and arbutus. Five hiking trails of varying degrees of difficulty and length cross the south and east face of Mount Newton. Explore here in spring to see a vivid display of wildflowers native to British Columbia, including drifts of blue camas lilies, which carpet the understorey, as well as red Indian paintbrush and white erythroniums. Wildlife flock to the food-rich forest, and from the top of Mount Newton, you can watch as ravens, red-tailed hawks, bald eagles, and turkey vultures put on a colourful display of soaring techniques. The summit of Mount Newton is renowned as the place to watch some of the best sunsets in British Columbia. To find the park, head west from Hwy 17 on McTavish Rd to East Saanich Rd, then south on East Saanich to Dean Park Rd and follow this road to its western terminus, where trails begin from the parking area.

So new is it that hikers are just beginning to make their way to **Gowlland Tod Provincial Park** in Saanich, where there are over 25 miles (40 km) of trails. In the afterglow of goodwill that followed Victoria's hosting of the 1994 Commonwealth Games, local and provincial governments, as well as interested private companies, joined together to create the Commonwealth Nature Legacy. The grand purpose of the project is to further protect the remaining natural spaces that surround the ever-expanding city. Gowlland Tod Provincial Park protects a significant part of the Gowlland Range, one of the last remaining natural areas in Greater Victoria, and a portion of the natural shoreline and uplands in Tod Inlet, which adjoins the Saanich Inlet south of Brentwood Bay near Butchart Gardens (see Attractions, below). Included in this park are representative examples of the rare, dry coastal Douglas fir habitat that features old-growth forest, wildflowers, and stands of arbutus and manzanita. Old mining and logging roads in the park now serve as hiking trails. There are three access points to the park, which shares a common boundary with **Mount Work Regional Park** (see Beaches/Picnics, above). For those hikers who enjoy easygoing trails coupled with access to Tod Inlet's shoreline, take Wallace Dr from either of its two intersections with Hwy 17A. The trailhead at the north end of the park is located on the west side of Wallis Rd opposite Quarry Lake. A second trailhead is located on Willis Point Rd west of Wallace Dr and is shared with Mount Work Regional Park. Trails provide seaside access to McKenzie Bight and climb to spectacular viewpoints and rocky outcroppings on Partridge Hills and Jocelyn Hill. The southern entrance to the park is reached by following Millstream Rd north from Hwy 1 to Caleb Pike Rd, then a short distance west to the trailhead. From here trails lead to Holmes Peak, Mount Finlayson, and Jocelyn Hill.

For a map of the hiking trails in Gowlland Tod Park, contact BC Parks, (250) 391-2300, or stop by BC Park's headquarters in Victoria at 800 Johnston St to pick one up. An excellent general map of the Victoria region, which highlights these and other trails, is published by Canadian Cartographics in cooperation with the British Columbia Automobile

Association. Call (250) 389-6700, or (800) 663-1956 toll-free in British Columbia, or stop by their office in Victoria at 1075 Pandora Ave.

Bear Hill Regional Park is paired with Elk and Beaver Lakes Regional Park (see Beaches/Picnics, above). Over 11 miles (19 km) of easygoing hiking trails link Eagle Beach with popular North Beach on Beaver Lake. For a more vigorous workout, head for Bear Hill Regional Park. The trailhead is located on Bear Hill Rd east of Oldfield Rd north of Elk Lake. The extensive park features more than 1,000 acres (400 ha) of lush wetland, tranquil forest, and panoramic hilltop vistas of the Saanich Peninsula.

Wildlife

The **Swan Lake/Christmas Hill Nature Sanctuary** is located beside the Galloping Goose Trail (see Biking, above) in Saanich. Its broad marshland is a welcome refuge for wildlife in the midst of Hwy 17 and neighbouring streets. A 1.5-mile (2.5-km) viewing trail loops through the marshland and lake, assisted in places by floating boardwalks. Spend some time quietly observing from one of the bird blinds in the sanctuary. Statuesque **great blue heron** stalk the marshland year-round, while their more diminutive relative, the much rarer **green heron,** is in residence during summer months. Waterfowl abound—**widgeons, grebes, teals**—while **ring-necked pheasants** forage in the nearby fields, caterwauling like Siamese cats. On sunny days you may also spot rows of **turtles** sunning themselves where they have hauled up on logs. These hardy creatures have been released here by owners whose pets have outgrown their living quarters or who have grown weary of feeding chores. Interpretive displays and talks are given at the nature house on a regular basis. Trail maps and bird identification guides are also available here. Call (250) 479-0211 for current information. The nature sanctuary is located on Rainbow Rd off McKenzie Ave and is well marked.

Albert Head Lagoon Park in Metchosin is one of three parks along a short stretch of Metchosin Rd that offer intimate glimpses of wildlife in a coastal setting. From Hwy 14, take Metchosin Rd west to Far Hill Rd. Turn south at the park sign and west on Lower Park Dr. This is a designated wildlife sanctuary that attracts a variety of birds journeying along the Pacific Flyway, including larger birds such as **swans, herons, and turkey vultures.** Stretch out on the cobble beach as you train your binoculars on the coastline. This is an exposed headland, so dress accordingly.

Witty's Lagoon Regional Park (see Beaches/Picnics, above) is a natural resting place for migrating birds such as **osprey** before they attempt the 13-mile (21-km) crossing of the Strait of Juan de Fuca to the Olympic

Peninsula. Other birds, such as the **belted kingfisher, orange-crowned warbler,** and **dark-eyed junco** overwinter in the shelter of the lagoon. In spring, the open meadows above the lagoon contain a brilliant array of wildflowers including **camas lilies, saxifrage,** and **nodding onions.** Displays of natural history can be found at the park's information centre on Metchosin Rd, about 12 miles (20 km) west of Victoria. There are several entrances to the park, including Tower Point. Turn south off Metchosin Rd on Duke Rd, then west on Olympic View Dr to reach the trailhead. A short trail leads to a small beach at Tower Point where the ocean has hollowed **tide pools** in the granite outcropping. A rich variety of marine life shelter in the pools and stand revealed at low tide. Bring your rubber boots. You'll also be rewarded with good views from here of aptly named Haystock Islands, where long, thick strands of grass grow in the shape of old stooks. Farther out in the strait are the Race Rocks, Canada's most southerly point on the west coast. Hurricane Ridge predominates on the distant southern horizon. At low tide you can wade across from the point to the long stretch of beach that fronts the lagoon; otherwise, approach the beach from the Sitting Woman Falls entrance on the road just south of Tower Point. A short walk past the falls brings you to an intertidal backwater, where the waters of Metchosin Creek mingle with the Pacific, and then to the beach cluttered with driftwood, excellent for building shelters from the cold wind while you bird-watch. The quiet backwater lagoon surrounded by Garry oak and arbutus is popular with **seals,** too. To reach the park, take the Old Island Hwy (Hwy 1A) to Sooke Rd. Follow Sooke Rd to Metchosin Rd and turn south. Follow along until you see the well-signed entrances to the park. For more information, including a bird-watching guide and map of Witty's Lagoon, as well as maps of other regional parks around Greater Victoria, call (250) 478-3344, or stop by the Capital Regional District Parks office, 490 Atkins Ave.

A short distance west of Witty's Lagoon in Metchosin on William Head Rd (an extension of Metchosin Rd) is **Devonian Regional Park,** a small parcel of farmland that now acts as a wildlife sanctuary, tucked into the gently rolling landscape. This part of the world was opened for farming in the 1860s to provide fresh produce for the burgeoning population of gold miners and attendant settlers in the nearby Victoria region. As such, the natural ambience here is pastoral. Despite the absence of marshland, many of the migratory birds seen at Witty's Lagoon Regional Park also use this park as a staging area, including **sandpipers, turnstones,** and **surfbirds,** all of whom work the cobble beach for all it's worth.

The annual salmon spawning run in **Goldstream Provincial Park** (see Parks/Camping, above) begins in October and lasts through December. Successive schools of **chum, coho, and chinook** return from the sea to lay their roe in their ancestral spawning grounds and then die. The transformation in their body colouring and shape, as well as their fervour and determination, make this event both vivid and poignant. At this time of year the Freeman King Visitors Centre hums with activity, as busloads of students and tourists arrive to learn more about the life cycle of this creature that has been vitally important to people of the coast since ancient tribes first arrived on these shores. Naturalists and volunteers conduct informative lecture tours along the river, which is a short walk from the centre.

Diving

With an artificial reef slowly taking shape offshore from Brentwood Bay in the Saanich Inlet, there's plenty of diving action locally. Much of the diving activity in Greater Victoria is based in Sidney. Air, equipment, charts, dive charters, and general information can be found at Boathouse Marine and Dive Centre, 2-2379 Bevan Ave, (250) 655-3682; Deep Cove Ocean Sports, 10990 Madrona St, (250) 656-0060; or Frank White's Dive Stores, 2200 Keating Cross Rd, (250) 652-3375.

Scenic Drives

Marine Scenic Drive begins on Dallas Rd at the south end of Douglas St near the Victoria harbour and follows the coastline east and north for about 20 miles (32 km) to Sayward Rd in Saanich. The well-marked route follows Dallas, Beach, Arbutus, and Cordova Bay Rds, always within sight of the ocean.

outside in

Attractions

Romantic as Victoria may be, with its delightful natural harbour and the Olympic Mountains of Washington State on the horizon, the provincial capital of British Columbia is less a museum piece nowadays than it is a tourist mecca. Visitors pour in to view vast sculpted gardens and London-style double-decker buses, to shop for Irish linens and Harris tweeds, to sip afternoon tea, and to soak up what they believe is the last vestige of British imperialism in the Western Hemisphere. Raves in the travel press have brought new crops of younger residents to upset Victoria's reputation as a peaceful but dull sanctuary for retiring civil servants from eastern Canada. The quality and variety of restaurants has improved as a result, and no longer are Victoria's streets silent after 10pm.

First stop should be **Tourism Victoria,** a well-staffed office dispensing useful information on the sights; 812 Wharf St, (250) 953-2033. The **Royal British Columbia Museum** is one of the finest of its kind in the country, offering dramatic dioramas of natural landscapes and full-scale reconstructions of Victorian storefronts. Of particular interest is the Northwest Coast Indian exhibit, rich with spiritual and cultural artifacts. Watch for special seasonal and touring exhibitions and an intriguing "undersea" show. The museum is open every day, at Belleville and Government Sts, (250) 387-3701. The **Art Gallery of Greater Victoria** houses one of the world's finest collections of Asian art (including the only Shinto shrine in North America), with special historic and contemporary exhibits on display throughout the year. It is open every day, 1040 Moss St, (250) 384-4101. The free *Monday Magazine* offers the city's best weekly calendar of events; pick it up at various locations throughout the city.

Crystal Garden is a turn-of-the-century swimming-pool building converted into a glass conservatory with a tropical theme (lush greenery, live flamingos, and macaws)—a fine place to spend a rainy day; admission is $7. Open every day, 713 Douglas St, (250) 381-1213.

Butchart Gardens, 13 miles (21 km) north of town, shows what can be done with reclaimed limestone quarries. The 50 acres (20 ha) of gardens are lovely, beautifully manicured displays in many international styles; they're lighted after dark. Take the time to look beyond the profusion of blooms to the landscape structure and its relationship to the setting of rocky bays and tree-covered mountains. In the summer it's best to go in late afternoon, after the busloads of tourists have left. Concerts, fireworks on Saturday evenings in summer, a surprisingly good afternoon tea, and light meals provide diversions. Open every day, (250) 652-5256.

Craigdarroch Castle puts you back into an era of unfettered wealth and ostentation. Vancouver Island coal tycoon Robert Dunsmuir built this 19th-century mansion to induce a Scottish wife to live in faraway Victoria. Open every day, 1050 Joan Crescent, (250) 592-5323. You can also visit five of the better-restored Victoria **heritage homes,** (250) 387-4697: Helmcken House, behind Thunderbird Park, east of the Royal British Columbia Museum; Point Ellice House, at Bay St and Pleasant St; Craigflower Manor, 110 Island Hwy; Craigflower Schoolhouse, at Admirals and Gorge Rd W; and Carr House, at Government and Simcoe. Admission to all five is $3.25.

For British woolens, suits, gifts, and sweets, the downtown area north from the Empress Hotel on Government St is the place to **shop.** W & J Wilson Clothiers sells English wool suits and women's clothes; Sasquatch Trading Company Ltd. offers some of the best of the Cowichan sweaters;

EA Morris Tobacconist Ltd. carries a very proper Victorian mix of fine pipes and tobaccos; Munro's, a monumental 19th-century bank-building-turned-bookstore, has a thoughtful selection; Murchie's Teas and Coffee offers the city's finest selection of specially blended teas and coffees; and don't forget Roger's Chocolates and the English Sweet Shop for chocolates, almond brittle, black-currant pastilles, marzipan bars, and more; and Bernard Callebaut Chocolaterie for picture-perfect chocolates in the Belgian style. Market Square is a restored 19th-century courtyard surrounded by a jumble of shops, restaurants, and offices on three floors. A few blocks farther on at Fisgard St, the entrance to Victoria's small and seemingly shrinking **Chinatown** is marked by the splendid, lion-bedecked Gate of Harmonious Interest. Visit the tiny shops and studios on Fan Tan Alley and check out Morley Co. Ltd., a Chinese grocery. Antique hunters should head east of downtown, up Fort St to **Antique Row**—block after block of shops, the best of which are the Connoisseurs Shop and David Robinson Ltd., with excellent 18th-century English pieces. Visit Bastion Square for sidewalk restaurants, galleries, the **Maritime Museum,** the alleged location of Victoria's old gallows, and a great gardener's shop called Dig This; and Windsor Court for boutique items and gifts.

Restaurants

Barb's Place It's truly spartan alfresco dining, but the fish doesn't get any fresher than this. Terrific fish (halibut or cod in a light, crisp batter) and homemade chips heads the menu, but burgers have been added. A perfect place for families. *310 St. Lawrence St (Fisherman's Wharf), Victoria; (604) 384-6515; $.*

Camille's ☆☆ Still Victoria's most romantic basement, with soft lights, music, and wine from a selection of over 200 varieties. The menu is based on fresh ingredients from Vancouver Island farmers and growers. Wine-tasting dinners are highly popular. *45 Bastion Square (Fort and Langley), Victoria; (250) 381-3433; $$.*

Carden Street Cafe ☆☆ Here, incredible soups in enormous bowls put a Western twist on an Eastern theme. Wonderful curries with fragrant basmati rice hold appeal for meat eaters and vegetarians alike. *1164 Stelly's Cross Rd (corner of W Saanich Rd), Victoria; (250) 544-1475; $$.*

Chez Daniel ☆☆☆ Unquestionably one of Victoria's finest French restaurants. Although off the beaten path in Oak Bay, it's definitely worth a visit. Chez Daniel boasts an award-winning wine list, and the pâté maison puts all others in town to shame. *2524 Estevan Ave (Estevan and Beach, 10 minutes from downtown), Victoria; (250) 592-7424; $$$.*

Don Mee Seafood Restaurant ☆☆ Located in Chinatown, Don Mee has the most extensive dim sum offered in Victoria. There is no menu, just a never-ending variety, served from carts that ceaselessly circle the room. *538 Fisgard St (at Government), Victoria; (250) 383-1032; $.*

Herald Street Caffe ☆☆☆ There are a lot of East-meets-West dishes, especially those made with pasta, and the kitchen takes full advantage of the abundance of fresh local seafood. *546 Herald St (at Government, 1 block past Chinatown), Victoria; (250) 381-1441; $$.*

John's Place ☆ John's Place is a haven for the younger set, but its reasonable prices make it appealing to any age. The eggs Benedict and the Belgian waffles are justifiably famous, but the Thai spring rolls vie for attention. *723 Pandora Ave (at Douglas), Victoria; (250) 389-0711; $.*

Millos Restaurant ☆☆ Its cool blue tiles evoke the Aegean influence, which has helped make this restaurant a favourite. Try the appetizer platter: it offers everything from spanakopita to calamari, dolmathes, taramasalata, and more. *716 Burdett St (at Douglas), Victoria; (250) 382-4422; $$.*

Re-bar ☆ Victoria's original vegetarian health-food and smoke-free restaurant is as popular as ever. Delicious pizzas are specialties, along with pastas, Asian salads, and black bean chili. Breads are all homemade. *50 Bastion Square (at Langley), Victoria; (250) 361-9223; $.*

Sam's Deli ☆☆ This 20-year-old restaurant offers the most bang for your buck in the city. Sam's is generous on everything, from large tureens of a daily soup to a ploughman's lunch, which can be eaten in or taken out for a picnic down by the Inner Harbour. *805 Government St (between Humboldt and Courteney), Victoria; (250) 382-8424; $.*

Siam ☆☆ Siam is a large restaurant, but delicate details give it an intimate Asian ambience. Share a tureen of tom yum koong, hot and sour soup with prawns and Thai spices—it's Thai magic! *512 Fort St (near foot of Fort St), Victoria; (250) 383-9911; $$.*

Spice Jammer Restaurant ☆☆ At this pretty little East Indian restaurant, pride of place on the menu goes to the tandoori dishes, but every dish, from vindaloo to marsala, is a jewel in the crown. You're here for the curries or you're not here at all. *852 Fort St (at Quadra), Victoria; (250) 480-1055; $$.*

Tomoe Japanese Restaurant ☆☆ Very fresh sushi is the order of the day in this above-average Japanese restaurant, but sashimi is the star of the show—eye-catching and mouth-watering, with delicate little morsels of the freshest fish. *726 Johnson St (at Douglas St), Victoria; (250) 381-0223; $$.*

The Victorian Restaurant (Ocean Pointe Resort) ☆☆☆ Here's an elegant space with an unsurpassed view, located in one of Victoria's finest hotels. Everything on this menu is superb and the emphasis is low fat without sacrificing flavour. *45 Songhees Rd (across Johnson St Bridge from downtown), Victoria; (250) 360-2999; $$$.*

The Windsor House Tea Room ☆☆ This joyful restaurant tucked away in Oak Bay is quintessentially English. Soups are sensational, and so are the wonderful homemade steak-and-kidney pie and chicken potpie. *2540 Windsor Ave (at Newport), Victoria; (250) 595-3135; $.*

Cheaper Eats

Beacon Drive-In Locals line up at the Beacon for burgers and British Columbia's best soft-serve ice cream. Summer bonus: outside tables and a "regular" breakfast that will have you wondering why you gave up crispy bacon and eggs. *126 Douglas St, Victoria; (250) 385-7521; $.*

Italian Foods Import Favourite foods here: prosciutto, Asiago cheese, calamata olives, Baci chocolates, and amaretto biscuits. On rainy days order lasagne at the small lunch bar, then treat yourself to some gelati. *1114 Blanshard St, Victoria; (250) 385-7923; $.*

Rebecca's Food Bar It's tempting to eat inside this waterfront heritage building, but Rebecca's daily specials and imaginative West Coast cuisine are ideal for a picnic basket—especially if you're en route to Fort Rodd Hill Park. *1127 Wharf St, Victoria; (250) 380-6999; $.*

Sally Cafe Head to Sally's for healthy soups, sandwiches (try the curried chicken and apricot), salads, decadent desserts, and breakfast goodies. *714 Cormorant St, Victoria; (250) 381-1431; $.*

17-Mile House You'll find lots of colourful locals at this former stage stop. The $29 Sunday platter of scallops, crab, shrimp, prawns, potatoes, and rice easily serves two. Pool, darts, checkers, crib, and backgammon keep you occupied as you wait for your meal. *5126 Sooke Rd, Victoria; (250) 642-5942; $.*

Lodgings

Abigail's Hotel ☆☆☆ The Tudor-style Abigail's is all gables and gardens and crystal chandeliers, with three floors of odd-shaped rooms. It combines the beauty of the Old World with the comforts of the New. (The hotel also manages a two-bedroom beach house that's perfect for families.) *906 McClure St (at Vancouver), Victoria, BC V8V 3E7; (250) 388-5363 or (800) 561-6565; $$$.*

The Beaconsfield ☆☆☆ Of all the imitation-England spots, this is the best. It's meant to convey a sense of romance and does, with nine antique-filled bedrooms, all with private baths. *998 Humboldt St (at Vancouver), Victoria, BC V8V 2Z8; (250) 384-4044; $$$.*

Craigmyle Guest House ☆ Built as a guest house early in the century, the Craigmyle stands next to Craigdarroch Castle and close to the Art Gallery of Greater Victoria. Reasonably priced, the Craigmyle is one of the few guest houses in Victoria that allows children. *1037 Craigdarroch Rd (off Fort), Victoria, BC V8S 2A5; (250) 595-5411 or (888) 595-5411; $.*

The Empress ☆☆ The hotel that once stood as the quiet dowager of the Inner Harbour had a $45 million facelift a decade ago. Unfortunately, rates in high season are astonishing, and because it's so big, service is hard-pressed to live up to expectations. Nevertheless, the Empress is the most notable landmark in town and is worth a stroll. *721 Government St (between Humboldt and Belleville), Victoria, BC V8W 1W5; (250) 384-8111 or (800) 441-1414; $$$.*

The Haterleigh ☆☆ Built in 1901, this inn has been well preserved and well restored. Geared towards romance, the rooms are generously sized and charmingly decorated. We especially like the Secret Garden Room, which has a lovely view of the Olympic Mountains. *243 Kingston St (at Pendray), Victoria, BC V8V 1V5; (250) 384-9995; $$$.*

Laurel Point Inn ☆☆☆ The Inn's angular construction means that all of the 200 rooms and suites offer views of the harbour or the ship channel. We prefer the junior suites in the newer south wing; all are beautifully appointed, with graceful Japanese accents and private decks. *680 Montreal St (at Belleville), Victoria, BC V8V 1Z8; (250) 386-8721 or (800) 663-7667; $$$.*

Oak Bay Beach Hotel ☆☆ Presiding over the Haro Strait, this Tudor-style hotel is in the loveliest part of Victoria, a nice place to stay if you want to be removed from downtown. The best rooms are those with private balconies and a water view. And do enjoy the hotel's afternoon tea. *1175 Beach Dr (near Oak Bay Ave), Victoria, BC V8S 2N2; (250) 598-4556 or (800) 668-7758; $$$.*

The Prior House ☆☆ No imitation here: this grand B&B occupies an English mansion built during the Edwardian period for the King's representative in British Columbia. Families with children older than 9 years may stay in one of the lower-level Garden Suites, which have private entrances and full kitchens. *620 St. Charles (at Rockland), Victoria, BC V8S 3N7; (250) 592-8847; $$$.*

Swans Hotel ☆ Behind the traditional facade of this 1913 building hide 29 modern suites, complete with kitchen facilities and living areas. The two-bedroom suites are an especially good deal for families. *506 Pandora Ave (at Store), Victoria, BC V8W 1N6; (250) 361-3310 or (800) 668-7926; $$.*

Cheaper Sleeps

Battery Street Guest House This 1898 B&B offers six spacious, homey downstairs rooms for guests. Some rooms boast ocean views; most of the guests share two bathrooms. This reasonably priced guest house is located just around the corner from Beacon Hill Park. *670 Battery St, Victoria, BC V8V 1E5; (250) 385-4632; $.*

Cherry Bank Hotel This 26-room Victorian house is a congenial spot that caters to a working-class crowd. Guest rooms lack TVs and telephones, but they're clean, comfortable, and surprisingly quiet, considering there's a pub and restaurant below. *825 Burdett Ave, Victoria, BC V8W 1B3; (250) 385-5380; $.*

Crystal Court Motel Built in 1950, the Crystal Court was the first motel in downtown Victoria—and it's still one of the city's best bargains. It's only a block from Crystal Gardens, the Royal British Columbia Museum, and the Inner Harbour. Every other room has a fully equipped kitchen. *701 Belleville St, Victoria, BC V8W 1A2; (250) 384-0551; $.*

University of Victoria Housing and Conference Services From May to August, the university opens campus dormitory rooms to visitors. Play it safe and book ahead for the single (about $32) or twin-bed rooms ($34), although some drop-in units may be available. *Parking Lot 5 off Sinclair Rd, Victoria, BC V8W 2Y2; (250) 721-8395; $.*

The Vacationer How many B&Bs let you know you're welcome to invite friends over for a visit? This pleasant inn is walking distance to bordering Beacon Hill Park. Better yet, borrow one of the bikes for a spin. Four-course breakfasts are served, too. *1143 Leonard St, Victoria, BC V8V 2S3; (250) 382-9469; $.*

Victoria International Hostel Victoria's youth hostel is housed in a wonderful late-19th-century heritage property just steps from the waterfront, in the heart of downtown. The men's and women's dormitory rooms together number 109 rooms. A night in a bunk will cost only about $19, and family rooms are available. *516 Yates St, Victoria, BC V8W 1K8; (250) 385-4511; $.*

More Information

BC Forest Service, South Island Forest District, Port Alberni: *(250) 724-9205.*

BC Parks: *(250) 391-2300; reservations (800) 689-9025.*

Capital Regional District Parks: *(250) 478-3344, or (250) 474-PARK.*

Department of Fisheries and Oceans (tidal waters): *(250) 746-6221.*

Fish and Wildlife Conservation Office (freshwater): *(250) 746-1236.*

Sidney InfoCentre: *(250) 656-3616.*

Victoria Travel InfoCentre: *(250) 953-2033; Web site: http://www.travel.bc.ca.*

West Shore Chamber of Commerce (representing the CRD communities of Colwood, Highlands, Langford, Metchosin, and View Royal): *(250) 478-1130.*

Sooke Basin and the West Coast Trail

The thin strip of Vancouver Island's southwestern coastline between Sooke and Port Renfrew, including French Beach, China Beach, and Botanical Beach Provincial Parks and the southern terminus of the West Coast Trail.

The exposed waters of Vancouver Island's southwestern coast quickly dispel any notion that an ocean is an ocean is an ocean. The true personality of the Pacific is revealed as you traverse the slopes of San Juan Ridge as the Strait of Juan de Fuca makes its entrance from the open water of the Pacific. Conditions shift dramatically from the sheltered, rain-shadowed waterways of the Strait of Georgia with its gaggle of tranquil islands. Here you face the open ocean, where nothing breaks the rolling swells or deflects the sting of winter storms. For those who listen for the voice of the West Coast, here it begins to speak up, way up. Many a dark chapter has been written about ships and crews that perished in the violent storms that rake the raw shoreline. This is the Pacific Davy Jones's Locker. Thrown up on the beach, survivors considered themselves blessed if they could reach the nearby West Coast Lifesaving Trail. As harsh today as then, less-endangered people willingly subject themselves to this legendary trail's test of endurance. Such a reputation adds a wild spice to adventuring here. Do not treat this environment lightly. Each year some unfortunate soul ventures too close to the ocean and pays the ultimate price. Venture with care and you'll come away with wonderful memories of your time spent by the shoreline, where many creatures live in splendid harmony with the ocean's deep rhythms.

Getting There

Owing to the ruggedness of the region, access is limited to the paved coastal Highway 14 and several unpaved backroads. Highway 14 begins in the Victoria suburb of Colwood Corners. It links the village of Sooke on the west side of Sooke Basin with Port Renfrew on the south shore of Port San Juan (actually a wide bay), a distance of 45 miles (70 km). To the north, the Harris Creek Mainline and Hillcrest Mainline Logging Roads link Port Renfrew with Mesachie Lake on Cowichan Lake, and from there with Highway 18 and the Cowichan Valley.

Adjoining Areas

NORTH: **Nanaimo and the Cowichan Valley**

EAST: **Greater Victoria**

Hiking/Backpacking

The **West Coast Trail** runs for almost 48 miles (77 km) along the west side of Vancouver Island between the hamlets of Port Renfrew in the south and Bamfield in the north, and lies within the southern boundaries of Pacific Rim National Park. The trail was originally created in 1907 to assist in the rescue of shipwrecked passengers and crews who ran aground in an extremely rugged area that, with more than 60 ships lost over the past two centuries, has deservedly earned the reputation as one of the graveyards of the Pacific.

These days the West Coast Trail is perceived as more of a 7- to 10-day adventure trek than an escape route, a sought-after trophy that draws hikers from around the world. (It also draws ultrafit marathoners who have run the route in less than 15 hours. Parks Canada does not condone this potentially dangerous activity.) Ironically, most rescue work on the trail now involves assisting hikers in distress rather than marooned sailors. Parks Canada reports that of the 8,000 hikers who attempt the trail annually, the Coast Guard is called upon to evacuate an average of 60 in distress. The cost of such rescues accounts, in part, for the **user-fee** of $70 currently being charged by Parks Canada to those who wish to attempt the trip. A **reservation fee** of $25 is charged for those who wish to plan in advance, which is recommended, as only 52 people per day are allowed on the trail. If you're serious about doing the trail, be ready to call when the reservation line opens on March 1. Call toll-free, (800) 663-6000. About 12 places per day are held on a first-come basis. If you arrive without reservations you may find yourself waiting a day or more in line for one of these places to become available. Official hiking **season** on the West Coast Trail is from May 1 to September 30. Parks Canada maintains offices in both Port Renfrew and Bamfield where hikers should register before setting off; the offices are also good sources for trail maps and tide tables. (Recent reports on the poor condition of the trail indicate that the offices are all that Parks Canada *is* maintaining.)

If you are planning to begin from Port Renfrew, you must make arrangements to be transported across Port San Juan to the trailhead at the mouth of Gordon River. Native Canadians from the nearby Pacheedaht First Nations Reserve provide a **shuttle service** from the federal wharf in Port Renfrew to the trailhead from April to September. Call (250) 647-5521 for information. Another boat ride is necessary near the north end of the trail to cross the Nitinat Narrows. Total cost of boat transportation along the trail is about $20.

Many hikers begin from Port Renfrew in order to cover the most challenging section of the trail first. A total of 70 sets of **ladders,** 130 **bridges,** and 4 hand-powered **cable cars** (which may or may not be operational, depending on maintenance and water levels) assist hikers across some of the most formidable obstacles. A pair of ski poles will provide invaluable help in stabilizing yourself when fording creeks in the rain forest (not to mention in the knee-deep mud). There are no amenities of any kind along the trail, and hikers must travel completely self-contained, including garbage bags to pack out all refuse. Hypothermia is the biggest threat faced on the trail; remaining dry and warm for the week or so that it takes to complete the trek is the major challenge.

Finally, opinions on the difficulty of the West Coast Trail range between those who have covered it and feel that the difficulties are exaggerated, and those hikers who found the challenge overwhelming. What is obvious is that this is an adventure for which you must be fully prepared, and certainly not one on which you'd choose to break in a new pair of hiking boots. Better to search out somewhere with conditions similar to those you're bound to encounter on the West Coast Trail, such as East Sooke Regional Park's Coast Trail (see Greater Victoria chapter), but with the option of being able to fall back into the welcoming arms of civilization at day's end.

For additional **information** on the West Coast Trail, call Parks Canada's Pacific Rim National Park West Coast Trail information offices at (250) 728-3234 in Bamfield, or (250) 647-5434 in Port Renfrew. Unless you are planning to make a round trip of the trail (few do), you'll have to arrange **transportation** from either Bamfield or Port Renfrew to return you to your vehicle or transportation of choice. Bus transportation from

Victoria to Port Renfrew and Bamfield leaves almost every day during hiking season; call (250) 477-8700 for information, or visit the Web site, www.pacificoast.net/~wcte. Charter bus service is available between Port Renfrew and Bamfield; call Pacheedaht Bus Service, (250) 647-5521, or Western Bus Line, (250) 723-3341. The MV *Lady Rose* provides a pleasant alternative to land travel; daily sailings connect Bamfield with Port Alberni, from where bus service links with Nanaimo and Victoria. Call (250) 723-8313 for information.

Finally, there are several time-honoured **guidebooks** on the West Coast Trail experience, at least one of which should be consulted before leaving home. The list includes *The Pacific Rim Explorer* by Bruce Obee, *The West Coast Trail and Nitinat Lakes* by Tim Leadem, and *Hiking on the Edge: Canada's West Coast Trail* by Ian Gill. Tide charts are useful in predicting the best times to cross beaches. Also valuable are detailed topographic maps, such as NTS series 92C/10/11/12/13/14.

The **Juan de Fuca Marine Trail and Provincial Park** (which includes access points at Botanical Beach, Parkinson Creek, Sombrio Beach, and China Beach Provincial Park) leads for almost 30 miles (48 km) along the southwestern coast of Vancouver Island, from Botanical Beach Provincial Park to China Beach Provincial Park. This ambitious trail has been opened only since 1995 and is still in its formative stages. Intended to be an alternative to the increasingly popular West Coast Trail, long stretches of the Juan de Fuca Marine Trail lead through clear-cut slopes above the Strait of Juan de Fuca. Campsites and beach access points are limited; conditions along large portions of the trail are often extremely wet. Dozens of small creeks pour down off the open slopes of San Juan Ridge, many of which become impassable after several days of heavy rain. Although with time this trail will improve, there are still many obstacles to be overcome. The easiest section of the trail is near its northern terminus in **Botanical Beach Provincial Park** (see Wildlife, below). A boardwalk leads hikers across wetland and makes the prospects appear quite promising. Unfortunately the trail quickly reveals its true nature as it climbs away from the beach and begins to lead through miles of abandoned logging roads. Views of the beach are cut off by a narrow perimeter of dense rain forest. Orange balls suspended from tree branches mark entry points to the beach from the trail. Exercise extreme care on the often steep, slippery approaches to the shoreline. Once there, be wary of "rogue" or "snap" waves that could sweep you out to sea. These waves are much larger than usual and occur most often in storm season, but can come out of nowhere at any time of the year. High tides and storms may completely cut off some beaches from the trail. (For this reason, camp only where designated.) Summer is the best time to visit here, but be prepared for rain and cold, and damp mists year-round. Campsites along the trail are evenly spaced—about 4 miles (7 km) between each—and include Payzant Creek, Little Kuitshe Creek, Sombrio Beach, China Beach, Bear Beach, and Mystic Beach. The longest and most difficult section of the trail lies between **Sombrio Beach** and **Bear Beach,** a distance of 11 miles (18 km). Easier sections include the 4 miles (7 km) between **Botanical Beach** and **Payzant Creek,** and the 5.5 miles (9 km) between **Bear Beach** and **China Beach.** If you just want to get a feel for the trail, try either the short boardwalk section at the south end of Botanical Beach or the 1.2-mile (2-km) section between China and Mystic Beaches (accessed via China Beach Provincial Park or via the Mystic Beach Trail from Hwy 14), which involves crossing a suspension bridge. For more information on Juan de Fuca Marine Trail, including a detailed map, contact BC Parks, (250) 391-2300.

The **Kludahk Forest Recreation Trail** runs along San Juan Ridge for 18 miles (30 km). The trailheads are located at the western terminus of the Galloping Goose Trail (see Greater Victoria chapter) in Sooke and at Parkinson Creek Provincial Park on the Juan de Fuca Marine Trail east of Port Renfrew. The trail, much of which is composed of former logging roads, follows San Juan Ridge through the Jordan Meadows in a subalpine region dense with avalanche lilies in springtime and four varieties of blueberries later in the summer. Four cabins are located along the trail (parts of which are still not complete) and are open to all. Built by volunteers from the Sooke Kludahk ("home of the elk") Club over the past decade, the trail is particularly popular in winter with snowshoers and cross-country skiers. For more information on the trail, contact Maywell Wickham of the Sooke Kludahk Trail Club at Sooke Marine, (250) 642-3523. Contact the BC Forest Service's South Island district office in Port Alberni, (250) 724-9205, for a recreation map of the region.

In comparison with the convoluted coastline on the south side of Vancouver Island, the southwestern side is positively razor-edged. So few are the protuberances that it even has a phantom point—Point No Point—that can be seen from certain angles but not others. In a series of indentations, the shoreline gradually sweeps east from Point No Point to Juan de Fuca Point—the real thing—which makes a bolder impression.

A trail leads out to **Juan de Fuca Point** from Hwy 14, an easy 10-minute walk. Look for the wide pulloff on the south side of the highway between French Beach Provincial Park (see Camping, below) and Point No Point. Gentler trails lead for shorter distances along the coastline, and often offer sheltered viewing of the ocean, even in storms.

From the little teahouse at **Point No Point,** which has since the early days of this century occupied this location west of Sooke, about 2 miles

(3.5 km) north of French Beach Provincial Park, a pathway runs downhill. The salal grows so tall and thick that it forms a canopy above the trail as it leads towards the beach. A chunky log bridge that spans part of the headland presents a question: How did it ever get here? Inquiring at the teahouse will give you a chance to look at some archival photographs of the beach, the trail, and the changes this spot has endured.

Despite the thoroughness of logging in the rain forest surrounding Port Renfrew, a number of solitary examples of extraordinarily large old-growth trees remain. As well, a grove of Sitka spruce are protected in undeveloped **Loss Creek Provincial Park** beside Hwy 14, just south of the turnoff to Sombrio Beach (see Beaches, below). A short drive north of Port Renfrew stands the **Red Creek Fir,** Canada's largest-known Douglas fir and possibly the largest of its kind in the world. A 24-acre (10-ha) buffer zone of trees has been left around the giant by the forest company that clear-cut the surrounding slopes (and in the process did irreparable damage to the San Juan River). You can drive to within a short distance of the Red Creek Fir, then walk the remaining distance, passing three large western red cedar along the way. To find your way there, follow the Red Creek Mainline Logging Rd, which begins just east of Port Renfrew on Hwy 14. Look for a sign, "Red Creek Fir 17 km" (10.5 miles) that marks the entrance to the gravel road. The road is not well maintained but negotiable by most vehicles. Stay left when the road forks at the 6-mile (10-km) point. The road deteriorates beyond here, and it's up to you to decide how much farther to drive before proceeding on foot. You should be able to make it to the clearing at the 9-mile (14.5-km) point, a good place to leave your vehicle. Walk left on the level road beyond the parking area, then turn right onto the marked trail, which switchbacks uphill to an old road. Turn left and you will pass a trio of sturdy western red cedar just as the Red Creek Fir comes into view. Having occupied this site for a millennium and having weathered countless storms that have snapped its crown and shattered its limbs, the giant still shows signs of remarkable vitality. At present it measures over 41 feet (12 m) in circumference, with a height of 241 feet (72 m), although at one time it must have been about 320 feet (96 m) high before losing its spire to wind or lightning.

Beaches

If there's one landscape most associated with oceans, it's beaches. Finding the best ones along the southwestern coast is not difficult, as almost all of them have been protected as provincial parks. Beginning at French Beach, a necklace of sites is strung north to Port Renfrew, where the most fabulous of all—Botanical Beach—is located. Although they are situated within a fairly narrow range, each one has its own personality.

French Beach Provincial Park (see Camping, below), about 14 miles (22 km) west of Sooke, is more protected than the rest from the full force of the ocean by the Olympic Peninsula, on the south side of the Strait of Juan de Fuca. It's also the easiest to reach. You can drive to within a short distance of the beach here, whereas a 10- to 45-minute walk is required to reach the other beaches, depending on the location. A wide swath of lawn fronts this pea-gravel beach where you can picnic, swim, beachcomb, and watch for wildlife. Above all, your attention will be drawn to the pulse of the waves as they break, race up the beach, and grab some gravel to take back with them. The stirring sound of the wind in the trees high above tells you that you've left the inner coast behind.

The hillsides above most beaches here plunge down San Juan Ridge. The trails to **China Beach** (see Hiking/Backpacking, above) and **Mystic Beach** are surprisingly steep, whereas those to **Sandcut Beach, Sombrio Beach** (see Surfing, below), and **Botanical Beach** (see Wildlife, below) are gentler. Once you reach these beaches, however, it's as if you've suddenly been let in on the action hidden behind the scenes in nearby Victoria. Even at the busiest times you'll have plenty of beach to yourself, though you might be surprised to find how calm the ocean can get for weeks at a time in summer. These are the long, lazy, endless days when the Pacific itself becomes laid-back. It becomes so relaxed that even the signposts take a break. Although you'll find the approaches to **China Beach Provincial Park** and **Botanical Beach Provincial Park** well marked off Hwy 14, others such as **Sandcut, Mystic,** and **Sombrio** may be more elusive. Sandcut is 1.2 miles (2 km) south of Jordan River; Mystic is just north of China Beach, and the turnoff for Sombrio is just north of Loss Creek Provincial Park. With the exception of Sombrio Beach, which has its own parking lot downhill from Hwy 14, park beside the highway and follow the trail to the beach.

If you have time to visit only one beach, **Sombrio** is a standout. A rough road leads downhill from Hwy 14, 11 miles (18 km) south of Port Renfrew, to an open parking space. A well-worn trail leads to the beach in 5 minutes. Until recently, a community of squatters lived here, as this is one of the few beaches where freshwater is guaranteed year-round. You'll have to cross Sombrio Creek and pass through a salal hedge to reach the fine gravel beach. Driftwood is in plentiful supply for use as backrests, picnic tables, and temporary shelters.

A steep trail leads to **Mystic Beach,** rougher than the one to nearby **China Beach** but just as enchanting. Plan on 15 minutes to walk to each. Part of the charm of visiting these beaches is admiring the rain forest that thrives in this moist climate. Thick moss coats the forest floor, while wispy strands of Spanish moss trail from the trunks and limbs of second-growth Douglas fir, Sitka spruce, western hemlock, and western red cedar. Salal, Oregon grape, and evergreen huckleberries form much of the under-brush, while in damp areas a variety of ferns adds to the riot of growth that feeds on the nutrient-rich ocean air. Aptly named Mystic Beach conjures an image of foggy mornings, paisley sunsets, and reverberating surf. You'll find that and more here, including twin caves at the north end of the beach that are neat to explore at low tide, along with broad, flat, multihued rock outcroppings covered with a zillion green life forms.

One of the **best views** anywhere on southern Vancouver Island of the Olympic Mountains occurs along Hwy 14 almost 5 miles (8 km) west of China Beach Provincial Park. To get maximum enjoyment, head a short distance uphill on one of the logging roads that lead off the highway in this vicinity. In a clear-cut, there's nothing to block your view.

The easiest beach to reach by far is that at **Jordan River** (or River Jordan, as shown on some maps), a small settlement between French Beach and China Beach, and home of the West Coast Surfing Association (also called the Jordan River Surf Club). Hwy 14 makes one of its only approaches to the ocean here before beginning to climb San Juan Ridge once more. You'll find picnic tables here at a small recreation site.

Surfing

Surfing on Vancouver Island is a dicey proposition at the best of times. Inconsistent wave conditions, big weather, bone-rattling water temperatures, and poor access all conspire to ensure that a summer safari to the real West Coast is a bruising experience. In winter, the climatic environment intensifies, and wave riding is best left to addicts, fools, and cryogenic researchers. Although the epicentre of surfing on Vancouver Island is in Tofino, there is a hard-core clique of riders centered in Jordan River. Storms originating in the Gulf of Alaska generate most of the tastier surf that lashes British Columbia's coast from late September through March. Other swells come from Japan and more localized weather systems. This is in marked contrast to the summer, when distant Southern Hemisphere swells have a minimal effect, blocked entirely from the southernmost areas of Vancouver Island by Washington's Olympic Peninsula.

Jordan River lies about 19 miles (30 km) south of Sombrio Beach and is home to the informal **Jordan River Surf Club** (see also Beaches, above). Locals tend to be turf conscious (make that *surf*-conscious) and are touchily protective of their place in the lineup. Any attempt to drop in out of turn risks a wrathful encounter. At first glance the ocean around Jordan River in winter looks grey and barren. The surprise, once you get out into it, is how alive it actually is. Seals pop up in the kelp beds to check your style, while black cormorants cruise around outside the take-off zone. Waves average 2- to 4-foot sets of rights that break off the point. When it's cold and raining, with the water temperature in single Celsius digits and a sky growing darker as the day wears on, you may well have the swells to yourself. The ideal board for British Columbia conditions is slightly longer (in the 7-feet-6-inches range) and wider than normal, and with three fins, which makes catching and controlling waves easier in less-than-optimum conditions.

If you decide to join the lineup offshore from **Sombrio Beach** (see Beaches, above), expect heavy conditions as you drift in the swells next to huge kelp beds. A gigantic rock commands the base of the breaking wave at Sombrio and dominates the path that faces a surfer after takeoff. A persistent mist often enshrouds the locale, creating a spooky ambience.

Wildlife

Botanical Beach Provincial Park is one of the most amazing places on the entire West Coast, particularly at low tide. This is when visitors can walk a long way out across flat sandstone and granite outcroppings to view tide pools filled like jewel boxes with brightly coloured marine animals. Purple, red, and orange **starfish** and **sea urchins**, blue **mussel** shells, white **gooseneck barnacles**, and green **sea anemones** and **sea cucumbers** only begin to hint at the spectrum of intertidal life that thrives here. So significant is this location that a research station was first established here in 1900 by a team from the University of Minnesota.

Visitors find their way to the beach along the same rough road used for most of this century. The distance from the dock in Port Renfrew to the beach is 3 miles (5 km). Only four-wheel-drive vehicles with high clearance should attempt the rough road past the parking area close to the 2-mile (3-km) point. Beyond here the road narrows, parking is limited, and turning around is all but impossible. Better to bike or walk in. Allow 45 minutes on foot from the parking lot. As you near the beach the trail divides: take the right fork to reach Botany Bay; go left for Botanical Beach and the tide pools.

Ridges of shale and quartz jut up through the basalt at Botanical Beach to create immense tableaus in places such as the awe-inspiring **Devil's Punchbowl.** The Punchbowl, flanked by smaller bowls on either side, features a gallery of caves rising above two huge cedar logs and a field of driftwood kindling. Although you wouldn't want to be anywhere near here at high tide, it's staggering to imagine how conditions must boil in there during winter storms. These formations are located at the north end of the sandy beach and require some scrambling to reach. Wear rubber boots, as the going is always wet. Even during the lowest tides of the year—December and January, June and July—the prospect of being caught out here will make your adrenal gland flutter.

Plan ahead so that you visit here when the tide is falling. At this point on the coast there is often only one major tide per day, and you can spend several hours waiting for it to recede if you arrive at the wrong time. The best local tide chart to consult is the one issued for Tofino. The store at the Port Renfrew Hotel is a good local source; so is Parks Canada's West Coast Trail office in Port Renfrew, (250) 647-5434, as well as the Sooke InfoCentre, (250) 642-6371.

Killer whales (or orcas, the largest members of the dolphin family) and **grey whales** are often seen swimming offshore from French Beach, China Beach, and Botanical Beach Provincial Parks. Although orcas live in these waters year-round, the best time for spotting grey whales is during their annual migration in March and April, when they are en route to Alaska from their breeding grounds in Baja, Mexico. **California and Steller sea lions** appear from August to March as they follow migrating fish stocks. You'll almost always spot from these beaches the smooth-domed head of a curious **harbour seal** bobbing offshore.

It's not unusual to spot **black bears** in early spring on some of the beaches as well, particularly around China and Mystic Beaches. Bears are unpredictable creatures, especially when they emerge hungry from winter denning. If you see one, back away slowly. Do not leave food or garbage lying around: a fed bear is a dead bear.

Camping

Campsites are limited along this section of the coast, in part because of the rugged terrain but also because of its isolation. **French Beach Provincial Park** (69 vehicle/tent sites; (250) 391-2300, reservations (800) 689-9025) is the place many visitors head for camping. It's conveniently close to Sooke and a good place to stage explorations to a number of beaches farther north along Hwy 14 (see Beaches, above). Campsites are well spaced and sheltered by a thick rain-forest canopy, as well as dense salal thickets above the beach.

Fairy Lake Forest Recreation Site is located a short drive north of Port Renfrew on the Harris Creek Mainline Logging Rd. Numerous rough sites have been used for decades by holidaying forestry workers, fishers, and rowdy punks. Weekdays are usually fine but summer weekends could find the heavy-metal crowd setting up their boom boxes on either side of you. For more information on Fairy Lake and other Forest Service recreation sites in the region, call BC Forest Service in Duncan, (250) 746-2700, or in Port Alberni, (250) 724-9205. If you're reluctant to take a chance, check out the **Pacheedaht First Nations Campground** on the shores of nearby San Juan Beach. The Pacheedaht First Nations Campground in Port Renfrew is located next to a wide swath of log-covered beach. West Coast Trail hikers overnight here before catching a ride to the trailhead. Call (250) 647-5521 for reservations.

Kayaking

For those who have paddled only in sheltered passages, sea kayaking along the outside waters of Vancouver Island is another world, one where you go big or you go home. However, if you pick your time, particularly in summer months, you'll find that the Pacific can be as well behaved as a sleeping giant. The 37-mile (60-km) ocean route between Sooke and Port Renfrew, with its string of beaches to touch on, can be paddled in a lengthy summer day. Of course, you don't have to do the entire length of this coast to enjoy an outing. Pick your launch locations, such as from **French Beach Provincial Park** (see Camping, above), one of the few beaches where you can drive to within a short distance of a launch site. Two other good locations include **Jordan River** (see Beaches, above) and **Pacheedaht Beach** in Port San Juan.

There's paddling in the sheltered waters of the **San Juan River**, a beautiful stretch of which can be reached from the Forest Service recreation site at Fairy Lake (see Camping, above). Hand-carried boats can be launched from the beach here. The lake drains into the golden-hued, sandy-bottomed river. A leisurely paddle upstream will bring you to a salmon-rearing station. Although heavy-handed logging has had a terrible impact on the San Juan River, destroying critical salmon spawning habitat and choking parts of the river with debris, the tranquillity of the tree-lined section around Fairy Lake is a reminder of happier, healthier times before the arrival of industry. The San Juan River empties into Port San Juan near Port Renfrew, creating an intertidal wetland at Harris Cove beside the Pacheedaht First Nations Reserve.

Fishing

The Sooke Basin is the staging ground for much of the salmon-fishing activity on the southwestern coast of Vancouver Island. As always, the best approach is to stop in at one of the local marine businesses for the latest advice on where the fish are running and biting, and what lures and bait they're attracted to. Several good sources of information include Sooke Harbour Marina, (250) 642-3236, and Sunny Shores Resort and

Marina, (250) 642-5731 (both have boat launching facilities), in Sooke, and the Port Renfrew Marina, (250) 647-5430, in Port Renfrew. Sooke Rentals in Sooke, (250) 642-5841, rents canoes, boats, outboard motors, crab traps, and other marine-related items.

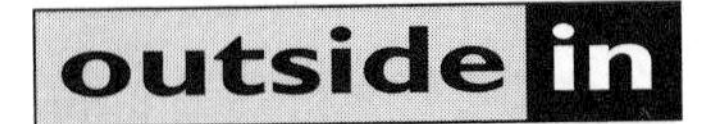

Attractions

Royal Roads University, on the road to Sooke, is a Dunsmuir family castle turned provincial university; the beautiful grounds are open to the public each day 10am to 4pm; (250) 391-2511.

Sooke Region Museum mounts some interesting displays of logging and pioneer equipment, Native artifacts, and a fully restored historic cottage showing turn-of-the-century lifestyles. The museum also sponsors British Columbia's largest juried fine-arts show, held every August in the Sooke Arena. Open Tuesday to Sunday; call (250) 642-6351 for more information.

For local crafts, organic vegetables, and children's activities, stop by the **Sooke Country Market,** every Saturday, May through September, at the Sooke Elementary School.

Restaurants

Country Cupboard Cafe ☆☆ The menu is a simple, welcome, herb-and-garlic-laced anomaly out here in Deep-Fried Country. Pastas and stir-fries shine at dinner, and lunch offerings include creatively composed sandwiches. *402 Sheringham Point Rd (at West Coast Rd), Sooke; (250) 646-2323; $$.*

Good Life Restaurant and Bookstore ☆ The food at this funky establishment is quite good and well priced. Seafood and chicken star at dinner. *2113 Otter Point Rd (downtown), Sooke; (250) 642-6821; $$.*

Cheaper Eats

Mom's Cafe Mom's dishes out real food—from hot meatloaf sandwiches with mashed potatoes for $8 to Bluenose chowder served in a bread basket for $5. Leave room for the homemade blackberry pie. *2036 Shields Rd, Sooke; (250) 642-3314; $.*

Lodgings

Fossil Bay Resort ☆☆ Expect all the comforts of home and a few luxurious extras at these immaculate, modern ocean-front cottages. This clutch of six studio-type dwellings is the perfect answer for those seeking solitude. *1603 West Coast Rd (15 miles/24 km west of downtown Sooke on Hwy 14), Sooke, BC V0S 1N0; (250) 646-2073; $$$.*

Hartmann House ☆☆☆ If you're going to choose a B&B in Sooke, this should be it. This is a stunning, English-style, country garden setting (and very, very private) with distant views of the water. *5262 Sooke Rd (3.75 miles/6 km east of Sooke), Sooke, BC V0S 1N0; (250) 642-3761; $$$.*

Ocean Wilderness ☆ This log cabin (with a nine-room wing for guests) is a good choice if you want to leave pretensions behind. The rooms are big and filled with an odd assortment of nice furnishings. Many guests come for the location, set back in a cove with a nice trail to the beach. *109 W Coast Rd (10 minutes west of Sooke), Sooke, BC V0S 1N0; (250) 646-2116 or (800) 323-2116; $$$.*

Point No Point Resort ☆ These 20 reasonably priced rustic cabins are set on a wild, undeveloped cliffside facing the Strait of Juan de Fuca and cater to those who seek remote beauty and tranquillity. *1505 West Coast Rd (Hwy 14, 15 miles/24 km west of Sooke), RR 2, Sooke, BC V0S 1N0; (250) 646-2020; $$$.*

Richview House ☆☆ This farmhouse is a 3-minute walk from its famous neighbour, the Sooke Harbour House, and a pleasant, low-key alternative to the often-booked inn. Three matching guest rooms are nestled upstairs in the farmhouse's B&B addition. *7031 Richview Dr (take Whiffen Spit Rd to Richview Rd, turn right), RR 4, Sooke, BC V0S 1N0; (250) 642-5520; $$$.*

Sooke Harbour House ☆☆☆☆ This waterside 1931 clapboard farmhouse, one of British Columbia's finest inns, features three spectacular suites and sits adjacent to another house with 10 rooms. The country-cozy dining room offers a stunning view and is famous for its lavish (and expensive) meals. The owners also lease a farm cottage on a 40-acre (16-ha) "gentleman's farm"—a perfect escape for city slickers. *1528 Whiffen Spit Rd (at very end of road), RR 4, Sooke, BC V0S 1N0; (250) 642-3421 or (800) 889-9688; $$$.*

Cheaper Sleeps

Blackfish Bed & Breakfast A bargain bed with an oceanfront location and a spectacular, secluded pebble beach—could it be true? The rooms aren't as special as the outdoor scenery, but at these prices, who's complaining? *2440 Blackfish Rd, Sooke, BC V0S 1N0; (250) 642-6864; $.*

Dutch Retreat Country Cottage This quaint, self-contained, one-bedroom cottage overlooking Sooke River is home to many happy geese and ducks. The cottage is close to the Galloping Goose hiking and cycling trail, too. *2882 Sooke River Rd, Sooke, BC V0S 1N0; (250) 642-3812; $.*

Mrs. Lewers Farmhouse Bed & Breakfast Who can resist the bucolic cherry orchard surrounding this B&B with two very private and cozy guests rooms? (Psst . . . the rooms literally were former chicken coops.) Although the bathroom is shared, you get your own farm-fresh eggs. *5526 Sooke Rd, Sooke, BC V0S 1N0; (250) 642-3150; $.*

More Information

BC Forest Service, South Island Forest District, Port Alberni: *(250) 724-9205.*

BC Parks: *(250) 391-2300; reservations (800) 689-9025.*

Discover BC: *(604) 663-6000 from Vancouver, or (800) 663-6000.*

Juan de Fuca Chamber of Commerce: *(250) 478-1130 or (250) 478-3242.*

Pacheedaht Band Office, Port Renfrew: *(250) 647-5521.*

Parks Canada (Pacific Rim National Park/West Coast Trail):

Port Renfrew: *(250) 647-5434.*

Ucluelet: *(250) 726-7211.*

Sooke InfoCentre: *(250) 642-6371.*

Sooke Marine Industries: *(250) 642-3523, for map of Kludahk Forest Service Trail.*

Nanaimo and the Cowichan Valley

North across the Malahat Ridge from Victoria through the Cowichan and Chemainus Valleys to Nanaimo and Parksville, including a cross-island trip to Carmanah-Walbran Provincial Park.

This slice of southern Vancouver Island covers the country between Port Renfrew and Bamfield on the west coast and Malahat and Parksville on the east side. Most of the population lives along the east coast, where farming in the lush, rolling Cowichan and Chemainus Valleys has gone hand in hand with logging since Vancouver Island was an independent Crown colony. The heart of agriculture lies south of Nanaimo, the Hub City, and this pastoral atmosphere persists as you make you way north towards Parksville. However, it's hard to ignore the slopes of the Vancouver Island Mountains that begin to nudge travellers closer to the coastline for wont of wide valley bottoms. Most roads west peter out quickly in the face of this granitic tour de force. The exception is the cross-island mélange of paved highway and gravel logging roads that link the sheltered Cowichan Valley with the storm-battered community of Bamfield on the west coast. A greater contrast is hard to find, which is what makes exploring this region so fascinating. There's plenty of easygoing adventuring to be found by sticking to the main routes, although everyone should treat themselves to a backroad or two where the valleys meet the Strait of Georgia. There are beaches here the likes of which are found nowhere else on the coast, with views that engender intimacy with the landscape, yet emphasize its isolation.

Getting There

The most westerly section of the 4,850-mile (7809-km) Trans-Canada Highway (Highway 1) runs north-south through southern Vancouver Island between Victoria and Nanaimo, a distance of 70 miles (113 km). Highway 14 runs 22 miles (35 km) north of Nanaimo to Parksville, and beyond to the northern end of Vancouver Island. Highway 4 links Parksville with Port Alberni, Ucluelet, and Tofino on the west side of Vancouver Island. Highway 18 is an 18-mile (29-km) stretch of blacktop that runs east-west from Highway 1 through the Cowichan Valley between Duncan and Youbou. From Youbou a series of logging roads leads 67 miles (108 km) west to Bamfield on the west coast of Vancouver Island. Ferry service from Brentwood Bay on the Saanich Peninsula with Mill Bay at the north end of Malahat Drive also connects with Highway 1. BC Ferries connects the Lower Mainland with Nanaimo's Departure Bay from the Horseshoe Bay terminal in West Vancouver, and Duke Point from the Tsawwassen terminal in Delta. BC Ferries also connects with southern Vancouver Island at Crofton from Vesuvius Bay on Salt Spring Island, and with Chemainus from Thetis and Kuper Islands.

Adjoining Areas

NORTH: **North Vancouver Island**

SOUTH: **Greater Victoria**

EAST: **Greater Vancouver**

WEST: **Tofino and Pacific Rim National Park Reserve**

inside out

Kayaking/Boating

Memory Island Provincial Park is located on the southern half of **Shawnigan Lake.** It only requires a short 0.6-mile (1-km) paddle to reach this tranquil little park. A boat launch is located on the west side of the Malahat Dr section of Hwy 1. Put in here and paddle up the lake to reach Memory Island, the largest of a small chain. Come ashore to picnic, stretch your legs and do a little laid-back bird-watching. You could also launch from West Shawnigan Lake Provincial Park (see Beaches/Picnics, below) but be prepared to paddle for several miles to reach the island.

The municipal boat launch in the centre of **Ladysmith,** south of Nanaimo, is the place to begin exploring the 5-mile (8-km) length of **Ladysmith Harbour. Dunsmuir** and **Woods Islands** on the north side of the harbour are good destination in summer, while the marshy lagoon at the head of the harbour attracts migrating birds in spring and fall.

As much as the ocean dominates the landscape near Nanaimo, there are several freshwater lakes where paddlers will find serenity in a rural setting. You can put in at Hemer Provincial Park on **Holden Lake** or at nearby **Quennell Lake.** Holden's shape is rather straightforward, with only one major bay. In comparison, Quennell is nothing *but* bays. The action at both is a good excuse for some paddling and perhaps cutthroat trout fishing. A short network of forested trails leads through the woods from the parking lot at Hemer Provincial Park to the west side of Holden Lake. Follow the signs a short distance east from Hwy 1 to reach Hemer Park. A backroad leads south of Holden Lake to Quennell Lake near Yellow Point.

There's a public boat ramp at **Pipers Lagoon Regional Park** (see Beaches/Picnics, below) in Nanaimo. It's one thing to putt-putt around the sheltered lagoon, but quite another to brave the open water of Horswell Channel on the east side of the narrow headland that shelters the lagoon. To reach the park, from Hwy 19 take Departure Bay Rd, which follows the natural arch of the coastline around the north arm of Departure Bay. Turn east onto Hammond Bay Rd and watch for signs to the park. The boat launch is at the end of Charlaine Rd, one of two well-marked entrances to the park.

There are at least four places on 20-mile-long (32-km) **Cowichan Lake** with boat launch ramps. The one suited to large boats is located at Gordon Bay Provincial Park (see Camping, below). Two others are found at Pine Point and Maple Grove Forest Service Recreation Sites (see Camping, below) on the north shore of Cowichan Lake. The ramps at these two are limited to boats up to 14 feet (4 m) in length. You can also launch a hand-carried boat at the Forest Service site at Nixon Creek (see Camping, below). The area around Cowichan Lake's south arm is a heat trap and boasts the highest average maximum summer temperature (75°F/24°C) in Canada. Small wonder that the lake attracts swimmers, boaters, and water-skiers in droves.

For those travelling to the west side of the island, you'll find a gravel boat launch at the Forest Service site on **Nitinat Lake** (see Windsurfing, below) suitable for car-top boats. Boaters must beware of the stiff winds that blow on Nitinat Lake.

Beaches/Picnics

There are several locations on Shawnigan Lake where good beaches and picnicking go hand in hand. Just walk a short distance from the parking lot to the beach and picnic tables at **West Shawnigan Lake Provincial Park.** The beach here is very popular with young families. The park is located 10 miles (16 km) west of Hwy 1 along West Shawnigan Lake Rd on the northwest corner of the lake. **Shawnigan Lake Municipal Beach** is located on Renfrew Rd in the quaint town of the same name beside the Esquimalt & Nanaimo Railway on the east side of the lake. Highway 1 goes right past the park.

Directly east of Shawnigan Lake and just south of the Mill Bay ferry terminal is **Bamberton Provincial Park** (see Camping, below). A large swath of sandy beach, complete with changing facilities, fronts on the Saanich Inlet here. Dozens of picnic tables sit on the terraced slopes above the beach, shaded by a fir-and-arbutus (madrona) forest. This is one of the more scenic locations on the inlet, and from here you look east towards Mount Baker on the mainland. Water in the inlet can be quite chilly year-round, but on this part of the inlet, temperatures are much warmer.

Both Osborne Bay Regional Park's **Crofton Beach,** in Crofton, and **Transfer Beach,** in Ladysmith Harbour, offer warm saltwater swimming to pass the time between bouts of picnicking. Follow the signs to Crofton and you'll find the beach. A ferry links Crofton with Vesuvius Bay on Salt Spring Island. As short distance farther north off Hwy 19 near the coastal hamlet of Yellow Point is **Roberts Memorial Provincial Park.** A peaceful walk on this sandstone beach is its own reward. Like many small parks that were gifted to the province in remembrance by area families, an atmosphere of transcendent serenity permeates the park, broken only by the barking of sea lions offshore and the mewling of sea gulls, great blue heron, and the occasional Pacific loon.

Pipers Lagoon Regional Park in Nanaimo has both a sheltered and an exposed side. Take your pick of beaches on either one. The lagoon drains so dry that at low tide you can wander out to nearby Shack Island. The eastern shore of the park faces the Strait of Georgia, where a stiff wind is often blowing. Hunker down and watch the heroics as small boats battle their way towards the mouth of Departure Bay. BC Ferries vessels entering and leaving the harbour normally don't feel the wind's sting, but even they can get slapped around during the worst winter blows. That's when the action at Pipers Lagoon is often the most dramatic. If you like storm watching, this is a great vantage point. A forest of Garry oak predominate on the narrow headland that shelters the lagoon. Wildflowers are profuse here in springtime and attract Columbia black-tailed deer out onto the beach. Pipers Lagoon Park lies nestled at the foot of Sugarloaf Mountain, 3 miles (5 km) north of the BC Ferries Departure Bay terminal off Hammond Bay Rd. The best approach to the beach is from the main parking lot at the foot of Place Rd.

From Nanaimo north to Parksville, the eastern coastline of Vancouver Island softens considerably. There are no islands along this stretch to interrupt the views across the Strait of Georgia to the snow-covered peaks of the Coast Mountains as they rise above the Sunshine Coast. Both **Departure Bay** in Nanaimo and Parksville's **Community Park** offer great lengths of public beach on town shoreline. Pick a location that appeals to you, park in one of the many access points, and stroll out onto the hard-packed sand. Also on the Nanaimo waterfront are **Maffeo Sutton Park** and **Swyalana Lagoon Park.** Although these two aren't in the same league as some of the larger stretches of waterfront farther north, they do provide convenient beach and picnicking locations on Nanaimo's sheltered inner harbour, are beside a seawall walking, cycling, and in-line skating route, and lie with easy walking distance of the Scotch Bakery on Commercial St. This is the home of the Nanaimo Bar, a regional specialty that is actually a form of chocolate fridgecake. No picnic here would be complete without one.

Just south of Parksville, the beaches in **Rathtrevor Beach Provincial Park** (see Camping, below) are a short drive east of Hwy 19. So vast is its sandy, shallow shingle, particularly when the tide is low, that you can spend hours beachcombing and bird-watching here beneath the wide-open sky. The waters of the Strait of Georgia warm up quickly when the tide rises over these sun-baked expanses. Seals often approach the beach, following the salmon that follow the needlefish that follow the zooplankton. Join the chain!

Just as popular as Rathtrevor Provincial Park is **Gordon Bay Provincial Park** (see Camping, below) on Cowichan Lake. The lake relies on the sunshine that floods this bright valley to warm its broad waters. The south arm of the lake acts as a heat trap and the water temperature rivals that of the air, which makes for a perfect beach combo. A log boom calms the inside water of Gordon Bay and protects the beach as well. No surf here, and no pesky Jet-skis either.

Smaller beaches on Cowichan Lake are located at a number of Forest Service recreation sites, including **Spring Beach, Maple Grove,** and **Nixon Creek** (see Camping, below).

Fishing

Vancouver Island waterways are characterized by relatively short watersheds. The **Cowichan River** is an exception to this general rule. Anglers can cover much of the **Cowichan River Footpath**'s 12 miles (19 km) of trails beside one of Vancouver Island's most popular fly-fishing locales in one of British Columbia's best fishing rivers and, according to knowledgeable sources, one of the world's best salmon and trout rivers. To find the trailhead, head west of Hwy 1 in Duncan on Allenby Rd, then south on Indian Rd, then make three successive right turns onto Glenora, Vaux, and

Robertson Rds. The trail begins from the parking lot of the Cowichan Fish and Game Association, (250) 746-1070. Brown, rainbow, and steelhead trout, as well as vigorous salmon runs, make fishing here legendary. Brown trout were successfully introduced here about a century ago and coexist with the native stocks. Local fishing guide Joe Saysell is noted for his intimate relationship with the river. Much of the year, he fishes from a Mackenzie drift boat, a popular West Coast design that originated in Seattle. Altogether, the oxygen-rich water supports **ten species of trout, salmon, and char.** A controversial weir controls the outflow of water from Cowichan Lake into the river and guarantees stable streamflow conditions for most of the year. Big rainbow trout come down out of the lake to feed on salmon roe and overwinter in the river before returning to the lake by June. Chinook, coho, and steelhead that school in Cowichan Bay enter the river to spawn in November and December. There's also a steelhead run in March. For more information, contact Joe Saysell, (250) 749-3062.

One of the best places to launch a boat when fishing in **Cowichan Lake** is at Gordon Bay Provincial Park (see Kayaking/Boating, above). There are dozens of parking places next to the ramps from which anglers pursue rainbow and cutthroat trout and dolly varden char. Springtime is best for trout fishing, before the lake really warms up. Keep it simple: use a float and a worm and a light spinning outfit. If you're casting a fly or other artificial lure, a small boat or float tube helps you cover the water.

Although it's hard to match the calibre of fishing in the Cowichan River, there are times when trolling or casting in a small lake suits the mood. You'll find many such spots dotted around Vancouver Island. In Nanaimo and the Cowichan Valley, anglers seek out any of the locations mentioned below. **Quamichan Lake** east of Duncan has good trout fishing. You can launch a car-top boat at Art Mann Park on the lake. To reach the park, follow Trunk Rd east of downtown Duncan to Tzouhalem Rd, then Maple Bay Rd to Indian Rd, which leads to the park. **Quennell Lake** (see Kayaking/Boating, above) near South Wellington is known for its good smallmouth bass and trout fishing, as is **Holden Lake** (launch at Hemer Provincial Park) near Yellow Point. **Long Lake** and **Brannen Lake** are situated 3 miles (5 km) north of Nanaimo centre. They're both easy to locate on opposite sides of Hwy 14. Follow Norwell Dr east of the highway to Louden Park on Long Lake or Dunster Rd west of the Nanaimo Pkwy to Brannen Lake. There are trout and smallmouth bass at Long Lake; cutthroat and rainbow trout at Brannen.

Spectacle Lake Provincial Park north of Malahat is regularly stocked with rainbow trout, which means that you must get there early in the season for best results. As you look down through the lake's incredibly clear water, you'll see crayfish scuttling along the lake bottom. Spectacle

Lake is located about 1 mile (2 km) west of Hwy 1 at Malahat Summit. The waters of the **Saanich Inlet** just east of Spectacle Lake are noted for their sport salmon fishing. You can launch a hand-carried boat from the beach at Bamberton Provincial Park (see Beaches/Picnics, above) to explore the inlet. For those in search of a boat ramp on the inlet, head north to **Cowichan Bay,** located 3 miles (5 km) east of Hwy 1. Launch beside the Pier 66 Marina, (250) 748-8444, on Cowichan Bay Rd, where you can pick up much useful information, bait, fuel, and supplies. There's also a boat launch at end of Handy Rd off Mill Bay Rd north of Bamberton Provincial Park. Finally, though this is not the last word in fishing in these environs by any means, launch from the ramp at Crofton Beach in Osborne Bay Regional Park (see Beaches/Picnics, above) for saltwater fishing in **Stuart Channel.**

For more information on fishing and **charters,** contact Sealand Tackle, 1840 Stewart Ave, (250) 754-1432; The Dock Shoppe in Pioneer Waterfront Plaza at the boat basin in Nanaimo's inner harbour, (250) 741-0990; Poby's Charter, (250) 245-3373, in Ladysmith; or the Tourism Nanaimo InfoCentre, 266 Bryden St, (250) 756-0106 or (800) 663-7337. For saltwater sportfishing information on licences, limits, and closures, contact the Fisheries and Oceans field offices in Nanaimo, (250) 754-0230, or in Duncan, (250) 746-6221. Visit their Web site: www.pac.dfo.ca/comm/.

Camping

Gordon Bay Provincial Park on Cowichan Lake east of Duncan is a large park with 130 vehicle/tent sites. Reservations are recommended in July and August, when the sun shines brightest on this southern exposure. The lay of the land here traps heat, and daytime temperatures are hot by coastal standards. Evidence of this is found on the hillsides above the park where Rocky Mountain juniper flourishes, one of the few locations west of the Rockies where this fragrant evergreen grows. The rewards for being here in April and May in advance of the summer crowds include having your choice of campsites and witnessing the spectacular display of wildflowers that begin blooming in April. For more information, contact BC Parks, (250) 391-2300. For reservations, call (800) 689-9025. To reach the park, travel west of Duncan on Hwy 18 to the town of Lake Cowichan, then follow South Shore Rd for 11 miles (18 km) to the park entrance. Campsites 1–14 are closest to the lake.

Bamberton Provincial Park is located just south of the Mill Bay ferry terminal beside Hwy 1. The 47 vehicle/tent sites are located beside Johns Creek on the hillside above Sechelt Inlet. Reservations are a necessity in summer, unless you are at the park entrance at noon when a number of first-come spaces may be available, depending on turnover. The one-two punch of a superb view and a sandy beach (see Beaches/Picnics, above) makes this park a knockout for lucky visitors. September is one of the best times to stay here, once the opening of school draws many families back to the homefront. This is also the time when the arbutus trees shed their bark, and their strawberry-hued trunks shine like a well-oiled handrail. For more information, contact BC Parks, (250) 391-2300. For reservations, call (800) 689-9025.

Rathtrevor Beach Provincial Park south of Parksville has acres of campsites to match its 1.3 miles (2.1 km) of beaches. If you're lucky enough to be travelling in the off-season (September to June) you'll have plenty of choice from among the 175 vehicle/tent sites. Otherwise, phone ahead for reservations, particularly on weekends. So good does the living get here that some families spend their entire vacations at Rathtrevor Beach, where the maximum stay permitted is 14 consecutive days. Small wonder, when all the comforts of home, such as hot showers, gas barbeques in covered beachside picnic shelters, and firewood, are included in the camping fee of about $15 per night per site. For more information, call BC Parks, (250) 954-4600; reservations, (800) 689-9025.

Ivy Green Park and Campground in Ladysmith was formerly a provincial park and is now run by the Chemainus First Nations, (250) 741-4985. The campground enjoys a beautiful location on Ladysmith Harbour, with a beach and shoreline nature trails.

There are five Forest Service recreation sites located on Cowichan Lake and along the Nitinat Main Logging Rd. Two small sites—**Spring Beach** and **Bald Mountain**—are located on the north side of the lake across from Gordon Bay Provincial Park and are limited to those campers who arrive by boat or on foot. You could launch at Gordon Bay (see Kayaking/Boating, above) or hike in from the Marble Bay entrance to the park. Allow 90 minutes to make the 4-mile (6-km) trek. Two spacious sites—**Pine Point** and **Maple Grove**—are situated on the north shore of the lake west of the town of Youbou, while a third is located at **Nixon Creek** on the southwest side of the lake. All are easily reached by following either North or South Shore Rds west of the community of Lake Cowichan.

The Forest Service recreation site at **Nitinat Lake** (see Windsurfing, below) has the international cachet that you'd also find in select places such as the Gorge in Oregon or the Squamish Spit (see Whistler and the Sea to Sky Highway chapter). Vans and trucks carrying board sailors from around the world and decked out with roof racks for windsurfing equipment occupy many of the rustic campsites beside the lake. You don't have to brave the winds; just driving the logging roads west of Cowichan Lake qualifies you to stay here. This campsite is busy almost year-round. If it's not the windsurfers, it's the visitors to nearby Carmanah-Walbran Provincial Park (see Hiking/Backpacking, below).

Hiking/Backpacking

In the late 1980s and early 1990s **Carmanah-Walbran Provincial Park** was the site of a heated confrontation between logging heavyweight MacMillan-Bloedel and a coalition of conservationists led by the Vancouver-based Western Canada Wilderness Committee. Even now, years after a provincial government decision created the 8,875-acre (3550-ha) Carmanah Pacific Park in the lower half of the valley (and more recently added to it the upper Carmanah Valley and neighbouring Walbran Valley), friction still exists between the company and visitors to the woodland. In order to reach Carmanah-Walbran Provincial Park, visitors must travel on active logging roads. Travellers on the Carmanah Mainline and Rosander Mainline Rds during logging hours must take great care. Although the roads are adequate for two-way traffic, in some sections there is a terrifyingly steep drop-off to the shores of Nitinat Lake far below. Tree Farm 44 presents a foreground of clear-cut stumps, with the Pacific's broad, grey sweep far off to the west. The persistent sight of such vast devastation only serves to heighten the relief when the entrance to the provincial park comes into view, announced by a large wooden sign with the carved and painted likeness of the marbled murrelet, a small seabird that requires old-growth forest for its habitat. Until recently, only a handful of this mysterious bird's nests had been located worldwide. In August 1990, researchers sited a marbled murrelet's nest in the Walbran Valley adjacent to the Carmanah, the first-ever identification of its kind in British Columbia.

Although you're unlikely to see a marbled murrelet, it hardly matters. Just to know that they might be resident in the misty upper realm of the moss-covered evergreens is enough. Visitors come to Carmanah to be entranced by the spell cast around big trees—trees so large that you have to expand your consciousness in order to assimilate the almost overwhelming impression made by such enormous biomass. Only an **annual rainfall** of almost 10 feet (3 m), frequent dense fog, and a nutrient-rich sea breeze could create an environment such as the one found here. When packing for the trip, head-to-toe waterproofing is advisable.

Sturdily built **Valley Mist Trail** (easy; 1.6 miles/2.6 km return) leads from the parking area down into the valley and links with the **Upper Valley Trail** (easy; 10 miles/16 km return), which runs through the valley beside Carmanah Creek. Although the forest floor rarely dries out at even the warmest time of year, boardwalks and compacted gravel paths keep hikers above the muck. You can make a quick descent into the valley for a day trip or pack in camping gear. Most visitors are here just for several hours rather than for the night. The majority either drive in from the east side of Vancouver Island via Cowichan Lake, or stay at the east end of Nitinat Lake. A limited number of spaces are available for vehicle camping in the parking lot beside the trailhead. Freshwater is also available here.

Once in the Carmanah Valley, an aura of calm and tranquillity surrounds you. Giant Sitka spruce rise like stately columns linking heaven with earth, while the forest floor is richly covered—false lily-of-the-valley's white blossoms, ferns, and fungi. Bring a tent and camp on one of the soft gravel bars exposed when water levels in the creek are low, and be serenaded by the hermit thrush's call as it drifts through the walls of the forest. There's as much to admire in the mystery of Carmanah's hidden side as there is in that which thrusts up before you.

In a ceremony held in the park on June 15, 1995, **Heaven's Grove,** an area of Carmanah on the Upper Valley Trail that contains some of the largest examples of Sitka spruce, was renamed in memory of author and environmental conservationist Randy Stoltmann, who died in an avalanche in 1994. It was Stoltmann who originally brought the Carmanah and Walbran Valleys to public attention. His books include *Hiking Guide to the Big Trees of Southwestern BC* and *Written by the Wind* and continue to be an invaluable resource and inspiration.

To reach Carmanah-Walbran Provincial Park, take Hwy 18 west from Hwy 1 near Duncan to Cowichan Lake. Follow either South Shore or North Shore Rd around Cowichan Lake. Both roads merge with the gravel-surfaced Nitinat Lake Rd west of Cowichan Lake. Be sure to stop at the BC Parks Travel Information kiosk on Nitinat Lake Rd to check current road conditions and safety information. Watch for signs to Carmanah-Walbran Provincial Park and Nitinat Lake. Nitinat Lake and the Ditidaht Nation Visitors Centre is about 25 miles (40 km) west of Cowichan Lake. Carmanah-Walbran Provincial Park is a well-signed, 18-mile (29-km) drive west of the Nitinat River Bridge and takes about 45 minutes to reach. For a detailed map of Carmanah-Walbran Provincial Park, contact the BC Parks office in Victoria, (250) 391-2300. Other good maps include the Forest Service recreation maps for both the Duncan and Port Alberni Forest Districts. Call (250) 724-9205 for copies. Yet another good map to consult on Carmanah-Walbran Provincial Park is published by ITMB Publishing and is available from World Wide Books and Maps, 736A Granville St, Vancouver.

If you are interested in joining a group tour of Carmanah-Walbran Provincial Park, Coastal Connections in Victoria offers both day and overnight **interpretive nature hikes** in the region throughout the summer. Packages include one with a seaplane ride from Victoria along the outer coast of Vancouver Island to Nitinat Lake, then by van to the park. On overnight trips, accommodation with the Ditidaht Nation includes a traditional salmon barbeque hosted by Native elders. Contact Coastal Connections, (800) 840-4453.

The **Cowichan River Footpath** (see Fishing, above) runs along the north and south sides of the Cowichan River, and although primarily used by anglers, it also provides a pleasant 12-mile (19-km) ramble through newly created **Cowichan River Provincial Park.** Highlights include salmon runs in fall and the large, open recreation site at **Skutz Falls.** There aren't many waterfalls as easily approached as Skutz Falls. To reach the falls, head west of Hwy 1 on Hwy 18 for almost 12 miles (19 km) to Skutz Falls Rd. Drive south along this road for almost 2 miles (3 km) to the Mile 12 section of the footpath.

Petroglyph Provincial Park at the south end of Nanaimo, where the Nanaimo River empties into Northumberland Channel, presents a look back in time to a prehistoric period perhaps a millennium ago. Mythological creatures—sea wolves in particular—and symbolic designs have skillfully been outlined in the sandstone surface of the rock. Examples of this art form exist elsewhere, but rarely in such concentration as viewed here. A short, wheelchair-accessible walkway leads from the parking lot on the east side of Hwy 1 to an interpretive display of concrete moulds taken from the nearby petroglyphs. Visitors who would like to take away an example of this artwork can make rubbings on paper of the coffee-table-size moulds. The originals are just a short distance farther along the walkway on a hill that overlooks the Nanaimo harbour.

Wildlife

Spring and fall present remarkable opportunities to view birds as they travel along the Pacific Flyway. Some of the protected areas where they pause and refresh themselves include **Hecate Regional Park** in Cowichan Bay, 3 miles (5 km) east of Hwy 1, about 30 miles (50 km) north of Victoria; **Art Mann Park** on Quamichan Lake (see Fishing, above) near Duncan, and nearby **Somenos Lake,** where the Nature Trust of BC maintains a waterfowl nesting and wintering habitat. Not to be outdone, BC Wildlife Watch has a viewing station at the **Morrell Wildlife Sanctuary** in Nanaimo. The sanctuary is located northwest of the Nanaimo Pkwy's intersection with Nanaimo Lakes Rd. Call (250) 753-5811 for more information.

Wildflowers don't return in the fall like birds, so you must be on site in the spring to appreciate them. The south side of Cowichan Lake is a particularly pretty place to be, including the **Honeymoon Bay Wildflower Ecological Reserve,** where pink easter lilies begin blooming in late

April, surrounded by dozens more blossoms that continue to perfume the air and colour the landscape throughout the summer. The reserve is located 9 miles (15 km) west of Cowichan Lake on South Shore Rd near Gordon Bay Provincial Park.

The beaches around Parksville and neighbouring Qualicum have been the site of an annual migration of tens of thousands of **brant geese** since well before the settlement of the town. With the establishment of the **Brant Goose Feeding Area** by the Mid Island Wildlife Watch Society, the arrival of the geese has been the trigger for annual festivities in mid-April. By then, thousands of the black-hued, duck-size sea geese touch down on the beaches and marshlands surrounding Parksville and Qualicum to rest and feed on the algae, eel grasses, seaweeds, and especially herring roe. Most of the migrating birds are travelling from Mexico to the Yukon-Kuskokwim delta of western Alaska. Guided tours of the feeding areas take visitors to special viewing locations, or you can simply walk out on the beach with a pair of binoculars and stalk them (and the more than 200 other bird species passing through at the same time). For information on tours and festival dates, call (250) 248-4117, or visit their Web site: qb.island.net/~bfest/.

Mountain Biking

The **Koksilah River/Burnt Bridge/Eagle Heights** region offers some incredible mountain-biking trails just west of Shawnigan Lake. This is the site of the annual Burnt Bridge Classic Race Loop and the Can-Am Trails. Lose yourself for hours or even days in this challenging, but not overly technical, area. Head west of Hwy 1 on Shawnigan Lake Rd where the highway divides at the south end of the lake. Take West Shawnigan Lake Rd to the north end of the lake, then go west on Renfrew Rd, which becomes a gravelled logging road as it follows the Koksilah River. Park at the three-way intersection near the site of an old burnt bridge that has been replaced by a new concrete-and-steel structure. To find the **Burnt Bridge Classic Race Loop,** bear left on the main road once across the bridge and pedal for about 2.5 miles (4 km). Bear left again after passing beneath some power lines, then right onto a trail that soon begins to narrow. Follow the tread marks from here as the trail descends to a log jump, crosses a log bridge, turns right, then left as it passes a clear-cut in the Wild Deer Creek drainage. Eventually you'll find yourself at a gated entrance to the main logging road, from where you return to your vehicle.

To ride the **Can-Am Trails,** turn right after pedalling across the new bridge from the parking area and right again at the first fork, about 1.5 miles (2.5 km) from the outset. Continue until a single-track trail appears on your left, which descends to an intersection where you go left again to reach a viewpoint on the Koksilah River. Retrace your tracks from here.

Both Nanaimo and Parksville have well-organized mountain-bike trail-building groups. In Nanaimo, the **Ultimate Abyss** is perhaps the best-known trail on Vancouver Island because of its notorious technical challenge. The semi-loop trail begins next to the SPCA shelter on Harewood Mines Rd. At the outset, the trail follows a string of power lines. The entrance to the trail begins beside power tower #24-2. Stay on the main trail and ignore all diversions. Much easier riding is found nearby in the **Westwood Lake** area, reached by following Jinglepot Rd and then Westwood Rd west of the city centre. More demanding trails lead off from the north end of the lake along **Westwood Ridge.**

Parksville is the site of one of the major mountain-bike competitions on Vancouver Island, the **Hammerfest.** In addition to the difficult race course, the Arrowsmith Mountain Bike Club has created the **Top Bridge Mountain Bike Park,** where more moderate adventuring awaits. To find the park, turn west off Hwy 14 at the weigh scales at Kay Rd, then turn onto Chattell Rd and follow it to its end, where the fun begins.

For more information on mountain-bike trails in the region, contact Iguana Cycles, (250) 748-6803; Experience Cycling Ltd., (250) 746-4041; or Howling Dawg Cycles, (250) 748-0404, all in Duncan. You can contact Bastion Cycle, (250) 758-2453; Pacific Rim Bicycle, (250) 754-1430; or Chain Reaction, (250) 754-3309, all in Nanaimo. In Parksville, contact Arrowsmith Mountain Cycles, (250) 248-5575; or Ocean Cycle Bicycle Specialists, (250) 248-0200. Good books to consult include *Mountain Biking British Columbia* by Darren Polischuk, and *Bicycling the Pacific Coast* by Tom Kirkendall and Vicky Spring.

Windsurfing

Some of the finest windsurfing in North America draws devotees to **Nitinat Lake** from around the globe. You have to be dedicated to make the long journey to the west side of Vancouver Island, and you have to be good to handle the constant thermal winds that sweep across the lake at speeds upwards of 30 mph (50 kph). Don't wait until you get to the lake to begin building upper-body strength. You're going to need all the buff you can bring with you. To reach Nitinat Lake, take Hwy 18 west from Hwy 1 near Duncan to Cowichan Lake. Follow either South Shore or North Shore Rd around Cowichan Lake. Both roads merge with the gravel-surfaced Nitinat Lake Rd west of Cowichan Lake. Be sure to stop at the BC Parks Travel Information kiosk on Nitinat Lake Rd to check current road conditions and safety information. Watch for signs to Nitinat

Lake. Nitinat Lake and the Ditidaht Nation Visitors Centre is about 25 miles (40 km) west of Cowichan Lake. For information on Nitinat Lake, contact the Ditidaht Nation Visitors Centre at (250) 745-8124. Good maps include the Forest Service reaction maps for both the Duncan and Port Alberni Forest Districts. Call (250) 724-9205 for copies.

A more easily reached windsurfing locale is **Pipers Lagoon Regional Park** (see Kayaking/Boating, above) in Nanaimo, where you'll often find just as stiff a breeze offshore as at Nitinat Lake.

Scenic Drives

The **Malahat Summit** on Hwy 1 lies about 9 miles (15 km) north of Goldstream Provincial Park (see Greater Victoria chapter). The highway climbs and descends both sides of this mountain that the Malahat people call Yos, one of the most sacred First Nations sites on southern Vancouver Island. The views from the summit are stunning and you will find pull-outs beside the road where you can gain inspiration from the sight of so much landscape. About a mile (2 km) farther north on Hwy 1 is the **Gulf Islands Viewpoint.** It will test your geographic skills to fit all the pieces in the island puzzle together from the views of ridges and shorelines that are visible from here.

Golfing

Nanaimo and the area to the north have seen the proliferation of golf courses with a view. Most noteworthy is the Nanaimo Golf Club, 3 miles (5 km) north of the city, a demanding 18-hole course with beautiful views of the water; (250) 758-6332. Others include Pryde Vista Golf Club in Nanaimo, (250) 753-6188; FairWinds at Nanoose, (250) 468-7766; and Morning Star, (250) 248-2244, and EagleCrest, (250) 752-9744, near Parksville/Qualicum.

Walking/Bungee Jumping

In Nanaimo, the **waterfront promenade** extends from the downtown harbour, past the modern seaplane terminal, through Swy-a-lana Lagoon Park (Canada's only man-made tidal lagoon), over the new pedestrian bridge, by the Nanaimo Yacht Club, and as far as the BC Ferries Terminal. For those who prefer falling over walking, Nanaimo claims itself as the home of North America's first (and only) bridge built specifically for bungee jumpers. You can watch or jump ($95) from this 140-foot (42-m) bridge above the Nanaimo River; contact Bungy Zone, (250) 753-5867.

Attractions

Nanaimo, a former coal-mining town, has evolved into something very different, with a clean, accessible waterfront, cultural festivals in the summer, a university campus with a marvellous view, and vastly improved dining. At The Bastion, built in 1853 and one of the few Hudson's Bay Company bastions still standing, there's a cannon-firing every day at noon in the summer. The Nanaimo District Museum, 100 Cameron Rd, (250) 753-1821, has a replica of a Chinatown street, among other displays. The Bastion Street Bookstore, 76 Bastion St, (250)753-3011, houses an impressive collection of children's books, natural history texts, guidebooks, and books by Canadian authors. On nearby Commercial St, the Scotch Bakery concocts the namesake Nanaimo bar. Head up the hill to Heritage Mews, off Bastion St, to sample coffee bars, restaurants, clothing shops (new and used), and home-decorating emporia. Or, for $4.50, ferry over to the Dinghy Dock Pub, a very nautical floating bar off Protection Island.

The Cowichan Valley is a gentle stretch of farmland and forest from Shawnigan Lake in the south to Chemainus in the north. A few **wineries** and a cider-maker grow grapes and apples and make their products south of Duncan; for tastings, visit the Cherry Point Vineyards (840 Cherry Point Rd, Cobble Hill, (250) 743-1272); Vigneti Zanatta (5039 Marshall Rd, Glenora, (250) 748-2338); Blue Grouse Vineyards (Blue Grouse Rd, off Lakeside Rd, (250) 743-3834); or Merridale Cider Works (1230 Merridale Rd, Cobble Hill, (250) 743-4293).

Wander through **Cowichan Bay,** a laid-back seaside community with restaurants (try the seafood chowder or the pie and coffee at The Bluenose, or the seafood quesadilla at The Inn at the Water), craft stores, and marinas. The Wooden Boat Society display and the hands-on exhibits at the Maritime Centre are well worth a visit.

In **Duncan,** the Native Heritage Centre is a must-see for admirers of Native arts and crafts. In summer you can watch the creation of the famous Cowichan sweaters as they are hand-knit in one piece, their unique patterns reflecting the knitter's family designs (some even spin their own wool). The Centre also features an open-air carving shed, where Native carvers with handmade tools craft traditional 12- to 20-foot totem poles, each pole representing the carver's interpretation of a tribal design. An excellent art gallery/gift shop has many Native carvings and prints for sale. The Native Heritage Centre is at 200 Cowichan Way, (250) 746-8119; call for the schedule. There are 66 **totem poles** in Duncan, both downtown and along a half-kilometre section of the Trans-Canada Hwy.

Faced with the shutdown of its mill, the logging town of **Chemainus** bucked up and hired artists to paint murals telling the story of the town—all over everything. Chemainus is now a tourist attraction, and with each passing year it takes on more class and less tackiness, managing to project an air of old-fashioned small-town charm. Check out the Dinner Theatre—(250) 246-9820 or (800) 565-7738—with a classy buffet before a theatre presentation.

Restaurants

Crow and Gate Neighbourhood Pub ☆ One of the first neighbourhood pubs in the province, this spot offers a good variety of draft beers, and patrons share the huge fireplace and long tables. But the real attraction is the food (especially the steak-and-kidney pie and pan-fried oysters). *2313 Yellow Point Rd (about 8 miles/13 km south of Nanaimo), Ladysmith; (250) 722-3731; $.*

Delicado's ☆ These people were into wraps before they became the latest cooking rage. The cafe/deli attracts a mixed Birkenstock, yuppie, and student crowd, who savour solid soups or burritos and enchiladas, and who finish up with a wildberry chocolate square. Take-out, too. *358 Wesley St (on hill west of hwy), Nanaimo; (250) 753-6524; $.*

La Fontana A pair of refugees from the Whistler scene created a cozy Mediterranean bistro in downtown Nanaimo, with dishes from all around that sea: Italian, French, Spanish, Greek, Moroccan. Share appetizers with a group of friends. Service can be slow. *99 Chapel St (off Church St, downtown), Nanaimo; (250) 755-1922; $$.*

The Mahle House ☆☆ This 1904 house is off the beaten track, but once discovered, it impresses. Three elegant rooms are the setting for a menu that emphasizes fresh, locally produced ingredients. There are a dozen daily specials and more than 200 wines. *RR 4 (corner of Cedar at Hemer Rd), Nanaimo; (250) 722-3621; $$–$$$.*

The Quamichan Inn ☆☆ Set amid several acres of lawn and garden, this comfortable turn-of-the-century home has been nicely transformed into a bed-and-breakfast-cum-dinner-house. *1478 Maple Bay Rd, RR 5 (just east of Duncan), Duncan; (250) 746-7028; $$$.*

The Waterford Inn & Restaurant Ltd. ☆☆ The finest dining for the thinnest dollar in this neck of the woods. Service is personal and prompt, and the food more than lives up to its billing. Dinner is more formal. *9875 Maple St (a few blocks from downtown), Chemainus; (250) 246-1046; $$.*

The Wesley Street Cafe ☆☆ The owner does exactly what she likes here, and that's fine with us. The menu is imaginative and fresh (try the rack of lamb), and the atmosphere is relaxed—brown butcher paper over the tablecloths, muted light, gentle jazz music. *321 Wesley St (from downtown, head uphill on Bastion St, then turn left on Wesley), Nanaimo; (250) 753-4004; $$–$$$.*

Cheaper Eats

Dot's Cafe Built in 1941, Nanaimo's first diner still serves up fish 'n' chips and burgers, but it's the fresh-baked pies that keep folks coming from miles around. *25935 North Island Hwy, Nanaimo; (250) 390-3331; $.*

Mom's Diner Prepare to be mothered by Fjola Roberts when you check out this original dining-car-style diner. She serves the island's best breakfasts—and her hearty portions keep you fuelled for most of the day. *9338 Trans-Canada Hwy, Chemainus; (250) 246-1461; $.*

Olde Firehall Coffee Roasterie Hand-painted church pews and brick walls set the scene for this roasterie with its 37 types of coffees, 27 types of teas, and housemade sandwiches and treats. Upstairs, build your own pasta meal at Pagliacci's; (250) 754-3443. Call for directions. *#2-34 Nicol St, Island Hwy, Nanaimo; (250) 754-7733; $.*

Red Rooster Coffee Shop Seven dinner entrees priced at about eight bucks is something to crow about in this rooster-themed restaurant. And be sure to save room for dessert: fresh cheesecake or the incredible banana-cream pie. *8432 Trans-Canada Hwy, Westholme; (250) 246-9342; $.*

Lodgings

The Aerie ☆☆☆ This European-style luxury resort looks as if it had been transplanted from Monte Carlo. The Aerie has 23 spacious rooms and suites in three buildings, and prices soar. Though the resort has grown, the dining room still feels intimate and the meal is a seven-course prix-fixe affair. *600 Ebedora Lane (take Spectacle Lake turnoff from Trans-Canada Hwy); PO Box 108, Malahat, BC V0R 2L0; (250) 743-7115; $$$.*

Best Western Dorchester Hotel ☆☆ There's little hint of the past at this refurbished Nanaimo landmark. The rooms are tastefully decorated; many have lovely harbour views. The restaurant offers good food at reasonable rates, and a view. Service is attentive; the wine list gets kudos. *70 Church St (at Front St), Nanaimo, BC V9R 5H4; (250) 754-6835 or (800) 661-2449; $$.*

Bird Song Cottage ☆ In this cottage a block from the water, the owners have created a dramatic air from the new veranda to the piano and harp music they play while guests breakfast. Several rooms have views, window seats, and private baths. *9909 Maple St (from Chemainus Rd, go downhill on Oak St to Maple, turn left, and look for white cottage); PO Box 1432, Chemainus, BC V0R 1K0; (250) 246-9910 or (250) 246-2909; $$.*

Coast Bastion Inn ☆☆ All 179 rooms of this popular hotel have views of the restored Bastion and the harbour; all are tastefully styled. There's a formal meeting room, a sauna, a hot tub, and a trio of formula eateries: a cafe, a lounge, and a deli. *11 Bastion St (at Front St), Nanaimo, BC V9R 2Z9; (250) 753-6601 or (800) 663-1144; $$$.*

Fairburn Farm Country Manor ☆☆ Originally an Irish millionaire's country estate, it's now a 130-acre (52-ha) organic sheep farm and country inn overlooking a vista reminiscent of southern England. Six large guest rooms feature Jacuzzi tubs, and a cottage is available in summer. *3310 Jackson Rd (7 miles/11 km south of Duncan); RR 7, Duncan, BC V9L 4W4; (250) 746-4637; $$–$$$.*

Inn of the Sea The nicest feature is the scenery, especially the stretch of beach along Stuart Channel. Deluxe suites have kitchens and balconies (but many rooms are smaller than standard). A range of beach and boating activities is offered, as well as a heated pool and a pier for boat moorage. *3600 Yellow Point Rd (9 miles/14.5 km east of Ladysmith); RR3, Ladysmith, BC V0R 2E0; (250) 245-2211 or (800) 663-7327; $$.*

Yellow Point Lodge ☆☆☆ This charming lodge sits on a forested promontory overlooking Stuart Channel. Most sought after are the rustic beach cabins, available May to October (no heat). And there are also popular beach barracks, built right on the shoreline rocks. *Yellow Point Rd (9 miles/14.5 km east of Ladysmith); RR3, Ladysmith, BC V0R 2E0; (250) 245-7422; $$–$$$.*

Cheaper Sleeps

Buccaneer Motel It doesn't have a waterside setting, but it has ocean views and a huge mural of a buccaneer, and it's only blocks from the ferry terminal. Rooms are cheery and offer stocked kitchenettes, and guests have access to barbeques and picnic tables. *1577 Stewart Ave, Nanaimo, BC V9S 4E3; (250) 753-1246; $.*

Carey House Bed and Breakfast The friendly proprietress offers inexpensive rooms (about $50 for two or $35 for a single lodger) with bathrooms down the hall. But a shared bath is a small price to pay in exchange for these rates and the opportunity to enjoy the award-winning garden. *750 Arbutus Ave, Nanaimo, BC V9S 5E5; (250) 753-3601; $.*

Chemainus Hostel Renovated with the budget traveller in mind ($15 a bunk for nonmembers), this hostel is an easy walk from the murals, the bus, and the railway. It's a clean, bright lodging, with a well-equipped kitchen and separate dorms for men and women. *9694 Chemainus Rd, Chemainus, BC V0R 1K0; (250) 246-2809; $.*

Horseshoe Bay Inn This cozy, family-run place is a good bet for decent, inexpensive lodgings located between Duncan and Nanaimo. Some rooms have a private bath; others share. The pub downstairs attracts a lively local crowd, and the adjoining restaurant serves reasonably priced fare. *9576 Chemainus Rd, Chemainus, BC V0R 1K0; (250) 246-3425; $.*

More Information

Brentwood-Mill Bay Ferry: *(250) 386-3431.*
BC Forest Service, South Island Forest District, Port Alberni: *(250) 724-9205.*
BC Parks, Victoria: *(250) 391-2300 or (250) 954-4600; reservations (800) 689-9025.*
Chemainus and District Chamber of Commerce: *(250) 246-3944.*
Cowichan Lake District Chamber of Commerce: *(250) 749-3244.*
Crofton InfoCentre: *(250) 246-2456.*
Duncan-Cowichan Chamber of Commerce InfoCentre: *(250) 746-4636.*
Ladysmith InfoCentre: *(250) 245-2218.*
Mill Bay Infocentre/Cowichan Chamber of Commerce: *(250) 743-3566.*
Nanaimo Tourist and Convention Bureau: *(250) 756-0106.*
Parksville and District Chamber of Commerce: *(250) 248-3613.*

Tofino and Pacific Rim National Park Reserve

Across the spine of the Vancouver Island Mountains from the inland sea to the open ocean, including Pacific Rim National Park Reserve.

In the decades before Pacific Rim National Park Reserve was born in 1970, this moss-laden landscape of mist and surf was a little-known outpost, a world apart. If adventurers managed to coax a vehicle across the tortuous road that led west from Port Alberni to the isolated sister ports of Tofino and Ucluelet, finding a bed was a simple matter at one of the few local inns. The alternative was constructing a driftwood shelter on one of the fabulous beaches nearby.

One million visitors a year now make this same journey on black-topped Highway 4 (Pacific Rim Highway) to experience the romantic isolation of the region. It's a tribute to the scale of this environment that so many travellers can be absorbed into it and still leave it so (apparently) empty. The open ocean stretches off unbroken and vacant, while the elemental forces at play here—the winds and tides, the sun and rain—excite within visitors a deep-seated resonance, a sense of *belonging* to this place. Undoubtedly, the same chaos that reigns in winter during gale-force storms mimics, on a microcosmic scale at least, the fury of the Big Bang. And on eternal summer evenings, when a magenta sunset ignites the ocean's serene surface, there's a peace so prevalent that you could almost bottle it and call it salvation. Take your pick of moods; they're both soul-satisfying.

Getting There

Just west of Parksville on the east coast of Vancouver Island, Highway 4 (Pacific Rim Highway) begins to wind across island to Port Alberni, Ucluelet, and Tofino, all three of which are sheltered harbours. Port Alberni sits at the head of the Alberni Inlet, a long indentation that reaches so far inland that it comes within 30 miles (50 km) of Parksville. Although the island is only about 60 miles (100 km) wide at this point, allow two to three hours to make the journey. The road must make its way around and over several natural obstacles, such as Sproat Lake and the rugged Vancouver Island Mountains, and is only two lanes wide for most of the distance. Passing lanes help, but patience is the key to a safe journey. During stormy months the section between Sproat Lake and the west coast can be extremely wet, so much so that your windshield wipers will have to work overtime to keep up with the deluge. Sometimes it's better just to pull over and wait for the lashing to abate.

Parksville is about 22 miles (35 km) north of Nanaimo's Departure Bay ferry terminal, which links Vancouver Island with Horseshoe Bay on the Lower Mainland. Highways 19A and 19 (The Island Highway) link Parksville with northern Vancouver Island. Two branches of Highway 4 lead west of Parksville (Craig's Crossing on the town's south side or Qualicum Beach just to the north). Both branches unite after a short distance and run for about 90 miles (140 km) to both Ucluelet and Tofino. Along the way, the highway passes through Port Alberni, about 30 miles (50 km) west of Parksville. Once on the west side of the island, Highway 4 (Pacific Rim Highway) divides and runs 5 miles (8 km) south to Ucluelet and 21 miles (34 km) north to Tofino.

This route connects visitors with the three major components of Pacific Rim National Park Reserve: the West Coast Trail's northern terminus near Bamfield, the Broken Group Islands in Barkley Sound, and the Long Beach Unit of bays and beaches between Tofino and Ucluelet. Although the West Coast Trail and the Broken Group Islands are remote and wild, the Long Beach Unit is readily accessible by road and much more welcoming to visitors. A park-use fee of about $5 per day is in effect for visitors to the Long Beach Unit from mid-March to mid-October.

Adjoining Areas

NORTH: **Nootka Sound and Strathcona Provincial Park**

SOUTH: **Sooke Basin and the West Coast Trail**

EAST: **Nanaimo and the Cowichan Valley**

Parks/Camping

With almost one million visitors a year to **Pacific Rim National Park Reserve,** it's important to have somewhere for them to camp, especially after they've driven all that way. With this in mind, Parks Canada maintains campgrounds in the park for both those who wish a formal site and those who wish to make contact with the wilderness. At the **Green Point** Campground on Long Beach, about 6 miles (10 km) north of the Tofino-Ucluelet junction on Hwy 4, you'll find 94 vehicle/tent sites and 54 walk-in sites on the beach, sheltered by thick stands of salal. Parks Canada runs an information service located in the park, open between May and October, (250) 726-4212 or (250) 726-7721 year-round. BC Parks' reservation line also handles sites in the national park (for drive-in sites only). Call (800) 689-9025 from March 1 to September 15.

In addition, there's wilderness camping in the Reserve at **Pachena Bay Campground,** about 3 miles (5 km) south of Bamfield. Fashion your own rough campsite here on the sandy surf beach at the north end of the West Coast Trail (see Hiking/Backpacking, below). Be sure to bring a tarp or two (plus plenty of rope) to help create a dry shelter for yourself. For more information on the campground, including fees, contact the Huu-ay-aht First Nation Administration Office, (250) 728-3414, or Parks Canada's West Coast Trail information office, (250) 728-3234, both in Bamfield.

Englishman River Falls Provincial Park (105 vehicle/tent sites) is tucked away in the sheltering Douglas fir forest 8 miles (13 km) southwest of Parksville. Turn off Hwy 4 at Errington Rd and follow signs 5.5 miles (9 km) to the park entrance. There's great picnicking, summer swimming, and a 2-mile (3-km) walking trail that passes through a stand of maple trees to an impressive waterfall and gorge. Ocean beaches are nearby at Parksville and Qualicum Beach. For reservations call (800) 689-9025. Call BC Parks for more information and a map of the provincial parks of Vancouver Island; (250) 954-4600 or (250) 248-3931.

Little Qualicum Falls Provincial Park (91 vehicle/tent sites), 12 miles (19 km) west of Parksville on Hwy 4, is quite similar in feel to Englishman River Falls Provincial Park. A wonderful quiet pervades here beside the Little Qualicum River and Cameron Lake. Although the two parks are quite close together, the forests that surround them are noticeably different. Here at Little Qualicum, the soil is much sandier and drier (hence the lovely beach), which means that pine trees thrive better here than fir. As at Englishman River Falls Provincial Park, there are short walking trails to view the Little Qualicum Falls beside the clear green waters of the river. Swimming is excellent—except near the falls. Heed the warning notices. For more information, call (250) 954-4600.

Port Alberni hums with visitor activity, especially during fishing season. The town operates the **Dry Creek Municipal Park and Campground** (52 vehicle/tent sites) close to the waterfront on Napier St in a pleasantly forested environment. Call (250) 723-6011 for information.

Stamp Falls Provincial Park (22 vehicle/tent sites, 250-954-4600) lies about 9 miles (14 km) north of Port Alberni. Take Beaver Creek Rd north of Hwy 4 from the centre of Port Alberni, an easy drive. This park is often used by anglers who come to fish for salmon in the Stamp River. As at Englishman River Falls Provincial Park, there is a beautiful waterfall here that is sure to soothe even the most jangled nerves.

Sproat Lake Provincial Park (59 vehicle/tent sites) lies 8 miles (13 km) west of Port Alberni on Hwy 4. The park overlooks an expansive body of freshwater with Mount Anderson rising to the south. The park sits beside a sheltered bay at the northeast corner of Sproat Lake. Many of those who camp here come to take advantage of the triple boat launch and large public marina. In fact, there are twice as many boat slips as campsites. As much as visitors are drawn west by the magnetism of Long Beach on the coast, Sproat Lake Provincial Park has a fine beach of its own and much warmer water than the ocean. Call BC Parks for more information, (250) 954-4600.

Taylor Arm Provincial Park is a forested site on the north shore of Sproat Lake about 9 miles (15 km) west of Port Alberni on Hwy 4. The park features an astounding number of undeveloped campsites, and is particularly popular with groups such as the Boy Scouts. Hiking trails lead beside the lake and onto the mountain ridges above the park, which are slowly beginning to regenerate after having being clear-cut in the 1970s.

Fishing

There's excellent bank casting for rainbow and cutthroat trout on the **Englishman River,** either near the river mouth on the Strait of Georgia near Parksville or in **Englishman River Falls Provincial Park** (see Parks/Camping, above). There's a steelhead run as well in the river. Unfortunately, a decline in salmon stocks has forced closures on fishing for a number of species, so be sure to check in advance with the Wildlife Conservation Officer in Port Alberni, (250) 724-9290. Information on fishing in tidal waters is available from the Fishery Officer in the Department of Fisheries and Oceans in Port Alberni, (250) 724-0195.

Over the past century, brown trout have been successfully introduced to a number of Vancouver Island rivers such as the Cowichan (see Nanaimo and the Cowichan Valley chapter) and **Little Qualicum.** The best access to the river for bank casting is at Little Qualicum Falls Provincial Park. You'll also find good trolling and boat casting in **Cameron Lake,** part of which also lies within the park. There's a boat launch at the picnic grounds on Cameron Lake (see Parks/Camping, above).

Port Alberni's harbour district is thick with tackle shops, boat rentals, and fishing charters. This is definitely one of the major hubs for angling on Vancouver Island and is the best resource centre for information on fishing locally in both saltwater and freshwater. The **Alberni Inlet** is a long, narrow flute that leads 25 miles (40 km) inland from the open ocean of Barkley Sound. Salmon school in the inlet before ascending to the spawning grounds. Timing is crucial if you wish to take advantage of their presence. One day they're here; the next, they're gone, so plan ahead. In general, the Alberni Inlet and Barkley Sound offer year-round fishing. Salmon is the prize catch in these waters but so too are halibut. Actively feeding spring salmon (also called blackmouths) begin appearing in March as they follow the bountiful herring and anchovy spawning runs. Springs linger into May, when they are replaced by early-run tyee (also called chinook) salmon migrating in the Alberni Inlet. Sockeye salmon succeed the early-run tyee in late June and are joined by late-run tyee, the largest of all salmon, in July and August. Call the Alberni Valley Chamber of Commerce for details; (250) 724-6535. For **charter salmon-fishing tours** and saltwater-angling information generally, contact Kelray Salmon Charters, (250) 723-8689, Sandpiper Charters, (250) 723-6947, Port Alberni Salmon Charters (250) 723-8022, and Pacific West Charters, (250) 723-1101, all in Port Alberni. One of the chief staging areas for fishing the Alberni Inlet is **China Creek,** 9 miles (14 km) south of Port Alberni on the road to Bamfield. You'll find a marina, a private campground, a boat launch, and quite possibly a salmon or two. China Creek is now designated as a provincial park. Primary fish runs in China Creek include cutthroat trout from January to March, and steelhead from October to December. Call (250) 954-4600 for a salmon update. For information on privately operated China Creek Provincial Park marina and campground, call (250) 723-9812.

Port Alberni has a freshwater side that would be the envy of any fishing town anywhere. The **Somas River** runs through the heart of town. Bank casting is possible from a number of locations beside Hwy 4 and along Hector Rd off Hwy 4 west of Port Alberni, including the privately operated Arrowvale Campground (30 vehicle/tent sites), 5955 Hector Rd, (250) 723-7948. Just north of Port Alberni, the **Stamp River** (see Parks/Camping, above) would probably make every chinook and steelhead angler's Top Ten.

Beginning in January and lasting through March, a winter run of steelhead occurs in the Stamp, while April and May are good months for steelhead in Sproat Lake. In late summer, upwards of a half-million salmon make their way to the spawning grounds near the Stamp River Hatchery. Bank casting is permitted downstream from the hatchery. Follow Beaver Creek Rd about 7.5 miles (12 km) north from Hwy 4 to Stamp River Provincial Park, (250) 954-4600. Watch for pullouts beside the river along the way. Nearby **Sproat Lake** (see Parks/Camping, above) also has a solid reputation for rainbow-trout angling, particularly June through September. Use the boat launch here to head out for some trolling or casting. For more information on freshwater angling here, call the Wildlife Conservation Officer in Port Alberni, (250) 724-9290. For more information on both freshwater and saltwater angling, as well as guided charter tours, contact Pacific Rim Outdoors, (250) 724-1541; Alberni Top Rods, 5245 Argyle St, (250) 723-7438; Lox & Lures, 5104 River Rd, (250) 723-9333; and Stamp Pacific Sportsfishing, (250) 723-2772, all in Port Alberni.

Open-ocean fishing occurs far offshore from **Ucluelet** and **Tofino.** The continental shelf runs west of the two ports for almost 20 miles (30 km) to La Pérouse Bank, an undersea plateau that forms the leading edge of British Columbia's coastline. This is where the action happens, where the currents, swells, and weather combine. It will take you almost two hours of bucking the swells to reach the nutrient-rich waters, so prepare yourself with warm clothing and antinausea protection. For information on fishing, licences, tackle, and bait, contact Ocean West Marina, (250) 725-3251, in Tofino; and Camper Jack's Esso, (250) 726-2331, and Eagle Marine Petro Canada, (250) 726-4262, in Ucluelet. **Charter fishing companies** include Quest Charters, (250) 726-7532, Subtidal Adventures, (250) 726-7336, Sea Fin Charters, (250) 726-2104, and TK Charters, (800) 667-3346, in Ucluelet; and Chinook Charters, (250) 725-2360, Cypre Prince Tours, (800) 787-2202, and Weigh West Marine Resort, (800) 655-8922 or (250) 725-3277, in Tofino. The Nuu-Chah-Nulth Booking Centre in Tofino will also arrange sportfishing charters; (800) 665-9425.

Beaches/Picnics

As you make your way across the island, Hwy 4 passes beside a number of fine locations for picnicking and swimming. You'll find both at the **Cameron Lake** and **Beaufort** provincial picnic grounds adjacent to the campground in Little Qualicum Falls Provincial Park (see Parks/Camping, above). Picnic tables are arranged beside the beach. Strong winds blow here in the afternoon, which attracts windsurfers but definitely deters those in small boats.

You can spend days walking the beaches between Ucluelet and Tofino, and in the process discover why some folks spend their whole lives caught up in the surf and tidal rhythms here. Radar Beach, Long Beach, Combers Beach, and Wickaninnish Beach run successively from north to south and stretch for 15.5 miles (25 km) between Cox and Quisitas Points. Together they comprise the **Long Beach Unit of beaches.** Radar Beach is rugged and puts up a fight when pummelled by the surf. Exercise great caution within range of the surf anywhere on these beaches.

If you only have a short amount of time, head directly to **Long Beach,** the most easily accessible and also the longest—6 miles (10 km) long! Depending on the season and the height of the swells in Wickaninnish Bay, not to mention the thickness of the mist, you may see surfers, sea kayakers, cyclists, kite flyers, hackey-sackers, disc tossers, swimmers, joggers, and walkers at play on the hard-packed sand. The scene here is as alive as you want to make it, and there's room to spare. Something about the enormity of Long Beach just makes you goofy. Take Hwy 4 north towards Tofino. The highway runs beside the beach—you'll recognize it on sight. There is parking on the south end at Green Point Campground (see Parks/Camping, above), as well as at the north end of Long Beach. The short trail that leads from the parking lot at Green Point passes a long row of picnic tables sheltered by the salal and stunted Sitka spruce, and deposits visitors at the halfway point on Wickaninnish Bay. To the north are Radar Beach and Long Beach; to the south are **Combers Beach and Wickaninnish Beach.**

Rocky headlands bookend Wickaninnish Bay, but south and north of it are four equally beautiful sandy expanses, each with a variation on the overall mood of isolation that characterizes these "outside" waters. **Wreck Beach** on Florencia Bay is 3 miles (5 km) long and lies at the south end of the Long Beach Unit. It's easily reached from Hwy 4, 3 miles (5 km) north of the Tofino-Ucluelet Junction. Turn west onto Long Beach Rd, then south at the first fork. (The Wickaninnish Bay Interpretive Centre lies nearby at the end of Long Beach Rd.)

Cox Bay, Chesterman, and **MacKenzie Beaches** lie to the north of the Long Beach Unit, between the northern boundary of Pacific Rim National Park Reserve and Tofino. There's public access to each of them, though you'll have to do some backroad driving to find it. A small park on Mackenzie Beach is a good place to begin. Take Mackenzie Beach Rd west of Hwy 4 (Pacific Rim Hwy) and watch for a small roadside parking area and picnic table at the end of the road. Chesterman Beach is reached via Lynn Rd, which loops west from Hwy 4. Cox Bay Beach is reached by following the road to the Pacific Sands Resort west of Hwy 4.

Ucluelet has two beaches in particular that welcome picnickers. A trail leads from Bay St to **Big Beach.** You'll find picnic tables near the trailhead and then a lengthy walk to the beach. A much shorter approach leads through **He-Tin-Kis Park** to **Terrace Beach** near the Amphitrite Point lighthouse at the south end of Peninsula Rd.

Ahous Beach on **Vargas Island** (see Kayaking/Boating, below), north of Tofino, is now part of a new provincial park. To reach it you must either paddle to the sheltered east side of the island and walk across to it on an old telegraph trail, or brave the swells and head right for the beach itself on the exposed west side of the island. Once on the beach you'll be able to explore for hours. Small coves filled with blue mussel shells brighten the scene at Ahous Beach. Two small islands offshore stand landlocked to Vargas at low tide and have done battle with the elements for thousands of years; they are windshaped into the appearance of gladiator helmets. An intertidal lagoon fills and empties throughout the day. Depending on the height of the tide, you can cross the mouth of the lagoon to explore farther north along the beach. Be cautious so that your return won't be blocked by high water.

Wildlife

One of the joys of visiting Pacific Rim National Park Reserve is participating in a **grey whale observation tour** led by a park naturalist. Start at the Wickaninnish Interpretive Centre, located beside a lengthy stretch of windswept and surf-pounded beach on Combers Beach on **Wickaninnish Bay.** The entrance is well marked adjacent to Hwy 4 at the end of Long Beach Rd. You'll find telescopes mounted on an observation deck at the centre, plus numerous displays inside that introduce visitors to the geographical and natural history of the Pacific Northwest. Numerous privately led whale-watching expeditions set forth from Tofino daily. Be prepared for a cold, wet, bone-jarring journey most days as part of the cost for a close-up view. Even viewing from the shore can be hazardous. Beware "snap" or "rogue" waves when approaching the coastline. Stay well back from the tideline when exploring rocky headlands.

Hiking/Backpacking

The northern terminus of the **West Coast Trail** is located at Pachena Bay, 2 miles (3 km) south of Bamfield in Pacific Rim National Park Reserve. See Sooke Basin and the West Coast Trail chapter for detailed information on this spectacular route.

This 7- to 10-day journey is more often begun from Port Renfrew to the south in order to clear the steepest sections first. However, for those who wish to sample a smaller section of the trail, you can hike from

Pachena Bay to the **Nitinat Narrows** (strenuous; 40 miles/64 km return) and back in three days. There's camping on open beach or nearby at a Huu-ay-aht (Ohiaht) First Nation's site. For information on the West Coast Trail, call the Pacific Rim National Park West Coast Trail information offices at (250) 728-3234 in Bamfield. Transportation from Bamfield to Pachena Bay is also arranged through the Huu-ay-aht (Ohiaht) First Nation Administration office in Bamfield, (250) 728-3414. Bamfield is reached from either of two directions, both of which require several hours' drive on gravel logging roads, 76 miles (123 km) west of Lake Cowichan via Nitinat Lake (see Nanaimo and the Cowichan Valley chapter) or 63 miles (102 km) south of Port Alberni.

Della Falls, northwest of Port Alberni, is Canada's highest waterfall (1,444 feet/440 m). Along with Mount Waddington, British Columbia's highest mountain, it's one of the most awesome and least visited sites in the province. You'll have to dedicate a week to reaching it via 18-mile (29-km) **Great Central Lake** (see Kayaking/Boating, below) and the historic **Drinkwater Trail** (moderate; 20 miles/32 km return). For a detailed description, consult *Adventuring around Vancouver Island* by Lebrecht and Noppe. As Della Falls lies within Strathcona Provincial Park, call BC Parks for a map; (250) 337-2400. An alternative to paddling to the trailhead is the water taxi that transports hikers up Great Central Lake from Ark Resort, (250) 723-2657, located 8 miles (13 km) west of Port Alberni off Hwy 4 on Great Central Lake Rd. Boat and canoe rentals are also available here on a limited basis. (Note: Payment is cash only.) Western Wildcat Tours, (250) 753-3234, leads three-day treks to Della Falls.

Both **Englishman River Falls** and **Little Qualicum Falls Provincial Parks** (see Parks/Camping, above) have rambling trails that lead beside the clear waters of these pristine rivers. A walk to the falls is a big part of a visit to either park.

Windstorms during the winter of 1997 toppled hundreds of trees in **MacMillan Provincial Park,** a small park on Hwy 4 (formerly known as Cathedral Grove Provincial Park) that showcases the old-growth Douglas fir forest that once flourished throughout this region between Parksville and Port Alberni. The trailhead is easy to find. It begins next to an interpretive display that describes the history of the forest. Because of blowdowns from violent winter storms, picking your way along the trails will be a bit tricky, but worth it, especially when you find a scenic spot beside the Cameron River. Evidence of a forest fire that roared through here 300 years ago is still visible on the thick bark of the tallest Douglas fir, some of which are 800 years old.

At Kennedy Lake, the **J. N. Godfrey Nature Trail** leads to a small sandy cove at the Clayoquot Arm Beach Forest Service Recreation Site on the northwest corner of the lake and is reached via the West Main Logging Rd. The turnoff from Hwy 4 is well marked but it helps to consult the Port Alberni District Forest Service recreation map. For a free copy call (250) 724-9205, or stop by the office, 4227 Sixth Ave in Port Alberni.

Many of the trails in Pacific Rim National Park Reserve provide short, easygoing walks. The **Wickaninnish Trail** (easy; 6 miles/10 km return) involves a much longer excursion between the beaches on Wickaninnish and Florencia Bays. It begins beside the Wickaninnish Centre and follows the same route as the South Beach Trail, before striking off on its own towards Florencia Bay. This is one of the best rain-forest trails in the park.

Numerous short trails lead through the salal and Sitka spruce forest and along the beaches of **Pacific Rim National Park Reserve.** Some of the trails follow pathways that have been tunnelled through the overhanging salal; others follow wooden boardwalks. During the rainy season, take extra care when walking on slippery wooden surfaces. Many of the trails lead through interpretive zones where plaques describe the biodiversity in the surrounding rain forest. From mid-March to September, park naturalists are on hand at the Wickaninnish Interpretive Centre to answer questions and lead tours. In the off-season, take one of the self-guided trails such as the **Shoreline Bog Trail** (0.5-mile/0.8-km loop), the **Rain Forest Trail** (two 0.6-mile/1-km loops), and the **Spruce Fringe Trail** (1-mile/1.5-km loop). The wooded **Willowbrae Trail** (1.7-mile/2.8-km loop) follows an old trail that homesteaders once used to reach either Florencia or Half Moon Bay. The trail begins from an unmarked gravel road opposite Willowbrae Rd, about 1 mile (2 km) south of the Ucluelet-Tofino Junction. As the level boardwalk trail nears the coast it divides, and a series of steep ramps and staircases leads to the beaches below. The **Gold Mine Trail** (2 miles/3 km return) leads visitors to Wreck Beach on Florencia Bay from Hwy 4. It passes through an old gold mining site. The **South Beach Trail** (1 mile/1.5 km return) leads from the Wickaninnish Centre across a rocky headland with ocean vistas to Lismer and South Beach. As the motion of the surf rolls the pebbles on the beach back and forth, it produces a percussive, musical sound. Be cautious here in winter storms. Towards the north end of Long Beach, the **Schooner Cove Trail** (1 mile/2 km return) leads through the rain forest and down a staircase to a secluded beach from Hwy 4.

For a real taste of a rain-forest trail, take an excursion around **Clayoquot Sound** from Tofino to Meares, Vargas, or Flores Islands. On **Meares Island** (also called **Wah-nah-juss/Hilth-hoo-iss** by the Tla-O-Qui-Aht and Ahousaht First Nations), the **Big Cedar Trail** (moderate; 2-mile/3-km loop) is marked by yellow ribbons and can be quite muddy. Boardwalks and stairs assist hikers over some of the boggiest sections but can themselves be treacherous when wet. Use caution and enjoy the experience of being in a pristine, temperate rain forest, where moss grows as deep as snowdrifts. Reaching the trailhead on Meares Island (part of the Tla-O-Qui-Aht and Ahousaht First Nations' traditional territory) requires a 10-minute water-taxi ride from the main government wharf in Tofino. Transportation (and, if desired, a guided tour) may be arranged with the Tin-Wis Resort Lodge, (250) 725-4445 or (800) 661-9995, or the Nuu-chah-nulth Booking and InfoCentre, (800) 665-9425, in Tofino.

Farther north on **Flores Island,** an ambitious trail-building project is underway to complete the **Ahousaht Wild Side Heritage Trail** (moderate; 20 miles/32 km return). The ambitious project links the Nuu-chah-nulth community of Ahousaht (Marktosis) with gorgeous, unpopulated white-sand beaches on the island's south and west sides as it traverses the slopes of Mount Flores. Flores Island lies 12 miles (20 km) north of Tofino and is accessible by water taxi, kayak, or floatplane. For more information on the trail, to arrange a guided tour, and to arrange water-taxi transportation, call (250) 670-9531 or (250) 670-9602 in Ahousaht, or the Nuu-chah-nulth Booking and InfoCentre, (250) 725-2888, in Tofino.

An old telegraph trail runs the width of **Vargas Island** (see Kayaking/Boating, below) between its east and west coasts. The **Ahous Trail** (3 miles/5 km return) has recently been protected as **Vargas Island Provincial Park.** The trail begins behind the Vargas Island Inn (see Lodgings, below), and if you have trouble locating the trail, just ask the affable owners to point the way. The Ahous Trail takes about an hour to walk each way, most of it across the tussocky bog that characterizes much of the landscape inland from the beaches along the west coast. An ancient corduroy road runs through meadows of pink western bog laurel, kinnikinnick, and Labrador tea, the hummocks of peat carpeted with moss in shades of strawberry and gold. So thick is the perimeter of salal through which the trail tunnels that the entrance on the other end at Ahous Beach is difficult to locate. A pile of beach refuse is the only clue to its presence. Mark this location well in your mind or, better yet, arrange some driftwood that you will recognize upon your return before setting out to explore the vastness of this magnificent beach.

The **Clayoquot Valley Witness Trail** (strenuous; 36 miles/58 km return) is an ambitious undertaking on the part of the Western Canada Wilderness Committee with permission from the Tla-O-Qui-Aht First Nation. No greater contrast imaginable exists between the clear-cut logging around the trailheads and the ancient rain forest the Clayoquot Valley Witness Trail traverses. The trail begins a short distance west of Hwy 4 and is best done in a south-to-north direction. Hikers should come well prepared for a minimum four-day excursion. No services are available along the route, and in summer freshwater may not be available. Day hikes are best done from the north trailhead. To reach the south trailhead, turn north off Hwy 4 on Kenquot Main Logging Rd, about 7 miles (11.5 km) west of Sutton Pass. As the gate on Kenquot Main is normally locked, park and hike in from here. The south trailhead is at the end of Kenquot Main, about 4.3 miles (7 km) beyond the gate. The north trailhead is reached via the Upper Kennedy Logging Rd, which begins 28 miles (45 km) west of Port Alberni, about 0.25 mile (400 m) west of the Sutton Pass road sign on Hwy 4. Drive 4.7 miles (7.5 km) to the end of Upper Kennedy Logging Rd to reach the north trailhead. To receive a copy of the trail map complete with detailed directions, contact the Western Canada Wilderness Committee, (800) 661-9453 or (604) 683-8220, in Vancouver.

Kayaking/Boating

Barkley Sound and the **Broken Group Islands** comprise one of the three main recreational components in Pacific Rim National Park Reserve. The popularity of these islands with paddlers and boaters has soared over the past decade, much to the dismay of longtime observers. One of the main reasons that the Broken Group Islands are so popular is that they provide a true west coast experience in sheltered water. Barkley Sound is not normally subject to the extreme ocean conditions farther west in the open waters around Ucluelet and exposed sections of the West Coast Trail and the Long Beach Unit, the two other areas that attract visitors to Pacific Rim National Park Reserve. The ease with which less-experienced sea kayakers can reach the Broken Group Islands on the MVs *Lady Rose* and *Frances Barkley* from Port Alberni and Ucluelet (see below) contributes greatly to their allure and charm.

Kayakers usually begin their exploration at **Gibraltar Island** and make their way through the chain, stopping at campsites on **Gilbert, Benson, Clarke, Turret, Willis,** and **Hand Islands.** All of these sites are easily reached within a day's paddle (or less) of each other. The best marine charts for this area are #3671 Barkley Sound and #3638 Broken Group (Barkley Sound).

Numerous **kayak operators** lead tours through the Broken Group Islands, including Gulf Islands Kayaking, (250) 539-2442, on Galiano Island; Pacific Rim Paddling Company, (250) 384-6103, in Tofino; and Wild Heart Adventure Tours, (250) 722-3683, Web site: www.island.net/~wheart, in Nanaimo. For a general overview of ocean-kayaking tour operators in British Columbia, including those who visit the Broken Group Islands, visit the Web site of *Wave~Length Paddling* magazine, interchange.idc.uvic.ca/~wavenet/guides.html. For a schedule of sailings aboard the MVs *Lady Rose* and *Frances Barkley,* call Alberni Marine Transportation, (800) 663-7192. Canoe and kayak rentals may also be arranged with the company. If you must visit here in July and August, be sure to reserve space for your kayak or canoe on deck well in advance.

Two ships, the MV ***Lady Rose*** and the MV ***Frances Barkley,*** are based in Port Alberni. Their routes lead through the Broken Group Islands in Barkley Sound to the fishing ports of Bamfield and Ucluelet. In the course of a day's trip the sturdy wooden packet freighters drop mail, groceries, supplies, and the occasional passenger along the way at float homes and the Sechart Whaling Station.

At times you'll definitely feel the motion of the ocean swells, but the better part of the journey through Barkley Sound is not as exposed as that experienced when you travel on the *Lady Rose*'s and *Frances Barkley*'s sister ship, the MV *Uchuck III* (see Nootka Sound and Strathcona Provincial Park chapter). The trip makes a pleasant outing in itself or can be a link for paddlers to the Broken Group Islands.

Visitors here please take note: Paddlers are increasingly being blamed for the trashiness around many of the more popular campsites. Except at the seven designated camping sites, garbage and toilet facilities are nonexistent, which should be a major consideration for visitors. Plan how you're going to deal with these factors in advance of your journey here so as not to further tarnish an already dismal situation. Practice random acts of kindness by removing litter where you find it as well as packing out all of your own refuse. Consult books such as *How to Shit in the Woods* by Kathleen Meyer to learn new approaches to the delicate subject of backcountry hygiene. Consider adventuring here in any month other than July and August, particularly if you value solitude.

Great Central Lake, 8 miles (13 km) northwest of Port Alberni, reached via Hwy 4 on Great Central Lake Rd, is a long (21-mile/34-km), skinny (1.25 miles/2 km wide) stretch of challenging paddling from east to west. You can adventure here either for the joy of paddling or couple the journey with a lengthy hike to Della Falls (see Hiking/Backpacking, above). The easiest approach to the lake is via the boat launch at Ark Resort near the Robertson Creek Fish Hatchery.

Grice Bay is a sheltered niche of ocean waterway tucked in beside Meares Island in the backwater of Clayoquot Sound. At low tide, the bay drains so low that it takes on the appearance of a green marshland. Eelgrass covers much of the mudflats in Browning Pass, which links Grice Bay with Tofino to the north. A boat launch is located at the end of Grice Bay Rd, which leads east from Hwy 4, almost 9 miles (14 km) south of Tofino. Grice Bay lies within the northern limits of the Long Beach Unit of Pacific Rim National Park Reserve.

As intimidating as the ocean can be at **Long Beach,** there are wonderfully long, calm days in summer when boaters and paddlers can safely enjoy an excursion offshore. A boat launch is located beside the parking lot at the north end of Long Beach beside Hwy 4.

Boating and paddling in the waters of **Clayoquot Sound** is one of the most rewarding ways to experience this environment. Depending on your skill level, you can either plan a trip on your own or join up with one of the tour operators that use Tofino as their base. Day trips close to town include **Meares, Stubbs, Wickaninnish,** and **Vargas Islands,** all within sight of the federal dock in Tofino. Far afield is **Flores Island.** The sandy beach on Stubbs Island makes it an ideal getaway within sight of Tofino. You can land on the east coast of Vargas Island, a 3-mile (5-km) paddle north from Tofino, and make the one-hour journey across island on foot to Ahous Beach (see Hiking/Backpacking, above). If you paddle to Ahous rather than hike, be prepared for a stretch of open ocean as you round the exposed southwest corner of Vargas. If it's blowing too hard, check out isolated **Medallion Bay** on the south end of the island, a delightful place to land. Nothing on Vargas, however, tops Ahous Beach's lengthy expanse, which rivals Long Beach in size. So vast is its hard-caked, sandy surface that light planes occasionally land here.

For more information on exploring the Tofino-Ucluelet region by water, contact the Pacific Kayak Centre, (250) 725-3232, or Seaside Adventures, (800) 222-3588, in Tofino. For information on **tours** as well as **rentals,** contact Tofino Sea Kayaking Company, (250) 725-4522. Sea Fin Charters, (250) 726-2104, offers sea-kayaking transportation in Barkley Sound from Ucluelet. The best marine map to consult on the region is Canadian Hydrographic Chart #3640. For a detailed description of some of the inside and outside routes in Clayoquot Sound, consult *Sea Kayaking Canada's West Coast* by John Ince and Hadi Köttner.

Windsurfing/Surfing

Stiff winds funnel through the Alberni Inlet and make **China Creek Provincial Park** (see Fishing, above) a hot place to be for serious windsurfers. The only problem is the numerous boaters who also flock to the park in fishing season in July. Because of its wide expanse and western exposure, **Long Beach** (see Beaches/Picnics, above) in Pacific Rim National Park Reserve is the beach of choice for freewheeling, Maui-style windsurfing when the ocean gets riled.

There are only two locations on Vancouver Island where you'll find a surfing community. Jordan River is one (see Sooke Basin and the West Coast Trail chapter), and **Tofino** the other. A small but dedicated group of aficionados lives here year-round, while another coterie safaris over as often as possible, particularly in winter months when storm season produces the best peeling surf. As the ocean temperature here hovers at a constant, chilly 42–44°F (6–7°C) year-round, it hardly matters what month it is: it's the waves that count. Tofino does boast the highest annual mean temperature in Canada (coincidentally, the same as the water temperature), which may help remove some of the sting if you think about it hard enough while you're paddling out to catch one more wave.

The closest shop to Long Beach is Live to Surf, (250) 725-4464, nearby on Hwy 4 (Pacific Rim Hwy), while in downtown Tofino you find Ocean Surf, (250) 725-3344. Both shops rent boards (surf and body styles) and wet suits. They'll also fill you in on local etiquette when joining the manners-conscious lineup offshore. Adam Smallwood teaches surfing on Vancouver Island. A four-hour guided lesson costs $100 and includes transportation from Tofino to nearby Chesterman or Cox Bay Beach, the use of a surfboard, and lunch. Contact him at Blue Planet Guiding Company, (250) 725-2182. Island Sauvage, a Sayward-based adventure company, runs heli-surfing camps on Vancouver Island. Call (800) 667-4354 for details.

Diving

A vast tableau of marine life that thrives in the nutrient-rich waters in **Dawley Passage Provincial Park** is arrayed underwater northwest of Tofino. This park is a popular local dive site. Strong currents surge through a narrow passage, which makes for clear water but sketchy conditions. Check with Ocean West Marina, (250) 725-3251, in Tofino. They fill tanks and dispense local dive information.

outside in

Attractions

Literally at the end of the road, **Tofino,** once a timber and fishing town, has become a favoured destination for Northwest and European travellers alike. Local environmentalists and artists have banded together to suspend destruction of one of the last virgin timberlands on the west coast of Vancouver Island and halt the rapid development for which the area is ripe. It boasts miles of sandy beaches to the south, islands of old-growth cedar, migrating grey whales, hot springs, sea lions, and a temperate climate. Between mid-March and early April the Pacific Rim Whale Festival is held; call (250) 726-4641 or (250) 725-3414 for information.

Various guided tours and water taxis explore the wilds of the west coast from Tofino (see Inside Out sections, above); consider a trip to Hot Springs Cove, an oasis north of Tofino where you can stay overnight at **Hot Springs Lodge,** a six-room lodge operated by the Hesquiaht First Nation, (250) 724-8570. Or, in town there are two excellent Native-run **galleries:** the hand-hewn longhouse, Eagle Aerie Gallery, (250) 725-3235, which displays Tsimshian artist Roy Henry Vickers's work, and the House of Himwitsa, which includes a gallery, restaurant, and lodging facilities, (250) 725-2017 or (800) 899-1947.

Head for Alberni Harbour Quay, at the foot of Argyle St in **Port Alberni,** a friendly conglomeration of restaurants, galleries, and tour operators. Drop by the Blue Door Cafe for a coffee-and-cholesterol breakfast (served 5am to 3:30pm) and a friendly slanging match with the waitresses, or see if watercolourist Penny Cote is painting at the Argyle Gallery (5304 Argyle, (250) 723-9993). In summer, the steam locomotive *Two Spot* departs from the station at the head of the quay for a tourist tour along the waterfront.

Bamfield is a tiny fishing village, heavily populated by marine biologists. The gravel logging road in takes about two hours to travel, and it's mostly used by logging trucks during the week, so those unused to industrial traffic might prefer to take the MV *Lady Rose* from Port Alberni (see Kayaking/Boating, above). The **Bamfield Marine Station,** open for tours on summer weekends, is a biological research station with scientific and historical displays; (250) 728-3301.

The **Wickaninnish Interpretive Centre,** (250) 726-7333, in Pacific Rim National Park Reserve has interesting oceanic exhibits and an expansive view, 6 miles (10 km) north of Ucluelet off Hwy 4. The same building houses the Wickaninnish Restaurant, with its spectacular setting overlooking the surf: slow service, often crowded, good food, closed in winter (not to be confused with The Pointe Restaurant in the Wickaninnish Inn in Tofino; see review below).

In **Ucluelet,** pick up a sandwich at the Grey Whale Ice Cream and Deli (1950 Peninsula Rd) and picnic on the rocks at Amphitrite Point lighthouse.

Restaurants

Common Loaf Bake Shop ☆ A town meeting place with wonderful cinnamon buns and peasant bread year-round (and pizza in summer). Line up at the counter for your food and carry it upstairs to the log tables and benches. *180 1st St (just behind the bank), Tofino; (250) 725-3915; $.*

Himwitsa Lodge and the Sea Shanty Restaurant ☆☆ The House of Himwitsa, a First Nations–run enterprise, takes in the Sea Shanty Restaurant, Himwitsa Lodge, and a Native art gallery, all in a log building on the waterfront. The menu is Northwest Coast with a French twist; upstairs are five rooms. *300 Main St (across from main dock); PO Box 176, Tofino, BC V0R 2Z0; (250) 725-2902 (restaurant), (250) 725-3319 (lodge), or (800) 899-1947; $$ (lodging $$$).*

The Pointe Restaurant (Wickaninnish Inn) ☆☆☆☆ The inn and restaurant opened in 1996, and have been garnering praise ever since. The chef has set a new standard on the island, both for food and for elegant presentation. The Pointe's view is outstanding, and guest rooms share the view and have fireplaces and balconies. *Osprey Lane at Chesterman's Beach (off Hwy 4 north of Long Beach); PO Box 250, Tofino, BC V0R 2Z0; (250) 725-3100 or (800) 333-4604; $$$.*

Surfside Pizza/Clayoquot Catering Surfside delivers right to you (by car, boat, or plane). Ask what's good tonight—they're open until midnight—and let the owners help you decide (perhaps pesto pizza, chicken Sichuan stir-fry, or a salad). Look for the menu almost anywhere in Tofino. *Delivery only; (250) 725-2882; $.*

Swale Rock Cafe This bright and busy seafood eatery at the entrance to the quay caters to office workers, boat crews, and tourists. At lunch, seats fill quickly, but you won't have long to wait. Evening meals are less rushed; a specialty is the mammoth seafood platter for two. *5328 Argyle St (near harbour quay), Port Alberni; (250) 723-0777; $$.*

Cheaper Eats

Alley Way Cafe Craving a vegetarian burrito? The chef whips up a mean, big burrito and other mucho-gusto-size portions of tasty ethnic-inspired health-conscious fare at this funky eatery. *305 Campbell St, Tofino; (250) 725-3105; $.*

Coffee Pod Tofino's local version of Starbuck's, the Pod dishes up atmosphere as well as homemade soups and their celebrated Podwich—their take on panini. *461 Campbell St, Tofino; (250) 725-4246; $.*

Weigh West Marine Resort Solid pub food is served here. And it's tough to beat a cold beer, a half crab, the local colour, and the waterfront setting overlooking the inlet. *634 Campbell St, Tofino; (250) 725-3277; $.*

Lodgings

Canadian Princess Fishing Resort ☆ A retired survey ship has been converted to 30 cabins and a below-decks dining room. Bypass the cramped cabins for one of the 46 roomier shoreside units. The galley serves reasonable food; this place serves as a base for fishermen. Closed

October through February. *1948 Peninsula Rd (in boat basin); PO Box 939, Ucluelet, BC V0R 3A0; (250) 726-777; $–$$.*

Middle Beach Lodge ☆☆☆ There's a whole new lodge called The Headlands, with rooms and cottages south of the original Middle Beach Lodge (now called The Beach). Choose a spacious new lodge room or a cabin. The original resort has smaller rooms—half face the forest, half the beach. *400 MacKenzie Beach Rd (south of Tofino off Rt 4, look for signs); PO Box 413, Tofino, BC V0R 2Z0; (250) 725-2900; $$.*

Ocean Village Beach Resort It's the best value of the on-the-beach motels. All family-size units face the beach, and there's a heated indoor pool and hot tub. *555 Hellesen Dr (2.5 miles/4 km south of Tofino; look for signs); PO Box 490, Tofino, BC V0R 2Z0; (250) 725-3755; $$.*

Paddler's Inn Bed and Breakfast ☆ The bookstore and espresso bar that the owner runs in her bed-and-breakfast-cum-sea-kayaking-company-headquarters make a good place even better. The five rooms in Tofino's original hotel are as basic and lovely as the town itself: no phones, no TVs, down comforters, shared bath. *320 Main St (just above 1st St dock); PO Box 620, Tofino, BC V0R 2Z0; (250) 725-4222; $.*

A Snug Harbour Inn ☆☆ Outside, the inn looks nice, but not extraordinary. Inside, the living room has a giant wood-burning fireplace and looks out onto a deck with a fantastic view and a hot tub. Steps lead to the private cove below. A continental breakfast is served, and guests can arrange for heli-tours. *460 Marine Dr (through the village and right on Marine Dr), Ucluelet, BC V0R 3A0; (250) 726-2686 or (888) 936-5222; $$$.*

Vargas Island Inn You're a couple of hours by kayak or a half-hour by skiff from Tofino, so expect a few sacrifices: there are no showers (except in summer) and no chef, but a nearby store is stocked. There are rooms in the main house, two cabins, a "beach studio," and camping sites. *Accessible only by water taxi or private boat from Tofino; PO Box 267, Tofino, BC V0R 2Z0; (250) 725-3309, or call the Village Gallery, (250) 725-4229; $.*

Wilp Gybuu (Wolf House) Bed & Breakfast ☆☆ A clean, shining contemporary home with comfortable beds and absolutely all the amenities. Every room has its own entrance. The hosts are extremely warm and welcoming, and offer a delicious breakfast. *311 Leighton Way (Hwy 4 turns into Campbell, turn left onto 1st, right on Arnet Rd, left onto Leighton Way); PO Box 396, Tofino, BC V0R 2Z0; (250) 725-2330; $$.*

Wood's End Landing Cottages ☆ These lodgings overlooking Bamfield Inlet were built with salvaged driftwood and recycled timber, and the cottages and suites are set in old gardens. Each cabin has a spacious living/cooking area and loft bedrooms. The owner runs nature adventure tours and fishing expeditions. Bring your own food. *168 Wild Duck Rd (across inlet from government dock), Bamfield, BC V0R 1B0; (250) 728-3383; $$.*

Cheaper Sleeps

Midori's B&B An international clientele tends to book this B&B's three guest rooms, each with a private bath. Guests share a common room and deck. Midori's is particularly convenient if you're limited to schlepping around by bus. *370 Gibson St, Tofino, BC V0R 1Z0; (250) 725-2203; $.*

Netty's Bed & Breakfast The amiable host is a great resource on Tofino, and her home is a short walk from the beach, offering a guest room with twin beds and a loft that sleeps four. Ask her about renting a cabin in the area and about off-season rates. *2384 Lynn Rd, Chesterman Beach, Tofino, BC V0R 2Z0; (250) 725-3451; $.*

More Information

Alberni Marine Transportation Company, Port Alberni: *(250) 723-8313, toll-free April-Sept (800) 663-7192; MV* Lady Rose, *canoe and kayak rentals.*

Alberni Valley Chamber of Commerce/InfoCentre: *(250) 724-6535.*

Bamfield Chamber of Commerce: *(250) 728-3228.*

BC Forest Service, South Island Forest District, Port Alberni: *(250) 724-9205.*

BC Parks, Strathcona District: *(250) 954-4600, (250) 248-3931, reservations March-Sept 15 (800) 689-9025.*

Department of Fisheries and Oceans: *(250) 724-0195 (saltwater angling).*

Huu-ay-aht (Ohiaht) First Nation Administration Office, Bamfield: *(250) 728-3414.*

Nuu-chah-nulth Booking and Information Centre, Tofino: *(800) 665-9425 or (250) 725-2888.*

Pacific Rim National Park Reserve Information Centre: *seasonal (250) 726-4212; year-round information (250) 726-7721.*

Tofino–Long Beach Chamber of Commerce: *(250) 725-3414.*

Ucluelet Chamber of Commerce: *(250) 726-4641.*

Wildlife Conservation Officer: *(250) 724-9290 (freshwater angling).*

Parksville and the Comox Valley

Highway 19 (Island Highway) runs beside the open water of the Strait of Georgia, from Parksville in the south through the Comox Valley and north to Campbell River, including Miracle Beach Provincial Park and the Mount Washington winter recreation area.

As you drive the Island Highway (Highway 19), it's always a treat to look across the Strait of Georgia at landmarks on the mainland as the spires of the Coast Mountains rise on the eastern horizon. One such scenic view is the profile of the Howe Sound Crest as revealed when you look back towards the city of Vancouver from Parksville. The farther north you head towards Courtenay and Campbell River, however, the more the peaks and glaciers of Vancouver Island's ranges, principally the imposing Comox Glacier, Forbidden Plateau, and Mount Washington, rise in the west and vie for equal attention.

As the highway winds past well-kept farms, this is a serenely rural part of the journey. Flowers abound in the gardens that front many of the homes along the way. Small rivers such as the Little Qualicum and the Englishman, as well as mightier ones such as the Puntledge and the Campbell, empty into the strait. From the highway you catch glimpses of quiet green forest settings on the banks that line each river's course. Come late summer, these streams teem with spawning salmon.

Offshore to the east of Parksville lies Lasqueti Island, the first of several northern Gulf Islands that you catch glimpses of as the Island Highway heads north towards Courtenay and Campbell River. Farther off in the distance is the dark profile of Texada Island.

Other islands closer at hand are Denman and Hornby south of Courtenay, and Quadra across Discovery Passage from Campbell River.

For much of the way between Courtenay and Campbell River the Island Highway runs beside Qualicum Bay, an area rich in seafood. Pullouts beside the road give easy access to the bay's sand and pebble beaches. At several places you can buy fresh seafood, brought to the docks daily from local waters.

Take your time as you meander through this laid-back region. Its rhythms are subtle, but with gentle probing they reveal themselves, showing greater complexity than first meets the eye.

Getting There

As the new Island Highway (Highway 19) takes shape, it's beginning to supersede the old Island Highway (Highway 19A) as the way to move quickly between Nanaimo and Campbell River. Parksville, 23 miles (37 km) north of Nanaimo's Departure Bay ferry, lies just east of the new Island Highway. Although much of the route between Parksville and Courtenay is now complete, it will be some time yet before the 30-mile (50-km) Courtenay-to-Campbell River link is open. For those wishing to make time, the new four-lane route will be a blessing. For those wishing to take their time, this will mean fewer cars tailgating along the scenic ocean drive. Highways 19 and 19A link Parksville with southern Vancouver Island. Highway 4 links Parksville with Port Alberni, and with Tofino and Ucluelet on the west side of Vancouver Island.

Approaching from the north, Highway 19 links Campbell River with the northern half of Vancouver Island. Campbell River may also be reached by BC Ferries from Quathiaski Cove on Quadra Island, a 10-minute ride. For more information on ferry routes, schedules, and fares, call (888) 223-3779.

Adjoining Areas

NORTH: **North Vancouver Island**

SOUTH: **Nanaimo and the Cowichan Valley; Tofino and Pacific Rim National Park Reserve**

Parks/Camping

Miracle Beach Provincial Park (193 vehicle/tent sites) is located 14 miles (23 km) north of Courtenay beside Hwy 19. It's a 10-minute walk from the campsites to the extravagant expanse of cobblestone beach that gives way to hard-packed sand flats at low tide where herons stalk, seals bark, and ravens and eagles call. What a chorus! The beach seems to stretch forever in each direction. From the covered picnic shelter (featuring two gas barbeques) visitors look east out onto Elma Bay. Watch for harbour porpoises, Steller sea lions, California sea lions (much smaller), harbour seals, and killer whales. The campsites are located in an second-growth forest of gnarly Douglas fir, western red cedar, and western hemlock. Wildflowers bloom throughout the park from early spring to the end of summer. Black Creek flows through the park and past the Miracle Beach Nature House, which has natural-history displays. Beachcombers will find a tide chart posted here daily from late May to September. Pick up a brochure here and take a self-guided nature walk through the park. For more information, contact BC Parks, (250) 337-2400. For reservations, call (800) 689-9025.

Beaches

Qualicum Beach, about 7.5 miles (12 km) north of Parksville beside Hwy 19A, gently spreads in front of one of the most pleasant small towns on east side of Vancouver Island. Pause here at any of the numerous beachside pullouts and smell the salt air intermingled with the perfume from the many private and public floral displays. From this point on, the pace of Vancouver Island slackens noticeably. Not that the southern portion is any more hurried, it's just that there are more people and more congestion. From here north, there is less traffic, and what habitation there is clings to a narrow coastal plain beside the ocean.

Spider Lake Provincial Park is a small lake located 5 miles (8 km) west of Hwy 19A near Horne Lake. There is a lovely stretch of beach beside the warm, clear waters of the lake, on which no motorized boats are allowed. If you're looking for a respite from travel, spend an hour or two picnicking here at any time year-round; take a dip in summer and toss in a hook if you like smallmouth bass. The lake is indented by a number of bays, particularly at its north end, which makes for quiet exploring in a canoe or rowboat.

The beaches around **Comox** are usually overlooked by visitors, which is a shame. Take the time to drive east of Hwy 19 as it passes through Courtenay and follow the signs to the BC Ferries terminal in Comox. (Sailings from here link central Vancouver Island with Powell River on the northern Sunshine Coast.) Miles of sandy shore lead off both north and south of the quiet little coastal town, whose charm has not been overwhelmed by either the nearby Canadian Forces Air Base or the more recent influx of arrivals that south Vancouver Island has experienced. **Kye**

Bay, 3 miles (5 km) north of Comox off Lazo Rd, has a long, sandy beach, as does **Goose Spit Regional Park,** which noses out into Comox Harbour at the west end of Hawkins Rd. **Kin Beach Park** on Kilmorley Rd south of the ferry terminal is a good spot to pass time if you're waiting for a sailing. Texada Island's dark form lies in the strait directly east of Comox, while Denman Island lies to the south.

A broad stretch of sandy beach stands revealed at low tide in **Seal Bay Regional Park** on Bates Rd. Also called Xwee Xwhya Lug, "a place with an atmosphere of serenity," by the Comox Native Band, a 0.6-mile (1-km) walk from the parking area through a forested ravine leads to this wide beach. The Comox Valley Ground Search and Rescue Association publishes a detailed map of the Comox Valley that provides invaluable assistance in finding all of these beaches. It is available throughout the Comox Valley, including from Blue Heron Books, 1775 Comox Rd, (250) 339-6111, in downtown Comox.

As you pass through **Campbell River,** it's hard not to notice strollers and cyclists meandering along **Oyster Bay Shoreline Regional Park,** a shoreline bike-and-walking trail with gravel beaches and great views across to Quadra Island. Pulverized oyster shells speckle the gravel with a bright, white hue. The trail winds for much of the distance from the town's southern perimeter to the central harbour, passing the new museum on the hillside above the beach. The occasional picnic table and park bench invite travellers to pull over and join the fun.

Caving

There are several hundred significant caves to explore on Vancouver Island, including those at **Horne Lake Caves Provincial Park,** 9 miles (15 km) west of Hwy 19A near Qualicum Beach. A small fee is charged for tours in July and August, conducted by knowledgeable guides from the Canadian Cave Conservancy, a nonprofit organization devoted to proper management, protection, and interpretation of Canada's cave resources. If you're here in summer, plan on joining the challenging Karst Trail and Riverbend Trail (about 0.25 mile/0.4 km) tours, which last about two hours. Tours leave the trailhead on the hour between 10am and 4pm. You can take a self-guided tour of Main Cave and Lower Main Cave throughout the year. Although the distance covered isn't great—about 0.1 mile (0.2 km)—you'll have to bend, duck, and squeeze your way through a series of narrow passages. No matter when you arrive, prepare yourself for a tour by dressing warmly, wearing sturdy boots, and carrying a bright flashlight. (Helmets and lights are provided on guided tours. For those with a lust to squeeze deeper into the cave system, the three- to four-hour

Riverbed Bottoming trip leads down through a series of vertical pits, the deepest of which is nearly 60 feet/19 m). For more information, contact the Conservancy at (250) 757-8541, or BC Parks, (250) 337-2400 or (250) 954-4600. Guided tours are also offered by Island Pacific Adventures in Courtenay, (250) 248-7829 or (250) 757-8687. Horne Lake Caves Provincial Park is located north of Qualicum Beach. A gravel road leads to the parking area and trailhead at the far end of Horne Lake, about 9 miles (14 km) west of Hwy 19A. A footbridge spans the Qualicum River, from where a rough limestone trail leads to the Main Cave.

Mountain Biking

The **Comox Valley** (which comprises the towns of Courtenay, Cumberland, and Comox) is blessed with a plethora of multiuse and mountain-biking trails. Many of the trails revolve around the Puntledge River and Comox Lake. A network of nine moderate-to-difficult trails, known collectively as the **Comox Lake–Puntledge River Trails** near Courtenay, for instance, starts at the dam on Comox Lake. Most of the trails here are hard-core singletrack, so if you find yourself chewing dirt, you can't say we didn't warn you. To find your way to the parking lot and trailhead, follow Cliffe Ave north of Hwy 19 from the centre of Courtenay. Turn west on Fifth St and drive about 1 mile (1.6 km) to Lake Trail Rd. Follow Lake Trail Rd west for about 6 miles (10 km) to Comox Lake. The parking lot is on the west side of the dam at the mouth of the lake. For an alternate approach, take Royston Rd west of Hwy 19 to Cumberland. Turn north on Bevan Rd, which connects with Lake Trail Rd just east of Comox Lake. Trails begin just west of the dam. Ride west on this gravel road and take the first road (B21) north. About 15 minutes uphill is a trail that leads off to the right. This is called **Puntledge Plunge,** and you'll figure out why in the first few seconds of a near-vertical descent. More moderate trails begin off both Lake Trail and Bevan Rds east of the dam. Watch for a stone pillar marked with the sign "Number Four Mine" on Bevan Rd. Ride along a fire road that begins here. The first fork on the left leads to an old mine site where mounds of tailings define the terrain and provide the challenge (i.e., the fun) for riders. The most detailed map of the Courtenay-Cumberland-Comox region is the Comox Valley Regional Map published by the Comox Valley Ground Search and Rescue Association, available at most local gas stations. A good mountain-bike trail guide to consult is *Mountain Biking British Columbia* by Darren Polischuk.

For those who like their ascents easy, and their descents long and sweet, you can't get any easier or sweeter than catching the Blue chairlift up **Mount Washington** (see Skiing, below) and riding down. Check with the Mount Washington Ski Resort, (250) 338-1386, for hours of operation and costs. The mountain-biking season here generally begins by July 1 and extends through August. Mount Washington is 5,216 feet (1590 m) above sea level. At the end of the day you can take a long time making your descent back into the Comox Valley. Follow the signs to Mount Washington from Hwy 19 at the north end of Courtenay, a distance of 15.5 miles (25 km).

North of Comox, **Seal Bay Nature Park** doesn't have a lot of downhill, but then, it doesn't have a lot of uphill, either. This is a nature park, but if you're trying to find some easy cranking and some peace of mind, you could do a whole lot worse than the multiuse trails here. All trails are well marked and begin from the park's main trailhead on Bates Rd. To find the park, follow the coastline north of Comox to Bates Rd, or take Ryan Rd west of Hwy 19A from the Courtenay Bypass to Anderton Rd. Turn north on Anderton, which turns into Waveland Rd and leads to Bates Rd. Follow the signs from here.

The Dump is another area located next to a landfill. Unlike the pleasant-smelling Hartland Surplus Lands near Victoria, these ones, quite frankly, stink in places. But if you can put up with the occasional olfactory assault, the riding's pretty sweet. The Dump is located by the Pigeon Lake Landfill on Bevan Rd in Cumberland. To find it, take Royston Rd west of Hwy 19 towards Cumberland, then turn north on Bevan.

The folks at Blacks Cycle, 274A Anderton Rd, (250) 339-3925, or Simon's Cycles, (250) 339-6683, in downtown Comox, and Spokes, (250) 334-2217, Pedal Pusher Cycles, (250) 334-4845, or Cyclepath (250) 338-0886, in the heart of Courtenay, can probably point you to all these and more trails in the Courtenay-Comox region.

There's some good biking around **Campbell River.** Nestled in a nook between Iron River Rd and Campbell River itself is an area known as the **Pump House Trails.** To reach this easygoing network of well-marked single-track trails, turn west off Hwy 19 in Campbell River onto Hwy 28. Follow Hwy 28, then turn north onto Duncan Bay Main and cross the Campbell River. A trailhead is located just south of the intersection of Duncan Bay and Iron River Rd. Another trailhead is located west of Duncan Bay Rd on Iron Bay Rd.

Farther to the north and west of Campbell River on Hwy 28, a trail leads from a parking lot on the right of Loveland Bay Rd (on the way to the Loveland Bay Provincial Campground) and into mountain-bike heaven, the **Snowden Demonstration Forest.** Trails here are suited to all levels of mountain-bike riding skills and include the **Frog Lake System**'s five major routes and the **Lost Lake Trail System**'s four main routes. Trails runs from 1 to 5 miles (2 to 8 km) in length and frequently feed from one into the other to create longer rides. Some of the easier-going routes follow the railbeds left from logging shows here in the 1920s. This is some of the finest intermediate mountain biking on Vancouver Island, and is a sign of things to come as Forest Renewal BC funds are channelled into rehabilitating old logging roads as recreational trails. Detailed maps of the trails in the Snowden Demonstration Forest are available from the BC Forest Service district office in Campbell River, 370 S Dogwood St, (250) 286-9300. Other good sources of information include Pedal Your World Sports, Merecroft Village Shopping Centre, (250) 287-2453; Pro-line Cycle, (250) 286-1110; Urban Lemming, (250) 286-6340; and Endurance Cycle, (250) 923-2313, all in Campbell River.

Skiing

The **Mount Washington Ski Area** lies 19 miles (31 km) west of Hwy 19 in Courtenay on Mount Washington Rd. The snow here is often deeper than anywhere else in British Columbia, and occasionally anywhere else in the world! That was Mount Washington's claim to fame in late 1995. Try as they might, no matter where the staff called, no one could beat the more than 21 feet (655 cm) of snowpack that just kept falling and falling. Mount Washington (elevation 5,216 feet/1590 m) has long been known for having good snow conditions from early in winter to well past Easter, despite the fact that the top of the mountain isn't as high as the peaks of Blackcomb or Whistler Mountains. In 1995, Mount Washington had more snow than any other ski resort in the world. This accounts, in part, for Mount Washington being the second-busiest winter recreation destination in British Columbia, behind Whistler/Blackcomb.

By far the majority of visitors comes from Vancouver Island, primarily from the Victoria area, a three-hour drive south of Courtenay. Visitors from the Lower Mainland account for about 10 percent of the total. Visitors can arrange to stay in either the on-hill accommodations or in the nearby Comox Valley. It doesn't take long to discover why this part of the province continues to attract new arrivals from across the country. With a temperate coastal climate, it's possible to ride bicycles on local trails year-round, yet be up in the snowfields with a half-hour drive.

And what a drive. A steep, winding road leads west from Hwy 19 in Courtenay to Mount Washington. Not that other winter play places don't also have such roads. Most of them just don't have the snowfall in such quantities. If you're not into driving, shuttle buses to the mountain run from a number of hotels in Courtenay.

A great deal of Mount Washington's charm comes from its location. On a clear day, visitors look out across the Strait of Georgia at a panorama of the Sunshine Coast, from Powell River to Sechelt, with the peaks of the Coast Mountains rising in a long march behind. Closer at hand, the many peaks adorning Strathcona Provincial Park's Forbidden Plateau region look suitably magnificent. A total of five chairlifts, two of which are high-speed quads, service the mountain, which has a vertical rise of 1,657 feet (505 m). In total there are 42 alpine runs, 25 percent beginner, 40 percent intermediate, and 35 percent expert. A variety of equipment-rental and lesson packages are available. For more information on rates and hours, call (250) 338-1386, or visit their Web site, www.vquest.com/alpine/. To arrange on-hill accommodation, call (800) 699-6499 or (888) 837-4663.

Mount Washington's **cross-country ski trails** extend from the private ski area out into **Strathcona Provincial Park** (see Nootka Sound and Strathcona Provincial Park chapter). Self-sufficient skiers intent on winter camping use these trails as starting points for exploring the Battleship Lake and Lake Helen MacKenzie region (see Hiking, below) and beyond.

From the cozy, cross-country day lodge at Mount Washington, a series of loop trails offers workouts between 2 and 7 miles (3 and 12 km) long across the gentle terrain of **Paradise Meadows.** All told, there are over 22 miles (35 km) of skating-style and double-track cross-country trails around Mount Washington. Intermediate and advanced nordic skiers can take advantage of a specially priced lift ticket for the **Red Chair,** from which you can descend into the upper **West Meadows** along 6 miles (10 km) of tracked trails.

There's an unhurried nature to cross-country skiing here. Families that have diverse interests within their group will appreciate the convenience of having both alpine and nordic facilities within a short walking distance of each other. While some members are riding the six lifts into an alpine area laced with a variety of predominantly intermediate runs, others can be exercising in the quiet of the backcountry. Some of the best views of Mount Washington's alpine terrain are from out in Paradise Meadows. **Snowshoes** and **tow sleds** are also available from the cross-country rental shop.

For information on Mount Washington, phone (250) 657-3275, or visit their Web site, www.vquiest.com/alpine/. For snow reports, call (250) 338-1515. For information on backcountry ski touring in Strathcona Provincial Park, call BC Parks, (250) 337-5121 or (250) 337-8181. Mount Washington is located 15.5 miles (25 km) west of Hwy 19 on Mount Washington Rd in Courtenay.

Forbidden Ski Area is a modest version of its neighbour, Mount Washington, but, having opened in the 1920s, can lay claim to being Vancouver Island's first ski operation. Forbidden (named for Forbidden Plateau in nearby Strathcona Provincial Park) has the advantage of being closer to Courtenay. It's a 14-mile (23-km) drive to the lodge from Hwy 19 via well-marked Mount Washington and Piercy Rds. A chairlift and two T-bars handle the crowds here, which include those who come to slide on the Wood Mountain Luge Centre's 2,100-foot (640-m) track. You can rent a **luge sled** and take a ride yourself. You'll never come down a mountain faster. Forbidden Plateau operates from Friday to Sunday. It features 1,150 feet (350 m) of vertical rise, with 40 percent beginner, 50 percent intermediate, and 10 percent advanced terrain spread over 21 runs. Call (250) 334-4744 for more information, and (250) 338-1919 for a snow report.

Good sources for information on winter recreation in the Comox Valley include Mountain Meadow Sports, 368 Fifth St, (250) 338-8999; Ski Tak Hut, 267 Sixth St (250) 334-2537; and Ski & Surf Shop Outfitters, 333 Fifth St, (250) 338-8844, all in downtown Courtenay.

Hiking

There's a catch to hiking in **Strathcona Provincial Park** via Mount Washington Resort and Forbidden Ski Area: depending on the amount of snowfall from the previous season, you must often wait until midsummer for the meadows to dry out before attempting these routes. See Hiking in Nootka Sound and Strathcona Provincial Park chapter for a complete description of these trails.

Fishing

The annual fall salmon run at the mouth of **French Creek** as it enters the Strait of Georgia 3 miles (5 km) north of Parksville attracts anglers to the French Creek Marina, (250) 248-4431, and public boat launch adjacent to the federal dock and Lasqueti Island ferry (see Northern Gulf Islands chapter). French Creek is located on Hwy 19A and is well marked.

Spider Lake Provincial Park (see Beaches, above) northwest of Qualicum Beach is renown locally for its smallmouth-bass and trout fishing. The lake is stocked regularly, so for best results come in early spring before it warms up, or wait until fall to try your angling luck once temperatures begin to drop. No motorized boats are allowed on the lake. Launch car-top boats from the beach beside the parking lot. Follow the signs west of Hwy 19A on Horne Lake Rd to reach Spider Lake Provincial Park. After passing Spider Lake, the road follows the shoreline of **Horne Lake** to the headwaters of the Qualicum River. The lake is 5 miles (8 km) long and about 1 mile (1.5 km) wide, and features good boat fishing year-round for cutthroat, rainbow, and kokanee trout.

North of Qualicum Beach is the small oceanside community of **Deep Bay,** a town seemingly devoted to angling. Mapleguard Point is the elbow of an arm and spit that protect Deep Bay's natural harbour beside much larger Qualicum Bay. Rich salmon grounds lie in the bay near the Norris Rocks, Chrome Island, and Eagle Rock. Check with Seaside Charters, B&B and Boat Rentals, 5513 Deep Bay Dr, (888) 878-2200, in Bowser; or Ship and Shore Marine, 180 Chrome Point Rd, (250) 757-8750, and Deep Bay Fishing Resort, 5315 Deep Bay Rd, (250) 757-8424, in Deep Bay for more information on fishing these waters, where chinook salmon in the 20-pound range top the scales each year. Just north of Deep Bay on Hwy 19 you'll find **Rosewall Creek Provincial Park** (see Kayaking/Canoeing, below), a small roadside park devoted to riverbank casting at the entrance to Qualicum Bay.

Comox Lake, west of Cumberland on Comox Lake Rd, has good freshwater fishing for trout and char year-round. Boaters must beware of the strong winds that rise in the afternoon on the large, dammed lake. You'll find a boat launch at the west end of Comox Lake Rd.

Some of the best saltwater fishing on the island, particularly for salmon, can be found in the waters of the **Strait of Georgia** north of the Puntledge River Estuary between Courtenay and Comox, and off of Cape Lazo, King Coho, and Bates Beach, just north of Comox. Because of its sheltered location and an absence of dangerous currents, the shoreline around Comox is well suited for rod fishing in a small boat. If the weather does change, you can see it coming and quickly make for shore. Shore angling for salmon is popular in Comox Bay from August to November.

For more information on fishing in the Comox Valley, contact the Crowsnest Marine Supplies, 204-1797 Comox Ave, (250) 339-3676, in Comox; the Adventure Store, (250) 338-1203, in Courtenay; or the Comox Valley Visitor InfoCentre, (250) 334-3234. For details on licences, closures, and limits, contact the Department of Fisheries and Oceans, (250) 339-2031. For guided **salmon fishing charters,** contact Denverlene Charters, 1784 Dogwood Ave in Comox, (250) 339-5137, or visit their Web site, //mars.ark.com/~denverle/. Boat rentals, tackle, fishing charters, and a launch ramp are available at King Coho Resort, (250) 339-2039, in Comox. Also visit the BC Fishing Resorts and Outfitters Association Web site, www.oppub.com/bcfroa/bcfroa.html, or call (250) 374-6836.

The closer you get to Campbell River, the better the salmon fishing becomes. Tidal flows in Discovery Passage churn up clouds of nutrients that sustain a complex food chain, which includes, near the top, tasty salmon. You'll find a boat launch at Pacific Playgrounds Resort's marina, 9082 Clarkson Dr, (250) 337-5600, at **Saratoga Beach** in the town of Black Creek, 10.5 miles (17 km) north of Courtenay on Hwy 19, and another at aptly named **Salmon Point** in Black Creek. Fly-fish for coho in September at the mouth of **Black Creek,** which flows through **Miracle**

Beach Provincial Park (see Parks/Camping, above) into the Strait of Georgia as well as farther north at **Oyster River** on Hwy 19.

Campbell River justifiably bills itself as "Salmon Capital of the World." One of the four main fishing centres on Vancouver Island, the city is internationally famous for both its ocean and freshwater fishing. The twice-yearly steelhead runs on the **Quinsam** and **Campbell Rivers** are as well known as that on the Cowichan River, while the year-round salmon fishing in Discovery Passage is unmatched. (For more information on fishing in Discovery Passage, see Northern Gulf Islands chapter.) The Quinsam flows into the Campbell just inland from the Strait of Georgia. As it meets the ocean at the north end of town, the Campbell broadens into an intertidal estuary. The fishing calendar here has a summer steelhead run scheduled from June to October, with a winter run between November and April. Chinook (king) salmon are in residence year-round in Discovery Passage, which also hosts successive runs of coho (June to September), tyee (July to September), sockeye (August), pink (August and September), and finally chum (September to November).

The wealth of the salmon fishery in **Discovery Passage** between Campbell River and Quadra Island is so legendary that a special ritual has grown up around it over the past century. Called *tyee* fishing, this method has stringent requirements, but success buys instant membership in the exclusive Tyee Club of BC. Tyee is the appellation given a chinook (king) salmon when its weight exceeds 30 pounds (13.5 kg). Anglers must abide by regulations that stipulate a minimum catch weight of 30 pounds, hooked with an artificial single-hook lure fastened to a maximum 20-pound (9-kg) test line. Oh, and you have to be in a rowboat. (Considering the size of an average tyee, make sure it's a *big* rowboat.) The official weigh-in station is at the Tyee Club House beside the boat launch on Tyee Spit, east of Hwy 19 on Spit Rd in Campbell River.

The waterfront in Campbell River appears to be one massive marina. In fact, there are three saltwater marinas, as well as a freshwater marina at the mouth of the Campbell River. Government Marina and Discovery Pier are located at the south end of the harbour on South Island Hwy (Hwy 19). Almost as many salmon are caught off this pier that juts out into Discovery Passage as farther offshore. Local ritual requires that at the cry of "fish on," all other anglers reel in and stand aside as the lucky soul manoeuvres the (unlucky) salmon ashore.

Sportfish Discovery Marina is located slightly north of the Government Marina on Discovery Crescent next to the Quadra Island ferry slip. Discovery Harbour Marina, the commercial hub of Campbell River's harbour, and Argonaut Wharf lie just slightly farther north off Hwy 19 on Old Spit Rd. Freshwater Marina, with public parking and public boat launch, is located on the north side of the Campbell River Estuary. Turn east of Hwy 19 on Baikie Rd to reach it.

There are dozens of **fishing-charter operators** in Campbell River. The trick is finding the right one for your style, whether it be boat trolling, bank casting, or drift fishing. Several sources to consult include Calypso Charter, 384 Simms Rd, (250) 923-5121; North Passage Ventures, (250) 287-7092; Harry's Classic Tackle and Guide Service, (250) 923-2236; Drift Fishing Adventures, (250) 923-7084; Bailey's Charter and Marine Apparel, (250) 286-3474; and the Sportfish Centre, (250) 287-4911, all in the Campbell River region. For information on boat rentals, call Big Bear Rentals, 2250 Island Hwy, (250) 286-8687; CR Sportfishing Rentals, (250) 287-7279; Campbell River Sportfishing Rentals, (250) 287-7279; or Rub-a-Dub-Dub Boat Rentals, (250) 287-4999, all in Campbell River. One of the oldest tackle, guide referral, and information resources in Campbell River is Tyee Marine, 880 Island Hwy, (250) 287-2641. Weekly fishing reports are posted on Campbell River's Web site: www.vquest.com/crtourism/.

Kayaking/Canoeing

The eastern coastline of central Vancouver Island is the polar opposite of its western counterpart. Comox Harbour presents the one major indentation in a smooth stretch of the shoreline between Parksville and Campbell River. Paddle out from one of the easily reached beaches along Hwys 19 and 19A to enjoy the view of the Beaufort Ranges, one of the most dramatic of all the Vancouver Island Mountains.

The federal dock at **French Creek** on Hwy 19 north of Parksville (see Fishing, above) is sheltered by a sturdy breakwater, a hint that conditions do get breezy here on occasion, most notably in winter months when winds blow from the southeast. When conditions are favourable, this is a good place to launch.

Two sites particularly suited to launching a canoe, kayak, or lightweight boat are the **Little Qualicum River Estuary** in Qualicum Beach beside Hwy 19A, where you'll find easygoing paddling in the **Marshall Stevenson Wildlife Preserve** and **Qualicum National Wildlife Area.** Don't blink or you'll miss often-overlooked **Rosewall Creek Provincial Park** (see Fishing, above) located 15 miles (24 km) north of Qualicum Beach on Hwy 19A. Put in here or at **Deep Bay,** a natural harbour on Qualicum Bay protected by the curve of Mapleguard Point.

The Comox Valley is the hub of recreational kayaking and canoeing activity in these parts. Travellers who want to explore the waters of north Vancouver Island often stage out of Courtenay. For more information, including rentals and routes, contact Comox Valley Kayaks, (250) 334-2628 or (800) 545-5595; Tree Island Kayaking, 3050 Comox Rd, (250) 339-0580; or Ski & Surf Shop Outfitters, 33 Fifth St, all in Courtenay.

Windsurfing/Surfing

Goose Spit Regional Park (see Beaches, above) in Comox is one of the best windsurfing locations on the central coast. A long neck of sand curves out into Comox Harbour, where a strong wind rises most afternoons as winds funnel off the Strait of Georgia and up the flanks of Forbidden Plateau. To find the park, head south of Comox on Comox Rd, then turn left on Pritchard Rd and right on Balmoral to Lazo Rd, beyond which Balmoral becomes Hawkins Rd and leads out to the spit.

You'll also find good windsurfing in the protected waters of **Deep Bay** beside Hwy 19, directly west of Denman Island's south end. Check with Seaside Boat Rentals, (888) 878-2200, as to the best place to launch. You can also rent windsurfers here.

One of British Columbia's more esoteric adventure companies is located in Campbell River. Island Sauvage, (250) 286-0205, leads **heli-surfing** expeditions to remote beaches on the west side of Vancouver Island.

Wildlife

The **trumpeter swans** come in low over the treetops, two or three at a time. With an 8-foot (2.5-m) wingspan, the world's largest waterfowl exemplifies aerodynamic magnificence. Mimicking the landing gear of a plane, pairs of wide, webbed feet drop down at the last instant to break their fall with a finesse that would make the best bush pilot burn with envy. Seconds after landing, the new arrivals come to a quick halt, fold their wings, arch their necks like bass clefs, and drift regally off to join other swans already on site for the night. An aristocratic bugling call and response rises among them that makes the homely honk of Canada geese and the quotidian quack of mallards sound decidedly plebian.

This scene is repeated twice daily on lakes and ponds throughout the Comox Valley. Over the past decade, as population numbers of trumpeter swans have continued to rebound remarkably from a dismal low of several hundred in the 1960s to well over 10,000 today, many Comox Valley farmers put out winter feed for the swans. This is part of a coordinated plan not only to provide for the birds' welfare but also to protect the sensitive grassland on which livestock depend for summer grazing. A hefty, 22-pound (10-kilo) swan has a big appetite. More than a thousand of them remain to winter here and form the largest colony on the west coast of North America. Smaller flocks settle in the Lower Mainland, while others fly as far south as Oregon. As you drive around the valley, signs alert visitors to participating farms in the **Trumpeter Swan Management Area.** One such spread—Knight Farm, one of the oldest in the valley—lies just inland from Cape Lazo. A good book to consult on trumpeter swan viewing areas is *Nature Viewing Sites in the Comox Valley and Environs* by the Comox Valley Naturalists Society. Augmented by the Comox Valley Ground Search and Rescue Society's detailed regional map, these materials will fully equip you to prowl the backroads in search of more wildlife. Trumpeter-swan viewing sites abound in the valley, including along the well-marked scenic route on Comox Rd between Courtenay and Comox. (The route is equally well suited to driving and cycling.) Shoreline sites include Point Holmes and Cape Lazo as well as Kin Beach, Singing Sands, and Seal Bay Parks. For more information on trumpeter swans, contact the Comox-Strathcona Natural History Society, (250) 338-0380, or the Comox Valley Chamber of Commerce InfoCentre, (250) 334-3234. For books and maps, consult Blue Heron Books in downtown Comox, 1775 Comox Rd, (250) 339-6111.

Seal Bay Regional Nature Park is a BC Wildlife Watch viewing site where **California and Steller sea lions, seals,** and **migratory birds** hang out at this sunny stretch of coastline. Spring is a time of increased activity, when the sea lions arrive as they follow the annual herring and eulachon migration. (Eulachon are a small, sardine-sized fish.) To reach the Seal Bay Regional Nature Park, follow signs to the Powell River ferry from Hwy 19A in Courtenay, then head north on Waveland Rd to Bates Rd. Trails begin from the north end of the road and lead to a staircase that descends to the beach. Call BC Wildlife Watch, (250) 334-6000, for more information.

If you can arrange to journey by boat to **Mitlenatch Island Provincial Park,** you'll find a bird-watching and wildflower paradise 8 miles (13 km) northeast of Miracle Beach Provincial Park (see Parks/Camping, above). Mitlenatch is home to the largest seabird colony on the Strait of Georgia, principally 3,000 pairs of **glaucous-winged gulls.** Other nesting species include **pelagic cormorants, pigeon guillemots,** and **black oystercatchers.** Specially designed trails for wildlife viewing lead across the middle of the island between Northwest and Camp Bays to an observation blind. This area is characterized by open meadows that were cleared by the island's former owners a century ago. Access is restricted to other parts of the island where rocky uplands are forested with **trembling aspen,** a species more frequently seen in the British Columbia Interior. Their presence, along with **prickly pear cactus,** are a result of the semi-arid conditions here in the rain shadow cast by the Vancouver Island Mountains. For more information on Mitlenatch Island Provincial Park, including a map, contact BC Parks, (250) 337-2400. Check with the marina in Deep Bay (see Fishing, above) for transportation.

About 12 miles (19 km) south of Campbell River, you'll find exceptional birding in **Woodhus Slough.** Viewing trails lead out into the slough from the parking lot in Oyster River Regional Park. To reach the park, turn east on Glenora as it follows the north side of the Oyster River. For more information, contact BC Wildlife Watch, (250) 334-6000.

Diving

There's no wreck like an old wreck. That's what the HMCS *Columbia,* scuttled by Artificial Reef Society near Maud Island in Discovery Passage just north of **Campbell River,** is fast becoming. Divers should check with dive shops and marinas in Campbell River for more details, including Sea-Fun Divers, (250) 287-3622; Beaver Aquatics, (250) 287-7652; and Big Rock Boat Rentals, (888) 233-3377 (also the official location for the Underwater Archeological Society of BC).

You don't actually have to dive in order to enjoy an unusual underwater experience on the Campbell River. Snorkelling here from July to September provides an opportunity to watch from the surface as salmon, some as large as 50 pounds (28 kg) school in the estuary in advance of spawning. For guided **snorkel tours,** contact CR Snorkel Tours, (250) 286-0030, in Campbell River.

outside in

Restaurants

The Fanny Bay Inn This is a real roadhouse: local clientele, a fine fireplace, the obligatory collection of tankards, a dart board, and hearty pub fare (great hamburgers). Fanny Bay oysters are famous—try some. A low-key, convenient stop on the trek north from Parksville. *7480 Island Hwy (south end of town), Fanny Bay; (250) 335-2323; $.*

La Crémaillère ☆☆ This restaurant, housed in a two-storey Tudor-style building with a river view, relies on the chef's culinary skills (which transform the region's delicacies into fine French cuisine) and an intimate ambience. *975 Comox Rd (cross the river on 17th St Bridge, turn left towards Campbell River, then left onto Comox Rd), Courtenay; (250) 338-8131; $$$.*

Old Dutch Inn This motel and dining room has a spectacular view of Qualicum Bay. The rooms are comfortable, but the real draw is the Dutch cuisine (the chef has cooked for Queen Elizabeth). Try a special sandwich and save room for dessert. *2690 W Island Hwy (on old Island Hwy, centre of town), Qualicum Beach, BC V9K 1G8; (250) 752-6914 or (800) 661-0199 (from Canada only); $$.*

The Old House Restaurant ☆☆ This pioneer-style home set amid flower gardens creates an air of simple, rough-hewn charm. Actually two restaurants—a formal upstairs dining room and the more casual downstairs restaurant—it's quite popular, especially at lunchtime. At night, the menu goes upscale. *1760 Riverside Lane (turn right towards 17th St Bridge to Comox/Campbell River, then take first right, just before bridge), Courtenay; (250) 338-5406; $$.*

Cheaper Eats

Cola Diner and Cola Emporium Step into this diner and you step back in time to the '50s. Nostalgia buffs will love the authentic decor as they sip cherry cokes or ice-cream floats. Don't miss the adjacent Emporium. *6060 W Island Hwy, Qualicum Bay; (250) 757-2029; $.*

Crown and Anchor Pub Just the spot to grab a pint and a tasty, inexpensive lunch or dinner. Show up on a Saturday and take advantage of the special: a draft, burger, and chicken wings for only $1.49 each. *6120 Island Hwy, Qualicum Bay; (250) 757-9444; $.*

Lodgings

Greystone Manor ☆ Convenient to Mount Washington and Forbidden Plateau, and midway between Nanaimo and Campbell River, this elegant three-room B&B is a welcome respite. Authentic Victoriana and other period furnishings abound. *4014 Haas Rd (3 miles/5 km south of Courtenay on Island Hwy; watch for signs), Courtenay; mail: 4014 Haas Rd, Site 684, Comp 2, Courtenay, BC V9N 8H9; (250) 338-1422; $$.*

Quality Inn and Suites—Kingfisher Set off the highway, this motel with its cedar-shake roof is inviting. Rooms are spacious with simple furnishings and decks with views. There's an outdoor pool, a tennis court, and a whirlpool. Plans are afoot for a big new development here. *4330 S Island Hwy (5 miles/8 km south of Courtenay), Courtenay; mail: RR 6, Site 672, C-1, Courtenay, BC V9N 8H9; (250) 338-1323 or (800) 663-7929; $$.*

Ships Point Beach House ☆☆ This seaside retreat has views of the sound and mountains. One of the owners cooks up a storm for breakfast and guests can pick oysters, dig clams, fish, or sea kayak. *7584 Ships Point Rd (follow signs from old Island Hwy towards water, 5 miles/8 km north of Deep Bay), Fanny Bay; mail: Site 39, Comp 76, Fanny Bay, BC V0R 1W0; (250) 335-2200 or (800) 925-1595; $$$.*

Tigh-Na-Mara Hotel ☆ This complex of lodge units, cottages, and condos (all with fireplaces and views, some with Jacuzzis) is spread out along a beach and among acres of arbutus and fir. There's an indoor pool, outdoor tennis courts, and a restaurant with an increasingly adventurous menu. 1095 E Island Hwy *(1.25 miles/2 km south of Parksville on old Island Hwy), Parksville, BC V9P 2E5; (250) 248- 2072 or (800) 663-7373; $$.*

Cheaper Sleeps

Quatna Manor This civilized, Tudor-style home has gorgeous grounds, a grape arbour, and wonderfully cushy lodgings in an elegant, old-world ambience. Choose from a room with a private or shared bath. *512 Quatna Rd, Qualicum Beach, BC V9K 1B4; (250) 752-6685; $.*

St. Andrews Lodge and Glen Cottages Sandwiched between the beach and the highway, this lodging is spotlessly clean and a true bargain. The proprietor's been here since 1938, when her family began building the little ocean-view cottages, which are the best units. *W Island Hwy, Qualicum Beach, BC V9K 2B3; (250) 752-6652; $.*

More Information

BC Ferries: *(888) 223-3779.*
BC Forest Service, Campbell River Forest District, Campbell River: *(250) 286-9300.*
BC Parks: *(250) 337-2400 or (250) 954-4600.*
Campbell River and District Chamber of Commerce: *(250) 287-4636.*
Campbell River Regional Parks: *(250) 334-4452 or (250) 287-9612.*
Canadian Cave Conservancy: *(250) 757-8541.*
Comox-Strathcona Natural History Society: *(250) 338-0380.*
Comox Valley Chamber of Commerce: *(250) 334-3234.*
Department of Fisheries and Oceans: *(250) 339-2031.*
Mitlenatch Field Naturalist Society: *(250) 337-8180 or (250) 285-3859.*
Mount Washington: *(250) 338-1386; snow report (250) 338-1515.*
Parksville and District Chamber of Commerce: *(250) 248-3613.*
Qualicum Beach Chamber of Commerce: *(250) 752-2923.*
Strathcona Wilderness Institute: *(250) 337-8220 or (250) 337-8180.*

Nootka Sound and Strathcona Provincial Park

Highway 28 runs the width of central Vancouver Island, linking Campbell River on the east coast with Gold River and Nootka Sound on the west, including Strathcona Provincial Park in the middle.

The mountains and islands of central Vancouver Island have a mysterious sense about them, as if they're always trying to hide some secret. It's true: you do have to travel farther afield here in order to penetrate its cloud-laced valleys, coastal rain forest, and the open ocean waters of its two sounds, Nootka and Kyuquot. Some of this landscape's mysteries lie tucked away inside the vaulted domes of underground caverns. Afloat in a sea kayak on an open sound, or deep inside the Quatsino cave system, be prepared to experience a blend of connectedness and jubilation, isolation and terror, when adventuring here. One thing is guaranteed: at the end of the day, you'll sleep well.

Getting There

Highway 28 originates from Highway 19 just north of Campbell River and leads west for 57 miles (92 km) to Gold River. Highway 19 to the north of Campbell River leads to Port Hardy. Highways 19 and 19A lead south of Campbell River to Courtenay. Travel to ports in Nootka Sound and neighbouring Kyuquot Sound to the north is via the MV Uchuck III, *a working freighter based in Gold River that provides year-round passenger and freight service.*

Adjoining Areas

NORTH: **North Vancouver Island**

SOUTH: **Tofino and Pacific Rim National Park Reserve**

inside out

Parks/Camping

Elk Falls Provincial Park (122 vehicle/tent sites), on Hwy 28 6 miles (10 km) west of its junction with Hwy 19A, is near the union of the Quinsam and Campbell Rivers. The park has two distinct sections. The picnic/day-use area is located near the waterfalls on the Campbell River as it enters John Hart Lake. Campsites are situated 4 miles (6.5 km) away on the Quinsam River. A large stand of Douglas fir surrounds Elk Falls, which present a lively sight during spring runoff. A 1.5-mile (2.5-km) hiking trail runs from the riverside campsites to the nearby Quinsam River Hatchery, which is open daily for tours. For more information, call BC Parks, (250) 954-4600.

Strathcona Provincial Park can be approached from several different sides; however, its headquarters and campgrounds are reached via Hwy 28, about 28 miles (45 km) west of Campbell River and Hwy 19. You'll find a total of 161 vehicle/tent campsites in two locations, Ralph River (76 campsites) and Buttle Lake (85 campsites). **Ralph River Campground** requires a 15.5-mile (25-km) drive south from Hwy 28 along the east shore of Buttle Lake; you'll find the well-marked turnoff from Hwy 28 on the east side of the bridge that spans Buttle Narrows, where Buttle Lake merges with Upper Campbell Lake. An old-growth Douglas fir forest shelters the peaceful setting of the campsites at Ralph River. **Buttle Lake Campground** is farther west, and just a short distance south of Hwy 28 at the junction of Upper Campbell and Buttle Lakes in a pleasantly forested, riverside location. There's good swimming, in season, at both campgrounds. For more information, including a map, contact BC Parks, (250) 954-4600.

Kayaking/Boating

Boat launches are situated at two locations on slender, steep-sided **Buttle Lake** in Strathcona Provincial Park. One is located beside the Auger Point picnic tables in the Buttle Lake Campground (see Parks/Camping, above); the other is located about 15 miles (25 km) south of the campground near the Karst Creek picnic area. Note: Buttle is a flooded lake, and along the shoreline submerged deadheads are an ever-present threat. Beware of the sudden winds and storm conditions that can quickly channel through this mountainous region. Boaters can head to four **wilderness marine campsites** on the western shore of Buttle Lake, as well as a site on **Rainbow Island** just offshore from the Buttle Lake campground at the north end of the lake; call BC Parks, (250) 954-4600, for more information on these sites.

The sheltered waters of **Muchalat Inlet** run like a long corridor through steep-sided fjords. Landing places are few. Once in **Nootka Sound,** however, a much more weather-beaten landscape begins to reveal itself. **Bligh Island Provincial Marine Park** (part of the Spanish Pilot Group) sits at the mouth of Muchalat Inlet. The MV *Uchuck III* (see below) stops nearby at Friendly Cove (Yuquot) or will drop off kayakers beside Bligh Island by prior arrangement. There's much to explore in this group of six islands, scattered where Muchalat Inlet converges with two adjacent inlets and their channels. The waters in this region can get choppy, so small craft must cross with care. Large Bligh Island is named for a much-maligned British Navy captain who sailed here with the equally well-known Captain Cook in 1788. A cairn at Resolute Cove on the southeast coast of the island commemorates the landing. Contact BC Parks, (250) 954-4600, for more information on paddling and camping in Bligh Island Provincial Marine Park. Good maps of this region include Canadian Hydrographic Chart #3662 (Nootka Sound to Esperanza Inlet) and #3664 (Nootka Sound), and the Campbell River Forest Service recreation map. Contact the Forest Service for a copy, (250) 286-9300. Ecomarine Ocean Kayak Centre on Granville Island in Vancouver offers week-long **sea-kayaking tours** of Nootka Sound in late summer. For an itinerary, contact them at (604) 689-7575.

MV *Uchuck III* Tour

Many visitors to the west side of Vancouver Island may never have had the chance to boat in the wind, the rain, and the ever-rolling seas that characterize the world of the "outside" waters, as the open ocean here is often called. One of three freighters (or "coasters") that ply the waters of Vancouver Island's Barkley, Nootka, and Kyuquot Sounds is based in **Gold River,** at the western terminus of Hwy 28. Barkley Sound is not as exposed as **Nootka** and **Kyuquot Sounds,** where the MV *Uchuck III* makes its rounds. (The *Uchuck III*'s sister ships, the MV *Lady Rose* and the MV *Frances Barkley,* are based out of Port Alberni on central Vancouver Island and sail through Barkley Sound; see Tofino and Pacific Rim National Park Reserve chapter.) Exploring the outside waters aboard the *Uchuck III* as the former World War II minesweeper makes a weekly two-day round-trip voyage to the fishing hamlet of Kyuquot can be an adventure. For many passengers, particularly in storm season, the high (or low) point of the journey is the two-hour stretch each way spent tossing about on the open ocean waters between Port Eliza and Kyuquot. From the moment the 136-foot-long freighter leaves the dock in Gold River and begins its 10-hour journey the big question is whether your constitution can handle the rise-and-fall motion of the ship in high seas. (At such times it helps to remember that the word *uchuck* translates as "healing waters.")

On a typical voyage, ocean swells can run in the 6- to 9-foot (2- to 3-m) range: plenty chaotic for most voyagers, though the skipper will go out in anything short of 25 feet (8 m) to make his rounds. Although the *Uchuck III* has sometimes had to wait out a blow in Kyuquot or Port Eliza, she's never foregone a regularly scheduled trip since 1982, when she was assigned to the Kyuquot run. (Most of the crew worked on the *Lady Rose* before coming to Gold River, and are clearly distressed at the trashing of the Broken Islands by campers in Barkley Sound. Despite the ever-present signs of similar treatment of the forest by logging companies along the *Uchuck III*'s route, most crew members feel Nootka and Kyuquot Sounds are a cut above their former assignment.)

If you're inclined to be right in on the action during a bout on the high seas, the wheelhouse is the place to be. Although not the roomiest place aboard, there is space for several passengers to stand inside with the skipper and first mate. When ocean waters are too rough north of Port Eliza to negotiate a tricky inside passage called the Rolling Roadstead north towards Kyuquot, the *Uchuck III* heads west of Vancouver Island into the vastness of the open water.

In storm season, winds often blow at 30 to 50 knots from the southeast, while ocean swells run from the west; large breakers roll in from all directions. The slender nose of the *Uchuck III* is the thin edge of the proverbial wedge—a wave cutter *par excellence*. The nose of the *Uchuck III* rises as the horizon line falls, then slams down on a cresting wave. The horizon rises as the *Uchuck III* drops into a trough, then rises again. The skipper looks like a defensive lineman on a football team, braced for the onrush of yet another surge. The mate scans the radar, recording the ship's position in a logbook.

After two hours of this, it's a relief to suddenly see the **Mission Islands** and **Nicolaye Channel**'s narrow entrance, beyond which lies Kyuquot. As the *Uchuck III* passes **Aktis Island,** there are signs of a clearing and several homes. This is the original village site where more than 2,000 Natives lived in the years before contact with the Europeans. Today there are fewer than 30 full-time residents here, who, by choice, shun such conveniences as telephones and electricity, except that provided by a limited-use generator.

The village of **Kyuquot** is home to 300 Natives and others, whose homes are built into the forest above the tideline. To turn into a small bay and find civilization after rocking and roiling for several hours in open water heightens Kyuquot's value. Much of the architecture here is identifiably Canadian West Coast style: modern and well kept, a testimony to good years in the fishing industry. Despite the overwhelming sense a visitor feels that the logging industry is the only employer around, brought on by endless patches of clear-cut on all sides coupled with an absence of other marine traffic, fishing is the predominant vocation in Kyuquot. Here on **Walters Island,** in a series of small bays just beyond reach of the spirits of wind and water, people have sheltered and drawn a living from the ocean for generations. In recent years, with the fishing season becoming more limited, tourism is seen by some residents as a viable alternative profession.

In winter months, cargo aboard the *Uchuck III* consists of goods destined for a dozen or more logging camps (more commonly referred to as logging "shows"). Come warmer weather, when logging shuts down due to the threat of fires, ferrying passengers is the staple business of the *Uchuck III*. Instead of off-loading heavy equipment, in summer the ship's deck is lined with kayaks and its towering Union rigging is busy wet-launching oceangoing adventurers. Although much of the coastline is rocky and rugged, there are choice campsites on beaches near Kyuquot, including **Rugged Point Provincial Marine Park.** Not everyone comes this far. At other times of the week, the *Uchuck III* makes day trips in the sheltered waters of Nootka Sound to **Tahsis** or **Friendly Cove,** the site of Captain James Cook's first contact with the Native people of Vancouver Island in 1778. Today only one family remains in the settlement of Yuquot at Friendly Cove on Nootka Island (see Hiking/Backpacking, below).

The MV *Uchuck III* sails from Gold River to Kyuquot every Thursday morning at 7am. Gold River is a comfortable, four-hour, 155-mile (250-km) drive from Nanaimo. Cost of the round trip to Kyuquot is $154 single, $260 double, which includes bed-and-breakfast accommodation in Kyuquot. Shorter **day trips** aboard the *Uchuck III* include the Tahsis Day Trip, which departs every Tuesday year-round. This trip will take you through Nootka Sound to Tahsis (about five hours one way), with stops as required to deliver passengers and cargo at logging camps and settlements. A one-hour stop in Tahsis allows enough time for a walking tour of the village. Costs are currently $45 for adults, with reduced rates for seniors and children 6 to 12 years of age. The Nootka Sound Day Trip includes a brief stop at Resolution Cove and a 90-minute stop at Yuquot (Friendly Cove). Costs are $35 for adults, with reductions for seniors and children. (Note: The fare does not include a landing fee at Friendly Cove, the proceeds of which go to the Mowachaht Band for redevelopment of this historic site. The landing fee for adults is $7, with reduced rates for seniors and children.) **Reservations** are a must for all sailings. Contact Nootka Sound Service in Gold River at (250) 283-2325. The Gold River Lions Campground is situated nearby. At least one motel—the Ridgeview, (250) 283-2277—operates a free shuttle service for guests from the town of Gold River, located about 9 miles (14 km) east, to the dock.

Hiking/Backpacking

The **Snowden Demonstration Forest** is located west of Campbell River and north of Hwy 28 near Loveland Bay Provincial Park. You'll find almost 19 miles (30 km) of easygoing hiking trails here. Logging was carried out in this forest from the 1920s to the 1950s, and the Snowden Demonstration Forest is in various stages of recovery. Early on, logs were brought out by railway. Their gentle grades (minus the ties) crisscross the forest in places such as the Frog Lake Trail System's **Old Rail Trail** (easy; 2.5 miles/4 km return) and **Lookout Loop** (easy; 2 miles/3.2 km return). These two feed into each other. Access is from parking lots at either the north or south ends of **Elmer Lake.** To reach Elmer Lake, turn north off Hwy 28 at Elk Falls Provincial Park. Follow well-marked Lower Campbell Lake Rd about 2.5 miles (4 km) west of Elk Falls Provincial Park towards Loveland Bay Provincial Park. Elmer Lake lies about 1 mile (1.6 km) along a secondary road that leads north from Lower Campbell Lake Rd. **Enchanted Forest Trail** (easy; 2.5 miles/4.3 km return) leads through some of the lushest growth in the forest and begins from the south end of Elmer Lake. The Snowden Demonstration Forest is about 10 miles (16 km) west of Campbell River. Follow Hwy 28 west of town for about 4 miles (7 km) to the turnoff for Loveland Bay Provincial Park. Stay left after crossing the John Hart Dam, from where a well-signed gravel road leads to the Snowden Demonstration Forest.

The **Nootka Island Trail** (also called the Friendly Cove/Yuquot Trail) rambles between Louie Bay on the north side of Nootka Island and Yuquot (Friendly Cove) on the south. Along the way, the trail crosses exquisite beaches and tidal shelves, as well as leading inland to bypass rocky headlands and deep river mouths. This 22-mile (35-km) trail is gradually becoming a choice hiking destination, and is a complement to the West Coast Trail. By comparison with the West Coast Trail, the Nootka Island Trail is poorly marked and infrequently maintained. Be prepared to bushwhack around fallen trees brought down by the frequent, savage winter storms that pound this section of coast. In order to avoid an exhausting amount of bushwhacking, consult tide charts for the most opportune times to cross beaches. Allow seven days to complete the hike one way. Hikers must be completely self-contained and are advised to carry a handheld marine radio, as the sole source of help is from the lighthouse staff at Yuquot. Hikers are also well advised to register with the Royal Canadian Mounted Police detachment in Gold River before starting out; (250) 283-2227. Note: There is a large population of bears on Nootka Island, and chances are good that hikers will encounter them along the beaches. At present, these bears do not associate hikers with food. Cache all supplies well out of reach of these animals. The best maps to consult for route finding are nautical chart #3662 or topographic chart 92E/10. Access to Louie Bay is by floatplane from Gold River or Tofino; to Yuquot, by the MV *Uchuck III* (see Kayaking/Boating, above). For information on Yuquot (Friendly Cove), contact Ahaminaquus Information, (250) 283-7464, 7 miles (12 km) south of Gold River on Pulp Mill Rd, to arrange transportation, cabins, and camping at Yuquot. For more information on air travel to Nootka Island, contact Tofino Air, (250) 725-4454, in Tofino, or Nootka Air, (250) 283-2255, in Gold River. Maxie Water Taxi operates between Gold River and Nootka Island, (250) 283-2282. One of the best ways to explore the Nootka Trail is to join a guided tour. Sea to Sky Trails leads **hiking tours** of Nootka Island. For information, call (604) 594-7701, or toll free (800) 990-8735, or visit their Web site: www.travel.bc.ca/seatosky/.

Strathcona Provincial Park was created in 1911 and is the original park in the provincial system, which now numbers over 450 protected sites. At the time, the 544,000 acres (200 000 ha) seemed like a fabulous amount of land to set aside. It still does, especially to those who like to hike in the middle of the rugged, heavily glaciated Vancouver Island Mountains. The park was created for those who seek adventure in remote wilderness surroundings. It may be easier to reach the trailheads, but the routes still remain as challenging as ever. To really experience the beauty of this park, come prepared to explore the backcountry.

You'll find trailheads at three locations in the park, including those at Great Central Lake for the Della Falls Trail (see Tofino and Pacific Rim National Park Reserve chapter for details on this route). Hiking routes also originate in the Forbidden Plateau region to the summit of **Mount Becher** (moderate; 6 miles/10 km return) and to **McKenzie Meadows** (strenuous; 22 miles/35 km return). Other trails in Forbidden Plateau begin from the **Paradise Meadows** trailhead on nearby **Mount Washington.** Forbidden Plateau is located 14 miles (23 km) west of Hwy 19 in Courtenay, via well-marked Mount Washington and Piercy Rds. Somewhat gentler, these trails range from a short loop through Paradise Meadows (easy; about 3 miles/4.5 km return) to an extended 5-mile (8-km) loop around **Lake Helen McKenzie** and **Battleship Lake.** Much lengthier exploring is possible using Lake Helen Mackenzie and Kwai Lake as a base. The **Helen McKenzie–Kwai Lake–Croteau Lake Loop** (moderate; 5 miles/8 km return) leads to a series of subalpine lakes in the beautiful alpine amphitheatre of Forbidden Plateau. Farther afield, the **Circlet Lake Trail** (strenuous; 12 miles/19 km return) leads from Lake Helen McKenzie past **Hairtrigger Lake** to a wilderness campsite at Circlet Lake. Stunning views of the rugged nearby mountain peaks, as well as the unending string of Coast Mountains to the east on the Lower Mainland, reward hikers for their efforts. Die-hard enthusiasts can hike still farther from Circlet Lake to **Moat** and **Amphitheatre Lakes,** eventually reaching the summit of **Mount Albert Edward.**

More than a dozen more hikes and walks originate from the Buttle Lake area of the park. Trailheads are found at both the north and south ends of the 9-mile (15-km) lake, as well as additional trails that lead off elsewhere around the lake. From the park entrance on Hwy 28, the **Elk River Trail** (moderate; 13.5 miles/22 km return) leads through the Elk River Valley to aptly named **Landslide Lake.** Careful of your footing here and on the **Crest Mountain Trail** (moderate; 6 miles/10 km return), which climbs to a variety of scenic viewpoints farther west. The Crest Mountain trailhead is located on the north side of Hwy 28, about 15 miles (24.5 km) west of Buttle Narrows Bridge.

One of the park's gentler hikes begins at the south end of Buttle Lake and leads to **Upper Myra Falls** (moderate; 4 miles/6 km return). Don't be fooled by the seemingly short distance. The lower part of this trail crosses a steep hill with sections of loose rock. A series of shorter hikes and walks leads from Hwy 28 to viewpoints at **Lady Falls, Elk River,** and **Lupin Falls.** A fascinating look at weathering appears along the **Karst Creek Trail** (easy; 2.5 miles/4 km return), which begins beside the picnic area on the east side of Buttle Lake. The **Wild Ginger** and **Shepard Creek** walking trails originate in the Ralph River Campground (see Parks/Camping, above).

Hiking trails in Strathcona Provincial Park as well as additional trails on central Vancouver Island are detailed in *Hiking Guide to the Vancouver Island Backbone* by Phil Stone, and *Hiking Trails III: Central and Northern Vancouver Island* by the Outdoor Club of Victoria. Excellent trail descriptions are also available from the BC Parks ranger station in Black Creek, (250) 337-2400, or Strathcona District headquarters in Miracle Beach, (250) 954-4600.

For a fascinating description of yet another approach to Strathcona Provincial Park, this time from the west coast north of Tofino through newly minted **Megin Provincial Park,** read *Written by the Wind* by Randy Stoltmann. This book also contains a gripping description of wilderness hiking in **Kyuquot Sound** (see Kayaking/Boating, above).

Western Wildcat Tours in Nanaimo, (250) 753-3234, leads **hiking tours** through Strathcona Provincial Park. For even more information and supplies, visit Strathcona Outfitters, 888 Island Hwy, in Campbell River, (250) 287-4453.

Caving

The **Upana Caves,** all 100 or so of them, are located about 10 miles (about 17 km) west of Gold River on Head Bay Forest Rd. They provide an awe-inspiring adventure for those who like to explore the interior of the earth. Dress warmly, as these caves, the deepest north of Mexico, extend more than 2,000 feet (610 m) into the honeycombed limestone rock. You can take a self-guided tour through a network of caves or join a guided tour. Contact Cave Treks, (250) 283-7144, in Gold River for more information.

Rock Climbing

Strathcona Provincial Park is a climber's dream. Over 100 routes exist in the **Crest Creek Crags** alone. Use the Crest Mountain trailhead (see Hiking/Backpacking, above) to reach the routes. For more information, check with Strathcona Park Lodge's Outdoor Education Centre on Hwy 28, just east of the Buttle Lake Campground, (250) 286-2008. The centre offers rock-climbing courses from May to October.

Attractions

A town of over 20,000 people, **Campbell River** is big as Vancouver Island cities go. It's completely ringed with shopping malls, yet the city centre still looks and feels as it undoubtedly did in the '50s. Here you'll find some of the best fishing outfitters on the island; during the Salmon Festival in July, the town is abuzz with famous and ordinary sports fisherfolk. The Museum at Campbell River, housed on the highway south of the town centre, is well worth a visit for its collection of Northwest Coast Native masks and other art (470 Island Hwy, (250) 287-3103). For information on the town and region, call the Chamber of Commerce, (250) 287-4636.

Restaurants

Gourmet-by-the-Sea ☆ The good food, reasonable prices, and oceanside location here have been attracting diners for years. The clientele is mostly local, seafood is utterly fresh, and all the tables look out to a magnificent view. *4378 S Island Hwy (9 miles/14.5 km south of Campbell River on Discovery Bay), Campbell River; (250) 923-5234; $$.*

Koto ☆☆ It makes sense: a very fresh sushi bar smack in the middle of fishing country. Locals are now fond of the sushi specialties and other Japanese fare, from teriyaki to sukiyaki. It's a good meal. *80 10th Ave (behind Bank of BC building), Campbell River; (250) 286-1422; $$.*

Vincenti's ☆ This simple Italian family restaurant isn't fancy—regulation red-check tablecloths and minimal decor—but with satisfying pastas and main courses, and wonderful service, it seems set for a long run. *702 Island Hwy (opposite Discovery Pier), Campbell River; (250) 287-3737; $–$$.*

Cheaper Eats

Beehive At breakfast time, make a beeline for a table with a view of the fishing boats docked in the marina, Discovery Passage, and the islands. The thick French toast is a good bet. *921 Island Hwy, Campbell River; (250) 286-6812; $.*

The Ideal Cafe Truckers and locals know it, and now you do, too: the Ideal serves the best cheap eats ($7.50 a plate, plus an extra buck for soup and dessert). Portions are more than generous (half portions are available, too) and the friendly staff is quite attentive. *2263 N Island Hwy, Campbell River; (250) 287-9055; $.*

Lodgings

Painter's Lodge ☆ Old photos of big-name types and their fish line the lobby. At 4am, seaplanes and motorboats pick up anglers (and shatter any nonfisherman's sleep). There are four buildings, plus the main lodge and cottages. Dinners may be inconsistent. Open April through October. *1625 McDonald Rd (at Island Hwy, 2.5 miles/4 km north of Campbell River); Box 460, Dept 2, Campbell River, BC V9W 5C1; (250) 286-1102 or (800) 663-7090; $$–$$$.*

Strathcona Park Lodge A week-in-the-woods experience on a lake. Amenities are simple—camper-style cabins or modest lodge units—but there are lots of outdoor programs perfect for families (canoeing, day hikes, lake play). Limited facilities in winter. *At the edge of Strathcona Park, 28 miles/45 km west of Campbell River; PO Box 2160, Campbell River, BC V9W 5C9; (250) 286-8206 or (250) 286-3122; $$.*

Cheaper Sleeps

Haig-Brown House This restored farmhouse, one of Vancouver Island's top lodgings, offers character, an amiable host, and a riverfront setting. In season, snorkel down the Campbell River while the salmon make their way upstream—it's an amazing experience. *2250 Campbell River Rd, Campbell River, BC V9W 4N7; (250) 286-6646; $.*

Passage View Motel Tucked unobtrusively among a string of expensive highwayside resorts, this spot offers pleasant, colourful rooms with a view. You can even access the beach via the small yard in back. *517 Island Hwy, Campbell River, BC V9W 2B9; (250) 286-1156; $.*

Pier House Bed & Breakfast Built in 1924, it's the oldest house in town and stands at the entrance to Campbell River's famous fishing pier. This B&B is a charming mix of old curiosity shop and museum—examine the many relics. *670 Island Hwy, Campbell River, BC V9W 2C3; (250) 287-2943; $.*

More Information

Ahaminaquus Information: *(250) 283-7464.*
BC Forest Service, Campbell River Forest District, Campbell River: *(250) 286-9300.*
BC Parks: *(250) 954-4600 or (250) 337-2400.*
Gold River Chamber of Commerce: *(250) 283-2202 or (250) 283-7418; Web site: www.Goldrvr.island.net/~goldriv/.*
Nootka Sound Service: *(250) 283-2515 or 283-2325.*
Tahsis InfoCentre: *(250) 934-6667.*

North Vancouver Island

The northern portion of Highway 19 from Campbell River to Port Hardy and Cape Scott, including Alert Bay, Telegraph Cove, Brooks Peninsula Provincial Park, and Cape Scott Provincial Park.

As 97 percent of the population lives on the southern half of Vancouver Island, outdoor recreationists in search of solitude come north. Much of Vancouver Island once looked as the north still does today. Thanks to recent government protection, some of the remaining wilderness, such as Brooks Peninsula, a stubby, 8.5-mile-long (14-km) projection on the northwest coast of the island, has been preserved. Other places, such as the most northerly tip of the island, are sheltered by the elements from the preying eye of industry. Cape Scott Provincial Park is one of the wildest, windiest, most woebegone locales in the province for human habitation. Journeying to either Brooks Peninsula or Cape Scott is only for those whose mettle has been tested by repeated exposure to the bellows and blast-furnace of nature in the raw. Gentler conditions prevail in the sheltered waters of Johnstone Strait, where the Kwakwaka'wakw First Nations are the traditional gatekeepers. To experience a tranquillity that passes all description, paddle these waters where whales rub and salmon run in summer months.

Getting There

The top half of 280-mile-long (450-km) Vancouver Island is served by a maze of logging roads and Highway 19 (North Island Highway), which links Campbell River with Port Hardy, the southern terminus of BC Ferries' Inside Passage and Discovery Coast routes. BC Ferries links the north and central coasts (Prince Rupert and Bella Coola, respectively) with Vancouver Island at Port Hardy. For more information, contact the Campbell River Visitor InfoCentre, (250) 287-4636, or stop by their office in the Tyee Plaza, 1235 Island Highway.

Adjoining Areas

SOUTH: **Nootka Sound and Strathcona Provincial Park**

inside out

Kayaking

The federal dock in **Fair Harbour,** about 22 miles (35 km) northwest of Zeballos, is the launching point for exploring Kyuquot Sound (see Nootka Sound and Strathcona Provincial Park chapter), Checleset Bay Ecological Reserve, and Brooks Peninsula Provincial Park. This is a vast, windswept, sea-sprayed section of Vancouver Island's northwest coast. The snout of Brooks Peninsula offers some protection for Checleset Bay from the winter storms that blow south from the Gulf of Alaska. Sea kayakers should beware the fury of the winds and surf that build around its protruding bulk, especially at Cape Cook and Clerke Point. The rewards for making the journey are the solitude provided by the surroundings and the sight of magnificent stands of Sitka spruce, the only species of tree able to thrive under the constant salt- and magnesium-loaded spindrift that the winds whip from the tops of the swells and carry ashore in the breeze. In the sheltering forest, marbled murrelets nest in the deep moss that enshrouds the thick branches of the spruce. Herds of Roosevelt elk graze in the lush, green understorey, while black bears forage in the berry-laden bushes. If you are among the few visitors who make their way here each year, you will be treated to one of the last remaining environments on the west coast where logging has been held mercifully at bay. **Brooks Peninsula Provincial Park** is huge, 127,528 acres (51 631 ha) of wilderness that is best explored with the help of a guide.

West Coast Expeditions offers six-day tours of Kyuquot Sound, Checleset Bay Ecological Reserve, and Brooks Peninsula Provincial Park from May to September. Established in 1974, the company is operated by marine biologist Rupert Wong, who also acts as the conservation warden for the Checleset Bay Ecological Reserve (see Wildlife, below). Originally based in Barkley Sound, West Coast Expeditions moved north into Kyuquot Sound in the early 1980s. Separate sea-kayaking tours are offered for novice, advanced, and all-women groups from a base camp on **Spring Island.** For more information, contact West Coast Expeditions, (800) 665-3040. For a map of the region, contact BC Forest Service's Port McNeill district office, (250) 956-5000. Good marine charts of the area are #3682 (Kyuquot Sound) and #3683 (Checleset Bay.) For more information on

Brooks Peninsula Provincial Park, call BC Parks, (250) 949-2816, in Port Hardy, or (250) 954-4600 (Strathcona District Headquarters). Fair Harbour is located about 22 miles (35 km) northwest of Zeballos, which lies about 26 miles (42 km) west of Hwy 19 on gravelled logging roads. Call (250) 934-7623 to check on winter road conditions.

Good sea kayaking is also found in the protected waters off the east side of Vancouver Island. There are several staging areas, including **Beaver Harbour** in **Fort Rupert (Kwakiutl),** south of Port Hardy. Head east of Hwy 19 on Beaver Harbour Rd to the marina and boat launch beside the federal wharf on Storey's Beach Rd. Kayak rentals can be arranged either here, or at North Island Boat, Canoe & Kayak Rentals, (250) 949-7707, in Port Hardy and also in Telegraph Cove (see Boating/Canoeing, below). For more information, contact North Island Tours, (250) 949-7707, in Port Hardy. For information on touring the Robson Bight area (see Wildlife, below) of **Johnstone Strait,** contact Wildheart Adventure Tours, (250) 722-3683, Web site: www.island.net/~wheart, in Nanaimo.

Boating/Canoeing

The **Sayward Forest Canoe Route** covers almost 30 miles (50 km) of lakes west of Campbell River. Allow three to four days to complete the circuit, which begins on Campbell Lake. Wisdom has it that the best approach to the route is to journey in a counterclockwise direction, putting in at the boat launch on Mohun Lake in Morton Lake Provincial Park. The well-marked route continues through 10 lakes before returning to the park. Road access to most of the lakes within the canoe route means that paddlers can pick and choose from a variety of put-in and take-out points. Portages range in distance from a stone's throw across a log jam at Brewster Bridge to about 1.4 miles (2.2 km) between Surprise and Brewster Lakes. BC Forest Service publishes a detailed map of the route. Call (250) 286-9300 to request a copy, or stop by the Campbell River office at 370 S Dogwood St. To reach the Mohun Lake boat ramp in Morton Lake Provincial Park, travel west of Hwy 19 via the Menzies Bay Mainline Logging Rd and then the Mohun Lake East Rd. For more information, including rentals, contact C.V. Sea Kayaks and Canoes, (250) 287-2650, in Campbell River.

Morton Lake Provincial Park (see Fishing, below) is trumpeted as the gateway to the Sayward Forest Canoe Route. **Loveland Bay Provincial Park** lies close by and is the more rustic of the two. Paddling is possible at both, though the main attraction in these parts is much larger **Mohun Lake:** a section of its shoreline lies within Morton Lake Provincial Park. Car-top boats can be launched at Morton Lake and Loveland Bay, and there is a boat ramp on Mohun Lake. Morton Lake Provincial Park lies west of Hwy 19 via the Menzies Bay Mainline Logging Rd and then the Mohun Lake East Rd. Loveland Bay on Campbell Lake is reached from Hwy 28 west of Campbell River on the John Hart Dam Rd and then the Camp 5 Logging Rd. Mohun Lake is accessed via the Mohun Lake East Rd. For more information, contact BC Parks, (250) 954-4600.

North of Sayward, you'll find good paddling on the **Klaklakama Lakes.** Travel 4 miles (7 km) south of Hwy 19 along a rough logging road that initially leads towards Schoen Lake Provincial Park (see Parks/Camping, below). The best place to launch is from the Forest Service recreation site on Upper Klaklakama Lake (5 vehicle/tent sites). You'll also find a small Forest Service recreation campground (4 vehicle/tent sites) at the south end of Upper Klaklakama Lake, as well as a good picnic spot on Lower Klaklakama Lake near Hwy 19, when you're in need of a break from driving.

Telegraph Cove is the place to begin exploring **Johnstone Strait** and **Robson Bight** (see Wildlife, below). You'll find a boat launch and moorage, as well as fishing licences, tackle, and bait for sale at Alder Bay Campsite, (250) 956-4117. This is also a prime staging area for whale-watching tours and kayak departures. Long-term parking can be arranged here for those setting out on extended boating trips in Johnstone Strait. Other good contacts around Telegraph Cove include Telegraph Cove Resorts, (800) 200-4665 or (250) 928-3131, which has a wooded campground, a boat launch and marina, boat rentals, and fishing licences, and serves as a staging area for whale-watching and salmon-fishing tours. Telegraph Cove, one of the last boardwalk communities on eastern Vancouver Island, is worth a visit even if you're not planning to do any offshore exploring.

Fishing

The saltwater fishing in **Discovery Passage** off Campbell River is legendary (see Parksville and the Comox Valley chapter). In addition, dozens of small, freshwater lakes are scattered throughout the north island. Many lakes can be reached only by the logging or gravel roads that lead off east and west from Hwy 19. Stop at one of the many tackle shops and marinas in Campbell River for advice on where the fish are biting. For more information, contact the Campbell River Visitor InfoCentre, (250) 287-4636, or stop by their office in the Tyee Plaza, 1235 Island Hwy. You can rent boats and buy fishing licences and tackle at Campbell River Fishing Village, (250) 287-3630, Salmon Point Marina, (250) 923-6605, and Rod and Reel Resort, (250) 923-5250, among others located in town.

Near Campbell River, you'll find good trout and char fishing at Morton Lake Provincial Park (see Boating/Canoeing, above). To reach the park, turn west off Hwy 19 17 miles (27) km north of Campbell River, then journey 12 miles (20 km) on good gravel road to **Morton** and **Mohun Lakes.** As well, **Roberts Lake,** 20 miles (32 km) north of Campbell River, also has good fishing close to Hwy 19. Car-top boats can be launched from its sandy beach, a short walk from the road on a Forest Service trail. Many small fishing lakes such as **McCreight Lake** feature rustic Forest Service campsites and the occasional boat launch. For a map, contact the Forest Service district office at 370 S Dogwood St in Campbell River, (250) 286-9300.

Near Sayward, the **Salmon River** is one of the better-known destinations for steelhead fishing on Vancouver Island. Drive east of Hwy 19 towards Sayward and Kelsey Bay. En route, Sayward Rd crosses the Salmon River at several points, offering access. Cabins and angling information are available at either Fisherboy Park, 1546 Sayward Rd, (250) 282-3204, or the quaint Cable House Café on the east side of the one-lane bridge on Sayward Rd that crosses the Salmon River.

For more information on Sayward and Kelsey Bay, call (250) 282-3265, or stop by the information centre a short distance west of Hwy 19 on Sayward Rd at Sayward Junction.

The water offshore from **Zeballos** (see Kayaking, above) boasts excellent saltwater sportfishing for salmon and rock cod, one of the smoothest, sexiest-tasting fish when fresh, before being doused with smoke (the usual treatment for most cod sold in BC stores.) For information on marinas, fishing charters, and accommodation, contact the Zeballos Village Office, (250) 761-4229, or Zeballos Board of Trade, (250) 761-4261.

There's a good salmon run on the **Marble River,** which lies 8 miles (13 km) west of Hwy 19 on the road to Port Alice. This logging road also provides access to **Alice, Victoria,** and **Kathleen Lakes,** which offer good cutthroat trout and dolly varden fishing. Campsites and a boat launch are located in the mill town of Port Alice, where you'll find full facilities for exploring the profusion of sheltered inlets in **Quatsino Sound.** For more information, contact the Village of Port Alice, (250) 284-3391, or the Port Alice InfoCentre, (250) 284-3318. Contact the Forest Service district office, 2217 Mine Rd in Port McNeill, for a detailed map of fishing and camping recreation sites in the region; (250) 956-5000.

In **Port Hardy,** a good place to begin a fishing trip in Queen Charlotte Strait is the Quarterdeck Marina, (250) 949-6551, which has bait, tackle, and fishing licences for sale, and features a boat launch as well.

Hiking/Backpacking

The trailhead for the **Ripple Rock Trail** (easy; 5 miles/8 km return) is located on the east side of Hwy 19 about 4 miles (6 km) north of the Ripple Rock Rest Area, which is just north of Campbell River. The roadside parking area is well marked. The trail leads hikers through abundant second-growth forest (with a few spectacular examples of old-growth Sitka spruce and Douglas fir on the east side of Menzies Creek) to a viewpoint of the treacherous waters in **Seymour Narrows.** Despite the blasting away in 1958 of the twin peaks of Ripple Rock, which lies underwater directly east of the viewpoint, large boats are still harassed by the rip tides, swirling currents, and whirlpools that constantly agitate the surface of the narrows. A map of the trail is available from the Forest Service, 370 S Dogwood St in Campbell River, (250) 286-9300.

Other hiking trails of the same distance and difficulty that lead off from Hwy 19 include the **McNair Lake Trail,** 22 miles (35 km) north of Campbell River, and the **Dalrymple Creek Trail,** 35 miles (57 km) north of Campbell River.

Wildlife

Robson Bight Provincial Park, 12 miles (20 km) south of Telegraph Cove in Johnstone Strait, provides ocean adventurers with a sure thing when it comes to **whale watching.** In this case it's actually killer-whale (large dolphins called orca) watching. Pods of orcas come to this part of Johnstone Strait each summer to rub on the barnacle-encrusted rocks at Robson Bight. As the top predator on the inland-water food chain, they are also attracted by the annual salmon runs that funnel through the strait beginning in late June. One of the best ways to approach killer whales is quietly aboard a sailboat. Contact Seasmoke/Sea Orca Expeditions in Alert Bay, (250) 974-5225, to join one of their watching and wildlife-viewing tours. For more information on Robson Bight Provincial Park, contact BC Parks, (250) 954-4600.

Between 1969 and 1972, almost one hundred **sea otters** were relocated to the waters of **Checleset Bay** (north of Kyuquot Sound and south of Brooks Peninsula) from the Aleutian Islands as part of an experiment to replenish a once-thriving population that had been hunted to the point of extinction on the west coast of Vancouver Island. Checleset's remoteness, coupled with an abundance of shallow reefs and a good food source (primarily sea urchin) have brought sea-otter numbers to a current level of more than 600 animals. In addition, sea otters have spread out from the 81,500-acre (33 000-ha) **Checleset Bay Ecological Reserve** and have been spotted as far south as Barkley Sound and north of the rugged

Brooks Peninsula. For more information, contact Rupert Wong, ecological warden for Checleset Bay, at West Coast Expeditions, (800) 665-3040; see also Kayaking, above.

Windsurfing

The Nimpkish Speed Slalom Windsurfing Weekend, held in early August, is the highlight of the season at slender **Nimpkish Lake.** Bring your wet suit and everything else you may need, as the nearest town is Port McNeill, a long drive from the large Forest Service recreation site at the south end of the 15-mile (24-km) lake. Strong, reliable winds rise here on summer afternoons. If they don't, you can still lie back enjoy the views of the rugged mountainscape that surround the lake. It's the west coast way. Hwy 19 parallels the entire east side of the lake, so make sure to strut your stuff for the passersby.

Parks/Camping

With no public campground located beside Hwy 19 from Campbell River north to Cape Scott, travellers must go farther afield to seek out a provincial or regional park or Forest Service recreation site if they want an alternative to a private campground.

Pockets of Forest Service sites occur around **McCreight Lake** (see Fishing, above) as well as nearby **Pye** and **Stella Lakes.** To reach McCreighton Lake, take Rock Bay Rd east of Hwy 19, about 23 miles (37 km) north of Campbell River. Both Pye and Stella Lakes are located short distances south of Rock Bay Rd, and their respective turnoffs are well-marked. For a detailed map of these and other sites in the Campbell River Forest District, call (250) 286-9300, or stop by the Forest Service's office, 370 S Dogwood St in Campbell River.

Marble River Provincial Park (33 vehicle/tent sites) is west of Hwy 19 on the **Port Alice** road near the north end of Alice Lake. It is nestled in a beautiful forest, and campers will find a boat launch and beach for swimming. For more information, contact BC Parks, (250) 954-4600.

Link River Regional Park (30 vehicle/tent sites) lies 30 miles (50 km) west of Hwy 19 on the Port Alice Rd near the south end of Alice Lake. Two Forest Service sites are located on the east side of the lake and at a series of nearby lakes. For more information on Link River and other regional parks, contact the Mount Waddington Regional District, (250) 956-3301.

North of Port Hardy, look for small sites off Hwy 19 at **Georgia** and **Nahwitti Lakes** on the way to Cape Scott. For a detailed map and description of these sites, contact the Port McNeill Forest District, (250)

956-5000, or stop by their office at 2217 Mine Rd in Port McNeill.

Schoen Lake Provincial Park (10 vehicle/tent sites) is located about 7 miles (12 km) south of Hwy 19, north of Sayward. Set in the Nimpkish Valley, this one of the most beautiful camping areas on the island. One of the best ways to experience this park is from one of the **wilderness campsites** on Schoen Lake. Launch a car-top boat from the end of Davie Rd beside the formal campsite and start paddling. Toss in a line. You might get lucky and catch your supper, though in these cold waters the trout rarely outgrow the frying pan. Mounts Schoen and Adam rises above the landscape and are best appreciated from out on the lake. Take topographic map #92L/01 with you for a detailed look at the crook-shaped lake and surroundings. Hikers face a challenging climb on **Mount Schoen.** Trails are vaguely marked at best but, as always, hikers are rewarded for their efforts with panoramic vistas. For more information on the backcountry around Schoen Lake Provincial Park and newly minted, even more undeveloped **Woss Lake Provincial Park** farther west, contact BC Parks, (250) 949-2816 in Port Hardy. Consult *Hiking Trails III: Central and Northern Vancouver Island* by the Outdoor Club of Victoria for information on backcountry trails in Schoen Lake Provincial Park.

Raft Cove Provincial Marine Park is located about 5 miles (8 km) south of Cape Scott Provincial Park, about 26 miles (42 km) west of Port Hardy. The road forks as it nears both parks. Bear to the left to reach Raft Cove. Dense western hemlock and Sitka spruce blanket the shoreline, where you'll find wilderness sites on nearby beaches. A rough trail leads from the parking lot to the beach. Allow 30–45 minutes to make the journey one way. This is an extremely exposed area. Come prepared to wear waterproof clothing on top of your waterproof clothing in an attempt to stay dry. Raft Cove is located just south of San Josef Bay. A good topographic map of this region is #1021/09. For more information, contact BC Parks, (250) 949-2816.

Cape Scott Provincial Park lies 37 miles (60 km) west of Port Hardy on a well-maintained gravel road. It's only a short, 1.5-mile (2.5-km) hike to **San Josef Bay,** where most backpackers set up on sandy beach fronted by sea stacks. More experienced hikers face an eight-hour slog through some of the muddiest, most tortuous terrain of any trail in British Columbia to reach **Cape Scott,** a distance of 17 miles (27 km) from the parking lot. The heavier your pack, the less likely you are to be swept away by the winds that brew around the cape, but don't count on it. A storm once blew so hard that it turned the lighthouse here sideways. No matter what time of year you choose to visit this park, come equipped for storms. Carry a pair of high-top rubber boots in addition to wearing waterproof hiking boots. Expect to spend considerable amounts of time changing between the two. Be particularly careful on boardwalk sections, which can be quite slippery. In winter months, average rainfall is 9–14 inches (22–35 cm) per month, while in summer the average lightens to 3–4 inches (8.5–10 cm). A good map to carry is NTS #1021/09 and hydrographic chart #3624 (Cape Cook to Cape Scott).

From the park's main parking lot, historic trails traverse the upland areas in two directions, either north to Cape Scott or southwest to San Josef Bay. In order not to be cut off from hiking routes by incoming tides, be sure to carry and consult tide tables if you are engaged in extended exploration along the shoreline. There are more than 35 miles (60 km) of ocean frontage within the park, composed of rocky headlands and promontories interspersed with wide, sandy beaches such as at Nels Bight. The north coast extends about 11 miles (18 km) from Cape Scott to the park's eastern boundary. It features three large bays at **Experiment Bight, Nels Bight,** and **Nissen Bight,** where backcountry explorers will find white sandy beaches interspersed with smaller bays that have steeper gravel beaches. The western (Pacific) coast is vulnerable to southwesterly storms, which makes it a more rugged, exposed shoreline. The three sandy beaches here at **Guise, Hansen,** and **Lowrie Bays** are smaller than the northern ones and are separated by long stretches of rocky coast.

Shellfish occur in abundance and can be harvested at low tide from the beach. Dig for razor, sand, mud, butter, and littleneck clams. A feast on these and a taste of hot clam broth will help ward off the chill while softening the memory of your trek. This park is home to both wolves and bears; food should be well cached. Cape Scott's strategic location means that it is a natural gathering place for migratory birds, particularly waterfowl, and sightings include sandhill cranes, trumpeter swans, pelagic cormorants, snipes, sandpipers, and plovers. **Hansen Lagoon** stretches for 3 miles (5 km) inland from the west coast and forms a large saltwater marsh and tidal mudflats where large numbers of birds gather.

For more information on Cape Scott Provincial Park, contact BC Parks, (250) 949-2816 in Port Hardy.

Caving

Little Hustan Cave Regional Park, on Zeballos Rd, 13 miles (21 km) west of Hwy 19, offers visitors a chance to view the Quatsimo System, a network of caves that honeycomb Vancouver Island between here and the Strathcona Provincial Park–Gold River region. If you've never experienced the sensation of spending time underground, it's like mountaineering in the dark with the sight of a smooth, white world revealed in the beam of your headlamp. Cave climates are damp and clammy, so dress accordingly. Little

Hustan's caves are a good place to begin caving or even to begin considering the possibility. A short trail leads from the parking lot to a view of several caves through which the Atluck River bores. For a guided caving tour of the park, contact Mountain Line Tours and Travel, (250) 956-4827, in Port McNeill. For more information on Little Hustan Regional Park, contact Mount Waddington Regional District, (250) 956-3301.

Diving

God's Pocket Provincial Park is a brand-new provincial park where the focus is on diving and habitat protection for wildlife. God's Pocket Provincial Park is made up of a group of islands, the largest of which are **Bull and Hurst Islands,** about 12.5 miles (20 km) due north of Port Hardy. Most diving takes place in nearby Browning Pass, an area highly rated by the late underwater explorer Jacques Cousteau as one of the best diving locales in the world. For more diving information, contact God's Pocket Resort, (250) 949-9221, which is located on Hurst Island. For more information on the park, contact BC Parks, (250) 949-2816 in Port Hardy.

Picnics

Ripple Rock Rest Area just north of Campbell River on Hwy 19 offers a fine view of **Seymour Narrows.** This is a harbinger of the vistas along the Inside Passage from here north to Prince Rupert (see Inside Passage and Discovery Coast chapter). An interpretive marker here describes the maritime history of the region since it was first charted by Captain George Vancouver in 1792. The tidal rip offshore is so vicious that when viewed through binoculars it has the appearance of a writhing mass of snakes.

There's romantic picnicking just south of the **Adam River Bridge** on Hwy 19 51.5 miles (83 km) north of Campbell River. As you feast, enjoy the view of Mounts Romeo and Juliet, the snowmelt from which fills Adam and Eve Lakes, from which two rivers of the same names flow east into Johnstone Strait. Equally impressive is the sight of Jagged Mountain and Mount Cain, which dominate the skyline north of here.

Just north of **Port McNeill** beside Hwy 19 near the "375 Km" marker is a panoramic lookout south along **Broughton Strait** past the Pultenay Point lighthouse towards Alert Bay, and east across Queen Charlotte Strait to the mainland. There are no telephone or power lines and no clear-cuts to intrude on the view, which is simply ga-ga.

outside in

Attractions

Interesting stops along the North Island Hwy include a short side trip to **Sayward,** a small coastal settlement on Kelsey Bay, from where the Inside Passage ferry sailed until 1978, when Hwy 19 was extended to Port Hardy. Fresh seafood is often available from one or more boats tied up at the federal wharf here. A good source of information (and wildlife watching) in Sayward is Robson Bight Charters, (250) 282-3833 or (800) 658-0022 (British Columbia only) or visit their Web site: oberon.ark.com/~robsonbi/. Sayward is located about 6 miles (10 km) east of Hwy 19 at the Km 233 road marker.

About 18 miles (30 km) south of Port Hardy is **Port McNeill.** Logging and marine-supply stores are the predominant features here, but so too is the waterfront, from where ferries to nearby Cormorant and Malcolm Islands sail. The towns of **Alert Bay** and **Sointula,** located respectively on each island, are both worthy destinations for day-tripping foot passengers. The U'mista Cultural Centre in Alert Bay, an inspiring Kwakwaka'wakw museum, examines cultural origins and potlatch traditions. Seasonal hours: call (250) 974-5403. Near the ferry slip in Port McNeill is the office of Western Forest Products, whose Japanese-inspired architecture and beautifully landscaped grounds warrant a visit. The turnoff for the BC Ferries terminal is located about 2 miles (3 km) south of **Port Hardy,** a town composed of single-storey company houses built into a low-slung ridge. A sign near the waterfront advertises fresh shrimp for sale at the town dock. The going price here (and elsewhere on the journey) is $10 per pound for headless, medium-size scampi. You can cook them up at a pleasant picnic site on Hardy Bay next to the ferry.

Stubbs Island Charters, (250) 928-3185, in **Telegraph Cove** can accommodate groups of five or more in a cluster of modest harbourfront cabins, and also takes groups out for morning and afternoon whale-watching cruises.

Restaurants

For recommended restaurants, see Adjoining Areas to this chapter.

Lodgings

Hidden Cove Lodge ☆☆ This retreat sits in its own secluded cove on 9.5 acres (4 ha): no TV or phone—just acres of woodsy, waterfront property. The hosts might sign you up for a whale-watching trip or a no-holds-barred heli-venture. Rooms are simply furnished, and accommodations can include continental breakfast or three meals. A window-lined lounge invites convivial gatherings and wildlife sightings. *From Hwy 19, take Beaver Cove/Telegraph Cove cutoff and watch for signs; PO Box 258, Port McNeill, BC V0N 2R0; (250) 956-3916; $$$.*

More Information

Alert Bay Band Office (Cormorant Island): *(250) 974-5213.*

BC Ferries: *(888) 223-3779 in Victoria; (250) 339-0444 in Port McNeill (Alert Bay–Sointula); Web site: www.bcferries.bc.ca.*

BC Forest Service, Campbell River Forest District: *(250) 286-9300.*

BC Forest Service, Port McNeill Forest District: *(250) 956-5000.*

BC Parks, Port Hardy: *(250) 949-2816.*

BC Parks, Strathcona District Headquarters: *(250) 954-4600.*

Fish and Wildlife Conservation Officer, Campbell River: *(250) 286-7630, for information concerning freshwater fishing regulations.*

Kyuquot Band Office: *(250) 332-5259.*

Mount Waddington Regional District: *(250) 956-3301 or (250) 956-3161; good source of maps on the north island.*

North Island Reservations and Information: *(250) 949-7622.*

Port Alice InfoCentre: *(250) 284-3318 or (250) 284-3391.*

Port Hardy and District Chamber of Commerce InfoCentre: *(250) 949-7622.*

Port McNeill InfoCentre: *(250) 956-3131.*

Sayward Chamber of Commerce: *(250) 282-3833.*

Sayward–Kelsey Bay InfoCentre: *(250) 282-3265.*

Tahsis Chamber of Commerce: *(250) 934-6667; (250) 934-6344; winter road information, (250) 934-7623.*

Telegraph Cove Tourist InfoCentre: *(250) 928-3185.*

Zeballos Village Office: *(250) 761-4229.*

Southern Gulf Islands

From Saturna and Pender Islands on the Canada-US border north to Gabriola Island near Nanaimo, including Portland, Galiano, Mayne, and Salt Spring Islands, and Ruckle and Montague Harbour Provincial Marine Parks.

There are seven major islands in the southern half of the Strait of Georgia (also referred to as the Gulf of Georgia, a holdover from an erroneous assumption on the part of early English explorers). Among them, Galiano Island has always enjoyed the reputation as being the most welcoming to visitors. This is due in large part to the limited amount of farmland on Galiano in comparison to other islands. Of necessity, early settlers here opened their homes to tourists as a way of earning a living. Today, Galiano is the hub for sea-kayak trips and the site of Montague Harbour Provincial Marine Park, one of the largest provincial parks on any of the islands.

This isn't to say that residents of other islands won't be just as pleased to see you disembark at the dock. Indeed, tourism is important to the livelihood and economic well-being of most of the Gulf Islands, although some are better prepared for it than others. Decide in advance which island suits your purposes best, then consult a BC Ferries schedule to see if you can manage the connections in the course of a day's visit or will have to seek overnight accommodation. Except in summer months, ferry service to many islands is restricted to one or two sailings a day. You may find that in order to catch a ride you'll have to start your day well before dawn and return home late in the evening. The trade-off is that you'll find far fewer visitors sharing the roads, waterways, and parks with you as you travel at off-peak times.

Getting There

A variety of BC Ferries vessels sails to Salt Spring, Galiano, Mayne, and Pender Islands from Tsawwassen on the Lower Mainland and Swartz Bay on Vancouver Island. In addition, BC Ferries sails from Village Bay on Mayne Island to Saturna Island, from Crofton on southern Vancouver Island to Vesuvius on Salt Spring Island, as well as from Nanaimo on southern Vancouver Island to Gabriola Island. If you're in a car, don't expect simply to arrive at the terminal and drive aboard. The perplexing web of schedules, routes, and fares makes advance planning (and, often, reservations) a must. Or spare yourself the stress and expense by leaving your car at home; most inns and B&Bs will pick you up at the dock. Interisland ferries ply the waters of the southern Gulfs, operating on a first-come, first-served basis.You can reserve a space for your vehicle in advance of departure on the most popular runs by calling BC Ferries toll-free in Canada at (888) 223-3779, or (250) 386-3431. Kayaks and canoes are considered hand luggage while a small fee is charged for those bringing bicycles. Most Gulf Islands have maps and tourist information available at the ferry dock when you arrive. It's best to orient yourself from these locations. A good books about the islands is The Gulf Islands Explorer *by Bruce Obee. You'll find an extensive selection of such material in the bookstores located aboard all but the smallest BC Ferries.*

Adjoining Areas

NORTH: **Northern Gulf Islands**

SOUTH: **Greater Victoria**

EAST: **Greater Vancouver**

WEST: **Nanaimo and the Cowichan Valley**

inside out

Camping/Parks

Salt Spring Island is the most densely populated of the Gulf Islands and is also home to the biggest Gulf Island provincial campground. **Ruckle Provincial Park** (80 walk-in sites) is located 5.5 miles (9 km) northeast of Fulford Harbour. (BC Ferries links Fulford Harbour with Swartz Bay on Vancouver Island.) The park features an interesting blend of easily reached sites in a wooded setting overlooking Swanson Channel, with North Pender Island on the far shore. The Ruckle family first homesteaded here over a century ago. Although they donated most of their property to the province for a park in 1974, the Ruckles still raise sheep on private land at the entrance to the campground. Visitors are welcome to visit the grounds where many old buildings have been restored. Also on Salt Spring is **Mouat Provincial Park** (15 vehicle/tent sites) in Ganges, 8 miles (13 km) north of Fulford Harbour. Just a short walk uphill from the commercial heart of Salt Spring, these campsites are functional but lack Ruckle's seaside ambience. (There's a BC Ferries dock in nearby Long Harbour with links to both Swartz Bay on Vancouver Island and Tsawwassen on the mainland.)

Across the water on **North Pender Island** there's camping at **Prior Centennial Provincial Park** (17 vehicle/tent sites; reservations recommended), as well as paddle or boat-in sites at **Beaumont Provincial Marine Park** (12 rustic sites). Prior Centennial may be more accessible but Beaumont's setting is tops. Prior Centennial is located about 4 miles (6 km) southeast of the ferry dock at Otter Bay on the west side of Canal Rd. Launch sites for Beaumont include Medicine Beach on North Pender and the government dock at Bedwell Bay on South Pender. Allow 30 minutes to make the 1-mile (1.6-km) paddle from either location. BC Parks publishes a detailed brochure on Beaumont Provincial Marine Park. To receive a copy, call (250) 391-2300.

Although **Montague Harbour Provincial Marine Park** (19 vehicle/tent sites, 21 walk-in) on the west side of **Galiano Island** was British Columbia's first marine park, it has become just as popular with drive-in and cycle-in visitors as with boaters. In fact, you can make reservations for both vehicle/tent and walk-in sites from April to September. Call BC Parks, (800) 689-9025, to secure a spot. The park lies 5 miles (8 km) north of the BC Ferries dock at Sturdies Bay. Some of the walk-in sites are located in an ultrapicturesque wooded setting on a small ridge above the harbour. Until a disputed right-of-way reopens, you'll have to boat to Galiano's northeastern tip to reach **Dionisio Point Provincial Park** (15 vehicle/tent sites, 25 walk-in), 22 miles (35 km) from Sturdies Bay. Much of this park has a weathered-limestone shoreline, characteristic of both Galiano and Gabriola Islands. Boaters can choose to land at pebble beaches on either side of Dionisio Point and thus avoid the tidal currents in Porlier Pass. To check on current road conditions, call BC Parks, (250) 391-2300.

Farther north, you'll find 18 walk-in campsites on **Newcastle Island Provincial Park** (see also Picnics/Parks, below). The entire island is park and can be reached by foot-passenger ferry from Nanaimo's inner harbour near the dock from which the car ferry sails to Gabriola Island. It only takes several minutes to walk from the dock on Newcastle Island to the campsites. Note: The public ferry to Newcastle runs during summer months only; otherwise, catch a ride with one of the private water taxis that whisk travellers around the harbour.

There are no public or private campgrounds on either Mayne or Saturna Islands. For more information on all of the provincial parks on the Gulf Islands, call BC Parks, (250) 391-2300.

Picnics/Parks

Saturna Island is tucked away at the southern end of the island chain. **East Point Park** is one of two public spaces on the island. Over the past few years, islanders have lobbied hard for the creation of this serene day park beside the East Point lighthouse. Depending on the height of the tides, you'll find more or less of the shoreline revealed during your visit, just as, depending on the clouds, you'll see more or less of Mount Baker's magnificent snow cone rising above the eastern horizon. The lower the ocean, the more there is to explore here. Walk the weathered snout of East Point and discover the many colours revealed by erosion in the smooth-shaped limestone. Offshore, the curious eyes of harbour seals will follow you around. If you've brought a hand-carried boat, you can launch from the beach to explore the shoreline, but beware the tidal currents that churn through Tumbo Channel. To find the park, head south from the ferry dock at Saturna Point along East Point Rd and follow it to its end. **Winter Cove Provincial Marine Park** is only about a mile from the ferry dock at Saturna Point. Paddle to it from the federal dock, about 30 minutes one way, or follow East Cove and Winter Point Rds to reach it. Picnic tables are placed about an open, grassy field beside the cove, a sunny location in which to enjoy yourself.

Mount Maxwell's Baynes Peak is crowned by a forest of mature grand fir and Garry oak. A provincial ecological reserve has been created here to protect the enclave and provide biologists an opportunity to study this vibrant ecosystem. **Mount Maxwell Provincial Park,** adjacent to the ecological reserve, gives visitors the chance to stand on the top of Baynes Peak and enjoy the best views of anywhere on the islands.

Spread out before you to the south is one of the very few open fields on the Gulf Islands, stretching all the way to Fulford Harbour. That's only the beginning. The farther you look, the more you see, as your eyes search out landmarks that distinguish this part of the Pacific Northwest: Mount Baker, the plains of western Washington, the San Juan Islands, and snow-gripped Hurricane Ridge in the Olympic Mountains. Just as obvious are the broad waters of Haro Strait and the Strait of Juan de Fuca, the vast shipping lanes through which supertankers journey between the refineries in Whatcom and Skagit Counties, and through which the Alaskan oilfields and freighters carry wheat, lumber, sulfur, and automobiles between the docks in Vancouver and Asian markets. Find a sheltered ledge and lean back to drink in all this. Ravens ride the updrafts off the face of the mountain and rise and dive as they cavort with each other. The approach to the park is on Cranberry Rd as it leads west from Fulford-Ganges Rd and links with Maxwell Rd. Drive slowly, as the road is rough but passable.

Galiano Island's Bellhouse Provincial Park is named in honour of the first innkeepers on the island. Besides the small beach here, the park's main attractions are the wildly shaped limestone formations on the shoreline of Active Pass and the parade of large ferry boats that squeeze through the waterway that separates Galiano and Mayne Islands. This is a dream location for photographers. Bellhouse is only a short walk north from the ferry dock at Sturdies Bay and is well marked. Pause here to rest and picnic before heading uphill to **Bluffs Park** (see Hiking, below), another good picnic location at the south end of Galiano.

Perhaps the most interesting limestone formation on the Gulf Islands is located just south of the beach and picnic grounds at **Gabriola Sands Provincial Park** on **Gabriola Island** near Nanaimo. This grassy, open, breezy location on Taylor and Pilot Bays is rather unique on the islands for its manicured ambience. It's an easy 1.2-mile (2-km) jaunt from the ferry dock at Descanso Bay to the park along Taylor Bay Rd. Walk the beach at Taylor Bay to the limestone formations called the Malaspina Galleries. An easier approach to them from the park is via Malaspina Dr, which leads east off Taylor Bay Rd. A trail leads from the drive's end to Malaspina Point and the Galleries.

Also reached from Nanaimo harbour is **Newcastle Island Provincial Marine Park** (see Camping/Parks, above) a delightfully adventurous location for a picnic. Part of the thrill is riding the foot-passenger ferry to the island, which gives visitors a feeling for activity in the harbour. As you move away from Nanaimo, the Vancouver Island Mountains come into view as they rise above the town. Once on the island, you find trails leading off in many directions, including to the well-organized picnic ground beside the Pavilion, a grand leftover from the dance-hall era. Newcastle was the site of commercial activity before it was turned into a park. Explore the old limestone quarry where the columns for the US Federal Mint in San Francisco were shaped. An unfinished one remains as an example of the work done here. Just as interesting is the site of a fish-salting plant nearby.

Beaches/Swimming

As you explore from island to island, you'll find dozens of small beaches along the convoluted shorelines. While all shoreline is public land in

British Columbia, not all of it is easily reached, nor does much of it provide a pleasant place to relax while watching the ebb and flow of the tides. Here's a sampling of some of the best and most readily accessible places in the southern Gulf Islands.

One of the prettiest beaches on all the islands is at **Salt Spring Island**'s **Ruckle Provincial Park** (see Camping/Parks, above). A trail leads down to the secluded beach from the nearby campground. It's easy to imagine generations of island families making their way here on hot summer days when the Ruckle farm was in full swing. A tall forest surmounts the beach, much of it sturdy first-growth Douglas fir, but there are also a number of hardwood species planted by the Ruckles that are a delight come fall. This beach is a wonderful refuge from the outside world, a place to find a sturdy piece of driftwood for a backrest and relax.

Drummond Park at the head of nearby Fulford Harbour has a more exposed pebble beach to explore. Look for the ancient pictograph image carved in the face of one of the larger boulders on the beach. Although the wooded setting at **Weston Lake,** about 2 miles (3 km) north of Fulford Harbour, is less picturesque than by the ocean, there is a sandy beach here where you can enjoy a freshwater swim.

One of the best beaches on the **Pender Islands** is at **Mortimer Spit,** close to the canal between the two islands. A snout of sand where you'll find plenty of room and few visitors to share the beach with juts out into Navy Channel. A more popular spot is just north at **Hamilton Beach** at Port Browning. You'll find a more festive atmosphere here in summer with a pub, marina, cafe, and picnic tables beside the beach. On the far shore, visible from Hamilton, is a sandy strip of beach at **Razor Point.** Take Bedwell Bay Rd south from the ferry dock at Otter Bay to reach Hamilton Beach. Follow Razor Point Rd east of Port Browning to find the small beach on the point.

If you take the time to travel to the very end of South Pender Island, you'll find the small beach park at **Gowlland Point Park,** the prettiest of all the beaches on the two Penders. A pebble beach slopes down to an indented shoreline. During winter storms, which pound this exposed coast with regularity, the ocean moves the cobblestones around with percussive effect. From the beach, you look due south into the San Juan Islands, west across the Strait of Juan de Fuca to Hurricane Ridge on Washington State's Olympic Peninsula and east to Saturna Island's Monarch Head, with Mount Baker rising above the mainland. To reach the park from the ferry dock, follow Bedwell Bay, Canal, Spalding, and finally Gowlland Point Rd to its southern terminus. If you want solitude, this is where to find it.

Much of the beach at **Miners Bay** on **Mayne Island** is composed of a gently sloping shelf of smooth rock. At low tide much of this table rock is revealed and makes for interesting exploration. Miners Bay is the commercial hub of Mayne Island and is anchored by the historic Springwater Lodge (see Cheaper Eats, below). Make your way from the ferry dock along Village Bay Rd, an easy walk or bike ride (see Biking, below). A beautiful sand-and-pebble beach is located on Mayne Island's east side at **Campbell Bay.** The trail leading down to the beach is not well marked but isn't difficult to locate. Follow Georgina Point Rd east of Miners Bay to its junction with Waugh Rd. Head south on Waugh, and as the road rounds Campbell Bay, watch for a shady trail that runs down the embankment to the ocean below. An overhanging forest shades the beach, providing a cool place to relax out of the sun. Big pieces of driftwood sit mired in the sand, ready to prop you up to enjoy the view as you look due east across the strait towards Vancouver.

Fishing

St. Mary Lake, near the north end of **Salt Spring Island,** is an anomaly. There are few freshwater lakes on any of the islands. St. Mary Lake is large enough to hold the rest of them put together. Stocked with trout and smallmouth bass, the lake is reached from a small beach and boat launch at the junction of Upper and Lower Ganges Rds and Vesuvius Bay Rd. Powerboats are not permitted here, except those with electric motors. For more information on fishing on Salt Spring Island, contact Salt Spring Marina at Harbour's End in Ganges, (250) 537-5810. They even rent tackle.

Owing to the strength of the tidal currents coursing through **Active Pass** between Mayne and Galiano Islands, there are plenty of nutrients in the water to attract marine life. Salmon feed in these waters, although in recent years the large chinook have all but disappeared. It's not as easy to purchase fresh seafood on the islands as you might imagine. Most islanders do their own crabbing and shrimping, but at **Horton Bay** on **Mayne Island,** you may find such delicacies for sale. Although the availability is seasonal, stop by the federal dock between 4 and 6pm and look for a truck with the personalized licence plates "CRAB 4U," which says it all. For more information on fishing in the waters of Active Pass around Mayne and Galiano Islands, contact Viable Marine Service, (250) 539-3200, and Active Pass Auto & Marine, (250) 539-5411, in Miners Bay on Mayne Island; and the Corner Store, (250) 539-2986, in Sturdies Bay on Galiano.

Saturna Island's **East Point Park** (see Picnics/Parks, above) is a good place to spin-cast for salmon that feed in back eddies created by the swirling currents.

One of the best places to begin a boating fishing trip in the Gulf

Islands is from **Silva Bay** at the south end of **Gabriola Island.** The nearby **Flat Top Islands** are a guaranteed hotspot to mooch for salmon. It's hard to keep a secret. You can tell where the fish are biting by looking to see where boats are congregating.

Other good contacts for information on salmon fishing in the southern and central Gulf Islands include Pacific Shoreline Adventure, (250) 629-9970, toll-free (800) 714-9260, and Otter Bay Marina, (250) 629-3579, on North Pender Island.

Kayaking/Boating

One of the most soulful ways to explore the Gulf Islands is in a sea kayak. Safer and more stable than a canoe, sea kayaks allow you to travel in comfort, with as much gear and goodies as you can manage to stow into the ample storage compartments fore and aft. If you bring your own kayak or canoe with you, BC Ferries treats them as hand baggage and there is no charge. Plan to launch from any of the ferry docks or federal wharfs on the Gulf Islands and paddle off towards the nearest provincial marine park. In most cases distance are quite short—less than 5 miles (8 km)—and benefit from protected waters. Tidal currents only present difficulties in several places, most notably Active and Porlier Passes, at the south and north end of Galiano Island, respectively. Consult tide tables to determine the most favourable times to negotiate these routes. (Note: As Active Pass is used by BC Ferries, use extreme caution when navigating here.) As a general rule, camping is only permitted in designated sites in the Gulf Islands. A ban on campfires is in effect in the Gulf Islands from April to October, and freshwater and toilet facilities are extremely limited, so plan accordingly.

Some of the more popular and easier-to-reach parks—all described above, in Camping/Parks—include **Montague Harbour Provincial Marine Park** and **Dionisio Provincial Park** on Galiano Island, and **Beaumont Provincial Marine Park** on the Pender Islands, as well as **Winter Cove Provincial Marine Park** on Saturna Island (no camping here though; see Picnics/Parks, above). Other marine parks include **Cabbage Island,** off the northeast coast of Tumbo Island east of Winter Cove Marine Park, and the large **Princess Margaret Marine Park** on Portland Island between Salt Spring and the Pender Islands. Maps and paddling information for each of these parks are available from BC Parks, (250) 391-2300.

Galiano Island is the centre for sea kayaking in the southern islands. You won't have to walk farther than the first intersection north of the ferry dock at Sturdies Bay to reach Gulf Island Kayaking, (250) 539-2442, Web site address: www.seakayak.bc.ca/tour, which offers **guided tours** of the islands and rents kayaks and canoes.

On Mayne Island, across the water from Galiano, contact Mayne Island Kayak and Canoe Rentals, (250) 539-2667 or 539-0077, for information on touring and camping. On North Pender Island, try Mouat Point Kayaking, (250) 629-6767. Salt Spring Island Kayaking, (250) 537-4664, is located on the wharf at Fulford Harbour, a great launch spot for exploring nearby Portland Island. A reliable contact on Gabriola Island is Gabriola Cycle and Kayaking, (250) 247-8277. Nearby in Nanaimo, Western Wildcat Tours' "Kayak Shack" rents kayaks and canoes; (250) 753-3234.

Good marine charts to consult for the waters around the Gulf Islands are #3441 Haro Strait, Boundary Pass, and Satellite Channel; #3442 North Pender Island to Thetis Island; and #3452 Thetis Island to Nanaimo. To get a good feel for adventuring by sea kayak in the Gulf Islands, consult *Sea Kayaking Canada's West Coast* by John Ince and Hadi Köttner.

For those who come with car-top or hand-carried boats, there are numerous places to launch throughout the islands, beginning with any number of public wharfs and federal docks. Suitable locations include Horton Bay on **Mayne Island** (see Biking, below); Montague Harbour Provincial Marine Park (see Camping/Parks, above) and Retreat Cove on **Galiano Island;** Grimmer Bay, Hope Bay, Port Browning, and Miracle Beach (see Camping/Parks, above) on **North Pender Island;** Bedwell Harbour and Gowlland Point (see Beaches/Swimming, above) at the foot of Craddock Rd on **South Pender Island;** and Silva Bay (see Biking, below) on **Gabriola Island.**

Biking

It's easy to imagine that you're **cycling** along rugged mountain tops as you pump your way around any of the Gulf Islands. You can count on hills, hills, and more hills, as well as narrow roads that are often inadequate for the increasing amount of traffic as island populations rise. All of the routes are "do-able," provided you have enough time.

Mayne Island is perhaps the most pleasant one to cycle. You can tour the whole island in the course of an easygoing day (about 18.5 miles/30 km), with stops around its perimeter at Miners Bay (see Beaches/Swimming, above), the Georgina Point lighthouse (visiting hours 1–3pm daily), Campbell Bay (see Beaches/Swimming, above), Horton Bay (see Fishing, above), and the BC Ferries dock at Village Bay. As with all islands, freshwater is a precious and often rare substance. One of the few places to fill your water bottles is at **Dinner Point Community Day Park,** a short ride south of Village Bay. A detailed road map of the island is available at the information kiosk at the dock. If you want to stay overnight on the island, there are many bed-and-breakfasts as well as a private campground run by

Mayne Island Kayaking, (250) 539-2667 or 539-0077.

A ride around **Gabriola Island** is lengthy—the island is about 12 miles (20 km) long—but touches on a variety of good beaches, including Gabriola Sands Provincial Park (see Picnics/Parks, above), Sandwell and Drumbeg Provincial Parks, roadside picnic tables at Brickyard Beach, and the sheltered enclave at Silva Bay, a popular stopover for marine traffic in summer and a good place to wet your whistle. Pedalling Gabriola is a fairly straightforward endeavour: North and South Rds loop around opposite sides of the island and meet at Silva Bay. For a special insight into the aboriginal mythology of the Cowichan Nation, take time to view the petroglyphs carved in the rock face of a field behind Gabriola United Church on South Rd. Follow a trail behind the church through the forest to an open field and begin exploring the rock face for ancient images. For more information on cycling Gabriola Island, contact Gabriola Cycle and Kayaking, (250) 247-8277.

Other sources of cycling information include Island Spoke Folk, (250) 537-4664, and Sports Traders, (250) 537-5588, in Ganges on Salt Spring Island, and Brett's Bicycle Base on the Pender Islands, (250) 629-3888.

Of all the southern islands, **Galiano Island** has the most well-organized mountain-biking trail system. Galiano Bicycle Rental and Repairs in Sturdies Bay, (250) 539-9907, is a good place to visit when exploring the rugged, spiny island. You'll pass the shop at the corner of Sturdies Bay and Burrill Rds on the way to **Bluffs Park,** the site of some spectacular views and the beginning of a network of trails and roads around Mount Galiano. From Sturdies Bay Rd, go south on Burrill to Bluff Rd, then west from here to the park and beyond.

Bicycles are allowed on both the **Kanaka Bay Trail** and **Mallard Lake Trail** in **Newcastle Island Provincial Marine Park** (see Camping/Parks, above). These are gentle, wide pathways shared with pedestrians.

Wildlife

Along the crest of **Galiano Island**'s long sandstone spine, the **Bodega Ridge Trail** (3 miles/5 km return) loops through a rare coastal habitat of Douglas fir, hairy manzanita, and Garry oak. Following the 1,076-foot-high (328-m) ridge, the first half of the trail encompasses a panorama that includes the Trincomali Channel, the hilly profile of Salt Spring Island, and the shadowy outline of the mountains of Vancouver Island. In contrast, the second half of the trail loops beneath the shade of tall Douglas firs, along paths and old logging roads heavily overgrown with hip-high salal, nettles, and brambles. Saved by the determination of the island's 950 permanent residents, the trail and the 368-acre (150-ha) **Bodega Ridge**

Nature Preserve—with its nesting **bald eagles** and **peregrine falcons**, and a separate 5-mile (8-km) section along the shore—could have been lost in perpetuity. However, in July 1995 the federal and provincial governments, together with The Nature Conservancy of Canada, purchased the land, and with the help of the newly established Pacific Marine Heritage Legacy agreement, the preserve has been saved.

The well-used trail starts at the faded Bodega Ridge Nature Trail sign at the end of Cottage Way. Cottage Way is off Porlier Pass Rd, about 12 miles (19 km) north of the Sturdies Bay ferry terminal. **Turkey vultures** call Galiano Island's Bodega Ridge home. There's a good chance that if you walk up on the ridge you'll see them circling on the updrafts. Others sit hunched at the top of skeletal Douglas fir trees and look down with beady eyes. Even if you've never seen a turkey vulture at close quarters, you'll instantly recognize its bald, red head, which definitely does look like a turkey.

The Bodega Ridge pathway has its own "self-appointed hostess," or so the sign outside her house says. Meghann is an old Irish setter that lives in a house on Cottage Way at the foot of the trail. She likes to accompany hikers going onto the ridge and is often found bounding around beneath the arbutus trees and Douglas firs. Five minutes of gentle, uphill walking through salal growing under a canopy of Douglas firs brings you to a clearing of Scotch broom. At the far end of the clearing, a sign cautions, "Proceed at your own risk. Steep rugged terrain." Just past the sign, the trail divides. Bear left here. Farther along the trail, past another sign warning of the impending dangerous terrain, the ridge drops away dramatically, revealing a magnificent view across the islands, mountains, and water. Far below, Wallace Island sits squat in the middle of Trincomali Channel. The Secretaries, Mogli, Norway, Hall, and Reid Islands lie like stepping stones in the narrow strait between Galiano and Salt Spring Islands. Farther northwest, beyond Kuper and Thetis Islands, lurk the shadowy outlines of the mountains of Vancouver Island. Spreading in a soothing collage of blues, greys, and greens, the unfolding scenery is balm to citified eyes.

Heading north along the edge of the ridge between the arbutus trees and clumps of hairy manzanita—this shrub grows more profusely on Bodega Ridge than anywhere else in the Gulf Islands—you'll reach a large slab of sand right on the ridge edge. Less than 2 miles (3.22 km) from the trailhead, you may well have spotted a turkey vulture or two by now. At a distance it's easy to confuse immature bald eagles with turkey vultures. Both birds soar in a similar way, and even with binoculars it is difficult to make out the red heads of the vultures. (In the US, Cherokee Indians call turkey vultures "peace eagles" because of their similarity to eagles, but soften the name because, unlike eagles, vultures don't kill prey.)

There's a good chance of spotting **killer whales** from Saturna Island's East Point Park (see Picnics/Parks, above) and South Pender Island's Gowlland Point Park (see Beaches/Swimming, above), particularly from May to October.

Newcastle Island Provincial Park (see Camping/Parks, above), in Nanaimo harbour, is renowned as a bird-watcher's paradise. Thousands of **shorebirds** throng its coastline year-round, including such hard workers as the red-billed **black oystercatcher.** For the best viewing, follow the Shoreline Trail (about 2.5 miles/4 km return) from the ferry wharf counterclockwise around the island to Brownie and Kanaka Bays.

Upswelling currents bring cold, nutrient-rich water to the surface around narrow passages between islands, such as in Active Pass, which divides Galiano and Mayne, and Porlier Pass, between Galiano and Valdes. In April and early May, thousands of **Bonaparte's gulls,** decked out in their black-headed breeding plumage, gather to feed on tiny shrimp or krill that float on the surface of Active Pass. Herring runs at this time of year attract **California sea lions** and **bald eagles** as well as hundreds of jet-black **Pacific loons** and **Brandt's cormorants.** One of the best places to observe all this action is from the deck of a BC Ferries vessel as it reduces speed when moving through Active Pass.

Hiking

Because the Gulf Islands are so tightly configured, it's often difficult to determine where one begins and another leaves off, especially as Vancouver Island provides such a big backdrop that it takes on the appearance of a mini-mainland. One of the best ways to sort things out is to take a hike to some of the higher viewpoints. There aren't as many hiking trails found in the islands as on the mainland. In part, this is a reflection of size, steepness, and also choice: most visitors come to the islands to indulge in activities centred around the water. You will find good hiking and walking trails, however, on **Galiano Island**'s **Bluffs Park** and the **Bodega Ridge Trail** in the Bodega Ridge Nature Preserve (see Wildlife, above).

Another viewpoint worth seeking out is on **South Pender Island.** Mount Norman dominates the southern half of the twin islands, forcing traffic to divert around its north flank. Take Canal Rd west where it divides and continue a short distance to the trailhead for **Mount Norman Regional Park.** From here it's a steep 1-mile (1.6-km) walk uphill along an old logging road. The detritus left behind from recent logging is not a pretty sight, and it will be some time before reforestation masks the damage. Make the journey only on a day when you're guaranteed a good view.

Once on top you'll find an observation platform with a wooden bench on which to rest while you get out your binoculars. The views from here are directly west over Bedwell harbour towards Salt Spring Island, Victoria, and southern Vancouver Island and south across Boundary Pass into Washington. Follow a rough trail from the viewpoint boardwalk through the salal to the east side of Mount Norman for a view of the sun-weathered flanks of Saturna Island, and beyond to Vancouver and the British Columbia–Washington mainland. For more information on Mount Norman Regional Park, contact Capital Regional District Parks, (250) 478-3344; Web site: http://www.crd.bc.ca/parks/index.

Almost 12 miles (20 km) of trails loop around **Newcastle Island Provincial Park** (see Camping/Parks, above) and lead to the grandest viewpoint at Giovanda Lookout. From the ferry wharf on Newcastle's south end, follow the Mallard Lake Trail and then the Nares Point Trail. The lookout is located along the Nares Point Trail near the northwest tip of the island. Cliffs drop away dramatically in front of the lookout with views stretching across the Strait of Georgia to the Lower Mainland. Continue back to the wharf via the Kanaka Bay and Shoreline Trail (see Wildlife, above).

The most challenging hiking of all is found on **Salt Spring Island,** where rough trails lead to the tops of both **Bruce Peak** (2,326 feet/709 m) and **Mount Tuam** (1,975 feet/602 m), the tallest points of land on the Gulf Islands. From Fulford Harbour at the south end of the island, follow the Fulford-Ganges Rd north to Jones Rd, then west on Jones to reach the Bruce Peak trailhead. Alternatively, take Musgrave Rd west from Fulford Harbour to reach them both, though eventually by different routes. One leads north off Musgrave to Bruce, while another leads south to Tuam. You'll find great views from both down onto the Saanich Inlet and Peninsula, and across Satellite Channel to Cowichan Bay. If you make this hike in summer, take plenty of drinking water with you as these open slopes are baked by the sun.

A good map to consult is the Gulf Islands Recreation Map by World Wide Books and Maps, (604) 687-3320. Good books to consult for information on these and additional trails include *Hiking the Gulf Islands* by Kahn and *The Gulf Islands Explorer* by Bruce Obee. See also More Information at end of chapter.

outside in

Attractions

Development in the Gulf Islands is sparse—a shop or two at the ferry terminal, some farms and pastureland, a scattering of lodgings. Well-stocked stores, bank machines, gas stations, and even restaurants are scarce to nonexistent on most of the islands, so plan accordingly. **Canadian Gulf Islands Bed & Breakfast Reservation Service,** (250) 539-5390, has maps of the islands, which indicate B&B locations.

Despite being the first stop off the Tsawwassen ferry, **Galiano Island** retains an undeveloped, secluded character. Dedicated residents have worked hard to protect the natural features that extend along the island's narrow, 19-mile (30-km) length. Pick up a map onboard the ferry (check the brochure rack) or ask at the island ferry dock. With barely 1,200 permanent residents, Galiano has one gas station, no bank, and a few stores, including some interesting **craft galleries,** all clustered at the southern end. Eateries are scarce, although you'll find hearty pub food and local colour at the popular Hummingbird Inn (junction of Sturdies Bay and Georgeson Bay Rds, (250) 539-5472). Drop by the Trincomali Bakery and Deli, just up the hill from the ferry dock, for coffee and a bun while you peruse the latest real estate listings and dream about your island hideaway.

Named for the cold and briny springs on the north end of the island, **Salt Spring Island** is the largest, most populated, and most visited of the Gulf chain. It's serviced by three ferry routes: Tsawwassen–Long Harbour, Crofton-Vesuvius, and Swartz Bay–Fulford. The island is known for its **sheep-raising;** be sure to tour the rolling pastures on the north end (visit in the spring, and you'll never order rack of lamb again). Salt Spring is also known as a centre for arts and crafts; pick up a map of the **studios** from the tourist bureau, (250) 537-5252.

All roads lead to **Ganges** here, the biggest and most bustling town in the Gulfs. There are more stores, services, restaurants, and galleries (not to mention tourists and cars) crammed into Ganges than exist on any other island. Even nonshoppers, however, enjoy historic **Mouat's Mall,** a rickety white-and-green building where you can browse a fine art collection at Pegasus Gallery, (250) 537-2421. Walk down to the water for lunch at Alfresco's, where you'll find marvellous bread and up to five different soupes du jour (if you're lucky, they'll have the roasted garlic and Spanish sausage); then stop next door at the Naikai Gallery for more art and crafts; (250) 537-4400. On Saturday mornings in the summer, wander the **farmers' market** in the park; head any summer day to the **crafts market** at Mahon Hall on Lower Ganges Rd.

Fulford, at the island's southern end, consists mostly of a few crafts shops, a Mexican cafe, the ferry terminal, and a decidedly laid-back atmosphere. Next to the ferry dock at the island's northern end is Vesuvius Inn, (250) 537-2312. The food ranges from good to so-so, but the view from the veranda fully compensates: this is one of the few ferry docks where you can park your car in line, then wander over and quaff a beer while you wait for your ship to come in.

Rolling orchards and warm rock-strewn beaches abound on **Mayne Island,** a rustic 5-square-mile (13-square-km) spot. It's small enough for a day trip, but pretty enough for a lifetime. Drop by the lighthouse, watch the frantic activity as fishermen wait till the last minute to get out of the ferry's way in Active Pass, or stroll up to the top of Mayne's mountain for a view of the Strait of Georgia—and you'll begin to discover what Mayne is all about.

North and South Pender Islands are separated by a canal and united by a bridge. Much of the islands is green and rural, but a massive subdivision on North Pender was one of the catalysts for the creation of the watchdog Islands Trust in the 1970s, as Gulf Islanders worried that similar development could spell an end to the islands' charm. The population is decidedly residential; don't expect many restaurants, lodgings, or shops. The ferry lands at the dock in Otter Bay, where the Stand, (250) 629-3292—an unprepossessing trailer—grills the best burgers (try the venison or the oyster burgers) around. If you can get a group of 10 to 30 people together, Clam Bay Country Estate, (800) 626-5955, is well worth checking out. This 100-acre (40-ha) farm estate, with cabins and cottages in the woods and on the beach, is getting excellent reviews as the location for a company or group retreat, but they accept only groups.

Rural, sparsely populated, and difficult to reach, **Saturna Island** is easily the least spoiled of the Gulf Islands. Saturna's big social event is the annual **lamb barbeque,** held on Canada Day (July 1).

Although **Gabriola Island,** the most accessible of the chain, has become a bedroom community for nearby Nanaimo (20 minutes by ferry), it manages to remain fairly rustic and beachy.

Restaurants

House Piccolo ☆☆ Some of the best food in Ganges can be had at this cozy house/restaurant right in the middle of things. The menu is European with a decidedly Scandinavian slant. Don't miss dessert. *108 Hereford Ave (heading north, it's at second main intersection in town, near Thrifty Foods), Ganges; (250) 537-1844; $$.*

La Berengerie ☆ This quaint restaurant is run by an owner/chef/hotelier who offers a four-course menu. Service and atmosphere are casual, but reservations are a must. In summer there's a vegetarian-only outdoor dining cafe (Cafe Boheme). Four modest guest rooms, too. Closed November through March. *Montague Harbour Rd (corner of Clanton Rd), Galiano Island, BC V0N 1P0; (250) 539-5392; $$.*

Pomodori ☆ "Eclectic" describes just about everything at this restaurant, which serves Mediterranean farmhouse cuisine and is filled with whitewashed tables and overstuffed couches. The view is enchanting. Two rooms are also rented out. *375 Baker Rd (take Vesuvius Bay Rd north from Ganges and watch for Booth Bay/Pomodori sign), Salt Spring Island; (250) 537-2247; $$$.*

Saturna Lodge ☆☆ Diners boat in from other islands for the prix-fixe menu, which is a steal at $20 a head—three courses, three choices with each course, and a well-chosen wine list. The B&B rooms upstairs are contemporary, with private baths and views. Reservations are essential. *130 Payne Rd (follow signs from ferry); PO Box 54, Saturna Island, BC V0N 2Y0; (250) 539-2254 or (888) 539-8800; $$–$$$.*

Cheaper Eats

The Flying Saucer Cafe The cafe is quickly becoming a favourite for vegetarian food at island-friendly prices. The decor is friendly-funky-artsy: ditto for the food. A perfect spot to curl up with a book and a mug of tea. *112 Hereford Ave, Salt Spring Island; (250) 537-0500; $.*

Lighthouse Pub For a casual nosh, head to this spot beside the ferry terminal, for lunch and dinner specials. The food is so-so, and the atmosphere is a trifle rough around the edges, but the setting, with its views of Lyle Harbour, is gorgeous. *102 E Point Rd, Saturna Island; (250) 539-5725; $.*

Moby's Marine Pub There are pubs. And then there are great pubs. Moby's falls into the latter category, with the tastiest, most imaginative pub menu on the islands. Natives and visitors jostle for elbow room in the lively atmosphere. *120 Upper Ganges Rd, Salt Spring Island; (250) 537-5559; $.*

Rodrigo's Is this place so popular because the food is great and cheap, or because it's so handy to the ferry terminal? We're not sure, but the Mexican-style food is tasty, portions are generous, and the company is colourful and friendly. Pastries are memorable. *2921 Fulford-Ganges Rd, Salt Spring Island; (250) 653-9222; $.*

The Salt Spring Roasting Company For the best coffee on these islands (and the best people-watching on Salt Spring) plus great pastries, sandwiches, and pizza, you can't beat this spot in downtown Ganges, where coffee is roasted fresh each morning. *109 McPhillips Ave, Salt Spring Island; (250) 537-0826; $.*

Springwater Lodge For reliable, inexpensive food, you could do worse than to sink your teeth into a burger here. Funky rusticity is the general decor theme, but the setting and the genial, low-key atmosphere make this an appealing choice. Inexpensive lodgings available, too. *400 Fernhill Rd, Mayne Island; (250) 539-5521; $.*

White Hart Pub This spot, on the doorstep of the ferry landing, is a convenient place to grab a bite, either on the deck or amid the dark pub atmosphere. There's a pool table and a decent selection of beers. Expect standard pub fare. *1 South Rd, Gabriola Island; (250) 247-8588; $.*

Lodgings

The Beach House on Sunset Drive ☆☆ This extraordinary property is in a league of its own, and the owners were born to be B&B hosts. The sprawling home is right on the ocean; the four-course breakfasts are legendary. Two guest rooms are in the main house, but best is the cozy boathouse. *930 Sunset Dr (up Sunset Dr from Vesuvius Bay), RR 1, Salt Spring Island, BC V8K 1E6; (250) 537-2879; $$$.*

Beddis House Bed and Breakfast ☆ It isn't easy to find a B&B on the water, but this charming farmhouse sits close to a private beach on Ganges Harbour. The three rooms offer claw-footed tubs, country-style furniture, and decks or balconies. *131 Miles Ave (follow Beddis Rd from Fulford-Ganges Rd, turn left onto Miles Rd), Salt Spring Island, BC V8K 2E1; (250) 537-1028; $$$.*

Bedwell Harbour Island Resort This sprawling resort complex includes a marina, rooms, cabins, villas in a condo building, a pub, and a restaurant (and there may be more in the works). Condos are newer and more luxurious than cabins. The waterfront pub offers typical pub fare. Closed winters. *9801 Spalding Rd (follow Canal Rd from bridge to Spalding, Spalding to Bedwell Harbour), South Pender Island, BC V0N 2M3; (250) 629-3212 or (800) 663-2899; $$.*

Bodega Resort ☆ On a high bluff is a Western-style resort, ideal for families or large groups. There are seven two-storey chalets, each with three bedrooms, a fully equipped kitchen, and decks, plus horseback riding, a trout pond, and hiking trails. *120 Monasty Rd (follow Porlier Pass Rd 14 miles/22.5 km north of Sturdies Bay to Cook Rd, then to Monasty Rd);*

PO Box 115, Galiano Island, BC V0N 1P0; (250) 539-2677; $$.

Corbett House B&B ☆ A fine B&B in a beautiful pastoral setting. All the rooms are all equally cozy (but one has a full bath and private balcony). The hosts provide an ample breakfast. Long country walks fit in well here. *4309 Corbett Rd (0.5 mile/0.3 km from ferry on Corbett Rd; call ahead for directions), RR1, Pender Island, BC V0N 2M0; (250) 629-6305; $$.*

Green Rose Farm and Guest House ☆☆ The hosts have restored this 1916 farmhouse on acres of orchard, meadow, and woods, and the result is classic and inviting. Decor is farmhouse-nautical, with painted pine floors and handsome pinstriped wallpaper. All three guest rooms have private baths. *346 Robinson Rd (take Upper Ganges Rd, stay right until Robinson), Salt Spring Island, BC V8K 1P7; (250) 537-9927; $$$.*

Hastings House ☆☆☆☆ It aspires to be the ultimate country retreat, and nearly achieves that goal. Farm buildings and a cottage, surrounded by meadows and gardens, overlook a cove, and the suites are beautifully furnished. Whether you stay here or not, reserve a place at the table d'hôte dinner. Dinner begins with cocktails, and progresses through five expertly prepared courses. *160 Upper Ganges Rd (just north of Ganges), Salt Spring Island, BC V8K 2S2; (250) 537-2362; $$$.*

Mount Galiano Eagle's Nest ☆☆ This unusual home is nestled at the foot of Mount Galiano and it sits on 75 acres (30 ha) of land and a kilometre of waterfront—all abutting the Galiano Mountain Wilderness Park. The garden is a work of art, as is every breakfast. The three rooms are lovely. *2-720 Active Pass Dr (call for directions), Galiano Island, BC V0N 1P0; (250) 539-2567; $$.*

Oceanwood Country Inn ☆☆☆ This fine island inn continues to garner rave reviews for its facilities, its location, its cuisine—but most of all, for the hospitality of its owners. Breakfasts are innovative and hearty, dinner is a set four-course menu. *630 Dinner Bay Rd (right on Dalton Dr, right on Mariners, immediate left onto Dinner Bay Rd; look for sign), Mayne Island, BC V0N 2J0; (250) 539-5074; $$$.*

The Old Farmhouse ☆☆☆ The German-born hosts have turned their heritage farmhouse into an inn worthy of *House Beautiful*. Four guest rooms, each with a patio or balcony, are charmingly decorated. An elegant and copious breakfast is served. *1077 North End Rd (2.5 miles/4 km north of Ganges), RR4, Salt Spring Island, BC V8K 1L9; (250) 537-4113; $$$.*

Pauper's Perch ☆ This is one of the best views you'll find on Salt Spring, from 1,000 feet (300 m) above the sea. All three rooms are comfortable, and the host sometimes presents Mexican dishes for breakfast. Closed winters. *225 Armand Way (Fulford-Ganges Rd to Dukes Rd, up hill to Seymour Heights, then onto Armand Way—don't give up), Salt Spring Island, BC V8K 2B6; (250) 653-2030; $$$.*

Spindrift ☆ Perfect: a place on the ocean, secluded, quiet, with forest walks outside your door. The oceanfront cottages on the peninsula all have ocean views and full kitchens. No telephones, no televisions, no hot tubs—just quiet. *255 Welbury Dr (on Welbury Point, near Long Harbour ferry terminal), Salt Spring Island, BC V8K 2L7; (250) 537-5311; $$–$$$.*

Stone House Farm Resort ☆☆ This farmhouse perched above a bay transports you to a 17th-century English inn with its gardens, Tudor construction, and period furniture. Three guest rooms have balconies, and a cottage sleeps eight. 207 *Narvaez Bay Rd (from ferry, take East Point Rd to Narvaez Bay Rd, follow nearly to end); Box 10, Saturna Island, BC V0N 2Y0; (250) 539-2683; $$$.*

Woodstone Country Inn ☆☆☆ The host is anxious to indulge, and the setting, overlooking field and forest, is relaxing. Each room is spacious and bright; all have sitting rooms. The dining room ranks high with its reasonably priced table d'hôte dinner. Closed January. *Georgeson Bay Rd (bear left off Sturdies Bay Rd, follow signs to turnoff), RR1, Galiano Island, BC V0N 1P0; (250) 539-2022; $$$.*

Cheaper Sleeps

Cliff Pagoda Bed and Breakfast This Oriental-style B&B stands out for its design and breathtaking views. Bicyclists are rewarded with bicycle racks. Rooms are small and bathrooms are shared, but with the porch and hot tub, why stay in your room? *2851 Montague Harbour Rd, Galiano Island, BC V0N 1P0; (250) 539-2260; $.*

Cusheon Creek Hostel The only official hostel in the islands rents basic, clean accommodations in a variety of configurations: two dorms, a family room, three tepees, and a treehouse (showers and washrooms are shared). Only a short hike from lake and beach. *640 Cusheon Lake Rd, Salt Spring Island, BC V8K 2C2; (250) 537-4149; $.*

Inn on Pender Island For its wooded location, its clean, comfortable rooms, and a few amenities that go beyond the minimum, the Inn gets our vote. Ten more bucks buys a larger room with a sofa. There's also a decent restaurant and pizza bar. *4709 Canal Rd, North Pender Island, BC V0N 2M0; (250) 629-3353 or (800) 550-0172; $.*

Surf Lodge You'll find a very relaxed atmosphere at this rustic lodge across from the beach, with a saltwater pool and outdoor recreational facilities. Accommodations include rooms or cabins, some with kitchens. The lodge has a restaurant and a lounge. *855 Berry Point Rd (RR 1, Site 1, C17), Gabriola Island, BC V0R 1X0; (250) 247-9231; $.*

The Tides Inn This spot in the centre of Ganges is one of Salt Spring's rare bargains. There's not much of a view from the bedroom windows, but the rooms are charming and immaculate with character. Bathrooms are shared. *132 Lower Ganges Rd, Salt Spring Island, BC V8K 2S9; (250) 537-1097; $.*

More Information

See also Getting There at beginning of chapter.

BC Ferries: *(250) 386-3431 or toll-free in Canada, (888) 223-3779.*

BC Parks: *(250) 391-2300.*

Capital Regional District (CRD) Parks: *(250) 478-3344, Web site: http://www.crd.bc.ca/parks/index.*

Galiano Island InfoCentre: *(250) 539-2233.*

Gulf Islands Recreation Map: *Published by World Wide Books and Maps, 736A Granville St, Vancouver, V6Z 1G3, (604) 687-3320; as well as presenting a detailed 1:50,000 scale look at the southern Gulf Islands, it's also loaded with pertinent names and addresses of destinations, accommodations, boat launches, docks, marinas and wharves, grocery stores, lighthouses, museums and historic places, campgrounds, parks and beaches, as well as galleries and artisans on each island.*

Salt Spring Island Chamber of Commerce: *(250) 537-4223.*

Northern Gulf Islands

From Lasqueti Island near Parkville north to Quadra and Cortes Islands near Campbell River, and from Texada Island near Powell River north to Savary and the Copeland Islands near Lund, including Jedediah Island Provincial Park.

These islands, part of the chain of 6,000 islands that shelter the British Columbia coastline between Washington and Alaska, lie beyond the quick-access range of Vancouver and Victoria. The fleet of BC Ferries that services some of them is not as large nor are the sailings as frequent. Others can only be reached by private transportation such as water taxis, kayaks, canoes, or powerboats, and occasionally airplanes. Visitors will find that the farther north in the Strait of Georgia they explore, the fewer fellow travellers they'll encounter. The wonderful silence that envelops these islands is characteristic of the ambience in remote central coast locales. It wasn't always this way. In the heyday of fishing and logging camps, the population on the more isolated islands was surprisingly higher than it is today. Evidence of this can be seen in abandoned cabins, ancient villages, and overgrown logging roads. Explore by car, kayak, mountain bike, or on foot. Find a location that appeals to you, and within this microcosm experience the wonder and magic that pervades life here.

Getting There

Lasqueti Island is reached by foot ferry from French Creek, a short distance north of Parksville on Vancouver Island's Hwy 19A. Turn right when you arrive at the wharf and drive to the south end to where a ramp leads down to the Centurion VII. *Unload here. Get a boarding pass, particularly at busy times. A book of them hangs from a kiosk on the wharf beside the ferry. (This is equally important when returning to Parksville from Lasqueti.) You must pay an overnight* *parking fee of $2.50 if you are leaving a vehicle in the lot. The Lasqueti Island ferry departs for False Bay on Lasqueti's northwest corner at 9:30am, 2:30pm, and 5:30pm every day except for Tuesday and Wednesday. Kayaks up to 15 feet in length can be taken on as cargo at a charge of $10. A one-way ticket for foot passengers is $4.50. The crossing takes about an hour. For fares and schedule information, call Western Pacific Marine in Vancouver, (604) 681-5199. Access to Jedediah Island Provincial Park is by private boat from Lasqueti Island.*

Denman Island is reached by BC Ferries from Buckley Bay on Vancouver Island. BC Ferries also links Gravelly Bay on Denman's east side with Shingle Spit on Hornby Island's west side. Ferries to both islands transport vehicles. Travel time from Vancouver Island to Denman Island, and from Denman Island to Hornby Island, is a brief 10–15 minutes. Sandy Island Provincial Marine Park, off the north end of Denman Island, can only be reached by private boat.

Quadra Island's Quathiaski Cove is reached by BC Ferries from Campbell River on Vancouver Island. BC Ferries also links Heriot Bay on Quadra and Whaletown Bay on Cortes Island. Both ferries transport vehicles. Sailing time between Campbell River and Quathiaski Cove is a mere 10 minutes, but the route to Cortes Island is a 45-minute journey.

Texada Island is reached by BC Ferries from Powell River on the Sunshine Coast. This ferry transports vehicles to Blubber Bay at the north end of the island. Travel time is approximately 15 minutes.

For fares and schedules on all BC Ferries routes, call (888) 223-3779.

Savary Island and the Copeland Islands Provincial Marine Park are only accessible by private boat or water taxi from Lund on the Sunshine Coast.

Air transportation is available to all islands, with the exception of Jedediah, Sandy, and the Copeland Islands. For information on flights to the Gulf Islands contact KD Air, (604) 688-9957; Coval Air, (604) 681-0311; and Coast Western Airline, (800) 839-3422, all in Vancouver. Charter service is also available from Nanaimo, Comox, and Campbell River on Vancouver Island and Powell River on the Sunshine Coast, among other areas.

Adjoining Areas

NORTH: **Inside Passage and Discovery Coast**

WEST: **Parksville and the Comox Valley**

EAST: **The Sunshine Coast**

inside out

Kayaking/Boating/Canoeing

Those who venture out on the water are rewarded with sheltered provincial wilderness campsites on several marine park islands. It's difficult to overstate how pleasant it is to stay at any of them. Most of the year, those who make the effort to paddle beyond a Gulf Island federal dock soon have the ocean to themselves. Come warmer weather and mellower seas, hundreds of visitors a day flock to provincial marine parks, such as **Jedediah Island Provincial Park** (which nearby Lasqueti Island residents refer to jokingly as "Club Jed"). Not that there isn't plenty of room; it's just that from October to May, it feels truly luxurious to have so much space in which to play. Part of Jedediah Island's charm is that it is not easy to reach.

The best approach is from Lasqueti Island. Plan on taking six hours to paddle the 11-mile (18-km) route from False Bay on Lasqueti to Jedediah Island. A good map to consult is Canadian Hydrographic Service Chart L/C 3512, Strait of Georgia. Kayaks may be rented on Lasqueti from Dancing Waters Kayaks. Call (250) 333-8704 for reservations. The going rate is $35 per day for singles, $55 for doubles. For a small fee, owner Bob Fawkes transports kayakers across island from the dock at False Bay to Tucker Bay on the east side of the island, which cuts a few hours off paddling time to Jedediah Island.

What sets Jedediah apart is its size (about 600 acres/240 ha)—one of the largest island parks in the province—and the fact that visitors can camp on it. Most island parks are intended as way stations and provide sheltered anchorage for those travelling in live-aboard boats. Reaching the park can prove harder than you would imagine. After all, you can see Jedediah from Lasqueti. All that is required is to cross **Bull Passage,** a 30-minute, 1-mile (1.6-km) paddle in calm water. Gales occasionally gather from out of the south; Lasqueti's steep-sided coastline (typical of much of the Gulf Islands) offers few safe places to put in along Sabine Channel and the more sheltered waters of Bull Passage. Assess the weather before setting out.

Once across the channel, the best approach is to enter Long Bay where park headquarters are located. (Note: To obtain a guide to the island's bays and trails, contact BC Parks, (250) 954-4600.) Jedediah's north and south ends are rocky and hilly; most visitors will be content to explore the trails that run through the middle section of the island. An old road crosses the island, linking Long and Home Bays. Unlike many of the nearby islands, Jedediah has never been subjected to wholesale logging; much of the forest cover through which visitors walk is old growth. An ageing, strawberry-coloured horse and a herd of feral sheep and goats graze in the fields that surround a farmhouse standing above the shoreline at Home Bay. The horse was brought to Jedediah in the 1980s and stayed on after the owners sold out. The weathered house is boarded up now, as are all the outbuildings, but there is still a definite feeling of a working homestead about the place. A shed houses antique farm equipment beside an orchard of gnarled trees that continue to blossom. The scene is an unusual one to find in a provincial park, and reminiscent of Ruckle Provincial Park (see Southern Gulf Islands chapter) at the south end of Salt Spring Island, site of one of British Columbia's first family farms.

Visitors are free to camp anywhere on Jedediah. Some of the best sites are near the shoreline around Long Bay, particularly as the drumming sounds of diesel-driven marine traffic in Sabine Channel don't reach this side of the island. Informal campsites abound around the sheltered shores of both **Long** and **Home Bays.** As well as sites on the clearings above the beaches at both bays, look for a series of trails that runs around Long Bay and a short distance through the forest to several small bays on the east side of the island. There are more campsites along here that may provide more privacy at the height of kayak-touring season. Home Bay is semi-sheltered by Mother Goose Island, which lies just offshore, but it lacks the tranquillity of Long Bay. Both bays teem with shellfish: when the tide goes out, the exposed mudflats are ripe for clam raking. (Sections of Long Bay are posted as a private oyster lease, so leave these areas undisturbed.)

For those who journey past the south end of Lasqueti Island, there's good reason for putting ashore at **Squitty Bay Provincial Marine Park.** Not only is there freshwater from a pump in the park's picnic area, there's also an interesting adjacent ecological reserve. Walk out on the headland to a rock cairn, from where you look southeast to Vancouver and distant Mount Baker, and west to the Comox Valley, surmounted by the white expanse of the Comox Glacier. Be careful where you walk and sit, as ground-hugging prickly pear cacti grow here alongside Rocky Mountain juniper, far from its montane habitat. Sunny weather and sandy soil are what attract it here, as it keeps company with some magnificent old-growth Douglas fir. When foxglove and yellow cornflowers bloom here in early summer, this is a delightful place to visit. Despite its prickly appearance, please respect the delicacy of this special environment.

There are several places around the northern straits where an open canoe is just as handy as a kayak to reach one of the provincial marine parks. For example, you can paddle from **Denman Island** to nearby **Sandy Island Provincial Marine Park.** Although it's possible on a calm day to launch from the wharf at Buckley Bay on Vancouver Island, cross **Baynes Sound** to the west side of Denman, and then make your way north to the park, you can reduce your travel time by taking the 10-minute ferry ride to Denman, then launching from there. Paddling distance from Denman's ferry dock to Sandy Island is about 6 miles (10 km); half that if you launch from the public beach access farther north on Denman. To reach this location, follow Northwest Rd to Gladstone Way, and park at the west end of Gladstone. A trail winds a short distance to the beach. If the tide is out you'll have to carry your canoe or kayak over oyster-encrusted rocks to reach the ocean. Wear beach shoes and tread carefully to avoid damaging the shellfish. The park is less than a 2-mile (3-km) paddle from here.

As you make your way you may well be accompanied by seals, dolphins, or loons. Tall blue herons stand posted like sentries on the rocky outcroppings exposed at low tide. A long spit of land—Longbreak Point—curves out from Denman towards Sandy Island and provides a calming breakwater.

As soon as you set foot on Sandy Island and a clam kneecaps you with a jet of seawater, you'll experience the magic of the place. Underfoot, small mussels the colour of lapis lazuli keep company with bleached geoduck, scallop, and oyster shells. Black and white sand dollars, enough to retire the national debt, stand banked up against the rest. Shorebirds in their hundreds work the waters for their meals. At low tide, deer emerge from nearby Denman's forests to nibble at moss growing on fallen logs, occasionally crossing between the two islands. As you explore Sandy Island, you'll see matted evidence of deer beds in the long grass. In the evening the lights of Comox and Courtenay twinkle over on Vancouver Island, and overhead, as the last light fades from the peaks of the Vancouver Island Mountains, the stars begin to appear like popcorn, first one, then another, and finally a barrage from the Milky Way as it spreads out like sea foam.

Sandy Island Provincial Marine Park is located so close to the north end of Denman Island that at low tide you can wade to the park from the tip of Longbeak Point. These islands are a holdover from a distant time when the entire Strait of Georgia was filled with sand. In more recent geological times, glaciation gouged out the trench that is now filled with seawater. At the centre of Sandy Island (or Tree Island on some maps) a mighty stand of Douglas fir shelters a small number of rustic campsites. Bring your own water and cookstove as fires are not allowed. When you sleep, cushioned by the soft sand, you'll enjoy a contentment known by those adventurers who, having made the effort, find safe haven in nature.

Copeland Islands Provincial Marine Park and **Savary Island** both lie offshore from **Lund** on the Sunshine Coast's Malaspina Peninsula. You can see the white sand beaches on Savary beckoning in the distance (see

Beaches/Picnics, below) while the Copelands (or Raggeds as they are also known locally) lie out of sight to the north. To reach Savary, paddle south from Lund along the peninsula's shoreline to the closest point to Savary, then paddle west for 30 minutes, or about 1 mile (1.6 km). To reach the Copelands, head north from Lund, hugging the steep-sided coastline. Marine traffic in Thulin Passage can kick up a sizable chop; thus, it's best to set out as early in the day as possible before many large pleasure craft begin to ply these waters. Pick your opening and paddle hard to cover the 0.6 mile (1 km) between the peninsula and the most southerly island in this chain. Once in the vicinity of the Copelands, you'll find sheltered paddling that you'll have to share only with the numerous seals that haul up on little islets when not fishing for their next meal. Shellfish are particularly abundant. Although the seven major islands in the Copelands are quite rugged, with limited level terrain, a handful of campsites are tucked away on the sheltered north side of the third from the top of the chain. There are no facilities here, no freshwater, and campfires are prohibited. Pack out everything except your oyster shells, though you'll probably want to keep one as a memento.

For more information, contact Powell River Sea Kayaks, (604) 483-2410, or Eagle Kayaking Adventures in Lund, (604) 483-3454 or 483-4012. Canoes and kayaks are available for rent from Ocean Kayak Rentals and Accessories, (604) 483-3223, in Lund; and from Powell River Boat Rentals, (604) 485-7322, and Sunshine Coast Fitness & Sports, (604) 485-6969, in Powell River.

Octopus Islands Provincial Marine Park is both remote and accessible at the same time. Nestled among the maze of islands through which the waters of Johnstone Strait funnel into the Strait of Georgia, the Octopus Islands are most easily reached from **Quadra Island.** From the ferry dock at Quadra's Quathiaski Cove, journey east across island to Heriot Bay, where another ferry connects to Cortes Island. This is one of two good places to launch, along with Village Bay farther north. Tidal currents around Quadra Island are notorious for their strength, particularly at **Surge Narrows** on the east and **Seymour Narrows** on the west. Paddlers should avoid Seymour Narrows completely and only transit Surge narrows at slack tide. In addition, you should be well versed in the reading of tidal-current charts to safely explore the fascinating waters around tightly packed Quadra, Cotes, Maurelle, Read, and Sonora Islands. The best nautical charts to study include Canadian Hydrographic Service Maps #3594, #3596, #3524, and Tidal Current Chart #23. For more information, consult *Sea Kayaking Canada's West Coast* by Ince and Kittner.

An alternative to saltwater paddling around Quadra is a small chain of freshwater lakes in the interior of the island that are perfectly suited to canoeing. In summer, the water in the lakes warms up as levels drop. You may well find that you'll have to haul your canoe through a narrow channel connecting **Village Bay Lake** and **Mine Lake.** You can bypass this section by launching directly into Mine Lake and heading for the prettiest part of the route that leads from Mine to **Main Lake,** the largest of the lakes in this chain. Sandy beaches on small islands and in cozy bays are delightfully welcoming spots to land and pass a sunny day, with hardly any other paddlers with which to share this slice of paradise. If you land on the northeast side of Main Lake, you'll find not only a sandy beach but also a short walking trail that follows an old logging road to Yeatman Bay, north of Surge Narrows on Quadra's coastline.

To reach the launch site, take West Rd north from the ferry landing at Quathiaski Bay to Heriot Bay. Keep heading north on first Hyacinths Bay Rd and then Village Bay Rd. Launch at the bridge in Village Bay or continue another 1.5 miles (2.5 km) farther north along Surge Narrows Rd to Miners Bay.

Camping/Parks

Because of certain inhibiting conditions—lack of water and garbage facilities, as well as tinder-dry forests in summer months—many islands have no public campgrounds. In most places, private accommodation must be arranged. In summer, reservations are highly recommended. There are, however, public campgrounds on Denman, Cortes, and Texada Islands.

Denman Island's **Fillongley Provincial Park** (10 vehicle/tent sites) is not particularly large and fills up quickly in July and August. There is no telling in advance whether you'll find room here. The campground is located in a forested setting on the east side of the island, about 2.5 miles (4 km) from the ferry dock to Vancouver Island. Although the campsites are tightly packed together with only concrete dividers to separate them, the sand and pebble beach that fronts the park is spacious and provides ample opportunity for exploring and, in season, hunting for shellfish for dinner.

After going to the effort to reach **Cortes Island,** your reward is finding a campsite on the southwestern corner at **Smelt Bay Provincial Park** (22 vehicle/tent sites), a heavenly setting on this picturesque island. Follow the island road 13 miles (21 km) from the ferry dock to the park, which is near Manson's Landing Provincial Marine Park (see Beaches/Picnics, below). Smelts are a green-and-silver, sardine-sized fish that frequents these waters in huge numbers and attracts salmon. Not difficult to net, they make a tasty meal. For information on Fillongley and Smelt Bay Provincial Parks, call BC Parks, (250) 954-4600.

If you'd like to savour a Mediterranean-like climate, head for **Texada Island's Shelter Point Regional Park** (47 vehicle/tent sites). Texada may be a rugged island, but it does possess this jewel of a regional park midway along its west side, 17 miles (27 km) south of the Blubber Bay ferry terminal. Note: It's best to avoid Shelter Point on the July weekend when the regional baseball tournament's in full swing. Call (250) 483-3231 or (250) 486-7228 for details. Douglas fir and western red cedar trees provide a fitting accompaniment to the beauty of the nearby beach with its exotic-looking sand dollars, sea anemones, and oversized moon snail shells. Most of the campsites are set back from the expansive sand and polished pea-gravel beach. A breeze blows almost constantly across the Strait of Georgia, but Shelter Point comes by its name honestly. Camping is especially good between April and October, when there are plenty of clear, warm days.

Beaches/Picnics

Even though there are no public campgrounds on some islands, there are attractive parks especially for picnickers, located where you can take best advantage of the seaside environment. Whether you're on the island just for the day or have made arrangements for private overnight accommodation, you'll want to head for these places to complement your visit.

Every island is invested with magic. Those who visit **Hornby Island** have really bought into the dream, as it takes two ferries to reach. Once there, head for the picnic grounds at **Tribune Bay** or **Helliwell Provincial Parks** (see Walking/Hiking, below). The latter sits on a headland forested with a beautiful stand of old-growth Douglas fir. If you arrive here in spring you'll be treated to a dazzling wildflower display. The rewards of visiting later in summer are the huckleberries and dark blue salal berries that cloak the hillside above the beach. Tribune Bay boasts eroded hoodoo formations and a sandy beach that vies with any in the Gulf Islands as the most ideal place to frolic and swim.

You'll get to tour **Quadra Island** on the way to your picnic in **Rebecca Spit Provincial Marine Park.** The park lies on the east side of the island at sheltered Drew Harbour, almost 6 miles (9 km) from the ferry landing. There are more picnic tables here than on any other island, and a prettier sandy beach than almost anywhere else on Quadra. Anglers launch from the ramp here, and it's a good place to pick up word on the health of fish stocks.

Cortes Island is blessed with both a provincial campground at Smelt Bay (see Camping/Parks, above) and a sublime picnic and fishing location at **Mansons Landing Provincial Marine Park.** If they aren't biting in the saltchuk ("chuk" is a Native word for water) just turn your attention to the fish in Hague Lake, a freshwater lake located within the park, a rarity in the provincial marine park system. A wide, sandy beach beckons to those who just wish to spread a blanket beside a driftwood backrest and dig into the cooler.

For those who journey the length of Lasqueti Island (see Mountain Biking, below), there's picnicking and swimming at **Squitty Bay Provincial Marine Park,** 9 miles (15 km) south of the ferry dock at False Bay. You'll be ready to drink from the freshwater pump by the time you arrive here. Picnic tables are arrayed among the spray-shaped forest of Douglas fir and strawberry arbutus (madrona). This idyllic location overlooks two narrow coves where the water is clear, green, and warm in summer months. A portion of the park is fenced off to protect it from the feral sheep that graze all over the island. Years ago, a small meadow was cleared above the beach at Squitty Bay, where there are still signs of a old orchard.

Without doubt, the best beaches in the entire inland sea are found on **Savary Island** offshore from Lund on the Sunshine Coast. Unfortunately, few visitors travelling without a boat will get the opportunity to stroll them. Savary is not serviced by public ferry so transportation is limited to water taxi or airplane. If you do have a boat, kayak, or canoe (rentals can be arranged in Powell River and Lund; see Kayaking/Boating/Canoeing, above), the First or Second Beaches on the island's north side are the easiest to reach. It's debatable which side of the snout-shaped island has the best beaches—when you're in heaven, it doesn't matter which side of the street you walk on.

Walking/Hiking

A nature walk along the forested shoreline of **Shelter Point Regional Park** (see Camping/Parks, above) on **Texada Island** takes visitors through a setting that could have been the inspiration for author J. R. R. Tolkien's giant marching trees featured in his *Lord of the Rings* trilogy. Long branches from two groves of Douglas fir spread like muscled arms above each end of the trail. Although sturdy, most of their tops have been cropped by winter storms. Eagles and osprey rest in the tallest boughs when they aren't out cruising the coastline for a meal. Others also have drawn sustenance from these waters for many generations. When the tide is out, look carefully from the promontory at the south end of the nature trail and you may be able to discern an ancient V-shaped rock fishing weir, fashioned by Indians of the Sliammon Nation. (Once frequent visitors to Texada, their traditional village was located where the Powell River pulp mill complex now stands.) Near the south end of the trail stands the gnarliest Douglas fir of them all, a full 7 feet (2.1 m) in diameter. As you look west from here across the Strait of Georgia at the Comox Glacier's broad white expanse, you get one of the best views of central Vancouver Island. Lasqueti Island lies off to the southwest. The trail loops back from its southern terminus at a gravel road through the forest to the giant fir. You can also choose to walk partway on a rough shoreline trail that branches away from the main trail and leads past arbutus and western red cedar. Also watch for the wild honeysuckle vines that entwine themselves around tree trunks in several places. The 2-mile (3-km) loop trail begins south of the entrance to the park's newly expanded campsite area. Although not well marked, the trail is easy to locate.

A forested trail leads through **Boyle Point Regional Park** at the south end of East Rd on **Denman Island.** Although not a lengthy walk, this 1-mile (1.6 km across) excursion will give your legs a good workout, and you will be rewarded at the end of the trail with views of Hornby Island (the ferry from Gravelly Bay on Denman to Shingle Bay on Hornby is a short distance north of the park) as well as the strategically located lighthouse on Chrome Island just offshore. Cliffs precipitously drop off below the lookout at trail's end, and you may not be tempted to follow a rough route down to the shoreline. One noticeable difference between the waters of the north and south ends of Denman is the presence of sea urchins around Boyle Point, but not at Longbeak Point and the waters around Sandy Island Provincial Marine Park.

Owing to the low elevation of most Gulf and Discovery Islands, walking routes are neither lengthy nor challenging. Some of the best trails are on **Hornby Island** and lead around **Helliwell Provincial Park.** A 3-mile (5-km) loop trail follows the bluffs that rise above the beach and lead through open fields and stands of magnificent old-growth Douglas fir. One of the best times to be here is in late April and early May, when wildflowers carpet the hillside above the beach.

Mountain Biking

Exploring **Lasqueti Island** by mountain bike (or even on skinny tires) makes a delightful day trip. You can easily ride the 11 miles (18 km) from False Bay at the north end of the island to Squitty Bay Provincial Marine Park (see Beaches/Picnics, above) on the southern tip in less than two hours. There is a small convenience store and pub at the bike-friendly Lasqueti Island Hotel next to the wharf at False Bay, (250) 333-8846.

On the ferry ride from Denman Island over to **Hornby Island,** you can't help but notice the spectacular cliffs that drop almost to the ferry landing. Imagine the exhilaration of travelling atop those cliffs on your mountain bike. Then ride the **Bench Trail,** which is atop the cliffs, and feel your knees go wobbly, and not just from the 1,000-foot (305-m) ascent to get there. Trails crisscross the island in all directions, and though the Bench Trail offers the best views, they are all worth exploring, especially the **No Horses Trail,** a half-pipe-like trail that follows an old riverbed. Hornby Island Off-Road Bike Shop, (250) 335-0444, has the skinny on all the trails on Hornby. Keep an eye out for members of Team Orb while you're there, either on the trail or in the shop. Team Orb is the best collection of trails riders in British Columbia, and they are easy to spot. They're the ones doing things you thought couldn't be done with mountain bikes.

Fishing

The waters around **Quadra Island** have yielded some of the largest **salmon** ever caught on BC's west coast. Although much of the activity is centred in nearby Campbell River on Vancouver Island, there's plenty of action around Quadra, particularly at **Quathiaski Cove,** where the ferry linking Quadra and Campbell River docks. Boaters must be extremely cautious in the waters of Discovery Passage. Anglers congregate in the waters off Cape Mudge, Copper Bluffs, April Point, and at the entrance to Quathiaski Cove around Grouse Island. Good fishing is also found in the protected waters around **Rebecca Spit Marine Provincial Park** (see Beaches/Picnics above), where a popular public boat ramp is located.

Inland on Quadra, **cutthroat trout** are numerous in the freshwater regions of **Village Bay, Mine,** and **Main Lakes** (see Kayaking/Boating/Canoeing, above). For more information on fishing on Quadra Island and Discovery Passage, contact Discovery Charters, (250) 285-3146 or (800) 668-8054, April Point Lodge, (250) 285-2222, or Big Spring Sports Fishing Resort, (800) 663-4400, all on Quadra Island.

outside in

Attractions

Quadra Island is a 10-minute ferry ride from Campbell River. Resident artists and craftspeople make the island a fine place to sleuth around for pottery and other wares. Ask in Quathiaski Cove, just up the road from the ferry dock, for a detailed map of the island, or pick one up at the **Kwagiulth Museum,** (250) 285-3733, 2 miles (3 km) south of the ferry dock on Green Rd. Their outstanding collection of Native American masks, blankets, and carvings rivals displays in the finest international museums.

Tranquil and bucolic, **Denman Island** and **Hornby Island** sit just off the east coast of Vancouver Island. Denman, the larger of the two (10 minutes by ferry from Buckley Bay, south of Courtenay), is known for its pastoral farmlands and its population of talented **artisans.**

Texada Island has been a mining site for the last century, which is obvious as you pull into the ferry dock at Blubber Bay. Fortunately, as you leave the dock, you also leave behind the sight of limestone and heavy equipment. Just before you reach Shelter Point, the road passes through Gillies Bay, one of Texada's two commercial centres. There's a food and liquor store here, a gallery featuring local art, and a **farmers' market** on Sundays in summer.

Cheaper Eats

Hollyhock Seminar Centre It's open to the public for breakfast ($8), lunch ($9), and dinner ($15)—so go! The buffets are so beautiful, eating becomes almost a sacrament. Everything from papadams to curries and chocolate-chip cookies is served. Reservations recommended. *Highfield Rd, Cortes; (250) 935-6576 or (800) 933-6339; $.*

Old Floathouse Restaurant The Floathouse overlooks the water, and sharing a main course or even an appetizer is just fine by the staff, which makes this spot wonderfully affordable. Prices are lower in the off-season. *Gorge Marina Resort, Hunt Rd, Cortes; (250) 935-6631; $.*

Lodgings

April Point Lodge ☆☆☆ This resort draws fisherfolk from all over. Also offered are bike and kayak rentals, horseback riding, and golf. Choose a house, room, suite, or a cabin; the main lodge is cheerful, and food is very good. Full service offered April through October; cabins available off-season. *April Point Rd (10 minutes north of ferry dock; follow signs), Quadra Island; PO Box 1, Campbell River, BC V9W 4Z9; (250) 285-2222 or (888) 334-3474; $$$.*

Sea Breeze Lodge Catch the ferry from Denman and stay in one of 13 beachside cottages at this comfortable family retreat. In summer, rates include three meals; the rest of the year, reserve a cabin with a kitchen. *Tralee Point; mail: Big Tree 3-2, Hornby Island, BC V0R 1Z0; (250) 335-2321; $$.*

Sonora Resort and Conference Centre ☆☆ Sonora is big and posh—a resort catering to those who want to fish from the lap of luxury. You'll pay a *lot*, but everything is included: airfare from Vancouver, guided fishing, gourmet meals, drinks, fishing rods, rain gear, and more. *On Sonora Island*

(30 miles/48 km north of Campbell River, accessible by boat or plane only); mail: 625-B 11th Ave, Campbell River, BC V9W 4G5; (250) 287-2869; $$$.

Tsa-Kwa-Luten Lodge ☆☆ The Cape Mudge Band of the Kwagiulth built this lodge on 110 acres, and Native arts are showcased. All units overlook Discovery Passage. Staff can arrange boat cruises, scuba diving, kayaking, or transportation. Closed winters. *Lighthouse Rd (about 10 minutes south of ferry dock; look for signs), Quadra Island; PO Box 460, Quathiaski Cove, BC V0P 1N0; (250) 285-2042 or (800) 665-7745; $$–$$$.*

Cheaper Sleeps

Blue Heron Bed and Breakfast This charming waterfront property is in a blissfully peaceful setting within earshot of the ocean's waves. The three guest rooms are in a separate wing with a private entrance. *Potlatch Rd, Cortes Island, BC V0P 1K0; (250) 935-6584; $.*

Joha Eagle View This house sits on the cove overlooking Discovery Passage just minutes from the ferry dock. Two guest rooms offer brass beds and stained-glass windows. Guests share the bathroom and the broad veranda. A lower unit is a good deal for a group. *Quathiaski Cove, Quadra Island, BC V0P 1N0; (250) 285-2247; $.*

More Information

BC Ferries: *(250) 277-0277 or (250) 286-1412.*

BC Fish and Wildlife Branch Conservation Office (freshwater fishing), Campbell River: *(250) 286-7630.*

BC Forest Service, Campbell River Forest District, Campbell River: *(250) 286-9300.*

BC Parks: *(250) 954-4600.*

Campbell River and District Chamber of Commerce (information on Quadra Island): *(250) 287-4636.*

Department of Fisheries and Oceans (Tidal Fishery Officer), Campbell River: *(250) 287-2151 or (250) 287-2101.*

Hornby & Denman Islands Tourist Association: *(250) 335-2321.*

Powell River InfoCentre (information on Texada Island): *(604) 485-4701.*

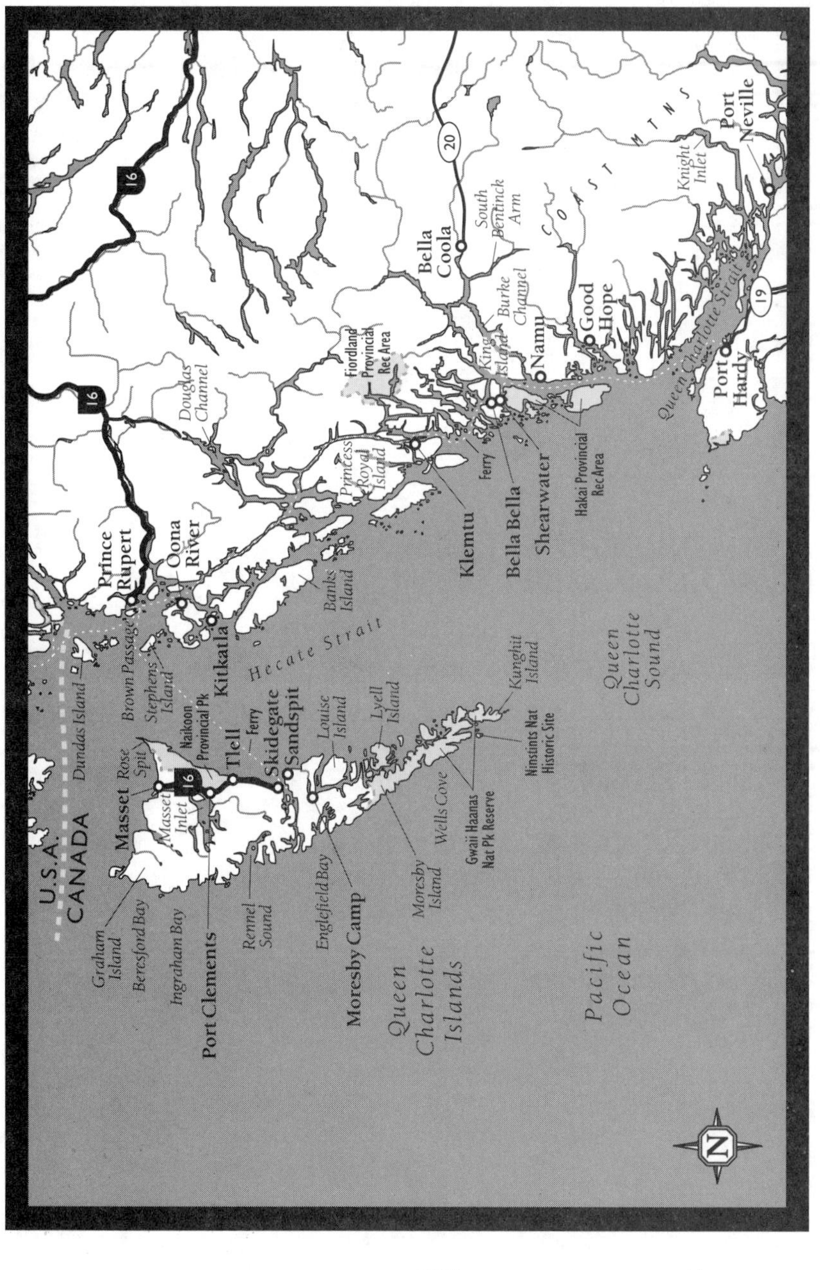

Central and Northwest Coasts

Inside Passage and Discovery Coast 389

Queen Charlotte Islands (Haida Gwaii) 403

Inside Passage and Discovery Coast

From Port Hardy to Prince Rupert through the protected waters of British Columbia's central and northern coastline, and from Port Hardy to Bella Coola on the Central Coast, including Namu, McLoughlin Bay, Shearwater, Klemtu, and Ocean Falls, and Hakai Provincial Recreation Area.

There are some places, luckily, that are still inaccessible by road. British Columbia's Central Coast is one of them. Until BC Ferries launched its Discovery Coast Passage run in the summer of 1996, the Central Coast was also largely inaccessible by water. Now, to the delight of adventurers and locals alike, from June to September the *Queen of Chilliwack* connects the community of Port Hardy, at the northeastern end of Vancouver Island, with Bella Coola, at the head of the North Bentinck Arm, making regular stops along the way.

For kayakers and campers, RVers and backpackers, the Discovery Coast Passage service opens up a brand-new circle tour through some of the province's most beautiful terrain. From Bella Coola, Highway 20 leads across the Chilcotin Plateau to the Cariboo, from where any number of routes lead back to the Lower Mainland. But one of the bonuses of this trip is that you needn't take a (four-wheeled) vehicle at all. Kayakers, backpackers, and cycle tourists can choose their destination, explore some territory, then reboard the ferry on a subsequent day. Planning your trip, which involves detailed study of the ferry schedule, is half the fun. As yet, the Discovery Coast Passage remains largely *un*discovered. Book soon.

When European explorers arrived along this coast in the 18th century, it was inhabited by Natives from several cultural groups.

Although hunters and gatherers like the tribes of the Interior, the coastal natives, due to their abundant food supply, were able to establish permanent villages. Their complex cultures were distinguished by an emphasis on wealth, a refined artistic tradition, and a rich spirit life. Travel along the coast was accomplished via cedar dugout canoes that could be impressive in their length. Although there's nothing more inspiring than to see one of these massive canoes in action, they are only brought out for ceremonial occasions, such as a paddle trip to Vancouver or the Olympic Peninsula in Washington. These days, aluminum-hulled, high-speed boats are the vessels of choice among all inhabitants of the coast.

Explorers from Russia, Britain, France, and Spain converged on this coastline in the last quarter of the 18th century, motivated by trade possibilities or—in the case of Spain—a desire to protect territorial waters. Two British explorers, Captain James Cook in 1778–79 and Captain George Vancouver in 1792–93, did the most systematic charting of the coast. After an international tussle, the British eventually gained control of what would later become the coast of British Columbia. Colonization and settlement began in the 19th century, although British Columbia's Central and Northern Coast is still not heavily populated. Logging, fishing, and tourism are the primary industries, though with the decline in stocks and automation in the forest, fewer people live here now than in previous decades. After a disastrous decline in Native populations (by as much as 90 percent in some nations) that began over a century ago due to infectious diseases such as smallpox and tuberculosis, today's numbers match those of precontact times.

Getting There

The Queen of Chilliwack, *377 feet (115 m) long, carrying 115 vehicles and 375 passengers, sails from its southern terminus in Port Hardy, 250 miles (400 km) north of Nanaimo on Highway 19. The drive from Nanaimo to Port Hardy takes four to five hours. Bella Coola, the ferry's main northern terminus, is 283 miles (456 km) west of Williams Lake on Highway 20. Wilderness Air, (604) 276-2635, has scheduled flights to Bella Coola (airport at Hagensborg) from Vancouver Airport, South Terminal. North Vancouver Air, (604) 278-1608, has scheduled flights between Vancouver and Bella Bella. Pacific Coastal Airlines, (800) 663-2872, in Vancouver offers scheduled service into both Port Hardy and Bella Bella.*

The Queen of the North *(capacity 700 passengers) also sails from Port Hardy. The ferry's northern terminus, Prince Rupert, is 450 miles (725 km) west of Prince George on Highway 16. The turnoff for the Port Hardy BC Ferries terminal is almost 2 miles (3 km) south of town.*

Adjoining Areas

SOUTH: **Northern Gulf Islands; North Vancouver Island**

EAST: **The Bella Coola Road (Highway 20); The Bulkley and Skeena River Valleys**

WEST: **Queen Charlotte Islands (Haida Gwaii)**

inside out

Ferry Riding

Queen of the North

Numerous cruise ships ply the waters of the 314-mile (507-km) **Inside Passage** en route to Alaska. BC Ferries' largest vessel, the *Queen of the North,* may not rival the *QE II* in size, but is majestic enough to carry freight trailers, family sedans, recreational vehicles, motorcycles, and touring bicycles. Passengers boarding in **Port Hardy** for the trip to **Prince Rupert** include the usual manifest of adventure-hungry world travellers you'd expect to find boarding a ferry in British Columbia, bolstered, depending on the season, by a contingent of tree planters. By the conclusion of the journey, you'll probably be on nodding, if not full-blown speaking, terms with many of your fellow passengers.

Aside from a short stretch of open ocean between Vancouver Island and Rivers Inlet, where the Central Coast archipelago begins, the route north to Prince Rupert leads through a narrow maze of channels, passes, and reaches. Snow and ice coat the peaks of the mountains, and their shoulders plunge to the tideline. So rugged is most of this coast that if you were exploring here by kayak, you'd be challenged to find a welcoming landing site. Passengers should keep their eyes peeled for a whale or dolphin in **Queen Charlotte Sound.** With luck you might even see a white-coated Kermode bear on Princess Royal Island's lengthy shoreline.

As no one is allowed on the car deck while the ferry is at sea, it's important to stake out a seat inside, even if you plan to occupy it only while sleeping. Most chairs come equipped with fold-out footrests, which provide tired travellers with a soothing position in which to snooze. These chairs are far more comfortable than those found on airlines and as wide as those on trains. In fact, the motion of the ferry, accompanied by the deep vibration from its drumming diesels, is surprisingly similar to that which comes with riding the rails.

With a draw of 16 feet (4.9 m), the *Queen of the North* is the largest ferry in the 40-vessel BC Ferries fleet. Stops at **Ocean Falls** and **McLoughlin Bay** in early spring and late fall prolong the daylong journey, but also lead to enjoyable scenery as the *Queen of the North* threads her way through the Inside Passage. Services aboard the ferry include a dining room with a full buffet, a licenced lounge, a cafeteria, cabins, a children's playroom, public showers, and a video arcade.

Come the end of May, when ferry service to ports on the Central Coast is shouldered by the *Queen of Chilliwack* (on the Discovery Coast Passage route, inaugurated in 1996; see below), there are no stops between Port Hardy and Prince Rupert, with its connections to the Queen Charlotte Islands and Alaska. That's a good thing. The ferry has become so popular with summer travellers that everything needs to click in order to keep to the demanding schedule. Timing is crucial for the *Queen of the North*'s arrival at tricky sections along the route, such as the treacherous passages around Boat Bluff and Ormiston Point, if the ferry is to avoid a standoff with one of the many Alaskan cruise ships in the narrow waterways.

Eighty-four crew members work the Inside Passage run in winter. Their numbers double in summer when the *Queen of the North,* commissioned in 1969, comes out of winter dry dock and into summer service. (In winter, a smaller vessel, the *Queen of Prince Rupert,* handles the entire Inside Passage route. During summer months, her sole assignment is the run between Prince Rupert on the mainland and Sandspit on the Queen Charlotte Islands.) The crew ranges from deckhands to cooks to the elite who staff the bridge. Whatever their calling, they work a demanding schedule of two weeks onboard, followed by two weeks ashore.

Between June 1 and October 16, the *Queen of the North* departs Port Hardy for Prince Rupert on odd-numbered days (except in August, when it sails on even-numbered days) at 7:30am and arrives in Prince Rupert at approximately 10:30pm. In early spring and late fall, the *Queen of the North* sails from Port Hardy to Prince Rupert on Saturdays and Wednesdays at 6pm. Depending on the season, the approximate sailing time is between 15 and 17 hours. Connections to the Queen Charlotte Islands from Prince Rupert are timed to coincide with the *Queen of the North*'s arrival.

If you are travelling with a vehicle, **reservations** are a must. For more details and reservations, contact BC Ferries in Canada at (888) 223-3779 or (250) 386-3431. Information and travel arrangements can also be made at the BC Ferries Web site: www.bcferries.bc.ca.

Queen of Chilliwack

As cruises go, the **Discovery Coast Passage** is hardly lavish. The *Queen of Chilliwack* is a working freight boat, serving the needs of the local communities. It's just as well that luxuries aboard this refurbished Norwegian vessel don't distract from the scenery, which is spectacular, with long fjords and narrow channels forming the backdrop to the Inside Passage. The roughest portion of the trip is just out of Port Hardy, as the ferry navigates the unprotected waters of Queen Charlotte Sound. This is a good time for a nap. The most stunning scenery is between **Bella Bella** and **Bella Coola.** With the setting sun behind you, the monolithic rock formations looming over the narrow Burke Channel give the cruise a European flavour. You'll get an even better look at the scenic **Dean Channel** during daylight hours if you board the ferry in Bella Coola for the southbound sailing. Weather permitting, the ship's two upper decks are an excellent vantage point from which to watch for the logging camps, barge houses, and abandoned settlements that indicate a human presence on this rugged coastline. Although Natives have inhabited the area for thousands of years, the inhospitable terrain has limited development and exploration by European settlers until comparatively recently. Wildlife viewing—the ferry slows for **orcas**—is another bonus of this trip. Don't forget your binoculars.

Facilities aboard the *Queen of Chilliwack* include reclining sleeper seats, a cafeteria, and small licenced lounge, a gift shop and—a boon for kayakers—pay showers. Service is friendly, the food is better-than-average for BC Ferries, and there is a staff member dedicated to customer service who can assist you with your onboard needs or travel plans. See **reservations,** above, for information on BC Ferries.

Kayaking

Many parts of the so-called Discovery Coast are relatively unknown to kayakers. It will appeal to resourceful paddlers who seek a sense of pioneering, which includes laying some groundwork, discovering new fishing spots, wildlife watching, dealing with unknown tidal currents, and finding new campsites. Canoes and kayaks can be rented by the day or week from North Island Boat Canoe & Kayak Rentals, (250) 949-7707, located in Port Hardy.

Approximately 80 miles (130 km) north of Port Hardy and 6.2 miles (10 km) west of Namu is the **Hakai Provincial Recreation Area,** British Columbia's largest marine park and one of the better-known paddling areas. This 304,000-acre (123 000-ha) area encompasses a large archipelago of outstanding natural beauty and recreational value. From fully exposed shorelines to rolling, forested hills and 3,000-foot (1 000-m) peaks, Hakai offers some of the most varied and scenic coastline in the province. Special features such as lagoons and reversing tidal rapids, beaches, all-weather anchorages, tombolos, and an intricate network of coves, inlets, and channels make it an ideal area for boaters, anglers, scuba divers, naturalists—and experienced sea kayakers. Winds during the summer are usually westerly or southwesterly, and on sunny days are often light or nil in the early morning, pick up midday to late afternoon, then die down in the evening. They can be extremely strong in the coastal inlets such as Burke Channel. Weather information can be picked up on VHF Channel 21B (161.65MHZ).

One of the better areas to paddle within Hakai is **Spider Anchorage,** southeast of **Spider Island,** which consists of sheltered bays, white sand beaches, and a multitude of marine life. Another popular anchorage is **Pruth Bay** on the north side of **Calvert Island,** reached via Kwakshua Channel. The recreation area has no developed facilities and has wilderness campsites only. Freshwater is available at some beaches, but creeks dry up during summer, and visitors are advised to carry a supply.

Kayakers must be well prepared for poor weather and rough seas, which may occur at any time of the year. Fog can roll in very quickly, necessitating navigation by compass, and sea conditions can change from flat calm to 12- to 20-foot (4- to 6-m) seas within a matter of hours. The west coast of Calvert Island can be hazardous due to strong surf and should not be approached without knowledge of the locale, and then only under ideal conditions.

Kayakers wishing to explore this remote wilderness can access it by sea or by air. BC Ferries' *Queen of Chilliwack* stops at **Namu,** the closest settlement. Hakai is located across Fitz Hugh Sound from Namu, a busy shipping route also frequented by Pacific white-sided dolphin. **Fuel and groceries** are available at Bella Bella, Namu, and Dawsons Landing (Rivers Inlet). Private or **chartered boats** can be arranged from Vancouver, Port Hardy, and Bella Coola. Chartered and scheduled flights are available from Vancouver, Port Hardy, Bella Bella, and Bella Coola. The nautical charts for this region are #3727, #3728, and #3786. For more information about Hakai, contact BC Parks' office in Williams Lake, (250) 398-4414.

Those who seek expert guidance (and safety in numbers) might want to contact one of the companies offering **group trips** to Hakai. They include Hakai Lodge Sea Kayaking, (604) 685-3732 or (800) 538-3551 in Vancouver; Island Expeditions, (604) 325-7952, in Courtenay; and Gistala Adventures, (250) 957-2652, in Shearwater.

Paddlers can enjoy the many small straits, exposed coastline, and islands accessible from the communities of **Bella Bella** and **Shearwater,** such as the **Goose Group** in the western reaches of the Hakai Provincial Recreation Area. There is good camping on the south end of Campbell Island as you make you way through Hunter Channel towards Goose. Be prepared to paddle 5 miles (8 km) through the open water in Queens

Sound between Campbell and Goose, the largest by far of the five islands gathered here. At the north end of **Goose Island** is a pure white beach composed largely of pulverized clam shells that when walked upon with bare feet emit a squeak not unlike the squeal of a sneaker on a gymnasium floor. This is truly an enchanted island. Note: There is no freshwater in the Goose Group. For more information on sea kayaking the Bella Bella archipelago, contact Gistala Adventures, (250) 957-2652, in Shearwater. A good nautical chart to consult is #3727 (Cape Calvert to Goose Island).

Paddlers can also disembark from the *Queen of Chilliwack* at Klemtu on **Swindle Island,** the ferry's most northerly port of call. From Klemtu, it's possible to paddle to **Princess Royal Island,** 7.5 km (12 km) farther north, home of the legendary Kermode or Spirit Bear. You can keep your fingers crossed for a sighting, but you'd be very lucky to spot one of these gorgeous blonds. The gaping fjords and inlets around Swindle and Princess Royal Islands are stunning, but be warned that campsites in this area are few and small, and by midsummer, most have a meagre water supply.

As in Hakai, paddlers here should be experienced and self-sufficient. Besides sea fog, strong currents represent a potential hazard. Crossings or exposed coasts can be dicey (with surf landings). High tides may make camping difficult, so try to schedule your trip for between full moons. Periodically strong outflow and inflow winds can be a problem in the steep-sided fjords. Because weather conditions can delay trips, give yourself plenty of time (and bring plenty of reading material). For more information, contact the Klemtu Tourist Office, (250) 839-2346.

Klemtu is also the staging area for trips to the **Fiordland Provincial Recreation Area,** a 224,770-acre (9100-ha) paradise for sea kayakers approximately 60 miles (100 km) north of Bella Coola by air—a magical world of inlets, bays, islands, and fjords. Waterfalls and glaciers are set amid the passages of a complex coastline. Some of the mountains are thickly cloaked with old-growth Sitka spruce and coastal western hemlock forests; others are monolithic domes, exhibiting their bare granite faces. Located in the Kitimat Ranges of the Coast Mountains, Fiordland is an exceptionally scenic area, with rich estuaries at the base of sharply plunging glacier-topped mountains. Salmon spawn in the many coastal rivers and creeks.

The three primary inlets represented here—**Mussel, Kynock,** and **Roscoe**—are outstanding locations of provincial and international significance. There are a number of excellent beaches and interesting upland features, including glaciers, waterfalls, lakes, and rivers, along with wonderful hiking and wildlife-viewing opportunities. Sitka deer, salmon, and grizzlies have shared this magnificent area with the Heiltsuk people for centuries. Trapping, hunting, fishing, and other traditional food-gathering activities have richly sustained these people over the years. There are a number of archaeological sites located here, particularly along the shorelines.

Unfortunately for paddlers, campsites are few due to the steep topography of the area. As in other parts of the Central Coast, winds can pick up quickly, resulting in hazardous conditions for small vessels. The recreation area is an important habitat area for both black and grizzly bears, which can make travel on shore risky. The chart for the region is #3962. For more information, contact BC Parks, (250) 398-4414.

From **Swindle Island,** adventurous paddlers can plot a 50-mile (80-km), 10-day course south, rejoining the ferry at **McLoughlin Bay.** (The charts required for such a trip are #3720, #3728, #3734, and #3737.) Head for the exposed west coast of **Price Island,** where you might see cruise ships passing in Laredo Sound. Again, campsites may be hard to find without exploring the many tiny bays behind the mass of rocky islets guarding the coastline.

This jumble of bays and tiny islets is characteristic of the west side of Price Island. Stunted trees, blown landward by the winter storms all their lives, give evidence of the ferocity of the weather that routinely batters this coastline. The east coast of the island may give more shelter, but ferocious horseflies (they bite!) can be a nuisance. Fishing can be rewarding, as long as the halibut isn't too big to land from a kayak. Vancouver Rock and Boulder Head, farther south, are both great spots for rock fish, red snapper, and halibut.

The tidal race through Gale Passage, between **Athlone** and **Dufferin Islands,** can be very strong. Wait for the slack tide. A small cove at the southern tip of Athlone provides a jewel of a campsite—freshwater and a beach of small but smooth flat rocks, offering a sunrise and view south to Potts Island and Goose Island in the distance. From here, aim for a tiny island to the northeast of Cape Mark with a flashing navigational marker, the island itself unnamed on the chart. The island has a sandy beach, and mussels can be harvested off a low granite cliff, even if the crashing Pacific breakers make this a bit of a challenge. Rock crabs lured by fish heads make a gourmet feast, provided they're of legal size.

Joassa Channel is not particularly attractive or significant: no enticing bays or beaches, just vegetation to the rocky edge. By comparison, **Gale Passage** is scenic and varied, and offers a choice of beaches for lunch and/or camping, albeit without freshwater. A big sheltered bay immediately to the east of Denniston Point may not offer much camping room at high tide but has a good source of freshwater. From here, it's only a few miles to the ferry terminal just south of Bella Bella. For more information about kayaking the waters around Klemtu, including equipment rentals, contact the Klemtu Tourist Office, (250) 839-2346.

Camping

Those taking the Discovery Coast Passage should be aware that, depending on their departure time and length of trip, they may have to "camp" one night **aboard ship.** A sleeping bag or warm blanket will enhance your comfort in one of the reclining seats. Alternatively, bring along a camping mattress and stretch out on the floor. A small number of cots and blankets are available onboard. Hardy types are also permitted to pitch their (self-supporting) tents on the deck.

As the *Queen of the North*'s summer sailings are scheduled in the early morning, you will probably wish to spend the night nearby in either Port Hardy or Prince Rupert. For the *Queen of Chilliwack*'s mostly early-morning departures from Port Hardy and Bella Coola, it's wise to book accommodation nearby.

In Port Hardy, **private campgrounds** are available half a mile (1 km) north of the ferry dock at Sunny Sanctuary Campground, (250) 949-8111, as well as at Wild Woods, (250) 949-6753, on the road to the ferry. Quatse River Campground, (250) 949-2395, is another private campground in Port Hardy.

In Prince Rupert, the Park Avenue Campground, (250) 624-5861, and **Prudhomme Lake Provincial Park,** (250) 798-2277, are two of the limited options for camping close to the ferry.

In Bella Coola, the nearest campground to the ferry terminal is the friendly Gnome's Home RV Park & Campground in Hagensborg, (250) 982-2504, 10 miles (16 km) east of Bella Coola. Bailey Bridge Campsite, (250) 982-2324, and Glacier View Resort, (250) 982-2615, are both located on the Bella Coola River east of Hagensborg.

McCall Flats, a Forest Service recreation site on the Bella Coola River east of Firvale on the western edge of Tweedsmuir Provincial Park (see The Bella Coola Road (Highway 20) chapter) has 5 vehicle/tent sites.

Camping is available at McLoughlin Bay near the ferry in Bella Bella, and in Klemtu at the Kitasoo Campground, which has room for 12 RVs or 24 tents.

In summer, accommodations fill up quickly at both ends, so reservations are recommended. For more information, consult Tourism BC's Accommodations or Super Camping guides, which are available from a variety of tourist information sites, or call (604) 689-9025.

Fishing/Boating

For those who'd "rather be fishing" than riding a ferry, BC Ferries allows passengers to fish over the side of the *Queen of Chilliwack* at the various stops. You can use your own tackle or rent gear from BC Ferries. Just don't hook the anchor!

Hakai Pass in the Hakai Provincial Recreation Area (see Kayaking, above) is world-famous for its salmon fishing, particularly for **chinook** (spring), which are commonly caught on cut-plug herring. The area has a number of commercial **floating fish camps** and resorts. Besides salmon, there's good fishing here for halibut, lingcod, and rockfish.

A relaxing and memorable fishing trip can be had aboard the *Breeze*, a converted deep-sea tug that anchors at Hakai Pass for the fishing season. Charter flights to the *Breeze* can be organized for a group of 10 or 12 from Vancouver; charter or scheduled flights can be arranged out of Port Hardy. Call (250) 656-6311. A similar operation is run aboard the *Ocean Explorer*, a 110-foot (33-m) vessel that moves with the salmon from June to September. For information, call Intercoast Adventures, (604) 870-0677.

For further information about fishing in Hakai Pass, consult the annual *Tidal Waters Sport Fishing Guide*, a free publication available from the federal Department of Fisheries and Oceans and most sporting-good stores.

Midcoast **fishing-charter operators** are located at Shearwater and Ocean Falls. Sportfishing adventures in Hakai can be arranged through Whiskey Point Fishing Charters on Denny Island, (250) 957-2723, in Shearwater; Hakai Lodge, Inc., (206) 784-4454 or (800) 538-3551 (U.S.); Joe's Salmon Lodge, (604) 244-9549; Ole's Lodge, (250) 287-2311; or Hakai Beach Resort, (604) 231-3721. Besides saltwater fishing, Ocean Falls Fishing Lodge, (800) 661-7550, offers freshwater fly-fishing for trout in nearby Link Lake, and Twin Lakes, a 20-minute ride away (by four-wheel-drive vehicle), has dolly varden, cutthroat trout, and kokanee.

Pleasure **boaters** have always appreciated the pristine beauty of the Central Coast; however, many have been reluctant to transit the open waters around Cape Caution, the only part of the Inside Passage not sheltered by offshore islands. Now boaters can bring their crafts by ferry to any of the coastal communities and launch from there. The ferry has a hosting service available for a small charge. Should you choose to put your boat in at Klemtu, for instance, and travel to Shearwater, the ferry can bring your vehicle and trailer down to meet you. Now that's service! For information about moorage and other facilities, contact BC Ferries, (250) 386-3431, or toll-free in Canada, (888) 223-3779.

Wildlife

The midcoast is **bald eagle** country, and kayakers will also have the company of the ubiquitous kingfisher, common loon, cormorant, and sandpiper. In the **Hakai Provincial Recreation Area** (see Kayaking, above), over **100 species of birds** have been identified, ravens and ospreys among them. Feeding flocks of gulls, auklets, murres, and murrelets are numerous in the waters of Kildidt and Queens Sounds. Black oystercatchers, pelagic cormorants, surf birds, and both black and ruddy turnstones are also common.

The intertidal waters are home to an amazing number of marine life form, and their existence and activities are controlled by the rhythmic movements of the tides. Every **tide pool** has its own distinctive inhabitants: mollusca, crabs, starfish, anemones, sea urchins, and many others.

Marine mammals to watch for include harbour seals, sea lions, beavers, river otters, orcas, and humpback whales. Offshore waters are home to minke, gray, and humpback whales, as well as porpoises and dolphins. Terrestrial wildlife includes black-tailed **deer, mink,** and **wolves,** as well as **black, Kermode,** and (on the mainland) the largest **grizzly bears** in the province.

Diving

The waters of the **Hakai Provincial Recreation Area** (see Kayaking, above) are among the finest in the world for underwater exploration, with exceptional viewing opportunities year-round. There are wrecks along virtually the entire Central Coast, making it a magnet for divers. (Three good wrecks are just off **Atli Point,** near Shearwater.) Consult *Diver Magazine* regarding dive spots in the area; **Namu** is particularly popular. For **charter dive tours,** contact Intercoast Adventures in Abbotsford, (604) 870-0677. Their 110-foot (33-m) vessel, the *Ocean Explorer,* is outfitted with diving tanks and wet suits, and is based on the Central Coast between June and September.

Hiking

Shearwater features a couple of good trails to nearby lakes, including **Croil Lake** (1 mile/1.6 km return), **Eddie Lake** (4 miles/6 km return), and **Gullchuk Lake** (6 miles/10 km return). A rudimentary map is available from the Shearwater Marine Resort.

There are plenty of trails and roads in and around **Ocean Falls** for hikers and mountain bikers. Those who are fit might want to hike up and around **Link Lake** behind the dam, or just hike around the remains of the old community and try to imagine what it was once like. Information can be obtained at the courthouse adjacent to the ferry terminal.

For trails around **Bella Coola,** see The Bella Coola Road (Highway 20) chapter.

Depending on your route, your trip aboard the *Queen of Chilliwack* may include an offshore photo stop at "Mackenzie's Rock," 24 miles (39 km) east of Ocean Falls on the north shore of the Dean Channel. Of inspirational significance for hikers, this marks the western terminus of Alexander Mackenzie's historic overland passage, where he inscribed the following message: *Alex Mackenzie, from Canada, by land, the twenty-second of July, one thousand seven hundred and ninety-three.* An engraved plaque commemorates the first-ever transcontinental journey, achieved by this employee of the North West Company, and the small **Sir Alexander Mackenzie Provincial Park** surrounds the site. This is also the formal western terminus of the Alexander Mackenzie Heritage Trail (see The Bella Coola Road (Highway 20) chapter).

outside in

Attractions

You'll feel as though you're on the edge of the world in **Port Hardy**—to venture any farther north, you'll need a boat or a plane. It's a town of loggers, fishermen, and miners, as well as travellers stopping long enough to catch the ferry to Prince Rupert or to Bella Coola. Reserve accommodation in Port Hardy ahead in summer; motels are usually packed the night before the Prince Rupert boat leaves and the night after it arrives.

The famous Edward S. Curtis film *In the Land of the War Canoes* was filmed near Port Hardy at **Fort Rupert,** a good place to purchase authentic Native American art.

North of Port Hardy at the confluence of the Burke Channel and Fitz Hugh Sound is an abandoned cannery called **Namu,** meaning "place of high winds" or whirlwind. Established in 1893 as a fish-processing plant and cannery, a fire levelled the community in the 1960s. The cannery was subsequently rebuilt and operations continued until the late 1980s, when high transportation costs and low fish prices forced the plant to close. You can still see structures built on wharves over the water, interconnected by boardwalk. A short trail leads to nearby Namu Lake, which has long expanses of sandy beaches and good fishing.

Bella Bella (also called Waglisla) is located approximately 40 miles (62 km) north of Port Hardy on Campbell Island and about 2 miles (3 km) north of McLoughlin Bay, where the *Queen of Chilliwack* docks. It is home to the Heiltsuk Native Band and is the largest community on the Central Coast (population 1,400). Although it was the former site of the Hudson's Bay Company's Fort McLoughlin in the 1830s, nothing remains of the fort. Services in Bella Bella include a bank, a large general store, a police station, and the only hospital and pharmacy on the Central Coast. A Native interpretive centre and "big house" explaining the history of the Heiltsuk peoples are located in McLoughlin Bay.

Three miles (5 km) from Bella Bella is the original site of the Heiltsuk encampment, **Shearwater,** on Denny Island. The current townsite was developed as an antisubmarine bomber reconnaissance unit in 1941, but disbanded in 1944. It was subsequently purchased by the Widsten family and developed into a full-service marina and fishing resort, the Shearwater Marine Resort; all that remains of the air force base is the hangar, the tarmac, and a few bunkers. Besides a Pacific Canadian fish plant, there are a couple of bed-and-breakfast lodgings, fishing-charter operators, moorage for pleasure boaters, a small store and post office, and regular water taxi service to Bella Bella.

On Swindle Island in Finlayson Channel, approximately 136 miles (219 km) north of Port Hardy, is **Klemtu,** home of the Kitasoo Native Band and the original site of summer camps where the Xais-Xais and Kitasoo peoples came to fish and hunt. A permanent settlement emerged in the 1870s with the advent of coastal steamer service. The China Hat Cannery constructed in 1925 by Todd & Sons is now owned and operated by the band, along with an experimental aquaculture farm, and is the village's main employer. The 200 residents live along the waterfront, which has a long boardwalk, and commercial activities center around the public Transport Canada wharf. A hot kayaking and dive spot, services here include a well-equipped general store, a cafe, post office, a modern fuel facility with a full range of marine and auto fuels, and a community health clinic. Note: Klemtu is a "dry" community (no liquor available).

The town of **Prince Rupert** began as a dream. Founder Charles Melville Hays saw the island on which it sits as the perfect terminus for rail as well as sea travel and trade. Unfortunately, on a trip back from Europe, where he was rustling up money to help finance his vision, he met with an untimely death aboard the *Titanic*. Seventy-five years later, a number of local folks rekindled Hays's dream, and by the mid-1980s, Prince Rupert had two major export terminals and a booming economy. With this newfound prosperity have come culture and tourism. The **Museum of Northern British Columbia** has one of the finest collections of Northwest Coast Indian art you're likely to find anywhere; First Ave E and McBride, (250) 624-3207.

Prince Rupert is also a common jumping-off point for trips to the Queen Charlottes (see Queen Charlotte Islands (Haida Gwaii) chapter) as well as to Alaska. The Alaska ferry winds north through the panhandle to Skagway; call (800) 642-0066 for Alaska Marine Highway information.

For information on Bella Coola, see The Bella Coola Road (Highway 20) chapter.

Restaurants

Smile's Seafood Cafe ☆ Since 1922, Smile's Cafe has been tucked unobtrusively among the fish-processing plants beside the railroad. Favourites still include the fresh Dungeness crab, halibut, and black cod, and service is small-town friendly. *131 Cow Bay Rd (follow 3rd Ave into George Hills Way), Prince Rupert; (250) 624-3072; $$.*

Lodgings

For recommended lodgings, see Adjoining Areas to this chapter.

More Information

BC Ferries: *(888) 223-3779 in Canada or (250) 386-3431; Web site: www.bcferries.bc.ca.*

BC Forest Service, Mid Coast Forest District: *(250) 982-2000.*

BC Parks, Central Coast/Hakai Provincial Recreation Area: *(250) 398-4414.*

BC Parks, Port Hardy region: *(250) 248-3931.*

BC Parks, Prince Rupert region: *(250) 847-7565.*

BC Travel InfoCentre: *(800) 667-1994.*

Bella Coola InfoCentre: *(250) 982-0008.*

Klemtu Tourist Office: *(250) 839-2346.*

Port Hardy Chamber of Commerce: *(250) 949-7622.*

Prince Rupert InfoCentre: *(800) 667-1994.*

Skeena Valley Wilderness Adventures: *(250) 624-5700, for advice on outdoor exploration and guided tours in the Prince Rupert region.*

Tourism BC: *(604) 689-9025.*

Queen Charlotte Islands (Haida Gwaii)

A scimitar-shaped archipelago of about 150 islands in a chain 155 miles (250 km) long, including Graham and Moresby Islands, Naikoon Provincial Park, and Gwaii Haanas National Park.

They lie on the edge of the province's collective memory like a dream scarce remembered; mythical and elusive, full of meaning and beauty, yet incomprehensible to the waking mind. Impossible not to marvel at, and revel in, these are the Queen Charlotte Islands, arguably one of the most beautiful and diverse landscapes in the world. Sometimes called Canada's Galápagos, they form a distinctive ecosystem. The animals are familiar yet different. The black bears here, for instance, have a longer snout than elsewhere. They're also bigger, flying in the face of the so-called "island rule" of evolution, that large animals get smaller when trapped on an island (a rule that was conceived, incidentally, by naturalist Bristol Foster while studying evolutionary patterns in the Queen Charlottes).

The Charlottes are about 60 miles (100 km) off the mainland, and are made up of about 150 islands. Two islands, Graham to the north and Morseby to the south, comprise the majority of the land mass. Most of Moresby is inaccessible by car except via logging road (a far, far too common feature of the Charlottes) or an alternative form of transportation, such as chartered boat, sea kayak, floatplane, or foot. Wildly undeveloped and unprotected, much of the land mass is open to resource-based exploitation.

The English name for these islands is prosaic, almost boring.

Named for the wife of King George III, or rather, for the ship that was named for her, the name hardly serves to capture their elusive quality. The Haida name that the islands go by now is hardly better: Haida Gwaii, the place of the people. It's a name that was given after the land was taken away from the Haida, and then part of it given back, grudgingly, after European diseases destroyed an entire culture and reduced the population of 30,000 Haida to a mere 600.

There is an older name for this place, a name that comes from the mists of time and seems to be the most appropriate name of all: Xhaaid-lagha Gwaayaai, Islands at the Boundary of the World.

Getting There

There are only 75 miles (120 km) of paved roads in the Queen Charlotte Islands, and the cost of transporting your car on the ferry is prohibitive, so we suggest leaving your car behind and letting boats, foot, or taxi be your mode of transport. Take the six- to eight-hour ferry crossing from Prince Rupert to Skidegate Landing on Graham Island (BC Ferries, (250) 386-3431, (888) 223-3779 in Canada); fly from Vancouver (Canadian Airlines International, (800) 665-1177) or Prince Rupert (Harbour Air Seaplanes, (604) 278-9897) to Sandspit on Moresby Island; or utilize charter air routes from the mainland. On Graham, Highway 16 (all of which is paved) runs north from Queen Charlotte City, the navel of the Charlottes, for 70 miles (113 km) to Masset on the north coast. Across Skidegate Inlet, a logging road runs 25 miles (40 km) south from Alliford Bay to Moresby Camp, or via Sandspit and Gray Bay, the first 9 miles (15 km) of which are paved. Contact the Sandspit Visitor Information Centre for more information; (250) 637-5362.

Adjoining Areas

NORTH: **The Stewart-Cassiar Highway (Highway 37)**

SOUTH: **North Vancouver Island**

EAST: **Inside Passage and Discovery Coast**

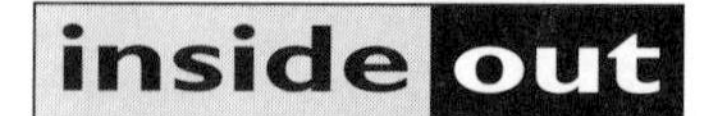

Parks/Camping

There are two large parks in the Charlottes: Naikoon Provincial Park in the north, and Gwaii Haanas National Park in the south. Gwaii Haanas is comprised of 138 separate islands, including the southern tip of Moresby Island.

Naikoon Provincial Park gets its name from a corruption of the

Haida term for "long nose," which was the Haida name for **Rose Spit,** one of the most prominent features in the park. The interior of the park remains undeveloped. There are two campgrounds: **Misty Meadows Campground** (30 vehicle/tent sites) near park headquarters in Tlell, and **Agate Beach Campground** (41 vehicle/tent sites). There are also three small shelters along the east coast of the park, a popular backpacking trip. Naikoon is 22 miles (35 km) north of Skidegate. For information, contact the park supervisor, (250) 557-4390, or BC Parks' Skeena District Office, (250) 847-7320.

There are 15 vehicle/tent sites plus several walk-in campsites at **Haydn Turner Park** on the west side of Queen Charlotte City. **Kagan Bay Forest Service Recreation Site,** just west of Queen Charlotte City, has 4 campsites. It's located 3 miles (5 km) west of town on Honna Forest Service Rd. A second road heads north and then west across Graham Island, to the west coast and a pair of Forest Service campgrounds on Rennell Sound. The **Cone Head Forest Service Recreation Site** has space for 2 vehicles/tents, and is about 9 miles (15 km) north past the 9-vehicle **Rennell Sound Forest Service Recreation Site.**

Across Skidegate Inlet on Moresby Island lie four Forest Service campgrounds. To find them, drive 9 miles (15 km) east from the ferry landing at Alliford Bay to Sandspit. Follow the main road south from there as it leads to two Forest Service campgrounds on the island's more sheltered east coast. The **Gray Bay Campground** 13 miles (21 km) southeast of Sandspit has two locations and space for 20 vehicles. A smaller, 2-vehicle campground on **Sheldens Bay** is located about 7 miles (11 km) farther south. Southwest of Allsford Bay are an 11-vehicle recreation site on **Mosquito Lake,** 27 miles (44 km) from Sandspit, and the 7-vehicle site at **Moresby Camp,** 4.5 miles (7 km) beyond. For more information and a map, contact the BC Forest Service, Queen Charlotte District Office, 1229 Cemetery Rd, (250) 559-6200 in Queen Charlotte City.

Elsewhere in the Charlottes, camping is not organized. There are no formal campgrounds in **Gwaii Haanas National Park Reserve and Haida Heritage Site** (managed by both Parks Canada and the Council of the Haida Nation), because there is no road access to the park. The park was formed in 1987 amidst a tense confrontation that divided the island's population, as well as public opinion across Canada and around the world. There are perhaps only 6,000 permanent residents in the Charlottes, but 3 million people pledged their support to see logging stopped in this area. At the height of the confrontation, 72 Haida were arrested and charged with criminal contempt of court, an act that shocked the international community. In a gesture of good faith, the Canadian government passed a resolution to support the Haida's wishes, and Gwaii Haanas was formed. Haida Gwaii Watchmen (Haida-appointed park wardens) have established **interpretive centres** at significant visitor stopping places such as Skedans, or K'una (outside park boundaries), Tanu (T'anuu), Windy Bay (Hlk'waah), Hotspring Island (Gandla'kin), and Ninstints on Anthony Island. For more information on ancient Haida villages, contact the Haida Gwaii Watchmen, (250) 559-8225, located beside the Haida Gwaii Museum at Qay'llnagaay near BC Ferries' Skidegate landing.

Random camping is the rule in Gwaii Haanas. You camp where you please, preferably on sand or stone, or wherever else you will have as little impact as possible. Camping is not permitted at T'anuu Village, or on Gandla'kin (Hotspring), Ata Naa (House), Copper, Jeffrey, Rankine, or Skung Gwaii (Anthony) Islands, or Slug Islet. These areas are particularly sensitive cultural sites or important bird-nesting areas. If in doubt, ask at any of the Watchmen base camps. There is no camping at any Haida Gwaii Watchmen site in the park except for **Windy Bay,** or Hik'yaah, where the stand against logging was taken by the Haida Nation back in the 1980s. For information, contact the Haida Gwaii Watchmen, (250) 559-8225.

Anthony Island, home of the old Haida village of **Ninstints,** is located within the boundaries of the park and is a UNESCO World Heritage Site. For people wishing to visit Gwaii Haanas, there are mandatory **orientation sessions** daily at the Queen Charlotte Visitor Information Centre, Queen Charlotte City (Graham Island), and at the Sandspit Visitor Information Centre (Moresby Island). Call (250) 559-8818 to determine exact times of sessions at each locale. A parks permit ($15) is needed to visit many areas within the park. Call (800) 663-6000 to make a reservation or for further information.

Kayaking

The kayak is a boon to the free spirit. It offers flexibility and mobility to the person who doesn't wish to be hampered by destination-driven travel schedules or a timetable other than the rhythm of the tides. Such is the lure of kayaking around Haida Gwaii. What need is there of a specific destination where every place is as magical as the next, save those coastlines ravaged by logging? The southeastern side of the Charlottes, rife with tiny islands, secluded coves, and lots of sheltered coastline, is the most popular kayaking destination. Because the Charlottes are perched on the edge of the Americas, plan on prohibitive conditions on at least a few—if not most—of the days you are out. The exposed west side of the islands receives the brunt of the open ocean, but any place can suffer a good buffeting by **severe weather.** Flexibility and spare time are two of the most important safety features you can bring with you.

Anyone planning on doing any serious kayaking needs the appropriate charts, a compass, and the knowledge of how to use them. Kayaking is one of the best ways to explore the Charlottes, but without a firm grounding in open-water kayaking or an experienced guide, it can also be one of the most dangerous. Wicked currents, unpredictable weather patterns, thick kelp beds, and submerged rocks or reefs all can, and have, claimed kayaks and kayakers. (The Coast Guard does not issue small-craft warnings for this area because small-craft-warning conditions are considered to be present at all times.)

The entire cluster of islands has been circumnavigated by kayak, and is open to the seafaring explorer. That said, **Gwaii Haanas National Park Reserve** is by far the most popular kayaking playground, with such destinations as **Hotspring Island, Burnaby Narrows, Windy Bay, Anthony Island (Ninstints), Tanu, All Alone Stone, Rose Harbour, St. James Island, Flatrock Island, Echo Harbour** . . . the list goes on and on. Many kayak trips start at Sandspit, although a less exposed route starts from Moresby Camp. From Moresby Camp to the northern boundary of the park reserve is a two-day, 22-mile (35-km) paddle, weather permitting. You could spend months, even years, exploring the coasts in Gwaii Haanas, stopping to investigate the many onshore and inland attractions, and still not feel that you knew the place. But that's part of the magic and appeal of the Charlottes.

Marine **charts** of Gwaii Haanas are available from the Hydrographic Chart Distribution Office, Department of Fisheries and Oceans, P.O. Box 6000, 9860 W Saanich Rd, Sidney, BC V8L 4B2. Topographic **maps** are available from the Geological Survey of Canada, BC Ministry of Crown Lands, in Victoria and the BC Government Agent in Queen Charlotte City. Tide tables published annually by the Hydrographic Service provide instructions on the use of tables to determine daily tides (time and height) for specific locations. For the Queen Charlotte Islands, you should obtain: *Canadian Tide & Current Tables Volume 6 (current year), Barkley Sound and Discovery Passage to Dixon Entrance* (available from Supply and Services Canada). Charts include #3808, #3809, #3825, #3853, #3894, and #3897. For detailed accounts of paddling routes around Moresby Island, consult *Sea Kayaking Canada's West Coast* by John Ince and Hadi Köttner.

If you are not travelling with a guide or guided tour, file a trip plan with the Canadian Coast Guard in Prince Rupert. Call collect, (250) 627-3082. Be sure to contact them as soon as you return. If you don't, you may be held responsible for any unnecessary search and rescue initiated on your behalf.

For information on **guided sea-kayak tour operators,** contact Parks Canada, Gwaii Haanas, (250) 559-8818, which maintains a directory.

Fishing

Fishing is the most common sport in the Queen Charlottes, there being ready access to superb freshwater and saltwater fishing. On many streams, high tide can easily push inland a mile (1.6 km) or more. As catch limits vary for tidal and nontidal waters, tidal boundaries are posted on streams where regulations are subject to change. Salmon fishing is seasonal. Check with the Department of Fisheries and Oceans, (250) 559-4413, for regulations and seasons. Fishing for just about everything else is a year-round sport. Catch cutthroat, rainbow trout, or dolly varden inland, or get out onto the ocean to jig for lingcod, red snapper, or halibut. Anglers fishing for the latter have been known to swamp smaller boats trying to land these large fish, so be careful if you snag a big one.

There are a number of outfitters, guides, and resorts on the Charlottes. For more **information,** contact the Queen Charlottes InfoCentre, (250) 559-4742. If you are interested in renting a boat, the InfoCentre can point you in the right direction.

There's a boat launch at **Mayer Lake** in Naikoon Provincial Park and wilderness camping along the lakeshore for people making extended fishing voyages. Mayer Lake and **Tlell River** are the most accessible freshwater fishing spots in Naikoon. **Yakoun Lake,** about 15 miles (25 km) northwest of Queen Charlotte City, is another popular freshwater fishing destination.

On Moresby Island, the best lake fishing is found in **Mosquito** and **Skidegate Lakes.** Both lakes are near Moresby Camp. Mosquito Lake is closer, about 3 miles (5 km) northwest, while Skidegate Lake is about 6 miles (10 km) beyond.

If you don't have a fishing rod, you can try your hand (and shovel) at digging for **razor clams** (a 12-clam-per-person limit is in effect; no licence needed) at low tide at **North Beach** in Naikoon Provincial Park. The clams are found between the high and low tide lines. Quarter-sized depressions in the sand show where clams most likely are. If the sand moves when tapped, there's a clam below. The trick is to dig fast enough to catch up with the clam, which is burrowing for safety. It takes a few tries to get the hang of it, and you have to be quick; these puppies are fast.

Hiking

There are four trails running through Naikoon Provincial Park, and hiking time ranges from a few hours to a few days. The longest trail is the **East Beach Trail.** It's 55 miles (90 km) from the Tlell River Bridge to Rose Point, a three- to four-day hike along mostly level terrain. There are three shelters along the route. It's recommended that you hike the trail south to north to avoid fighting prevailing winds. Strong hikers can do the East Beach Trail from the Tlell River Bridge to **Cape Ball River** and back (8.5 miles/14.5 km one way) in a day. A second trail runs 3 miles (5 km) one way from the Tlell River Bridge and leads to the **Pesuta,** an old log barge that was wrecked here in 1928. Two trails start from Tow Hill on the north side of the park. The first leads to the summit of **Tow Hill,** an easy 0.6-mile (1-km) uphill climb. You can see Alaska from the top. A second trail leads 6 miles (10 km) to **Cape Fife** on the east coast. From here it is possible to hook up with the East Beach Trail, and hike a two-day, 13-mile (21-km) loop back to Tow Hill.

Many of the Forest Service recreational sites on Graham Island (see Parks/Camping, above) are located along beaches, with long stretches of open sand before your wandering feet. If level, sandy beaches aren't your cup of tea, try the **Sleeping Beauty Trail,** which leads up to the top of Mount Genevieve near Queen Charlotte City. It's not a long trail, but it is steep. To reach the trailhead, go north of the Forest Service office on 1229 Cemetery Rd and follow Honna Forest Rd for 3 miles (5 km). The trailhead is well signed. Allow 90 minutes to reach the summit of Mount Genevieve. For more information and directions, check with the Queen Charlotte Visitor Information Centre, (250) 559-8316, or the Forest Service, (250) 559-6200.

Over on Moresby Island, **The Gray Bay–Cumshewa Head Trail** leads 3 miles (4.5 km) from the end of the Forest Service road near Sheldens Bay along the shoreline to Cumshewa Head, one of the easternmost points on Moresby.

For more information, consult *A Guide to the Queen Charlottes* by Neil Carey, now in its 12th edition.

Wildlife

The Queen Charlottes are rich in wildlife in the sky and sea, and on the ground. Many of the animals are native, but some—**blacktail deer, elk, beavers, raccoons,** and even **wild cows** in Naikoon Provincial Park—are introduced. Among the native species, expect to see **black bears** and **river otters,** birds such as **bald eagles, Steller's jays,** and **peregrine falcons,** and all kinds of ocean creatures, from **grey and killer whales** to **jellyfish** and **starfish.**

One of the best places to see the latter is in Burnaby Narrows on the east side of Moresby Island, accessible only by boat from Moresby camp. Also known as Dolomite Narrows, the waterway connects Juan Perez Sound with Skincuttle Inlet. The narrows are about half a mile (1 km) long, about 160 feet (50 m) wide, and quite shallow, especially at low tide.

The bottom is coloured with a cornucopia of **sea life:** starfish, sea urchins, moon snails, clams, needlefish, sea cucumbers, sea blubbers, red crab . . . the list goes on and on. Because of the high nutrient content in the water, the aquatic life is almost impossibly large and vibrant. From a kayak or other small boat the viewing is good; with a mask and snorkel, it's even better. At low tide it is possible to walk along the shore, but as this can't be done without treading on delicate life forms, it is discouraged.

It can be reached only by boat or plane, but nothing is more idyllic than relaxing in a hot spring on Hotspring Island and watching a pod of orcas swim past. Killer whales, or **orcas,** are often sighted in the Juan Perez Sound region. Best time for whale watching is late spring and early summer.

Eagles are a common sight, as are dozens of other birds scattered about the islands. A good place to go is the Delkatla Wildlife Sanctuary near Masset, at the head of the Delkatla inlet. **Sandhill cranes** stop here in spring and fall on their migratory routes, and **tundra swans** stay for the winter. Dozens of other birds—coots, snipe, and various species of duck and geese among them—can be found here at different times of the year. Another common resting spot for migrating birds is the Rose Spit Ecological Reserve in Naikoon Provincial Park.

Fully one third of the province's **sea lion** population calls the Charlottes home. A large colony hauls up on Joseph Rocks, off the west coast of Graham Island, miles away from the nearest point of road access (the Cone Head Forest Service Site; see Parks/Camping, above). This is a trip best made by boat or kayak. Only experienced paddlers should attempt travelling along the exposed west coast of the Charlottes, though. A second, water-access-only site for viewing sea lions is located at the southernmost tip of the Charlottes, on a string of islands called the Kerouards. All manner of seabirds, including the **horned puffin,** can also be seen. Visitors in this area can never be sure what manner of creature will show up. A pod of orcas, a grey or a humpbacked whale, or perhaps a gang of **Dall's porpoises,** numbering up to 300 strong, may escort you as you sail or paddle along in the southern section of Gwaii Haanas.

Beaches

When you stand on the west coast of the Charlottes, nothing lies between you and Japan except the great expanse of the North Pacific. Currents from across the ocean kiss the shores of Haida Gwaii, washing up all kinds of interesting treasure. The most common find on the beaches used to be the glass floats used on Japanese fishing nets, but lately all kinds of artifacts have washed up, from enough dead jellyfish to make it look like a freak snowstorm has hit the beach, to hockey pads and Nike shoes spilled from passing freighters. Glass floats make great souvenirs; dead jellyfish don't. Occasionally, you'll find the bleached bones of a dead whale, or a thick knot of rope. Litter on the beaches, such as the ubiquitous empty dish detergent bottles, are reminders that the world is awash in plastic. The west side of the Charlottes is dotted with pocket coves and beaches, most of which are cannot be reached by road, but you can spend a day combing beaches around **Rennell Sound.** To reach these shores, travel north from Queen Charlotte City on gravelled Skidegate Main Line Forest Rd for about 25 miles (40 km). The road divides north and south along Rennell Sound. Watch for beach access points in either direction. For more information, contact the Forest Service office in Queen Charlotte City, (250) 559-6200.

outside in

Attractions

A microcosm of the British Columbia coast—often referred to as the Galápagos of the Northwest—these sparsely populated, beautiful islands offer an escape to a rough-edged (and often rainy) paradise. There are countless beaches, streams, fishing holes, coves, and abandoned Indian villages to explore. Many unique subspecies of flora and fauna share these islands with the 6,000 residents.

This string of islands is the ancestral home of the Haida, a nation legendary for its art. Many visitors come to the islands to see the abandoned villages on Moresby Island, accessible only by boat, and reservations are necessary (check with BC Parks, (250) 847-7320, before you visit any of the protected sites). The Haida quarry and carve rare black argillite, found only on these islands, into miniature totem poles, jewelry, and boxes. A few artist's studios may be open for you to visit (ask around upon your arrival), or purchase the art at one of several gift shops, including the one at the **Haida Gwaii Museum,** (250) 559-4643.

Food and lodging are available, mainly on Graham Island, but most people who come camp. For information, call the local Chamber of Commerce, (250) 559-8188, or call Kallahin Expeditions (out of Queen Charlotte City) for **island-related excursions**—everything from a bus-tour package to a pickup for you and your kayak; (250) 559-8070. Pacific Synergies offers sailing excursions in the area, (604) 932-3107. Or explore the island via kayak or sailboat with the help of Ecosummer, (604) 669-7741.

Lodgings

Spruce Point Lodge The lodge, on Skidegate Inlet, attracts families and couples alike—and, most often, kayakers. There are seven clean rooms. Reasonable rates include a continental breakfast, and adventurers on a budget will appreciate the hostel rooms. *609 6th Ave (3.5 miles/5.5 km west of ferry, left after Chevron station, then second left); PO Box 735, Queen Charlotte City, BC V0T 1S0; (250) 559-8234; $.*

Copper Beech House ☆☆☆ The garden's a bit tangled at this old home, but come spring it smells wonderful, and come morning, so does breakfast. Upstairs are three guest rooms, but most visitors prefer to spend time at the dinner table where the owner's culinary improvisations abound. *1590 Delkatla (right by fishing boat docks, at Collison); Box 97, Masset, BC V0T 1M0; (250) 626-5441; $.*

More Information

BC Forest Service, Queen Charlotte District: *(250) 559-6200.*
BC Parks, Skeena District: *(250) 847-7320.*
Department of Fisheries and Oceans: *(250) 559-4413.*
Gwaii Haanas National Park Reserve and Haida Heritage Site: *(250) 559-8818.*
Haida Gwaii Watchmen: *(250) 559-8225, for information on ancient Haida villages, located beside museum at Qay'llnagaay near BC Ferries' Skidegate landing.*
MacMillan-Bloedel: *(250) 559-4224 (Queen Charlotte City), (250) 557-4212 (Juskatla), for information on logging roads on Graham Island.*
Masset Information: *(250) 626-3982.*
Queen Charlottes InfoCentre: *(250) 559-4742.*
Queen Charlotte Visitor Information Centre: *(250) 559-8316.*
Sandspit Visitor Information Centre: *(250) 637-5362.*
TimberWest: *(250) 637-5323 for information on logging roads on Moresby Island.*

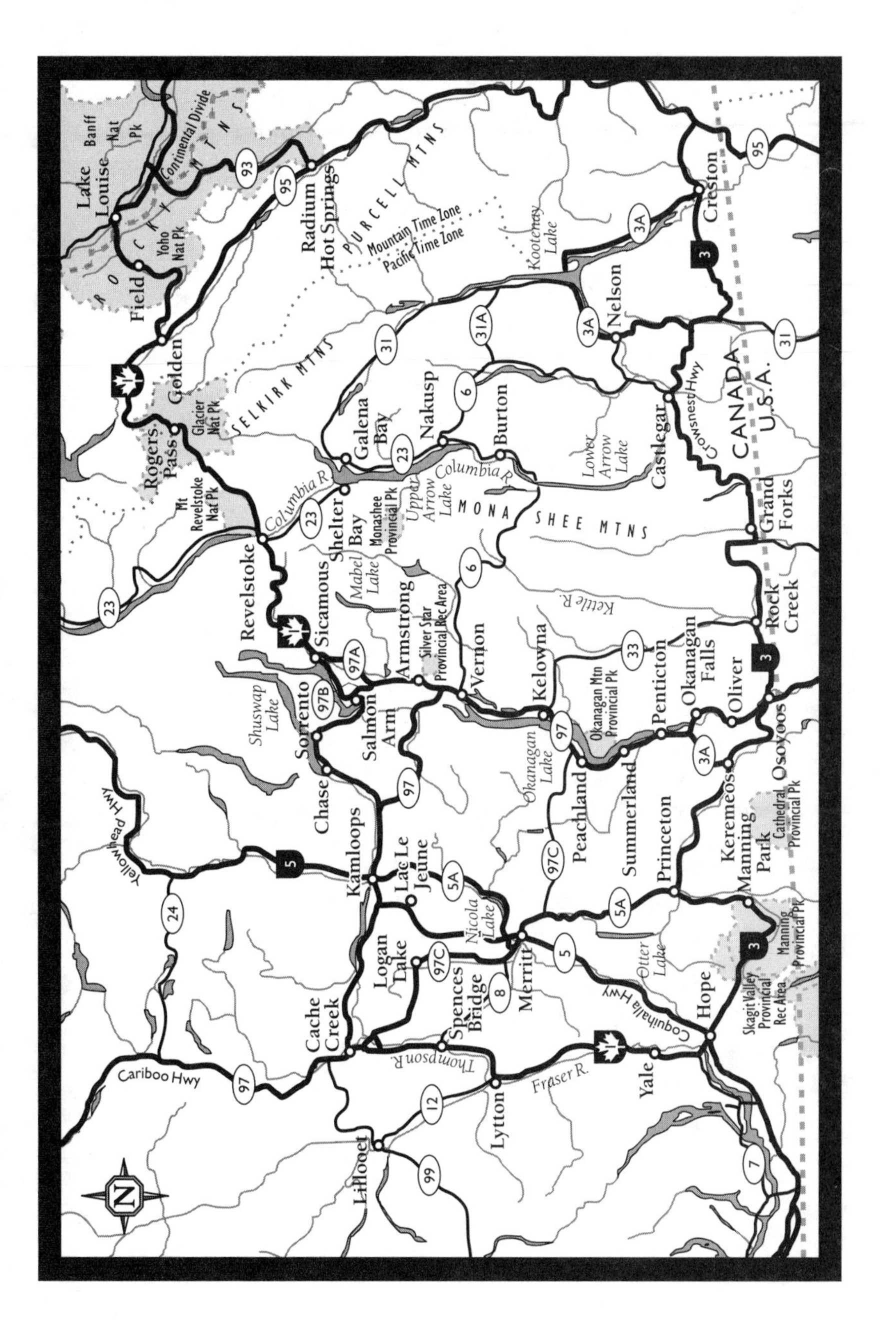

Southern Interior

The Trans-Canada Highway 415

Manning Provincial Park 435

Crowsnest Highway: South Okanagan Valley 441

The Coquihalla Highway 450

Okanagan Valley 458

Kettle Valley 478

Southern Interior

The Trans-Canada Highway

The Trans-Canada Highway (Highway 1) spans the Southern Interior of the province, linking the eastern end of the Fraser Valley with the Rocky Mountains at Golden, including Stein Valley Nlaka'pamux Heritage Park, Shuswap Lake and Roderick Haig-Brown Provincial Parks, and Mount Revelstoke, Glacier, and Yoho National Parks.

The 4,849-mile (7821-km) Trans-Canada is this country's mythic highway, starting (technically) at Mile 0 in St. John's, Newfoundland, and ending in Victoria, British Columbia. More than 500 miles (800 km) of the Trans-Canada run through the Southern Interior, Lower Mainland, and Vancouver Island regions. You can't really say you know British Columbia until you've travelled the area covered here, certainly one of the liveliest. Once you leave the Fraser Valley north of Hope, you're suddenly into some great driving. When you pass delightfully named Spuzzum (don't blink), you know that you're on your way towards Golden, a distance of about 350 miles (560 km). In the short space of 25 miles (42 km) a series of seven tunnels, interspaced by long sections of heavily forested roadway, leads through the rock walls of the Fraser Canyon at Yale, Saddle Rock, Sailor Bar, Alexandra, Hell's Gate, Ferrabee, and China Bar (at 2,000 feet/610 m, one of the longest highway tunnels in North America).

In 1986, the opening of the Coquihalla Highway (Highway 5) sharply reduced traffic on the stretch of Highway 1 between Hope and Kamloops. Today this drive is much easier to explore without fear of holding up a convoy of 18-wheelers. Truckers surely don't miss this winding road through the canyon. However, anyone interested in a real motoring experience (instead of putting the car on cruise control) should drive this section of Highway 1. You'll be doing so in the spirit of many pioneers who've gone before you under much more trying circumstances.

Once east of the Fraser Canyon, the Trans-Canada climbs onto the open Thompson Plateau. The arid, eroded windswept countryside here is one of the most unusually beautiful landscapes in British Columbia, and that's saying a great deal. Thanks to widespread irrigation you'll find roadside fruit and vegetable stands between Lytton and Cache Creek.

A series of gentle mountain ranges rolls between the Thompson Plateau in the west and the Shuswap Highlands to the east, then rises dramatically in the Selkirk and Monashee Mountains between Revelstoke and Golden near the British Columbia–Alberta border. Travellers between the two towns must negotiate Rogers Pass (elevation 4,534 feet/1382 m), one of the great mountain crossings in the province and certainly the Trans-Canada Highway's crowning glory. The lofty sensation of crossing Rogers Pass is one of the rewards for travelling here.

Getting There

Almost every main road or highway in British Columbia intersects with the Trans-Canada at some point. To get to Yale, the westernmost point mentioned in this chapter, take Highway 1 from Hope or Highway 3 from Princeton. Highway 12 links Lytton with Lillooet. Highway 97 links the Central Interior with Highway 1 at Cache Creek. Highway 5 links Merritt in the Okanagan-Boundary to the south and Barrière in Central Interior to the north with Highway 1 at Kamloops. Highway 97 links Vernon in the north Okanagan Valley with Highway 1 at three points: Monte Creek, Salmon Arm, and Sicamous. Highway 23 links Shelter Bay in the West Kootenays with Highway 1 at Revelstoke. Highway 95 links Radium Hot Springs in the East Kootenays with Highway 1 at Golden. Kamloops (population 77,500), Salmon Arm (population 15,000), Revelstoke (population 8,400), and Golden (population 4,000) are the four major urban areas along this route. Kamloops is served by Air BC (Air Canada's regional branch), (800) 663-3721; Canadian Airlines International, (800) 665-1177; and Via Rail, (800) 561-8630. Greyhound Bus Lines, (800) 663-8868, offers daily service to all towns along the Trans-Canada Highway.

Adjoining Areas

NORTH: **The Cariboo Highway; The Yellowhead Highway**

SOUTH: **Okanagan Valley; Crowsnest Highway: The West Kootenays**

WEST: **The Fraser Valley**

inside out

Camping/Parks

Historic **Emory Creek Provincial Park** (34 vehicle/tent sites, reservations) has a small campground situated at the former townsite of Emory City, which was a tiny but bustling trading settlement in the mid-1800s. When the Canadian Pacific Railway decided that nearby Yale would be its major centre, Emory was left to "sigh and die." Conveniently located beside Hwy 1 and the Fraser River, this park fills up quickly in summer. Take Hwy 1 north from Hope for 11 miles (18 km). For reservations, call BC Parks, (800) 689-9025, between March 1 and Sept. 15. For more information on Emory Creek Provincial Park, call BC Parks' district office in Cultus Lake, (604) 824-2300.

The scent of sagebrush fills the air in **Skihist Provincial Park** (56 vehicle/tent sites), yet another park with a historical flavour. Situated high above the junction of the Thompson and Fraser Rivers, the park encompasses a section of the old Cariboo Wagon Road, used by early settlers and travellers here in the heart of the Thompson First Nation. The best things about this park are the Saskatoon berries, which you can munch on when they're in season, and the **whitewater river-rafting.** Arrange a trip at nearby Lytton or Spences Bridge (see Rafting, below). Go about 5 miles (8 km) north of Lytton on Hwy 1. For more information, call BC Parks' district office in Kamloops, (250) 851-3000.

Right on the Thompson River, **Goldpan Provincial Park** (14 vehicle/tent sites) is the park of choice for anglers. The Thompson Nation has fished here for centuries, and still do. It's great for steelhead during the busiest time—mid-October to December. If you're river rafting, you might overnight here, as Goldpan Provincial Park is used as a rest stop for many commercial river-rafting companies. Swimming is fun here, too. Take Hwy 1 for 6 miles (10 km) south of Spences Bridge. For more information, call BC Parks, (250) 851-3000.

Anglers and swimmers alike gravitate to **Juniper Beach Provincial Park** (30 vehicle/tent sites). Juniper Beach is one of the few access points to the **Thompson River** between Savona and Spences Bridge. One of the newest parks in British Columbia, it was created to help protect a desert landscape. Some of the world's best steelhead fishing is found here. In July, you'll be able to watch sockeye salmon as they travel upstream to spawn in the Adams River. Visitors can pretend to join them by taking a plunge in a large, natural pool that is separated from the river for swimming. Take Hwy 1 east from Cache Creek for about 12 miles (19 km). For more information, call BC Parks, (250) 851-3000.

Steelhead Provincial Park (32 vehicle/tent sites), a recently created park, is located on the southwest shore of Kamloops Lake. Summer recreation draws a crowd, but at other times you'll have this park and its wonderfully eroded landscape to yourself. This is an angling hot spot, too. Take Hwy 1 about 22 miles (35 km) east of Cache Creek. For more information, call BC Parks, (250) 851-3000.

Niskonlith Lake Provincial Park (30 vehicle/tent sites) offers camping in a lushly forested environment, sheltered by towering cottonwoods. (Allergy sufferers beware in June.) Spring wildflowers bloom in extraordinary profusion, as birds make their northern migration through this area of the Shuswap Highlands. Come fall, the birds are back again. The park is open from April to October. Fishing and easygoing hiking are both good reasons to camp here. Take the mostly gravel road off Hwy 1 about 9 miles (15 km) northwest of Chase. For more information, call BC Parks, (250) 851-3000.

Shuswap Lake Provincial Park (272 vehicle/tent sites; reservations) is wildly popular. Everything you need for summer fun is right here: camping, picnicking, fishing, boating, paddling, swimming, hiking, windsurfing, sailing, houseboating, water-skiing, nature study, photography, visitor programs, and bicycling. With 7 miles (12 km) of paved trails, Shuswap Lake may also be the cycling capital of the BC Parks system. The park is open in the fall during the Adams River salmon run. (Don't confuse this park with Shuswap Lake Provincial Marine Park; see Boating/Canoeing, below). Take Hwy 1 about 56 miles (90 km) east of Kamloops, turn off towards Scotch Creek, then go about 12 miles (20 km) farther. For reservations, call (800) 689-9025; for more information on Shuswap Lake Provincial Park, call (250) 851-3000.

Silver Beach Provincial Park (20 vehicle/tent sites, 10 walk-in sites) is located at the end of a long, gravel road at the head of **Seymour Arm** on **Shuswap Lake.** Its size and distance from Hwy 1 keep many visitors at bay. Check it out for yourself; it's worth it. This part of the lake is as blessed with sandy beaches. Houseboaters come here to get away from it all. The park's forest setting is lovely—Douglas fir interwoven with aspen. Paddle around the mouth of the Seymour River to watch the salmon spawn from mid-August to mid-September. Also nearby are the remains of a gold-rush town. Go almost 11 miles (17 km) on Hwy 1 from Chase northeast to Scotch Creek, then take the 40-mile (65-km) logging road to the park. For more information, contact BC Parks, (250) 851-3000.

Herald Provincial Park (51 vehicle/tent sites; reservations) is also situated along the shore of **Shuswap Lake,** on **Salmon Arm.** The park is very popular and fills up quickly during July and August. For these months, reservations should be made well in advance. If you can't make a reservation, put your name on the waiting list for the small number of first-come, first-served sites that are available each day at noon. Campsites are located both at lakeside and a short distance uphill in the cool forest. Swimming, fishing, and bird-watching are the order of the day here. For picnickers looking for a break from Hwy 1, it's worth the short drive to reach the park, situated on the grounds of an old homestead; there's a feeling about the place as if you've come to visit your grandparents. Take Hwy 1 east of Tappen for about 7 miles (12 km). For reservations, call (800) 689-9025 between March 1 and September 15. For more information on Herald Park, call BC Parks, (250) 851-3000.

Yard Creek Provincial Park (90 vehicle/tent sites) lies just east of Sicamous on Hwy 1. Despite its roadside location, the park offers quiet, shady camping from June to September and is a pleasant stopover camp or even base camp when exploring the Shuswap. The icy temperature of Yard Creek precludes swimming on even the hottest days. Conversely, for much of the year, moist conditions prevail here in the eastern reaches of the Interior wetbelt. Take Hwy 1 almost 10 miles (15 km) west of Sicamous. For more information, contact BC Parks, (250) 851-3000.

Martha Creek Provincial Park (28 vehicle/tent sites) is a pleasant spot north of Revelstoke. The campground's western exposure on **Revelstoke Lake** provides scenic views as the Selkirk and Monashee Mountains are reflected in the lake's long, narrow surface. Excellent hiking and fishing await travellers who wish more than an overnight stay. Take Hwy 23 north of Revelstoke for 12 miles (19 km). For more information, contact BC Parks' district office in Nelson, (250) 825-3500.

Blanket Creek Provincial Park (64 vehicle/tent sites) is located on an old homestead where Blanket Creek enters the Columbia River. From here, the mighty river empties into Upper Arrow Lake on its way south. In fall, kokanee spawn at the mouth of the creek. The park offers good lake and stream fishing for dolly varden, kokanee, and rainbow trout. Thick stands of western hemlock, western red cedar, and white pine cover the slopes of the Monashees, which rise and roll off to the west. A brief five-minute walk leads from the campground to the delightful and beautiful 40-foot-high (12-m) **Sutherland Falls.** This park is also handy to the Shelter Bay ferry, which takes travellers into the West Kootenays. Take Hwy 23 15 miles (25 km) south of Hwy 1 in Revelstoke. For more information, contact BC Parks' district office in Nelson, (250) 825-3500.

For those of you who don't want to tackle camping in provincial or national parks, try **Golden Municipal Campground** (70 vehicle/tent sites). It's right on the shores of the lively **Kicking Horse River** in the middle of Golden. Call (250) 344-5412 for more information.

Tucked in between Harrison Lake and the Fraser Canyon is the

Nahatlatch Lake and River system. The river flows from a series of three lakes—**Nahatlatch, Hannah,** and **Frances**—12 miles (20 km) upstream from the Nahatlatch's confluence with the Fraser River. To reach the Nahatlatch, turn west off Hwy 1 at the main intersection in Boston Bar and drive downhill to the river. A bridge links Boston Bar with North Bend on the far shore. West Side Rd leads 11 miles (18 km) upriver from North Bend to the Nahatlatch River Bridge. Short trails descend to the river on both sides of the bridge. If you explore the south side of Nahatlatch below the bridge, you'll find open spots for fishing and backwater pools for swimming. The lakes themselves lie beside the narrow Nahatlatch Lakes Forest Rd that runs for 12.5 miles (20 km) west of the Nahatlatch River Bridge. As the Nahatlatch Forest Rd climbs above the Nahatlatch Canyon, you'll see groups of whitewater rafters (see Rafting, below) tackling this very powerful river and its tremendous series of rapids. A series of 10 Forest Service recreation sites lies along this road, most having access to either the river or the lakes. There is a car-top boat launch on each lake. Most sites are suited to only one or two vehicles, so just keep driving until you reach an empty spot. For a detailed map of the Nahatlatch River Forest Service recreation sites, contact the Chilliwack district office, 9880 S McGrath Rd in Rosedale, (604) 794-2100 or (800) 665-1551.

National Parks

Three national parks—Mount Revelstoke, Glacier, and Yoho—present themselves in succession beside Hwy 1 in the eastern reaches of the Southern Interior. Being national parks, they are by definition *big*, and you'll find much to do in each. Many of their attractions are described in subsequent sections. What follows here is a short description of each park and its camping facilities. For detailed on-line information on these parks, visit Parks Canada's Web site: http://parkscanada.pch.gc.ca. For information on fees and park passes, call (800) 748-7275.

Mount Revelstoke National Park offers no developed camping facilities, although a few primitive backcountry sites are available. This park welcomes hikers, cross-country skiers, and picnickers at a variety of day-use areas along Summit Rd and Hwy 1 as they weave through the park. Similar in its geographical features to Glacier National Park (where travellers will find overnight camping), Mount Revelstoke is extremely beautiful, with a mile-high rolling alpine plateau and spectacular views of the Monashees and Selkirks. This is one of the few places in Canada where it is possible to drive right into an alpine meadow. **Summit Road** winds 16 miles (26 km) up to the top of this 6,094-foot (1860-m) mountain. Unfortunately, this trip is possible only during the summer. Take Hwy 1 east from Revelstoke. For more information on Mount Revelstoke National Park, contact Parks Canada, (250) 837-7500. Park information is available at the Rogers Pass Visitor Centre, about 43 miles (70 km) east of Revelstoke, or about 50 miles (80 km) west of Golden. Information is also available from the Mount Revelstoke National Park administration office, 301C Third St W in Revelstoke.

Glacier National Park offers challenging outdoor experiences, including wilderness camping and hiking, mountaineering, and Nordic and alpine skiing. Until recently, there were three campgrounds in Glacier National Park, but now there are only two. Mountain Creek Campground has been closed as a result of widespread root rot in the trees; so severe is the damage that the area may have to be clear-cut. **Illecillewaet Campground** (58 vehicle/tent sites) is centrally located near Hwy 1 and has kitchen shelters and washrooms with flush toilets (no electrical hookups or RV sani-station). **Loop Brook Campground** (19 vehicle/tent sites) is farther west than Illecillewaet and has similar facilities. The interpretive program of Glacier and Mount Revelstoke National Parks, located in the Rogers Pass Visitors Centre at the summit of Rogers Pass on Hwy 1, depicts the human history of the region through fascinating accounts of first climbs, last spikes, lives lost, and railway lines laid. Hwy 1 winds for more than 27 miles (44 km) through Glacier National Park. The park's west gate is about 30 miles (48 km) east of Revelstoke, while its east gate is 24 miles (40 km) west of Golden. For more information on Glacier National Park, contact Parks Canada's office, 301C Third St W in Revelstoke, (250) 837-7500, or visit the Rogers Pass Information Centre, located at the park's west gate.

Yoho National Park has a total of 262 campsites that range from vehicle/tent to walk-in wilderness. **Kicking Horse Campground** (86 vehicle/tent sites), located 3 miles (5 km) west of Field on the British Columbia–Alberta border, could be considered the "main" site, with its playground, amphitheatre, and nearby grocery store; however, there are no water, sewer, or electrical hookups. **Hoodoo Creek Campground** (106 semiprivate vehicle/tent sites) is in a heavily wooded area and is near several trailheads. It's 15 miles (23 km) west of Field. **Chancellor Peak Campground** (58 semiprivate vehicle/tent sites) is also 15 miles (23 km) west of Field on the north side of Hwy 1 from the Hoodoo Creek Campground. **Takakkaw Falls Campground** (35 semiprivate walk-in only sites with wooden pallets for tents) is about 10 miles (16 km) up the Yoho Valley Rd from Field. This site has a great view of the 2,211-foot (675-m) falls and affords access to many of the trails in the Yoho Valley. **Lake O'Hara Campground** (30 semiprivate, walk-in only sites) is 7 miles (11 km) up the Lake O'Hara Rd from Hwy 1 on the east side of Spiral Tunnels, followed by an 8-mile (13-km) hiking trail. If you'd rather not walk in, you can access this campground by bus. The bus operates from June 19 through October 1. Reservations for campsites at Lake O'Hara and the bus must be made in advance, (250) 343-6433; inquire at the park office in Field. Hwy 1 runs through Yoho National Park. The park's western border is about 10 miles (16 km) east of Golden. To the east, Yoho borders Banff National Park and to the south it borders Kootenay National Park. The park information centre is located on Hwy 1 in Field. Call (250) 343-6783 for more information.

A final note about **national park permits:** a park pass is required for all visitors to national parks. This pass is available at the park gates or, for the credit-card endowed, by calling (800) 748-7275. You can choose between a $25 annual-entry permit, a $9 four-day permit, or a $4 daily-entry permit. In addition, there is a daily camping fee in summer. Note: Permits are good in national parks throughout Canada, including Alberta's Banff and Jasper National Parks, which are adjacent to British Columbia.

Hiking/Backpacking

The **Stein Valley** (see also Pemberton and Lillooet chapter) is one of the last untouched watersheds in the southwestern part of the province. **Stein Valley Nlaka'pamux Heritage Park** was officially protected in 1995 and is jointly managed by the Lytton First Nation and BC Parks. A very rewarding (if demanding) 46.5-mile (75-km) hike runs the full length of the valley. This hike is suitable only for very fit, experienced hikers who are prepared to be totally self-sufficient. Sudden changes in the weather can result in a whiteout, making route finding by compass a necessary skill, and it's important to remember that once you are at **Stein Lake,** the halfway point, you are at least two days away from any assistance. This is not a trip to be undertaken lightly. There are other hikes available here, however, which vary in difficulty and length. Wilderness campsites occur at regular intervals in the park. The main trailhead into the park is located north of Lytton near the mouth of the Stein River's confluence with the Fraser. To reach it, follow Hwy 12 north from its junction with Hwy 1 in Lytton and turn west on Lytton Ferry Rd to reach a free, 2-vehicle ferry, a total distance of 1 mile (1.6 km). The ferry operates between 6:00am and 10:15pm, with half-hour breaks at 10:30am and 6:30pm. Crossings take several minutes and waits are rare. Sailings may be affected by ice or spring runoff. For current information, contact the Ministry of Transportation and Highways, (604) 660-9770, in Vancouver. Follow West Side Rd north for 3 miles (5 km); the well-marked trailhead is 0.6 mile (1 km) west of West Side Rd on a dirt road that crosses Lytton First Nation land.

Call Lytton First Nation at (250) 455-2304 or BC Parks at (250) 851-3000 for more information and to get a report on conditions. For a detailed look at all of the features in the Stein Valley, including hiking trails, consult *The Stein Valley Guide* by Gordon White.

The Fraser Canyon contains the trailhead of a tortuous (and historic) trek made by fur traders in the 1840s. The **First Brigade Trail** (strenuous; 8 miles/13 km return) is the one to seek out, a gruelling ascent followed by an equally punishing descent through some of the steepest terrain in the Lower Mainland. The trailhead is located just north of the old Alexandra Lodge, about a mile (2 km) north of Alexandra Bridge Provincial Park (see Picnics/Scenic Drives, below). Take plenty of water.

In the Shuswap Highlands region east of Kamloops, hike the gentle trails in **Niskonlith Lake Provincial Park** (see Camping/Parks, above) in fall to see a host of migratory birds. Head to **Herald Provincial Park** (see Camping/Parks, above) for some interesting hiking: two distinct topographical units (upland and flat delta) have created a great terrain; there are also Native Canadian pithouse depressions, or *kekuli*, in the area west of the creek, as well as some old Native cache pits. **Roderick Haig-Brown Provincial Park** (see Wildlife, below) has several beautiful walks and low-key hikes; the **Lower Trail System** provides access to viewing the salmon run along the Adams River. You shouldn't miss the **Reinecker Creek** self-guided nature walk here, which leads to Margaret Falls. **Eagle River Nature Park,** about 7 miles (12 km) east of Sicamous, has 10 miles (16 km) of hiking and cross-country trails.

Mount Revelstoke National Park (see Camping/Parks, above) has a few primitive campsites sprinkled beside its backcountry trails. Some easy rambles, all of which begin from trailheads along Summit Rd as it climbs the flanks of Mount Revelstoke, include the **Eva Lake Trail** (easy; 7.5 miles/12 km return), which runs through both subalpine and alpine tundra zones. There's a backcountry cabin at Eva Lake, but visitors must register with the park warden before using it overnight. By far the most popular trail in the park is also its shortest: **Mountain Meadows Trail** (easy; 0.6 mile/1 km return) leads from the south side of the Heather Lake parking lot at the upper end of Summit Rd through nearby subalpine meadows that run riot with wildflowers in late July and early August. You can hike longer and harder if you want to by following **Lindmark Trail** (moderate; 10 miles/16 km return) for a day, a route that leads to Eagle and Balsam Lakes, which are pleasant resting spots. You'll find the most challenging hiking in the park on the **Summit Trail** (difficult; 16 miles/20 km return). Early residents blazed this hiking trail a century ago. Note: You must obtain a backcountry pass to explore in national parks.

Hiking in **Glacier National Park** (see Camping/Parks, above) is far more extensive and at higher elevation than in Revelstoke National Park. Glaciers cover much of the challenging terrain in the park, which is dominated by 10 peaks ranging from 8,530 to 11,120 feet (2600 to 3390 m) in height. By comparison, the highest peak in Mount Revelstoke National Park, Mount Coursier (elevation 8,681 feet/2646 m), is hard pressed to compete. **Illecillewaet Glacier** on the **Great Glacier Trail** (moderate; 6 miles/9.5 km return) has been a "must-see" destination for over a century. The trailhead is located behind the Illecillewaet campground (see Camping/Parks, above) on the east side of the Illecillewaet River. Cross the bridge next to the campground to reach the trailhead, which is located a short distance farther on the left. Over a half-dozen other hiking routes lead through the park from the Illecillewaet campground, including the **Avalanche Crest Trail** (moderate; 5 miles/8 km return), which offers some of the most dramatic views in this region of the park overlooking Rogers Pass. Icefields forever is the scenic byword here. The **Mount Sir Donald Trail** (strenuous; 5 miles/8 km return) and the **Perley Rock Trail** (strenuous; 7 miles/11 km return) begin from the same trailhead but diverge after 1.5 miles (2.5 km). The Sir Donald Trail brings hikers close to Vaux Glacier, while the Perley Rock Trail leads to the summit of Perley Rock from where hikers look out in awe at the crevassed expanse of the Illecillewaet Névé. Other trails in this area include the **Asulkan Valley Trail** (strenuous; 8 miles/13 km return), the **Glacier Crest Trail** (strenuous; 6 miles/9.5 km return), **Meeting of the Waters Trail** (easy; 1.2 miles/2 km return), and the **Marion Lake Trail** (easy; 2.7 miles/4.5 km return). The **Abbot Ridge Trail** (strenuous; 6 miles/10 km return) is an extension of the Marion Lake Trail and provides experienced hikers with some of the most challenging alpine trekking in the park short of donning crampons.

For more information on hiking routes in both Mount Revelstoke and Glacier National Parks, consult *Glacier Country* by John Woods.

There's extensive hiking along the almost 250 miles (400 km) of trails in **Yoho National Park** (see Camping/Parks, above), a park characterized by rock walls and waterfalls. Many of the trails begin beside or near Hwy 1 as it leads through the park. The park's west gate is located about 16 miles (26 km) east of Golden. Hwy 1 parallels the Kicking Horse River here as it winds through a beautiful, broad valley. By the time Hwy 1 reaches the park's headquarters in Field, a distance of about 18.5 miles (30 km), the tone of the landscape shifts to one of glaciated Rocky Mountain peaks. The east gate of the park is at the British Columbia–Alberta border on the Continental Divide. Total distance between the two gates is about 30 miles (48 km). About 1.5 miles (2.5 km) west of Field, Emerald Lake Rd leads north from Hwy 1 for 5 miles (8 km) to the parking lot beside Emerald

Lake, the largest lake in Yoho National Park. The **Emerald Lake Trail** (easy; 3-mile/5-km loop) leads around the lake, on which the faces of surrounding peaks and glaciers are reflected in stunning detail. The **Emerald Basin Trail** (moderate; 5.25 miles/8.5 km return) initially follows the Emerald Lake Trail for 1 mile (1.5 km), then climbs steeply through old-growth Douglas fir and western red cedar into the open alpine zone. As the trail approaches Emerald Peak, there are grand views of a hanging glacier on the limestone flanks of the peak. A much easier hike is the **Deerlodge Trail** (1.75-mile/2.8-km loop) where you can admire elegantly shaped hoodoos. The well-marked trailhead is located a short distance beyond the entrance to the Hoodoo Creek Campground (see Camping/ Parks, above). A 1-mile (1.6-km) hiking trail leads to a view of **Wapta Falls** and then descends to the gravel beach fanned out below the cataract. To reach the trailhead, turn south off Hwy 1 onto Wapta Falls Rd near the park's west gate and follow it for 1 mile (1.6 km). An even shorter trail leads to the foot of **Takakkaw Falls,** the third highest in Canada and emblematic of Yoho National Park. In the Cree language, *takakkaw* means "it is wonderful," which, coupled with *yoho,* "awe and wonder," expresses the exhilaration that most hikers will experience during a visit to the park. To reach the Takakkaw Falls trailhead, turn north on the narrow, winding Yoho Valley Rd located off Hwy 1, 2.3 miles (3.7 km) east of Field. Follow Yoho Valley Rd for 8.7 miles (14 km) to the parking lot from where the trail begins. The more demanding **Laughing Falls Trail** (moderate; 6 miles/9.5 km return) begins from the Takakkaw Falls parking lot and leads to the wilderness campground near Laughing Falls. Along the way, short side trips lead off to **Angel's Staircase, Point Lace Falls,** and **Duchesnay Lake.**

A good guide to hiking routes in Yoho National Park is *Backcountry Guide to Yoho National Park,* available at the Yoho Visitor Centre in Field. For **guided hiking tours** in Yoho National Park, contact Mountain Ramblers Hiking Tours, (250) 348-2336, in Parsons or the Four "H" Buffalo Ranch, (250) 344-5825, in Golden.

One of the most precious natural resources in Yoho National Park is its deposits of fossils. The remains of more than 120 species of marine animals from the Middle Cambrian epoch (about 515 million years ago) were unearthed in the early decades of this century by Charles Walcott, Secretary of the Smithsonian Institution in Washington, D.C. At the time of his discovery in Yoho National Park, Walcott was the world's leading authority on Cambrian rocks and fossils. Returning from an outing one day in the Yoho Valley, he split open a slab of shale that was blocking the Burgess Pass. Inside were the fossilized remains of soft-bodied organisms, preserved in greater detail than had ever been thought possible. Between

1909 and his death in 1927, Walcott collected and shipped fossils back to the Smithsonian for classification. Visitors to the Smithsonian can still see them on display, and visitors to Yoho National Park can view a sampling at the park's Information Centre. Each year a select group of visitors to Yoho can retrace Walcott's footsteps. In order to protect the delicate landscape in **Walcott's Quarry** and the **Trilobite Beds,** visitors are allowed access only as part of a guided tour. The hikes are led by licenced guides and limited to groups of 15. Hikes to both locations are lengthy, strenuous all-day endeavours on the steep, scree-covered slopes of Mount Field above Emerald Lake. The tours are given beginning in June and continuing through October, weather permitting. For fees, schedules, and reservations, contact the Yoho Burgess Shale Foundation, (800) 343-3006. For more information on the Burgess Shale, consult *Wonderful Life: The Burgess Shale and the Nature of History* by Stephen Jay Gould, or *Western Journeys* by Wood and Sinclair.

For more information on Yoho National Park, call the Yoho Information Centre, (250) 343-6783, or Yoho Park Administration, (250) 343-6324, both in Field.

Picnics/Scenic Drives

Alexandra Bridge Provincial Park, about 14 miles (22 km) north of Yale on Hwy 1, provides an interesting place to stop in the Fraser Canyon. An interpretative display gives picnickers an idea of the canyon's history. The canyon was a major obstacle to transportation developers who needed to link Interior locales with the rapidly urbanizing coastal settlements, and it has seen the passing of Simon Fraser; the road building of the Royal Engineers; the fur brigade; thousands of gold seekers; railway, highway, and bridge builders; and early truckers. Since the Cariboo gold-rush days of the 1860s, a strategically located bridge has spanned the Fraser River here. The original, Joseph Trutch's spectacular suspension bridge, opened in 1862. A second Alexandra Bridge washed out in the flood of 1887; a subsequent replacement built in 1925 is now a neglected relic.

Since 1965, travellers on Hwy 1 cross the river downstream from the park over a four-lane, orange-arched beauty. Look up the canyon from here and you'll get a quick glimpse of its silver-coated predecessor, which still has some flash left in its boiler-plate finish. The old bridge leads nowhere and, like a monument desecrated by rebellion, has been stripped of officialdom. Graffiti-scratching day trippers took over when the old bridge was decommissioned. One of oldest of the many well-preserved markings reads, "Eddie's getting married '65."

If you've got a morning or afternoon to dally away, picnic on the old

Alexandra Bridge's honeycomb plated-steel deck or at one of the picnic tables in the park. They are sheltered by towering Douglas fir, whereas the bridge sits in the open. Take your pick. A road leads from the parking lot to the old Alexandra Bridge, a five-minute walk from the picnic area. For more information, contact BC Parks' district office in Cultus Lake, (604) 824-2300.

Hwy 12 from **Lytton to Lillooet** runs along the Fraser River, a good way to see this important waterway. Hwy 8, 40 miles (65 km) in length from **Spences Bridge to Merritt,** winds through the Nicola Valley, with plenty of rest stops and opportunities for swimming in the cool and shallow Nicola River, in the sage-scented air.

Stop just north of Lytton on Hwy 1 for a must-see view at the confluence of the **Thompson and Fraser Rivers.** For a great view of **Shuswap Lake,** stop at the **Shuswap Rest Area,** 13 miles (21 km) east of **Salmon Arm** on Hwy 1.

Near the west end of Kamloops Lake, **Savona Provincial Park** offers a pretty spot for a picnic and a swim. Hwy 1 runs right by the park.

Columbia View Park, on Hwy 23 just north of Revelstoke is quite close to the Trans-Canada Hwy, and is worth stopping at for its excellent view of the Columbia River and the massive **Revelstoke Dam.**

If you're not going to camp in Yoho National Park but feel like stopping for a couple of hours, go to the **Faeder Lake Picnic Area,** the **Finn Creek Picnic Area,** or one of several roadside picnic sites beside the Kicking Horse River, all on Hwy 1.

Boating/Canoeing

Idling around the waters of the three lakes in the **Nahatlatch** system (see Camping/Parks, above) is serene, with the sound of loons, the still surfaces of the water, and the view of Mount Maston (7,548 feet/2317 m) in the distance. Boat launches are located on the shores of each lake at Forest Service recreation sites on the Nahatlatch Forest Rd. It's possible to paddle between the three lakes in the course of a morning or afternoon excursion.

Shuswap Lake Provincial Marine Park is among of the most popular boating and canoeing locations in the Southern Interior. One of the best places to begin exploring Shuswap Lake is at **Sicamous,** the "houseboat capital of Canada" and the service centre for Shuswap marine park. Marinas and watercraft rentals are located here. Of note is the MV *Phoebe Ann*, which can hold 40 passengers (and canoes or kayaks) and acts as a vehicle barge. This vessel stops at numerous lakeside locations year-round, except when ice makes travel impossible.

Shuswap Lake is shaped like an addled H and is made up of four large arms: the Shuswap Lake Main Arm, Salmon Arm, Anstey Arm, and Seymour Arm. The product of the glacial scouring that also rounded the surrounding Shuswap Highlands, all four arms converge at Cinnemousun Narrows, northeast of Sicamous. Those mariners interested in an extended visit will find 14 campsites, some vehicle-accessible but most the preserve of boaters and paddlers. Good vehicle-access sites on **Shuswap Lake** include Shuswap Lake Provincial Park, about 12 miles (20 km) northeast of Hwy 1 at Squilax. On **Salmon Arm,** launch at the public wharf in Canoe, about 4 miles (6 km) east of Salmon Arm on Hwy 1, or in Sicamous, 13 miles (21 km) farther east on Hwy 1. There's also gravel-road access from Hwy 1 to Seymour Arm at Silver Beach Provincial Park (see Camping/Parks, above). Wilderness campsites with basic facilities include **Two Mile Creek, Albas,** and **Fowler Point** on the northeast shore of Seymour Arm; **Anstey View** on the northwest shore and **Four Mile Creek** and **Anstey Beach** on the south shore of Anstey Arm; and **Marble Point** on the south shore and **Hermit Bay** on the north shore of Salmon Arm.

For more information on Shuswap Lake Provincial Marine Park, including a detailed map of the region, contact BC Parks, 1210 McGill St in Kamloops, (250) 851-3000.

Fishing

There are few fishing runs as legendary—or as threatened—as the **steelhead** run on the **Thompson River** and one of its main tributaries, the **Nicola.** Steelhead are an oceangoing species of trout (or salmon, depending on whom you consult) famous for their size, speed, stamina, and tremendous strength. In order to surmount obstacles in the Fraser Canyon before entering the Thompson near Lytton, steelhead must possess all these characteristics. In fall, anglers head for two places in particular: **Goldpan Provincial Park** (see Camping/Parks, above), located on the Thompson River, and **Spences Bridge,** located on Hwy 8, about 0.6 mile (1 km) west of Hwy 1, 23 miles (37 km) north of Lytton. Anglers can readily access both the Thompson and the Nicola Rivers from Spences Bridge. For information on steelhead fishing regulations, contact the Fish and Wildlife Conservation Officer in Kamloops, (250) 374-9117. For **guided fishing trips** on the Thompson and Nicola Rivers, contact The Steelhead Inn, (800) 665-7926 or (250) 458-2398, in Spences Bridge. For an insight into the Thompson River steelhead run, as well as portraits of 10 other British Columbia rivers, consult *The Run of the River* by Mark Hume.

As well known as the steelhead are the **Kamloops trout.** Kamloops trout are a unique strain of trout that put on a eye-popping, acrobatic performance for fly-fishers skilled enough to hook one. These wild rainbow trout, native to central and south-central Interior regions of the province, are the prize in **Niskonlith Provincial Park** and **Silver Beach Provincial Park,** at Seymour Arm at Shuswap Lake (see Camping/Parks, above). For more information on angling in the Kamloops region, contact the Kamloops InfoCentre, (800) 662-1994 or (250) 372-7722. Local fishing guides include Carlos Tallent, (250) 372-8783, Wilderness Fly-Fishing Outfitters, (250) 372-3311, Fish n' Float Guided Tours, (250) 851-3141, or Coquihalla Outpost Sporting Clay Resort, (250) 828-0870, all in the Kamloops region. Good tackle shops in Kamloops include Fine Flies for Fishermen, (250) 828-6149, Surplus Herby's, (250) 376-2714, and Yosh's Hook and Tackle, (250) 554-3311.

The **Eagle River** system, which begins at **Griffin Lake,** has a total of five lakes along a 12-mile (20-km) stretch of Hwy 1 between Sicamous and Revelstoke. This system includes **Three Valley, Victor, Clanwilliam, and Wetask Lakes,** all good fishing spots for rainbow trout and easily accessed from Hwy 1.

Along Highway 23 north and south of Revelstoke are a series of campgrounds and boat launches where anglers congregate, including **Shelter Bay Provincial Park** near the ferry that links Shelter Bay with Hwy 6 at Galena on the east side of Upper Arrow Lake (see Slocan Valley and Upper Arrow Lake chapter). A boat launch and beach welcome visitors.

Your best bet for a combination of camping and fishing is at **Blanket Creek Provincial Park** (see Camping/Parks, above), midway between Shelter Bay and Revelstoke. This park is an easy 15-minute drive along Hwy 23 from Hwy 1. You can fish for **kokanee,** which spawn at the mouth of Blanket Creek where it flows into Upper Arrow Lake, as well as dolly varden and rainbow trout. **Martha Creek Provincial Park** (see Camping/Parks, above) is the destination for anglers trying their luck on **Lake Revelstoke.** And in **Roderick Haig-Brown Provincial Park** (see Wildlife, below), angling for rainbow trout, dolly varden, and whitefish is popular, with the canyon and the river mouth being among the most productive sites. Note: The **Adams River** is closed to salmon fishing year-round, and in spring is also closed to rainbow trout fishing. For more information on licences, openings, and regulations, contact the Fish and Wildlife Conservation Officer in Vernon, (250) 549-5558, or the Department of Fisheries and Oceans in Salmon Arm, (250) 832-8037.

Wildlife

Roderick Haig-Brown was a magistrate, writer, angler, and conservationist dedicated to preserving, among other wildlife, the sockeye salmon so key to British Columbia's economy. He even wrote a poem about salmon, which appears in its entirety on a plaque in the park named in his honour: **Roderick Haig-Brown Provincial Park.** This 2,440-acre (988-ha) park encompasses the entire length of the Adams River, the site of the largest **sockeye salmon** run on the West Coast. There's an excellent interpretive area that explains the whole phenomenal trek. A "dominant" run happens every four years, followed by years of much smaller runs. The next dominant run will be in 2002, and the sockeye will be joined by **chinook, coho, and pink salmon.** The exact dates of the late summer–early fall salmon run depend on temperature, rainfall, and water levels; if you want to see it at its best, call BC Parks' district office in Kamloops. Many wild critters live in this park, among them **bears, beavers,** and **river otters.**

To get to Roderick Haig-Brown Provincial Park, travel east on Hwy 1 from Kamloops for 41 miles (66 km) to Monte Creek. Follow the signs north to Squilax. The park is about 3 miles (5 km) north of here. For more information, including a detailed map, contact BC Parks, 1210 McGill Rd in Kamloops, (250) 851-3000.

In the town of Salmon Arm, the mouth of the Salmon River is alive with breeding and nesting **birds,** especially **Clark's** and **western grebes,** from April to June. Downtown, the Rotary Peace Park and Public wharf has a BC Wildlife Watch viewing area and picnic site, and offers good access to the river and its birds.

Skiing

Larch Hills Cross-Country Area, near Salmon Arm, has an impressive 87 miles (140 km) of cross-country trails, about 25 miles (40 km) of which are groomed. To reach the trailhead, drive 11 miles (17 km) south of Salmon Arm on Hwy 97B, turn left on Grandview Bench Rd and go 3 miles (5 km), and turn left on Edgar Rd and drive 1 mile (2 km) farther. For more information, call the Larch Hills Ski Club, (250) 832-6247. The club maintains a chalet, which is open to all, the site of the annual "loppet," or cross-country ski race. A map of the Larch Hills trails ($4) is available at the Salmon Arm and District InfoCentre, (250) 832-6247 on Hwy 1.

In the 1920s, world championship ski jumping was a passion in Revelstoke, the site of one of North America's tallest jumps. Since those heady days in 1914 when the citizens of Revelstoke successfully lobbied to have their unique (and popular) area declared a national park, cross-country and downhill skiing have spread to nearby valleys and mountains. Parks Canada no longer maintains any winter facilities in Mount Revelstoke National Park, but don't let that deter you. There's still wonderful, ungroomed backcountry skiing in the park, particularly via the popular 15.5-mile (25-km) Summit Rd. For more information on routes, contact

Parks Canada's Mount Revelstoke Park administration office, 301C Third St W, (250) 837-7500, in Revelstoke.

Over 11 miles (18 km) of groomed cross-country trails can be found on **Mount MacPherson.** The trailhead parking lot is about 3.7 miles (6 km) south of Revelstoke on Highway 23. Trails are rated as moderate to strenuous. The Revelstoke Nordic Ski Club maintains a cabin on the Main Loop Trail where skiers are welcome to warm up while digging into their pack lunches. Those looking for a gentle workout should head to the Revelstoke Golf Club, where 3 miles (5 km) of groomed trails run beside the Columbia River. Set among giant firs, this makes an enchanting setting for a moonlight ski outing. Trails here and on Mount MacPherson are maintained by the Revelstoke Nordic Ski Club, and use is by donation. Skiers will find an honour box at the trailhead. For more information and a trail map, contact the Revelstoke InfoCentre, (250) 837-5345. For snow conditions, call nearby Mount Mackenzie Ski Area. (250) 837-5268. **Mount Mackenzie Ski Area** has downhill as well as helicopter- and sno-cat-assisted skiing for the diehards. Mount Mackenzie lies almost 4 miles (6 km) south of Revelstoke's city centre on Airport Way, then east on Westerburg Rd. You'll find steep, fall-line skiing here over a 2,000-foot (610-m) vertical drop, serviced by two double chairlifts and a lengthy T-bar. Sno-cats carry skiers to higher elevations above the chairlifts.

The powder doesn't come any lighter than that at **Whitetooth Ski Area** in **Golden,** where there is downhill skiing in addition to more than 12 miles (17 km) of cross-country trails. Call (250) 344-6114 for information on this area.

For the serious skier, Revelstoke serves as a **heli-skiing** base camp to some amazing runs in and around the Albert Icefields. The catch: You need a helicopter to get there. The answer: Selkirk Tangiers Helicopter Skiing Ltd., (250) 837-5378. For a few grand, Canadian Mountain Holidays, (800) 662-0252 or (250) 837-9344, will take you out, for a week at a time, to one of their fully staffed lodges in remote hideaways for some great skiing and hiking. Expert skiers can sign on to ski 25 scenic peaks and 14 glaciers with Selkirk Mountain Experience, (250) 837-2381, or Selkirk Lodge, (800) 663-7080.

Rafting

The **Nahatlatch, Fraser, and Thompson Rivers** are all justifiably well known for their river-rafting experiences. Of the three, the Fraser and Thompson are more prominent, though not necessarily more challenging than the Nahatlatch. In fact, the Nahatlatch provides more excitement in its varied run than either of the others. Both the Thompson and the

Nahatlatch flow into the Fraser within a short distance of each other. The season begins in May, once water levels become manageable. The later in summer you try the Nahatlatch, the better your chances of being able to run the narrow **Nahatlatch Canyon,** a Class IV–V mind-altering experience. Although it's entirely possible to run these rivers unaccompanied, the majority of paddlers opt for the services of a certified guide, at least the first time. For more details, contact the following: Hyak Wilderness Adventures, (604) 734-8622 in Vancouver, (206) 382-1311 in Seattle, or (800) 663-7238 for information on the Fraser and Thompson Rivers; REO Rafting Resorts, (604) 684-4438, in Vancouver, for information on the Nahatlatch and Thompson Rivers; Ryans Rapids Rafting, (800) 665-7926, in Spences Bridge, or Kumsheen Raft Adventures in Lytton, (604) 609-3966, for information on the Thompson and Fraser Rivers. For information on water levels, contact the Forest Service's Chilliwack district office, (604) 794-3361, or the Lillooet district office, (250) 256-1200.

The **Kicking Horse River** cuts a wild swath through the Yoho Valley before spilling through a narrow stretch of canyon east of Golden. Along the way it displays both a gentle and a ferocious side. Because river rafting can be quite physically demanding, it's good to have calm stretches of water where you can relax while admiring the breathtaking Rocky Mountain scenery before plunging back into Class IV+ rapids. One of the most popular sections of the river runs for about 12 miles (20 km) west of the Crozier Bridge. Popular put-in locations are at the intersection of Beaverfoot Rd and Hwy 1, and at Hunter Creek's confluence with the Kicking Horse River beside Hwy 1. To experience the power of this whitewater, contact one of the local outfitters: Wild n' Wet Adventures, (250) 344-6546 or (800) 668-9119, or Whitewater Voyageurs, (250) 762-9117 or (800) 667-7138, both based in Golden; or Hydra River Guides, (800) 644-8888, in Banff, Alberta.

outside in

Attractions

Revelstoke's history is tied to the building of the Canadian Pacific Railway, which you can delve into at the Revelstoke Railway Museum, 719 Track St, (250) 837-6060. Towering mountains rise all around Revelstoke, and it's clear the town is trying to build a tourist industry that appeals to hikers and skiers. The four-block-long downtown on MacKenzie Ave makes a nice stroll; a map for a self-guided heritage walking tour is available at the Revelstoke Museum, 315 W First St, (250) 837-3067. Free tours of the Revelstoke Dam, five minutes north of Revelstoke, are offered from mid-March to late October; call (250) 837-6515 for hours. The Canyon Hotsprings, (250) 837-2420, are 21 miles (34 km) east of Revelstoke on Trans-Canada 1, and have a mineral-water hot pool and a mineral-water swimming pool, but are open summers only.

In a region made famous by its gold rush, you too can pan for gold. The Cariboo stampede of the 1850s and '60s may be just a memory, but that doesn't keep the Fraser from washing down a few more grains and nuggets each spring onto these shores. The staff at the **Lytton InfoCentre** can assist you in your search at Lytton's **Gold Panning Recreation Reserve** on the Fraser River. For more information, call (250) 455-2523.

Restaurants

Black Forest Inn Fondue Provençal, British Columbia salmon fillets, and a variety of beef tenderloins round out a rather extensive menu; we recommend one of the Bavarian dishes such as sauerbraten or schnitzel. *3251 Weirdwood Rd (3 miles/5 km west of Revelstoke on Trans-Canada Hwy), Revelstoke; (250) 837-3495; $$.*

The 112 Located in the Regent Inn downtown, The 112 is a unanimous favourite among locals. The chef specializes in veal dishes, but the cioppino and the lamb Provençal also come highly recommended. *112 E 1st St (at McKenzie), Revelstoke; (250) 837-2107; $$.*

Lodgings

Emerald Lake Lodge ☆☆☆☆ In the heart of Yoho National Park, surrounded by stunning mountain views, sits this complex, which includes 24 buildings as well as the cozy main lodge. Most people opt for horseback riding, trout fishing, canoeing, or hiking. Come winter, there's cross-country skiing. *In Yoho National Park, 5 miles/8 km north of Trans-Canada Hwy (no parking at lodge; leave car at parking lot and call bellhop for transport); PO Box 10, Field, BC V0A 1G0; (250) 343-6321 or (800) 663-6336; $$$.*

Sundance Ranch ☆☆ This dude ranch is set in high plateau country, with a river to the west. Low buildings contain handsome rooms. The rustic public rooms are great for socializing and the pool is grand, but the real attraction is the corral's 100 horses. Closed winters. *Off Kirkland Ranch Rd (5 miles/8 km south of town); PO Box 489, Ashcroft, BC V0K 1A0; (250) 453-2422; $$.*

3 Valley Gap Motor Inn The best thing about the 3 Valley Gap is that the front door opens right onto the beach of Shuswap Lake. The season here is short, since the motel is located where deep winter snows pile up. Revelstoke is 12 miles (19 km) west, but there's a family restaurant onsite. *On Trans-Canada Hwy 1 east of Revelstoke; Box 860, Revelstoke, BC V0E 2S0; (250) 837-2109; $$.*

More Information

Ashcroft Information: *(250) 453-9232.*
BC Forest Service, Chilliwack District: *(604) 794-2100 or (800) 665-1551.*
BC Forest Service, Kamloops District: *(250) 371-6500.*
BC Forest Service, Kamloops Regional Office: *(250) 828-4131.*
BC Forest Service, Salmon Arm District: *(250) 833-3400.*
BC Parks, Cultus Lake: *(604) 824-2300.*
BC Parks, Kamloops: *(250) 851-3000.*
BC Parks, Nelson: *(250) 825-3500.*
Cache Creek Chamber of Commerce: *(250) 457-6237.*
Chase and District InfoCentre: *(250) 679-8432.*
Field InfoCentre: *(250) 343-6783.*
Golden Chamber of Commerce: *(250) 344-7125.*
Kamloops InfoCentre: *(250) 372-7722 or (800) 662-1994.*
Lytton and District Chamber of Commerce InfoCentre: *(250) 455-2523.*
Mount Revelstoke and Glacier National Parks: *(250) 837-7500.*
North Shuswap InfoCentre: *(250) 955-2113.*
Parks Canada: *(250) 837-7500; Web site: http://parkscanada.pch.gc.ca.*
Revelstoke InfoCentre: *(250) 837-5345; (250) 837-3522.*
Salmon Arm and District InfoCentre: *(250) 832-6247.*
Sicamous and District InfoCentre: *(250) 836-3313.*
Siska First Nation (near Lytton): *(250) 455-2219.*
Sorrento Chamber of Commerce InfoCentre: *(250) 675-3515.*
Yale Museum (town information): *(604) 863-2324.*
Yoho National Park: *(250) 343-6783.*

Manning Provincial Park

More than 162,700 acres (66 220 ha) of rugged wilderness in the heart of the Cascade Mountains, immediately north of the Canada–US border.

If you're looking for a getaway less than three hours' drive from Vancouver, Manning Provincial Park is it. Named for E. C. Manning, chief forester of British Columbia from 1935 to 1940, the park has rain forests on its west side and grassland slopes on its east. Between the two extremes lies a land of wild rivers, crystal lakes, towering peaks, and alpine meadows that is brimming with recreational opportunities year-round.

Manning Provincial Park features tremendously diverse landscapes and plentiful flora and fauna. Hiking trails are its chief draw, but the park also offers horseback riding, swimming, canoeing, fishing, mountain biking, and, in winter, cross-country and downhill skiing.

Lying between the moist coast and the dry interior, Manning contains examples of 5 of British Columbia's 14 biogeoclimatic zones. Lush coastal growth gives way to dryland stands of pine and, near the timberline, stands of alpine larch. One of the most spectacular is on Mount Frosty's eastern shoulder, where some of the trees are nearly a yard (1 m) in diameter. Conifers such as Douglas fir, western red cedar, western hemlock, subalpine fir, Englemann spruce, and lodgepole pine may be seen in the park, as well as aspen and cottonwood.

The park is perhaps best known for its magnificent midsummer displays of subalpine flowers, but there are other flora worth watching for. Rhododendron Flats, near the park's western entrance, has a substantial colony of pinkish-red rhododendrons, a protected indigenous species that blooms early to mid-June. The California or red rhododendron is rarely found as far north as British Columbia. Strawberry Flats boasts a profusion of wild strawberries and rich variety of plant species. Orchids and other bog flora can be viewed June through July along the Rein Orchid Nature Trail.

Manning Provincial Park makes nature's wonders available to everyone. Short self-guided nature trails allow visitors to experience the fascinating world of the subalpine zone or view magnificent stands of western red cedar and Douglas fir in a half-hour or less. Almost all of the park's important features are easily reached from Highway 3. Small wonder, then, that Manning is the third most popular park in the province. Among the best times to visit are in May, once the snow has left the ground and before the biting insects become aggressive, and in September, when the first frosts trigger autumn colours here where the Cascade and Coast Mountains meet. No matter what the season, magic always freshens the mountain peaks at sunrise and sunset.

Getting There

Manning Provincial Park straddles Highway 3 between Hope and Princeton. The park's western entrance is 16 miles (26 km) east of Hope, its eastern entrance 30 miles (48 km) southwest of Princeton. Allison Pass, at an elevation of 4,403 feet (1342 m), is the high point of Highway 3 as it traverses the park. The Manning Provincial Park Visitors Centre, situated just over 0.6 mile (1 km) east of the Manning Provincial Park Resort on Highway 3 and open daily throughout the year, has displays depicting the natural and human history of the region. During the summer months, interpreters offer a variety of special programs ranging from nature walks to evening slide shows. For more information, call (250) 840-8836.

Adjoining Areas

NORTH: **The Coquihalla Highway**

EAST: **Crowsnest Highway: South Okanagan Valley**

WEST: **The Fraser Valley**

inside out

Hiking/Backpacking

Manning Provincial Park boasts numerous trails to suit both novice and experienced hikers. North of Hwy 3, the **Blackwall Peak** and **Three Brothers Mountain** area offers Canada's finest and most extensive example of subalpine meadows accessible by vehicle. A partly paved, partly gravel road winds up the mountain to the parking area just below the 6,768-foot (2063-m) Blackwall Peak. At this level, the snow stays until late June and returns in September; as a result, all kinds of plants rush into flower. The magnificent floral displays peak from late July to mid-August, when the meadows provide a kaleidoscope of colours.

The short **Paintbrush Trail** (easy; less than 1 mile/1.6 km) beginning at the naturalist hut introduces visitors to the fascinating world of the subalpine zone. To experience more extensive floral displays and better views of the mountain peaks, hike along part or all of the **Heather Trail** (moderate; 26 miles/42 km return) to Nicomen Ridge. In places, the carpets of flowers spread 3 miles wide; in others, they condense into massive mats of arctic lupines speckled with Indian paintbrushes and subalpine daisies. A park booklet helps with flower identification en route. Plants, of course, should never be damaged or removed, and hikers must not venture off the trail. Wilderness camping areas are located along the Kicking Horse Trail at **Kicking Horse,** at about 8 miles (13.5 km), and **Nicomen Lake,** at just over 14 miles (23 km). This area has a permanent ban on open fires, so backpacking stoves should be used for all cooking. Overnighters can return the same way or, with the use of two vehicles, along **Grainger Creek Trail** and **Hope Pass Trail** (moderate; 7.5 miles/12 km), coming out on Hwy 3 at **Cayuse Flats,** about 15 miles (24 km) west of Manning Provincial Park headquarters.

Shorter trails in the park include one to the top of **Windy Joe Mountain** (moderate to difficult; 9.3 miles/15 km return), where an old fire lookout with interpretive panels identifies the surrounding mountains. **Frosty Mountain Loop** (difficult; 17 or 18 miles/28 or 29 km return, depending on route) is most colourful in the fall, when its beautiful larch forest is on fire with autumnal shades. The highest peak in the park at 7,900 feet (2408 m), Frosty offers fabulous views of the North Cascades.

Awe-inspiring peaks and wildflower meadows can be experienced along the **Skyline I Trail** (difficult; 12.7-mile/20-km loop) and **Skyline II Trail** (difficult; 7.8 miles/12.5 km to Mowich Camp), which heads west towards the Skagit Valley Provincial Park (see The Fraser Valley chapter for details). Manning Provincial Park also contains a section of the Canada-wide **National Trail,** which enters the park in its southeast corner as **Monument 83 Trail** from Cathedral Provincial Park (see Crowsnest Highway: South Okanagan Valley chapter). For real long-distance hiking buffs, Manning is the start of the **Pacific Crest Trail,** which runs for 2,480 miles (4000 km) to Mexico. Detailed descriptions of all park trails are available at the visitors centre.

Camping

Water, toilets, and firewood are located near each unit in the park's four camping areas: **Hampton Campground** (99 vehicle/tent sites), **Mule Deer Campground** (49 vehicle/tent sites), **Coldspring Campground** (64 vehicle/tent sites), and **Lightning Lake Campground** (143 vehicle/tent sites). The latter is especially popular during the summer months; reservations (recommended) for any site can be made by calling (800) 689-9025. Wilderness camping is permitted in designated areas, but open fires are not encouraged. A group campground can be reserved by calling the Manning Provincial Park visitors centre, (250) 840-8836.

Horseback Riding

Horse use has been traditional on the **historic trails** in Manning Provincial Park. Staging areas for horses have been cleared at **Cayuse Flats,** the **Dewdney** trailhead, and the **Monument 83** parking area. Trail riders can camp overnight at **Grant Camp,** at the intersection of the Hope and Grainger Creek Trails, and at **Paradise Valley,** in the Cascade Recreation Area (access via Manning Provincial Park). Trail rides are available during summer months and hay rides during winter. For more information, contact the Manning Provincial Park Corral, (250) 840-8844.

Wildlife

Manning Provincial Park provides excellent wildlife-viewing opportunities. Small mammals, including **marmots, beavers,** and **chipmunks,** share the wilderness areas with **black bears, mule deer,** and **coyotes. Beavers, elk,** and **moose** reside in the park but are seldom seen. **Birdlife** is abundant, especially in summer, with 206 species to watch for. Early morning is the best time for observing birds and mammals. As always in wilderness areas, hikers and campers should be alert for wild animals, especially bears, and take the necessary safety precautions (see the British Columbia Outdoors Primer at the start of this book). For a guide on wildlife, stop at the park's visitors centre.

Winter Recreation

Manning Provincial Park offers more than 62 miles (100 km) of ungroomed beginner, intermediate, and advanced **cross-country ski trails,** as well as **snowshoeing** opportunities. For **downhill skiers** and **snowboarders,** the **Gibson Pass Ski Area,** a private operation located in the park, offers a variety of slopes and runs with its two chairlifts, T-bar and beginners' handle tow. It also features a ski school, groomed and track-set cross-country ski trails, equipment rentals, a day lodge, and day care. Total vertical drop here is 1,417 feet (431 m). For more information, call (250) 840-8822.

Winter camping for self-contained units is available at the Lightning Lake day-use area, and for tenters there is the Lone Duck winter camping area. The extensive trail system of the Cascade Provincial Recreation Area, which is accessed from Hwy 3 in Manning Provincial Park, provides the opportunity for ski touring, but no huts or shelters are available.

Mountain Biking

Half a dozen trails in the park, as well as designated vehicle roadways, are open to mountain bikers. The shortest is the **Lone Duck Trail** (easy; less than 1 mile/1.6 km one way), between the Lightning Lake campground and 20 Minute Lake. There are also three 2-mile-long (one way) trails beside Lightning Lake for intermediate to advanced riders. For the more advanced rider, there is the 9.3-mile (15-km) return ride on the **Windy Joe Trail** from the Beaver Pond over the top of Windy Joe Mountain. For a full list of mountain-bike trails, cyclists should obtain a park brochure and map from the visitors centre.

Swimming/Canoeing

A chain of lakes flows southwest from Manning Provincial Park's **Lightning Lake,** the biggest in the series, where there is an unpatrolled beach and swimming area. Visitors are urged to mind their water safety: Never swim alone and be vigilant when children are near or in the water. Pets must be leashed at all times and are not allowed in beach and picnic areas.

Lightning Lake also provides good canoeing (there is a launch ramp at the day-use area), but powerboats are prohibited in the park.

Fishing

Fly-fishing for **rainbow trout** in **Lightning and Strike Lakes** is usually good though the trout in these cold, nutrient-poor waters rarely exceed 2 pounds (1 kg). The **Similkameen and Sumallo Rivers** have dolly varden, and rainbow and cutthroat trout. Watch for good casting spots as Hwy 3 runs beside both rivers on its journey through the park. You will need a British Columbia angling licence if you plan to fish in Manning Provincial Park. For information, contact the Fish and Wildlife Conservation officer at Princeton, (250) 295-6343.

Restaurants

For recommended restaurants, see Adjoining Areas to this chapter.

Lodgings

Manning Provincial Park Resort This simple lodge within pretty Manning Provincial Park gives you easy access to hiking trails and Lightning Lake. Besides the 41 motel rooms, the low-key resort includes a restaurant, coffee shop, cabins, and triplexes—all in the same plain, functional style. *Just off Hwy 3 in Manning Provincial Park; Box 1480, Manning Provincial Park, BC V0X 1R0; (250) 840-8822; $$.*

More Information

BC Fish and Wildlife Conservation Officer, Princeton: *(250) 295-6343.*
BC Parks, South Coast Region: *(604) 924-2200.*
Gibson Pass Ski Area: *(250) 840-8822.*
Manning Park Corral: *(250) 840-8844.*
Manning Provincial Park Visitors Centre: *(250) 840-8836.*

Crowsnest Highway: South Okanagan Valley

From Hope at the east end of the Fraser Valley east on Highway 3 (Crowsnest Highway) to Grand Forks on the western edge of the Kootenays, through the Cascade Mountains and Manning Provincial Park and across the desertlike southern Okanagan Valley, including Princeton, Keremeos, and Osoyoos.

Sometimes called the Crowsnest Route or the Route of the Crow, Highway 3 is a memorial to a young engineer who came to Canada in 1859. An Englishman from Devonshire, 24-year-old Edgar Dewdney arrived in Victoria with little more than a letter of introduction to Governor James Douglas. To keep himself alive during his first few months in the west, he found work surveying for the Royal Engineers.

When the discovery of gold in the Similkameen River prompted Governor Douglas to build a trail to the Interior through British territory, Edgar Dewdney and Walter Moberly won the contract. They completed the section from Fort Hope to Vermilion Forks, now Princeton, in 1861. A few years later, gold was discovered in Wild Horse Creek, and Dewdney was given the job of continuing the trail into the Kootenays. Fighting towering mountain ranges, wild rivers, and bottomless bogs, Dewdney and his crew completed the 366-mile-long (590-km) trail in seven months at a cost of a mere $75,000. Dewdney's hard work and ambition later served him well in provincial and federal politics. He became lieutenant-governor of British Columbia before he retired in 1897.

As you descend into the Okanagan Valley on Highway 3, a desert panorama broken by regular patterns of green spreads out before you. The area from the United States border north to Skaha Lake is known as Canada's "pocket desert," although it is slightly too cold and wet to qualify for official designation as such. Instead, climatologists classify it as a midlatitude steppe. However, outside the sweep of the irrigation sprinklers, greasewood, sagebrush, and prickly pear cactus are visible reminders of the desertlike environment, while western rattlesnakes and scorpions lurk out of sight.

Getting There

The western approach to the Okanagan Valley is from Hope, a small town on the Fraser River two hours' drive east of Vancouver. Among the towns passed along the way east of Hope are the mining town of Princeton, 80 miles (130 km) east of Hope; Keremeos, about 40 miles (65 km) east of Princeton; Osoyoos, about 30 miles (45 km) east of Keremeos; and Grand Forks, about 78 miles (125 km) east of Keremeos. Access to Highway 3 from the north is via Merritt, about 53 miles (85 km) north of Princeton on Highway 5A; from Penticton, about 23 miles (37 km) north of Keremeos on Highway 3A and about 30 miles (50 km) north of Osoyoos on Highway 97; and from Kelowna, about 125 miles (200 km) north of Grand Forks via Rock Creek on Highway 33.

Adjoining Areas

NORTH: **The Coquihalla Highway**

EAST: **Crowsnest Highway: The West Kootenays**

WEST: **The Fraser Valley**

inside out

Camping

Aside from the four campgrounds in Manning Provincial Park, there are six additional provincial parks that offer camping to travellers in the southern Okanagan Valley region.

Bromley Rock Provincial Park, 13 miles (21 km) east of Princeton on Hwy 3, is a popular swimming hole with 17 vehicle/tent sites in a pleasantly forested site along the Similkameen River. Hiking in the area (just outside the park) affords good views of the Similkameen Valley. Canoeing is also popular here, providing a downstream route to **Stemwinder Provincial Park.** This park is located at Hedley on Hwy 3, about 22 miles (35 km) east of Princeton. Open year-round (as is Bromley Rock), it has 27 vehicle/tent sites. **Cathedral Provincial Park,** 30 miles (48 km) southeast of Princeton off Hwy 3, offers three campgrounds in its core area: Quiniscoe Lane (30 tent sites), Pyramid (12 tent sites), and Lake of the Woods (28 tent sites). Fires are allowed only at Quiniscoe Lake, and private vehicles aren't permitted in the core area of Cathedral so you must hike in or arrange transportation with Cathedral Lakes Lodge (see Hiking/Backpacking, below). For information on these parks, contact BC Parks' Okanagan District office in Summerland, (250) 494-6500.

Johnstone Creek Provincial Park, located near Rock Creek on Hwy 3, about 30 miles (45 km) east of Osoyoos, is only open May through September. Its 16 vehicle/tent sites are situated in a scenic, peaceful area forested with Douglas fir, pine, and aspen. There is a picturesque waterfall on Johnstone Creek near its confluence with Rock Creek. Visitors can fish as well as hike. For information, contact BC Parks, (250) 494-6500.

Also open May to September, **Conkle Lake Provincial Park,** about 19 miles (30 km) west of Greenwood, can be reached by three different routes. However, all three are over rough, narrow, winding roads not suitable for motor homes, low-clearance vehicles, or towed trailers. Named for an early settler in the nearby Kettle River Valley, W. H. Conkle, this secluded park is a perfect place for a quiet vacation. It features 24 vehicle/tent sites set in a forest of western larch, lodgepole pine, alder, and willow, and is a favourite with sunbathers, swimmers, and anglers. It is reached by travelling about 10 miles (16 km) west of Hwy 33 at Westbridge; 16 miles (26 km) from Hwy 3, about 4 miles (6 km) east of Bridesville; or almost 22 miles (35 km) east from Hwy 97 at Okanagan Falls. For information, contact BC Parks in Nelson, (250) 825-3500.

Just over 3 miles (5 km) north of Rock Creek on Hwy 33, the **Kettle River Provincial Recreation Area** is named for the river that runs through it. It also contains the abandoned right-of-way of the Kettle Valley Railway, which makes an excellent hiking trail. (See also Mountain Biking, below). Open May through September, this recreation area features 53 vehicle/tent sites and a picnic/day-use area, as well as an amphitheatre and a visitors program. Remains of gold and silver mines that once brought thousands of people to this now peaceful area can be seen on the river's eastern bank. For more information, contact BC Parks, (250) 825-3500.

You can camp beneath the cottonwoods at **Boundary Creek Provincial Park,** about 2 miles (3 km) west of Greenwood on Hwy 3, just north of the US border. This tranquil park offers 18 vehicle/tent sites and the chance for patient anglers to catch rainbow and brook trout. Nearby are the remains of the old BC Copper Company smelter, which employed about 400 men from 1901 to 1918. For more information, contact BC Parks, (250) 825-3500.

Hiking/Backpacking

Trails are so plentiful and wonderfully diverse in this section of the Cascade Mountains that only a few can be mentioned here. (See also Manning Provincial Park chapter.) The **Skagit River Trail** (easy; 9 miles/15 km one way) can be accessed from Hwy 3 at Sumallo Grove, about 6.5 miles (10.5 km) from Manning Provincial Park's western entrance. From the junction of the Sumallo and Skagit Rivers, the trail follows the latter's beautiful valley bottom along the original Whatcom Trail (see below) into the Skagit Valley Recreation Area (see The Fraser Valley chapter).

The **Cascade Provincial Recreation Area** is located on the north side of Hwy 3, adjacent to Manning Provincial Park. Situated in the magnificent Cascade Mountains, largely within the Hozameen Range, it contains such spectacular landscapes that an early Hudson's Bay Brigade Trail explorer named its Paradise Valley area the "Garden of Eden." Unlike Manning Provincial Park, it contains no road network. Access is chiefly via trail from two parking lots along Hwy 3 in Manning Provincial Park, at Snass Creek (just east of Rhododendron Flats) and Cayuse Flats.

In the late 1850s, gold was discovered on the Columbia, Fraser, Thompson, and Similkameen Rivers. The Cascade Provincial Recreation Area contains three important **historic trails** dating from this period—the Dewdney, Whatcom, and Hope Pass Trails—any one of which constitutes an all-day hike.

Originally designed to be a mule trail to the Similkameen, the **Dewdney Trail** became a wagon road between Fort Hope and Snass Creek. A moderate 10-mile (16-km) section leading from Hwy 3 follows Snass Creek to Dry Lake and Paradise Valley.

The **Whatcom Trail** (difficult; 10.5 miles/17 km one way) was built by the citizens of Whatcom, Washington, who wanted a trail from the gold fields through their town. Also accessed from the Snass Creek parking lot, it veers northeast and climbs steeply through forest and meadows to Whatcom Pass and the Punchbowl, continuing on to Paradise Valley. Hiking up on the Dewdney Trail and returning on the Whatcom Trail makes an interesting two-day loop.

The **Hope Pass Trail** was an alternative to the Dewdney Trail built by the Royal Engineers. From the junction of the Sumallo and Skaist Rivers (at the Cayuse Flats parking lot), it follows the Skaist River to its source, then crosses the divide at Hope Pass and heads northeastward along Whipsaw Creek to the Similkameen. With proper transportation arrangements, one could complete this strenuous 16-mile (26-km) hike by coming back on Hwy 3 at 41-Mile Creek, 30 miles (48 km) east of the Manning Provincial Park visitors centre.

Cathedral Provincial Park, located 30 miles (48 km) southeast of Princeton off Hwy 3, is in the transition zone between the dense, wet forests of the Cascade Mountains and the arid, desertlike Okanagan Valley. This mountainous park presents a wealth of variety in its terrain, flora, and fauna, as well as hiking opportunities suitable for both the novice and the seasoned climber. The five major lakes in the heart of Cathedral are like azure gemstones, surrounded by jagged peaks mantled with alpine and subalpine wildflowers. There are more than 230 plant species in the park, including over 20 that are rare in British Columbia. Fascinating rock formations with names like Smokey the Bear, the Devil's Woodpile, and Stone City make hiking in this park a thrilling adventure. No water is available other than from lakes and streams as you cross the 20 miles (32 km) of hiking trails. You'll find overnight parking at the trailheads and six info shelters, where detailed information on the park is displayed. Experienced, well-equipped hikers might want to tackle a section of the **Centennial Trail,** which runs about 250 miles (400 km) from Osoyoos all the way to Burnaby. Many other trails wind through the park, most starting in the core area around **Quiniscoe Lake** (see also Camping, above). All the trails are detailed in the park brochure available at the info shelters, and more information can be obtained by calling the Okanagan District office of BC Parks, (250) 494-6500. Transportation to Quiniscoe Lake along the rough gravel road from the park's Ashnola River entrance on Hwy 3 can be arranged with the Cathedral Lakes Lodge, (888) 255-4453. Note: This road is closed to all but lodge and BC Parks vehicles. From Hwy 3 a rough gravel road skirts the north and most of the west boundary of the park. Access roads are not maintained.

Located just to the east of Hope, the **Coquihalla Canyon Provincial Recreation Area** allows visitors to explore an engineering marvel. The **Othello Tunnels** were built from 1911 to 1918 to complete the Kettle Valley Railway. They were cut through solid granite to allow the railway to span the 300-foot-deep (90-m) Coquihalla Canyon, at a whopping cost (for the time) of $300,000. Plagued by washouts and rock slides, the railway line was closed in 1959. The impressive chain of tunnels, linked by a suspension bridge and a wooden bridge, is a major attraction during summer months. A leisurely walk (2.5 miles/4 km return) on the abandoned railway grade will take you though the tunnels and the spectacular Coquihalla Canyon gorge. Flashlights are useful inside the tunnels. Traffic heading northeast should enter Hope and follow Kawkawa Lake Rd and Othello Rd east for about 5 miles (8 km) to reach the park. Southwestbound traffic on Hwy 5 (the Coquihalla Hwy) should take exit 183. Pit toilets and picnic tables are available near the parking lot.

Swimming/Canoeing

Beautiful forest enhances **Kawkawa Lake Provincial Park,** which features a large picnic/day use area. Less than 2 miles (3 km) northwest of Hope off Hwy 1, its proximity to town and a warm-water lake make it popular with boaters, anglers, and swimmers.

For a refreshing dip or paddle in the cool waters of the **Similkameen River** on a hot summer day, stop at **Bromley Rock** or **Stemwinder Provincial Parks** (see Camping, above). At Stemwinder, only very good swimmers should brave the fast waters. Watch out for poison ivy along the riverbank. Bromley Rock features a large picnic/day use area, and Stemwinder is also popular as a picnic stop for travellers along Hwy 3. Swimming is a favourite activity at **Conkle Lake** Provincial Park (see Camping, above), where there is a beach.

In summer, the **Kettle River,** accessible from the Kettle River Provincial Recreation Area (see Camping, above), is excellent for canoeing and inner-tubing, although potential hazards such as submerged sweepers do exist. Don't attempt this river during spring runoff.

Fishing

Conkle Lake (see Camping, above) is a bit of a trek to reach, but once there you'll find good car-top-boat fishing for rainbow trout in an idyllic setting. It's so quiet here that you'd think it was a library.

Jewel Lake is an almost 2-mile-long (3-km) lake in the Monashees that offers great opportunities for water sports. Rainbow trout can be caught by fly-casting in summer or ice fishing in winter. There are no services or maintenance staff at Jewel Lake Provincial Park, so visitors are asked to keep the area clean for themselves and others. It's located 6 miles (10 km) north of Greenwood off Hwy 3.

For **fly-fishing instruction and guided trips** in the west Boundary region, contact Drifters Rod 'n River Adventures in Rock Creek, (800) 301-3611 or (250) 446-2442.

Mountain Biking

The Kettle Valley Railway, a Canadian Pacific Railway spur line, opened in 1915–16, completing the link between southern Alberta and the Pacific coast. Prior to that time, the southern Okanagan Valley did not have direct rail access to the West Coast but depended heavily on US railways and river boats for transporting goods and people. Communities such as Greenwood, Penticton, and Princeton needed reliable Canadian transportation routes to the west in order to flourish.

The Kettle Valley Railway discontinued service between Beaverdell and Penticton in 1973, and the track was removed between Midway and Penticton in 1979–80. Much of the 370 miles (600 km) of abandoned right-of-way now serves as the **Kettle Valley Mountain Bike Trail,** accessible from many places along Hwy 3, including the Kettle River Provincial Recreation Area (see Camping, above). For a detailed look at the route, consult *Cycling the Kettle Valley Railway* by Dan and Sandra Langford.

Other than the rail-trail routes, the terrain around **Grand Forks** caters to hardy cyclists only. (See Crowsnest Highway: The West Kootenays chapter.) For more information, contact Silver Barn Bike & Board on Hwy 3 in Grand Forks, (800) 667-1196 or (250) 442-8006.

Cross-Country Skiing

There are more than 20 miles (33 km) of interconnected loops for cross-country skiers of all levels at **China Ridge,** just west of Princeton. Follow Tulameen Rd a short distance north from Hwy 3 in Princeton, then west on Snowpatch Rd to reach the trailhead and skiers' chalet, a total of more than 4 miles (7 km). These trails are popular with hikers and mountain bikers in the summer. A map is available from the Forest Service district office, 315 Vermilion St, (250) 295-3106, in Princeton, or the Merritt Forest District office at the intersection of Hwy 5A and Airport Rd in Merritt, (800) 665-1511.

In winter, cross-country skiing and snowshoeing are favourite pastimes in the **Kettle River Provincial Recreation Area** (see Camping, above).

Wildlife

If you're travelling Hwy 3 during the early morning, watch for a **mountain goat** colony that inhabits the exposed, rocky north side of the highway between Hedley and Keremeos.

Attractions

Osoyoos bills itself as "the Spanish capital of Canada," but not because of any pioneer ethnic roots. It's purely a gimmicky town theme selected by city fathers. The climate is Canada's driest, with 10 inches of rain a year, and Osoyoos Lake is reportedly Canada's warmest freshwater lake.

The name Osoyoos, or more correctly Sooyuss, comes from a Native word meaning "the place where two lakes come together." Here the ancestors of the Okanagan Salish Indians trapped the salmon swimming up the Okanagan River. David Stuart, a Scotsman working for the American-based Pacific Fur Company in 1811, was one of the first white explorers to visit this area. For nearly half a century, Osoyoos was on the north-south fur trade route. Then, after a lull, it gained importance as a border entry point for cattle drives to the gold miners in the Cariboo.

Commercial fruit growing started in the early 1900s, but Osoyoos grew slowly until the railway reached it from the north in 1944. Today the dry, sunny climate and long growing season make the South Okanagan the fruit basket of Canada, with Osoyoos as its capital city.

Restaurants

Diamond Steak & Seafood House ☆ Locals like this casual steak, seafood, and pizza house. The decor carries out the town's ersatz Spanish theme better than most, and the pizzas are quite good, if you like super-crispy crust. The wine list has labels from valley wineries. *Main St (near 89th), Osoyoos; (250) 495-6223; $$.*

Cheaper Eats

Campo Marina Oddly enough, the two best restaurants in this Spanish-style town serve Italian and Greek food. You'll find superb pasta dishes at this intimate yet bustling little bistro. On hot summer nights ask for a seat on the patio. *Main St, Osoyoos; (250) 495-7650; $.*

Lodgings

Cathedral Lakes Resort ☆☆ Remote? That's an understatement. It takes an hour in a four-wheel-drive vehicle to get here. The resort is heavy on recreation (hiking, canoeing, fishing) and light on modern conveniences. Choose a cabin or a room—all have views. Three big meals are served. Make reservations early. Open June through October. *Call ahead for directions. mail: RR1, Cawston, BC V0X 1C0; (250) 226-7560 or (888) 255-4453; $$$.*

Inkaneep Point Resort The best thing about this unassuming resort is its location on a peninsula in Osoyoos Lake. All beach-level rooms face south for maximum sun and are only feet away from water's edge. Accommodations are a bit campish, but families love it. Closed winters. *About 2 miles (3 km) north of Osoyoos off Hwy 97; RR 2, Osoyoos, BC V0H 1V0; (250) 495-6353; $.*

Reflections Guesthouse ☆ Behind this bed and breakfast are apple orchards, and out front is a small lake. The four suites have kitchens and balconies. Guests can sit in the garden, or soak in the hot tub. *From*

Osoyoos, take Hwy 97 south to 74th Ave, turn west at 103rd St, follow signs; RR 2, Site 82, Comp 7, Osoyoos, BC V0H 1V0; (250) 495-5229; $.

Cheaper Sleeps

Avalon Motel The centrally located Avalon is just a walk away from Lion's Park, Gyro Park, and Legion Beaches. The amiable owner offers 12 guest rooms at reasonable rates. A continental breakfast is part of the package. *9106 Main St (PO Box 92), Osoyoos, BC V0H 1V0; (250) 495-6334; $.*

More Information

Artistic Endeavours (topographic maps): *7442 4th St, Grand Forks, (250) 442-3113.*

BC Forest Service, Boundary Forest District, Grand Forks, *(250) 442-5411.*

BC Forest Service, Merritt Forest District Office: *(800) 665-1511 in Canada only or (250) 378-8400.*

BC Forest Service, Princeton Field Office: *(250) 295-3106 or (250) 378-8400.*

BC Parks, Manning Park Office: *(250) 840-8836.*

BC Parks, Okanagan District Office, Summerland: *(250) 494-6500.*

BC Parks, West Kootenay Office, Nelson: *(250) 825-3500.*

Fish and Wildlife Conservation Officer, Grand Forks: *(250) 442-4310.*

Fish and Wildlife Conservation Officer, Kelowna: *(250) 861-7670.*

Hope InfoCentre: *(604) 869-2121.*

Keremeos InfoCentre: *(250) 499-5225.*

Princeton InfoCentre: *(250) 295-3103.*

The Coquihalla Highway

From Hope north to Kamloops via Merritt on Highway 5 (the Coquihalla Highway), including Monck and Lac Le Jeune Provincial Parks.

The Coquihalla Highway climbs through the Great Bear Snow Shed, crests the summit of Coquihalla Pass (elevation 4,068 feet/1240 m), then crosses the top of the Thompson Plateau, with side roads leading off into rolling countryside speckled with fishing lakes. This is the only toll road in British Columbia, but you don't need to pay a toll to drive the Hope section and enjoy the wonderful mountain scenery.

Avalanche chutes scar the mountainsides and are a visible reminder of the steep terrain that surrounds the highway. Avalanche guns mounted on platforms beside the highway battle the elements to keep the highway open in winter. Travellers must weigh the pros and cons of this route: 75 minutes' driving time can be saved between Kamloops and Hope (and there is the convenience of connecting to the Okanagan), but the severe winter snow and winds threaten even the most experienced and best-equipped drivers. At least the roads are well plowed. In summer, because of the steady uphill grade of the highway, motorists must monitor their vehicles for overheating. Highway patrols are frequent should you encounter engine problems.

Highway 5 follows the Coquihalla River to Merritt and is particularly scenic in the early fall, when rolling fields and forest foliage take on a golden glow. The surrounding Merritt Forest District supports stands of Engelmann spruce, lodgepole pine, and subalpine fir at higher elevations; Douglas fir and ponderosa pine are found on the lower benchlands. Extensive grasslands also occur at low-elevation areas, particularly toward Merritt. Moose, mule deer, bears, and grouse are the main wildlife species here, while small numbers of elk and mountain goats find refuge in the south.

Getting There

Hope, at the eastern end of the Fraser Valley, is the hub for three major routes leading north: Highway 1, Highway 3, and Highway 5. The latter, the Coquihalla Highway, is a toll route ($10 per vehicle) to Merritt and Kamloops. The toll booth is located near the summit of the Coquihalla Pass. Prior to reaching it, a variety of gravel roads lead off into the bush on both the Hope and the Merritt sides of the pass. For a map of the side roads, contact the BC Forest Service for a map of the Merritt Forest District, (800) 665-1511. An alternate approach to Kamloops via Princeton and Merritt is Highway 5A, the route that predates the Coquihalla, which opened in 1986. Merritt is a hub, where three highways—5, 5A, and 8—converge. Kamloops (population 77,000) is 10 times the size of Merritt and Hope. Highways 1 and 5 intersect here at the confluence of the Thompson and North Thompson Rivers.

Adjoining Areas

NORTH: **The Trans-Canada Highway**

SOUTH: **Manning Provincial Park; Crowsnest Highway: South Okanagan Valley**

EAST: **Okanagan Valley**

WEST: **The Fraser Valley**

inside out

Camping

The largest and most northerly provincial campground in this area is **Lac Le Jeune Provincial Park,** located 23 miles (37 km) southwest of Kamloops. From Hwy 5, take the Lac Le Jeune exit. An alternate access route is an 18-mile (29-km) paved road from Hwy 1. Open mid-May through September, this lakeside park with 144 vehicle/tent sites is surrounded by lodgepole pine and pinegrass forests. Besides camping and water sports, it provides lakeshore hiking opportunities, horseshoe pitches, and visitor-program activities in its amphitheatre. The park also contains two archaeological sites. For more information on Lac Le Jeune and other provincial parks in this region, call BC Parks, (250) 851-3000. For campsite reservations in Lac Le Jeune, call the BC Parks reservation line, (800) 681-9025, from March 1 through September 15.

Also accessible via the Lac Le Jeune exit from Hwy 5 is **Walloper Lake Provincial Park,** 18.6 miles (30 km) southwest of Kamloops. This former Forest Service recreation site is being operated to Forest Service standard (rustic) until further developed by BC Parks. You'll find 10 walk-in sites beside a popular boat launch. For more information, contact BC Parks, (250) 851-3000.

Stake-McConnell Lakes Provincial Recreation Area contains two former Forest Service recreation sites also awaiting development; only McConnell Lake has one with camping facilities (15 rustic sites with pit toilets). Fishing, hiking, and mountain biking are all possible here. For more information, contact BC Parks, (250) 851-3000. The area is just over 11 miles (18 km) southwest of Kamloops on access from Hwy 1, or take the Lac Le Jeune exit from Hwy 5.

Closer to Merritt is **Monck Provincial Park,** with 71 vehicle/tent campsites. Located on the northwest side of **Nicola Lake,** 13.6 miles (22 km) north of Merritt, this is a good park for the entire family. From Hwy 5, a 7.4-mile (12-km) paved road follows the northwest side of the lake to the park, which is open May through October. Hiking trails, including an interpretive walk to some lava beds, provide spectacular views of the valley and surrounding countryside. The park features a visitor program and amphitheatre, boat launch, horseshoe pitches, and three archaeological sites.

This area of the Nicola Valley was a winter encampment for Natives for centuries before European settlers arrived. Pithouse depressions remain near the park's beach as evidence of their habitation. The name Nicola was given to the famous chieftain Hwistesmetxquen by the early fur traders for the obvious reason that they couldn't pronounce his Native name. When they tried it phonetically, it sounded vaguely like Nicholas or Nicola, and their mispronunciation has remained.

The vegetation of this part of the Thompson Plateau is chiefly ponderosa pine, Douglas fir, and black cottonwood. Tule and cattail, both used in Native mat making, grow in dense patches round the shore of Nicola Lake. For more information on Monck Provincial Park, contact BC Parks, (250) 851-3000. For campsite reservations in Monck, call the BC Parks reservation line, (800) 681-9025, from March 1 through September 15.

In addition to the campsites detailed above, the BC Forest Service maintains numerous **small, rustic campsites** in this region. They are located near lakes and rivers, blending in with the natural surroundings. Although these sites do not offer sophisticated amenities such as power hookups and piped water, they include basic sanitary facilities, fire rings, picnic tables, and, where appropriate, boat-launch ramps. Access is mostly via narrow unpaved roads, not always suitable for large RVs. Three popular sites with two-wheel-drive access via gravel road are those at **Harmon**

Lake West (16 vehicle/tent sites), **Harmon Lake East** (18 sites), and **Kane Lake** (5 sites), and can be reached from Hwy 5 or 5A. To find them, drive about 12 miles (20 km) south of Merritt on Hwy 5A, then about 5 miles (8 km) west on the Kane Valley Forest Rd. A brochure/map indicating these sites and many others is available from the Merritt Forest District, (800) 665-1511, in Merritt.

Fishing

Good river access for fishing makes the Coquihalla River Provincial Recreation Area a popular spot. However, there are spawning channels alongside the **Coquihalla River** in the vicinity of this park, so be sure to get the newest fishing regulations. This recreation area, located 15.5 miles (25 km) northeast of Hope on Hwy 5, was closed to private vehicles in early 1998, but fishers can reach it by parking nearby and walking in. Southbound highway traffic will find it easy to reach the park (via the Carolin Mines exit before the tollbooths). Northbound traffic should take Othello Rd from Hope to the Dewdney Creek intersection, then a sharp right turn onto the park access road. Leave your vehicle here.

Coldwater River Provincial Park is just north of the summit on the Coquihalla Hwy. Nearby are the Coquihalla Lakes, where both the Coquihalla and Coldwater Rivers have their sources. The **Coldwater River** runs north alongside the highway. It is shallow and gravel-bottomed, a good steelhead spawning area. There is a small Forest Service campsite at Zum Peak beside the river. Follow Zum Peak Forest Rd for 5 miles (8 km) west from the park to reach the Zum Peak campsite. Coldwater River Provincial Park is located 31 miles (50 km) south of Merritt on Hwy 5, just north of the tollbooths, with north and south access ramps.

For more information on fishing in the Coquihalla Lakes region, including boat and equipment rentals, contact Coquihalla Lakes Lodge, (250) 378-0038.

The waters of **Lac Le Jeune** are famous for producing fighting rainbow trout. Fly-fishing is also possible in the **Stake-McConnell Lakes** Provincial Recreation Area (see Camping, above). Call BC Parks for more information, (250) 851-3000.

"A lake a day as long as you stay" is no idle boast for the Nicola Valley. Close to 50 percent of the province's total freshwater sportfishing occurs in the Thompson-Nicola region. Relative to its size, this region is unsurpassed in British Columbia for its sports fishery. The **Thompson and Nicola Rivers** are historic salmon-spawning tributaries of the Fraser River, and the **smaller tributary streams** are where rainbow trout, dolly varden, and kokanee lay their eggs. It's the lakes, however, that are the main attraction for anglers. **Chapperon, Douglas, and Nicola Lakes** have long been noted for their ample fish stocks. Nicola Lake, renowned for its depth, is said to harbour 26 varieties of fish, some weighing up to 20 pounds (9 kg). Nicola Lake is the easiest to reach and is located about 4 miles (7 km) east of Merritt on Hwy 5A. Use the boat launch at Monck Provincial Park (see Camping, above) for access to the big lake. Douglas and Chapperon Lakes are located about 12 miles (20 km) and 18.5 miles (30 km), respectively, east of Hwy 5A on the Douglas Lake Rd. Angling is the most popular form of sportfishing in the Nicola area lakes, but ice fishing, spear fishing, and set-lines methods are also used.

For **information** about permits, contact the Fish and Wildlife Conservation officer at Merritt, (250) 378-9377. For a Forest Service recreation map, contact the Merritt district office, (800) 665-1511, or stop by their office at the intersection of Hwy 5A and Airport Rd. Maps are also available at the Merritt InfoCentre at the junction of Hwys 5 and 5A. For information on fishing in Douglas Lake, contact the Douglas Lake Ranch, (800) 663-4838. Licences, tackle, and sound advice are available in Merritt at Denis' Small Engine, 2626 Nicola Ave, (250) 378-2416; McLeod's Department Store, 2088 Quichena Ave, (250) 378-5191; Nicola Valley Chevron, 3043 Voght St, (250) 378-2525; and Powder Keg Outdoor Supply, 2052 Nicola Ave, (250) 378-9211. For **fly-in fishing,** call Float Plane Adventures, (250) 378-9444, in Merritt.

Picnics/Walking

The **Coquihalla Summit Provincial Recreation Area's** Boston Bar site has picnicking facilities, and photography buffs might want to document the sheer rock faces towering skyward at Zopkios Ridge. There are hiking trails for the travel-weary, as well as information shelters to assist in nature study. The recreation area is located 26 miles (42 km) northeast of Hope on Hwy 5, just east of the tollbooths. Travellers can also stretch their legs at **Coldwater River Provincial Park** (see Fishing, above), which features walking trails.

The Merritt Forest District has two interpretive trails. The **Harmon Lake Trail** (easy; about 2 miles/3 km), located in the Kane Valley, demonstrates forest-management practices. To find the trail, drive about 12 miles (20 km) south of Merritt on Hwy 5A, then about 5 miles (8 km) west on the Kane Valley Forest Rd. The **Godey Creek Trail** (easy; 1.5 miles/2.5 km return), adjacent to the Merritt Visitor Centre, was built in 1990 by a fire-suppression crew. Plaques explaining various aspects of forestry are located along the trail.

A comprehensive guide to this region is *Coquihalla Country* by Murphy Shewchuk.

Boating

The various parks around **Lac Le Jeune** (see Camping, above) offer plenty of opportunities for canoeing. Lac Le Jeune is one of the bigger lakes in a region characterized by hundreds of pocket-sized ponds, many of which provide serenity in the midst of splendid isolation. Get a Merritt Forest District recreation map and pick out a recreation site that appeals to you. Call (800) 665-1511, or stop by their office in Merritt at the intersection of Hwy 5A and Airport Rd. For information on boating in Lac Le Jeune Provincial Park, call BC Parks in Kamloops, (250) 851-3000.

Occasional strong winds make **Nicola Lake** a popular place to go windsurfing and sailing. (For boat launch, see Monck Provincial Park in Camping, above). Nicola Lake is home to the Kamloops Sailing Association, which operates the Quilchena Sailing Centre on the lake, a facility with moorage, docking, and boat-storage facilities. For more information, contact (250) 378-6166 or (250) 378-5432.

Although the Coquihalla River itself is much too cold, **swimming** is popular during the summer in Lac Le Jeune, Nicola Lake, and the Nicola River.

Biking

How about a ride down the **Coquihalla Highway** from the tollbooths to Hope? It's a 40-mph (65-kph) blast! If that's a little too rambunctious, you'll find standard-issue, single-track, mountain-bike trails at **Stake Lake** in the **Stake-McConnell Lakes Provincial Recreation Area** (see Camping, above) near Lac Le Jeune.

The many cross-country ski trails in the **Kane Valley** (see Cross-Country Skiing, below) cover varied terrain and double as mountain-bike trails in summer. For more information, contact the Kane Valley Nordic Ski Club, (250) 378-6328. A map of the trail system is available from the Merritt Forest District office at the intersection of Hwy 5A and Airport Rd, (800) 665-1511, or at many local hotels in Merritt.

A branch line of the **Kettle Valley Railway** leads between Hope and Merritt, passing the Coquihalla Tunnels and Brookmere, a distance of about 87 miles (140 km). Due to washouts and the construction of the Coquihalla Hwy, not all of the line is suitable for biking. One of the best places to begin is Coquihalla Canyon Provincial Recreation Area (see Crowsnest Highway: South Okanagan Valley chapter). Much of the railbed north to Brookmere is intact. For a detailed description of this route, consult *Cycling the Kettle Valley Railway* by Dan and Sandra Langford. For **guided tours** and bike rentals, contact Guichon Creek Outdoor Adventures, 322 Guichon Ave, (250) 378-2065, in Lower Nicola. For **fly-in backcountry mountain-bike trips,** contact Float Plane Adventures, (250) 378-9444.

Cross-Country Skiing

The **Kane Valley,** about 11 miles (17 km) east of Merritt, has been a paradise destination for cross-country skiers for more than 30 years. Portions of the valley have been farmed since the 1890s and selectively logged since the 1960s. The more than 25 miles (40 km) of trails, some of them groomed, follow old roads and skid trails through open timber and across natural grassy slopes. These ski trails (beginner to intermediate) are accessible even during colder weather because they are sheltered from the winter wind. They are managed cooperatively by the BC Forest Service and the Nicola Valley Nordic Ski Club of Merritt, (250) 378-6328. A map of the trail system is available from the Merritt Forest District office or at many local hotels.

Although there are no developed ski trails at **Lac Le Jeune** or **Walloper Lake Provincial Parks,** they are used by cross-country skiers willing to cut their own tracks. Cross-country skiing is also popular at **Stake Lake** in winter months. (See Camping, above.)

Horseback Riding

The open grassland around Merritt is a delight for those who like to trail ride. This is ranching country, home to the Douglas Lake Ranch, one of British Columbia's oldest and largest working ranches. It lies east off Hwy 5A from the crossroads settlement of Quilchena. (Stop at the old hotel here to get a whiff of life as it once was in the Nicola Valley.) For information on horse-trail riding, contact the Douglas Lake Ranch, (800) 663-4838, the Grant Ranches, (250) 378-4004, or Winding River Ranch, (250) 378-6534, all in the Merritt region.

outside in

Restaurants

For recommended restaurants, see Adjoining Areas to this chapter.

Lodgings

Corbett Lake Country Inn ☆ Catering to lovers of fly-fishing in the summer and cross-country skiers in the winter, the inn is run by a French-trained owner and chef, and aside from outdoor activities, the food's the thing here. Dinner is by reservation only and is a wonderful, four-course affair. *7.5 miles/12 km south of Merritt on Hwy 5A; Box 327, Merritt, BC V0K 2B0; (250) 378-4334; $$.*

Quilchena Hotel ☆☆ This remote hotel captures the ambience of southwestern British Columbia's cattle country. It attracts a motley assortment, from moneyed urbanites to cattle barons. Guests share bathrooms and dine together. Ride horses, golf on the adjacent course, or search the nearby fossil beds. *Take second Merritt exit off Coquihalla Hwy; Box 1, Hwy 5A, Quilchena, BC V0E 2R0; (250) 378-2611; $$.*

More Information

BC Forest Service, Kamloops Regional Office: *(250) 828-4131.*
BC Forest Service, Merritt Forest District: *(800) 665-1511 in Canada only or (250) 378-8400.*
BC Parks, Lower Mainland District: *(604) 824-2300.*
BC Parks, Thompson River District: *(250) 851-3000.*
Kamloops InfoCentre: *(250) 372-7722 or (800) 662-1994.*
Merritt InfoCentre: *(250) 378-2281.*

From the Canada–US border and Keremeos north along Highway 97 through the Okanagan Valley to Vernon, including Silver Star and Apex Mountain Provincial Recreation Areas and Okanagan Mountain Provincial Park.

The Okanagan Valley is almost dry enough to warrant being called a desert. After even one visit to this spectacularly diverse area, you'll understand why superlatives are constantly used to describe it. Beloved by thousands of visitors and inhabitants alike for the unparalleled variety of its climate and landscape, the Okanagan Valley has something for everyone: hoodoos, orchards, vineyards, mountains, valleys, lakes, highlands, ski slopes, and trails. This is truly one of the most desirable locales in the province for year-round outdoor fun.

Starting in the south, near the US border, you'll find spectacular backcountry, with the remains of old mining settlements dotting the highway. After you pass through the arid Osoyoos and Oliver regions and head north up the valley, you will encounter orchards and vineyards, evidence of some of the best fruit- and vegetable-growing land in the world.

Dozens of parks surround Okanagan Lake, an outdoor adventure playground where the only difficulty is deciding what to do with your time. Ski at Silver Star, Big White, or Apex? Wilderness camp at Okanagan Mountain, or farther north at Monashee? Mountain bike at Kalamalka, or at Silver Star? Wait, wasn't that where you were thinking of skiing? As you can see, the choice is dizzying: Many of the spots you love in one season offer a whole new set of opportunities in another. To put it simply, this is one area worth spending some serious time in.

Getting There

There are a variety of entry points to the Okanagan Valley, which is about 155 miles (250 km) in length: from the west along Highway 3 via Keremeos and then Highway 3A; from the south along Highway 97 via Osoyoos; from the northwest along Highway 97C (the Coquihalla Connector) or along Highway 5 (the Coquihalla), both via Merritt; from the west or east along Highway 1 (the Trans-Canada); from the southeast along Highway 33; from the northeast along Highway 1 via Sicamous and then south along Highways 97A or 97B. Airline service to the Okanagan is through Kelowna. Air BC and Canadian Airlines both have daily scheduled flights to Kelowna.

Adjoining Areas

NORTH: **The Trans-Canada Highway**

SOUTH: **Crowsnest Highway: South Okanagan Valley**

EAST: **Kettle Valley**

WEST: **The Coquihalla Highway**

inside out

Parks/Camping/Picnics

You could spend months exploring the Okanagan Valley region. There are more than 60 provincial parks, and dozens and dozens of recreation sites. If you want the basic campground, with pit toilets, campsites, and firewood, the provincial parks will satisfy. They are popular, however, and souls looking for more undisturbed places will not want to miss wilderness camping in some of the remote areas, such as **Okanagan Mountain Provincial Park** (see Hiking/Backpacking, below). For details on a particular region, consult the list of telephone numbers at the end of this section; for provincial parks call (250) 494-6500 directly. Here's your briefing on the parks that are a good destination for day trips, easy camping, and picnics, from north to south along Hwy 97.

About two minutes south of Osoyoos on Osoyoos Lake, considered the warmest lake in Canada, is **Haynes Point Provincial Park** (41 vehicle/tent sites). Its namesake is Judge John Carmichael Haynes, a jurist who brought law and order to the gold fields of Wildhorse Creek in the 1860s. The deep valley was formed primarily by glacial erosion. Its steep, arid hillsides receive only a tiny amount of precipitation annually, and are vegetated by desert-loving plants such as sagebrush, greasewood, and ponderosa pine. The park is open from March until October and is so popular, the staff assign numbers to those in line, put them on a reservation list, and then call the numbers in the afternoon, when you must be present to get a site. Part of the attraction here is the park's rainbow trout and bass fishing (there's a boat ramp) and its wildlife. A little more than 12 acres (4.8 ha) of the park are covered by a marsh and sandy spit lined with cottonwoods, making it great place for observing some of nature's fascinating creatures and their habits. Swimmers will like it too, and the lake-frontage campsites are the ones to aim for. For more information, contact BC Parks' district office in Summerland, (250) 494-6500. To reserve a campsite in advance, call the BC Parks reservation line, (800) 689-9025, March 1 to September 15.

Inkaneep Provincial Park (7 vehicle/tent sites), 4 miles (6 km) north of Oliver on Hwy 97, is a cool riverside respite from the Okanagan sun. A trail provides access to the Okanagan River and some good spots for camping, fishing, and canoeing, but take binoculars; the area's thickets are a well-known habitat for birds such as the black-headed grosbeak, American redstart, northern oriole, and many others. Some unique flora and fauna are present in the nearby ecological reserve. For more information, call BC Parks, (250) 494-6500.

There are 160 campsites in two separate campgrounds on the west side of the lake in **Okanagan Lake Provincial Park,** 15 miles (24 km) north of Penticton. This is a scenic, well-developed site, with sandy beaches along the lake backed by uplands of ponderosa pine and sagebrush. The park is open year-round and is suitable for day use and picnics, but campers should be prepared for crowds during the peak season. To reserve a campsite here, call BC Parks' reservation system, (800) 689-9025, March 1 to September 15. For general information on Okanagan Lake Provincial Park, call (250) 494-6500. Across the lake (accessible by boat) is over 24,700 acres (10 000 ha) of wilderness in Okanagan Mountain Provincial Park (see Hiking/Backpacking, below). Take Hwy 97 15 miles (24 km) north of Penticton.

If you're looking for a short break from the central Okanagan's summer heat, **Bear Creek Provincial Park** (122 vehicle/tent sites at two locations) may be the place to visit for easy camping and picnics. Here, 15 minutes from downtown Kelowna, is everything from soft beaches to a wild, rocky canyon. On the lakeshore are beautiful, sandy beaches and a parkland campground with showers and a horseshoe pit. In the open hillside behind the campsites are 14 miles (23 km) of trail to explore. Bear Creek flows through the bottom of the tree-walled canyon, bringing with it small flakes of placer gold. Along the trails above the canyon, ponderosa pine and Douglas fir compete with juniper, bunchgrass, and prickly-pear cactus for the area's meagre rainfall. Below, moistened by the mist rising off the waterfalls, is yet another world, one of maple and birch, wild rose, horsetail, and moss. Wildlife abounds here. Take Hwy 97 6 miles (9 km) west of Kelowna. The park's on the west side of Okanagan Lake. For more information, contact BC Parks in Summerland, (250) 494-6500. To reserve a campsite here, call (800) 689-9025 from March 1 to September 15.

Fintry Provincial Park (50 vehicle/tent sites) is a getaway with a historical flavour. Located on the west side of Okanagan Lake, its site was the transportation hub of the valley; Hudson's Bay Company fur brigade traders passed through here. Easy walking through the park will bring you to the waterfalls and deep pools of Shorts Creek, as well as a suspension bridge and the remains of irrigation and power generation structures. Other features from the past are a ferry wharf from which freight boats operated, and a preserved Manor house, caretakers' house, and several barns. The surrounding hillsides have a canopy of ponderosa pine and Douglas fir. In addition to the campsites, there is a large picnic and day-use area. Take Westside Rd off Hwy 97 (south of Kelowna) and drive north for 21 miles (34 km) north of Kelowna on Westside Rd. To reserve a campsite here, call the BC Parks' reservation service, (250) 689-9025, from March 1 to September 15. For general information, call BC Parks in Summerland, (250) 494-6500.

The rocky, forested headlands and sheltered, sandy bays of small **Ellison Provincial Park** (5 sites) await you on the east side of Okanagan Lake, just a few miles south of Vernon. Walking trails provide access to the headlands that separate two beautiful bays, offering boulder-climbing excitement and wildflower photo opportunities. The bays are good fishing spots, attracting carp, burbot, kokanee, and trout. (A car-top boat launch is located just north of the park, and a full boat-launch facility is about 5 miles (8 km) north of the park.) This is an area of undulating benchland dominated by stands of ponderosa pine and Douglas fir, set between the rolling hills of the Thompson Plateau to the west and the peaks of the Monashee Mountains to the east. The climate is dry and warm, and this is one of the prime fruit-growing and agricultural areas of the province. There are six archaeological sites within the park. Take Hwy 97 for 10 miles (16 km) south from Vernon; there is paved access from Vernon only. For more information, contact BC Parks in Summerland, (250) 494-6500.

Located northeast of Vernon at the southeast end of Mabel Lake, **Mabel Lake Provincial Park** (81 vehicle/tent sites) is situated in a valley formed by the glaciers of the last ice age. The Shuswap Highlands to the east grade into the impressive Monashee Mountains. The park's sandy shoreline is backed by a forest of hemlock, red cedar, and birch, in sharp contrast to the drier ponderosa pine and Douglas fir forests of the Thompson Plateau to the west. Summer camping here is ideal for those who prefer a cooler locale than the Okanagan Valley. You might spot a deer or black bear; you'll definitely see a variety of waterfowl and other birdlife. The lake offers good rainbow-trout fishing. There is an archaeological site here. From Vernon, take Hwy 6 east to Lumby, then go northeast. It's 50 miles (76 km) to the park; the last 22 miles (35 km) are gravel. For more information, contact BC Parks in Summerland, (250) 494-6500.

Yet another popular, scenic spot in the north Okanagan is **Echo Lake Provincial Park** east of Lumby, with its large group campground, boat rentals, cabins, and campsites at Echo Lake Resort, (250) 547-6434, within the park. For information, contact BC Parks, (250) 494-6500.

Beaches/Swimming

Christie Memorial Provincial Park is a very popular day-use site on **Skaha Lake.** The park is located at the town of Okanagan Falls on Hwy 97. There are three developed beaches on **Okanagan Lake** at **Kickininee Provincial Park:** Kickininee, Pyramid, and Soorimpt (which features a boat launch). Take Hwy 97 about 9 miles (14.5 km) north of Penticton and bring your snorkelling gear to explore the lake's treasures. **Sun-Oka Beach Provincial Park,** 4 miles (6 km) south of Summerland on Hwy 97, has one of the most superb beaches in the valley and features two public boat launches nearby. Its name combines the words "sunny" and "Okanagan." **Kelowna City Waterfront Park** and **Bertram Creek Regional Park** are both good swimming spots in Kelowna.

Kalamalka Lake Provincial Park, 5 miles (8 km) south of Vernon off Kalamalka Rd and Hwy 6, has year-round appeal, especially if you're looking for a north Okanagan getaway that doesn't involve really getting away. On the northeast side of Kalamalka Lake (Lake of a Thousand Colours), this park is a well-preserved remnant of the natural grasslands that once stretched from Vernon to Osoyoos. Its easy walking trails wind through the grassland slopes and along lightly forested ridges. Scenic clifftop viewpoints overlook a rocky shoreline indented with bays and tiny coves. From the spectacular wildflower display in the spring to the relative seclusion of the beaches and boating spots in summer; from the golden-hued forests in autumn to the rolling, cross-country ski trails in winter, this park is a favourite with visitors year-round. Two archaeological sites lie within park boundaries, and you may see coyote, deer, or black bear but are most likely to observe Columbian ground squirrels and yellow-bellied marmots. Pacific rattlesnakes, shy creatures who wish only to be left alone, are an important part of this fascinating ecosystem.

Mara Provincial Park, at Mara Lake north of Enderby, has a broad beach and boat launch. Take Hwy 97A to reach the park, which is situated along the east side of Mara Lake.

Wildlife

For a special wildlife-viewing experience, take a day to visit Vaseux Lake Provincial Park, about 15 miles (25 km) south of Penticton on Hwy 97. Here, the Vaseux Lake Nature Trust operates the **Vaseux Wildlife Centre** in a multiagency cooperative project. In addition, there is a Canadian Wildlife Service wildlife sanctuary adjacent to the park and two Wildlife Management Units ensuring protection of critical **bighorn sheep** winter range. The cliffs surrounding the park include spring and winter range of California bighorn sheep, and the area is famous for **bird-watching.** Grasses, reeds, willows, and shrubs along the shore afford a home to many varieties of birdlife. Waterfowl, including **trumpeter swans, widgeons, Canada geese, wood ducks,** and **blue-winged teal,** are common. In spring, the beautiful **lazuli bunting** has been seen. Other bird species present include chukar partridge, wrens, swifts, sage thrashers, woodpeckers, curlews, and dippers. **Mammal species** found here include beavers, bats, cottontail rabbits, muskrats, deer, and mice. **Rattlesnakes, toads,** and **turtles** also live in this area. Considerable populations of largemouth bass, rainbow trout, and carp make their home in the water, and in winter, the frozen lake offers excellent conditions for ice fishing as well as other ice-related activities. For more information on the Vaseux Wildlife Centre and Vaseux Lake Provincial Park, contact BC Parks, (250) 494-6500.

If you're in the town of Kelowna itself, you can watch kokanee salmon spawning mid-September to mid-October in Lion's Park from a BC Wildlife viewing area off Springfield Rd or during a guided tour; and you can take advantage of another BC Wildlife migratory **bird-viewing site** at Bertram Creek Regional Park (see Beaches/Swimming, above). For more information, contact Kelowna Regional District Parks, (250) 860-3938 or (250) 763-4918, or BC Wildlife Watch, (250) 387-9896 in Victoria.

Fishing

Darke Lake Provincial Park is about 20 miles (35 km) northwest of Penticton off Hwy 97 on Prairie Valley Rd (12 miles of gravel road). It has a small campground (5 vehicle/tent sites), with good rainbow and brook trout fishing. In winter, the lake is the site of ice fishing and skating. From Darke Lake, it's only 2.5 miles (4 km) farther to **Eneas Lakes Provincial Park,** a lovely undeveloped area consisting of four lakes on a fir- and pine-forested plateau. It's 13 miles (20 km) west of Peachland; road access is limited and rough, and four-wheel-drive vehicles are recommended.

Pennask Lake Provincial Park, 35 miles (56 km) northwest of Peachland off Hwy 97, is a source of much of the province's rainbow trout eggs, which are used for restocking purposes. Fishing is excellent here, and the park has a boat launch. The road in is not suitable for recreational vehicles: it's rough for 30 miles (50 km) from Peachland and then gravel into the park. **Kekuli Bay Provincial Park** ("kekuli" refers to the semi-subterranean homes built by the Interior Salish natives), on the west side of Kalamalka Lake, 7 miles (11 km) south of Vernon, is located on a lovely bay. The only development so far is the access road, parking lot, and boat launch, but the launch is already deemed the best on Kalamalka Lake, and the sandy beach promises to become a lure visitors. **Wood Lake,** between Okanagan Centre and Oyama on Hwy 97, has a solid reputation for its kokanee and rainbow trout fishing. The large lake sits just south of Kalamalka Lake on the east side of Hwy 97 south of Vernon. Fishing is also good at **Ellison Provincial Park** on Okanagan Lake, about 10 miles (16 km) southwest of Vernon (see Parks/Camping/Picnics, above). It features a car-top boat launch about 1 mile (2 km) north of the park and a full boat-launch facility about 5 miles (8 km) north of park. Anglers will find a cheery welcome, information on rainbow trout fishing, licence, boat rentals, bait, and tackle in **Echo Lake Provincial Park** (see Parks/Camping/Picnics, above) north of Lumby at Echo Lake Resort, (250) 547-6434.

For information on fishing in the Kelowna region, contact Harv's Outdoor Sports, 2903 Pandosy St, (250) 762-4278; Benshona Custom Rods and Tackle, 361 Bernard St, (250) 860-4244; Bear Creek Sports, 2012B Springfield Rd, (250) 861-4838; or Rutland Sports Centre, 154 Asher Rd, (250) 765-6956, or their fishing information line, (250) 491-0132. In Penticton, contact Ray's Sports Den, 215 Main St, (250) 493-1216.

Hiking/Backpacking

The Okanagan's open terrain makes for ideal hiking, with little or no bushwhacking required. The parks mentioned below offer remoteness, breathtaking landscapes, and challenging outdoor adventure. Unless otherwise noted, these parks are open year-round. For more information, contact the BC Parks district office in Summerland, (250) 494-6500.

Okanagan Mountain Provincial Park (48 wilderness walk-in sites) is located on the east side of Okanagan Lake just opposite Peachland. There's no road access to the park, but secondary roads from Kelowna offer access to parking lots on the park's northeastern boundary. To reach the parking lots, travel 9 miles (15 km) south of Kelowna on Lakeshore Rd. Just east of the park, Lakeshore Rd continues west to the north parking lot, while Rimrock Rd leads south to the Golden Mile–Boulder Trail parking lot. An alternative approach is from Penticton via Naramata on Chute Lake Rd, a rough 15.5-mile (25-km) route to the south parking lot.

This park is well suited to backwoods camping. Wilderness campsites are located at Divide, Victor, and Baker Lakes and at Buchan Bay. From the north parking lot, follow **Golden Mile–Boulder Trail** (moderate; 2 miles/3.5 km) to the **Wildhorse Canyon Trail** (moderate; 3 miles/5 km) and finally the **Buchan Bay Trail** (easy; 1 mile/1.6 km) to reach the wilderness campsites at Buchan Bay. Wilderness campsites are located near the south parking lot. More sites are located at Divide Lake on Okanagan Mountain, reached via the **Divide Lake North Trail** (10 miles/16 km return) from the Rimrock Rd parking lot, or via the **Mountain Goat Trail** (6 miles/10 km return) from the south parking lot. The campsites at Baker and Victor Lakes are reached by following the **Baker Lake Trail** (moderate; 2.5 miles/4 km return) from Divide Lake.

Hiking trails provide an excellent opportunity to ramble around and see unique plants and animal life in this semidesert wilderness region. The lake and mountain views are good from the top of Okanagan Mountain, but wear sturdy footwear (this park is in rattlesnake country) and carry water between camping areas if you're hiking in summer. In addition to the backcountry campsites, facilities also include horse-loading ramps in the north and south parking lots, as well as marine campsites and mooring buoys on Okanagan Lake. Hike to the top of Okanagan Mountain on the **Divide Lake North Trail** (moderate; 10 miles/16 km return) from the Rimrock Rd parking lot for beautiful views of the lake to the west and the Monashees to the east, and check out the four archaeological sites in the park. For more information, including a detailed map, contact BC Parks in Summerland, (250) 494-6500. A good topographic map to consult is NTS 82E/12.

Another undeveloped wilderness area that hikers and cross-country skiers will find rewarding is **Nickel Plate Provincial Park.** Nearby Lookout Mountain rises above the Nickel Plate Lake region, studded with huge erratics (boulders deposited by receding glacial ice). There's soft camping on the lake's sandy beaches. Blueberries and other edible berries grow in the forested surroundings, as does Labrador tea, with its white blossoms and fuzz-backed leaves, used by Native Canadians and early settlers to make a relaxing drink. Nickel Plate is 18 miles (29 km) northeast of Hedley, near Apex Resort, and is accessed by a gravel road off Hwy 3A. For more information and a map, contact the BC Parks in Summerland, (250) 494-6500 or the Forest Service district office in Penticton, 102 Industrial Pl, (250) 490-2200 or (800) 661-4099.

Bear Creek Provincial Park (see Parks/Camping/Picnics, above) features a moderate 14-mile (24-km) hiking trail as well as a 6-mile (10-km) easygoing hiking trail. Trails begin from a common trailhead at the entrance to the park. Wear sturdy footwear because the prickly pear cacti on the more exposed rocky slopes of the upland region of the park can puncture skin even through clothing and running shoes. (Rattlesnakes abound here. Visitors are asked to stay on the trails in Bear Creek Provincial Park.) This area is a feast for the senses, with its expansive views of the lake and canyon; its scent of cottonwood, pine, and fir forests; and its splashes of colourful wildflowers. Bear Creek Provincial Park is located 5 miles (9 km) west of Kelowna on the west side of Okanagan Lake off Hwy 97. For more information, contact BC Parks, (250) 494-6500.

Silver Star Provincial Recreation Area, 14 miles 22 (km) north of Vernon, is superb for winter activities (see Skiing/Snowboarding, below), and is also a great place to visit in summer for hiking and nature rambling. In summer, Silver Star Mountain operates a chairlift for visitors to ascend to hiking trails in the subalpine zone with fabulous views of the Monashees in the north and east, the Shuswap Highlands in the north and west, and the Okanagan Plateau in the south. For more information, call Silver Star Mountain Resort, (250) 542-0224, or visit their Web site: www.silverstarmtn.com.

Walking tours in the Okanagan include **Okanagan Valley International Peace Park** in Oliver and **Historic Vernon and Okanagan Landing** in Vernon. Maps are available from the Oliver InfoCentre on Hwy 97, (250) 498-6321, and Vernon Tourism on Hwy 97, or the Vernon Chamber of Commerce, (800) 665-0795 or (250) 542-1415.

Hardy Falls Park in Peachland is a cool oasis in what can sometimes be a hot landscape. A pleasant walking trail (easy; 2 miles/3 km return), complete with seven footbridges, leads to a splendid little waterfall hidden away at the head of a narrow canyon. The shade and the cool water attract a wide variety of wildlife as well as human visitors. In the spring, wildflowers brighten the canyon walls and the underbrush along the trail. Carp spawn in the creek and dippers nest in the cracks of the waterfall. In October, crimson kokanee dart among the riffles in the creek. Harry Hardy was one of the first orchardists in the Westbank area, and Hardy Falls Park is named in his honour. The park is adjacent to **Antlers Beach Park,** where you can head for a dip after your walk.

You can walk or hike as much or as little of the **Kettle Valley Railway Trail,** south of Kelowna, as you feel inclined to tackle. Stamina, more than conditioning, will determine if you complete the 15-mile (24-km) round trip between the trailheads on the Little White and Myra Forest Service Rds. As the trail follows an abandoned railbed, the grade is moderate. This was one of the more challenging sections of the route to engineer, and required 18 trestles and two tunnels. Washrooms are available at the trailheads as well as near the middle of Myra Canyon. Pack along water and wear sturdy shoes. To reach the Little White trailhead, go south of Hwy 97 (also called Harvey St) in downtown Kelowna on Pandosy St, east on K.L.O. road, then south on Spiers, June Springs, and Little White Forest Service Rds, all of which interconnect and lead to the railbed. To reach the Myra trailhead, travel east of Pandosy St on K.L.O road to McCulloch Rd, which joins the Myra Forest Service Rd and leads to the railbed. A detailed map of Kelowna and the trail is available at Outdoor Adventure Gear, 2013 Harvey Ave, (250) 860-9481, in Kelowna.

Skiing/Snowboarding

Apex Mountain Resort near Apex Mountain Provincial Recreation Area is located 20 miles (32 km) southwest of Penticton off Hwy 97. Justly renowned in western Canada as one of the three prime ski and snowboard destinations in the Okanagan Valley, it's fast becoming a popular destination for summer hikers and mountain bikers. The provincial recreation area covers **Mount Riorda** and **Beaconsfield Mountain.** From the summits of these mountains, you will enjoy the vistas of Manning and Cathedral Provincial Parks, Peachland Hills, and the rolling Okanagan Highland. More than anything else, skiers and snowboarders will love the fluffy powder snow that accumulates here. Powder fills the gun barrels of twelve steep chutes that lead skiers down from the peak of Beaconsfield Mountain (elevation 7,187 feet/2178 m), reached by the high-speed quad Westbank chairlift. The mountain is also served by a triple chair and a T-bar. Total vertical rise from the base to the peak is 2,000 feet (605 m). The 50 trails at Apex are divided between 16 percent novice, 48 percent intermediate, 18 percent advanced, and 18 percent expert ability levels. Almost anything's possible when you have ideal conditions, and light crowds to boot. Apex Alpine also offers 7.5 miles (12 km) of **cross-country trails.** The trailhead is located beside the resort's RV park. Skiing is free on the cross-country trails. For information on on-hill accommodation, fees, lessons, and snow conditions, call Apex Mountain Resort, (800) 387-2739, (250) 292-8111, (250) 492-2880, or visit their Web site: www.apexresort.com. For information on snow conditions, call (250) 492-2929.

Just 3.7 miles (6 km) from Apex Mountain Resort is the **Nickel Plate Nordic Centre** in Nickel Plate Provincial Park (see Hiking/Backpacking, above). Access to the 18.6 miles (30 km) of groomed and track-set trails here is from Hwy 97 in Penticton on the Apex Mountain Rd or northeast of Hedley via a 20-mile (30-km) gravel road off Hwy 3A. The weather conditions that make downhill skiing at Apex such a joy provide light powder snow at Nickel Plate. For snow and road conditions, call Apex

Mountain Resort, (250) 492-2929, or BC Parks, (250) 494-6500.

Silver Star Provincial Recreation Area in the Shuswap Highlands is home to **Silver Star Mountain Resort,** the most northerly winter playground in the Okanagan Valley. The park and resort are located north of Vernon on Hwy 97, then east on well-marked Silver Star Rd, for a total distance of 14 miles (22 km). Skiers and snowboarders will find a year-round resort here, built on a 1890s Gaslight Era theme in keeping with architecture found in the north Okanagan Valley a century ago. Hotels, restaurants, a saloon, lounges, and a grocery store are all clustered at the base of the resort's chairlifts. There's no need of a vehicle once you arrive here, as everything is within easy walking (or skiing) distance. The resort expanded its ski operation *up* the slopes of Silver Star Mountain (elevation 6,280 feet/1915 m) in the 1980s, and when it wanted to expand in the 1990s, there was nowhere to go but *down.* Fortunately, Silver Star Resort sits high enough up the mountain (village elevation 5,280 feet/1584 m) that it could afford to create a new set of trails between the village and Putnam Creek (3,780 feet/1155 m). As a result, skiers and snowboarders here have 2,491 feet (760 m) of vertical drop in which to defy gravity. The 84 designed trails are designated as 20 percent easy, 50 percent more difficult, 20 percent most difficult, and 10 percent extreme. In addition to the trails, there are 400 acres (162 ha) of open bowls and lightly forested glades. The mountain is serviced by two high-speed quad chairlifts, a quad and double chairlift, and two T-bars.

Cross-country skiers receive just as much welcome here as do other winter enthusiasts. Beginning from the trailhead at the entrance to the resort, the 23 miles (37 km) of tracked and groomed trails fan out through the park. An additional 30 miles (50 km) of groomed trails lead through the adjacent **Sovereign Lake** area. The trailhead for the Sovereign Lake cross-country area is located just west of the entrance to the resort and has its own parking area. A fee is charged for cross-country skiing here and at the resort.

The **National Altitude Training Centre,** a world-class sport and recreation facility, is also located at Silver Star. The centre, in addition to being a professionally equipped facility with a weight room and a wax room (bring your own waxing equipment), has been host to a number of downhill and cross-country ski and mountain-bike competitions, and is the year-round training base for several ski, bike, and luge teams. For more information, call (250) 558-6017.

For information on skiing and snowboarding lessons, equipment rentals, lift and cross-country fees, as well as accommodation at Silver Star Mountain Resort, call (800) 663-4431 or (250) 542-0224, or visit their Web site: www.silverstarmtn.com. For current snow conditions in Silver

Star Provincial Park, including the Sovereign Lake area, call (250) 542-1745. Connector bus service is available to Silver Star Mountain Resort from the Kelowna airport, about 60 miles (100 km) south of Vernon. Call the resort to make travel arrangements. For information on winter recreation as well as equipment rental in Vernon, contact the Jim Attridge Ski Centre, 2707 48th Ave, (250) 558-5575 or (800) 416-5794.

Mountain Biking

The Okanagan Valley area is great for mountain biking. Here's a summary of some of the more notable trails and roads here, starting at Vernon in the north and ending at Keremeos near the Canada–US border.

A trip to **Vernon** is not complete without a spin down **Spanky's,** possibly the most popular ride in Vernon. The trailhead is right across from the Sovereign Lake cross-country ski area in Silver Star Provincial Recreation Area, which can be reached via the Silver Star Rd east of Hwy 97. Spanky's features a 2,625-foot (800-m) vertical descent, spread over 8 miles (13 km) of trail. If you can't arrange a ride to the trailhead and don't feel like slogging all the way up the mountain, call Vernon Taxi, (250) 545-3337, or Jim's Limo, (250) 542-6119.

If you're feeling ambitious, take your bike up the chairlift at Silver Star Mountain Resort (see Skiing/Snowboarding, above) and spend time bombing around the peak of **Silver Star Mountain** first before starting your descent. Maps of the mountain are available at the resort or by calling (250) 542-0224. Silver Star is one of the more "mountain-bike-friendly" provincial parks. The National Altitude Training Centre and Silver Star Mountain Resort have hosted the 1994 Grundig/UCI World Cup Finals, the sixth event of the Canada Cup series in 1996, and the 1997 Canadian Mountain Bike Festival. Several trails are designated as bike-only. Silver Star offers bike rentals, guided tours, mountain-bike camps, and national and world mountain bike competitions. Bring extra clothes along. At 6,000 feet (1830 m), it can be chilly here, even on a warm day. The Silver Star Mountain Bike Club hosts bike clinics and stages mountain-bike races on Wednesday evenings in July and August. Daily mountain-bike tours for all ages and abilities are offered by the club, which is based at the National Altitude Training Centre. For more information, call (250) 558-6017.

If Spanky's doesn't seem ambitious enough, try the **Trinity Ricardo Trail System,** which runs north from Silver Star Mountain Resort to Ashton Creek, a small town east of Hwy 97 at Enderby. This trail is a whopping 24 miles (40 km), almost all of it downhill. The Trinity Ricardo Trail System is popular among the snowmobiling crowd, but is practically unknown to mountain bikers. For more information, call (250) 558-5575.

Check with Vernon Bike World, 3106 32nd St, (250) 545-0140; Sport Tech, 3003 29th Ave, (250) 549-1199; or Olympia Cycle, 3102 31st Ave, (250) 542-9684, in Vernon, for more information on local trails. Detailed descriptions of some rides appear in *Mountain Biking British Columbia* by Darrin Polischuk.

Kalamalka Lake Provincial Park (see Beaches/Swimming, above) south of Vernon is another bike-friendly area. A large portion of the park contains multiuse hiking, horseback riding, and mountain biking trails. A word of advice: Kalamalka Lake was an artillery range during World War II, so give any suspicious, bombshell-shaped objects a wide berth and report these objects to a park official. Maps of the trails are available from BC Parks, (250) 464-6500, or at the lake itself.

Around Kelowna, the **Glenmore Trails** in Knox Mountain Regional Park also offer interesting bike paths with great views over Lake Okanagan. One caution: This is an area in which you can easily get lost, so be forewarned. A paved road leads to the top of Knox Mountain (elevation 1,970 feet/600 m) from the park entrance off Clifton Rd. Once on top, a variety of unmarked trails lead off in several directions. Like most mountain-bike areas, it is a mix of logging roads (mostly up) and singletracks (mostly down). To get to the park, take Clifton Rd in Kelowna's Glenmore neighbourhood to Grainger Rd, then turn right and head to the dead end. Ride north and pick one of the trails that will appear in front of you. For more information on the mountain-bike trails in Knox Mountain Regional Park, call Kelowna Regional Parks, (250) 860-3938.

Just south of Kelowna is **Myra Canyon,** a lovingly restored section of the **Kettle Valley Railway Trail** (see Hiking/Backpacking, above). It weighs in at 12 miles (24 km) round trip, but there are no steep climbs or hairball singletracks—just some fun, casual riding. What makes the Myra Canyon section special are the 18 trestles and two tunnels you'll pass over and through. Exercise caution when riding across the trestles. The Myra Canyon section is part of the historic 133-mile (215-km) route (also known as the Carmi Subdivision) between Midway and Penticton. This is part of a much longer biking trip, other sections of which are described elsewhere in the Kettle Valley chapter. For more information, consult *Cycling the Kettle Valley Railway* by Dan and Sandra Langford. For more information on the Myra Canyon route, contact the Myra Canyon Trestle Restoration Society, (250) 860-6261, in Kelowna.

Okanagan Mountain Provincial Park, on the east side of Okanagan Lake (see Hiking/Backpacking, above), is good for mountain biking. Remember that there is no access to the park by road; it's boat, bicycle, or hike-in only. One of the most popular rides is a two-day excursion around the border of the park (just bring the spare tube and pump; it's a long hike back). Almost all the trails are open to mountain bikers. Popular trails include **Commando Bay Trail** (lengthy, moderate) and **Boulder Trail** (short, technical). Maps are available from BC Parks, (250) 494-6500.

The **Casa Loma Trails** (easy; 3 miles/4.5 km) provide an easy ride along the shores of Okanagan Lake. Get there by heading south on Hwy 97 from Kelowna, taking a left on Boucherie Rd, then taking a left again on Sunnyside. The trail starts at the end of Sunnyside. For more information on mountain biking in the Kelowna region, contact Kelowna Cycle, 2949 Pandosy St, (250) 762-2453; Cyclepath, 2169 Springfield Rd, (250) 868-0122; or Gerick Cycle, 1963 Harvey Rd, (250) 868-3007, all in Kelowna. For **guided bike tours,** contact Okanagan Bicycle Tours, (800) 991-3233 or (250) 766-4086; or Monashee Mountain Bike Tours, 1591 Highland Dr, North Kelowna, (250) 762-9253.

High above **Penticton,** along the Ellis Creek Canyon, is the **Ellis Ridge Trail.** From Carmi Ave in town, turn right at the cross-country area and take the trail from the parking lot 2 miles (3 km) past the cattle gate. If you are driving, park at the cattle gate. This isn't a difficult ride, but don't push your limits. The trail skirts the canyon in places, and you don't want to miss a turn.

Just to the north of Ellis Creek is **Campbell Mountain,** a maze of interconnected single- and doubletrack: not technically difficult, but not for the faint of heart, either. To reach it, take Reservoir Rd off Upper Bench Rd in Penticton. Take the right fork in Reservoir Rd to the parking lot at the foot of Campbell Mountain. For more information on mountain biking around Penticton, contact Sun Country Cycle, 533 Main St, (250) 493-0686; or Bike Barn, 300 Westminster Ave, (250) 492-4140. Ski areas that used to sit fallow during the summer have of late been appropriated by mountain bikers. **Apex Mountain Resort** (see Skiing/Snowboarding, above) operates a chairlift, but it is only open to mountain bikers on a guided tour. For more information on bike tours, call Apex Mountain Resort, (800) 387-2739. Soloists with iron lungs can always pedal up **Grandfather's Trail,** which leads right to the top of Beaconsfield Mountain from the resort's main parking area. Maps are available from the resort.

Riddle Road is located about 3 miles (5 km) from Penticton on Naramata Rd. If you take Riddle Rd to its end, you'll find another mountain-bike haven that gives credence to the oft-repeated Okanagan phrase: "Vancouver's got nothing to ride on compared to here." Great views, great singletrack, great downhill.

The International Bicycling and Hiking Society has developed a lovely little river ride between **Oliver** and **Osoyoos** (12 miles/20 km). To find it, just head east on any of the turnoffs from Hwy 97 between

McAlpine Bridge (the northern terminus of the trail) and Rd 22. This is an easygoing ride, perfect for a summer day.

The **Osoyoos Trails** are a great series of old jeep roads and single-track on the slopes west of Osoyoos. From town, head west towards the golf course and turn left on Fairwind. Park at the first cattle gate. The trail dances around the perimeter of the golf course. Most of the routes are quick and moderately easy, but frustratingly short for those looking for the eternal descent. For more information, contact Mitchell Sports, (250) 495-2013, in Osoyoos.

Golfing

Of the 37 golf courses scattered from Osoyoos to Vernon, Kelowna boasts 15. Most courses open in March, and some years golfers play into November. Fruit trees and water hazards challenge the patrons on many courses. Kelowna Springs Golf Course, (250) 765-4653, has seven natural spring-fed lakes, and more than a thousand apple trees grow on the fairways of Harvest Golf Club, (250) 862-3103. Gallagher's Canyon Golf & Country Club, (250) 861-4240, straddles Gallagher's Canyon, through which a river runs. Predator Ridge Golf Course, (250) 542-3436, has undulating greens and dozens of bunkers set on the dry and hilly terrain near Vernon. The T Times Central Booking Service, (800) 689-4653 or (250) 762-7844, will book tee times at most courses in the area.

Diving

When diving at **Paul's Tomb** in the **Knox Mountain Nature Park** in Kelowna (see Mountain Biking, above), you can see, at a depth of 25 feet (8 m), a replica of Ogopogo, a mythological creature reputed to inhabit the waters of nearby Okanagan Lake. For more information, contact the Kelowna Visitors Bureau, (800) 663-4345 or (250) 861-1515.

Otter Bay in **Ellison Provincial Park** in Vernon is the site of western Canada's first freshwater scuba-diving and snorkelling park. A number of objects have been sunk here to attract a variety of fish and other lake-dwelling creatures. For more information, contact BC Parks, (250) 494-6500. For sales, rentals, and service, contact Innerspace Dive & Kayak, 3306 32nd Ave, Vernon, (250) 549-2040.

outside in

Attractions

The Okanagan Valley, stretching from Osoyoos at the US border north to Vernon, is laden with orchards, making it especially appealing in spring when the **fruit trees** are in full bloom. The best time to pick up some of the valley's bounty is mid-August through early September; however, as early as the end of June, the fruit starts ripening: cherries (late June through mid-July), peaches (mid-July through September), pears (August through September), apricots (mid-July through mid-August), plums (September), apples (August through October), and grapes (September through mid-October). There are even free Tree Fruit Tours, (800) 665-5254.

Fruit aside, winemaking is the hot ticket in the Okanagan. British Columbians have long taken inordinate pride in their wines, even when those mostly came from a few largish factories like Kelowna's Calona, on Richter St, (250) 762-3332. But ever since the province authorized estate and smaller farmgate **wineries,** many excellent small wineries have popped up. Nearly three dozen wineries operate in the Okanagan Valley from Vernon to Osoyoos; some have tasting rooms. Most are open summers and through the wine crush in September. Maps for **self-guided tours** of the wineries are available from the British Columbia Wine Institute, 1855 Kirschner Rd, Kelowna, BC V1Y 4N7; (250) 762-4887.

Kelowna is the centre of the burgeoning wine industry. The biggest and best known of the Okanagan wineries is Summerhill, 4870 Chute Lake Rd, (800) 667-3538. Other notable Kelowna wineries include St. Hubertus Estate Winery, (800) 989-9463, and the excellent Quails' Gate Estate Winery, (800) 420-9463.

Okanagan Falls is a charming town best visited for its tasty pleasures: it's home to the increasingly famous chocolate factory Snowy Mountain Chocolate; the largest ice-cream cone seller in the valley, Tickleberry's; the world-famous fruit-snack producer, Okanagan Dried Fruit; and two prestigious wineries, Wild Goose Vineyards and LeComte Estate Winery. Samples of all these treats await you—enjoy.

Penticton takes full advantage of its dual lakefronts. The south end of town (with its go-cart tracks, amusement centres, miniature golf courses, water slides, and RV parks) touches the north shore of Skaha Lake. The north end of town sidles along the southern tip of 70-mile-long (113-km) Lake Okanagan. Visit the Dominion Radio Astrophysical Observatory, operated by the National Research Council, which draws astronomers from around the world. It's open to the public during daylight hours, and tours are available Sunday afternoons.

On the east side of Lake Okanagan, **Kelowna** is the largest and liveliest of the Okanagan cities, with some noisy nightlife, a bit of culture (an art museum and summer theatre), a range of continental and ethnic restaurants, a big regatta in July, and an interesting historical preserve at Father Pandosy's Mission, (250) 860-8369. Kelowna even has its own version of the Loch Ness monster: Ogopogo. Keep a lookout for him (her?) while supping on the gaily decked-out paddle wheeler *Fintry Queen* or touring aboard the *Okanagan Princess*. Call (250) 861-1515 for information on both tours.

Summerland is a theme town done in the same spirit as Osoyoos, only this time they chose to do it Tudor style. Old Summerland is down on the water, but most of the town's business now thrives up on the hill. Pick up the pamphlet "A Walking Tour of Summerland," available at the museum or InfoCentre. Also of note is the Agricultural Research Station, the only active agricultural research centre in the Okanagan. Its interpretive centre, research facilities, and ornamental gardens have become a draw for thousands of international visitors every year.

There are many **festivals** in this region—too many to mention here. For a complete listing, contact the InfoCentre of the area you're visiting.

Restaurants

The Country Squire ☆☆☆ Every meal is an event here—dinner might take four hours but the table is yours for the night. You choose from among several entrees when you reserve, and upon arrival a card details the courses to come. The food is good and the price is a flat $39.50. *3950 1st St (take Naramata Rd, left on Robinson, right on 1st), Naramata; (250) 496-5416; $$.*

De Montreuil ☆☆☆ Dinners here are ordered by the course—two, three, four, or five—but the fare is more rustic than pretentious. Everything on the menu bursts with flavours. The extra time and money for the five-course option is worth it. *368 Bernard Ave (corner of Pandosy), Kelowna; (250) 860-5508; $$$.*

Granny Bogner's ☆☆ One of British Columbia's best restaurants is also one of the most consistent, and it has just about everything—great food, great location, great building, and fantastic desserts. The menu covers a broad spectrum (halibut to prime rib), and presentation is exquisite. *302 Eckhardt Ave W (2 blocks south of Main), Penticton; (250) 493-2711; $$$.*

Kitchen Cowboy ☆☆ A mixture of Santa Fe style and the real Old West, this spot serves up a great breakfast and a stout cup of coffee. The dinner menu is more adventuresome, but is at its best with items like cornbreaded chicken and burgers. *353 Bernard Ave (near Pandosy), Kelowna; (250) 868-8288; $$.*

Schroth Wood Fire Bakery ☆ The best pizza in Kelowna comes out of the ovens of this bakery. Toppings change daily, but the crust is always thick. There are other options, too (pastries and fresh-baked breads even outshine the pizza). Service is cafeteria style, and ambience is nil. *2041 Harvey (on Hwy 97 in north Kelowna), Kelowna; (250) 762-2626; $.*

Shaughnessy's Cove The view of Lake Okanagan and an airy atmosphere are the strong suits here. The restaurant is tiered into four levels, with decks, skylights, and fireplaces, and the menu ranges from fish 'n' chips to stew. A free shuttle can pick customers up and return them home. *12817 Lakeshore Dr (in Old Summerland), Summerland; (250) 494-1212; $.*

Theo's ☆ This ever-popular spot sports sun-dappled interior patios. The rabbit and octopus are excellent, but the accompaniments could be a little more inspired. That said, by all means go—in the afternoon for an aperitif or at night to eat moussaka. *687 Main St (near corner of Eckhardt), Penticton; (250) 492-4019; $$.*

Vintage Room (Capri Hotel) ☆☆ Nobody wants to like this elegant, pricey restaurant because it's tucked back in a dark corner of the hotel. Maybe that's what makes it try so hard, and it usually succeeds. Service is impeccable, and some of the most sophisticated food around is served here. *1171 Harvey Ave (at Gordon), Kelowna; (250) 860-6060; $$.*

Cheaper Eats

Hog's Breath Coffee Company A local triathlete named his coffee bar after an Australian saloon. Now his place is a hangout for international triathletes, locals, and tourists. Try one of the quiches, salads, or sandwiches that make this spot popular. *202 Main St, Penticton; (250) 493-7800; $.*

Lodgings

Castle Rock B&B ☆ This massive log lodge above Okanagan and Skaha Lakes is *the* place to stay in Penticton—if you can get a room (the owners don't advertise and there are only four rooms). It's a great home base: borrow bikes and then swim in the heated pool. *2050 Sutherland Rd (just north of downtown, off Naramata Rd); mail: C22, S200, RR1, Penticton, BC V2A 6J6; (250) 492-4429; $$.*

Crawford View Bed and Breakfast ☆ All the rooms have private entrances, so it's easy to find solitude here. Enjoy the small apple orchard, the tennis court, and the outdoor swimming pool. The latter has an outstanding night view of Kelowna and the lake. *810 Crawford Rd (off Lakeshore Dr), Kelowna, BC V1W 4N3; (250) 764-1140; $–$$.*

The Grand Okanagan Lakefront Resort ☆☆ This posh resort dominates the eastern shoreline west of downtown with a 10-storey tower. It's not right on the water, but it has a waterfront park in front of the hotel. Facilities include a heated outdoor pool and fitness room. *1310 Water St (almost 0.5 mile/1 km west of Harvey St), Kelowna, BC V1Y 9P3; (250) 763-4500 or (800) 465-4651; $$$.*

Hotel Eldorado ☆☆ This is the best place to stay on Lake Okanagan. Because of a 1989 fire, the rebuilt manse feels new, yet has the grandeur of a bygone era. Most rooms have balconies and some have Jacuzzis. The restaurant is consistently excellent. *500 Cook Rd (follow Pandosy, which becomes Lakeshore, for 4 miles/6.5 km south of Okanagan Floating Bridge), Kelowna, BC V1W 3G9; (250) 763-7500; $$$.*

Lake Okanagan Resort ☆ The appointments at this 300-acre (120-ha) resort on the lake are not first-class (they're time-share units that also rent by the night), but sailing, swimming, golf, tennis, and horseback riding are all offered here, and there are several lodgings options. *2751 Westside Rd (10.5 miles/17 km north of Kelowna), Kelowna, BC V1Y 8B2; (250) 769-3511; $$$.*

Ponderosa Point Resort ☆☆ This compound of individually owned rental cabins sits on a peninsula extending out into Skaha Lake. There's a sandy beach, boat rentals, tennis courts, and playground. The cabins aren't plush but they're comfortable and clean. Closed winters; some minimum-stay requirements. *319 Ponderosa Ave (4 miles/7 km south of Penticton on Hwy 97), Box 106, Kalenden, BC V0H 1K0; (250) 497-5354; $$$.*

Sandy Beach Lodge ☆☆ This archetypal summer lodge on the lake has a wide, shaded lawn that slopes down to a cove. There are duplexes (request one near the lake) or lodge rooms, as well as tennis courts, a small pool, and rental boats. Reserve for summer *way* in advance. *4275 Mill Rd (off Robson), PO Box 8, Naramata, BC V0H 1N0; (250) 496-5765; $$.*

Cheaper Sleeps

Club Paradise Motel Across the street from Okanagan Lake's sandy beaches stands this 11-room motel. Some rooms have kitchenettes, and all have access to the indoor Jacuzzi. Use the picnic tables and barbeques or dine indoors at nearby Salty's Seafood. *1000 Lakeshore Dr, Penticton, BC V2A 1C1; (250) 493-8400; $.*

Idabel Lake Resort The lake is a great base camp for fishing, cycling, or hiking. The resort's cottages are a better deal than the more luxurious suites, and can sleep six. There are campsites, too. Canoes and rowboats are complimentary. Bring your own food. *12000 Hwy 33E, #4, Kelowna, BC V1P 4K4; (250) 765-9511; $.*

Penticton Youth Hostel This hostel sets standards that other local hostels can't even hope to match. Dorm, family, and couples' rooms are all offered, as well as dining facilities, a kitchen, a barbeque, a living room, and a laundry. Reserve early for summer. *464 Ellis St, Penticton, BC V2A 4M2; (250) 492-3992; $.*

More Information

Apex Mountain Resort: *(800) 387-2739 or (250) 292-8111; Web site: www.apexresort.com.*

BC Forest Service, Boundary Forest District, Grand Forks: *(250) 442-5411.*

BC Forest Service, North Okanagan District, Vernon: *(250) 558-1700 or (800) 665-1511.*

BC Forest Service, South Okanagan District, Penticton: *(250) 490-2200 or (800) 661-4099.*

BC Parks, Okanagan District, Summerland: *(250) 494-6500; reservations, (800) 689-9025.*

Corporation of the District of Peachland: *(250) 767-2647.*

Kelowna Visitors and Convention Bureau: *(250) 861-1515 or (800) 663-4345.*

Keremeos Chamber of Commerce: *(250) 499-5225.*

Mosaic Books (map source, Kelowna): *(250) 763-4418.*

Okanagan Falls Chamber of Commerce: *(250) 497-8222.*

Oliver InfoCentre: *(250) 498-6321.*

Osoyoos InfoCentre: *(250) 495-7142.*

Salmon Arm InfoCentre: *(250) 832-6247.*

Sicamous InfoCentre: *(250) 836-3313.*

Silver Star Resort: *(800) 663-4431 or (250) 542-0224; Web site: www.silverstarmtn.com.*

Summerland Chamber of Commerce InfoCentre: *(250) 494-2686.*

Tourism Penticton: *(250) 493-4055 or (800) 663-5052.*

Vernon Tourism: *(250) 542-1415 or (800) 665-0795.*

Kettle Valley

Highway 33 follows the old Kettle Valley Railway grade as it links Kelowna with Rock Creek, including the Kettle River Provincial Recreation Area, the Kettle Valley Railway Trail, and Big White Ski Resort.

Probably the first white man to travel through the Boundary area of the West Kootenays was David Douglas, a renowned botanist, after whom the Douglas fir was named. It has been said that he was a very religious man who read from the Bible every day and offered prayers giving thanks for the spectacular beauty of the new landscapes he encountered.

A series of major and minor gold rushes began at Rock Creek in 1859 and throughout the area over the next 10 years, and saw the sudden influx of more than 5,000 miners, most of whom were from the US. Governor James Douglas (not related to David Douglas) quickly ordered the rapid construction of the now-famous Dewdney Trail, going from the coast to the gold field just north of the border. When bigger strikes occurred in the Okanagan and the Cariboo, the miners left, but an important trade route remained. Later, as copper, silver, lead, and zinc ores were being mined in large amounts, the Kettle Valley Railway, a branch line of the Canadian Pacific Railway, was built so that ore and smelter traffic would remain in Canada instead of being shipped to the US, as had been the case. Remains of this early history are abundant. A backroad trip to a ghost town will colour your visit to this extremely beautiful region.

The area became more settled later, particularly by the Doukhobors (spirit wrestlers), a group of Russian religious pacifists who emigrated to Canada in 1898–99 with the assistance of writer

Leo Tolstoy and British and American Quakers. As the Boundary district was well suited to cattle ranching and agriculture, the Doukhobors found the pastoral serenity around Greenwood, Grand Forks, and Trail compatible with their values of respect for the land and peaceful self-sufficiency. In this regard, David Douglas (who died an untimely death in Hawaii) would have felt at home among them.

Getting There

This area is most directly approached either from the west or east along Highway 3 to Rock Creek (located just north of the Canada–US border and about midway between the Pacific coast and the British Columbia–Alberta border); or from Kelowna in the north, along Highway 97.

Adjoining Areas

NORTH: **The Trans-Canada Highway**

SOUTH: **Crowsnest Highway: South Okanagan Valley**

EAST: **Slocan Valley and Upper Arrow Lake**

WEST: **Okanagan Valley**

inside out

Parks/Camping

The **Kettle River Provincial Recreation Area** (also see Crowsnest Highway: South Okanagan Valley chapter) is named for the river that runs through it, and brings to mind one of Canada's most historic and scenic railway routes. The **Kettle Valley Railway** discontinued service between Beaverdell and Penticton in 1973, and the track was removed between Midway and Penticton in 1979–80, but the abandoned right-of-way runs through this recreational area—including a sturdy iron bridge spanning the Kettle River—and is an excellent trail. (See Hiking/Biking, below.)

The river is well suited to canoeing and inner-tubing, but potential hazards do exist, so be sure to do some preliminary scouting. In winter, cross-country skiing and snowshoeing are favourite pastimes. The recreation area is open May through September; there is a camping fee in summer. The facilities consist of 49 vehicle/tent sites, a picnic/day-use area, water, pit toilets, sani-station, firewood, trails, and an amphitheatre and visitor program. Follow Hwy 33 for 3 miles (5 km) north of Rock Creek. For more information, contact BC Parks' district office in Summerland, (250) 494-6500.

Providence Lake (also known as Marshall Lake) is located east of

Greenwood on Hwy 3. Summer campers and fishers will find 3 vehicle/tent sites at this lovely spot, and mountain bikers and hikers will enjoy the numerous old logging roads and abandoned railways that run throughout the area. Providence Lake cross-country ski trails begin here; pick up a trail map from the Forest Service's Boundary District Office, 136 Sagamore Ave, in Grand Forks, (250) 442-5411.

Arlington Lakes Provincial Recreation Area, 6 miles (17 km) north of Beaverdell on Hwy 33, features 12 small campsites on both sides of the southernmost lake. (There are three small lakes strung out in a row.) The area is good for biking and fishing, and a car-top boat launch is available, but visitors should be aware that the sites are heavily used, and although access is good for 2 miles (3 km) from Hwy 33, the road to the northwest site is narrow and not suitable for trailers or motor homes.

Hiking/Biking

The trailhead at **Midway Village** (just southeast of Midway on the Myers Creek Rd) has nearly 6 miles (10 km) of easy to difficult hiking and biking trails from Midway to a scenic viewpoint on the international border.

The route to **Thimble Mount Viewpoint** (moderate; 9 miles/14 km return) is well groomed and perfectly suited for hiking, biking, and horseback riding, with an abandoned turn-of-the-century mine site in the area. To reach the trailhead, turn north off Hwy 3 between Greenwood and Grand Forks on BC Mine Rd. The trailhead is located about 1.5 miles (2.5 km) on the east side of the road.

Aside from the parks mentioned above, the most interesting trail in the Boundary area has to be the abandoned **Kettle Valley Railway** itself (also see Crowsnest Highway: South Okanagan Valley chapter). Bikers, hikers, and horseback riders can pick up the trail at **Grand Forks, Greenwood,** or **Midway** (all along Hwy 3) or at **Rock Creek, Westbridge,** or **Beaverdell** (all along Hwy 33). The **Kettle River Provincial Recreation Area** (see Parks/Camping, above) makes a good staging area. This "rails-to-trails" route is for those who like difficulty measured in distance travelled rather than miles per second or wipeouts per trip. The trail is not formally managed, and doesn't have heart-stopping thrills or technically difficult riding, but your heart will beat a little faster crossing trestles nearly 200 feet (60 m) high (walk your bike). The river's eastern bank can be explored for the remains of gold and silver mines, but keep a sharp eye out for old mine shafts and adits (horizontal entrances or passages). Wondering about the name? A **kettle** is a peculiar geological formation left over from the most recent ice age. These steep-sided depressions (also known as potholes) mark the ground where ice boulders were once trapped between rocks. If you'd like to join a **group tour** of the railway trail, contact Okanagan Bicycle Tours, (800) 991-3233 or (250) 766-4086, Wildways Adventure Sports Tours, (800) 663-6561 or (250) 447-6561, or Monashee Mountain Bike Tours, (250) 762-9253. Silver Barn Bike and Board on Hwy 3 in Grand Forks, (800) 667-1196 or (250) 442-8006, is a good source of maps, parts, and general bike expertise. *Cycling the Kettle Valley Railway* by Dan and Sandra Langford is a comprehensive guide to the Kettle Valley Railway, as well as several other railway trails that have been converted to cycling, biking, and hiking trails, including the Columbia and Western Railway that runs from Castlegar to Midway.

Skiing

There are many reasons to go exploring but none more compelling than to see extraordinary natural phenomena. Imagine standing atop a mountain near sunset as the winter sky turns orange and the ground turns blue. Although such a sight might be commonplace in New Mexico, finding it on a ski hill in the Okanagan places it—and you—in the realm of the fantastic. When this occurs in a subalpine meadow, where you are surrounded by bowed treetops draped in mantles of snow, you are transported from the mundane into the zone of the truly sublime.

In the Okanagan, you will most likely find this phenomenon at **Big White Ski Resort,** 34 miles (54 km) southeast of Kelowna via Hwy 33 and Big White Rd on the western perimeter of the Monashee Mountains. You may have come here simply for the skiing and snowboarding, but when witnessing a sunset such as this, it seems as if you also made an unspoken appointment with nature to have your consciousness altered. The hoodoo-like bestiary that form each winter near the top of the snow-domed mountain are a distinctive feature at Big White. Once the snow has layered the exposed treetops, the wind begins its chiselling, and features emerge that resemble frozen creatures from the Jurassic period. Then you begin your final descent of the day, turning through the trees, leaving your mark on the untracked powder snow for which the Okanagan is renowned.

One of the advantages of staying here in the mountain village that boasts the highest elevation—5,450 feet (1661 m)—of any winter resort in the province is being able to ski right to the door of your accommodation, whether it be a condominium, a lodge, or your camperized vehicle. Once you've arrived at Big White, there's no choice but to leave your wheels behind, but this doesn't mean you have to hoof it around the village. Some streets are rather steep, so when the horse-drawn wagon that serves as the local transportation trots by, hop on. In return for a contribution, you can park yourself on a hay bale and let the team of vapour-snorting Percherons do the rest.

With the growth of nearby Kelowna fuelling expansion on the mountain, Big White now sports three quad express chairlifts in addition to five regular chairs and a T-bar lift that takes riders into the hoodoo zone. Almost 70 runs create an intricate network of routes to explore. Although there are a handful of extreme runs—particularly the double–black diamond free-fall slopes in the Parachute Bowl—the mountain is predominated by *pistes* designed to challenge snowboarders and skiers of intermediate ability. Big White Mountain (elevation 7,601 feet/2317 m) boasts one of the greatest snowpacks of any mountain in North America. From its peak, when the skies above the Okanagan clear up, it seems as if you can look halfway across the province, from the Cascade Mountains far off in the west to the Selkirk Mountains in the east. Visitors will enjoy the night skiing, but those with any reserves left after attacking the slopes may find nightlife somewhat limited on the mountain.

The 16-mile (26-km) network of **cross-country ski trails** around the forests and glades of Big White's lower perimeter should keep Nordic skiers busy. There is no charge for use of the Nordic trails, all of which can be reached from the village; Nordic skiers can also use the Plaza quad chairlift to return to the village free of charge. To get to Big White from Kelowna, take Hwy 33 southeast for about 25 miles (40 km) and turn east onto the 15-mile (23-km) side road that climbs up the mountain. The roads are paved and in good shape. For more information, contact Big White Ski Resort, (250) 765-3101; for a snow report, call (250) 765-7669.

outside in

Restaurants and Lodgings

For recommended establishments, see Adjoining Areas to this chapter.

More Information

BC Forest Service, Boundary District: *(250) 442-5411 or (800) 665-1511.*

BC Parks: *(250) 825-3500.*

Fish and Wildlife Conservation Officer, Grand Forks: *(250) 442-4310.*

Fish and Wildlife Conservation Officer, Kelowna: *(250) 861-7670.*

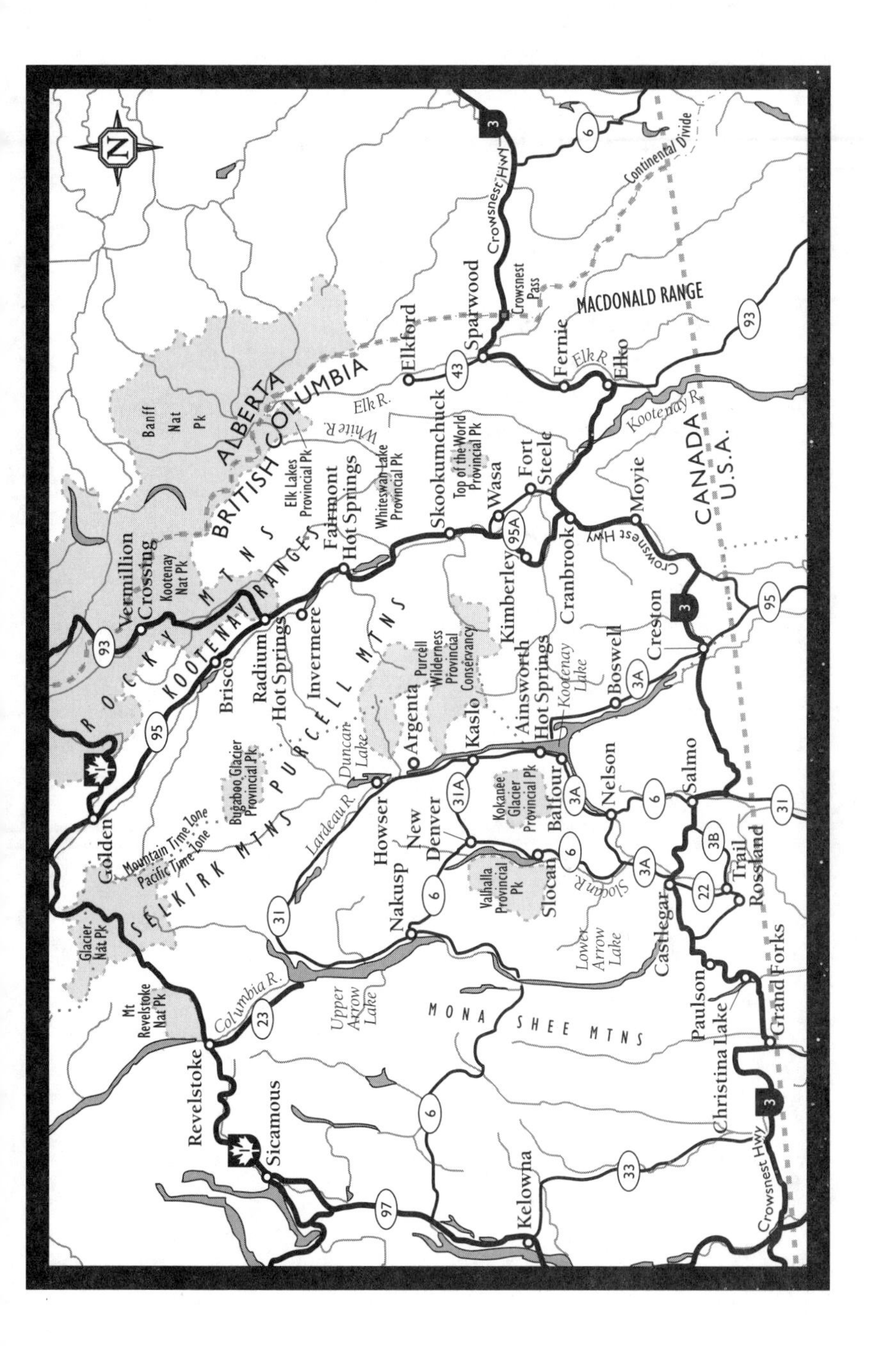

The Kootenays

Crowsnest Highway: The West Kootenays 485

Slocan Valley and Upper Arrow Lake 502

North Kootenay Lake and Selkirk Valleys 517

Crowsnest Highway: The East Kootenays 522

Columbia River Valley 529

The Kootenays

Crowsnest Highway: The West Kootenays

The Crowsnest Highway (Highway 3) winds its way through the Monashee and Selkirk Mountains for about 135 miles (220 km) between Grand Forks and Creston, including the Kootenay Summit (5,820 feet/1746 m), Red Mountain Ski Area, and Christina Lake, Nancy Greene, and Kokanee Glacier Provincial Parks.

Two geographical features dominate the Kootenays: mountains and water. Four parallel mountain ranges, running in a generally northwest direction, march successively across the southeastern British Columbia landscape. The most westerly are the Monashees, followed by the rugged Selkirks, defined on their western flanks by the Arrow reservoir system and Slocan Lake, and on the east by the spectacular waters of Kootenay Lake. These two mountain ranges and accompanying lake systems define this district. Farther east are the Purcells, then the Rockies, outlining the area known as the East Kootenays.

The other major north-south water system in this district is formed by Kootenay Lake (at more than 65 miles/105 km long, it's one of the province's largest freshwater lakes) and Kootenay River, which joins with the Columbia near Castlegar.

The Crowsnest Highway east of Grand Forks provides a good introduction to the often steep terrain of the West Kootenays. *Only* intrepid travellers need apply to drive what is the highest-elevation paved highway in Canada, the Skyway. But you'll want some time—and cooperation from the weather. During winter storms, avoid this route, particularly the stretch between Salmo and Creston, for avalanches are a fact of life and road closures inevitable. Alberta licence plates begin to appear more regularly in parks here; the Kootenays are almost equidistant from the Prairies and the West Coast.

Getting There

Travellers heading west on Highway 3 join this section of the Crowsnest Highway at Creston, just north of the British Columbia–Idaho border. From Creston, Highway 3A runs north along the east side of Kootenay Lake to Crawford Bay, where a free ferry at Kootenay Bay links with Balfour on the west side of the lake. Travellers approaching from the north may use this route or Highways 3A and 6 to link with Highway 3. So convoluted does the highway become that branches of it spin off and feed into each other in a tight knot in the Nelson, Castlegar, Trail, and Salmo loop. Travellers journeying south from the Slocan Valley on Highway 6 link with Highway 3A north of Castlegar, site of the only airport in the rugged Kootenays. Travellers heading south from the Okanagan on Highway 33 join Highway 3 at Rock Creek.

Adjoining Areas

NORTH: **The Trans-Canada Highway**

EAST: **Crowsnest Highway: The East Kootenays**

WEST: **Kettle Valley**

inside out

Parks/Camping

The biggest provincial campground in this part of the West Kootenays is **Kokanee Creek Provincial Park,** about 12 miles (19 km) east of Nelson on Hwy 3A, on the north shore of the west arm of Kootenay Lake. The park offers 112 vehicle/tent sites in two campgrounds, **Sandspit** and **Redfish.** Its extensive sandy beaches and delta area are backed by a gently rising upland, giving way to the forested slopes of the Slocan Range of the Selkirk Mountains. Open all year, Kokanee Creek has facilities that include hiking and ski trails, a visitor centre with displays, and a boat launch. Nearby is Kokanee Glacier Provincial Park, a mountain wilderness with an extensive trail system for day or longer hikes (see Hiking/Backpacking, below). For more information, contact the BC Parks office located in Kokanee Creek Provincial Park, (250) 825-3500.

Champion Lakes Provincial Park is another large campground, with 89 vehicle/tent sites, 30 of which can be reserved. Its three small lakes form the headwaters of Landis Creek, which flows northward to join Champion Creek, a tributary of the Columbia River. The lakes and Champion Creek are named for James W. Champion, an early settler and orchardist. Open June 1 to September 15, this 3,520-acre (1425-ha) park offers excellent fishing for rainbow trout, two beaches, many miles of hiking trails, weekend interpretation programs, and an adventure playground. There are two car-top boat launches for paddle boats only. For those who like to get away from it all in a civilized fashion, a golf course can be reached in five minutes. Champion Lakes Provincial Park is just over 11 miles (18 km) northwest of Fruitvale (east of Trail), off Hwy 3B. For more information, contact BC Parks, (250) 825-3500. For reservations, call the BC Parks reservation line, (800) 689-9025, from March 1 to September 15.

If you're looking to stay awhile and want plenty of things to do, one of the largest provincial campgrounds in this area is **Syringa Creek Provincial Park,** with 60 vehicle/tent sites, all available on a first-come, first-served basis. Located about 12 miles (19 km) northwest of Castlegar off Hwy 6 and Hwy 3A, Syringa is on the east side of Lower Arrow Lake at the foot of the Norns Range of the Columbia Mountains. The lake is actually part of the Columbia River that was widened and deepened through construction of the Hugh Keenleyside Dam, a short distance downstream. Across the lake from the park's broad sand and gravel beach rises the Christina Range of the Monashee Mountains. The park is named for Syringa Creek, which flows into Lower Arrow Lake, near the park's southern boundary. The "syringa," or mock orange, a shrub indigenous to the area, blooms in early spring and emits an enchanting bouquet as recognizable as an orange itself. Along with two boat ramps, hiking trails, an archaeological site, and outdoor nature displays, this park offers interpretive programs most afternoons and evenings from mid-June through the Labour Day weekend, and it's open May through September. For information on opening dates and fees, contact BC Parks, (250) 825-3500.

In the small-but-pleasant category is **Gladstone Provincial Park** (formerly Texas Creek) on Christina Lake, which has 33 informal campsites. The campsites are located in an open pine forest, giving pleasant shade from the summer sun. This waterfront park has many small pocket beaches, which provide splendid opportunities for solitude and privacy. Hiking trails lead north along the lakeshore. To reach the park, drive 6 miles (10 km) northeast of Christina Lake on Hwy 3, then 3.7 miles (6 km) to end of East Lake. For more information, contact BC Parks, (250) 494-6500.

Farther east along Hwy 3, **Nancy Greene Provincial Park** is a popular overnight stop with 10 parking-lot sites for RVs. It is a place to enjoy a cool night's rest away from the heat in the valley, and you can often catch your supper of rainbow trout. This park and a nearby provincial recreation area are named after Canada's world-famous Olympic skier Nancy Greene, who originated from the Rossland-Trail area. The setting of this park, which includes a subalpine lake encircled by a self-guided nature trail (powerboats are not allowed) is almost 22 miles (35 km) north of Rossland at the junction of Hwys 3 and 3B. For more information, contact BC Parks, (250) 825-3500.

Less than 14 miles (22 km) east of Trail on Hwy 22A, **Beaver Creek Provincial Park,** open mid-May to mid-September, has 15 vehicle/tent sites, a boat launch, and a picnic/day-use area. On the east side of the Columbia River near the US border, Beaver Creek offers an opportunity to observe the terraces formed by the retreating glaciers as the last great ice age waned. Fort Shepherd, a Hudson's Bay Company trading post and stop along the Dewdney Trail (see Hiking/Backpacking, below), once stood nearby. Two archaeological sites are located in the park. For more information, contact BC Parks, (250) 825-3500.

Lockhart Beach Provincial Park is a small, beautifully forested park on the east side of the south arm of Kootenay Lake. As well as a sandy beach, the park has a picnic/day-use area, a car-top boat launch, and 13 vehicle/tent sites. A hiking trail runs along Lockhart Creek through a mixed forest of Douglas fir, western red cedar, and ponderosa pine. It's about 35 miles (55 km) north of Creston on Hwy 3A. From the west, Hwy 3A connects across Kootenay Lake by ferry. For more information, contact BC Parks, (250) 825-3500.

In addition to the provincial parks in this region, the BC Forest Service maintains a number of smaller recreation sites, some of which permit camping. For a map showing these sites, contact the Arrow Forest District Office, 845 Columbia Ave, in downtown Castlegar, (250) 365-8600, or the Nelson Forest Region Office, 518 Lake St, in the heart of Nelson, (250) 354-6200, or visit the district Web site: www.for.gov.bc.ca/nelson/district/arrow.

Castlegar's **Pass Creek Regional Park** has 37 vehicle/tent sites and features swimming, hiking, and mountain biking. The park is located 1 mile (1.6 km) north of Castlegar off Hwy 3A. For more information, contact the Castlegar InfoCentre, (250) 365-6313.

Scenic Drives/Picnics

The **North Fork Scenic Drive** along the winding, forested **Granby River** runs for about 20 miles (30 km). Information on this scenic loop can be obtained from the Grand Forks InfoCentre, (250) 442-2833.

Grohman Narrows Provincial Park, 3 miles (5 km) west of Nelson on Hwy 3A, has no campsites but is the perfect spot for a picnic. Open year-round, it features walking trails beside the Kootenay River, Narrows Island, and an abandoned orchard.

Another place for a picnic is **King George VI Provincial Park,** south of Rossland, which has a picnic/day-use area with a shelter (and 3 vehicle/tent sites). Attractive scenery and the former right-of-way for the Red Mountain Railway can be found here. From before the turn of the century until just after World War II, the railway took ore from Rossland to Northport, Washington, for smelting. The park is just over 6 miles (10 km) south of Rossland off Hwy 22, which extends north from US Hwy 25 at the border. For more information, contact BC Parks, (250) 422-4200.

Hiking/Backpacking

The historic **Dewdney Trail** ran between Hope, at the east end of the Fraser Valley in the Lower Mainland, and Wildhorse, near Creston in the East Kootenays. Although much of the original 4-foot (1.2-m) pathway that Edgar Dewdney blazed in 1865 has been neglected, it's still possible to hike portions of it that have been maintained between Christina Lake and Rossland.

Dewdney was a young civilian surveyor who was originally hired by Colonial-Governor Douglas in 1860 to build a trail between Hope and the gold fields in the Okanagan Valley region. With the discovery of gold in Stud Horse Creek (later renamed Wild Horse Creek) Dewdney was asked to extend the trail east to Wildhorse in 1865. With help from the weather, he was able to complete the route through the Kootenays in five months. Dewdney's legacy can be touched in several places and by several modes of exploration as you explore this region. In addition to hiking, you can drive a section of the trail as Hwy 3B passes through Trail, which takes its name from the Dewdney Trail.

The BC Forest Service office in Grand Forks, (250) 442-5411, or in Nelson, (250) 354-6200, should be able to provide more information about this trail and others it maintains in this part of the West Kootenays, including the **Old Glory Trail** (see Horseback Riding, below).

Located in the Monashee Mountains on Hwy 3B just north of Rossland, the 20,000-acre (8100-ha) **Nancy Greene Provincial Park** is noted for its alpine and Nordic skiing, especially at Red Mountain (see Downhill Skiing and Cross-Country Skiing, below). During summer and fall, hikers can take advantage of the more than 12 miles (20 km) of low-elevation trails to view mule deer and black bear. A small band of mountain goats ranges along the west side of Old Glory Mountain until winter conditions drive them down into Sheep Creek. Other wildlife found here are pikas,

Columbia and golden-mantled ground squirrels, and other small rodents. Blue grouse, Clark's nutcrackers, juncos, Steller's jays, and red-tailed hawks are frequently observed. Many migratory songbirds are heard, if not seen, in the subalpine forests. For more information, contact BC Parks, (250) 825-3500.

Kokanee Glacier Provincial Park is located in the Slocan Range of the Selkirk Mountains between Slocan Lake and the north arm of Kootenay Lake, 18.6 miles (30 km) northeast of Nelson off Hwy 3A. It is a mountain wilderness of more than 74,000 acres (30 000 ha), most of which lies above 5,900 feet (1800 m), with half of it at elevations above 6,880 feet (2100 m). The glacier (for which the park is named) clinging to the slopes of 9,100-foot (2774-m) Kokanee Peak is almost in the park's centre.

The warm summers give way to cold winters, which can begin as early as October. Precipitation is fairly high, with about eight months of often heavy snowfall, and summer rains that can turn into light snowfall at any time. Always be prepared for below-freezing temperatures at the park's higher elevations.

The terrain is extremely rugged, the hard granitic rock having been sculpted into jagged peaks by the carving action of glaciers. Three of these—Kokanee, Caribou, and Woodbury Glaciers—are the source of many of the park's creeks, which have cut deep valleys across the landscape. Three biogeoclimatic zones are found in the park, although it is primarily in the Engelmann spruce/subalpine fir zone. At higher elevations, forests give way to alpine communities of dwarf blueberry, white rhododendron, and heather, interspersed with open grassy areas, wildflower meadows, and moss- and lichen-covered boulders.

The alpine slopes are the summer home of a wide variety of wildlife, including mountain goats, deer, black bears, and grizzlies. (Protection of significant grizzly bear habitat was the main reason for an expansion of the park in 1995.) More frequently observed, however, are smaller mammals like the hoary marmot, ground squirrel, and pika. Blue and Franklin grouse inhabit the forests, and dippers can be found around the many lakes. Raptors sometimes seen include the sharp-shinned hawk and the golden eagle.

The park offers excellent wilderness recreation in both summer and winter. Vehicular traffic is allowed only on access roads; some of these traverse avalanche zones, so caution must be exercised at all times. There is **wilderness camping** throughout the park, and three cabins for overnight use. Visitors are reminded that, as this is a wilderness area without supplies or equipment of any kind, they should be reasonably physically fit and well equipped for all conditions. And don't forget the chicken wire.

Believe it or not, for overnight stays it is recommended that you surround your vehicle with chicken wire to protect it from porcupines, which like to chew on rubber!

Trails within the park—there are more than 50 miles (85 km) of them—range from easy to difficult, with most falling into the moderate range. Many of these trails were built for miners hauling ore and supplies. For more information about the park and its trails, contact BC Parks, (250) 825-3500, or visit their Web site: www.env.gov.bc.ca. Five access roads, which may not be suitable for low-clearance vehicles, lead to trailheads in the central area of the park. For the southernmost route, from Hwy 3A, 12 miles (19 km) northeast of Nelson, drive up Kokanee Creek for 10 miles (16 km) to Gibson Lake. For more information about access to the park, see Slocan Valley and Upper Arrow Lake chapter.

For more information on some of the newer parks in this region, such as **Granby Provincial Park,** contact BC Parks, (250) 825-3500. For guided hiking tours of the region, contact Boundary Backcountry Tours, (250) 442-3556. Information on many local trails in regional parks such as **Pass Creek** (see Parks/Camping, above) in Castlegar can be easily obtained from Tourist InfoCentres and recreation departments in major towns. For telephone numbers, see More Information, below. For more information on hiking in the West Kootenays, consult *Classic Hiking Trails in the West Kootenays* by John Carter or contact Valhalla Pure Outfitters, 624 Baker St, (250) 354-1006, or the general outfitter Kootenay Experience, 306 Victoria St, (888) 488-4327 or (250) 354-4441, or visit their informative Web site: www.netidea.com/~kootexp/. Both are located in Nelson.

Mountain Biking

Most of the established trails around **Castlegar** are of the beginner to intermediate variety, including **Beaver Trails,** or Beev's, in local parlance. Located just northwest of the junction of Hwys 22 and 3, these are a mess of interconnected trails of varying difficulty. Snails Trail connects this series of trails with the slightly easier (and less developed) system of trails around **Merry Creek,** which can also be accessed from the Merry Creek Forest Service Rd, 2.5 miles (4 km) south of town towards Grand Forks on Hwy 3. The **Selkirk College Campus** in Castlegar has a system of beginner-friendly trails. This is short, easy singletrack for people who wouldn't find the **Viewpoint Trails** appealing. The latter are a fast, technical bit of singletrack, about 3 miles (5 km) long, near the Castlegar/Salmo viewpoint on Hwy 3. For a slightly longer ride, try the **CPR Railgrade,** from the Blueberry Paulson Bridge on Hwy 3 west, to the Celgar Pulp

Mill, or vice versa. It's 52.5 miles (86 km) one way. Bring along your bike light, as the trail passes through seven tunnels, the longest of which is nearly half a mile (1 km). There are many other trails in the area, and the folks at Gerick Cycle, (250) 365-5599, in Castlegar, or their shop in Nelson, 702 Baker St, (250) 354-4622, can direct you to them.

Former world champion mountain-bike downhiller Cindy Devine moved to Rossland from Whistler for the summer trail riding and winter backcountry powder. One of her summer haunts might be the **Paulson Cross-Country Ski Trails** (see Cross-Country Skiing, below). For information on other trails in the region, contact BC Parks, (250) 825-3500, or any of the BC Forest Service offices listed below under More Information.

Mountain biking around **Grand Forks** is done in grand, sweeping style. There's very little in the way of short, technical rides, and a great many epic, daylong adventures that will take you up some pretty big climbs, then down the same. Expect rides like the **Vertical (S)Mile,** which climbs 5,300 feet (1616 m). For most of these rides, you'll want to start early and know exactly where you're going. The Silver Barn Bike Shop on Hwy 3 in Grand Forks, (800) 667-1196 or (250) 442-8006, should be able to help, and if you're lucky, you can hook up with a few of the locals for a mondo ride . . . if you can keep up.

There's an extended ride to **Christina Lake** from Grand Forks known as the **Spooner Creek Route.** Fair warning, though: If you do ride out, chances are, you're not going to want to ride back unless you're a real goer. Best arrange for a pickup. Ride from town on Overton Rd to Sand Creek Rd. Go right on Sand Creek Rd through a logged area. Take the road that heads to the top of the logging block. Once through the block, climb to the top of Sand Creek. Follow this road until the next right, and go down 10 miles (14.5 km) on Stewart Creek Rd. Ride Stewart Creek Rd 5.5 miles (9 km) until you see the flagging on your left: this is where the Spooner Creek singletrack downhill *starts*! A few thousand feet downhill at Christina Lake, take the **Deer Point Trail,** an out-and-back excursion from the Texas Creek campgrounds. It's 3.5 miles (6 km) to Deer Point, and about 6 miles (10 km) to Troy Creek. The trail is an up-and-down affair, great riding married with great views of Christina Lake. You can also try the **Dewdney Trail** (see Hiking/Backpacking, above). It's about 5.5 miles (9 km) up Santa Rosa Rd (there's one left turn about 4 miles/ 7 km along), and there are some great views from the top. Dewdney Trail crosses the road. Take it left, and enjoy the ride back to the lake.

The aformentioned **Vertical (S)Mile** is 19 miles (31 km) east of Christina Lake. The road up starts in the Bonanza Gravel Pit. You've got a slog ahead of you, but the screaming downhill should more than make up for the effort.

Another place you can ride to directly from Grand Forks is **Morrisey Lookout.** Follow Morrisey Rd out of town, then right at the first junction. The third left will bring you all the way up (4,000 feet/1200 m) to a viewpoint overlooking Sunshine Valley.

The **Thimble Mountain Trail** begins about 13 miles (21 km) west of Grand Forks on Hwy 3. There's a pullout beside the highway to park your car. Cross the cattle guard, follow the gravel road to the first left turn. A short way down this road is a sign marking the Thimble Mountain Trail. Hours of pristine singletrack lay before you, so get moving.

Beaches

Christina Lake Provincial Park is located at the south end of Christina Lake, often referred to as one of the warmest, clearest lakes in Canada. The beach is long and sandy, and is backed by sweet-smelling cottonwoods and white-barked birches. Surrounded by the Christina and Rossland Ranges of the Monashees, the lake offers some of the best water-oriented recreation anywhere. The park is located 13 miles (21 km) east of Grand Forks on Hwy 3; it's also accessible by US Hwy 395 from Spokane. For more information, contact BC Parks, (250) 825-3500.

Kootenay Lake has some nice beaches; among them are those at **Kokanee Creek Provincial Park** and **Lockhart Beach Provincial Park** (see Parks/Camping, above). There is also a beach (and boat ramp) at **Kuskonnok Rest Area,** on the east side of Kootenay Lake, 15 miles (25 km) north of Creston on Hwy 3A.

Horseback Riding

In addition to the **Dewdney Trail** (see Hiking/Backpacking, above), horses are allowed on the **Old Glory Trail** north of Rossland. There is a BC Forest Service trail that leads to the lookout at the summit of Old Glory Mountain. The Old Glory Trail (6 miles/10 km) follows Unnecessary Ridge and also leads to the summit. The shorter **Plewman Trail** (5 miles/8 km) goes through the Plewman Basin. The two trails share a common trailhead on Hwy 3A east of Nancy Greene Provincial Park towards Rossland. The highway makes a big bend as it leads past Hannah Creek. Watch for the pullout and trailhead on the west side of the highway, about 100 yards (91 m) south of Hannah Creek. The trail divides a short distance from the trailhead, with Plewman Trail to the right and Old Glory to the left.

This area was used in times past by the Colville Indians from Washington state, who made regular trips here to pick huckleberries. Local place names such as Squaw Basin, Indian Flats, and Papoose Basin reflect this history. The former Forest Service lookout on Old Glory Mountain, the remains of a meteorological station, some stables, and the Old Glory Trail are remnants of the area's more recent history. Contact the BC Forest Service office in Castlegar, (250) 365-8600, for more information.

Fishing

It's hard to *escape* fish in this area of the West Kootenays. It seems that wherever there's water—whether lake, creek, or river—there is fishing. At **Christina Lake,** for starters (see Beaches, above), fishing for kokanee, rainbow trout, smallmouth bass, burbot, and whitefish is popular, and there are marinas and a public boat ramp in the vicinity.

Anglers frequently have good luck catching rainbow trout in **Nancy Greene Lake** (see Parks/Camping, above). The chain of three small lakes that make up the **Champion Lakes** (see Parks/Camping, above) has been regularly stocked with rainbow trout since the 1930s and makes for very good fishing. Development is concentrated around the third lake, which has deep, clear water and a regular shoreline. The others remain in their natural states. The third and second lakes have trout up to 10 inches (25 cm) in length, which will rise to the fly or trolling spoon, and to the persistent angler the first lake will yield fish up to 12 inches (30 cm) in length.

To the northwest, the **Arrow Lakes,** reached via Castlegar, form a dammed lake system 250 miles (400 km) long. Access to the grand **Columbia River** is from Hwy 22 between Castlegar and Trail. Boat rentals and fishing information on lingcod, char, trout, and pike can be had from Scottie's Marina, (250) 365-3267, or the Syringa Park Marina, (250) 365-5472, beside **Syringa Creek Provincial Park** (see Parks/Camping, above), which has boat-launching ramps for high and low water.

Kokanee Creek (see Parks/Camping, above) and **Kootenay Lake** maintain considerable populations of various fish species, including kokanee, rainbow and cutthroat trout, dolly varden, burbot, and whitefish. Kootenay Lake supports record-sized rainbow trout, and the world's largest recorded kokanee—almost 10 pounds (4.5 kg)—was taken from the lake. "Kokanee" means "red fish" in the Kootenay Indian language and is the name given to the land-locked salmon that spawn in large numbers in Kokanee Creek in the late summer. Rainbow trout are plentiful in **Lockhart Creek** (see Parks/Camping, above) on the east side of the south arm of Kootenay Lake.

Many of the more than 30 lakes in **Kokanee Glacier Provincial Park** (see Hiking/Backpacking, above) have been stocked with cutthroat trout. The streams also have rainbow and cutthroat trout and dolly varden.

For information on angling in Kokanee Glacier Provincial Park, contact Kokanee Park Marine at the entrance to the park on Hwy 3A, (250) 825-9235. Boat rentals are also available here. For information, boat rentals, and tackle on Kootenay Lake, contact Woodbury Resort and Marina on Hwy 31, 2.5 miles (4 km) north of Ainsworth Hot Springs, (250) 353-7717. For fishing supplies in Nelson, contact Nelson Mohawk Service, 702 Nelson Ave, (250) 354-4612. For information about **permits** required for fishing in the West Kootenays, contact a Fish and Wildlife conservation officer at one of the following numbers: Castlegar, (250) 365-8522; Nelson, (250) 354-6397; Creston, (250) 428-3220.

Canoeing/Kayaking

Christina Lake has a disposition as sweet as the rolling hills that surround this classic Kootenay beauty. Launch a canoe or kayak from the beach in Gladstone Provincial Park (see Parks/Camping, above) and enjoy a paddle around the northern half of this popular lake. You'll find wilderness campsites on sandy shores, if you care to spend a night under the stars. For information, contact BC Parks, (250) 494-6400, in Summerland. For **guided paddling tours** of Christina Lake, contact Wildways Adventure Sports and Tours, (250) 447-6561, in the town of Christina Lake.

If you're lured to spend more than a day on the water, tackle the three-day, 30-mile (50-km) paddle from Procter near Nelson to Kuskanook on the south arm of **Kootenay Lake.** There are dispersed camping locations at pocket beaches and creek mouths, as well as formal campsites provided by BC Parks and the BC Forest Service. Among these are Irvine Creek and Wilson Creek Forest Service Recreation Sites, and Drewry Point and Midge Creek Provincial Parks, all of which are marine access only. The lake can be windy, so an early-morning start is strongly recommended. For more information and a map, contact the BC Forest Service in Nelson, (250) 354-6200, or BC Parks at Kokanee Creek Provincial Park, (250) 825-3500. For canoe and kayak rentals, trail information, and repair service, contact Gerick Cycle and Sports, 702 Baker St, (250) 354-4622, in Nelson.

For a short trip on a big river, paddlers can access the **Columbia River** at the old ferry slip at Robson or Castlegar and take out in Trail at the municipal park, 0.6 mile (1 km) north of the bridge on the east side of the river. Allow one short day for this 18.5-mile (30-km), Class I or II trip. For a longer day, paddle on 12 miles (20 km) farther to Waneta, at the Canada-US border.

For information on **guided canoe and kayak adventures,** contact North Quest Adventures, (250) 354-7918, in Nelson.

Wildlife

There is a spawning channel in **Kokanee Creek Provincial Park** (see Parks/Camping, above) where visitors can observe the remarkable transformation that **spawning kokanee** undergo in late summer. Their bodies become a deep crimson colour and their heads turn emerald green. Like other Pacific salmon, after completing their fascinating spawning activities they die, drifting downstream to the lake, their dead bodies enriching (and perfuming!) the area. During this time, park interpreters offer daily programs focusing on this important phenomenon. For more information on spawning season, call park headquarters, (250) 825-3500.

The name alone is enough to draw visitors to **Stagleap Provincial Park,** 21 miles (34 km) west of Creston on Hwy 3 at the Kootenay Pass. The highway here, commonly called the Mile High Pass, is at an elevation of 5,820 feet (1774 m), the highest paved road in Canada. Bridal Lake, the focal point for both summer and winter activities, is surrounded by forests of subalpine fir. Visitors can enjoy the subalpine zone from the luxury of their car or go for a short walk around the lake. Call BC Parks, (250) 825-3500, for more information.

The park is named for the **woodland caribou** that migrate through this area. These large, majestic animals are related to reindeer and other members of the deer family. These Selkirk Mountains woodland caribou are actually the source of the only population in the United States, as they migrate through this part of BC and into northeastern Washington, northern Idaho, and occasionally into northwest Montana. They are on the US endangered species list. If you're not lucky enough to see any of the remnant herd that frequent the area, you can check out the park's interpretive display.

The **Creston Valley Wildlife Management Area,** a showplace of migratory waterfowl about 7 miles (11 km) west of Creston on Hwy 3, provides opportunities for hiking, biking, **bird-watching** (265 species), wildlife viewing, canoeing, and fishing. Its interpretive centre, open May to mid-October, offers a variety of wildlife activities and programs, and there is a campground nearby. For more information, call (250) 428-3259.

Downhill Skiing

In 1947, a progressive group of local skiers installed Western Canada's first chairlift at **Red Mountain.** Of course, if you had powder skiing at your door the way the folks in Rossland do, you too would want the newest-fangled technology to get you to it as quickly as possible. So fabled are the snow conditions in this town tucked away in the southeast corner of the province that a century ago, Red Mountain hosted the first Canadian Ski Jumping and Ski Racing Championships. One of the local Scandinavian miners, Olaus Jeldness, not only organized the championships but won the event.

There must be something in the water here, for in more recent times Rossland has produced two of the best women skiers to ever represent Canada, Nancy Greene and Kerrin Lee-Gartner, as well as several dozen national alpine ski team members, among them Felix Belczyk and Don Stevens. (Although the mountains around Rossland may not look formidable, the town itself is perched closer to the peaks. At an elevation of 3,385 feet (1023 m), it's higher than most other towns in Canada.)

Red Mountain is honeycombed with mine shafts tunnelled in the 1890s; most of these mines were exhausted by the 1930s. In many ways time has stood still here when compared with the upstart activity on ski slopes in the Okanagan Valley and at Whistler, especially over the past two decades. That suits the townsfolk here just fine. First-time visitors may feel slightly underwhelmed upon arrival at the base of Red and Granite, the round-shouldered sister mountains that stand side by side and are serviced by four chairlifts and a T-bar. There's always plenty of snow, but after driving through some of the province's more rugged ranges, such as the Coast Mountains, the Monashee Mountains look diminutive by comparison. (In geological terms the Monashees are a half-million years older and more worn down by successive periods of glaciation.) Be of good cheer: there's a vertical rise of 2,800 feet (853 m) between the base and the top of the Granite Mountain, the fourth largest in British Columbia.

When you know that there's more to a mountain than meets the eye, it's best to enlist the help of a local guide. One of Red Mountain's volunteer mountain hosts will gladly take you straight up the Silverlode triple chairlift, from which you'll sight fluffy untracked powder in the evergreens. The trees in the forested slopes surrounding the cleared runs are spaced just widely enough to provide room for quick turns. As gentle as the terrain appears from the bottom, there are challenging chutes aplenty through which to plummet, with lots of knee-high powder to slow your descent. Occasionally you'll pass one of the many funky old skiers' cabins tucked away in the woods.

For more information on Red Mountain, including lessons, rentals, schedules, and lift fees, call (250) 362-7384. For snow conditions, call (250) 362-5500.

Cross-Country Skiing

Hidden trails lead off from Red Mountain towards meadows on the sides of **Granite Mountain,** where snow trekkers with the benefit of climbing skins can spend their entire day. Red Mountain sells $10 single-ride tickets (compared to a regular adult $35 day pass) that enable skiers to ride to the top of the lift and head off into the backcountry.

A quick tour of both mountains will quickly reveal that the groomed slopes are only the most visible portion of a far vaster expanse of alpine and cross-country terrain. The **BlackJack Cross-Country Ski Club** lies just across the road from Red Mountain. Over 30 miles (50 km) of packed and tracked trails lead off from here through evergreen forests, across frozen lakes, and past abandoned homesteads. These are reminders that although today the population of Rossland (3,500) and surrounding communities in the Kootenays is on the rise, a century ago there were twice as many people living here.

In winter **Nancy Greene Provincial Park** (see Parks/Camping, above) is a popular location with cross-country skiers who like to cut their own tracks. For those who would rather enjoy groomed runs, the **Paulson Cross-Country Ski Trails,** directly adjacent to Nancy Greene Provincial Park on Hwy 3, are maintained by the BC Forest Service and the Nelson Nordic Club, and provide an extensive network (almost 28.5 miles/46 km) of easy to advanced cross-country trails. There are warming shelters and trail maps at strategic locations on this trail system (which also makes for good mountain biking in summer.) Watch for three pullouts on Hwy 3 from where the Paulson trails begin. For further information, contact Nelson Nordic Club representative Tom Johnson, (250) 352-7025.

Other BC Forest Service ski-trail networks include **Beaver Valley,** northeast of Trail, with 5 miles (8 km) of easy to advanced ski trails in the gently rolling hills of the Bonnington Range. The Beaver Valley Cross-Country Ski Club in Fruitvale maintains the trails, many of which are groomed. The trailhead is located about 11 miles (18 km) northeast of Fruitvale. Follow the paved road to Champion Lakes Provincial Park west of Hwy 3B and watch for signs just before the park boundary. For a more extended trip, try the alpine backcountry ski-touring route along the summits of the **Bonnington Range.** Contact the Forest Service in Castlegar, (250) 365-8600, or Kootenay Lake, (250) 825-1100, for details.

Snowshoeing and cross-country skiing are featured at **Champion Lakes Provincial Park** (see Parks/Camping, above), and there are ski trails at **Stagleap Provincial Park** (see Wildlife, above) and Nelson's **Clearwater Creek** (known locally as Apex).

For more information, consult *Ski Touring in the West Kootenays* by Trevor Holsworth or contact Snowpack Outdoor Experience, 333 Baker St, (250) 352-6411; or Kootenay Experience, 306 Victoria St, (888) 488-4327 or (250) 354-4441, or visit their Web site: www.netidea.com/~kootexp/. Both are located in Nelson.

Attractions

Rossland, a 1890s gold-rush town, has experienced a second boom recently. This time the gold is not in Red Mountain, but on it. Red Mountain Ski Area is one of the more challenging ski areas in British Columbia (see Downhill Skiing, above). In the summer, the colourful turn-of-the-century main street of tiny Rossland bustles with hikers bound for alpine lakes, mountain bikers en route to explore the numerous trails, or visitors seeking scenery. Gold Rush Books and Espresso, 2063 Washington St, (250) 362-5333, is a good place to linger over a latte and a good book. For something a little stiffer, stop by the Flying Steamshovel Inn and Onlywell Pub, 2003 Second Ave, (250) 362-7323, a favourite local watering hole named after the unfortunate fellow who piloted—and then crashed—the first helicopter in North America.

Tour the fascinating Le Roi Gold Mine, Canada's only hard-rock gold mine open to the public, at the junction of Hwy 22 and 3B in Rossland. It's not just another roadside attraction (open May through September), (250) 362-7722.

The tiny community of **Crawford Bay,** accessible via an hour's ferry ride from Balfour (19 miles/32 km east of Nelson), happens to be the home of one of British Columbia's finest golf courses, Kokanee Springs Golf Course; (250) 227-9226. Just up from the ferry dock is La Chance Swiss Restaurant, (250) 227-9477, a local hangout with a menu that leans towards Swiss and German fare; it's open April through October.

Restaurants

Elmer's Corner Since opening, Elmer's has won over locals with its funky atmosphere, homemade breads, and mostly (but not all) vegetarian entrees. The thin-crust pizzas are excellent; the desserts are not. *1999 2nd Ave (2 blocks up from Columbia, on Washington), Rossland; (250) 362-5266; $.*

Sunshine Cafe Virtually anybody will feel a bit of shine in Rossland's favourite cafe, which features a range of internationally inspired foods. The food doesn't try to be fancy, just good, and there's lots of it. Mealtimes are crowded; reserve ahead during ski season. *2116 Columbia Ave (in middle of town on main street), Rossland; (250) 362-7630; $.*

Cheaper Eats

Flying Steamshovel Inn The atmosphere is minimal, but the standard pub-style fare is good value for the dollar, with the expected burgers and sandwiches, pastas, and seafood, all under $10. An adjoining dining room opened recently, serving Mexican food. *2003 2nd Ave, Rossland; (250) 362-7323; $.*

Kootenay Rose Coffeehouse Be sure to stop in for a steaming cup of java; this is the only coffeehouse east of Kelowna that roasts its own beans. The strictly vegetarian menu offers soups and salads, quiches, and lasagne to help keep the jitters at bay. *129 N 10th Ave, Creston; (250) 428-7252; $.*

Lodgings

Angela's Place British transplant Angela Wright "guarantees" her accommodations. They're casual and fun, as they should be in this ski town. Prices are also flexible; Wright uses an honour-system sliding scale. Closed summers. *1520 Spokane St (4 blocks down hill from Uplander Hotel); Box 944, Rossland, BC V0G 1Y0; (250) 362-7790; $–$$.*

Destiny Bay Resort ☆☆ The German-born owners brought a bit of Europe to the little town of Boswell on Kootenay Lake. You stay in one of the five sod-roofed cabins or in one of the suites in the lodge. Closed winters. *11935 Hwy 3A (40 minutes from Creston); Box 6, Boswell, BC V0B 1A0; (250) 223-8455 or (800) 818-6633; $$.*

Ram's Head Inn ☆☆ This comfortable nonsmoking inn is the choice place to stay in this mountainous part of the province: it's just a few hundred yards' walk to the Red Mountain ski area. Of 12 rooms, the 4 in the addition are the plushest. *Red Mountain Rd (at base of mountain, 2 miles/3 km north of town); Box 636, Rossland, BC V0G 1Y0; (250) 362-9577; $$–$$$.*

Wedgwood Manor ☆☆ On 50 acres (20 ha) within sight of the Purcell Mountains, this 1910 home is one of the finest lodgings in southeastern BC. In summer, sit on the porch and look out at the Kokanee Glacier across the lake. Closed winters. *16002 Crawford Creek Rd (east of Nelson on Hwy 3A, take Balfour ferry to Kootenay Bay and head south); PO Box 135, Crawford Bay, BC V0B 1E0; (250) 227-9233 or (800) 862-0022; $$.*

Cheaper Sleeps

Red Shutter You don't walk to Red Mountain from here, you ski. This slopeside bed and breakfast is a comfy, kick-back kind of place, and summer rates are moderate. *Red Mountain Rd (PO Box 742), Rossland, BC V0G 1Y0; (250) 362-5131; $.*

Scotsman Motel It may be plain, but this motel has a hot tub that cures sore muscles, and the rooms are the right price. There's a multiroom suite that sleeps six and (off-season) may just be the best per-person deal in town. *Junction of Hwy 3B and Hwy 22 (PO Box 1071), Rossland, BC V0G 1Y0; (250) 362-7364; $.*

More Information

BC Forest Service, Arrow Forest District: *(250) 365-8600; Web site: www.for.gov.bc.ca/nelson/district/arrow.*

BC Forest Service, Boundary Forest District, Grand Forks: *(250) 442-5411.*

BC Forest Service, Kootenay Lake Forest District: *(250) 825-1100; Web site: www.for.gov.ca/nelson/district/kootenay.*

BC Forest Service, Nelson Forest Regional Office, Castlegar: *(250) 354-6200.*

BC Parks, Kootenay District, Wasa: *(250) 422-4200.*

BC Parks, Okanagan District, Summerland: *(250) 494-6500.*

BC Parks, West Kootenays District, Nelson: *(250) 825-3500.*

Castlegar InfoCentre: *(250) 365-6313.*

Creston InfoCentre: *(250) 428-4342.*

Grand Forks InfoCentre: *(250) 442-2833.*

Kootenay Lake Ferry Information: *(250) 229-4215.*

Nelson InfoCentre: *(250) 352-3433.*

Rossland InfoCentre: *(250) 362-5666.*

Trail InfoCentre: *(250) 368-3144.*

Slocan Valley and Upper Arrow Lake

From Salmo to Galena Bay via Highways 6 and 23, as well as a side trip to Kaslo on Highway 31A, including Valhalla and Monashee Provincial Parks.

This is a very pretty drive, not to be attempted in a rush. By their very nature, the Selkirk Mountains define this part of the Kootenays. Highway 6 links silvan Salmo with Highway 23 and stern-wheeling Nakusp, and forms alliances with branches of Highway 3 (Crowsnest Highway) to wrap all who journey here in a seductive embrace. Love at first sight is the reaction of many visitors to the Kootenays.

Two of British Columbia's major mountain wilderness parks, Valhalla and Kokanee Glacier, are situated here. Cody Caves, a unique area of karst topography, also occurs here. (A karst is a limestone region with underground drainage and many cavities and passages caused by the dissolution of the rock.) Serrated, glacier-cloaked granite peaks dominate the landscape. Huge lake-filled glacial valleys provide habitat for many kinds of wildlife and offer excellent opportunities for water-based recreation. The range of wilderness experiences offered throughout the West Kootenays is exhilarating and diverse. Hot springs, alpine meadows, spectacular winter recreation, wildlife observation, and photography are among the many reasons to visit.

Throughout both the East and West Kootenay regions winds the majestic Columbia River, with its source in Columbia Lake near the town of Fairmont Hot Springs on the Rockies' western slopes.

The river flows north for over 186 miles (300 km) before hooking west and south to begin its long journey—more than 250 miles (400 km)—to the US border. For nearly half this length it widens to form the Upper and Lower Arrow Lakes, vast reservoirs of water that moderate winter temperatures and help retain moisture in the local atmosphere, thus greatly influencing the types of vegetation found there. The river crosses the border just south of Trail and passes through Washington to its mouth at Astoria, Oregon.

Getting There

Highway 3 (Crowsnest Highway) leads west from Creston and east from Castlegar to Salmo. Highway 6 leads east from Vernon to Nakusp. Highway 23 leads south from Highway 1 at Revelstoke to Galena Bay via the Shelter Bay ferry.

Adjoining Areas

NORTH: **The Trans-Canada Highway**

SOUTH: **Crowsnest Highway: The West Kootenays**

EAST: **North Kootenay Lake and Selkirk Valleys**

WEST: **Kettle Valley**

inside out

Parks/Camping

Recently improved, **McDonald Creek Provincial Park,** 6 miles (10 km) southwest of Nakusp on Hwy 6, has 28 vehicle/tent sites on both sides of Upper Arrow Lake. The park is open May through mid-September, and all campsites are first-come, first-served. From most of the campsites, campers have direct access to their "own" beach (see also Beaches/Picnics and Fishing, below). For more information, contact BC Parks in Nelson, (250) 825-3500.

For a great view of the Valhalla Range to the west, pitch your tent or park your camper at **Rosebery Provincial Park.** Situated on the banks of Wilson Creek on the east side of Slocan Lake near New Denver, Rosebery offers secluded camping in 36 vehicle/tent sites. It is a good staging spot for backcountry exploration of Valhalla and Kokanee Glacier Provincial Parks. You can also explore the numerous mining ghost towns nearby or visit the developed or undeveloped natural hot springs in the area. The park is located on Hwy 6 between New Denver and Nakusp, about 4 miles (6 km) southeast of Rosebery. For more information, contact BC Parks, (250) 825-3500.

In addition to provincial campsites, there are number of recreation sites in the Arrow Forest District, maintained by the BC Forest Service, including several at **Wilson Lake,** directly east of Nakusp. For a map of these sites, call (250) 365-8600 or stop by the Arrow Forest District office at 845 Columbia Ave in Castlegar.

Hiking/Backpacking

East from Hwy 6, there are two approaches to **Kokanee Glacier Provincial Park:** 5 miles (8 km) south of Slocan at Lemon Creek, a gravel road runs 10 miles (16 km) to the park entrance; 9 miles (14.4 km) north of Slocan, an access road follows Enterprise Creek for 8 miles (13 km) to the trailhead. Another approach is from Hwy 31A, 3.7 miles (6 km) northwest of Kaslo, up Keen Creek for almost 15 miles (24 km) to the Joker Millsite trailhead. Yet another route is from Hwy 31, just over 6 miles (10 km) north of Ainsworth Hot Springs, up Woodbury Creek for 8 miles (13 km) to the trailhead. For a detailed description of hiking trails in Kokanee Glacier Provincial Park, contact BC Parks, (250) 825-3500, and see also Crowsnest Highway: The West Kootenays chapter.

Valhalla Provincial Park is a magnificent world-class wilderness area half again as large as Kokanee Glacier Provincial Park, including nearly 20 miles (30 km) of the pristine wilderness shoreline of Slocan Lake. According to Norse mythology, Valhalla was a palace roofed with shields, wherein lived the bravest of the slain Norse warriors. There, under the leadership of the god Odin, they lived a happy life waiting for the day when they would be rallied to march out of the palace and do battle with the giants. The spirit of Valhalla lives on in the splendour of this portion of southeastern British Columbia, where great palaces of rock call forth majestic images with names such as Asgard, Gimli, and Thor.

The Valhalla Range is a dramatically diverse area in the Selkirks. Deep river valleys, large subalpine lakes, and granite peaks of up to 9,275 feet (2827 m) grace this park. The peaks are truly magnificent. In the northwest, New Denver Glacier at 9,049 feet (2758 m) dominates the landscape, while the block-shaped Devil's Couch at 8,750 feet (2667 m) and Hela Peak at 8,914 feet (2717 m) define the central area. Along the southwestern boundary is an outstanding group of spires including Mount Dag, the Wolfs Ears, Gimli, Asgard, and Gladsheim, all over 8,700 feet (2660 m).

Boat access across Slocan Lake from Hwy 6 between Slocan and New Denver is required to reach most of this wilderness. Slocan, Silverton, and New Denver, the closest communities, all have boat launches. The lake can also be accessed from Rosebery, which has public access at the north end of the lake and, via the narrow Wragge Creek Forest Service Rd, which leads west from Hwy 6, at Wragge Beach on the western shore, where there is a medium-sized, forested, heavily used BC Forest Service campsite.

Commercial **water taxis** take visitors across the lake. Visitors who opt to canoe to the beaches and trails should note that strong crosswinds may blow up suddenly. Early-morning starts are recommended. The shoreline of Slocan Lake is for the most part a rugged combination of bluffs and large rocks interspersed with beautifully isolated pebble and sand beaches. Pictographs on the rock bluffs overhanging the lake are reminders of former Native inhabitants, while overgrown trails and logging flumes mark the passing of the local mining boom that brought Europeans to this area a century ago.

Three biogeoclimatic zones are found within Valhalla: interior cedar/hemlock, Engelmann spruce/subalpine fir, and alpine tundra. Due to a moist climate, interesting plant communities, such as yellow cedar, Engelmann spruce/fern associations, and coastal fern communities, are important features of the area. Mountain caribou, goats, black bears, and grizzlies roam Valhalla, and smaller mammals like marmots and pikas can occasionally be seen among the rocks. Alpine ptarmigans and golden eagles are favourite birds to watch for when hiking.

The hiking trails that cover a variety of distances and terrains lead from the six main drainages from the mountain heights to Slocan Lake below, and from the Hoder Creek Logging Rd past Drinnon Lake and Gwillim Lakes in the southwest. For information about these trails as well as boating opportunities in Valhalla Provincial Park, contact BC Parks, (250) 825-3500. For canoe and mountain bike rentals, contact Lemon Creek Lodge on Hwy 6 in Slocan, (250) 355-2403. Good topographic maps of this region include NTS# 82K/3W, 82F/13, and 82F/14.

Northwest of Nakusp, in the Monashee Mountains, **Monashee Provincial Park** is a wilderness area of mountains, lakes, and forests. It comprises several small untouched watersheds supporting substantial old-growth cedar, hemlock, and spruce forests and important habitat for grizzly bears. The area also features some of the oldest rocks in the province, a small threatened herd of caribou, and some rare specimens of coastal plant species.

The park is intersected by switchback trails, necessary in this steep terrain. The feelings of early explorers are manifested in the local place names Belly-Up Canyon and S.O.B. Gulch, and a large area at an elevation of 8,000 feet (2439 m) named Valley of the Moon. There are a number of trails for exploring this wonderful park. Climb up Fosthal Mountain for beautiful views of the Monashees and Okanagan Highlands, or go to the

Fawn Lakes, an interesting area of more than 100 "little puddles." Hikers can use the 10 wilderness campsites at Spectrum Lake to take day or longer trips.

There is no road access to Monashee Provincial Park, which is located 46.5 miles (75 km) northeast of Vernon. Take Hwy 97 to Vernon, then go east on Hwy 6 to Cherryville. Go northeast up Sugar Lake Rd to Spectrum Creek, where there is a parking lot. The climb to the park is a fairly stiff 7.5 miles (12 km). For more information and a map of the park's hiking trails, contact BC Parks, (250) 825-3500.

Hiking trails maintained by the BC Forest Service in this region of the West Kootenays include the **Kuskanax Creek Trail** (about 10 miles/16 km return) south of Nakusp, which leads to Kimbol Lake. To find the trailhead, drive 1.2 miles (2 km) south of Nakusp on Hwy 6. Turn east on Alexander Rd for 1.2 miles (2 km) and watch for trail signs posted beside the Nakusp Cemetery.

Other trails lead east of Hwy 6 in the town of New Denver. For a full list, contact the Arrow Forest District in Castlegar, (250) 365-8600, or (250) 265-3685 in Nakusp. The best guide to consult is *Classic Hiking Trails in the West Kootenays* by Trevor Holsworth. For an overview of back-country adventures in the West Kootenays, contact Kootenay Experience, 306 Victoria St in Nelson, (888) 488-4327 or (250) 354-4441, or visit their excellent Web site: www.netidea.com/~kootexp/.

Beaches/Picnics

McDonald Creek Provincial Park (see Parks/Camping, above) has a couple of miles of sandy beach on Upper Arrow Lake. Visitors can find a quiet spot or join in the fun at the main swimming area. The park has eight picnic tables as well as a boat launch.

A pleasant spot on a summer's day is **Grohman Narrows Provincial Park,** 3 miles (5 km) west of Nelson on Hwy 3A near the link with Hwy 6, which has a picnic/day-use area as well as nature, walking, and hiking trails. About 5 miles (8 km) south of Slocan is the **Lemon Creek Rest Area,** where there is a turnoff for Kokanee Glacier Provincial Park.

Although it's not on this section of Hwy 6, **Arrow Lakes Provincial Park** deserves a mention. Like the parks farther north on the Revelstoke Reservoir, it consists of a number of choice sites scattered along the length of the Upper and Lower Arrow Lakes reservoir system. These lakes are a widened portion of the Columbia River as it wends its way south to the US border.

The three sites on the northern end of Lower Arrow Lake—**Burton, Fauquier**, and **Eagle Creek**—off Hwy 6 have picnic/day-use areas and boat ramps. A free ferry crosses the lake from Fauquier to Needles on the west side. The **Shelter Bay** site, about 30 miles (50 km) south of Revelstoke on Hwy 23, near the ferry crossing on the west side of Upper Arrow Lake for Galena Bay, also has 13 vehicle/tent sites. All of the sites are open from May to September.

Travellers can picnic, stretch their legs, and refresh themselves with a short walk to a waterfall at **Ione Falls Rest Stop,** 11 miles (18 km) north of Nakusp on the east side of Hwy 23.

If you're hungry for a view, stop at the Slocan Lake Viewpoint, on Hwy 6 near New Denver. From here the "Silvery Slocan" displays itself in all its glory.

Possibly the best picnic viewpoint in the Slocan Valley, and certainly one of the easiest to reach (once the snow has left the road), is the **Idaho Peak Forestry Lookout** off Hwy 31A near Sandon. Follow the well-marked Idaho Peak Forest Rd for 7.5 miles (12 km) south of Hwy 31A. A hiking trail (easy; 1.7 miles/2.8 km return) leads from the parking lot to a Forest Service lookout (elevation 7,480 feet/2280 m). Wildflowers bloom in complete abandon here in late July and early August. A good map is available from BC Forest Service, Arrow Forest District, 845 Columbia Ave, in Castlegar. Call (250) 365-8600 or (800) 665-1511 for a copy.

One of the rewards for making a journey to the viewpoints in summer is savouring the abundant huckleberries that proliferate in clear-cut areas. Just be sure to wear long pants when you go picking, as the knee-high bushes are both lush and scratchy.

Mountain Biking

A battle for bragging rights is being waged among mountain bikers. Bikers from around Whistler say they've got the best riding in the province, at which folks from the Okanagan just laugh. But riders in **Rossland** sit back and smile, because they know that Rossland has the best trails, not only in British Columbia, but also in all of Canada. The **Dewdney Trail,** with its blisteringly fast 3,000-foot (1000-m) descent, is the trail that put Rossland on the mountain-bike map, and is still one of the best rides around. The start of the trail is up the **Old Cascade Highway** (a fair ride in and of itself, continuing south from Rossland to the US border and beyond), off Hwy 22 just west of the junction of Hwys 22 and 3B. The climb north is about 7.5 miles (12.5 km) before turning left onto the Dewdney downhill, which takes you *down*. The ride is about 11 miles (18 km) all totalled.

Another well-known trail is the **Rubberhead,** south of the golf course (access is at the end of the Golf Course Rd, just out of town on Hwy 3B to Trail). Rubberhead is also the name of the local mountain-bike festival, held every September, a three-day event, with fun for all ages and riding ability. The Rubberhead is one of a number of trails in this area that include easy rides such as the **Wagon Road,** a wide, sloping 2-mile (3.5-km) trail that used to be an old wagon trail, and the 5-mile (8-km) **Railgrade,** which used to be—wait for it—an old railway line. Then there is the more challenging **Whiskey Trail,** a technical masterpiece of logs, climbs, quick drops, and steep, rocky sections. Other well-established trails in the area include Dilley's, Technogrind, The Coffee Run, Drakes, Doukhobor Draw, Smugglers, .007 and Crown Point, which all interconnect. There are dozens of less established or secret trails in the area, too. Perhaps if you go asking around Alpine Cycle, (250) 362-9646, in Nelson, a local will lead you to some sweet singletrack that no outsider has ever seen before.

Like other areas in the Kootenays, in the **Nelson** area mountain biking is a matter of going straight up or straight down. Finding a level trail is tricky indeed. For those interested in the latter, the **Clearwater Creek Cross-Country Ski Trails** (see Skiing/Snowboarding, below), south of Nelson on Hwy 6 near the Whitewater Ski Area, allow mountain biking in the summer.

For something a little longer, try one of the rides west of Nelson, like the 8.5-mile (14-km) **Stanley Loop,** the 24.5-mile (40-km) **Rover Creek,** or the 27-mile (44-km) **Kenville Mine Road.** Most of these rides are on logging roads, but Stanley Loop offers some singletrack. If you're looking for capital 'H' Hard-core riding, the handful of trails just off **Mount Station Road** east of Nelson is rated psycho. They're not long, but they sure are tough, both vertically and technically.

For other trails in the area, talk to the folks at Coolsport, (250) 354-4674, or Gerick Sports, (250) 354-4622, in Nelson. For a preview of mountain-bike trails in the West Kootenays, visit the Radical Multimedia mountain-bike cyber-guide Web site: http://www.rideguide.com. For more information on outdoor recreation around Nelson, contact outfitters Valhalla Pure Outfitters, 624 Baker St, (250) 354-1006, in Nelson, or (250) 358-7755, in New Denver; or Kootenay Experience, (888) 488-4327 or (250) 354-4441, or visit their excellent Web site: www.netidea.com/~kootexp/. For **guided bike tours,** contact Revolution Adventure Tours, (250) 354-1566, in Nelson.

The **Wensley Creek Cross-Country Ski Trails** south of Nakusp (see Skiing/Snowboarding, below) on Hwy 6 at Box Lake also double as mountain-bike trails in the summer. Another popular ride is to the **Nakusp Hot Springs** (see Attractions, below) along the multi-use **Kuskanax Creek Trail** (10.5 miles/17 km return), which follows Hot Spring Rd east of Hwy 23 north of Nakusp. It'll take you an hour or so to get there, and about the same to get back to town. How long you spend at the commercially developed hot springs is up to you. If you don't want to pay to soak, there are a handful of other hot springs in the area. You can bike at least part of the way to most of the springs. Contact the Nakusp InfoCentre on Hwy 6 in Nakusp, (800) 909-8819, for more information.

East of New Denver off Hwy 31A, the **Kaslo & Slocan Railway Trail** is suitable for both hiking and mountain biking. This trail has two trailheads, at **Sandon** and **Three Forks.** From Sandon, a pleasant 3.8-mile (6.1-km) trail follows the abandoned rail grade past old mine workings to Payne Bluff. From Three Forks, an 0.8-mile (1.4-km) trail over a moderate grade leads up to the rail grade close to **Payne Bluff.** East of Payne Bluff, the abandoned grade is identifiable but not maintained as a trail. Northwest of Kaslo, the **Kaslo River Trailway** is a multi-use, nonmotorized trail parallel to and above Highway 31A. This 11-mile (18-km) trail, suitable for easygoing mountain biking, follows active roads for short sections; cyclists should watch for signs to redirect them onto the trail.

Boating/Kayaking/Canoeing

For boat launches on **Slocan Lake,** see Valhalla Provincial Park in Hiking/Backpacking, above. Boaters are warned that the lake can have treacherous winds; consult locals before setting out. Smaller motorboats should use the more protected areas. The adventurous might want to canoe the length of the lake (staying close to the western shore), which can take from two to five days. The 25-mile (40-km) shoreline has many attractive sand and cobble beaches to enjoy, and the park has nine camping areas with outhouses and bear-proof food caches. Contact BC Parks for a detailed map; (250) 825-3500.

The **Slocan River** is a small river, with occasional rapids, in a rural setting. Although none of the rapids is particularly difficult (nothing over Class III), experience in reading and running whitewater is definitely required. Paddlers should be adequately equipped, know their abilities and limitations, and reconnoitre unfamiliar territory.

Intermediate-level paddlers might want to get a taste of the river between Slocan and Crescent Valley, a Class II, 50-mile (80-km) trip that will take one long day. To shorten the trip, the river may be accessed at any of the bridges along Hwy 6, particularly between Perry Siding and Slocan Park. The most technical portion of the river (Class III) is just north of its confluence with the Kootenay River, a 3-mile (5-km) stretch between Crescent Valley and Shoreacres, a popular play spot for kayakers and canoers. Put in at Crescent Valley and take out at Shoreacres, just downstream of the railroad bridge. Allow one to three hours.

For more information, consult Valhalla Pure Outfitters, 624 Baker St,

(250) 354-1006, or Gerick Cycle and Sports, 702 Baker St, (250) 354-4622, both in Nelson. A good guide book to consult on paddling in the region is *The Silvery Slocan Outdoors Guide.*

Fishing

With so much water in this part of the West Kootenays, the fish are never far away. Fishing for kokanee, dolly varden, and rainbow trout is good in **Upper Arrow Lake,** accessible from McDonald Creek Provincial Park (see Parks/Camping, above). The various sites comprising Arrow Lakes Provincial Park (see Beaches/Picnics, above) also provide access to **Upper and Lower Arrow Lakes.**

There is a small lakeside Forest Service campsite at **Box Lake,** 6 miles (10 km) south of Nakusp on Hwy 6, where fly-fishing for rainbow trout is popular. The site has a boat launch, but boats are restricted to electric motors only. Farther south, try your luck for rainbow trout or dolly varden in **Wilson Creek,** at Rosebery Provincial Park (see Parks/Camping, above). For directions to other creeks and small lakes offering good fishing, get a brochure/map of the region from the BC Forest Service, (250) 365-8600. For information about fishing licences, contact the Fish and Wildlife office in Nelson, (250) 354-6397, or Nakusp, (250) 265-3714.

Caving

For an experience *under* this world, visitors shouldn't pass up the opportunity to visit **Cody Caves Provincial Park,** eight rough but well-marked miles (13 km) off Hwy 31 on the west side of Kootenay Lake about 2 miles (3 km) north of Ainsworth Hot Springs. Open mid-June to mid-September depending on the condition of the road, this unique park is dedicated to preserving a cave system and an underground stream flowing through ancient limestone formations. The access road is unsuitable for low-clearance vehicles.

The underground experience is available by guided tour only, at a cost of $12 for adults and $8 for children for a one-hour tour, complete with equipment such as coveralls, helmets, headlamps, and gloves. Visitors must come equipped with sturdy footwear and warm clothing.

The caves are fascinating. About 875 yards (800 m) of passageways are explorable, revealing impressive displays of various types of calcite formations, such as stalagmites, stalactites, moonmilk, soda straws, bacon strips, and rimstone dams. The park also has an outside display, a day-use area, and some hiking trails outside the caves. For further information, contact BC Parks, (250) 825-3500. HiAdventure Corporation, (250) 353-7425, in Nelson leads **guided caving tours.**

Skiing/Snowboarding

South of Nelson on Hwy 6 are the **Clearwater Creek Cross-Country Ski Trails** (known locally as **Apex),** an extensive system of groomed trails maintained by the Nelson Nordic Ski Club. For more information, contact club representative Shirley Turner, (250) 352-8239.

South of Nakusp off Hwy 6 at Box Lake, the **Wensley Creek Cross-Country Ski Trails** offer a variety of cross-country ski trails for beginner and intermediate skiers. There is a warming shelter at the midpoint of the 6-mile (9-km) network of trails. Cross-country trails have also been brushed out recently around the nearby **Nakusp Hot Springs** (see Attractions, below); several **wilderness hot springs** on the east side of Upper Arrow Lake, north of **Nakusp** off Hwy 23, can be reached on skis, snowshoes, or via snowmobile. There's nothing quite like the presence of steaming hot water in the midst of a snow-covered forest to warm your soul. (In non-snowy months you can drive into these wilderness springs.) Hot springs are found at **Halcyon** (above a ghost town on undeveloped private land but available to the public), **Halfway River,** and **St. Leon Creek** (privately owned). Contact the Nakusp InfoCentre for directions, current road conditions, and accessibility.

Your initial reaction to **Whitewater Ski Area** near Nelson will depend on what's important to you when it comes to a downhill skiing/snowboarding vacation. In an age of on-slope sushi bars and hand-crafted microbreweries at the base of the lifts, Whitewater represents a Zen approach to ski development. Simply put, Whitewater is four ski lifts strung up in the wilderness. There's nothing but big peaks; a ton of light, dry powder; and the rudimentary, no-nonsense lifts to get you to the top. Who needs those high-speed quads, anyway?

The Summit Chair rises a modest 1,300 feet (400 m) to the top of a ridge on Mount Ymir (elevation 7,884 feet/2403 m), where 10 out of 15 runs are rated expert. Whitewater's high base elevation of 5,400 feet (1640 m) ensures plentiful snow and very few midseason thaws. Snowfall is far more abundant than in nearby Nelson. The best powder at Whitewater is found in the trees. Catch Basin, Glory Basin, Terrorada, and the Trash Chutes will yield sick and twisted lines after a big storm. This is expert skiing only, and even good skiers should remember to ski in pairs and take avalanche equipment if straying beyond the boundary ropes. Local expert skiers here will show competent visitors where to go; Whitewater is one of the friendliest mountains in the province.

Intermediate-level skiers and snowboarders will find the tops of Quicksilver and Sleeper spacious. A series of fine cruising runs off the summit will also appeal to intermediates; the best bets here are Joker, Motherlode, Paydirt, and Bonanza. Novices have their own chairlift to play on, and with all of that soft powder to fall in, even the intermediate runs are not terribly imposing.

For skiers willing to forego "walk to the lifts" convenience, the Victorian town of Nelson offers a refreshing change from the plasticity of resort life. For more information, contact Whitewater Ski Area, (250) 352-4944; for the **snow report,** call (250) 352-7669. Whitewater is located in the Selkirk Range, about 12 miles (19 km) south of Nelson on Hwy 6.

Scenic Drives

Highway 31A, from New Denver to Kaslo, a distance of 29 miles (47 km), follows the railbed of the Kaslo & Slocan Railway, passing the **ghost towns** of Zincton, Retallack, Three Forks, and Sandon. Don't expect to make any time on this exciting, rock-and-rolling road. However, it provides a picturesque alternative route to Nelson via Kaslo and Ainsworth Hot Springs (see Attractions, below). For a side trip, take the two-hour (round-trip) Balfour ferry across Kootenay Lake to Crawford Bay. It's a pretty trip and happens to be the world's longest free ferry ride.

outside in

Attractions

Nestled in a valley on the shore of Kootenay Lake, **Nelson** sprang up with the silver and gold mining boom back in the late 1890s and has retained its Victorian character. Its main street has changed little in a century, luring more than one filmmaker to use its downtown as a set. More than 350 heritage sites are listed in this city of about 10,000 people. For the best overall view of Nelson, stroll through Gyro Park to the vista point on the hillside just north of the town centre. The park has picturesque gardens and a nice wading pool for children. An interesting pictorial exhibit of the region's history can be seen at the **Nelson Museum,** 402 Anderson St, (250) 352-9813, which is open year-round.

Nelson has raised afternoon browsing to a fine art. In addition to the many **galleries,** there is a plethora of other interesting **shops** in the downtown area. Outdoor enthusiasts should stop in at Snowpack, 333 Baker St, (250) 352-6411. For art and crafts by many regionally based artists, visit the Craft Connection, 441 Baker St, (250) 352-3006. The Kootenay Baker, 295 Baker St, (250) 352-2274, boasts one of the best selections of health foods in the region, including organic baked goods.

The variety of **arts programs** brought into Nelson by the town's arts council is well selected. From theatrical productions to wildlife lectures to classical guitarists to nationally known folk-rock groups, there's almost always something going on at the Capitol Theatre; (250) 352-6363. From June through August, the entire town turns into an art gallery, with artists' work exhibited in almost 20 shops, restaurants, and galleries. Pick up a map of **Artwalk Gallery Tours** at the Tourist Information Bureau, 225 Hall St, (250) 352-3433, or contact Artwalk, Box 422, Nelson, BC V1L 5R2, (250) 352-2402. For a calendar of weekly events, pick up a free copy of the *Kootenay Weekly Express,* distributed at businesses around town.

Don't miss **Ainsworth Hot Springs,** (250) 229-4212, where for $3–12 you can explore caves of piping-hot (112°F/44°C), waist-deep water, or swim in the slightly cooler pool (open 365 days a year). The restaurant here offers a stunning view of Kootenay Lake.

In **Kaslo,** tour the SS *Moyie*, (250) 353-2525, a stern-wheeler that plied the waters of Kootenay Lake from 1898 until 1957; open summers only, hours vary.

Another hot-springs option is at **Nakusp Hot Springs,** (250) 265-4528, which also has overnight accommodations in four A-frame cedar chalets. Although the Nakusp Hot Springs might lack some of the drama of the horseshoe-shaped tunnel at Ainsworth Hot Springs, they nonetheless provide an equally vivid hot-spring experience. The setting here is a narrow canyon through which runs the Kuskanax River. Surrounded by dense forest, the circular municipal outdoor pool is divided in two. The larger portion is deep enough for swimming, and its temperature is maintained at a comfortable 98.6°F (37°C). A smaller section is kept much hotter, at 106°F (41°C). You'll find that a difference of even a degree or two in water temperature affects the amount of time your body can tolerate the heat. Sit in the hottest section for awhile, then find a patch of snow in which to make a snow angel. There's no cold plunge pool here, just the air—which, in winter, is equally effective. Call the Nakusp and District Chamber of Commerce, (800) 909-8819, for information on other wilderness hot springs. (See also Skiing/Snowboarding, above.)

New Denver, a former mining town, is now noted mainly for its spectacular location on Slocan Lake, with the peaks of the Valhalla Mountains rising more than 7,000 feet (2100 m) on the opposite shore. During World War II, New Denver was the site of an internment camp that housed some 2,000 Japanese-Canadians displaced from their West Coast homes. This shameful period of history has been commemorated with the **Nikkei Internment Memorial Centre,** on Josephine St off Third Ave, (250) 358-2663; the centre is open during the summer only, and in the off-season by appointment. For such a small town, New Denver has a fine **bookstore:** The Motherlode, 317 Sixth Ave, (250) 358-7274.

Restaurants

Book Garden Cafe Cafe fare and books just seem to go together naturally, and this bookstore-eatery combination is no exception. You can always get a fresh salad here. During winter, the cafe's a perfect place to while away the hours with a good book. *556 Josephine St (1 block uphill from Baker St), Nelson; (250) 352-1812; $.*

Fiddler's Green ☆☆ Locals quibble over whether the food here is really the best in town, but they agree unanimously that this old estate house has the best atmosphere—and the only garden dining. *Lower 6 Mile Rd (on north lakeshore, 6 miles/9.5 km north of town), Nelson; (250) 825-4466; $$.*

The Rosewood Cafe The Rosewood draws clientele from as far away as New Denver and Spokane, Washington. Decor is casual, but the menu is ambitious, especially for the eastern reaches of British Columbia. Entrees range from blackened redfish to tortellini in curry sauce. *1435 Kaslo (at end of main street), Kaslo; (250) 353-7673; $.*

Cheaper Eats

The Glacier Gourmet The food leans to the pizza-by-the-slice end of the spectrum, with sandwiches and veggie rolls, pasta salads, and sweets rounding out the menu. No booze, but they stay open late for java junkies looking for an inexpensive place to hang. *621 Vernon St, Nelson; (250) 354-4495; $.*

Hungry Wolf Cafe It's worth the 28-mile (45-km) drive to tiny Winlaw in the Slocan Valley to stuff yourself at the famous Hungry Wolf Cafe. The eclectic menu ranges from an 8-ounce New York strip to pizzas, stir-fries, and vegetarian fare. *Hwy 6, Winlaw; (250) 226-7355; $.*

Main Street Diner This diner is one of the most popular spots in town. Locals congregate for Canadian classics like steak and fries or fish and chips, as well as such Mediterranean comfort foods as Greek salad, hummous, or souvlaki with warm pita bread. *616 Baker St, Nelson; (250) 354-4848; $.*

The Outer Clove This trendy spot is for those who believe that there's no such thing as too much garlic. Everything here, from tapas to soup to dessert(!), is garlic based. Fortunately, there's a skilled hand in the kitchen, and the results are a revelation. *536 Baker St, Nelson; (250) 354-1667; $.*

Treehouse Looking for great cheap eats in Kaslo? Do as the locals do and chow down at the Treehouse. This neglected-looking place has a surprisingly diverse menu that runs from Mexican to pasta, to Asian-style stir-fries, to better-than-average burgers. *419 Front St, Kaslo; (250) 353-2955; $.*

Lodgings

Emory House ☆ This pretty arts-and-crafts–style cottage at the north edge of downtown is perfectly situated for those who want to explore Nelson on foot. Opt for the rooms that overlook the lake. Breakfast is a main event. *811 Vernon St (at north end of street, downtown), Nelson, BC V1L 4G3; (250) 352-7007; $$.*

Inn the Garden ☆ Toronto expatriates bought this Victorian house (only a few blocks from downtown) and decorated it on a garden theme. Of the six guest rooms, three have views of the lake, and there is a two-bedroom suite. *408 Victoria St (1 block south of Baker St between Stanley and Ward), Nelson, BC V1L 4K5; (250) 352-3226; $$$.*

Silverton Resort ☆ These cabins on Slocan Lake are the place to stay if you like water play; bring your own canoe, windsurfer, or rowboat, or rent one. You stay in one of five hemlock-log cabins: some have sleeping lofts; all have kitchens and decks. *Lake Ave (on lakeshore); Box 107, Silverton, BC V0G 2B0; (250) 358-7157; $$.*

Sweet Dreams Guesthouse The old Craftsman-style former municipal building across the street from Slocan Lake has been renovated and transformed into a delightful B&B. All five rooms share the four bathrooms. Breakfast is so big it's served in the former courtroom. *702 Eldorado Ave (1 block off main street, across from lake); PO Box 177, New Denver, BC V0G 1S0; (250) 358-2415; $–$$.*

Willow Point Lodge ☆☆ You'll feel welcome in this large, rambling 1922 Victorian perched on a hill. The living room has a large stone fireplace. There are six guest rooms—the Green Room is our favourite. Breakfast is up whenever you are. *Taylor Dr (2.5 miles/4 km north of Nelson on Hwy 3A over Nelson Bridge to Taylor); mail: RR1, S-21, C-31, Nelson, BC V1L 5P4; (250) 825-9411 or (800) 949-2211; $$.*

Cheaper Sleeps

The Alpine This is the nicest little motel in town. The cheapest of the 30 rooms comes in at about $55. Families or ski-bum pals might consider the two-bedroom suite that's practically a small apartment. *1120 Hall Mines Rd, Nelson, BC V1L 1G6; (250) 352-5501; $.*

The Dancing Bear Inn This European-style hostel is so pleasant and inexpensive, it's almost too good to be true. Solo travellers may end up sharing a room with another guest, and everyone is free to use the communal kitchen and laundry facilities. *171 Baker St, Nelson, BC V1L 4H1; (250) 352-7573; $.*

Lemon Creek Lodge Located between Nelson and Slocan, the Lemon Creek is part lodge, part cabins, and part tent and RV sites. Sociable types will like the lodge rooms, where mingling is encouraged with reading nooks and family-style meals. The cabins are more private. *Kennedy Rd (PO Box 68), Slocan, BC V0G 2C0; (250) 355-2403; $.*

More Information

BC Forest Service, Arrow Forest District: *(250) 365-8600 or (800) 665-1511; Web site: http://www.for.gov.ca/nelson/district/arrow.*
BC Parks, Nelson: *(250) 825-3500.*
Galena Bay Ferry Information: *(250) 837-4375.*
Kaslo InfoCentre: *(250) 353-7323.*
Nakusp InfoCentre: *(250) 265-4234 or (800) 909-8819.*
Needles Ferry Information: *(250) 269-7222.*
Nelson InfoCentre: *(250) 352-3433.*
Salmo InfoCentre (seasonal): *(250) 357-2596.*
Slocan InfoCentre (seasonal): *(250) 355-2277.*
Whitewater Ski Area: *(250) 352-4944; snow report, (250) 352-7669.*

North Kootenay Lake and Selkirk Valleys

From Kaslo on the west side of Kootenay Lake north to Galena Bay via Highway 31A, including the northern tip of the lake, Argenta, the Purcell Wilderness Provincial Conservancy, and Goat Range Provincial Park.

The Kootenays wouldn't be complete without at least a backroad or two for those travellers with a little time on their hands and an inclination to search out wilderness backpacking destinations and fishing holes. This route leads through the Lardeau and Duncan Valleys, which are hemmed in by the Selkirk Mountains. Steep-sided valleys force the peaks' runoff into long, narrow lakes, from which fast-flowing rivers cascade south into Kootenay Lake. Dense stands of timber are constant reminders that here in the Kootenays, there's still plenty of untouched wilderness to explore.

About 100 years ago, prospectors came to the West Kootenays, attracted by its rich ore deposits. Mining ghost towns can be found now, silent relics of past treasures. Some backroad travel to these ghost towns will enhance your visit to this extremely beautiful region. Visitors can learn about the development and history of the area at mining museums in Kaslo and New Denver.

Getting There

Highway 31 leads north to Kaslo from the ferry terminal at Balfour on Kootenay Lake's west side, and beyond to the free-ferry terminal at Galena Bay on Upper Arrow Lake. Highway 23 links Galena Bay with Nakusp to the south and Revelstoke to the north. Highway 31A leads east to Kaslo from New Denver, on the east side of Slocan Lake.

Adjoining Areas

NORTH: **The Trans-Canada Highway**

SOUTH: **Crowsnest Highway: The East Kootenays**

EAST: **Columbia River Valley**

WEST: **Slocan Valley and Upper Arrow Lake**

inside out

Hiking/Backpacking

For those in good shape and desiring an extreme backpacking adventure, the **Purcell Wilderness Provincial Conservancy** can be explored along a 37-mile (60-km) stretch of trail that begins just south of the Kootenay Lake town of Argenta. From the **Earl Grey Pass** trailhead, the hiking or horseback route passes through some of the Purcell Mountains' most awe-inspiring peaks, some of which reach heights of more than 12,000 feet (3600 m), on its way to **Toby Creek,** just west of Invermere. For approaches from the east, see Columbia River Valley chapter.

In contrast to the forest-mantled Selkirk Mountains to the west, much of the Purcell Range rode out the last ice age above the glaciers. Thus, fossils are frequently found at elevations above 7,000 feet (2100 m). The high, rugged mountains are undisturbed by roads in British Columbia's only park classed as a "wilderness conservancy," where all forms of mechanized access (including helicopters) are prohibited. Hikers are rewarded with undisturbed views of some of the finest wildlife habitat in the southeastern region of the province. (Providing complete wilderness experience is the primary objective of the conservancy.)

Five biogeoclimatic zones are found here: interior cedar/hemlock, interior Douglas fir, montane spruce, Engelmann spruce/subalpine fir, and alpine tundra. There are grassy meadows at low elevations, which are crucial for elk and moose. Abundant wildflower and alpine meadows astound backcountry trekkers. Wildlife includes mule and white-tailed deer, moose, elk, black and grizzly bears, mountain caribou, and mountain goats. More than 68 species of birds have been recorded. Some of the streams contain native stock of cutthroat and rainbow trout, dolly varden, and mountain whitefish.

Information on the Purcell Wilderness Provincial Conservancy may be obtained from the BC Parks office at Wasa Lake, (250) 422-4200. The park is particularly attractive to climbers. For more information, consult *Classic Hiking Trails of the West Kootenays* by Trevor Holsworth.

Fry Creek Canyon Provincial Recreation Area is a wilderness area on the western slopes of the Purcell Mountains above the north arm of Kootenay Lake. From Argenta, a rough road leads south 7 miles (12 km) to Johnson's Landing, from where the recreation area can be reached via a 2.5-mile (4-km) trail. Besides wilderness campsites, Fry Creek Canyon has over 6 miles (10 km) of hiking trails. Splendid views of the canyon and surrounding peaks from an old miners' trail along the creek provide photographers with subjects aplenty. For more information, contact BC Parks in Nelson, (250) 825-3500.

Northwest of Argenta, the BC Forest Service maintains a small alpine campsite at **Meadow Mountain** that offers great views as well as access to meadows, small lakes, and an extensive alpine ridge system for hiking, horseback riding, or snowmobiling. Northeast of Argenta, a short trail (moderate; 4 miles/6.5 km; last 0.5 mile/0.8 km steep) leads to the base of the **MacBeth Icefield,** where there is a small lake and wilderness camping. You can get to it from Argenta by a rough road along Glacier Creek, accessible from the east side of Duncan Lake and suitable for both two-wheel-drive and four-wheel-drive vehicles.

North of Trout Lake off Hwy 31, there is an alpine and subalpine trail along **Silvercup Ridge.** Originally built as a mining trail, this 12-mile (20-km) trail provides great views and a two- to three-day backpacking trek. All roads to the trail are for high-clearance four-wheel-drive vehicles. For other Forest Service sites around Kaslo and along Hwy 31, contact BC Forest Service, Kootenay Lake Forest District, 1907 Ridgewood Rd off Hwy 3A between Nelson and Balfour, (250) 825-1100.

Camping

North of Kaslo on Hwy 31 is **Lost Ledge Provincial Park.** Situated on Kootenay Lake, it features great fishing from the shore or by boat, as well as 12 secluded campsites in the shade or right on the beach. This picturesque site is open mid-May to mid-September, with sites available on a first-come, first-served basis. For more information, call BC Parks in Nelson, (250) 825-3500.

Another dozen campsites, albeit rustic ones, are located farther north at **Davis Creek** in **Kootenay Lake Provincial Park,** just south of Lardeau on the west side of Kootenay Lake. Campers can swim at this semiprimitive site, which also offers good fishing off the creek mouth. For more information, call BC Parks, (250) 825-3500.

Howser Glayco is a medium-sized BC Forest Service campsite on the west shore of Duncan Lake off Hwy 31 that has a good beach and a boat launch. Swimming, fishing, and windsurfing make it a popular place in summer. Unusual for a Forest Service site, it has handicapped-accessible facilities. For a map and information on current conditions, contact the Kootenay Lake Forest Region Office, (250) 825-1100.

Entrance to the newly enlarged, massive, undeveloped **Goat Range Provincial Park** is from the old townsite of Gerrard at the southeastern end of Trout Lake, about 50 miles (80 km) north of Kaslo; call BC Parks at (250) 825-3500 for details. A dozen campsites are located at Gerrard, an abandoned railroad town. From 1900 until World War II, Gerrard was the terminus of the Arrowhead & Kootenay line of the Canadian Pacific Railway. The nearby Lardeau River once sustained an abundant stock of the world's largest rainbow trout (up to 50 pounds/23 kg in size), now endangered to the point where fishing this river is restricted (see Fishing, below). One of the primary reasons for including Trout Lake (Gerrard) Provincial Park in the newly expanded Goat Range Provincial Park is to protect these fish, as well as to provide undisturbed habitat for the area's bear, elk, deer, mountain caribou, and mountain goats.

Campbell Bay Provincial Park is one of the newer parks in the provincial system, located on east shore of Kootenay Lake, northeast of Kaslo. For more information, contact BC Parks, (250) 825-3500.

Skiing

Sno-cat skiing in the Great Northern and Thompson Mountains around **Trout Lake** is the best way to explore this region in winter. For information on backcountry adventure, contact Selkirk Wilderness Skiing at Meadow Mountain Lodge in Meadow Creek, (250) 366-4424, or Great Northern Lodge/Great Northern Snow-Cat Skiing Ltd in Trout Lake, (250) 369-2227, or (403) 287-2267 in Calgary, Alberta.

Fishing

In what must be one of the classic fisheries blunders, early this century fisheries officers at Gerrard erected a fence and trapping facility facing upstream to capture eggs from the mammoth **Lardeau River rainbow trout,** hoping to introduce these fish to other river and lake systems. Assuming that the fish dropped down from Trout Lake, they were dismayed to find fish accumulating on the downstream side of the fence in the spring of 1914. The fish were from Kootenay Lake.

Realizing their mistake, they developed an elaborate technique to catch the fish. Eggs were reared at Gerrard, Nelson, Kaslo, Lardeau, Argenta, and more distant British Columbia and US hatcheries. After 1939, most of them were not released to the Lardeau River, with the result that the population began to decline seriously. By the 1950s, the Gerrard run had been reduced to fewer than 50 fish! In spite of the fact that their fry had been released in other systems, they attained their maximum growth only in their original habitat at Gerrard. Heavy fishing pressure and logging activity were also major factors in the rapidly diminishing numbers of these spectacular rainbow trout.

To protect these fish today, the Lardeau River and associated tributary waters are permanently closed to fishing. The north end of **Kootenay Lake** is also closed from February through June to protect both upstream migrants and spawned-out downstreamers. However, fishing for char, burbot, and rainbow trout is possible on the aptly named **Trout Lake,** reached from the boat launch at the Gerrard campsite (see Camping, above) or the one at Trout Lake City, at the opposite end of this narrow, 17-mile (28-km) lake. Northwest of Trout Lake, you can fish for rainbow trout and whitefish in **Staubert and Armstrong Lakes.**

There's also good trout fishing at Duncan Dam, 26 miles (42 km) north of Kaslo. For more information, contact the Fish and Wildlife Conservation Office in Cranbrook, (250) 489-8570.

A good contact for fishing **information** plus licences, fuel, tackle, and bait is the Schroeder Creek Resort, 9 miles (15 km) north of Kaslo, (250) 353-7383; or the Lakewood Inn, 4 miles (6 km) north of Kalso, (250) 353-2395, which also has boats for rent. Several other private resorts near Kaslo maintain their own marinas, including Sunny Bluffs, (250) 353-2277. The Windsor Hotel on Kelly St in the town of Trout Lake carries fishing and boating supplies. Call (250) 369-2244.

outside in

Restaurants and Lodgings

For recommended establishments, see Adjoining Areas to this chapter.

More Information

BC Forest Service, Kootenay Lake Forest District: *(250) 825-1100 or (800) 665-1511.*
BC Parks, Nelson: *(250) 825-3500.*
BC Parks, Wasa Lake: *(250) 422-4200.*
Galena Bay Ferry Information: *(250) 837-4375.*
Kaslo InfoCentre (seasonal): *(250) 353-2525.*

Crowsnest Highway: The East Kootenays

From Creston in the Selkirk Mountains via Highway 3 to Cranbrook in the Purcell Mountains, and Crowsnest Pass and the British Columbia–Alberta border in the Rockies, including Moyie Lake Provincial Park, Fernie Snow Valley Ski Area, and the border-area provincial parks.

For outdoor enthusiasts, the route from Creston to Crowsnest Pass is a motherlode of *serious* adventure. The British Columbia–Alberta border parks—Height of the Rockies Provincial Park, Elk Lakes Provincial Park, and Akamina-Kishinena Recreation Area—present some truly extraordinary landscapes to explore.

The name Kootenay, used for the southeastern portion of the province, comes from the Kootenay First Nation, a group of linguistically distinct Native people. They occupy the East Kootenays, with their territory extending into northern Washington, Idaho, and Montana. The western portion of the district was also occupied by Interior Salishan Natives, linguistically and culturally related to the coastal people, or by Thompson River–Shuswap Natives, heavily influenced by the Athapaskan culture.

Getting There

This area can be approached from the Columbia River Valley in the north along Highway 93/95, from the west along Highway 3, or from the east along Highway 6 in Alberta.

Adjoining Areas

NORTH: **Columbia River Valley; North Kootenay Lake and Selkirk Valleys**

WEST: **Crowsnest Highway: The West Kootenays**

inside out

Parks/Camping

Yahk Provincial Park (26 vehicle/tent sites) sits just north of the British Columbia–Idaho border on the banks of the Moyie River. Yahk is a pleasant little campground, on the south side of Hwy 3, 22 miles (35 km) east from Creston. For more information, contact BC Parks' Kootenay District Headquarters located in Wasa Provincial Park, on Hwy 93/95 north of Cranbrook; (250) 422-4200.

Moyie Lake Provincial Park (104 vehicle/tent sites) occupies the north end of Moyie Lake, a large scenic lake on the eastern fringe of the Purcell Mountains. If you like cool, secluded picnics beside a welcoming lake on a hot summer day, this is the spot. When you want to explore after the tent is set up, there's a marsh with a fascinating community of plants and animals, plus the forested **Meadow Trail.** Fly-casting and trolling for trout and other fish are also fun here; the lake has a boat launch. The park is beside Hwy 3, 12 miles (19 km) south of Cranbrook. For more information, contact BC Parks, (250) 422-4200.

Jimsmith Lake Provincial Park (28 vehicle/tent sites), just south of Cranbrook, is a popular park for year-round outdoor recreation. It's centred on small Jimsmith Lake, a good ice-fishing site in winter. Once the ice thaws, the boat launch swings into action, but only nonmotorized boats are allowed on the lake. For information, contact BC Parks, (250) 422-4200. Jimsmith is located on Hwy 3, 2.5 miles (4 km) south of Cranbrook.

Mount Fernie Provincial Park (38 vehicle/tent sites) is a small park with a big personality. Black bear, deer, and elk are commonly seen in these parts, and if they drop by for a visit, you better be on your best behaviour. To take your mind off that, follow the trail that leads beside Lizard Creek. Let the small waterfall that the creek forms as it near its confluence with the Elk River do your thinking for you. You find this well-signed, semiwilderness park just off Hwy 3, about 2 miles (3 km) west of Fernie. For more information, contact BC Parks, (250) 422-4200.

If you're travelling with an RV, **Elkford Municipal Campground** may be best for you—60 vehicle/tent sites are featured in the freshest air in the Rockies. The campground is located on Hwy 43, 22 miles (35.5 km) north of Sparwood. Call (250) 865-2241 for more information.

Hiking/Backpacking

In the rugged East Kootenays, Hwy 3 is the link to three great backcountry and hiking sites that hold their own in any claim-to-fame competition.

Elk Lakes Provincial Park is about 30 miles (50 km) north of Elkford and borders the south side of Alberta's Kananaskis Park, nestled above the tree line in the Front Range of the Rocky Mountains. The scenery is breathtaking—there's just something about lakes set against massive cliff faces, headwalls, waterfalls, craggy summits, and hanging icefalls that makes you stop in your tracks and say a profound "wow." You'll need to stop, anyway, to rest—most of the hikes in Elk Lake justify the adjectives "strenuous," "demanding," and "very demanding." The one exception is the 0.5-mile (0.8-km) walk from the parking lot to **Lower Elk Lake.** Muscle-taxing hiking trails lead from the park entrance to **Elk Pass,** along the shoreline of **Upper Elk Lake,** and to **Petain Creek Falls,** and mountain climbing is also quite challenging here. Horseback riders will enjoy this park—there are extensive, well-established, and durable trails. However, winter recreation is somewhat curtailed here, due to the park's remote location and unfavourable weather conditions. There are three areas of **wilderness camping,** located at the park entrance, at Lower Elk Lake, and at Petain Creek. To reach the park, take Hwy 43 north of Sparwood for 22 miles (35 km) to the town of Elkford. From Elkford, travel well-marked gravel roads on west side of the Elk River for about 27 miles (44 km) to where the road crosses the river and joins the Kananaskis Power Line Rd. It's 26 miles (43 km) from this crossing to the park. Call BC Parks, (250) 422-4200, to get details on road conditions and maps. For more information on these and other hiking trails in the East Kootenays, consult *Rumours, Routes and Rapids (Finding Your Way in the Elk Valley)* by Palmer and Short.

British Columbia's **Akamina-Kishinena Provincial Recreation Area,** together with Waterton Lakes National Park in Alberta and Glacier National Park in Montana, form the "Crown of the Continent," a combination of biological, geological, and climatic factors that occurs nowhere else in North America. And if that weren't enough, these parks are home to one of the densest grizzly bear populations in North America and the only specimens of Wyoming (Yellowstone) moose in Canada. Add unique geological features and the highest peaks in the Clark Range of the Rockies—Starvation and King Edward, clocking in at 9,301 feet (2837 m) and 9,186 feet (2802 m), respectively—and you have a royal park system indeed. It's likely that up to half of all the rare and endangered plant species in British Columbia occur in Akamina-Kishinena. To protect this delicate ecosystem, no motorized transportation is allowed in the park. Backcountry campsites are available, and the area is good for horseback riding and some fishing. Exercise caution: There really are many very big bears around here. Plan in advance for a trip to this area by contacting BC Parks, (250) 422-4200. Akamina-Kishinena Provincial Recreation Area is located in the extreme southeastern corner of the province, close to the Alberta and US borders. The only road to the park in Canada is gravel, south from Hwy 3 at Morrissey Provincial Park, or from the town of Michel south to Kishinena Creek Logging Rd. There's also trail access over Akamina Pass from the roadhead at Cameron Lake in Waterton Lakes National Park, Alberta.

Height of the Rockies Wilderness Area is a new, undeveloped site. One of its key characteristics is its variation of elevation—from 4,265 to 11,315 feet (1310 to 3474 m). It's a great place for hiking and horseback riding but, like the two wilderness parks mentioned, should be attempted by experienced hikers and mountaineers only. The 167,960-acre (68 000-ha) wilderness area is located in the Rocky Mountains and stretches northwest along the Continental Divide between the Elk Lakes Provincial Park in southeastern British Columbia, and Banff National Park and Peter Lougheed Provincial Park in southwestern Alberta. For a detailed map, call the BC Forest Service district office in Cranbrook, (250) 426-1700, or in Invermere, (250) 342-4200.

Picnics

Those who like to picnic at riverside should stop at the **Ryan Rest Area** on the **Moyie River,** just east of Yahk Provincial Park on Hwy 3.

Morrissey Provincial Park's picnic spot, 10 miles (16 km) southeast of Fernie on Hwy 3 on the banks of Elk River, has the river *and* the shade of tall cottonwoods *and* a historic atmosphere—nearby coke ovens are evidence of the area's early coal mines.

Crowsnest Provincial Park, 32 miles (51.5 km) east of Fernie on Hwy 3, is close to Crowsnest Pass (elevation 4,452 feet/1367 m), where the climate is somewhat dramatic because of a narrow flow of air through the pass from Alberta; the imposing Erickson and Loop Ridges of the Rockies stand nearby. You'll be so busy looking at them that you'll forget to eat.

Even if you're not planning an excursion to one of the parks but just want one last, great look at the Rockies before heading into Alberta, stop at the **Olsen Rest Stop** along Hwy 3 just 10 miles (16 km) east of Fernie. Here, you can gaze to your heart's content.

Skiing/Snowboarding

The craggy cleft of the Lizard Range above **Fernie Snow Valley Ski Area** is often likened to an open catcher's mitt. The sheer limestone faces tower above the lifts of the ski area, trapping snow-laden storms and making Fernie, along with Whitewater, near Nelson (see Slocan Valley and Upper

Arrow Lake chapter), and Powder King, near Prince George, a must-ski on British Columbia's powder circuit.

On weekends, the parking lot will likely have about three cars bearing Alberta plates for every one from British Columbia, as Fernie is well patronized by skiers from Calgary, a three-and-a-half-hour drive away. These savvy skiers have known about Fernie's bounty for years—photographers regularly descend after a major snowfall to take those great magazine cover shots.

The ski area rises about 3 miles (5 km) above the town of Fernie; you can see the massive bowls from Main St. Trails on the lower mountain cut through dense forest. Fifty named runs and countless other secret chutes and gullies drop a total of 2,400 vertical feet (730 m). Experts, intermediates, and novices can all get the chance to ski powder, since all levels of skier can utilize each lift.

Experts can follow North Ridge to the ultrasteep Boomerang Ridge, which offers heart-thumping glade skiing. Cedar Bowl is more open and less intimidating. Directly above the base lodge, Stag Leap, Decline, and Sky Dive provide knee-knocking mogul-skiing thrills. Backcountry skiers equipped with avalanche transceivers and other relevant safety equipment can traverse beyond the area boundary into bowls that are scheduled for future lift development. At this time, the runs here are unpatrolled and usually untracked.

For intermediates, the front face of the mountain offers great fall-line skiing on Power Trip and Lower Bear. The upper T-bar accesses several fine open runs to hone your powder-skiing technique. The novice trails near the bottom are vast, uncrowded, and well serviced by two lifts. Meandering runs like Meadow and Bambi won't strike fear into the hearts of too many skiers.

Fernie itself is more of a rough-and-tumble resource town than a typical ski resort. Après-ski action can get pretty wild at Buckaroos, especially when the powder hounds start howling. Now that Lake Louise owner Charlie Locke has bought the place, there's a major buzz that new lifts and on-mountain accommodation will follow in the next few years. For more **information,** contact Fernie Snow Valley Ski Area, (250) 423-4655, or visit their Web site: www.elkvalley.net/far. Fernie also features 9 miles (15 km) of groomed and track-set cross-country trails next to the resort.

The **Elkford Interpretive Trail** system has 25 miles (40 km) of cross-country trails. Maps are available at the Elkford InfoCentre right in town; call (250) 865-4362 for information. For maps and information on the many **forest recreation trails** suitable for cross-country skiing in the Cranbrook Forest District, call (250) 426-1700. A good book to consult is *Ski Trails in the Canadian Rockies* by Scott.

Horseback Riding

Elk Lakes Provincial Park, Akamina-Kishinena Provincial Recreation Area, and Height of the Rockies Provincial Park (see Hiking/Backpacking, above) all have great trails with unparalleled scenery. However, their ruggedness may make them better places to see on a horse rather than on foot! Rocky Mountain High Adventure in Sparwood can help you plan a horse-riding trip. Call them at (250) 423-7863. Other guide outfitters are easily located through BC Parks or a local Tourist InfoCentre (see More Information, below).

Canoeing/Kayaking

If you have the time, take a trip down the **Elk River** from Elkford to Elko, a weeklong journey of about 120 miles (193 km). There's excellent paddling throughout the East Kootenays, including the **Columbia and North and South Fraser drainages.** For a detailed account of these and other routes, consult *Canadian Rockies Whitewater* and *Canadian Rockies Whitewater/The Central Rockies* by Stuart Smith.

outside in

Attractions

Throughout British Columbia, diverse historic 19th-century forts have been preserved as reminders of how the west was settled by Europeans. **Fort Steele Heritage Town,** (250) 426-7352, near Cranbrook is undoubtedly the best example and is well worth a day's visit when travelling through the East Kootenays in summer months. (It's open from early May until the end of October.)

Restaurants and Lodgings

For recommended establishments, see Adjoining Areas to this chapter.

More Information

BC Forest Service: *(800) 331-7001 (from Vancouver only).*
BC Forest Service, Cranbrook Forest District: *(250) 426-1700.*
BC Forest Service, Invermere Forest District: *(250) 342-4200.*
BC Parks: Wasa Lake: *(250) 422-4200.*
Cranbrook Chamber of Commerce InfoCentre: *(250) 426-5414.*
Creston Chamber of Commerce InfoCentre: *(250) 428-4342.*

Elkford Chamber of Commerce InfoCentre: *(250) 865-4362.*
Fernie Chamber of Commerce InfoCentre: *(250) 423-6868.*
Fernie Snow Valley Ski Area: *(250) 423-4655.*
Kimberley Chamber of Commerce InfoCentre: *(250) 427-3666.*
Sparwood Chamber of Commerce InfoCentre: *(250) 425-2423.*

Columbia River Valley

From Cranbrook to Golden via Highway 93/95, following and including Columbia and Windermere Lakes, Fort Steele Heritage Town, Kootenay National Park, Mount Assiniboine and Whiteswan Lake Provincial Parks, the Purcell Wilderness Provincial Conservancy, Lussier Creek Hot Springs, and Panorama and Kimberley Ski Resorts.

The Rocky Mountain Trench (also known as the Columbia Valley) is surmounted by the Rocky Mountains on the east and the Bugaboos on the west. Both are impressively high and rugged ranges. Equally impressive is the Columbia River, which rolls through the southern part of the valley. The broad waterway is an important stopover on the semiannual migration route for wildlife and a joy to travel in any season.

Highway 93/95 links Cranbrook at the south end of the Columbia River Valley with Golden, about 140 miles (230 km) north. A steady stream of travellers pass through the region, but few are fortunate enough to make a home in this blessed setting. The land will sustain agriculture only at its south end, leaving vast tracts of wilderness for the enjoyment of those who love the outdoors. For additional adventure, explore the northeast section of Highway 93, which runs from Radium Hot Springs into Kootenay National Park.

Getting There

Highway 3 deposits travellers at its junction with Highway 93/95 in Cranbrook. The Trans-Canada Highway (Highway 1) does the same in Golden, where it meets Highway 95. Highways 93 and 95 part company in Radium Hot Springs. Highway 93 heads northeast to Alberta and meets the Trans-Canada at Banff, a distance of 65 miles (105 km).

Adjoining Areas

NORTH: **The Trans-Canada Highway**

SOUTH: **Crowsnest Highway: The East Kootenays**

WEST: **North Kootenay Lake and Selkirk Valleys**

Parks/Camping

Off the beaten path, **Norbury Lake Provincial Park** (46 vehicle/tent sites) is situated in the broad, rolling valley of the Rocky Mountain Trench, a remarkable feature extending north almost 750 miles (1210 km) from the US border through the Rockies and the Purcells. Not surprisingly, there's a spectacular view here of the Steeples (in the Hughes Range of the Rockies). The campsites are well spaced beside Norbury Lake. Nearby, Peckham's Lake offers good boating (self-propelled craft only) and swimming in summer. There aren't any winter facilities here, but cross-country skiing, ice fishing, and skating are all worth trying. For more information, contact BC Parks' Kootenay District Office, (250) 422-4200. From Cranbrook, Norbury Lake Provincial Park is about 24 miles (38 km) east; from Fort Steele, about 11 miles (17 km) southeast, off Hwy 93. The entrance is from Wardner–Fort Steele Rd.

Friendly **Wasa Lake Provincial Park** (104 vehicle/tent sites) sits at the northern end of Wasa Lake, one of the best recreational lakes in the East Kootenays (and one of the warmest in the province). The beaches here are very good, with sandy shores from which to launch car-top boats, and excellent swimming conditions. Two separate picnic/day-use areas are complemented by an amphitheatre and a self-guided nature trail. In winter, the cross-country ski trails are well groomed, and there's even a lit, maintained ice rink. For more information, call BC Parks, (250) 422-4200. For reservation at Wasa Lake Provincial Park, call the BC Parks reservation line, (800) 689-9025 between March 1 and September 15. Wasa is about a 13-mile (21-km) drive northeast from Kimberley via Hwys 95A/95 or north from Fort Steele on Hwy 93.

Thunder Hill Provincial Park (23 vehicle/tent sites) is a small, tucked-away roadside campground with spectacular views of Columbia Lake and the undulating terrain of the Rocky Mountain Trench. In the past, Kootenay Indians camped near this site and named it for the stormy natural phenomenon they experienced. Nearby are the remnants of the Thunder Hill mine tramway. For more information, call BC Parks, (250)

422-4200. Take Hwy 93/95 for 43 miles (69 km) north of Kimberley, just past Canal Flats.

Whiteswan Lake Provincial Park (88 vehicle/tent sites, 24 walk-in wilderness sites) is a favourite destination for anglers (see Fishing, below). Campsites are spread out among four locations in the park, primarily at **Alces Lake Campground, Packrat Point Campground,** and **Inlet Creek Campground,** all easily accessed from the Whiteswan Forest Rd. More sites are located at **Homebasin Campground,** reached via the Moscow Creek Forest Rd, which branches away from Whiteswan Forest Rd at the northwest corner of Whiteswan Lake. To reach the park, go south from Canal Flats on Hwy 93/95 to Whiteswan Forest Rd, then take Whiteswan Forest Rd about 12 miles (20 km) east. For more information, contact BC Parks, (250) 422-4200.

Kootenay National Park

Kootenay National Park blankets almost 350,000 acres (140 600 ha). Its lands were ceded to the federal government from British Columbia in 1919. In return, the federal government built the Banff-Windermere Rd (Hwy 93)—the first motor road through the Canadian Rockies. After severe construction difficulties, the road was completed in 1922; in 1952, it was rebuilt and repaved, and remains a favoured route for visitors.

Situated on the west side of the **Continental Divide,** Kootenay National Park extends across the valleys of the Vermilion and Kootenay Rivers, touches on the Rocky Mountain Trench at Radium Hot Springs, and straddles the Main and Western Ranges of the Rockies. Some of these peaks rise to 11,000 feet (3355 m). The 110°F (43°C) waters at Radium Hot Springs come out of the Redstreak breccia fault line, a unique area of red cliffs and shattered rocks, and, like most hot springs, these are well worth relaxing in. (You can also find mineral hot springs bubbling out of the canyon of Sinclair Creek.)

The park features three major campgrounds: the biggest one, **Redstreak Campground,** can only be approached from the south side of Radium Hot Springs, 2 miles (3 km) southeast of the park's western entrance at the junction of Hwy 93/95. There's a total of 242 sites; almost one-quarter of these include water, sewer, and electrical servicing—for a fee of about $13.50 per night. The 38 partially serviced (electricity included) sites are slightly cheaper, but the least expensive are the remaining unserviced sites. Prices here are in the $10 range. (All sites in the other two campgrounds are unserviced sites.) A 30-minute walking trail links the campground with Radium Hot Springs.

McLeod Meadows Campground (98 vehicle/tent sites) occupies a quiet, wooded area on the banks of the Kootenay River. The wildlife is plentiful; in early summer, it's a special treat to see the orchids bloom in the nearby meadows once the snow has melted. This campground is located 16 miles (26 km) north of Radium Hot Springs on Hwy 93. A dense subalpine forest is the setting for **Marble Canyon Campground** (61 vehicle/tent sites). It's 27 miles (43 km) north of McLeod (9 miles/ 14.5 km west of the park's east entrance).

Two major forest fires swept through the park this century, destroying more than 21,000 acres (8505 ha) and affecting the plant community. Glacial erosion has left fascinating patterns everywhere—cirques, moraines, hanging valleys, and more. Especially notable are deep cuts into the limestone at **Rockwall** and **Marble Canyons.** If you want the hottest and driest environment in the area, head south into the **Columbia** and **Lower Kootenay Valleys** and explore the forests. In the northern area around the **Upper Kootenay** and **Vermilion Valleys,** the summers are moderate and the winters severe. You'll find the alpine zone above 6,561 feet (2001 m) with its own beautiful flora. Some wetland communities have developed around ponds, beaver dams, and small lakes.

Wildlife is much in evidence. A band of Rocky Mountain bighorn sheep have their summer range near Radium Hot Springs; mountain goats can be spotted in the Mount Wardle area. Two words of warning about elk and bears: the elk population has grown, and in winter they migrate down the valley and congregate along the highway. Drive carefully. Ask for information on bears from an information officer or a warden: black bears are present throughout the park, and grizzlies frequent the avalanche slopes in the spring, digging for tender lily bulbs. (For proper bear etiquette, see General Introduction.)

Most of the park's waters are glacier-fed and are too cold to provide sufficient nutrients for fish growth; however, some of the lakes have been stocked, and you might try for whitefish and native dolly varden, or for stocked trout in the rivers.

Finally, on your rambles, you might justifiably feel a part of history. Archaeological evidence shows that the mountain passes and river valleys have been major trading routes for thousands of years for Natives, and **pictographs** near the hot springs suggest its role as a gathering place. Hudson's Bay Company traders also travelled through here.

Other facilities at the park include an aquacourt and fully developed pool area, picnic/rest stops along the highway, self-guided trails, warden stations and backcountry warden-patrol cabins, and more than 124 miles (200 km) of hiking and cross-country ski trails. Powerboats are not allowed anywhere in the park; other boating is permitted only on the Kootenay and Vermilion Rivers. (Note: Only experienced paddlers should attempt to canoe on the Kootenay.) For some activities, arrangements must be made in advance. Backcountry hikers, campers, and mountaineers require a park use **permit** from a park officer to make overnight trips. Registration is required at the park information office or with the warden for **group camping** at the **Dolly Varden Picnic Area,** for using the winter vehicle trails, and for winter camping and snowmobiling. Kootenay National Park is open year-round. The western entrance to the park is located in British Columbia at the junction of Hwys 93 and 95 in the town of Radium Hot Springs. Radium Hot Springs is located 64.5 miles (104 km) south of Golden and 88.5 miles (143 km) north of Cranbrook. The park's eastern entrance is located at Vermilion Pass in Alberta. For information, call Parks Canada, (250) 347-9505. From June to September contact the Kootenay National Park Information Centre, located at the western entrance to the park; (250) 347-9505.

If you can't get into **Kootenay National Park,** you might try **Dry Gulch Provincial Park** (25 vehicle/tent sites), just 5 miles (8 km) south of Radium Hot Springs on Hwy 93. Dry Gulch is frequently used as an overflow campground for the popular national park nearby. For more information, contact BC Parks, (250) 422-4200.

Hiking/Backpacking

Great hiking is available in **Kootenay National Park** (see Parks/Camping above). Two trails in particular are worth mentioning: **Floe Lake/Hawke Creek** (6 miles/10 km) leads west to a glacier-fed lake; **Stanley Glacier Trail** is a short, strenuous, 3-mile (5-km) hike that leads to a hanging valley and glacier.

There are many rewarding and beautiful hikes on the recreation trails throughout the **Revelstoke, Golden,** and **Invermere** Forest Districts. For a detailed map of trails and recreation sites in these areas, call the local BC Forest Service office (see More Information, below), or call toll free, (800) 665-1511.

Top of the World Provincial Park receives top marks as an alpine region of sublime beauty. Mount Morro (elevation 9,553 feet/2914 m) is the highest peak in the park. Many archaeological sites are located here, in what was once the traditional home of the Upper Kootenay First Nation. Forest cover is mostly spruce, pine, and some fir, and most of the plateau is carpeted with alpine flowers. Small populations of large mammals inhabit the park, and an abundance of birds live around **Fish Lake.** This lake is noted for its cutthroat trout and dolly varden fishery, but you must have a valid British Columbia fishing licence and a copy of the park's fishing regulations before casting a line. There are backcountry campsites available and rustic cabins. To arrange for their use, contact BC Parks at (250) 422-4200.

You'll find the access road to Top of the World Park on Hwy 93/95, just past Skookumchuk. Follow Sheep Creek Rd. It's very rough and not recommended for low-clearance vehicles. Alternatively, turn east off Hwy 93/95 about 3 miles (4.5 km) south of Canal Flats and travel southeast for about 32 miles (52 km) on the Whiteswan Forest Rd. Both routes are well marked.

Purcell Wilderness Provincial Conservancy is in a class of its own. Early in this century, Earl Grey, then Governor-General of Canada, crossed the Purcell Mountains from Invermere in the Columbia Valley to Argenta on Kootenay Lake. His route followed a trail up Toby Creek and down Hamill Creek over a 7,401-foot (2257 m) pass. This route, later named the **Earl Grey Pass Trail,** had already been well defined by the Shuswap Indians. Despite Grey's urging to set aside this magnificently scenic area as a park, not much was done until the 1970s, when the area was designated as a "roadless tract" in which the natural environment would remain undisturbed by any development. Consequently, there's no road access, and *all* forms of mechanized access are prohibited, including helicopters. Over 85 miles (137 km) of hiking trails, challenging mountaineering, horse riding, and winter recreation await backpackers in the five biogeoclimactic zones spread throughout this central portion of the **Purcell Mountains.** Use the western trailhead at Argenta on the northeast shore of Kootenay Lake (see North Kootenay Lake and Selkirk Valleys chapter), or **Toby Creek Trail** from Invermere on the east. For more information, including a detailed map of the Toby Creek Trail, call BC Parks, (250) 422-4200.

Bugaboo Glacier Provincial Park and Alpine Recreation Area is a first-class mountaineering region; its challenging peaks in the northern extremity of the Purcell Mountain Range have attracted climbers from around the world since the late 1880s. Particularly, the **North Howser "Tower"** and the **South Ridge of Bugaboo Spire** are considered very difficult. It's certainly breathtaking, but you shouldn't attempt to hike or climb this region unless you're experienced, well-equipped, and in good physical condition. The Bugaboos lie 28 miles (45 km) west of Hwy 95 at Brisco. There's good gravel road access, but the roads are used by logging trucks, so check with BC Parks, (250) 422-4200, regarding road use and condition before embarking.

Another park requiring experience and self-sufficiency, but offering many heavenly rewards, is **Mount Assiniboine Provincial Park,** located 30 miles (48 km) south of Banff and about 30 miles (50 km) northeast of Radium Hot Springs on the British Columbia–Alberta border. To get into the park you have to take one of four major hiking-access trails. Two of these originate in British Columbia. Most hikers take the **Lake Magog**

Trail (strenuous; 12 miles/20 km return) from Hwy 93 in Kootenay National Park (see Parks/Camping, above). The trailhead is located at the junction of the Simpson and Vermilion Rivers. An infrequently used route to Lake Magog leads about 9 miles (14 km) east from Hwy 93 along Settlers Rd in Kootenay National Park, then connects with the Cross River Forest Rd for another 15 miles (24.5 km) as it follows the **Cross** and **Mitchell Rivers.** Be particularly careful of mining trucks along the Mitchell River portion. From the trailhead beside an ore-mining operation the 18.5-mile (30-km) trail leads along the Mitchell River to Wedgewood Lake, and then Lake Magog. Visitors are strongly advised to pick up a park brochure and the National Topographic Series (NTS) map #82J/13 before going into the park. Once you're in the park, there are a number of trails to choose from, ranging in difficulty from easy to strenuous. There are also several undeveloped routes that lead to some of the most scenic areas in the park; ask a ranger for advice. Wilderness campgrounds, four alpine cabin shelters, a group-camping area plus other backcountry tent sites, climbing shelters, and ranger stations are available. For information, call BC Parks, (250) 422-4200.

Swimming

When you're swimming in **Canal Flats Provincial Park,** you're swimming in **Columbia Lake,** the source of the great Columbia River. The park sits on the south side of the lake, a short 2 miles (3 km) north of Canal Flats on Hwy 93/95.

The broad sandy beach at **James Chabot Provincial Park,** 2 miles (3 km) west of Hwy 93 at Invermere, attracts travellers searching for a pleasant, landscaped environment. The beach fronts **Windermere Lake.**

A short drive through **Kootenay National Park** (see Parks/Camping, above) east on Hwy 93 from Radium Hot Springs will bring you to several good picnic sites and swimming spots, including Sinclair Creek, Olive Lake, Kootenay River, Dolly Varden, Hector Gorge, Wardle Creek, Numa Falls, Paint Pots, Marble Canyon, and Tokumm Creek.

Lussier Hot Springs is located near the western boundary of Whiteswan Lake Provincial Park (see Parks/Camping, above). To find this delightful, undeveloped site, follow the signs from Hwy 93/95 near the town of Canal Flats to Whiteswan Lake Provincial Park, located about 13 miles (20 km) east of the highway on a rough road.

Wildlife

Wildlife is well represented and protected in this region, with opportunities for viewing wildlife not restricted to the **Purcell Wilderness Provincial**

Conservancy (see Hiking/Backpacking, above). The **Wasa Slough Wildlife Sanctuary** is certainly worth a visit and is easily located south of Wasa Lake along Hwy 93/95. Much of the roadside on Hwy 93/95 between Fort Steele and Wasa is wetland and provides resting, nesting, and feeding stops for large migratory birds such as **Canada geese, great blue herons, turkey vultures, ospreys, and eagles.**

More of these magnificent birds can be viewed at the **Columbia Wildlife Area,** a short drive west of Hwy 95 at Brisco. The **Great Blue Heron Rookery,** beside Hwy 95, 20 miles (30 km) north of Radium Hot Springs, is the second-largest colony of its kind in Western Canada.

Canada geese nesting platforms dot the marshier sections of the **Columbia River** on the 25-mile (40-km) stretch of Hwy 95 from Parson to Golden. Finally, **Animal Lick** beside Hwy 93 in **Kootenay National Park** is a natural salt lick, a big drawing card for ungulates.

Fishing

Fishing is the premier attraction at Premier Lake Provincial Park, located at the north end of Premier Ridge in the Hughes Range of the Rockies. **Premier Lake** and three other, smaller lakes offer great angling for trout—rainbow, eastern brook, and Gerrard rainbow (Gerrard giants). The Kootenay Fish Hatchery collects trout eggs from these lakes, and the Fish and Wildlife Branch has a fish trap here with an interpretive display. For more information, contact the Fish and Wildlife Conservation Officer in Invermere, (250) 342-4266, or Cranbrook InfoCentre, (250) 426-1464. Take Hwy 95 for 28 miles (45 km) northeast from Kimberley; access to the park is from Skookumchuk along a 9-mile (15-km) gravel road.

Abundant fish populations of **Whiteswan and Alces Lakes,** both wholly in Whiteswan Lake Provincial Park (see Parks/Camping, above), led to the establishment of this semi-wilderness park. Both lakes are managed for high-yield fisheries. Rainbow trout have been stocked in the lakes since 1961, with annual releases of about 30,000 fingerlings. Steps taken to make the fishery self-supporting include improvements to the spawning channel, prohibiting motorboats on Alces Lake, and restricting angling to fly-fishing only. Boat ramps are located at Whiteswan Lake beside the Packrat Point and Home Basin Campgrounds. Car-top boats can be launched at the Alces Lake Campground. To find the park, head 12 miles (20 km) east of Hwy 93/95, south of Canal Flats on a rough road.

Windermere Lake in Invermere has good trout fishing. You'll find a boat launch at James Chabot Provincial Park (see Swimming, above).

Scenic Drives

Where to start? The best way is to take a deep breath, and start driving. Watch for the **Dutch Creek Hoodoos** at the north end of Columbia Lake. The highway drives right past them. Nearby, Hwy 93/95 crosses the **headwaters of the Columbia River,** a river that flows from here to the Washington-Oregon border on the Pacific Ocean, a 1,200-mile (2000-km) journey.

The most overwhelming viewpoints in the East Kootenays are dotted along Hwy 93 between Radium Hot Springs and the British Columbia–Alberta border in **Kootenay National Park.** In fact, this entire stretch of highway is one big viewpoint. Standouts include the **Kootenay Valley Viewpoint,** about 9 miles (15 km) east of Radium Hot Springs on Hwy 93, the **Hector Gorge Viewpoint,** 29 miles (46 km) east of Radium on Hwy 93, and the main event, the Continental Divide, about 60 miles (95 km) east of Radium Hot Springs at the British Columbia–Alberta border. Simply put, with scenery like this, it should be illegal *not* to stop in the Columbia Valley north of Invermere.

Biking

For an easy, scenic ride, **West Side Road** is perfect. It's more than 16 miles (26 km) of paved road running along the west side of **Windermere Lake.** The road starts just north of Columbia Lake on Hwy 93/95 and heads north to Invermere.

Take Toby Creek Rd west out of Invermere to explore the **Panorama Resort** trails (see Skiing/Snowboarding, below).

Skiing/Snowboarding

There are three commercial winter areas in this region. **Fairmont Hot Springs Resort Ski Hills** has limited downhill skiing and snowboarding, with a vertical rise of about 985 feet (300 m), serviced by a T-bar and rope tow. In addition, there are about 12 miles (20 km) of groomed cross-country trail. Call (250) 345-6311 for more information. The resort is located on Hwy 93/95 in the town of Fairmont Hot Springs.

In a province of great, relatively unknown ski resorts, no place in British Columbia is as underrated or overlooked as **Panorama Ski Resort.** Because of its remote location in the Purcell Mountains, Panorama is more of a mountain retreat. Bed capacity at the resort is 1,500, while the mountain can comfortably handle 7,000 day-skiers.

Panorama has all the trappings of a tremendous destination resort: walk-to-lifts accommodation, high-speed quad chairlifts, and a relatively easy international gateway airport (Calgary, in this instance, about 300 miles/500 km away). The resort is owned and managed by the highly respected Intrawest Corporation (which has done wonders with Whistler/ Blackcomb in southwestern British Columbia and Mont Tremblant in Quebec), and customer service is generally excellent. There are even several outdoor hot tubs located right at the base of the lifts, in which you can soak your weary bones after a day on the slopes.

Then there's the mountain itself. With 4,300 vertical feet (1320 m) of skiing, Panorama is one massive piece of work. This is a mountain on which you can really find space to spread out; at the most, only 3,000 skiers and boarders show up on a busy day. The runs provide enough length and steepness to regularly host World Cup downhill races.

Starting from the top, Panorama's summit is just above tree line, reached via two T-bars. This is Panorama's Extreme Dream Zone, where expert skiers and snowboarders can plunge down gladed runs blanketed in dry, fluffy powder. In places such as Hopeful Sun Bowl and the bottom of the cliff band on Extreme Dream, the terrain opens up, providing dozens of untracked turns before picking up a cat-track back to the main core of the mountain. Panorama's terrain flattens considerably on the mountain's lower flanks, which provide ideal cruising runs on which you'll seldom encounter another rider. In fact, most of Panorama's more than 60 trails lean to novice/intermediate runs. All runs lead to a common base area, so there's little likelihood of getting lost.

Skiers looking to improve their form need go no farther than Panorama's famous **ski school,** managed by the husband-and-wife team of Don and Heather Bilodeau, two of Canada's top instructors. And there's great **cross-country skiing** on a network of 19 miles (30 km) of trails that winds its way through the woods at the base of the mountain.

Panorama Ski Resort is located in the Toby Creek Valley, a tributary of the mighty Columbia River, 11 miles (17 km) west of Invermere on Toby Creek Rd. The nearby towns of Invermere and Radium Hot Springs provide additional accommodation. For **information** on Panorama, call (250) 342-6941 or (800) 663-2929, or visit their Web site: www.panoramaresort.com.

At **Kimberley Ski and Summer Resort,** you relax on a bench in the Bavarian Platzl, sipping a cold Warsteiner. The accordion player serenades passing pedestrians as the pungent smell of bratwurst and sauerkraut fills your nostrils, its scent mingling with the crisply invigorating mountain air. With Teutonic precision, a Happy Hans figurine emerges from a cuckoo clock and marks the passing of another hour.

No, you're not in a hamlet in the Black Forest, but rather the funky mountain town of Kimberley, about 20 miles (32 km) northwest of Cranbrook on Hwy 95A. Two decades ago, this mining town decided to stake a tourism claim and undertook an ambitious Bavarian-style face lift of its downtown.

Kimberley's long, sunny, south-facing ridge offers a respectable 2,300-foot (700-m) vertical drop and 43 tree-lined runs and glades. The nearby mountains were once staked for mining claims, a history reflected in the names of the runs.

Experts will head to the Easter triple-chair and hop through the moguls under the lift line. There's great groomed cruising on Flapper, while powder-hounding tree riders will love Flush. For more adventure, take the Ridgeway traverse to precipitous thrills and spills on Magma, Twist, Maverick, and Vortex. These are the best places to powder ski after a storm.To the skier's right off the Rosa chair, a galaxy of well-groomed intermediate runs awaits on Telegraph Line, Dreadnought, and Rosa. The nearby Buckhorn chair takes you to sweeping, undulating challenges on Utopia, Stemwinder, and Twilight. Expert skiers will find double–black diamond steep shots through the trees on Jack the Bear, Quantrell, and White Pine. Novices can enjoy the broad boulevard of fall-line cruising on Main run (reached via the Rosa triple). Kimberley also boasts **night skiing and snowboarding** on some of the longest illuminated runs in North America. Located about 2.5 miles (4 km) from the centre of town, the resort's challenging runs and friendly local ambience draw skiers and snowboarders of all abilities. For information on Kimberley Ski Resort, call (250) 427-4881, or visit their Web site: www.Kimberleyski.infopages.com.

In addition to the downhill runs, there is also a 16-mile (26-km) network of groomed and track-set **cross-country ski** trails suited to all ability levels. The trailhead is located directly across from the Kirkwood Inn in Kimberley. A 2-mile (3-km) loop is lit for night skiing.

Windsurfing

Windsurfing can be an especially *elevating* experience when it takes place between the towering peaks of the Rockies and the serrated ridges of the Purcells. **Windermere Lake** is the place to go for this serene activity. Launch from the wide, sandy beach in **James Chabot Provincial Park** (see Swimming, above) in Invermere where strong winds arise with regularity on summer afternoons.

Nearby at **Canal Flats Provincial Park** (see Swimming, above), windsurfers can breeze along on Columbia Lake, getting a head start on the same waters that eventually flow through the Columbia River Gorge in Oregon, one of the preeminent windsurfing spots on the continent.

Attractions

Like many foundering mining towns in the early 1970s, **Kimberley** looked to tourism to bolster a faltering economy. At 4,000 feet (1200 m), Kimberley is the highest incorporated city in Canada. Views of the snow-capped Rocky Mountains are stunning, especially from the Kimberley Ski Resort (see Skiing/Snowboarding, above).

The town was named in 1896 after Kimberley, South Africa, because of a rich outcrop of minerals at the Sullivan Mine. Now owned by Cominco Ltd., Sullivan Mine is one of the largest **lead, zinc, and silver mines** in the world. It once employed 1,200 people; now half that many work there (the town's population is 6,700). The mountainside was initially mined as an open pit, and even though the pit has been filled in, it remains an ugly scar. Ore is now mined 2 miles (3.2 km) deep in the mountain and carried by railcar to the Cominco smelter in Trail. Gardeners shouldn't miss the teahouse, greenhouse, and immaculately kept **gardens,** once maintained by Cominco and now under the care of the city, on the grounds of the Kimberley District Hospital.

The Heritage Museum, 105 Spokane St, (250) 427-7510, has an excellent display of the town's mining history and memorabilia, such as hockey equipment from the town team that won the World Senior Amateur Hockey Championships in 1937. Accordion music is played on loudspeakers at the centre of the **Bavarian Platzl** (the town's three-block walking street). For a quarter, a yodeling puppet pops out of the upper window of Canada's largest cuckoo clock. For a nice selection of regional books, try Bookends, 100 Deer Park Ave, (250) 427-2500. The Bauerhaus Restaurant, 280 Norton Ave, (250) 427-5133, has an outstanding view of the mountains; however, the well-regarded restaurant, dismantled in Austria and reconstructed here, is open only during ski season and at the height of summer.

The town of **Radium Hot Springs** is little more than a support system for area vacation developments—gas stations, a couple of cafes, and a string of motels that grow denser as they near Radium Hot Springs. But people don't come here for the town; it's within the boundaries of Kootenay National Park (see Inside Out, above), which has the same mountain peaks and glaciers as Alberta's more famous Banff National Park.

Radium Hot Springs (the actual springs), on Hwy 93, 2 miles (3 km) from Radium Junction, (250) 347-9485, makes an ideal soaking stop at the base of the Kootenay Mountain Range. The **hot springs,** open to the public year-round, are equipped with two pools: one heated, the other cooler for more athletic swimming. Unlike some hot springs, these waters are free of odorous sulphur. The water temperature varies with the season; in spring, the snowmelt cools the thermally heated springs. Those staying in Kootenay or Banff National Park overnight need to stop at the park entrance and pay a use fee. (Bring the receipt into the hot springs resort; a $1 user fee is charged at the hot springs in addition to the entrance fees for those not staying in the park.) If you didn't pack your bathing suit, don't worry; they'll rent you one for a buck and a half.

Restaurants

Chef Bernard's Kitchen ☆ Originally a fresh-pasta eatery, Chef Bernard's also dishes up Louisiana specialties such as blackened catfish fillet and Gulf shrimp étouffée. The steaks are named for celebrities, but the fresh pasta's the thing here. *170 Spokane St (on Bavarian Platzl), Kimberley; (250) 427-4820; $$.*

The Snowdrift Cafe The local hangout for the young sporting crowd, this small eatery boasts plenty of healthful foods: homemade whole-wheat bread, vegetarian chili, spinach and caesar salads, and a good carbo-loading lasagne for skiers and cyclers. *110 Spokane St (on Bavarian Platzl), Kimberley; (250) 427-2001; $.*

Strand's Old House ☆☆ This 1912 house has been converted to an idyllic setting for fine dining. Everything is made from scratch, right down to the mayonnaise served with the steamed artichokes. Regional wines and beers and occasional evenings of live music add gusto. *818 12th St (in middle of town), Invermere; (250) 342-6344; $$.*

Lodgings

Inn West/Kirkwood Inn ☆ Three miles (5 km) from Kimberley, adjacent to the ski and summer resort, is the Inn West/Kirkwood Inn. There are hotel rooms, but we suggest opting for one of the condos instead, which have kitchens and fireplaces. *840 North Star Dr (at top of hill at Kimberley Ski Resort); PO Box 247, Kimberley, BC V1A 2Y6; (250) 427-7616 or (800) 663-4755; $$$.*

Panorama Resort ☆ More than a resort, Panorama is its own village—a sprawling establishment in the Purcell Mountains that contains a ski area, condos, a hotel, lots of restaurants and nightspots, and outdoor recreation. *11 miles (18 km) west of Invermere on Toby Creek Rd; PO Box 7000, Invermere, BC V0A 1T0; (250) 342-6941 or (800) 663-2929; $$.*

Springs at Radium Golf Resort ☆☆ Golf is the show at this resort—nearly all the rooms look out onto fairways or greens of the two 18-hole courses. The resort has 118 rooms, some of which are two-bedroom condos. Tennis, squash, raquetball, and a swimming pool are also offered. *South of Radium Hot Springs on Hwy 93; Box 310, Radium Hot Springs, BC V0A 1M0; (250) 347-9311 or (800) 665-3585; $$$.*

Storm Mountain Lodge ☆☆ Located on Vermilion Pass, the lodge was built in 1922 by the Canadian Pacific Railway. It's rustic, but loaded with alpine lodge ambience. Each of the single-room cabins has a fireplace and bathroom with shower. Fifty miles (80 km) of hiking trails are nearby. *At Vermilion Pass on Hwy 93; PO Box 670, Banff, AB T0L 0C0; (403) 762-4155; $$$.*

Cheaper Sleeps

Mountain Edge Resort Inn Though they're down the hill from the Kimberley Ski Resort, these one-bedroom condos are still within a hardy walking distance of the lifts. Some units have views of the Rockies; all condos have kitchen facilities. *930 Dogwood Dr (PO Box 98), Kimberley, BC V1A 2Y5; (250) 427-5381 or (800) 525-6622; $.*

More Information

BC Forest Service, Invermere Forest District: *(250) 342-4200.*
BC Forest Service, Revelstoke and Golden Forest District: *(250) 837-7611.*
BC Parks, Kootenay District, Wasa Lake: *(250) 422-4200; reservations, (800) 689-9025.*
Columbia Valley Chamber of Commerce InfoCentre: *(250) 342-6316 (seasonal); (250) 342-2844.*
Cranbrook InfoCentre: *(250) 489-5261 or (250) 426-5914.*
Golden InfoCentre: *(250) 344-7125.*
Invermere InfoCentre: *(250) 342-6316 or (250) 342-2844 (seasonal).*
Kimberley InfoCentre: *(250) 427-3666.*
Parks Canada: *(250) 347-9505.*
Radium Hot Springs InfoCentre: *(250) 347-9331.*

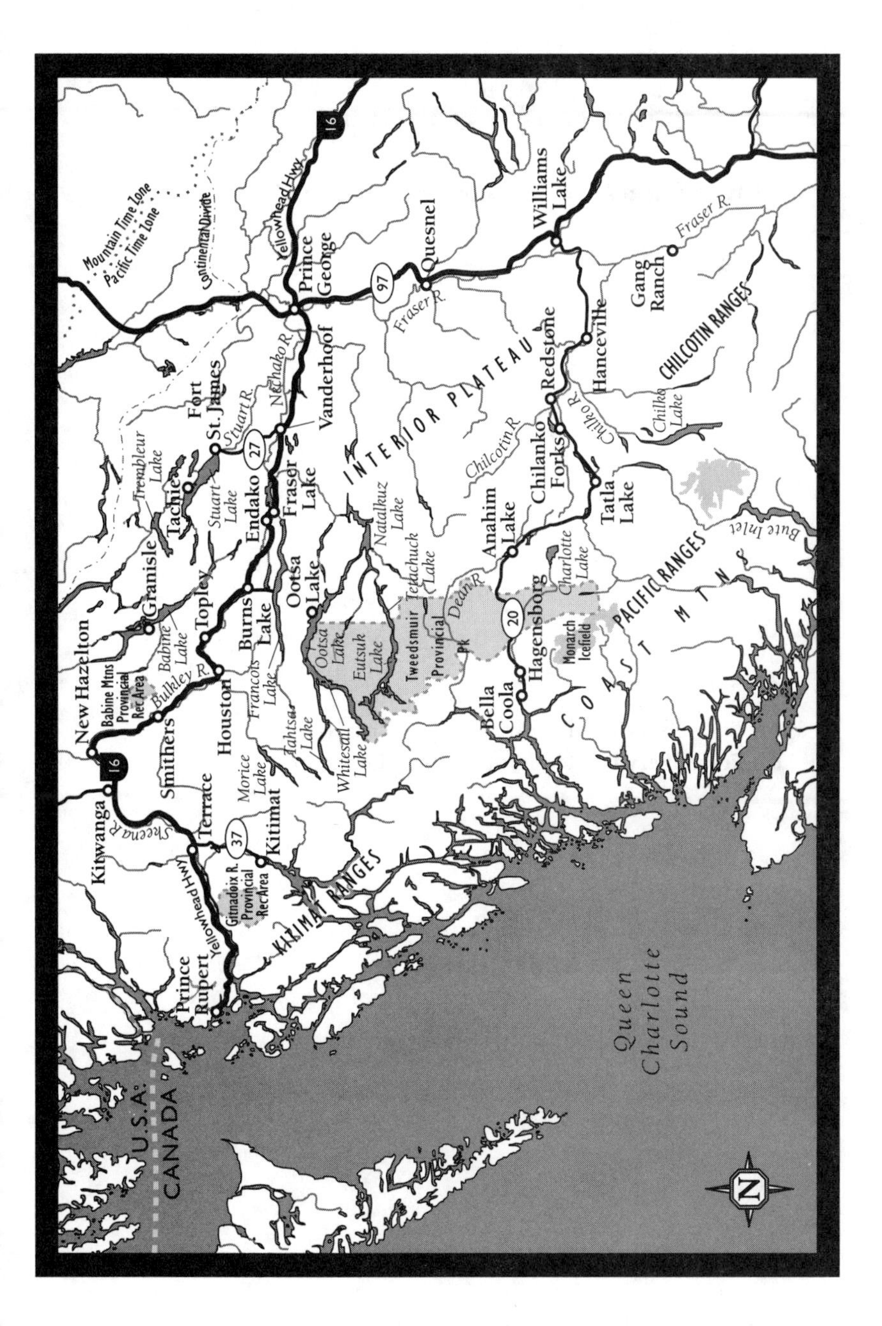

Northwest Interior

The Bella Coola Road (Highway 20) 545

The Bulkley and Skeena River Valleys 560

Fraser Plateau 572

Northwest Interior

The Bella Coola Road (Highway 20)

Highway 20 runs for 283 miles (456 km) from Bella Coola to Williams Lake, linking the Central Coast with the Central Interior as it crosses the Coast Mountains and the Chilcotin Plateau, including Tweedsmuir Provincial Park and Farwell Canyon.

Highway 20, also known as the Bella Coola Road, passes through diverse landscapes ranging from grassy plateaus and rolling meadows to picturesque canyons and high mountain peaks. The portion of the highway over Heckman Pass was completed only in August 1953—by the residents of Bella Coola themselves. They gained road access to the Chilcotin Plateau and Williams Lake and a newfound freedom; hence, the route's other nickname, the Freedom Highway.

Bella Coola (population 2,500) marks the western terminus of Alexander Mackenzie's trek across Canada in 1793, the first crossing of the country by land. Long the home of the Nuxalk people, the Bella Coola Valley became a route to the Cariboo gold fields in 1858, the location of a Hudson's Bay Trading Post in 1867, and a home for Norwegian colonists from Minnesota, who settled in nearby Hagensborg, in 1894. The colonists chose the area because the landscape reminded them of their homeland. Farming, lumber, and fishing industries began shortly after.

The Bella Coola Valley is of archaeological and historical significance in that it was a trade corridor between coastal and interior Native groups. The river had several villages along its length. Furs and leather were exchanged for salmon and eulachon grease, and were transported along what were called the "grease" trails. (You can still see, though you might not want to smell, the herring-sized eulachon being rendered into oil by the local Nuxalks at the right time of year.) Remnants of precontact Native culture include the site of Friendly Village, visited by Sir Alexander Mackenzie in 1793, pictographs near Big Rock, a burial ground and smokehouse near Stuie, and aboriginal trade trails. There are also obsidian quarries on Tsitsutl Peak.

Tweedsmuir Provincial Park and Recreation Area, at over 2.2 million acres (895 000 ha) one of British Columbia's biggest parks, is most easily accessed from Highway 20, which bisects the southern half of the park east of Bella Coola. Established in 1938 and since enlarged, it is named for the 15th Governor-General of Canada, John Buchan, Baron Tweedsmuir of Elsfield, who travelled extensively throughout the park in 1937 and was greatly impressed by its magnificence.

Roughly triangular in shape, **Tweedsmuir Provincial Park** is bounded on the north and northwest by the Ootsa-Whitesail Lakes Reservoir, on the west and southwest by the Coast Mountains, and on the east by the Interior Plateau. The park encompasses an astounding diversity of landscapes and conditions. Because access, facilities, and activities differ from north to south, the park is divided into two sections, with the Dean River acting as a natural boundary between the north and south. For information about the northern section of Tweedsmuir Provincial Park, see Fraser Plateau chapter.

Tweedsmuir Park South comprises many natural history features, as well as some incredibly diverse landscapes in the Coast Mountains and Interior Plateau regions. The Interior Plateau (which includes the Fraser, Chilcotin, and Nechako Plateaus), in the eastern portion of the park, is a rolling and hilly landscape. Within the park, the plateau is warped sharply upward to more than 6,560 feet (2000 m) and is largely covered with glacial drift. East of the park near Anahim Lake, the Interior Plateau abruptly gives way, at an elevation of about 4,430 feet (1350 m), to peaks of the Rainbow Range. The peaks of the Rainbow Range—Tsitsutl in the local dialect, meaning "painted mountains"—form an enormous dome of eroded lava and fragmented rock that presents an astonishing spectrum of reds, oranges, yellows, and lavenders. Contrasting with the vivid colouration and gentler slopes of the Rainbow Range are the higher and more rugged Coast Mountains. Vast glaciers sculpted these granite giants, leaving behind serrated peaks that are still being eroded by the alpine ice. A special feature in the upper Atnarko watershed is the magnificent Hunlen Falls, with its 853-foot (260-m) single drop over a sheer rock face. It is one of the highest waterfalls in Canada.

Four biogeoclimatic zones lie within the southern half of Tweedsmuir: alpine tundra, Engelmann spruce/subalpine fir, sub-boreal spruce, and coastal western hemlock. From the east, travellers on Highway 20 pass through the lower reaches of the Englemann spruce/subalpine fir zone in Heckman Pass (elevation 5,000 feet/1525 m) at the park's eastern boundary, about 223 miles (360 km) west of Williams Lake. The road drops quickly down the Bella Coola Hill, passing through dry lodgepole pine stands on Young Creek Hill to reach the Atnarko Valley, with its fir and cedar forests.

The low-lying Atnarko and Bella Coola Valleys have a more coastal climate and vegetation. Towering specimens of coastal hemlock, western red cedar, and some remnant Douglas fir, as well as a great deal of black cottonwood on the valley floors, thrive in forests carpeted with giant sword ferns and tangles of huckleberries, blueberries, raspberries, wild roses, thimbleberries, salmonberries, wild lilies, and orchids, to name but a few of the many plant species found here.

With all those berries, it's no wonder there are many bears. Both grizzly and black bears occupy the Atnarko and Bella Coola Valleys. In autumn they congregate along riverbanks to feast during the annual salmon spawning migrations.

Although you'll find cowboy boots and Stetson hats to be standard issue in many parts of the province, from Surrey in the Lower Mainland to Dawson Creek in the Northeast, the Chilcotin Plateau east of the Bella Coola Valley can rightfully claim to be the true bastion of the range rider in British Columbia. Very few of the roads are paved, restricting access to only the most adventuresome and savvy map readers. Vast expanses of the Chilcotin are worked by large outfits such as the Gang Ranch, at one time the largest ranch in North America with over 1 million acres (400 000 ha). The ranch epitomizes the spirit of this isolated region. Wherever you stop along the Bella Coola Road, there's always a pot of (mostly free) coffee brewing.

Getting There

BC Ferries' Discovery Coast Passage route from Port Hardy on the northeastern tip of Vancouver Island deposits and picks up travellers at Bella Coola. If you are trying to decide which approach to take, common wisdom has it that the north-south ferry route is preferable. The Queen of Chilliwack *sails from Bella Coola in the early morning, offering daylight views of the picturesque Dean Channel and a stop at Ocean Falls. Highway 97 links with Highway 20 at Williams Lake, which is 148 miles (238 km) south of Prince George and 126 miles (203 km) north of Cache Creek and Highway 1. Highway 20 is paved in sections, good gravel in others. The notorious stretch east of Bella Coola, known locally as "the Hill," is 27 miles (43 km) of steep, narrow road with sharp hairpin turns and two major switchbacks as the highway descends from the Chilcotin Plateau. Definitely not for drivers who suffer from a fear of heights, the Hill has a 5.6-mile (9-km) stretch of up to 18-percent grade. Westbound drivers towing heavy loads may wish to leave their trailers in the parking lot at the top of the Hill. Safety measures include using low gear on steep sections and stopping several times to allow your vehicle's brakes to cool. Information on highway conditions is available 24 hours a day from the BC Ministry of Transportation and Highways, (604) 660-9770.*

Adjoining Areas

NORTH: **Fraser Plateau**

EAST: **The Cariboo Highway**

WEST: **Inside Passage and Discovery Coast**

SOUTH: **Pemberton and Lillooet**

inside out

Guides and Outfitters

Due to the wild nature of this region, visitors who wish to get off the beaten track but lack backcountry experience would do well to hire a guide. In Anahim Lake, a Native community 61 miles (98 km) west of Williams Lake, contact local guides through the Tsilhqot'in National Government Office, (250) 392-3918. Tweedsmuir Air Services Ltd., (800) 668-4335, based in Nimpo Lake, offers canoe and cabin rentals at Tweedsmuir Wilderness Camp, Turner Lake; floatplane flights to Turner Lake; and sightseeing flights to the massive Monarch Icefield in the Coast Mountains just west of Tweedsmuir Provincial Park's southwestern border. Wayco Aviation Ltd., (800) 928-7688, also at Nimpo Lake (in the summer), offers customized adventures in the region. In Tatla Lake, information on exploring the region by floatplane is available at West Chilcotin Trading, (250) 476-1111. Guide services are also available from the Chilko Lake Resort, (250) 481-3333; the River Ridge Resort, (250) 398-7755; the Elkin Creek Guest Ranch in a Nemaiah Valley, (604) 984-4666; and Bracewells Alpine Wilderness Adventures, (250) 476-1169. Dream Factory Adventures, (800) 707-3363, located at Glacier View Resort east of Hagensborg, offers guided trips of the Alexander Mackenzie Heritage Trail as well as other land and sea adventures.

Hiking/Backpacking

Southwest of Bella Coola on Hwy 20, the **McGurr Lake Trail** (easy; just over 0.5 mile/1 km) offers access to local mountain hikes with spectacular views of the Coast Mountain ranges and fjords. Nearby, the **Gray Jay Lake Trail** crosses some sensitive wetland habitat on its way to a scenic viewpoint of local fjords.

The **Snooka Creek Trail,** developed by the BC Forest Service, is an easy to moderately challenging trail between Bella Coola and Hagensborg that accommodates hikers, mountain bikers, and horseback riders. It consists of two loops and one linear trail named (respectively) Snooka East Loop (easy; 3.5 miles/5.5 km), Snooka South Loop (moderate; 1 mile/1.7 km), and Snooka West (moderate; 4.7 miles/7.5 km return). To reach the trailhead, turn south off Hwy 20 across from the "Barb's Pottery" sign on the north side of the highway and drive for just over 0.5 mile (1 km) on the gravel Snooka Creek Forest Service Rd to the parking lot. For further details, contact the Forest Service's Mid Coast Forest District Office, (250) 982-2000.

Three miles (5 km) east of Hagensborg and about 12 miles (20 km) south of Hwy 20, **Odegaard Falls** is a fine destination for picnics or hiking. The turnoff is immediately west of the Nusatsum River Bridge, and the rough access road, with four short steep sections, takes about 40 minutes to drive under good conditions. The major attraction of this Forest Service recreation site is the outstanding view of the falls, which cascade about 600 feet (200 m) down into the East Nusatsum Valley. The Odegaard Glacier that feeds the creek is visible well above the timberline, at the head of the east fork of the Nusatsum River.

The **Odegaard Falls Trail** (easy; 2.4 miles/4 km return) begins at the nearby Nusatsum River Recreation Site about 0.5 mile (1 km) south, where you can watch the Nusatsum River flowing down a steep, narrow canyon. After snaking through beautiful hemlock, cedar, and balsam forests for 30 minutes, you'll begin a moderate, steady climb up to the falls. The last 900 feet (300 m) of the trail can be muddy and slippery when wet. There are also a number of small creek crossings.

South of the Nusatsum River Recreation Site is the **Ape Lake Trail.** Only 3.7 miles (6 km) of this planned 13.6-mile (22-km) trail have been developed so far. The trail now ends at a viewpoint of rugged ice-capped mountains averaging 8,000 feet (2500 m) in elevation.

The **Saloompt Forest Interpretive Trail** (easy; about 0.5 mile/1 km) north of Hwy 20 at Hagensborg takes you to an old-growth forest and riverside walk, with views of the local valley. A bit farther east, the **Lost Lake Trail** (easy; 0.5 mile/1 km) travels through an old-growth forest, up some moderately steep terrain, and ends at a small lake with a view of the

Bella Coola Valley. East of the Noosgulch River on Hwy 20, the **Capoose Summer Trail** (strenuous; 28 miles/45 km return) connects to the Alexander Mackenzie Heritage Trail. The Capoose Summer Trail has some steep and winding sections but can be completed by foot or on horseback. For a brochure/map showing these trails, contact the Forest Service's Mid Coast Forest District Office, (250) 982-2000.

Hikers with a historical bent would appreciate tackling some or all of the Alexander Mackenzie Heritage Trail, which stretches a full 260 miles (420 km) from the mouth of the West Road (Blackwater) River between Prince George and Quesnel to the Sir Alexander Mackenzie Provincial Park in Dean Channel west of Bella Coola. The trail's hiking terminus is at **Burnt Bridge Creek,** adjacent to the western boundary of Tweedsmuir Provincial Park, where it is intersected by Hwy 20.

Designated as the first heritage trail in British Columbia in 1985, the Alexander Mackenzie Heritage Trail is gaining international recognition among hikers who wish to make a three-week trip along this historic route. The trail includes local wagon roads, provincial highways, forest access roads, rivers, and coastal waterways. Approximately 186 miles (300 km) of this corridor is recreational trail, and about 62 miles (100 km) is well-preserved aboriginal footpath. The 50-mile (80-km) stretch of the trail in Tweedsmuir Provincial Park, which takes five to seven days to travel, is perhaps the most scenic of the entire route. A short section of the trail that offers views of the Bella Coola Valley and south to Stupendous Mountain can be reached in a one- to two-hour loop from Burnt Bridge Creek.

The heritage trail spans an area traditionally occupied by three culturally distinct Native groups: the Nuxalk people of the Bella Coola Valley, an enclave of the Salishan linguistic group; the Heiltsuk people of Waglisla (Bella Bella) and the Outer Coast, members of the Wakashan linguistic group; and the Southern Carrier people of the Interior Plateau, members of the Athapaskan linguistic group. There are a number of prehistoric cultural sites along the trail. Several are at Bella Coola and in Tweedsmuir Provincial Park, and about eight are located in the Upper and Lower Blackwater River areas. Portions of the trail itself have been in use for thousands of years.

The trail follows the route of Alexander Mackenzie, who trekked overland and by canoe from Lake Athabaska in 1793 on behalf of the North West Company in search of a trade route to the Pacific. His journey took him 72 days and covered over 1,240 miles (2000 km) of unmapped terrain. When he reached his westernmost terminus he painted a memorial to his labours on what is now called Mackenzie's Rock in the small provincial park named after him in Dean Channel (see Inside Passage and Discovery Coast chapter).

Since portions of this trail may be on or near private property (including Native reserves), trekkers should check with the BC Parks district office, 181 First Ave N in Williams Lake, (250) 398-4414, regarding access. Staff there can also supply information on current maps, local conditions, and available guides. An excellent 200-page trail guide ($18) as well as informative free brochures describing short walks from road-accessible trailheads are available from the **Alexander Mackenzie Trail Association,** PO Box 425, Station A, Kelowna, BC V1Y 7P1; (250) 762-4241.

West of Tweedsmuir Provincial Park's headquarters on Hwy 20 (just west of the sani-station at Mosher Creek) is the start of the **Tweedsmuir Trail,** which leads north about 22 miles (35 km) to the Rainbow Cabin on the Alexander Mackenzie Heritage Trail. The Tweedsmuir Trail can also lead you to the Rainbow Range. The **Hunlen Falls/Turner Lakes Trail** (strenuous; 36 miles/58 km return) along the Atnarko River begins at the Young Creek picnic site east of park headquarters. This trail passes through prime grizzly bear habitat, and hikers should use caution at all times. Hiking alone is not recommended. As always, be bear aware and avoid confrontations with these wild creatures (see General Introduction). Hikers should allow 10 to 12 hours to reach the north end of Turner Lake, where there is a primitive campground. West of Hunlen Falls, there is good alpine hiking along the **Ptarmigan Lake Trail** (moderate; 15 miles/24 km return), which ascends to Panorama Ridge. To the east is **Lonesome Lake** (19 miles/31 km from Young Creek), made famous by writer Ralph Edwards, who homesteaded here in 1912. His descendants still live in the area and operate the nearby Hunlen Wilderness Camp. The **Junker Lake Trail** (moderate; 13 miles/21 km return) starts at the north end of Turner Lake. Rolling pine flats and forest meadows make for an easy hike that leads to a delightful sandy beach on Junker Lake.

The **Rainbow Range Trail** (easy; 10 miles/16 km return) heads north from Hwy 20 near the park's eastern boundary, leading to an alpine environment. The trail starts in a lodgepole pine forest and climbs through stands of whitebark pine and alpine fir to a small alpine lake, offering an excellent viewpoint of the multihued Rainbow Range. Other trails in the area include the **Octopus Lake Trail** (moderate; 20 miles/32 km return), the **Crystal Lake Trail** (moderate; 31 miles/50 km return), and the **Capoose Trail** (moderate; 17.5 miles/28 km return). For information about these and other trails in Tweedsmuir Provincial Park, contact BC Parks in Williams Lake, (250) 398-4414, or stop at the park headquarters. Hikers should also consult *Hikes in Tweedsmuir South Provincial Park* by Scott Whittemore.

Itcha Ilgachuz Provincial Park is a new, roadless wilderness area north of Anahim Lake. The trailhead for this park is reached by travelling about 11 miles (18 km) north of Anahim Lake on Lessard Lake Rd, then about 40 miles (64 km) on a so-so gravel road (check conditions beforehand with BC Parks in Williams Lake, (250) 398-4414). Anahim Lake, where Hwy 20 starts its descent to the coast, is 86 miles (139 km) east of Bella Coola and 61 miles (98 km) west of Williams Lake.

In **Ts'yl-os** (pronounced sigh-loss) **Provincial Park** (see Camping, below), experienced hikers can undertake a four- to six-day loop trek through the **Yohetta Valley, Spectrum Pass,** and **Tchaikazan Valley.** The easiest approach is from the Tchaikazan trailhead. To reach the trailhead, turn south at Elkin Creek about 60 miles (100 km) southwest of Hanceville on Hwy 20. An alternative approach is via Chilko Lake and the Rainbow Creek Trail, which connects with the Yohetta-Spectrum-Tchaikazan Trail, a difficult 3-hour, 4-mile (6.5-km) hike. Boat service to the Rainbow Creek trailhead at the south end of Chilko Lake is available from the Xeni Gwet'in community in Nemaiah Valley, (250) 481-1149. Contact Larry Rudd, who will arrange drop-off and pick-up times and keep tabs on overdue hikers. To reach him, dial "0" and ask the operator for the radio phone operator in Prince George. Rudd's radio phone number is H422749 on the YJ Alexis Creek channel.

Also in the park at the north end of Chilko Lake, the well-marked **Tullin Mountain Trail** (easy; 7.5 miles/12 km return) starts at the Gwa Da Ts'ih campground. This excellent day hike has an elevation gain of 2,400 feet (730 m). Note: Since Ts'yl-os is a wilderness park with limited services, all hikers should be experienced in the backcountry and well equipped for route finding, first aid, and survival situations. The chance of encountering grizzly bears is much higher in Ts'yl-os Park than elsewhere in this region. Be bear aware. (See General Introduction for more information.) Topographic maps to consult are 92J/13, 92K/16, 92N/9, and 92O/12. For more information and a detailed map, contact BC Parks, (250) 398-4414, or stop by 281 First Ave N in Williams Lake.

There are also trails at **Puntzi Lake,** just over 4 miles (7 km) north of Hwy 20, about 35 miles (60 km) west of Alexis Creek, and hikers can explore the badlands of the Chilcotin Plateau on trails in the vicinity of **Farwell Canyon** (see Scenic Drives/Picnics, below).

Camping

Forest Service campsites located close to Bella Coola include those at **Odegaard Falls** and **Nusatsum River** (2 and 4 rustic sites, respectively; see Hiking/Backpacking, above). Just southwest of Bella Coola, **Blue Jay Lake** has 5 vehicle/tent campsites and 2 lakeside picnic areas. It's a popular spot for canoeing, angling, and swimming. A 12-foot-square (4-m^2) float is anchored about 150 feet (50 m) offshore for swimmers. For more information, contact the Forest Service's Mid Coast Forest District Office, (250) 982-2000.

On the Bella Coola River, near the western boundary of Tweedsmuir Provincial Park, **McCall Flats** is a Forest Service recreation site with 5 vehicle-only sites. No tenting is allowed because of the bear hazard. The main features of this site are its sandy riverside beach, sportfishing, and numerous roads and trails nearby for hiking, mountain biking, or horseback riding. Travel south from the park entrance/exit sign on Hwy 20 at Burnt Bridge for about 1.5 miles (2.5 km), then turn west onto the gravel Talchako Forest Service Rd. After crossing the Talchako Bridge, turn right (north) onto the Noomst Forest Service Rd at the west end of the bridge. Travel 0.5 mile (1 km), then turn right (east) at the sign indicating the site, which is just over 1 mile (2 km) from Hwy 20. For more information, contact the Forest Service's Mid Coast Forest District Office in Hagensborg, (250) 982-2000.

Campgrounds in **Tweedsmuir Park South** are located on the Atnarko River near park headquarters, at the bottom of the Hill (see Getting There, above) and farther west at Fisheries Pool, near Stuie. The Atnarko Campground (28 vehicle/tent sites, including 2 double sites) is situated in a grove of old-growth Douglas fir and is popular with anglers, as is Fisheries Pool Campground (14 vehicle/tent sites). Most trailers and RVs can be accommodated, although no hookups are provided. The park abounds with recreational opportunities for those who desire—and are prepared for—a wilderness experience. (See also Hiking/Backpacking, above, and Canoeing and other activities, below.) For more information about Tweedsmuir Park South, contact BC Parks, (250) 398-4414.

Ts'yl-os Provincial Park, a wilderness park south of Hwy 20 approximately 100 miles (160 km) southwest of Williams Lake, has two small campgrounds that tend to fill quickly in the summer months. There are two developed campgrounds located in the northern half of the park. Nu Chugh Beniz Campground (16 vehicle/tent sites) is situated at Chilko Lake's midpoint and is reached via Hanceville, 26 miles (42 km) west of Riske Creek (pronounced "risky") on Hwy 20. The approach is recommended for high-clearance vehicles only. Gwa Da Ts'ih Campground (8 vehicle/tent sites) is at the north end of the park on Chilko Lake, reached via Tatla Lake (150 miles/240 km west of Williams Lake) on a good gravel road. For more information, contact BC Parks, (250) 398-4414, or Ts'yl-os Park Lodge and Adventures, (800) 487-9567.

More campsites are available at **Bull Canyon Provincial Park,** about 6 miles (10 km) west of Alexis Creek off Hwy 20. This peaceful, forested park on the Chilcotin River has 25 vehicle/tent sites. It is a good place for fishing, and the aspen forest and wildflowers are beautiful.

For more detailed information, including maps of campgrounds in provincial parks, contact BC Parks, 281 First Ave N in Williams Lake, (250) 398-4414.

Scenic Drives/Picnics

The **Coast Mountains** begin about 18 miles (30 km) west of Anahim Lake and stretch to Bella Coola, at the mouth of Burke Channel's North Bentinck Arm. Heavy glaciation on these peaks is evidence that parts of British Columbia are still in grip of the most recent ice age. Viewpoints abound. Particularly notable are those at the summit of the **Bella Coola Freedom Road** (Hwy 20) at **Heckman Pass** near the eastern entrance to Tweedsmuir Provincial Park, and farther west at the Hill, which overlooks the Atnarko Valley. **Lee's Corner Rest Area,** about 56 miles (90 km) west of **Williams Lake** in Hanceville, offers the panorama of the Chilcotin Plateau, with the Coast Mountains in the distance to the west.

Good views of the **Upper Fraser Canyon** can be had from several locations along Hwy 20 near Williams Lake, including the Chilcotin Bridge, about 15 miles (25 km) west of Williams Lake. At Riske Creek, 32 miles (52 km) west of Williams Lake on Hwy 20, take a side trip 12 miles (19 km) south to **Farwell Canyon** for a look at ancient hoodoo rock formations and Native rock pictographs. Farwell Canyon Rd begins 28 miles (45 km) west of Williams Lake. A bridge spans the canyon carved by the Chilcotin River; the pictographs are on the cliff south of the bridge. This road will also take you through a California bighorn sheep reserve (see Wildlife, below).

Southwest of Bella Coola on the South Bentinck Arm, the **Big Cedar Tree** Forest Service Recreation Site protects one of the province's largest western red cedars. Measuring more than 16 feet (5 m) across, this old cedar stands as a monument to British Columbia's ancient forests. A short trail begins about 150 feet (50 m) from the roadside, and there is a picnic table nearby.

Picnic sites along Hwy 20 in Tweedsmuir Provincial Park include, from east to west, **Rainbow Range,** just inside the park's east entrance; **Young Creek,** a good place to take a break while driving the Hill; **Big Rock,** almost 7 miles (11 km) west of park headquarters; **Fisheries Pool,** in the middle of the Hwy 20 corridor through the park, where there is a covered picnic shelter; and **Burnt Bridge,** 16 miles (26 km) west of park headquarters near the park's western entrance.

Fishing

The **Bella Coola River** system is one of the most productive on the entire coast. East of the Bella Coola on the **Atnarko River,** steelhead and cutthroat trout; chinook, sockeye, coho, chum and pink salmon; and dolly varden are fished at various times of the year. There is easy access to both the Bella Coola and Atnarko Rivers from Hwy 20. Anglers must be familiar with the conservation regulations in effect throughout this system. For more information on freshwater fishing, contact the Fish and Wildlife Conservation Officer in Bella Coola, (250) 982-2626. For **guided river drift fishing** in the Bella Coola region, contact the Tweedsmuir Lodge, (250) 982-2402, in Bella Coola. Tackle and angling supplies are available from the Glacier View Resort, (250) 982-2615, in Hagensborg, about 17 miles (28 km) east of Bella Coola on Hwy 20.

North of Bella Coola, the **Dean River** and backcountry lakes and streams have productive rainbow trout fishing. The Dean River, reached by air from Anahim Lake, boasts world-record steelhead and full-service resorts. Contact the Anahim Lake Resort, (800) 667-7212 in the US, (250) 742-3242 in Canada; the Eagle's Nest Resort, (250) 742-3707; Escott Bay Resort, (250) 742-3233; or the Moose Lake Lodge, (250) 742-3535, all in the Anahim Lake region.

Charlotte Lake, situated between the southern part of Tweedsmuir Provincial Park and Hwy 20, to the east in the foothills of the Coast Mountains, has trophy-size rainbow trout. The turnoff from Hwy 20 is 40 miles (66 km) west of Tatla Lake. Follow Charlotte Lake Rd about 9 miles (15 km) southwest of Hwy 20. Contact the Chilko Lake Resort/Hotel, (250) 481-3333, for more information.

Approximately 37 miles (60 km) northwest of Tatla Lake on Hwy 20 lies **Nimpo Lake,** known as "the floatplane capital of BC." It's a major centre for air charters flying guests to remote fishing locations. In recognition of its reputation for rainbow trout fishing, Nimpo Lake was chosen as the location for the 1993 Commonwealth Fly-Fishing Championships. For more information, contact Tweedsmuir Air Service, (800) 668-4335; Wayco Aviation, (250) 742-3303; the Dean River Resort, (250) 742-3332; Pine Point Resort and Air Service, (250) 742-3300; Stewart's Lodge, (800) 668-4335; or Wilderness Rim Resort, (250) 742-3360, all in the Nimpo Lake region.

Kleena Kleene, almost 20 miles (30 km) west of Tatla Lake, is the departure point for flights to remote lakes such as One Eye, and rivers such as the Klinaklini. Charter flights are also available at **Tatla Lake** to nearby fishing lakes. For more information, contact White Saddle Air Service, (250) 476-1182, or Clearwater Lake Lodge and Resort, (250) 476-1150 in the Kleena Kleene region.

Fifty miles (80 km) long and glacier-fed, **Chilko Lake** is the largest natural, high-elevation freshwater lake in North America, and plays host to the third-largest chinook/sockeye salmon run, from August through

October. The salmon eggs are a major food source for rainbow trout and dolly varden. There is true trophy fishing here, with rainbow trout as big as 22 pounds (10 kg) and dolly varden as large as 24 pounds (54 kg). Whitefish also inhabit Chilko Lake. The lake is situated with the new Ts'yl-os Provincial Park (see Camping, above). There is a natural boat launch in the midlake area and a concrete ramp for powerboats at the lake's north end. Beware the strong winds that sweep down off the glaciated peaks surrounding the park: these make for treacherous boating conditions. For more information, contact Chilko Lake Resort, (250) 481-3333, Ts'yl-os Park Lodge and Adventures, (800) 487-9567, both in Ts'yl-os Provincial Park, as well as BC Parks, (250) 398-4414.

You can fish for trout and kokanee at **Puntzi Lake,** which features a fishing derby on the last weekend in June. The lake is about 4 miles (7 km) north of Hwy 20, about 35 miles (60 km) west of Alexis Creek. The ice fishing is also good, particularly for whitefish in January.

The **Chilcotin River** is a good spot for steelhead and sockeye. South of Lee's Corner (Hanceville) are numerous **Chilcotin lakes,** some with rough Forest Service recreation sites (picnic table, pit toilet). Obtain a map from the BC Forest Service office in Alexis Creek, (250) 394-4700, or Williams Lake, (250) 398-4341, or try the Williams Lake InfoCentre, (250) 392-5025. For **information** about licences required for freshwater fishing in the Chilcotin, contact the BC Ministry of Environment in Williams Lake, (250) 398-4530, or the Fish and Wildlife Conservation Officer in Bella Coola, (250) 982-2626. For more information on **fishing guides,** contact the Cariboo Tourism Association, 109 Yorston St in Williams Lake, (250) 392-2226 or (800) 663-5885.

Kayaking/Rafting

The **Chilcotin River** is rated among the best—and most challenging—in North America for kayaking and whitewater rafting. The **Chilko River,** a tributary of the Chilcotin that flows out of Chilko Lake, is also known for its whitewater activities. Not only will the Class IV–V whitewater get your adrenal glands fluttering, the landscape will too. The headwaters of the Chilcotin and the Chilko lie in the Coast Mountains near the southeast corner of Tweedsmuir Provincial Park. The rivers become runable in the subalpine regions, then they descend to the Chilcotin Plateau's sprawling grasslands and arid canyons. Some of the most spectacular scenery is found near the Chilcotin's confluence with the Fraser River, south of Riske Creek. This is an esteemed kayaking and rafting locale, but because of its isolation, the Chilcotin sees relatively few rafters and whitewater kayakers. For information, contact the Cariboo Tourism Association, (250) 392-2226 or

(800) 663-5885. For **guided rafting trips** on the Chilcotin, contact Rivers & Oceans Unlimited Expeditions, (800) 360-7238. For **information on water levels,** contact the BC Forest Service Office in Alexis Creek, (250) 394-4700, or Williams Lake, (250) 398-4345.

Canoeing

Within Tweedsmuir Provincial Park, the chain of lakes connected by Hunlen Creek provides the opportunity for an enjoyable canoe trip of three to five days. Leading from **Turner Lake** to **Sunshine Lake,** a distance of about 17 miles (27.5 km) one way, this route enjoys calm water, beautiful scenery, good cutthroat trout fishing, sandy beaches, and wilderness camping. With the exception of 7-mile (11-km) Turner Lake, the lakes are small. There are six easy, short portages, the longest taking 30 minutes. Although the canoe season begins in June, the best time to enjoy this delightful corner of Tweedsmuir Provincial Park is in September, once the first frost has brought an end to insect season. Canoes can be airlifted in or rented from Tweedsmuir Wilderness Camp on Turner Lake, (800) 668-4335, June 15–September 15. Contact Wayco Aviation for information on air charters, (250) 742-3303 in Nimpo Lake, or (250) 249-5358 in Quesnel. BC Parks provides detailed information on the route. Call (250) 398-4414 or stop by 281 First Ave N in Williams Lake.

There is a three- to four-day canoe route on the **Nazko Lakes** south of Alexis Creek. Campsites are located at Loomis and Deerpelt Lakes in the new **Nazko Lakes Provincial Park.** Total round-trip distance is about 30 miles (50 km). To reach the park, drive 28 miles (45 km) south of Alexis Creek on the Alexis Lakes Forest Service Rd. For more information, call BC Parks, (250) 398-4414.

Wildlife

Magnificent **trumpeter swans** winter at Lonesome Lake, south of Hwy 20 in Tweedsmuir Provincial Park (see Camping, above). A heartfelt description of a Chilcotin pioneer's relationship with these birds is recorded in *Ralph Edwards of Lonesome Lake* by Ed Gould.

The Chilanko Forks Wildlife Management Area, a protected marshland on Hwy 20 near Chilanko Forks, 38 miles (62 km) west of Alexis Creek, is home to more than 52 species of birds (among them **waterfowl, hummingbirds,** and **woodpeckers**) as well as **beavers.**

Puntzi Lake, about 4 miles (7 km) north of Hwy 20, about 35 miles (60 km) west of Alexis Creek, is a feeding area for **white pelicans** in the spring and summer and **trumpeter swans** from fall to freeze-up. Other viewing sites are on Alkali, Anahim, and Pantag Lakes. Never approach nesting white pelicans and keep well back when they are foraging; any encroachment may cause adult pelicans to abandon their nests or feeding grounds.

Nine miles (15 km) south of Hwy 20 on Farwell Canyon Rd (see Scenic Drives/Picnics, above) is the **California Bighorn Sheep Reserve,** a more than 1,000-acre (400-ha) game reserve at the confluence of the Fraser and Chilcotin Rivers. The reserve is home to 500 bighorns, one-fifth of the world's population. Watch for groups of them scaling the steep sandstone riverbanks.

Horseback Riding

Horses are permitted on many of the trails leading from the **Rainbow Range** trailhead in Tweedsmuir Provincial Park, 18.6 miles (30 km) west of Anahim Lake (see Hiking/Backpacking, above). The **Alexander Mackenzie Heritage Trail** also can be travelled on horseback. David Dorsey of Anahim Lake, (250) 742-3251, leads guided horse trips in the area. You'll also find good riding on the **Puntzi Lake** trails, 4.3 miles (7 km) north of Hwy 20, about 35 miles (60 km) west of Alexis Creek.

Cross-Country Skiing

For information about cross-country ski trails in the **Tatla Lake** region, contact West Chilcotin Trading, (250) 476-1111. Cross-country ski touring and winter camping are possible in **Itcha Ilgachuz Provincial Park** (see Hiking/Backpacking, above). Heckman Pass in Tweedsmuir Provincial Park is the home of the **Tweedsmuir Ski Club.** For more information, contact BC Parks' district office in Williams Lake, (250) 398-4414.

outside in

Attractions

The settlement of **Bella Coola,** located 298 miles (480 km) west of Williams Lake, is home to the Coast Salish Nuxalk. It's linked to Vancouver Island via BC Ferries; see Inside Passage and Discovery Coast chapter. A Hudson's Bay Company outpost was established in the valley in the 1860s, while at the turn of the century a group of Norwegians settled at Hagensborg, a town that still reflects this Norwegian heritage. The **Bella Coola Museum,** located in a former schoolhouse and open June to September, recounts the history of the Nuxalk Nation, as well as the area's Norwegian history and the building of the Freedom Highway by local residents.

The **Thorsen Creek Petroglyphs** are located 5 miles (8 km) east of Bella Coola; Norwegian explorer and writer Thor Heyerdahl suggested the Easter Islanders originated here because the incised rock symbols on the canyon face so resemble Polynesian stone carvings. A guide to the site is available at the Bella Coola InfoCentre, located in the Bella Coola Museum during summer months and in the senior citizens' centre (next to the co-op) at other times.

For more than a century, **general stores** throughout the Chilcotin region have played an important role as community centres and meeting places where hospitality is legendary and genuine. Stop in to get a taste of Chilcotin living today—and as it was in the past. Examples along Hwy 20 include the Riske Creek General Store, about 30 miles (47 km) west of Williams Lake; Lee's Corner (Hanceville) General Store, 56 miles (91 km) west of Williams Lake; the Chilanko Forks General Store, about 35 miles (56.5 km) west of Alexis Creek; the Kleena Kleene General Store, 19 miles (31 km) west of Tatla Lake; and the Anahim Lake General Store, about 60 miles (95 km) west of Tatla Lake.

More Information

BC Forest Service, Cariboo Forest Regional Headquarters: *(250) 398-4345.*

BC Forest Service, Chilcotin Forest District: *(250) 394-4700.*

BC Forest Service, Mid Coast Forest District: *(250) 982-2000.*

BC Forest Service, Williams Lake Forest District: *(250) 398-4341.*

BC Ministry of Environment: *(250) 398-4530.*

BC Ministry of Transportation and Highways: *24-hour road report (604) 660-9770.*

BC Parks, Bella Coola: *(250) 799-5255.*

BC Parks, Williams Lake: *(250) 398-4414.*

Cariboo Tourism Association: *(250) 392-2226 or (800) 663-5885.*

Williams Lake InfoCentre: *(250) 392-5025.*

The Bulkley and Skeena River Valleys

From Smithers through the Hazelton Mountains to Prince Rupert via Highway 16, including the Bulkley and Skeena Rivers, Kitimat, Terrace, the Kitlope Heritage Conservancy Protected Area, and Gitnadoix River Provincial Recreation Area.

There are many things this area isn't. It's not home to a major city such as Vancouver or even Prince George; it's not a hugely popular tourist destination such as the near-mythical Queen Charlottes or the cozy Okanagan Valley are; and it doesn't contain vast tracts of uncharted wilderness such as the north does. Therefore, it's easy to overlook or underappreciate what, on closer inspection, is an adventurer's playground. Accessible by paved road, ferry, and plane, this region is filled with both unique wilderness experiences and the "standard" British Columbia fare of deep fjords, dramatic canyons, sheer mountains, rivers thick with salmon, old-growth forests, and an abundance of wildlife.

Nestled up under the Alaska Panhandle, this is the province's northernmost coast. It's home to the Skeena, the second-largest river in British Columbia. Over five million salmon return to the Skeena every year, making this a premier salmon-fishing area. Prince Rupert, with its highway, rail, air, and ferry connections, serves as a gateway to pristine wilderness. Stop and stay awhile on your way through—there's room to relax and to play in this region, so rich in Native and pioneer history. And since this area includes the world's largest intact coastal rain forest, bring your rain gear, just in case!

Getting There

Highway 16 links Smithers with Prince George to the southeast. Highway 37 (Stewart-Cassiar Hwy) links Highway 16 with points north on the way to Yukon from Kitwanga, and Highway 37 links Highway 16 with Kitimat, 35 miles (58 km) to the south from Terrace. Highway 16 runs north and west from Smithers to Prince Rupert, a distance of about 220 miles (355 km). For ferry access to Prince Rupert, see Inside Passage and Discovery Coast chapter. There's regularly scheduled airline service to Prince Rupert, Terrace, and Smithers from southern British Columbia. Contact Air BC and Central Mountain Air, (800) 663-3721 (same number for both), and Canadian Regional Airlines, (800) 665-1177, for more information. For information on passenger rail service between Smithers and Prince Rupert, contact Via Rail, (800) 561-8630.

Adjoining Areas

NORTH: **The Stewart-Cassiar Highway (Highway 37)**

SOUTH: **Inside Passage and Discovery Coast**

EAST: **Fraser Plateau**

WEST: **Queen Charlotte Islands (Haida Gwaii)**

Parks/Camping

The Northwest features truly beautiful campgrounds, most of which are easily reached from the main highways. After a full day exploring the region, stroll through old-growth forests in search of wildlife, throw a line in the water, or just sit back and drink in the dramatic landscape. For information on all BC Parks campgrounds in this region, contact the Skeena District Office, 3790 Alfred St, Smithers, (250) 847-7320. For information on Forest Service campgrounds, contact the North Coast Forest District Office, 125 Market Pl, Prince Rupert, (250) 624-7460; the Ministry of Forest's Prince Rupert regional office, 3726 Alfred St, Smithers, (250) 847-7500; or the Bulkley-Cassiar Forest District Office, (250) 847-6300 in Smithers.

After Hwy 16 leaves Smithers heading west, the first campground is **Seeley Lake Provincial Park** (20 vehicle/tent sites), located 6 miles (10 km) west of New Hazelton. The Hazelton Mountains and the sheer pyramid of Mount Roche Deboule form a dramatic backdrop, and the lake provides trout fishing, canoeing, and wildlife viewing. You'll also find a fascinating Native legend about a mythological monster associated with Seeley Lake posted here. The tale was used to instruct children on the need to respect all of nature's creations, a lesson that is still timely today.

Kleanza Creek Provincial Park (23 vehicle/tent sites) is located 6 miles (10 km) east of Terrace on Hwy 16. Located in a truly lovely setting in a canyon beside a creek, and ideally suited for picnics, the park runs along one side of the Skeena River and both sides of Kleanza Creek. Hiking trails lead to views of the canyon and abandoned gold mines. Kleanza is one of the words associated with eulachon (see Wildlife, below).

Lakelse Lake Provincial Park (156 vehicle/tent sites) is located 12 miles (20 km) south of Terrace along Hwy 37. To get there, follow signs to the park from Hwy 16 on the Terrace–Kitimat Airport access road. This is a popular, well-developed campground, set in old-growth forests. Reservations are recommended in summer; call the BC Parks reservation line, (800) 689-9025, between March 1 and September 15.

Ferry Island Municipal Campground and Park (68 vehicle/tent sites) is located just east of Terrace near the junction of Hwys 16 and 37, on Ferry Island in the mighty Skeena River. For more information, call the Terrace and District Chamber of Commerce, (800) 499-1637.

Exchamsiks River Provincial Park (18 vehicle/tent sites, including several on the banks of the river) is one of the most beautifully situated parks in the region. A Sitka spruce forest towers above the campsites, picnic tables, and boat launch. The campground is located beside Highway 16, about 34 miles (55 km) west of Terrace.

Prudhomme Lake Provincial Park (24 vehicle/tent sites) lies 10 miles (16 km) east of Prince Rupert on Hwy 16 on a small lake, with a boat launch for anglers and paddlers. It's also the closest public campground for those connecting with BC Ferries' **Inside Passage** route (see Inside Passage and Discovery Coast chapter) and the Alaska ferry.

For a dip in refreshing water, sunbathing, or a walk along a rain-forest nature trail, **Diana Lake Provincial Park,** adjacent to Prudhomme Lake Provincial Park, is a much-frequented day-use area with facilities, close to Prince Rupert.

For a campsite farther from the highway, **Lachmach Forest Service Campground** is accessed via the Lachmach Forestry Rd; four-wheel-drive vehicles are recommended in heavy rain. Turn northeast off of Hwy 16 near the abandoned town of Haysport, near Prince Rupert. The roadside campsites are in a forested setting at the south end of Work Channel. The campground offers fishing, and the only facility provided is a primitive boat launch. For more information on Forest Service recreation campgrounds, see More Information at the end of this chapter.

The world's largest intact coastal rain forest is protected in the **Kitlope**

Heritage Conservancy Protected Area (Huchsduwachsdu Nuyem Jees). Kitimat is the closest settlement, about 84 miles (135 km) northwest of the protected area by water. The park covers a 784,000-acre (317 500 ha) valley, the ancestral home of the Haisla Nation, and includes stands of trees that are more than 800 years old. Three rivers—the Gamsby, Tezwa, and Tsaytis—feed into the Kitlope River, which then enters the head of the sinuous Gardner Canal. Drooping stands of western hemlock interspersed with Douglas fir cloak the domed mountains. As there are no developed trail or camping facilities, first-time visitors are advised to contact a guiding service (see Hiking/Backpacking, below).

Many parts of this region are worth a short visit, which is what picnics are all about. **Smithers Municipal Campground,** on Kathryn Lake Rd near Hwy 16 in Smithers, and **Ross Lake Provincial Park,** about 38 miles (62 km) west of Smithers on Hwy 16, are two such places. Ross Lake also offers canoeing, swimming, fly-fishing, and hiking.

For handy stopping spots with picnic tables and views of the beautiful Skeena River Valley along Hwy 16, check out the **Exstew Rest Area** on Hwy 16, about 25 miles (40 km) west of Terrace; the **Kasiks Rest Area,** about halfway between Prince Rupert and Terrace (complete with a boat launch); and the **Telegraph Point Rest Area,** about 34 miles (55 km) east of Prince Rupert.

Wildlife

If you can't find the mythical monster in Seeley Lake (see Parks/Camping, above), there's still a chance to see a legend in this region—a white black bear. Native legend in this area tells of a magical white bear that will help, rescue, and protect humans. One of the rarest bears in the world, the **Kermode bear,** a subspecies of the black bear, is found only in the Terrace area and on some islands in the Douglas Channel. Not an albino, it ranges from light chestnut blond to steel blue-grey, appearing almost white. These bears, once hunted nearly to extinction, are now under provincial protection. Harming the Kermode is strictly prohibited, but as the bears haven't signed a reciprocal agreement, remember to use the same caution around these animals as you would around any other bears (see General Introduction).

The **Gitnadoix River Provincial Recreation Area** is home to **mountain goats, moose, trumpeter swans,** and all **five species of salmon.** This classic, U-shaped valley contains the entire drainage of the Gitnadoix River, a major tributary of the Skeena, upriver from Prince Rupert. The ocean currents backing up into the Gitnadoix are so intertidal that seals pursue spawning salmon as far as 60 miles (100 km) upstream to Alastair

Lake. Alastair Lake is one of British Columbia's three known nesting sites for trumpeter swans, the largest waterfowl in the world. Getting to Alastair takes some effort. Unlike its southern sister, the Stein Valley, the Gitnadoix is not served by a little river ferry to help adventurers cross the *skookum* Skeena River. Charter aircraft or boat travel via the Skeena River from Prince Rupert is the way to go. Guided boat and hiking tours are available from Blue Heron Tours, (250) 624-5770, in Prince Rupert. Call BC Parks for more information, (250) 847-7320.

In recognition of the large bear population in this region, the first and only **grizzly bear** sanctuary in Canada was established 28 miles (45 km) northeast of Prince Rupert. As the Khutzeymateen/K'tzim-a-deen Grizzly Bear Sanctuary is a protected area, human activity is not encouraged. However, controlled viewing is permitted, although access is only by boat and floatplane. All visitors must register at the ranger station near the Khutzeymateen River estuary. Viewpoints look over the estuary and shoreline, and offer a chance to glimpse the **black bears, mountain goats, martens, wolverines, wolves, porcupines, river otters, beavers,** and **harbour seals** that share the sanctuary with the grizzlies. For a closer look, authorized groups with professional guides, such as Seachaser Charters, (250) 624-5472, in Prince Rupert, are allowed to enter the estuary. Overnight anchorage is permitted on the Khutzeymateen Inlet, but be aware of the drastic tides. Call the Prince Rupert Regional Travel InfoCentre, (800) 667-1994 or (250) 624-5637, for information, or call BC Parks, (250) 847-7320.

In March and April, **eulachon** run in the mouth of the Skeena River. Basalt Creek, in particular, offers good viewing. Turn off of Hwy 16 about 12 miles (20 km) east of Prince Rupert. This is a great opportunity to also watch the **seals, sea lions, eagles, and gulls** in the hundreds, which gather to feed on the small, silvery fish. Eulachon contain so much oil that they are easily ignited once dried. Try cooking one over a campfire on a thin, sharpened stick the same way that you'd cook a hotdog: they are so tasty that you can eat the whole fish, bones and all.

Fishing

In this glacier-carved ground, where the long fingers of fjords hold hands with rivers, and lakes collect in the gouged rock, the fishing is just about anything you want it to be. Freshwater fishing—for rainbow, cutthroat, and dolly varden trout; chinook, coho, pink, and sockeye salmon; and the feisty steelhead—can be done at both accessible and remote locations. For remote areas, there are charter operations, helicopters, and floatplanes. For accessible areas, there's the paved highway. Fly-fishing is excellent on

Ross Lake, best reached from **Ross Lake Provincial Park** (see Parks/Camping, above), on Hwy 16, 38 miles (62 km) west of Smithers, near New Hazelton. On a summer day, the park is popular with anglers, boaters (electric motors only), and swimmers alike. At **Seeley Lake** (see Parks/Camping, above), west of New Hazelton, cutthroat and rainbow trout fishing is a peaceful experience, as there is car-top-boat launching only. These trout average 1 to 3 pounds (0.5 to 1.5 kg).

If you're looking for just a bit more excitement, the **Skeena** watershed offers some of the largest steelhead and salmon in the world. The average chinook caught weighs in at 35 to 50 pounds (16 to 23 kg), but they can be 90 pounds (40 kg) or larger. Fish for coho in the Skeena and its tributaries, the **Kasiks, Gitnadoix, Exchamsiks, Exstew, Lakelse,** and **Kitsumkalum Rivers,** as well as the **Kitimat and Nass River systems.** Runs peak in September and October, although coho start to appear in July and don't completely disappear until December.

Farther upstream, the **Morice, Babine, Sustut,** and **Kispiox Rivers,** accessed from Hwy 16 and 37, are known for record steelhead (up to 37 pounds/17 kg); fish these rivers in September and October. In July, if you want company and action, fish for steelhead at **Idiot Rock** just downstream of Moricetown off Hwy 16 on the **Bulkley River.** For more information on fishing in this region, contact the Smithers Visitor InfoCentre, (800) 542-6673 or (250) 847-9854, or the Hazelton Visitor InfoCentre, (250) 842-6071 (May-September) or (250) 842-6571 (October-April), both on Hwy 16. For licences and full information on local fishing, contact Oscars Source for Sports, 1214 Main St, (250) 847-2136, in Smithers.

The waters around **Lakelse Lake** south of Hwy 16 near Terrace-Kitimat Airport (see Parks/Camping, above) support both trout and salmon. Fishing is also good in **Onion Lake,** off Hwy 37, south of Mount Layton Hot Springs. In the **Kitimat** area, productive spots include the Lower Dyke, Pumphouse Pool, Goose Creek, Coho Flats, Claybands, the Old Sawmill, 18 Mile Hole, and the Powerlines, all on or near the Kitimat River and easily reached from Hwy 37. For more information, contact Dream Catchers Guiding, (800) 234-4112; Northwest Fishing Guides, (250) 635-5295; Skeena Wilderness Fishing Charters, (250) 635-4686; or Rivers Edge Lodge, (250) 635-2540, all located in the Terrace-Kitimat region.

Now that you have a good sense of just how much freshwater fishing there is along this short stretch of highway, remember that this area, particularly **Prince Rupert,** is primarily a saltwater-fishing destination, and as such is virtually unbeatable. All the islands and inlets that protect this section of coast provide feeding grounds for fish that are easily persuaded to try nibbling on your line. Chinook can be found just minutes from

Prince Rupert's harbour. Coho and pink salmon are plentiful in August and September. If you're after something truly large, cautiously lower your line to the bottom. Ling cod weighing more than 60 pounds (27 kg) and halibut more than 250 pounds (114 kg) have been caught in these waters. Don't try to land one in a small boat! Information on popular areas, charts, and tide information can be found at any Prince Rupert tackle shop. The Prince Rupert Visitor Information Centre (see More Information, below) has details on available charters. For more information, contact Mystic Ventures, (250) 627-4529; Crest Adventure Charters, (800) 663-8150; or Seashore Charters, (800) 667-4393, in Prince Rupert.

The saltwater fishing around Kitimat also yields results, where **Douglas Channel** forms the end of British Columbia's longest inland fjord. May and June are good months in which to meet up with chinook salmon, while July and August are the time for coho. Halibut and cod can be caught in the channel almost year-round; several 200-pound (90-kg) halibut have been landed within 10 miles (16 km) of the dock. Charter fishing is big business in Kitimat and you'll have no trouble finding your way to the hot spots. It's an embarrassment of riches here. Angling guides in Kitimat include Hodson & Sons, (250) 982-2322, McCowan's Sporting Adventures, (250) 769-6931, and Spring King Charters, (250) 632-7431. Alt-BC Tours and Guiding, based in Alberta, (403) 288-1769, leads guided fishing tours in the **Kitlope Heritage Conservancy Protected Area** (see Hiking/Backpacking, below).

Skiing/Snowboarding

Downhill and cross-country skiing, as well as snowboarding, are popular in winter. **Ski Smithers** on **Hudson Bay Mountain,** (250) 847-2058, (800) 665-4299 (BC only), 14 miles (22 km) west of Smithers on Ski Hill Rd, has plenty of light, dry powder that's been enjoyed by locals since the 1920s, when the Smithers Ski Club began clearing runs. In 1980, the Smithers Ski Corporation was created to promote the mountain. The ski area has complete facilities for alpine skiing and snowboarding, including a triple chairlift and two T-bars that service 1,750 feet (525 m) of vertical rise and 18 runs. In good conditions, it is possible to ski up the south ridge close to the summit of Hudson Bay Mountain (8,300 feet/2530 m). By traversing the prairie in a northeasterly direction, it is feasible to ski or hike back to Smithers via Simpson Creek Rd, or you can travel in a westerly direction to join with the top end of Duthie Mine Rd. These routes are for experienced, equipped skiers only. Further inquiries can be made at the Smithers District Chamber of Commerce, (250) 847-5072 or (250) 847-9854.

Pine Creek Trails and **Smithers Community Forest, Smithers Golf Course, Tyee Lake Provincial Park,** and a dozen other areas offer nordic skiing in fine, dry, powder snow near Smithers. On the east side of the valley in the **Babine Mountains Provincial Recreational Area,** cross-country routes from trailheads along Driftwood Rd east of Hwy 16 lead to Driftwood Canyon, Silver King Basin, and Harvey Mountain. Skiers follow an old mining road in Silver King Basin for almost 7 miles (11 km) to reach the subalpine region. The Silver King Cabin is located about 8 miles (13.5 km) from the trailhead. There's room for about 12 people to overnight in the cabin on a first-come basis. For a detailed map of these trails, contact BC Parks, (250) 847-7320, in Smithers. If you like to be on your own in the outdoors, with the chance to spot a diminutive northern pygmy owl (one of the few owls that hunt by day), this is the perfect winter getaway in the "great white north."

The first year that **Shames Mountain Ski Area** was opened, it had to close. Seems they weren't expecting quite so much snow: the top of the ski lift got snowed under. Shames Mountain boasts the most accumulated snow of any ski hill in North America (but just try telling that to Mount Baker Ski Area in Washington state). Fifteen runs accommodate skiers of all levels on a vertical rise of 1,705 feet (520 m), and the ski resort offers equipment rental, multilevel ski lessons, snowboard lessons, a double chairlift, T-bar, and handle-tow services. Shames Mountain Ski Corporation is situated about 12 miles (20 km) west of Terrace on Hwy 16, then 9 miles (14 km) north on Shames Rd. Call (250) 635-3773 for more information and a snow report.

Walking

Walking tours are possible in many of the cities and towns in this region. **Prince Rupert** has Kinsmen's Linear Park, which consists of trails running along abandoned railway tracks. A City Walking Tour map is available at the Visitor's Bureau. **Kitimat** also has a walking tour. For a journey into the past, **Old Hazelton** offers a tour of restored heritage buildings. For a detailed visitor and walking tour guide to Hazelton's Old Town, ask at the village office on Field St.

Hiking/Backpacking

Wildlife viewing is a major attraction in the Kitlope Heritage Conservancy Protected Area (Huchsduwachsdu Nuyem Jees). Grizzly and black bears, moose, mountain goats, caribou, and a wide range of birds are found throughout the Kitlope. A trip to the Kitlope often begins from the river estuary at **Douglas Channel,** which is reached by boat or air, and then you can backpack through the forest to the alpine regions above. Summers here are often as wet as winters, so don't let weather influence your plans. One of the rewards of approaching by water is stopping at the Wewanie and Shearwater natural hot springs in Douglas Channel. Shearwater's are considered by some to be the best hot springs on the north coast. During summer months, the area is monitored by a group of Watchmen (similar to park wardens) based in the Kitlope. For more **information,** contact the Watchmen at the Na Na Kila Institute, (250) 632-3308, in Kitimaat Village. For information on **guided tours,** contact the Haisla Tribal Council, (250) 639-9382, for charter boat tours of the park. Kitlope is jointly managed by BC Parks and the Haisla Nation. Call BC Parks for more information, (250) 847-7320. BC Parks recommends the following ecotourism guides: Mystical Charters, (250) 632-4321; Exodus Adventure, (250) 639-9650; Haisla Charters, (250) 632-4173, in Kitimat; and Alt-BC Tours and Guiding, (403) 288-1769, in Alberta.

Four hikes near Prince Rupert—the Butze Rapids, Oldfield Meadows, Tall Trees, and Mount Oldfield Trails—all begin almost 4 miles (6 km) east of the city centre, on Hwy 16. The **Butze Rapids Trail** (easy; 6 miles/10 km return) has a few steep sections as it loops through old-growth forest, bogs, and wetlands to the tidal flats of Grassy Bay, where a reversing tidal rapid puts on a whitewater performance twice a day (check the tide book). Depending on who you consult, a rising tide or a falling tide is best for viewing the rapids, which are reminiscent of Skookumchuk Narrows on the Sunshine Coast. The **Oldfield Meadows Trail** (easy; 6 miles/10 km return) follows a cedar boardwalk through open meadows in a stunted bonsai forest. The granite that underlies much of the boggy terrain provides poor drainage, which accounts for the stunted growth in many of the low-lying coastal forests. The **Tall Trees Trail** (moderate; 4 miles/6 km return) begins by ascending a steep, almost 1,000-foot (300-m) boardwalk, then loops through a towering forest of Sitka spruce, western hemlock, balsam fir, and western red cedar. The trail crosses several creeks and finally leads to a view of Kaien Island. For those in search of a longer hike, the **Mount Oldfield Trail** (strenuous; 12 miles/20 km return) takes you to the summit with its 1,837-foot (560-m) elevation. You can get to this trail from the Tall Trees Trail or Oldfield Meadows Trails. The summit of Mount Hays can also be reached via the Tall Trees Trail. Maps for these well-marked trails are available from the Prince Rupert Visitor Information Centre (see More Information, below), and at the trailhead on Hwy 16.

The **Bornite Mountain Trail** (easy; 2.5 miles/4 km return) begins in Kleanza Creek Provincial Park (see Parks/Camping, above), just east of Terrace, and follows an old mining road to the site of an abandoned placer gold operation. Along the way, hikers get a view down into the Kleanza Creek Canyon.

The **Ferry Island Trail** (easy; 4 miles/6 km return), beside Hwy 16 near Terrace, provides travellers with a relaxing stroll that circles through the woods and along the shoreline of the Skeena River. The beauty of the landscape—the broad, brown river surmounted by snowcapped Coast Mountain peaks—is extraordinary and well worth a stop to enjoy.

In summer, the trails in the **Shames Mountain Ski Area** (see Skiing/Snowboarding, above), 22 miles (35 km) west of Terrace, lead hikers through meadows in full bloom and provides incredible mountainscape views. The well-marked ski trails serve as hiking trails, which vary from easy strolls to steep climbs. Maps are available at the day lodge and local sports shops. (Note: Hungry hikers can reward themselves at the Shames Mountain Tea Bar, which features scones and cinnamon buns and is open on weekends and holidays throughout the summer.)

The **Kitimat** area offers hiking as well. If you want a challenge, hike to the summit of **Mount Elizabeth.** Also recommended are the **Bish Creek Trail** and the **Hirsch Creek Falls and Canyon Trail.** Ask at the Kitimat Visitor InfoCentre for detailed information.

Just west of Smithers is some of the best hiking of all. **Glacier Gulch** and **Twin Falls** are must-see destinations. Look for the signs on Hwy 16, 2.5 miles (4 km) west of Smithers, that indicate the turnoff west to the falls and gulch. The road is unpaved and may still have snow on its upper reaches through May. A short, rocky path leads to a lookout platform close to the parking lot. From there a short trail leads to the base of the south falls. The trail to view **Lake Kathryn Glacier** is a challenging, three-hour climb. The glacier, left over from the last ice age, lies in a mile-wide (2-km) gorge. Waterfalls plunge 525 feet (150 m) down the sides of the gradually melting glacier and feed alpine streams, some of which you must ford to get here.

Also near Smithers, **Ski Hill Road** to Hudson Bay Mountain (see Skiing/Snowboarding, above) provides elevated views of the Bulkley Mountains; in summer, this road climbs to tree line, then hiking trails lead into alpine meadows.

At **Nisga'a Memorial Lava Bed Provincial Park,** about 60 miles (100 km) north of Terrace, adjacent to New Aiyansh on the Nass Valley Rd, arrangements can be made for a guided 2-mile (3-km) hike to a volcano's cone. Two centuries ago the volcano erupted, killing approximately 2,000 people. The pocked lava plain, 6 miles (10 km) long and 2 miles (3 km) wide, is an eerily moonlike landscape. If you want to circle around the park in your vehicle, take the Nass Forest Service Rd to join Hwy 37, and then meet Hwy 16 at Kitwanga. Watch out for logging trucks.

Boating/Canoeing/Kayaking

In this water-coursed area, one can get more places by boat than by car. Whether you're boating for transportation or for relaxation (or both), there's plenty of room to play. If you're going by paddle power, try **Ross Lake Provincial Park** (see Parks/Camping, above) near Hwy 16, 38 miles (62 km) west of Smithers (no powerboats), as well as **Seeley Lake, Diana Lake,** and **Lakelse Lake Provincial Parks** (see Parks/Camping, above).

For charter boat tours of **Kitlope Heritage Conservancy Protected Area (Huchsduwachsdu Nuyem Jees)** contact the Na Na Kila Institute, (250) 632-3308, or Kitlope Tours, (250) 632-7794, both in Kitimat. You'll also need a guide to explore **Gitnadoix River Provincial Recreation Area** (see Wildlife, above), which offers superb boating or paddling in a fully protected watershed that drains into Skeena River east of Prince Rupert; check in Prince Rupert for guided boat trips into the area. If you want to get out onto the ocean proper, **Prince Rupert** has a plethora of boats and guides available. To smell salt in the air around Kitimat, explore the Douglas Channel; check on charter boats and guides with the Kitimat Chamber of Commerce, (250) 632-6294 or (800) 664-6554.

During the summer, services are available for exciting half-day heli-rafting trips on the **Exchamsiks River.** For more information, contact the Terrace and District Chamber of Commerce, (800) 499-1637 or (250) 635-2063.

Windsurfing

Windsurfers can indulge themselves at **Diana Lake Provincial Park** (see Parks/Camping, above), 10 miles (16 km) east of Prince Rupert on Hwy 16. Windsurfing, waterskiing, and Jet-skiing are also popular on expansive **Lakelse Lake** (see Parks/Camping, above), off Hwy 37 near Terrace. Lakelse is a Tsimshian word for freshwater mussel; they thrive in these waters.

outside in

Attractions

An interesting stop in this region is the **North Pacific Cannery Village Museum,** (250) 628-3538, located about 7 miles (11 km) south of Hwy 16 on Skeena Dr from Prince Rupert via Port Edward; it's open mid-May to mid-September.

More Information

BC Fish and Wildlife Conservation Officer: *(250) 627-7389.*

BC Forest Service, Bulkley-Cassiar Forest District, Smithers: *(250) 847-6300.*

BC Forest Service, North Coast Forest District, Prince Rupert: *(250) 624-7460.*

BC Forest Service, Prince Rupert Regional Office, Smithers: *(250) 847-7500.*

BC Parks, Smithers: *(250) 847-7320; reservations, (800) 689-9025.*

Canadian Department of Fisheries and Oceans: *(250) 624-9137.*

Hazelton Visitor InfoCentre: *(250) 842-6071 (May-September) or (250) 842-6571 (October-April).*

Kitimat Chamber of Commerce: *(800) 664-6554 or (250) 632-6294.*

Kitlope Heritage Conservancy Protected Area (Huchsduwachsdu Nuyem Jees), The Haisla Tribal Council: *(250) 639-9382, information on tours of world's largest intact coastal temperate rain forest.*

Prince Rupert Visitor Information Centre: *(800) 667-1994 or (250) 624-5637.*

Skeena Valley Wilderness Adventures: *(250) 624-5700.*

Smithers Visitor InfoCentre/Smithers District Chamber of Commerce: *(800) 542-6673, (250) 847-5072, or (250) 847-9854.*

Terrace Tourism: *(800) 499-1637 or (250) 635-2063.*

A 230-mile (370-km) stretch of Highway 16 that runs across the Fraser Plateau west of Prince George and links the Central Interior with Smithers and the Northwest, including Babine Mountain and Tweedsmuir Provincial Park.

Like most Canadian provinces, British Columbia is bottom-heavy, with much of its population tucked away into its southwest corner. Vanderhoof, about 60 miles (100 km) west of Prince George on Highway 16, is the geographic centre of British Columbia, and yet is considered to be well ensconced in the northern half of the province. But then, for many people in the Lower Mainland, anything north of Whistler is the far north.

This is land steeped in history. Alexander Mackenzie walked this way in 1793, becoming the first European to cross North America by land. The Alexander Mackenzie Historical Trail weaves its way through the vast wilderness between Highways 16 and 20 to the south, and is one of the longest hiking trails in the province. Fort St. James, north of Vanderhoof, is one of the oldest white settlements in British Columbia. Every campground you visit, every trail you walk, every canoe route you travel likely has some history attached to it, from prehistoric fossils at Driftwood Canyon Provincial Park to century-old Native grease trails, to turn-of-the-century gold-rush and telegraph trails.

In the past, people had to walk, ride horses, or take canoes. Now, Highway 16 runs west from Prince George, carrying you through the north end of the Interior Plateau, a land rife with lakes of all sizes. Is it any wonder that this is fishing country, and that water sports are one of the most popular forms of summer recreation?

This is also a land of long, cold winters and short, hot summers. In winter, the temperature can drop to below -22°F/-30°C for weeks on end. In the summer, clouds of insects, most of them out for blood, swarm about in early evening. If you are planning on travelling in this area, know your enemies and come prepared.

Getting There

Highway 97 links Prince George with Cache Creek to the south and Dawson Creek to the north. Highway 16 connects Prince George and points west with eastern British Columbia at Tête Jaune Cache, as part of its four-province course between Portage La Prairie in Manitoba and Prince Rupert and the Queen Charlotte Islands on the west coast. Highway 27 leads north from Highway 16 at Vanderhoof and connects with Fort St. James on the shores of Stuart Lake, a distance of almost 38.5 miles (62 km). Highway 35 leads south from Highway 16 at the town of Burns Lake and connects with the town of Francois Lake, a distance of about 10 miles (16 km).

Adjoining Areas

NORTH: **The Northeast**

SOUTH: **The Cariboo Highway**

EAST: **The Yellowhead Highway**

WEST: **The Bulkley and Skeena River Valleys**

inside out

Parks/Camping

Once you're off the main highway, a huge selection of camping possibilities present themselves. There are many excellent, small, user-maintained Forest Service sites available to the explorer at no cost. Unfortunately, a good map, a strong sense of direction, a little luck, and occasionally a really big four-wheel-drive vehicle are necessary to find these pocket campgrounds. Maps of the Prince George, Vanderhoof, and Fort St. James Forest Districts are available from the Forest Service's Prince George Regional Office, 1011 Fourth Ave in Prince George, (250) 565-6100, while maps of the Lakes, Bulkley and Morice Forest Districts are available from the Forest Service's Prince Rupert Regional Office, 3726 Alfred Ave in Smithers, (250) 847-7500.

One of the easier Forest Service sites to find in this area is the **Hogsback Lake Forest Service Site.** The turnoff south of Hwy 16 is 6 miles (10 km) east of Vanderhoof. The lake is about the same distance beyond on Mapes Rd.

If you're not into searching back roads for Forest Service campsites, but instead want the formality provided (for a fee) by a provincial park, contact BC Parks' Skeena District Office, 3790 Alfred St in Smithers, (250) 847-7320; or the Prince George District Office, 4051 18th Ave, (250) 565-6340, in Prince George, for more information and a map. Maps are also available at Travel InfoCentres located in major towns along Hwy 16.

Follow the signs 35 miles (57 km) north of Vanderhoof on Hwy 27 to Fort St. James, and then on to your choice of two provincial parks on the 60-mile-long (100-km) Stuart Lake: **Paarens Beach Provincial Park** (36 vehicle/tent sites) or **Sowchea Bay Provincial Recreation Area** (30 vehicle/tent sites), located just 3 miles (5 km) west of Paarens Beach, both along Sowchea Rd. Reservations are possible at Paarens Beach Provincial Park by calling the BC Parks reservation line, (800) 689-9025, between May 1 and September 15. For general information, call (250) 847-7320. Note: Most parks in this region do not officially open until late May, once the snow has melted and the ice is gone from the lakes.

Beaumont Provincial Park (49 vehicle/tent sites) lies just off Hwy 16 on Fraser Lake near the community of the same name, 25 miles (40 km) west of Vanderhoof. The site has open views of the big lake, and the breeze that blows here helps keep the mosquitoes away. In the 1840s, Beaumont was the site of historic Fort Fraser, and there are still a few signs of the habitation around the park. For reservations, call the BC Parks reservation line, (800) 689-9025, between March 1 and September 15. For general information, call (250) 847-7320.

Ethel F. Wilson Provincial Park, (250) 847-7320, on Pinkut Lake, is located 14.5 miles (24 km) north of the town of Burns Lake via unpaved Babine Rd, and is popular with local anglers plying the waters for rainbow trout. There is no fee to stay at any of the 10 sites in this modestly developed campground.

About 7 miles (11 km) beyond the Ethel F. Wilson Provincial Park is the first of three campgrounds situated along the western shore of the massive Babine Lake. Camping at **Pendleton Bay Provincial Park,** (250) 847-7320, is primitive; consequently, there are no fees charged for the 20 vehicle/tent sites. Most people use this area as a starting point for excursions onto Babine Lake. Farther up the lake is **Red Bluff Provincial Park,** (250) 847-7320, named for iron-stained cliffs that plunge into Babine. There are camping fees in summer for use of the 27 campsites. The park is located 28 miles (45 km) north of Topley off Hwy 16 on paved Granisle Hwy. About 24 miles (40 km) beyond Red Bluff, past the community of Granisle, is **Smithers Landing Provincial Park,** (250) 847-7320. This is the most northerly of the parks on Babine Lake, and lies 34 miles (56 km) off Hwy 16 on Granisle Hwy. There are 6 primitive sites and very little development past the boat launch.

Tyhee Lake Provincial Park, (250) 847-7320, located just north of Telkwa, less than a mile (1 km) north of Hwy 16, is a lightly forested park in the Bulkley Valley and has 59 vehicle/tent sites. The main activities in the park are swimming, boating, fishing, and bird-watching.

Houston's **Steelhead Park** is one of the largest and most attractive municipal parks along Hwy 16. Look for it in the centre of town beside a giant fly-rod. Pretty catchy! In summer, the vehicle/tent site is surrounded by colourful shrubs and flowerbeds. For more information, call the Houston InfoCentre, (250) 845-7640.

Fishing

The corridor from Prince George to Smithers has some of the best fishing in the province—an oft-repeated claim, but in this case, categorically true. This truly is prime fishing country: far enough south to grow the big fish, but not far enough south that it has been overfished. The area between Vanderhoof and Houston is known as the **Lakes Forest District,** and almost every lake offers new fishing opportunities. To list all the good fishing holes would be to list all the lakes between Prince George and Smithers, and most of the rivers as well. To protect stocks, there are some restrictions in place. The two largest rivers in the province, the **Fraser** and the **Skeena,** both flow through this region, with excellent fishing in both the rivers and their tributaries, and quick access from Hwy 16.

Houston, 30 miles (50 km) southeast of Smithers on Hwy 16, is home of the largest fly-fishing rod in the world. The fishing is *par excellence* in the lakes and rivers that surround Houston, which can rightfully claim to be the steelhead capital of Canada. Local anglers are the best source of day-to-day information on where the fish are biting, and can usually be ambushed having coffee at the A&W Restaurant early in the morning. Fishing licences are available at Paradise Sports, (250) 845-2892, in downtown Houston. The Houston InfoCentre (250) 845-7640, located under the giant fly-rod, produces a pamphlet outlining more than two dozen steelhead fishing spots in the Houston area, including **Morice Lake,** 51 miles (84 km) southwest of Houston, **Morice River,** and **Collins Lake,** 34 miles (56 km) south of Houston, all along the Morice River Forest Rd.

Babine Lake is filled with huge fish. Rainbow trout grow as big as 12 pounds (5.5 kg), while char range up to 20 pounds (9 kg). Pendleton Bay, Red Bluff, and Smithers Landing Provincial Parks are all located on Babine Lake (see Parks/Camping, above). For boat rentals, bait, licences, and tackle, contact Babine Lake Resort, at radio phone N69-6674, with the assistance of the Prince George operator.

Hwy 16 follows the **Bulkley River** for more than 97 miles (160 km), from Rose Lake to Hazelton. Anglers can try for rainbow and cutthroat trout, dolly varden, steelhead, chinook, and coho in many fishing holes easily reached from the highway. A popular spot is at the confluence of the Bulkley and Morice Rivers, near Telkwa.

Paradise Lake, 24.5 miles (40 km) from Telkwa along rough road, is a trout angler's paradise. Turn north of Hwy 16, 5 miles (8 km) east of Telkwa. **Tyhee Lake,** 1 mile (2 km) north of Telkwa, is another great place to catch trout; there's a boat launch at Tyhee Lake Provincial Park (see Parks/Camping, above).

Near Fort St. James, fishing is centred around **Stuart Lake.** Sowchea Bay Provincial Recreation Area has a boat launch (see Parks/Camping, above). Beware the high winds on this vast lake. For a more remote fishing experience, try **Takla Lake Provincial Marine Park,** almost 84 miles (135 km) northwest of Hwy 27 in Fort St. James via a network of gravel Forest Service roads, or any of the **Nation Lakes,** north of Fort St. James and east of Takla Lake. For a detailed map of this region, contact the Fort St. James Forest District Office, (250) 996-5200. For more information on fishing, contact the Fish and Wildlife Conservation Officer in Vanderhoof, (250) 567-6304.

The **Nechako River** in the Lakes Forest District once boasted one of the strongest salmon runs in the province. Since the building of the Kenney Dam, stocks in the Nechako have been in decline, in part due to an insufficient and inconsistent amount of water released annually from the dam into the river. That being said, the **Nechako Reservoir** (see Kayaking/Canoeing, below) is still a popular place to fish. A freshwater fishing licence can be obtained at Burns Lake.

Most angling trips in the Lakes Forest District begin from the Forest Service boat launch at **Ootsa Lake,** south of Burns Lake. Ootsa Lake is part of the massive Nechako Reservoir system and marks the northern boundary of Tweedsmuir Provincial Park. A network of back roads leads to Ootsa Lake via **Francois Lake.** The quickest way across Francois Lake is on the free ferry, which runs frequently between the towns of Francois Lake and Southbank. The town of Francois Lake lies about 14 miles (23 km) south of Burns Lake on Hwy 35. Ootsa Lake lies a further 26 miles (42 km) south of Southbank, along well-marked gravel Forest Service roads. A variety of private operators provide guided fishing tours and accommodations on the reservoir. Note: All fish caught in **Tweedsmuir Provincial Park** must be registered at park headquarters on **Whitesail Lake.** For more information on fishing throughout the Lakes Forest District, contact Lakes District Air Services, (250) 692-3229, or Nanika Guiding, (250) 695-6351, in Burns Lake; Likkel's Lakeside Store & Resort,

(250) 694-3403, in Francois Lake; Spatsizi Wilderness Vacations, (250) 847-9692, Nass Headwaters Guiding and Outfitting, (250) 847-5011, Steelhead Valhalla Lodge, (250) 847-9351, or Kispiox River Tours, (250) 847-5002, in Smithers; and Omineca Lodges, (250) 563-8042, in Prince George, Web site address: www.pgonline.com/omenica. For a detailed map of the Lakes Forest District, call the Forest Service office in Burns Lake, (250) 692-2200, or the Prince Rupert Regional Office in Smithers, (250) 847-7500. For more information on fishing throughout the region, contact the Fish and Wildlife Conservation Officer in Burns Lake, (250) 692-7777.

Hiking/Backpacking

This region is littered with trails, both historical and modern. Unfortunately, many lie well off the beaten track along a maze of logging roads. Forest Service recreation maps of these areas are helpful and are available at the Prince George and Prince Rupert Forest District Offices, (250) 996-5200 and (250) 847-7500, respectively.

The defining backpacking trek in this region, and perhaps in the entire province, is the **Nuxalk-Carrier Grease Route/Alexander Mackenzie Heritage Trail.** Alexander Mackenzie is Canada's Lewis and Clark, both wrapped up into one intrepid explorer. Mackenzie was the first European to cross the Rocky Mountains, predating the aforementioned Lewis and Clark by 12 years. He travelled by canoe across much of Canada, but near Prince George, he set out on foot along pre-existing trading trails, established by Native British Columbians. The trails were used by First Nations primarily for trading eulachon grease, perhaps the most valued commodity in the northwest. It is not necessary to hike the 264-mile (420-km) route from Prince George to Bella Coola in one trek in order to get a feeling for what Mackenzie encountered. There are a number of access points to the trail, mostly in the first 60 miles (100 km) or so. The main trailhead begins next to a parking lot on Blackwater Rd, southwest of Prince George, near a viewpoint that overlooks the Blackwater River Valley. To reach it, travel about 37 miles (60 km) south of Hwy 16 on Blackwater Rd, which begins west of Prince George. You can also fly in via floatplane to points along the trail—or, rather, trails, as this is not so much a single trail wending over hill and dale as it is a network of interconnected trails, fragmenting into a dizzying array of routes in some places. Sometimes, these are just different routes around a lake, while at other points the trails lead to different destinations entirely. Proper maps and a compass are indispensable. To obtain a detailed map, contact the Forest Service's Prince George Regional Office, (250) 565-6100. The main trail stretches from the primary trailhead, just south of Prince George where Blackwater Forest Service Rd ends at the confluence of the Blackwater and Fraser Rivers, through Tweedsmuir Provincial Park and all the way to Bella Coola (see The Bella Coola Road (Highway 20) chapter), though not to the actual site Alexander Mackenzie reached. (To get there, you'll need to take a boat from Bella Coola to Mackenzie Rock to see the famous inscription: "Alexander Mackenzie, from Canada, by land, 22nd July 1793.")

If you do attempt to hike the entire trail in one fell swoop, bear in mind that experienced hikers can expect to take three weeks, and most of the trail runs through remote wilderness areas, far from civilization. The trail is best done in late summer or early fall. Any earlier, and the black flies and mosquitoes in some of the lower, wetter areas can be unbearable. No matter how much or little of the trail you want to hike, you must plan ahead. An excellent guide to the entire trail is *In the Steps of Alexander Mackenzie* published by the Alexander Mackenzie Trail Association, Box 425, Kelowna BC, V1Y 7P1.

The Alexander Mackenzie Heritage Trail runs through **Tweedsmuir Provincial Park,** but it's not the only trail of length in this park. Tweedsmuir is serious backcountry camping, and the only road access is to the southern half of the park via Hwy 20 from Hwy 97 near Williams Lake (see The Bella Coola Road (Highway 20) chapter for details). To reach the northern half of the park, you're limited to floatplane from the town of Burns Lake, jet-boat from Ootsa Landing, or by foot or horseback via the Alexander Mackenzie Heritage Trail.

Most of the northern half of Tweedsmuir is encircled by the lakes that comprise the **Nechako Reservoir: Ootsa** and **Whitesail Lakes** define the north and west boundaries of the park respectively, while **Eutsuk Lake** bisects the park, turning northern Tweedsmuir into a huge, unpopulated near-island (Eutsuk and Whitesail fall about a half-mile/1 km short of connecting). A series of trails start from **Wistaria Provincial Park,** (250) 847-7320, located on the north shore of Ootsa Lake about 80 km southwest of Burns Lake via Hwy 35, the Ootsa-Nadina Junction Rd, and the Wistaria Hwy. To hike this route, you'll need to get across nearly 3 miles (5 km) of open water on Ootsa Lake, which is notorious for sudden changes of weather and high winds. For this reason, canoeing across the lake is not recommended. Once across, though, hiking trails lead to **Sabina Lake, Chief Louis Lake, Nutli Lake,** and ultimately **Blanchet Lake,** 30 miles (50 km) beyond Ootsa Lake. Hikers can arrange to be dropped off and picked up by a local outfitter or tour operator, such as Tweedsmuir Park Guides and Outfitters in Vanderhoof, (250) 567-4399. Call BC Parks, (250) 847-7320, for more information on outfitters and a map of hiking trails in Tweedsmuir (North) Provincial Park. There is little margin for error in this wilderness area, and backpacking here is recommended for expert backcountry aficionados only.

The **Babine Mountains Provincial Recreation Area,** located about 9 miles (15 km) east of Smithers off Hwy 16 on gravel road, has an extensive interlinking trail system that leads into the open alpine regions. There are a lot of day-hike trails that can be knit together into two- or three-day loops through the park. For horseback, angling, and backcountry adventure tours, contact local guides and outfitters in the Smithers-Houston region such as Ray Makowichuk in Houston, (250) 845-2982. For more information, contact Bear Mountaineering School, (250) 847-3351, Suskwa Adventure Outfitters, (250) 847-2885, or Northern Sun Tours, (250) 847-4349, in Smithers. A good backcountry guide to consult is locally produced *Trails to Timberline in Western Canada* by Einar Blix. Populations are small in the northwest, and almost everyone knows everyone else. Contact the local Tourist InfoCentres in Smithers and Houston for more good contacts.

The trailhead of the **Mount Pope Hiking Trail** (moderate; 7.5 miles/12 km return) is 3 miles (5 km) northwest of Fort St. James on Stones Bay Rd. Allow a half-day for the hike to an old forestry lookout at top of 4,857-foot (1472-m) Mount Pope, from where you'll enjoy sweeping views of big Stuart Lake and the Interior Plateau. For more information and a map of hiking trails in the area, call the Fort St. James InfoCentre, (250) 996-7023, or stop by their office on Hwy 27 in town.

During the Klondike gold rush in the late 1890s, a telegraph line was constructed to connect the gold fields to the rest of civilization, which in those days began in central British Columbia around Prince George. The telegraph fell out of use in the 1930s with the advent of radio technology. Some parts of the old trail still survive; the longest of these connects Telegraph Creek to Atlin (see The Stewart-Cassiar Highway (Highway 37) chapter). A section of the **Telegraph Trail** west of Prince George off Hwy 16 runs from Hogsback Lake for about 6 miles (10 km), until it is lost under Blackwater Rd. To reach the trailhead, drive 10.5 miles (17 km) south of Hwy 16 on the Bobtail Forest Rd, then 5 miles (8 km) west on Blackwater Rd to Hogsback Lake.

The turnoff to Telegraph Rd is near Fort Fraser, west of Vanderhoof on Hwy 16. Telegraph Rd runs southeast, and connects with the Kluskus Forest Service Rd, which heads due south through the Nulki Hills for about 37 miles (60 km). There are a number of hiking trails along the way, including the **Home Lake Trail,** a 4-mile (6-km) trail to Home Lake. You can hike to the lake and back in a day but, as the Forest Service has been kind enough to build a cabin at the lake for you to use, why not stay the night? The trailhead is located at km 42.5 (about 26 miles) on the Kluskus Forest Service Rd. About 6 miles (10 km) beyond is the **Johnson Lake Trail.** There's no cabin here, but it's a pretty spot to pitch a tent and enjoy swatting mosquitoes as the sun sets. The trail is about 3 miles (5 km) one way. A short distance beyond that on the Kluskus Forest Service Rd is the **Gluten Lake Trail,** which leads 3.5 miles (6 km) east to Gluten Lake, past **Zippermouth Lake.** For more information on hiking trails in the Vanderhoof Forest District, contact their office, (250) 567-6363, for a map. Copies are also available at the Vanderhoof InfoCentre on Hwy 16.

Also in the Vanderhoof region you'll find a short interpretive trail in Beaumont Provincial Park (see Parks/Camping, above). Across Hwy 16 from the park is the **Fraser Mountain Trail.** It's about a 5-mile (8-km) return trip, from the bottom of an old ski hill to the top. This hike begins 25 miles (40 km) west of Vanderhoof. There's good hiking on the north side of Fraser Lake at the Peterson's Beach Forest Service Recreation Site. A perimeter road around Fraser Lake begins off Hwy 16 at the community of Stella. Follow this for about 12 miles (20 km) to reach the recreation site. On the other side of the road from Peterson's is the **Ormond Creek Trail,** a 16-mile (26-km) return trip to Ormond Lake through Ormond Creek Canyon. The first half-mile or so of the trail passes through a 300-year-old Douglas fir forest.

The **Morice Mountain Ski Trails** (see Skiing/Snowboarding, below) in the Silverthorne Lake area of the Houston Community Forest are open to hikers in the summer. There is about 24 miles (40 km) of trails; the longest runs 5.5 miles (9 km) to Morice Mountain. For guided hiking tours in the Houston region, contact Hungry Hills Adventures, (250) 845-7030, in Houston.

Babine Mountains Provincial Recreation Area, 9 miles (15 km) east of Smithers, is latticed with hiking trails ranging in length from 2 to 10 miles (3 to 16.5 km). This is an undeveloped wilderness area full of impressive mountains, glaciers, and broad alpine expanses. In winter, it's a very popular backcountry ski destination. Contact BC Parks in Smithers for more information, (250) 847-7565.

The northern part of **Tweedsmuir Provincial Park** is best travelled by jet-boat. There are **boat launches** on Ootsa Lake at Andrews Bay Provincial Park and Wistaria Provincial Park. It takes about two days to do the circuit route created by Ootsa, Whitesail, Eutsuk, and Tetachuck Lakes by jet-boat; a few more if you take the time to hike some of the Tweedsmuir trails. Trails start across from Wistaria Provincial Park and lead back into the heart of Tweedsmuir. Shorter trails are scattered about, mostly at the western end of the two western lakes. **The Chickamin Mountain Trail** (3 miles/5 km return), **Surel Lake Trail** (1.5 miles/3 km return), and **Musclow Lake Trail** (1.5 miles/3 km return) are off Eutsuk Lake, while the **Zinc Mountain Mining Road** leads up the north side of the Chikamin Range from Whitesail Lake. Contact BC Parks, (250) 847-7320, for a brochure outlining the trails.

Bring your colour film along when hiking the **Fort George Canyon Trail,** an almost 3-mile (4.5-km) ramble through flowers and shrubs to the banks of the Fraser River. To reach the trail, head for **West Lake Provincial Park** (see Picnics, below), west of Prince George, and continue for about 6 miles (10 km) along West Lake Rd. The trailhead is well marked.

Picnics

West Lake Provincial Park is located about 6 miles (10 km) west of Prince George on Hwy 16, then 9 miles (14 km) south on Blackwater Rd. There are tables and a covered shelter that doubles as warming hut in winter, as well as a sandy beach for swimming. Hiking trails around the north end of the lake double as cross-country trails in winter. **Paarens Beach Provincial Park** and **Sowchea Bay Provincial Recreation Area** (see Parks/Camping, above) both have picnic tables and firepits. Paarens Beach is 9 miles (15 km) west of Fort St. James on Stuart Lake; Sowchea Bay is 1.5 miles (3 km) beyond. **Red Bluff Provincial Park** (see Parks/Camping, above), 28 miles (45 km) north of Topley on the west shore of Babine Lake, is a pleasant spot to pull out the old basket. After lunch, go for a swim in Babine Lake. In the town of Telkwa, try **Eddy Park** beside the blue waters of the Bulkley River, or **Tyhee Lake Provincial Park** to the north off Hwy 16, with beachside picnic tables and a covered shelter. One of the more unusual parks in this region is **Driftwood Canyon Provincial Park,** on Driftwood Creek Rd, 6 miles (10 km) northeast of Smithers and Hwy 16. It is located in a fossil-lined canyon, ripe for exploring by the amateur paleontologist. Please, take only photographs.

The highest point on Hwy 16 is the **Six Mile Summit** on **China Nose Mountain,** about 25 miles (40 km) west of **Burns Lake.** As the road climbs to highest point on Hwy 16 (elevation 4,695 feet/1423 m), views of the rolling mountains in the Bulkley and Morice Ranges stand revealed. (Far from being a derogatory term, China Nose refers to a savvy Chinese miner who told area residents "China *knows*" where the gold is; hence, the corruption.)

The **Hungry Hill,** about 6 miles (10 km) west of Houston, has nice views of surrounding mountains from this roadside pullout, complete with a picnic table. The **Bulkley View Rest Area,** 27 miles (43 km) west of Houston, offers fine views of the **Bulkley Valley.**

Skiing/Snowboarding

In a land where winter lasts for what seems like most of the year, winter recreation is a necessity. There are more snowmobiles here than you would imagine possible, and cross-country **snowmobiling** is far and away the most popular winter pastime.

There aren't many big ski hills in the region, so **downhill skiers** and **snowboarders** must travel some distance to find the steep stuff. **Hudson Bay Mountain** (see The Bulkley and Skeena River Valleys chapter), 14 miles (22 km) west of Smithers, is the biggest hill in the area, with excellent powder skiing.

The only other option of any note is **Murray Ridge Ski Hill,** about 6 miles (10 km) east of Fort St. James. Murray Ridge has the longest T-bar in North America (6,500 feet/1980 m) and is open to downhill skiers and snowboarders. In February, the ski hill hosts the Great Bathtub Race, with an emphasis on fun rather than competition. If you're in the area when the race is on, make sure you check it out. Murray Ridge also has 12 miles (20 km) of cross-country trails. Call (250) 996-8513 or (888) 229-1155 for more information.

In the winter, lakes and rivers freeze, creating level playgrounds for **cross-country skiers.** During winter, ice can freeze 4 feet thick or more. Be careful when skiing on frozen surfaces, especially rivers, where moving water does not freeze as solidly as lake water does. Check with locals for ice conditions before heading out.

There are numerous cross-country trails around **Vanderhoof.** The Nechako Valley Sporting Association maintains some of the trails in this area, including 19 miles (30 km) of groomed trail at **Waterlily Lake,** located north of town off Hwy 16 on Sturgeon Point Rd. A detailed map of the trails is available from the Forest Service office in Vanderhoof, (250) 567-6363.

The **Morice Mountain Ski Trails,** in the Silverthorne Lake area of the Houston Community Forest, are track-set by the volunteer Morice Mountain Nordic Club. There is about 24.5 miles (40 km) of well-signed, groomed trails. There is also a 5.5-mile (9-km) trek along unmaintained trails to an overnight cabin just below the tree line on the slopes of Morice Mountain, a starting point for excursions into the alpine. The cabin is free to members and $10 a night for nonmembers; it must be booked in advance through Paradise Sports, (250) 845-2892. The trails are southwest of Houston on Buck Flats Rd.

The Omineca Cross-Country Ski Trails, 4 miles (6.5 km) south of Burns Lake on Hwy 35, consist of 15 miles (25 km) of groomed trails. There are also many, many ungroomed trails, such as hiking trails, that are open to cross-country skiers. **Babine Mountains Provincial Recreation Area,** 9 miles (15 km) east of Smithers off Hwy 16, has an extensive system of trails open to skiers and snowshoers. A popular overnighting destination is the **Silver King Cabin,** just over 8 miles (13.5 km) down the trail, but there are many routes in this area. Because this is mountain backcountry skiing, there is the danger of avalanches. Take the appropriate precautions (see BC Outdoor Primer). For more information on cross-country skiing in provincial parks, call BC Parks, (250) 847-7320, in Smithers.

Mountain Biking

Many of the cities in this region have discovered a very important concept: mountain biking is now a big part of outdoor exploration. Towns such as **Fort St. James** have grabbed this concept and run with it. Don't expect to find ripping singletrack just yet, but for the fat-tire tourist, there are a number of pleasing day rides, like the six- to seven-hour **Tezzeron Lake Return,** and a couple of extended trips, including **The Great Northern Circuit,** a six- to seven-day journey along northern logging roads. Other multiday trips include the **Fraser Lake Circuit** and the **Great Beaver Lake Circumnavigation.** A ride that should have any true bikepacker drooling is the **Spatsizi Overlander Adventure Ride,** an amazingly lengthy ride from Fort St. James to southeast Alaska. This isn't a formal bike trail, but for hard-core bike tourists, this is the ride to end all rides. There is no estimate of the time it will take you, but there is a challenge. Drop a postcard in the mail in Fort St. James addressed to yourself in Telegraph Creek (at the northern tip of Mount Edziza Provincial Park), and try to beat it there. For more information and a brochure outlining mountain-biking in this area, contact Fort St. James InfoCentre, (250) 996-7023.

Near **Vanderhoof,** the 19 miles (30 km) of the **Waterlily Cross-Country Ski Trails** (see Skiing/Snowboarding, above) are open to mountain bikes in the summer. A section of the **Telegraph Trail** (see Hiking/Backpacking, above) runs from Hogsback Lake for about 6 miles (10 km) until it is lost under Blackwater Rd. The trail connects to Blackwater Rd, making a 12-mile (20-km) circuit ride. The **Omineca Trail,** from Noonla to Stuart River, is 9 miles (15 km) long. This was the old route to the Omineca Gold Fields. Side trips include trails to McLeod Meadow and to Wonder and Expected Lakes. The trail is located just north of Vanderhoof, on the east side of Hwy 27. Note: Don't confuse this trail with the Omenica Cross-Country Ski Trails near Burns Lake.

Babine Mountains Provincial Recreation Area (see Hiking/Backpacking, above), 9 miles (15 km) east of Smithers, has many trails that are open to the mountain biker, including the Harvey Mountain Trail, The Silver King Basin Trail, Onion Mountain Rd, Cronin Creek Trail, and Higgins Creek Trail. Many of the trails are also open, at least partway, to four-wheel drives and ATVs.

The **Morice Mountain Ski Trails,** in the Silverthorne Lake area of the Houston Community Forest, are open to mountain bikes in the summer. There are about 24.5 miles (40 km) of trail, including the 5.5-mile (9-km) run to Morice Mountain (see Skiing/Snowboarding, above).

For more information on mountain biking in this region, contact the BC Forest Service office in Houston, (250) 845-6200.

Canoeing/Kayaking

There are dozens of fine canoe routes here. You can take a few hours to run a river, or a few weeks to run a chain of lakes. Many of the routes have been well documented by the phenomenal Northwest Brigade Canoe Club, one of the most active canoe groups in the province. If you're planning to spend a lot of time in this area, or even to make just one extensive trip, it would be a good idea to contact them at Box 327, Prince George, BC V2L 4S2, or pick up a copy of *Canoe and Kayak Trip Guide for the Central Interior of British Columbia,* put out by the canoe club. At the very least, get in touch with them for any new information on regional routes. Another helpful guidebook is *Canoe Routes British Columbia* by Jack Wainwright.

The **Stuart River** has rapids of up to Class IV, depending on water levels, but if you can handle that (or, in a pinch, portage), you can canoe the **Stuart and Nechako Rivers** from Fort St. James to Prince George. Alexander Mackenzie did this route, albeit going the other way, back in 1806 when he established Fort St. James. A lot of this route is flatwater, scarcely Class I, but watch out for occasional rapids and the usual litany of wild-water hazards: fallen trees, logs, etc. The entire trip runs for 119 miles (195 km), with rapids to Class III as well as one Class IV. Plan on taking three to six days to complete the journey one way.

The **Nechako River** is also paddleable well above its confluence with the Stuart River. From the **Cheslatta River Forest Service Site** (about 68 miles/110 km south of Vanderhoof and Hwy 16 via the Holy-Cross Forest Rd) to the mouth of the Stuart is about 87 miles (140 km), the first mile (1.6 km) of which is on foot to the base of Cheslatta Falls. Most of the river is Class II, with some rapids. Expect to take five days to reach the Stuart River, and another day to reach Prince George, 30 miles (50 km) beyond. Don't have a time for a weeklong trip? You don't have to do the entire route, you know. For detailed maps of these routes, contact the Vanderhoof Forest Service District, (250) 567-6363, and the Forest Service's Prince George Regional Office, (250) 565-6100.

Another option is the **Stellako River.** From the east end of **Francois Lake** to **Fraser Lake** is just 4 miles (7 km), the perfect way to spend an afternoon. The river is maximum Class II, with the exception of a Class IV waterfall. A short portage—less than 100 feet (30 m)—leads around the falls. Of course, if you don't want to deal with the rapids, you can always spend a lazy day paddling about Fraser Lake, and spend the night at **Beaumont Provincial Park** (see Parks/Camping, above).

In 1952, Alcan Aluminum built the Kenney Dam on the Nechako River, creating the **Nechako Reservoir,** a series of interconnected lakes that runs nearly 125 miles (200 km) east/west in two broad arms that connect near the dam at the easternmost end of the reservoir. The northern arm consists of **Ootsa** and **Whitesail Lakes,** while the southern arm, which bisects **Tweedsmuir Provincial Park,** consists of **Eutsuk** and **Tetachuck Lakes.** With a short portage between Whitesail and Eutsuk (a tramway has been built to haul bigger boats across), the lakes can be boated as a 170-mile (275-km) circuit that runs through the rugged peaks of the Coast Mountains in the west and rolling Interior Plateau hills in the east.

Canoeing or kayaking the Nechako Reservoir is not recommended, as the area was not logged out before it was flooded. Still, people do it, and no wonder. This is one of the longest circuit routes in the province, with only two portages (or one, if you travel counterclockwise and are comfortable shooting Class III). Prominent are the ghostly stands of trees, rising silent from the water, a legacy of the 165-foot (50-m) climb in water levels when the dam was built. **Redfern Rapids** (which can be navigated safely by powerboat) is one of the highlights of the trip, as are the **glaciers** at Eutsuk's western shoreline. With the deep green of the surrounding foliage, the white snow, and the blue sky, the reservoir is a photographer's dream.

The landscape surrounding the eastern section of the reservoir, particularly the stretch between the settlement of Ootsa Lake and Redfern Rapids, consists of the rolling, heavily forested slopes of the Fraser Plateau, but the western half features vast glacial expanses of Coast Mountains, for which Tweedsmuir Provincial Park is renowned.

For more information on the Nechako Reservoir, including boat **rentals** and lodgings, contact BC Parks, (250) 565-6340, and the Forest Service, (250) 996-5200. Good maps of the region included NTS #93E/01 and 92N/13. Once in the region, consult private operators such as Van Tine Fishing Camp, (250) 694-3359, among others for current information on navigation. The best time of the year to visit the Nechako Reservoir is in late summer, once water levels and insects have declined. Early autumn is a particularly beautiful season, when leaves turn the Fraser Plateau pure gold.

Plan on seven to ten days to paddle the 56-mile (90-km) **Nation Lakes,** north of Fort St. James, from one end to the other by canoe. The route begins at **Tsayta Lake,** and passes through **Indata, Tchentlo,** and **Chuchi Lakes.** There are 12 Forest Service recreation sites along the lakeshores. Make sure you stop by the **Tchentlo Lake Warm Springs** on your way through. They're within sight of the Tchentlo Lake Lodge on the opposite shore. The springs have a maximum temperature of 75°F/24°C. On a warm summer's evening, you won't want it much hotter. If you don't want to do the entire route, you can launch a canoe from the Tchentlo Lake Lodge, an 83-mile (133-km) drive from Fort St. James. Follow the signs from the Leo Creek Forest Service Rd in Fort St. James. Canoes can be rented from the lodge. To contact them, call the operator in Prince George and ask for radio-phone service on the Mount Dixon channel, then request radio phone #H425357. For more information on the Nation Lakes, contact the Fort St. James InfoCentre, (250) 996-7023. For a map of the Nation Lakes system, contact the Fort St. James Forest District office, (250) 996-5200, or the Forest Service's Prince George Regional Office, (250) 565-6100.

Depending on where you begin on Takla Lake, it will take you two to four days to canoe the **Takla Lake/Stuart Lake system.** The most common starting point is Takla Landing. It's 118 miles (190 km) from there to Stuart River Campground, just south of Fort St. James. The route travels south down **Takla Lake,** along the **Middle River** to **Trembleur Lake,** then takes the **Tachie River** to **Stuart Lake.** For a map, contact the Fort St. James Forest District Office, (250) 996-5200, or the Forest Service's Prince George Regional Office, (250) 565-6100.

It will probably take you over a week to canoe **Babine Lake,** British Columbia's longest (but not largest) lake at 110 miles (177 km) from tip to tip. You can also put in and take out at many places along the lake, including Fort Babine, Smithers Landing, Granisle, Topley Landing, or Pendleton Bay Provincial Park. Hug the shore of this huge lake; weather can change rapidly. For detailed recreation maps, contact the Lakes Forest District Office, (250) 692-2200, and the Morice Forest District Office, (250) 845-6200, or the Forest Service's Prince Rupert Regional Office, (250) 847-7500.

Located well off the beaten path is the **Nanika-Kidprice Portage Trails,** a wilderness canoe route through four lakes on the edge of the Coast Mountains. Round trip to **Nanika Falls** on **Kidprice Lake** is about 30 miles (50 km)—allow at least three days. Access to the lakes is difficult along Forest Service roads south of Houston. A detailed brochure of the route is available from Morice Forest District Office, (250) 845-6200.

For **more information** on boating and paddling in the region, consult Island Alpine, (250) 562-8445, or Backwater Paddling, (250) 964-7400, in Prince George; and Northern Sun Tours, (250) 847-4349, in Smithers. Also visit the Adventure Network Web site: www.bcadventure.com/.

Wildlife

The **Vanderhoof Bird Sanctuary** in Riverside Park is a **migratory bird** rest area on the Nechako River in Vanderhoof. Farther north, Tyhee Lake Provincial Park, near Smithers, has trails and a wildlife viewing platform in a marshy area on the popular lake—popular, that is, with **loons, grebes, beavers,** and, oh yes, swimmers and sunbathers in summer.

Climbing

Owen Hat near Houston is a local rockface with easy to moderate routes, including bolted routes rated from 5.6 to 5.9 and top-roped routes rated up to 5.1 in difficulty. It's an hour's drive from Hwy 16 on Morice River Rd, Morice Owen Rd, and finally Owen North Rd. Watch for the trailhead, about 37 miles (60 km) from Hwy 16. There's camping in the area around the base of Owen Hat. As it is one of the only places to rock-climb in the area, it has become an increasingly popular destination for local climbers and, therefore, a good place to find out more local lore. Contact the Houston InfoCentre for more information, (250) 845-7640.

More Information

BC Forest Service, Fort St. James Forest District: *(250) 996-5200.*
BC Forest Service, Lakes Forest District, Burns Lake: *(250) 692-2200.*
BC Forest Service, Morice Forest District, Houston: *(250) 845-6200.*
BC Forest Service, Prince George Regional Office, Prince George: *(250) 565-6100.*
BC Forest Service, Prince Rupert Regional Office, Smithers: *(250) 847-7500.*
BC Forest Service, Vanderhoof Forest District: *(250) 567-6363.*
BC Parks, Prince George: *(250) 565-6340;*
BC Parks, reservations: *(800) 689-9025.*
BC Parks, Smithers: *(250) 847-7320 or (250) 847-7565.*
Burns Lake InfoCentre: *(250) 692-3773.*
Fort St. James InfoCentre: *(250) 996-7023.*
Granisle Travel Information and Museum: *(250) 697-2248 or (250) 697-2248.*

Houston InfoCentre: *(250) 845-7640.*
Smithers InfoCentre: *(800) 542-6673 or (250) 847-9854.*
Telkwa Information: *(250) 846-5212.*
Tourism Prince George: *year-round, (250) 562-3700; seasonal, (250) 563-5493; toll free, (800) 668-7646.*
Vanderhoof InfoCentre: *(250) 567-2124.*

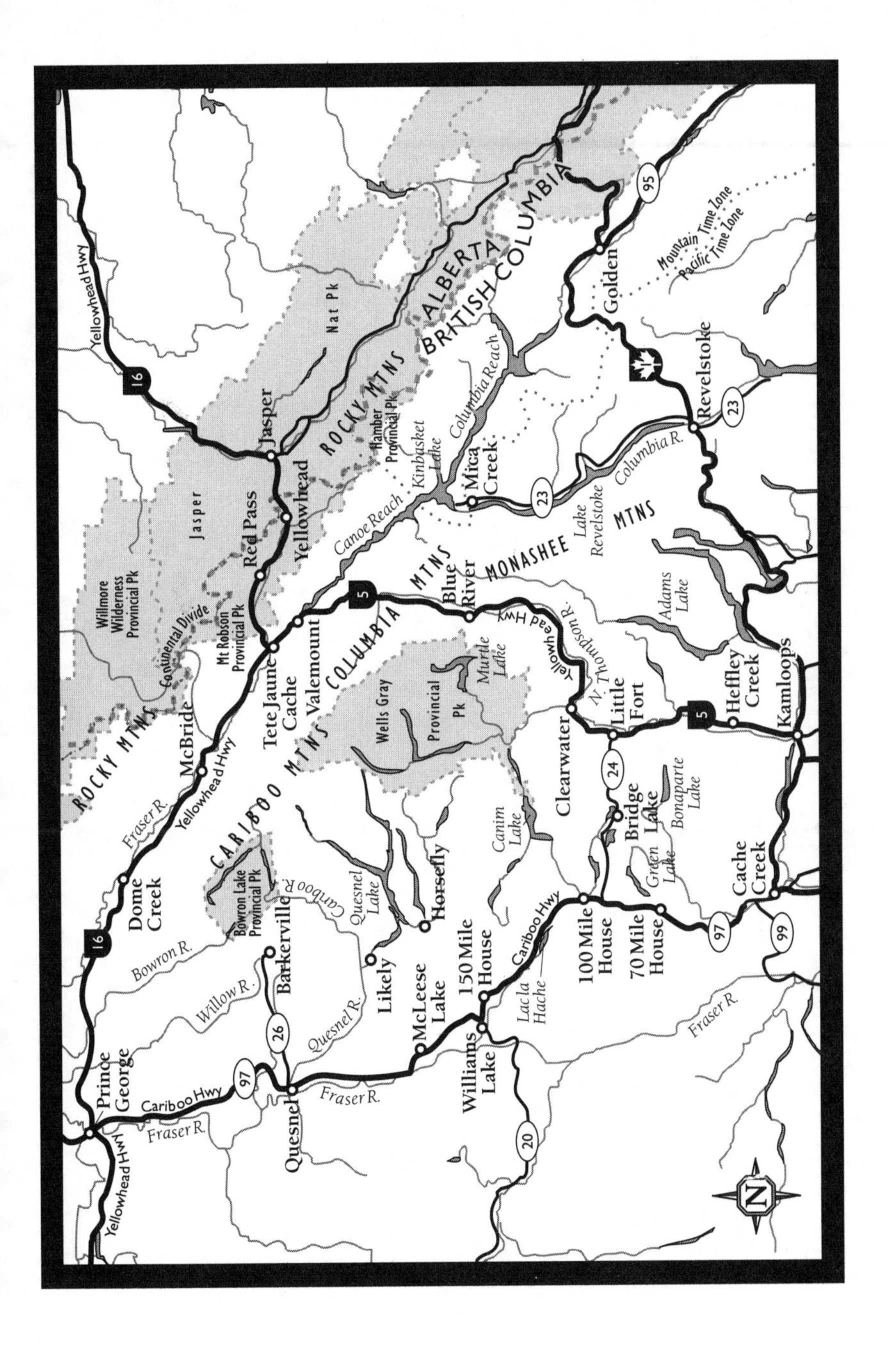

Central Interior

The Cariboo Highway 591

The Yellowhead Highway 602

Central Interior

The Cariboo Highway

From Cache Creek north on Highway 97 to Prince George across the lake-studded Fraser Plateau, including the Chasm, Green Lake, and Bowron Lake Provincial Parks, and the historic Gold Rush Trail from Lillooet (Mile 0) to Barkerville.

This is a classic 275-mile (445-km) ramble through the heart of the Cariboo region, with branch roads that lead west into one of British Columbia's most thinly populated outbacks, Chilcotin country. Many towns along the Cariboo Highway are helpfully referred to by distance from Lillooet (Mile 0) north along the Gold Rush Trail. Thus 70 Mile House, for example, marks the distance between Lillooet and this point, the original site of a pioneer roadhouse. Evidence of the days of the stampeders persists in delightful places such as the roadhouses at Hat Creek, 108 Mile Ranch, and Cottonwood Creek. Even more impressive is the landscape itself, with its rolling hills, deeply incised rivers, and many lakes.

There are several approaches one can take: hurried or slow, scenic or under cover of darkness, direct or circuitous. However, no matter which route you choose when heading to or from the Cariboo, all offer rewards along the way. After experiencing the peace that prevails in this region, and inspired by sights such as that of a canoe mirrored in the surface of a crystal lake or fresh ski tracks lit by a full moon, the glow of your adventure will make you drag your feet when the time to head home draws nigh.

Getting There

BC Rail parallels Highway 97 from Prince George to Clinton. In the south, Highway 1 links with Highway 97 at Cache Creek, the Cariboo Highway's southern terminus. To the west, Highway 20 links Bella Coola on the central coast with Highway 97 at Williams Lake, while Highway 16 links Prince

Rupert on the northwest coast with Prince George. To the east, Highway 24 links Highway 5 (the Yellowhead) with Highway 97 near 93 Mile House. Daily air, rail, and bus service to Prince George is provided by Air BC, (604) 688-5515, BC Rail (604) 984-5246, and Greyhound Canada, (604) 482-8747, respectively, from Vancouver.

Adjoining Areas

NORTH: **The Northeast**

SOUTH: **The Trans-Canada Highway**

EAST: **The Yellowhead Highway**

WEST: **The Bella Coola Road (Highway 20)**

Camping/Parks

There are plenty of provincial campgrounds within easy reach of the Cariboo Highway. Maps and detailed information on all of them are available from BC Parks' Cariboo district headquarters, 282 First Ave N, in Williams Lake, (250) 398-4414. For those parks where reservations are accepted, call (800) 689-9025 to request a campsite.

For a nice and easy start to a summer trip in the Cariboo, go just northeast of Cache Creek. **Loon Lake Provincial Park**'s 14 vehicle/tent sites are tucked into a mixed Douglas fir and ponderosa pine forest. Close by is Loon Creek hatchery, which raises kokanee salmon and rainbow trout. Take the paved secondary road off Hwy 97 for 17 miles (27 km) northeast of Cache Creek.

I once stood on the shores of the lake in **Big Bar Lake Provincial Park** for half an hour simply trying to memorize the view—the Cariboo encourages that kind of behaviour. Glaciers melting as recently as 10,000 to 20,000 years ago have left a hummocky landscape marked with lakes and ponds: a real treat for open-eyed adventurers. There are 33 vehicle/tent sites in this park, which opens in June—as soon as the snow melts! Swimming, fishing, and boating are popular activities here. To get there, take Hwy 97 north of Cache Creek and Clinton, turn off about 5 miles (8 km) north of Clinton. A gravel road leads about 13 miles (21 km) to the park.

Green Lake of **Green Lake Provincial Park** is wide and shallow, fed by two small creeks, lake-bottom springs, and upland runoff. Since its outlet only functions in high-water periods, there's lots of time for algae and other micro-organisms to form: hence the lake's greenish hue and its name. This lake is excellent for both summer and winter recreation. Swimming, boating, waterskiing, paddling, and horseback riding are all popular; the undulating plateau and highlands around the lake have become a cross-country skier's paradise; sandy beaches dot the irregular shoreline at five spots. There are 121 vehicle/tent sites at three locations, and reservations are recommended in summer. Call BC Parks' reservation service between March 1 and September 15: (800) 689-9025. Go 9 miles (15 km) northeast from Hwy 97 on Bonaparte Rd at 70 Mile House; there's an alternate approach from 83 Mile House.

The small but beautifully situated **Bridge Lake Provincial Park** is particularly popular with anglers looking for rainbow and lake trout. It will win the heart of anyone who has the good fortune to spend a night here, particularly in fall once the mosquito season has ended. A walking trail skirts the lake and provides an excellent afternoon's exercise. There are 19 vehicle/tent sites and 7 walk-in campsites. There are three ways to get to the park: take Hwy 24 east at 93 Mile House for 31 miles (50 km); or take Hwy 24 for 31 miles (50 km) west from Hwy 5 at Little Fort; or take a part-paved, part-gravel road for about 34 miles (55 km) east of 70 Mile House.

Despite the popularity of local angling, there is very limited camping at **Canim Beach Provincial Park** (7 vehicle/tent sites; 9 walk-in sites) at the beach on the south end of Canim Lake. Competition for these sites is intense, but should you find yourself frozen out there's plenty of private accommodation nearby. The park is located 27 miles (43 km) northwest of Hwy 97 at 100 Mile House, on paved road via Forest Grove.

Lac la Hache (Axe Lake) describes itself as "the longest town in the Cariboo." **Lac la Hache Provincial Park**'s 83 vehicle/tent sites are set in relatively open Douglas fir and aspen woodlands beside one of the biggest lakes seen from Hwy 97. Campsites are uphill from the highway, while the picnic site and boat launch are right on the lake. This park is great for afternoon munching, swimming, and boating. Take Hwy 97 north from Lac la Hache for 8 miles (13 km).

Set in the heart of what were once goldfields, the large lake here is now used mainly by anglers. **Horsefly Lake Provincial Park** has 22 vehicle/tent sites, a picnic/day-use area, and a boat launch. And, yes, the biting-insect population here is the reason for the lake's name. Take the part-paved, part-gravel road off Hwy 97 at either McLeese Lake or 150 Mile House; the park is 8 miles (13 km) northeast of Horsefly.

Most people, when they think of Barkerville, think of the gold-rush centre that was once the largest city west of Chicago and north of San Francisco. **Barkerville Provincial Park** is adjacent to the restored town, a very popular destination for tourists (see Attractions, below), and camping at the park may be a good alternative to seeking private accommodations. The park has 168 vehicle/tent sites and reservations are recommended. While visiting here, stretch your legs along one of the three hikes suitable for an afternoon ramble. The trail to Mount Agnes goes from Barkerville to Richfield, following the route of the original Cariboo Wagon Trail to Summit Rock. If Barkerville is full, you should try to get a campsite at the other nearby parks: **Forest Rose, Lowhee,** and **Government Hill,** all just north of the town. Take Hwy 26 for 55 miles (89 km) east of Quesnel; reservations, (800) 689-9025.

The large, backcountry **Bowron Lake Provincial Park** offers a wide variety of recreational opportunities: camping, canoeing, boating, kayaking, hiking, swimming, fishing, and winter recreation. Particularly notable is its canoe circuit (see Canoeing, below). Bowron lies across the boundaries of two regional landscapes. The western portion of the park is in the Quesnel Highlands (a subsection of the Interior Plateau) and the eastern portion is in the Cariboo Mountains. The Bowron and Spectacle Lakes waterway marks the boundary between these two landscapes. There are 25 vehicle/tent sites and 103 wilderness sites in the park. The entire park is a wildlife sanctuary, including prime habitat for grizzly bears, so be on your best backcountry camping behaviour. Use the bear caches near the wilderness campsites. The Bowron Lakes are also a major stopover on the bird migration route, so bring your binoculars. Take Hwy 26 east of Quesnel for 68 miles (110 km); at the end of Hwy 26, continue along the gravel access road for about 11 miles (18 km).

Ten Mile Lake Provincial Park was originally a milepost for the Pacific Great Eastern Railway. Abandoned railway grade can still be seen in the park, which is popular now for its recreational offerings. Among these are a fine sandy beach and a great lake for swimming, waterskiing, and boating. The park has 142 vehicle/tent sites, and reservations are recommended. There is a boat launch so that campers can get out and explore the lake (and get away from the bugs). (See Cross-Country Skiing, below.) Take Hwy 97 north of Quesnel for almost 7 miles (11 km).

For those of you who would like to camp in a quiet, unspoiled setting, **Cottonwood River Provincial Park** is perfect. Comfortably close to the main highway but away from the traffic at the same time, you'll find 15 vehicle/tent sites here. Take Hwy 97 north of Quesnel for 17 miles (27 km); then take the 4-mile (6-km) gravel road to the park.

Fishing/Boating

Fishing is great in the Cariboo; there are literally thousands of lakes, ponds, and rivers in this region. Among the best of them are **Loon Lake** (see Camping/Parks, above), a long, narrow, well-stocked rainbow trout lake that also contains kokanee and steelhead; **Big Bar Lake** (see Camping/Parks, above), which has rainbow trout, too; and **Bonaparte Lake and Valley,** the dominant lake and river system in the south Cariboo. There are two approaches to Bonaparte: either head west of Hwy 5 from Barrière or head east from Hwy 97 at 70 Mile House. In the **Interlakes District, Sheridan** and **Bridge Lakes** are the largest of hundreds dotted along Hwy 24 (the "Fishing Highway"), which runs about 60 miles (97 km) east to the North Thompson River and the town of Little Fort on Hwy 5. Sheridan Lake holds spectacular-sized rainbow trout in the 14- to 16-pound range. The best time to try your luck here is as soon as the ice is off the lakes in May. Mayfly hatch brings out the fly-fishers for rainbow trout as well as burbot.

Canim Lake, a large lake 27 miles (43 km) northeast of 100 Mile House (on paved backroad), is the angling centre of a region famed for the size of its char, or "laker," as the fish is referred to locally. Car-top boat launching is possible from the provincial park at the south end of the lake (see Camping/Parks, above). East of Hwy 97, on the road to Canim Lake, you can take your boat over to **Mahood Lake** (in Wells Gray Provincial Park; see The Yellowhead Highway chapter). This is the boat-only access route into 12-mile-long (19-km) Mahood, which offers good rainbow trout fishing. It's subject to winds, so be prepared (as good fishers always are). Look for the ancient pictographs on the rock face of both the north and south sides of the lake near its midpoint.

Lac la Hache (see Camping/Parks, above), a beautiful lake in a rolling Fraser Plateau setting, has many fishing lodges sprinkled along its perimeter. Fishing information is available at the 100 Mile House Info-Centre, (250) 395-5353, on Hwy 97. Both **Horsefly and Quesnel Lakes** are good fishing spots for rainbow trout, and nearby **Williams Lake,** which has a boat launch at **Scout Island Nature Centre,** has the added attraction of easy paddling around the island and marsh areas, which feature sublime scenery. The best place to begin fishing around Horsefly is Horsefly Lake Provincial Park (see Camping/Parks, above). There are healthy wild stocks of rainbow trout at **Dragon Lake,** just south of Quesnel on Hwy 97. A loop road runs around Dragon Lake. Finally, if you just want to drive a short way north out of Quesnel on Hwy 97 (about 15 miles/24 km), you'll find a boat launch at **Hush Lake Rest Area.**

The handiest guides to fishing in the region are the Forest Service recreation maps to the Cariboo, Quesnel, Williams Lake, Horsefly, 100 Mile House, and Chilcotin Forest Districts. For complimentary copies, contact regional headquarters in Williams Lake, (250) 398-4345, or any Tourist InfoCentre.

Canoeing/Kayaking

For canoe enthusiasts desiring a challenge, **Bowron Lake Provincial Park** delivers. Its extended 72-mile (116-km) canoe and kayak route through a chain of lakes, rivers, and creeks linked by portages is legendary, drawing visitors from around the globe. Plan on taking seven to ten days to complete the route, although it can be done in less time.

You must prepare for Bowron. That means three things: planning, physical fitness, and proper equipment (including food). You may have to share your campsites with other parties, so it's a good idea to limit the number in your group. If your number exceeds six, you must obtain prior permission from the District Manager to make the trip; reservations (for any size of party) are required in summer. I recommend canoeing here in September—there will be fewer people, fewer insects, and more beautiful colours than at other times. Also, even if you're planning to do the seven-day trip, it's a good idea to bring enough food for ten days. You may become stormbound for a day or two. There can be high winds on the lake in the afternoons, and the nights can be chilly. Finally, extra caution must be taken because of bears. But it's a great trip! Call (250) 992-3111 for reservations, and (250) 398-4414 for general information. Supplies, including **canoe rentals,** are available; contact Beckers Lodge, (250) 992-8864, or Bowron Lake Lodge and Resorts (250) 992-2733, for more information. The classic guide to the route is *Canoeing Bowron Lakes Provincial Park* by Richard Wright.

Cross-Country Skiing

The rolling landscape of British Columbia's Central Interior region was meant for cross-country skiing. Despite the extremely cold weather of the Cariboo in the harshest months of winter, there's still a very strong upside: no bugs, no bogs, just blue skies forever! And in the distance, the peaks of the Cariboo Mountains promise extended, untracked snow-trekking routes for experienced backcountry explorers.

Arguably the best track-set cross-country skiing in the Cariboo is found at **108 Mile Ranch,** the home of "Mr. Cross-Country," Gunner Rasmussen. Not that Rasmussen promotes himself as such. He'd much rather talk about going for an outing when the moon is full, his favourite time to be out on the trails. In the rest of the nordic ski community, Gunner is acknowledged as the single best representative of the spirit of skiing in the Cariboo. And the 120 miles (200 km) of community trails that loop between his home in 108 Mile Ranch and **99 Mile House** are unmatched anywhere else this side of Washington's Methow Valley.

Rasmussen came to the Cariboo from Denmark in the 1980s and

opened a ski and bike shop. A former cross-country ski and bike racer, he joined 100 Mile House's Nordic Club, one of the most active, well-organized ski clubs in British Columbia, with a roster of more than 150 hardcore members.

The trails are divided into two categories. Close to 108 Mile Ranch the terrain is gentle: perfect for the gliding style that makes cross-country skiing such a rhythmic experience. Beginner and intermediate skiers will find these groomed routes just their speed. Closer to 99 Mile House you'll discover 12 miles (20 km) of steep, high-performance trails with tight corners and a variety of technical sections suited to marathoners. Many of the trails in both 108 Mile Ranch and 99 Mile House are also lit for night skiing, though nothing tops moonlight. Over 20,000 visitors a year come to enjoy the cross-country skiing here. A user fee of $7 per day is charged, which includes the use of a large log chalet built by the 100 Mile Nordic Club four years ago.

100 Mile House is the home of the Cariboo Cross-Country Ski Marathon, run each February. To show that skiing is serious business here, the town's information centre is adorned with the world's largest pair of skinny skis, accompanied by a pair of 30-foot (9-m) poles, pointing skyward out in front of a modern peeled-log cabin.

For more information on cross-country skiing in the Cariboo, contact Gunner's Cycle and X-Country Ski Shop in 108 Mile Ranch, (250) 791-6537, or toll free (800) 664-5414. For information on 100 Mile House, contact the South Cariboo Chamber of Commerce, (250) 395-5353. Trail fees are collected at the 100 Mile House InfoCentre, 108 Mile Ranch, or on the honour system at a drop box at the 99 Mile House trailhead on Hwy 97.

Guest ranches in the Cariboo-Chilcotin are lively places in winter, when skiers come to explore the trails that many ranchers groom around their spreads. Nowhere do the trails match those of 108 Mile Ranch, but farther north in **Quesnel,** Forest Renewal BC seed money was recently used to upgrade the routes around **Bouchie Lake,** just west of Hwy 97. One thing that Quesnel or a village like **Wells,** an hour's drive east of Highway 97 in the Cariboo Mountains, has is an abundance of character that can't be replicated at a lodge or ranch. Quesnel's riverfront on the Fraser has the ambience of a city, while Wells has the ongoing gold-fever vitality that once invigorated nearby Barkerville. The *pistes de résistance* in Wells run through a beautiful, steep-sided valley where moose graze year-round in the open meadows and the tracks of ptarmigan and ravens, coyotes and rabbits, beaver and muskrat can all be seen as clearly as ski tracks in the snow. Most skiers can easily cover the 5-mile (8-km) route between Wells and Barkerville, or other trails that loop around Wells. More advanced cross-country skiers head from **Barkerville Historic Park** past the ghost town of Richfield and up **Mount Agnes,** where 14 miles (23 km) of trails lead through the heavily forested countryside around Groundhog Lake.

For information on Quesnel, call toll free (800) 992-4922, or (250) 992-8716. An excellent source of information on the trails around the Quesnel region is John Marien at Quesnel Ski, (250) 992-7065. For information on cross-country skiing in Wells, call the Wells Trails Society, (250) 994-0001 or (250) 994-2352. The annual **Wells Winter Carnival** takes place in January.

Purists looking to cut their own cross-country tracks in the Cariboo should head 58 miles (36 km) east of 100 Mile House to **Canim Lake** (see Camping/Parks, above). In summer, this is serious angling country. Once the big, 23-mile-long (37-km) lake freezes over, the landscape turns into significant backcountry touring turf. Several lodges at Canim Lake and nearby subalpine lakes remain open year-round, including Canim Lake Resort and Guide Outfitters, (250) 397-2355, Ponderosa Resort, (250) 397-2242, and the Wolf Den Country Inn, (250) 397-2108.

For a substantial cross-country ski experience, don't miss **Big Bar Road.** Located about 4 miles (6 km) west of Hwy 97 near Clinton, this road accesses over 35 miles (60 km) of ungroomed trails. The trails are also good at **Ten Mile Lake Provincial Park** (see Camping/Parks, above). **West Lake Provincial Park,** 18 miles (29 km) southwest of Prince George off Hwy 16, is a favourite spot for cross-country skiing, snowshoeing, and tobogganing. The 9 miles (14.5 km) of ungroomed trails are usually suitable for cross-country skiing from December until April, and its large picnic/day-use area has the added advantage, during those cold winter days, of an enclosed shelter for cooking.

The BC Adventure Network has an excellent Web site to visit for more information on **winter recreation** (and recreation in general) in the Cariboo-Chilcotin region: http://www.bcadventure.com.

Mountain Biking

Big Bar Road (see Cross-Country Skiing, above) doubles as a mountain-bike route in summer. For other routes, you should definitely check with the various Forest Region offices in the Cariboo (see More Information, below). Although the Cariboo Forest Region map doesn't list any mountain-bike trails *as such*, many locations have cross-country ski trails that could conceivably be accessible to mountain bikers in summer, and the region is full of hiking trails. Check with the district you'd like to visit for specific routes.

Pinnacles Provincial Park has mountain-bike trails in a spectacular setting just west of Quesnel. Follow the signs to Pinnacles Provincial Park west from Hwy 97 in Quesnel for 5 miles (8 km) to reach the trailhead. Follow the main trail from the parking lot to the park's viewing area, then pick up the rambling single-track trails that run from there. Quesnel itself has some lovely cycling paths that run beside the Fraser and Quesnel Rivers that feature pedestrian/cyclists-only bridges to help you across. There's easy access to the town's trails from the Quesnel Tourist Infocentre on Hwy 97.

Good contacts for more information on mountain biking in the Cariboo include Koops Bike Shop, 1733 Nicholson St, (250) 563-4828, and Ultra Sports, 1237 Fourth Ave, (250) 562-7930, both in Prince George; Quesnel Ski and Sport, (250) 992-7065, in Quesnel; and Red Shred's Bike & Board Shed, (250) 398-7873, in Williams Lake.

Wildlife

If **ospreys** and **eagles** are your kind of bird, go to Green Lake (see Camping/Parks, above). The shallow, reedy west end of the lake is attractive to waterfowl as a nesting and migratory resting area. At 100 Mile House (see Cross-Country Skiing, above), BC Wildlife Watch has a viewing site located in the marsh behind the InfoCentre. Look for **moose, sandhill cranes,** and **bald eagles,** as well as waterfowl by the thousands. At Williams Lake, the Scout Island Nature Centre focuses on the marshland and the superb birding in it. Spotting a **yellow-breasted blackbird** won't require much effort, but will make your visit here entirely worthwhile.

Scenic Drives

Meadow Lake Road, north of Clinton, leads west off Hwy 97 to one of the Chilcotin's (and British Columbia's) most fabled spreads, the Gang Ranch. If you don't want to backtrack along what is, at times, a most challenging dirt road, forge ahead from the ranch along **Dog Creek Road** to Hwy 20 and Williams Lake via Alkali Lake, a total of about 80 dusty miles (a just-as-dusty 130 km). Expect some confusion, but persevere.

The road to Horsefly and Quesnel Lakes and the settlement of **Likely** (which must be visited simply to reward the town for coming up with that name) leads to superb fishing country. The turnoff runs east from 150 Mile House for about 35 miles (60 km). Horsefly is one of the most important salmon-spawning sites for Fraser River stock; this road also leads to Horsefly Provincial Park (see Camping/Parks, above).

Finally, follow the historic **Gold Rush Trail** (also known as Hwy 26) to Barkerville. It begins north of Quesnel. A detailed map of all the historic sites along this route can be obtained from the Quesnel InfoCentre, (250) 992-8716, or toll free (800) 992-4922.

Horseback Riding

Freedom to move is one of the big attractions of small **guest ranches** in the Cariboo. Smaller places provide a spontaneity and intimacy missing from some of the larger guest ranches, where supervised horse tours are more the order of the day. If you want a horse adventure, this is the way to go. Wherever you plan to spend your time in the Cariboo, be sure to inquire about which approach a guest ranch offers when making your arrangements.

At the same time, clarify the financial terms of your stay. For example, many ranches operate on the "American plan." That is, everything—accommodation, three ranch-style meals daily, horses, riding lessons, hayrides, boats—is included in one fixed price, in the range of $95 to $125 per adult per day, depending on the season. For information on guest ranches in the Cariboo, call the Cariboo Tourism Association, (800) 663-5885, or the Thompson-Okanagan Tourism Association, (800) 567-2275.

Two typical small guest ranches that offer experienced riders the chance to **trail ride** on their own are the Crystal Waters Guest Ranch, (250) 593-4252, in Bridge Lake, and the Flying U Guest Ranch, (250) 456-7717, in Green Lake (see Camping/Parks, above). The Flying U rates the distinction of having its own whistle stop on BC Rail's Cariboo Dayliner run between Prince George and North Vancouver.

outside in

Attractions

Billy Barker found lots of gold in **Barkerville** in 1862, whereupon the town became the largest city north of San Francisco; then it became a ghost town; and now it's a place revived for the tourist trade. It's not bad, really: restored old buildings and a general store full of 5-cent jawbreakers and lots of retro '60s (that's 1860s) goods. The whole place shuts down after the summer season (May to September).

Restaurants

Wake Up Jake's There's nothing about this old-time saloon that isn't 1870s authentic: they don't use processed anything. Instead, it's all real:

soups, caribou stew, sourdough-bread sandwiches, steaks, flaky-crusted fruit pies, all amid historic saloon decor. Closed October to April. *In centre of town, Barkerville; (604) 994-3259; $.*

Lodgings

Best Western 108 Resort ☆ At what seems like the edge of civilization, this full-scale Best Western–owned resort covers thousands of acres of rangeland. In winter, the cross-country skiing is some of the best in the Northwest. *Hwy 97, 8 miles (13 km) north of 100 Mile House; Box 2, 108 Mile Ranch, BC V0K 2Z0; (250) 791-5211; $$.*

Flying U Guest Ranch ☆ It's a working ranch, ideal for families who like to ride horses. At the lodge, you can stay in log cabins and canoe on the nearby lake. Rates include three meals a day, all you can chow. *Twelve miles (20 km) east of 70 Mile House on N Greenlake Rd; Box 69, 70 Mile House, BC V0K 2K0; (604) 456-7717; $$.*

More Information

BC Adventure Network: *Web site: www.bcadventure.com.*

BC Forest Service: Cariboo Region Headquarters Forest District, *(250) 398-4345;* **Chilcotin Forest District,** *(250) 394-4700;* **Horsefly Forest District,** *(250) 620-3200;* **100 Mile House Forest District,** *(250) 395-7800;* **Quesnel Forest District,** *(250) 992-4400;* **Williams Lake Forest District,** *(250) 398-4341.*

BC Parks, Cariboo District, Williams Lake: *(250) 398-4414 or (250) 398-4414; reservations, (800) 689-9025.*

Cariboo Tourist Association, Williams Lake: *(250) 392-2226.*

Clinton and District Chamber of Commerce: *(250) 459-2640.*

Maps BC, Rathbone & Goodrich, Williams Lake: *(250) 392-2616. A good source for detailed topographic maps of the region.*

100 Mile House, South Cariboo Chamber of Commerce InfoCentre: *(250) 395-5353; Web site: www.netshop.net/100mile/sccofc.html.*

Quesnel InfoCentre: *(250) 992-8716; (800) 992-4922.*

Tourism Prince George: *(250) 562-3700.*

Wells and District Chamber of Commerce: *(250) 994-2352.*

Williams Lake and District Chamber of Commerce: *(250) 392-5025.*

The Yellowhead Highway

The southern portion of the Yellowhead Highway (Highway 5) links Kamloops on Highway 1 with Tête Jaune Cache as it follows the North Thompson River for much of the journey, including Wells Gray and Mount Robson Provincial Parks and Sun Peaks Resort.

This southern stretch of Highway 5, the Yellowhead Highway, follows the green-hued North Thompson River as it flows south through the forested hillsides and grasslands of the Thompson Plateau. This is a quiet, lightly populated region, and travellers along this route soon realize that they're sharing this part of British Columbia with relatively few people. Nothing is as arresting as the sight of snaggle-toothed Mount Robson or the sinuous, green-tinted surface of the North Thompson River. It's easy to go with the flow here.

The Yellowhead Pass (elevation 3,730 feet/1138 m), is 48 miles (77 km) east of Tête Jaune Cache on the British Columbia–Alberta border, and marks the border between Mount Robson Provincial Park and Jasper National Park. Both Tête Jaune Cache and Yellowhead were the nicknames of an early 19th-century fur trader and trapper—either François Decoigne, or Pierre Hatsinaton. Which of these blond fellows was it? Only the mountains know for sure.

Getting There

Highway 1 connects with Highway 5 in Kamloops from both the east and west. Highway 24 from 97 Mile House links with Highway 5 at Little Fort, and Highway 16 links with Highway 5 at Tête Jaune Cache, bringing traffic from Jasper National Park in Alberta to the east and from Prince George to the west.

Adjoining Areas

NORTH: **The Northeast**

SOUTH: **Okanagan Valley; Slocan Valley and Upper Arrow Lake**

WEST: **The Cariboo Highway**

inside out

Parks/Camping

The drive north along Hwy 5 from Kamloops brings you almost immediately past the turnoff to Paul Lake; from there on it's about 60 miles (100 km) until you reach a concentration of parks in the region of Wells Gray Provincial Park, which offers splendid camping opportunities. For more information on camping in all the provincial parks mentioned here, contact BC Parks' Thompson River District office in Kamloops, 1210 McGill Rd, (250) 851-3000. For parks where reservations are indicated, call (800) 689-9025 from March 1 to September 15.

Paul Lake Provincial Park lies just north of Kamloops. The park's 111 vehicle/tent sites are as popular with RVers as the extensive picnic grounds are with day trippers. The park features a car-top boat launch, and an easy, 8-mile (13-km) round-trip hiking trail leads to a great view of the lake and nearby Harper Mountain. Take Hwy 5 north of Kamloops; turn east off the highway and drive for about 11 miles (17 km) on paved road. The total distance from the city is about 17 miles (24 km).

North Thompson River Provincial Park includes a quiet campground with 78 vehicle/tent sites, open from May to September, on the banks of the North Thompson River. A riverside picnic area, a playground, and trails complement the campsites in a forested area near the confluence of the Clearwater and North Thompson Rivers. Canoeing and kayaking are superb, as is the hiking. Smooth depressions in the ground are evidence of former Native Canadian habitation in the park; check out the two archeological sites as well. Take Hwy 5 for 73 miles (118 km) north of Kamloops.

Visit **Spahats Creek Provincial Park** as much for the scenery as for a good night's rest. This small park (20 vehicle/tent sites) has a viewpoint from which you can see the 400-foot-deep (122-m) canyon carved by the creek as it cuts through the layers of lava that form the walls of the canyon. Nearby is a waterfall that spills from Spahats Creek into the Clearwater River. The park is popular with visitors on their way to Wells Gray Provincial Park, and in fall is bedecked with glorious colour. From Clearwater, take Hwy 5 north about 7 miles (11 km), and turn west on the paved road towards Wells Gray Provincial Park.

Valemount, between Wells Gray Provincial Park and Mount Robson Provincial Park at the north end of this route, has a good municipal campground beside Swift Creek, with 75 vehicle/tent sites. It features partial hookups for RVs and is open from April to October. Call (250) 566-4411 for more information.

Wells Gray Provincial Park

Wells Gray Provincial Park is one of British Columbia's largest (1,274,000 acres/515 785 ha) and most spectacular parks. Its area encompasses the greater part of the Clearwater River watershed. There are five major lakes here, as well as two large river systems, numerous small lakes, streams, and waterways, and a multitude of waterfalls, rapids, and cataracts. Although boating and paddling are major attractions for campers, the area has something for everyone. In winter, there are just as many opportunities for recreation as in summer, with the advantage of no bugs! This park is as ideal as any you will find in the province, with a climate and terrain varied enough to suit the most demanding backpacker or mountaineer.

It's not surprising that in a park this vast there are three distinct biogeoclimatic zones: the Interior cedar-hemlock zone (lowest); the subalpine zone (at elevations between 4,900 and 6,500 feet/1495 and 1985 m); and the alpine tundra zone (which covers about 65 percent of the total park area). Mineral springs, several waterfalls, and evidence of volcanic phenomena complement the many attractions of this park.

Worth special mention in Wells Gray are **Dawson Falls** (a short walking trail leads to the view); the **Mushbowl** and **Devil's Punch Bowl** on the Myrtle River; **Helmcken Falls** (a short walk brings you to the 450-foot/137-m falls, the fourth highest in Canada and the park's centrepiece); and **Murtle Lake,** considered one of the most beautiful wilderness lakes in BC and set aside for paddlers only. Its entrance is from the town of Blue River, and visitors must obtain a permit there, 66 miles (107 km) north of Clearwater (see Rafting/Canoeing, below).

There are four formal camping areas in the park: at **Dawson Falls Campground** (10 vehicle/tent sites, located 5 miles/8 km north of the Hemp Creek entrance), **Clearwater Lake Campground** (37 vehicle/tent sites), **Falls Creek Campground** (41 vehicle/tent sites at Clearwater Lake, 20 miles/32 km north of the Hemp Creek entrance), and **Mahood Lake Campground** (32 vehicle/tent sites at the west end of Mahood Lake, 55 miles/88 km east of Hwy 97 and 100 Mile House; see The Cariboo Highway chapter). There's also wilderness camping at various sites on Azure, Clearwater, Mahood, and Murtle Lakes. From Hwy 5 at Clearwater, go 25 miles (40 km) north on Clearwater Valley Rd to the park's Hemp Creek entrance. Hemp Valley Rd is paved for the first 19 miles (30 km), then gravelled to the entrance. From the park entrance, a paved road leads 6 miles (10 km) to Helmcken Falls. From the falls the road leads a further 14 miles (23 km) on gravel to Clearwater Lake. A second approach to the east side of the park begins 69 miles (112 km) north of Clearwater on Hwy 5 at Blue River. A gravel road runs about 15 miles (24 km) west to Murtle Lake. It's a 1-mile (1.6-km) hike from the parking lot to the wilderness sites and canoe launch here. Mahood Lake is accessible via 40 miles (65 km) of gravel road from Hwy 24 at Sheridan Lake. For more information on Wells Gray Provincial Park, including a detailed map, contact BC Parks in Kamloops, (250) 851-3000, or the Wells Gray Provincial Park office in North Thompson River Provincial Park in Clearwater, (250) 587-6150. Current information on conditions in Wells Gray Provincial Park are posted at the kiosk at the park's Clearwater Valley Rd entrance, about 23 miles (37 km) west of Hwy 5.

Mount Robson Provincial Park

The peak of **Mount Robson** is the highest in the Canadian Rockies, towering 12,972 feet (3954 m) over the western entrance to the park. As well as occupying a portion of the Main (Park) Ranges of the Rockies, the park, one of the oldest in British Columbia, also contains the headwaters of the **Fraser River,** and, in the northwest section of the park, the massive **Berg Glacier,** notable for being one of the few living (or advancing) glaciers in the Canadian Rockies. Before the discovery of Mount Waddington on the central coast in 1925, Mount Robson held the distinction of being the tallest mountain in British Columbia.

The superb scenery in the park makes it an excellent site for hikers, climbers, and backcountry enthusiasts (see Hiking/Backpacking, below). Fishing is generally poor because of the cold temperature of the waters and their high sediment load, but Yellowhead and Moose Lakes support populations of dolly varden and lake char, and kokanee and rainbow trout. To simply observe the fish, go to the west side of the park, where a lookout gives a view of **Rearguard Falls,** the furthest migration point possible on the Fraser for most returning Pacific salmon.

Three camping areas in the park have a combined total of 176 vehicle/tent sites at **Robson Meadows Campground** (125 vehicle/tent sites) and **Robson River Campground** (19 vehicle/tent sites), both near the western boundary, and **Lucerne Campground** (32 vehicle/tent sites), just west of the Alberta border. Reservations are recommended in summer; call (800) 689-9025. (Note: There are no RV hookups in the park.) Wilderness campsites are also located along the Berg Lake Trail (see Hiking/Backpacking, below). Concrete boat launches and ample parking are located at the east end of **Moose Lake** and at **Yellowhead Lake;** the latter also has a sandy beach. Take Hwy 16 east from its junction with Hwy 5 in Tête Jaune Cache into the park, which is adjacent to the Alberta border and Jasper National Park. Extensive information on the park's camping facilities and detailed descriptions of its recreational trails are available on request from BC Parks in Valemount, (250) 566-4325, or in Prince George, 4051 18th Ave, (250) 565-6340. Park headquarters are located on Hwy 16 at the Mount Robson Viewpoint on the western border of the park in the Mount Robson Visitors Centre. Specific information on Mount Robson Provincial Park, as well as general information on BC Parks, is available here. Park staff are on hand from May to September to provide current reports on conditions within the park.

Hiking/Backpacking

Wells Gray Provincial Park (see Parks/Camping, above) is laced with hiking trails, ranging in length from 1 to 15 miles (1.5 to 24 km) one way. The **Helmcken Falls Rim Trail** (easy; 5 miles/8 km return) leads from the Dawson Falls Campground on Clearwater Valley Rd and follows the rim of the falls for much of the way. The thunder of the falls grows louder as you approach them, gradually drowning out all other sounds. In winter this trail is open for snowshoeing and cross-country skiing for those who wish to see the falls covered with a thick mantle of ice.

Much of the park's topography is the result of glacial erosion and volcanic activity. One of the best hiking trails from which to observe this is the **Pyramid Mountain Trail** (moderate; 8 miles/13 km return), which leads to the summit of Pyramid Mountain, from where hikers enjoy spectacular views of the Premier Ranges across the north end of the park. The mountain itself exhibits fascinating volcanic characteristics. Geologists believe that Pyramid Mountain built up gradually beneath a thick glacial sheet as magma erupting beneath the ice was chilled and shattered into tiny fragments by cold water and ice. Over time, these fragments accumulated around the vent to form a mound-shaped structure. Hikers looking for an opportunity to journey deeper into the park should follow the **Horseshoe Falls Trail** (strenuous; 21 miles/34 km return), which shares the Pyramid Mountain Trail and then continues beyond to Horseshoe Falls. Wilderness campsites are located at the 5-mile (8-km) point and at the top of Horseshoe Falls. The well-marked trailhead is located about 3.75 miles (6 km) north of the park entrance on the east side of Clearwater Valley Rd.

Some of the best routes in the park feature lovely alpine hiking, with various huts to stop at along the way. (In winter, there is hut-to-hut skiing on these same trails.) For more information on **hut-to-hut hiking** and skiing, contact Wells Gray Back Country Chalets, (250) 587-6444 or (800) 754-8735. Detailed hiking guides of the park are available from BC Parks, (250) 587-6150 or (250) 851-3000. Good books to consult include *Nature Wells Gray* by Goward and Hickson, and *Exploring Wells Gray Park* by Roland Neave.

Several challenging hikes are possible in **Mount Robson Provincial Park,** as well as many easy walking trips: there's a hike for every skill level here. If you want a two-day hike past glaciers and waterfalls, take the very well-known and popular **Berg Lake Trail** (moderate; 27 miles/44 km return). The trailhead is at the parking lot beside the Robson River, close to the visitors centre. The trail leads to Kinney Lake and the base of Mount Robson, skirts the lake, and enters a valley heavily dotted with spectacular waterfalls and more than 15 glaciers before reaching Berg Lake, at an elevation of 5,341 feet (1628 m). From here the trail continues through Robson Pass into Jasper National Park. It's possible to make a loop via the Berg Lake and **Moose Rivers Trail,** a distance of about 65 miles (105 km), in approximately seven days. This route is particularly rigorous; only attempt it if you're a highly experienced backcountry hiker. (Note: The first half of the Berg Lake Trail as far as Kinney Lake is accessible by mountain bike. Some keeners have been know to bike to Kinney Lake and then hike to Berg Lake from there, making it back to the parking lot before sundown.)

Several other hikes are rewarding. The eastern portion of the park has trails ranging from easy to difficult. Some of the more challenging are **Mount Fitzwilliam** (moderate; 7.5 miles/12 km return to Rockingham Creek wilderness campground; 13.5 miles/22 km return to alpine lakes); **Moose River Route** (strenuous; 87 miles/140 km return; allow six days); **Fraser River Route** (strenuous; 30 miles/50 km return); and **Yellowhead Mountain Trail** (moderate; 10.5 miles/17 km return). The Mount Fitzwilliam Trail starts at Yellowhead Lake and continues for 4.4 miles (7 km) to the designated campsite at Rockingham Creek. An additional 4.3 miles (6.9 km) takes hikers up Fitzwilliam Creek to the wilderness campsite and several day-hike opportunities. All hikers should check with park staff regarding the condition of trails before starting off; hikers entering Jasper National Park must register with park officials beforehand. For detailed maps of hiking trails at Mount Robson, contact BC Parks, (250) 566-4325 or (250) 565-6340, or stop at park headquarters.

For the experienced backcountry hiker, **Hamber Provincial Park** offers extremely beautiful scenery in a wild and rugged locale. Tucked into the midpoint of Jasper National Park on the British Columbia–Alberta border, Hamber is accessible by foot only. (Hwy 93 in Alberta is the nearest highway.) There is a difficult 14-mile (22.5-km) hike in from Sunwapta Falls in Jasper, or you can reach the park by floatplane to **Fortress Lake.** Call Fortress Lake Wilderness Retreat for information on flights, (250) 343-6386. At high elevation and with pristine wilderness, this park has excellent angling opportunities and is prime grizzly and black bear country. For more information, contact BC Parks in Valemount, (250) 566-4325, or in Prince George, (250) 565-6340.

A challenging 8-mile (13-km) round-trip hike in **Mount Terry Fox Provincial Park** leads into the alpine zone from its trailhead north of Valemount. Staggeringly impressive views are everywhere along this route. Mount Terry Fox is located 6 miles (10 km) north of Valemount off Hwy 5.

It's best to visit **Trophy Mountain**'s self-guided trail, "To the Treeline and Beyond" (easy; 1.2 miles/2 km return) between the end of June and mid-August to see the wildflowers that carpet the subalpine meadows here. A lengthier hiking trail leads from the meadows to views of the Shuswap Highlands from Skyline Ridge (moderate; 7.5 miles/12 km return). Sudden changes in the weather occur even in summer, however, so wear layered clothing and bring waterproof gear (and sunscreen, just in case). This trail is documented in a charming brochure. Pick up a copy from the BC Parks office in Clearwater before heading out. The trailhead in Trophy Mountain Recreation Area begins just east of Spahats Creek Provincial Park (see Parks/Camping, above) off Clearwater Valley Rd. Follow gravelled Rd 80 east of Clearwater Valley Rd for about 1 mile (1.6 km), then turn north on Rd 10 for almost 2 miles (3 km), then turn east on Rd 201 for 2.7 miles (4.4 km) to reach the trailhead parking lot. For more information, call BC Parks, (250) 587-6150. For **guided hiking tours** in Trophy Mountain Recreation Area and nearby Wells Gray Provincial Park, contact Clearwater Adventure resort, (250) 674-3909.

Fishing

Paul Lake (see Parks/Camping, above), stocked with two species of rainbow trout, is easily accessed with a car-top boat. Farther north, **Heffley Lake** is a great location for rainbow trout. Ice fishing is also possible here. Heffley Lake Fishing Resort, (250) 578-7251, rents boats. Heffley Lake is located 19 miles (31 km) northeast of Kamloops off Hwy 5 on the road to Sun Peaks Resort.

The **Barrière Lakes** (North, South, and East) are all located about 60 miles (100 km) north of Kamloops and 10 miles (16 km) west of Hwy 5 on Barrière Lake Rd. Some of the best trout fishing in this region renowned for its fine fishing lakes can be found here. The Kamloops Forest District details over 60 medium-sized and small lakes for fishing. Call them at (250) 371-6500 for a map. North Barrière Lake Resort, (250) 672-9595, rents boats and motors. Caverhill Lodge on Barrière Lake, (250) 672-9806, offers fly-fishing and light spin casting for native Kamloops rainbow trout, and is so secluded it can only be accessed by boat.

You can fish at **Rearguard Falls Provincial Park,** approximately 3 miles (4.8 km) of east of Tête Jaune Cache on Hwy 16. The park is on the Upper Fraser River, and the falls are the final barrier to salmon migrating from the Fraser's mouth, some 744 miles (120 km) southeast at the Pacific Ocean. Salmon season begins in August and continues through September. For more information, contact BC Parks, (250) 565-6340, in Prince George, or the Fish and Wildlife Conservation Office in Valemount, (250) 566-4398.

For more information on fishing in this region, contact the BC Fishing Resorts and Outfitters Association, (250) 374-6836, or visit their Web site: www.oppub.com/bcfroa/bcfroa.html. **Fly-in fishing lodges** are located on some of the 700 lakes in the area; flights depart and return to the Kamloops Airport. For a list of lodges, contact the Kamloops Visitor InfoCentre, (800) 662-1994, or the BC Fishing Resorts & Outfitters Association, (250) 374-8646.

Skiing/Snowmobiling

Harper Mountain on Paul Lake Rd north of Kamloops (about 9 miles/14 km east of Hwy 5) offers downhill and cross-country skiing. A local operation here is geared to teaching families to ski. The mountain has one triple-chair and one T-bar, with 1,394 feet (425 m) of vertical. For more information, call (250) 372-2119.

Former world ski champion and Olympic gold medallist Nancy Greene Raine is the spokesperson and director of skiing for **Sun Peaks Resort** (located at Tod Mountain, north of Kamloops) in the Thompson Plateau. Greene Raine, who first skied at Sun Peaks in 1964 when the Canadian Alpine Championships were held there, describes the resort as mellow. Many visitors, particularly those from outside British Columbia, take a week at Whistler-Blackcomb for the big hit; then they want to come to a resort that has a more relaxed atmosphere.

The opening of three new hotels and a new base lodge at Sun Peaks, plus the installation of faster, covered lifts means that in the depths of winter, skiers won't require an infusion of hot chocolate to warm their blood after each run. After all, with 3,000 feet (1000 m) of vertical, Sun Peaks has some of the longest runs in the province. In the past, Tod Mountain was perceived as a place where a small group of rugged, wild-and-woolly skiers went to enjoy some of the best powder skiing in the province. Sun Peaks has finally brought the mountain to the attention of a wider group, something that's been promised here for decades. An extensive network of **cross-country trails** runs from the village, around the golf course, and through the surrounding forest, and is posted with trail markers and groomed regularly. A **skating rink** and a public outdoor hot tub also add to the winter ambience in the valley. Always known for its involvement with racing, Sun Peaks hosts the Grundig Snowboard World Cup. In mid-February, there is the BC Tel Nancy Greene Invitational Fundraiser, a ski race that benefits the local amateur ski club. Sun Peaks Resort is located 20 miles (32 km) east of Hwy 5 on Heffley Creek Rd (15 miles/24 km north of Kamloops); (250) 578-7842 or (800) 807-3257.

In winter, the world-famous Helmcken Falls in **Wells Gray Provincial**

Park (see Parks/Camping, above) forms a magnificent ice cone, a view of which is a reward for backcountry skiers willing to make a short trek. Another marvel here is the frozen crescent of Dawson Falls. Groomed and track-set trails lead cross-country skiers through the park past the Majerus homestead, King Meadow, and the always welcome sight of a warming hut. More challenging routes include the Corkscrew and the Roller Coaster. **Hut-to-hut backcountry skiing** provides an extended multiday winter adventure. For more information, contact Wells Gray Back Country Chalets, (250) 587-6444. Also contact Helmcken Falls Lodge, (250) 674-3657, located at the entrance to the park, or visit their Web site, www.profiles.net/helmcken.

Cross-country skiers should also check out the untracked backcountry routes in the region around **Blue River** on Eleanor Lake. Call Mike Wiegele Heli-Ski Village, (800) 661-9170 or (250) 673-8381, in Blue River when planning your trip. **Valemount** is the hub of the Cariboo, Monashee, and Rocky Mountains, and is the best base you can have for your **heli-skiing** and **snowmobiling** adventure. Robson Helimagic Inc., (250) 566-4700, in Valemount will help you plot a course.

Rafting/Canoeing

One of the "funnest" outdoor activities has got to be whitewater rafting, and you shouldn't miss the opportunity to indulge in it while you're in this chock-full-of-rivers region. The **outfitter** Interior Whitewater Expeditions, (800) 661-7238, in Clearwater has a good reputation, as does Clearwater Adventures Resort, (250) 674-3909.

For easygoing paddling, the **North Thompson River** is perfect. Use North Thompson River Provincial Park (see Parks/Camping, above) as your base. The current gently pulls paddlers downstream all the way to Kamloops, although you'll need several days to cover the entire distance.

For an even more peaceful experience, head to **Murtle Lake** in Wells Gray Provincial Park (see Parks/Camping, above). This lake has over 62 miles (100 km) of shoreline. Providing visitors with a quiet wilderness experience is the goal and motorboats and combustion engines are not permitted. Access is from Blue River (on Hwy 5) along a narrow, winding, 16-mile (27-km) gravel road. A parking lot at the end of this road is the trailhead for a 1-mile (1.5-km) portage to the canoe launch.

To canoe the long and skinny **Kinbasket Lake,** start at Canoe Reach at Valemount (near the north end of the lake, just south of Tête Jaune Cache on Hwy 5) and work your way south. Mount Robson Adventure Holidays can help plan a **guided paddling trip** in this region; call them at (250) 566-4386. There's a boat launch beside Hwy 16 in Mount Robson Provincial Park that provides access to **Moose Lake** and **Yellowhead Lake** in the park.

Horseback Riding

This is great country to see from the back of a horse. Many commercial **outfitters** offer guided trips: in Clearwater, call Stillwater Horseback Adventure at (250) 674-2997; farther east in Vavenby, call Vavenby Trail Rides at Shook Ranch, (250) 676-9598; in Valemount, ask at the town's visitor information centre, (250) 566-4846, about local outfitters.

Wildlife

BC Wildlife Watch **migratory bird, mammal, amphibian, and plant life** viewing sites, complete with trails and observation towers, are located in Valemount's **Starratt Wildlife Sanctuary** and **Hicks Regional Park.** Contact the Watch at (250) 387-9796.

At Jackman Flats, 3 miles (5 km) south of Tête Jaune Cache, visitors will find unique **botanical interpretive trails.** And August and September is the time to witness the always-amazing spectacle of the Fraser River **salmon run** in Rearguard Falls Provincial Park (see Fishing, above).

outside in

Attractions

A sprawling city of nearly 75,000 residents, **Kamloops** is midway between Vancouver (four hours west) and Banff National Park in Alberta (just three hours east on the Trans-Canada Hwy). With the forest industry waning, Kamloops is turning its attention to tourism. Outdoor enthusiasts will find enough activities here to keep them busy. Named after a Shuswap Indian word meaning "meeting place," Kamloops is at the confluence of the North and South Thompson Rivers.

Restaurants

Minos ☆ Service is friendly, prompt, and well informed, and the menu leans heavily towards Greek fare—souvlaki of lamb, chicken, and seafood. The atmosphere is warm and welcoming. *262 Tranquille Rd (0.5 mile/1 km north of Overlander Bridge), Kamloops; (250) 376-2010; $.*

Peter's Pasta ☆ What this narrow cafe lacks in ambience, it makes up for in the sauces. It's so popular you may run into a short wait for a table—even this far north. Diners choose from four pastas and a generous range of sauces. *149 Victoria St (downtown), Kamloops; (250) 372-8514; $.*

Lodgings

Lac Le Jeune Resort ☆ This lodge puts you right on a lake and at the edge of the wilderness. Several lodging options (lodge room, cabin, chalet) and a sauna, an adjacent downhill ski area, and 62 miles (100 km) of cross-country skiing trails are all offered. Closed winters. *650 Victoria St (off Coquihalla Hwy, Lac Le Jeune exit, 18 miles/29 km southwest of Kamloops), Kamloops, BC V2C 2B4; (250) 372-2722; $$.*

Sevinth Heaven B&B ☆ This spot is in a fantastic location. Fly-fishermen flock here, and in winter frozen Paul Lake—just outside the front door—offers a perfect surface for cross-country skiing, snowmobiling, and ice fishing. The host runs a small, one-guest-room operation, and does a wonderful job. *7007 Paul Lake Rd (east of town); mail: Site 1, Comp 42, RR5, Kamloops, BC V2C 6C2. (250) 573-7533; $.*

Sun Peaks Resort [*unrated*] This destination resort 33 miles (53 km) northeast of Kamloops continues to grow. Improvements have been made with high-speed chairlifts and new runs, and there's a challenging, nine-hole golf course as well. In 1998, on-mountain lodging options continue to open, as well as several restaurants. *Northeast of Kamloops; PO Box 869, Kamloops, BC V2C 5M8; (800) 807-3257; $$$.*

The Thompson ☆ It was named after the explorer David Thompson, but there's nothing adventuresome about this standard hotel fare. The rooms are pleasant, though, and amenities include a hot tub, fitness room, and a restaurant and bar, all close to downtown. *650 Victoria St (downtown), Kamloops, BC V2C 2B4; (250) 374-1999 or (800) 561-5253; $–$$.*

More Information

Barrière: *(250) 672-0013.*

BC Adventure Network: *Web site: www.bcadventure.com. A good source of information on the Central Interior and elsewhere.*

BC Forest Service: Clearwater Forest District, *(250) 587-6700;* **Kamloops Forest District,** *(250) 371-6500;* **Robson Valley Forest District,** *(250) 569-3700.*

BC Parks: *(250) 851-3000; Web site: www.env.gov.bc.ca.*

Clearwater and District Chamber of Commerce: *(250) 674-2646.*

Fish and Wildlife Conservation Office: *(250) 566-4398 in Valemount.*

Mount Robson Provincial Park: *(250) 566-4325.*

Valemount InfoCentre: *(250) 566-4846.*

Wells Gray Provincial Park: *(250) 587-6150.*

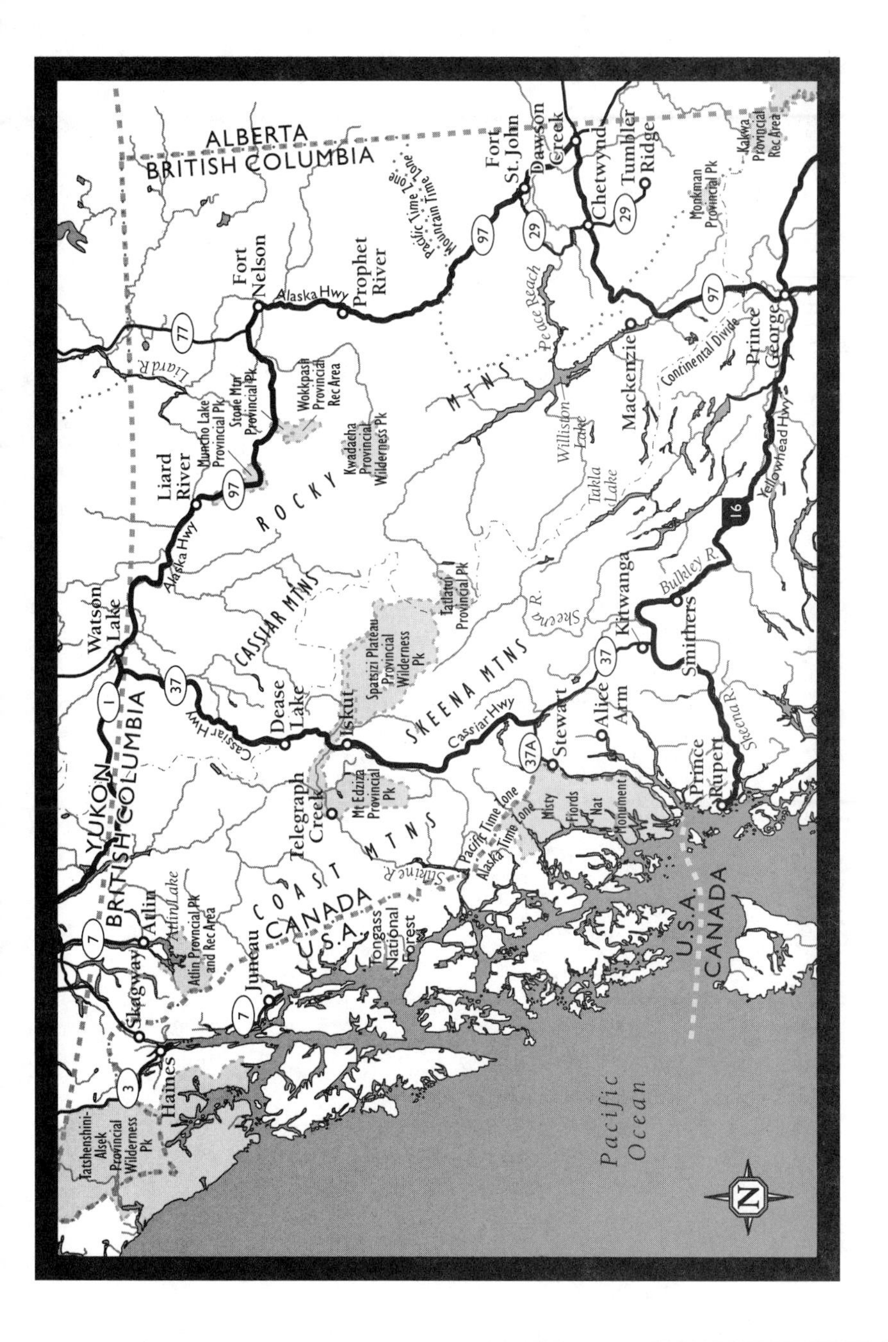

The Far North

The Northeast 615

The Stewart-Cassiar Highway (Highway 37) 639

The Northeast

From Prince George north via the Alaska Highway (Highway 97) to Watson Lake and the British Columbia–Yukon border, including Dawson Creek, Fort Nelson, and Monkman, Stone Mountain, Muncho Lake, and Liard River Hotsprings Provincial Parks.

When people think of the Rocky Mountains, they usually think of Banff and Jasper National Parks on the Alberta side of the British Columbia–Alberta border. It doesn't register that a major portion of these mountains spill across the Alberta border, cutting a vast swath across the northern half of British Columbia. The Rocky Mountains and their foothills dominate the Northeast, comprising roughly 20 million acres (8 million ha). There are no roads that cross the range north of Pine Pass (between Mackenzie and Chetwynd) until the Yukon border. The Northern Rocky Mountains are the largest roadless landscape south of the 60th parallel, as well as one of the richest and most varied intact large wildlife ecosystems remaining in North America. The area's wildlife population is so prolific that this portion of the Northern Rockies has been dubbed the "Serengeti of North America."

In the vast, highwayless gulf between the Alaska Highway, which begins in Dawson Creek at Milepost 0, and Hwy 37 to the west is an area that at its most expansive is 400 miles (700 km) wide and 750 miles (1200 km) long. To put that in perspective, you could drop Switzerland into this region and not have road access. This is big country. Most people don't venture more than a few miles off paved road. Some never make it off pavement at all, but if you do, a world of recreational opportunities awaits, whether you're a weekend adventurer or a trail-hardened backpacker. People who go out unprepared into this wilderness, however, don't come back. Ignorance and arrogance in the face of nature are the surest ways of getting yourself killed. Come prepared, and enjoy the rich and varied wilderness, a place where people are scarce, but the exploits plentiful.

Getting There

Highway 97 (John Hart Highway) links Prince George with Dawson Creek (about 250 miles/400 km); along the way, travellers may pursue a possible side trip on Highway 29 between Tumbler Ridge and Fort St. John, via Chetwynd. From Dawson Creek, Mile 0 on the Alaska Highway, Highway 97 winds north and then northwest to Watson Lake on the British Columbia–Yukon border, via Fort St. John and Fort Nelson, a distance of just over 700 miles (1140 km). These are the only highways that run through the Northeast, which remains mostly undeveloped and sparsely populated.

Prince George stands as the south-central gateway for the Northeast, at the junction of Highways 97 and 16. As the largest city in the Interior, it is well served by air, rail, and bus. BC Rail's Cariboo Limited makes daily runs between North Vancouver and Prince George. Via Rail provides service from Jasper and Prince Rupert.

Adjoining Areas

SOUTH: **The Yellowhead Highway; Fraser Plateau**

WEST: **The Stewart-Cassiar Highway (Highway 37)**

inside out

Parks/Camping

Northern British Columbia is strung with pocket parks and tiny campgrounds, many of which are only partially developed. Besides the region's provincial parks and Forest Service recreation sites, many towns maintain one or two civic campgrounds or parks, and new parks and campgrounds are opening all the time. Most campsites spring up at the confluence of roads and water—common in the river-laced and lake-bejewelled north. The easiest order to describe them is the same one in which they are discovered: just follow Hwy 97 north from Prince George.

The **Summit Lake Forest Service Recreation Site** lies about 1 mile (2 km) west of Hwy 97 on Caine Creek Rd. The turnoff is about 19 miles (30 km) north of Prince George. It is a popular campground with locals, and has space for 28 vehicles. This is a good launching point for canoeists heading down Crooked River (see Kayaking/Canoeing, below).

There is a rash of additional Forest Service recreation sites around

Crooked River near Davis Lake, including **Crystal Lake, Emerald Lake, 100 Road Bridge, Domino Lake, Caines Bridge, Merton Lake,** and **Davie Lake.** For more information on these and Summit Lake, contact the Prince George Forest Regional Office, (250) 565-6100, 1011 Fourth Ave in Prince George.

Crooked River Provincial Park is the biggest and most popular provincial park in the region. It is located 43 miles (70 km) north of Prince George along Hwy 97, and encompasses a number of lakes with sand beaches, including Bear, Skeleton, Hart, and Squaw Lakes. It has 90 vehicle/tent sites, more than all the Forest Service recreation sites listed above combined. Then again, the Forest Service recreation sites are free for the taking. For reservations at Crooked River Provincial Park, call BC Parks' reservation line, (800) 689-9025, from March 1 to September 15. For general information, call BC Parks, (250) 565-6340, or stop by the district office, 4051 18th Ave, Prince George.

The area around the **Tacheeda Lakes** is a popular getaway spot for locals, especially anglers. A circuit of lakes in a 5-mile (8-km) radius, including the Tacheeda Lakes, **Goose Lake, Cat Lake, Hambone Lake,** and **Fishhook Lake,** all sport their own Forest Service campgrounds (Tacheeda has three campgrounds, for a total of 28 vehicle/tent sites.) An eighth campground, the **Anzac Forest Service Recreation Site,** on the Parsnip River, insures that you'll probably find a place to pitch a tent *somewhere* in this area. The turnoff to the lakes is about 56 miles (90 km) north of Prince George. For more information on these campgrounds, contact the Forest Service's Prince George Regional Office, (250) 565-6100.

Whiskers Point Provincial Park (69 vehicle/tent sites), about 85 miles (138 km) north of Prince George, sits on the shores of **McLeod Lake,** a pleasant spot to pitch a tent or to park a trailer. Call BC Parks at (250) 565-6340 for more information.

A third pocket of campsites springs up near **Carp Lake Provincial Park** (see Kayaking/Canoeing, below). If there is one place that sums up the camping experience along the Hwy 97 corridor from Prince George to Mackenzie, this is it. There are 102 vehicle/tent sites, split between two campgrounds: one at **Kettle Bay** on Carp Lake itself and one on the smaller **War Lake.** If you've come prepared with watercraft, there are wilderness campsites on three of the islands that dot Carp Lake. Fishing, boating, canoeing, and swimming are the prime activities here. Even the attractions tend to involve water, whether it be a visit to **War Falls** (just north of War Lake), scouting the marshes for moose, or just watching the sun set across the lake. **Warhorse Lake, Sekani Lake, Munlo Lake, Turner Lake, Oldman Lake, Clarkston Lake,** and **Gates Lake** are all within 15 minutes' drive of the park, and all sport Forest Service recreation sites, but if you can find space, spend a day or two at Carp Lake. The park is 20 miles (32 km) southwest of the town of McLeod Lake. Call BC Parks in Prince George for information and a detailed map; (250) 565-6340. For more information on Forest Service campgrounds, contact the Prince George Regional Office, (250) 565-6100.

Tudyah Lake Provincial Park lies on the western perimeter of the Rocky Mountain Trench, between the Nechako Plateau on the west and the Hart Ranges of the Rockies to the east. Tudyah Lake is 97 miles (157 km) north of Prince George, near the junction of Hwys 97 and 39, and is the last stop Crooked River makes before becoming one with giant **Williston Lake.** It has 36 vehicle/tent sites to its credit. A smaller, 5-unit Forest Service campground lies farther north along the lake, accessible from the Finlay Forest Service Rd. The road continues beyond Tudyah Lake, and is the main access road for areas on the western side of Williston Lake, where hundreds of miles of arterial gravel roads, most of which eventually end in either bush or clear-cut, lead to nearly two dozen small Forest Service campgrounds scattered across the landscape, including a trio of sites around the popular **Germansen Lake.** If you're interested in visiting this area, perhaps to see if you can find the oddly named **Where Are We Lake** and **Here We Are Lake,** you can get a detailed Forest Service map from the Mackenzie Forest District office, (250) 997-2200, located in Mackenzie where the pavement ends on Hwy 39. For more information on Tudyah Lake Provincial Park, contact BC Parks in Prince George, (250) 565-6340.

There are no provincial parks along Hwy 39, but there are a number of small Forest Service recreation sites for campers to choose from. The exception to the small rule is the **Finlay Bay Forest Service Recreation Site,** about 58 miles (95 km) north of Mackenzie off Hwy 39, which boasts 20 sites and is located in one of the most scenic areas on Williston Lake, the largest man-made lake in North America. The lake stretches north and south from here, while to the east, the Peace Reach Arm leads nearly 60 miles (100 km) to the W. A. C. Bennett Dam off of Hwy 29, approximately 43 miles (70 km) north of Mackenzie. If you're planning on taking a boat out onto the water at Finlay Bay, be warned that the boat launch is steep. In bad weather, you will probably need a four-wheel-drive vehicle to retrieve a powerboat. To reach the campground at Finlay Bay, follow the unpaved Parsnip Forest Service Rd for about 46.5 miles (75 km) from the north end of Hwy 37 near Mackenzie.

On the way to Finlay Bay are two Forest Service recreation sites near **Dina Lakes,** a popular four-hour canoe route (see Kayaking/Canoeing, below). The first has 5 vehicle/tent sites, suitable for motorhomes, located at Dina Lake itself. The second is at nearby **Heather Lake.** Heather Lake is

11 miles (18 km) north of Mackenzie on Hwy 39, while Dina Lake lies about 2 miles (3 km) beyond. For more information on these campgrounds, contact the Mackenzie Forest District office, (250) 997-2200.

There is a dearth of campgrounds along Hwy 97 between the Mackenzie turnoff and Chetwynd. The exception is **Heart Lake Forest Service Recreation Site,** on the shores of small Heart Lake, about 2 miles (3 km) east of Hwy 97, about 22 miles (35 km) north of Pine Pass Summit. Watch for the West Pine Rest Area; the turnoff to Heart Lake is on the opposite side of the highway. Campsites are located next to Heart Lake's small beach and along the service road that leads around the perimeter of the lake. For more information and a map, contact the Dawson Creek Forest District Office, (250) 784-1200, or stop by the office at 9000 17th St in Dawson Creek.

The **Chetwynd Municipal Campground,** at the junction of Hwys 97 and 29 on the eastern edge of town, has 15 vehicle/tent sites at no charge to the camper. From here you can go south to Tumbler Ridge, east to Dawson Creek and Mile 0 on the Alaska Hwy, or north to Hudson's Hope and, ultimately, to Fort St. John. For more information, call the Chetwynd Chamber of Commerce, (250) 788-3345.

North of Chetwynd along Hwy 29, there are only a few campgrounds, the largest of which is **Moberly Lake Provincial Park,** on the south shore of Moberly Lake. The park hosts the usual variety of water-related activities—swimming, fishing, canoeing, boating, sailing—as well as boasting 109 vehicle/tent sites for overnighting. Moberly Lake is a popular getaway for residents and nonresidents alike, but there are usually a few spaces open for latecomers on all but the busiest of weekends. The park is located about 15 miles (25 km) north of Chetwynd on Hwy 29. You can reserve a campsite here by calling BC Parks' reservation line, (800) 689-9025. For more information and a map, contact BC Parks in Prince George, (250) 565-6340.

The halfway point between Chetwynd and Tumbler Ridge, 65 miles (105 km) south on Hwy 29, is marked by **Gwillim Lake Provincial Park** (49 vehicle/tent sites). Gwillim Lake is deep, blue, and cold. People with high metabolisms will find a dip in the lake refreshing; others will find it bone-chilling. More adventurous types can follow the unmaintained hiking trails that lead around the lake and deeper into the park, either as a day hike or as a short backpacking trek. The majority of people who come to Gwillim, though, come to kick back, relax, and get out on the water, in a canoe, kayak, or boat, where tremendous views open up west towards the Rocky Mountains. For more information, contact BC Parks, (250) 565-6340.

Flatbed Falls Campsite, located 3 miles (5 km) outside of Tumbler

Ridge, is surprisingly large and is a good place to stay if you're visiting people in town. However, if you're looking for a scenic place to camp, follow the Forest Service roads to **Monkman Provincial Park.** Up until a few years ago, just getting to Monkman was as big an adventure as exploring the park itself. Washed out Forest Service roads with nearly a dozen creek crossings kept access limited to four-wheel-drive vehicles, and only at certain times of the year. Though still fairly rough, the gravel road has been upgraded and bridges have been built, opening up the park to almost all vehicles. Follow the signs from Hwy 29 to Monkman's campground past the colourful Quintette Coal Mine, which employs nearly half the Tumbler Ridge work force. Watch out for logging trucks and wildlife on the roads.

One of the most outstanding features in Monkman Provincial Park is **Kinuseo Falls.** At 197 feet (60 m), Kinuseo Falls is slightly taller than Niagara Falls. Though it doesn't move the same volume of water as Niagara, it also lacks the tacky tourist get-up of the latter. The falls are located a short, but challenging, stroll from any of the 42 vehicle/tent sites in the wild Rocky Mountain foothills. The campground is also a departure point for people making further explorations into the park. To reach Monkman Provincial Park, travel 35 miles (60 km) south of Tumbler Ridge on Hwy 29. Call BC Parks in Fort St. John for more information, (250) 787-3407.

From Tumbler Ridge, you can take the back way—Hwys 52 and 2—directly to Dawson Creek. The middle section of this road is still unpaved. South of Dawson Creek are a handful of regional and provincial parks, the largest being **Swan Lake Provincial Park** (41 vehicle/tent sites), about 18 miles (30 km) south of the city along Hwy 2 in the high, flat prairies of northeastern British Columbia. For more information and a map of Swan Lake and other provincial parks in this region, contact BC Parks in Prince George, (250) 565-6340. For information on regional parks, contact the Dawson Creek InfoCentre, (250) 782-9595.

The **Alaska Highway** officially begins in Dawson Creek, and is one of the longest, loneliest stretches of road you'll ever have the pleasure of driving. Until you get to Fort St. John, about 50 miles (80 km) north of Dawson Creek, there is still a pretence of civilization. **Kiskatinaw Provincial Park,** about 22 miles (34 km) north of Dawson Creek, is not quite at the halfway point between the two. It lies 2.5 miles (4 km) off Hwy 97 on Rd 64, with 28 vehicle/tent sites to its credit. **Peace Island Regional Park** (20 vehicle/tent sites) is about 12 miles (20 km) beyond. For more information on Kiskatinaw Provincial Park, contact BC Parks in Prince George, (250) 565-6340. For information on Peace Island Regional Park, contact the Dawson Creek InfoCentre, (250) 782-9595.

Beatton Provincial Park (37 vehicle/tent sites) is located in the rolling eastern foothills of the Rockies on the east side of Charlie Lake.

The signed turnoff to Beatton is about 4 miles (6 km) north of Fort St. John and on the east side of Hwy 97. The park lies 6 miles (10 km) beyond, along a paved road. **Charlie Lake Provincial Park** (58 vehicle/tent sites) is a few miles farther north along Hwy 97, at its junction with Hwy 29 on the west side of Charlie Lake. Note: In summer, Charlie Lake has a high algae content. Swimming can be a less-than-pleasurable experience at certain times of the year. For information on Charlie Lake and Beatton Provincial Parks, call BC Parks in Fort St. John, (250) 787-3407; for reservations, call (800) 689-9025.

North of Charlie Lake, the Alaska Hwy of song and story begins in earnest. From here to Watson Lake just north of the British Columbia–Yukon border, there are only two directions: forward or backward. Forward leads to some truly amazing places. In the low foothills of the Rocky Mountains, the hundreds upon hundreds of miles of unbroken black pine and bog can get monotonous. That's why there are places to pull off and rest, such as **Buckinghorse River Provincial Park** (33 vehicle/tent sites), at Mile 173 (Km 281), and **Prophet River Provincial Recreation Area** (45 vehicle/tent sites), at Mile 217 (Km 350). The latter sports a lovely freshwater spring to revive your spirits. The spring spouts from the hillside where a trail leads down to the river. For more information, call BC Parks in Fort St. John, (250) 787-3407.

Andy Bailey Provincial Recreation Area (12 vehicle/tent sites) lies 17 miles (27 km) south of Fort Nelson. A gravel access road runs 7 miles (12 km) east of Hwy 97 to the park. In the summer, take a dip in the lake; in winter, break out the cross-country skis or toboggan. This is a popular playground for locals all year round, so join in the fun. For more information, call BC Parks in Fort St. John, (250) 787-3407.

You'll find that **Tetsa River Provincial Park** (25 vehicle/tent sites), 60 miles (100 km) north of Fort Nelson on Hwy 97, enjoys one of the prettiest locations this side of the Yukon border. Campsites here are spread out along the grassy shores of the Tetsa River. Easy walking through the poplar forest leads to river viewpoints and fishing holes. Call BC Parks in Fort St. John, (250) 787-3407, for more information.

For more information on camping in the region, contact Sports Traders in Fort St. John, (250) 785-7771, or Camp Sports in Fort Nelson, (250) 774-2944.

Summit Lake Provincial Campground (28 vehicle/tent sites) is located on the Alaska Hwy inside **Stone Mountain Provincial Park** (see Hiking/Backpacking, below). This is one of the most exposed campgrounds in the province and also one of the most beautifully situated. All sites sit within open view of each other, the highway, and the surrounding smooth summits of the Stone Mountain Range. The campground is located just north of the highest point of elevation on the Alaska Hwy (4,249 feet/1295 m), and also just north of one of the last remaining sections of unpaved highway. If you've been travelling north, this is a good place to pull off and relax. If you're here around sunset, the sight of the Stone Mountains reflected on the lake's surface is mesmerizing. (Note: There are three Summit Lakes in northeastern British Columbia: one near Prince George, another near Pine Pass between Prince George and Dawson Creek, and this one. Don't confuse the three; they are separated by many miles of highway.) For more information on Summit Lake Provincial Campground, contact BC Parks, (250) 787-3407.

One-Fifteen Creek Provincial Park lies a short distance north of Summit Lake Provincial Campground, on Hwy 97 beside MacDonald Creek. The 8 vehicle/tent sites here are occasionally closed when there's a rogue bear in the area.

Muncho Lake Provincial Park has two separate campgrounds situated on the shores of one of the loveliest big lakes anywhere. Muncho Lake displays a perpetually blue hue, the result of copper oxides leached from the bedrock. **Strawberry Flats Campground** (15 vehicle/tent sites) is located at the south end of the lake, while **MacDonald Campground** (15 vehicle/tent sites) sits roughly at the midpoint of the 7.5-mile-long (12-km) lake. There are small beaches at each location. Car-top boats can be launched at Strawberry; MacDonald has its own boat launch. The Terminal Range is on the west side of the lake, while the Sentinel Ranges, rising sharply above the campgrounds to the east, are near the northern limit of the Rockies. One of the best ways to appreciate them is to either get out on the lake in a boat or hike up into them from nearby trails. Beware the winds that rise on Muncho Lake and quickly whip up whitecaps. These same breezes will ensure that you wear a sweater on most days while camping here, even in the middle of summer. Wilderness campsites are located along the west shore of Muncho Lake for those willing to make the crossing by boat. Hwy 97 follows the east side of Muncho Lake and passes beside both campgrounds. For more information, contact BC Parks in Muncho Lake, (250) 776-3486, or in Prince George, (250) 565-6340.

Liard River Hotsprings Provincial Park (53 vehicle/tent sites), located about 12 miles (20 km) north of Muncho Lake on Hwy 97, is one of the few provincial campgrounds that remain open year-round along the Alaska Hwy, and with good reason. Even in the depths of winter (which lasts eight months here) the springs are hot enough to provide relief to weary adventurers, whether they've been hiking on foot or on skis. These springs are very popular with residents of the nearest town, Fort Nelson, 155 miles (250 km) south of the park, so be sure to reserve a space if you wish to overnight here. All sites are located in a heavily forested area of pine, trembling aspen, and cottonwood, a delightful environment at any time of year. Caution: Beware bears, even in areas where groups of campers are bathing. For more information, call BC Parks, (250) 565-6340; for reservations, call (800) 689-9025, from March 1 to September 15.

Hiking/Backpacking

There are numerous avid backpackers in northeastern British Columbia, but few marked trails. Bushwhacking is often the order of the day, which suits many people just fine, but goes beyond the scope of this book. If you really want to get into the remote areas, contact local backpacking clubs, Forest Service offices, or provincial park offices for detailed information.

For information on hiking in the Prince George region, visit Backwoods Industrial Revolutions, (250) 562-2185, 610 Richmond Rd, Prince George, or contact the Caledonia Ramblers, (250) 564-8887. They publish *The Prince George and District Trail Guide,* which provides dozens of walks in the Prince George region. Some of the more popular destinations include **Teapot Mountain,** just north of Summit Lake Forest Service Recreation Site (see Parks/Camping, above), a popular day-trip destination. The trail to the top is short and moderately steep. The trailhead is 3 miles (5 km) west of Hwy 97 on Caine Creek Forest Service Rd. Note: There are two other Summit Lakes in northeastern British Columbia, one located near Pine Pass between Prince George and Dawson Creek, and the other situated beside the Alaska Hwy in Stone Mountain Provincial Park (see below).

An esker is a long, narrow, steep-sided ridge of sand and gravel deposited by streams flowing between the icy walls of two glaciers, or through a meltwater tunnel inside a glacier. These glacial features dominate **Eskers Provincial Park** (see Skiing, below), a popular day-use area located 25 miles (40 km) northwest of Prince George near Ness Lake. The walking is easy here; the trail to Pine Marsh and Circle Lake is accessible even by wheelchair. There are about 9 miles (15 km) of trails wending their way around the many small lakes in the area. The longest trail runs almost 4 miles (6 km) to the tip of **Kathy Lake.**

Muskeg Falls Trail lies along 200 Rd, which is about 45 miles (72 km) north of Prince George. It's about that distance again to the parking lot. An easy walking trail leads to Muskeg Falls in less than an hour.

Recently, the 5-mile (8-km) **Giscome Portage Heritage Trail** was recognized by the provincial government as an important part of British Columbia's history. The creation of Giscome Portage Regional Park has been proposed to protect the existing trail, which formed a lengthy portage between Summit Lake near Prince George, whose waters flow north and east, eventually ending up in the Arctic Ocean, and the North Fraser River, whose waters flow west to the Pacific Ocean. Follow in the footsteps of earlier explorers along this trail, which dates back to the turn of the century. You could even carry a canoe on your back if it would help set the mood, though part of the trail is paved over as Hwy 97. The northern trailhead is vaguely located at the junction of Hwy 97 and Barney Rd; the southern terminus, on the banks of the North Fraser River in Hubble Farm Historic Regional Park, east of Hwy 97, is much easier to locate. Interpretive displays on the history of the trail are mounted here each summer. For more information on hiking the Giscome Portage Heritage Trail, call the Fraser–Fort George Regional District, (250) 960-4400.

Crooked River Provincial Park (see Parks/Camping, above) lies 43 miles (70 km) north of Prince George along Hwy 97. There is a pleasant 5.5-mile (9-km) hiking route around **Bear** and **Squaw Lakes** in the park.

East of Mackenzie is the **Morfee Mountain Trail** (moderate; 3 miles/5 km return), which leads down from the peak of Morfee Mountain to the headwaters of John Bennett Creek. The trail is short and steep; don't go down unless you know you can make it back up again. It's not the usual way to hike a mountain, that's for sure. The Morfee Mountain Rd goes almost 6,000 feet (1817 m) to the top, though access is restricted to summer. From the top of Morfee, visitors are treated to great views of Williston Lake, the Nechako Plateau, and the Rocky Mountain Trench. Follow Morfee Mountain Rd east of Hwy 37 in Mackenzie. The unpaved road begins just north of Morfee Lake. For more information, contact the Mackenzie Chamber of Commerce Travel InfoCentre, (250) 997-5459.

The **Baldy Mountain Trail,** an established but unmarked trail near Williston Lake, runs 42 miles (67 km) from Sylvester Creek north to the old gold fields at Manson Creek, with a 2.5-mile (4-km) spur running up to the peak of Baldy Mountain. It's part of a trail that used to run north from Vanderhoof (on Hwy 16 west of Prince George). It might take a bit of work to find either end, but once you've found it, it's distinct and well maintained by local trapper Oscar Swede. Be prepared for some boggy creek crossings, especially through Sylvester Creek. The trailhead is located west of Williston Lake along a network of Forest Service roads. Contact the Mackenzie Forest District Office for a recreation map of this area, as well as trail information, (250) 997-2200.

North of Mackenzie is **Kimta Trail** (strenuous; 14 miles/24 km return), which traverses three biogeoclimatic zones and diverse stands of trees to a viewpoint above Kimta Creek. It's a difficult hike, especially near the top, where the trail passes through dense brush. Expect to take seven to nine hours round trip. The trailhead is located in a Forest Service pull-out beside Kimta Creek on the east side of the Parsnip Forest Service Rd, about 21 miles (34 km) north of Hwy 37 in Mackenzie.

A steep, 3.1-mile (5-km) trail leads up to **Bickford Lookout,** a Forest Service fire-spotting tower with exceptional views of the Pine River Valley, just east of the Pine Pass Summit on the north side of Hwy 97, about 30 miles (50 km) west of Chetwynd. About 1.5 miles (3 km) beyond is **Bickford Lake.** The trail to the lake is unmarked, but follows a mountain ridge almost due north.

Kinuseo Falls are just the tip of the wilderness in large (79,000-acre/32 000 ha) **Monkman Provincial Park** (see Parks/Camping, above). Day trippers should try hiking from the campground to the **Murray River Crossing** (moderate; 9 miles/14 km return). Allow at least two days to hike the 15 miles (24 km) to the south end of **Monkman Lake.** Don't rush. Monkman is a place of stillness and beauty that should be savoured. From Monkman Lake you can hike into the surrounding mountains. Remember that the southeast corner of Monkman Provincial Park is prime grizzly bear habitat, and though it is not officially closed to visitors, it is recommended that you not head into this area, for the grizzlies' sake and your own. Extreme caution should be exercised everywhere in the park to prevent confrontations with the bears (see BC Outdoor Primer), and only experienced backpackers should hike beyond Monkman Lake. For more information on hiking in Monkman Provincial Park, contact BC Parks in Prince George, (250) 565-6340. The detailed map of the park is NTS #93I/11.

Monkman Provincial Park gets all the glory in the **Tumbler Ridge** area, but there are some excellent hiking trails nearby that are less lauded but equally pleasing. Multi-use trails surround the townsite, perfect for a day of hiking, mountain biking, or cross-country skiing. There is a clearing on the ridge that buttresses Tumbler Ridge's east side, which looks for all the world like a bald patch. No wonder it's known locally as the **Bald Spot.** To reach it, follow a power line that runs up the ridge to the viewpoint. It's a mighty steep scramble, but the views west over the town and to the Rocky Mountains beyond are worth it.

A little farther from town is the **Wapiti Onion Trail.** About 7 miles (12 km) west of Monkman Provincial Park as the raven flies lies **Onion Lake,** a small lake between two mountain ridges of peaks over 6,550 feet (2000 m) high on both sides. You can't get to it from Monkman (at least, not easily), but you can by following the Wapiti Onion Trail. The trail starts from the Wapiti Forest Service Recreation Site, located about 28 miles (45 km) south of Tumbler Ridge along Hwy 29, then right onto the Wapiti Forest Service Rd for 18 miles (30 km) to a fork. The Forest Service recreation site and trailhead are at the end of the right fork. It's 7 miles (12 km) from the trailhead to the shores of **Wapiti Lake,** a popular destination with day hikers. On the way to the lake, you'll pass an old cabin and a shrine, built by Father C. Mariman, who lived in this area, translating the bible for the Beaver and Slavey Indians. The trail is well marked, and it's another 18 miles (30 km) to Onion Lake. Don't let the first half of the hike fool you; it's a pretty stiff climb to Onion Lake once you get past Wapiti. Allow two to three days to complete the round trip.

Another multi-use trail runs for 22 miles (35 km) into the backcountry around Red Deer Creek from the Wapiti Onion trailhead and leads to **Red Deer Falls.** The falls lie 4 miles (7 km) along this lengthy route. Watch out for motorcycles and ATVs on the trail. For a detailed map of the Wapiti Onion Trail and the surrounding region, contact the Dawson Creek Forest District Office, (250) 784-1200.

For more information on trails around **Dawson Creek,** including information on popular trails to Mount Bickford, the Paradise Valley Trails, Salt Ridge Trails, and Salt Ridge Connectors, call the Dawson Creek Forest District Officer, (250) 784-1200, or the Dawson Creek InfoCentre, (250) 782-9595.

Chowade River Trail is an unmarked all-purpose trail that hikers should expect to share with off-road vehicles. From Hwy 97, turn west onto 187 Rd, just south of the community of **Pink Mountain,** and drive to the end. For a shorter trip, try the **Cypress Creek Trail.** Turn left 2 miles (3.5 km) past **Halfway River Forest Service Recreation Site** on Hwy 97 and drive to the end of the road. It's possible for active hikers to do the 10.5-mile (17-km) return journey in a day, but you probably should plan on spending the night on the trail. For more information, contact the general store at Pink Mountain Campsite and RV Park, (250) 774-1033.

North of Fort St. John, there are a handful of lengthy, easygoing trails. The longest trail in the area is the **Redfern Lake Trail** (50 miles/80 km return), which leads to a public cabin at Redfern Lake. The trail is unmarked but easy to follow, and open to ATVs and horses. Expect to take five to seven days there and back. Access to the trail is 3 miles (5 km) north of Buckinghorse River Provincial Park (see Parks/Camping, above) along Hwy 97. A good map to consult is NTS #94G/07.

There are so many truly immense wilderness areas in northern British Columbia that at just over 390,000 acres (158 475 ha), **Kwadacha Provincial Wilderness Park** seems modest compared to Spatsizi Plateau, Mount Edziza, or Tweedsmuir Provincial Park. However, this park's **Lloyd George Icefield** is the largest icefield in the Rocky Mountains north of the 54th parallel. As the Rockies head towards their northern limit at the 60th parallel (the British Columbia–Yukon border), they begin to diminish somewhat. In Kwadacha, though, they're still the Rockies: a number of peaks in and surrounding the park crest at 9,100 feet (2800 m).There is no road access into the park; it must be reached by air or on horseback. It's about 90 miles (150 km) of backpacking just to make it to the park from Hwy 97, with many treacherous river crossings: allow 12 to 14 days. There are a number of undeveloped trails in the park, and a few primitive campsites. Trails within this park are not maintained, and only experienced wilderness backpackers should venture here. This is beautiful but unforgiving country. Kwadacha Provincial Wilderness Park is located about 100 miles (160 km) southwest of Fort Nelson. For more information, contact BC Parks in Fort St. John, (250) 787-3407, or in Prince George, (250) 565-6340. For information on **charter airplanes and guide outfitters,** contact the Fort St. John Chamber of Commerce InfoCentre, (250) 785-6037, or the Fort Nelson–Liard Regional District Travel InfoCentre, (250) 774-6400. A good map to consult is NTS #94F/10.

Just south of **Tetsa River Provincial Park** (see Parks/Camping, above) on the opposite side of Hwy 97 is the **Teetering Rock Hiking Trail,** an 8-mile (12.5-km) trail that runs into the escarpments of the Alberta Plateau, providing expansive views of the northern Rockies. The trailhead begins from a viewpoint 10.5 miles (17 km) north of Steamboat Mountain on Hwy 97.

Stone Mountain Provincial Park is 87 miles (140 km) west of Fort Nelson along the Alaska Hwy. Much of the park lies in the alpine tundra biogeoclimatic zone, which means that trees are scarce and mountains of little more than solid rock reach for the sky. The contrast with the rolling, tree-covered foothills farther south is startling. Plan on 7 to 14 days to complete a 44-mile (70-km) loop through the headwaters of **MacDonald Creek** and the adjacent **Wokkpash Provincial Recreation Area.** Much of the route follows well-trodden game trails laid down by caribou but adhered to by all, as attested to by the wide variety of scat encountered along the way. A horse trail (moderate; 30 miles/50 km return) follows the north side of MacDonald Creek from the trailhead at Mile 400 (Km 645) on the Alaska Hwy.

Old Churchill Mine Rd leads into Wokkpash Provincial Recreation Area from **One-Fifteen Creek Provincial Park** (see Parks/Camping, above), on Hwy 97. Hoodoos in the **Wokkpash Gorge** are one of the scenic features at the 7.5-mile (12-km) point along this route. Other highlights in Wokkpash include **Forlorn Gorge,** an 80-foot (25-m)-wide, 490-foot (150-m)-deep canyon, whose steep-sided slopes should be attempted only with great caution. The nearest help is a long way off in the town of Toad River. For more information, contact BC Parks in Fort St. John, (250) 787-3407, or Prince George, (250) 565-6340. The best maps to consult include NTS #94K and #94K/07.

As well as offering tremendous wilderness hiking for the experienced backpacker, Stone Mountain Provincial Park also features several shorter hiking trails more suited to a quick day trip. These include the **Summit Peak Trail** (strenuous; 6 miles/10 km return) and the **Flower Springs Lake Trail** (moderate; 7 miles/12 km return), to an alpine lake sublimely situated in the folds of the Stone Mountains. Both trailheads are well marked and begin from pullouts on the east side of Hwy 97.

The 55-mile (90-km) drive through **Muncho Lake Provincial Park** (see Parks/Camping, above) has a reputation of being the most scenic part of the Alaska Hwy. It's also one of the most informative. Roadside pullouts appear frequently. Interpretive displays not only provide details on wildlife and geological features but also indicate hiking trails. Accessing higher regions of the Rocky Mountains is easy from here. Pick a wash, any wash, and up you go. For more information on hiking in the park, contact the park ranger in the town of Muncho Lake, on Hwy 97 or call (250) 776-3486 (June through September), or BC Parks in Prince George, (250) 565-6340.

Mountain Biking

Mountain biking, as it is understood in most of the province, is an unknown activity in northeastern British Columbia. Thousands of miles of logging road, both used and unused, stretch out before the fat tires that may be the first to leave an imprint here. Ski and snowmobile trails are plentiful, and see little action in the summer, occasionally for good reason: marshes freeze in the winter, eh? However, the intrepid mountain biker can follow cut lines, trap lines, and other trails that head into the bush. Very few trails have restrictions, so a hiking trail like **Baldy Mountain** or the trail to **Monkman Lake** in Monkman Provincial Park (see Hiking/Backpacking, above) can be turned into a mountain-biking trek, with no one to say otherwise. The Great Canadian Adventure Company in Edmonton, Alberta, leads five-day **bike tours** through Monkman Provincial Park. If you're interested in a trek, but don't want to plan it yourself or have no one to go with, contact them at (403) 913-7157, or visit their Web site: www.adventures.ca.

The area around the **Tumbler Ridge** townsite near Monkman is rife with multi-use trails. In winter, snowmobiles and cross-country skiers roam at will through the forest, but in summer, hiking and mountain biking are the order of the day. Some of the more popular trails start off Bergeron Crescent in Tumbler Ridge. For the extreme biker, these trails will be a walk in the park; enjoy the views over **Flatbed Creek** and the **Murray River** as you pedal along. More information on mountain biking around Tumbler Ridge can be obtained from Euphoria Canoe & Cycle, Tumbler Ridge, (250) 242-4112.

Bear Mountain near **Dawson Creek** is a popular mountain-biking area just southwest of town, where 15.5 miles (25 km) of trails run through this community forest. Trail maps are available from the Dawson Creek Forest Service District Office, (250) 784-1200.

For more information on mountain biking in northeastern British Columbia contact Velocity Sports, Box 85, Chetwynd, (250) 788-2234; Dan Beaudoin Mountain Bike Club in Mackenzie, (250) 997-4610; the Dawson Creek Recreation Department, (250) 782-3351; Westside Recreation, (250) 787-0208, in Fort St. John; the Prince George Cycling Club, (250) 563-3896, or Olympia Cycle & Ski, (250) 564-7479, in Prince George; and Taylor Recreation Centre in Taylor, (250) 789-3734.

Skiing

Okay, so sandblasting doesn't qualify as downhill skiing, but how else can it be classified? If you're overwhelmed by a desire for some skiing, and it's still the middle of summer, try **sandblasting,** a peculiar local sport that involves powering down the sandy cutbanks of the Nechako Plateau on Hwy 97 near Prince George. Just don't expect to use that pair of skis on snow again. There's even a competition for all the die-hard skiers every August.

There's more conventional winter recreation in the Prince George region. **Hart Highlands** is a small ski hill for beginners, children, and freestyle skiers. Call (250) 962-8006 for information. **Tabor Mountain Ski Area,** 15 minutes east of Prince George, is a lot bigger (800 feet/240 m vertical), with triple lift and a T-bar. It has a bus service on weekends, and is open seven days a week, including night skiing three times a week. Phone (250) 564-7669 for the Prince George snow report.

Prince George also has superb cross-country skiing. There are trails in **Cottonwood Island,** the **University of Northern British Columbia** campus, **Forests for the World,** and **Moore's Meadow.** You'll find maintained trails (for a modest fee) at **Otway Ski Trails** and **Tabor Mountain Ski Area.** Contact Caledonia Nordic Ski Club at (250) 564-3809. The Sons of Norway Ski Club organizes local and out-of-town tours and provides guides, maps, and services. Call (250) 563-0830 or (250) 964-6564. Cross-country skis can be **rented** from Olympia Cycle & Ski, (250) 564-7479. Also check with Sport and Ski Motors, 805 First Ave, (250) 563-8891, in Prince George.

There's cross-country skiing and snowshoeing on 9 miles (14 km) of trails in **Eskers Provincial Park** (see Hiking/Backpacking, above), west of Hwy 97 on Chief Lake Rd, about 25 miles (40 km) northwest of Prince George. The **Giscome Portage Heritage Trail** (see Hiking/Backpacking, above) offers 5 miles (8 km) of cross-country trails. There's 5.5 miles (9 km) of cross-country trails around Bear and Squaw Lakes in **Crooked River Provincial Park** (see Parks/Camping, above), north of Prince George.

For those more interested in downhill skiing and snowboarding, **Powder King Ski Village,** located right next to the **Pine Pass** summit on Hwy 97, offers, as the name suggests, some of the best powder skiing in the province. The 18 runs serviced by a chairlift, 2 T-bars and a Platter tow are located about 120 miles (200 km) north of Prince George on Hwy 97. Most of the terrain, spread over a vertical rise of 2,100 feet (640 m), favours intermediate-level skiers. For information on hill accommodation, lessons, schedules, fees, and equipment rental, call (250) 563-9428 in Prince George, or (250) 997-6323 at Powder King.

Around **Dawson Creek,** you can cross-country ski on the 15 miles (25 km) of the **Bear Mountain Forest Service**'s (see Mountain Biking, above) interpretive trails. Phone (250) 784-1200 for a map. Farther north, the hiking trails in **Beatton Provincial Park** (see Parks/Camping, above) near Fort St. John double as cross-country skiing and snowshoeing routes. **Andy Bailey Provincial Recreation Area,** about 24 miles (38 km) southeast of Fort Nelson, has some of the driest, fluffiest powder snow in the province, and there's hardly anyone to share it with. Cut your own track here. For more information and **rentals,** contact Griffin Sport & Ski Shoppe, (250) 782-5066, and City Source for Sports, (250) 782-5432, in Dawson Creek.

Fishing

In the far north, lakes may be either too shallow or too deep, and fish stocks don't do well. Shallow water freezes solid in winter, while deeper lakes never really warm up in summer, stunting fish growth. With that said, there are fish beyond count in these waters, both wild and introduced. Prime species include various types of trout, char, arctic grayling, dolly varden, Rocky Mountain whitefish, and northern pike. If you're into serious fishing and are looking for an **outfitter,** you might want to contact the BC Fishing Resorts and Outfitters Association, PO Box 3301, Kamloops, BC V2C 6R9, (250) 374-6836, or try their Web site: www.oppub.com/bcfroa/bcfroa.html. Licences and regulatory information can be obtained at local suppliers, like Northern Troutfitters Fly & Tackle Shop, 770 Central Ave, (250) 562-3597, or Canadian Tire, 1727 W Central, (250) 562-8258, in Prince George; Macleods True Value, 700 Mackenzie Blvd, (250) 997-4555, in Mackenzie; and Lonestar Sporting Goods, (250) 788-1850, in Chetwynd.

Almost every provincial park supports sportfishing, and many Forest

Service recreation sites were built specifically for anglers looking for a place to park near their favourite spot. Along Hwy 97, the lakes on and surrounding **Crooked River** provide good fishing. You'll find squawfish, char, and rainbow trout in **Summit Lake** and lakes along the Crooked River chain, while surrounding lakes also have brook trout, Rocky Mountain whitefish, and arctic grayling. In particular, try **Bear and Hart Lakes,** located within the borders of Crooked River Provincial Park (see Parks/Camping, above), 43 miles (70 km) north of Prince George along Hwy 97 (watch for powerboat restrictions).

Fifty-six miles (90 km) north of Prince George, along Hwy 97, is the turnoff to the **Tacheeda Lakes** (see Parks/Camping, above). Rainbow trout are the prime catch here; but if you're not having much luck, or Tacheeda is too crowded, try one of the other lakes in the area, including **Goose, Cat, Hambone,** or **Fishhook Lakes.** You can also drop a line into the nearby Parsnip River (see Kayaking/Canoeing, below), which runs all the way north to Williston Lake.

McLeod Lake, the lake, is located just south of McLeod Lake, the town. There's a boat launch at Whiskers Point Provincial Park (see Parks/Camping, above), and good arctic grayling, rainbow trout, and char fishing. **Carp Lake,** 20 miles (32 km) west of McLeod Lake (the town), boasts . . . guess what?

North of McLeod Lake is **Tudyah Lake Provincial Park** (see Parks/Camping, above), where you'll enjoy good squawfish angling, with some rainbow and bull trout. From here, a rat's nest of Forest Service roads bring the angler into a fisherman's paradise far too expansive (and too difficult) to describe without a good map. You can get a detailed Forest Service map from the Mackenzie Forest District Office, (250) 997-2200. Or you can just head for Finlay Bay on **Williston Lake** (see Parks/Camping, above). You can't miss it; it's the largest body of water in the province. Whether or not you can catch a fish here, well, that depends on your skill and if the fish are biting when you cast a line. Talk to local outfitters for information on where to catch what in this gigantic lake.

Hwy 97 follows the **Pine River** through the Pine Pass. Simply pick a Forest Service recreation site along the road and toss in a line. Further east, 15.5 miles (25 km) past Chetwynd, is East Pine Provincial Park, where the **East Pine** and **Murray Rivers** come together. There's a boat launch in the park, and the rivers offer good bull trout fishing.

Cast a line in the **Sukunka River** for dolly varden and arctic grayling. Watch for the turnoff for Sukunka Forest Service Rd, 12 miles (20 km) south of Chetwynd along Hwy 29. Continuing along Hwy 29, south of Gwillim Lake Provincial Park (see Parks/Camping, above), is **Moose Lake,** popular with the locals for lake trout.

The **Kiskatinaw River** flows along the east side of Dawson Creek, then bends north around the town. Kiskatinaw Provincial Park, which has access to the river, is right beside the historic bridge on Hwy 97, offering good fishing for pike, and possibly bull and rainbow trout, right near town. Even better fishing is found on the Peace River near its confluence with the Kiskatinaw. Use the boat launch at Blackfoot Regional Park, northeast of Dawson Creek near the town of Clayhurst. For more information, contact the Dawson Creek InfoCentre, (250) 782-9595.

Just north of Fort St. John is **Charlie Lake.** Walleye, northern pike, and yellow perch are found here, and there are boat launches at Beatton and Charlie Lake Provincial Parks, about 4 miles (6 km) north of Fort St. John. For information on angling in the Fort St. John region, contact Horseshoe Creek Outfitters, (250) 262-3218, in Charlie Lake, Klukas Lake Ranch, (250) 789-9224, in Taylor, and Sikanni River Outfitters, (250) 774-0932, in Pink Mountain.

For more information on fishing throughout the Northeast, contact the local BC Forest Service or BC Parks offices (see More Information, below) for maps and information on guides and outfitters. Other good sources of information are the local Fish and Wildlife Conservation Officers in Prince George, (250) 565-6420; Mackenzie, (250) 997-6555; Dawson Creek, (250) 784-2304; Fort St. John, (250) 787-3507; and Fort Nelson, (250) 774-3547.

Kayaking/Canoeing

Prince George has one of the biggest, most active paddling clubs in the province, the Northwest Brigade Canoe Club. They've even put out a book devoted to paddling in this neck of the woods, *Canoe and Kayak Trip Guide for the Central Interior of British Columbia.* Trips run from flatwater to Class V rapids, but don't expect to find much more than Class II in this easygoing guidebook. For anyone planning on spending time in this area, it's a good investment. At the very least, get in touch with the club for any new information on routes in the area. Write to them at Box 327, Prince George, BC V2L 4S2.

A spot near Prince George is **Eskers Provincial Park** (see Hiking/Backpacking, above). A series of tiny lakes linked by portages lets you experience a day or three of wilderness paddling in close proximity to Prince George. The only real danger here is getting lost, and with a bit of preparation even that is pretty easy to avoid. The park is located about 25 miles (40 km) northwest of Prince George on Chief Lake Rd. Simon Fraser himself paddled through this area more than 100 years ago.

Class II is as stiff as it gets along the **Crooked River,** the link running through a chain of lakes from Summit Lake, north of Prince George on Hwy 97, all the way to Williston Lake. Most people only go as far as Kerry Lake (five hours) or McLeod Lake (two easy days). The river is best run in early summer, unless you think you might enjoy walking your canoe for the first 6 miles (10 km); the river can get fairly low later in the year. Watch for the Crooked River Canyon Forest Service Recreation Site on your way downstream, which can be reached only by canoe.

On the east side of Hwy 97 is the **Parsnip River,** named for the giant cow parsnips that grow along its banks. The name is amusing, but the paddling is serious. It'll take you two days to do the 35 miles (57 km) from the old Anzac Mill site to Windy Point, where the Parsnip crosses Hwy 97 to meet Williston Lake. Tacheeda Lakes Rd is 56 miles (90 km) along Hwy 97 from the John Hart Bridge; the launch site is 17 miles (27 km) beyond on gravel road.

You can follow part of Simon Fraser's route by paddling the 5 miles (8 km) of **McLeod River** that link War and Carp Lakes in **Carp Lake Provincial Park** (see Parks/Camping, above). Once you hit Carp Lake, spend a day exploring, then a night at a designated campsite on one of the islands that dot the lake.

It's recommended that you *not* put a canoe in **Williston Lake,** the largest lake in the area, and indeed, in the province. The lake is man-made, and the area wasn't logged before it was flooded. Jams, floaters, and ice-sharpened snags can make this a dangerous lake to canoe, though that doesn't stop many people. Consider this fair warning. If you are planning on canoeing Williston, there's a put-in at Finlay Bay Forest Service Recreation Site at the end of Hwy 39. Instead, try canoeing down what used to be the Peace River Valley. Now that it's been flooded, it's called the **Peace Reach.** Don't expect to do the reach in a day, though. It stretches 37 miles (60 km) east to the W. A. C. Bennett Dam.

If such warnings put you off the big lake, try the **Dina Lakes Canoe Circuit,** a route through a number of small lakes that should take about four hours to complete. Access to the lakes is about 12 miles (20 km) north of Mackenzie. Best time to do the Dina Lakes route is in early June, once the portages have been brushed out. The longest portage on this route is about 230 feet (70 m). Maps of the route are available at the Mackenzie Chamber of Commerce, or the Mackenzie Forest District Office, (250) 997-2200.

Depending on where you put in and how fast you paddle, canoeing the **Murray River** near **Tumbler Ridge** can be a few hours or a few days. You're going to need someone to drop you off and pick you up, or leave a vehicle at the end. Follow the Forest Service road toward Monkman Provincial Park (see Parks/Camping, above). There are two bridges over the Murray on the way to Monkman, or if you can handle the portage down (it's a killer), you can launch from near the base of **Kinuseo Falls.** Watch for an old trappers cabin as you head down the river. The best place to take out is near the second bridge from Tumbler Ridge along Hwy 29 to Chetwynd. If you pass the BC Rail shops heading north, you've gone too far. Another popular put-in point is at **East Pine Provincial Park** (see Fishing, above) where the East Pine River flows into the Murray, 15.5 miles (25 km) east of Chetwynd.

For more information on paddling in the region contact Euphoria Canoe & Cycle in Tumbler Ridge, (250) 242-4112, and Lone Star Sporting in Chetwynd, (250) 788-1850.

Since the **W. A. C. Bennett Dam** was built, the **Peace River** has lost what spunk it once had. The dam was built at the end of the roughest sections of the river, and flooded out the entire river valley for hundreds of kilometres back. The 600-foot (183-m) monstrosity is a wonder of modern engineering, a half-mile wide at its base; when the floodgates are opened in early spring, the gushing water is truly an impressive sight. Past the dam, the Peace flows gently east through the foothills of the Rockies and on into the Prairies. You could float east from **Hudson's Hope** to Hudson's Bay, with not much more than the occasional weir to worry about. Shorter trips include a five-day paddle from Hudson's Hope to **Taylor Landing Provincial Park,** or 10 days to Dunvegan, Alberta. Or you could just spend a day canoeing around Taylor Landing Provincial Park, along Hwy 97, 24 miles (38 km) north of Dawson Creek.

Rafting

The Northeast gets short shrift when it comes to river rafting; rivers farther west such as the Stikine and the Skeena get all the glory. But being less popular means being less crowded. There are very few companies that make regular runs in this area, but as other rivers become too crowded this will change. Canadian River Expeditions, based in Whistler, leads **rafting trips** down the **Gataga** and **Kechika Rivers.** Contact them at (800) 898-7238. The River League, (604) 687-3417, based in Squamish, leads 11-day tours down the **Turnagain** and **Tuchodi Rivers.** One local company that guides river-rafting expeditions in the area is Backcountry Adventures in Fort St. John. They will tailor river-rafting trips to suit your abilities. Call (250) 787-5359.

Scenic Drives/Photography

Bijoux Falls, an attractive cascade of water just off Hwy 97, offers a brief respite from your journey and is a lovely place to stop for lunch. Bijoux

Falls is located just west of the Pine Pass, about 18 miles (30 km) north of Hwy 39's junction with Hwy 97. The **Pine Pass** summit on Hwy 97 is particularly pretty, and offers great views down the Burnt River Valley and, through the pass, views of towering mountains and the sparkling Pine River. You can even climb to the top of **Mount Bickford** for a different camera angle. As Hwy 97 crosses Pine Pass, there are a number of places to pull off to the side of the road and admire the scenery. This is the shortest pass through the Rockies, and the big mountains stand in stark contrast to the gentler terrain on either side. In addition, **Peace Foothills Area Map and Rest Area,** on Hwy 97 near Hassler Flats, features a sweeping look at the western foothills of the Rockies.

The **Alaska Highway** has long stretches of rolling hills and lodgepole pine, but there are a number interesting viewpoints along the way where you can break out your camera. During the wildflower bloom, **Pink Mountain** looks, well, pink from a distance because of all the blossoms. If you miss this phenomenon, you can still take pictures of the surrounding landscape from the peak of Pink, or continue on for 6 miles (10 km) for views of Lilly Lake, Moose Lick Creek, and Halfway River. The turnoff to the mountain is at Mile 147 (Km 237) of the Alaska Hwy, 4 miles (6.5 km) north of the hamlet of Pink Mountain. Viewpoints continue along the Alaska Hwy from here.

Wildlife

It is almost impossible not to observe wildlife as you travel through the Northeast, the so-called "Serengeti of North America." The area's spectacular wildlife fauna consists of eight species of wild ungulates, namely **Stone sheep, mountain goats, bison, moose, elk, caribou, and white-tailed and mule deer;** plus at least seven species of large and medium-size carnivores including **wolves, coyotes, foxes, grizzly bears, black bears, lynx, and wolverines.** Deer, moose, bears, and elk frequent clearings alongside roads, foraging for food. In some areas, salt licks have been placed near the road to attract ungulates. Be careful when driving these roads, especially at night; if you were to hit a moose, chances are good that your vehicle would come out of the encounter in worse shape than the moose. Honest.

Eskers Provincial Park (see Hiking/Backpacking, above) near Prince George has wheelchair-accessible facilities to Pine Marsh and Circle Lake. Pine Marsh in particular is a great place for **bird-watching,** but moose and beavers also inhabit the park. To reach the park, travel about 25 miles (40 km) west of Hwy 97 on Chief Lake Rd.

Pink Mountain (see Scenic Drives/Photography, above) is a designated viewing area for wildlife in this region, and places have been cleared to provide browsing territory for ungulates. One of the rarer browsing species is the **plains bison,** but almost all the ungulates are represented, as well as several carnivorous species. Pink Mountain's real claim to fame is the high population of rare **Arctic butterflies.**

Brand-new **Muskwa-Kechika Management Unit** is 10.8 million acres (4.4 million ha) in size, and comprises 50 intact watersheds. The Big E, as it's known (E is for Environment), is the largest of its kind in British Columbia. The Muskwa-Kechika wilderness consists of three major components: the Northern Rocky Mountains and associated foothills, the Rocky Mountain Trench, and the Cassiar Mountains. This is a predator-prey ecosystem that doesn't have to be fixed, because it isn't broken, and is being maintained as inaccessible. Under a plan put forward by a coalition of interest groups, including such diverse partners as trappers, miners, oil companies, and a host of conservation groups, roads can be put in on a temporary basis, then taken out when no longer needed. Of the 10.8-million-acre (4.4-million-ha) protected area, more than 2.5 million acres (1 million ha) are permanently protected with the creation of 11 new parks. For outdoor enthusiasts willing to make the long journey into the Northeast, the new parks run a gamut from the mammoth 1,593,000-acre (645 000-ha) **Northern Rockies Protected Area** to the diminutive 445-acre (180-ha) **Prophet River Hot Springs Protected Area.** Visit the provincial government's Land Use Coordination Office Web site, where you'll find a brief description of the new Muskwa-Kechika protected area. Go to www.luco.gov.bc.ca and view the Land Use Plans page, where you'll also find a map of the new region (you'll have to download the map to read the fine print). Hum a few bars of "Home on the Range" to get yourself in the mood. In the 21st century, this may be one of the few places on earth where large mammals and their predators continue to survive and evolve. Access to the newly protected areas is from Hwy 97 between Fort St. John and the British Columbia–Yukon border. For more information, contact BC Parks in Fort St. John, (250) 787-3407, or in Prince George, (250) 565-6340.

The defining feature of **Stone Mountain Provincial Park** (see Parks/Camping, above) is the mountains: great humps of raw stone rising from the valleys below, where only the barest plant life—lichen, grasses, moss—survive. You wouldn't expect to find much in the way of wildlife here, and in truth, you won't find much on the bare slopes. But the valleys are a different matter. **Mountain caribou** and **Stone sheep** winter in some of the lower valleys, and mountain goats, moose, and grizzly and black bears also frequent the valleys. A number of bird species live in the park, none more magnificent than the **golden eagle.** Watch for Stone sheep beside the Alaska Hwy between here and Liard River Hotsprings.

For information on wildlife and nature observation in the Prince George region, contact the Prince George Naturalist's Club, (250) 967-4288. For **guided wildlife viewing** in the Northeast, contact Pink Mountain Outfitters, (250) 694-3406, in Burns Lake; Kyllo Brothers, (250) 783-5248, or Christina Falls Outfitters, (250) 783-9455, in Hudson's Hope; Peace Country Wilderness Adventures, (250) 788-1980, in Chetwynd; and G. F. Moore Enterprises, (250) 782-2908, in Dawson Creek.

outside in

Attractions

Prince George, the fourth-largest city in the province, is the hub of northern and central British Columbia, and the departure point for brave souls heading up the Alaska Hwy. The city sits between two mountain ranges on a dry plateau at the confluence of the Nechako and Fraser Rivers, on the traditional trading route of the Carrier and Sekani tribes. Forestry is the main industry here, and loads of logging roads take adventurers back into remote and bountiful spots. Adjacent to the Cottonwood Island Nature Park is the **Prince George Railway Museum,** (250) 563-7351. Two city **galleries** are of interest: Prince George Art Gallery, (250) 563-6447, features regional and national exhibits monthly; Native Art Gallery, (250) 562-7385, exhibits local Native art and crafts.

The town of **Dawson Creek,** an agricultural community near the Alberta border, is probably most famous as the location of **Mile 0** on the Alaska Hwy, found in the centre of town on 10th St. Another worthwhile attraction in town is the Northern Alberta Railways Station Park, (250) 782-9595, which features an award-winning restoration job on a **historic train station.** A farmer's market is also held here, May through October.

Toad River (Mile 422 Alaska Hwy/Hwy 97) is a town of 60 with a collection of 4,580 hats—one for every mile between the Yukon and the continental United States, plus a few extras for every head in town.

At the Yukon border in Watson Lake, **Signposts Forever** is a must-photograph stop, with 9,000-plus signs pointing the way home from the 60th parallel.

Lodgings

Esther's Inn This Polynesian-style hotel brings the tropics to the North, with palm trees and waterfalls that cascade around the indoor swimming pool (there are also water slides spiralling into a separate pool). Rates are reasonable—so what if they lay it on a little thick? *1151 Commercial Dr (off Hwy 97 at 10th Ave), Prince George, BC V2M 6W6; (250) 562-4131; $$.*

The Inn on Ferry Breakfasts here are legendary, at least in northern British Columbia. There's plenty of room to spread out in this 5,000-square-foot (450-m^2) house; guests can use the lounge and library. *1506 Ferry Ave (just off Hwy 97 bridge across Fraser River), Prince George, BC V2L 5H2; (250) 562-4450; $$–$$$.*

Westhaven Cottage-by-the-Lake B&B Guests can stay in a rustic cottage or one guest room in the adjacent house. Both are on the shores of West Lake, a small lake that's more popular among canoers than with fishermen. There are canoes for rent, too. *23357 Fyfe Rd (12 miles/19 km west of Prince George on Hwy 16), Prince George, BC V2N 2S7; (250) 964-0180; $$.*

More Information

BC Forest Service, Dawson Creek Forest District: *(250) 784-1200.*
BC Forest Service, Fort Nelson Forest District: *(250) 774-3936.*
BC Forest Service, Fort St. John Forest District: *(250) 787-5600.*
BC Forest Service, Mackenzie Forest District: *(250) 997-2200.*
BC Forest Service, Prince George Forest District: *(250) 565-7100.*
BC Forest Service, Prince George Regional Office: *(250) 565-6100.*
BC Parks: *reservations, (800) 689-9025.*
BC Parks, Fort St. John: *(250) 787-3407.*
BC Parks, Muncho Lake: *(250) 776-3486.*
BC Parks, Prince George: *(250) 565-6340.*
Chetwynd Chamber of Commerce: *(250) 788-3345, (250) 788-3655.*
Dawson Creek and District Chamber of Commerce: *(250) 782-4868.*
Dawson Creek InfoCentre: *(250) 782-9595.*
Fort Nelson–Liard Regional District InfoCentre: *(250) 774-6400 or (250) 774-2541 (off-season).*
Fort St. John Chamber of Commerce InfoCentre: *(250) 785-6037 or (250) 785-3033 (summer only).*
Fraser–Fort George Regional District: *(250) 960-4400.*
Groundbirch General Store: *(250) 780-2334. North of Dawson Creek on Hwy 97; a good source of information on outdoor recreation in the region.*
Mackenzie Chamber of Commerce InfoCentre: *(250) 997-5459.*
Taylor InfoCentre: *(250) 789-9015 or (250) 789-3392.*
Tourism Prince George: *toll free, (800) 668-7646; (250) 562-3700; (250) 563-5493 (seasonal).*

The Stewart-Cassiar Highway (Highway 37)

From the junction with Highway 16 north to the Yukon border, including the Trail of the Totems, the Spatsizi Plateau Provincial Wilderness Park, Stikine River Provincial Recreation Area, Mount Edziza Provincial Park, Atlin Provincial Park, and Tatshenshini-Alsek Provincial Wilderness Park.

The linchpin between the Yellowhead and Alaska Highways (finally completed in 1972), the Stewart-Cassiar Highway is the only road that delivers adventurers to this awe-inspiring wilderness. Part of the Cassiar Highway doubles (or trebles) as an emergency landing strip—duck, sucker! Sections are still unpaved and services are few; be prepared for any eventuality, including a passing bear asking for a hand-out. There's a long, 115-mile (186-km) stretch with intermittent gravel from Bell–Irving River Bridge to Kinaskan Lake, but on a clear day nothing can spoil the stupendous views. Two roads branch west of Highway 37 and connect with Stewart and Telegraph Creek, respectively. And for those who must find the real edge, Highway 7 south from Jakes Corner on Highway 1 (Alaska Highway) in Yukon nips through the extreme northwestern corner of the province to Atlin. Along the way it runs alongside the immense, uninhabited wilderness of the Tatshenshini-Alsek Provincial Wilderness Park, which is in turn bordered on the north by Yukon's Kluane National Park and on the south by Alaska's Glacier Bay National Park. Up here, it's a tight little world of parks.

The far northwest offers explorers huge areas of unspoiled wilderness. But such isolation comes at a price: this is a dangerous place to be if you don't know what you're doing. Long winters and short summers keep many areas out of reach, and mosquitoes the size of small jet planes can terrorize the unprepared into cursing the day they ever set foot in this region. Vehicle access is limited to Highway 37 and logging roads. The Coast Mountains grow larger and larger as you travel farther north. The Central Coast's Mount Waddington, at 13,176 feet (4016 m) is the largest peak in the province; Mount Fairweather, in Tatshenshini-Alsek on the British Columbia–Alaska border, is even taller, at 15,299 feet (4663 m).

Nature, it seems, conspires to keep this region a secret, but for those who are prepared, the Stewart-Cassiar Highway supplies unimaginably rich rewards. A handful of wilderness parks—Mount Edziza, Spatsizi Plateau, Tatlatui, Atlin, and Tatshenshini-Alsek—cover some of the toughest territory on the continent. Getting off the beaten path—even as meagre a one as Highway 37— is a must for explorers; many areas can be reached only by foot, horseback, helicopter, or floatplane. Those seeking solitude can go for days or weeks in some areas without sharing this rugged beauty with anyone else. Forged in fire, carved with ice, coloured with sprawling verdant forests, crystalline blue lakes, and fragile alpine meadows: welcome to the backcountry.

Getting There

Kitwanga lies just west of Hazelton on Highway 37, about 2.5 miles (4 km) north of the junction of Highway 16 and Highway 37, about 280 miles (450 km) northwest of Prince George and about 760 miles (1225 km) from Vancouver. Upper Liard lies just north of the British Columbia–Yukon border at the junction of Highway 37 and the Alaska Highway (Highway 1), 447 miles (720 km) from Kitwanga. Highway 37 is also called the Stewart-Cassiar connector (as it connects Stewart and the entire Cassiar district to the rest of the province). Stewart is an "easy" hour's drive (38 miles/62 km) from Meziadin Junction, 88 miles (142 km) north of Kitwanga; Telegraph Creek is a much more demanding two hours southwest of Dease Lake, a distance of 70 miles (113 km). Tatshenshini-Alsek Provincial Wilderness Park, at the northwestern tip of mainland British Columbia, is one of the most difficult yet rewarding parks to reach in the province. (You don't come this far expecting anything less.) Road access is via Yukon Highway 3 and BC–Alaska Highway 7, south from the Alaska Highway (Highway 1) in Yukon.

Adjoining Areas

SOUTH: **The Bulkley and Skeena Valleys**

EAST: **The Northeast**

Parks/Camping

Organized camping is sparse in the great wilderness of the northwest. There are some small, 2- or 3-vehicle Forest Service recreation sites in the first 60 miles (100 km) north along Hwy 37 from Kitwanga, and a handful more east of the highway along Forest Service roads. Most Forest Service recreation sites in this region are small, with room for at most 10 vehicles, but there are a few larger sites, including **Morchuea Lake,** which has a boat launch and good views of Mount Edziza, about 43 miles (70 km) south of Dease Lake. This campground borders the Stikine River Provincial Recreational Area and is an excellent starting point for trips into this vast area. **Allen Lake Forest Service Recreation Site,** a medium-size campground, is located next to the town of Dease Lake. Watch for the **Sawmill Point Forest Service Recreation Site,** also a medium-size campground, just west of Hwy 37, about 25 miles (40 km) farther north along majestic Dease Lake.

A rough Forest Service road runs southwest from the town of Dease Lake, skirts the Grand Canyon of the Stikine River, and connects with the must-see town of Telegraph Creek. A few miles downriver from Telegraph Creek is a trio of Forest Service recreation sites on the banks of the Stikine: **Glenora, Witner Creek,** and **Dodjatin Creek.** Together, these provide space for more than 40 vehicles on the banks of this spectacular river.

French Creek Forest Service Recreation Site, a medium-size campground on the banks of the Dease River, is located 15 miles (25 km) north of Boya Lake. It holds the distinction of being the last campsite on Hwy 37 before Yukon, 30 miles (50 km) beyond. The Forest Service site that is farthest north, however, is **Morley Lake Forest Service Recreation Site,** located about 120 miles (200 km) west of the junction of Hwys 37 and 97. The junction is in Yukon, but the Alaska Hwy dips south into British Columbia for a few miles, and Morley Lake Forest Service Recreation Site is located on the very border. The lake itself is in Yukon, but the medium-size Forest Service site is under British Columbia's jurisdiction.

Hwy 7 makes its way south from Jakes Corner in Yukon to **Atlin** and **Atlin Provincial Park and Recreation Area.** There's a half dozen Forest Service recreation sites within a 30-mile (50-km) radius of the town of Atlin, the largest of which are **Surprise Lake,** about 20 miles (35 km) east of Atlin on a Forest Service road, and **Warm Bay,** just south of Atlin on Atlin Lake. But if you've made it to Warm Bay, you might consider going a few more miles to try to find a site at **The Grotto,** about 12 miles (20 km) beyond Atlin. There's space only for a few overnight vehicles (it's primarily a day-use site), but the warm springs here should encourage you to make an effort to secure a spot. If not, the springs are easily reached from the other Forest Service recreation sites.

For a detailed **map** of all Forest Service recreation sites in northwestern British Columbia, contact the Prince Rupert Regional Office, 3726 Alfred Ave, (250) 847-7500, in Smithers; the Kispiox Forest District Office, (250) 842-7600, in Hazelton; the Cassiar Forest District Office, (250) 771-4211, in Dease Lake; the Kalum Forest District Office, 5220 Keith Ave, (250) 638-5100, in Terrace; the Stewart Field Office, (250) 636-2663; or the Atlin Field Office, (250) 651-7638, in Atlin. For information on provincial park campgrounds, contact BC Parks' Skeena District Office, 3790 Alfred Ave, (250) 847-7320, in Smithers.

For information on Atlin Provincial Park, contact BC Parks, (250) 847-7320, in Smithers. For **guided camping tours** in Atlin Provincial Park, contact Norseman Adventure, (604) 651-7535, in Mission.

BC Parks does not maintain campgrounds in any of its large wilderness parks in the northwest. If you plan on camping in these parks, make sure you bear-proof your site, and camp where you will have the least impact on the environment. However, there are three fine provincial parks with camping that most of us only dream about. **Meziadin Lake Provincial Park** (42 vehicle/tent sites), about 96 miles (155 km) north of Kitwanga, fills up quickly in summer; many of its picturesque campsites are right at lakeside. **Kinaskan Lake Provincial Park** (50 vehicle/tent sites) is located 225 miles (365 km) north of Kitwanga. The campsites in this park are enough to make you drool: killer views west across the wide lake to Mount Edziza Provincial Park. The other campground of substance is **Boya Lake Provincial Park,** (45 vehicle/tent sites), 27 miles (45 km) northeast of Cassiar and about 45 miles (75 km) south of the British Columbia–Yukon border. The blue waters of this lake coupled with the sight of the Horseranch Range and the Cassiar Mountains will make you cry. For more information, contact BC Parks, (250) 847-7320, in Smithers.

Hiking/Backpacking

Many of the trails in the Stewart area (along Hwy 37A) follow old mining routes, like the **Sluice Box/Barney's Gulch Trail,** a short, moderately difficult trail that follows an old railway bed and a historic sluice box to a viewpoint overlooking Stewart. This trail starts on the southeast corner of town. Another is the **United Empire Loyalist Trail,** also short and moderately difficult, which leads from the townsite of Stewart to a viewpoint overlooking Stewart and Bear Valley. Beyond the viewpoint, a more difficult, unkempt route continues on to the United Empire Loyalist Mine site. The Forest Service is currently working with local trail builders to connect the United Empire Loyalist Trail to the **Titan Trail,** a moderate to difficult hike to Titan Mine, located (barely) on the Alaska side of the British Columbia–Alaska border. When the route is finished (and it should be finished soon), it will be an international trail (22 miles/36 km return). At present, the trailhead for Titan Trail is located 6 miles (10 km) north of Hyder, Alaska, on the Salmon River Rd. The **Ore Mountain Trail** starts from the Clements Lake Forest Service Recreation Site on Hwy 37A, about 6 miles (10 km) north of Stewart, and climbs steeply up Ore Mountain to alpine viewpoints overlooking the Bear Valley. The trail is only 6 miles (10 km) return, but with difficult sections where a great deal of elevation is gained. Spend a day hiking to **Bear Glacier,** 15 miles (24 km) west of Meziadin Lake Provincial Park (see Parks/Camping, above) on Hwy 37A. The name says it all. Follow the trail from **Strohn Lake,** and watch out for bears—black and grizzly—they're everywhere.

There are two moderately short hiking trails in the **Stikine River Provincial Recreation Area** on Hwy 37. The first leads from a pullout near the northern park border to a viewpoint overlooking the **Tuya River Valley.** About 6 miles (10 km) beyond, a trail leads to the floor of the valley and on to the confluence of the Tuya and Stikine Rivers. For detailed descriptions of hiking trails in this area, call BC Parks, (250) 847-7320.

The most common modes of transportation into **Mount Edziza Provincial Park** are by horseback and floatplane, but you can also hike in. **Mowdade Lake Trail** leads 15 miles (24 km) from the trailhead at Kinaskan Lake Provincial Park (see Parks/Camping, above) to Mount Edziza Provincial Park, but you'll need a boat to get across the Iskut River at the trailhead. The **Klastline River Trail** begins at the A-E Guest Ranch farther north at Iskut and follows the Klastline River to Buckley Lake. From here, the trail hooks up with the **Buckley Lake Trail,** which leads out of the park to (or into the park from) Telegraph Creek, or rather, the south banks of the Stikine River, across from Telegraph Creek. A trail runs from Mowdade Lake west to Coffee Crater, and then north, where it hooks up with the Buckley Lake Trail, though trail is perhaps too strong a word. Route would be more accurate, as these are unmarked, uncleared, undeveloped . . . well, routes. From Mowdade Lake to Buckley Lake is approximately 37 miles (60 km). Expect to take six to seven days to backpack in. Weather is unpredictable. Temperatures can hit 86°F (30°C) in the day, and drop below freezing in the evening, causing snowstorms. Only experienced backcountry travellers should attempt these routes without an experienced guide. For information on **guided trips** into

Mount Edziza Provincial Park, contact BC Parks in Smithers, (250) 847-7320, or the Iskut Band Administration Office, (250) 234-3331.

Telegraph Creek gets its name from an overland telegraph line to Yukon, the assembly of which was started in 1866. The project was stopped when the first trans-Atlantic submarine cable was laid, then started again during the Klondike gold rush. The cable was finished in 1901, and abandoned in 1936, when wireless radio killed it. Though the **Yukon Telegraph Trail** is mostly grown over to the south of Telegraph Creek, a 161-mile (265-km) stretch still survives between Telegraph Creek and Atlin, and is open to the serious backpacker. The best contact for anything related to outdoor adventure around Telegraph Creek is Stikine River Song Lodge, (250) 235-3196, complete with cafe, general store, and **outfitters.**

"Spatsizi" means "red goat" in the tongue of the original inhabitants of the area around Spatsizi Plateau, the Tahltan. The goats aren't really red, but roll in iron-oxide dust, coating their otherwise white coats. The **Spatsizi Plateau Provincial Wilderness Park** is the second-largest park in the province, weighing in at 1,693,890 acres (656 785 ha).To get there, turn east off of Hwy 37 onto the Ealue Lake Rd at Tatogga Lake. Follow the road for 13.5 miles (22 km), crossing the Klappan River, where it then intersects the BC Rail grade. The grade parallels the southwestern boundary of the park for 68 miles (112 km) and is rough but driveable for most vehicles. From here the park must be accessed by foot, horseback, or canoe. The two trails that lead into the park, the **McEwan Creek Trail** and the **Eaglesnest Creek Trail,** follow well-marked routes and connect to a number of other trails, some easier to follow than others. There are well over 100 miles (160 km) of trail in the park. An old outfitters' cabin is available for public use at Cold Fish Lake. Call BC Parks for more information, (250) 847-7320, or the **outfitter** Spatsizi Wilderness Vacations, (250) 847-2909, in Smithers. Many local guides are also based in Iskut, strategically (and breathtakingly) placed between Mount Edziza and Spatsizi. The best source of information here is the Iskut Band Administration Office, (250) 234-3331.

Tatlatui Provincial Park rubs noses with Spatsizi's southeast corner. This is the only contact that Tatlatui has with anything. The closest road is well over 50 miles (80 km) away, leaving you to reach the park by air, horseback, or foot. If you're planning on hiking this region, it is strongly recommended that you have a guide, as trails are not marked. Information on **outfitters** can be obtained from BC Parks in Smithers, (250) 847-7320. The same goes for backpacking in **Atlin Provincial Park,** as there are no marked routes in this park either.

Near Atlin, the **Monarch Mountain Trail** is a 6-mile (10-km) return climb of Monarch Mountain, with views of Atlin Lake. The trailhead is located at the Palmer Lake Forest Service Recreation Site, just south of Atlin.

Marking the extreme northwest corner of the province is the **Tatshenshini-Alsek Provincial Wilderness Park,** which is nestled between Kluane National Park in Yukon and Glacier Bay and Wrangell–St. Elias National Parks in Alaska. The park—the largest in British Columbia—covers 2,366,260 acres (958 000 ha) of rugged north-coast wilderness and, together with the other three adjacent national parks, comprise the largest contingent area of protected wilderness in the world, at around 21 million acres (8.5 million ha). The Tat, as it is known to people who have difficulty pronouncing the full name, is also designated by the United Nations as a World Heritage Site.

The blood that flows through the Tat's veins is the icy cold water of hundreds of streams that feed that **Tatshenshini and Alsek Rivers.** There are two established entries into the park along the Haines Hwy (Hwys 3 and 7) from Yukon or Alaska and these provide access for hikers, backpackers, and mountain bikers. There are a very few trails in the park; for the most part, you have to make it up as you go along. Fortunately, game trails are plentiful. For information on **guided backpacking tours** into the park, contact BC Parks, (250) 847-7320, or the Atlin Visitors Association, (250) 651-7522 or (250) 651-7470.

Fishing

The recently established **Swan Lake–Kispiox River Provincial Park** contains a chain of undeveloped lakes and rivers just waiting for anglers in search of rainbow trout. The park is located 8.5 miles (14 km) east of Hwy 37 along a rough road that begins at Mile 68 (Km 110) north of Kitwanga and leads to a small boat launch at the north end of **Brown Bear Lake.** From there, visitors must paddle (no powerboats) and portage to other lakes in the park. Please keep in mind this is a remote area; come prepared for wilderness travel. For more information, contact BC Parks in Smithers, (250) 847-7320, and the Fish and Wildlife Conservation Officer in Hazelton, (250) 842-5319.

There's good whitefish, rainbow trout, and dolly varden fishing at **Meziadin Lake.** A boat launch is located in Meziadin Lake Provincial Park (see Parks/Camping, above), but the best fishing is off the gravel bars at the mouths of many of the creeks that drain into the lake.

You would expect good fishing in a creek called Fish, and, indeed, you can catch some of the biggest chum salmon on the coast in **Fish Creek** and in the **Portland Canal.** Road and boat access is from Hwy 37A near **Stewart.** It's catch-and-release only in the creek, though; make sure you have a camera so you can prove that you caught the monster.

North of the Hwy 37A turnoff, Hwy 37 runs parallel to the **Bell-Irving River,** then the **Ningunsaw River,** then **Kinaskan and Eddontenajon Lakes,** then . . . well, you get the picture. There are numerous points where road and water meet, or come close to meeting, that offer many opportunities to pull off the road and break out the fishing rod.

For less spur-of-the-moment-style fishing, there are many **outfitters** and guides who would be more than willing to take you into some of the more remote lakes in the **Spatsizi Plateau Provincial Wilderness Park** and **Tatlatui Provincial Park.** A good source of fishing and outdoor information in this region is Arctic Sun Wilderness Adventure Tours, (250) 234-3456, in Eddontenajon. (See Hiking/Backpacking, above, for more information on guides and outfitters.)

It was once said that every cast in the **Firesteel River** in Tatlatui Provincial Park would yield a catch. Unfortunately, that could only go on for so long, and recently the fishing hasn't been as good, which is to say you'll only catch a fish on every second cast. Fortunately, people are becoming more conservation minded, protecting this area for anglers in years to come. For more information, contact the Fish and Wildlife Conservation Officer, (250) 771-3566 in Dease Lake.

Broad **Dease Lake** and curvaceous **Boya Lake** offer angling for char and a variety of northern specialties: burbot and whitefish; while **Dease River,** which flows north from Dease Lake, through Boya Lake Provincial Park and north to the **Liard River,** has good grayling fishing. Access is from the town of Dease Lake, from pullouts beside Hwy 37, and from Boya Lake Park's boat ramp.

Atlin Provincial Park surrounds the southern third of **Atlin Lake,** the largest natural lake in the province (even though part of it is in Yukon). Atlin Lake contains lake trout, grayling, and dolly varden. There are dozens of smaller lakes in the Atlin region.

Contact BC Parks in Dease Lake, (250) 771-4591, for information on **guides and outfitters.** A good place to begin is Norseman Adventures, (250) 651-7535 or (604) 823-2259, which rents boats and sells fishing licences in Atlin.

Kayaking/Canoeing/Rafting

Swan Lake–Kispiox River Provincial Park contains a chain of undeveloped lakes, rivers, and swamps that provides an outstanding opportunity for water-related adventure. The park is located about 8 miles (14 km) east off Hwy 37. Entry is from Mile 74 (Km 120). There is a small boat launch at the north end of **Brown Bear Lake.** From there, canoeists must paddle and portage to Swan Lake and beyond. For more information, contact BC Parks, (250) 847-7320, or the outfitter Northern Sun Tours, (250) 847-4349, both in Smithers.

There is a series of five lakes in the **Bonney Lakes Canoe Route,** which starts 21 miles (34 km) off Hwy 37 on Brown Bear Forest Service Rd at Meziadin Junction. The route starts and ends in Bonney Lake, with portages of 100 feet (30 m) to 2,300 feet (700 m) along cleared but undeveloped portage routes. Expect to take two to four days to complete the route. For more information, consult the Kalum Forest District Office, (250) 638-5100, in Terrace.

For those wishing simply to paddle around a lake for a few hours while in this neck of the woods, **Meziadin Lake** in Meziadin Lake Provincial Park (see Parks/Camping, above) is good to float about on.

Don't even think about canoeing or kayaking the **Stikine River** into the Grand Canyon of the Stikine, a 61-mile (100-km) stretch of impassable waters that charge through canyons 1,000 feet (300 m) deep. It has only once been bested. Be content with the waters that are runable: for instance, the 160-mile (260-km) stretch between Tuaton Lake in the **Spatsizi Plateau Provincial Wilderness Park** (see Hiking/Backpacking, above) and the Hwy 37 bridge over the Stikine. If you wish, you can pick up the trip on the other side of the Grand Canyon of the Stikine, continuing downriver from **Telegraph Creek** all the way to Wrangell, Alaska, for a fortnight's travel of 280 miles (459 km). This is a trip for experienced backcountry paddlers only. Tuaton Lake can be reached by floatplane.

A second canoe route starts in the Spatsizi Plateau Provincial Wilderness Park, and is accessible via a 3-mile (5-km) portage from the BC Rail grade to the **Spatsizi River.** There are no major rapids on the Spatsizi River, but once the Spatsizi flows into the Stikine, expect some rough water and rapids, especially at higher water levels. Plan on 7 to 10 days for canoeing either the Stikine (Tuaton to Hwy 37 bridge) or the Spatsizi/Stikine routes. Less-experienced paddlers can still experience the wonder of the Stikine. Dozens of river-rafting companies offer treks through this wilderness paradise. Contact BC Parks, (250) 771-4591, for information on **guides and outfitters.**

The **Dease River** from Dease Lake to Liard River used to be one of the most important water highways in the province, and saw its last great use during the construction of the Alaska Hwy. Nowadays, the river is experiencing a bit of a renaissance, as paddlers discover this 162-mile (265-km) waterway. It's mostly Class I and II, with some Class III rapids. Expect to take about seven days to complete the one-way paddle.

Though the usual route for rafting expeditions on the **Tatshenshini**

River starts in the Yukon and ends in Alaska, much of the river's path is through British Columbia's Coast Mountains. The full 161-mile (260-km) river-rafting trek will take 14 days, though it is possible to do smaller 6- and 8-day trips on the Upper Alsek River. Altogether, there are three routes on the Y-shaped river system that lend themselves to exploration in this World Heritage site. The Tatshenshini and its heftier counterpart, the Alsek, run south through the St. Elias Mountains, home to some of the tallest peaks in Canada, many of which reach elevations of 15,000 feet (4575 m). The two rivers merge just inside the western boundary of Tatshenshini-Alsek Provincial Wilderness Park, then flow as the Alsek through Alaska to meet the Pacific at Dry Bay. Contact BC Parks, (250) 771-4591, for information on **guides and outfitters.** Canadian River Expeditions, (800) 898-7238 or (604) 938-6651, in Whistler, is acknowledged as the most experienced rafting company operating in the Tatshenshini-Alsek watershed, which is often referred to as the "Holy Grail" of rafting. For information on access from Yukon, contact Cloudberry Adventures, (403) 668-7711, in Whitehorse, Yukon.

There are paddling adventures to be had on **Atlin Lake** in Atlin Provincial Park and Recreation Area. The massive lake is reached from the town of Atlin on Hwy 7, and is subject to sudden, strong gusts of wind, so be careful not to paddle more than 110 feet (30 m) offshore. Although there are no developed facilities, there are many sheltered locations to beach a canoe and pitch a tent. For a detailed map of the lake, contact BC Parks in Smithers, (250) 847-7320. For information on guided canoe and kayak trips in Atlin Provincial Park, contact Sitka Tours, (250) 651-7691, in Atlin, or Cloudberry Adventures, (403) 668-7711, in Whitehorse, Yukon.

Wildlife

There's a fish ladder at the south end of **Meziadin Lake** in Meziadin Lake Provincial Park (see Parks/Camping, above), where the Nass River flows out. **Chinook** spawn here in late summer, and it's truly an impressive sight. Fish of up to 30 lbs (13.5 kg) leap into the air as they navigate the ladder. Across Hwy 37 from Meziadin Lake is the Hanna Creek Salmon Viewing Area. Best viewing time is late summer–early fall.

The four contingent parks around the Stikine River—Tatlatui, Spatsizi Plateau, Stikine River Recreational Area, and Mount Edziza—are home to hundreds of animal species. Lands within Spatsizi Plateau Provincial Wilderness Park and Tatlatui Provincial Park support a large population of wildlife. The Spatsizi Plateau is one of the most important habitats for **woodland caribou** in British Columbia, while both parks support a variety of wildlife, including **moose, grizzly and black bears, wolves, beavers, hoary marmots,** and more than 140 species of **birds,** including **gyrfalcons.**

At last count, the Grand Canyon of the Stikine, located in the Stikine River Recreational Area, is home to more than 360 **mountain goats,** which use the sheer canyon walls as effective protection from all natural predators. Their greatest threat is BC Hydro, which is planning a massive hydroelectric project that would flood out this natural wonder, displacing the mountain goats. **Mount Edziza Provincial Park** also supports a large population of mountain goats, as well as **Stone sheep, moose, Osbourn caribou, grizzly and black bears,** and **wolves.**

Nearly 250 miles (400 km) to the northwest is the **Tatshenshini-Alsek Provincial Wilderness Park.** The Tat supports more than 53 species of mammals, including **wolverines, blue (or glacier) bear** (thought to be a variation of the black bear and found nowhere else Canada), and **grizzlies.** About 200 of the known 400 **Dall's sheep** in the province have their range year-round in this area. The park provides an important travel route for **waterfowl,** with at least 40 bird species known to use the region. These include **trumpeter swans, peregrine falcons, great grey owls,** and **bald eagles.**

Mountain Biking

There are very few mountain-bike trails in the northwest, and many multi-use trails are too overgrown to make mountain biking any fun. A pleasant surprise for the avid fat-tracker is that, unlike most provincial parks in this region, and indeed, in the province, the **Tatshenshini-Alsek Provincial Wilderness Park** is open to mountain bikers. There are two main trails for mountain bikers to follow: the Parton River Trail and the Chuck Creek Trail. The **Parton River Trail** begins just south of Stanley Creek. A road heads west from Hwy 7 to the trailhead on the Tatshenshini River. If the river is running high, good luck getting across without a raft (probably not a bad idea to have one anyway). There are no bridges here, and this is only the first of two numbing river crossings. Best bring a pair of waders; the water here is cold! The second river crossing quickly follows the first, this time across the Parton River. The trail runs about 18 miles (30 km) to an old airstrip, with a 1-mile (2.5-km) side trail to the Shinney Lakes. The **Shinney Lakes Trail** to the lakes heads right from the main trail near the 9-mile (15-km) point.

The **Chuck Creek Trail** begins just past Chuck Creek, beside a big **Tatshenshini-Alsek** park sign. An old road leads into the park to an old gypsum mine, but the best views of the **Samuel Glacier** come shortly after fording **Clear Creek,** at the 4-mile (7-km) point.

For more information on these trails, contact BC Parks, (250) 847-7320 in Smithers.

Scenic Drives

One of the most unique scenic drives in the province leads around a well-marked circuit in the Hazelton Valley called the **Trail of the Totems Tour.** First, stop to view the ceremonial poles in the village of **Kitwanga,** one of several locations in the Hazelton region where such poles are situated. The dozen poles here face the Skeena River beside a century-old wooden bell tower and church. The weathered poles are carved with an array of animal and humanlike images. Then head north for about 12 miles (20 km) along the Cassiar Hwy (Hwy 37) to the small village of **Kitwancool** to see what are reputed to be the oldest and finest examples of poles. Here are more than 20 poles, some old, but also a trio of new ones. All are intricately carved and very thought-provoking. Some of the tallest poles have been left uncarved on their top halves and are surmounted by images of raven, bear, eagle, wolf, or humans. Nearby, a shed houses some of the oldest poles, which have been laid to rest, beautifully weathered, almost beyond recognition, with just an eye or a beak left to suggest the original design. The three new poles mounted together directly in front of the Gitanyow Band Council office are among the most intricately designed ones of the whole group and demonstrate that the carving tradition here is stronger than ever. (Note: The Gitanyow have placed a ban on taking photographs or video recordings of their poles. Please respect their wishes.)

Back on Hwy 17, stop again, this time at **Kitseguecla,** a small Skeena River settlement near **Hazelton,** to see their two poles, which are as wonderfully unique as any in the region. Large sculptures grace the front yards of several homes in the community. Drive slowly and smile—you're part of their view.

End the Totem Tour with a quick detour through Hazelton and Kispiox. Pull into the **'Ksan Historical Village and Museum** in Hazelton. The village was originally called the Skeena Treasure House, and with good reason, judging from its rich display of totems, jewelry, and clothing. A museum in one of the long houses honours the Gitksan ancestors, who were graced with such abundance that they had time to beautify the items they carved for everyday use. Seven lovingly decorated long houses are grouped together here at the confluence of the Skeena and Bulkley Rivers. Several of the long houses are open to visitors at no charge, while guided tours are offered of the Fireweed, Wolf, and Frog clan houses for a small fee.

The **Kispiox** ceremonial poles are the most animated of all, with carved tears dripping off the faces of some figures whose eyes are inlaid with abalone. On one, a human character holds a grease bowl in its arms, a reminder that not only is this a modern-day trail, but also that it was once part of a coastal "grease trail" along which highly valued fish grease obtained from eulachon (a sardine-sized fish whose body contains such a high percentage of oil that it burns like a torch when dried) was transported from the coast to the Interior. The views of the Skeena River from here are staggering. Kispiox is built on high ground, about 18 miles (30 km) north of Hazelton on a paved side road, and its 18 poles have the appearance of being held in the palm of the Creator.

For more information on the Hazeltons, including the self-guided Tour of the Totems and Hands of History tours, contact the Hazelton InfoCentre on Hwy 16, (250) 842-6071 (June-September) or (250) 842-6571 in the off-season. To learn more about 'Ksan Historical Village and Museum, call (250) 842-5544.

More Information

Atlin Visitors Association: *(250) 651-7522 or (250) 651-7470.*
BC Forest Service: Prince Rupert Regional Office, *(250) 847-7500.*
BC Parks, Dease Lake: *(250) 771-4591.*
BC Parks, Smithers, *(250) 847-7320.*
Dease Lake InfoCentre: *(250) 771-3900 (seasonal).*
Hazelton InfoCentre: *(250) 842-6071 (June-September) or (250) 842-6571 (off-season).*
Iskut Band Administration Office Information: *(250) 234-3331.*
Stewart Chamber of Commerce InfoCentre: *(250) 636-9224.*

Index

Abbotsford, information, 105
Acadia Beach, 13
Ahous Beach, 302
Ainsworth Hot Springs, 513
Akamina-Kishinena Provincial Recreation Area, hiking, 524–25
Alaska Highway
- camping, 620–23
- scenic drives, 628, 635
- *See also* Cariboo Highway; Highway 97 (John Hart Highway)

Alastair Lake, wildlife, 564
Albert Head Lagoon Park, 252
Aldergrove Lake Regional Park
- cycling/skating, 81–82
- mountain biking, 86–87

Alert Bay, attractions, 352
Alexander Mackenzie Heritage Trail
- guides/outfitters, 548
- hiking, 550–51, 577–78
- horseback riding, 558

Alexandra Bridge Provincial Park, picnics, 426–27
Alice Lake/Alice Lake Provincial Park
- boating/canoeing/kayaking, 174
- camping, 145–46
- fishing, 180
- hiking, 154–55
- mountain biking, 168
- swimming, 179

Alouette Lake
- beaches, 68
- boating/canoeing/kayaking, 76
- camping, 63
- hiking, 92
- picnics, 71
- *See also* Golden Ears Provincial Park

Alouette River, fishing, 87–88
Ambleside Park, 131
- hiking, 117
- picnics, 137–38

Anderson Lake, boating/canoeing/kayaking, 201
Andy Bailey Provincial Recreation Area
- camping, 621
- skiing, cross-country, 630

Apex Mountain Resort
- mountain biking, 471
- skiing/snowboarding, 467

Arlington Lakes Provincial Recreation Area, camping, 480
Arrow Lakes/Arrow Lakes Provincial Park
- beaches/picnics, 506–7
- fishing, 494
- *See also* Upper Arrow Lake

Ashcroft, lodgings, 433
Ashlu Creek, camping, 146
Atlin, information, 638
Atlin Lake,
- canoeing/kayaking/rafting, 648

Atlin Provincial Park and Recreation Area
- camping, 641, 642
- fishing, 646
- hiking, 644

Atnarko River, fishing, 554–55
Atnarko Valley, 547

Babine Lake
- camping/parks, 574
- canoeing/kayaking, 586
- fishing, 575

Babine Mountains Provincial Recreation Area, 583–84
- hiking, 579, 580
- skiing, 567, 583

Backpacking. *See* Hiking
Baden-Powell Trail, 110–13, 116
Balfour, ferry, 512
Bamberton Provincial Park
- beaches/picnics, 279
- camping, 282–83

Bamfield
- attractions, 310
- hiking, 263–64
- information, 313
- lodgings, 312–13

Barkerville
- attractions, 600
- restaurants, 600–1

Barkerville Provincial Park, camping, 593–94
Barkley Sound, boating/kayaking, 306–7
Barnet Marine Park
- beaches, 14–15
- boating/canoeing/kayaking, 23

Barnston Island, cycling, 49–50
Barrière Lakes, fishing, 608
Beaches
- Burnaby, 14–15
- clothing optional, 13–14
- Comox, 316–17
- Fraser Estuary, 42–46
- Fraser Valley, 68–70
- Gulf Islands, northern, 381–82
- Gulf Islands, southern, 358–60
- Island Highway (Highway 19), 316
- Malaspina Peninsula, 213–14
- North Shore, 130–32
- Okanagan Valley, 462–63
- Pacific Rim Highway (Highway 4), 300
- Pemberton/Pemberton Valley, 205–6
- Queen Charlotte Islands, 410–11
- Sechelt, 212
- Slocan Valley, 506–7
- Sooke Basin, 267–69
- Sunshine Coast, 212–14
- Tofino, 301–2
- Ucluelet, 300
- Vancouver, 12–15
- Victoria, 240–43
- West Kootenays (Crowsnest Highway), 493
- West Vancouver, 130–31
- *See also* Parks; Swimming; *individual entries for parks and bodies of water*

Beaconsfield Mountain, skiing/snowboarding, 467
Bear Creek Provincial Park
- camping, 460–61
- hiking, 465–66

Bear Hill Regional Park, hiking, 252
Bear Mountain, mountain biking, 85–86
Bears, xi–xii
Beatton Provincial Park
- camping, 620–21
- cross-country skiing/snowshoeing, 630

Beaumont Provincial Marine Park
- boating/kayaking, 361
- camping, 356, 574

Beaver Creek Provincial Park, camping, 488
Belcarra Regional Park
- beaches, 15
- canoeing/kayaking, 23
- diving, 26
- fishing, 24–25
- hiking/walking, 16–17

Bella Bella
- air service, 390
- attractions, 400–1

Bella Coola
- air/boat service, 390, 547
- attractions, 558–59
- directions, 547–48
- information, 402
- petroglyphs, 559

Bella Coola River, fishing, 554–55
Bella Coola Road (Highway 20), 545–59
- adjoining areas, 548
- attractions, 558–59
- camping, 552–54
- canoeing, 557
- fishing, 554–55
- guides/outfitters, 548
- hiking, 549–52
- horseback riding, 558
- information, 559
- kayaking/rafting, 556–57
- scenic drives/picnics, 554
- skiing, cross-country, 558
- wildlife, 557–58
- *See also* Bella Coola; Bella Coola Valley; Chilcotin Plateau

Bella Coola Valley, 545–47
Bellhouse Provincial Park, 358
Big Bar Lake/Big Bar Lake Provincial Park
- boating/fishing, 595
- camping, 592

Big White Ski Resort, skiing/snowboarding, 481–82
Biking. *See* Cycling; Mountain biking

Bird-watching. *See* Wildlife
Birkenhead Lake/Birkenhead Lake Provincial Park
boating/canoeing/kayaking, 201
camping, 191–92
fishing, 203
hiking, 196
Birkenhead River
canoeing/kayaking, 202
fishing, 203
Blackcomb
information, 188
paragliding, 166
skiing/snowboarding, 161–63
See also Whistler
Blanket Creek Provincial Park
camping, 419
fishing, 429
Bligh Island Provincial Marine Park, boating/kayaking, 333
Blowdown Lake, camping, 193–94
Blowdown Pass, hiking, 196
Blue Mountain, mountain biking, 85
Blue River, skiing, cross-country, 610
Boat tours
MV *Frances Barkley*, 307
MV *Lady Rose*, 307
MV *Uchuck III*, 333–36
See also Ferries
Boating
Bulkley/Skeena River Valleys, 570
Cariboo Highway (Highway 97), 594–95
Central/Discovery Coast, 398
Cheakamus Lake, 175
Chehalis Lake, 77–78
Clayoquot Sound, 307–8
Coquihalla Highway (Highway 5), 455
Cowichan Valley, 278
Fraser Valley, 73–79
Gulf Islands, northern, 375–80
Gulf Islands, southern, 361–62
Horseshoe Bay, 134
Howe Sound, 173
Malaspina Peninsula, 216–18
Nanaimo, 277–78
Nootka Sound, 333
North Shore, 132–34
Pacific Rim National Park Reserve, 306–7
Pemberton/Pemberton Valley, 201–3
Sasquatch Provincial Park, 78
Sechelt Peninsula, 214–15
Slocan Valley, 509–10
Squamish River, 173–74
Strathcona Provincial Park, 332–33
Sunshine Coast, 214–18
Trans-Canada Highway (Highway 1), 427–28
Vancouver, 22–24
Vancouver Island, North, 344–45
Victoria, 243–44
Whistler, 175–77
See also Canoeing; Kayaking; Sailing
Bodega Ridge Nature Preserve, wildlife, 365
Boise Valley, mountain biking, 84
Bonaparte Lake, boating/fishing, 595
Bonney Lakes, canoeing/kayaking, 647
Border crossings, 4–5
Boswell, lodgings, 500
Botanical Beach Provincial Park
hiking, 265–66
wildlife, 270–71
Boundary Bay Regional Park
beaches, 42–43
wildlife, 53–54
windsurfing, 55
Boundary Creek Provincial Park, camping, 443
Bowen Island
mountain biking, 127–28
parks, 129–30
Bowron Lake Provincial Park
camping, 594
canoeing/kayaking, 596
Boya Lake/Boya Lake Provincial Park
camping, 642
fishing, 646
Boyle Point Regional Park, hiking, 383
Brackendale, lodgings, 187
Brackendale Eagle Reserve, 181
Bradner, attractions, 103–4
Bralorne, directions, 190
Brandywine Falls Provincial Park
camping, 146
hiking, 156
skiing, cross-country, 163–64
swimming, 179
Bridge Lake Provincial Park, camping, 593
Bridge River, canoeing/kayaking, 202–3
British Columbia Forest Service districts, information
Arrow, 501, 516
Boundary, 449, 477, 482, 501, 516
Bulkley–Cassiar, 571
Campbell River, 341, 353, 386
Cariboo, 559, 601
Central Coast, 402
Central Interior, 612
Chilcotin, 559, 601
Clearwater, 612
Cranbrook, 527, 542
Dawson Creek, 638
Fort Nelson, 638
Fort St. James, 587
Fort St. John, 638
Fraser Valley, 105
Golden Forest, 542
Horsefly, 601
Invermere, 527, 542
Kamloops, 457, 612
Kootenay Lake, 501, 516
Lakes, 587
Mackenzie, 638
Merritt, 449, 457
Mid Coast, 559
Morice, 587
Nelson, 501, 516
North Coast, 571
North Okanagan, 477, 482
North Shore, 141
100 Mile House, 601
Prince George, 587, 638
Prince Rupert, 571, 587, 651
Princeton, 449
Quesnel, 601
Revelstoke, 542
Robson Valley, 612
South Okanagan, 477, 482
Squamish Forest, 187, 207
Sunshine Coast, 234
Vancouver Island (south), 261, 275, 294, 313
Vanderhoof, 587
Williams Lake, 559, 601
See also Provincial forests
British Columbia Parks districts, information
Bella Coola, 559
Cariboo, 601
Central Coast, 402
Dease Lake, 651
Fort St. John, 638
Fraser Valley, 105
Garibaldi-Sunshine Coast, 187, 207, 234
Gulf Islands, 373, 386
Kettle Valley, 482
Kootenay, 501
Lower Mainland, 457
Manning, 449
Muncho Lake, 638
Nelson, 516
North Shore, 141
Okanagan, 449, 477, 501
Port Hardy, 402
Prince George, 587, 638
Prince Rupert, 402
Smithers, 571, 587, 651
South Coast, 440
Strathcona, 313
Thompson River, 207, 457
Vancouver Island, 261, 275, 294, 330, 341, 353
Wasa Lake, 527, 542
West Kootenays, 449, 501
Williams Lake, 559
See also Provincial parks; *individual parks*
Brohm Lake
boating/canoeing/kayaking, 174
camping, 146
swimming, 179
Brohm Lake Interpretive Forest
hiking, 155–56
mountain biking, 168
Broken Group Islands, boating/kayaking, 306–7
Bromley Rock Provincial Park
camping, 442
canoeing/swimming, 446
Brooks Peninsula, 342
Brooks Peninsula Provincial Park, kayaking, 343–44
Browning Lake, fishing, 180
Buccaneer Bay Marine Park, boating/canoeing/kayaking, 215–16

Buckinghorse River Provincial Park, 621
Bugaboo Glacier Provincial Park and Alpine Recreation Area, hiking, 534
Bulkley River, fishing, 565, 576
Bulkley/Skeena River Valleys, 560–71
adjoining areas, 561
attractions, 570
boating/canoeing/kayaking, 570
camping/parks, 561–63
directions, 561
fishing, 564–66
hiking, 567–69
information, 570
skiing/snowboarding, 566–67
wildlife, 563–64
windsurfing, 570
Bull Canyon Provincial Park, camping, 553
Bungee jumping, Nanaimo, 289
Buntzen Lake Recreation Area, 15, 21, 24
Burke Mountain, mountain biking, 83
Burnaby
beaches, 14–15
hiking, 16
information, 38
mountain biking, 21
parks, 11
photography, 25–26
Burnaby Lake Regional Park, 11–12
Burnaby Mountain/Burnaby Mountain Park
mountain biking, 21,
photography, 25–26
Burns Lake, information, 587
Burrard Inlet, 22
Buttle Lake
boating/kayaking, 332–33
camping, 332

Cabbage Island, boating/kayaking, 361
Cal-Cheak Forest Service Recreation Site, camping, 146
California Bighorn Sheep Reserve, wildlife, 558
Callaghan Lake, boating/canoeing/kayaking, 174–75
Campbell Bay Provincial Park, camping, 520
Campbell River
attractions, 339
beaches, 317
directions, 315
diving/snorkeling, 328
fishing, 323–24
heli-surfing, 326
information, 330
kayaking/canoeing, 51
lodgings, 340–41
mountain biking, 319
restaurants, 339–40
snorkeling, 340–41
Campbell Valley Regional Park
hiking, 97–98
horseback riding, 101
picnics, 72
Camping
Bella Coola Road (Highway 20), 552–54
Bulkley/Skeena River Valleys, 561–63
Cal-Cheak Forest Service Recreation Site, 146
Cariboo Highway (Highway 97), 592–94
Cat Lake, 146
Central/Discovery Coast, 397
Columbia River Valley, 530–33
Comox Valley, 315–16
Coquihalla Highway (Highway 5), 451–53
Cowichan Valley, 282–84
East Kootenays (Crowsnest Highway), 523
Fraser Estuary, 57
Fraser Plateau, 573–75
Fraser Valley, 63–68
Garibaldi Provincial Park, 146–49
Golden Ears Provincial Park, 63–64
Gulf Islands, northern, 380–81
Gulf Islands, southern, 355–57
information, x
Inside Passage, 397
Kettle Valley, 479–80
Kootenay Lake, 519–20
Lillooet, 193–94
Lillooet Lake, 192
Manning Provincial Park, 438, 439
North Kootenay Lake/Selkirk Valleys, 519–20
Northeast British Columbia, 616–23
Okanagan Valley, 442–43, 459–62
Pacific Rim Highway (Highway 4), 297–98
Pacific Rim National Park Reserve, 297
Pemberton/Pemberton Valley, 191–94
Point Roberts (WA), 57
Port Alberni, 298
Powell River, 211
Queen Charlotte Islands, 404–6
reservations, ix
Sasquatch Provincial Park, 64–65
Skagit Valley, 66–68
Slocan Valley, 503–4
Sooke Basin, 271–72
Squamish/Squamish Valley, 145–46
Stewart-Cassiar Highway (Highway 37), 641–42
Strathcona Provincial Park, 332
Sunshine Coast, 210–11
Trans-Canada Highway (Highway 1), 417–22
Upper Arrow Lake, 503
Vancouver Island, North, 348–50
Victoria, 239–40
West Kootenays (Crowsnest Highway), 486–87
Whistler, 146–47
Yellowhead Highway (Highway 5), 603–6
See also Hiking; Parks; *individual entries for parks, regions, and geographic features*
Canal Flats Provincial Park
swimming, 535
windsurfing, 539
Canim Beach Provincial Park, camping, 593
Canim Lake
boating/fishing, 595
skiing, cross-country, 598
Canoeing
Bella Coola Road (Highway 20), 557
Bulkley/Skeena River Valleys, 570
Cariboo Highway (Highway 97), 596
East Kootenays (Crowsnest Highway), 527
Fraser Estuary, 50–51
Fraser Plateau, 584–87
Fraser River, 50–51, 77
Fraser Valley, 73–79
Gulf Islands, northern, 375–80
Howe Sound, 173
Malaspina Peninsula, 216–18
Manning Provincial Park, 439
North Shore, 132–34
Northeast British Columbia, 632–34
Okanagan Valley, southern, 446
Pemberton/Pemberton Valley, 201–3
Sechelt Peninsula, 214–15
Slocan Valley, 509–10
Squamish River, 173–74
Stewart-Cassiar Highway (Highway 37), 646–48
Sunshine Coast, 214–18
Trans-Canada Highway (Highway 1), 427–28
Tweedsmuir Provincial Park, 557
Vancouver, 22–24
Vancouver Island, North, 344–45
West Kootenays (Crowsnest Highway), 495
Whistler, 175–77
Yellowhead Highway (Highway 5), 610
See also Boating; Kayaking; Rafting; *entries for individual parks, towns, regions, and bodies of water*
Cape Scott Provincial Park, camping, 349–50
Capilano Regional Park, hiking, 111
Capilano River
boating/canoeing/kayaking, 133–34
fish hatchery, 134–35
hiking, 117–18
Capilano River Regional Park

hiking, 117–18
picnics, 138
Caren Provincial Park, bird-watching/wildlife, 229
Cariboo, information, 559, 601
Cariboo Highway (Highway 97), 591–601
adjoining areas, 592
attractions, 600
boating, 594–95
camping/parks, 592–94
canoeing/kayaking, 596
directions, 591–92
fishing, 594–95
horseback riding, 600
information, 601
lodgings, 601
mountain biking, 598–99
scenic drives, 599–600
skiing, cross-country, 596–98
wildlife, 599
See also Alaska Highway; Highway 97 (John Hart Highway)
Carmanah-Walbran Provincial Park, hiking, 284–86
Carp Lake Provincial Park
camping, 617
canoeing/kayaking, 633
Cascade Provincial Recreation Area, hiking, 444
Castlegar
information, 501
mountain biking, 491–93
Cat Lake, camping, 146
Cathedral Lakes, lodgings, 448
Cathedral Provincial Park
camping, 442–43
hiking, 445
Caulfeild Park, 131
Caves
Cody Caves Provincial Park, 510
Horne Lake Caves Provincial Park, 317–18
information, 330
Little Hustan Cave Regional Park, 350–51
Upana Caves, 339
Central/Discovery Coast, 389–402
attractions, 400–1
boat service, 389–390, 392–93
boating, 398
camping, 397
diving, 399
fishing, 397–98
hiking, 399–400
information, 402
kayaking, 393–96
whale watching, 391, 393
wildlife, 398–99
See also Inside Passage
Champion Lakes/Champion Lakes Provincial Park
camping, 486–87
cross-country skiing/snowshoeing, 498
fishing, 494
Charlie Lake/Charlie Lake Provincial Park
camping, 621
fishing, 631
Charlotte Lake, fishing, 555
Cheakamus Lake, boating/canoeing/kayaking, 175
Cheakamus River
canoeing/kayaking/rafting, 176–77
fishing, 180
Checleset Bay Ecological Reserve, wildlife, 347–48
Chehalis Lake, boating/canoeing/kayaking, 77–78
Chehalis River, rafting/kayaking, 78
Chemainus
attractions, 291
information, 294
lodgings, 293–94
restaurants, 291–92
Chetwynd,
camping, 619
information, 638
Chilanko Forks Wildlife Management Area, wildlife, 557
Chilcotin Plateau, 547
attractions, 559
fishing, 556
Chilcotin River, kayaking/rafting, 556–57
Chilko Lake, fishing, 555–56
Chilko River, kayaking/rafting, 556–57
Chilliwack
information, 105
restaurants, 59
Chilliwack Lake
beaches, 70
fishing, 90
hiking, 94–95
windsurfing, 102
Chilliwack Lake Provincial Park
camping, 66
hiking, 94–95
Chilliwack River
fishing, 89–90
hiking, 95–96
rafting/kayaking, 78, 79
skiing, cross-country, 102
China Beach, 268–69
China Creek Provincial Park, windsurfing, 308
Christie Memorial Provincial Park, beaches/swimming, 462
Christina Lake/Christina Lake Provincial Park
beaches, 493
camping/parks, 487
canoeing/kayaking, 495
fishing, 494
mountain biking, 492
Clayoquot Sound
boating/kayaking, 307–8
hiking, 304–5
Clayoquot Valley, hiking, 305–6
Clearwater, information, 612
Climbing, Owen Hat, 587
Clinton, information, 601
Cloverdale, attractions, 58
Coast Trail, hiking, 248–49
Cody Caves Provincial Park, caves, 510
Coldwater River Provincial Park
fishing, 453
walking, 454
Coles Bay Regional Park, beaches/picnics, 241–42
Columbia Lake
swimming, 535
windsurfing, 539
Columbia River
canoeing/kayaking, 495, 527
fishing, 494
Columbia River Valley, 529–42
adjoining areas, 530
attractions, 540–41
biking, 537
camping/parks, 530–33
directions, 529
fishing, 536
hiking, 533–35
information, 542
lodgings, 541–42
restaurants, 541
scenic drives, 537
skiing/snowboarding, 537–39
swimming, 535
wildlife, 535–36
windsurfing, 539
Columbia Valley, cycling, 82–83
Columbia Wildlife Area, wildlife, 536
Comox
beaches, 316–17
windsurfing, 326
Comox Lake, fishing, 323
Comox Valley, 314–30
adjoining areas, 315
camping/parks, 315–16
canoeing/kayaking, 325–26
caves, 317
fishing, 322–25
information, 330
mountain biking, 318–20
wildlife, 326–28
Conkle Lake Provincial Park
camping, 443
fishing, 446
swimming, 446
Coopers Green Regional Park, beaches/picnics, 212–13
Copeland Islands Provincial Marine Park, boating/canoeing/kayaking, 378–79
Coquihalla Canyon Provincial Recreation Area, hiking, 445
Coquihalla Highway (Highway 5), 450–57
adjoining areas, 451
boating, 455
camping, 451–53
cycling/mountain biking, 455
directions, 451
fishing, 453–54
horseback riding, 456
information, 457
lodgings, 456–57
picnics/walking, 454
skiing, cross-country, 456
Coquihalla River, fishing, 453
Coquihalla River Provincial Recreation Area,

picnics/walking, 454
Coquitlam, information, 105
Cortes Island
beaches/picnics, 381
camping/parks, 380
restaurants, 385–86
Cottonwood River Provincial Park, camping, 594
Courtenay
directions, 215
lodgings, 329
restaurants, 328–29
Cowichan Bay, attractions, 290
Cowichan Lake
beaches/picnics, 280
boating/kayaking, 278
camping, 283
fishing, 281
information, 294
Cowichan River, fishing, 280–81
Cowichan River Provincial Park, hiking, 286
Cowichan Valley, 276–94
attractions, 290
beaches/picnics, 277–80
boating/kayaking, 278
camping, 282–84
directions, 277
fishing, 280–82
golfing, 289
hiking, 284–86
information, 294
mountain biking, 287–88
scenic drives, 289
wildlife, 286–87
windsurfing, 288–89
Cranbrook, information, 527, 542
Crawford Bay
attractions, 499
ferry service, 512
lodgings, 500
Crescent Beach, 56
Crescent Beach Park, 43–44, 51
Creston Valley Wildlife Management Area, wildlife, 496
Creston
information, 501, 527
restaurants, 500
Crippen Regional Park, 129–30
picnics, 138
Crofton
beaches/picnics, 279
information, 294
Crooked River
camping, 616–17
canoeing/kayaking, 632–33
Crooked River Provincial Park
camping, 617
hiking, 623
skiing, cross-country, 630
Crowsnest Highway (Highway 3). *See* East Kootenays (Crowsnest Highway); Okanagan Valley, southern (Crowsnest Highway); West Kootenays (Crowsnest Highway)
Crowsnest Provincial Park, picnics, 525
Cultus Lake
beaches, 69–70
boating/canoeing/kayaking, 79
waterskiing, 79
See also Cultus Lake Provincial Park
Cultus Lake Provincial Park
beaches, 70
camping, 65–66
hiking, 93–94
See also Cultus Lake
Cycling
Columbia River Valley, 537
Columbia Valley, 82–83
Coquihalla Highway (Highway 5), 455
Fraser Estuary, 46–50
Fraser Valley, 79–83
Gulf Islands, southern, 362–63
Malaspina Peninsula, 218–19
North Shore, 124–25
Pemberton/Pemberton Valley, 198–99
Sea to Sky Highway (Highway 99), 172
Sechelt Peninsula, 218
Squamish/Squamish Valley, 171–72
Sunshine Coast, 218–19
Surrey, 49–50
Vancouver, 17–19
Victoria, 245–47
See also individual entries for towns and parks
Cypress Falls Park, hiking, 115–16
Cypress Provincial Park
hiking, 111, 112–15
mountain biking, 126–27
picnics, 138
skiing/snowboarding, 135–36

D'Arcy
cycling, 199
festivals and events, 190
picnics, 204–5
Darke Lake Provincial Park, fishing, 463
Davis Bay, beaches/picnics, 212
Dawley Passage Provincial Park, diving, 309
Dawson Creek
attractions, 637
hiking, 626
information, 638
mountain biking, 629
skiing, cross-country, 630
Dean River, fishing, 555
Deas Island Regional Park
camping, 57
canoeing/kayaking, 50
fishing, 57
hiking/walking, 56
picnics, 55
Dease Lake
camping, 641
fishing, 646
information, 651
Dease River, canoeing/kayaking/rafting, 647
Deep Bay, fishing, 322–23
Deer Lake, 65
Delta
cycling, 47–48
directions, 41
hiking, 57
information, 60
Denman Island
attractions, 385
boating/canoeing/kayaking, 377–78
camping/parks, 380
ferry service, 375
hiking, 383
information, 386
Derby Reach, 69
Derby Reach Regional Park
camping, 65
fishing, 89
Desolation Sound, attractions, 231–32
Desolation Sound Marine Park, boating/canoeing/kayaking, 217
Devonian Regional Park, bird-watching/wildlife, 253
Dewdney Trail, hiking/biking, 489, 492, hiking/biking, 507
Diana Lake Provincial Park
boating/canoeing/kayaking, 570
camping, 562
windsurfing, 570
Dina Lakes, canoeing/kayaking, 633
Dionisio Point Provincial Park
boating/kayaking, 361
camping, 356
Discovery Coast. *See* Central/Discovery Coast
Discovery Park, 9
Discovery Passage, fishing, 324–25, fishing, 345
Diving
Campbell River, 328
Central/Discovery Coast, 399
Dawley Passage Provincial Park, 309
information, 26
Kelowna, 472
Malaspina Peninsula, 228
North Shore, 137
North Vancouver Island, 351
Okanagan Valley, 472
Porteau Cove Provincial Park, 180
Sechelt Peninsula, 227–28
Sunshine Coast, 227–28
Tofino, 309
Vancouver, 26
Victoria, 254
Whytecliff Marine Park, 137
Douglas Channel
fishing, 566
hiking, 567–68
Driftwood Canyon Provincial Park, picnics, 581
Dry Gulch Provincial Park, camping, 533
Duncan
attractions, 290–91
information, 294
lodgings, 294
restaurants, 291

Eagle River system, fishing, 429
East Kootenays (Crowsnest Highway), 522–28

adjoining areas, 522
attractions, 527
camping/parks, 523
canoeing/kayaking, 527
directions, 522
hiking, 523–25
horseback riding, 527
information, 527–28
picnics, 525
skiing/snowboarding, 525
East Lion, hiking, 150–52
East Pine Provincial Park, canoeing/kayaking, 634
Echo Lake Provincial Park
camping, 462
fishing, 464
Elk and Beaver Lakes Regional Park
beaches/picnics, 241
boating/kayaking, 243
walking, 248
Elk Falls Provincial Park, camping, 332
Elk Lakes Provincial Park, hiking, 524
Elk River, canoeing/kayaking, 527
Elkford
information, 528
skiing, 526
Ellison Provincial Park
camping, 461
diving, 472
fishing, 464
Emory Creek Provincial Park, camping, 417
Eneas Lakes Provincial Park, fishing, 463
Englishman River Falls Provincial Park
camping, 297
fishing, 298
hiking, 303
Eskers Provincial Park
canoeing/kayaking, 632
cross-country skiing/snowshoeing, 629
hiking, 623
wildlife, 635
Ethel F. Wilson Provincial Park, camping, 574
Everett Crowley Park, 20–21
Exchamsiks River Provincial Park
camping, 562
boating/canoeing/kayaking, 570

Fair Harbour, kayaking, 343
Fairmount Hot Springs Resort Ski Hills, skiing/snowboarding, 537
Fairy Lake Forest Recreation Site, camping, 271–72
False Creek, 22–23
Fanny Bay
lodgings, 329
restaurants, 328
Farms, Fraser Estuary, 58
Fernie, 526
information, 528
Fernie Snow Valley Ski Area, skiing, 525–26
Ferries
Balfour, 512
Brentwood-Mill Bay, 294
British Columbia, 38, 234
Galena Bay, 516
Gulf Islands, 373
Denman Island, 375
information, viii
Kootenay Lake, 501, 512
Needles, 516
Vancouver Island, 353
See also Boat tours
Fillongley Provincial Park, camping, 380
Fintry Provincial Park, camping, 461
Fiordland Provincial Recreation Area, kayaking, 395–96
Fishing
Bella Coola Road (Highway 20), 554–55
Bulkley/Skeena River Valleys, 564–66
Campbell River, 323–24
Cariboo Highway (Highway 97), 594–95
Central/Discovery Coast, 397–98
Columbia River Valley, 536
Comox Valley, 322–25
Coquihalla Highway (Highway 5), 453–54
Cowichan Valley, 280–82
Discovery Passage, 324–25, 345
Fraser Estuary, 57
Fraser Plateau, 575–77
Fraser Valley, 87–90
Gulf Islands, northern, 384
Gulf Islands, southern, 360–61
Horseshoe Bay, 135
information, xii–xiv
Inside Passage, 397–98
Lakes Forest District, 575–77
licences, 24
Malaspina Peninsula, 226–27
Manning Provincial Park, 439
Murrin Provincial Park, 180
Nanaimo, 282
North Kootenay Lake/Selkirk Valleys, 520–21
North Shore, 135
Northeast British Columbia, 630–32
Okanagan Valley, 463–64
Okanagan Valley, southern, 446
Pacific Rim Highway (Highway 4), 298–300
Pemberton/Pemberton Valley, 203–4
Port Alberni, 299–300
Powell River, 226
Queen Charlotte Islands, 408
Sechelt Peninsula, 225–26
Sidney, 244
Slocan Valley, 510
Sooke Basin, 272–73
Squamish/Squamish Valley, 180–81
Stewart-Cassiar Highway (Highway 37), 645–46
Sunshine Coast, 225–27
Trans-Canada Highway (Highway 1), 428–29
Ucluelet, 300
Vancouver, 24–25
Vancouver Island, North, 345–46
West Kootenays (Crowsnest Highway), 494–95
Whistler, 181
Yellowhead Highway (Highway 5), 608–9
See also Shellfish; *individual parks, town, bodies of water*
Flat Top Islands, fishing, 361
Flores Island, hiking, 305
Forbidden Ski Area, skiing/luge, 321–22
Fort Langley
attractions, 103
restaurants, 105
Fort Nelson, information, 638
Fort Rupert, attractions, 400
Fort St. James
information, 588
mountain biking, 583
Fort St. John, information, 638
Fort Steele Heritage Town, 527
Fossils, Yoho National Park, 425–26
Frances Barkley (MV), 307
Francis/King Regional Park, walking, 247
Francois Lake, fishing, 576
Fraser Canyon, hiking, 423
Fraser Estuary, 40–60
attractions, 58
beaches, 42–46
bird-watching, 51–54
camping, 57
canoeing, 50–51
cycling, 46–50
directions, 41
farms, 58
fishing, 57
hiking, 56–57
information, 60
kayaking, 50–51
lodgings, 59
parks, 42–46
photography, 54
restaurants, 59
swimming, 42–44
wildlife, 51–54
windsurfing, 55
See also Fraser River
Fraser Lake, camping/parks, 574
Fraser Plateau, 572–88
adjoining areas, 573
camping/parks, 573–75
canoeing/kayaking, 584–87
directions, 573
fishing, 575–77
hiking, 577–81
information, 587–88
mountain biking, 583–84
picnics, 581
rock climbing, 587
skiing/snowboarding, 582–83
snowmobiling, 582
wildlife, 587
Fraser River
beaches, 69
boating/canoeing/kayaking, 77

canoeing/kayaking, 527
fishing, 575
gold panning, 433
kayaking/canoeing, 50–51
rafting, 431–32
scenic drive, 426–27
See also Fraser Estuary
Fraser River Heritage Regional Park, picnics, 71
Fraser River Park (Burnaby), 15, 16, 23–24
Fraser River Park (Vancouver), 15, 16, 23–24
Fraser Valley, 61–106
adjoining areas, 63
attractions, 103–4
beaches, 68–70
boating, 73–79
camping, 63–68
canoeing, 73–79
cycling, 79–83
directions, 62
fishing, 87–90
gliding/hang gliding, 101–2
hiking, 90–98
horseback riding, 98, 101
information, 105–6
kayaking, 73–79
mountain biking, 83–87
parks, 63–68
picnics, 70–72
skating, 79–83
skiing/snowboarding, 102
wildlife, 98–100
windsurfing, 102
Fraser–Fort George, information, 638
French Beach Provincial Park
beaches, 268
camping, 271
kayaking, 272
French Creek
canoeing/kayaking, 325
fishing, fishing, 322
Fry Creek Canyon Provincial Recreation Area, hiking, 519
Fulford, attractions, 368

Gabriola Island
attractions, 368
boating/kayaking, 362
cycling, 363
fishing, 361
lodgings, 372–73
parks/picnics, 358
restaurants, 370
Gabriola Sands Provincial Park, picnics, 358
Gale Passage, kayaking, 396
Galiano Island, 354
attractions, 367
boating/kayaking, 361–62
camping, 356
hiking, 365
information, 373
lodgings, 370–72
mountain biking, 363
parks/picnics, 358
restaurants, 369
wildlife, 363–65
Galloping Goose Trail Regional Park, biking, 245–46
Ganges
attractions, 367–68
restaurants, 368
Garden Bay, lodgings, 234
Gardens, Vancouver, 29
Garibaldi Provincial Park
camping, 146–49
hiking, 156–61
mountain biking, 169, 170
skiing, cross-country, 163–64
Georgia, Strait of, fishing, 323–25
Gibson Pass Ski Area, downhill skiing/snowboarding, 438–39
Gibsons
attractions, 231
information, 234
lodgings, 233
restaurants, 232
Gitnadoix River Provincial Recreation Area
boating/canoeing/kayaking, 570
wildlife, 563–64
Glacier National Park
camping, 421
hiking, 423–24
information, 434
Gladstone Provincial Park, camping, 487
Gladstone-Elliot Park
canoeing/kayaking, 24
hiking/walking, 16
Glen Valley Regional Park, fishing, 89
Gliding, Fraser Valley, 101–2
Goat Range Provincial Park, camping, 520
God's Pocket Provincial Park, diving, 351
Gold Bridge
directions, 190
lodgings, 207
Gold River
directions, 335
information, 341
MV *Uchuck III*, 333
Upana Caves, 339
Gold Rush Heritage Trail, 195
Golden
camping, 419
information, 542
Golden Ears Provincial Park
camping, 63–64
hiking, 91–93
horseback riding, 101
mountain biking, 84–85
picnics, 71
See also Alouette Lake
Goldpan Provincial Park
camping, 417
fishing, 428
Goldstream Provincial Park
camping, 239
cycling, 246–47
fishing, 244
hiking/walking, 247–50
picnics, 241
wildlife, 253–54
Golfing
Cowichan Valley, 289
Kelowna, 472
Nanaimo, 289
Okanagan Valley, 472
Vancouver, 8
Goose Spit Regional Park
beaches, 317
windsurfing, 326
Gordon Bay Provincial Park
beaches/picnics, 280
boating/kayaking, 278
camping, 282
fishing, 281
Gowlland Tod Provincial Park, hiking, 251
Graham Island
attractions, 411
camping, 405
hiking, 408–9
See also Queen Charlotte Islands
Granby Provincial Park, hiking, 491
Grand Forks
information, 501
mountain biking, 492–93
Granite Falls Regional Park, 133
Granite Mountain, skiing, cross-country, 497–98
Grant Narrows Regional Park, boating/canoeing/kayaking, 73–74
Granville Island Waterpark, 29
Great Central Lake
boating/kayaking, 307
water taxi, 303
Greater Vancouver Regional District, 74
Green Lake Provincial Park, camping, 592–93
Grohman Narrows Provincial Park, picnics, 488–89, 506
Grotto, The, warm springs, 641–42
Grouse Mountain
hiking, 109, 123–24
mountain biking, 127
skiing/snowboarding, 136
Gulf Islands, 354–86
information, 373, 386
See also Gulf Islands, Northern; Gulf Islands, Southern; *individual islands*
Gulf Islands, northern, 374–86
adjoining areas, 375
air service, 375
attractions, 384–85
beaches/picnics, 381–82
boating/canoeing/kayaking, 375–80
camping/parks, 380–81
ferry service, 374–75
fishing, 384
hiking, 382–83
information, 386
lodgings, 385–86
mountain biking, 383–84
restaurants, 385
Gulf Islands, southern, 354–73
adjoining areas, 355
attractions, 367–68
beaches/swimming, 358–60
boating/kayaking, 361–62
camping/parks, 355–57
cycling, 362–63

ferry service, 355
fishing, 360–61
hiking, 365–66
information, 373
lodgings, 370–73
parks/picnics, 357–58
restaurants, 368–70
whale watching, 365
wildlife, 363–65
Gwaii Haanas National Park Reserve and Haida Heritage Site, 412
camping, 405–6
information, 412
kayaking, 407
Gwillim Lake Provincial Park, camping, 619

Haida Gwaii. *See* Queen Charlotte Islands
Hakai Provincial Recreation Area
diving, 399
fishing, 398
kayaking, 393–95
wildlife, 398–99
Halfmoon Bay, lodgings, 233
Hamber Provincial Park, hiking, 606–7
Hang gliding, Fraser Valley, 101–2
Harper Mountain, skiing, 609
Harrison Hot Springs, 65, 69
attractions, 104
information, 105
lodgings, 105
restaurants, 105
Harrison Lake, 64–65
beaches, 69
mountain biking, 86
Harrison River, boating/canoeing/kayaking, 77
Haynes Point Provincial Park, camping, 459–60
Hayward Lake
beaches, 68–69
boating/canoeing/kayaking, 76
Haywire Bay Regional Park
beaches/picnics, 214
camping, 211
Hazelton, information, 571, 651
Hazelton Valley
scenic drives, 650–51
totem poles, 650–51
Hecate Regional Park, wildlife, 286
Height of the Rockies Wilderness Area, hiking, 525
Heli-skiing
Albert Icefields, 431
Valemount, 610
Whistler, 166
Helliwell Provincial Park
beaches/picnics, 381
hiking, 383
Hemer Provincial Park, boating/kayaking, 278
Hemlock Valley, mountain biking, 86
Hemlock Valley Ski Area, 102
Herald Provincial Park
camping, 418–19
hiking, 423
Hicks Lake, 65
Highway 1. *See* Trans-Canada Highway
Highway 3. *See* Crowsnest Highway
Highway 4. *See* Pacific Rim Highway
Highway 5. *See* Coquihalla Highway
Highway 19. *See* Island Highway
Highway 20. *See* Bella Coola Road
Highway 37. *See* Stewart-Cassiar Highway
Highway 97 (John Hart Highway)
camping, 616–23
canoeing/kayaking, 633
fishing, 631
hiking, 623–28
scenic drives, 634–35
See also Alaska Highway; Cariboo Highway (Highway 97)
Highway 99. *See* Sea to Sky Highway
Hiking, x–xii
Alexander Mackenzie Heritage Trail, 548, 550–51, 577–78
Baden-Powell Trail, 110–13, 116
Bella Coola Road (Highway 20), 549–52
Bulkley/Skeena River Valleys, 567–69
Burnaby, 16
Capilano River, 117–18
Centennial Trail, 445
Central/Discovery Coast, 399–400
Coast Trail, 248–49
Columbia River Valley, 533–35
Coquihalla Highway (Highway 5), 454
Cowichan Valley, 284–86
Dewdney Trail, 489
East Kootenays (Crowsnest Highway), 523–25
Fraser Estuary, 56–57
Fraser Valley, 90–98
Gold Rush Heritage Trail, 195
Gulf Islands, northern, 382–83
Gulf Islands, southern, 365–66
Howe Sound, 152–53
Kaslo & Slocan Railway Trail, 509
Kettle Valley, 480–81
Kettle Valley Railway Trail, 466–67, 479, 480–81
Malaspina Peninsula, 224–25
Manning Provincial Park, 96–97, 436–37
Nootka Island Trail, 336–37
North Kootenay Lake/Selkirk Valleys, 518–19
North Shore, 109–24
North Vancouver, 117–24
Northeast British Columbia, 623–28
Okanagan Valley, 464–67
Okanagan Valley, South, 444–45
Pacific Rim Highway (Highway 4), 303
Pacific Rim National Park Reserve, 302–3, 304
Pemberton/Pemberton Valley, 194–96
Powell River, 224–25
Queen Charlotte Islands, 408–9
Sea to Sky Highway, 150–61
Sea to Sky Trail, 170, 195–96
Sechelt Peninsula, 221–24
Slocan Valley, 504–6
Sooke Basin, 263–67
Squamish/Squamish Valley, 154–55
Stewart-Cassiar Highway (Highway 37), 642–47
Strathcona Provincial Park, 303, 322, 337–38
Sunshine Coast, 221–25
Trans-Canada Highway (Highway 1), 422–26
Vancouver, 10, 16–17
Vancouver Island, North, 347
Victoria, 248–52
West Coast Trail, 263–65, 302–3
West Kootenays (Crowsnest Highway), 489–91
West Vancouver, 112–17
Whistler, 156–61
Yellowhead Highway (Highway 5), 606–8
See also Beaches; Camping; Parks; *individual entries for towns, parks, regions, and geographic features*
Holden Lake, boating/kayaking, 278
Hollyburn Mountain, hiking, 113–14
Honeymoon Bay Wildflower Ecological Preserve, 286–87
Hope, information, 105
Hornby Island
attractions, 385
beaches/picnics, 381
hiking, 383
information, 386
lodgings, 385
mountain biking, 383–84
Horne Lake Caves Provincial Park, caves, 317–18
Horseback riding
Alexander Mackenzie Heritage Trail, 558
Bella Coola Road (Highway 20), 558
Cariboo Highway (Highway 97), 600
Coquihalla Highway (Highway 5), 456
East Kootenays (Crowsnest Highway), 527
Fraser Valley, 98, 101
Manning Provincial Park, 438
Pemberton/Pemberton Valley, 204
Squamish/Squamish Valley, 182
West Kootenays (Crowsnest Highway), 493–94
Yellowhead Highway (Highway 5), 611
See also individual parks
Horsefly Lake Provincial Park,

camping, 593
Horseshoe Bay
attractions, 139
boating/canoeing/kayaking, 134
directions, 107–8
fishing, 135
Hot springs
Ainsworth Hot Springs, 513
Grotto, The, warm springs, 641–42
Harrison Hot Springs, 65, 69, 104
Hot Springs Cove, 310
Hotspring Island, 410
Liard River Hotsprings Provincial Park, 622–23
Lussier Hot Springs, 535
Nakusp Hot Springs, 508–9, 511, 513
Pitt River, 84
Radium Hot Springs, 540
St. Agnes Well Hot Spring, 195
Shearwater Hot Springs, 568
Tchentlo Lake Warm Springs, 586
Wewanie, 568
Hot Springs Cove, 310
Houston
camping/parks, 575
fishing, 575
information, 588
Howe Sound
boating/canoeing/kayaking, 173
camping/parks, 144–45
hiking, 152–53
Hozameen, camping, 67
Hudson Bay Mountain, skiing/snowboarding, 566

Ice climbing, 206
Indian Arm Provincial Marine Park, boating/canoeing/kayaking, 132–33
Information
camping, x
ferries, viii
fishing, xiii–xiv
roads, viii
sea kayaking, xiv
skiing, xv
weather, viii–ix
See also individual entries for activities, regions, towns, and parks
Inkaneep Provincial Park, camping, 460
Inland Lake, beaches/picnics, 214
In-line skating. *See* Skating
Inside Passage
boat service, 390, 391–92
camping, 397
fishing, 397–98
kayaking, 393–96
See also Central/Discovery Coast
Invermere
information, 542
restaurants, 541
Iona Beach Regional Park, 45–46
photography, 54
hiking, 57
Island Highway (Highway 19), 314–30
beaches, 316
camping/parks, 315–16
Island View Beach Regional Park
beaches/picnics, 241
biking, 246
boating/kayaking, 243
Itcha Ilgachuz Provincial Park
hiking, 551–52
skiing, cross-country, 558
Ivy Green Park, camping, 283

James Chabot Provincial Park
fishing, 536
swimming, 535
windsurfing, 539
Jedediah Island Provincial Marine Park, boating/canoeing/kayaking, 376–77
Jericho Beach Park
beaches/festivals, 13,
fishing, 24–25
windsurfing, 26
Jewel Lake Provincial Park, fishing, 446
Jimsmith Provincial Park, camping, 523
Joffre Lakes/Joffre Lakes Provincial Recreation Area
boating/canoeing/kayaking, 202
camping, 192
fishing, 203
hiking, 196
ice climbing, 206
John Dean Provincial Park
hiking, 250–51
picnics, 242
John Hart Highway. *See* Highway 97
Johnstone Creek Provincial Park, camping, 443
Johnstone Strait, boating/canoeing, 345
Jordan River
beaches, 269
kayaking, 272
surfing, 269–70
Juan de Fuca Marine Trail and Provincial Park, hiking, 265–66
Juniper Beach Provincial Park
camping, 417
fishing, 417

Kalamalka Lake/Kalamalka Lake Provincial Park
beaches/swimming, 462
mountain biking, 470
Kalenden, lodgings, 476
Kamloops
attractions, 611
information, 434, 457
lodgings, 612
restaurants, 611
Kanaka Creek
fish hatchery, 99
fishing, 88
Kanaka Creek Regional Park
boating/canoeing/kayaking, 75–76
hiking, 90–91
picnics, 70–71
Kane Valley
mountain biking, 455
skiing, cross-country, 456
Kaslo
attractions, 513
information, 516
restaurants, 514
Kaslo & Slocan Railway Trail, hiking/biking, 509
Katherine Lake Regional Park
beaches/picnics, 213
camping, 211
Kawkawa Lake Provincial Park
beaches, 70
canoeing/swimming, 446
Kayaking, xiv
Bella Coola Road (Highway 20), 556–57
Bulkley/Skeena River Valleys, 570
Capilano River, 133–34
Cariboo Highway (Highway 97), 596
Central/Discovery Coast, 393–96
Clayoquot Sound, 307
Columbia River, 495
Cowichan Valley, 278
East Kootenays (Crowsnest Highway),527
Fraser Estuary, 50–51
Fraser Plateau, 584–87
Fraser River, 50–51, 77
Fraser Valley, 73–79
Gulf Islands, northern, 375–80
Gulf Islands, southern, 361–62
Horseshoe Bay, 134
Howe Sound, 173
Ladner, 50
Malaspina Peninsula, 216–18
Nanaimo, 277–78
Nootka Sound, 333
North Shore, 132–34
Northeast British Columbia, 632–34
Pacific Rim National Park Reserve, 306–7
Pemberton/Pemberton Valley, 201–3
Queen Charlotte Islands, 406–7
Sechelt Peninsula, 214–15
Slocan Valley, 509–10
Sooke Basin, 272
Squamish River, 173–74
Stewart-Cassiar Highway (Highway 37), 646–48
Strathcona Provincial Park, 332–33
Sunshine Coast, 214–18
Vancouver, 22–24
Vancouver Island, North 343–44
Victoria, 243–44
West Kootenays (Crowsnest Highway), 495
Whistler, 175–77
See also Boating; Canoeing;

Rafting; *entries for individual parks and bodies of water*
Kekulia Bay Provincial Park, fishing, 464
Kelowna
attractions, 474
beaches/swimming, 462
diving, 472
fishing, 464
golfing, 472
information, 477
lodgings, 476–77
mountain biking, 470
restaurants, 474–75
wildlife, 463
Keremeos, information, 449, 477
Kettle River, canoeing, 446
Kettle River Provincial Recreation Area
camping, 443, 479
skiing, cross-country, 447
Kettle Valley, 478–82
adjoining areas, 479
camping/parks, 479–80
directions, 479
hiking/biking, 480–81
information, 482
skiing/snowboarding, 481–82
Kettle Valley Railway Trail, 446–47
hiking, 466–67, 479, 480–81
mountain biking, 455, 470, 479, 480–81
Khutzeymateen/K'tzim-a-deen Grizzly Bear Sanctuary, wildlife, 564
Kicking Horse River, rafting, 432
Kickininee Provincial Park, beaches/swimming, 462
Kilby, attractions, 103
Kilby Provincial Park
beaches, 69
boating/canoeing/kayaking, 77
camping, 65
picnics, 72
Killarney Lake, hiking, 130
Kimberley
attractions, 540
information, 528, 542
lodgings, 541–42
restaurants, 541
Kimberley Ski and Summer Resort, skiing/snowboarding, 538–39
Kinaskan Lake Provincial Park, camping, 642
Kinbasket Lake, canoeing, 610
King George VI Provincial Park, picnics, 489
Kiskatinaw Provincial Park, camping, 620
Kiskatinaw River, fishing, 631
Kitimat
fishing, 565, 566
hiking/ walking, 567-9
information, 571
Kitlope Heritage Conservancy Protected Area
boating/canoeing/kayaking, 570
camping, 562–63
fishing, 566
information, 571
Kitsilano Beach, 12
Kitsilano Beach Park/Kitsilano Point, beaches, 12–13
Kleanza Creek Provincial Park
camping, 562
hiking, 568–69
Klein Lake, beaches/picnics, 213
Klemtu
attractions, 401
information, 402
kayaking, 395
Kludahk Forest Recreation Trail, hiking, 266
Kokanee Creek, fishing, 494
Kokanee Creek Provincial Park
beaches, 493
camping, 486
wildlife, 496
Kokanee Glacier Provincial Park
hiking, 490–91
hiking, 504
fishing, 494–95
Kootenay Lake
beaches, 493
camping/parks, 486, 488, 519–20
canoeing/kayaking, 495
ferry service, 501, 512
fishing, 494
See also North Kootenay Lake/Selkirk Valleys
Kootenay Lake Provincial Park, camping, 519
Kootenay National Park
camping, 531–33
hiking, 533
scenic drives, 537
swimming, 535
wildlife, 532, 536
Kwadacha Provincial Wilderness Park, hiking, 626–27
Kyuquot Sound
boat tour, 333–36
directions, 331
Kyuquot, 334–36

Lac la Hache/Lac la Hache Provincial Park
boating/fishing, 595
camping, 593
Lac Le Jeune
boating, 455
lodgings, 612
Lac Le Jeune Provincial Park
camping, 451–52
fishing, 453
skiing, cross-country, 456
Ladner
kayaking/canoeing,
lodgings, 59
Lady Rose (MV), 307
Ladysmith
beaches/picnicking, 279
boating/kayaking, 277
camping, 283
information, 294
lodgings, 294
restaurants, 291
Lake Lovely Water Provincial Park, hiking, 155
Lake Revelstoke, fishing, 429
Lakelse Lake
fishing, 565
waterskiing/windsurfing, 570
Lakelse Lake Provincial Park, camping, 562
Lakes Forest District, fishing, 575–76
Langley
cycling/skating, 80–81
information, 105, 106
Larch Hills Cross-Country Area, skiing, cross-country, 430
Lasqueti Island
beaches/picnics, 381–82
ferry service, 374–75
mountain biking, 383
Levette Lake, swimming, 179
Liard River Hotsprings Provincial Park, camping, 622–23
Licenses, fishing, 24
Lighthouse Park, 128
picnics, 137–38
Lillooet, 189–207
adjoining areas, 190
attractions, 206–7
camping/parks, 193–94
directions, 144, 190
fishing, 203–4
hiking, 194–96
information, 207
mountain biking, 198
rock/ice climbing, 206
Lillooet Lake
beaches, 205
boating/canoeing/kayaking, 201–2
camping/parks, 192
Lillooet River, canoeing/kayaking, 202
Link River Regional Park, camping, 348
Little Hustan Cave Regional Park, caves, 350–51
Little Qualicum Falls Provincial Park
camping, 297
fishing, 299
hiking, 303
Lockhart Beach Provincial Park
beaches, 493
camping, 488
Lockhart Creek, fishing, 494
Lodgings. *See specific cities for listings*
Long Beach Unit, 301
boating/kayaking, 307
information, 313
windsurfing, 308
Loon Lake, boating/fishing, 594–95
Loon Lake Provincial Park, camping, 592
Loss Creek Provincial Park, hiking, 267
Lost Ledge Provincial Park, camping, 519
Loveland Bay Provincial Park, canoeing, 344–45
Luge, Forbidden Ski Area, 322
Lund, attractions, 231–32
Lussier Hot Springs, 535
Lynn Canyon Park, 128–29
Lynn Headwaters Regional Park

hiking, 118–21
skiing, cross-country, 136–37

Mabel Lake Provincial Park, camping, 461–62
Mackenzie, information, 638
Mackenzie (Sir Alexander) Provincial Park, 400
MacMillan Provincial Park, hiking, 303
Madeira Park, lodgings, 233
Mahood Lake, boating/fishing, 595
Malahat, lodgings, 292
Malaspina Peninsula
beaches/picnics, 213–14
boat launches, 217–18
boating/canoeing/kayaking, 216–18
cycling, 218–19
diving, 228
fishing, 226–27
hiking, 224–25
mountain biking, 221
wildlife, 229–30
Manning Provincial Park, 435–40
adjoining areas, 436
camping, 438, 439
canoeing, 439
directions, 436
fishing, 439
hiking, 96–97, 436–37
horseback riding, 438
information, 440
lodgings, 440
mountain biking, 439
skiing/snowboarding/snowshoeing, 438–39
swimming, 439
wildlife, 438
Mansons Landing Provincial Marine Park, beaches/picnics, 381
Maple Ridge
attractions, 104
information, 105
Maple Ridge Park and Campground, 64
Mara Provincial Park, beaches/swimming, 462–63
Marble Canyon Provincial Park
camping, 193
ice climbing, 206
picnics, 205
Marble River Provincial Park, camping, 348
Marine parks
Barnet Marine Park, 14–15, 23
Beaumont Provincial Marine Park, 356
Beaumont Provincial Marine Park, 361
Bligh Island Provincial Marine Park, 333
Buccaneer Bay Marine Park, 215–16
Copeland Islands Provincial Marine Park, 378–79
Desolation Sound Marine Park, 217
Dionisio Provincial Park, 361
Indian Arm Provincial Marine Park, 132–33
Jedediah Island Provincial Marine Park, 376–77
Mansons Landing Provincial Marine Park, 381
Montague Harbour Provincial Marine Park, 356, 361
Newcastle Island Provincial Marine Park, 356–57, 358, 363, 365, 366
Octopus Islands Provincial Marine Park, 379
Princess Margaret Marine Park, 361
Princess Margaret Provincial Marine Park, 240, 243
Raft Cove Provincial Marine Park, 349
Rebecca Spit Provincial Marine Park, 381, 384
Sandy Island Provincial Marine Park, 377–78
Shuswap Lake Provincial Marine Park, 427–28
Sidney Spit Provincial Marine Park, 240, 241, 243
Simson Marine Park, boating/canoeing/kayaking, 215
Smuggler Cove Provincial Marine Park, 210, 216
Squitty Bay Provincial Marine Park, 377, 381–82
Takla Lake Provincial Marine Park, 576
Whytecliff Marine Park, 131, 135, 137–38
Winter Cove Provincial Marine Park, 357, 361
Martha Creek Provincial Park
camping, 419
fishing, 429
Masset
information, 412
lodgings, 412
Matheson Lake Regional Park, boating/kayaking, 244
Matsqui Trail Regional Park
cycling/skating, 82
fishing, 89
hiking, 98
picnics, 72
Mayne Island
attractions, 368
beaches/swimming, 359
boating/kayaking, 362
cycling, 362–63
fishing, 360
lodgings, 371
restaurants, 370
McDonald Beach, fishing, 57
McDonald Creek Provincial Park
beaches/picnics, 506
camping, 503
McDonald Provincial Park, 239–40
McKee Peak, mountain biking, 87
McLoughlin Bay, boat service, 391–92
Meares Island, hiking, 304–5
Memory Island Provincial Park, boating/kayaking, 277
Merritt
information, 457
lodgings, 456
Metchosin, wildlife, 252
Meziadin Lake/Meziadin Lake Provincial Park
camping, 642
canoeing/kayaking, 647
fishing, 645
wildlife, 648
Mill Bay, information, 294
Millstream Highlands, mountain biking, 246
Minnekhada Regional Park, hiking, 90
Miracle Beach Provincial Park, camping, 315–16
Mission
attractions, 104
cycling/skating, 82
picnics, 71–72
Mitlenatch Island Provincial Park, wildlife, 327
Moberly Lake Provincial Park, camping, 619
Monashee Provincial Park, hiking, 505–6
Monck Provincial Park, camping, 452
Monkman Provincial Park
camping, 620
hiking, 625
mountain biking, 628
Montague Harbour Provincial Marine Park
boating/kayaking, 361
camping, 356
Morchuea Lake, camping, 641
Moresby Island
camping, 405
fishing, 408
hiking, 409
information, 412
See also Queen Charlotte Islands
Morice Mountain Ski Trails
hiking, 580
mountain biking, 584
skiing, cross-country, 582
Morrell Wildlife Sanctuary, 286
Morrissey Provincial Park, picnics, 525
Morton Lake Provincial Park
canoeing, 344–45
fishing, 345–46
Mouat Provincial Park, camping, 356
Mount Assiniboine Provincial Park, hiking, 534–35
Mount Edziza Provincial Park
hiking, 643–44
wildlife, 649
Mount Fernie Provincial Park, camping, 523
Mount Mackenzie Ski Area, downhill skiing, 431
Mount MacPherson, skiing, cross-country, 431
Mount Mary Ann, mountain biking, 86
Mount Maxwell Provincial Parks, parks/picnics, 357–58
Mount Norman Regional Park,

hiking, 365–66
Mount Revelstoke National Park
camping, 420–21
hiking, 423
information, 434
Mount Riorda, skiing/snowboarding, 467
Mount Robson Provincial Park
camping, 605–6
canoeing, 610
hiking, 606–7
information, 612
Mount Seymour, skiing/snowboarding, 136
Mount Seymour Provincial Park
hiking, 122–23
mountain biking, 126
picnics, 138–39
Mount Terry Fox Provincial Park, hiking, 607
Mount Washington
mountain biking, 318–19
skiing, 320–21
Mount Work Provincial Park, hiking, 251–52
Mountain biking, xii
Cariboo Highway (Highway 97), 598–99
Columbia River Valley, 537
Comox Valley, 318–20
Coquihalla Highway (Highway 5), 455
Cowichan Valley, 287–88
Dewdey Trail, 507
Fraser Plateau, 583–84
Fraser Valley, 83–87
Gulf Islands, northern, 383–84
Gulf Islands, southern, 363
Kaslo & Slocan Railway Trail, 509
Kettle Valley Railway Trail, 446–47, 455, 470, 479, 480–81
Malaspina Peninsula, 221
Manning Provincial Park, 439
Nanaimo, 288
North Shore, 125–28
Northeast British Columbia, 628–29
Okanagan Valley, 469–72
Okanagan Valley, South, 446
Pemberton/Pemberton Valley, 197–98
Sea to Sky Highway, 168–70
Sea to Sky Trail, 197
Sechelt Peninsula, 219–20
Slocan Valley, 507–9
Squamish/Squamish Valley, 168–70
Stewart-Cassiar Highway (Highway 37), 649–50
Sunshine Coast, 219–21
Vancouver, 19–22
Victoria, 245–47
West Kootenays (Crowsnest Highway), 491–93
Whistler, 169–71
See also individual entries for parks, towns, and geographic features
Mowat Bay Park, beaches/picnics, 213–14
Moyie Lake Provincial Park, camping, 523
Muncho Lake Provincial Park
camping, 622
hiking, 628
scenic drives, 628
Murray River, canoeing/kayaking, 633–34
Murrin Provincial Park
fishing, 180
picnics, 150
rock climbing, 166–67
swimming, 178
Muskwa-Kechika Management Unit, wildlife, 636
Mystic Beach, 268

Nahatlatch Lake and River system
boating/canoeing, 427
camping, 420
rafting, 431–32
Naikoon Provincial Park
camping, 404–5
fishing/shellfish, 408
hiking, 408–9
Nairn Falls Provincial Park, camping, 191–92
Nakusp
information, 516
mountain biking, 507–8
Nakusp Hot Springs, 508–9, 511, 513
Namu, attractions, 400
Nanaimo, 276–94
attractions, 290
beaches/picnics, 279–80
boating/kayaking, 277–78
bungee jumping, 289
directions, 277
fishing, 282
golfing, 289
information, 294
lodgings, 292–94
mountain biking, 288
restaurants, 291–92
walking, 289
Nancy Greene Lake, fishing, 494
Nancy Greene Provincial Park
camping, 487–88
hiking, 489–90
skiing, cross-country, 498
Nanika-Kidprice Portage Trails, canoeing/kayaking, 586
Naramata
lodgings, 476
restaurants, 474
Nation Lakes, canoeing/kayaking, 586
National parks
information, 275, 542
permits, 422
reservations, ix
See also individual entries
Nazko Lakes Provincial Park, canoeing, 557
Nechako Reservoir
canoeing/kayaking, 585
fishing, 576
Nechako River, canoeing/kayaking, 584–85
Neilson Regional Park
boating/canoeing/kayaking, 76
picnics, 71–72
Nelson
attractions, 512–13
information, 501, 516
lodgings, 515
mountain biking, 508
restaurants, 514
New Denver
attractions, 513
lodgings, 515
New Westminster
information, 38
parks, 12
Newcastle Island Provincial Marine Park
biking, 363
camping, 356–57
hiking, 366
picnics, 358
wildlife, 365
Nickel Plate Nordic Center, skiing, cross-country, 467
Nickel Plate Provincial Park, hiking, 465
Nicola Lake
boating/sailing/windsurfing, 455
camping, 452
fishing, 454
Nicola River, fishing, 428, 453
Nicola Valley
camping, 452–53
fishing, 453–54
horseback riding, 456
Nicomekl River, kayaking/canoeing, 51
Nicomen Island, cycling/skating, 80
Nimpkish Lake, windsurfing, 348
Nimpo Lake, fishing, 555
Nisga'a Memorial Lava Bed Provincial Park, hiking, 569
Niskonlith Lake Provincial Park
camping, 418
fishing, 429
hiking, 423
Nitinat Lake
boating/kayaking, 278
camping, 283–84
windsurfing, 288–89
Nootka Island Trail, hiking, 336–37
Nootka Sound, 331–41
adjoining areas, 331
boat tour, 333–36
boating/kayaking, 333
directions, 331
information, 341
Norbury Lake Provincial Park, camping, 530
North Hill Regional Park, hiking, 250
North Kootenay Lake/Selkirk Valleys, 517–21
camping, 519–20
directions, 517
fishing, 520–21
hiking, 518–19
information, 521
skiing, 520
North Shore, 107–41
adjoining areas, 109

attractions, 139
beaches/swimming, 130–32
boating/canoeing/kayaking, 132–34
cycling, 124–25
directions, 107–8
diving, 137
fishing, 135
hiking, 109–24
information, 141
mountain biking, 125–28
parks, 128–30
picnics, 137–39
skiing/snowboarding, 135–37
snowshoeing, 137
wildlife, 134–35
See also North Vancouver; West Vancouver
North Thompson River, canoeing/rafting, 610
North Thompson River Provincial Park, camping, 603
North Vancouver
boating/canoeing/kayaking, 132–34
cycling, 124–25
directions, 108
fishing, 135
hiking, 117–24
information, 141
lodgings, 140–41
restaurants, 139–40
See also North Shore; West Vancouver
Northeast British Columbia, 615–38
adjoining areas, 616
attractions, 637
camping/parks, 616–23
canoeing/kayaking, 632–34
directions, 616
fishing, 630–32
hiking, 623–28
information, 638
mountain biking, 628–29
photography, 634–35
rafting, 634
scenic drives, 634–35
skiing, 629–30
wildlife, 635–37
Northern British Columbia. *See* Northeastern British Columbia; Stewart-Cassiar Highway (Highway 37)
Northern Rockies Protected Area, wildlife, 636
Northwestern British Columbia. *See* Stewart-Cassiar Highway (Highway 37)
Nuxalk-Carrier Grease Route, hiking, 577–78

Ocean Falls
boat service, 391–92
hiking, 399
Octopus Islands Provincial Marine Park, boating/canoeing/kayaking, 379
Odegaard Falls, 549
Okanagan Falls
attractions, 473
information, 477
Okanagan Lake
beaches/swimming, 462
camping, 461–62
See also Okanagan Lake Provincial Park; Okanagan Valley; Okanagan Valley, South (Crowsnest Highway)
Okanagan Lake Provincial Park, camping, 460
Okanagan Mountain Provincial Park
camping, 459
hiking, 464–65
mountain biking, 470–71
Okanagan Valley, 458–77
adjoining areas, 459
attractions, 473–74
beaches/swimming, 462–63
camping/parks/picnics, 459–62
directions, 459
diving, 472
fishing, 463–64
golfing, 472
hiking, 464–67
information, 477
mountain biking, 469–72
skiing/snowboarding, 467–69
wildlife, 463
wineries, 473
See also Okanagan Valley, South (Crowsnest Highway)
Okanagan Valley, South (Crowsnest Highway), 441–49
adjoining areas, 442
attractions, 447–48
camping, 442–43
canoeing, 446
directions, 442
fishing, 446
hiking, 444–45
information, 449
lodgings, 448–49
mountain biking, 446–47
restaurants, 448
skiing, cross-country, 447
swimming, 446
wildlife, 447
See also Manning Provincial Park; Okanagan Lake; Okanagan Valley
Okeover Arm Provincial Park, camping, 210–11
Old Hazelton, walking, 567
Oliver
hiking, 466
information, 477
mountain biking, 471–72
One-Fifteen Creek Provincial Park
camping, 622
hiking, 627
100 Mile House
information, 601
skiing, cross-country, 596–97
108 Mile Ranch
lodgings, 601
skiing, cross-country, 596–97
Ootsa Lake, fishing, 576
Osoyoos
attractions, 447–48
lodgings, 448–49
mountain biking, 471–72
restaurants, 448
Osoyoos Lake, camping/parks/picnics, 459–60
Othello Tunnels, hiking, 445
Owen Hat, climbing, 587
Oyster Bay Shoreline Regional Park, beaches, 317

Paarens Beach Provincial Park
camping, 574
picnics, 581
Pacheedaht Beach, 272
Pacific Rim Highway (Highway 4)
camping, 297–98
beaches/picnics, 300
fishing, 298–300
hiking, 303
Pacific Rim National Park Reserve, 295–313
adjoining areas, 296
attractions, 310
boating/kayaking, 306
camping, 297
directions, 296
hiking, 302–3, 304
information, 313
West Coast Trail, 263–65
whale watching, 302
wildlife, 302
windsurfing, 308
Pacific Spirit Regional Park, 9–11, 16, 18, 20
Paleface Creek Campground, 66
Panorama Ski Resort
lodgings, 541
mountain biking, 537
skiing/snowboarding, 537–38
Paradise Lake, fishing, 576
Paragliding, Blackcomb, 166
Parks Canada. *See* National parks; *individual entries*
Parks
Bulkley/Skeena River Valleys, 561–63
camping reservations, ix–x
Cariboo Highway (Highway 97), 592–94
Columbia River Valley, 530–33
Comox Valley, 315–16
East Kootenays (Crowsnest Highway), 523
Fraser Estuary, 42–46
Fraser Plateau, 573–75
Fraser Valley, 63–68
Gulf Islands, northern, 380–81
Gulf Islands, southern, 355–58
Kettle Valley, 479–80
Lillooet, 193–94
Lillooet Lake, 192
North Shore, 128–30
Northeast British Columbia, 616–23
Okanagan Valley, 459–62
Pemberton/Pemberton Valley, 191–94
Queen Charlotte Islands, 404–6
Slocan Valley, 503–4
Squamish/Squamish Valley, 145–46
Stewart-Cassiar Highway

(Highway 37), 641–42
Trans-Canada Highway
(Highway 1), 417–22
Upper Arrow Lake, 503
Vancouver, 5–12, 60
Vancouver Island, North,
348–50
Victoria, 239–43
West Kootenays (Crowsnest
Highway), 486–87
West Vancouver, 128
wheelchair accessible, 219
Whistler, 146–47
Yellowhead Highway (Highway
5), 603–6
See also Beaches; British
Columbia Parks; Camping;
Hiking; Marine parks;
National parks; Picnics;
individual parks
Parksville, 314–30
adjoining areas, 315
canoeing/kayaking, 325
directions, 296, 315
fishing, 322
information, 294, 330
lodgings, 329–30
mountain biking, 288
wildlife, 287
Parsnip River, canoeing/kayaking,
633
Pass Creek Regional Park,
camping, 488
Paul Lake/Paul Lake Provincial
Park
camping, 603
fishing, 608
Peace Arch Provincial Park, 54, 55
Peace Island Regional Park,
camping, 620
Peace River, canoeing/kayaking,
634
Peachland, hiking, 466
Pemberton/Pemberton Valley,
189–207
adjoining areas, 190
attractions, 206–7
beaches/swimming, 205–6
boating/canoeing, kayaking,
201–3
camping/parks, 191–94
cross-country
skiing/snowshoeing,
199–200
cycling, 198–99
directions, 190
fishing, 203–4
hiking, 194–96
horseback riding, 204
information, 188, 207
lodgings, 207
mountain biking, 197–98
picnics, 204–5
rock climbing, 206
wildlife, 200–1
Pender Harbour, attractions, 231
Pender Islands, North and South
attractions, 368
beaches/swimming, 359
boating/kayaking, 361–62
camping, 356
hiking, 365–66
lodgings, 370–72
Pendleton Bay Provincial Park,
camping, 574
Pennask Lake Provincial Park,
fishing, 464
Penticton
attractions, 473–74
fishing, 464
information, 477
lodgings, 475–77
mountain biking, 471
restaurants, 474–75
Petroglyph Provincial Park,
hiking, 286
Pink Mountain, wildlife, 635–36
Pinkut Lake, camping/parks, 574
Pinnacles Provincial Park,
mountain biking, 599
Pipers Lagoon Regional Park
beaches/picnics, 279
boating/kayaking, 278
windsurfing, 289
Pitt-Addington Marsh Wildlife
Management Area, wildlife,
98–100
Pitt Lake
boating/canoeing/kayaking, 73,
75
Pitt Meadows, information, 106
Pitt River
fish hatchery, 84
fishing, 87
hot springs, 84
mountain biking, 83–84
Playground of the Gods, 25
PoCo Dike Trail, cycling, 79–80
Point Roberts (WA)
camping, 57
cycling, 48
whale watching, 54
Porpoise Bay Provincial Park
beaches/picnics, 212
camping, 210
Port Alberni
attractions, 310
camping, 298
directions, 296
information, 313
Lady Rose/Frances Barkley
(MV), 307
restaurants, 311
Port Alice, information, 353
Port Coquitlam, information, 106
Port Hardy
attractions, 352, 400
camping, 397
fishing, 346
information, 353, 402
Port McNeill
attractions, 352
information, 353
Port Moody, 38
parks, 19
Port Renfrew
camping, 271–72
directions, 263
hiking, 263–64
Porteau Cove/Porteau Cove
Provincial Park
boating/canoeing/kayaking,
173
camping, 144–45
diving, 180
picnics, 149
swimming, 178
Portland Island, boating/kayaking,
361–62
Post Creek Campground, 66
Powder King Ski Village,
skiing/snowboarding, 630
Powell Forest Canoe Route,
canoeing/kayaking, 216–17
Powell River
attractions, 231
camping, 211
diving, 228
fishing, 226
hiking, 224–25
information, 234
lodgings, 232–33
restaurants, 232
Premier Lake Provincial Park,
fishing, 536
Prince George
attractions, 637
canoeing/kayaking, 632
hiking, 623
information, 588, 601
lodgings, 637–38
skiing, 629
wildlife, 637
Prince Rupert
air service, 561
attractions, 401
boat service, 390, 391–92
boating/canoeing/kayaking,
570
camping, 397
fishing, 565–66
hiking/walking, 567-8
information, 571
restaurants, 402
Princess Margaret Provincial
Marine Park
boating/kayaking, 243, 361
camping, 240
Princess Royal Island, kayaking,
395
Princeton, information, 449
Prior Centennial Provincial Park,
camping, 356
Prophet River Hot Springs
Protected Area, wildlife, 636
Prophet River Provincial
Recreation Area, camping, 621
Providence Lake, camping,
479–80
Provincial forests, reservations, x.
See also British Columbia
Forest Service
Provincial parks, reservations, ix.
See also British Columbia
Parks; *individual entries*
Prudhomme Lake Provincial Park,
camping, 397, 562
Puntzi Lake
fishing, 556
hiking, 552
horseback riding, 558
wildlife, 557–68
Purcell Wilderness Provincial
Conservancy
hiking, 518, 534
wildlife, 536

Quadra Island
attractions, 384
beaches/picnics, 381
boating/canoeing/kayaking, 379–80
ferry service, 375
fishing, 384
information, 386
lodgings, 385–86
Qualicum, wildlife, 287
Qualicum Bay, restaurants, 329
Qualicum Beach, 316
canoeing/kayaking, 325
information, 330
lodgings, 330
restaurants, 328
Quatsino Sound, fishing, 346
Queen Charlotte City, lodgings, 412
Queen Charlotte Islands, 403–12
adjoining areas, 404
air/boat service, 404
attractions, 411
beaches, 410–11
camping/parks, 404–6
fishing, 408
hiking, 408–9
information, 412
kayaking, 406–7
lodgings, 412
whale watching/wildlife, 409–10
See also Graham Island; Moresby Island
Queen Charlotte Strait, boat service, 389–90
Queen Elizabeth Park, 8–9, 16
Queen of Chilliwack, 389–90, 392–93, 397, 399–400
Queen of the North, 390, 391–92
Queen's Park, 12, 16
Quennell Lake, boating/kayaking, 278
Quesnel, skiing, cross-country, 597–98
Quilchena, lodgings, 457

Radium Hot Springs (hot springs), 540–41
Radium Hot Springs (town)
attractions, 540
information, 542
lodgings, 542
Raft Cove Provincial Marine Park, camping, 349
Rafting
Bella Coola Road (Highway 20), 556–57
Cheakamus River, 176–77
Chehalis River, 78
Chilliwack River, 78, 79
Fraser River, 431–32
Kicking Horse River, 432
Nahatlatch River, 431–32
Northeast British Columbia, 634
Skihist Provincial Park, 417
Squamish/Squamish Valley, 177
Stewart-Cassiar Highway (Highway 37), 646–48
Thompson River, 431–32
Whistler, 176–77
Yellowhead Highway (Highway 5), 610
See also Canoeing; Kayaking
Rathtrevor Beach Provincial Park
beaches/picnics, 280
camping, 283
Rearguard Falls Provincial Park, fishing, 608
Rebecca Spit Provincial Marine Park
beaches/picnics, 381
fishing, 384
Red Bluff Provincial Park
camping, 574
picnics, 581
Red Creek Fir, 267
Red Mountain
downhill skiing, 496–97
lodgings, 500–1
mountain biking, 85–86
Reifel (George C.) Migratory Bird Sanctuary, 51–52, 55
Reservations, camping, ix
Restaurants. *See specific cities for listings*
Revelstoke
attractions, 432–33
information, 434
lodgings, 433–34
restaurants, 433
skiing, 430–31
Revelstoke Lake, camping, 419
Richmond
cycling, 46–47
directions, 41
hiking, 57
information, 60
lodgings, 59
restaurants, 59
River of Golden Dreams, boating/canoeing/kayaking, 175–76
Riverfront Park, 16, 24
Road conditions, information, viii
Roberts Creek
attractions, 231
lodgings, 233–34
restaurants, 232
Roberts Creek Provincial Park
beaches/picnics, 212
camping, 210
Roberts Memorial Provincial Park, beaches/picnics, 279
Robson Bight/Robson Bight Provincial Park
boating/canoeing, 345
whale watching, 347
Rock climbing
Fraser Plateau, 587
Pemberton/Pemberton Valley, 206
Sea to Sky Highway, 166–68
Squamish/Squamish Valley, 167–68
Strathcona Provincial Park, 339
See also Ice climbing
Rocky Point Park, 19
Rodeos, 190
Roderick Haig-Brown Provincial Park
fishing, 429
hiking, 423
wildlife, 429–30
Rolley Lake/Rolley Lake Provincial Park
beaches, 68
camping, 64
canoeing/kayaking, 76
fishing, 88
hiking, 93
Rosebery Provincial Park
camping, 503
fishing, 510
Rosewall Creek Provincial Park, fishing, 323
Ross Lake Provincial Campground, 67
Ross Lake Provincial Park
boating/canoeing/kayaking, 570
camping, 563
fishing, 565
Rossland
attractions, 499
information, 501
lodgings, 500–1
mountain biking, 492, 507–8
restaurants, 499–500
Ruby Lake, boating/canoeing/kayaking, 216
Ruckle Provincial Park
beaches/swimming, 359
camping, 355–56
Ruskin Recreation Area, fishing, 88
RV parks, North Shore, 141. *See also* Camping

Saanich
mountain biking, 246
walking, 247
Safety, outdoor, x–xii, xv
Sailing
Vancouver, 26
Whistler, 178
See also Boating; Windsurfing
St. Agnes Well Hot Spring, 195
Salmo, information, 516
Salmon, fishing, xiii–xiv. *See also* Fishing
Salmon Arm
information, 434, 477
wildlife, 430
Salmon River, fishing, 346
Salt Spring Island
attractions, 367–68
beaches/swimming, 359
boating/kayaking, 362
camping/parks, 355–57
fishing, 360
hiking, 366
information, 373
lodgings, 370–73
restaurants, 368–70
Saltery Bay Provincial Park
beaches/picnics, 213
camping, 210
diving, 228
San Juan River, kayaking, 272
Sandspit, information, 412
Sandy Island Provincial Marine Park,

boating/canoeing/kayaking, 377–78
Sargeant Bay Provincial Park
beaches/picnics, 212
wildlife, 229
Sasamat Lake, 15, 16–17
Sasquatch Provincial Park
boating/canoeing/kayaking, 78
camping, 64–65
fishing, 88–89
hiking, 93
mountain biking, 86
wildlife, 100
Saturna Island
attractions, 368
boating/kayaking, 361–62
fishing, 360
lodgings, 372
parks/picnics, 357–58
restaurants, 369
whale watching, 365
Savary Island
beaches/picnics, 382
boating/canoeing/kayaking, 378
Savona Provincial Park, picnics, 427
Sayward
attractions, 352
information, 353
Sayward Forest Canoe Route, canoeing, 344
Scenic drives
Alaska Highway, 628, 635
Bella Coola Road (Highway 20), 554
Cariboo Highway (Highway 97), 599–600
Columbia River Valley, 537
Cowichan Valley, 289
Highway 97 (John Hart Highway), 634–35
Northeast British Columbia, 634–35
Slocan Valley, 512
Stewart-Cassiar Highway (Highway 37), 650–51
Trans-Canada Highway (Highway 1), 426–27
Victoria, 254
West Kootenays (Crowsnest Highway), 488–89
Schoen Lake Provincial Park, camping, 349
Sea kayaking. *See* Kayaking
Sea to Sky Highway (Highway 99), 142–88, 190
adjoining areas, 144
camping/parks, 144–49
cycling/skating, 172
directions, 144
hiking, 150–61
mountain biking, 168–70
picnics, 149–50
rock climbing, 166–68
skiing, cross-country, 163–65
See also Whistler
Sea to Sky Trail, 170, 195–96
mountain biking, 197
Seal Bay Regional Nature Park
beaches, 317
wildlife, 327
Sechelt
attractions, 231
beaches/picnics, 212
information, 234
restaurants, 232
Sechelt Inlets Provincial Marine Recreation Area
boating/canoeing/kayaking, 215
diving, 227
Sechelt Peninsula
boat launches, 216
boating/canoeing/kayaking, 214–15
cycling, 218
diving, 227–28
fishing, 225–26
hiking, 221–24
mountain biking, 219–20
skiing, cross-country, 229–30
wildlife, 228–29
Seeley Lake/Seeley Lake Provincial Park
camping, 561–62
fishing, 565
Selkirk Valleys. *See* North Kootenay Lake/Selkirk Valleys
Semiahmoo Park, 44, 51
Serpentine Wildlife Management Area, 52–53
Seton Lake/Seton Lake Reservoir
camping, 193
beaches, 206
70 Mile House, lodgings, 601
Seymour Demonstration Forest
cycling/skating, 124
hiking, 121–22
mountain biking, 125–26
Seymour River
boating/canoeing/kayaking, 134
fish hatchery, 135
swimming, 132
Shames Mountain Ski Area
hiking, 569
skiing, 567
Shannon Falls Provincial Park, picnics, 150
Shawnigan Lake
beaches/picnics, 278–79
boating/kayaking, 277
Shearwater, attractions, 401
Shearwater Hot Springs, 568
Shellfish
Copeland Islands Provincial Marine Park, 378–79
North Vancouver Island, 350
Queen Charlotte Islands, 408
See also Fishing
Shelter Bay Provincial Park, fishing, 429
Shelter Point Regional Park
camping, 380–81
hiking, 382–83
Shuswap Lake
camping, 418
fishing, 429
lodgings, 433–34
See also Shuswap Lake Provincial Park
Shuswap Lake Provincial Marine Park
boating/canoeing, 427–28
camping, 418
See also Shuswap Lake
Sidney
fishing, 4
information, 261
Sidney Spit Provincial Marine Park
beaches/picnics, 241
boating/kayaking, 243
camping, 240
Silver Beach Provincial Park
camping, 418
fishing, 429
Silver Lake Provincial Park
camping, 67
windsurfing, 102
Silver Star Mountain Resort
mountain biking, 469–70
skiing/snowboarding, 468–69
Silver Star Provincial Recreation Area, 466
Silvertip Provincial Campground, 67
Silverton, lodgings, 515
Similkameen River
fishing, 439
swimming, 446
Simson Marine Park, boating/canoeing/kayaking, 215
Singing Pass, hiking, 158–59
Skagit River, fishing, 90
Skagit Valley Provincial Park, 67
hiking, 96–97
wildlife, 100
Skagit Valley, camping, 66–68
Skaha Lake
beaches/swimming, 462
lodgings, 476
Skating
Fraser Valley, 79–83
Squamish/Squamish Valley, 171–72
Vancouver, 17–19
Skeena River
fishing, 565, 575
See also Bulkley/Skeena River Valleys
Skihist Provincial Park
camping, 417
rafting, 417
Skiing, cross-country, xiv–xv
Bella Coola Road (Highway 20), 558
Bulkley/Skeena River Valleys, 566–67
Cariboo Highway (Highway 97), 596–98
Coquihalla Highway (Highway 5), 456
East Kootenays (Crowsnest Highway), 525–26
Fraser Plateau, 582–83
Fraser Valley, 102
information, xv
Kettle Valley, 481–82
Manning Provincial Park, 438–39
North Kootenay Lake/Selkirk Valleys, 520
North Shore, 135–37
Northeast British Columbia,

629–30
Okanagan Valley, 467–69
Okanagan Valley, South, 447
Pemberton/Pemberton Valley, 199–200
Sechelt Peninsula, 229–30
Slocan Valley, 511
Squamish/Squamish Valley, 163–64
Sunshine Coast, 229–30
Trans-Canada Highway (Highway 1), 430–31
West Kootenays (Crowsnest Highway), 497–98
Whistler, 164–65
Yellowhead Highway (Highway 5), 609–10
See also Skiing, downhill; Snowshoeing; *entries for individual parks, towns, and skiing areas*
Skiing, downhill, xiv–xv
Blackcomb, 161–63
Bulkley/Skeena River Valleys, 566–67
Columbia River Valley, 537–39
East Kootenays (Crowsnest Highway), 525–26
Fraser Plateau, 582–83
Fraser Valley, 102
information, xv
Kettle Valley, 481–82
North Kootenay Lake/Selkirk Valleys, 520
North Shore, 135–37
Northeast British Columbia, 629–30
Okanagan Valley, 467–69
Slocan Valley, 511–12
Trans-Canada Highway (Highway 1), 430–31
West Kootenays (Crowsnest Highway), 496–97
Whistler, 161–63
Whitewater Ski Area, 511–12
Yellowhead Highway (Highway 5), 609–10
See also Heli-skiing; Skiing, cross-country; Snowboarding; *entries for individual parks, towns, and skiing areas*
Skookumchuk Narrows, boating/canoeing/kayaking, 215
Skookumchuk Narrows Provincial Park, hiking, 223–24
Slocan, information, 516
Slocan Lake
boating/canoeing/kayaking, 509–10
lodgings, 515
Slocan River, canoeing/kayaking, 509–10
Slocan Valley, 502–16
adjoining areas, 503, 518
attractions, 512–13
beaches/picnics, 506–7
boating/canoeing/kayaking, 509–10
camping/parks, 503–4
caves, 510
directions, 503
fishing, 510
hiking, 504–6
information, 515
lodgings, 515–16
mountain biking, 507–9
restaurants, 514
scenic drives, 512
skiing/snowboarding, 511–12
Smelt Bay Provincial Park, camping, 380
Smithers
air service, 561
camping, 563
hiking, 569
information, 571, 588
skiing/snowboarding, 566–67
Smithers Landing Provincial Park, camping, 574–75
Smoke Bluffs, rock climbing, 167–68
Smuggler Cove Provincial Marine Park
boating/canoeing/kayaking, 216
camping, 210
Snorkeling, Campbell River, 328, 340–41
Snowboarding, xiv–xv
Blackcomb, 161–63
Bulkley/Skeena River Valleys, 566–67
Columbia River Valley, 537–39
East Kootenays (Crowsnest Highway), 525–26
Fraser Plateau, 582–83
Fraser Valley, 102
Kettle Valley, 481–82
North Shore, 135–37
Okanagan Valley, 467–69
Slocan Valley, 511–12
Whistler, 161–63, 166
Yellowhead Highway (Highway 5), 609–10
See also Heli-skiing; Skiing, downhill
Snowden Demonstration Forest, hiking, 336
mountain biking, 319–20
Snowmobiling
Fraser Plateau, 582
Valemount, 610
Whistler, 165–66
Snowshoeing
Champion Lakes Provincial Park, 498
Mount Washington, 321
North Shore, 137
Pemberton/Pemberton Valley, 199–200
Stagleap Provincial Park, 498
Whistler, 166
Sointula, attractions, 352
Sombrio Beach, 268
surfing, 270
Sonora Island, lodgings, 385
Sooke
attractions, 273
information, 275
lodgings, 274–75
restaurants, 273
Sooke Basin, 262–75
adjoining areas, 263
beaches, 267–69
camping, 271–72
directions, 263
fishing, 272–73
hiking, 263–67
information, 275
kayaking, 272
surfing, 269–70
whale watching, 271
wildlife, 270–71
Sooke Potholes Provincial Park, picnics/swimming, 243
Sooke River, fishing, 244
South Chilcotin Wilderness
camping, 194
horseback riding, 204
South Okanagan Valley. *See* Okanagan Valley; South
Sowchea Bay Provincial Recreation Area
camping, 574
picnics, 581
Spahats Creek Provincial Park, camping, 603
Sparwood, information, 528
Spatsizi Plateau Provincial Wilderness Park
canoeing/kayaking/rafting, 647
fishing, 646
hiking, 644
wildlife, 648–49
Spectacle Lake Provincial Park, fishing, 281–82
Spences Bridge, lodgings, 187
Spider Lake Provincial Park
beaches, 316
fishing, 322
Spring Island, kayaking, 343
Sproat Lake Provincial Park
camping, 298
fishing, 300
Squamish River, boating/canoeing/kayaking, 173–74
Squamish/Squamish Valley, 143
Squamish/Squamish Valley
camping/parks, 145–46
cycling/skating, 171–72
fishing, 180–81
hiking, 154–55
horseback riding, 182
information, 187–88
lodgings, 186–87
mountain biking, 168–70
photography, 182
rafting, 177
rock climbing, 167–68
skiing, cross-country, 163–64
swimming, 178–79
wildlife, 181–82
windsurfing/sailing, 177–78
Squitty Bay Provincial Marine Park
beaches/picnics, 381–82
boating/canoeing/kayaking, 377
Stagleap Provincial Park
cross-country skiing/snowshoeing, 498
wildlife, 496
Stake Lake, skiing, cross-country, 456

Stake-McConnell Lakes Provincial Recreation Area
camping, 452
fishing, 453
mountain biking, 455
Stamp Falls Provincial Park, camping, 298
Stanley Park, 5–8
beaches, 12,
biking/skating, 17–18,
fishing, 25
hiking/walking, 16,
Stave River, fishing, 88
Stawamus Chief Mountain
hiking, 153
rock climbing, 167
Stawamus Chief Provincial Park, camping, 145
Steelhead Provincial Park, camping, 418
Stein Valley Nlaka'pamux Heritage Park, hiking, 195, 196, 422–23
Stemwinder Provincial Park
camping, 442
canoeing, 446
Steveston
attractions, 58
fishing, 57
Stewart
fishing, 645–46
hiking, 642–43
information, 651
information, 651
Stewart-Cassiar Highway (Highway 37), 639–51
adjoining areas, 640
camping/parks, 641–42
canoeing/kayaking/rafting, 646–48
directions, 640
fishing, 645–46
hiking, 642–45
information, 651
mountain biking, 649–50
scenic drives, 650–51
wildlife, 648–49
Stikine River
canoeing/kayaking/rafting, 647
wildlife, 648–49
Stikine River Provincial Recreation Area, hiking, 643
Stone Mountain Provincial Park
camping, 621–22
hiking, 627–628
wildlife, 636–37
Strait of Georgia. *See* Georgia, Strait of
Strathcona Provincial Park, 331–41
boating/kayaking, 332–33
camping, 332
hiking, 303, 322, 337–38
lodgings, 340
rock climbing, 339
skiing, cross-country, 321
Stuart Lake
camping/parks, 574
canoeing/kayaking, 586
fishing, 576
Stuart River, canoeing/kayaking, 584
Sumallo River, fishing, 439
Summerland
attractions, 474
information, 477
restaurants, 475
Summit Lake Forest Service Recreation Site, camping, 616
Sun Peaks Resort, skiing, 609
Sun-Oka Beach Provincial Park, beaches/swimming, 462
Sunshine Coast, 208–34
adjoining areas, 209
attractions, 231–32
beaches/picnics, 212–14
boat launches, 216, 218
boating/canoeing/kayaking, 214–18
camping, 210–11
cycling, 218–19
directions, 209
diving, 227–28
fishing, 225–27
hiking, 221–25
information, 234
mountain biking, 219–21
skiing, cross-country, 229–30
wildlife, 228–30
Surfing
Campbell River, 326
Sooke Basin, 269–70
Tofino, 308–9
See also Windsurfing
Surrey
bird-watching, 52
cycling, 49–50
directions, 41
information, 60
kayaking/canoeing, 51
Swan Lake/Christmas Hill Nature Sanctuary, 252
Swan Lake–Kispiox River Provincial Park
canoeing/kayaking, 646–47
fishing, 645
Swan Lake Provincial Park, camping, 620
Swimming
Columbia River Valley, 535
Gulf Islands, southern, 358–60
Manning Provincial Park, 439
North Shore, 130–32
Okanagan Valley, 462–63
Okanagan Valley, South, 446
Pemberton/Pemberton Valley, 205–6
Squamish/Squamish Valley, 178–79
Whistler, 179
See also Beaches; *entries for individual bodies of water*
Swindle Island, kayaking, 395–96
Syringa Creek Provincial Park
camping, 487
fishing, 494

Tabor Mountain Ski Area, skiing, 629
Tacheeda Lakes
camping, 617
fishing, 631
Tahsis, information, 341, 353
Takakkaw Falls, 425
Takla Lake/Takla Lake Provincial Marine Park
canoeing/kayaking, 586
fishing, 576
Tatla Lake
fishing, 555
skiing, cross-country, 558
Tatlatui Provincial Park
fishing, 646
hiking, 644
wildlife, 648–49
Tatshenshini River, canoeing/kayaking/rafting, 647–48
Tatshenshini-Alsek Provincial Wilderness Park
hiking, 645
mountain biking, 649–50
wildlife, 649
Taylor, information, 638
Taylor Arm Provincial Park, camping, 298
Tchentlo Lake Warm Springs, 586
Telegraph Cove
attractions, 352
boating/canoeing, 345
information, 353
Telegraph Creek
camping, 641
hiking, 643–44
Telkwa, information, 588
"Ten Essentials," x–xi
Ten Mile Lake Provincial Park
camping, 594
skiing, cross-country, 598
Tennis, Vancouver, 8
Tenquille Lake
camping, 192
fishing, 203
hiking, 194
Terrace
air service, 561
camping, 562
hiking, 569
information, 571
Tetrahedron Provincial Park, skiing, cross-country, 229–30
Tetsa River Provincial Park, camping, 621
Texada Island
attractions, 385
camping/parks, 380–81
ferry service, 375
hiking, 382–83
information, 386
Thetis Lake Regional Park
beaches/picnics, 242
boating/kayaking, 243–44
Thompson River
camping, 417
fishing, 417, 428, 453
rafting, 431–32
Thunder Hill Provincial Park, camping, 530–31
Toad River, attractions, 637
Tofino, 295–313
adjoining areas, 296
attractions, 309–10
beaches/picnics, 301–2
boating/kayaking, 306–7
directions, 296
diving, 309
festivals and events, 309

fishing, 300
information, 313
lodgings, 312–13
restaurants, 310–11
surfing/windsurfing, 308–9
Top of the World Provincial Park, hiking, 533–34
Trans-Canada Highway (Highway 1), 415–34
access, 416
adjoining areas, 416
boating/canoeing, 427–28
camping/parks, 417–22
fishing, 428–29
hiking, 422–26
picnics/scenic drives, 426–27
skiing, 430–31
wildlife, 429–30
Tribune Bay Provincial Park, beaches/picnics, 381
Trophy Mountain Recreation Area, hiking, 608
Trumpeter Swan Management Area, 327
Ts'yl-os Provincial Park
camping, 553
hiking, 552
Tsawwassen, 49, 55. *See also* Boundary Bay Regional Park
Tudyah Lake Provincial Park
camping, 618
fishing, 631
Tumbler Ridge, mountain biking, 628
Tweedsmuir Provincial Park, 546–47
camping, 553
canoeing, 557
fishing, 576
hiking, 578, 580–81
horseback riding, 558
picnics, 554
skiing, cross-country, 558
wildlife, 557
Tyhee Lake/Tyee Lake Provincial Park
camping, 575
fishing, 576
picnics, 581
skiing, cross-country, 567
Tynehead Regional Park, 53

Uchuck III (MV), 333–36
Ucluelet
attractions, 310
beaches/picnics, 301–2
boating/kayaking, 306–7
directions, 296
fishing, 300
information, 313
lodgings, 311–12
Upper Arrow Lake, 502–16
camping/parks, 503
fishing, 510
See also Arrow Lakes/Arrow Lakes Provincial Park
Upper Lillooet Headwaters
hiking, 194
wildlife, 201

Valemount
camping/parks, 603
heli-skiing/snowmobiling, 610
information, 612
wildlife, 611
Valentine Mountain, picnics, 213
Valhalla Provincial Park, hiking, 504–5
Vancouver, 3–39
adjoining areas, 5
attractions, 26–30
beaches, 12–15
canoeing, 22–24
cycling, 17–19
directions, 4–5
diving, 26
fishing, 24–25
gardens, 29
golf, 8
hiking, 10, 16–17
information, 38–39
kayaking, 22–24
lodgings, 36–38
mountain biking, 19–22
parks, 5–12
photography, 25–26
restaurants, 30–36
sailing/windsurfing, 26
skating, 17–19
Stanley Park, 5–8
swimming, 12
tennis, 8
waterparks, 12, 29
See also Greater Vancouver Regional District; North Shore; North Vancouver; West Vancouver
Vancouver Island, North, 342–53
adjoining areas, 343
attractions, 352
boating/canoeing, 344–45
camping/parks, 348–50
caves, 350–51
directions, 342
diving, 351
fishing, 345–46
hiking, 347
information, 353
kayaking/sea kayaking, 343–44
lodgings, 352–53
picnics, 351
wildlife, 347–48
Vanderhoof
hiking, 579–80
information, 588
mountain biking, 583
skiing, cross-country, 582
wildlife, 587
Vanier Park, 9
Vargas Island/Vargas Island Provincial Park
beaches, 302
hiking, 305
Vaseux Lake Provincial Park/Wildlife Centre, wildlife, 463
Vedder Peak, mountain biking, 87
Vermilion Pass, lodgings, 542
Vernon
golfing, 472
hiking, 466
information, 477
mountain biking, 469
Victoria (and environs), 237–61
adjoining areas, 239
attractions, 254–56
beaches/picnics, 240–43
bird-watching/wildlife, 252–54
boating/kayaking, 243–44
camping, 239–40
cycling, 245–47
directions, 238–39
diving, 254
fishing, 244
hiking/walking, 247–52
information, 261
lodgings, 258–60
mountain biking, 245–47
parks, 239–43
restaurants, 256–58
scenic drives, 254
Victoria Gorge
boating/kayaking, 244
fishing, 244

Walking. *See* Hiking
Walloper Lake Provincial Park
camping, 452
skiing, cross-country, 456
Wapta Falls, 425
Wasa Lake Provincial Park, camping, 530
Wasa Slough Wildlife Sanctuary, wildlife, 536
Waterskiing, Cultus Lake, 79. *See also* Boating
Weather, information, viii–ix
Wedgemount Lake, hiking, 160–61
Wells
festivals and events, 598
information, 601
skiing, cross-country, 597–98
Wells Gray Provincial Park
camping, 604–5
canoeing, 610
hiking, 606
information, 612
skiing, cross-country, 609–10
West Coast Trail, 262–75
hiking, 263–65, 302–3
West Kootenays (Crowsnest Highway), 485–501
adjoining areas, 486
attractions, 498
beaches, 493
camping/parks, 486–88
canoeing/kayaking, 495
directions, 486
downhill skiing, 496–97
fishing, 494–95
hiking, 489–91
horseback riding, 493–94
information, 501
mountain biking, 491–93
picnics/scenic drives, 488–89
skiing, cross-country, 497–98
wildlife, 496
See also East Kootenays (Crowsnest Highway)
West Lake, lodgings, 638
West Lake Provincial Park
hiking, 581
picnics, 581
skiing, cross-country, 598
West Lion, hiking, 150–52

West Shawnigan Lake Provincial Park
beaches/picnics, 278–79
boating/kayaking, 277
West Vancouver
beaches, 130–31
cycling, 124–25
directions, 108
hiking, 112–17
information, 141
lodgings, 140–41
parks, 128
restaurants, 139–40
See also North Shore; North Vancouver
Westholme, restaurants, 292
Wewanie Hot Springs, 568
Whale watching
Central/Discovery Coast, 391, 393
festivals and events, 309
Gulf Islands, southern, 365
Pacific Rim National Park Reserve, 302
Point Roberts (WA), 54
Queen Charlotte Islands, 409–10
Robson Bight Provincial Park, 347
Sooke Basin, 271
See also Wildlife
Wheelchair accessible
parks, 219
wildlife viewing, 635
Whiskers Point Provincial Park, camping, 617
Whistler, 142–88. *See also* Sea to Sky Highway
adjoining areas, 144
attractions, 182
boating/canoeing/kayaking, 175–77
camping/parks, 146–47
dogsledding, 166
fishing, 181
heli-skiing/boarding, 166
hiking, 156–61
ice skating, 166
information, 187–88
lodgings, 185–87
mountain biking, 169–71
picnics, 150
restaurants, 182–85
skiing, cross-country, 164–65
skiing/snowboarding, 161–63
snowboarding, 166
snowmobiling, 165–66
snowshoeing, 166
swimming, 179
windsurfing/sailing, 178
winter sports, 165–66
See also Blackcomb
Whistler Interpretive Forest, 157
hiking, 157
mountain biking, 170
White Rock
information, 60
parks, 44–45
restaurants, 59
White Rock Beach, 45
Whiteswan Lake Provincial Park
camping, 531
fishing, 536
Whitetooth Ski Area, skiing, 431
Whitewater Ski Area, downhill skiing, 511–12
Whytecliff Marine Park, 131
diving, 137
picnics, 137–38
wildlife, 135
Widgeon Creek, boating/canoeing/kayaking, 74
Wildlife
Bella Coola Road (Highway 20), 557–58
Bulkley/Skeena River Valleys, 563–64
Cariboo Highway (Highway 97), 599
Central/Discovery Coast, 398–99
Columbia River Valley, 535–36
Comox Valley, 326–28
Cowichan Valley, 286–87
Fraser Estuary, 51–54
Fraser Plateau, 587
Fraser Valley, 98–100
Gulf Islands, southern, 363–65
Malaspina Peninsula, 229–30
Manning Provincial Park, 438
North Shore, 134–35
Northeast British Columbia, 635–37
Okanagan Valley, 463
Okanagan Valley, South, 447
Pacific Rim National Park Reserve, 302
Queen Charlotte Islands, 409–10
Sechelt Peninsula, 228–29
Sooke Basin, 270–71
Squamish/Squamish Valley, 181–82
Stewart-Cassiar Highway (Highway 37), 648–49
Sunshine Coast, 228–30
Trans-Canada Highway (Highway 1), 429–30
Upper Lillooet Headwaters, 201
Vancouver Island, North, 347–48
Vanderhoof, 587
Victoria, 252–54
West Kootenays (Crowsnest Highway), 496
wheelchair-accessible facilities, 635
Yellowhead Highway (Highway 5), 611
See also Whale watching; *individual entries for towns, parks, and geographic features*
Williams Lake, information, 559, 601
Williston Lake
camping, 618
canoeing/kayaking, 633
fishing, 631
Wilson (Ethel F.) Provincial Park, camping, 574
Windermere Lake
cycling, 537
fishing, 536
swimming, 535
windsurfing, 539
Windsurfing
Boundary Bay Regional Park, 55
Bulkley/Skeena River Valleys, 570
Chilliwack Lake, 102
Columbia River Valley, 539
Comox, 326
Cowichan Valley, 288–89
Fraser Estuary, 55
Fraser Valley, 102
Nicola Lake, 455
Pacific Rim National Park Reserve, 308
Silver Lake Provincial Park, 102
Squamish/Squamish Valley, 177–78
Tofino, 308–9
Vancouver, 26
Vancouver Island, North, 348
Whistler, 178
See also Sailing; Surfing
Winlaw, restaurants, 514
Winter Cove Provincial Marine Park
boating/kayaking, 361
picnics, 357
Wistaria Provincial Park, hiking, 578
Witty's Lagoon Regional Park
beaches/picnics, 242–43
bird-watching/wildlife, 252–53
walking, 248
Wokkpash Provincial Recreation Area, hiking, 627
Wood Lake, fishing, 464
Woss Lake Provincial Park, camping, 349
Wreck Beach, 13–14

Yahk Provincial Park, camping, 523
Yard Creek Provincial Park, camping, 419
Yellowhead Highway (Highway 5), 602–12
adjoining areas, 602
attractions, 611
camping/parks, 603–6
canoeing/rafting, 610
directions, 602
fishing/fly-in fishing, 608–9
hiking, 606–8
horseback riding, 611
information, 612
lodgings, 612
skiing/snowmobiling, 609–10
wildlife, 611
Yoho National Park
camping, 421–22
fossils, 425–26
hiking, 424–26
information, 434
lodgings, 433
picnics, 427

Zeballos, 353
fishing, 346